COMPLETE BOOK OF BALLETS

Some other Books by Cyril W. Beaumont

ANTHOLOGY
A Miscellany for Dancers

BIBLIOGRAPHY
A Bibliography of Dancing

COSTUME AND SETTING
Design for the Ballet

DICTIONARY
A French-English Dictionary of Terms used in Classical Ballet

HISTORY
A Short History of Ballet
A History of Ballet in Russia (1613-1881).

STUDIES
Enrico Cecchetti
Serge Diaghilev
Fanny Elssler
Michel Fokine and his Ballets
Three French Dancers of the 18th Century
Three French Dancers of the 19th Century
Alicia Markova
The Monte Carlo Russian Ballet
Vaslav Nijinsky
Anna Pavlova
The Vic-Wells Ballet

TECHNIQUE
A Primer of Classical Ballet for Children
A Second Primer of Classical Ballet for Children
A Manual of the Theory and Practice of Classical Theatrical Dancing
The Theory and Practice of Allegro in Classical Ballet

TRANSLATIONS
Vaslav Nijinsky by F. de Miomandre
Orchesography by Thoinot Arbeau
Letters on Dancing by J. G. Noverre
The Dancing-Master by P. Rameau
Marie Taglioni by André Levinson
The Romantic Ballet as seen by Théophile Gautier

ALICIA MARKOVA IN "LE LAC DES CYNGES"

Complete Book
Of Ballets

A GUIDE TO THE PRINCIPAL BALLETS
OF THE NINETEENTH AND
TWENTIETH CENTURIES

BY

Cyril W. Beaumont

GROSSET & DUNLAP *Publishers*

NEW YORK

To

LYDIA LOPOKOVA

In Friendship and Admiration

CONTENTS

ILLUSTRATIONS

XV

PREFACE

ONE of the most surprising events in the theatrical world during recent years has been the extraordinary and ever-increasing popularity of ballet. This art, which for many years relied for its support on a special public, is now enjoyed by audiences drawn from all classes. Interest in ballet has led to a desire for information which has resulted in many additions to the bibliography of dancing. None the less there are still several gaps to be filled and not the least is the lack of a comprehensive work on the ballets themselves. The present book has been planned to meet that need.

It is a collection of the stories of the principal ballets of the 19th and 20th centuries, grouped together in chronological order under their choreographers. This arrangement enables the reader to study the work of a choreographer as a whole, or to compare the achievements and theories of one with those of another, and so determine the value and interest of their respective contributions.

My chief concern has been to describe the principal ballets which have had their first performance in London, Paris, or St. Petersburg; nevertheless, I have included the stories of several ballets which have had their first performance at Moscow, Milan, Budapest, or Vienna. Not only are the works of the masters of the past described and those of famous contemporary choreographers, but also the principal productions of the Soviet *maîtres de ballet* and of the rising new school of English choreographers.

My original intention was to begin with the first romantic ballet, *La Sylphide* (1832), but, to make clear the entirely new conception effected by that production, I have added some specimens of the works of pre-Taglioni choreographers. While I have restricted the scope of the book to stories of works intended to be presented through the medium of the technique of the classical ballet, I have occasionally departed from that plan in order to include such productions as Jooss's *The Green Table* and Harangozó's *Perhaps To-morrow!* because of their special importance and interest.

xxi

While every endeavour has been made to provide as complete and informative a work as possible, and its 866 pages are, I submit, sufficient proof of that endeavour, I have been compelled to exercise a measure of selection in order to keep the book within reasonable bounds. I have, however, attempted to describe almost every production given at the three centers of ballet stated, during the last hundred years, which can fairly be classed as important under one or more of the following heads: (1) for its popularity; (2) for its association with a particular dancer; (3) for the interest or originality of its theme; (4) for marking a definite stage in the development of ballet; (5) for the introduction of a new theatrical effect; (6) for being the reflection of some subject of topical interest; (7) for its association with a new movement in art, music, or literature; (8) for marking a development in setting or costume for the ballet.

In the case of ballets given after 1910 the majority have been described from actual observation, or from information supplied by the choreographer responsible for the work. The stories of ballets presented before that date have been compiled partly from a study of the original scenario, partly from contemporary records and notices.

Certain of the famous old ballets still performed, such as *Giselle, Le Lac des Cygnes, La Belle au Bois Dormant,* and the like, I have described at some length, because they are particularly dear to the ballet-goer. I have also recorded very fully certain of the ballets of Fokine and Massine from notes made by me while actually witnessing the first and subsequent performances, in the hope that my descriptions may give those who did not have that privilege at least a faint impression of how such ballets were originally presented.

I must ask the reader's indulgence for a certain lack of uniformity in the length and treatment of the various ballets, which results from a number of causes, particularly the varying amount of material available. Again, ballets which consist mainly of abstract movement, or possess little or no theme, can only be described briefly, or must, of necessity, be omitted.

Apart from the description of a ballet, I have endeavoured to give full particulars of the author of the theme, the designer of the costumes and scenery, the composer of the music, the date and place of the first performance, and the original cast. There are also occasional notes on the origin of a ballet, its history, the names of the dancers associated with the principal roles, and some account, based on contemporary impressions and notices, of how the principal dancer danced and how the ballet was received. In the case of modern ballets I have added critical notes of my own.

Read as a whole this book is not only a record of the principal ballets of the 19th and 20th centuries but, indirectly, an informal history of the ballet of that period. As the reader turns over these pages he will have a glimpse of that great panorama of choreographic achievement; he will see the mythological ballet give place to the romantic ballet, the romantic exchanged for the topical ballet, the topical succeeded by a revival of the symphonic or abstract ballet; he will see the long ballet of five acts, with a theme as involved and highly coloured as a novel by Alexandre Dumas, give place to the one-act ballet with a highly concentrated theme, which, in turn is replaced by the ballet with only the vestige of a story; he will see the most modernist movements in art, literature, and music, bent to the service of the ballet; and, against this ever-changing, vari-coloured background, he will see the great dancers of the past and present, and those young artistes destined perhaps to be "stars" in the years to come.

For my description of some of the ballets of Fokine and Massine I have drawn upon my *Impressions of the Russian Ballet, Michel Fokine and his Ballets,* and *The Monte Carlo Ballet,* while the stories of *Giselle, La Diable Boiteux,* and *Ondine* are based partly on the descriptions in *Les Beautés de l'Opéra* (1845) and partly upon the contemporary notices of Gautier and other writers.

In the transliteration of Russian names, I have, in general, adopted the system advocated by Prince D. S. Mirsky in his *History of Russian Literature.* I have occasionally departed from this practice when a name so transcribed might take on too unfamiliar an appearance; thus, I have written Tchaikovsky in place of Chaikovsky, and Toumanova instead of Tumanova. All names of ballets are given in their English equivalent, except where I considered them to be more familiar in the French title; but in many such cases the English equivalent is given in a footnote. All dates of performances in Russia are given in both the "old style" and the "new style," the former being twelve and thirteen days behind in the 19th and 20th centuries respectively.

In conclusion I desire to record my deep appreciation of the assistance extended to me by several friends in the preparation of this book. Most especially must I express my grateful thanks to six helpers: to my wife, who read through the whole of the proofs; to Mme. Lydia Lopokova, who procured for me transcriptions of certain Russian ballets which, to the best of my belief, exist only in manuscript; to Mr. Serge Leslie, who not only placed his fine collection of *scenarii* at my disposal, but checked up dates and casts for me in Paris, and gave me the most valuable help in tracking down certain material which I required for illustrative purposes; to Mr. H. S. Sibthorp, who compiled the index, which adds much to the usefulness of the volume as a work of reference; to Dr. Walter Toscanini, of Milan, well known for his researches in the history of ballet in Italy, who most generously allowed me to draw upon his collection of material relating to Viganò and Manzotti; and to Mr. De V. Payen-Payen, who read through my renderings of contemporary notices of French ballets and gave me several valuable suggestions.

In connection with *scenarii* written in languages other than French it has been necessary to render them into English for the purpose of study. My translators were as follows: Russian—M. V. Virkow; Italian—Sig. Gino Gario and Miss C. Allardice; German—Miss Derra de Moroda and Herr T. Schuler; Hungarian—Dr. Sima and M. A. Schwitzer.

For courtesies in connection with the examination of material in various public collections I desire to record my indebtedness to M. Rolf de Maré and Dr. Pierre Tugal, director and curator respectively of the Archives Internationales de la Danse, Paris, who also loaned me many important photographs of productions; to Mr. A. I. Ellis, Superintendent of the Reading Room, British Museum; to Mme. Horn, of the Bibliothèque de l'Arsenal, Paris; to M. J. G. Prod'homme, of the Bibliothèque de l'Opéra, Paris; to Mrs. Gabrielle Enthoven and Miss Helen Brown of the Enthoven Theatrical Collection, Victoria and Albert Museum; and to Miss Dorothy Lawton, of the Music Library, New York Public Library.

I have also to thank the following for the loan of material: The Soviet Embassy, London; Col. W. de Basil; M. René Blum; Mr. L. J. Bradley; M. Victor Dandré; Miss Derra de Moroda; Mr. Anton Dolin; Dr. Paolo Fabbri; the Hon. Grania Guinness; Miss Theresa Heyman; the Imperial Society of Teachers of Dancing; Mr. Lincoln Kirstein; Mr. Philip Richardson, editor of the *Dancing Times;* and Miss A. E. Twysden.

Last, but by no means least, I have to thank my publishers for their unfailing encouragement and support throughout this onerous task.

CYRIL W. BEAUMONT.

October, 1937.

COMPLETE BOOK OF BALLETS

DAUBERVAL

JEAN BERCHER, professionally known as Dauberval, some-times written D'Auberval, was born at Montpellier on August 19th, 1742. He was a pupil of Noverre, who said of him that he was fashioned by the Graces, and endowed with wit, good taste, and intelligence. He made his *début* at the Opera, Paris, on June 12th, 1761, and two years later attained the rank of *premier danseur de demi-caractère*. In 1770 he became *premier danseur noble*. He also studied choreography and became assistant first to Noverre and later to Pierre Gardel; but, owing to differences with the last-named, he retired in 1783 with a pension of 3,500 francs.

From Paris he went to Bordeaux where from 1785 to 1791 he produced several ballets which attained great success, for instance: *La Fille Mal Gardée, Le Deserteur, L'Epreuve Villageoise, Télémaque,* and *Le Page Inconstant.* Many of these were revived at Paris by his pupil, Jean Aumer.

Dauberval was an excellent dancer in the *demi-caractère* style and a mime of the first rank. As a choreographer he composed few ballets, but they were all distinguished for their artistic conception and skilful arrangement, and required fine artistes for their interpretation. He was a great admirer of the *ballet d'action* and did much to develop Noverre's theories. In fact, Dauberval might be termed the inventor of the comedy ballet.

He was a man of witty conversation and charming manners, whose chief pleasure, apart from the theatre, was the chase, to which he attributed his good health and slender figure.

Dauberval died at Tours on February 14th, 1806.

LA FILLE MAL GARDÉE

Pantomime Ballet in 2 Acts and 3 Scenes. Book: Dauberval.
Choreography: Dauberval. First produced: Bordeaux, 1786.

CHARACTERS

Mother Simone, a rich farmer . . . .
Lise, her daughter . . . . . .
Colas, a young farmer, in love with Lise .
Thomas, a vine-grower . . . . .
Alain, his son . . . .
The Village Notary . . . . . .
Villagers, Harvesters, etc.

Act. I. Scene I. A small village. In the left foreground is
Simone's house. Facing it is a small dairy. Dawn is just breaking.

At the rise of the curtain, harvesters are seen passing in the
background. Lise comes out of the house with an air of mystery
and seems surprised and disappointed that her sweetheart, Colas, is
nowhere in sight. She opens the dairy, goes inside, and reappears
with a bowl of cream, which she sets on the ground by the door.
She decides to go indoors but, to prove to Colas that she did not
forget their tryst, she takes a ribbon from her bodice and hangs it
on a tree.

Hardly has she vanished when Colas arrives, accompanied by
some harvesters. He sends them away and, tip-toeing towards the
door, listens anxiously. Hearing nothing, he is about to depart,
when he sees the ribbon. He kisses it and attaches it to his stick.
Leaning towards Lise's window he is about to blow her a kiss
when Simone surprises him in the act.

Furious, she shakes her fist at Colas. Then she throws her bonnet
at him, and is about to follow it up with a basket, when Lise opens
the door and warns him to be off. Colas dodges the basket and
takes to flight. Simone descends to rate her daughter who, picking
up the basket and bonnet, restores them to her. But Simone is not
deceived and demands an explanation.

A number of villagers arrive and apply for work as harvesters.
Simone engages them and gives each a sickle, while Lise prepares
a basket of provisions. She is about to leave with them when her
mother calls her back.

Colas appears in the distance, but Lise signs to him to hide behind the farm. She continues her explanations which her mother

reruses to accept and forbids her to go out. When Simone goes to fetch a churn, Colas slips into the dairy. Simone returns and, giving Lise some cream, tells her to beat it into butter. Lise obeys, and Simone goes towards the dairy and is about to open the door when she sees the bowl of cream left by Lise. She rates her for her carelessness and departs.

Hardly has she gone when Colas darts to Lise's side. He holds out his hand to her, but she fears to take it. He is about to leave in a temper, when she pulls him back by the ribbon. She takes it off the stick and pins it on his waistcoat. Delighted with this favour, he attempts to steal a kiss, which she modestly refuses.

She shows him the task set her and Colas wishes to help her make the butter, but, as their glances meet, their thoughts wander, and the task is forgotten. There is a noise of footsteps and Colas makes off, while Lise resumes her task.

A number of village girls arrive and try to induce Lise to go to the harvest, when Simone appears and drives them away. She reproaches Lise for the little she has done.

Enter Thomas and his son, Alain. Simone, aware of the reason for their visit, sends Lise indoors. Then Thomas proposes that Alain shall be Simone's son-in-law. His proposal is accepted. Lise returns to try and overhear the conversation, but it is concluded and she cannot understand the reason for the prevailing good-humour. Her mother then gives her permission to accompany her to the harvest. Alain offers her his arm. She rejects it and takes the arm of Thomas. Simone is escorted by Alain.

Act I. Scene II. A vast field filled with harvesters. Noon strikes.

Colas arrives and orders a meal to be served. Simone, Lise, Thomas, and Alain go to the house. Colas greets his neighbours. Alain goes to sit with the girls, but Colas places him at a table with his father.

After the repast there are several dances, and at the end Simone herself takes part. Colas takes the opportunity to sit by Lise, but Simone surprises him. Thomas and Alain are jealous and leave in ill humour.

Another villager replaces them and his pleasant manner animates all the young girls. He plays on his flageolet and the dances are resumed. Presently he joins in, but one of the girls runs off with his flageolet and he hastens in pursuit.

The *divertissement* becomes general until it is suddenly interrupted by a distant clap of thunder. The storm breaks and the frightened villagers hastily cover up their work and leave in disorder. Colas follows his sweetheart, but Simone sees him and he runs away. Lise, Simone, and the harvesters depart.

Act II. The interior of Mother Simone's farm. To the left is a wooden staircase leading to a room, the window of which faces the spectator. In the background, to the right, is the entrance door, at the top of which is an opening, protected by wooden bars.

Enter Simone and Lise, each carrying a sheaf. The former, exhausted, drops in the first chair at hand. She decides to busy herself with her spinning wheel. Lise hastens to fetch it for her, while Simone, realizing that she has left the door open, goes to close it.

Lise brings the wheel and two distaffs. They begin to work but her mother soon grows drowsy. Lise then tries to take the door-key, but her mother wakes up and proposes that Lise should dance, while she accompanies her on a tambourine. Lise dances, but Simone soon falls asleep.

During the dance Lise has espied Colas through the wicket and goes to speak with him. But Simone wakes with a start and bangs her tambourine. Lise hurriedly resumes her dance and Colas vanishes. Now mother and daughter dance together.

There is a knock at the door and the peasants bring in the sheaves and receive their wages. The men ask for a drink and Simone leads them to her cellar, taking care to lock in Lise while she is gone.

Lise peers through the window and is disappointed not to see Colas. But when she goes to the pile of sheaves to pick up her distaff, Colas comes out from behind them. He had entered with the harvesters and hidden himself behind the sheaves until Simone went out.

Lise is greatly alarmed at being shut up with her lover and she forbids him to approach her. He respects her wishes. But the struggle is hard and love sorely tempts the young people. Lise tries to resume her work, but begins to cry, and the distaff falls to the floor. Colas, thinking Lise has fainted, runs to her assistance. He takes off his neckerchief and dries her tears. She gives him her neckerchief in exchange. They become affectionate when Simone is heard returning. Colas bounds up the staircase while Lise pretends to be asleep in a chair.

Simone is duped, but asks Lise where she obtained her neckerchief. She replies that it is one belonging to her mother. Simone, suspecting that Lise has been talking to Colas through the wicket, orders her to go to the room where Colas is hidden.

end for his kindness. The Governor proposes
⁝ip be strengthened still further by asking him to
⁝ marry Nina. The Comte had never expected to
⁝atch, yet he does not wish to disappoint Germeuil.
⁝ matter over he feels it would be ungrateful to refuse
⁝ffer and he accepts. The parents seal the bargain
⁝-shake. The Comte, however, begs the Governor to
⁝tter secret for a little while. Blinval, however, does not
⁝ndition, for he has already sped to Nina to ask her for

⁝ceives the declaration in astonishment and looks at her
⁝r an explanation. The Comte has no alternative but to
⁝his approval of the match which will unite their two
⁝.

⁝a, struck speechless, bursts into tears, then kneels to her
⁝ and entreats him to alter his decision, but he induces her to
⁝nd orders Elyse to take her indoors.

⁝e Governor and his son are bewildered by this scene, but the
⁝nte explains that Nina's sorrow is due to the possibility of her
⁝ng separated from her father. He invites the Governor and his
⁝n to join in the festivities.

The Comte goes into the summer-house where he writes a note
⁝ Germeuil, advising him of the projected marriage and request-
⁝ng that he will leave the castle. He gives Georges the message and
⁝nstructs him that Germeuil is not to be admitted to the castle.

Germeuil, disturbed at the disappearance of Nina and the Comte,
⁝mes to look for them. He meets Georges who gives him the let-
⁝er, the contents of which distress him greatly.

Elyse comes out of the summer-house and observes Germeuil
walking up and down in agitation. Seeing her, he begs Elyse to
help him to bid farewell to Nina. This request is overheard by
Blinval, who is concealed in the grove. In the meantime Germeuil
takes his departure.

The villagers return, dancing gaily. Georges signals to them to
cease and tells them of Germeuil's expulsion and Nina's despair.
Meanwhile, Victor and Georgette return. Georges seizes Victor
and forbids him to speak with Georgette. The Mayor approves his
action, since he finds it absurd that a peasant should pretend to
Georgette's hand. Instead, he offers himself as a much more
suitable spouse. Georges agrees, but when the Mayor approaches
Georgette, she flees into the park.

The Governor and his son return and enter the castle, while
Georges goes in search of his daughter.

Now Thomas, Alain, and the village notary arrive to draw up
the marriage contract. Everything is settled and Alain calls the villagers to share in his happiness. Simone accords him the pleasure
of fetching his bride, but, just as he sets foot on the ladder, Colas
emerges from the room and bars the way.

Simone is greatly distressed, but Colas and Lise kneel and
entreat her to let them marry. The notary and the villagers take
their part, the former convincing Simone that it is best for the
lovers to marry. She agrees and to the chagrin of Thomas and his
son gives her consent.

The ballet ends with a village festival.

*

This ballet is said to have originated in a curious manner.
Charles Maurice, in his *Histoire Anécdotique du Théâtre,* asserts
that Dauberval happened to stop one day in front of a glazier's
shop. Glancing at the window he saw "a crude coloured print depicting a village youth fleeing from a cottage, with an angry old
woman throwing his hat after him, while a peasant girl shed tears.
At the end of a very short interval, the ravishing ballet *La Fille
Mal Gardée* was evolved."

La Fille Mal Gardée is the oldest ballet still given to-day, for it is
still included in the repertory of the Soviet Ballet. This ballet,
although produced at one time or another in most European capitals, has had its greatest success in Russia where, under the title of
Useless Precautions, it has been continually performed and served
as a test for aspiring dancers.

It was last produced in London by the Anna Pavlova Company
when Pavlova took the part of Lise, and Novikov that of Colas, or
Colin, as the part is sometimes called. The role of Mother Simone
was often played by Enrico Cecchetti, for this character, which is
slightly burlesque, is, in accordance with tradition, nearly always
taken by a man.

LOUIS MILON

LOUIS JACQUES JESSÉ MILON was born in 1765. He studied at the academy of dancing attached to the Opera, Paris, and made his *début* in 1790. Three years later he became the understudy for the *premier danseur* and soon afterwards attained the rank of *premier sujet*. He is said to have been a fine dancer in the classic style and an excellent mime.

About 1815 he became assistant *maître de ballet* under Pierre Gardel and produced a number of ballets at the Opera such as *Hero et Léandre* (1799), *Pygmalion* (1800), *Les Noces de Gamache* (1801), *Lucas et Laurette* (1803), *Le Retour d'Ulysse* (1807), *L'Enlèvement des Sabines* (1811), *Nina ou la Folle par Amour* (1813), *L'Epreuve Villageoise* (1815), *L'Heureux Retour* (1815), *Le Carnaval de Venise* (1816), *Les Sauvages de la Mer de Sud* (1816), *Les Fiancés de Caserte* (1817), *Zéloïde* (1818), and *Clari* (1820).

His ballets were noted for their invention and novelty, and particularly for their dramatic quality which was often highly effective and deeply moving.

Milon retired in 1827 and died in November, 1849.

NINA OU LA FOLLE PAR AMOUR[1]

Ballet Pantomime in 2 Acts. Book: L. J. Milon. Music: Persius. Choreography: L. J. Milon. First produced: Théâtre de l'Académie Impériale de Musique, November 23rd, 1813.

CHARACTERS

The Comte, Nina's father	M. Milon
Nina, his daughter	Mlle. Bigottini
Germeuil, in love with Nina	M. Albert
The Governor of the Province	M. Mérante

[1] *Nina, or the Girl driven mad by Love.*

6

Blinval, the Governor's son an[d] . . . suitor 7

Georges, the Comte's steward .

Elyse, Nina's governess . . . .

Georgette, daughter of Georges .

Victor, a peasant, in love with Georget[te]

The Mayor . . . .

Lords, Ladies, Retainers, the Comte's es[-] cort, Sailors, Villagers, Peasa[nts]

The action passes near Marseille, in the [s] the sea-coast.

Act I. To the right the Comte's castle, with [a] park a little further back. In the distance can be see[n] washes a terrace, protected by a balustrade running [ ] the stage. To the left, an iron gate leads to the count[ry] the foreground is a grassy bank surrounded by a grove.

Villagers, superintended by Germeuil and Georges, [are] paring for the festival which the Comte has ordered in hon[our of] the Governor. Georgette fashions a garland of flowers. Vic[tor is] busy on the opposite side, but he often goes to Georgette and g[azes] tenderly at her, until she orders him back to work. Germeuil b[eats] a drum to summon the tenants, whom he arranges in differe[nt] groups.

Nina comes out of the summer-house and gives each girl a rib[-] bon similar to the one she wears herself. While Elyse distribu[tes] the ribbons Germeuil offers Nina his hand and shows her th[e] various preparations for the festival. They sit on the grass and ex[-] change tender vows.

The Comte comes out of the castle and, inspecting the decora- tions, arrives at the grove, where he pretends to be surprised t[o] see the lovers. They ask him to consent to their union. He [is] about to consider the matter when the Governor's arrival is si[g-] nalled. The Comte, Nina, and Germeuil hasten to meet him.

The Governor and his escort arrive at the terrace, where th[ey] are simultaneously met by the villagers, headed by the Mayor. [The] Governor announces that his sovereign has conferred on the Co[mte] the rank of Grand Officer and he proceeds to invest him with [the] decoration. The festival follows and after a number of d[ances] and games the villagers go to the park where the banquet has [been] prepared.

The Comte remains with the Governor and his son, Blinva[l,]

As night approaches Blinval returns and hides near the summer-house. When Germeuil appears to bid Nina farewell, Blinval asks him by what right he is in the castle grounds. The rivals draw swords and a violent duel ensues. Germeuil, disarmed, bares his breast to the victor's sword, when Nina runs up. Her cries of distress rouse the Comte and the Governor, who hasten to her side.

The Comte, furious at Germeuil's presence, orders him to leave. Blinval confesses that he was the aggressor. Nevertheless the Comte reiterates his order. The distracted lover, overwhelmed with grief and humiliation, runs to the terrace and throws himself into the sea.

Nina falls to the ground in a dead faint. Blinval and some sailors hurry to rescue Germeuil, while the tocsin is rung to summon the villagers.

The Comte runs to Nina and sets her down on the grassy bank. Slowly she opens her eyes, which look fixedly as if trying to remember what had happened. When her father tries to console her, she draws back in terror and flees from his presence. The Comte, filled with despair, refuses all attempts to calm him.

At last Nina recovers and seems less troubled. She smiles and believes she is dancing with Germeuil at the festival. But, suddenly conscious that he is absent, she searches for him, only to grow distressed at her failure.

Her father tries to approach her in the hope that she will recognize him, but she hides behind the villagers, then, opening the gate, flees into the countryside, signing to Elyse to follow. The bystanders, full of apprehension, hasten after her.

Act II. The countryside. To the right, the entrance to a great avenue; to the left a turf seat beneath a thicket. In the distance a path leading to the village.

Nina sleeps on the seat, guarded by the Comte, Georges, and Elyse. Nina begins to stir and the Comte is forced to leave, because he has become an object of horror to his daughter. Georges and Elyse gently lead him away.

Nina awakes and looks anxiously about, but smiles on seeing the posy beside her, which she will give to her lover when he returns. She listens for his steps, but he does not come.

Elyse returns with some young girls who wish to keep their mistress company. She asks them if they have seen her lover and, when they shake their heads, she asks them to pray with her for his return.

Afterwards Nina feels more hopeful and she gives the girls all the money in her purse. Since there is none left for Georgette, Nina offers her a diamond ring. The girl refuses it saying that she would be content with the plain gold ring which Nina wears on another finger. But Nina will not part with this, since it was a present from Germeuil. This love-token reminds Georgette of her own trouble and of the impossibility of her marrying Victor. Suddenly the strains of a bagpipe are heard.

It is Victor passing in the distance. He sees Georgette, yet dare not go near her. But Nina orders him to do so, promising to induce their parents to consent to the marriage. The lovers recover their spirits. Victor plays his bagpipe and the girls, led by Nina, begin to dance. But she soon grows weary and returns to her gloomy reflections. The Comte, who secretly watches all that takes place, is distressed to see his daughter resume her sad mood.

At this moment Georges and the Mayor return from the village; they seem to be engaged in important business. The former is furious on seeing Victor with Georgette. But Nina intervenes and points out to Georges that he will destroy his daughter's happiness. The Comte, greatly affected by her arguments, orders the Mayor to retire and signs to Georges to unite Victor and Georgette.

Nina sees the Comte and asks who he is. He tells her that he is her father. Immediately she recoils from him and hastens to the path leading to the village. She is accompanied by all except the Comte and Georges.

Now the Governor enters from the avenue; he is followed by Blinval and Germeuil. The Comte, astonished and delighted, runs towards Germeuil and embraces him, and calls him his son. Germeuil looks from one to the other as if he were dreaming.

At this juncture Georges announces Nina's return. Everyone hides. Elyse tells her that her beloved will soon return. She looks round and Germeuil emerges from the avenue. He walks slowly towards her and clasps her hands. But while Nina greets him with pleasure, she is still uncertain of his identity.

He leads her to the grassy seat and takes the posy he finds there. But she tells him that it is for her beloved. When he offers to return it she does not reply. He tells her about Germeuil, how they met and loved, and exchanged tokens, and then he kisses her. All at once she remembers everything and recognizes her father. She kneels before the Comte who unites her to Germeuil. She cannot believe in her happiness and warmly expresses her gratitude to the Governor and his son.

The Governor promises Germeuil his protection and everyone kneels and renders thanks to God.

The ballet ends with a gay festival.

*

Nina is a well-constructed dramatic ballet which might with advantage be revived. It is based on the comedy of the same name in one act—words by Marsollier, music by Dalayrac—first produced at the Théâtre de la Comédie Italienne, Paris, on May 15th, 1786. The text was soon afterwards translated into Italian and furnished with new music by Paisiello, when it was given in 1787, under the title *Nina o la Pazza per Amore,* first at the Caserta Theatre near Naples, and later at Naples itself.

The first act is of particular interest, for certain of the dramatic scenes have much in common with those in *Giselle.* Nina's sudden coming upon the duel between Blinval and Germeuil causes her to swoon from terror. On regaining consciousness she has lost her reason. She recovers a little and believes herself still to be dancing with Germeuil at the recent festival. This succession of incidents is so similar to those in the first act of *Giselle* as to suggest that Vernoy de Saint Georges received inspiration from *Nina* for some of his situations.

The *Journal de l'Empire,* reviewing *Nina,* declares: "This composition will add still more to the well-deserved reputation that M. Milon has won by his ballets *Les Noces de Gamache, Hero et Léandre, Ulysse,* and *L'Enlèvement des Sabines.*

"The music is by M. Persius, who has most tastefully selected from well-known melodies those best suited to the theme.

"Mlle. Bigottini played the part of Nina with considerable dramatic effect, feeling, and expression."

Nina had an excellent success and was continually revived until 1837.

*

Nina was first produced at London, at the King's Theatre, on May 4th, 1821, with Noblet in the title-role. John Ebers in his Reminiscences[2] has recorded an interesting impression of her performance.

"Nina is a young woman loving and beloved. An obstacle apparently permanent to the current of her affection, deprives her of her senses; and never was the touching sadness of the worst of

[2] *Seven Years of the King's Theatre.*

maladies more truly delineated than in the mute eloquence of Noblet's performance. The madness of Nina is not the phrenzied excitement of ungovernable despair, but the melancholy estrangement of a mind retaining, in its ruin, the sweetness and benevolence of its unshaken state. In portraying the workings of this affliction, not a gesture of this affliction, not a movement of Noblet was idly wasted. Everything was true to nature—everything contributed to the feeling of the piece. Her countenance, expressive as her action was graceful, kept time to every inflection of feeling, and harmonized with all the speaking graces of her deportment."

CHARLES DIDELOT

CHARLES LOUIS DIDELOT was born at Stockholm in 1767. His father, a Frenchman, was *premier danseur* at the Royal Theatre, Stockholm, and taught dancing to the pupils of the elementary class. He dreamed that his son would be crowned with laurels, for he was well-formed, strong, intelligent, and of lively disposition.

When only six years old Charles accompanied his father to the rehearsal-room, where he amused himself in endeavouring to copy the dancers' leaps and bounds. While still a child he caught small-pox, which marred his features, and the father saw all his hopes ruined.

Fate, however, changed the situation. The brother of the King of Sweden, Gustavus III, wished to appear at a Court masquerade as a Savoyard. At the last moment he could not find his marmot, and Didelot was asked to select from his pupils a small and intelligent boy who could take the part. There were, however, no little boys in the class, and, being desperate, the father had his son dressed in a skin with a marmot's head. Charles sustained the part in a droll manner that captivated all present.

This initial success decided Didelot to have his son trained as a dancer, and he placed him in the care of a dancing master called Frossard. The King, pleased with the child's progress, directed that he should be sent to Paris, to study under Dauberval. But, not long after Charles's arrival, Dauberval left the capital, and handed over his pupil to Lany, a dancing master of high repute. The latter, seeing that Charles's attire did not accord with those of his other pupils, who were drawn from the highest members of society, politely asked him to choose another master, and suggested Deshayes. The last named, delighted with his pupil's ability, eventually recommended him to Audinot, director of the Théâtre de l'Ambigu, who promptly engaged him. Charles was then twelve years old.

A little later King Gustavus visited Paris and, having seen Didelot dance, suggested that he should go back to Sweden. In 1781 he

13

returned to Stockholm, where he executed some *pas* of his own composition, which pleased greatly. As a consequence, he, despite his youth, was charged to compose the dances for a ballet called *Freya,* which achieved considerable success.

He was then again sent to Paris where he studied first under Noverre and later with Auguste Vestris. The celebrated Noverre made a contract with Didelot for London, by which he received the sum of £400 for the season. The latter produced there his own ballet *Richard Cœur de Lion,* and, on account of its favourable reception, his contract was renewed for several years.

Didelot made his first appearance at the Paris Opera in 1790, with Mlle. Guimard, in Maximilien Gardel's ballet *Le Premier Navigateur.* He then made a short appearance at the Théâtre Montansier, and went to Lyon and London, where he was well received. Unfortunately, the performances given at the Montansier had a better reception than those given at the State Theatre, and Didelot was accused of conspiracy and put in prison. Happily influential persons interested themselves in his case and secured his release.

In 1796 Didelot was back in London, where he produced his best ballet, *Flore et Zéphire,* which earned for him a great reputation. In this production, Didelot, for the first time, made use of wires for the purpose of enabling dancers to simulate aerial flight, producing effects which astonished the audience. He returned to Paris and again danced with Mlle. Guimard at the Opera, and also appeared at Bordeaux and Lyon.

In 1801 Paul I of Russia commanded the Director of the Imperial Theatres to engage Didelot in the triple capacity of dancer, *maître de ballet,* and professor of dancing. In September he arrived at St. Petersburg, where he contributed considerably to the development of the national ballet. He produced *Apollo and Daphnis* in 1802, then *Faun and Hamadryad, Cupid and Psyche, Laura and Henry,* and *Roland and Morgana.* His ballets did not require special funds from the directorate, and they attracted a large public, partly on account of their beauty, partly on account of the novelty of their stage effects.

Didelot married a French dancer, Rose Colinette, well known in Russia, who bore him a son, called Charles, like his father. He became a talented dancer, but was forced to give up his career as the result of ill health.

However, notwithstanding his fame and excellent position in Russia, Didelot longed to be acclaimed in Paris as a *maître de ballet.* Accordingly, in 1811, he set out for that capital, but on his journey from St. Petersburg to Lübeck he suffered shipwreck, lost all his music, and narrowly escaped with his life.

He went to London, where he produced several ballets, yet always cherished his ambition to show his *Flore et Zéphire* at Paris; but Gardel, who was in high favour at the Opera, was jealous of the ballet's renown, and, as a result of his intrigues, months, even years, passed before Didelot achieved his aim. The management having raised all manner of polite objections, finally informed him that his ballet would be too expensive to mount, and that they could not produce it unless he would guarantee to pay all the expenses in advance.

Didelot was much offended, but agreed. Now it was necessary to have a special scene made to conceal the wires used for the effects of flying. The scene was painted, but some days later at the dress rehearsal he was astonished to see it used as the setting for a short opera, which was to precede the ballet. He protested and quarrelled, but without avail. His patience exhausted, he determined to leave Paris; but his friends, promising him success, forced him to remain.

Eventually the ballet was produced on December 12th, 1815, and its reception compensated the weary *maître de ballet* for all his sufferings. It was much admired, and Louis XVIII, who was present, invited Didelot to his box and commanded him to be given a present of 2,000 francs.

But when the choreographer went to the treasurer he received a bill for expenses amounting to 2,400 francs, so that, instead of having money to receive, he owed 400 francs. Didelot paid the account, and, though offered a profitable engagement at the Opera, returned to Russia, being afraid of the omnipotent Gardel.

Didelot arrived at St. Petersburg in 1816 and was appointed *premier maître de ballet*. During his second period he produced more than twenty ballets: *Atys and Galatea* (1816), *The Unexpected Return* (1817), *The Young Dairymaid* (1817), *Carlos and Rosalba* (1817), *The Hungarian Hut* (1817), *Theseus and Ariadne* (1817), *Flore et Zéphire* (1818), *The Young Girl from the Island* (1818), *Faun and Hamadryad* (revived 1818), *Hunting Adventures* (1818, at Hermitage Theatre), *The Caliph of Bagdad* (1818), *Raoul de Crequis* (1818), *Hensi and Tao* (1819), *Laura and Henry* (revived 1819), *Charles and Lisbeth* (1820), *Cora and Alonzo* (1820), *Alceste* (1821), *Roland and Morgana* (revived 1821), *The Wooden Leg* (1821), *The Prisoner of the Caucasus* (1823), *Phædra and Hippolytus* (1825), and *Dido* (1827).

Didelot retired in 1829 owing to a quarrel with Prince Gagarin,

the director of the Imperial Theatres. At a certain performance
the interval between the acts was too long and the Prince commanded the next act to begin earlier and the dancers to change
their costumes quicker. Didelot received the order haughtily, and
in consequence the Prince threatened him with arrest. The
maître de ballet gave way, but the next day tendered his resignation, which was accepted.

In 1836 Didelot's health showed signs of failing and he went to
South Russia to recuperate. On November 1st he was taken seriously ill at Kiev, where he died six days later.

*

What were the particular attractions of Didelot's ballets? Contemporary Russian writers paid high tributes to the master. Pushkin himself declared that "Didelot's ballets are invested with a rich
imaginative quality and an amazing charm." But none of those
writers has left a prose picture of his ballets which enables us to
visualize one.

An English critic who witnessed the performance of Didelot's
La Reine de Golconde at the King's Theatre, London, in June,
1812, has summed up his impressions thus: "The art of Mr. Didelot is admirably displayed in his living pictures—every part of his
scene is animated—below, above, everywhere we see life and motion, and every creature, as well as every part of the decoration, is
employed or placed as the subject requires. The eye is not only attracted by the variety, the business, the interest of the spectacle, but
when the first emotion of agreeable surprise is gone off, the mind
rests upon the investigation of the contrivance with new delight."

Didelot remained faithful to the lessons he imbibed from Noverre; he omitted no opportunity of acquiring knowledge which
he might turn to account in the composition of his ballets. He
was well read and versatile, for he not only composed the dances
for his ballets, but wrote the synopses, which he often provided
with a preface setting forth his theories of production; selected the
music; planned the scenery and costumes, with or without the collaboration of artists; and devised the machinery for the realization
of a stage effect he had visualized. He worked quickly and effi-
ciently, and with a careful regard for style-atmosphere.

He selected his themes from a variety of sources. Some were derived from the pages of Greek mythology, some were based on historical episodes, others were taken from contemporary life. He
based one of his ballets on Racine's *Phèdre,* and another on Pushkin's *The Prisoner of the Caucasus.* Sometimes he chose a theme

which afforded opportunities for exotic dances; for instance, *Cora and Alonzo* deals with the customs and pastimes of Peru, while *Hensi and Tao* is concerned with China.

In the actual composition of his ballets, Didelot insisted on technique being subordinated to the exigencies of the theme. Dances were not introduced as a mere excuse for the execution of *tours de force,* but only when contributory to the action. He disliked the "star" system and devised something of interest for each member of the company. He paid particular attention to mime so that the actions of the dancers should be clearly understood by all.

He had a particular aptitude for groups which he planned with loving care to form attractive patterns, the effect being sometimes suggested by a famous painting or piece of sculpture. For instance, in the second act of *Hunting Adventures,* he reproduced a painting by Teniers in the Hermitage Collection. He also made use of mirrors on the stage, so placed that the spectators could see the dancers from two viewpoints.

Didelot introduced several reforms. He is credited with the invention, during his first years in Paris, of fleshings, and, in *Ariane et Bacchus,* in which he portrayed Bacchus, he appeared at the Opera wearing fleshings, with a tiger's skin over one shoulder and a garland of vine-leaves about his head. In *Corisande,* in which he took the part of a Sylph, he appeared in a muslin tunic.

Mention has been made of Didelot's invention of "flying" by means of wires. He continually developed this effect during his long residence at St. Petersburg. In his early ballets he used only one or two "flying" dancers; later, however, he employed numbers of "flying" dancers who, at a given moment, formed a group which harmonized with the other groups on the stage. In *Alceste,* demons flew from the depths of the scene to above the footlights, and waved their flaming torches over the spectators in the stalls. In *Cupid and Psyche,* given at the Hermitage Theatre in honour of the Peace of Tilsit, Didelot made Venus appear in an aerial chariot drawn, apparently, by fifty doves. Each bird was fitted with an elastic belt carrying a length of fine wire which was attached to the car.

Apart from his talents as a choreographer, Didelot was a fine dancer and a teacher of rare ability. Here is a prose portrait of him. A Russian contemporary, describing a *ballet-divertissement* given in December, 1806, mentions a *pas de deux* performed by Didelot and Ikonina, respectively as Apollo and Diana. He declares that the famous dancer was "as thin as a skeleton, had a very long red nose, wore a light-red wig with a laurel wreath on his head, and danced with a lyre in his hand, with great success."

Didelot was always in a bustle and his expression constantly varied. He was very excitable and became quite carried away by his emotions when in the throes of composition. The slightest opposition to his wishes or failure to realize his conception of a step would rouse him to ungovernable fury, as the following example will serve to show. One day, while rehearsing a ballet at the Hermitage Theatre, he noticed that one of the dancers had no lyre. Mad with rage he rushed out of the room and along the Nevsky Prospect until he reached the property store, then, having seized a lyre, he dashed back again.

In the classroom he ruled his subjects with a rod of iron. According to A. Y. Golovacheva-Panaeva, "the children returned home with bruises on their arms and legs; even his son was not exempt from such treatment".

"It was very amusing," she continues, "to see Didelot behind the scenes watching his pupils. Sometimes he swayed from side to side, smiled, and took mincing steps and stamped his foot. But when the little pupils danced he shook his fist at them, and, if they missed the figures, he made their lives a misery. He pounced on them like a hawk, pulled their hair or ears, and if any ran away he gave them a kick which sent them flying. Even the solo dancers suffered from him. Being applauded, a dancer went behind the scenes, when Didelot seized her by the shoulders, shook her with all his might and, having given her a punch in the back, pushed her on to the stage as if she were recalled.[1]"

Outside the theatre Didelot was very kind to his pupils, and helped and kissed those whom he had punched but an hour before. These were the conditions under which the ballet was formed and, however cruel and unjustifiable they may seem, it is of interest to note that the members of the *corps de ballet* were uniformly talented. The "flying" of some of the groups was wonderful; the dancers could soar forward and stop at the very edge of the footlights. Apart from the *corps de ballet,* Didelot formed many talented soloists such as Danilova, Istomina, Likhutina, Zubova, and Teleshova.

Didelot exerted a great influence on the development of the Russian Ballet, so much so that the history of Russian choreography may be divided into two periods—before Didelot, and after Didelot.

[1] Quoted Pleshchayev. *Nash Balet.*

FLORE ET ZÉPHIRE [2]

Ballet-Divertissement in 1 *Act. Book: C. L. Didelot. Music: Cesare Bossi. Scenery and machinery: Liparotti. Choreography: C. L. Didelot. First produced: King's Theatre, London, July 7th, 1796.*

CHARACTERS

Cleonisa, a nymph	MME. HILLIGSBERG
Flora, a nymph	MME. ROSE
Shepherdesses . . . . . . {	MLLE. PARISOT
	MME. BOSSI
Zephyrus	M. DIDELOT
Cupid	MASTER MENAGE
A little cupid	MISS HILL

Shepherds and Shepherdesses.

Cleonisa is discovered, sleeping on a grassy bank. Zephyrus descends from Heaven, holding Cupid in his arms. He begs him to put an end to his sufferings by inspiring Chloris with the same flame that consumes him. Here, he expresses, Chloris comes every morning; this is the grove she tends; this rose tree her own hand waters every day. But while admiring the tree, he perceives Cleonisa, and the inconstant Zephyrus already becomes unfaithful. Cupid reminds him of Chloris, but she is absent, and Cleonisa is present. Zephyrus cannot resist the pleasure of awakening her, and begs Cupid to watch for the coming of Chloris. Cupid complies, but warns him that he will repent his inconstancy.

Zephyrus, unmoved, continues to flutter about Cleonisa, and, with the motion of his painted wings, wantonly agitates her flaxen tresses. The nymph awakes, and Zephyrus boldly declares his passion, but with little success. The sportive Cleonisa answers with a laugh, and only thinks of dancing. Zephyrus is obliged to submit to her caprice and they mutually join in a measure. Suddenly the nymph stops and Zephyrus, amazed at her thoughtful countenance, inquires the reason. She has seen his shadow on the wall of a temple, and conceives the plan of drawing the contours of it.

She desires Zephyrus to resume the same attitude. He yields to her entreaties. His shadow appears again, and Cleonisa, with a bodkin, delineates the outline.

[2] The description of this ballet which follows is a condensed version of a contemporary synopsis.

Cupid runs in to inform Zephyrus that Chloris is near. Zephyrus takes to flight, leaving Cleonisa astonished, and her task unfinished.

She looks after him and seems divided between anger and mirth at his abrupt departure; but her good humour prevails, for she is delighted with her discovery of the art of painting. She departs for Mount Helicon to render homage to the God of Arts for his gift.

Chloris arrives, with a vase on her head and a pruning-knife in her hand. She gazes on her beloved rose tree, and fills her vase, then waters the plant, dancing round it the while. She remarks the image of Zephyrus and seems to say: "How charming he would be, had he no wings."

Suddenly the rose tree opens, Cupid springs out of it, and the amazed Chloris is encircled by the fires of the God, who disappears as quickly as he came. The marvel is repeated and Chloris endeavours to extinguish the torch carried by the God. But it is too late, for already her heart is warmed with the flame of love. She refills her vase and then feels a touch on her arm. She turns and perceives Zephyrus.

Zephyrus declares his passion and promises to love her for ever. But she reminds him that he is a winged being. Cupid, overhearing her, devises a plan at once to punish Zephyrus for his inconstancy and complete his happiness. He runs in, pulls off Zephyrus's wings, and presents them to Chloris. Zephyrus cries out with pain and, seeing his wings in Cupid's hands, dashes forward to recover them; but a band of little cupids bar his way while Cupid fastens the wings to Chloris's shoulders. She, wishing to see what the sky is like, bids Zephyrus good-bye, and soars into the air.

Zephyrus, wingless, cannot follow her, and, distressed at his double loss, reproaches Cupid and threatens to destroy the empire of flowers. Cupid laughs at his threats and offers to restore him to happiness, if he will engage to be constant. Zephyrus promises, but Cupid demands an oath, which the God must write on the wall of the temple. At Cupid's dictation Zephyrus swears to be constant if Chloris, henceforth to be Flora, agrees to share with him the empire of flowers, and to receive immortality.

Cupid embraces Zephyrus and declares that Chloris will soon be in his arms. Hardly has he spoken when the nymph is seen flying in the air. Zephyrus and Cupid hide behind a fountain.

Chloris descends to earth and is surprised to find neither Cupid nor her lover. She runs to the fountain, the basin of which serves her as a mirror, and views her image with delight. Then Zephyrus comes from his hiding-place and grasps the tips of her wings, while Cupid, standing before her, shows her the oath taken by the God, whose happiness she alone can complete. She accepts Zephyrus's love with delight.

The amorous couple express their passion in a dance, and now Flora returns Zephyrus his wings, since he swears to use them only to fly after her.

Shepherds and shepherdesses come and congratulate the happy pair. Cleonisa presses Flora in her arms and the ballet ends with a general dance.

*

Flore et Zéphire, as already stated, is noted for being the first ballet in which wires were used to enable the dancers to simulate aerial flight. The production achieved a great success and was frequently revived.

I have not been able to discover an account of the first performance of this ballet, which records the effect of this invention upon the audience. Here, however, is an account of the first performance of the ballet at Paris, at the Opera, in 1815, as reported in the *Journal des Débats*.[3]

"These kinds of works do not lend themselves to a close analysis; this ballet is a series of pictures, attractive scenes, and elegant poses; and of gay, ethereal, and voluptuous movements. It is easier to enjoy in advance the pleasure of the dancer's performance; it is sufficient to recapitulate the names of the distinguished artistes who take part in the ballet. There is Albert who plays Zéphire—and no other dancer is worthier than he to represent that God whom poets invest with all the graces of youth and beauty—gliding up to the sky with an ethereal grace. Such a picture which hitherto has been conceived in the imagination only was yesterday realized before the astonished eyes of the spectators.

"There have often been admirable flights at the Opera. In *Psyche,* for instance, another Zéphire bore Psyche to the Palace of Love and vanished with her amid the clouds. The machine was well devised and produced an excellent effect; but you see, or imagine you see, the apparatus. Didelot's Zéphire is much more wonderful: alone, apart, without any followers to distract the attention, he rises from the centre of the stage by his own strength; with disdainful foot he spurns the earth that he forsakes, soars for several minutes into space, grazes with the tips of his wings the greenish tops of the trees, and at last majestically disappears amid the azure vault.

[3] December 14th, 1815.

"At a spectacle so novel and at which all the witnesses are still far from fathoming the secret, the public could not control its emotion; the applause was prolonged far into the interval and broke out with redoubled vigour when Zéphire, returning in the same way as he ascended, rose a second time bearing Flore in his arms. This marvel, even more striking than the first, raised the enthusiasm to its height.

"The elder Mlle. Gosselin is naturally Flore when Albert is Zéphire. The younger Mlle. Gosselin is in turn Venus and Shepherdess, and always equally good in her double role. Mlle. Delisle has the figure of a Bacchante, and admirably expresses mad passion."

Flore et Zéphire was first produced at St. Petersburg, at the Hermitage Theatre in January, 1808.

*

It is of interest to note that *Flore et Zéphire* was the ballet in which Marie Taglioni made her first bow to an English audience. This event took place at the King's Theatre, London, on June 3rd, 1830.

The Times' critic asserts that the music by Venua [4] "is generally of inferior merit. In other respects it is a very pleasing spectacle, being, unlike the greater number of mythological ballets, animated throughout. It has also the merit of being not too long." [5]

Of Taglioni the same writer observes: "Supreme elegance, grace, picturesque attitudes, and lightness of step, are the characteristics of her style of dancing. Her person is rather tall, slender, and well formed; but we find that her other personal attractions have been greatly exaggerated in some of the descriptions of them which we have seen in both French and English papers. Mademoiselle Taglioni met with a most favourable reception, and received and deserved great applause throughout her dancing. The house was crowded to excess before the rising of the curtain."

The *Examiner* [6] declares: "Signora Taglioni is the most perfect specimen of grace and elegance, as a dancer, we ever beheld. Her movements are all a series of classical studies. Not only does it seem a matter of perfect indifference whether she be standing on one foot or on two feet, but every evolution is accomplished with such extraordinary ease, and with the airiness of thistledown, that it

[4] The original music by Bossi was evidently not retained.
[5] June 4th, 1830.
[6] June 6th, 1830.

would scarcely have increased our wonder and delight had she ascended like a spirit."

There are no engravings of *Flore et Zéphire,* although there are some lithographs by Chalon showing Taglioni as Flore. It is possible, however, to gain some interesting impressions respecting the ballet from the bitter caricatures of Taglioni and her partner by W. M. Thackeray in his *Flore et Zephyr, Ballet Mythologique,* published under the *nom de plume* "Théophile Wagstaff" at Paris, 1836.

SALVATORE VIGANÒ

SALVATORE VIGANÒ was born at Naples on March 25th,
1769. He came of a family of dancers, for his father, Onorato,
was a well-known dancer and *maître de ballet,* and his father's
brothers were dancers likewise. His mother was also a dancer, and
the sister of the famous composer Boccherini.

Salvatore, although he received a strictly professional education,
did not at first display any particular disposition for the dance; he
was more interested in literature; and, had he concentrated on that
branch of the arts, he might, in the opinion of Monti, have become
a second Ariosto. From his mother, Salvatore inherited a great
love for music, of which he made a close study, having formed a
transitory ambition to become a composer like his uncle. At the
age of seventeen he composed an *intermezzo* which was performed at Rome. But, gradually the dance claimed his interest,
and he made his *début* at that city in women's roles, for at Rome
women were still prohibited from taking part in theatrical representations.

He accompanied his uncle, Giovanni, to Madrid, in order to take
part in the festivals organised in connection with the coronation of
Charles IV. There he became enamoured of a beautiful Spanish
dancer, called Maria Medina, whom he married. He also made the
acquaintance of Dauberval who, charmed with the young man,
induced him and his wife to accompany him to London.

Doubtless it was from Dauberval that he received his first inspiration for his dance dramas, for that choreographer, a pupil of
Noverre, attached the greatest importance to mime, and always
sought to make his dances expressive of the theme. As he observed,
"it is not enough for me to please the eye, I wish to interest the
heart." [1]

In 1790 Viganò returned to Italy and danced at the San Samuele
Theatre, Venice, where his father was director. The following

[1] Quoted Blasis (C.) *Traité de la Danse,* 1820.

24

year he produced on that stage his first ballet, *Raul, Signor de Crequi*. In 1792 he produced Dauberval's comedy-ballet, *La Fille Mal Gardée*.

In 1793, Viganò and his wife visited Vienna, where they gave a series of performances which caused a furore. Maria Medina danced in a dress of clinging semitransparent material which revealed to advantage the lovely proportions of her figure. Her dancing had a voluptuous quality which drew the town, and shopkeepers of every kind attempted to profit by her popularity by styling the best of their products *à la Viganò*. The couple remained at Vienna until 1795 when they made a tour of central Europe. They returned to Italy about 1798, and again went to Vienna where they remained until 1803. During this period Viganò composed further ballets, such as *La Figlia dell' Aria, I Giochi Istmici,* and *Il Noce di Benevente*.

At this period Viganò became estranged from his wife and left for Milan, where he composed *Coriolano, Gli Spagnuoli all' isola Cristina,* and *Sammete e Tamiri;* then *Ippotoo* at Padua (1809), and *Gli Strelizzi* at Venice (1809). In this last named ballet he began to strike out a new road. Instead of the ballet consisting of mimed scenes varied with dances, he conceived the plan of expressing the theme in terms of dramatic movement harmonised exactly with the rhythm and colour of the music.

From 1812 Viganò lived permanently in Milan where he was appointed *maître de ballet* at the Scala, in succession to Gaetano Gioja. A lady admirer left him a considerable fortune, and, his father having died, he resolved to dance no longer himself but concentrate all his energies on attempting to realise his theories. He seems to have worked slowly, methodically, and with difficulty. Once in the throes of composition, he rehearsed his artistes regardless of fatigue or the passing of time, until he was satisfied with the effect he wished to produce. Stendhal informs us that a particular manifestation of Viganò's genius was his patience. "Surrounded by eighty dancers on the stage of the Scala, with an orchestra of ten musicians at his feet, he composes and pitilessly rehearses the whole afternoon ten bars of his ballet which seem to him to be lacking in some particular.[1]" Stendhal also tells us that Viganò began his *Dedalo e Icare* on August 4th (1818) and completed it on December 25th, "by rehearsing from ten in the morning to six, and from ten at night to four in the morning.[2]"

Viganò's ballets seem to have been in the nature of dance dramas. The principal sources of information regarding his pro-

[2] *Rome, Naples et Florence.*

ductions are his biography, by Carlo Ritorni[3], and the essays and letters of Stendhal, his fervent admirer. For pictorial evidence we have the wonderful scenic designs by Sanquirico, wherein the grouping of the figures suggests that the artist saw the rehearsals, or was fully conversant with Viganò's intentions.

In Viganò's ballets no longer did the dancers express some emotion with their arms all disposed at the same height, a form of expression which Noverre had sought to abolish; instead the choreographer presented an animated and continually changing picture in which each dancer, each unit, *seemed* to be actuated by his or her own feelings, and yet contributed to form a striking whole. Remember, too, that all these changing poses and groupings were most delicately attuned to the mood and rhythm of the music.

But Viganò's compositions remained dominated by his classical education. Whatever the period or the costumes demanded by the theme, the gestures and attitudes of the dancers are those of the sculptures and paintings bequeathed to us by the artists of ancient Greece and Rome.

There can be no doubt about Viganò's genius for composition and dramatic effect; one is immediately sensible of those qualities on reading the programmes of his ballets. It requires no great effort of the imagination to picture the attitudes that might result from the emotions engendered by the development of the action.

As to the effect of his ballets, Stendhal, referring to *Prometeo,* declares: "Doubtless there are parts in *Prometeo* which are absurd, but, after ten years, the memory of it is as fresh as on the first day, and still astounds me.[4]" Again, in a letter to the Baron de Mareste, Stendhal, describing *I Titani,* asserts: "Two great men, that is to say, Monti and I, are raving about the first two acts. . . . In the fourth, the evils which come out of the iron vase, which contains bracelets, a sword, and a diadem . . . are the highest form of art[5]." If we were to seek a modern analogy it is possible that certain portions of Fokine's *Don Juan* and *L'Épreuve d'Amour,* of Massine's *Choreartium* and *Symphonie Fantastique,* and of Jooss's *Green Table* and *The Mirror* would have affinities with the compositions of Viganò.

Yet there were not wanting critics who did not always see "eye to eye" with Viganò. Rossini complained to Stendhal that Viganò's ballets contained "too much mime and not enough dancing."

[3] *Commentarii della Vita e delle Opere Coredrammatiche di Salvatore Viganò,* Milan, 1838.
[4] *Op. cit.*
[5] Letter dated November 2nd, 1819.

Petracci, in his pamphlet on *La Vestale,* supposes a dialogue between Viganò and a stranger. When the latter reproaches the choreographer for producing ballets in which the dancers do not dance, he replies that there are dances in all his ballets when the theme demands them, and instances the Ritual Dance in *La Vestale* and the Furlana in *Otello.* He also points out that the mimed scenes are not "walked" but danced. He admits that he has considerably curtailed the *pas de deux* and *soli* beloved of the French school, but excuses this on the ground that they tend to retard the development of the action.

The music of Viganò's ballets is rarely, if ever, by one composer. The score of a ballet consists of a skilful piecing together of airs drawn from the work of such composers as Haydn, Mozart, Beethoven, Rossini, and Spontini, interpolated with portions written by contemporary composers of another grade.[6] Viganò's musical training stood him in good stead; indeed, when he could not find a piece of music to suit his purpose, he would compose the melody himself.

He had an excellent company of artistes at the Scala, headed by the famous dancer-mime, Antonia Pallerini, and Nicola Molinari; and for scene-designer he had Alessandro Sanquirico, whose quality may be judged from an examination of the reproductions of his settings which follow.

Viganò composed over 40 ballets, the majority being dance dramas comprising from three to six acts. His best known works are *Il Noce di Benevente, Gli Strelizzi* (1809), *Dedalo* (1813), *Prometeo* (1813), *Mirra* (1817), *Psammi, Re d'Egitto* (1817), *Otello* (1818), *La Spada di Kenneth* (1818), *La Vestale* (1818), and *I Titani* (1819).

Viganò died from an affection of the lungs on August 18th, 1821. He was accorded an impressive funeral and the most famous poets of Italy vied with each other in composing epitaphs in honour of his achievements. So passed the inventor of the dance drama, whose tomb bears the inscription "the greatest of all choreographers," and whose imaginative genius Stendhal likened to that of Shakespeare.

[6] For instance, the score of *La Vestale* includes music by Weigl, Lichtental, Rossini, Viganò, Spontini, Beethoven, Mozart, and Carafa.

GLI STRELIZZI [7]

Mimodrama in 6 Acts. Book: Salvatore Viganò. Scenery: Alessandro Sanquirico. Choreography: Salvatore Viganò. First produced: Teatro La Fenice, Venice, 1809.

CHARACTERS

Peter I, Tsar of Russia	M. Salvatore Vigano
Princess Sophia, Regent, his sister .	M. Gaetana Abrami
Shukanin, Commander of the Streletsy	M. Antonio Silei
Elizabeth, his daughter, in love with the Tsar	Mlle. Amalia Muzzarelli-Cesari
Lefort, Peter's minister and confidant	M. Luigi Gucci

Nobles, Ladies, Officers and Men of the Streletsy, German Officers and Soldiers, Citizens, etc.

The action passes at Moscow.

Act I. A large courtyard in the Kreml, Moscow. On one side can be seen the windows of the inner apartments.

Princess Sophia, standing at the head of a staircase, receives through Shukanin the homage of the *Streletsy,* who wish her to become Queen. Delighted, she accepts a loyal address, and presents to one of the principal officers a parchment inscribed with the honours she proposes to confer upon them.

Suddenly cannon shots are heard and an officer announces the arrival of the Tsar. The company, much against their will, are obliged to make obeisance to him.

The Tsar enters accompanied by soldiers and citizens. He thanks the German troops for having crushed the revolt of the Ukranian *Streletsy* and rewards them with honours. The *Streletsy* are presented to him as prisoners of war. He ignores them and invites the nobles and ladies to a great feast, then leaves with his sister. The act concludes with a dance by the soldiers.

Act II. The banqueting-hall in the Kreml. The main scene is masked by a curtain.

Princess Sophia enters in a state of great agitation to converse

[7] *The Streletsy.* A Russian word meaning, literally, Archers. It implies the standing army.

with Shukanin, who almost immediately arrives with his daughter, Elizabeth, who is the Tsar's mistress. The Princess entreats the minister to keep his promise and make her Tsarina, and gossips about his daughter's friendship with the Tsar. Peter comes in and, out of friendship for Elizabeth, requests his sister to confer on Shukanin the collar of the Order of Saint Andrew.

The Princess, inwardly raging, agrees. Shukanin, although he detests Peter, pretends to be deeply grateful for the honour conferred upon him. The Tsar and Elizabeth do not conceal their mutual affection for each other.

Lefort enters and declares the banquet ready. At this juncture the curtain rises and reveals the banqueting hall filled with the nobility. Everyone toasts the Tsar and then the dances begin. Peter and Elizabeth leave in opposite directions and a little later return in European costume, and dance a *pas de deux*. Some members of the guests take umbrage at the Tsar's appearing in foreign dress, but take care not to voice their disapproval.

During the dance the Princess accidentally drops a letter. The Tsar signs to Lefort to bring it to him. Peter reads the letter and sees that it is a list of conspirators. The Tsar, greatly disturbed, stops the dancing and orders everyone to leave. Amid great excitement the guests depart, the adherents of the Regent assuring her of their fidelity.

Act III. Shukanin's private chamber in the Kreml.

Shukanin enters with Elizabeth. He orders her to renounce her royal lover and kill him with a dagger which he gives her. When she refuses, her father threatens to kill the Tsar himself. While they are arguing, Peter is announced. The minister hurriedly departs and Elizabeth is left in great confusion to meet her lover.

The Tsar goes to kiss her, but she is so upset that she does not respond with her usual tenderness. Saddened by his cold reception Peter sits in an armchair, holding his head in his hands. Shukanin appears from behind a door and aims a pistol at the Tsar. Elizabeth, seeing her father, snatches the pistol from his hands. But the weapon goes off, and the Tsar and those who have hurried to his assistance, seeing the pistol in Elizabeth's hand, conclude that she had attempted to kill him. Their suspicions are confirmed by Shukanin, who basely accuses his daughter of having attempted the life of the Tsar. Peter orders her to be imprisoned, although she tearfully protests her love for him.

Act IV. A corridor leading to the prison.

The jailer receives Elizabeth and, moved by her charm and distress, gives her materials to write a letter to the Tsar. While she is engaged in writing the letter, he enters. Since she cannot accuse her own father, she entreats Peter to sign a pardon for an unknown person, whose name she will disclose later, promising that when the document is signed she will reveal the truth.

He refuses to sign a pardon, but orders Elizabeth to be liberated, and restores her to the Court circle.

Act V. A large underground hall in the Kreml.

The chief officers of the *Streletsy* are assembled to plot the death of the Tsar. Among the conspirators are Peter and Lefort, disguised as *Streletsy*. Shukanin proposes that the Tsar shall be stabbed and offers a dagger for the purpose. But only one of the conspirators agrees to undertake the deed. When Peter sees this lack of determination, he reveals his presence to the *Streletsy,* who are so afraid that they permit him to leave with Lefort.

No sooner has the Tsar departed than the *Streletsy* swear to kill him. Suddenly they hear the beating of drums and the screams of the crowd gathered about the Kreml. Believing that the people have revolted, they decide to join them.

Act VI. A square in Moscow.

Amid the noise of tumult the square fills with people, led by the *Streletsy*. But Peter's troops arrive and, after a fight, capture the *Streletsy*.

The Tsar orders the prisoners to be executed, but Elizabeth arrives and entreats him to spare her father's life. He consents and commands that Princess Sophia and the chiefs of the *Streletsy* shall be banished to Siberia, while Shukanin and his daughter must leave the country. He tells Elizabeth that he had intended to marry her, but must renounce his plan now that he knows that her father had attempted to kill him.

The confusion of the vanquished, the surprise of the victors, the mortification of Shukanin and the Princess, and the contrast between the two lovers form a striking group with which the action ends.

OTELLO

Ballet in 5 Acts. Book: Salvatore Viganò. Scenery: Alessandro Sanquirico. Choreography: Salvatore Viganò. First produced: Teatro alla Scala, Milan, February 6th, 1818.

CHARACTERS

The Doge . . . . M. CARLO BIANCIARDI
Brabanzio, a Venetian nobleman . M. CARLO NICHLI
Othello, General of the Venetian Republic . . . . M. NICOLA MOLINARI
Cassio, Othello's lieutenant . . M. FILIPPO CIOTTI
Iago, Othello's officer . . . . M. GIUSEPPE BOCCI
Rodrigo, a Venetian nobleman . . M. PIETRO TRIGAMBI
Montano, Othello's predecessor . . M. GIROLAMO PALLERINI
Desdemona, Brabanzio's daughter and Othello's wife . . . . MME. ANTONIA PALLERINI
Emilia, Desdemona's confidential maid . . . . MLLE. MARIA BOCCI
Venetian Ladies, Procurators, Senators, Gondoliers, Sailors, Guards, Citizens, etc.

The action takes place in Venice.

Act I. A small piazza in Venice. On one side the Ducal Palace, on the other several buildings. In the background the lagoon covered with small craft, some surrounding Othello's galleon.

Amid the booming of cannon and the plaudits of the citizens, Othello disembarks from his galleon, fresh from his victory at Cyprus. Desdemona, his wife, escorted by numerous friends, goes to welcome him. When they have exchanged greetings, Othello leaves for the Ducal Palace, there to give an account of his battle to the Doge and the Senate.

Meanwhile, the citizens give expression to their joy in dances. Rodrigo alone holds aloof from the celebrations for, passionately in love with Desdemona, he sees all his hopes shattered with the return of Othello. Nevertheless, he seizes a favourable opportunity to declare his love to Desdemona, and the more distant her manner grows, the more he urges his suit.

Othello returns with the Doge and Senators who nominate him Governor of Cyprus. The Doge and Senators depart and Othello tenderly embraces his wife, a demonstration which moves all present. Then the couple, at the request of their friends, return to their palace, acclaimed by the crowd.

Act II. A street leading to Othello's palace.

Rodrigo and Montano are seen in deep conversation; they are jealous of Othello's success. Iago, who also hates Othello in secret, joins in the conversation in the hope of furthering his plans. He tells Rodrigo that Desdemona has refused his suit because she loves Cassio, and he urges him to advise Othello of his wife's unfaithfulness, so that in a moment of jealousy he may commit an act which will ruin both his reputation and his position, which should belong to Montano. The last named at first disapproves of the plan, but in the end is persuaded to join in the conspiracy.

Cassio is seen to leave Othello's palace and Iago, wishing to fan Rodrigo's hate, cries: "Look! Here comes the elegant and fortunate lover." "Truly," sneers Rodrigo, "he looks more the gallant than the soldier."

Cassio pales with anger at this insult and in an instant swords are drawn. Iago treacherously tries to stab Cassio in the back, but Montano prevents him from doing so. The noise of the conflict causes a crowd to collect and finally Othello himself appears on the scene. He demands to know who began the fight. "Cassio," replies Iago. Othello, highly indignant that such a brawl should take place before his palace, orders the Guard to arrest Cassio. He recommends the wounded Rodrigo to Montano and departs.

Iago secretly rejoices at Cassio's distress, then, pretending to take pity upon him, urges him to enlist the help of Desdemona, who can obtain anything from her husband. Cassio thanks Iago and, taking affectionate leave of him, hastens to plead his cause before Desdemona. Iago, delighted at having deceived Cassio, enters Othello's palace.

Act II. A garden of Othello's palace.

Slaves are busily engaged in preparing for their master's arrival. Iago enters and asks for Emilia, who is evidently in love with him, while he, deceiving her with promises of marriage, induces her to consent to arrange a meeting between her mistress and Cassio.

Now come Othello and Desdemona, accompanied by Brabanzio and several ladies and gentlemen. After partaking of refreshment all save Othello and Iago leave for the dance to be given in celebration of the victory.

Iago converses with Othello and seizes the opportunity to hint at his wife's infidelity and her love for Cassio. At this moment the last named is announced. Iago suggests to Othello that they hide behind a fountain. No sooner are they concealed than Emilia, meeting Cassio, leads him to Desdemona's chamber. Othello, enraged, wishes to follow, but Iago restrains him.

Desdemona emerges from the room. She bids Cassio farewell and promises to do all in her power to gain his pardon. Cassio kisses her hand in gratitude and leaves, accompanied by Emilia.

Desdemona seeks for Othello and finds him in a corner in earnest conversation with Iago. Othello is about to accuse his wife when Brabanzio arrives. Thwarted of his purpose Othello grinds his teeth and falls fainting to the floor. Everyone runs to his aid, while Desdemona, weeping in her anxiety, drops her handkerchief.

Presently Othello revives, but his actions show the disordered state of his mind. He gives Emilia a bag of gold which he forces her to accept. Brabanzio reasons with Othello and takes him with his wife to the ball, where the Doge is awaiting them. Iago remains behind and gleefully retrieves Desdemona's handkerchief which, despite Emilia's entreaties, he refuses to give up.

Act IV. The ballroom in the Ducal Palace.

The Doge, Senators, and members of the Venetian nobility are assembled to honour Othello. Dancing begins and all eyes gaze admiringly upon the beautiful Desdemona.

Meanwhile Iago goes to Cassio and, giving him the handkerchief, bids him offer it to Desdemona and remind her of her promise. Then the villain seeks out Othello and shows him Desdemona and Cassio conversing together; he points out that Cassio holds her handkerchief, which she has surely given him as a love token.

Othello, recognising the handkerchief as a gift from himself, can no longer restrain his rage. He rushes at Cassio, snatches away the handkerchief, and, reviling his wife, orders her to leave with him immediately.

Desdemona's parents demand to know the reason for Othello's outburst, but he only replies with further insults, dragging his wife with him.

Brabanzio, bitterly offended at this treatment of his daughter and at the insults offered to the guests, entreats the Doge's aid. The Doge declares Othello discharged of his office and orders Cassio to arrest him, and further charges him to restore Desdemona to her father's keeping.

Act V. Desdemona's chamber, with a bed in an alcove, where she is sleeping. Night.

After a brief interval, Othello enters with a sword in one hand and a lantern in the other. His features reflect his tortured mind and he swears to kill his unfaithful wife. Fearing that her beauty may deter him from carrying out his vengeance, he extinguishes the lantern.

At this point Desdemona awakes and, seeing her husband, greets him with affection. But Othello, staring fiercely into her eyes, cries: "Pray to heaven to pardon your sin, for I have no wish to slay your soul."

Astonished, Desdemona leaves her bed and asks her husband why he threatens her. He shows her the handkerchief and, accusing her of having given his gift to her lover, orders her to prepare for death. She denies having given the handkerchief and takes heaven to witness that she is innocent.

Othello calls his wife a perjurer and swears vengeance on her lover. He draws the bed curtains that he may shut out from his gaze the couch he believes her to have dishonoured. Desdemona bursts into tears, which Othello interprets as fear for her lover's safety. Enraged at this thought he determines to kill her. She hides in the alcove but he follows her and the deed is done. He emerges with his sword all bloody.

Voices are heard outside the room and Othello is at a loss for what to do. Blows rain upon the door which is forced open, and a number of Senators burst into the room, followed by Brabanzio, Montano, Rodrigo, Emilia, Cassio, and Iago at the head of the Guard.

No sooner does Othello see Cassio than he goes to kill him, but the crowd intervenes. The Senators inform Othello that he has been discharged from office, and Brabanzio demands his daughter.

Othello points to the alcove. Emilia runs to the bed and lifts the curtains. Everyone recoils in horror. Then Othello relates how, through Iago, he discovered his wife's intrigue with Cassio. Cassio and Emilia declare Desdemona to be innocent and reveal Iago's plot.

Overcome with remorse, Othello runs to the alcove, takes a last look at Desdemona, and stabs himself to the heart. The bystanders are filled with consternation, while Iago is placed under arrest.

*

Stendhal, in his biography of Rossini [8], draws an interesting com-

[8] *Vie de Rossini*, 1823.

parison between that composer's opera, *Otello,* and Viganò's ballet on the same theme. "Viganò," says he, "displays much more genius in his ballet *Otello,* which he had the hardihood to begin with a Furlana. In the second act Viganò had again the wit to place a big scene in the noble and quiet style; an evening festival which Othello gives in his gardens; it is during that festival that he becomes jealous. So, on reaching the last act of Viganò's ballet, we did not experience a satiety of the dreadful and shocking; and soon tears filled every eye. I have very rarely seen anyone shed tears at Rossini's *Otello.*"

LA VESTALE

Tragedy Ballet in 5 Acts. Book: Salvatore Viganò. Scenery: Alessandro Sanquirico. Choreography: Salvatore Viganò. First produced: Teatro alla Scala, Milan June 9th, 1818.

CHARACTERS

Julius Silanus, a Consul	M. CARLO BIANCIARDI
Licinius Murena, a Consul	M. CARLO NICHLI
Metellus Pius, the High-Priest . .	M. GIUSEPPE BOCCI
Decius, son of the Consul Murena .	M. NICOLA MOLINARI
Claudius, friend of Decius	M. GIUSEPPE VILLA
Emilia, a Vestal Virgin	MME. ANTONIA PALLERINI

Senators, Priests, Athletes, Dancers, Lictors, Soldiers, Citizens, Vestals, Slaves, etc.

The action passes at Rome.

Act I. The Circus.

In celebration of the Feast of Ceres a number of contests are to be held in the presence of the Consuls, Senators, and Roman people. The tiers of the great circus fill with sightseers draped in their togas and mantles. In the distance can be seen chariot races (with real horses). The games at an end, the Vestals enter to a slow measured rhythm, bearing the palms and crowns destined for the victors. The movements of the Vestals are inspired by the victories which adorn Roman triumphal arches. After ceremonial libations and prayers the prizes are distributed. Among the winners is Decius who, going to claim his prize, notices the Vestal called Emilia. Their eyes meet and each is enamoured of the other.

The act concludes with a sacred bacchanale danced by maenads, satyrs, and youthful bacchantes.

Act II. *A room in the house of the Consul Murena.*

Decius, moody and preoccupied, returns home. His victory affords him no pleasure, for he is obsessed with his new born love for Emilia, and, realising the utter hopelessness of such a passion, gives way to despair.

Enter the Consul, attended by his suite. Overjoyed at his son's triumph, he is surprised to find Decius plunged in gloom. He enquires the reason and Decius pretends that he is merely tired from the contest. The Consul accepts his explanation and orders a banquet to be prepared in honour of the occasion. When the guests have left, Decius tells his friend, Claudius, of his love for Emilia, and that he is minded to destroy himself. Claudius, horrified at this revelation, informs him that he knows of a secret passage leading to the Temple of the Vestals, and that he will take him thither on the following night. Decius, enraptured, embraces his friend with delight

Act III. *Interior of the Temple of the Vestals. A sacred flame burns before the statue of the Goddess.*

It is Emilia's turn to watch and tend the sacred fire. In solitude she meditates upon her unhappy fate. Aware of her affection for Decius she knows that, being a Vestal, she must renounce all earthly love. In despair she kneels before the statue of the Goddess and invokes her aid. She rises and a vision of Decius appears to her. She tries to dispel this apparition, but in vain.

At this moment Decius enters with Claudius, who keeps watch at the entrance. Emilia, seeing her lover in the flesh, turns to flee, but Decius restrains her and urges the Vestal to depart with him. Emilia, alarmed by his passionate pleading, kneels before the statue and prays for protection.

Decius, believing his love to be rejected, is almost in despair when Emilia swoons. He goes to her aid and swears to obey her wishes.

Claudius returns to warn Decius of the approach of some Vestals and urges him to flee immediately. Emilia, ashamed and terrified, falls to the ground in a faint. Decius and Claudius hide in the shadow.

The Vestals arrive and are horrified to find the sacred flame is not burning, and that two men are in the sanctuary, while Emilia is lying on the ground.

Decius implores the Vestals to keep silent respecting what they have seen. Claudius, however, fearing for his friend and himself, leads Decius out of the Temple.

No sooner have they gone than the High Priest and Priestesses arrive, attracted by the noise. The Vestals in their innocence relate what has occurred, whereupon the High Priest, furious at the profanation of the sanctuary, orders the culprit to be seized and put to trial. Amid the tears of her companions, Emilia is led away for judgment.

Act IV. A hill overlooking the sacred wood.

Decius and Claudius, concealed, await the trial of Emilia. Claudius goes to reconnoitre and returns quickly with the news that the Priestesses are arriving and hence they must leave immediately. Decius decides to save Emilia or die with her, and goes with Claudius to prepare his plans.

The Priestesses and Vestals enter, then the Consuls, to whom the High Priest details the case. Emilia is brought in by soldiers, interrogated, and found guilty. In vain do the judges try to discover the name of her lover.

Decius goes to his father and implores him to pardon Emilia. The bystanders are moved to tears by his pleading. But the High Priest condemns Emilia to death, tears off the sacred insignia, and, covering her with a black veil, tells the Consul that his son is well aware of the futility of his request.

The High Priest, attended by the Vestals, departs in one direction, while the Consuls and their suites leave in the opposite direction. Murena shows clearly his distress at his son's conduct.

Act V. The execution ground.

All Rome has heard of the death sentence passed upon the Vestal, and citizens arrive from all quarters to witness her execution.

Presently there enters a grim procession, consisting of the High Priest, the Vestals, the Consul Silanus and a body of soldiers, and, last of all, Emilia, surrounded by guards.

The High Priest prays to the Gods to pardon the sacrilege that has been committed, then accompanies Emilia to the tomb in which she is to be buried alive. When the prisoner is in the hands of the executioner, the High Priest turns his back on her. The

Vestal is placed in the tomb, which is closed with a slab of marble.

Decius enters with an armed band, determined to rescue Emilia. He pleads with the High Priest, then, finding him obdurate, attempts to kill him, but is cut down by the guards.

The Consul Murena arrives at this moment, hoping to restrain his son's impetuosity, but, seeing what has happened, remains at a distance, horror-stricken.

Decius staggers towards Emilia's tomb, and, calling out her name, expires, greatly pitied by the sorrowing bystanders.

*

La Vestale is based on the well-known opera of the same name by Spontini, for which Jouy wrote the libretto, produced at the Opera, Paris, 1807. The ballet, *La Vestale,* is generally regarded as the finest of Viganò's compositions.

Ritorni[9] gives a very interesting description of Pallerini's miming as Emilia in the third act, which I reproduce. "She stands leaning against the altar, absorbed in her thoughts. She rouses herself and tends the fire. She turns a little sideways and, musing upon what has happened to her, seems to listen to the voice of her new-born love. She first tries to subdue it by appealing to her own common sense. She reminds herself of her sacred calling, her duty, and her religion. Finally she believes it will be more efficacious to go to the Goddess and beseech her to deliver her from this sinful love. . . . While she descends the altar steps on which she has prayed, a vision reveals to her the features of Decius. She wishes to banish this apparition, but in vain. She lowers her eyes to the ground and tries to absorb herself in a prayer. When she rises, the vision is still there. She can resist no longer and extends her arms, but immediately recoils in horror. She flees to the altar, a prey to remorse. She prays, but in vain; you feel that she desires with all her being the return of the wraith, vanished at last. At this moment Decius appears, accompanied by Claudius."

[9] *Op. cit.*

Photo: Fischer, St. Petersburg

RYATSOV AND FEDOROVA IN "LA FILLE MAL GARDÉE", ACT II.

Production under Imperial Russian Ballet, early 20th century

SOME POSES TAKEN BY MARIE TAGLIONI IN "LA SYLPHIDE"
From the lithographs of A. E. Chalon

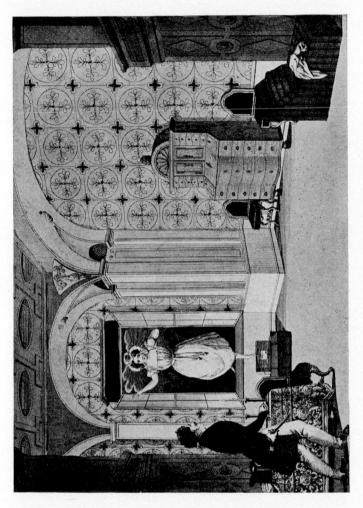

SCENE FROM "LA SOMNAMBULE", ACT II.
From the engraving by Zinke after Schoeller

MARIE TAGLIONI IN "LA BAYADÈRE"
From the lithographs by A. E. Chalon

MARIE TAGLIONI IN "LA SYLPHIDE"

From the painting by Lepolle

SCENES FROM "LA SYLPHIDE", ACT II.
From the wood-engravings in "Les Beautés de l'Opéra", 1845

MARIE TAGLIONI IN "LA GITANA"
From the lithograph by A. E. Chalon after the painting by Mme. Soyer

MARIE TAGLIONI IN "LA GITANA"

From the lithograph by Blau

JEAN CORALLI
From Saint-Léon's "La Stenochorégraphie"

THE THREE GRACES

*The print represents Taglioni in "La Sylphide," Fanny
Elssler in "Le Diable Boiteux," and Grisi in "La Jolie Fille de Gand"
From the lithograph by and after Lejeune*

CARLOTTA GRISI IN "GISELLE"

From the lithograph by J. Brandard

ANNA PAVLOVA IN "GISELLE"

FANNY ELSSLER IN "LA TARENTULE"
From the lithograph by Bouvier

SCENES FROM "GISELLE", ACTS I. AND II.
From the wood-engravings in "Les Beautés de l'Opéra", 1845

CARLOTTA GRISI IN "LA PÉRI"
From the lithograph by J. Brandard

SCENE FROM "LA PÉRI", ACT I.

Showing Carlotta Grisi making her famous leap in the "Pas du Songe"
From the lithograph by Alophe

ADÈLE DUMILÂTRE AND JEAN CORALLI IN "LA GYPSY", ACT II.

From the drawing by Deveria

FANNY ELSSLER IN "LA GYPSY"

From the lithograph by Haguental

JULES PERROT AND CARLOTTA GRISI IN "ESMERALDA"
From the lithograph by J. Bouvier

CARLOTTA GRISI AND LUCIEN PETIPA IN "PAQUITA"
From the lithograph by J. Brandard

AMALIA FERRARIS IN "LES ELFES"
From the lithograph by Alophe

SCENE FROM "MARCO SPADA", ACT III. SC. III.

SCENES FROM "ONDINE", SCENES I. AND II.
From the wood-engravings in "Les Beautés de l'Opéra," 1845

FANNY CERITO IN THE PAS DE L'OMBRE IN "ONDINE"
From the painting by G. A. Turner

LUCILE GRAHN IN "CATARINA", ACT I. SC. I.
From the lithograph by J. Brandard

LE PAS DES DÉESSES

From the lithograph by Jules Bouvier

Cerito   *Saint-Léon*   *Taglioni*   *Rosati*

JULES PERROT AND LUCILE GRAHN IN "CATARINA"
From the lithograph by J. Brandard

LE PAS DE QUATRE, 1845
From the lithograph by A. E. Chalon
Grisi   *Taglioni*   *Grahn*   *Cerito*

SCENE FROM "LE PAPILLON", ACT I. SC. II.

PAUL TAGLIONI

ADÈLE DUMILATRE AND LUCIEN PETIPA IN "THE MARBLE MAIDEN"
From the lithograph by J. Brandard

ARTHUR SAINT-LÉON AND FANNY CERITO IN "LE VIOLIN DU DIABLE"

I TITANI [10]

Ballet in 6 Acts. Book: Salvatore Viganò. Scenery: Alessandro Sanquirico. Choreography: Salvatore Viganò. First produced: Teatro alla Scala, Milan, October 11th, 1819.

CHARACTERS

Jupiter	M. Luigi Sidini
Hyperion	M. Nicola Molinari
Theia	Mlle. Maria Bocci
Selene, their daughter . . .	Mme. Antonia Pallerini
Helios, their son	Mlle. Adelaide Grassini
Eone, a beautiful girl	Mlle. Teresa Oliviera
Nereus, a handsome youth . .	M. Giovanni Bianchi

The Gods of Olympus, Men, Women, and Children, the Nymph Melia, Titans, Giants, Cyclops, Children of Night, and the Virtues.

Act I. A fertile plain in springtime, with a profusion of flowers and fruit-trees. In the centre a small hill. In the background a stream.

The Virtues are seated with Theia on a hill, where they converse together. Melia dances about Cupid and tries to ensnare him with a garland of roses. Cupid endeavours unsuccessfully to escape. Groups of men, women, and children sport among themselves and frolic with lambs, birds, and rabbits.

Selene places chains of flowers about Hyperion, who is sleeping. Helios picks fruit from the trees.

A group of children chase butterflies.

Hyperion awakes and embraces his children, Helios and Selene. They take him by the hand and lead him to Theia, their mother.

Enter Eone and Dori, two beautiful virgins, followed by Selene and Helios. Nereus falls in love with Eone, but is too shy to approach her. Cupid, freeing himself from Melia, goes to Nereus and urges him to be bolder with Eone and declare his love.

Then Cupid goes from man to man, and from woman to woman, and bids them love each other. Follows a general dance expressive of pure and simple love.

Cupid becomes tired and goes under a tree to rest. Various children wish him to play with them, but he tells them that, although

[10] *The Titans.*

he looks so young, he is really grown up. They mock him and he runs away, pursued by the children.

At a signal from Hyperion and Theia, everyone gathers about them. Theia expresses her sorrow for her brothers, whom Jupiter has relegated to Tartarus. She obtains Hyperion's permission to go and visit them. Selene and Helios give her fruit and flowers for the Titans.

Hyperion and others go with Theia to set her on her journey.

When all have vanished from sight Cupid enters, followed by the children. Exulting in the thought that he will soon be their prisoner, they almost catch up with him when, to their chagrin, he flies over their heads.

Act II. An enormous space in Chaos. Here lives Atlantis who carries the Earth on his shoulders. All is dark and savage.

This is the abode of Night, who is seated, covered with clouds. She is surrounded by her children: Calamity, Fate, Death, Nemesis, Sin, Deceit, Discord, and so on. Three Giants—Cottys, Briareus, and Gyges—are lying down, but the Titans and Cyclops go round and round in the darkness.

One of the Titans asks the Giants why they do not aid them with their mighty strength to revolt against Jupiter. They also accuse Saturn of failing to help them. Saturn places the blame on another, and so Giants and Titans quarrel with a terrible noise. The children of Night incite the combatants to greater fury.

But Fate stops the conflict and declares that so long as the inhabitants of the Earth live in peace and happiness, and are protected by the Virtues, so long will they be unassailable. But, if they can conquer the mortals with evils, then they will be victorious.

The Titans, profiting by this counsel, prepare three vases respectively made of silver, copper, and iron, into which they put various evils.

Now Theia arrives and offers gifts of fruit and flowers to the Titans, who in exchange offer her the vases as presents for her children.

Theia departs and the Titans try to imagine what effect the vases will have upon the world.

Act III. A pleasant glade.

Selene enters, fondling a graceful deer. Helios follows and embraces Hyperion who, arriving at this moment, is delighted to see his children so happy.

Theia returns from Tartarus and is welcomed by a crowd of people. She gives her children the vases she received from the Titans.

Helios opens his vase, the silver one, which emits a dense black vapour, and causes the trees and flowers to wither. Hyperion strives to close the vase, but in vain. The people are filled with distress.

Suddenly joyful music is heard, and Cupid enters with Pan and a number of fauns and satyrs. They play and dance, and give the mortals implements to till the soil and restore the glade to its former beauty.

These gifts are received with delight, when Cupid and his company depart, while the crowd go away in various directions. Hyperion alone remains. The copper vase has been overturned and from it arises a red vapour. He fears that other misfortunes will result. Noticing that the iron vase is the only one that remains, he resolves to conceal it.

He begins to till the soil and Selene comes to help her father. As they work, snow falls lightly at first, then in heavy flakes. Hyperion, overcome with the cold, sinks to the ground. Selene, in despair, calls for help.

Nereus and others arrive, clothed in the skins of wild animals, but they refuse their aid; they have grown hard-hearted and selfish.

Now come Helios and Eone. The former goes to help Hyperion, but he is dying.

Eone, seeing that Hyperion is dead, claims the implements; this leads to a quarrel. Hearing the uproar Theia enters, and is surprised and furious at what she sees. Failing to calm the dispute and observing that the iron vase is unopened, she places it under her arm and steals quietly away, followed by Selene.

The others, continuing their quarrel, fail to notice Theia's departure.

Act IV. A deep grotto through the back of which can be seen Mount Otri, the pinnacle of which is white with snow.

Enter Theia and Selene wearing the skins of animals. Theia, aided by Selene, hides the vase beneath some stones, and forces her daughter to swear that she will never reveal its position.

Theia leaves and is seen kneeling in the open, praying to the Gods to help her children.

Selene remains alone in the grotto. Unable to resist temptation she opens the vase, from which she pours gold, silver, and jewels, and a dagger. She replaces the dagger, which fills her with fear, and decks herself with the ornaments.

Nereus, Eone, and others enter. Surprised to see the radiant Selene, they worship her as a goddess. She goes out, followed by the crowd and Nereus.

Eone remains behind and Nereus, failing to see her, returns and finds her in tears. She confesses that she is jealous of Selene, for she fears he will prefer Selene to her.

Nereus, in the hope of calming Eone, goes to the vases to ascertain if any gold remains, and finds the dagger. Eone is seized with alarm. Nereus tells her that the dagger will make him master of everyone. Eone agrees with him and they go and hide in the depths of the grotto.

Theia returns, but ignores Selene, because she has broken her oath. Cupid takes Selene by the hand and forces her to kneel before her mother. Theia orders her to take off her ornaments, but, divided between the wish to please her and the desire to retain the treasures, she falls into a swoon.

Nereus emerges from the grotto, armed with his dagger. Everyone recoils before him. He goes to Selene and asks for her ornaments. When she refuses, he stabs her with the dagger. Then he gives the ornaments to Eone, who puts them on.

Helios wishes to defend Selene's body, but he is forced aside by Nereus's friends.

Theia leaves and implores the aid of the Gods.

A light fades from the summit of Mount Otri, signifying that the Virtues have left the Earth. Simultaneously the Titans come out of the grotto and attack the mortals.

Theia again appeals to the Gods and is taken to heaven in a cloud.

Justice appears and, seeing what the Titans are doing, decides to appeal to Jupiter. The Titans, seeing that they cannot do any more harm to the mortals, commence to pile the mountains one on top of the other, to reach the sky where the Gods reside. The Cyclops and Giants help the Titans.

Act V. The throne-room of Jupiter.

Jupiter is seen enthroned. Muses beguile him with music and *amorini* offer him wine in a cold cup. Genii burn perfumes before him. The Hours dance and an eagle is tranquil beside him.

The Virtues arrive from the Earth in great consternation and tell of the Titans' intention to climb to the sky. Jupiter calmly arises from his throne and prepares to defend the sky with his lightnings.

Act VI. The pile of mountains erected by the Titans, Cyclops, and Giants.

The Titans slowly climb the mountains and approach the sky. Suddenly, Jupiter hurls his lightnings. The mountains, split in twain, topple over, carrying with them the invaders, who are buried beneath the great masses of rock.

*

According to contemporary evidence, *I Titani* was an unequal production. The first act, which represents the Golden Age of Innocence, was so beautiful in the poetry and harmony of the dancers' movements that the fall of the curtain provoked a tornado of applause. The third act seemed long. The fourth again aroused the interest of the audience, but the fifth and sixth acts were found to be tedious.

JEAN AUMER

JEAN PIERRE AUMER was born at Paris in 1776. He was the son of a simple workman and received but a modest education. While still a youth he happened to make the acquaintance of Dauberval who, attracted by the boy's intelligence and enthusiasm, offered to train him as a dancer.

When Dauberval went to Bordeaux as *maître de ballet,* Aumer accompanied him and made his *début* under his direction. Unfortunately he began to grow tall and, fearing that he might not be able to continue dancing, resolved to prepare himself to become a choreographer, to which end he studied Dauberval's methods of composition and neglected no effort to acquire a knowledge of the related arts, such as music and painting.

In 1798 Aumer went to the Opera, Paris, and made his first appearance on May 15th in *Le Deserteur.* Eight years later he was permitted to produce a ballet for the Théâtre de la Porte Saint-Martin. This composition, *Jenny ou La Mariage Secret,* his first venture, achieved considerable success. It was followed by the production of *Les Deux Créoles,* which was also well received.

In 1807 he went to Lyon as *maître de ballet* where he revived the two ballets mentioned and produced a new dramatic ballet called *Antoine et Cléopâtre.* The reader will be able to judge of the author's sense of dramatic effect and the ingenuity of construction of this ballet which, except for a little compression, is given as originally written. The success of this ballet brought Aumer an engagement from King Jerome to act as *maître de ballet* at Cassel, where he remained for some seven years.

In 1815 Aumer went to Vienna where he had under his direction such well-known artistes as Mlles. Bigottini and Chévigny, and MM. Petit and Deshayes. Aumer's ballets were very popular in the gay capital, the most admired being *Les Pages du Duc de Vendôme.*

He returned to the Opera, Paris, in 1820, where he produced several ballets such as *La Fête Hongroise* (1821), *Alfred le Grand* (1822), *Aline, Reine de Golconde* (1823), *Le Page Inconstant*

44

(1823), *Astolphe et Joconde* (1827), *La Somnambule* (1827), *La Belle au Bois Dormant* (1829), and *Manon Lescaut* (1830).

Aumer died at Saint-Martin in 1833, aged fifty-seven.

LES DEUX CRÉOLES

Ballet Pantomime in 3 Acts. Book: Jean Aumer. Music: Darondeau. Choreography: Jean Aumer. First produced: Théâtre de la Porte Saint-Martin, Paris, June 28th, 1806.

CHARACTERS

Théodore	MME. QUÉRIAU
Zoé	MLLE. CAROLINE
M. de la Martinière, governor of the island .	M. LEFEBRE
Mme. de Sénange, Zoé's mother . . .	MLLE. ALINE
Marianne	MME. DESCUILLÉS
Dominguo	M. ROBILLON
Dorival, a planter	M. MÉRANTE
An Old Man, living on the island . .	M. FUSIL
The Pastor	M. AUGUSTE
An Overseer	M. SÉVIN
Marie, a negress	MME. BELLEMENT
Zobi, her child	MLLE. DESCUILLÉS
A Negress	MLLE. DEGVILLE

Negroes, Negresses, Planters, Creoles, Officers, Sailors.

Act I. A sugar plantation in the Ile de France, showing the banks of a large stream, which crosses the road. The water is low and the rocks jutting out of the stream permit it to be crossed in safety. To the right is a date tree.

At the rise of the curtain a number of negroes are seen working on the plantation. The overseer, pleased with their labours, allows them a rest period. A negro and two negresses dance the Bamboula; the onlookers applaud with hand-claps. Suddenly thunder is heard and the negroes hurriedly seek shelter.

When the storm is nearly over Théodore and Zoé arrive and stand under the date-tree. Presently Théodore leaves the tree and observes that the storm is over. But Zoé is tired, so they sit on the grass and eat. The repast over, Théodore begs a kiss which Zoé refuses. But when he sulks she promises him one, if he will procure her some dates. Overjoyed, he climbs a tree and throws down some dates. Zoé wafts him a kiss which he declares the wind blew away. He climbs down, holding a bunch of dates, but, when she goes to take them, drops the bunch and kisses her instead. Zoé, a little shocked, wishes to go; but Théodore induces her to stay and asks her pardon. He is forgiven and the lovers express their happiness in a dance.

They are interrupted by the arrival of a negress bearing a child on her shoulder. On seeing them she is about to flee, but they calm her fears and lead her to a grassy bank. Zoé and Théodore seeing that the pair are exhausted, give the mother and child all their provisions and are delighted to see them revive a little. The mother tells how she has fled from a severe master who ill treated her because she refused to give up her child. She wishes to kneel to her benefactors but they make her sit beside them. Remarking that her feet are injured, the lovers propose to take her to their home. But when they find she is too weak to walk, Théodore tears down some branches and makes a shelter for her.

Some negroes approach with Dorival, their master. The negress is terrified, but Théodore and Zoé conceal her. Dorival asks the lovers if they have seen a slave. They remain silent. Dorival, seeing that Zoé is pretty, stares at her so intently that Théodore can hardly restrain his temper. Zoé begs Dorival to pardon the slave if he finds her. No sooner has he consented than she shows him where the negress is hidden.

Dorival orders his negroes to seize the slave. Zoé implores him to respect his promise and at last he gives way. The negroes demonstrate their joy, and the lovers thank Dorival, who seems loath to leave. Zoé and Théodore beseech Dorival to free the slave. The negroes add their entreaties and promise to do her work. The master finally agrees and the negress is overjoyed. Dorival looks tenderly at Zoé and departs with his men.

The negress can hardly credit her happiness. She kneels and calls down blessings on the lovers. But now they are anxious to return home, although doubtful as to which road to take. Théodore takes Zoé on his shoulder and steps from rock to rock; he is followed by the negress carrying her child. But when they get half-way Théodore is obliged to turn back. Zoé begs Théodore to go on alone and calm their mothers, but he refuses to leave her. While the lovers consider what to do, the negress offers to seek help, if they will take care of her child. She is about to start when Dominguo appears on the opposite bank. He is delighted to see his young master and mistress.

He crosses the stream and reproves the lovers for having caused their mothers such anxiety. They shed tears of remorse. Dominguo seems surprised to find the negress but, on learning how the young people rescued her from slavery, he praises their kindness.

Now they make a second effort to cross the river. Dominguo agrees to carry Théodore on his shoulder, who will carry the baby, while the negress carries Zoé. As they are about to go, a number of negroes cross from the opposite bank. Then they take the branches used for the shelter and form it into a litter in which Zoé is placed. They wish to place Théodore beside her, but he insists on the negress and her child being carried. Dominguo takes Théodore on his shoulders and so the party crosses the stream and passes from view.

Act II. On one side Mme. de Sénange's hut with two cocoa-trees at the entrance; on the other side Marianne's hut: in the distance the church of La Pampeleuse. The background is formed by rocks and trees.

Mme. de Sénange enters to see if her children have arrived. Marianne follows and tries to console her, but she gives way to profound grief. An old man, a neighbour of Mme. du Sénange, enters and, seeing the distress of the two women, sympathizes. Suddenly Dominguo runs in to tell of the arrival of his young master, and the procession files in. Théodore runs to greet his mother, Marianne: Mme. de Sénange kisses Zoé and grumbles at the pair for having caused her such anxiety. They ask her forgiveness and show the negress and her child, whom they have rescued from slavery. Mme. de Sénange kisses the baby and they all sit down to a meal, after which the negroes are given refreshments. Afterwards the negroes dance and Théodore and Zoé take part in their games.

An officer brings Mme. de Sénange a letter from her aunt, asking for Zoé to be sent to her. Consternation is general. Marianne begs her not to separate the young people, who are so fond of each other. Mme. de Sénange sends the children indoors while she discusses their future. The old man proposes that they should marry, but Mme. de Sénange fears to disobey her aunt. However, she agrees to the plan and they go in search of a missionary.

Théodore returns and asks Dominguo where the ladies have gone. Dominguo remains silent, not wishing to betray the happy secret. Zoé comes in and Théodore asks her to discover the secret, but Dominguo refuses to speak, until she becomes so filled with anxiety that he feels compelled to confide in her. But all at once distant music is heard and Dominguo breaks into a dance. When they ask him the reason, he pretends to be angry and drives the children into their respective huts.

At the same moment Mme. de Sénange and Marianne return with the pastor and the old man. The negroes dance before the huts and the old man fetches first Zoé and then Théodore, and places them before the pastor, who, to their astonishment, asks each in turn if it is their desire to be united to each other. When they reply in the affirmative, Creole girls place a white crown and veil on Zoé's head. The young people kneel at their mothers' feet and receive the pastor's blessing. But, just as he is about to lead them to his church, the Governor and his officers arrive with various coffers.

The Governor is astonished to learn of the betrothal of Zoé to Théodore and, expressing his displeasure, shows Mme. de Sénange the order he has received to send her daughter back to France; for which purpose he has brought her a supply of money and necessaries. Everyone entreats him to allow Zoé to stay, but he refuses. However, not entirely unmoved, he asks the pastor to use his influence to induce her to obey him.

Théodore and Zoé beg the old man to protect them, but Mme. de Sénange fears to disobey her aunt. Théodore seizes Zoé in his arms and refuses to be separated from her, and declares that their happiness is being destroyed for the sake of riches. Mme. de Sénange tries to calm him but he refuses to listen to her. The pastor reproves him, but as he is about to ask her pardon, he is overcome with sadness and falls into the old man's arms. The pastor bids Marianne go into her hut; Zoé wishes to follow but the pastor restrains her.

Mme. de Sénange seems determined not to permit the unfortunate journey, but the pastor points out all the advantages she will lose by opposing her aunt's wishes and tries to persuade Zoé to go. He tells her that it is God's will and that she must not shrink from sacrifices in His service. Sobbing deeply, Zoé agrees to go, and the pastor hastens to inform the Governor of her resolution, while Dominguo, in despair, goes to tell Théodore the fatal news.

Théodore returns and reproaches Zoé for leaving him. He implores her to give up the proposed journey and reminds her of all the happy times they have spent together. She runs to his arms but suddenly a cannon booms; it is the signal for the vessel to depart. Zoé kisses Théodore, who swears he will go with her. But Marianne implores her son not to forsake her. So he is divided between his love for Zoé and his affection for his mother. Drums roll and the Governor arrives.

As soon as Théodore sees him he grasps Zoé and defies everyone to take his sweetheart. Marianne implores the Governor to revise the order he has received, but he declares he must obey orders. When Zoé refuses to go, he orders his officers to separate the lovers. Théodore opposes the officers with the courage of despair, but is obliged to give way. Zoé is about to be carried to the ship when she slips away and the lovers run into each other's arms. They try to escape, but Zoé is recaptured and carried to the beach. Mme. de Sénange sobs bitterly during this affecting scene, while Dominguo beats his breast with despair.

The sailors place Zoé in a canoe and row her out to sea. She throws her handkerchief, wet with tears, to Théodore who kisses it and falls into the arms of his mother and the old man, who carry him back to the hut. Everyone leaves in the utmost despair.

Act III. The sea coast. On one side a very high rock. In the foreground a pawpaw tree, carved with the initials of Théodore and Zoé.

The vessel is leaving the shore. Zoé is on the deck with the Governor beside her. Dominguo, Marie, the negress and the baby are standing on the bank waving good-bye. The vessel is decked with flags and sails away to the accompaniment of cheers. Dominguo and Marie climb the rock to catch the last glimpse of the vessel.

Théodore runs in asking for Zoé. When he sees from the sadness of the negress that she has really gone, he falls at the foot of the tree. Then he catches sight of their initials and grows calmer at the recollections they bring, only to become oppressed by the deepest despair. Dominguo, Marie, and the child succeed in soothing him. The negro takes the opportunity to give him a ring which Zoé had left for him. Then he leads him up to the rock to see the vessel, but already it is lost to view. Yet Théodore, believing he can still see his beloved Zoé, blows her kisses until, conscious of his error, he bursts into tears. Then, assisted by Dominguo, he descends the rock.

Mme. de Sénange enters, accompanied by the old man and Marianne. They look for Théodore who, on seeing them, hides his face in his hands. He is about to flee when Mme. de Sénange holds him back. The old man begs him not to leave his mother so he runs to Marianne; but when he sees Mme. de Sénange he turns away.

Suddenly the sky darkens, the clouds gather, and a terrible storm ensues. Théodore kneels and prays that no harm may befall Zoé; his example is followed by all present. A cannon booms and warns those on shore that the ship is in peril.

A number of soldiers, led by an officer, run in bearing torches. Sailors climb the rock and send life-lines towards the vessel. Inhabitants arrive and run about in the greatest agitation. Mme. de Sénange and Marianne are stricken with anguish.

Now the vessel is seen making for shore, firing a distress warning every moment. The bridge is crowded with people.

Zoé, holding the mast with one hand, signals for help. Théodore, unable to contain his anxiety, resolves to swim to her assistance. He embraces his mother and dives into the sea. Now he nears the ship, now he is swept back by a giant wave. At last he reaches the vessel as the Governor climbs into a boat and is about to help Zoé beside him. Suddenly the lightning flashes, the stricken ship bursts into flame, and sinks in full view of the helpless spectators.

A boat puts to land, the Governor steps to the ground, greatly distressed at having caused the death of Zoé. He entreats the sailors to make an effort to rescue Théodore and Zoé, and begs the mothers not to abandon hope.

At last Théodore and Dominguo, supporting Zoé, are seen swimming towards the shore. Sailors help them to land. Zoé is unconscious and so pale that Théodore believes her dead. Having vainly tried to revive her he seems on the point of losing his reason, when Dominguo, feeling Zoé's heart beating, calls him to her side. He lavishes every care on her and gradually she revives and they embrace. They go to their mothers who receive them with the utmost delight.

The Governor congratulates Dominguo on his devotion and, in appreciation of his courage, gives him a purse of gold, which he passes to the negress's baby. Then the Governor begs Mme. de Sénange to unite Théodore to Zoé, and, promising his protection, places his castle at their service for the wedding. Mme. de Sénange consents, and Théodore and Zoé kneel in gratitude to the Governor. Théodore and Zoé are placed in a palanquin, the Governor gives his hand to Mme. de Sénange, and they depart, followed by the negroes, who dance in token of their delight.

*

Les Deux Créoles is the second of two ballets inspired by, and founded upon, Bernardin de Saint Pierre's celebrated romance,

Paul et Virginie, the first being *Paul et Virginie,* produced by Pierre Gardel at the Paris Opera on June 25th, 1806.

Geoffroy, an ardent admirer of Gardel, severely criticises in the *Journal de l'Empire*[1] Aumer's conception. He asserts that the situations are the same in both ballets yet the two productions are very different, "because the theatres, choreographers, styles, and players have nothing in common." *Les Deux Créoles,* he asserts, "is merely a parody, or rather a burlesque, of *Paul et Virginie.*" He then proceeds to draw comparisons.

"At the Opera, Virginie is becomingly modest, although lively and witty. At the Porte Saint-Martin Theatre, this Virginie, under the name of Zoé, is cold and foolish, but much less scrupulous regarding propriety; she lightly accepts the attentions of an unknown planter whom she meets by chance; it is true that her intentions are good; for it is to rescue an unfortunate negress that Zoé enters into conversation with him.

"As for Paul, so simple, so innocent, and so well brought up by Mr. Bernardin de Saint Pierre, here, in *Les Deux Créoles,* he is an enterprising and determined libertine called Théodore. . . .

"At the Opera it is a negro who flees with his two children to escape his master's cruelty; at the Porte Saint-Martin, it is a negress with a single child. The Opera neglects the incident of Paul's likeness, which Virginie carries next to her heart; at the Porte Saint-Martin some importance is attached to this sentimental trifle; but one great difference between Paul and his representative Théodore is that Paul is a man and Théodore a woman; although that woman is Mme. Quériau she sustains the illusion no longer, and the love of one woman for another is scarcely affecting. . . .

"Those young people who would place *Les Deux Créoles* on a level with, or above, *Paul et Virginie,* preferring Aumer to Gardel, and a boulevard theatre to the first lyric stage in the world, would greatly wrong Aumer, his ballet, and the Porte Saint-Martin Theatre. This choreographer has himself too much intelligence, perception, and modesty not to be distressed at the indiscretion of some foolish persons who dare to prefer him to a man he looks upon as his master. Aumer's ballet, considered in regard to the theatre for which it is intended, seems to achieve its object; it entertains the frequenters of the Porte Saint-Martin . . . but, compared with *Paul et Virginie,* it is a hotch-potch. . . . In short, Aumer's ballet is to Gardel's as the Porte Saint-Martin is to the Opera."

The critic of the *Courrier des Spectacles*[2] offers a different opin-

---

[1] July 4th, 1806.
[2] June 30th, 1806.

ion. *"Les Deux Créoles,"* says he, "should be as profitable to the management . . . as *Jenny*. It relates adventures so moving, offers pictures so striking and so varied, that, in suppressing three or four of its *pas,* it would be no less successful, for each situation is adroitly introduced, all the scenes are most effective, and the climax is skillfully contrived. The author has neglected nothing which could render his characters interesting. . . . Few pieces have been played with such a cast, and in one only, that of *Jenny,* does Mme. Quériau display as much talent. In *Les Deux Créoles* she plays the part of Théodore, and invests it with all the warmth, abandon, and pathos of which she is capable. I do not know how she can support so many shocks. As the climax approaches, at the moment when she appears exhausted, she seems to acquire new strength.

"The same tribute must be paid to Mlle. Caroline Soissons, who showed herself a worthy rival of Mme. Quériau in the interesting role of Zoé.

"Mlle. Aline and Mme. Descuillés portray with much feeling the characters of the two mothers, and Mme. Bellement, as the unfortunate negress, won applause. In regard to this part we shall offer a small criticism: the pitiable plight of the negress is a little overprolonged. It would be better if, after having obtained her pardon, the request from Théodore and Zoé, that she should be freed, did not expose her afresh to her master's anger and blows . . . a repetition of the previous episode. This little blemish can easily disappear, this scene would not produce any the less effect. One of the most interesting roles in this piece is that of the negro Dominguo . . . M. Robillon invests it with all the gaiety and feeling which it demands. . . .

"There is little dancing . . . because everything is in action from the first act to the last; nevertheless, the *pas negre* in the first act, the execution of which is perfect, was much applauded. M. Sévin, who leads this troupe of negroes, was noticeable for the strength and skill with which he managed the bamboo.

"The settings of this work are very beautiful and the music appropriate to the theme."

LES AMOURS D'ANTOINE ET DE CLÉOPÂTRE[3]

Historical Ballet in 3 Acts. Book: Jean Aumer. Music: Kreutzer. Choreography: Jean Aumer. First produced: Théâtre de l'Académie Royale de Musique, Paris, March 8th, 1808.

CHARACTERS

Antony, Triumvir	M. C. Vestris
Octavia, Antony's consort	Mlle. Chevigny
Her two children	Mlle. Hullin / Mlle. Legallois
Cleopatra, Queen of Egypt	Mlle. Bigottini
Octavius, Triumvir, Octavia's brother . .	M. L'Huillier
An Egyptian Ambassador	M. Dodefroi
Two of the Ambassador's Officers . .	M. Seuriot / M. Paul
The High Priest of the Temple of Peace .	M. L'Enfant
Charmian, Cleopatra's friend and confidant	Mme. Elie
Iras, an attendant	Mlle. Laurence
A Peasant	M. Godefroi

Cleopatra's suite, Egyptian soldiers, Antony's suite, Roman soldiers, Three Young Girls personating Graces, a Child representing Cupid, Young Egyptian Girls as Nymphs, Children as Sylphs, Cupids, Zephyrs, and so on.

Act I. The city of Tarsus. On one side is a Temple of Peace; in front, a Tribunal; in the background, the river Cydnus.

Antony, seated in his tribune, surrounded by lictors, receives the Egyptian ambassador, who brings the olive branch and presents a scroll containing the terms of the intended treaty. Antony refuses his acquiescence. The ambassadors expostulate and implore his clemency; but he remains inflexible and orders them to retire. •

He summons his chief courtiers and bids them prepare for war. His troops express a strong desire for conquest, and the multitude seem to be inspired with the same warlike feeling.

A messenger brings Antony intelligence of Cleopatra's arrival. Filled with curiosity the people run to meet the Queen, and Antony is almost forsaken. He wonders at his people's eagerness to

[3] The description which follows is a condensed version of a contemporary translation of the original synopsis.

see the Queen and gives instructions for her to be invited to his presence.

Cleopatra, elegantly attired, is borne in a rich galley. Cupids flutter about her, Zephyrs clasp the rigging. Some of her attendants, dressed as Graces and Nereids, steer the vessel, others row it with silver oars, while Tritons, with their conches, join the delightful harmony of various instruments. On landing, the Queen proceeds to the public square. Zephyrs lead the procession, strewing the Queen's path with flowers.

The Queen and her attendants bow to Antony, who, overawed by so much magnificence, is unable to resist her charms and invites her to sit by his side. Cleopatra bows in token of submission, but her looks already proclaim her happiness at having made him her conquest. Some Egyptians bring presents, which she offers him as so many pledges of friendship. Antony orders the Temple of Peace to be opened.

The High Priest, wearing an olive crown, stands on the threshold of the temple, where he receives from Antony the rich offerings of Cleopatra. After he has poured libations, Antony and Cleopatra promise inviolable fidelity to one another at the altar of the Deity. The Egyptians and Romans fraternize with mutual protestations of amity. The people pay homage to the Queen. Sports and dances follow.

The festival is interrupted by the arrival of Octavia, with her two children, and preceded by a chosen bodyguard. Antony expresses his astonishment. Cleopatra becomes alarmed at the prospect of losing his affection; her attendants seem to share her fears.

The High Priest re-enters the Temple.

Octavia approaches. The strictest morals prevail among the attendants of Octavia, while voluptuousness is the characteristic of Cleopatra's retinue. No sooner do the two children perceive their father, than they overwhelm him with tokens of affection. Antony is moved and filled with parental tenderness.

Octavia is agitated; Cleopatra is jealous. Antony introduces his children to Cleopatra, who pretends to receive them with affection, but, when thinking herself unobserved, shows her hatred of them and their mother. Octavia wishes to embrace Antony, but he is indifferent. He inquires the reason for her journey; she explains that it was prompted by her ardent desire to see him.

Antony is grateful but Octavia, unable to bear his coldness, turns to her children, and embraces them tenderly. Hardly able to bear her endeavours to regain his affections, he turns away his eyes and looks at Cleopatra. Octavia, indignant, demands a private audience, which he feels compelled to grant. He invites Cleopatra to go to the Temple where he will follow her later. Cleopatra consents and withdraws, casting a loving glance upon Antony.

The High Priest and people attend the Queen.

Octavia reproaches her husband for having forsaken her and warns him not to be deceived by the arts of the Egyptian Queen. Antony tries to dissipate her fears. She reminds him of the children she has borne him and entreats him not to forsake her. Antony is moved, and Octavia and the children kneel at his feet and endeavour to effect a reconciliation, when Cleopatra comes out of the Temple.

Antony is confused, Octavia overwhelmed with grief. Cleopatra, inwardly raging with jealousy, ironically congratulates him on his attachment to Octavia. He is swayed between his duty and his passion for the Egyptian Queen. The latter pretends to withdraw.

Antony is about to follow when Octavia and her children restrain him. Cleopatra, seeing him ready to yield, summons her attendants. The Graces, Zephyrs, and Cupids come forward with garlands of flowers. Octavia calls down the vengeance of the gods upon her rival. Antony, seduced by the pleasures offered to him, blindly follows Cleopatra.

Octavia, overwhelmed with sorrow, swoons on the Temple steps: her children endeavour to revive her; when she recovers she hurries in search of her husband.

Act II. Scene I. *Cleopatra's inner apartments.*

Cleopatra is seen reclining on a couch. Nymphs announce the approach of Antony. He enters, attended by Graces; enraptured with love he is ready to fall at the Queen's feet. She reproaches him for his attachment to his wife and advises him to leave the Egyptian Queen to her misery. He replies that his heart is hers alone. Then she confesses her love. Sylphs, Cupids, and Zephyrs entwine Antony and Cleopatra with garlands of flowers and lead them to a couch. Nymphs offer them baskets of fruit; some burn perfumes, others crown them with roses; while Graces present cups of wine to the Queen and her lover.

Antony is intoxicated with delight. Dances begin and he wishes to take part. Zephyrs take off his cloak. Cleopatra, ever ready to anticipate his wishes, consents to gratify them. She advances with the most graceful attitudes. Groups of cupids express the sentiments by which they are animated.

Cleopatra, aware that Antony is fond of appearing as the Conqueror of India, orders a crown of vine leaves to be brought, a thyrsus, and a panther's skin, as if to celebrate a festival of Bacchus. Antony takes these attributes and is hailed as the son of Jupiter. The Queen invites him to go to the Temple where he is to receive the honours due to him as a god. Zephyrs, Nymphs, and Sylphs precede the lovers.

Act II. Scene II. A spot sacred to Bacchus. In the distance hills covered with vines; here and there statues dedicated to Pan.

The music of cymbals and flutes is heard and youths dressed as satyrs enter, followed by girls attired as bacchantes; among the latter is Octavia, who has disguised herself in order to watch over her husband.

A car enters drawn by satyrs and cupids, in which Antony is seated with Cleopatra. A young girl, representing Erigone, beats her tambourine in the ears of Silenus, borne by satyrs, who holds two cups into which bacchantes press the juice of grapes.

The High Priest welcomes Antony and Cleopatra and is impressed by the majestic appearance of the former, as much as if he were Bacchus himself. The company prostrate themselves before Antony, who is overwhelmed with all this adoration. Antony and Cleopatra sit near the altar, and are entertained with dances.

The lovers are invited to join in the dance. The Queen expresses her love for Antony. She flutters round him like a bacchante, now clasping him in her arms, now feigning to flee from him. Antony pursues and overtakes her, and burns with love. The music increases in volume and passion.

Suddenly one of Antony's officers appears. He looks anxiously for the Emperor. As Antony advances to receive him, he is amazed at finding him engaged in such frivolous pastimes when his presence with the army is imperative. The officer informs him of the arrival of the Roman troops, commanded by Octavius, come to protect and avenge his sister, Octavia. Antony, ashamed of his conduct, orders the officer to assemble his troops.

The Queen endeavours to regain her domination, but Antony tears off his crown and garlands, and upbraids Cleopatra for her beauty, which has become so fatal to his glory. But she stays him with a gesture and seems to say: "Can he think that Cleopatra would abandon him, when his life and honour are in danger?"

She orders her attendants to retire. Egyptian soldiers arrive and range themselves beside her, brandishing their lances and shields. She goes to Antony and returns to him his sword, helmet, and armour, then holds out her hand which he kisses. The troops, headed by Antony and Cleopatra, set out to meet the enemy.

Act III. Scene I. The interior of Cleopatra's palace.

Cleopatra anxiously awaits the result of the battle. Her attendants vainly attempt to calm her. In this hour of uncertainty a cry of victory is heard from the besiegers.

Charmian informs the Queen that Antony is in flight. She is seized with despair but, collecting herself, seems to say to her attendants: "If you wish to preserve the honour of your Queen, set fire to this palace the moment Octavius attempts to chain me to his triumphal car."

Then she gives secret instructions to Charmian, who shudders at their import. In vain does she try to turn her from her purpose. Charmian retires. The clash of arms is heard and Cleopatra retires to the inner part of the palace.

Antony, deserted by his troops, arrives wounded, pursued by Octavius's soldiers, who attempt to enter the palace. Octavia, going to welcome her brother, meets Antony; she entreats the soldiers to spare his life. Antony staggers and falls. Opening his eyes he is surprised to see Octavia and her children, and, overcome with remorse, reproaches himself for his infidelity.

Cleopatra returns and is grieved to find Antony wounded. But he throws himself into his wife's arms and reproaches Cleopatra for his downfall. The Queen, furious at this ingratitude, curses Octavia, who listens with tears in her eyes, while the children, pointing to their father, reproach Cleopatra for their father's death. Antony clasps his wife and children. Cleopatra tries to obtain a last look of forgiveness from her former lover, but he calls down the vengeance of heaven upon her. Enraged, she orders Antony to be removed. Octavia and her sons bear him away.

The Queen, alone, gives vent to tears, until interrupted by the arrival of a peasant who brings her a basket of fruit and flowers, which she receives with eagerness. The tramp of armed men heralds Octavius, who enters with his guard. Cleopatra signs to her attendants and assumes a graceful pose.

Octavius enters and Cleopatra endeavours to charm him, in the hope of being spared the indignity of captivity. Her attendants assume voluptuous groups, but Octavius regards them coldly. He declares that Cleopatra must attend him to Rome. The Queen entreats him to permit her to return to her own land, there to end her days. He refuses. Then the Queen pleads for a few minutes' delay, and orders her diadem and jewels to be brought.

Octavia enters and, hastening to her brother, informs him of the imminent death of her husband. Octavius goes to Antony. Cleopatra commands her attendants to proceed with her plan, then she seizes the basket and hurries away.

Octavius returns overwhelmed with sorrow and holding Octavia's children by the hand; he vows vengeance on Cleopatra. Surprised at not seeing her he speaks to one of his guards, who tells him that she has retired to an inner chamber. Octavius is about to enter it when Cleopatra emerges, supported by two of her faithful attendants. She seats herself on a couch and listens calmly to the reproaches of the conqueror.

Gradually her expression changes and an ironical smile appears on her lips. Avowing her affection for Antony she uncovers her arm and shows the asp entwined about it. Octavius is struck dumb that he should be deprived of the gratification of leading her away a captive.

Cleopatra gazes compassionately at Antony's children and now wishes she could save them from the vengeance that is preparing; her strength forsaking her, she falls into the arms of Charmian and Iras.

At this moment the palace bursts into flames. Octavius seizes the two children and attempts to flee with them, but is stopped by the fall of a wall which reveals the whole palace in flames, and women running hither and thither with lighted torches.

Octavia, half distracted, comes to find her children; approaching near Cleopatra she observes her dead. She would like to render thanks to the gods for having answered her prayers, but she is anxious for the safety of her children. At last she finds her brother and her sons; she runs through the flames to meet them. She sees them overwhelmed in the ruins yet, by her undaunted exertions, saves both her brother and her children.

The soldiers are in full flight; the palace is utterly destroyed.

*

"The arrangement and composition of this ballet," declares the *Journal de l'Empire*[4]: "reveal the touch of an accomplished master. However, this would avail little were the execution unequal to the invention; but what ensures the brilliant success of this work is the combination of the rarest artists to whom the mimed portions have been entrusted.

"Mlle. Chevigny is a really astounding artist in this style; her features are the faithful mirror of the passions which succeed one

[4] March 10th, 1808.

another with incredible rapidity; no one can express tenderness, jealousy, spite, hate, and contempt with greater truth and force; there was one opinion only on the admirable manner in which she rendered the part of Octavia, which she may be said to have created.

"Vestris, already known and distinguished in the same art of depicting the passions with movements of the face and body, surpassed himself. The character of Antony is perfectly adapted to his powers and physique; he is admirably cast; and the various situations in which the Roman General finds himself, enable the actor to display all his rare talent for expression. Struggling with remorse in the midst of pleasure, dying a victim of his follies and debauches, Vestris knew how to depict in turn conjugal love, paternal tenderness, the transports of passion, the intoxication of joy, and the depths of sadness and despair. This role has brought his reputation to its climax.

"Mlle. Clotilde worthily represented Cleopatra by the elegance of her figure, her seductive manners, and by the grace which animates all her movements. These three artists form a triumvirate undoubtedly much less important but much more pleasing in its results than that of Octavius, Antony, and Lepidus."

*

The ballet, under the title of *Cléopâtre Reine d'Egypte,* was produced at London, at the King's Theatre, on April 16th, 1825, the principal parts being taken as follows: M. C. Vestris (*Antony*), Mme. Ronzi-Vestris (*Octavia*), Mme. Le Gros (*Cleopatra*), and M. Boisgirard (*Octavius*). While the presentation was excellent the settings and mechanical effects seemed to have left much to be desired, as will be seen from the following comments in *The Times*[5]:

"In some—but not in all—of the qualities by which a good ballet should be distinguished, the present may be said to excel. The story is very intelligently told; the dances are various and appropriate; the grouping of large masses of figures is managed so as to produce an imposing and elegant effect; the music (a selection from Kreutzer and other eminent composers) is selected with taste; the dances are not only splendid, but, in general, appropriate. Here our praise must end.

"The scenery is not remarkable for its beauty. The opening scene, representing part of Tarsus, and the river Cydnus, is a

[5] April 17th, 1825.

glaring production; the interior of Cleopatra's residence is glittering and tawdry, and the concluding scene, with the illuminated garden, and farthing candle conflagration is contemptible. The best scene is that of a spot sacred to Bacchus. Here, however, the great charm is not to be found in the design, but in the picturesque beauty with which the bacchanals and bacchantes are grouped. . . .

"The two finest dances in the ballet are that in which the Romans and Egyptians, when the heart of Antony has been subdued by the wiles of Cleopatra, unite and bury their dissensions in mutual kindness; and next, when the bacchanals and bacchantes give loose to 'tipsy dance and jollity.' The arrangement of each of the dances was exquisitely harmonious.

"We cannot pay too high a tribute of praise to the graceful movements of Madame Le Gros, who personated Cleopatra. She spoke, so far as action can be made to speak. Her *pas de deux* with Mons. C. Vestris, the elegant Antony of the ballet, was a *chef d'œuvre* of the art. Octavia, the consort of Antony, was represented by Madame Ronzi-Vestris in an enchanting style."

LES PAGES DU DUC DE VENDÔME

Ballet in 1 Act. Book: Jean Aumer. Music: Gyrowitz. Choreography: Jean Aumer. First produced: Kaernthner Thor Theatre, Vienna, October 16th, 1815.

CHARACTERS

The Duc de Vendôme . . .	M. Aumer
The Comte de Muret . . .	M. Rehberger I
Marimon, an old Colonel . .	M. Destasa
Victor, his son ⎱	Mlle. T. Aumer
Auguste ⎰ Pages . .	Mlle. Horschelt I
Philippe ⎱	Mlle. Roiter
Eugène ⎰	Mlle. Neuwirth
Madame de Saint-Ange, the Duc's Sister	Mme. Horschelt
Elise, her niece	Mlle. J. Aumer
Pedrillo, a miller	M. Aichinger
His Wife	Mme. Pfeiffer
Babette,[6] their daughter . . .	Mlle. Horschelt II

Officers of the Duke, Soldiers, Valets,
Peasant Girls, Villagers.

[6] In the Paris production of 1820 the part of *Babette* is called *Rosine*.

Scene. A village in Castile. One one side is the dwelling of Mme. de Saint-Ange, on the other some trees and grassy slopes. In the background a cottage, and an eminence crowned with a mill.

Mme. de Saint-Ange and her niece are seen seated before the door of their house. A number of villagers are gathered about them. Mme. de Saint-Ange reads a letter announcing the imminent arrival of the Duc de Vendôme. Elise takes the opportunity surreptitiously to peruse a letter from her sweetheart, Victor, one of the Duke's pages. Her aunt instructs her to give the village girls flowers and the youths branches of laurel with which to greet the Duke and his officers.

To the gay rhythm of drums beating, the Duke and his staff arrive. He greets Mme. de Saint-Ange and embraces his ward, who is sad at not seeing Victor. But to her joy he enters bearing a flag captured from the enemy. His father, Colonel Marimon, embraces him proudly.

The Duke makes a number of promotions, among those rewarded being the Comte de Muret, whom he presents to Mme. de Saint-Ange as her niece's future husband. Elise cannot conceal her vexation, but Victor, confident of her love, receives the announcement with indifference.

Mme. de Saint-Ange invites the Duke and his staff to witness a little entertainment prepared in his honour. First, the village girls and youths dance, then the pages join in. Afterwards Victor asks Elise for the favour of a dance. They perform a bolero, which is imitated by the other pages and their partners. During the dancing Victor arranges to meet Elise outside her window, at nightfall.

Suddenly an officer arrives with the news that the outposts have been attacked. The Duke orders Marimon to repulse the enemy. Victor wishes to accompany him, but his request is refused. The Duke orders the pages to take six hours' rest, and then goes into his tent.

The girls leave with regret. Eugène follows Babette and tries to creep into her cottage, but her father shuts the door in his face. Undaunted, he prowls round the dwelling.

The pages sup and toast their sweethearts. Meanwhile, Babette steals out of her cottage and looks to see if Eugène is still present. He remains in hiding until she approaches the mill, when he shuts her parents in the house and runs after the girl, who is forced to seek refuge among the pages, each of whom tries to kiss her. Victor, however, contrives to protect Babette until Eugène comes to claim her.

The parents are seen raging at their imprisonment. At last the father manages to get out and rushes to rescue his daughter; but Eugène and Babette run to the mill. When the father dashes back to the mill, Eugène leaves by another path and returns to his companions, who applaud his dexterity.

With the approach of night, Victor recalls his rendezvous with Elise. He suggests to his companions that they should put up their tent and retire for the night. They are surprised at his choice of camping-ground and suggest that he wishes to be as near as possible to his sweetheart. He confesses that is so, but implores them to be discreet. The tent is erected, sentries are posted, and the pages go to sleep, wrapped in the captured flags.

No sooner are the pages asleep than Victor rises and steals towards Elise's house. He claps his hands and she answers with a few chords on her harp. Then Victor climbs on to the balcony and Elise appears at the window. Unexpectedly the Duke chooses this moment to go the rounds. Victor hurriedly hides behind the balcony while Elise closes the window.

The Duke has been attracted by the sound of the harp. Surprised to see the pages' tent and, suspecting some plot against his ward, he determines to call on Mme. de Saint-Ange. As he passes under the balcony Victor leaps over his head and takes to flight.

But the Duke has recognized one of his pages and observes him returning to the tent. Unwilling to compromise Elise he goes to the tent where, recognizing Victor, who feigns to be asleep, he takes off his aiguillette as a means of identification and departs.

Victor, troubled by the Duke's action, takes off his companions' aiguillettes and, showing them to Elise, indicates that he is saved. His mimed messages of love are interrupted by the appearance of Mme. de Saint-Ange, come to look round before retiring. She is surprised at the proximity of the pages' tent and is about to go indoors when Auguste, who has been awakened by Victor's return, seeing Mme. de Saint-Ange and taking her for a girl, rises and makes love to her before she can disclose her identity.

Victor, observing Auguste's error, takes the opportunity to go to Elise, who has followed her aunt at a short distance. At last Auguste recognizes his companion and takes to flight. Presently two other pages fall into the same trap, and the good lady is astonished to see her one admirer become two. She tells them who she is, when they run away so quickly that Elise and Victor have hardly time to separate.

The Duke returns with the Comte de Muret. Mme. de Saint-Ange tells the former of the pages' pranks. To her astonishment he replies that he is acquainted with their lapses. He summons the pages who form in a line. But when she tells him that there are three culprits, it is his turn to be surprised.

He orders the Comte to seize the page without an aiguillette, but finds it difficult to repress a smile when the Comte reports that none of the pages have aiguillettes. Then the Duke reprimands the pages for appearing without so honourable a badge. The pages look at their shoulders and are amazed to find they have no aiguillettes. They immediately go to their tent to search for them.

Mme. de Saint-Ange is horrified to learn from the Duke that one of the pages had entered her house during the night. She goes indoors to look for Elise. Meanwhile the Duke warns the pages that he will break them if they do not find their aiguillettes within an hour. Then he goes into Mme. de Saint-Ange's house.

The Comte tries to find the culprit, but the pages mock him and he retires. When he has gone Victor confesses his stratagem and wishes to return his companions their aiguillettes, but they will not hear of it. While they strive to discover a means of avoiding punishment, the Duke returns. The pages flee, all save Victor, who hides behind a tree.

The Duke calls him, but Victor hesitates. Elise, accompanied by her aunt, witnesses her lover's embarrassment, and becomes greatly agitated. The Duke looks suspiciously at Victor, who disconcerts him by producing an aiguillette from under his coat. Mme. de Saint-Ange suggests that possibly the Duke is mistaken. Then he takes an aiguillette from under his coat and places it in his jacket pocket. Victor adroitly filches it, and, while the Duke and Mme. de Saint-Ange are engaged in conversation, shows it triumphantly to Elise.

The Duke turns to Victor and asks him if he knows the culprit. He replies in the affirmative, but declares that honour prevents his naming him. The Duke orders the page to withdraw.

Enter the Comte de Muret who asks the Duke if he may have the honour of his ward's hand in marriage. Her aunt signs approval. But Elise informs the Comte that she does not love him. He bows and retires. The Duke and Mme. de Saint-Ange are greatly incensed. Her aunt orders Elise to name the page who has the pretension to aspire to her hand. She remains silent. The Duke orders the Comte to summon the pages.

They arrive and form in a line. To the Duke's astonishment they are all wearing aiguillettes. He goes to take the aiguillette from his pocket but finds it gone. Furious, he orders Victor to name the culprit. Each page raises his hand.

Then the Duke plays his last card. He takes Elise by the hand and, presenting her to the pages, asks her to indicate the one she needs to complete her happiness. The pages immediately congratulate Victor, who kneels before the Duke, and Elise does likewise. The Duke is about to vent his rage on the lovers, when Marimon returns victorious.

The Duke shows him his son under arrest for having compromised his niece's reputation. The old Colonel is saddened by this news. The Duke offers to pardon Victor, but the old man refuses the favour. Then the Comte de Muret entreats the Duke to consent to the union of Victor and Elise. His anger soothed by this request, he gives his consent, which is confirmed by Mme. de Saint-Ange.

The captured flags are formed into a trophy, beneath which sit the Duke and his officers. The ballet ends with dances by the villagers and soldiers in honour of the festive occasion.

*

Les Pages du Duc de Vendôme is based on the comedy of the same name by Dieulafoy and Gersin, which was very popular early in the 19th century. A comic opera on the same theme and similarly entitled, with music by Gyrowetz, was performed at the Imperial Opera, Vienna, in 1808.

The ballet was produced at Paris, at the Théâtre de la Salle Favart, on October 18th, 1820. Contemporary opinion expressed the view that the ballet was overloaded with dances so that the development of the action was hindered. "Two *divertissements* in one act," observes the critic of the *Journal des Débats*[7], "is at least one to many, and if the choreographer had retained only the first, I should still advise him to shorten it." The same writer suggests that a choreographer "should devise a varied theme in which pictures of different styles fall naturally into place and present . . . a succession of scenes which harmonize with the plot and serve at once to point and embellish it."

Commenting on the first *divertissement* the critic declares: "No one could witness without delight the scene in which the pages set upon and struggle with the village girls, and, with the petulance of youth and the privilege of their uniform, endeavour to steal kisses from them." The character dances by Ferdinand and Mlle. Aimée, and a *pas* danced by Mlles. Bigottini and Fanny Bias, were highly praised. But the second *divertissement* at the end of the ballet was thought to be superfluous. However, despite these

<hr>

[7] October 20th, 1820.

shortcomings, the piece achieved a complete success and was frequently revived.

The ballet, under the title *The Pages of the Duke de Vendôme,* was produced at London, at the Theatre Royal, Drury Lane, on May 21st, 1833. The cast was Mr. Gilbert (*Duke de Vendôme*), Mr. Howell (*Count de Muret*), Mr. Halton (*Marimon*), Mr. Bartlett (*Pedrillo*), Miss Bell (*Elise*), and Mlle. Augusta (*Victor*).

LA SOMNAMBULE OU L'ARRIVÉE D'UN NOUVEAU SEIGNEUR [8]

Pantomimic Ballet in 3 Acts by Scribe and Jean Aumer. Music composed and arranged by Hérold. Scenery: Ciceri. Choreography: Jean Aumer. First produced: Théâtre de l'Académie Royale de Musique, Paris, September 19th, 1827.

CHARACTERS

Edmond, a wealthy farmer . . .	M. FERDINAND
Thérèse, his fiancée, an orphan girl who has been brought up by Mother Michaud	MME. MONTESSU
Mother Michaud, a miller, Thérèse's foster-mother	MME. ELIE
Madame Gertrude, a young widow and inn-keeper	MLLE. LEGALLOIS
M. de Saint-Rambert, a young Colonel of Musketeers and lord of the manor	M. MONTJOIE
Olivier, a trumpeter of Musketeers and Saint-Rambert's servant . .	MLLE. BROCARD
A Notary	M. MÉRANTE
Marceline, a servant at the inn . .	MME. LAURE

Lords, Ladies, Peasants.

The action passes in Provence, in the island of La Camargue, near Arles.

Act I. A village cross-road. To the right is the entrance to Edmond's farm; to the left is an inn with the sign "The True Lover's Knot." In the distance, forming an angle with the inn, is a dwelling with the name "Michaud, Miller." A ladder stands against Mother Michaud's corn-loft, at the edge of which is a sack of

---

[8] *The Sleepwalker or the Arrival of a New Lord of the Manor.*

wheat. To the right is a sign-post with two arms, marked respectively: "To Arles" and "To Tarascon." To the left is another sign-post lettered "To the Castle."

The curtain rises on a rural scene. It is the rest-hour during a day of hay-making. Farm-hands are eating or resting; young girls and boys are enjoying a dance. Edmond is seen giving instructions.

From time to time he returns to Thérèse and Mother Michaud, looking at the former with love and at the latter with gratitude. Thérèse dances with the girls, but her eyes are on Edmond, and she always comes back to dance with him. In their innocent gaiety they express their mutual love and happiness.

Gertrude comes out of the inn and cannot conceal her spite at such proceedings. She conveys her suspicions to Mother Michaud, who ridicules them. Meanwhile Thérèse and Edmond gaze frequently in the direction of the castle as if expecting someone. At last they see the notary and run to welcome him. The dancing stops.

They reproach the notary for being so late and he explains that he has been awaiting the arrival of the new lord of the manor who would seem to be not coming after all. Seeing Gertrude, the notary pays her compliments, which she acknowledges with an affectionate curtsey.

Edmond, eager to have the marriage-contract drawn up, orders a table to be brought out. Thérèse induces the notary to sit down. Gertrude, piqued against Thérèse, wishes to leave, but Edmond begs her to witness the contract. When all the parties are seated the villagers gather round.

The terms settled, the lovers append their signatures. Mother Michaud makes her cross and Edmond proffers the pen to the widow, who can scarcely hold the pen for rage. But, seeing all eyes fixed upon her, she slowly writes her name and protests her friendship for Thérèse. Edmond asks the villagers to resume work and invites them to the wedding on the morrow.

The villagers depart and Edmond and Thérèse, lingering behind, find themselves alone. They dance together and Edmond places an engagement ring on her finger. Then he gives her a posy which she kisses and places in her bosom. He wishes to kiss her, but she bids him wait until to-morrow. He climbs the ladder to look at the wheat, descends, and leans the ladder against one of the windows of the inn; then he leaves Thérèse, having exacted a kiss from her.

Gertrude enters and reproaches Thérèse for her conduct, but Edmond pleads for her not to be jealous so that they may be good friends. He dances with the two women, forces them to kiss him, and then kisses each in turn. At this moment Saint-Rambert appears, accompanied by his servant, Olivier.

He greets Edmond with a familiarity which surprises him, so that he asks him his business. The stranger begs to be directed to the castle, but, learning that his destination is two leagues away, declares he is too exhausted to go any further.

Edmond invites him to stay the night, but asks him to forgive his house being a little crowded as he has many guests, for he is to be married to-morrow. "Is this your fiancée?" asks the stranger, pointing to Thérèse. "Yes," replies Edmond. "And who is this lady?" continues Saint-Rambert, looking at Gertrude. The latter cannot conceal her annoyance.

Saint-Rambert thanks Edmond for his courtesy but declares that he could not think of intruding upon him. "Here is an inn?" he observes, "I will stay there." Olivier takes Saint-Rambert aside and reminds him that they are expected at the castle. His master insists that he must rest and bids his servant go to the castle and explain that he will arrive to-morrow.

Edmond invites Olivier to go to the farmhouse where he will find a glass of wine, but, seeing the sprightly maid at the inn, he is about to direct his steps there, when his master reminds him that he is taking the wrong direction. Olivier salutes, but Saint-Rambert bids him hold his tongue so that he is not recognized.

Evening falls and the old women of the village form a circle and gossip while the old men play games and drink. They are joined by Olivier. In the centre the young men and girls dance and play at blindman's buff.

The dancing over, Mother Michaud announces that it is time for everyone to go to bed. Gertrude, frightened of catching cold, sends Marceline to fetch her red scarf, which she places over her shoulders. Saint-Rambert goes to the inn.

Olivier, a little fuddled, goes into the farm-house. Edmond follows Thérèse to the mill, but Mother Michaud bids Edmond go to his own home, since they will not be wed until the morrow.

Everyone has retired except Gertrude and the notary. Edmond comes out with a great piece of news and tells Gertrude that the guest she has slighted is the new lord of the manor, for the trumpeter has been talking in his cups. Gertrude hastens to enter the inn and put matters right. The notary is displeased at her sudden departure as he had planned a surprise for her. Edmond gazes at

Thérèse's window and bids the notary goodnight. The worthy
man, greatly preoccupied, strolls homeward.

*Act II. A room in the inn; two side doors. To the right, in the
foreground, is a bed and an armchair; to the left a table.*

Saint-Rambert is seen looking over his room; he sits in an arm-
chair and muses on the events of the evening. Marceline enters
with a candle which she places on the table. Gertrude follows and,
reproving the maid for her lack of attention towards her guest,
places two fine candlesticks on the table. She sends the maid away
and announces that she will wait on him herself. Saint-Rambert,
astonished at his hostess's change of manner, takes advantage of
the occasion to make love to her. She feigns to retire, but, when
Saint-Rambert restrains her, she struggles so violently that he releases her. Gertrude, seeing herself unmolested, leaves so slowly
that Saint-Rambert grasps her shawl; but she escapes leaving the
shawl in his hand; he throws it in the armchair and kneels at
Gertrude's feet. Hearing a noise at the window Gertrude darts
into the room at the right, while Saint-Rambert goes to the window, which suddenly opens to reveal Thérèse.

She is wearing a nightdress and her arms and feet are bare.
Above the window-sill can be seen the head of the ladder left by
Edmond. Thérèse is sleep-walking. She walks slowly to the centre
of the room and seems to be dreaming of her recent dances. She
believes herself to be playing blindman's buff. She flees from an
imaginary pursuer and, taking Saint-Rambert for Edmond, gives
him her hand to kiss. Losing his head, Saint-Rambert runs to
bolt the door. At this moment Gertrude enters and, seeing a
woman in white, retires in indignation.

Saint-Rambert goes to Thérèse who, dreaming of her marriage,
swears to be ever faithful to her husband. Recalled to his senses
Saint-Rambert opens the window and the moonlight streams in.
Thérèse lies down on the sofa as if to sleep. Saint-Rambert gazes
at her for a moment, climbs through the window, and disappears.

Now the door opens softly and the notary, Edmond, Mother
Michaud, and a number of villagers enter bearing posies. They go
to the couch and are amazed to see Thérèse. Edmond is furious.
The noise awakens Thérèse, who does not know where she is or
what is happening.

Mother Michaud gives a cry, seizes the shawl on the sofa, and
wraps Thérèse in it. Meanwhile, Gertrude emerges from the
room. She mingles with the villagers and her indignation exceeds

their own. Thérèse, quailing under her gibes and her foster-mother's reproaches, begs Edmond to defend her. But he repulses her and tells her that their marriage cannot now take place. Every-one goes out. Thérèse, half dead with anxiety, is led away by Mother Michaud.

Act III. A beautiful landscape in Provence. In the background is a mill with a tiled roof; the mill is driven by a river which winds through the grass-land. To the left is a platform prepared for the musicians; here and there are garlands of flowers and interlaced initials.

Young boys and girls decked with ribbons and flowers enter. They attach flowers to Thérèse's door and pass from view.

Mother Michaud and Thérèse come out of the mill. The latter protests her innocence. Her foster-mother calms her and reminds her that her difficulty is to convince Edmond (who now ap-proaches) of her faithfulness. Edmond is sad and moody. Thérèse goes to him and asks him why he treats her so cruelly. He tells her that she has been unfaithful to him. Thérèse kneels at his feet, but he turns his back on her.

Enter Saint-Rambert followed by lords and ladies of the castle and the villagers, who offer him their congratulations. He signs to some of his servants who offer Mother Michaud a beautiful trous-seau for Thérèse. Seeing the two lovers in despair, Saint-Rambert asks everyone else to withdraw. He explains to Edmond how Thérèse, while sleep-walking, innocently entered his room. But Edmond refuses to accept his explanation and declares that were not Saint-Rambert the lord of the manor he would be revenged upon him; since, however, that right is denied him, he will marry someone else. Thérèse is horrified. Seizing her hand Edmond draws off his ring. She swoons into the arms of her foster-mother, who carries her into the mill.

Saint-Rambert is overcome with sadness. He implores Edmond to delay his new marriage for he is sure that Thérèse's innocence will soon be established. Edmond refuses and announces that he is to marry Gertrude, the most virtuous woman in the village. Rec-ognizing his hostess, Saint-Rambert finds it difficult to hide a smile as she approaches in wedding-dress, accompanied by her maid. He is minded to reveal all to Edmond, but Gertrude stays him with a warning gesture.

Preparations for the new wedding are hurried forward. Ed-mond tears down the flowers on the mill and orders the initial

"T" to be replaced by a "G." Then he presents Gertrude to the company as his intended wife. The notary makes a wry face and, when Olivier is asked to lead the musicians, he refuses, since Thérèse is not to be the bride.

Mother Michaud comes out of the mill and shakes her head over Edmond's new choice. She denounces Gertrude and displays the shawl which she found on Saint-Rambert's bed. Edmond is enraged at this new obstacle to his plans. Saint-Rambert reminds him that he had already declared Thérèse innocent, and when Edmond asks him to prove his words, he points to the mill.

Everyone looks in that direction and is horrified to see Thérèse walking in her sleep on the edge of the roof. Edmond wishes to run to her help, but Saint-Rambert holds him back, explaining that she must not be awakened but must seek her own safety. Everyone watches her in terror.

The musicians stop playing. Thérèse continues to walk round the edge. At one moment she is about to rest her foot on the moving sails of the windmill and everyone kneels in prayer, including Gertrude, who is overcome with remorse. At one part of the roof there is the remains of a wall which forms a natural staircase, and by this Thérèse descends to the ground. She listens and believes she hears the bells ringing for Edmond's marriage. She kneels and prays for his happiness. She is sad at the loss of his ring, but consoles herself with the thought that his image is engraved on her heart.

Gertrude, greatly moved by this scene, implores Saint-Rambert to unite in marriage Thérèse and Edmond. Edmond kneels at Thérèse's feet and replaces his ring on her finger. Saint-Rambert opens the basket containing the trousseau. Gertrude places the wedding veil on Thérèse's head, while Saint-Rambert adds a wreath of orange blossom. He signs to the musicians to make ready.

The dancers take their places. Edmond takes Thérèse's hand and, as the music strikes up, the sleeping girl awakes. She thinks she is dreaming and cannot believe in so much happiness, and when she gradually realizes that it is true she can scarcely speak for joy.

Saint-Rambert, having united the happy couple, takes the notary aside and, having disposed of his doubts, induces him to ask for Gertrude's hand, to which she gives her consent. At the same time Olivier becomes engaged to Marceline.

Tables are laid for the wedding-feast and the company take their places. While Thérèse's health is toasted a little boy shows the garter he has filched from the bride. Thérèse blushes, but Edmond reassures her. Everyone struggles to obtain a piece of the ribbon and joyful dances end this happy day.

*

"This is by no means an ordinary ballet," declares *Le Corsaire,* "it is a little drama, perfect as a whole, delightful in detail, characterized by two situations, one lively and bold, the other moving and pathetic, which would have ensured the success of a real play. The music, part adapted, part original, does credit to M. Hérold's taste and ability. The *pas* in the first act were thought to be a little drawn out, it will be easy to curtail them. Mme. Montessu dances and mimes the part of Thérèse with a perfection that our foremost actresses might envy. The success was complete. Tears and applause proved it.

"Many dancers of this theatre could claim the principal role because, notwithstanding her intelligence, Mme. Montessu is perhaps a little too small for a stage so vast, and night-attire does not become her figure. In our opinion, simple dresses would have greatly enhanced the appearance of certain opera nymphs; nevertheless, Mme. Montessu deserved the applause which greeted her from time to time; but her real forte is always dancing, and the tip of her toe will always know more than the tip of her finger.

"Ferdinand carried off the honours of the evening. To appreciate fully the artistry of his mime, you should see him in the first act, effecting a reconciliation between Thérèse and Gertrude, inducing them to kiss each other. Although this is not the most important episode, it is perhaps the one which requires the most skill.

"The first act is perhaps a little long and is composed solely of *pas de trois* and *ensembles*; generally speaking, the dances are not well placed except towards the end of the work; elsewhere, they induce tedium, and their conclusion is awaited impatiently because the audience is anxious to make acquaintance with the somnambulist, and her part does not begin until the second act."

La Somnambule was successfully revived in 1835 and again in 1857 with Pauline Leroux and Carolina Rosati respectively in the title-role.

FILIPPO TAGLIONI

FILIPPO TAGLIONI was born at Milan in 1778. His father, Carlo Taglioni, was a well-known Italian dancer; his mother, whose maiden name was Petrachi, was a member of a well-known family resident at Pisa. There were five children of the marriage—Giuseppa, Luigia, Salvatore, Lorenzo, and Filippo —all of whom attained distinction in the dance, with the exception of Lorenzo whose bent was mechanical invention. The Taglionis had one common characteristic; they all lived to a great age.

Filippo made his *début* as a dancer in 1794 at Pisa, and for the next five years appeared as *premier danseur* at Livorna, Florence, and Venice, often in company with his sisters.

In 1799 he went to Paris and studied with Coulon. He made his *début* at the Académie Royale de Musique on September 17th of the same year in *La Caravane*.

In 1803 he went to the Theatre Royal, Stockholm, as *premier danseur* and *maître de ballet*. He became a friend of the Swedish dramatic author and singer, Christopher Karsten, and fell in love with his daughter, Anna, whom he married on July 9th. They had two children: Marie, born on April 23rd, 1804, and Paul, born on January 12th, 1808. The first was to be the precursor of the romantic school of ballet and the high priestess of the *danse d'élévation*; the second became a talented dancer and choreographer.

During the next thirty years F. Taglioni devised a great number of ballets, variously produced at Cassel, Milan, Turin, Stockholm, Vienna, Paris, Stuttgart, Berlin, and London, of which the most successful were *La Laitière Suisse* (1831) with Fanny Elssler, *La Sylphide* (1832), *La Révolte au Sérail* (1834), and *La Fille du Danube* (1836), in which last three ballets his daughter created the principal roles.

In 1837 Taglioni and his daughter accepted an excellent engagement with the Imperial Russian Theatres; these visits were renewed annually until 1842. During this period Taglioni composed several new ballets of which *La Gitana* (1838) and *L'Ombre* (1839) were the most important.

Taglioni retired in 1852 and built a villa called *Mon Désir* on the banks of Lake Como, where he lived peacefully until he lost his sight, which, happily, was later restored to him as the result of an operation. His wife passed away in 1862 and, oppressed with loneliness, he sought relief in travel. He died at Como on February 11th, 1871, at the age of ninety-four.

Since none of Taglioni's ballets have come down to us to-day it is not easy to assess his value as a choreographer, for his contemporaries are divided as to his merits. From the viewpoint of style his ballets seem to have been *divertissements* linked together with mimed episodes to provide excuse and atmosphere for the succeeding dances.

His greatest contribution to the dance was his daughter, Marie, whose extraordinary elevation and rare lightness he turned to excellent account. Indeed, his chief concern was to devise suitable ballets for the exploitation of those qualities.

La Sylphide, the most successful of Taglioni's compositions, and the one with which his daughter's name is inseparably linked, was the first romantic ballet. This work exerted an enormous influence for not only did it largely abolish the mythological ballet so popular in the eighteenth century, but it opened the door to a new ballet world and a new conception of ballet. Gods and heroes were replaced by supernatural beings who came from dark forest and misty pool, or descended from some poetic heaven to bring romance into the lives of mortals; while the ballet, instead of being a vehicle for voluptuous and provocative poses, was ennobled, spiritualized, elevated almost to the height of a religion

LE DIEU ET LA BAYADÈRE

Opera Ballet in 2 Acts. Book: Scribe. Music: Auber. Choreography of dances by Filippo Taglioni. First produced: Théâtre de l'Académie Royale de Musique, Paris, October 13th, 1830.

CHARACTERS

The Unknown	MM.	Nourrit
Olifour		Levasseur
The Tchop-Dar . . .		Alexis
Captain of the Guard . . .		F. Provot
Chief of the Slaves . . .		Pouilley
A Eunuch		Trevaux

Ninka . . . . . . MMES. CINTI-DAMOREAU
Fatme . . . . . . NOBLET
Zoloe . . . . . . MARIE TAGLIONI

Act I. The principal square in the town of Cashmere. The background is formed by the city gate and the ramparts planted with banyan trees. In the far distance rises a range of mountains. To the left is a pagoda, to the right the Chief Judge's palace. In the centre of the square is a dais surrounded by ushers. The townsfolk are ranged about the dais. To the left is the Unknown, dressed simply and wrapped in a cloak.

The people are impatiently awaiting the judge's arrival. Presently Olifour, preceded by slaves, comes out of his palace. The people approach him with petitions, but the judge is musing on the splendid repast he has just enjoyed.

At last he takes his seat and prepares to administer justice when the sound of dance music is heard. The judge questions an official and is informed that a band of *bayadères* is approaching. No sooner has he spoken than there emerge from the pagoda Ninka with a group of singing *bayadères,* while Zoloe heads a number of dancing *bayadères.* Olifour, offended at the interruption, orders the women to be arrested, but they easily elude the officials who pursue them. Then they return and form a group about Olifour. He speaks to Zoloe who remains silent. Then Ninka explains that she is a stranger and cannot speak the Indian tongue, although she understands it. Olifour asks her what her profession is; she replies with a series of steps. He then inquires what her consolation is in the hour of grief. She dances and her companions follow her example.

Olifour observes that he should punish her, but offers to pardon her if she will be kind to him. Zoloe dances away from him. Then the judge asks the reason for her refusal. She intimates that he is old and ugly. "Who then should I resemble to please you?" he inquires. Zoloe looks round and indicates the Unknown. Ninka implores Zoloe to be prudent.

The judge orders his men to arrest Zoloe. The Unknown challenges the judge's authority and is arrested instead. Zoloe kneels before Olifour and offers to accept his attentions if he will set free the Unknown. The judge consents, declares the court closed, and, having seen Zoloe escorted to the pagoda, goes into his palace.

A little later Zoloe emerges and goes to the Unknown. He thanks her for the great service she has rendered him and gives her a gold bracelet from his arm which, at first, she refuses, then accepts and presses to her heart. He is about to go but she signs to him to remain.

Olifour's slaves come out of the palace bearing caskets of jewels and precious stuffs which they set before Zoloe. Ninka and her *bayadères* watch the scene with interest. The Unknown looks at the presents and is about to depart when again Zoloe entreats him to stay. She gives all her presents to Ninka and her companions. The *bayadères* seize the lovely materials and, draping them about their bodies, form innumerable pictures. The dance grows more and more animated until suddenly interrupted by a trumpet-blast.

The Captain of the Guard and his soldiers enter and announce that a large reward will be paid for information leading to the arrest of a stranger, while death shall be the penalty for any person found sheltering him. The soldiers march away followed by an excited populace.

Zoloe, realizing that the Unknown is the wanted person, urges him to flee through the city gate, but the exit is guarded by soldiers and escape is impossible. Zoloe bids the Unknown hide in a cluster of banyan trees.

Music is heard and Olifour enters, attended by numerous slaves. A rich palanquin is brought forward and Olifour, taking Zoloe's hand, invites her to sit beside him. Suddenly a messenger arrives with a letter. The judge reads the missive, which is a summons for him to attend the Grand Vizier. At first he is minded to ignore it, but, fearful of the consequences, Olifour follows the messenger, telling Zoloe that he will return soon.

No sooner has he gone than Zoloe signs to her companions, and the Unknown, shielded by them, steps into the palanquin, where he is joined by Zoloe. She waves a greeting to Olifour, who has just returned, and the palanquin, surrounded by dancing *bayadères* and escorted by soldiers, passes through the city gate.

Act II. Zoloe's hut, furnished with a table, bed, and two chairs. To the left a hammock attached to the wall. In the background a door.

Zoloe and the Unknown enter cautiously. She begs her guest to be seated. He staggers and confesses that he is starving and thirsty. The *bayadère,* having no food to offer him, takes her jewels from a coffer and, bidding the Unknown remain, darts through the door.

Presently she returns accompanied by Ninka and Fatme bearing provisions. Ninka and Fatme wish to leave, but the Unknown implores them to share the repast. They eat heartily, all save Zoloe who is sad and pensive. The Unknown begs Ninka to sing, and when she has finished expresses his delight. Afterwards Zoloe is asked to dance, but she refuses. Then Ninka asks Fatme to dance. The Unknown is delighted and Zoloe, filled with jealousy, dances first with Fatme, then alone. The Unknown praises Fatme and affects to ignore Zoloe, who gives way to tears. Seeing her distress, Ninka withdraws with Fatme.

The Unknown goes to Zoloe and asks why she is tearful. She confesses her love for him and implores his pardon for her presumption. She kneels to him, but he begs her to rise.

He tells her that he is sleepy and must rest. She prepares the hammock for him into which he climbs. Believing him asleep she tip-toes forward and watches him tenderly. As he seems to be stifled with the heat, she opens a window and fans him. The Unknown opens his eyes and Zoloe, fearful at having awakened him, kneels and begs forgiveness. Suddenly there is a loud knock at the door.

The voice of Olifour is heard, demanding admittance. Zoloe runs and shuts the door, then returns to the Unknown. The judge peers through the open window and is furious to see the two lovers.

A trumpet-blast announces the arrival of the Captain of the Guard and his soldiers.

Zoloe shows the Unknown a secret cave and implores him to flee for her sake. At first he refuses, then consents. Meanwhile the door quivers under the blows rained upon it, then splits into two. The Captain asks Zoloe where her companion is. She indicates that he has fled.

The Captain orders her to be seized and burnt. Soldiers chop the door into pieces and build a pyre on which Zoloe is placed. The wood is fired and immediately thunder rolls and lightning flashes. Zoloe is surrounded by leaping flames when the Unknown, now seen to be the God Brama, shining like the sun, appears at her side and takes her in his arms. Together they rise towards the clouds where gleams the Indian paradise. The clouds close over them and the lovers pass from sight.

*

This ballet is a dramatization of Goethe's ballad and is interesting in that it marks a return to the eighteenth century convention in opera-ballet, when the dancing was combined with the action expressed by the singers. Another point of interest is the dance competition between the two *bayadères* for the favours of

the Unknown. This incident is revived in many ballets, for instance in *La Sylphide,* where the Sylphide and Effie compete for
Reuben's love.

Hippolyte Lecomte's designs for the costumes, which may be
seen in the Bibliothèque de l'Opéra, Paris, are distinguished by a
rare sense of style and atmosphere. But if the lithograph which
accompanies the original libretto is any criterion, the costume-
designs were subjected to many crude "improvements."

Le Dieu et la Bayadère was frequently revived and, reviewing a
production in 1844, Gautier makes some interesting observations
on the theme. "The mute character of the *bayadère,* in conjunction
with the action which persons sing or speak, offers certain difficulties which a piece contrived entirely in pantomime would not
possess. Often the character must hold the stage with nothing to
do, while the others give vent to trills and flourishes. This mixture of conventions produces a disagreeable effect. It may well be
conceded that, by looking at things from a certain angle, singing
and dancing can be the means of expression of a certain group of
persons; but this is more difficult of acceptance when a reply expressed in dancing is made to a question that is sung."

Speaking of Taglioni, who took the role on this occasion, the
critic concedes that she has overcome this obstacle "with an infinite good fortune and skill. By the expressive and touching play
of her features in all manner of ways she links herself with the
action that forsakes her, and demonstrates that she understands
every word the actors say, although they do not speak the same
tongue."

Gautier also reviewed an earlier production of *Le Dieu et La
Bayadère* in 1837, with some pertinent comments on the costumes
then worn. "In this ballet opera the *bayadères* are divided into
bayadères who sing, and *bayadères* who dance. These two classes
are subdivided into two others: flesh coloured *bayadères,* and others
coloured like half-castes. The last-named . . . wear long gloves
of floss-silk on their arms, and silk or cotton gloves of an incredible
shade on their hands. Their faces are carelessly daubed with ochre
or liquorice, which makes them look more like chimney-sweeps
than those voluptuous enchantresses gilded by the sun's rays, who
sound the silver bells of their bracelets before the door of the hot
rooms and on the steps of the pagodas. It seems to us that it would
be an easy matter to make up a dye warm enough in tone to afford that beautiful amber yellow shade characteristic of oriental
complexions, in which the eyes open like black flowers. This
method would obviate that awful chocolate hue and those floss-

silk gloves, unlovely even to the most short-sighted; or else we must presume quite frankly that negresses are white. For our part we would willingly admit this convention, the red skins in *Les Mohicans* and the yellow skins in *La Bayadère* have disgusted us with colour."

*

Le Dieu et La Bayadère was first produced at London, on November 16th, 1833, under the title of *The Maid of Cashmere,* at the Theatre Royal, Drury Lane. The cast was Mr. Wood (The Unknown), Mr. Seguin (Olifour), Miss Betts (Leila), Miss Cawse (Zilia), Mlle. Duvernay (Zelica), and Mlle. Augusta (Fatima).

"It is excellently got in every department," declares *The Times.*[1] "The dances are numerous and they are exceedingly well performed. Mademoiselle Duvernay, as the heroine, exhibited much elegance and grace in her movements. Her style of dancing is unambitious but it is expressive. Her dumb-show answers to the old judge, in the first interview with him, spoke as plainly as it is possible for mere action to speak. The *tableau* at its conclusion, is as beautiful as it is unique."

Thackeray, however, was enthusiastic concerning Duvernay's dancing. "When I think of Duvernay prancing in as the Bayadère —I say it was a vision of loveliness such as mortal eyes can't see nowadays. How well I remember the tune to which she used to appear! Kaled used to say to the Sultan: 'My Lord, a troop of those dancing and singing girls called Bayadères approaches,' and, to the clash of cymbals, and the thumping of my heart, in she used to dance! There has never been anything like it—never. There never will be—I laugh to scorn old people who tell me about your Noblet, your Montessu, your Vestris, your Parisot—pshaw, the senile twaddlers[2]!"

LA SYLPHIDE

Ballet in 2 Acts. Book: Adolphe Nourrit. Music: Jean Schneitzhoeffer. Scenery: Ciceri. Costumes: Eugène Lami. Choreography: Filippo Taglioni. First produced: Théâtre de l'Académie Royale de Musique, Paris, March 12th, 1832.

[1] *November 17th, 1833.*
[2] *Roundabout Papers.*

La Sylphide	MLLE. MARIE TAGLIONI
James Reuben, a Scots peasant	M. MAZILIER
Anna Reuben, his mother .	MLLE. BROCARD
Effie, a peasant, Anna's niece	MLLE. NOBLET
Gurn, a Scots peasant . .	M. ELIE
Old Madge, a Sorceress . .	MME. ELIE
A Sorceress	MLLE. ROLAND
Sylphides	MLLES. ALEXIS, LEROUX, PERCEVAL

Peasants, Witches, Sylphides.

Act I. The interior of a farmhouse in Scotland. In the background is a large window, to the left of which is a staircase, leading to an upper room. The day is just dawning.

In the corner of a vast chimney lies Gurn, sleeping heavily. James, seated in a chair by the fireside, dreams of a charming vision. A Sylphide, the object of his dream, kneels beside him and contemplates his features with affection. She flutters around him and over his head, cooling the air he breathes by agitating her wings. James, still asleep, appears to follow her movements. Then she leans over him and lightly kisses his forehead. He awakes with a start and pursues the phantom, which vanishes through the chimney.

Unable to determine whether he was awake or asleep, James calls Gurn and plies him with questions. But Gurn was dreaming of the lovely Effie, who is to be married to James that morning.

There is a knock at the door and Effie enters with James's mother. Gurn offers her bashfully the feathers of a heron he has killed. She thanks him and, observing James still deep in thought, reproaches him for being sorrowful on their wedding-day. He protests his love and kisses the hand she extends to him. Gurn advances to do the same, but she will not permit him to do so. James laughingly threatens his rival and Gurn retires. Sad at heart, he can scarcely control his tears as he sees the betrothed couple kneel and receive a blessing from James's mother.

Now Effie's friends arrive with gifts; the young girls congratulate James and laugh at Gurn, who begs them to plead for him. Effie thanks her friends and adorns herself with their presents. James, thinking of the Sylphide, unwittingly draws near the chimney and gazes at the place where she vanished. But what does he see—a hideous old hag known as Madge, reputed a sorceress.

He bids her begone, but the girls entreat him to let her remain so that she can read their hands. Effie asks her if she will be happy in wedlock. "Yes," replies Old Madge. "Does James love me truly?" she continues. "No," is the answer. Now Gurn offers his hand and Madge declares that he loves Effie. James, enraged, drives the hag away. Gurn asks Effie to pay heed to Madge's words, but the girls mock him and Effie assures James that she does not believe what the fortune-teller said.

Mother Reuben bids Effie prepare for the ceremony and escorts the young bride up the staircase, followed by the girls.

James, alone, is divided between Effie and the Sylphide. Suddenly the window opens and James sees the Sylphide standing on the window ledge. Perceiving that she is sad he questions her, and gradually, unwillingly, she confesses that she loves him. She tells him how in the depths of night she protects him from evil and sends him sweet dreams. James is deeply touched but replies that he is betrothed to Effie.

The Sylphide is in despair. She bids James farewell, for she wishes to die. James calls her back and confesses in his turn that her image is always with him. The Sylphide, overjoyed, flutters about James and urges him to go with her. He refuses. Then the Sylphide dons a plaid left by Effie and kneels at his feet. James, greatly moved, takes her in his arms and kisses her lips.

Gurn, a witness of this scene, hastens to tell Effie and her friends. Hearing the noise, James places the Sylphide in his armchair and covers her with the plaid. Gurn and Effie raise the plaid, but the sprite has disappeared. The girls laugh and Effie reproaches Gurn for having accused James unjustly. Now the villagers arrive to join in the festival; the old people drink, the young dance.

James, still distracted by recent events, forgets to invite his bride to dance; it is she who invites him. But always the pale Sylphide, seen by James alone, flits in and out of the dancers, vainly pursued by James. The company think him bereft of his senses.

The dancing ceases and the wedding ceremony begins. Effie receives the virginal crown and nosegay, and Mother Reuben gives her a wedding ring. James takes off the ring from his own finger and is about to exchange it with Effie's, when the Sylphide glides from the chimney and seizes the ring. She swears that she will die if he marry Effie. James is fearful for her welfare and she takes this opportunity to induce him to go with her. They disappear behind Effie's friends.

Effie is ready and now James is called. But, to the general consternation, there is no reply. Gurn declares that he has seen him flying towards the mountains with a young woman. Effie is heart-broken. Mother Reuben is angry, and everyone expresses the utmost indignation. Gurn again urges his love and the girls speak in his favour. But Effie cannot reply for despair. Mother Reuben takes her in her arms while Gurn kneels at her feet.

Act II. A forest. To the left is a rock and a cavern. In the foreground is a great tree. It is night and the air is heavy with mist.

Old Madge is seen engaged in casting spells. She traces a magic circle in the centre of which she places a cauldron. She walks three times round the cauldron and strikes it with a spoon. Immediately evil witches hurry to her side. With fiendish glee they dance about the cauldron, which begins to boil. Presently they take from the vessel a spangled scarf of sinister purpose which is entrusted to Madge. At dawn the witches glide into the cavern.

The mist clears before the rising sun and now it is possible to see the wooded landscape. James enters the glade, bearing a bird's nest which he wishes to offer to the Sylphide. Suddenly she is beside him. She dances gaily about James while he watches her with enraptured gaze.

She asks him what he carries in his hand. He offers her the nest, but the Sylphide, alarmed to find it is a living gift, hastens to return the nest to a tree-top.

Quickly she returns and the lovers walk blissfully, hand in hand, through the forest. The Sylphide summons her sisters and a band of sylphs appear and encircle them. The Sylphide vanishes and James tries to recapture her, but time and again he finds he has only captured a sister. Exhausted by his efforts he is about to fling himself on the ground, when the Sylphide again stands beside him, and his distress is calmed. One by one the sylphs vanish until finally he is alone.

James, in despair, thinks regretfully of Effie and wonders if he has relinquished material happiness for a vain chimera. He cannot bear the fleeting visits of the Sylphide and would compel her constant presence.

Old Madge comes out of the cavern and crosses his path. He takes the opportunity to beg her forgiveness for his insults. She airily waves aside the apology and asks if he desires help. He grasps eagerly at her suggestion and she produces the spangled scarf. "Twine this about her," Madge directs, "and her wings will fall; unable to fly, she is thine for ever." James overwhelms the hag with thanks and escorts her to the cavern.

As he returns the Sylphide flies to meet him. James, eager to test the efficacy of his talisman, invests her with the fatal scarf. The sparkling wings drop to earth and at the same instant the Sylphide places her hand on her heart, as if struck by a mortal blow. James clasps her in his arms, but she repulses him and swoons at his feet. Her breathless farewell is drowned by a hoarse laugh from Old Madge, come to gloat upon the tragedy.

Sad music fills the air and the sylphs descend from the trees and surround their sister, who expires in their arms. James kneels beside her, stricken with remorse. The mourning sylphs bear their dead companion away, up and up, towards the tree tops, where they pass from sight.

The silence of the forest is broken by the stirring music of a bagpipe, mingled with the joyful ringing of bells. Through the trees can be seen a bridal procession. Gurn, triumphant, is leading to the altar Effie, already consoled.

*

La Sylphide occupies a unique position in the history of ballet, for its production marked the beginning of a quite new era in choreography. The Romantic Movement which had its inception in 1830 saw its choreographic expression in La Sylphide. Its success was immediate and its influence immense. As Gautier remarked: "After La Sylphide, Les Filets de Vulcain and Flore et Zéphire were no longer possible; the Opera was given over to gnomes, undines, salamanders, elves, nixes, wilis, peris—to all that strange and mysterious folk who lend themselves so marvellously to the fantasies of the maître de ballet. The twelve palaces in marble and gold of the Olympians were relegated to the dust of the store-rooms, and the scene-painters received orders only for romantic forests, valleys illumined by the pretty German moonlight reminiscent of Heinrich Heine's charming ballads. Pink-coloured tights always remained pink, because there could be no choreography without tights; only the Greek cothurnus was exchanged for satin shoes."

La Sylphide, personified in the rare grace and lightness of Marie Taglioni, caused the Ballet to become ennobled and spiritualised; the voluptuous dancing and poses characteristic of the eighteenth century ballets, which tradition persisted in the early nineteenth century ballets, gave place to a seeking after a sublime and chaste ethereality; the danseuse was transformed from a woman into a wraith.

The plot of La Sylphide served as the model for numerous other ballets, for the vogue of the Romantic Ballet was to endure for a long decade, to be reborn in later years in such productions as *Le Lac des Cygnes.* The key situation is always the same, a female being of supernatural origin visits the earth and becomes enamoured of a male mortal; discord ensues as a result of her lover's earthly ties and interests clashing with her own demands. The situation is repeated in *Giselle, La Péri, Ondine, Eoline,* and similar ballets, only the setting is varied so that sometimes the visitor comes from the air, sometimes from depths of lake or sea, and sometimes from a forest glade.

La Sylphide also marks a revolution in stage costume. The dancers of the Empire wore high waisted tunics, pleated to reveal the figure. Eugène Lami, the designer of the costumes for this ballet, created a costume of white muslin to suggest the vaporous quality of the Sylphide. The dress consisted of a tight fitting bodice, leaving the neck and shoulders bare, bell shaped skirt reaching midway between the knee and the ankle, and pale pink tights and satin shoes; the only adornments were a pale blue ribbon about the waist, a pair of tiny wings between the shoulder blades, a posy at the breast, a pearl necklace and bracelets, and a garland of convolvuli to frame the hair.

*

On February 28th, 1831, Dr. L. Véron undertook the direction of the Opera. His first important production was Meyerbeer's opera *Robert le Diable,* which contains the famous ballet of the nuns, specially written for Taglioni.

Soon after its first performance on November 22nd of the same year, Adolphe Nourrit, the celebrated tenor at the Opera, brought to the director a *scenario* for a ballet—to be world-renowned as *La Sylphide*—which he had composed on Charles Nodier's fantastic tale *Trilby ou le Lutin d'Argail* (1822). Nodier is, of course, famous for his romantic stories, which tell how the lives of mortals are affected by the visitations of elves and goblins. In 1821 Nodier had visited Scotland in the company of Baron Taylor and presumably *Trilby* was the outcome.

It has been customary to consider Nourrit's *scenario* as simply an arrangement of certain incidents in Nodier's story. This is not so. *Trilby* is the story of a Scots fisherman and his wife whose happiness is destroyed by the visitations of a handsome male sprite who continually appears before the latter, whispering declarations of love into her ear. Now, in the ballet, there is a sprite too, a sylphide, a female sprite. The sylphide, like the sprite in *Trilby,* has a partiality for making appearances from the chimney. The scene, too, is laid in Scotland; but otherwise the plot is different entirely.

Nourrit never seems to have had his just share of the credit for the success of *La Sylphide*. Whether, as in so many modern ballets, the audience thought only of the ballet for its association with the dancer and scarcely gave a thought to the unseen writer of the *scenario*; or whether Nourrit preferred to remain anonymous (for his name does not appear on the poster advertizing the first performance), having earned by his magnificent singing laurels enough and to spare; the fact remains. The majority of the printed stories of the ballet quite falsely attribute the authorship to Filippo Taglioni.

Dr. Véron read through Nourrit's synopsis, and heartily approved for, as he said: "the action was simple, easy to follow, and the end most touching." He took the *scenario* to Filippo Taglioni and his daughter, who were both enchanted with it and eager to begin rehearsals at once. It was decided to call the ballet *La Sylphide,* and Véron tells us that "the better to justify the title, numerous flights of sylphides were devised, and, above all, a circling flight; there was fantasy in this ballet; the first act, which contrasted with the poetic setting of the second, diverted the spectator by more than one surprise. A scene of sorcerers preceded the forest spectacle; but as M. Duponchel was already very keen on the devilries in *La Tentation* (an opera ballet by Cavé), then in course of preparation, he stole some of M. Taglioni's devils, and this *maître de ballet* often came to me in tears about the meanness of his hell and the few sorcerers that were left him.[3] "

The first performance of *La Sylphide* was announced for March 12th (1832). The director could not sleep the night before, so much did he fear an accident might befall one or other of the twelve or fifteen *figurantes* suspended by wires from the "flies." At every rehearsal he had carefully examined the "flying" apparatus to make certain that all was in order. The "flying" dancers were given a bonus of ten francs apiece, but there was no lack of volunteers; every member of the *corps de ballet,* both women and children, begged the favour of being hooked on the wires.

Owing to the careful production, the first performance went without a hitch, and the part of the Sylphide found its first and greatest exponent in the person of Marie Taglioni. Her wings of pale blue gauze seemed a part of her body and not a detail of stage costume, for she soared and hovered with the grace and ease of a bird.

---

[3] *Mémoires d'un Bourgeois de Paris.*

As to the ballet's reception, it is sufficient to quote De Boigne who says, *"Robert le Diable,* sung by Nourrit, Levasseur, Damoreau, Dorus, and danced by Taglioni, had an immense, prodigious, and astounding success, which still endures and will always endure. *La Sylphide,* borne on the wings of Taglioni, soared to the skies.[4]"

It is true that some critics saw fit to reproach the scene of "flying" as being only a repetition of one of the effects in Didelot's *Flore et Zéphire,* which had remained in the repertory. But, in the Didelot ballet, the principal dancers did not risk themselves on the wires, their parts were doubled by others; and there were only two dancers on wires, whereas, in the second act of *La Sylphide,* there were some twelve or fifteen, *including the première danseuse.*

And what of Taglioni herself? An anonymous critic wrote of her thus: "The telegraph wires and the geometrical figures disappeared; no more of those laboriously voluptuous poses, no more of those would-be lascivious scenes, played with smiles and sidelong glances; no more pointed elbows, broken wrists, detached little fingers; in a word, nothing which made one feel the labour of a profession, the artifice of a craft, the characteristics of a school. All her proportions are full of harmony, she forms in her *ensemble,* deliciously rounded contours or lines of an admirable purity. In all her person there is a remarkable suppleness, in all her movements a lightness which keeps her from the ground; if it may be so expressed, she dances everywhere as if each one of her limbs were carried by wings.[5]"

All Paris spoke of the dancer as "Our Sylphide." The ballet created a new fashion. Taglioni, both on the stage and in private life, favoured dresses of white muslin, as a result of which this material became the rage. The Maison Maurice Beauvais brought out, in her honour, a new head-dress style "The Sylphide." All the ladies sought to emulate her airiness. They adorned their costumes with a profusion of ribbons to make them seem ethereal with their flutterings and rustlings.

*

La Sylphide was first produced in London on July 26th, 1832, at the Theatre Royal, Covent Garden. The parts were taken as follows: Marie Taglioni (*La Sylphide*), Paul Taglioni (*James*), and his wife, Amalia Galster-Taglioni (*Effie*). The character of the Sorceress was played by Laporte, the director of the theatre. The

---

[4] *Petits Mémoires de l'Opéra.*
[5] *Les Adieux à Mademoiselle Taglioni,* Paris, 1837.

scenery was by Grieve, and, in addition to the original score, one episode was accompanied by music taken from Paganini's *Witches Dance*.

The ballet was received "with thunders of applause." *The Times* described *La Sylphide* as "a new ballet in which Taglioni convinces the most fastidious critic that dancing is an art worthy to rank with poetry and painting—that motions can convey to the mind, not only the most beautiful and picturesque forms, but also the most enchanting fancies. No description of a sylph ever imagined by poet, or delineated by painter, could come up to the embodied realization presented by this wonderful artist."

La Sylphide was first produced at St. Petersburg on September 6/18, 1837, with Taglioni, who made her *début* before a Russian public. The *Svernaya Pchela* (*Northern Bee*), records: "Yesterday, November 6th, Marie Taglioni made her first appearance in *La Sylphide* and the public, which received her with acclamation and applause, was not disappointed in its expectations. Marie Taglioni was recalled at the end of the first act, after her dance in the second act, and three times at the end of the ballet."

La Sylphide was first produced at Milan on May 29th, 1841, at the Teatro alla Scala, with Taglioni in the title-role.

The ballet enjoyed a great vogue and was constantly produced and revived in most European capitals, sometimes with the original choreography, and sometimes with new versions composed by other *maîtres de ballet*. Most of the prominent dancers of the day attempted the famous role, but none succeeded in effacing the memory of its creator.

La Sylphide has a considerable iconography; there must be not far short of a hundred representations of the ballet and its principal interpreters.

NATHALIE OU LA LAITIÈRE SUISSE[6]

Ballet in 2 Acts. Book: Filippo Taglioni. Music: Gyrowitz and Caraffa. Scenery: Ciceri. Choreography: Filippo Taglioni. Produced: Théâtre de l'Académie Royale de Musique, Paris, November 7th, 1832.

CHARACTERS

Lord Rewena	M. Montjoie
Lady Rewena, his wife . .	Mme. Roland
Oswald, his brother . . .	M. Mazilier

[6] *Nathalie or The Swiss Milkmaid.*

Bettemberg, a farmer on Lord Rewena's estate . . .	M. Mérante
Charlotte, his wife . . .	Mme. Elie
Henriette	Mlle. Pauline Leroux
Nathalie	Mlle. Marie Taglioni
Karll, Henriette's fiancé . .	M. Simon
Walther, Oswald's confidant .	M. Desplaces
Zug, a goat-herd, a kinsman .	M. Elie

Musicians, Sportsmen, Huntsmen, Villagers.

The action passes in Switzerland, on Lord Rewena's estate.

Act I. A farm. To the right is the main entrance of the farmer's residence, which is a continuation of the farm buildings. Opposite is an elegant summer-house which Lady Rewena has built as a hunting-box for her husband. In the background is a smiling and picturesque Swiss landscape. Dawn is just breaking. Shepherds are seen leading their flocks of goats to pasture, while villagers are setting out gaily to their work.

Farmer Bettemberg comes out of his house and delights in the promise of fine weather. Astonished to see no one about, he shouts towards the stalls. Immediately farm-hands enter drawing wheel-barrows or carrying farm implements; others sweep the ground and tidy up.

Women emerge from the dairy with pails of milk which they carry to the farm; all is bustle and movement. The farmer scolds and gives his orders. Henriette, his eldest daughter, bids him good-day and having kissed her he tells her to take the milk to various houses. She is about to leave on her errand when Karll, her fiancé, arrives, impatient to see her. After greeting Bettemberg he asks his permission to give Henriette a posy. The farmer consents but almost immediately bids the lovers attend to their tasks.

Nathalie comes, dragging a little wheel-barrow. She runs to her father and kisses him. It is easy to see that she is his favourite. He inspects the milk she has brought and the flowers she has gathered for Lady Rewena, and tells her to return as soon as possible. She sets out for the castle.

Other peasants come hurrying up and Bettemberg berates them for being late. They make excuses and go into the cattle-shed.

Now comes the farmer's wife, followed by servants carrying large baskets. She tells her husband that she is going to the fields to superintend the work and serve breakfast. Bettemberg thanks her. The latest arrived workers come out of the sheds with large cheeses, which they are told to take to various markets.

Just as Bettemberg is about to leave, Zug arrives and asks for Nathalie. Charlotte tells him that she has gone to the castle. Bettemberg urges Zug to his work and everyone leaves.

Young Oswald, Lord Rewena's brother, enters with his confidant, Walther. The former looks towards the castle, then hides with Walther. Nathalie, radiant, enters with an empty wheelbarrow. Oswald goes towards her; surprised at his sudden appearance, she remains motionless. But seeing him minded to come nearer she leaves the wheel-barrow and runs to the farmhouse. Oswald leaps over the wheel-barrow and reaches the door just as Nathalie closes it.

Oswald tells Walther of his love for Nathalie and asks him to carry her off. Walther refuses but, on being offered a purse of gold, promises his aid. Oswald begins to explain his plan when footsteps are heard and the plotters return to the castle.

Enter Zug, breathless with running back from the market. Delighted to see Nathalie's wheel-barrow he wheels it to the shed. At the same moment Nathalie opens the door and looks to see if Oswald is still there.

Zug goes to her and reproaches her for her coldness towards him. At first she laughs, then, soothing him, consents to dance with him.

Bettemberg and his wife return from the fields just as Walther arrives to announce that Lord Rewena is going to hunt and desires breakfast at his pavilion before leaving. The farmer is delighted with this news and busies himself with the necessary preparations.

Walther returns to the castle and the farmer and his wife give various directions. Some peasants are told to summon the village; others, under Henriette, prepare the breakfast. Nathalie is sent to warn the young girls to be ready to receive Lady Rewena; Zug and Karll are dispatched to the millers to ask them to put on their best clothes.

Nathalie comes with the girls; Zug and Karll have collected a number of musicians; the farmer and his wife bring out baskets of flowers which Nathalie and her friends are to present to Lady Rewena.

A lively march announces the arrival of Lord and Lady Rewena, accompanied by their friends and Oswald. The villagers dance gaily and fling their hats into the air. Lord and Lady Rewena thank the farmer and his wife for their charming reception and Lady Rewena distributes a number of presents to the young girls, Nathalie being given a gold chain. Oswald tries to approach Nathalie, but always she evades him.

Nathalie and her friends, delighted with their presents, demonstrate their joy in graceful dances and by offering flowers to their lord and lady.

Oswald, greatly moved by Nathalie's charm and grace, reminds Walther of their compact. A huntsman announces that breakfast is ready. The party move off to the pavilion and the villagers dance for their entertainment. The repast ended, the party sets out for the chase.

Bettemberg and his wife bid the villagers good-bye and invite them to the wedding of Henriette and Karll, soon to take place. The farmer sends Karll indoors to read the marriage contract, while Charlotte sends Henriette and Nathalie to tidy the pavilion and close it.

Walther, who has feigned to follow the hunt, waits for an opportunity favourable to the execution of his project. Zug offers to help Nathalie, but the sisters, who wish to send him away, finally accept his assistance on condition that he carry everything to the farmhouse, in consequence of which he is soon loaded like a mule. Charlotte comes to the door of the farm and calls to Henriette to sign the contract. She joyfully obeys, promising to return shortly.

Nathalie closes the windows and Walther, seeing her alone, engages her in conversation. But Nathalie indignantly refuses his proposals. He tries to hold her, but she slips from his grasp and runs to the farmhouse. Alas, her escape is barred by Walther's men, whom he has previously placed in concealment. Frightened at their appearance she swoons and is quickly carried off.

Zug, not finding Nathalie, searches for her and finds on the ground the gold chain which Lady Rewena gave her. Walther returns to look for the chain and sees Zug considering it. For the moment he does not know what to do, but, seeing Zug enter the pavilion, he quickly locks the door and flings the key away.

Zug, finding himself shut in, makes such a noise that everyone comes to see what is the matter. They are astonished to see Zug at one of the windows. They run to the door but the key is missing. Zug, furious, climbs through the window and tells the farmhands of his discovery. Consternation is general. The farmhands form search-parties and Bettemberg, attended by a number of villagers, hastens to acquaint Lady Rewena of his misfortune.

Act II. An elegant room in Lord Rewena's castle. It is presented to communicate with Oswald's apartment. In the background, a little to the left, is a large drapery which conceals an alcove containing a life-size statute of Oswald; to the right is a window with a door at the side.

Oswald and Walther bring in Nathalie, still unconscious. Oswald directs her to be carefully placed on a sofa and, sending away the men, after having handsomely rewarded them, he places Walther behind the curtain.

Oswald looks at the girl with admiration but becomes alarmed that she does not come to. He goes to the curtain and tells Walther to fetch a bottle of smelling-salts, with which he tries to revive Nathalie. When she shows signs of returning consciousness Oswald hides behind the curtain and watches her movements.

With mingled surprise and fear Nathalie looks upon the splendour of her surroundings and tries to recollect how she came to be there. Then she remembers how she was captured and resolves to escape. Glancing in a mirror she is frightened, thinking that she is not alone, but, discovering her mistake, she contemplates her image with delight. Seeing the door she tries it only to find it locked. She goes to the curtain and Oswald withdraws.

Nathalie lifts the curtain softly and, to her fright, sees Oswald placed in the middle of the alcove. She runs behind the sofa and begs him not to approach her. Hearing nothing she goes towards Oswald and, reassured by his immobility, places her hand on his heart and seems annoyed that it does not beat. She goes to the sofa and sulks. Meanwhile Oswald places a posy in the statue's hand. Startled by the noise she turns round and is astonished at the appearance of the flowers, but she comes to the conclusion that she must have overlooked them. Taking the posy she dances. Oswald seizes the opportunity to move the statue and take its place.

Nathalie goes to the supposed statue and amuses herself by placing the posy upon it in various ways until, growing tired, she sits at the statue's feet. This position incites Oswald to express his love, but, seeing her conscious of his gestures, he resumes his former immobility. Reassured, Nathalie goes to place the posy in the supposed statue's hand and feels the heart beating. Astonished at this marvel she dances for joy.

Oswald, unable to contain his emotions, throws himself at her feet. Nathalie, seized with apprehension, kneels facing him and implores him to save her. Oswald calms her and succeeds in inducing her to listen to him. He asks for her hand which at first she refuses, then finally surrenders. A loud banging at the door interrupts this scene of love.

Oswald runs to open the door and there enter Lord and Lady Rewena, followed by the farmer and his wife, and a number of villagers. Lord Rewena expresses his displeasure at Oswald's conduct and demands an explanation. Oswald pleads his overmaster-

ing love. Lord Rewena is dissatisfied with this excuse. Oswald
then offers to make every reparation and turning to Bettemberg
asks for his daughter's hand in marriage. Everyone is astonished
and Lord Rewena asks him to repeat his words.

Nathalie is confused. Lady Rewena asks her if she is willing to
marry Oswald. She consents. Joy is universal. Lady Rewena gives
Nathalie to Oswald. Bettemberg approves the union and clasps
the couple in his arms.

Zug is in despair but Karll consoles him. Lady Rewena suggests
that everyone should go to the farm and celebrate this happy ending, a suggestion which is unanimously approved.

The scene changes to that of the first act and the ballet concludes
with a succession of dances in which all take part.

*

Nathalie ou la Laitière Suisse was first produced by F. Taglioni
for Fanny Elssler at Vienna, on February 4th, 1831. He revived
the piece for his daughter at Paris in 1832. A ballet, however, based
on the same theme, was given by the *maître de ballet* Titus in 1832.

The production had a good reception in Paris, due to the merits
of the dancers taking part in it, rather than to any particular merit
of the theme, which depends on the far-fetched assumption that
the heroine mistakes her lover for a statue, and *vice versa*.

The settings, according to *Le Constitutionel*,[7] were "very beautiful, the costumes new and elegant."

"Mlle. Taglioni's artlessness, grace, and lightness," continues the
same writer, "approach the prodigious in the new part which she
has just played; she danced like a bird in the first act, when she
makes fun of the goat-herd Zug while eluding his attentions, and
revealed herself a perfect actress in the statue scene. . . .

"Nothing less than Mlle. Taglioni's marvellous talent is required
to ensure the success of this choreographic work. That virtuoso
remains constantly on the stage and when she does not dance, you
see the pick of the other dancers. . . . Daumont with Mlles. Noblet and Dupont, Perrot and Mlle. Leroux, Emile and Mlle.
Taglioni. . . ."

The *Journal des Artistes*[8] acclaims Taglioni as an admirable
dancer, but asks whether she merits the same praise as mime.
"Certainly," he declares, "Mlle. Noblet and Mme. Montessu would
have done better, and it is to be regretted that one sees them so
seldom in mimed roles of the first rank."

[7] November 9th, 1832.
[8] November 11th, 1832.

Nathalie was produced at London, at the King's Theatre, on May 9th, 1833, with Taglioni in the title-role. *The Times*, however, dismisses the ballet in a single line as being "very insipid."

LA RÉVOLTE AU SÉRAIL [9]

Ballet in 3 Acts. Book: Filippo Taglioni. Music: T. Labarre. Scenery: Ciceri, Léger, Feuchère, and Despléchin. Costumes: Duponchel. Choreography: Filippo Taglioni. First produced: Théâtre de l'Académie Royale de Musique, Paris, December 4th, 1833.

CHARACTERS

Mahomet, King of Granada .	M. MONTJOIE
Ismaël, Commander of the Army	M. MAZILIER
Zulma, his betrothed . . .	MLLE. MARIE TAGLIONI
Myssauf, Chief Eunuch . .	M. SIMON
Zeir, the King's Page . . .	MLLE. PAULINE LEROUX
Mina, a Negress	MLLE. ELIE
The Spirit of Womankind, in the guise of a Slave	MLLE. LEGALLOIS
An Iman	M. DÉSPLACES.
A Black Slave	M. GUÉRIOT

The King's Wives, the King's suite, Ismaël's suite, Pages, Slaves, Amazons, Attendants on the Spirit of Women.

The action passes in Spain, in the kingdom of Granada, at the period of the Moorish domination.

Act I. The audience hall at the Palace of the Alhambra, Granada. To the left are circular tiers of seats. The main entrance permits a view of the Court of Lions. Above is a gallery leading to a mosque. To the right a door, covered with a rich hanging, leading to the women's apartments. Above the door is a balcony leading to the same quarters.

At the rise of the curtain the principal officers of state are seated in tiers, while Mahomet, enthroned, reads a communication which evidently affords him the greatest pleasure.

There is a burst of martial music and Ismaël enters, followed by a numerous suite who lay at Mahomet's feet the standards and trophies captured from the vanquished Spaniards. As Ismaël enters, Mahomet and his officers rise. The monarch greets the

[9] *The Revolt in the Harem.*

general and congratulates him on his victory. Having given details of the battle, Ismaël requests permission to retire, as he wishes to visit his betrothed. Mahomet consents but asks him to remain a little while at the palace and share in the festival that has been prepared in his honour. Forced to obey, Ismaël has to sit beside the king, who signs for the festival to commence.

The curtain guarding the women's apartments is drawn aside and slaves dance before the king, who is surprised not to see Zulma, his favourite. Zeir informs him that she is sad, but the king orders her to dance. Zeir communicates this desire to Myssauf who hastens to fetch the slave.

Presently Zulma enters with Mina, her negress. She is sad at heart, fearing never to see her beloved again. She walks towards the throne with eyes downcast. Raising her eyes she perceives Ismaël, who is horrified to find that his beloved is the king's favourite. Zulma appears to indicate that her situation is due to no fault of her own. Ismaël is furious while Zulma burns to justify herself, but Mina signs to the lovers to be silent. Mahomet is delighted to observe Ismaël's appreciation of Zulma. The monarch asks him if his mistress is as beautiful, then orders Zulma to dance.

Pages bring in a cushion on which Ismaël kneels. At a sign from the king Zulma removes the warrior's aigrette and replaces it with another fashioned of diamonds. The dance continues during which Mina whispers to Ismaël where he may meet Zulma.

Then the king offers Ismaël a magnificent sword, but he prefers his own victorious weapon. Mahomet offers him two of his prettiest slaves, but Ismaël declines them with a tender glance at Zulma. Then the king declares that he will give him anything he desires. Ismaël asks him to set free his slaves. The monarch, surprised, refuses this request.

The women entreat the king to grant them their liberty, but he orders Myssauf to take them back to their quarters. Ismaël, annoyed, prepares to go, when Mahomet stays him. Catching sight of the trophies which fill the room, he is reminded of his general's great valour, and consents to free the slaves. He signs an edict accordingly and hands it to Ismaël, who, overjoyed, wishes to proclaim the news to all Granada. As he leaves, Mahomet asks him to return soon, that they may visit the mosque together and offer thanks for the victory.

The king summons Zulma, whom he has decided to retain. He loves her with an ardour which is not returned. Zulma hurries in hoping to find Ismaël, but is dismayed to discover herself alone with her master. He tells her that he has decided to renounce all his women, with one exception—herself. He will marry her and she will share his throne and wealth. Zulma replies that her heart is given to another. Furious at the thought of a rival, Mahomet summons a eunuch and orders him to punish the insolent slave. Zulma kneels and bows her head to receive the fatal blow.

Suddenly Zeir enters and informs the king that Ismaël is returning with a vast concourse of people. At this moment the general enters followed by a crowd of people. The guards bar their way, but Mahomet orders them to be admitted. Men, women, and children pour into the hall until interrupted by solemn music which heralds the arrival of Imans who descend the staircase and invite Mahomet and Ismaël to enter the mosque. A procession is formed. Some of the king's women dance in the procession, others throw flowers from the balcony. Amid the tossing banners and fumes of burning incense, and the acclamations of the populace, Mahomet leads Ismaël towards the Court of Lions.

Act II. A splendid bathing place. In the centre, beneath a kiosk surrounded by frail columns, is a circular bath of white marble, able to hold a dozen bathers. There are two side doors; that on the right leads to the women's quarters, that on the left leads to the interior of the palace. In the background is a secret door masked by a gold curtain.

Zulma and her friends sport in the water. Slaves burn perfumes, others prepare to dress the king's wives. Zulma emerges first and is enveloped in a light veil behind which she makes her toilet. Soon her companions follow her example and dress in the same manner. Then the women dance and admire themselves in mirrors, forming a succession of the most captivating pictures, which centre upon the beautiful Zulma.

Myssauf enters with a number of female slaves who bear fruit and ices. The women follow them through the right-hand door, all save Zulma, who remains behind. At the same time one of the slaves staggers and drops a vase she is carrying. Myssauf threatens the culprit, but Zulma declares that it was her fault. Myssauf bows and retires.

In token of gratitude the slave offers Zulma a bunch of faded flowers which she picks from among the pieces of the broken vase, telling her that it is a talisman in the hour of danger.

Zulma, alone, takes Ismaël's portrait from her bosom and gazes at it with tenderness. At this moment the secret door opens and Ismaël enters, followed by Mina. The negress touches Zulma who, seeing Ismaël, runs to his arms. but he repulses her.

Then she tells him how, desperate at the lack of news, she went in search of him, and, while journeying, encountered the king, who proposed that she should become his favourite. She refused, but was captured by the king's guards and placed in the harem, where she is continually courted.

Mina confirms her statements and adds that Mahomet offered to share with Zulma his throne and kingdom, and, when she refused, would have put her to death.

Ismaël is furious but Zulma calms him. He tells her that she will soon be freed and displays the edict given him by Mahomet. A distant trumpet call is heard which Ismaël informs her is the proclamation setting the women free. Mina, hearing footsteps, hurries the general away.

The king's wives enter, full of curiosity. The palace officers arrive and announce the wives free, all save Zulma. She compares the edict with the parchment held by Ismaël and perceives that they do not correspond. She bids her companions leave her to her fate, but they swear that all or none shall be free. Zeir hastens to tell the king of this development.

Meanwhile Zulma proposes to the women that they should rebel, but her companions ask where they are to obtain weapons. They kneel in prayer when Zulma drops the posy from her girdle. She picks it up and suddenly the flowers bloom again, while the wainscot opens and reveals stands of arms.

The women seize the weapons and execute a warlike dance. Myssauf, hearing the noise, hurries in and is amazed at the spectacle that greets his eyes. Terrified, he runs for help. But, before he can return with soldiers, Zulma waves her bouquet and the lances become lyres, and the warlike measure changes to a graceful dance.

The soldiers mock Myssauf for his fears and retire. The eunuch is stupefied. At a sign from Zulma the women seize and bind him with their scarves to one of the columns.

The lyres change back into lances and Zulma ties the posy to her weapon, which thus becomes a standard. Meanwhile the women raise the far curtain to reveal a golden gate, through which can be seen the waters of the Xenil.

Zulma touches the gate with her lance and it opens immediately. She calls to the passing women and entreats them to join in their revolt against the despotism of man. The women of the people applaud and run to the boats drawn up on the beach. There is no time to lose for some of the soldiers have gone to the palace to give the alarm.

The king, Ismaël, and their attendants hurry into the harem. Mahomet rushes towards the women, but the gate closes. Mad with rage the king watches the boats put off, while Ismaël is secretly overjoyed at seeing his beloved escape from Mahomet's persecution.

Act III. Scene I. A savage landscape in the Alpuxaras. In the background is a chain of steep mountains where gleam bivouac fires. To right and left are hastily erected palisades. Moonlight.

The women of the people, who wear a special uniform, construct palisades. Others mount guard. A warlike march is heard and the women seize their weapons. But, as the music increases in volume, women armed with muskets enter from all sides and are drawn up in battle array.

Zulma enters with her staff and reviews the troops, after which she orders them to pile arms and rest, then she also lies down to sleep. From time to time the sentries are relieved, otherwise all is quiet.

Presently a cloaked man glides among the sleepers seeking here and there until he reaches Zulma, whom he recognizes by the posy she wears at her girdle. He takes the flowers, kisses them, and places the posy in his breast. Zulma awakes and recognizes Ismaël, who commands silence. He tells of the dangers that threaten and urges her to fly with him. But she refuses to forsake her companions.

Ismaël threatens to leave her if she will not follow him. Distressed at the thought she consents to go, and Ismaël, kneeling at her feet, takes off her helmet and armour. Zulma embraces him and allows herself to be led to the confines of the camp when a trumpet sounds. She remembers her duty and hastens to rouse her companions. Meanwhile Zulma directs Mina to guide Ismaël out of the camp.

It is daybreak and a party of women announce the arrival of a messenger, who is led in with eyes bandaged. He proves to be Zeir, who announces that he comes from the king and summons Zulma to surrender. She indignantly refuses, whereupon the emissary explains that Mahomet wishes to discuss peace terms with her.

Zulma calls her lieutenants to a council of war. After deliberation it is decided to allow Mahomet and his suite to enter, provided they come unarmed. Zeir departs with this decision while Zulma draws up her troops ready to receive the king.

Presently Mahomet and his counsellors enter, bearing olive branches. Zulma states her terms: first, that eunuchs shall be abolished; second, that women shall be free to give their hearts to whom they please. The king consents. Then Zulma declares that she will marry the man she loves and she indicates Ismaël.

Mahomet is furious but appears to approve the union. In token of friendship he orders his slaves to bring forth coffers filled with jewels and precious stuffs which he offers to the women. Excited by such dazzling treasures they break their ranks and discard their weapons, eager to take their choice. Meanwhile Mahomet's guards glide behind the women and seize their weapons. Zulma and her defenceless troops are quickly surrounded, likewise Ismaël.

Zulma raises her sword and plucks at her girdle for the magic posy which has disappeared. Horrified, her arm drops. Mahomet offers to spare Ismaël if she will be his alone. Zulma, for the sake of her lover, agrees. Ismaël, enraged, snatches the posy from his breast and flings it at her feet. She seizes it with joy and waves it in the air. Thunder rolls with deafening peals so that everyone kneels in terror; darkness falls.

Act III. Scene II. Gradually the scene grows light, revealing the beautiful gardens of Generalife. In the background rises a terrace where stands the Spirit of Womankind, surrounded by a brilliant court.

The Spirit goes to Zulma, who recognizes her as the former slave who gave her the magic posy. He orders the king to consent to the union of Zulma and Ismaël, and forbids him to oppress women in the future, since, by treating them fairly, he will have two armies where before he had but one. The curtain falls on a series of manœuvres performed by Zulma's troops and ending in a final group.

*

La Révolte au Sérail is the first and, for a century, remained, the only ballet to deal with the emancipation of women. Taglioni was acclaimed with fervour and the ballet much applauded, particularly the military evolutions in the final scene. But contemporary notices of the Paris production yield little of value in so far as enabling one to conjure up something of the dancing and miming.

The extraordinary success of the ballet caused some lively apprehension among the correspondents to English ladies' journals, lest *La Révolte au Sérail* should be produced at London. "It is a very silly and unnatural affair," observes the correspondent of *The World of Fashion*,[10] "there is something very indelicate and unbecoming in females marching about the stage and aping military men, that we sincerely hope such things will be confined to the French Theatre."

The ballet, however, was produced at the Theatre Royal, Covent Garden, on February 5th, 1834, with the following cast: M. Silvain (*Ismaël*), Mlle. Pauline Leroux (*Zulma*), Mlle. Larche (*Zeir*), Mlle. Vagon (*Zelika*), Mlle. Celeste (*Atargol*), Mlle. Cara (*Mina*), and Mlle. Kenneth (*The Genius of the Harem*).

The ladies' journals were dismayed by the Bathing Scene, and the *World of Fashion* characterized the ballet as "one of the most miserable and wretched attempts that have ever disgraced our stage." [11]

This opinion would seem to be inspired by excessive prudery, for *The Times*[12] declares that "upon the whole the ballet is eminently successful, and is entitled to the praise of being a very gay, novel, and an agreeable production got up with great splendour and good taste."

The Amazon army was to have many imitators, for having demonstrated that few costumes set off the female form to better advantage than a fanciful military dress, and that a manner of military drill has an excellent stage effect, *La Révolte au Sérail* must be held responsible for the introduction of the armies of comely young women bearing sword, lance, or musket, who have since been the mainstay of so many spectacular productions.

Here is an impression of the famous third act as recorded by *The Times*[13]: "The painting of this scene is one of the happiest displays that has perhaps been made in the theatre. The distance gives a very extensive moonlight view, and is of extraordinary beauty. The groups of sleeping Amazons, the piled arms, the watch-fires, and the sentinels on duty, are arranged with great skill. . . . There are in this scene, we should think, about 150 armed females, who march and countermarch, deploy, and form into line and square, and go through their manœuvres in a style which is highly creditable to such recruits."

The ballet became very popular and was frequently revived, the part of Zulma being later taken by Clara Webster, one of the most promising of English dancers. It was while taking this part that

[10] January, 1834.
[11] *World of Fashion,* March, 1834.
[12] February 6th, 1834.
[13] February 6th, 1834.

she lost her life as the result of a tragic accident which occurred on December 14th, 1844. This occurred in the second act, when Zulma and her friends are frolicking in the bath. There were two baths, one before the other; the dancers stood in an opening about three feet wide. There were some oil lamps a little beneath the stage, and it was thought that the dancer's gauzy dress touched the flame of one of the lamps and so became ignited. The whole episode lasted barely two minutes. But the dancer was found to be severely burnt and after much suffering expired a few days later.

It is extraordinary to record that, notwithstanding so terrible an accident to the principal dancer, the ballet, after some delay, was continued and concluded in the usual way.

LA FILLE DU DANUBE

Pantomimic Ballet in 2 Acts and 4 Scenes. Book: Filippo Taglioni. Music: Adolphe Adam. Scenery: Ciceri, Despléchin, Diéterle, Feuchère, and Séchan. Choreography: Filippo Taglioni. First produced: Théâtre de l'Académie Royale de Musique, Paris, September 21st, 1836.

CHARACTERS

Fleur-des-Champs (The Daughter of the Danube)	MLLE. MARIE TAGLIONI
Baron Willibald	M. MONTJOIE
Rudolph, his squire	M. MAZILIER
Irmengarde, Fleur-des-Champs's foster-mother	MLLE. FLORENTINE
The Nymph of the Danube . .	MLLE. LEGALLOIS
A Young Girl	MLLE. PAULINE LEROUX
An Officer	M. QUÉRIAU
The Danube	M. RAGAINE

Young Girls of the Valley of Flowers, Undines, Nymphs, Lords, Ladies, Pages, Heralds, Soldiers, Peasants.

Act I. Scene I. The valley of Donaueschingen.

When the curtain rises, a young girl known as Fleur-des-Champs is seen kneeling amid the forget-me-nots, making offerings of flowers to the Danube by the light of the rising sun. It was in this very spot that she was found by Mother Irmengarde who adopted her; and the orphan's girl friends gave her the name of Fleur-des-Champs in honour of her mysterious origin.

Enter young Rudolph, Baron Willibald's squire, who loves this strange maiden. He fashions a garland of forget-me-nots which he places on her brow. Then the Nymph whom the spirit of the Danube has chosen to watch over Fleur-des-Champs comes from the river attended by undines. She breathes softly on the eyes of the two lovers and they fall asleep. Then she places a ring on the finger of each and marries the perfume of their breaths.

They awake and embrace, but Irmengarde surprises the lovers and drives Rudolph away, for she dreams of a noble husband for her adopted daughter. The squire leaves in distress but Fleur-des-Champs soothes him with a look. No sooner has he departed than trumpet-calls summon the villagers.

Heralds appear and announce that Baron Willibald desires to take a wife and invites all young girls of marriageable age to present themselves at his castle. He will choose his bride from among their number.

The parents are delighted at the splendid opportunity afforded their daughters, especially Irmengarde. Rudolph, alarmed by the news he has heard, runs to Fleur-des-Champs, who whispers that she will be so awkward that the Baron will take no interest in her. She recalls the dream in which a nymph united her to Rudolph.

Act I. Scene II. A room in the baron's castle, prepared for a festival. Through a large window can be seen the limpid waters of the Danube.

The Baron enters with a splendid suite and greets his noble guests. He wonders the while whether the maidens of the Valley of Flowers will accept his invitation. He is soon assured for a herald announces the immediate arrival of the young girls.

They enter and the Baron is pleased. But the nobles are indignant that he should choose a wife from those of lowly birth. The young girls in their plain white dresses adorned with flowers contrast strangely with the rich costumes and jewels worn by the ladies of the Court.

The Baron invites the maidens to take part in the ball and, watching the dancers closely, chooses Fleur-des-Champs for his bride. Rudolph is hard put to it to restrain his sorrow, while Irmengarde can scarcely contain her joy.

The dances end and the ladies of the Court, trembling with indignation, are glad to retire. But the Baron, as if to provoke them still more, bids them remain and witness his happiness.

He asks Fleur-des-Champs for her hand, but she declines the

honour. Rudolph implores the Baron not to marry her, since she loves him. Enraged, Willibald thrusts Rudolph aside and tries to grasp the hand of Fleur-des-Champs, but she eludes him and leaps on to the balcony overlooking the river.

The onlookers are terrified. Then Fleur-des-Champs curses the Baron, throws her posy of forget-me-nots to Rudolph, and flings herself into the Danube.

The ladies of the Court take a cruel delight in the tragedy; the companions of Fleur-des-Champs are overcome with sadness, Rudolph is overwhelmed, and the Baron is distraught.

Act II. Scene I. Same as Act I. Scene I.

Rudolph, who has lost his reason as a result of the self-destruction of Fleur-des-Champs, wanders along the banks of the Danube, as if asking the waters for news of his beloved. Nothing can lessen his sorrow, neither Irmengarde's tears nor the Baron's entreaties. Still hopeful of recovering Fleur-des-Champs, Rudolph grows calmer, and, taking from his breast the posy, which was her farewell gift to him, he kisses it and is about to leap into the water, when the Nymph appears attended by undines. Fleur-des-Champs is close beside her.

Rudolph, scarcely able to believe his eyes, falls on his knees and entreats her to return to him. In a moment she is beside him, but she is now a shade, intangible, and always evades him. Hearing a footstep Rudolph turns his head and the phantom disappears. It is the Baron and his friends come to watch over Rudolph.

Then Willibald conceives a plan for restoring Rudolph's reason. One of the girls with him wears a dress similar to that worn by Fleur-des-Champs, and he asks her to wear a veil and show herself to Rudolph.

Rudolph wishes to flee from the Baron, but guards prevent his doing so. Then he seizes a sword from a soldier and is about to strike the Baron when the veiled girl runs between them. Rudolph, thinking he sees his beloved, drops the weapon, and Willibald and his friends withdraw to watch the result of the ruse.

Rudolph kneels at the girl's feet and implores her to raise her veil. He reminds her of their tender meetings. The girl turns as if to invite him to follow her, but, as he does so, her veil is drawn aside and Rudolph realizes his error. He takes the cherished posy from his breast, kisses it, and throws himself into the Danube.

Act II. Scene II. Beneath the Danube.

Rudolph, unconscious, is borne by a group of undines to the

grotto of the Danube. The Nymph restores him to life and gives him back his reason. His love is to be put to the proof once more. Veiled nymphs try to captivate him with their grace and beauty, but he repulses them. Still others tempt him with beautiful shells and the rarest plants, but in vain. His posy is a talisman which enables him to distinguish the false from the true. Then he espies a nymph whom he feels sure is Fleur-des-Champs; he pursues her and in a trice they are clasped in each other's arms.

The lovers kneel before the Nymph of the Danube and beseech her to restore them to the world from whence they came. The Nymph points the way, undines surround the lovers and restore them to the outer world.

*

La Fille du Danube "is the very poetic sequel of *La Sylphide,*" observes Jules Janin. "All elements are the province of Mlle. Taglioni, save the earth. Yesterday in the skies, to-day in the depths of the roaring Danube, but whether daughter of the air, or daughter of the waters, she is always ethereal and graceful. She treads a wave as she flies in the air.

"The dances in this ballet, which was highly applauded, are devised with considerable artistry, many *pas* are very charming. The galop in the first act will be all over the town in a fortnight. The mingling of baronesses and village girls has a most piquant effect. The veil dance in the last scene is very poetic. M. Taglioni has never been so inventive.

"As for Taglioni herself, so ethereal and so sad, so passionate and so calm, she executed with the most natural air the most wonderful *tours de force* in dancing that the world has ever seen." [14]

It should be observed that Janin was as ardent a Taglionist as Gautier was an Elsslerist. The critics were not undivided in their opinions as the following will show.

The *Revue du Théâtre*[15] says "M. Cicéri's settings are very old-fashioned, particularly that of the last act, which is mean; on the other hand, the scene representing the depths of the Danube, peopled with its charming inhabitants, has a better effect. The plan of using gauzes to suggest submarine effects is very good.

"Be not deceived by the hyperbole in certain newspapers which inform you that Mlle. Taglioni caused tears to flow at the moment she flung herself into the river. . . . Nothing could be less true. No tears flowed. Mlle. Taglioni put delicacy and archness into the

[14] *Journal des Débats,* September 23rd, 1836.
[15] No. 231, 1836.

scene where she hides behind a veil; and, apart from the fact that she only repeated her former *pas,* with merit, it is true, she drew all she could from the dull and stupid plot which her father had written, but it was of no great account."

The critic of the *Tam-Tam*[16] declares, "If, to ensure the success of a ballet, it suffices to have splendid settings, cleverly composed music, and some *pas* danced with considerable grace and ethereal lightness, *La Fille du Danube,* which includes all these qualities, would have completely succeeded; but, in addition, it is essential to have an ingenious plot and simple and expressive miming, and, unfortunately, it is just this which is lacking in the new ballet, hence it was most coldly received by the public. Mlle. Taglioni made us yearn for Mlle. Fanny Elssler and *Le Diable Boiteux;* however, it is not her fault, since she displayed all her talent, but that of the choreographer, who proved to be lacking in skill."

*

La Fille du Danube was produced at London, under the title of *The Daughter of the Danube,* at the Theatre Royal, Drury Lane, on November 21st, 1837.

The Times[17] comments as follows: "The celebrated French ballet, called the *Daughter of the Danube,* has been produced in vast splendour at this theatre. It would be vain to attempt any description of the numerous and magnificent scenes that are introduced into the piece; these and the other striking merits with which it abounds must be seen to be properly appreciated. On Tuesday night and last night it was received with the most enthusiastic applause by crowded audiences; there can be no doubt that it will have, as it deserves to have, a long run."

La Fille du Danube was produced at St. Petersburg by Mlle. Taglioni and her father, in 1837, the year of their first visit.

L'OMBRE

Ballet in 2 Acts. Book: Filippo Taglioni. Music: Maurer. Scenery: W. Grieve. Choreography: Filippo Taglioni. Produced at Her Majesty's Theatre, London, June 18th, 1840.

Having failed to discover the *scenario* of this ballet, which perhaps may not exist in a printed or MS. version, I cite a contem-

---

[16] September 25th, 1836.
[17] November 23rd, 1837.
[18] June 19th, 1840.

porary notice from *The Times*,[18] which gives a good idea of the ballet's content.

"The idea of the ballet is beautiful and poetical in the highest degree, but the ballet itself is needlessly spun out and encumbered. . . .

"Taglioni in this ballet is a ghost; she is always a creation of air, a being that flies rather than walks; and here she is a *bona fide* ghost—the spectre of a murdered lady. Her lover bewails her, and she is ever before his eyes; she steps on flowers and they do not bend with her weight, she stands on a revolving spinning-wheel, bounds along the water which sustains her aery form, and dances with her lover with melancholy playfulness.

"None but Taglioni could have embodied this idea; she was wafted in all directions—she became a spiritual ubiquity, peering through every tree—a pure being with still a gentle love for earth. This is the first time we recollect a voluptuousness given to terror, excepting in Goethe's ballad *Die Braut von Corinth*.

"In the first act, which represents the death of the lady by smelling a poisoned bunch of flowers, the narrative being conveyed in the form of a dream, a singular effect is produced. A large mirror is placed at the back of the stage, and while the business of the toilette goes forward in front, a reflection is performed by another set of actors. This was very well done, though M. Guerra's reflection might have represented the motions of M. Guerra himself a little more speedily—looking-glasses are good timists.

"The ballet was beautifully got up and loudly applauded."

The artistes taking part in the ballet, in addition to Taglioni, were Mlles. Pierson, Keppler, and Briestoff, and MM. Guerra and Gosselin.

*

L'Ombre was first produced at St. Petersburg, in a three act version, Taglioni taking the title-role, on November 28th (O.S.), 1839. The scenery was designed by Fedorov, Serkov, Shenian, and Roller; the costumes were by Mathieu.

A Russian critic declared that Taglioni's resemblance to a shade was perfect. "It is impossible to describe the suggestion she conveyed of aerial flight, the fluttering of wings, soaring in the air, alighting on flowers and gliding over the mirror-like surface of a river."

A version of the ballet under the title of *Le Pas de l'Ombre* was presented at Paris on the occasion of Taglioni's farewell performance in June, 1844.

"The *Pas de l'Ombre,*" records Gautier,[19] "is one of the most charming choreographic compositions we have seen. And, what is rare in a *pas,* it has a theme; the poses do not succeed one another at random and without reason. The scene represents a wild land-scape where a vague moonbeam filtering through the clouds causes a bluish twilight, in which glisten, like dewdrops, the spangles with which the Shadow's tunic is starred. Mlle. Taglioni evapo-rates, condenses in the form of mist, glides over the lake like a wreath of fog blown by the wind, and displays so many captivating graces that her lover follows her under the cascade of foam, with-out thinking that his body, however light it may be, cannot follow a sprite; but it is only faith that saves him; and, if one believes that one can walk firmly on water, one will do so. Thus, instead of falling into the black depths of the abyss, he falls into a fairy para-dise gleaming with light, such as a lover of Leyden and Haarlem might dream of, because it is full of enormous tulips, variegated with fabulous stripes. It is true that maniacs do not amuse them-selves by dreaming of a paradise. The fairy leaps on to these tulips painted by a scenic artist, who has doubtless fashioned them to the measure of her foot, and seems to propose to reward her lover with a chaplet of flowers which he strives to seize, and which she with-holds from him for a little while with an admirable skill. The passage in which, while dancing, she picks up the flowers that have fallen to the ground, was much applauded; however, we much prefer the first to the second part of the *pas.*"

AGLAË OU L'ÉLÈVE DE L'AMOUR [20]

Ballet Divertissement in 1 Act. Book and Choreography by Filippo Taglioni. Produced at Her Majesty's Theatre, London, July 8th, 1841.

CHARACTERS

Aglaë	MLLE. MARIE TAGLIONI
Cupid	
The Faun	M. MATHIEU
The Youth	M. ALBERT

The following account is taken from *The Times,* July 9th, 1841.

"Though called a *divertissement,* it was in fact a short ballet, and one of the very best which has been produced for some time,

---

[19] *La Presse,* July 1st, 1844.
[20] *Aglaë or Cupid's Pupil.*

having just plot enough to connect and give a meaning to the dances, without those encumbrances, such as processions, etc., which a more weighty subject requires. Taglioni is *l'élève de l'Amour,* and from her the piece is named.

"A dear little Cupid has to instruct her, step by step, in the art of dancing, while the pupil soon outstrips the minute preceptor, for steps that he tottered through as he gives his lesson, she achieves with matchless grace and brilliancy.

"When she is thoroughly accomplished, a Faun, who has been watching the lesson, becomes enamoured of her, and contemplates with rapture the movement of her feet. He catches her with a wreath, and she allows a flirtation as far as a *pas de deux,* but from the black beard of the gentleman, it is easy to perceive that he will not be the happy man.

"Presently a beardless youth in an innocent white tunic appears, and Taglioni smiles, and he smiles, and the little Cupid joins them in a *pas de trois,* and suffers himself to be fondled in the arms of both, and now there is no doubt that the lucky man is before us.

"The Faun would damage the happy youth, but a number of ladies entangle him in various wreaths, so that he cannot free himself, but is obliged to sue for mercy, and is forgiven."

*

"The whole of the ballet is of a soft and voluptuous character. It is got up with a quiet elegance, without splendour, while the groups are novel and effective, particularly those in which the young Cupid is lifted in various attitudes by the other dancers.

"Taglioni has never been more brilliant—we may say so brilliant —as on this occasion. The style of her dancing has been so essentially different from that of Cerito, to whom we have now become accustomed, that the public had begun to assume that Taglioni's was necessarily a quiet style, while all the displays of power were to be looked for from Cerito alone.

"Last night Taglioni seemed to strive against this notion, and while she exhibited all her usual graces, executed *tours de force* with a vigour and energy that equalled those of her young rival, and which, from her first appearance this season, we had supposed to be scarcely in her power."

*

Aglaë, ou l'Élève de l'Amour was produced during Taglioni's visits to Russia (1837-1842), but whether this preceded or followed the London performances I am unable to state with certainty.

LA GITANA

Ballet in a Prologue, 3 Acts, and 5 Scenes. Book: Filippo Taglioni. Choreography: Filippo Taglioni. First produced: Bolshoy Theatre, St. Petersburg, November 23/December 5, 1838.

CHARACTERS

PROLOGUE

The Duke of Medina-Celi
The Duchess, his Wife
Lauretta, their Daughter (aged 7)
Don Alonso, her brother (aged 19)
Perez, the Duke's Majordomo
Parembo, Chief of the Gipsies
Masetto, a young peasant
Pachita, his fiancée
  Ladies and Gentlemen, Pages, Servants, Gipsies.

TEN YEARS LATER

The Duke of Medina-Celi
The Duchess, his Wife
Lauretta, their daughter . . . . MLLE. MARIE TAGLIONI
Don Alonso
Perez
Parembo
Masetto
Pachita
Smouroff, Governor of Nijni Novgorod
Ivan, his Son . . . . . . M. N. O. GOLTZ
Olova, a Gipsy Woman
Mina, a Gipsy
A Peasant
 Gipsies, People of all Nations, Cossack Officers and Soldiers,
       Masks.

Prologue. A gallery, overlooking the gardens, in the Duke of Medina-Celi's castle, near Madrid.

Perez is directing the decoration of the gallery in honour of the Duchess's birthday. His plans are being approved by Don Alonso, when Lauretta hastens to her brother in great alarm, for some evil persons have tried to steal her gold necklace.

Her fears are increased by the entrance of the gipsy Parembo, accompanied by some of his band, who offers to provide dances in connection with the festival. Perez is minded to engage him, but Lauretta forbids him to do so. Parembo leaves, but conceals himself in the garden, where he keeps close watch.

The entertainment is rehearsed and Lauretta practises the Spanish dance she has been learning for the occasion, until, annoyed by Perez's comments, she runs into the garden. A page summons Alonso to his father.

Lauretta returns to the gallery and tries a few steps. As she is about to leave, Parembo darts from his hiding-place, snatches her up, and carries her off, throwing to the ground her necklace and garland of flowers.

The guests fill the gallery and the Duchess, accompanied by the Duke and Alonso, thanks her husband for the festival he has planned for her. While she is receiving gifts from her guests, she asks for Lauretta. Alonso is about to search for her, when Masetto rushes in with Lauretta's garland and necklace, which Pachita has found in the garden. The Duchess implores the Duke and Alonso to hasten in search of her daughter, who she fears has been kidnapped.

Act I. Scene I. The Fair of Nijni Novgorod, ten years later. The central square is decked out for the occasion. A few Chinese shops make a separate quarter, parallel to another line of Russian and Turkish shops. At the sides are various amusements and shows, both European and Oriental.

The Governor and his son, Ivan, are surrounded by merchants and strolling players craving permission to ply their business at the fair. Gradually the square fills with visitors of all nationalities, among whom is Alonso. At noon the shops open and music is heard, and several dances are performed.

Parembo appears and asks the Governor's permission to give his entertainment. The Governor, preoccupied with visitors, at first ignores him. But Ivan and Alonso, seeing the celebrated name of the Gipsy Girl on his bill, entreat the Governor to grant the necessary authorization. He consents and Parembo goes to fetch his troupe. Soon the gipsies enter, heralded by wild music. Immediately the square is filled with spectators, while others appear at the windows and even on the roofs of the shops.

When several dances have been given, the Gipsy Girl appears and charms everyone with her dancing. Ivan and Alonso throw her flowers and she picks up Ivan's posy. When she is about to depart, Ivan begs her to tell his fortune. She looks at his hand and tells him that he loves a woman he can never marry, and that he must renounce this passion. He refuses.

Alonso also wishes to have his hand read. But when the gipsy mocks him, he tries to kiss her. Ivan takes offence and Alonso, annoyed at this opposition, lays hold of the Gipsy Girl. Then Parembo flings him aside. There is an outcry and the Governor orders the gipsy to be arrested, but he disappears. Then the Governor orders the Gipsy Girl to be apprehended, but Ivan objects and allows her to escape.

The Governor, furious that his son should flout his authority, orders his arrest. But in the confusion that follows Ivan slips away in pursuit of the Gipsy Girl. The Governor and the rest of the company dash after him.

Act II. Scene I. A hill-slope in a forest in Catalonia, on the southern slope of the Pyrenees. Six months later.

Gipsies cross the stage and disappear into the forest. For a time the stage is empty, then Ivan appears; he seems uncertain of his way. A peasant passes by and Ivan asks him where the gipsies are encamped. At first he refuses to answer, but, won over by Ivan's proffered reward, he agrees to lead him to the desired spot.

Act II. Scene II. In the forest. On both sides are valleys with wide paths running down them, watered by torrents that are spanned by rustic bridges. Cloths are hung from tree to tree, forming rough tents. It is moonlight.

Gipsies are sitting about, eating, drinking, and smoking. Parembo appears to be planning something, as he waits for the remainder of his band to arrive.

After their meal, the gipsies dance until, at a sign from the Chief, they cease. Parembo bids them make ready to move on at dawn; everyone makes the necessary preparations.

The Gipsy Girl appears, lost in thought. She stops on the bridge, smiling at her reflection in the moonlit stream, then sits upon a tree-trunk. She draws Ivan's posy from her bosom and is about to place it to her lips, when she feels that her love is hopeless. Yet she has a feeling that she is not really a gipsy. She strives to remember the past, but, failing to do so, gives way to tears.

Her friend, Mina, glides to her side, and, taking up a lyre, plays one of her favourite melodies. The Gipsy Girl turns round and

sees Mina, who continues playing. The Gipsy Girl sobs as if overcome by deep emotion.

The music, at first melancholy, becomes gay and awakens in the
Gipsy Girl a desire to dance. But a gipsy outpost runs in and warns
Parembo that a stranger is approaching the camp. At the Chief's
command, some of his men lie down, others contrive an ambush.
Only the Gipsy Girl remains where she is, filled with vague
presentiments.

Ivan appears and the gipsies make him prisoner. But the Gipsy
Girl orders them to withdraw. So imperious is she that they obey.
Parembo remains hidden among the trees.

The Gipsy Girl cannot conceal her joy at meeting the constant
object of her thoughts, while Ivan tells her how he has sought her
for months past. He urges her to go with him so that she can
shine in some great city. But she does not wish to leave her companions, who found her as an abandoned child, and have always
befriended her.

Ivan is overjoyed to learn that she is not a gipsy by birth and declares his resolution to share her life and become one of the tribe.
At this proof of devotion she confesses her love and shows him the
posy. He kneels at her feet.

Parembo, who has seen all and fears to lose the Gipsy Girl, goes
to Ivan to find out if he really means what he says. The Chief
calls the gipsies who form various groups, expressive of the hard-
ships and hazards of gipsy life. But Ivan is undeterred and, giving
a purse to Parembo for his keep, takes the oath that binds him to
the tribe.

The sky lightens, it is time to leave. The camp breaks up and
the gipsies file down a winding path, to be lost in the distance.

Act III. Scene I. Same as that of the Prologue.

Perez, who is beginning to feel his age, is making preparations
for a masked ball which the Duke and Duchess are giving in
honour of their son's return from his travels.

Alonso is announced and welcomed by his father. Together they
go to visit the Duchess.

Some servants drag in a gipsy who has been found in the
gardens; it is Ivan. Perez orders him to be taken before the
magistrate.

They have hardly gone when the Gipsy Girl appears. She has
escaped from Parembo to follow Ivan. Exhausted, she sinks into a
chair. The Chief, who has followed her, is uneasy on recognising
the scene of the kidnapping.

She rises and prepares to enter the rooms, but Parembo bars her way and orders her to follow him. When she refuses to leave without Ivan, he tries to carry her off by force. At this moment the Duke enters and the Chief takes to flight. The Gipsy Girl kneels at his feet.

The Duke gently questions her and she explains how her *fiancé* came to be arrested in the garden, to which he had been attracted by the announcement of the festivities. The Duke's pity is aroused and he orders the gipsy to be released. As Perez brings in Ivan, she rushes to his side, then stops, struck by the majordomo's expression; she seems to be trying to remember where she has seen him before. Perez watches her with intense interest.

Alonso recognizes the gipsy of the Nijni Novgorod Fair. She looks from Perez to the Duke, as if trying to recollect some former association with them. A fragment of melody springs to her mind. She tries a few steps, but is too upset and buries her face in her hands.

The Duke sends for the Duchess, and Perez instructs Masetto to fetch a small casket in which are preserved Lauretta's garland and the dress she was to have worn.

The Gipsy Girl raises her tearful eyes, which encounter those of Perez, and, all at once, she begins to recollect the childhood she passed in this gallery. Alonso hums the bar of music she had been trying to remember. Suddenly Masetto and Pachita appear before her. Then she recalls the dance she was to have performed and how she was kidnapped. She flings herself into the Duke's arms and then goes to her mother, whom she has at last remembered.

Ivan kneels at Lauretta's feet, and Alonso, who has recognized his friend in spite of his gipsy attire, presents him to the Duke as the son of the Governor of Nijni Novgorod. The Duke and Duchess are delighted at this revelation, give their blessing to the lovers, and all go into the ballroom.

Act III. Scene II. A magnificent ballroom, brilliantly illuminated.

The ballroom is thronged with guests in fancy dress. The Duke and Duchess, with their son and daughter, enter and take their places, whereupon the dances begin.

Quadrilles are formed and various dances given. Suddenly a charming melody is heard and everyone waits to see what is going to happen.

Then Lauretta, richly dressed, steps out to perform the dance which she had intended to give eleven years before. The festivities conclude with a general dance.

*

This ballet was produced during the first visit of Taglioni and her father to Russia; they arrived at St. Petersburg in the autumn of 1837. The famous dancer had a splendid reception, and, when *La Gitana* was announced, thousands of persons stood at the entrance to the theatre from early morning. After the performance the dancer became so popular that all kinds of articles were named after her. There were Taglioni caramels, Taglioni cake, *coiffures à la* Taglioni, and so forth. The ballet pleased greatly, especially one dance in which Taglioni as the Gipsy lifted the veil from her face.

I have not been able to find the distribution of the roles, but the following dancers took part: Mlles. M. Taglioni, Dur, Teleshova II, Bertrand, Reutova, Ivanova, Samoylova, Shiryaeva, Apollonskaya, and MM. M. O. Goltz, Lashouque, Frédéric, Shelikhov I, Artemiev, Fleury, and Spiridinov.

*

La Gitana was produced at London, at Her Majesty's Theatre, on June 6th, 1839. *The Times* acclaims it as "one of the most beautiful ballets ever produced. How shall we do justice to the incomparable dancing of Taglioni? Every term of admiration has been exhausted, and it is vain attempting to describe the grace, the lightness, and at the same time the perfect chasteness of her dancing." [21]

N. P. Willis[22] records a fine impression of the great dancer in this ballet as follows: "In the new ballet of *La Gitana,* the music is based upon the mazurka. The story is the old one of the child of a *grandee* of Spain, stolen by gipsies, and recovered by chance in Russia. The gradual stealing over her of the music which she had heard in her childhood was the finest piece of pantomimic acting I ever saw. But there is one thing, the Cachuca, introduced at the close of the ballet, in which Taglioni has enchanted the world anew. It could only be done by herself; for there is a succession of flying movements expressive of alarm, in the midst of which she alights and stands poised upon the points of her feet, with a look over her shoulder of *fierté* and animation possible to no other face, I think, in the world. It was like a deer standing with expanded nostril and neck uplifted to its loftiest height, at the first scent of his pursuers in the breeze. It was the very soul of swiftness embodied in a look! How can I describe it to you?"

[21] June 24th, 1839.
[22] *Famous Persons and Famous Places,* 1854.

JEAN CORALLI

JEAN CORALLI PERACINI, of Bolognese extraction, was born at Paris on January 15th, 1779. He became a student of the School of Ballet attached to the Opera and made his *début* in 1802. His first essays in choreography were made at Vienna in 1800, where he produced *Paul et Rozette, Les Abencérages, Le Calif Genéreux, Les Incas,* and *Hélène et Pâris.*

During 1815 to 1822 he produced a number of ballets at Milan, Lisbon, and Marseille, the principal being *Hymen Defié, La Folie de la Danse, Lisbett, L'Amour et l'Hymen au Village, Armide,* and others. He returned to Milan in 1824 and produced *L'Union de Flore et Zéphire* (1824) for Paul, and *La Statue de Vénus* (1825) for Héberlé.

Towards 1825 he was appointed *maître de ballet* to the Théâtre de la Porte Saint-Martin, Paris, where he composed several ballets such as *La Neige, Léocadie, Le Mariage de Raison,* and *Les Artistes.*

In 1831 he was attached to the Théâtre de l'Académie Royale de Musique, then under the direction of Dr. Véron, where he composed *L'Orgie* (1831), *La Tempête* (1834), *Le Diable Boiteux* (1836), *La Tarentule* (1839), *Giselle ou les Wilis* (1841), *La Péri* (1843), *Eucharis* (1844), and *Ozaï* (1847). Of these *Le Diable Boiteux, La Tarentule, Giselle,* and *La Péri* achieved considerable success, and have been produced at one time or another by most of the principal ballet companies, and frequently revived. *Le Diable Boiteux* provided Fanny Elssler with an opportunity to make her first outstanding success, while *Giselle* is inseparably linked with Carlotta Grisi.

Little is recorded of Coralli's characteristics, except that he appears to have been at once the most courteous and most irascible of choreographers. According to Saint-Léon, his style of composition "was essentially French, that is to say, refined, delicate, and poetic."

As a teacher he formed a number of pupils, among whom may be cited his son, Eugène, who became·a noted mime.

Jean Coralli died at Paris on May 1st, 1854, aged seventy-five.

LE DIABLE BOITEUX [1]

Pantomimic Ballet in 3 Acts. Book: Burat de Gurgy and Jean Coralli. Music: Casimir Gide. Scenery: Feuchères, Séchan, J. Diéterle, Philastre, and Cambon. Choreography: Jean Coralli. First produced: Théâtre de l'Académie Royale de Musique, Paris, June 1st, 1836.

CHARACTERS

Asmodeus, the Devil on Two Sticks .	MM.	BARREZ
Cleophas, a student of Alcala . . .		MAZILIER
Captain Bellaspada, Doña Dorotea's brother		MONTJOIE
Don Gil, a Spanish nobleman . . .		ELIE
The Ballet-Master		CHATILLON
The Doctor		L. PETIT
The Hair-dresser		CORALLI
The Call-Boy		PÉQUEUX
The Stage Manager		VINCENT
The Inspector		FAUCHER II
A Valet		PAUL
Florinda, a Dancer	Mmes.	FANNY ELSSLER
Doña Dorotea, a young widow . .		LEGALLOIS
Paquita, a young girl		LEROUX
Florinda's maid		ROLAND

Masks, Servants, Sprites, Tradesmen, Noblemen, Corps de Ballet, Musicians, Mountebanks, Representatives of the various provinces of Spain.

Act I. Scene I. The resplendent foyer *of the Theatre Royal, Madrid, prepared for a masked ball.*

The ball is at its height. Don Gil arrives escorting an elegant "pilgrim"; a short distance away is the Captain, with a pink domino, and Cleophas, flirting with a white domino. The scholar hands his mask a passionate love poem and receives a ring in exchange. Now the pilgrim leaves Don Gil for Cleophas; he offers her a similar poem and receives a flower in return. Don Gil, who is jealous, reclaims his mask. But the fickle scholar espies a pink domino, to whom he presents a third copy of his verses; she allows him to abstract a knot of ribbon.

---

[1] *The Devil on Two Sticks.*

But Bellaspada, the lady's escort, and Don Gil decide that Cleophas shall be beaten by their servants. Fortunately Cleophas is advised of their intentions by the white domino, and, donning feminine guise, succeeds in getting himself asked to supper by his two rivals. Excited by the wine they ask Cleophas to unmask, and are amazed to see the visage of their rival. Seeing Cleophas is unarmed the gentlemen demand satisfaction. Cleophas seizes Don Gil's sword and defends himself against the Captain. There is a general disturbance and the police enter, but Cleophas escapes, aided by the pink domino, the pilgrim, and especially the white domino.

Act I. Scene II. An alchemist's laboratory. To the left are giant bottles; to the right is a high window, and a table laden with books of magic, a globe, and sundry phials.

Cleophas appears at the window and, having made sure that he is not followed, lowers himself into the room and inspects his surroundings with considerable curiosity. Hearing a groan from a large bottle he smashes it with a hammer. A black vapour escapes to give place to a deformed dwarf who stands with a crutch in one hand and a silver bell in the other. Cleophas is terrified by this apparition. But Asmodeus, such is the devil's name, thanks the scholar for having liberated him from the alchemist's conjurations, and promises to serve him well.

Cleophas, desirous of testing the devil's power, asks to see the three masked ladies he met at the ball. Asmodeus waves his crutch and they instantly appear. Another wave of his crutch and the masks and dominoes fall off and the scholar sees the ladies in their usual attire. The first is Paquita, a simple work-girl; the second is Florinda, a dancer; and the third is Dorotea, a young widow.

Asmodeus tells Cleophas that the ladies are coming to consult the alchemist. He invites the student to don the magician's cloak and receive them in his stead.

Paquita enters first. She wishes to know if the cavalier who courted her at the ball really loves her, and, since she can neither read not write, she shows the supposed magician the note. Cleophas, little pleased with this conquest, tells her that her cavalier has already forsaken her for another, and returns her the ring, which he asserts he has secured by means of his magic art. Paquita leaves in despair, but Asmodeus bids her not to lose hope; and when she has gone he reproaches Cleophas for rejecting so worthy a love.

Now Dorotea appears, accompanied by her brother the Captain, and Don Gil. She complains of languor. Cleophas prescribes a husband. Don Gil approves, since he aspires to the widow's hand, but Cleophas, taking the lady aside, advises her not to marry anyone but the cavalier who, on the night of the ball, stole a knot of ribbon from her. Dorotea is incredulous, but when Cleophas shows her the ribbon, she believes him.

Don Gil kneels at her feet and begs her to marry him. At this moment Florinda arrives and expresses her displeasure at seeing her swain at Dorotea's feet. The widow leaves in a temper, followed by the Captain and Don Gil.

Cleophas, alone with Florinda, reveals his true self, and is making a favourable impression, when Don Gil returns. Florinda pretends to faint and Cleophas sends his rival to fetch this restorative and that, during which time he comes to a perfect understanding with the dancer. Then Florinda opens her eyes and pardons Don Gil, meanwhile Cleophas filches the key of her dressing-room. Afterwards the dancer permits Don Gil to escort her home. Cleophas responds by kissing the flower she gave him and the stolen key.

He thanks Asmodeus for his aid and asks him how he can succeed with the widow and the dancer, since he is a penniless student. The demon waves his crutch and in an instant there is a splendid mansion.

Act I. Scene III. A magnificent park, with a palace in the Moorish style. On every side are the noble trees and scented flowers of Spain.

Splendid lackeys parade for their master's approval. Cleophas is charmed with all this luxury, but has a sudden desire to eat. In an instant a table laden with silver dishes and the choicest foods rises from the ground, and from every bush come forth beautiful girls bearing fruit and flowers. Cleophas seats himself at the table and as he dines is entertained with music and dances. The repast ended, a sedan-chair is brought forward, in which he takes his place. The chair is carried by splendid footmen, escorted by numerous pages and servants.

Act II. Scene I. The Green-room at the Opera House, Madrid.

The ballet-master is taking a class when Cleophas and Asmodeus enter, but the intruders are ejected. Then Asmodeus glides through the fire-place, makes the ballet-master disappear, and, assuming his likeness, continues the class without anyone's being aware of the change.

The hair-dresser enters with Paquita who wishes to join the *corps de ballet* in the hope of encountering Cleophas, whom she believes to be in love with Florinda. Paquita is accorded an immediate audition, but her simple country dance is received with derision, and when the pretended ballet-master tells her that she will never become a dancer, the poor girl is so distressed that Florinda and Don Gil try to console her.

Meanwhile various gentlemen enter and greet their favourites. Paquita is delighted to see Cleophas but he pretends not to know her, and, behind her back, exchanges meaning glances with Florinda.

It is time for the *prima ballerina* and her partner to dance, but, finding her partner's *pas* so infinitely superior in arrangement to her own, she demands that hers be altered. Asmodeus refuses and Florinda declares that she will not dance. The bystanders take sides and the discussion grows heated. But the call-bell rings and everyone hastens to her post.

Paquita goes to Florinda and Cleophas, but the former repulses her, and the latter ignores her. Asmodeus alone whispers "Patience."

Act II. Scene II. The stage of the Opera House, Madrid, seen from behind.

The curtain is down and the dancers can be observed taking their places. The orchestra strikes up the overture and presently the curtain rises to disclose the auditorium crowded with spectators. The *corps de ballet* dance a *divertissement,* with their backs to the real audience. Next follows the new *pas de deux.*

Florinda's apprehensions prove to be well-founded, for while her rival is rapturously acclaimed, she is scarcely noticed. To save the situation Florinda pretends to sprain her ankle and falls to the ground. The stage-manager rings down the curtain.

Act II. Scene III. The dancer's dressing-room. It is an elegantly furnished apartment with a french window opening on to a balcony.

Florinda's hair-dresser and maid are gossiping when **Don Gil** announces the accident to their mistress.

Asmodeus and Cleophas glide through the wall of the dressing room just as Florinda is carried in and placed on a sofa. **Don Gil,** who accompanies her, sends everyone away and leaves her maid to attend to her, while he goes to fetch a doctor. Florinda, enraged with herself, orders her maid to lock the door. Cleophas chooses this moment to appear.

The dancer is amazed at his appearance, but he shows her the key he had appropriated. Florinda sends her maid away and, after pretending to be angry, grows very affectionate towards the scholar. But the maid returns to announce the ballet-master. Cleophas hides behind a screen.

Florinda reproaches the ballet-master for her failure, but in the end they become reconciled, and the dancer pardons him with a kiss.

There is another knock and this time it is Don Gil and the doctor. Cleophas retires behind the screen. The doctor reassures Don Gil and retires. The nobleman, thinking he is alone with Florinda, makes an impassioned declaration, so much so, that Cleophas, losing all discretion, throws down the screen and confronts his stupefied rival.

Florinda enjoys the surprise and anger of the two men, and, despite the angry denials of Cleophas, persuades Don Gil that the student is her maid's lover. The nobleman calls his valet to chastise the intruder, but, thanks to Asmodeus, Cleophas makes good his escape.

Act II. Scene IV. The drawing-room in Florinda's house. At the back are three doors which give entrance to the dining-room.

Florinda has invited her admirers to supper. The repast ended, the hostess and her guests go from the dining room to the drawing room. To celebrate the occasion Florinda is asked to dance the Cachuca, which she does to perfection. Meanwhile, Asmodeus has lifted off the roof so that Cleophas can look down upon his fickle charmer. The student, enraged, throws down the rose she gave him at the ball. Florinda, overcome, recognizes her gift.

Act III. Scene I. A square in Madrid. To the left is Dorotea's house, with a projecting balcony.

Cleophas, surrounded by musicians, is serenading the widow. Dorotea appears on the balcony and seems delighted at the compliment paid her. But at this moment Don Gil comes in and hastens to summon her brother, Bellaspada. At the same time the widow returns to her room.

Now Florinda's maid brings Cleophas a letter which the student tears up, without even troubling to look at it. The maid, disconcerted at her reception, retires. While Cleophas is paying the musicians, Don Gil and Bellaspada arrive.

The latter demands an explanation. Cleophas replies that he is a man of immense wealth and aspires to the honour of being his (Bellaspada's) brother-in-law. The Captain is flattered and, ignoring Don Gil, who signs to him to chastise the student, promises to speak to Dorotea in his favour.

Asmodeus, seeing Cleophas overjoyed, tries to make him understand that it is his wealth alone that makes him acceptable, but the student turns a deaf ear to his warnings.

Paquita comes with a new hat for the widow and, seeing Cleophas, pleads her cause with such sincerity that he is moved in spite of himself. Then in the midst of his doubts a lackey brings an invitation from Dorotea to call upon her, and all his thoughts turn to the widow. But, as he is about to enter the house, Florinda, disguised as an officer, declares her love for Dorotea and challenges the student to a duel. The adversaries cross swords, but Paquita throws herself between them, and the fight is broken off. Then Cleophas calmly goes into the widow's house.

Presently Florinda recognizes Paquita, and the two women, having exchanged confidences, join forces against the widow, and discover a further ally in Asmodeus.

Act III. Scene II. A sumptuous room in Dorotea's house, with tables arranged for play.

A bell rings and Cleophas is ushered in. Bellaspada welcomes him warmly and conducts him to a side room. Another ring and Paquita enters, followed by the "officer," who hides beneath the tablecloth. Paquita is asked to take her wares into a neighbouring room, while the widow completes her toilet. Florinda seizes this opportunity to make an impassioned declaration of love to the widow, who, carried away, grants the supposed officer a kiss. At this moment Cleophas returns. He restrains his anger and sits down to play, but loses all his money.

Then Dorotea proposes to the company to go to a fair which begins on that day. The suggestion is eagerly accepted and the party set out. But now that Cleophas is penniless he has to drag in the rear, for Dorotea and her brother are seeking fresh fields to conquer. Too late, he realizes the truth of Asmodeus's warning.

Act III. Scene III. A landscape on the banks of the Manzanares, with the bridge of Toledo spanning its waters. It is a day of festival and here are mingled all those fantastic elements which form a Spanish crowd.

The *tambour de basque* is heard, the castanets begin their sonorous murmur, the guitar tinkles, and the natives of each province display their local music and dances.

Florinda enters accompanied by Paquita, who executes a national dance with a charming grace and elegance. Asmodeus comes in, disguised as a gypsy, and tells fortunes. He predicts happiness to Paquita, pulls off Florinda's moustache, and denounces Cleophas as a penniless impostor.

The stall-holders attack Cleophas, and Bellaspada retires with Dorotea, who has decided to marry Don Gil. But Florinda remains and presents Paquita with a purse of gold for, touched by her sincerity, she has renounced all thoughts of Cleophas.

The student and Paquita are united, while Asmodeus restores his friendship to Cleophas and presents him with a magic bell, by which he may be summoned at any time. The demon vanishes, but Cleophas tinkles his bell and brings him back. He thanks Asmodeus, who signs for the dances to recommence, and on this gay scene the curtain falls.

*

Le Diable Boiteux was hailed as a ballet quite out of the ordinary, with an ingeniously contrived plot, several well contrasted scenes of humour and intrigue, and many new theatrical effects. "The author," asserts the critic of *Le Tam-Tam*[2], "has the art of making episodes and passions speak as clearly as the plainest and most precise language."

The same writer records a curious incident. He declares that the *libretti* sold at the theatre had their title-pages torn out, because the authorship of the ballet was ascribed jointly to Burat de Gurgy and Coralli; in the same way the former's name was removed from the bill for the second performance. He asks for an explanation since he is well aware that de Gurgy is the sole author of the synopsis.

The settings are said to have been of a rare magnificence and of an enchanting truthfulness. The costumes, however, were thought to be more remarkable for their variety than for their taste and richness.

The choreography, according to the same critic, was not equal to the libretto. "The crowds of supers and the *corps de ballet* generally move in confusion. The *maître de ballet* of the Opera lacks in great measure the grasp of choreographic strategy, of which Henri at the Théâtre Nautique has given such remarkable examples."

[2] June 5th, 1836.

Of the interpretation of Florinda, the same writer observes: "Never has Mlle. Fanny Elssler displayed so much skill and such grace; not only has she henceforth no rivals in the Dance, but she revealed in this ballet an ability to mime which is beyond all praise."

The character of Florinda was ideally suited to Fanny, for the ballet contained many opportunities for subtle by-play to which she gave the utmost point and piquancy. In the second act she put the crowning touch to the rising tide of applause by her rendering of the Cachuca, a sparkling impression, full of life and vigour, spiced with a dash of naturalness, which her sense of style enabled her to keep within the bounds of propriety.

Gautier has left us a delightful prose portrait of Fanny in this dance: "She comes forward in her pink satin basquine trimmed with wide flounces of black lace; her skirt, weighted at the hem, fits tightly over the hips; her slender waist boldly arches and causes the diamond ornament on her bodice to glitter; her leg, smooth as marble, gleams through the frail mesh of her silk stocking; and her little foot at rest seems but to await the signal of the music. How charming she is with her big comb, the rose behind her ear, her lustrous eyes and her sparkling smile. At the tips of her rosy fingers quiver ebony castanets. Now she darts forward; the castanets begin their sonorous chatter. With her hand she shakes down great clusters of rhythm. How she twists, how she bends! What fire! What voluptuousness! What precision! Her swooning arms toss about her drooping head, her body curves backwards, her white shoulders almost graze the ground. What a charming gesture! Would you not say that in that hand which seems to skim the dazzling barrier of the footlights, she gathers up all the desires and all the enthusiasm of the spectators?"

It is of interest at this point to quote Charles de Boigne's impression of the effect produced on the general public by this dance. "A certain number of performances were required to accustom the real public to the Cachuca. Those swayings of the hips . . . those provocative gestures, those arms which seemed to reach out for and embrace an absent being, that mouth which asked to be kissed, the body that thrilled, shuddered, and twisted, that seductive music, those castanets, that unfamiliar costume, that short skirt, that half-opening bodice, all this, and, above all, Elssler's sensuous grace, lascivious abandon, and plastic beauty were greatly appreciated by the opera-glasses of the stalls and boxes. But the public, the real public, found it difficult to accept such choreographic audacities." Nevertheless, despite the doubts and fears of the more prudish members of the audience, the critics were loud in their praise of Elssler's dancing.

The splendid reception accorded the ballet and its continual success animated the whole company so that they danced like persons possessed, and once a measure was executed with such zest that one of the dancers was whirled into the well of the orchestra.

*

Le Diable Boiteux, rendered as *The Devil on Two Sticks,* was first produced in London on March 16th, 1836, at the King's Theatre, with Pauline Duvernay as Florinda. *The Times'* critic, apologizing for not being able to devote more space to the ballet, concludes: "We cannot, however, omit to notice the admirable dancing of Mademoiselle Duvernay in the Cachuca dance, one of the most celebrated of the dances of Spain, which was executed by her with as much spirit as gracefulness."

The Cachuca became so popular that it was frequently introduced into other ballets, for example, *Beniowsky* (revived March 16th, 1837). Duvernay made a great success in this dance, for there are at least six representations of her in the Cachuca, three being frontispieces to arrangements of the music of the dance for the piano. One of the copies in the writer's possession is over-printed "thirty-first edition," a convincing proof of the popularity of both the dancer and the dance.

LA TARENTULE

Pantomimic Ballet in 2 Acts and 3 Scenes. Theme: Scribe and Jean Coralli. Music: Casimir Gide. Choreography: Jean Coralli. First produced: Théâtre de l'Académie Royale de Musique, Paris, June 24th, 1839.

CHARACTERS

Luigi . . . . MM.	MAZILIER
Omeopatico	BARREZ I
The Constable ⎱	L. PETIT
The Sacristan ⎰	
Lauretta . . . . MLLES.	FANNY ELSSLER
Mathea, her mother, a post-mistress .	ROLAND
Clorinde	FORSTER
A Nun	DELAQUIT

Hunters, Harvesters, Peasants, Village Girls, Postillions, Servants, Nuns, Children, Choir-Boys, etc.

Act. I. A village in Calabria. On the left is an inn, with a balcony overlooking the street. On the right is a church. The landscape is completed with a few stray houses, a road leading to a mountain, and lastly the mountain itself.

Luigi, a young peasant, has risen at daybreak to serenade his beloved Lauretta. He knocks up his friends that the serenade may be complete, and, armed with guitars, triangles, and mandolines, they begin their preparations.

Lauretta opens her window and, seeing Luigi and his companions, withdraws to her room to listen. But just as the serenade is to begin the noise of many footsteps is heard. Luigi signs to his friends to go indoors, while he hides behind a tree. Soon a party of brigands, loaded with plunder and bearing with them a number of prisoners, including a blindfolded woman on a horse, pass cautiously through the village.

Luigi calls his friends and tells them what he has seen. They resolve to attempt a rescue and, fetching their muskets, go in pursuit of the brigands.

Lauretta, surprised that the serenade has not begun, looks over the balcony and is amazed to see the musicians departed. She descends into the street and is still more surprised to find the musical instruments left lying on the steps. She takes up a mandoline and begins to play it herself. The village girls, hearing the music, come into the street and, following her example, take up the other instruments and strum on them.

The post-mistress, hearing the noise, opens her window, but Lauretta and her friends hide beneath the balcony. Then Mathea, believing Luigi to be responsible, descends to rate him and is surprised to find the girls. She reproaches them for idling and, finding that Lauretta has Luigi's mandoline, snatches it from her and flings it on the ground, declaring that she shall never marry the poorest youth in the village. Lauretta bursts into tears. Her mother orders her indoors, but the village girls dance about her and prevent her going. Suddenly musket-shots are heard and everyone looks towards the mountain.

Luigi and his friends enter with some captured brigands and a number of their former prisoners, now freed. The rescued lady, the Signora Clorinde, shows her gratitude to Luigi by offering to reward him. He thanks her, but says that he has only one ambition, that is, to marry Lauretta, but her mother will not give her consent because he is too poor.

The Signora gives a wallet of notes to Luigi and tells Mathea that, if she will give her blessing to his marriage with Lauretta, she will double the sum. Mathea agrees. Luigi, overjoyed, invites everyone to his wedding, which he declares shall take place that very evening.

The nuns offer to lodge Clorinde in their convent, an invitation she accepts, while the villagers invite the other travellers to share the shelter of their huts.

The post-mistress is about to go indoors when she sees a post-chaise approaching. She calls her men to attend to the traveller and not keep him waiting. Hardly has she spoken when the vehicle drives up. The postillions dismount and help out a gay old man, who is none other than the celebrated Dr. Omeopatico.

He is tired and minded to rest awhile. But his eyes light up on seeing Lauretta. He would like to give her a consultation, and even goes so far as to put his arm round her waist and hold her hand, with a view to trying her heart and testing her pulse. But she soon escapes from his grasp. Then the Doctor, whose crape band on his hat proclaims that he is newly widowed, proposes marriage. Lauretta replies by introducing Luigi, whom she is to marry that evening.

Lauretta's friends come upon the scene and, impatient to dance, begin the wedding festivities without more ado. Inspired by all this youth the old buck feels quite young again.

Lauretta returns in her wedding dress, a green bodice adorned with silver, and a short white muslin skirt, and dances the tarantella. The dance ended, the revellers wander off. The sacristan is late and Luigi goes in search of him. No sooner has he gone than the sacristan arrives, and now Lauretta goes to fetch Luigi.

The doctor takes the opportunity to tell Mathea of his love for her daughter. The post-mistress is angered that the chance of marrying Lauretta to a rich man should have come just too late. At this moment Lauretta, pale, breathless, and with distracted gaze, walks on the stage with all the signs of the most violent terror. People press round her and inquire the reason for her despair. Luigi has just been bitten by a tarantula.

Luigi, restrained with difficulty by his companions, crosses the stage with spasmodic *cabrioles,* and soon falls exhausted into the arms of Lauretta and her mother. Dr. Omeopatico is coldly indifferent to the youth's sufferings.

Lauretta, seeing that Luigi is about to expire, offers to marry the doctor if he will save her beloved. He agrees and places a phial of elixir to Luigi's nose; his spasms gradually become calmer.

Luigi is carried into the post-house to recover, while Omeopatico escorts Lauretta to the church.

Act II. Scene I. Lauretta's room in the post-house. In the background is a window, with doors to right and left, and a clock. In the right foreground is a dressing room and mirror; to the left a fire-place and arm-chair.

Luigi is helped into the room by several village-girls and placed in the arm-chair. They assure him that Lauretta will soon be with him. She enters and he greets her with joy, but the girls hold him back.

He looks at her with love and pride. She bursts into tears. He goes to comfort her, but she recoils in horror. Luigi, astonished, asks if she loves him no longer. Then she confesses that in order to induce the doctor to save his life, she consented to marry him, in proof of which she displays the marriage contract. Luigi, enraged, declares the contract worthless as it was made under threat. He will go at once to ask counsel of the lady he rescued.

Lauretta asks him how long he will be. He points to the clock and promises to return within two hours. Lauretta promises to gain that time. Her mother calls to her, and Luigi, hearing footsteps on the stairs, climbs through the window.

Mathea and several girls fetch Lauretta to prepare her for her wedding-night. The doctor enters with a noisy throng of villagers, whom he dismisses with a present of money. Then he knocks on the door of the dressing-room and awaits his wife.

The pale victim is brought in; her wedding garments fall to the ground one by one until she remains standing in a simple dimity bodice and muslin petticoat, her tumbled skirts at her feet. This scene takes place behind a gauze screen which Lauretta's friends interpose between the modesty of the young girl and the impatience of her husband.

As soon as she is left alone with her spouse she asks leave to pray. As she prays, she smiles at her thoughts, and, rising, goes to the mantelpiece. All at once she claps her hand to her foot and announces that she has been bitten by a tarantula. The doctor, having the antidote, is little disturbed and watches the young girl leap about the room. She quickens the pace and the doctor decides to administer the antidote. But when he goes to place the phial under her nose she sends it flying, and the bottle breaks into a thousand pieces. The doctor, thoroughly alarmed, tries to seize his wife, who bounds and dances with ever increasing rapidity, in the course of which she contrives to administer a number of painful little kicks.

Omeopatico, breathless, flings himself into a chair. Lauretta falls into another chair. The girls rush in and press round Lauretta who whispers to them to contradict her in nothing. She feigns death. The village youths, apprised of the terrible news, beat the doctor with their staves, so that he takes to flight.

Act II. Scene II. A mountain landscape dominated by a convent.

Luigi and Clorinde, escorted by a nun, are seen descending the mountain-side. Luigi explains the situation and implores his patron's help. She bids the nun go to the doctor and inform him that a lady wishes to consult him.

The head of a funeral procession enters with Lauretta borne on a litter. Luigi is horrified to recognize his beloved. Lauretta, seeing him so downcast, smiles and bids him hold his peace. The litter is set down before the convent chapel and all retire. Luigi goes to Lauretta and gives her a kiss. He urges her to depart with him.

Now the nun returns with the doctor. She presents him to Clorinde who is veiled. She raises her veil and shows herself to be the wife whom he had thought to be killed by the bandits.

Lauretta, who has witnessed this scene, approaches the couple and amazes the doctor, who thought her dead. Luigi rings the convent bell. Enter the villagers and Mathea who embraces her daughter. Lauretta's marriage is annulled and she is happily reunited to Luigi, while Omeopatico and his restored wife drive away in the post-chaise.

*

La Tarentule, observes the critic of *La France Musicale*[3], "is one of the most graceful ballets we have seen since *La Sylphide.* Its great merit is its extreme simplicity."

The music by Gide was an arrangement of selected airs rather than an original composition, and it was complained that the melodies chosen were too modern and too well known. However, M. Gide was praised for "his good taste, happy choice of themes, and the elegant simplicity of his orchestration."

"There are . . . several *pas* whose invention does honour to M. Coralli," declared another writer. "Among others, a *pas de trois,* danced by the sisters Dumilâtre and Mlle. Albertine, which, while not being very original, is, however, in very good taste; then

[3] June 30th, 1839.

another *pas* for Mabille and Mmes. Maria, Alexis, and Nathalie Fitzjames. We have also noticed a well-planned scene danced amid hoops of flowers made to bend and unbend in a thousand shapes, each more graceful than the other. It is one of the happiest inventions of M. Coralli, who has devised so many other beautiful things.[4]"

"The success of the ballet is due to Mlle. Fanny Elssler and M. Mazilier. In the first act, when Lauretta comes to say that Luigi has been bitten by a tarantula, Mlle. Elssler is sublime in her terror. . . . This genuinely tragic episode makes you shiver; never did actress express fear and despair with more energy and passion. Previous to this admirable scene, Mlle. Elssler, sprightly and animated, dances a tarantella which gladdens and excites you. In turn coquettish, passionate, witty, she depicts with wonderful intelligence that ardent character which is only found in Italy. Beautiful in her lovely Italian costume, she recalls the suave models of Veronese and Titian; full of suppleness in her movements, sometimes artless, sometimes energetic, always inspired and always expressive, Fanny Elssler has never before risen to such heights as mime and dancer.[5]"

Gautier tells us that Elssler was "graceful, light, moving, witty, terrible as an ancient sibyl when she conveyed the convulsions of her sweetheart after he had been bitten by the tarantula, malicious as the Columbina of the Commedia dell'Arte when she led her old bridegroom a dance—she transformed a burlesque into comedy, and glossed over with admirable tact all that the ballet contained in the way of impossible or risky scenes.[6]"

*

La Tarentule was first performed at London on March 21st, 1840, at Her Majesty's Theatre, with Elssler in her original role. The scenario was revised for London, which could not have been expected to approve of a mock funeral procession on the stage.

The Times' critic observes: "Picturesque effects, elaborate groupings, and *coups d'œil* are less studied than usual, and the design is to represent a little farce by action alone, to give a sort of *pièce de conversation* without a line of conversation being spoken. . . .

"The ballet should end more effectively; a postillion walks in to tell the doctor that his carriage is ready, and the curtain falls with-

---

[4] *Journal de Paris*, June 25th, 1839.
[5] *La France Musicale*, June 30th, 1839.
[6] *La Presse*, July 1st, 1839.

out anything like a *groupe* being formed. This was a kind of
damper, the audience scarcely knew whether all was over or not,
and for fear of applauding in the wrong place, at first did not applaud at all. However, a chosen few enlightened their understand-
ings by calling for Fanny Elssler; applause once begun caught
like wildfire, and the charming *danseuse* made her appearance,
and smiled amid the loudest acclamations."

Of Fanny as Lauretta, the same writer says she is the ballet's
"centre and its circumference. It was all Fanny Elssler, and the
little *pas* without her were merely to give her breathing time. Such
a continued flow of animation, such a long deep draught of inspiration, is rarely seen. The manner in which she darted between two
danseuses in the first act, and went through one of the wildest figures with almost a ferocity of spirit, was electrifying, it was a complete abandonment of self to impulse during a few moments, and
when it was all over, and she gave her usual arch acknowledgment
to the audience, she seemed herself astonished at what she had
gone through.

"The pause was but momentary; off she bounded with a tarantella to the tune well known in the concert room as La Danza, and
figured against her companions with all the petulance of this
eccentric dance. For a few minutes she retired, and returned to
describe by action her lover's misfortune. Here was a new field,
she had to illustrate the tarantula bite, and represented the combination of trembling and dancing in a manner quite indescribable.

"In the second act, where she is supposed herself to be under the
influence of the bite, she has an entirely new *pas*—to idealize, as it
were, the notion of agony, and render it picturesque, becoming a
Philoctetes in a ballet. The lameness gives an opportunity for some
elegant movements on one foot, while the other is trembling suspended, the paroxysms, when she drags the doctor about, and
drives him round the tables and chairs, are a new display of that
immense spirit in which Fanny Elssler stands alone."

And here is Chorley's impression of Elssler as Lauretta, as
recorded in his *Musical Recollections*: "She put off in it all her
mimic power, all that audacious and exuberant execution which
made the critics say that if Taglioni was 'the Poetry,' she was 'the
Wit' of motion.

"The manner in which she wrought its whimsical scenes up to a
climax, the grace, the daring, the incessant brilliancy, the feverish
buoyancy, and the air of sly humour with which she managed to
let the public into her secret that her madness was only feigned,
raised this ridiculous farce to the level of a work of art."

GISELLE OU LES WILIS

Fantastic Ballet in 2 Acts. Book: Vernoy de Saint-Georges, Théophile Gautier, and Jean Coralli. Music: Adolphe Adam. Scenery: Ciceri. Choreography: Jean Coralli and Jules Perrot. First produced: Théâtre de l'Académie Royale de Musique, Paris, June 28th, 1841.

CHARACTERS

Albrecht, Duke of Silesia . . .	MM.	L. Petipa
The Prince of Courland . . .		Quériau
Wilfrid, the Duke's Squire . . .		Adice
Hilarion, a game-keeper . . .		Coralli
An Old Peasant		L. Petit
Bathilde, the Duke's fiancée . . .	Mlles.	Marquet
Berthe, Giselle's mother . . .		Aline
Giselle, a peasant girl		Carlotta Grisi
Myrtha, Queen of the Wilis . . .		A. Dumilâtre

Vine-gatherers, Huntsmen, Lords, Ladies, Wilis.

Act I. A corner of the Rhine at vintage time. To the left is a thatched cottage, half-hidden by the clustering vines and flowering shrubs. To the right is a similar dwelling. The background is formed by hillocks weighed down with russet vines, while, far in the distance, perched on the summit of a grey rock, can be seen the white turrets of a feudal castle. The dawn is just breaking.

Hilarion enters and peers about him as if in search of someone. He gazes at Giselle's cottage with tenderness and at its neighbour with anger. The door of the latter opens mysteriously and Albrecht, disguised as a peasant and calling himself Loys, emerges, accompanied by his squire, Wilfrid. The latter seems to be urging the former to renounce some project, but he is dismissed. Wilfrid bows low and retires.

The game-keeper, astonished to see so splendidly attired a youth making obeisance to a peasant, is filled with suspicion.

Albrecht goes to the cottage where resides Giselle, with whom he is in love, and who loves him no less ardently in return. He knocks on the door and Giselle runs to meet him. She tells him that she has had an evil dream, in which a noble lady wearing a rich dress was about to be married to Loys, who was dressed like a prince. Loys does his best to reassure her, but Giselle, still uneasy, questions the marguerites as to her lover's fidelity. The oracle is unfavourable, but Loys, taking the flowers from her hand, repeats the test, which this time is satisfactory. Overjoyed, the lovers express their pleasure in a dance.

Hilarion, enraged to see Giselle in Loys's arms, reproaches her for her conduct, but she turns her back on him. Loys warns him not to annoy Giselle or it will be the worse for him, to which Hilarion replies with a threatening gesture.

Now some village-girls arrive, laden with baskets, ready to gather in the grapes. But Giselle suggests to them that it would be much more pleasant to dance. She dances herself and, inspired by her example, the girls put down their baskets and join her. But Berthe, Giselle's mother, trembles for her daughter and cautions her, saying: "You will dance yourself into your grave, and even then find no rest, for you will become a Wili." But Giselle pays no heed, dancing is her passion and she means to indulge it to the full.

Distant trumpet-calls announce the proximity of a hunting-party. Loys, alarmed at the thought of who it may be, hastily leads the girls to their work in the vineyards. Giselle and her mother go into their cottage. Hilarion, now alone, takes the opportunity to steal into Loys's hut.

Enter the hunting-party led by the Prince of Courland and his daughter, Bathilde, who, weary from the chase, come to seek a little rest in Giselle's cottage.

Giselle, with a timid and charming grace, hastens to set out on a rustic table refreshments for her noble guests. She approaches Bathilde with cat-like tread and, in a rapture of artless admiration, ventures to touch the rich velvet of her dress. The Princess, charmed by Giselle's modesty, places her gold chain about her neck and wishes to take her into her service. Giselle thanks her profusely, but replies that she wants nothing more in the world but to dance and be loved by Loys.

The Prince and his daughter withdraw into the cottage to rest, the former having informed his huntsmen that a call on his horn will be the signal for them to return.

While Giselle looks to see if Loys is returning, Hilarion steals out of his cottage carrying a splendid sword and knightly mantle. Exulting in his knowledge, he awaits but a suitable moment to denounce his rival. Loys returns and is relieved to find that the hunt has passed on. Giselle runs to his arms, at the same moment gay music heralds the return of the vine-gatherers. Giselle, elected by common consent as Queen of the festival, is crowned with vine-leaves and carried in triumphant procession. The vintage is celebrated with gay dances.

Joy is at its height when Hilarion appears, carrying the sword and mantle found in Loys's hut. Mad with jealousy he denounces Giselle's lover as an impostor, a nobleman in disguise. When Giselle replies that he is dreaming, Hilarion produces the sword and mantle. Loys rushes at the game-keeper who seizes the Prince's horn and blows it like a madman. The huntsmen run up, and the Prince and Princess come out of the cottage, amazed to see Albrecht in such guise.

Giselle, recognizing Bathilde as the beautiful lady of her dream, can doubt her misfortune no longer. Her heart swells, her head swims, her feet tremble and start; she repeats the measure she danced with her lover. She places Albrecht's hand on her heart and then repulses him with horror. Then she seizes Albrecht's sword and tries to thrust it into her heart. He dashes the sword aside, but too late. In her final agony the poor girl seeks relief in a mad, frenzied dance, then she suddenly stops, makes a few trembling steps, and falls dead in the arms of Bathilde and Berthe, to the despair of Albrecht and the bitter remorse of Hilarion. The villagers gather about the dead girl in varied attitudes of pity and sorrow.

Act II. A forest on the banks of a pool. There are tall pale trees with interlaced branches, whose roots spring from the grass and the rushes; the water-lily spreads its broad leaves on the surface of the placid water, which the moon silvers here and there with a trail of white spangles. Reeds with their brown velvet sheaths shiver and palpitate beneath the intermittent night breeze. A bluish mist hovers about the trees, converting them into so many spectres. At the foot of a cypress is a mound covered with moss and wild flowers, on which stands a marble cross. A sudden gleam of moonlight playing on the cross reveals the name: Giselle.

Fitful flashes of lightning give warning of an approaching storm. A party of huntsmen, led by Hilarion, enter in search of refuge. Hilarion frightens his companions by telling them that the surroundings are supposed to be haunted by Wilis. The hour of midnight tolls in the distance and from the long grass and tufted reeds dart will-o'-the-wisps; the startled huntsmen flee.

The reeds part and a pale vapour is exhaled, which, gradually condensing, becomes the slender form of a young girl. With melancholy grace, she frolics in the moonlight, then plucking a branch of rosemary, she summons the Wilis, her subjects, who come from plant and flower to take part in the dance. Myrtha, such is the Queen's name, stays the fantastic ball and announces that they are to admit another sister that night.

She extends her sceptre over the new-made grave, from which rises a rigid form wrapped in a winding-sheet. The shroud falls and vanishes, and Giselle, still benumbed, makes a few faltering steps and does homage to the Queen. A glittering star is placed on Giselle's forehead and from her shoulders spring a pair of wings. Inspired by the silvery moonlight she bounds for rapture at her release.

Footsteps are heard and the Wilis hide behind the trees. It is a party of merry-makers, homeward bound. The Wilis try to urge them into the magic circle, but, warned by a wise greybeard, who knows the legend, the villagers escape.

Hardly have they gone when Albrecht appears, attended by Wilfrid. He has come to visit the grave of his beloved. Giselle cannot resist so touching a picture of profound grief and flies towards him. He wishes to take her into his arms, but the Wilis return. Giselle is fearful for Albrecht, but, fortunately for him, they espy the luckless Hilarion, who, distracted by remorse, has retraced his steps. In a trice he is surrounded, passed from hand to hand, forced to join in the dance, and whirled nearer and nearer the water. Giddy and spent, he stumbles and topples headlong into the pool to drown.

Seeking for fresh sport, a Wili finds Albrecht. The Queen orders Giselle to entice him forth. Her pleas on his behalf being ignored, she draws her lover towards the tomb she has left, then signs to him to cling to the cross and never forsake it.

Now Myrtha commands Giselle to dance the most seductive *pas*. Albrecht, more and more enchanted, leaves the protecting cross and goes to his beloved. The other Wilis encircle the lovers and Albrecht is soon seized with the fatal madness. But four o'clock strikes and dawn breaks. The Wilis vanish and Giselle is drawn towards her cold retreat. Albrecht clasps her in his arms and rests her slight form upon the flowered mound, which parts and engulfs her.

The young man rises, plucks some of the flowers, which he presses to his lips, and falls fainting into the arms of Bathilde and Wilfrid, who have been anxiously seeking him.

*

The *scenario* of *Giselle,* has an interesting origin, which Gautier reveals in his notice of the ballet, which is addressed to a brother poet. "My dear Heinrich Heine, when reviewing, a few weeks ago, your fine book *De l'Allemagne*[7], I came across a charming passage—one has only to open the book at random—the place where you speak of elves in white dresses, whose hems are always damp [8]; of nixes who display their little satin feet on the ceiling of the nuptial chamber; of snow-coloured Wilis who waltz pitilessly; and of all those delicious apparitions you have encountered in the Harz mountains and on the banks of the Ilse, in a mist softened by German moonlight; and I involuntarily said to myself: 'Wouldn't this make a pretty ballet?'"

What is this legend regarding the Wilis? Here is what Heine says: "There is a tradition of nocturnal dancing known in Slav countries under the name of *Wili*. The *Wilis* are affianced maidens who have died before their wedding-day; those poor young creatures cannot rest peacefully in their graves. In their hearts which have ceased to throb, in their dead feet, there still remains that passion for dancing which they could not satisfy during life; and at midnight they rise up and gather in bands on the highway, and woe betide the young man who meets them, for he must dance until he drops dead.

"Attired in their bridal-dresses, with garlands of flowers on their heads, and shining rings on their fingers, the *Wilis* dance in the moonlight like the Elves; their faces, although white as snow, are beautiful in their youthfulness. They laugh with such a deceptive joy, they lure you so seductively, their expressions offer such sweet prospects, that these lifeless Bacchantes are irresistible."

Gautier's first problem was to devise a logical theme, suitable for expression in terms of dancing and mime, which would ensure the death of his heroine in the first act, so that she could play her part as a *Wili* in the second act. He planned a first act consisting of a mimed version of a poem by Victor Hugo. "One would have seen a beautiful ballroom belonging to some prince; the candles would have been lighter, flowers placed in vases, buffets loaded, but the guests would not yet have arrived; the *Wilis* would have shown themselves for a moment, attracted by the joy of dancing in a room glittering with crystal and gilding in the hope of adding to

---

[7] This work, written in French, appeared first in a Paris journal called *Europe Littéraire*, during 1833. In the same year it appeared in German under the title, *Zur Geschichte der neueren schönen Literatur in Deutschland*. The first French edition, called *De l'Allemagne*, was published in 1835.

[8] It is the tradition in fairy mythology that water-spirits, however they seek to disguise themselves, can always be detected because a portion of their dress invariably appears to be wet.

their number. The Queen of the *Wilis* would have touched the floor with her magic wand to fill the dancers' feet with an insatiable desire for contredanses, waltzes, gallops, and mazurkas. The advent of the lords and ladies would have made them fly away like so many vague shadows. Giselle, having danced all the evening, excited by the magic floor and the desire to keep her lover from inviting other women to dance, would have been surprised by the cold dawn like the young Spaniard, and the pale Queen of the *Wilis,* invisible to all, would have laid her icy hand on her heart."

Not altogether satisfied with his conception, Gautier went that evening to the Opera, still haunted by the white forms of the Wilis. There he encountered Vernoy de Saint-Georges, the celebrated librettist, to whom he imparted the tradition of the Wilis, which Heine had recorded. Three days later the ballet, *Giselle ou les Wilis,* was written and accepted. By the end of the week the composer, Adolphe Adam, had improvised the music; the scenery was almost ready; and Coralli had the ballet in rehearsal. Even in these days of speed things do not move so quickly.

*

Giselle achieved an outstanding success, "the greatest obtained by a ballet at the Opera," says a contemporary,[9] "since *La Sylphide* of glorious and triumphant memory."

The music by Adam was considered to be superior to the usual run of ballet music, not only for the attractiveness and novelty of its melodies, and for its well-produced fugue, but particularly for the close relation of the music with the varied situations of the theme. The haunting melodies, sweet sadness, and dramatic quality of the score do not fail of their appeal even in this sophisticated age, as the comparatively recent revival of the Vic-Wells Ballet has proved.

The settings by Ciceri, well known for his representation of landscapes, were regarded as masterpieces of perspective and detail.

Coralli's choreography can be judged to some extent by the several revivals of the ballet lately seen in London. It is at once poetic and dramatic; the principal episodes being the tense scene of Giselle's madness and death at the end of the first act, and the greater part of the second act, which has many charming *ensembles*.

It is doubtful, however, whether Giselle's dances were com-

---

[9] *Moniteur des Théâtres,* June 30th, 1841.

posed by Coralli, as the following extracts from contemporary
notices will show: "Apart from the authors cited in the programme . . . there is a fifth collaborator unnamed—Perrot, Carlotta's husband and teacher, who has arranged all the *pas* in the
scenes for his wife.[10]" Again, "It is well to add, for the sake of
fairness, since the bill makes no mention of it, that M. Perrot has
himself arranged all his wife's *pas,* that is to say, he is the author
of a good part of the new ballet.[11] "

And what of Grisi? Gautier tells us that, "Carlotta danced with
a perfection, lightness, boldness, and a chaste and refined seductiveness, which place her in the front rank, between Elssler and
Taglioni; as for pantomime, she exceeded all expectations; not a
single conventional gesture, not one false moment; she was nature
and artlessness personified."

The critic of the *Moniteur des Théâtres*[12] is still more enthusiastic, for he styles Grisi the true Queen of the Festival. "What a
charming dancer," he continues, "and how she dances! . . . Imagine then that, from one end of *Giselle* to the other, she is perpetually *en l'air* or *sur les pointes.* In the first act she runs, flies,
bounds over the stage like an amorous gazelle; so much so that
the peace of the tomb does not seem too deep for so many races
and such expenditure of effort. And yet this is nothing compared
with what the second act has in store for her. There, not only
must she dance again as just now, but in addition she must be a
thousand times more ethereal and intangible, so to speak, because
she is a shade. She has no ground to stand upon, no point of support. She cleaves the air like a swallow, perches on the rushes, and
leans from the tree-tops, which is the literal truth, to cast flowers to
her lover. Do you remember the Sylphide's swift and sudden appearances? . . . 'Giselle is a sylphide who has not a single moment's rest.'

"Mlle. Taglioni has certainly found a successor. . . . Undoubtedly Carlotta Grisi has not so much technical skill as Mlle. Taglioni, nor such a wealth of stage experience, which is only natural
since Carlotta is but twenty . . . but Mlle. Taglioni's qualities,
her most precious qualities—precision of movement, graceful
bearing, lightness, and suppleness—are possessed by Carlotta in
the highest degree. And in addition she has an indefinable provocativeness, but yet a modest provocativeness, if I may so express
myself, which contributed to Fanny Elssler's success. Yes, for my

[10] *La France Musicale,* July 4th, 1841.
[11] *Moniteur des Théâtres,* June 30th, 1841.
[12] July 3rd, 1841.

part, I have no hesitation in stating that the very different qualities of Taglioni and Fanny Elssler are combined in Carlotta Grisi."

*

The principal role, as in most ballets of the Romantic Period, is vested in the *prima ballerina,* who must not only be able to dance, but also be capable of miming; the full extent of the latter demand can only be grasped by a study of the number of the ballets of this type, when it will be seen that the requirements are considerable.

Perhaps the actual demands on acting ability in *Giselle* are not so great as in some other ballets, but there is no doubt but what the title-role is the most emotionally exhausting of all parts in the repertory of classical ballet, for that character is to the *danseuse* what Hamlet is to the actor. It is imperative that the interpreter of Giselle shall be not only a dancer equipped with a first-rate technique, but one able to mime moments of comedy and tragedy; moreover, she must be able to act *while dancing.*

For all these reasons the part of Giselle has always been something of a lodestar to dancers, and there have been few dancers of eminence since 1841 who have not at one time or another essayed the role. It swings between the two poles of lyricism and drama, and so each *ballerina,* according to her temperament, inclines to one or the other; thus Grahn's rendering of Giselle was lyrical, and that of Elssler dramatic. But the technique and dramatic ability essential to success, to say nothing of the difficulties consequent on the sudden transition from the realism of the first act to the fantasic world of the second, make the part of Giselle a severe test. Among the numerous successors to Grisi may be cited Grahn, F. Elssler, Cerito, Taglioni, Andreyanova, Bogdanova, Ferraris, Rosati, Muravieva, Grantsova, Kemmerer, Karsavina, Pavlova, Spessivtzeva, Nemchinova, and Markova. Of recent interpretations the most dramatic was that of Pavlova, and the most technically perfect that of Spessivtzeva; but the performance of our own dancer, Markova, has several claims to consideration, particularly for the poetic and intangible quality with which she invests her dancing in the second act.

The latest addition to this noble line is Margot Fonteyn, the youthful *ballerina* of the Vic-Wells Ballet, who invests the Giselle of the first act with a rare sweetness and charm; but her treatment of the mad scene and the very difficult second act still requires those final touches which can only be acquired as the result of long experience of the role.

The part of Albrecht offers considerable opportunity to the artist-dancer. The gay sentimentality of the first act, which is so suddenly shattered by tragedy, is in sharp contrast with the ineffable pathos of the second act, in which the Prince, unutterably sad and lonely, seeks consolation in the contemplation of the tomb of his beloved, who, issuing forth as a phantom, fills him with bitter-sweet rapture, since he pursues the imagined woman only to grasp a wraith, who finally returns to her tomb, and leaves him once more overwhelmed with grief. Here again is required not only a fine dancer who can act while dancing, but one who can convey the poetry and nobility of his grief, and the pathos of his disillusionment, without becoming ridiculous. Among the more recent interpreters of the role may be mentioned Njinsky, Mordkin, Novikov, Lifar, Dolin, Judson, Obukhov, and Helpmann.

Giselle is the only ballet which has an unbroken tradition of performance since its first production, now covering a period of nearly a hundred years. It was first produced in London on March 12th, 1842, at Her Majesty's Theatre,[13] the title role being taken by Grisi, but the choreography would seem to have been revised since it is ascribed to Deshayes and Perrot; in Moscow on December 18/30, 1842; and in Milan on January 17th, 1843, at the Teatro alla Scala. In the case of the last-named new music was written by N. Bajetti and new choreography composed by A. Cortesi.

LA PÉRI

Fantastic Ballet in 2 Acts and 3 Scenes. Book: Théophile Gautier and Jean Coralli. Music: Burgmüller. Scenery of Act I by Séchan, Diéterle, and Desplèchin; that of Act II by Philastre and Cambon. Choreography: Jean Coralli. First produced: Théâtre de l'Académie Royale de Musique, Paris, July 17th, 1843.

CHARACTERS

Achmet	MM.	LUCIEN PETIPA
Roucem . . . . {		BARREZ
		ELIE
A Slave-dealer		CORALLI

[13] The Paris success of *Giselle* inspired a writer, William Moncrieff, to attempt a drama in 2 acts and 8 scenes on the same theme. This production, entitled *Giselle or The Phantom Night Dancers,* and styled "A Dramatic, Melo-dramatic, Choreographic, Fantastique [*sic*], Traditionary Tale of Superstition," with selections from the music of Adam, was first presented at the Theatre Royal, Sadler's Wells, on August 23rd, 1841. The similarity of title has led to the erroneous statement that this was the first London production of the ballet.

The Pasha	RAGAINE
A Eunuch	ADICE
A Jailer	QUÉRIAU
The Peri, afterwards Leila . . .	MLLES. CARLOTTA GRISI
Nourmahal, the favourite sultana . .	MARQUET I
Avesha	PIERSON

Slaves, Odalisques, Almées, Peris, Negro Boys, Dumb-mutes,
Eunuchs, Executioners, Officials, Musicians, Soldiers, etc.

*Act I. The interior of a harem, with marble columns, mosaic
pavements, and fretted walls like lace. Here and there are tapestry hangings, and flowers placed in tall vases. In the background
is a fountain with high-flung crystal thread. In the left foreground
is a divan covered with a lionskin.*

At the rise of the curtain the women of the harem are seen busily
engaged, under the direction of the chief eunuch, Roucem, in
adding artificial beauties to their natural charms, the better to
please their master.

A slave-dealer arrives and tells Roucem that he has for sale four
European women of great beauty. "What do you ask?" asks
Roucem. "A high price," replies the dealer. The transaction is
concluded after an amusing scene in which the eunuch decries the
merchandise as much as the dealer extols it.

Achmet enters with an air of boredom, leaning on a slave.
Roucem, hoping to afford his lord a pleasant surprise, contrives a
tent formed of flowing scarves borne by slaves, which parts to reveal the four new women: a Spaniard, a German, a Scotswoman,
and a Frenchwoman. The first dances a bolero, the second a
waltz, the third a jig, the fourth a menuet. Achmet, momentarily
interested, soon resumes his air of boredom.

The truth is Achmet is something of a poet. He is weary of
earthly pleasures and dreams of celestial amours. He seeks happiness in an artificial paradise. Dismissing the women, he calls for
his opium-pipe. Then, reclining on the divan, he fills his lungs
with the smoke and falls into a stupor.

As the drug affects his brain, the harem dissolves in mist to give
place to an immense, fairy-like oasis. "A mystic radiance, which
is derived from neither the moon nor the sun, bathes the valleys,
illumines the lakes like a pale silver cloud, and diffuses itself into
the glades of magic forests; the dew glitters on unknown flowers,
whose calixes smile like vermilion mouths; pools and water-falls
glitter beneath the branches; it is a real dream of Arabia—all ver-
dure and freshness."

Peris, oriental fairies, are grouped about their Queen, who stands amid the prostrate court. A starry crown gleams on her forehead; wings, shot with gold, azure, and purple, quiver on her shoulders; a light muslin skirt envelopes her in a silvery mist.

The peris cross the boundary that divides the ideal from the real world. They gather about Achmet who dreams on, oblivious of their presence. But when the Queen kisses his forehead, he wakes, rises, and perceives the ideal beauty of his dreams. He pursues her, but always she eludes his grasp.

She strives to induce Achmet to follow her into her domain, but, since he cannot fly, she resolves to give him a talisman by which he can summon her at will.

At her bidding the flowers in the vases fall into her hand to form a bouquet, to which she adds a star taken from her crown. "You have but to kiss the star," she says, "and I will appear." Since Achmet is incredulous, the Peri hides; he presses the star to his lips and in a flash she stands before him. Then she takes a tender farewell of the astonished and delighted young man.

With the departure of the Peri, Achmet falls to sleep again. Later, Roucem enters and awakes his master, who tells him of his wonderful experience. But the eunuch tells him that he has been dreaming. Achmet, half-convinced by Roucem, gives way to doubt. He summons his women and Nourmahal uses all her wiles to arouse her master's former love for her. He is about to throw the handkerchief to her when the Peri, an invisible witness of this scene, seizes the handkerchief, and places the mystic bouquet in Achmet's hands.

He remembers and places the star to his lips. At the same moment the Peri appears. She reproaches him, saying: "You are not worthy of an immortal's love. Farewell!" Then she disappears, taking the bouquet with her.

Nourmahal, astonished at this scene and at the coldness which succeeds Achmet's ardour, gives way to tears and reproaches. Achmet, weary of her complaints, repulses his slave and sells her to the dealer.

The Peri re-appears, delighting in her triumph, and restores the bouquet to Achmet. Nourmahal, threatening vengeance, leaves with the merchant.

Act II. Scene I. The terrace of Achmet's palace, which offers a birdseye view of Cairo, with its myriad domes, turrets, and frail minarets, while in the far distance loom the three giant pyramids of Gizeh. It is night and the moon shines strongly on one of the palace windows.

The Peri's companions flutter about Achmet's palace, reviving the flowers with dew poured from golden urns. The Peri herself peers through the gleaming window in search of Achmet, as if to spy upon his actions. One of the peris urges her to renounce this foolish love for a mortal and return to her proper sphere. She hints that Achmet is only in love with her power. The Peri is troubled at the thought of such a possibility.

There is a sudden clamour and it is possible to see a running figure in white, hotly pursued by armed men. The Peri and her companions watch the scene with interest. The woman, as the figure is now seen to be, makes a desperate bound and reaches the terrace, only to be shot by one of the soldiers. She is a fugitive slave from the Pasha's harem.

The Peri resolves to enter the body of the dead slave and in this humble guise test Achmet's love. The transformation is accomplished and the Peri becomes the slave, Leila.

Achmet and Roucem enter and find Leila. They restore her to consciousness and she tells them that she has fled the Pasha's harem, because she cannot return his love. She asks for Achmet's protection and swears eternal fidelity to him.

The women of the harem, filled with curiosity, run in to see the stranger. Some consider her charming, others find fault with her. Achmet, fearful of the Peri's jealousy, treats Leila with reserve, which gradually softens as he becomes aware of her resemblance to that being. He asks her what talents she possesses. She replies that she can play on the gusla, and dance. Achmet tests her abilities and, charmed by her artistry, commands a festival in her honour. The odalisques seek to rival the newcomer in the graces of the dance. Measure succeeds measure, but Leila triumphs by her interpretation of the famous *Pas de l'Abeille,* which victory her master acknowledges by covering her forehead and bosom with gold pieces. He bids Leila sit with him and dismisses the other women.

The more Achmet studies Leila, the closer he finds her resemblance to the Peri, but to all his inquiries she replies that she is only a humble slave.

Nourmahal, filled with a burning desire for revenge, makes her way into the palace. She draws a dagger from her girdle and attempts to stab Achmet, but Leila seizes her wrist and turns the weapon aside. Then Nourmahal turns upon Leila, who is saved by Achmet. The former favourite is threatened with death, but Leila intercedes for Nourmahal and secures her pardon.

Suddenly a negro enters in a great fright and declares that the Pasha claims Leila in order to put her to death. Achmet confides her to Roucem who makes her descend into a subterranean passage. There is a tense atmosphere of confusion and alarm.

Act II. Scene II. A prison in a fortress. In the background is a solitary barred window.

Achmet, now a prisoner of the Pasha, attempts in vain to bribe his jailer. Dismayed by his failure he muses sadly on his unhappy lot. All at once the prison wall opens and the Peri appears. She urges him to give up Leila, of whom she pretends to be jealous, and share eternal happiness and power with her. Achmet refuses and the Peri departs in feigned anger.

Now the Pasha summons Achmet for the last time to surrender Leila, and, when he declines, orders the executioners to throw him out of the window, where his body will be torn to death in its descent by the sharp hooks fixed in the wall. Hardly has Achmet disappeared from view when the prison-walls vanish to give place to banks of clouds peopled with peris. The clouds part to reveal a wonderful paradise to which Achmet climbs, holding the hand of his beloved.

*

Gautier having, in his capacity of dramatic critic to *La Presse,* to write a notice on the ballet of which he was part author, gives some interesting details concerning its genesis. He begins his article by contrasting the happiness of his friend, Gérard de Nerval, then on holiday in Egypt, with himself, forced to labour in Paris. As a solace he determines to create an Orient for himself, since, although a Frenchman, he is convinced that in reality he is a Turk, not from Constantinople, but from Egypt. He proves this by the witty observation that "when, at Carnival-time, I disguise myself in a real caftan and tarboosh, I think I am putting on my proper clothes. I am always surprised that I do not understand Arabic readily; I must have forgotten it.[14]"

In this preoccupation with the Orient, he continues: "I had begun, doubtless as a reaction, a kind of little Turkish or Persian poem. . . . Then I threw my stanzas into the wastepaper basket, and seizing a fresh sheet of paper, took as my subject the pretty little feet which turned four lines of Heine into the last act of *Giselle.*"

La Péri enjoyed a success which fell little short of that accorded to *Giselle.*

The music by Burgmüller was pronounced by Gautier to be

[14] July 25th, 1843.

"elegant, delicate, full of adroit and lilting melodies which linger in one's memory like the waltz from *Giselle*.[15] "

The settings were likewise praised. Of the scenery for the first act Gautier observes: "If you have visited the cafés of opium-smokers and dropped the glowing paste into the porcelain bowl, I doubt if your dreamy eyes could conjure up a more brilliant mirage than the fairy oasis painted by MM. Séchan, Diéterle, and Despléchin, who seem to have rediscovered the soft colours of Breughel the Elder, the painter of paradise." Of the setting for the second act, the same critic remarks: "You would never believe that MM. Philastre and Cambon have never been to Egypt . . . nothing is wanting, the panorama is complete. I doubt if I should see more if I went there myself." [16]

Coralli's choreography and groups were found to be novel and graceful. The cashmere kiosk was held to be a charming conception, and the *pas de quatre,* which occurs in the second act, to be full of originality and colour.

Gautier gives a beautiful description of Grisi in two of her dances—the *Pas du Songe* from the first act, and the *Pas de l'Abeille* from the second—which must be reproduced.

"Carlotta's *Pas du Songe* was a real triumph; when she appeared in that luminous halo, with a child-like smile, her eyes betokening astonishment and delight, her poses like those of a bird who seeks to alight but whose wings carry her away in spite of herself, unanimous applause burst from every corner of the house. What a marvellous dance! I should very much like to see real peris and fairies! How she glides over the ground without touching it, just like a rose-leaf wafted by the breeze; and, moreover, what nerves of steel reside in that frail leg . . . how she alights on the tip of that slender toe, like an arrow falling on its barb!

"This *pas* includes a certain fall which will soon be as famous as the Niagara Falls. The audience wait for it in awed curiosity. At the moment when the vision is about to end, the Peri falls from the top of a cloud into her lover's arms. If it were only a *tour de force* we should not mention it; but this perilous leap forms a group so full of grace and charm that it suggests a dove's feather drifting downwards, rather than a human being leaping from a platform."

This leap, as Gautier foresaw, became one of the great moments in the ballet. Alberic Second declared the leap so dangerous that "I calculate that Carlotta Grisi risks her life each time she attempts it.

[15] *La Presse,* July 25th, 1843.
[16] *La Presse,* July 25th, 1843.

Let M. Petipa be clumsy or merely distracted and Carlotta will fracture her head on the stage. I know an Englishman who never misses a single performance. . . . He is convinced that the ballet is destined to be fatal to Carlotta, and not for anything in the world would he be absent for a single evening.[17]"

Of the *Pas de l'Abeille* Gautier remarks, "If you only knew with what modest embarrassment Carlotta takes off her long white veil; how she poses, while kneeling beneath its transparent folds, like Venus of old smiling in her pearly shell; with what child-like fright she is seized as the angry bee comes out of the calix of the flower; how well she expresses the hopes, the anxieties, all the phases of the struggle, as the bodice and scarf, and the skirt which the bee attempts to pass through, fly quickly to right and left and disappear in the whirl of the dance.[18]"

*

Le Péri was first produced in London on September 30th, 1843, at the Theatre Royal, Drury Lane; the principals were Grisi and L. Petipa, as at Paris. The ballet followed the first performance of Balfe's opera, *The Siege of Rochelle,* which was a failure.

The Times critic reports, "We never saw an audience so completely turned round from an ill-humour to a state of perfect delight as Saturday's audience were by the dancing of Carlotta Grisi. There is a great deal of tedious pantomime in this piece which should at once be curtailed, but all that is done by Carlotta Grisi is worthy of the highest praise. Her grand achievement is the *pas de deux* with Petipa, in the first act. She introduces several evolutions, totally unlike anything that has been seen before; such are a flying movement from one side of the stage to the other, in which she is supported by Petipa, but seems as if supported by air alone; such is a terrific spring she takes from an eminence at the back of the stage, which she continues by a brilliant advance to the lamps. The applause of the audience at these feats was a perfect storm that has rarely been equalled.[19]"

OZAÏ

Ballet in 2 Acts and 6 Scenes. Book: Jean Coralli. Music: Casimir Gide. Scenery: Ciceri. Choreography: Jean Coralli. First produced: Théâtre de l'Académie Royale de Musique, Paris, April 26th, 1847.

[17] *Les Petits Mystères de l'Opéra.*
[18] *La Presse,* July 25th.
[19] October 2nd.

CHARACTERS

M. de Bougainville	MM.	Elie
M. de Surville		Desplaces
An Abbé . . . ⎫		Coralli
Bidgi, a negro cabin-boy ⎬		
A Sailor		Adice
Another Sailor		Quériau
A Financier		Monet
The King of France		Lenfant
The Minister of Marine		Petit
A Page		Wiéthof I
Ozaï	Mlles.	A. Plunkett
Mlle. de Bougainville		C. Emarot
Mme. de Bougainville		Delaquit
La Guimard		Zélie
A Maid		Pézé
The Marquis		Maria
A Guardsman		

Tahitans, Naval Officers, Seamen, Lords, Ladies, Provençales, Bayaderes, Almées, Americans, Peasants

Act I. Scene I. An island in the South Seas. On one side is a grotto, its entrance half-hidden by lianas; on the other side are clumps of trees and masses of rock, from which pour sparkling cascades of water. The background is formed by the sea, which reflects the burning sunlight.

At the rise of the curtain the scene is filled with native girls, some bathing, some resting on the grass, some dressing their hair with flowers. In the foreground a group of young girls perform their native dances. Sometimes they put on artificial wings and imitate the movements of birds in flight; sometimes they dance with bamboos. A number of girls dance about a mast, from the top of which depend a dozen gaily-coloured streamers. During these dances the men fish from canoes. The natives eat and depart, fanning themselves with large leaves.

Ozaï, making sure that she is alone, goes to the grotto and, parting the curtain of lianas, lightly claps her hands. Surville, a naval officer, the sole survivor of a shipwreck, comes forth. Ozaï places food before him and makes him sit beside her. But, despite her tenderness, he seems sad and preoccupied. When she asks him the reason, he points to the sea which separates him from his country.

At last, vanquished by the girl's entreaties and concluding that he will never again see Mlle. de Bougainville, whom he had hoped to marry, he declares Ozaï is his wife in the sight of heaven, in proof of which he hangs a cross about her neck and places his ring on her finger. At this moment several natives appear in the distance. Ozaï hides Surville in the grotto and leaves with her companions.

A vessel appears on the horizon and gradually approaches nearer. A boat puts off for the island and M. de Bougainville, its captain, steps ashore and takes possession of it in the name of France. Then he sends his men to see if they can find any traces of the wreck of a French ship. He intimates that he will rest until their return.

Ozaï enters and is surprised to see the officer asleep. Half-hesitating, she goes to look at him. Attracted by his shining musket, she tries to divine its use. She plays with the trigger and suddenly there is an explosion. M. de Bougainville springs to his feet in alarm and is astonished to see a young girl lying unconscious.

Hearing the report, officers and men run to the aid of their commander, who reassures them. With a flask of brandy they revive Ozaï, who is terrified to see so many strange faces.

The captain calms her and orders the sailors to dance for her amusement. Other natives draw near and are given presents. Ozaï, wishing to imitate the sailors, dances with the utmost vivacity until, drowsy from the liquor, she sinks to the ground and falls asleep.

A cannon-shot recalls the landing-party. As the sailors prepare to leave, the captain orders them to put Ozaï into the boat, then embarks with his officers. The boat is escorted by a number of natives in their canoes.

When all is silent, Surville comes from his grotto and sees, to his grief, the flag which marks the arrival of a French ship. He gazes out to sea, and, perceiving the vessel, is torn between an intense desire to see his native land and his duty to Ozaï. He resolves to swim to the ship and return to the island for his wife. The decision made, he plunges into the sea. At this moment natives enter and gradually fill the clearing.

Act I. Scene II. The captain's cabin on board M. de Bougainville's command.

Ozaï is carried in and laid on a couch. A little later she turns in her sleep and rolls to the floor. Amazed at her surroundings, she examines with interest the various articles in the cabin. She finds a bell and rings it.

Bidgi runs in and, expecting to see the captain, is amazed to meet Ozaï. At first mutually afraid, they become reassured. Ozaï amuses herself by making the negro put on different portions of the captain's uniform. Suddenly M. de Bougainville enters and feigns anger at seeing Bidgi wearing his clothes. Bidgi runs out and Ozaï explains that the boy was only doing her bidding.

The captain is interested in Ozaï and asks her if she is glad to leave the island. She replies that she misses her companions, especially a shipwrecked sailor whom she loves. The captain promises to restore her later to her country.

Bidgi returns and announces that a man has swum from the island and is being hoisted on board. Surville appears, supported by sailors. As they help him to his feet, a miniature falls from his clothes; the captain, unperceived, retrieves it, and is astonished to find the miniature a portrait of his daughter. Ozaï is overjoyed at being restored to her lover.

Act II. Scene I. A dressing room in M. de Bougainville's mansion. A year later.

Mme. de Bougainville and her daughter have finished dressing and go to help Ozaï, who remains at heart a simple native.

A marquis, a financier, and a lawyer enter to pay compliments to the ladies. The lawyer offers Ozaï a bouquet; he also gives her a bottle of scent which she throws away, after having sniffed its contents. The lawyer, at first annoyed, offers her a box of sweets, which is received with delight.

The financier next approaches and, extending his fingers, dazzles her with his glittering rings. He produces a snuff-box and takes a pinch of snuff. Ozaï follows his example and is almost suffocated. She is furious with the financier, who calms her with the gift of a beautiful ring.

La Guimard arrives to give Mlle. de Bougainville a dancing-lesson. Her pupil dances a gavotte and a rigaudon, and is congratulated by her friends.

M. de Bougainville enters with Surville who, he announces, has just been promoted to lieutenant. Everyone applauds except Ozaï, who is only interested in his shining epaulettes, with which she toys. She caresses him, but Surville appears ill at ease.

A maid announces that the carriage is waiting and everyone leaves. The financier offers his arm to the mistress of the house, and Surville gives his to Mlle. de Bougainville; but Ozaï slips between them and takes her lover's arm instead. M. de Bougainville announces that he intends to celebrate his nephew's promotion by a ball, which will be held that evening.

Act II. Scene II. The gardens of M. de Bougainville's mansion. The rear portion is curtained off. At the side is a lattice-work pavilion.

The illuminated gardens are thronged with guests of every nationality. The quadrilles are formed and Surville and Mlle. de Bougainville distinguish themselves in a measure in which dancers symbolical of the four quarters of the world take part. Ozaï is jealous of Mlle. de Bougainville's grace and Surville's evident admiration for her. Suddenly the curtains are drawn to reveal a painting which represents the lately discovered island, with Ozaï surrounded by her companions. This surprise, devised by Surville, is received with great applause.

But M. de Bougainville is displeased, fearing that his nephew's love for Ozaï will prevent Surville marrying his daughter. The festival ended, the guests take leave of their host, who is left alone with Surville and Ozaï.

The lieutenant is about to depart when M. de Bougainville expresses a desire to speak with him. Ozaï, full of apprehension, feigns to leave, but hides behind a grove in order to overhear their conversation.

M. de Bougainville asks Surville his intentions towards his daughter. He replies that he loves her deeply, but cannot break his word to Ozaï. The poor girl, learning that Surville is attached to her for honour's sake and not from love, falls to the ground in a faint. Astonished, M. de Bougainville calls his servants and orders Ozaï to be carried indoors. Presently she recovers and Surville leads her away.

Act II. Scene III. The King's study at Versailles.

The King is seen receiving numerous officers and granting them various commissions, when M. de Bougainville is announced. The King welcomes his visitor, who presents his nephew. Afterwards the King appoints M. de Bougainville to command a second expedition to the South Seas.

Act II. Scene IV. The Port of Marseille. The dock is full of vessels and preparations are being made for an embarkment.

Naval troops mount a guard of honour, which presents arms as M. de Bougainville arrives, escorted by his family and friends.

Presently Ozaï arrives in native dress. She goes to Surville and with dignity takes off his ring and cross, and hands them back to him, indicating that she releases him from his vow. Surville, aghast, is about to go to her. But she stops him, takes M. de Bougainville's hand and places it in that of Surville. She embraces Mme. de Bougainville and kneels to the captain, who gently raises her. Then, with a gesture of farewell, she leaps into the boat that is putting off to the ship. The spectators are deeply moved by this scene of renunciation.

*

Ozaï is mainly interesting for its theme, the voyages of the celebrated French explorer, M. de Bougainville (1729–1814), which serves as a basis for the introduction of native dances.

The ballet achieved a moderate success. The critic of *La France Musicale* declares M. Gide's music to be charming. "It abounds in elegant motifs and provides a whole succession of waltzes and contredanses. The whimsical scene with the negro is perfectly handled. In the second scene particularly the melodies are fresh and original; all the music for the ball scene is capital. M. Gide is an excellent musician, his new score is a worthy successor to *Le Diable Boiteux*.[20] "

The settings, according to the same critic, "are nothing wonderful; nevertheless they are not unworthy of the great stage of the Académie Royale de Musique. The costumes, very varied, very splendid, and very new, offer a pleasing spectacle." The critic of *Le Corsaire* finds the final scene, representing the port of Marseille, "very beautiful.[21] "

The references to the dancers are confined to such commonplaces as: "Mlle. Plunkett, very piquant in her native costume, and very pretty with powdered hair, dances gracefully and prettily."

[20] May 2nd, 1847.
[21] April 28th, 1847.

ALBERT

FERDINAND ALBERT DECOMBE was born at Bordeaux on April 15th, 1789. He was the son of a retired calvary officer.

Albert was ten when he first began to study dancing in his native town, but, dissatisfied with his progress, he had almost made up his mind to abandon his chosen profession, when Vestris came to dance at Bordeaux. His ambition rekindled at the sight of that great artist, Albert laboured unceasingly and to such purpose that he obtained an engagement as *premier danseur* at the Théâtre de la Gaité, Paris. There he studied under Coulon and later returned to Bordeaux as principal dancer.

In 1803 he became a member of the ballet company attached to the Paris Opera. One of his earliest successes was gained in Gardel's ballet *Paul et Virginie,* in which Mlle. Bigottini and he played the two lovers. Some of his principal roles were Zéphire (*Flore et Zéphire*), Mathieu (*La Servante Justifiée*), and Mectal (*Le Seducteur au Village*). Albert's fine figure, attractive features, and virile yet graceful dancing, greatly endeared him to the public. He attained the rank of *premier danseur* in 1817.

Albert was appointed *maître de ballet* in 1829. He produced a number of ballets for the principal European theatres. The most successful of his compositions were: *Le Seducteur au Village* (1818), *Cendrillon* (1823) and *La Jolie Fille de Gand* (1842).

Albert died at Fontainebleau in 1865.

LA JOLIE FILLE DE GAND

Pantomimic Ballet in 3 Acts and 9 Scenes. Book: Vernoy de Saint-Georges and Albert. Music: Adolphe Adam. Scenery: Ciceri, Philastre, and Cambon. Choreography: Albert. First produced: Théâtre de l'Académie Royale de Musique, Paris, June 22nd, 1842.

CHARACTERS

The Marquis de San Lucar . . .	MM.	ALBERT
Cesarius, a wealthy goldsmith of Ghent		MAZILIER
Zephiros, *maître de danse* . . .		CORALLI
Bustamente, a Spaniard and friend of the Marquis		ELIE
Benedict, Cesarius's nephew . . .		PETIPA
Count Leonardo		QUÉRIAU
A Farmer		ADICE
A Gypsy		ADICE
A Notary		L. PETIT
A Provost		BEGRAND
Diana, *première danseuse* at the Fenice Theatre	MMES.	L. FITZJAMES
Beatrix, Cesarius's daughter, betrothed to Benedict		C. GRISI
Julia, Cousin to Beatrix and Agnes . .		MARIA
Agnes, Cesarius's younger daughter .		A. DUMILÂTRE
A Farmer's Wife		ALINE
A Gypsy		ALINE
Beatrix's waiting-maid		PERES

The action passes at Ghent.

Act I. Scene I. Cesarius's shop. The background is formed by a central glazed door, with a stained-glass window on either side, looking on to the main street.

At the rise of the curtain Zephiros is giving a dancing-lesson to Beatrix and her sister, Agnes. The former makes good progress, but the latter dances clumsily. Zephiros repeats the poses and gestures she must learn, but she only laughs at his grotesque airs.

Julia enters and greets her cousin and Zephiros, who presents her as his best pupil. To please him she dances with Agnes and Beatrix. The lesson is interrupted by Benedict, who offers a bouquet to Beatrix, his *fiancée*. But she receives it indifferently. Julia mocks Benedict, but Agnes tries to console him. Meanwhile Julia takes Beatrix aside and shows her a letter from a nobleman who courts her; and when Beatrix refuses to look at the letter, Julia reads it to her.

Enter Cesarius, followed by a notary. The former affectionately greets his daughter and Benedict, but salutes Julia coldly. He announces that Benedict and Beatrix are to be married on the morrow. Benedict is overjoyed, but Beatrix is troubled. Agnes congratulates her sister, although, as Julia observes cynically, she likes Benedict too.

Fanfares announce the commencement of a fête, and Benedict goes to dress and fetch Beatrix's friends; Zephiros follows him.

No sooner are they gone than two noblemen enter the shop, the Marquis and his friend, Don Bustamente. Julia points out the former to Beatrix, but she has already seen him. The noblemen ask to see various jewels, and, while Cesarius and Julia are attending to their customers, the Marquis makes love to Beatrix. He chooses a rich jewel-casket for himself, then purchases some other trinkets which he offers to the girls, who are overwhelmed at his generosity.

Benedict returns, dressed in his best, and Cesarius presents him to the Marquis as his future son-in-law, who is marrying Beatrix on the morrow. The Marquis is chagrined. But Julia whispers: "Have patience, she does not love him."

The sound of gay music increases in volume and a band of fiddlers appear, followed by a number of girls, led by Zephiros, come to call for their friends. The Marquis offers to drive Cesarius and his family to the Kermess. Julia accepts with delight for Beatrix and her cousins. Benedict finds himself left alone, but Agnes sees his plight and, returning, accompanies him to the fête. The crowd follows in merry disorder.

Act I. Scene II. The main square in Ghent.

The church bells ring out and a drum calls the people of Ghent to the Kermess, and soon a motley crowd fills the square. Enter the town company of crossbowmen, followed by representatives of the town guilds, allegorical cars, and, lastly, a band of young girls in white. Zephiros, Benedict, and the fiddlers lead in other groups of dancers. Benedict searches in vain for Beatrix.

A fresh movement among the crowd announces the arrival of the Marquis and his party. Benedict runs to meet Beatrix and makes her sit in an arbour, to watch the crossbowmen shooting for the prize—a crown of white roses, suspended from a tall mast. The crossbowmen miss the target so Bustamente tries his hand, only to launch a bolt through Zephiros's wig. Benedict tries and all but touches the mark. He is about to be awarded the prize, when the Marquis shoots the crown from the pole. He presents the crown to Beatrix which vexes Benedict, but Cesarius consoles him by saying: "What does it matter, to-morrow she will be your wife." Julia, however, does not lose the opportunity to enlarge on the Marquis's merits. "Be quiet," cautions Beatrix, "here is the

key of my room, come and see me to-night and then we will talk."
The Marquis observes the passing of the key.

A rustic ball follows, but it is suddenly interrupted by a storm.
The frightened dancers flee. The Marquis tries to run off with
Beatrix, but Benedict is before him. Then, seeing Julia, under
pretext of shielding her, he secures the key. The storm increases
in volume.

*Act I. Scene III. Beatrix's room. In the left background is a
bed, and a window overlooking the countryside. Doors at the side.
A* prie-dieu, *crucifix, and wooden clock.*

Beatrix enters with her father and Benedict. She is sad and preoccupied. Cesarius gently reproaches her for her coolness towards
Benedict. Seeing the latter almost in tears, she tries to console him.
Cesarius blesses the couple and gives Beatrix a medallion containing his portrait. She thanks him warmly. Cesarius embraces her
and leaves, followed by Benedict. Left alone, Beatrix ponders and
decides to be dutiful and marry Benedict.

Then she takes off her crown of roses, which reminds her of the
Marquis, who persists in her thoughts. She begins to undress
when she hears the noise of a key in the lock. Thinking it to be
Julia she goes to open the door and finds herself face to face with
the Marquis. Terrified, she runs towards her bed and wraps herself in its curtains. She entreats the Marquis to go, but he calmly
closes the door. Beatrix takes the opportunity to throw a mantle
about her shoulders and again implores him to leave. He kneels
at her feet and begs her to listen to him. Again the door opens
and Julia appears.

Beatrix explains how the Marquis came into her room and
how pleased she is that Julia has come. The Marquis also expresses
his pleasure at her arrival, for he hopes for her support. He re-
doubles his protestations of love, and Julia urges his nobility and
wealth. In despair, the Marquis produces a dagger and swears he
will kill himself if Beatrix should belong to another. The two
women rush towards him and wrench the dagger from him. At
this moment there is another knock at the door. While Beatrix
gives herself up for lost, Julia hides the Marquis behind the bed
curtains; then Beatrix goes to open the door.

The visitor is Agnes, who has come to tell Beatrix that her marriage is fixed for six o'clock on the morrow. She is astonished at
the frightened expressions of Beatrix and Julia, who explain that
they have been discussing Beatrix's marriage. Agnes embraces

Beatrix and leaves, signing to Julia to follow her. Julia takes the opportunity to help the Marquis to climb through the window. Hardly is he outside when Agnes returns for Julia. The former bids her sister good-night, saying: "The marriage is at six o'clock in the morning," which the Marquis repeats from behind the window, drawing Beatrix's attention to the clock. The girls leave, and door and window close at once.

Left alone once more, Beatrix kneels and offers a prayer of thanksgiving. Then she rises and goes to bed.

Act II. Scene I. A splendid boudoir in the palace of the Marquis de San Lucar, at Venice.

Beatrix has been carried off by the Marquis and is now his mistress. She reclines on a sofa and listens to his words of love. Merchants bring in beautiful shawls and jewels which the Marquis offers her. But she tells him that she is satisfied with his love, for which she has renounced everything.

Some of the Marquis's friends arrive and pay court to Beatrix. They are followed by Zephiros, who is going to give a ball that evening and wishes to secure the Marquis's patronage. He is delighted to see Beatrix and, much to her embarrassment, congratulates her on her marriage. He inquires if she is keeping up her dancing, and, when she replies in the negative, immediately proceeds to give her a lesson.

Julia appears and, embracing Beatrix, announces that she has become a dancer. Zephiros claims her as his pupil, and presents her to the Marquis. Julia is accompanied by a nobleman with whom she seems to be on intimate terms. "But," asks Beatrix, "what has happened to Don Bustamente?" Julia is embarrassed and replies: "The only one I love is Count Leonardo," and she indicates her companion. Beatrix appears displeased and Julia seems to say, "One day you will do the same as I."

Enter Bustamente accompanied by Diana, the *première danseuse* of the Fenice Theatre. The former ignores Julia and presents Diana to the Marquis, who is much taken with her. Beatrix reproaches him, and Julia is furious with Bustamente. Bustamente and Leonardo threaten each other, and the two young dancers quarrel violently. At the height of the tumult, Zephiros tries to calm the disputants, whereupon he is accused of being the cause of all the trouble. Finally, the Marquis succeeds in making peace.

Now the joyous music of the carnival is heard. Zephiros invites his guests to the ball and the girls surround the Marquis and beg him to take them there. Beatrix looks sadly at her medallion. But the Marquis soothes her and orders his lackeys to bring in some carnival costumes. Each guest chooses a mask and domino, and escorted by torch-bearers and led by Zephiros, the party set out for the ball.

Act II. Scene II. A magnificent ballroom, with a large orchestra in the background.

A crowd of masked revellers, among whom is Beatrix and the Marquis, cross and re-cross the floor, while fashionably-dressed spectators look down on the scene from boxes. Now a circle is formed and Zephiros announces the commencement of the entertainment.

Diana dances at the head of a band of nymphs. San Lucar warmly congratulates her, to Beatrix's displeasure. Follow several character dances, then Beatrix appears as the goddess Diana. At first hesitating, she finally dances so brilliantly as to achieve a triumph. In token of reconciliation she plucks a rose from the flowers showered upon her and presents it to San Lucar.

The dancing becomes general and, at the end of a mad *Galop,* the Marquis places a garland of flowers on his mistress's head. But a mysterious domino hurls the garland to the ground, and, unmasking, reveals the stern, condemning features of Cesarius. Beatrix kneels for pardon, but her father orders her to leave the ballroom. Two more dominoes unmask and prove to be Agnes and Benedict; they ask pardon for the culprit. San Lucar places himself in front of Beatrix. Benedict is about to draw his sword on him, but Cesarius tells him that the Marquis's conduct is beneath contempt.

Cesarius orders his daughter to choose between San Lucar and himself. She hesitates and her father curses her.

Beatrix, unable to support this terrible blow, swoons into· San Lucar's arms, while the bystanders, stupefied by this moving scene, give passage to Cesarius, leaning heavily on Agnes and Benedict.

Act III. Scene I. The park of San Lucar's villa. In the background is the Brenta, whose moonlit waters lap the boundaries of the park. The gardens are illuminated with groups of coloured fairy lamps.

Young noblemen and women dressed as nymphs and bacchantes are seated at tables laden with rich fare. Other groups are reclining or fast asleep on the grass. The Marquis, Beatrix, Bustamente, Diana, Julia, and Zephiros have a table to themselves.

The Marquis, seeing Beatrix sad and indifferent, gives a signal and the women dance a voluptuous *pas*. This is followed by gaming, at which Zephiros loses all his money to Julia.

Beatrix and San Lucar, who have been strolling in the park, reappear, arm in arm. The Marquis shows Beatrix the rose she gave him after the dance as Diana, and which he wears in his domino. He kisses the rose as if it were a symbol of herself.

Bustamente invites San Lucar to join the play, but, at Beatrix's entreaties, he refuses. But when his friend insists, he surrenders. He plays high and loses all. Beatrix tries to console him by saying that the jewels he gave her will keep them. He takes her jewels and loses those too. Then Bustamente offers to wager his winnings against the possession of Beatrix. San Lucar, after agonising moments of indecision, stakes the rose from his cloak. He throws the dice but loses. Horrified, he takes to flight, while Bustamente places the flower—symbol of Beatrix—in his coat.

Seeing her approaching he puts on his mask and lowers the hood of his domino, which is blue like that of San Lucar. Beatrix, thinking from the rose he wears that the mask is the Marquis, begs him to leave the gaming table. He pretends to hesitate then, signing to the noblemen near by not to undeceive her, leads her to a gondola which glides away. The guests, highly diverted by Bustamente's successful ruse, drink to his success.

Act III. Scene II. Same as Act II. Scene I, but now lighted by the moon.

Bustamente, still masked, leads Beatrix into the room. She asks him to remove his mask, but he refuses and embraces her with ardour. Seized with misgivings she snatches off her lover's mask, and is made aware of her error.

At this moment San Lucar darts in with a drawn sword. He is about to kill Bustamente when Beatrix intervenes. The Marquis curses his friend, who replies that he won Beatrix at the gaming-table. Beatrix, shocked at his words, gazes in horror at the Marquis, who remains silent, then flies at Bustamente. The latter draws his sword and a terrible fight ensues, as a result of which Bustamente receives a mortal wound and topples over the balcony into the water below.

Beatrix flies in horror, while the Marquis, who has lost his reason, runs madly in the opposite direction.

Act III. Scene III. A pretty village square on the outskirts of Ghent. In the background is a precipice with steps cut into the rock. To the left is a charming house; to the right, a church.

Enter Agnes and Benedict, followed by a notary and a group of villagers who present the bride with bouquets. Then Benedict goes into the house, followed by Agnes, the notary, and his old governess.

The villagers dance and presently they are joined by a band of gypsies led by Zephiros, who gives a performance. The principal dancer is Julia.

Meanwhile, Beatrix enters. Exhausted and hardly able to stand, she sits on a stone bench. Julia recognizes her cousin and asks her to join the troupe, but she refuses.

Benedict reappears to take his bride to the altar. He throws money to the crowd, but does not recognize Beatrix, who is greatly distressed in consequence.

The villagers and gypsies depart, and Beatrix, left alone, gives way to despair at finding herself among the familiar scenes of her childhood.

The goldsmith's door opens and the wedding procession forms and goes towards the church. Surprised not to see her father, Beatrix seizes the governess's hand and asks after him. For answer, the governess points to a tomb inscribed CESARIUS.

The shock of the announcement is such that Beatrix loses her reason. She climbs up the rocky path and, to the terror of the on-lookers, throws herself into the abyss.

Act III. Scene IV. Same as Act I. Scene I.

Beatrix is asleep in her bed. Suddenly she opens her eyes and looks fearfully about her; then, seeing her crown of roses, she falls on her knees and prays. At the same moment the clock strikes six and there is a tap at the window.

It is the hour at which she had decided to elope with the Marquis, but the memories of her dream are too strong for her. She opens the window and, seeing San Lucar, rushes to the door. The door opens and Cesarius appears, followed by Agnes and Benedict in their wedding-clothes.

The Marquis makes a furious gesture and disappears.

Father and daughter embrace, and Benedict kneels at his fiancée's feet, while Agnes places the crown of roses on her head.

Cesarius places Beatrix's hand in that of Benedict and the wedding procession is formed.

*

La Jolie Fille de Gand is based on the drama *Victorine ou la Nuit porte Conseil* by Dumersan, Gabriel and Dupeuty.

"The ballet is well planned," says the critic of *La France Musicale*[1], "the dances are tastefully composed. . . . There are, however . . . moments when the action drags."

"The music by Adolphe Adam," observes the same writer, "is very remarkable. . . . In the piece which opens the Kermess there is heard a very novel bell-like effect, which wonderfully expresses the bustle and gaiety of the festival. The March which follows is one of M. Adam's most original inspirations. The rhythm is brilliant, the melody very infectious. The peal of bells danced by Carlotta Grisi and Petipa is charming and full of character; the accompaniment of little bells in the orchestra again emphasizes the principal melody, which should become popular.

"Among the numerous *pas* in the second act we shall mention that which opens the ball, delicious in its animation and go; the *Cracovienne*; the *pas* of the three-legged man, the music of which is as droll as the dance; the ravishing andante for harps and flutes, to which Mlle. Fitzjames dances; the *Pas de Diane* by Carlotta Grisi; and, lastly, the Galop, whose finale is full of new and unexpected effects.

"In the third act, in the orgy scene, there is a delicious andante for clarinet, then the *Pas de Saltimbanques,* whose lively music contrasts so well with the dramatic scenes that follow.

"As for the music of the mimed scenes, the end of the second act, in which energy and passion are carried to the furthest degree, was particularly applauded.

"This score lacks the misty quality of that of *Giselle,* but it has more brilliance and warmth, as required by the difference in theme."

Gautier declares the music to be "written with all that care the composer bestows on his ballet music. It contains enough themes for three comic operas; the *Pas des Clochettes* . . . and the galop of the masked ball, which will become as popular as the galop from *Gustave,* are pieces charming in melody and very happy in rhythm.[2]"

Of Grisi as Beatrix, Gautier reveals that it was feared "that the dramatic and violent scenes in the piece would be unsuited to her simple and poetic nature. She exceeded all expectations. Her

---

[1] June 26th, 1842.
[2] *La Presse,* July 2nd, 1842.

chaste astonishment at the sight of all the orgies and quarrels she encounters, her penetrating sensitiveness, her energy in dramatic moments; her lively and pathetic terror at the paternal curse, left nothing to be desired.

"From the first act, the scene of the Kermess, her success was already assured. How she flies, how she rises, how she soars! How at home she is in the air! When, from time to time, the tip of her little white foot skims the ground, it is easy to see that it is out of pure good nature, so as not to drive to despair those who have no wings. We must say that the music of this *pas* is deliciously original; peals of sparkling notes burst like rockets through the orchestral arrangement, affording a ravishing imitation of those Flemish clocks which inspired Victor Hugo to write a pretty piece of poetry in *Les Rayons et les Ombres*. In fact, Carlotta resembles the ethereal dancer whom the poet sees descend and ascend the crystal staircase of melody in a deep-toned mist of light. She succeeds without a quiver in attaining the last rung of that ladder of silver filigree which the composer has built for her, as if to defy her lightness, and the public, amazed, furiously applauded her when she came down again. . . . It is impossible to dance with greater perfection, vigour, and grace, with a profounder sense of rhythm and time, with happier or more smiling features. No fatigue, no effort; no perspiration or gasping; these wonders accomplished, Carlotta went to sit beneath the great noble trees of the principal square in Ghent, like a young lady who has just danced a *contredanse* in a ballroom."

*

La Jolie Fille de Gand was first produced in London, on February 15th, 1844, at the Theatre Royal, Drury Lane, under the title of *The Beauty of Ghent,* with Albert as the Marquis di San Lucar, and Louise Fleury as Beatrix.

The Times' critic observes: "There is plenty of substance in this ballet. We have two or three *pas* to applaud—we have some beautiful scenes and a marvellously fine procession to admire—we have abundance of lengthy pantomime to make us yawn. No want of magnificence, nothing like parsimony, but a palpable want of compactness. It should, however, be observed, that the ballet improves as it goes on, and that the first part is decidedly the dullest. A heavy affair that first act! . . .

"But then, in the second act, we had a ballroom illuminated with gas in the *Alma* style and enlivened by the *pas de deux* of Petit Stephan and Huguet Vestris, and the *Diane Chasseresse* of Fleury;

and, in the third act, the 'business' of the piece became interesting and the pantomime effective; and there was, moreover, a very pretty scene of a villa, with elegant groups disposed on the stage."

Of Fleury as Beatrix the same writer observes: "Her pantomime . . . is well conceived and striking; her starts, her exhibitions of terror, are all well managed. Whether she has really more genuine feeling than two years ago, or whether she has merely learned the mute language by which emotion is represented in ballet, we do not undertake to decide, but yet incline to believe that the latter is the case, and that she has rather cultivated the routine of pantomime than penetrated into the depths herself.

"As a dancer Mademoiselle Fleury has less passion than Petit Stephan who on Saturday danced a beautiful *pas de deux* (with Huguet Vestris) with a voluptuous tenderness which for a moment recalled the remembrance of Carlotta Grisi. All that Fleury does exhibits a very careful training, an innate grace, an unwavering determination to give a high finish to her performance.

"The chief *pas* was a *Diane Chasseresse*. . . . The slow movement is very beautiful, its chief characteristic being given by the series of classical attitudes into which the dancer falls. The gracefulness with which Fleury poised on one toe, bent forward with extended bow, and in that attitude slowly revolved, was very striking, and the bouquets that were thrown to her were not unmerited.

"The performance throughout, if not of the most astonishing kind, was very pleasing and interesting; an artless expression of face adds charm to her achievements, and when she was called for with very loud plaudits at the end of the ballet, there is no doubt that a feeling of real gratification was represented on the part of the audience."

MAZILIER

MAZILIER was born at Bordeaux, where he began his career as a dancer. In 1822 he came to Paris and danced first at the Théâtre de la Porte Saint-Martin, later he appeared at the Opéra. He was appointed *premier danseur de caractère* in 1833 and *maître de ballet* in 1839. It was said of him that he could compose a ballet a day and dance every night. A Russian critic asserts that he was very inferior to Perrot, especially in *ensembles* and *ballabili*. The latter criticism is borne out by Charles de Boigne, who declares that "Mazilier was not so bad at building up a scene, but he understood nothing of the handling of masses. He did not know how to bring them on the stage, how to get them off, or how to make them move. He struggled with himself, taxed all his ingenuity in vain, he produced nothing but a muddle."

He composed a number of ballets of which the following are the best known: *La Gypsy* (1839), *Le Diable Amoureux* (1840), *Le Diable au Corps* (1845), *Paquita* (1846), *Betty* (1846), *Vert-Vert* (1851), *Jovita* (1853), *Les Elfes* (1856), *Le Corsaire* (1856), *Marco Spada* (1857).

Some of these compositions were very successful and were reproduced by the principal ballet companies; moreover, many dancers won renown or added to their laurels through the opportunities which these ballets afforded—for instance, Fanny Elssler in *La Gypsy*, Grisi in *Paquita*, Ferraris in *Les Elfes*, and Rosati in *Le Corsaire*.

LA GYPSY

Pantomimic Ballet in 3 Acts and 5 Scenes. Book: H. Vernoy de Saint-Georges and Mazilier. Music: Benoist, Thomas, and Marliani. Scenery: Philastre and Cambon. Choreography: Mazilier. First produced: Théâtre de l'Académie Royale de Musique, Paris, January 28th, 1839.

Act I. Scene I. A beautiful landscape a few miles from Edinburgh. To the left is the principal entrance to Lord Campbell's castle. Opposite is a statue of Charles II, above which waves a banner crowned with flowers and bearing the words: Accession of Charles II. In the background are two immense rocks between which flows a torrent. On the left is a staircase hewn out of the rock. A fir-tree thrown across the rocks serves as a primitive bridge. The horizon is dominated by a forest of tall fir-trees.

Lord Campbell, an ardent Royalist, is celebrating the accession to the throne of Charles II. The clan are assembled and the festival is to begin with a hunt in the mountains.

Lord Campbell comes out of his castle and greets his followers. He is accompanied by his only child, Sarah, attended by Meg, her nurse. Narcisse de Crakentorp, Lord Campbell's nephew, a conceited fool, tells him that he will look after Sarah while he goes hunting. The hunting-party, led by Lord Campbell, climb the rocks and are soon lost to sight.

Hardly have they gone when Stenio, a fugitive Roundhead, enters. Hard pressed, he is endeavouring to make his escape. At the same moment a band of gypsies under Trousse-Diable make their appearance. Stenio asks if he may join them, which request is granted. A gypsy reports the arrival of a party of soldiers. "They are looking for me," declares Stenio. In an instant his clothes are taken from him and he is dressed as a gypsy, during which a roll of parchment falls from his pocket. "What is that?" asks Trousse-Diable. "It is my officer's commission," replies Stenio, "my sole possession," and he hides it in his new clothes.

The soldiers enter but are told that the fugitive has climbed up the rocks. On this news the soldiers follow in pursuit. Trousse-Diable bids Stenio wait while he and his band depart on some errand. The hunting-calls ring out louder and nearer and a wild beast is seen to cross the bridge and go down the pathway where are Meg, Sarah, Narcisse, and the villagers. Narcisse and the peasants retire in a great fright and tell Stenio that Lord Campbell's daughter and her nurse have been attacked and doubtless killed. Stenio snatches up Narcisse's gun and dashes up the rocky pathway. Presently he fires and disappears from view.

Hearing the report, Lord Campbell and his huntsmen come running in. At this moment Stenio returns, supporting Sarah, who is about to faint and whose arm is lacerated. Meg falls on her knees and tells her lord how Stenio saved his daughter. Trousse-Diable is thunder-struck that Stenio should have rendered such a service. A doctor is summoned and asserts that Sarah is in no danger. Meg carries the girl into the castle and her master, thanking Stenio for the great service he has rendered him, invites him to the banquet, which servants are engaged in setting out. Stenio declines, but is induced to take his place at the table.

Meanwhile the nurse appears at one of the rooms in the castle, whose open window faces the spectator. She is seen with Sarah on her knees; having soothed her, she places her in bed.

Various dances take place on the castle lawn and then the national anthem is played. All the guests rise, when Lord Campbell, looking towards the statue, toasts the King. Noticing that Stenio remains seated, Lord Campbell pours out a glass of wine and begs him to drink the King's health. Stenio takes the cup and pours the wine on the ground. There is an uproar and swords are drawn. But Lord Campbell reminds his guests that the stranger has just saved his daughter's life. Trousse-Diable, furious, insults Lord Campbell and is arrested. Stenio, who refuses with dignity the purse of gold that is offered him, takes his departure. Trousse-Diable tries to follow, but is taken into the castle.

The festival is resumed. The nurse informs her master that Sarah is sleeping peacefully. All at once and while the villagers are enjoying an animated dance, a man is seen climbing down a side of the castle. He lowers himself until he reaches the window of the room in which Sarah sleeps. He climbs through the window and closes it. A little later the window is thrown open, and the nurse, who has hastily returned to watch over Sarah, cries out that her charge has disappeared.

Lord Campbell is thunderstruck at this news. He dashes into the castle and presently himself appears at the window and shows the empty cradle. He returns to his guests who vainly strive to console him. Then Meg espies Trousse-Diable climbing the rocky path, with the child in his arms.

Lord Campbell and his friends run madly in pursuit; but, no sooner has Trousse-Diable crossed the narrow bridge, than he pushes the tree into the abyss. Then, wrapping the child in his cloak, he disappears into the depths of the forest.

Act II. Scene I. Twelve years have passed and the scene shifts to a vast tent erected in a street in Edinburgh. It is evening. The tent is lit by a lamp, the street by a brilliant moon. All is quiet, except for the sounds of revelry which come from a tavern. The tent, which faces the spectator, is the dwelling of Mab, queen of the gypsies.

The street is deserted. Sarah, now eighteen, is resting on a pile of tiger-skins. A patrol of the town-watch marches down the street. They are succeeded by a number of gypsies led by Trousse-Diable, who suggests that they should rob the nobleman drinking in the tavern.

Narcisse, now Lord Campbell's heir, comes out of the tavern. As he passes by, Trousse-Diable asks him the time. He takes out his watch to ascertain and Trousse-Diable seizes it and puts it in his own pocket. The gypsy then bids him hand over his rings. Narcisse reaches for his sword but the other gypsies leap on him and rob him of his all, while Trousse-Diable escapes with a miniature.

Mab appears and orders them to give back to Narcisse everything they have stolen. They obey. Narcisse, after thanking his rescuer, asks for the miniature. "Trousse-Diable had it," cries one, "but he ran off." Mab escorts Narcisse to his home.

The noise awakens Sarah who comes out of the tent. Stenio, who watches over her, runs to her side. She tells him that she dreamt that she was rich but that he loved her just the same. Stenio takes her in his arms, but she cries out and shows the scar on her arm. He tells her the story of his fight with the wild animal and is about to reveal the secret of her birth when, in an access of love, he kneels at her feet.

At this moment the back of the tent parts and Mab appears. She is in love with Stenio and threatens Sarah for daring to be her rival. Sarah asks Stenio to choose between them and he goes to her, then she calls out to the gypsies who come running in.

She tells them that she loves Stenio and wishes to be his wife.

Mab, as queen of the gypsies, is forced to unite Sarah and Stenio.

A gypsy tells Mab that a festival is about to take place and they should be there. The gypsies take their departure. Mab, seeing Trousse-Diable, asks him where he obtained a miniature he is wearing. He refuses to reply, but the queen forces him to give it to her.

While the gypsies surround Trousse-Diable, who harangues them, Sarah comes out in the most charming costume. She holds a tambourine in her hand and is followed by gypsies wearing Scottish plaids.

The queen bids the gypsies depart, but, led by Trousse-Diable, they refuse. Sarah begs them to come and again they refuse. Then she begins to dance with such vivacity that they cannot withhold from imitating her steps and end by dancing after her. Mab, furious at Sarah's success, follows in the rear.

Act II. Scene II. The great fair of Edinburgh in the market-place. To the left is an imposing building on the pediment of which is inscribed: "Town Hall."

A crowd, on pleasure bent, move noisily among the various stalls. A band of gypsies dart upon the people and force them to give room. The band divide in two and Mab emerges at the head of a number of girls. The spectators gather round.

First the gypsies dance an *ensemble,* then Mab and Sarah dance, after which they make a collection. Meanwhile Lord Campbell walks across the square. He is greeted by Narcisse who draws his attention to Sarah's dancing. Now follows a *Pas Cracovien* and the dances conclude with an *ensemble* executed by Mab and the gypsies.

As the dancers disperse Narcisse tries to speak with Sarah. He pays her compliments and tries to kiss her, but she slaps his face to the amusement of Stenio, who is about to come to her aid. Narcisse retires and, in passing, is recognized by Mab as the victim of the previous night. Seeing an opportunity for revenge she runs after Sarah, congratulating her on her dancing, and presents her with the miniature, which she places about her neck. Sarah is delighted and thanks her warmly.

The festival ended, the gypsies leave the market-place. Suddenly Narcisse catches sight of the miniature. He runs to Sarah and accuses her of having stolen it. She replies that it was given to her by the queen.

Narcisse calls to his friends, who recognize the miniature. Sarah looks for Mab but she cannot be found. The gypsy is surrounded and Stenio tries to protect her. The sheriff's officers arrive on the scene. There is a fierce struggle with the gypsies, but Sarah is arrested and taken before the sheriff, while Stenio is detained. Mab glides from behind one of the stalls, making a gesture of triumph at the downfall of her rival.

Act II. Scene III. A room in the house of Lord Campbell, sheriff of Edinburgh. There is a door in the background, and doors to the side. The window in the background overlooks the market-place. To the right is a full-length portrait of Sarah at the age when she was kidnapped.

Lord Campbell enters, sad and preoccupied, for Sarah's dancing reminds him of his lost daughter. A sheriff's officer announces that there is a case of theft to be tried. Sarah is ushered in, followed by Narcisse, her accuser. She denies the charge and, while she is being examined, Stenio, escaped from his guards, forces his way into the room. He is surprised to see Lord Campbell.

Sarah swears that she is innocent. But when Lord Campbell is forced to find her guilty, she draws a dagger from her scarf and tries to stab herself. Lord Campbell swings up her arm and, in doing so, catches sight of the scar. He shows Meg the scar and asks Sarah the origin of it. She repeats the story Stenio told her. Lord Campbell doubts no longer and acclaims her as his long-lost daughter. Stenio, hiding his face in his hands, is led away by Trousse-Diable.

Act III. Scene I. A dining-room in Lord Campbell's castle. A window in the background overlooks a park. To the right is the door of a study.

Lord Campbell is to give a brilliant ball in honour of the recovery of his daughter. Sarah enters in a beautiful ball-dress, but appears overwhelmed with sadness. Her father enters and is charmed with his daughter's beauty. Narcisse arrives and offers Sarah a bouquet, but she turns her back on him. Lord Campbell and Narcisse go to receive their guests.

As soon as Sarah is alone she goes to the study and brings out her gypsy clothes and her tambourine. The window opens and Trousse-Diable climbs into the room. He is followed by Stenio, who is overjoyed to find that Sarah still loves him. At the same moment the doors open and Lord Campbell enters with his guests. She has just time to hide Stenio in the study while Trousse-Diable slips out of the window.

Narcisse invites Sarah to dance a minuet to which she unwillingly consents. The company joins in. While they are dancing, Meg, seeing the gypsy clothes on the sofa, goes to put them away in the study. Sarah, fearing that her lover will be discovered, leaves off dancing and forbids her to enter the study.

At the same moment there is an uproar outside, the doors are flung open, and a veiled woman enters. It is Mab, Sarah's rival. She goes to Lord Campbell and tells him that his daughter has a gypsy lover concealed in the castle, and indicates the study. Sarah attempts to restrain her father, but he goes to the study and discovers Stenio. Sarah, alarmed to see her rival, takes Stenio by the arm and presents him to her father as her husband.

Lord Campbell, enraged, bids Stenio begone. Mab slips her arm into his to lead him away, but Sarah stops Stenio and implores her father to listen to her. Mab, furious in her turn, leaves, followed by the guests, who are amazed at the scene they have just witnessed.

Sarah begs her father not to separate her from her husband. But Lord Campbell is horrified that his daughter should be married to a gypsy, a beggar. Stenio cannot support this insult and declares that, although a rebel, he is of noble blood. So saying he displays his commission. Lord Campbell holds out his hand. During this scene of reconciliation Mab appears at the window followed by a gypsy. She points to Stenio and the gypsy whips out a pistol and fires. Stenio falls to the ground.

At the sound of the pistol-shot the guests dash into the room. Lord Campbell lavishes every care on Stenio, but he is past human aid. Sarah, motionless, seems oblivious of what is going on about her. Mab comes forward with an air of triumph.

Sarah, mad with rage, becomes a gypsy. She seizes a dagger and stabs her rival. Then she runs to Stenio and, finding his hand cold, her gaze wanders; she grasps at her heart as if to tear out her life, then swoons into her father's arms. Meanwhile the gypsy who shot Stenio is arrested by Lord Campbell's men, while Mab, who is also surrounded, glares defiance.

*

La Gypsy, according to Gautier,[1] was the first ballet to be composed by Mazilier. It is "gracefully arranged and the *pas* are new. Its only defect in our opinion is that all the dances are placed in the first scenes, while the latter ones are given up entirely to mime.

"The music is written by three composers, MM. Benoist, Thomas,

[1] *La Presse,* February 4th, 1839.

and Marliani. The act composed by M. Thomas seems to us far above the others, both in the novelty and the elegance of its arrangement. But everything—book, music, dancing—obtained the greatest success."

The critic of *La France Musicale*[2] observes, in regard to the music: "With the exception of the third act, which belongs entirely to M. Marliani, and which is the least good of the three, the two others seemed to us hardly more than some competent arrangements by two distinguished musicians, MM. Benoist and Ambroise Thomas: so there are three composers for one ballet. The innovation is not to be recommended; moreover, the three musicians have chosen the most celebrated composers for collaborators."

Of Fanny Elssler as Sarah, Gautier declares: "She has surpassed herself. She has combined Florinda and Fenella; the *Pas de la Cracovienne* affords her a triumph which will make the ballet's fortune. She dances in the most coquettish and roguish costume that could be imagined: an officer's tunic sparkling with buttons and a *vivandière's* skirt, boots with steel spurs, and a black necktie framing a delightful chin—the whole crowned with a triumphant, sprightly little plume, the prettiest you ever saw. It is impossible to describe this dance: it is rhythmic precision mingled with a charming ease, a muscular and bounding agility which cannot be imagined; the metallic clicking of the spurs, a kind of castanets on the heels, emphasizes each step and gives the dance a quality of joyous vivacity which is quite irresistible. This *pas* is encored every evening. . . .

"In the dramatic part of the ballet, Mlle. Fanny Elssler rises to the most sublime heights of dramatic art; a noble pride in innocence, energy, tears, grief, love, intoxicating joy, she runs through the whole gamut of human emotions; only Miss Smithson or Mme. Dorval could attain such pathetic transports, such forceful miming.

"Mlle. Theresa Elssler invested the difficult part of Mab . . . with a quite remarkable aged and symbolic character; Mazilier is graceful and pathetic; Elie is a delightful Narcisse, and Simon, in a very picturesque costume, played the part of Trousse-Diable in a vigorous and realistic manner."

*

La Gypsy, with Fanny Elssler in the title-role, was first produced at London at Her Majesty's Theatre on June 24th, 1839, where its original success was repeated.

[2] January 31st, 1839.

The Times reports that "F. Elssler introduced a delightful mazurka, which she danced in a fantastic military dress, and with a naïveté and piquancy which caused it to be tumultously encored.[3]"

Chorley, in his *Recollections,* records some interesting impressions of Elssler as Sarah. "It was not till *The Gypsy* was produced that Mdlle. Fanny Elssler's full genius was known. This ballet, given on a reduced scale in London . . . as seen in Paris, was a performance never to be forgotten. Much of the lovely music of Weber's *Preciosa* was used in it; the Bolero which opens his overture was allotted to a scene where the gypsy girl compels her sulky mates to dance. When she appeared on the stage of Paris the folk lay couched in fifties, huddled together in their wild and picturesque clothes, as only the French stage-managers know how to group forms and colours. How she moved hither and thither, quick and bright as a torch, lighting up one sullen heap of tinder after another, gradually animating the scene with emotion, till at last the excited rout of vagabonds trooped after her with the wild vivacity of a chorus of bacchanals, made a picture of many pictures, the brightness and spirit of which stand almost alone in the gallery of similar ones. There have been Gitanas, Esmeraldas, Mignons by the score, but no Gipsy to approach Mdlle. Fanny Elssler.

"In the next act of the ballet came the scene of the minuet danced by the heroine to gain time, and to distract attention from her lover in concealment hard by, whose life was imperilled. Lord Byron, when speaking on his own dramas, has subtly dwelt on the power of suppressed passion. Few things have been seen more fearful than the cold and measured grace of Mdlle. Fanny Elssler in this juncture, than the manner in which every step was watched, every gesture allowed its right time, so that neither flurry nor faltering might be detected, than the set smile, the vigilant ear, the quivering lip controlling itself. It is in moments like these that genius rises above talent. It was by representations such as these that Mdlle. Fanny Elssler gradually established a fame among the few as well as the many, which could have been built up by no *pirouettes* and *entrechats,* but in right of which she is enrolled among the great dramatic artists of the century."

[3] June 25th, 1839.

LE DIABLE AMOUREUX

Pantomimic Ballet in 3 Acts and 8 Scenes. Book: Vernoy de Saint-Georges and Mazilier. Music: Benoist and Réber. Scenery: Philastre and Cambon. Choreography: Mazilier. First produced: Théâtre de l'Académie Royale de Musique, Paris, September 23rd, 1840.

CHARACTERS

Beelzebub	MM.	Montjoie
Frédéric		Mazilier
Hortensius . . .		Barrez I
Simplice } The Grand Vizier } . .		Elie
Bracaccio		Simon
Grand Bailiff . . .		Quériau
A Nobleman . . .		Coralli (jun.)
A Pirate		Adice
Another Pirate . . .		Desplaces (jun.)
A Priest		L. Petit
Phœbe	Mmes.	Noblet
Urielle		Pauline Leroux
Lilia		Nathaniel Fitzjames
Thérésine . . .		Mazilier
Janetta		Adèle Dumilâtre
A Female Demon . . .		Roland

Peasants, Lords, Ladies, Pirates, Creditors, Fishermen, Male and Female Demons, Eunuchs, Merchants, Negroes, Bayadères, Odalisques, etc.

Act I. Scene I. The park of Phœbe's villa. To the right is an elegant kiosk placed at the head of some steps; in the centre is a gaming-table.

Phœbe, seated in the kiosk and attended by numerous admirers, watches the dances of the peasants on her estate. Count Frédéric, Phœbe's lover, pays court to her while his tutor, old Dr. Hortensius, looks on the scene with obvious displeasure. Lilia, one of the dancers, attracts the Count's attention and he goes to speak with her, but Phœbe forces him to return to her side.

After a final dance the company disperse through the gardens and the guests follow Phœbe. Frédéric pretends to join them, but presently returns to speak with Lilia, who has stayed behind with her mother. Frédéric tells Lilia that he is sure he has seen her before. She replies that they played together as children, when her mother was his nurse.

Phœbe returns and is jealous at this exchange of memories. She bids him dismiss Lilia with a money present, but instead he gives her a ring from his finger. As soon as Phœbe is alone with Frédéric, she reproaches him for his infidelity. The Count is indifferent and Hortensius is delighted at this rift.

But when Phœbe's admirers return and she receives their advances with every pleasure, Frédéric is furious. In a fit of temper he tries his luck at the gaming-table, only to lose his fortune. Then Lilia returns him his ring and offers him her gold cross. He accepts the cross which he presses to his lips and accuses the players of having cheated him. Swords are drawn, but Phœbe parts the combatants. Lilia sheds tears and Frédéric is led away by Hortensius.

Act I. Scene II. An ancient library in the gothic tower of a deserted castle belonging to Count Frédéric. Painted above the great fire-place is a picture representing a legend associated with one of the Count's ancestors, to whom, in exchange for his soul, Beelzebub gave a devil as a page. The room is lighted by the moon's rays which stream through a large open window.

Janetta, a servant, carrying a lantern, enters in fear, followed by Simplice, her sweetheart. He pesters her to kiss him, when a bell rings loudly. The servants are frightened. But Janetta opens the door and admits two drenched travellers, Frédéric and Hortensius.

Janetta helps them to remove their cloaks and hastens to light a fire. Simplice offers his services to the Count, who expresses a preference for Janetta, which rouses the youth's jealousy. Then Hortensius dismisses the servants.

Frédéric, left alone, tells his tutor of his ruin. Hortensius takes some books from the shelves and begs him to calm himself by reading. The Count studies the pages with little interest until he comes across a manuscript dealing with black magic. To the doctor's horror he determines to follow his ancestor's example and summon the aid of Beelzebub. The Count makes the prescribed incantations. Thunder rolls, lightning flashes, and the fire-place is struck by a spear of light through which stalks Beelzebub, with Urielle, a female demon, crouching at his feet. Hortensius flees.

The Lord of Evil commands Urielle to obey the Count. She goes to the swooning Frédéric and, attracted by his youth, seems to implore Beelzebub to spare him. But with an angry gesture he changes her into a page. There is a burst of infernal music and Beelzebub vanishes.

Frédéric asks the page who he is and Urielle replies that she has come to do his bidding. He asks that a splendid supper may be served for himself and the doctor. The wish is granted and, when Hortensius returns, Frédéric invites him to dine, which he fearfully accepts. The page continually replenishes their glasses with wine and presently the Count falls asleep. Since Hortensius continues to keep awake, Urielle makes a sign which sends him to sleep likewise.

Urielle goes to Frédéric. Her page's costume vanishes and her true female form is discerned beneath a gauze dress. She dances before the Count in the most captivating manner imaginable, while Frédéric, still asleep, shows evidence of his delight. Then Urielle kisses him on the brow and he awakes. The demon takes to flight while the Count vainly searches for the phantom of his dream. He rouses Hortensius and forces him to help. The tutor opens a chest and there they find the page.

A bell rings loudly. Hortensius rushes to the window and tells Frédéric that a party of creditors have come to claim their dues. The page lets them in and when all are assembled renders them motionless. Urielle makes another sign and the chest is covered with bags of gold. She makes a third sign, places a bag in the hands of each creditor, and awakens them. But when they open the bags to count the pieces, only a little smoke comes from each. Enraged, they rush at Frédéric, but Urielle shows them their receipts, overturns them with a single gesture, and goes out with Frédéric, laughing in their faces.

Act II. Scene 1. A drawing room in Count Frédéric's palace.

The curtain rises on a scene of orgy. Frédéric, now rich and happy, allows his passions to run riot. Drinking and gaming are in full swing, and courtesans dressed as bacchantes and nymphs entertain the guests with dances. Urielle adds to the tumult by mocking the players who have lost and embroiling lovers.

Simplice and his betrothed, Janetta, greet Frédéric. The Count draws Janetta apart and makes love to her. Urielle, jealous, draws Simplice's attention to the Count, who bids him take a walk. But when Frédéric wishes to kiss Janetta, Urielle causes the lights to dim and takes her from the Count. When Frédéric finds Janetta, Urielle restores the light and shows Phœbe in the background. The last named reproaches him for having forsaken her. The

Count ignores his mistress, but, when she pretends to cry, consoles her.

The festival is resumed and Urielle joins in the dancing. The page begs Phœbe to dance. She consents and is so fascinated by Urielle that she falls in "his" arms, to the amazement of the Count and his friends.

Frédéric, enraged, dismisses the page, who refuses to leave. When he menaces Urielle, she pretends to go, but in reality hides behind a sofa. The Count grows ardent towards Phœbe, when the jealous page makes a sign; a door opens in the background and reveals Lilia. The Count rushes towards her, and, when the image vanishes, runs out of the room. Phœbe, furious at being left alone, goes out.

Now the real Lilia and her mother enter on a visit. The page makes love to Lilia just as Frédéric returns. The Count kisses Lilia but now Phœbe enters. Furious, she is about to stab the Count, when Lilia darts forward and receives the blow instead.

Simplice enters and calls the guard. Everyone rushes in, including Thérésine, who hastens to her daughter's aid. Phœbe disappears in the crowd. Lilia is carried away and, just when Frédéric is about to follow her, Simplice returns, accompanied by the bailiff and his men.

The bailiff arrests the Count, who vainly protests his innocence. But while his captor turns his back to place guards at the doors, the page takes Frédéric by the hand and leads him through the wall, which divides and closes behind them.

The bailiff, astonished to find his prisoner vanished, orders his men to arrest the unfortunate Simplice and takes him away.

Act II. Scene II. To the right is a small fisherman's hut. In the background is a rock with a chapel on its summit, to which access is gained by steps cut out of the rock.

A boat manned by pirates is beached on the sands. The chief, Bracaccio, and his men, spy out the land. Janetta and her companions return from fishing. The chief is much taken by Janetta and dances with her. The hut door opens and the pirates hide among the rocks.

Lilia comes out supported by her mother and Hortensius. Frédéric rushes in without at first seeing Lilia, and when he does so they are delighted to meet again. He asks her hand in marriage which he wishes to take place that day. Urielle appears. Lilia goes into the cottage to prepare for the wedding.

A veiled woman arrives in a litter. It is Phœbe who, seeing the supposed page, asks for news of the Count. The demon causes a window to open so that the scene of preparation is revealed. Phœbe is enraged.

The pirates come from their hiding places. Phœbe calls Bracaccio and bribes him to kidnap Lilia. The chapel-bells ring merrily and Lilia emerges. The chief seizes her and places her in his boat. Then Urielle draws Bracaccio aside and offers him a still larger bribe to carry off Phœbe, to which he agrees. The boat puts off and disappears, followed by Urielle's laughter.

Frédéric and Hortensius knock at the door of the hut. The door opens and a veiled woman emerges, followed by young girls in bridal array. But while Frédéric goes in search of Thérésine, the woman's veil slips aside to disclose the features of Urielle. The Count returns and Urielle, much to her discomfort, is forced to kneel to Thérésine and receive her blessing.

As the procession moves toward the chapel, Urielle grows more and more agitated. The chapel door is opened to reveal the altar, surrounded with glittering candles. The sky darkens, thunder peals, and the priest recoils in horror, as if impelled by some supernatural force. The candles go out and a flash of lightning strikes the false bride. The onlookers, terror-stricken, take to flight. Frédéric lifts the victim's veil and is horrified to see in place of Lilia the features of Urielle.

Simplice appears and recounts the kidnapping of Lilia. Frédéric leaps into a boat and, accompanied by a number of men, goes in pursuit of the ravisher. Thérésine and all the women kneel in prayer, while the body of Urielle bursts into flame and disappears into the ground.

Act III. Scene I. A sombre grotto. To the right is a rock; to the left a subterranean staircase leading into the depths of the earth.

In the centre of the grotto stands Beelzebub, surrounded by prostrate demons of both sexes. Near him is the unconscious Urielle, whom he awakens with a touch of his sceptre. He asks her if she has accomplished her mission. She confesses that she failed to seduce Frédéric because he loved another, and she, too, was in love with him. Beelzebub is furious and, presenting her with a parchment deed, commands her to obtain the Count's signature to it so that his soul may belong to him.

The female demons entreat Beelzebub to let one of their number take Urielle's place. But, fired with jealousy, she swears to accomplish her mission. She begs to be allowed to return to the earth, whereupon Beelzebub makes a sign, the grotto opens, and Urielle disappears through the opening. At the same moment Beelzebub and his demons disappear into the ground.

Act III. Scene II. The interior of a slave-market at Ispahan.

Merchants are appraising their living wares, *bayadères* are dancing, jugglers are performing tricks, dervishes are turning round—all is colour and movement.

Bracaccio and his men, disguised as merchants, bring in veiled women for sale. The owners force them to dance, during which a cannon-shot is heard, marking the arrival of a European vessel. Passengers disembark, including Frédéric and a number of sailors. He espies Lilia who runs to him for protection. But Bracaccio puts her up for sale. There are many eager buyers. The Grand Vizier arrives in a palanquin and outbids Frédéric. Urielle appears and the Count, driven to desperation, asks her to find him gold. She refuses. The Grand Vizier therefore buys Lilia. The Count is furious with Urielle, who promises to aid him if he will sign the parchment deed. He consents.

Urielle asks Frédéric to detain the Vizier. He runs to do so and Urielle lets fall her burnous and appears in the costume of a *baya-dère*. She dances so delightfully that the Vizier desires to purchase her. But she tells him that Frédéric is her master. Then the Vizier asks him what he will take for the dancer. "Lilia," he replies. The Vizier refuses, but when Urielle dances more seductively than ever he agrees to the exchange.

Frédéric, overjoyed, takes Lilia to his ship. Urielle climbs into the palanquin, but, no sooner is the Vizier beside her, than she disappears. The Vizier is dumbfounded and begins to despair. At this moment Bracaccio appears with Phœbe whom he offers to the Vizier. The old man throws the chief his purse and places the courtesan in his litter.

Act III. Scene III. Same as Act I. Scene II.

It is night and the eve of the marriage of Lilia and Frédéric. The latter is seated at a table deep in thought. Lilia is kneeling on a *prie-dieu*. The lovers embrace and Lilia returns to her room.

Hardly is the Count alone when the clock strikes midnight. There is a knock at the door and Urielle enters with the deed in her hand. She commands the Count to follow her, but he refuses. He pleads that tomorrow he is to be married to Lilia, a statement which enrages the demon. She insists on the Count's following her, which some supernatural power forces him to do. At this moment Lilia runs to her lover's side. The Count then declares that the demon shall have his dead body only; he draws a dagger and is about to plunge it in his side when Urielle holds his arm.

This act rouses her good nature and she tells Frédéric that she will suffer eternal death for his sake. She tears up the parchment bond and causes it to burst into flames. No sooner is the deed consumed than Urielle grows weaker and weaker. She begs the Count to place his hand on her heart, which he does, and expires.

Lilia prays that Urielle may be forgiven, and Frédéric, taking the rosary and cross which Lilia gave him, places them on the dead body and flees with his betrothed.

Act III. Scene IV. An immense canopy of fire covers a burning lake which fills the stage. A flaming rock dominates this terrifying abyss. In the background are giant steps which give entrance to this abode of horror.

Beelzebub, surrounded by his court, awaits the unfortunate Urielle, whom a giant demon bears in his arms and sets down at his master's feet. The demons are about to rend the body to pieces, when an angel appears on the highest rock and, stretching out his arms, restores Urielle to life. Horrified to see herself surrounded by demons, she holds out Lilia's cross and rosary, before which Beelzebub and his demons recoil. Then Urielle mounts the steps towards the angel who takes her in his arms.

*

Le Diable Amoureux is based on a story by Cazotte.

Commenting on the scenery, the critic of *La Sylphide*[4] declares: "The villa of the first scene; the chapel with the great flight of steps cut out of the rock; the fourth, the Bazaar at Ispahan; the seventh; and, finally, the last, of Heaven and Earth; are perhaps the most remarkable settings which have been painted by MM. Philastre and Cambon.

"The music," says the same writer, "is generally pretty, often grandiose, and always appropriate to the situations which it is its business to explain or translate."

This ballet was the vehicle chosen for the return appearance of Pauline Leroux, whom an accident had forced temporarily to leave the stage. The critic of *La Sylphide* informs us that she made

[4] September 26th, 1840.

her reappearance with "a splendour, an appropriateness, and an animation of which the remembrance will long be treasured. It seems that absence, instead of having being prejudicial to Mlle. Pauline Leroux, has increased, developed that airiness, that poise, and those precious traditions of the noble school, of which she has always been one of the most gracious interpreters.

"By turn page and woman, lover and *bayadère,* she has known how to accord each scene the character which suits it, while losing nothing of her delicate prettiness; she has known how to conceive each disguise and each role with an incomparable fitness and nicety.

"In some sort Mlle. Pauline Leroux is the whole of the ballet, the *deus intersit* of the plot: it is she who makes the piece go, entering by one trap, making her exit through another, changing from man to woman in a second, sometimes going down into hell, sometimes ascending to heaven, beautiful and witty, everywhere and always. Because here is a French *danseuse* who mimes with our wit, who dances with our spirit, lively, petulant, full of provocation and malice, but, above all, full of despair and love."

*

Le Diable Amoureux was first produced at London, at Her Majesty's Theatre, on March 11th, 1841. Perhaps something of its novelty was diminished by an operatic ballet burletta on the same theme, entitled *Santanas and the Spirit of Beauty,* which had been presented earlier in the year at the Theatre Royal, Adelphi.

The part of Urielle was taken by Mlle. Guy Stephan who made her London début in this ballet, which, however, *The Times* critic notices but briefly: *"Le Diable Amoureux . . .* was got up with great splendour as a ballet, which would be much improved by condensation. A new dancer, Mademoiselle Guy Stephan, made her appearance; a stoutish young lady, with a pretty face, who moves with great flexibility, and dances with an easy careless grace that is very pleasing, without representing any sentiment by her movements, or displaying any remarkable agility.[5]"

The ballet, under the title of *The Devil in Love,* was revived on November 20th, 1843, at the Theatre Royal, Drury Lane, with Pauline Leroux in her original part. *The Times* critic declares it to be "well put on the stage. A scene of a chapel, with a high flight of steps by the sea-shore, is a good piece of stage building, and we have a fine glittering view of an Eastern bazaar. The pruning-knife should be used pretty freely as the length of the ballet is

[5] March 12th, 1841.

rather formidable at present, and then a tolerable 'run' may be anticipated."

Of Leroux the same writer says she "does nothing to electrify an audience like Carlotta Grisi; there is no wonderful feat to record, no new gesture is impressed on the memory. Nevertheless, she is still a beautiful dancer, with a great deal of elasticity, and as a pantomimist she is excellent. The impassioned manner in which she contemplated the sleeping Count, her haughty entrance when she came to demand a fulfilment of the terms of the contract, her sudden relenting, her terror at the sight of the priest, when on one occasion she was about to be married to Albert, in the disguise of the peasant girl, and felt the repugnance of an evil spirit to the appearance of holiness, were very artist-like.

"The *pas de fascination,* by which she lured the Vizier, was a nice specimen of pantomime dancing. Now she became playful and animated, now retiring and sentimental; now she crept slowly and noiselessly round the Vizier, fixing her eyes upon him till he seemed absorbed into an atmosphere of fascination. When at last she dropped on her knee, with head flung back, and with raised tambourine, a shower of bouquets was thrown, and an encore loudly demanded.[6]"

LE DIABLE À QUATRE

Pantomimic Ballet in 2 Acts. Book: De Leuven and Mazilier. Music: Adolphe Adam. Scenery: Ciceri, Despléchin, Séchan, and Diéterle. Choreography: Mazilier. First produced: Théâtre de l'Académie Royale de Musique, Paris, August 11th, 1845.

CHARACTERS

The Count Polinski	M. Petipa
The Countess, his wife	Mlle. Maria
Mazourki, a basket-maker . . .	M. Mazilier
Mazourka, his wife	Mlle. Carlotta Grisi
Yvan, house-porter at the Count's castle	M. H. Desplaces
Yelva, the Countess's maid . . .	Mlle. Célestine Emarot
A Blind Old Man	M. Elie
The Dancing-Master	M. Coralli (jun.)
The Butler	M. Quériau

[6] November 21st, 1843.

A Fairy . . . . MLLE. ALINE
    Guests, Lords and Ladies, Game-keepers, Vassals, Soldiers,
             Sprites, and Gnomes.
    The action passes at Poland on Count Polinski's estate.

*Act I. A circular prospect in front of the Count's castle. To the
left the castle entrance; on the same side a summer house, belonging to the castle, with a window facing the public. To the right a
basket-maker's hut, with a casement facing the spectators. In the
distance a fine landscape.*

A huntsman emerges from the castle and blows his horn to summon the game-keepers. He tells them that the Count is to give a
hunting party and that there will be many guests.

Yvan comes out with Yelva whom he introduces to the game-
keepers as his future wife. They congratulate him and he invites
them to the wedding.

The Count greets his retainers and going to Yelva gives her a
purse of gold for her dowry. The couple kneel in gratitude to their
master. Yelva begs the Count to let them give a little ball in the
open air to celebrate the betrothal. He willingly consents and
Yvan goes to invite the villagers, while Yelva enters the castle to
attend on her mistress.

The Count's friends arrive and are warmly greeted by him.
The huntsmen are called with joyous fanfares and soon all are
ready to set out. Suddenly Yelva enters in great alarm. She tells
the Count that the fanfares have awakened the Countess who is
furious and forbids the hunting party.

Enter the Countess in a morning wrap. Pale with anger she
reproaches the Count for always leaving her and thinking of
nothing but the chase. The Count, horrified at this domestic
scene taking place before his guests, tries to soothe her. His friends
try to intervene and she reproaches them bitterly for taking her
husband from her. Pitying the husband, they are about to withdraw, when the Count announces that he will be master. The
party shall take place and he invites them to a festival on the morrow, at which the Countess will do the honours in compensation
for the ill humour she has just displayed. He gives the signal to
depart.

The Countess, stupefied at her husband's firmness, retires in
tears to the summer-house. Yelva shuts the window.

Meanwhile Mazourka appears in the distance. She carries a basket of provisions. Seeing her husband is nowhere in sight she

begins to dance. Mazourki comes out of the hut carrying a bottle of wine. He reproaches his wife for having been gone so long and for dancing. She reproves him for being too fond of wine. He wishes her to plait a basket. She agrees on condition that he will not touch the bottle of wine, while she will put aside all thoughts of dancing. The pact is made and for a time they work hard. But Mazourki, unable to control his thirst, seizes the bottle and takes a drink.

Mazourka immediately stops work and begins to dance.

Yelva comes out of the summer-house and meets Yvan, who tells her that he has issued all the invitations. The *fiancés* invite Mazourki and his wife, who accept with pleasure.

"And where is the fiddler?" inquires Mazourka.

Yvan leads forward a blind old man who has promised to play in exchange for his food and drink.

The Count and his friends return from the hunt which has been a complete success. At his suggestion the village festival begins. The fiddler strikes up and Mazourka dances. The proceedings grow more and more animated.

Suddenly the door of the summer-house flies open and the Countess rushes out and upbraids the company for dancing while she is sad. She goes to the blind fiddler who is still playing and, snatching away his violin, flings it on the ground and breaks it.

The retainers take to flight. Mazourki and his wife run to their hut. The Count's friends retire, much aggrieved. The Count leads the Countess indoors. As Yvan and Yelva follow them into the castle, Mazourka peeps out to see if the Countess has gone.

As soon as she has disappeared Mazourka comes out of her hut and gives the old fiddler some money in compensation for the loss he has suffered. He thanks her and announces that he will read her future.

He takes Mazourka's hand and tracing the lines informs her that she will become a great lady. She will have servants and carriages and own the beautiful castle that stands before her.

"But what about the Countess?" inquires Mazourka.

"She will become the wife of Mazourki."

Mazourka refuses as she does not wish to leave her husband. The fiddler assures her that it will only be for a day to punish the wicked Countess. Mazourka laughs at the future he predicts.

The fiddler declares that if she will follow his instructions all will take place as he has said. She hesitates, then consents.

Immediately the fiddler changes into a magician. Mazourka, terrified, runs to her hut, where, at his command, she falls asleep.

The window of the summer-house opens and the Countess is seen sleeping on her bed.

The magician makes another gesture and a spirit appears to whom he gives his orders. He extends his arms towards the summer-house and then towards the hut. Immediately Mazourka is wearing the fine clothes of the Countess, while the latter is clad in Mazourka's simple dress. Sprites enter the summer-house and transport the Countess to the hut, while they place Mazourka on the couch in the summer-house.

Act II. Scene I. Interior of the basket-maker's hut; in the background a window opening on to the countryside. To the right a rustic bed with green serge curtains. To the left a table laden with half-finished baskets and bottles: a settle and stools.

Day has not yet dawned. Mazourki is asleep with his head resting on the table. The bed curtains are closed.

Mazourki gradually awakes and is surprised to find he is not in bed until he sees the bottles strewn near him. The basket-maker opens the curtains, revealing the Countess asleep, but wearing Mazourka's clothes. Mazourki is about to waken her when he remembers the bottles, which he hides. Then he taps the Countess on the cheek; she stretches out her hand to pull the bed cord, but Mazourki drags her up with a jerk.

The Countess sits up and rubs her eyes with astonishment at her lowly surroundings. Alarmed, she leaps out of bed. Mazourki laughs and seizes her hand, which she indignantly refuses. She demands to know who placed her in this wretched hut, and announces her intention of immediately returning to the castle. Mazourki, thinking his wife bereft of her senses, locks the door as she goes to open it. The Countess falls in despair on the settle. Suddenly there is a knock at the door and Mazourki goes to open it.

Yvan and Yelva have come to invite Mazourki and his wife to their wedding. The basket-maker is profuse in his thanks and calls his wife to congratulate the young couple. The Countess, recognizing her servants, orders them to inform Mazourki of her name and rank. But the lovers only smile. Then the Countess tears off Yelva's wedding-veil. Mazourki, furious at this attack, wishes to force his supposed wife to beg Yelva's pardon on her knees, but the bride asks him to forgive his wife for what was only a moment of temper. The couple leave and Mazourka, having relocked the door, prepares to dress.

The basket-maker reproaches his wife for her rudeness. She pretends to be ill, but, when he approaches her, slaps his cheek This is too much for Mazourki who takes up a stick and pursues the Countess, who upsets everything in her flight. At last, he promises to forgive her if she will kiss the cheek she struck. At first she refuses, but finally kisses Mazourki on each cheek.

The basket-maker, having recovered his good humour, orders his wife to dance. When she refuses he again threatens her with his stick. So she essays a few *pas de menuet*. But he soon tires of this and forces her to dance a rustic measure with him until she sinks exhausted on the settle.

Mazourki announces that he must dress for the wedding and orders his wife to bring him his clothes and dress his hair. The Countess flatters him to get him to look in a mirror, then causes a big basket to fall over his head. Quickly she unlocks the door and dashes out of the hut, with Mazourki in hot pursuit.

Act II. Scene II. The Countess's boudoir in the castle.

Mazourka, dressed in the Countess's clothes, is resting in a splendid bed. The magician stands beside her. He raises his arm and she awakes and looks with delight at her reflection in a mirror. The magician tells her that she must act like a great lady. She thinks it will be difficult but promises to do her best. The magician shows her a jewel case, then vanishes. Yelva and a number of maids enter the boudoir.

Yelva enters nervously, fearful of being scolded. Mazourka bows to her. Yelva is stupefied. Mazourka signs to her to approach and, taking her hand, looks at her with an air of gentle approval.

Yelva calls the maids to assist her in dressing the Countess. Mazourka seems to say: "Am I not fine enough already?" But Yelva intimates that a new dress has been specially prepared for her.

Mazourka makes Yelva sit down and wishes to help her with her own dress.

A butler and several valets enter to receive the Countess's wishes. Breakfast is brought in and placed on a table, but Mazourka invites Yelva to share it with her. A valet announces the arrival of the Count. Mazourka rises in the utmost trepidation.

Yelva runs to the Count and tells him that his wife has changed and become an angel. The Count, delighted, signs to the maids to retire.

Then he goes to Mazourka who makes him many curtseys

The Count compliments her and induces her to sit beside him. When he leans forward to kiss her, she draws back her chair as he advances his. He is inclined to be annoyed, but she holds out her hand and says: "Let us be good friends." He takes her hand astounded at these new ways.

He announces that a ball will be held on the morrow and begs her to receive his friends. She is delighted and begins to dance for joy.

The maids return and show their mistress a number of costumes so that she may choose one for the ball. She selects a nymph's costume.

The dancing-master enters. He has come to teach the Countess a new dance for the ball. Mazourka is greatly embarrassed, but the Count begs her to try. The dancing-master takes her hand but to the Count's surprise she cannot master any of the steps. Annoyed, she begins a rustic dance, but the Count explains that this is unsuitable.

At this moment the magician returns and extends his hand towards Mazourka. Immediately she executes the dance in the most distinguished manner. But she does not stop, she improvises a waltz which carries her out of the room. The Count follows her in delight, while the dancing-master feels that, compared with his pupil, he is only a student.

Act II. Scene III. A splendid gallery forming a green-house fitted with the rarest flowers.

The Count and his wife receive the guests. Music strikes up and the ball begins.

Suddenly a disturbance is heard; the valets are trying to prevent the real Countess from gaining admittance.

The real Countess, mad with rage, and still dressed in simple clothes, is stupefied to see Mazourka, richly dressed and doing the honours of her position. Mazourka looks at the Countess in astonishment. The Count and his friends cannot understand why this peasant woman is present.

There is a fresh disturbance at the door. Mazourki threatens the lackeys with his stick. As soon as he sees his wife he rushes towards her. The Countess begs her husband to protect her. Mazourki explains to the Count that the woman is his wife, and it is she who has beaten him.

The Countess protests that she is not the basket-maker's wife but the mistress of the mansion. Everyone laughs. The Count turns to Mazourki who explains that his wife is light-headed. He taps his stick significantly and asserts that he has a remedy.

Mazourka forbids Mazourki to beat his wife and makes him take a solemn oath to that effect. Then she implores the Countess to be kind and considerate. The Countess is much touched by her compassion for her.

The Count signs to Mazourki to take his wife away, but the Countess falls on her knees and implores the Count's forgiveness. The Count is moved by this scene, when Mazourki, impatient, takes the Countess's arm to lead her away.

Mazourka, who has withdrawn for a few moments, returns with the musician and begs him to use his power in favour of the Countess. The latter, escaping from Mazourki, hastens to the Count and begs, as a last favour, that he will grant her a kiss.

The Count agrees, but Mazourki opposes the favour. Then Mazourka goes to the basket-maker and declares that if the Count kisses his wife, she will permit him to kiss her. Mazourki consents and the couples are re-united.

At this point the magician extends his arm and Mazourka becomes a peasant again, while the Countess is once more dressed as befits her station.

Everyone is stupefied at this metamorphosis, but the magician explains everything to the Count. The Countess kisses Mazourka and promises to look after her. She declares that she will never more be proud and haughty, in proof of which she begs Mazourka to join in the festival, which concludes with a national dance in which all the guests take part.

PAQUITA

Pantomimic Ballet in 2 Acts and 3 Scenes. Book: Paul Foucher and Mazilier. Music: Deldevez. Scenery: Philastre, Cambon, Diéterle, Séchan, and Despléchin. Choreography: Mazilier. First produced: Théâtre de l'Académie Royale de Musique, Paris, April 1st, 1846.

CHARACTERS

Lucien d'Hervilly . . . . . MM.	Petipa
Inigo, chief of a band of gypsies . .	Elie
Don Lopez de Mendoza, the Spanish Governor of the province . . .	Coralli
The Comte d'Hervilly, a French General, and Lucien's father . . .	Monet

A Stone-mason	PETIT
Paquita	MMES. CARLOTTA GRISI
Dona Seraphina	ZÉLIE PIERSON
The Comtesse, the General's mother .	DELAQUIT
A Young Gypsy	DABAS I

Gypsies, Peasants, French Officers, Spanish Officers,
Hussars, Ladies of the Court, Children.

*Act I. Scene I. The valley of the bulls in the neighbourhood of
Saragossa. The valley takes its name from the great rudely-carved
bulls which line the hill-sides. To the right, in the distance, are
immense rocks over which winds a zig-zag of steps cut out of the
stone, while at the side is a camp of gypsies.*

At the rise of the curtain a mason is seen chiselling an inscription
on a marble tablet, watched by Spanish peasants lounging in the
sun. Enter a French General, accompanied by the Spanish Governor and his sister Seraphina. The General's son, Lucien, escorts
his grandmother.

The Comte d'Hervilly, in a mimed episode, explains that the
tablet is erected in memory of his brother who, some years ago,
was killed on this spot by a party of bandits. The Governor intervenes with the news that a village festival is about to take place.
Don Lopez does the honours of his country while the General
takes Seraphina's hand and places it in that of his son. She offers
no opposition, but her father's manner suggests resignation from
political necessity rather than approval.

Gay music heralds the arrival of a company of gypsies who descend the mountain side. Inigo, the chief, noting that Paquita is
absent, is about to go in search of her, when she appears. Inigo,
furious at the delay, vents his rage upon her, and orders the gypsies
to prepare to dance.

But he calls Paquita to him and tells her that, if she wishes, the
master she fears can become her slave. Paquita makes no reply and
begins to dance as if to banish her thoughts. Inigo tries to stop
her, but she looks at him with such contempt that he retires.

Paquita, alone, draws from her bosom a miniature which she
believes to portray her father, and which is related to some terrible
event which still lingers in her memory. This very place seems
familiar to her, but her sad reflections are disturbed by the arrival
of the crowd and she goes into the tent to prepare to dance.

The place is crowded and the General, his mother, Seraphina,
and the Governor take their allotted places. The gypsies come out
of the tent wearing their gala costumes and give their dances.

At the conclusion of the entertainment, Inigo bids Paquita go round with the hat. She does so unwillingly. In the course of her collection she makes a great impression on Lucien, but, despite his generous contribution, Inigo is dissatisfied with the takings. He orders Paquita to dance once more so that she can go round with the hat again. But she shrinks from playing the part of beggar, and refuses. Inigo threatens to strike Paquita, but Lucien protects her.

As he endeavours to soothe Paquita, he is struck by her delicate complexion. He questions her, and cannot believe that she was born among the gypsies. She wishes to show him the miniature, but Inigo, foreseeing the trend of the conversation, has filched it.

Paquita is greatly distressed at her loss and accuses Inigo of having stolen her miniature. Lucien wishes to have him arrested, but his family and the Governor intervene. The young officer calms himself but enjoins Inigo not to force Paquita to dance against her will. But now she wishes to dance to please Lucien, and, inspired by his presence, dances with a captivating vivacity which overwhelms him.

The Governor is very interested in this course of affairs and, at the conclusion of the dance, invites the French family to dine with him before leaving. He asks them to precede him as he must remain until the end of the festival.

Left alone with Inigo he tells him that he may kill Lucien with impunity, for he is opposed to the officer's marrying his daughter. He suggests Paquita as the bait to snare Lucien in the trap. Paquita returns and the Governor goes to join his guests. At the same time Inigo collects his troupe together.

No sooner is Paquita alone than Lucien hurries to her side. He offers her a bulky wallet and proposes that she shall go with him. But, mindful of the distance that separates a gypsy from an officer, she declines. "At least give me that posy as a remembrance," says Lucien, pointing to the flowers she is wearing. But Paquita refuses, and Lucien goes away, disappointed.

The Governor returns in advance of his guests. Inigo, who has watched the lovers from a hiding-place, tells him of their meeting. The Governor announces that the French General is about to leave and asks the villagers to offer him a tribute in the form of a basket of flowers, but he retains Paquita's posy which he gives to a young gypsy girl, with certain instructions.

The General, his grandmother, and Seraphina prepare to depart. Lucien is about to follow them when the gypsy hands him Paquita's posy, which he recognizes with delight. He questions the gypsy who tells him how to find her dwelling, which is not far off. The elated young man tells his parents that he will rejoin them at Saragossa on the morrow, when a big ball is to be given in honour of his forthcoming marriage.

The villagers dance a farewell round about the departing guests, while the gypsies, with Inigo and Paquita at their head, wind their way about the rocks. Lucien follows in the rear.

Act II. Scene I. The interior of a gypsy dwelling. In the background a fire-place; to the left, a cupboard; between the cupboard and the fire-place is a shuttered window. To the right, a door, a rustic clock, chairs, etc.

Paquita enters alone, dreaming of the officer whom she will probably never see again. Her meditations are interrupted by a noise outside. She opens the shutter and, to her astonishment, sees a masked and cloaked man coming towards her abode. Suspecting some mischief, she hides behind the cupboard.

Inigo enters with the cloaked man who, on removing his mask, proves to be the Governor. He bids Inigo be relentless, and the latter shows him the sleeping draught he has prepared. The Governor, satisfied with this preparation, gives Inigo a piece of money. Then he calls through the window to four men, to each of whom he gives a payment on account. Midnight is the hour fixed for the murder. Inigo hides two men in the fire-place, which turns on itself.

Paquita takes the opportunity to creep to the door, but her foot catches in a chair and Inigo turns round. He runs to her, fearful lest she shall reveal the plot, but she tells him that she has only just come in. Inigo posts one of the remaining men by the door, the other climbs out through the window.

There is a knock at the door and Lucien enters, overjoyed to see Paquita again. He asks Inigo to accord him shelter for the night, a request which is granted with humility. Paquita appears surprised by Lucien's visit, but he shows her the posy which he carries under his cloak. He gives his sword to Inigo, who promptly hides it, and hands his cloak to Paquita who drops it over Inigo's head, and warns Lucien by signs of the threatened danger, which he refuses to credit. Inigo invites him to sup, and goes out with Paquita to prepare the meal.

Lucien, left to himself, takes stock of the situation. He finds the window shuttered and the door double-locked. His sword is missing.

The door opens and Paquita enters bearing plates. Inigo follows and the supper is served. The chief of the gypsies is just going out when Paquita signs to Lucien to keep him. He asks Inigo to join him at supper, which invitation is accepted. Inigo pours out a glass of wine for his guest. Paquita signs to Lucien that he may drink and while waiting at table removes the percussion caps from the pistols in Inigo's belt. She cajoles Inigo who asks her to dance. Inigo pours out a second glass of wine for Lucien, although his own is still untouched. Then he seems to recall a special bottle of wine in the cupboard and goes to fetch it.

Paquita warns Lucien that it is drugged. Inigo pours out a glass of the new bottle, which the officer is about to refuse when Paquita drops a pile of plates. Inigo turns round, enraged at the damage done, and Paquita profits by this diversion to change the glasses. Lucien invites the gypsy to drink with him. He does so, then dances with Paquita. While dancing she conveys to Lucien the number of assailants and warns him that the hour of danger approaches. He tries to kiss Paquita as she passes, but she bids him pretend to be sleepy.

Inigo mocks his apparently defenceless rival, but at the same moment becomes drowsy and sinks in his chair. He drags at his clothes the better to breathe and Paquita's miniature falls on the table.

Paquita tells Lucien to rise quickly as the fatal hour is at hand. He seizes Inigo's pistols but she tells him that they are useless. Seeking for a weapon he finds his sword. Midnight strikes and the chimney piece begins to revolve.

Paquita has an idea, and she and Lucien stand against the wall which, turning on its axis, places them outside the hut at the same moment as it deposits the ruffians inside. They are astonished to find Inigo alone and asleep. They succeed in arousing him and he is furious to find his victims have escaped.

Act II. Scene II. A magnificent ballroom in the residence of the French commander at Saragossa. The architecture is Moorish with embellishments in the Empire style. A large portrait of an officer hangs on the wall. Among the numerous guests are aged generals and young officers, representative of all arms, in the splendid uniforms of the period. Apart from the military there are French officials in court dress, ladies in evening dress, and members of the Spanish nobility in national costume.

The Comte d'Hervilly appears with his future daughter-in-law and the Governor The General's mother who accompanies them, is alarmed at Lucien's non-arrival. The Comte reassures her but, as the time passes, he himself grows anxious. Suddenly the dancers part in astonishment and Lucien appears with Paquita. The surprise of the Comte and his mother is equalled only by their joy, when he describes the danger he has escaped. The Governor cannot conceal his annoyance at this blow to his plans.

Lucien declares that he owes his life to Paquita's courage and devotion. The General is astounded. Paquita wishes to withdraw, but Lucien tells her that if she runs away he will follow her. The Comte and his mother promise to take Paquita under their protection, but remind Lucien that he is betrothed to Seraphina.

Suddenly Paquita catches sight of the Governor and, recoiling in horror, announces that he bribed the men to murder Lucien. At this revelation the Governor and his suite are placed under arrest. Paquita wishes to take to flight when she comes face to face with the portrait on the wall. She draws the miniature from her bosom and, comparing the portraits, finds that they are alike. The officer is her father and she, the sole survivor of the massacre in the valley of the bulls, had been retained by Inigo.

The General embraces Paquita and his mother takes her away to dress in accordance with her station. Then he orders the ball to continue. Towards the conclusion Paquita reappears and dances a *pas* which is the prelude to a final *ensemble*.

*

Paquita was an attempt to vary the conventional choreographic backgrounds by setting the story in Spain and, in the last scene, by reviving the glories of the First Empire.

"This ballet," declares Gautier, "the theme of which is a little too melodramatic, was a complete success. The splendour and strangeness of the Empire costumes, the beauty of the scenery, and, above all, the perfection of Carlotta's dancing, brought about its success:" [7]

The critic of *La France Musicale*[8] asserts that "the new ballet succeeded very well and, in default of thrilling interest, M. Paul Foucher's story provides situations favourable . . . to the arrangement of groups and the composition of picturesque dances. Among a number of very pretty *pas* devised by M. Mazilier, we must mention the *pas de trois* danced by Mlles. Robert, Emarot, and Barré; the gypsy festival, inspired by the *ensembles* danced last year by the Danseuses Viennoises, in which Caroline and

[7] *La Presse*, April 6th, 1846.
[8] April 5th, 1846.

Dimier showed much gracefulness; and all the *pas* designed to set off Carlotta Grisi's original and animated talent; and, lastly, the ravishing *pastiche* of a French Ball under the Empire."

Commenting on the music by Deldevez, the same writer observes: "Ideas, knowledge, drama, and a marked sense of theatrical effect—such are the qualities which distinguish the music of the new ballet; add to these an unusual skilfulness, an unfailing tact, and a rare moderation in employing the different orchestral instruments.

"The numbers in the score which have been the best and most justly applauded were, in the first act, Carlotta Grisi's *pas de trois,* and the Spanish dances led by Caroline and Dimier; during the second act, the symphonic work which depicts so clearly the development of the plot hatched against Lucien, and, lastly, the rococo dances in the *divertissement."*

Of Grisi as Paquita, *Le Corsaire-Satan*[9] declares: "It is impossible to display more grace, more airiness, more seductiveness, more adroitness, and more animation. Mlle. Grisi, or rather Paquita the gypsy, is constantly on the stage, and her tiny birdlike feet have not a single moment's rest. Ravishing in all three of her costumes, she mimes with rare intelligence and dances with an astonishing perfection. All her *variations* are followed by many rounds of applause, almost each step, each gesture of the tireless artist, is accompanied by a bravo."

Gautier has a charming description of Grisi's dance in the gypsy festival. "Never did foot so small support a more supple body, and never did castanets chatter more gaily at the tips of more agile fingers. How lightly she bounds and quickly escapes the enticements of the two gypsies who are her partners, poor devils who think to be able to pinch her waist or kiss her hand! She darts away like an adder, smiling maliciously over her shoulder, and the pursuit begins all over again! Her dance at an end, all breathless and palpitating, she stretches out her tambourine to catch the rain of money which falls from all hands."

The reader of the synopsis will recall how Lucien, greatly attracted by Paquita, entreats her to give him a posy she is wearing. It is of interest to note that in the Romantic Ballet, such a quest has a deeper significance than this apparently innocent favour would seem to imply, for it symbolizes that the wearer of the flower should surrender herself to her admirer. The invitation is answered modestly or passionately by the withholding or giving of the posy.

[9] April 3rd, 1846.

Grisi's last *pas* is described by Gautier as "full of intrepidity and innumerable difficulties, such as a kind of *sauts à clochepied sur la pointe,* with a sudden turn round executed with a dazzling vivacity, which inspires a delight mingled with fear; because the movements seem impossible of performance, although she repeats them some eight or ten times. Thunders of applause acclaimed the dancer, who twice had to repeat the *pas* after the fall of the curtain."

*

Paquita was first produced at London on June 3rd, 1846, at the Theatre Royal, Drury Lane, with Grisi in the title-role.

"Considered as a drama," observes *The Times'* [10] critic, "this is a neat piece, without much novelty . . . the ballet is free from heaviness, while the ball scene, with which it concludes, is excellently mounted, and affords a scope for some admirable dancing. Perhaps it would not be wrong to reckon this scene as a substantial part of the ballet, and the rest as a sort of preface.

"Among the *pas d'ensemble* may be mentioned a very clever one called the *Pas des Manteaux,* danced by the peasants. One would think that all groups depending upon the arrangement of scarves, and other spreading articles of attire, had been exhausted, but the thick red mantle now folded round the figure, now extended wide is a new material, and is turned to account."

Of Grisi as Paquita, the same writer declares: "The vivacity and piquancy with which she danced the gypsy chief into a stupor, after he had swallowed the opiate, was inimitable, while the *pas seul* in the ball-room, with which the whole ballet concluded, was an admirable specimen of brilliancy in her art. The broad sweeping bounds, the little sparkling steps, all were given to perfection. The last 'variation' of this *pas seul* was rapturously encored by the whole house; and the fair *danseuse* was tumultuously called for after the fall of the curtain."

BETTY

Pantomimic Ballet in 2 Acts. Book: Mazilier. Music: Ambroise Thomas. Scenery: Ciceri and Rubé, Despléchin, Diéterle and Séchan, Philastre and Cambon. Choreography: Mazilier. First produced: Théâtre de l'Académie Royale de Musique, Paris, July 10th, 1846.

[10] June 4th, 1846.

CHARACTERS

Prince Charles (afterwards Charles II, King of England)	M. L. Petipa
The Duke of Rochester	M. Coralli (jun.)
Coop, an old sailor, proprietor of the Grand Admiral Inn	M. Mazilier
Edward, Charles's page	Mlle. Maria
Princess Catherine of Portugal (wife of Prince Charles)	Mlle. Emarot
Lady Clara, maid of honour . . .	Mlle. Pierson
Betty, Coop's daughter	Mlle. Sofia Fuoco
A Constable	M. Petit

Lords and Ladies, Constables, Sailors, Men and Women.

The action passes in London towards the end of the
reign of Charles I.

*Act I. Scene I. A little room in Prince Charles's palace. To the
right is a door leading to the Prince's apartment, and another door,
further back, leading out of the room. To the left is a door leading
to the Princess's apartments.*

Charles's page, Edward, is sleeping beside a table, on which lie
the clothes of a simple citizen. Ten o'clock strikes. Edward wakes
up, collects the clothes, and hurries out to dress.

Enter Lady Clara and Rochester. He wishes to marry her but
she reproaches him for leading Prince Charles into evil ways.
Rochester protests that he does not approve of the Prince's actions
and accompanies him purely for friendship's sake. Now the
Princess passes through the room, attended by pages and maids of
honour, on her way to church. Lady Clara presents Rochester and
announces that she has converted him to better ways. The Princess
congratulates her.

While Rochester escorts the two ladies, Edward returns in disguise. Rochester surprises him and demands to know the reason
for his attire. The page confesses that he is in love with a tavern-
keeper's daughter and goes to see her disguised as a dancing-
master. Rochester thinks that if he can inveigle the Prince in a
tavern brawl it may teach him a lesson. He summons a valet and
orders him to procure two sailor's costumes. Edward goes out, ill-
pleased at these preparations.

Prince Charles enters fresh from the chase. Ministers approach
with documents which require his signature. Exhausted, he signs

them without a glance at their contents. The Princess returns and expresses the hope that he is not over-working himself. She reminds him that she is giving a ball that evening and hopes that she may have the pleasure of a few moments of his company. The Prince replies that he will take good care not to be absent. The Princess thanks him and, with a meaning glance at Rochester, goes into her apartment.

Charles, moved by the Princess's sweetness, reproaches himself for his neglect of her. Rochester congratulates him on turning his steps towards the path of virtue and remarks that in consequence he will not mention a little plan he had in mind for his diversion. Charles insists on being told of the plan and, delighted at the proposed disguise, goes off with Rochester.

Act I. Scene II. A picturesque locality on the banks of the Thames. To the right is the Grand Admiral Tavern.

Sailors and men and women of all classes are walking past or sitting down at a table set in front of the tavern. Some are drinking, some are playing dice. Presently there is a quarrel. Coop and his daughter, Betty, come out of the tavern. They compose the disturbance and the sailors promise to patronize the tavern on their return.

Alone with her father, Betty seems anxious. Coop tells her that she is thinking about her dancing master, and if she wishes to marry him, he is ready to give his consent. Betty, overjoyed, embraces her father.

Edward enters and Betty reproaches him for not having been there for several days. He apologizes for his non-arrival. The lovers are inclined to quarrel but Coop, smoothing matters over, suggests that Edward should give Betty her dancing-lesson, for a ship is due to arrive at any moment, and there will be a festival in which he wishes Betty to dance her best.

The lesson is given and Edward is proud of his pupil. Some cannon-shots announce the vessel's arrival. The crowd rush to greet their friends, and an entertainment, in which dancing plays a prominent part, is soon in full swing.

Now Charles and Rochester arrive, disguised as sailors, and begin kissing wives and daughters. There is another outcry which Coop composes and afterwards the supposed sailors invite him to drink with them. Edward recognizes the "sailors" and wishes to fly, but Rochester stops him. Rochester presents Betty to Charles. The Prince invites her to dance, but Edward raises objections.

Then Charles bids Rochester entertain Edward while he dances with Betty. Rochester takes the page aside and forces him to contain his anger.

Charles escorts Betty back to her seat and kisses her. Coop is angry but Betty calms him. Charles drinks punch with Coop, but, in taking out his handkerchief to wipe his forehead, drops his purse without being aware of it. Rochester signs to Edward to leave.

The ship's bell summons the sailors to return and Charles and Rochester are left alone, drinking punch. Coop wishes to close and hands Charles the reckoning. While he is looking at it, Rochester steals away. Charles says that his friend will pay, but Edward declares that his friend has gone. Furious, Charles wishes to go in search of him, but Coop reminds him of his bill. The Prince goes to take out his purse but cannot find it. He declares that he has been robbed. Coop, very indignant, observes that such a thing is impossible in his tavern, for all his customers are honest men. Charles, going through his pockets again, finds his watch, which he offers as security. Coop, finding it strange that a simple sailor should possess so splendid a watch, declares that Charles has stolen it.

Edward asks to look at the watch and points out the royal arms on it. "Ha!" cries Coop, "you have stolen this watch from a prince." Charles, alarmed at the turn matters are taking, demands his watch back, but Coop refuses and declares that he himself will restore the watch to the Prince. Charles, beside himself with annoyance, springs at Coop to recover the watch; but the old sailor holds him and, with the help of passing sailors, takes him into the tavern, where he proposes to hold him prisoner until the patrol arrive.

Act II. Scene I. Coop's room inside the tavern.

Charles is brought into the room, the doors are locked, and guards posted. Betty and Edward enter to console the prisoner. Charles promises them all kinds of rewards if only they will help him to escape. He wins over Betty by playing on her sympathy and afterwards secures the assistance of Edward by giving him a precious ring. They tell him that the only way of escape is through the window. The noise of the approaching patrol is heard, and the lovers urge Charles to hurry. They take off his belt and, fixing it to the window, help him to climb down into the street.

Hardly has Charles disappeared when Coop enters with the patrol. Betty pretends to have swooned and Edward declares that Charles threatened them with a dagger and made his escape. Coop reprimands the lovers for their cowardice and runs after Charles. Edward points to the opposite direction from that taken by the Prince, and then himself hurries back to the palace.

Act II. Scene II. A splendid room in the palace, closed to view by rich hangings. To the right is a door leading to the Prince's apartments. Everything is prepared for a brilliant ball.

Edward enters hurriedly, wearing his page's costume. He is followed by Rochester and Lady Clara, who is very amused at the story of his adventure. Rochester and Lady Clara hide behind some columns, while Edward sits in an arm-chair placed in front of the Prince's room and pretends to be asleep.

Charles, still wearing his sailor's dress, enters furtively by means of a secret door. Astonished at the resemblance between Edward and the dancing-master he has just left, Charles tries to pass behind his chair. But Edward awakes and cries: "Who goes there?" Lady Clara runs to the page's aid and pretends to be astonished to see the Prince in such a guise.

Charles mumbles an excuse and tries to slip into his room, but Lady Clara declares that she has come at the Princess's command and would be glad if he would append his signature to a document, which she presents to him. The Prince signs hurriedly to be rid of her, but, just as he is about to enter his room, Rochester bows low. Charles is furious, but the signal for the ball is heard and he hastens to change his dress.

The curtains at the back are drawn aside, showing a splendid gallery decorated with flowers and plants. The Princess enters with her suite. Rochester and Lady Clara tell her of the Prince's adventure.

A little later Charles appears in a rich costume and takes his place beside the Princess. Rochester greets him with a deep obeisance, but Charles frowns angrily. Edward informs Rochester that Coop and Betty desire to restore to the Prince a watch which has come into their possession. Rochester asks the Prince's pleasure. Charles says that he has not lost a watch. But the Princess, feigning to be astonished at this strange conversation, begs the Prince to permit Coop and Betty to enter.

The unexpected visitors make their way through the splendid Court. Edward goes to Coop and tells him that he will present him to the Duke of Rochester. Coop and Betty are astonished at Edward's likeness to the dancing-master, and still more amazed to encounter Rochester. The Duke presents Coop and Betty to

Charles. Amused at their embarrassment the Prince receives them
with a kindness that reassures them. He tells the Princess that he
is to blame and offers to explain everything. But the Princess tells
him that she knows all.

"It was a plot, then," observes Charles.

"Yes," replies the Princess, "and it has succeeded so well that I
ask your pardon for the conspirators."

"Not for Rochester," asserts the Prince.

Lady Clara then shows him the pardon which he has unwittingly
signed.

"Will you not confer happiness on Betty by marrying her to
her dancing-master?" inquires the Princess.

"No," says Charles, "he is unworthy of her. He accepted my
ring to help me to escape."

"And that ring I now return, Your Highness," observes Edward,
presenting him with his purse and ring.

"So it was my page," cries Charles. "Since there is no one to
punish, it is I who must cede for pardon."

The Princess takes Charles's hand in token of reconciliation and
the ball ends with a *divertissement* in which Betty and Edward
play their part.

*

Betty was inspired by the play, *La Jeunesse de Henri V,* by
Alexandre Duval. The critics are generally unanimous in condemning the increasing practice to transpose a play or opera into a
ballet by the simple process of replacing vital dialogue with gesture. Gautier offers some interesting comments on this practice, as
follows: "Ballet is a particular type of entertainment, which demands themes of a quite special nature, in which dancing enters
forcibly, imperiously, and is even used to explain the story. A play
translated into terms of mime and accompanied by a *divertissement*
is not a ballet. This fact is very often forgotten. Craftsmen skilled
in dramatic joinery err in applying their usual methods to choreography. A poet explaining his ideas to an artist who expresses
them in sketches, that is the best combination for the production
of a fine theme for a ballet, a much rarer occurrence than would be
believed, because it is difficult to make a theme perpetually clear
by means of graceful forms." [11]

The critic of *Le Corsaire-Satan* observes: "It must not be forgotten that these hastily arranged pictures are only an excuse to
present the very youthful person who comes to us from Milan.

[11] *La Presse,* July 20th, 1846.

The gracefulness, vigour, precision, and ease displayed by the *débutante* are a sufficient attraction to fill the house and prolong the run of *Betty*." [12]

"The costumes and settings," asserts the critic of *La France Musicale*," [13] produce the most beautiful effect and the music is a real treasure. . . . I found great pleasure in listening to that music, animated, attractive, always distinguished, always in keeping with the theme, orchestrated in a masterly manner with brilliance but without excess, with variety but without affectation, and with taste and knowledge."

Gautier declares: "Mlle. Fuoco, who makes her *début* in this ballet, bears a name of happy augury—*fire!* It might have been invented for her. . . .

"From her first appearance, Mlle. Sofia Fuoco made a distinct impression. She has the merit of originality, so rare in the dance, a limited art if ever there was one; she does not remind one of either Taglioni, Elssler, Carlotta, or Cerito.

"Her *pointes* in particular are astounding; she executes the whole of an *écho* without once lowering her heel to the ground. Her feet are like two steel arrows rebounding from a marble pavement; not a moment of weakness, not a vibration, not a tremor; that inflexible toe never betrays the light body it supports.

"Other dancers have been said to have wings, to have roamed the air amid clouds of muslin; Mlle. Fuoco flies too, but grazing the ground with the tip of her nail, alive, quick, dazzling in her rapidity.

"Dancing, it will be said, does not consist entirely of *pointes* and *taquetés*. True, but, in everything executed by Mlle. Fuoco, we have remarked that neatness, that finish, that precision which are to the dance what style is to poetry, we also believe that she possesses other qualities, in a lesser degree, undoubtedly, but sufficient. Mlle. Fuoco is very young; she is seventeen at most, as is proved by a certain slenderness of her arms and shoulders. Her features, without being exactly pretty, have a certain attraction and vivacity; she is happy when dancing and her lips part in a natural smile. A few months hence, Mlle. Fuoco will know how to dress her hair better, to put on her clothes more tastefully; she will have acquired French coquetry, and her worth will be doubled. Each night, the public applauds and recalls her, and justly; because hers is one of the most brilliant *débuts* in dancing that we have had to notice for a long time."

[12] July 14th, 1846.
[13] July 19th, 1846.

VERT–VERT

Pantomimic Ballet in 3 Acts. Book: De Leuven and Mazilier.
Music: Deldevez and Tolbecque. Scenery: Cambon and Thierry.
Choreography: Mazilier. First produced: Théâtre de l'Académie
Nationale de Musique, Paris, November 24th, 1851.

CHARACTERS

Vert-Vert	MLLE. PLUNKET
Colombus, his tutor	M. BERTHIER
The Marquis de Luzy	MLLE. MARQUET
The Comte de Montbazon . . .	MLLE. MATHILDE
The Baron de Guebriant . . .	MLLE. SAVEL
The Court Maître de Ballet . . .	M. FUCHS
A Servant	M. LEVASSEUR
Blanche, the Queen's maid of honour .	MLLE. PRIORA
Mme. de Navailles, Governess of the maids of honour	MLLE. LAURENT
Euphémie	MLLE. PIERRON
Batilde	MLLE. NATHAN
Berthe	MLLE. LACOSTE
A Stage-Manager	M. MATHIEU
A Commissioner	M. CORNET
The Innkeeper	M. GONDOIN
Sylvia	MLLE. EMAROT
Rosamonde	MLLE. BOUVIER
Harlequin	M. MATHIEU
Pierrot	M. ADICE
Pierrette	MLLE. EMAROT
Columbine	MLLE. CAROLINE

Maids of Honour, Servants, Dragoons, Dancers, Players,
Travellers, Spectators, Harlequin's Children, Pierrot's
Children.

Act I. The private gardens of the Queen's maids of honour at
Fontainebleau. To the left is a table on which stands a gold cage,
half-covered with a cloth. The time is just before dawn.

Three maids of honour enter and listen anxiously. A hunting-
horn sounds and three pages come to talk to the ladies. But footsteps are heard and the frightened courtiers hide behind some
flower boxes. Mme. de Navailles appears, preceded by a gardener

carrying a lantern. She makes her round of inspection and when she has gone the pages emerge from their hiding-places. But she returns and there are anxious moments until the pages find further concealment.

Dawn breaks and the pages court the ladies. But the latter induce them to leave in exchange for a kiss. The maids of honour go out and Blanche enters.

She dances for joy carrying a little basket which she places on the table. She lifts the cloth from the cage and, taking a biscuit from her basket, offers it to the bird, which remains motionless. Blanche, alarmed, takes the bird in her hand and is horrified to find it dead. She lays it on a cushion and rings a bell.

The maids of honour run in and Blanche shows them the dead bird. They are very grieved at the loss of their companion which is laid to rest beneath the flowers.

At this moment Colombus and Candide enter reading. They sit down and appear to be absorbed in their books. Blanche tries to attract the attention of the latter who is unmoved until she offers him a biscuit from her basket. He cannot resist such temptation. Then the other ladies offer him sweets until he is obliged to plead for mercy. Blanche tells the maids that Candide shall be their new Vert-Vert, such was the parrot's name. She then teaches him the menuet. Meanwhile Colombus has not ceased to read.

Enter the pages, one of whom brings a message for Mme. de Navailles. Seeing Vert-Vert they mock him until Blanche takes his part. The governess enters accompanied by the Court *maître de ballet* and receives the message. She reads it and announces that the maids are to dance in the King's quadrille. The *maître de ballet* tells them that they must rehearse the dance in costume. The excited maids hasten to change their dresses.

While the governess confers with the *maître de ballet,* the pages conceal their love letters in the flower boxes. But Vert-Vert betrays them to Mme. de Navailles who finds the letters and forbids the pages to visit the maids. She gives Colombus a bunch of keys and orders him to exercise the strictest surveillance. He calls to Vert-Vert and the two make a solemn exit, reading, as on their entrance.

The maids return and the *maître de ballet* begins the rehearsal. At first all is confusion, but, at last, the dances improve and conclude with a brilliant measure.

Colombus returns with Vert-Vert and is stupefied to see the maids in their short skirts. He is minded to bandage his pupil's eyes, but the maids pet their new Vert-Vert.

A servant approaches the governess and tells her that Vert-Vert

is required by his mother. He is loath to leave Blanche until Mme.
de Navailles exercises her authority. She bids Colombus watch
over his precious charge during which injunction the maids fill
their pet's pockets with dainties, and kiss his forehead in turn.
Vert-Vert is surprised not to see Blanche whom he wishes to kiss
most of all, but his tutor drags him away. All gradually go out.

Blanche enters alone, dressed for a journey. She cannot bear the
thought of Vert-Vert's absence and has decided to follow him.

*Act II. The hall of an inn. On each side is a staircase leading to
a gallery with numbered doors. To the left, in the background, is a
great entrance door, through which can be seen a river.*

The hall is filled with musketeers and dragoons, some seated at
tables, some standing, some playing cards and drinking. A coach
is seen arriving and a number of travellers step down.

Enter the three pages, then two dancers, Sylvia and Rosamonde,
other members of the company and their stage-manager. The
latter distributes bills announcing a new ballet to be performed that
evening in the hall. Then he puts up an immense bill, headed:

HARLEQUIN AND PIERROT
OR THE TRICKSTERS
PANTOMIME-BALLET

Everyone applauds and hastens to purchase seats. The manager
goes out followed by Rosamonde and his company.

Enter Colombus with Vert-Vert. The seven pages recognize and
mock him. Sylvia, although joining in the laughter, makes a fuss
of Vert-Vert, while his tutor does his best to protect him from the
dancer.

She begs Vert-Vert to dance and after some hesitation he dances
very badly a few *pas de menuet* that he had learnt from the maids
of honour. His clumsiness arouses more laughter, but Sylvia announces that she will educate Vert-Vert. She wishes to take him
away, greatly to the consternation of the tutor, who asserts his
authority. Sylvia goes out laughing, followed by the pages, who
poke fun at Vert-Vert.

Vert-Vert, vexed at the treatment to which he has been subjected,
sighs for Blanche. While waiting for the coach to change horses,
Colombus gives his pupil a book to study, but he rejects it.

Enter Blanche, in fear of pursuit. She recognizes Vert-Vert and
the lovers fall into each other's arms. Colombus, scandalized,

orders Blanche to return to Mme. de Navailles, but the lovers pay no heed to the tutor's threats.

The pages come in and recognizing Blanche begin to ogle her. The manager returns, followed by his troupe, delighted at having sold all his tickets. The hall is cleared and seats set out for the performance.

Sylvia comes in with Rosamonde who limps in pain. The manager is in despair that she cannot dance. Vert-Vert tells the manager that Blanche dances beautifully, whereupon he entreats her assistance, to which she consents.

The pages ask that Vert-Vert shall take part in the piece, disguised as a woman. They help him to dress, despite his tutor's protestations.

The spectators arrive and take their seats, the traditional three knocks are given, and the performance begins.

HARLEQUIN AND PIERROT

Harlequin enters and indicates that he is awaiting his sweetheart. Pierrette appears and Harlequin makes love to her.

Pierrot glides in and surprises his wife with the amorous Harlequin. Furious, he threatens the lovers.

Columbine runs in and Pierrot tells of his discovery. But she makes light of the incident and proposes that they change husbands. Harlequin takes Pierrette in his arms and Pierrot embraces Columbine. But it is not enough to change wives, they must exchange their children too.

Pierrette's children enter from one side, and those of Harlequin from the other. Each parent counts his offspring and it is found that Pierrot has one more than Harlequin. The former does not wish to take the baby Harlequin and suggests that each party takes half. But in the end Pierrot accepts him whole, as a make-weight.

The company dance, in the course of which the husbands find themselves dancing with their true wives, whom they come to the conclusion they prefer, and so both parties return to their original state. The piece ends with a *divertissement* in which Blanche and Vert-Vert take part.

Now servants bring in a table which is set in the centre of the hall. One of the pages is going to give a supper in honour of the dancers.

Vert-Vert, Sylvia, Blanche, and Colombus enter. Blanche is congratulated on her success and given the place of honour. Sylvia asks Vert-Vert to sit beside her. Bottles of champagne are opened and Vert-Vert is offered a glass. But Colombus takes it from him and drinks it himself. Another glass is handed to Vert-Vert and the same thing happens. At last, however, Vert-Vert is successful in drinking the wine.

One of the pages discovers some foils and teaches Vert-Vert how to fence; another, sitting beside Sylvia, shows him how to make love; a third teaches him how to smoke. The pupil grows lively and kisses Sylvia. The pages, delighted, take Vert-Vert with them, while Colombus, fast asleep, gradually slips under the table.

Act III. Scene I. A little salon leading to the dormitory of the maids of honour, which is concealed by a large curtain. To the right is a window; to the left is an entrance door and a smaller door. On the table are lighted candles. The room is filled with rich dresses.

Three maids of honour, under the watchful eye of their governess, are examining with delight the ball-dresses they are to wear that evening. A commissioner brings in Blanche who looks down. The maids greet her warmly, but the governess forbids them to talk to Blanche. They beg Mme. de Navailles to forgive her, but she refuses. Then they rebel, but a burst of music announces the commencement of the festival and they become calm at the thought of how they are going to enjoy themselves.

The governess, however, informs them that they shall not go to the ball as they have been so ill-mannered. She sends the costumes away and orders the maids to go to bed. She leads Blanche to the little room and locks the door on her, then, having seen the maids enter the dormitory, she leaves with her attendants. The door to the salon is heard to be double-locked.

As soon as the governess has gone the window opens and in climbs Vert-Vert, followed by the three pages. He draws back the curtain and shows them the dormitory. The young men are delighted. But a noise is heard and they quickly hide.

Mme. de Navailles enters and, having assured herself that her charges are asleep, retires, having locked the door as before.

Vert-Vert and the pages come from their hiding-places. Acting on his instructions each page goes to a bed and knocks three times. Heads look through the curtains and, seeing the young men, are quickly withdrawn. The pages draw the curtains but the girls have disappeared. Then they espy them at the further end of the dormitory, banded together for self-protection.

Vert-Vert tries to find Blanche, but, not seeing her, goes to the little door on the left, and, using a key borrowed from his tutor, opens it.

Meanwhile the pages go to the window and hoist up Colombus, who arrives, pale and unsteady, with a basket of bottles of wine in one hand, and a basket of cakes in the other.

Vert-Vert enters with Blanche, who runs to the aid of her companions. The girls prepare for defence, while Vert-Vert masses his troops for the attack. Each page takes a box of sweets or cakes from Colombus's basket and soon wins over the enemy, and presently all join in a gay dance.

At the height of the merriment the governess returns and is scandalized at the scene. She asks the pages who let them in, but Vert-Vert takes the responsibility. The governess reprimands him, but he laughs and kisses Blanche, and then tries to kiss the governess, who recoils in horror. Then, to her intense indignation, she perceives Colombus, who can scarcely stand.

Vert-Vert, with a finger to his lips, warns her of the inadvisability of creating a scandal. Colombus echoes his advice. But the governess repulses him with indignation.

Mme. de Navailles resigns herself to the inevitable and a fresh burst of music is heard. The maids of honour entreat the governess to pardon them and let them go to the ball. She consents and all hasten to prepare for the festival.

Act III. Scene II. A hall in the palace of Fontainebleau.

The ball is in full swing. There is a shepherd's quadrille in which Vert-Vert as a shepherd and Blanche as a shepherdess dance a *pas de deux*. Then follows a Hungarian waltz, in which everyone joins and which brings the ball to a joyful conclusion.

*

Vert-Vert is based on the vaudeville by De Leuven and Desforges, performed at the Théâtre de la Palais Royal in 1841, which is founded on Gresset's well-known poem of the same name.

"The music," says the critic of *La France Musicale*,[14] "is the work of two composers, one very distinguished who has already proved his abilities, the other is the brother of a composer of quadrilles, which are the delight of persons of taste. Whatever one may say, it is not very easy to write ballet music. M. Deldevez has covered with rubies and pearls that part of the theme which has been entrusted to him. M. Tolbecque has adorned his portion with gold spangles. Waltzes, quadrilles, polkas, jostle together and follow one another in quick succession. . . . The waltz in the first

[14] November 30th, 1851.

act, the harlequinade in the second, and the *pas hongrois* in the third, are certainly by M. Deldevez, whom I congratulate sincerely."

But the production of the ballet is principally associated with the *début* of Mlle. Priora. The same writer declares: "I hasten to say that not since Taglioni have I seen a dancer so accomplished as the young and beautiful native of Bologna. Although not yet eighteen, she has already attained the pinnacle of her art.

"Hers is an unusual talent which does not permit of analysis. She was trained by her father, an excellent choreographer, but she owes very much more to nature than to training. Imagine a head like an antique cameo set amid a mass of hair, black as ebony; thick eyebrows even darker; large eyes at once animated and velvety, admirably formed arms, a perfect figure, and you will still have a very incomplete idea of that ravishing creature.

"At fifteen she had already danced at the principal theatres of Italy, at Florence and at Rome, where she was nicknamed 'La Taglioni-Elssler.' Mlle. Priora has justified the brilliant reputation that had preceded her at Paris, her success in the part of Blanche has been brilliant, immense, and entirely deserved. She is the star of Venus amid the constellations in the Opera firmament.

"Mlle. Plunkett, who portrays Vert-Vert, has been inspired by the traditions bequeathed by the inimitable Dejazet in that part at the Palais Royal. She is a charming demon of roguishness, of animation, and elfish grace. This pleasing creation places Mlle. Plunkett among the best mimes the Opera has possessed. She shared Mlle. Priora's success."

*

Vert-Vert was first produced at London on February 6th, 1852, at the Theatre Royal, Drury Lane, with Adeline Plunkett in her original part of Vert-Vert, and Carlotta de Vecchi as Blanche.

The *Illustrated London News* observes: "The incidents *of Vert-Vert* are not very animated or ingenious, but the figures of some of the *pas* and groupings are exceedingly novel and clever. Mdlle. Plunkett's *pas de deux* with Durant and the *pas Espanol,* drew down thunders of applause, and Mdlle. de la Vecchi quite sustains the glory of the Italian school. Since the first night of *Vert-Vert* . . . it has been much curtailed in its four *tableaux*. Besides the *pas* we have specified, the *Pas des Trois Graces* danced by Mesdlles. Adèle, A. Payne, and D'Antoine; a *Pas Chinois,* executed by Messrs. Marshall and some coryphées, and a *galop général,* are greatly applauded."

The Times' [15] critic, contrary to his French colleague, describes the music of the ballet as "neither remarkable for originality nor for spirit.

"Among the *pas d'ensemble,* the most attractive and the most applauded was the *Pas des Trois Graces,* a well-constructed dance, executed with great skill by Mlles. Adèle, A. Payne, and D'Antoine. The 'Galop General' at the conclusion was also a lively affair."

The same writer declares of the two principals: "Mlle. Plunkett, who, not less sprightly, vivacious, piquant, and fascinating as Vert-Vert than in Paris, although with so much less favourable an *entourage,* supported the chief weight of the ballet with admirable talent and unabated zeal. Mlle. Carlotta de Vecchi, who assumed the part of Blanche, although 'from the San Carlo at Naples,' must be regarded as a *débutante*—one of distinguished promise, nevertheless, with youth and physical qualifications remarkably in her favour. Her deportment is graceful, and there is a peculiar modesty in her appearance that tells greatly in her behalf. In the mechanical part of her art Mlle. de Vecchi already displays a singular facility, and, though she has yet much to learn, it is more than probable that she will acquire it with ease and promptitude. Her *pas seul* in the first act was much applauded, and her *pas de caractère* with Mlle. Plunkett in the last was equally well received. The great hit of the ballet as a Terpsichorean display, was a *grand pas de deux* between Mlle. Plunkett (attired in her female costume) and M. Durand. This was vociferously applauded. Mlle. Plunkett exhibited an extraordinary degree of agility, quite divested of effort or affectation; while M. Durand—according to the bills 'the most eminent dancer in Europe'—turned round once, twice, and thrice, with a rapidity that thoroughly astonished the occupants of the higher gallery."

JOVITA OU LES BOUCANIERS

Pantomimic Ballet in 3 Scenes. Book: Mazilier. Music: Théodore Labarre. Scenery: Despléchin, Thierry, and Cambon. Choreography: Mazilier. First produced: Théâtre Impérial de l'Opéra, Paris, November 11th, 1853.

[15] February 7th, 1852.

CHARACTERS

Don Jose Cavallines	. . . .	MM.	Lenfant
Don Altamirano, a naval officer	. .		Merante
Don Alvar	. . . . . .		Bauchet
Zubillaga, chief of the buccaneers	. .		Petipa
Cardoval, a buccaneer	. . . .		Berthier
Gil, a buccaneer	. . . . .		Petit
Diego	. . . . . .		Mazilier
Jovita Cavallines	. . . . .	Mmes.	Carolina
			Rosati
Amalia	. . . .		Besson
Ines	. . . .		Emarot
Catalina	. . . . . .		Caroline

Creoles, Buccaneers, Slaves, Nobles, Pages, Negroes,
Mexicans.

*Scene I. A plantation in Mexico at the beginning of the 17th
century. To the right is the master's house, to the left a number of
slave huts. Daybreak.*

The slaves are busy decking their huts with flowers, others are
erecting a banner, inscribed—To Jovita. Don Jose enters and urges
the workers to hurry.

Jovita comes in and embraces her father. Then each slave offers
her a bouquet. She bids them drink her health and dance.

There is a roll of drums and a party of soldiers under the command of Altamirano post a notice offering a large reward for the
capture of Zubillaga, a buccaneer chief.

The officer greets Jovita tenderly, but she receives him coldly,
since he has forgotten it is her birthday. She welcomes her friends
Amalia, Ines, and Catalina, and their brother Don Alvar. To complete Altamirano's discomfiture she will dance only with Alvar.

Enter an old bearded man walking with the aid of a stick. He
begs for hospitality which is granted, and sits facing the notice,
which he reads with interest.

Altamirano, enraged at Jovita's conduct, courts Amalia to such
purpose that Jovita is forced to relent and the lovers become reconciled. Don Jose watches this scene and when Jovita and her friends
go into a room where a repast is to be served, he draws the officer
aside and informs him that he could not accept a mere lieutenant
for a son-in-law.

He replies that he hopes soon to be captain, for he is going to
capture Zubillaga and his band. At these words the old man rises

and warns him that he has chosen a dangerous task, but, if he wishes, he will lead him to the buccaneer's retreat. His offer is accepted and he promises to return at sunset.

Jovita returns and tells her father that the guests are awaiting him. The officer tells her father that Don Jose has consented to their marriage when he is made captain, which he hopes to become that evening.

But Jovita is apprehensive when she learns that he is going to attack Zubillaga. She changes her tone and invites Altamirano to join in the festivities.

Musicians arrive and the slaves execute their local dances; then the masters follow with European dances. So the time passes pleasantly until sunset.

The beggar returns armed with a long sword. The officer summons his men and they begin their march. Altamirano, seeing that the old man appears tired, offers him a horse. But he replies that they have only a short way to go.

When the officers asks for an explanation, the beggar tears off his wig and, unsheathing his sword, defies him, saying, "I am Zubillaga!" The soldiers level their muskets at the bandit, but the officer tells them not to fire as he wishes to take him alive. Zubillaga raises his hand and a horde of buccaneers rush in and disarm the officer and his men.

The slaves endeavour to take to flight but, finding their retreat cut off, beg for mercy. Slaves and masters are driven together into one group. Zubillaga orders Don Jose to be bound to a tree and replaces the notice with a new one which reads: Zubillaga will not surrender Lieutenant Altamirano except on payment of four hundred ounces of gold. The bandits depart with their spoils and Don Jose tries to exchange a parting glance with his daughter, but cannot see her.

When the buccaneers have gone she creeps from beneath a pile of matting and frees her father. She is distressed at the capture of her lover, but her father, reading the notice, offers to ransom him. Jovita reminds him that the buccaneers have plundered everything.

Rising, she walks quietly to and fro and finds a dagger on the ground. She picks it up and swears to rescue her lover. Her father tries to dissuade her but she runs out of the plantation.

Scene II. A grotto in the Cordilleras. It has only one entrance, and it is here that Zubillaga conceals his captives and his plunder.

The buccaneer has sold the slaves and retained only Altamirano, the three sisters, and some Europeans. They divide the booty and drink the bumpers poured out for them by their pretty captives. Altamirano is enraged at his powerlessness.

Scouts warn Zubillaga of the approach of a stranger. He goes to reconnoitre and returns with the information that the stranger is a woman.

Jovita enters, dressed as a gypsy, and bearing a tambourine. The buccaneers welcome her with acclamation and the three sisters run towards her. But she receives them coldly and with astonishment. Altamarino greets her too, but she replies that she does not know him.

Zubillaga looks keenly at Jovita and asks the reason for her visit. She replies that she wished to entertain such brave men. "And afterwards?" inquires the chief. "I shall leave," she answers. Zubillaga informs her that she must remain, since she would be able to reveal their hiding place. Then she offers to accompany the bandits and share their trials.

The chief, still suspicious, orders a number of his men to search the rocks for possible enemies. Then, observing Altamirano looking closely at the visitor, he pretends to leave, but hides behind a rock where he can observe the couple.

As soon as Zubillaga has departed, Altamirano and the other prisoners say to the visitor, "Are you not Jovita Cavallines?" She, divining the chief's ruse, replies in the negative.

The buccaneer, reassured by this statement, returns, and, announcing that he had been listening, declares his confidence in her. He invites her to be his wife and attempts to embrace her, but she slips from his grasp, allowing him to hold her arm.

Altamirano, watching the gypsy, sees that she wears his ring. He draws her aside and swears that he will kill her rather than that she should be submitted to such insults. He seizes a stool and tries to strike Zubillaga, but his men fell the officer.

The chief orders the officer to be shot, but Jovita observes that it would be a pity to waste such a ransom. Zubillaga agrees and the officer is bound and placed in a cavern.

The bandits return and announce that there is no ambush. Then they ask the gypsy to give her promised dance. She dances a *pas* which excites the onlookers to such frenzy that Zubillaga reminds his men that he has asked her to be his wife. But they resent his action and demand that the gypsy be drawn for. Zubillaga agrees and promises that he will write each man's name on a slip of paper, and the gypsy shall belong to the first name drawn.

Jovita protests to the chief that she does not wish to belong to any of the men. Zubillaga replies that his men cannot read and so he has written his own name on each slip.

Jovita, while talking to the chief, cuts the end of his power-flask and tips the contents beside a barrel of powder. Then she goes to the officer, cuts his cords, and, telling the prisoners to stand by him, seizes a lamp and hurls it at the powder. There is a tremendous explosion and the face of the rock collapses, carrying the buccaneers with it. The captives, saved by a miracle, offer a prayer of thanksgiving.

Scene III. A ball given by the Viceroy at his palace in Mexico, in honour of the exploit of Jovita Cavallines.

To the ringing of bells and the boom of cannon Jovita makes her entrance in a car drawn by white horses. She is received by the Viceroy and his officers, from whom she receives the reward she claims—a captain's commission for Altamirano.

LE CORSAIRE

Pantomimic Ballet in 3 Acts and 5 Scenes. Book: H. V. de Saint-Georges and Mazilier. Music: Adolphe Adam. Scenery: Despléchin, Cambon, Thierry, and Martin. Choreography: Mazilier. Machinery: Sacré. First performed: Théâtre Impérial de l'Opéra, Paris, January 23rd, 1856.

CHARACTERS

Conrad, a Pirate . . . . . MM.	SEGARELLI
Seyd, Pasha of the Isle of Cos . . .	DAUTY
Isaac Lanquedem, owner of a bazaar at	
Adrianople	BERTHIER
Birbanto, Conrad's lieutenant . . .	FUCHS
Chief Eunuch of Seyd Pasha's harem .	PETIT
Second Eunuch	CORNET
Medora, a young Greek girl . . . MMES.	CAROLINA ROSATI
Zulmea, the Pasha's favourite sultana .	L. MARQUET
Gulnare, the Pasha's slave . . .	COUQUI
A Moldavian slave	CAROLINE
An Italian slave	NATHAN
A French slave	QUÉNIAUX
An English slave	LEGRAIN

A Spanish slave . . . . . .   L. MARQUET
A Negress . . . .   ALINE
Eunuchs, Pirates, Slaves, Imans, Dealers, Buyers, Guards,
Sailors, Almées, Odalisques etc.

*Act I. Scene I. A square in Adrianople. In the centre of the
square is a slave-market.*

The slave-market is thronged with dealers and buyers. A band
of pirates led by Conrad, their chief, mingles with the crowd. A
young girl, Medora, appears on the balcony of one of the houses
and throws a flower to Conrad, as a token of her love. A little
later Medora and her guardian, Isaac Lanquedem, a slave-dealer,
appear in the bazaar. Conrad and Medora exchange a significant
glance.

A rich litter heralds the arrival of Seyd Pasha, a wealthy old
roué, desirous of adding to his harem. The dealers bring out their
choicest wares for his inspection, but none pleases him. Then he
espies Medora and wishes to purchase her. The Jew at first refuses
to sell his ward, but, dazzled by the price offered, he finally
consents.

The Pasha ogles the girl who, frightened, runs to Conrad for
protection. He signals to his men who surround the Jew and dance
with the *almées* while Conrad departs with Medora, despite the
protests of Isaac and the rage of the Pasha. Another sign and the
pirates seize the women and Isaac and carry them off, to the consternation of the Pasha and his eunuchs.

Act I. Scene II. A vast underground palace filled with treasures.

Conrad enters with Medora, who examines her surroundings
with mingled curiosity and fear. He offers to give her all his
treasures and renounce his mode of living in exchange for her love.
They go out together.

Birbanto and the pirates bring in Isaac and place themselves
about the grotto. A curtain rises to disclose Conrad seated on a
tiger's skin, smoking his chibouk, while he gazes tenderly at
Medora seated at his feet. The women captured in the market are
brought in for his inspection, but he has eyes for Medora only. The
women beg for mercy but he pushes them away and orders them
to join Medora in a dance.

At the conclusion she entreats Conrad to free the women, to
which he consents. But Birbanto and the other officers protest that
they are entitled to share them. Feeling runs so high that the

pirates become mutinous. But Conrad seizes Birbanto and forces
him to his knees. The women are set free. Conrad and Medora go
out followed by the submissive officers.

Birbanto and some pirates remain with Isaac. They tell him that
he must buy back Medora. When he protests that he has no
money, the pirates shake his clothing, from which fall jewels and
coins. Birbanto tells him that Medora will soon be free. When the
Jew is incredulous, the pirate plucks a lotus from a shrub and,
drawing a phial from his breast, pours the contents on the flower.
He approaches the sentinel before Conrad's room and gives him
the flower to smell. Immediately he falls asleep.

Pirates bring in a table laid with a splendid repast. Conrad reappears with Medora, whom he invites to sup with him. But she
prefers to wait on him. While she alternately waits upon him and
dances for his delight, a young girl enters bearing a gold plate with
the drugged lotus. Guided by Isaac she hands the flower to Medora, who in turn offers it to Conrad. The pirate presses it to his
lips and falls asleep.

Now pirates glide into the room and threaten Medora with their
daggers. But she draws a dagger from Conrad's girdle and, when
Birbanto tries to disarm her, stabs him in the arm. A noise is heard,
and, while the pirates investigate, Medora scribbles a note to Conrad, which she places in his hand. Hardly has she done so when
the pirates return, throw a veil over her head, and bear her away,
followed by the gleeful Isaac.

*Act II. Scene I. The Pasha's Palace in the Island of Cos. The
bathing-place of the Pasha's women surrounded by magnificent
gardens. The bathing-place is screened by immense draperies.*

As the curtain rises the women come out of the bathing-pool and
make their toilet.

Zulmea, the favourite sultana, disdainfully accepts the attentions
of the *odalisques,* who grumblingly wait upon her and dance for
her delight.

Enter Gulnare who incites her companions to disobey the commands of her rival, Zulmea.

In the midst of this disturbance there arrives Seyd Pasha, furious
at his discomfiture in the bazaar. He is immediately the subject of
complaints from all sides. He orders the women to obey Zulmea,
but Gulnare laughs at the Pasha and dancing in front of him so
charms the old tyrant that he throws his handkerchief to her.
Gulnare picks up the handkerchief with mock humility and hands

it to one of her companions, who throws it to another, until it finally reaches an aged negress. The Pasha is furious with Gulnare but she takes to her heels, followed by her friends. The Pasha reprimands the eunuch for his inability to keep order, and commands that he shall receive the *bastonnado*.

Now Isaac arrives, dragging with him a veiled woman, who proves to be Medora. The Pasha is overjoyed, but Zulmea bitterly resents this new rival. Medora demands justice, but the Pasha merely orders that the Jew be paid the price agreed. Then Medora seizes the Pasha's dagger and strikes at Isaac who takes to his heels.

A messenger announces the arrival of a party of pilgrims bound for Mecca. The chief is an old and pious man who begs the Pasha's hospitality, which is granted. But the Pasha delights in tempting the old man by showing him his women and making them dance for him.

Night falls and the Pasha orders a eunuch to take Medora to his room. At the same moment the old man flings off his cloak and is revealed as Conrad the pirate. He blows his horn and the supposed pilgrims change into armed pirates. The Pasha, his guards, and his women take to flight; Conrad clasps Medora in his arms.

Gulnare, pursued by Birbanto, runs to Conrad for protection. Medora, remembering the scene in the cave, accuses Birbanto of having delivered her to Isaac, which is proved by the wound on the pirate's arm. Conrad forces Birbanto to his knees and is about to blow out his brains with a pistol when Medora stays his arm. The pirate seizes the opportunity to make his escape.

Medora, overcome with emotion, is about to faint, but Gulnare and Conrad revive her. At this moment, the Pasha, encouraged by Birbanto, arrives with reinforcements and surrounds the little group. Conrad is disarmed and told to prepare for death, despite the entreaties of Gulnare and her companions.

Act III. Scene I. The Pasha's rooms situated in an elegant kiosk, overlooking the sea. There is a large door at the rear.

Seyd Pasha is surrounded by his Court. He orders Medora to be brought in.

He says to her: "Accept my throne, my hand, and the life of the one you love." She refuses.

A funeral march is heard and in the background passes Conrad in chains being taken to his execution. At this terrible spectacle Medora begs the Pasha to suspend the execution. He agrees but bids her acquaint Conrad of the terms on which his life is to be spared. At a signal from the Pasha, the prisoner is brought in and the lovers embrace. The Pasha and his suite withdraw.

Medora explains the Pasha's conditions to Conrad, which he indignantly rejects. The lovers resolve to die together.

Gulnare glides into the kiosk and whispers to the lovers to accept the terms offered and she will contrive a means to evade them.

The Pasha returns and demands an answer. Conrad declares that his love cannot compare with the throne offered, and Medora makes a sign of submission. The Pasha, delighted, transmits his joy to the assembly. Meanwhile Conrad, Gulnare, and Medora make their plans, by which Conrad is to return at midnight. The Pasha orders Conrad to be set free, who departs with a meaning glance at Medora.

The Pasha commands a festival and Gulnare retires to prepare Medora for her marriage. Overjoyed, he orders coffers of jewels and gold trinkets to be brought, which he distributes to the eager women.

A wedding march is heard and ministers, eunuchs, and slaves enter and group themselves about the Pasha. The procession is preceded by *almées* throwing flowers, and incense-bearers wafting clouds of perfume. The bride is covered with a long veil of muslin, which, in passing, she raises slightly to reveal the features of Gulnare. The ceremony concluded, the Pasha places a ring on his bride's finger, and conducts her to his apartments.

Preparations are made for the wedding night. The Pasha orders flowers and incense to be brought, and presently the bride is ushered in by her women. Seyd dismisses them, and raises his wife's veil to disclose not Gulnare, but Medora. She dances to the Pasha to make the time pass more quickly. She pretends to be frightened of the dagger and pistols which he carries in his belt, and he surrenders them to her. Then he tries to clasp her in his arms, but she escapes from his grasp. He falls on his knees and begs her to listen to him. As he extends his arms she laughingly pretends to make him her prisoner by binding them with her scarf.

On the stroke of midnight the window glides upwards and Conrad enters. Seyd, frightened at this sudden apparition, sees Medora hand the pirate his dagger. The Pasha runs to summon help but Medora threatens to shoot him with his pistols. Then, slowly backing towards the window, the lovers escape. Seyd, having freed his hands, strikes a gong.

Guards and women run in from all sides. The Pasha points to the window. At the same moment three distant cannon shots are heard. The fugitives have reached Conrad's ship. Seyd bewails the loss of his bride, but Gulnare contradicts him and, showing her ring, declares that she is his wife. Immediately the women kneel before her.

Act III. Scene II. The scene shows an immense ship floating on a calm sea. The horizon is cloudless.

Conrad is seated on the bridge with Medora in his arms. He orders a cask of rum to be broached so that the sailors may drink in honour of their escape. While the men carouse, some women slaves dance about Medora.

Suddenly the wind springs up, darkness falls, and distant thunder peals. The men run hither and thither to shorten sail. But the storm increases in intensity and the waves mount steadily higher, shaking the vessel from stem to stern. There is a terrific explosion and a thunderbolt strikes the ship, rending her in two. The water pours in and engulfs the vessel and all aboard her.

Epilogue

The storm ceases and, as the scene grows lighter, two figures are seen clinging to a piece of wreckage. They are borne towards land. It is Conrad and Medora. They kneel and offer up a prayer of thanksgiving for having been delivered from dire peril.

*

Le Corsaire is founded on Byron's poem of the same name, but the resemblances are slight. An earlier ballet on the same theme, with music by Bochsa and choreography by Albert, was produced at London, at the King's Theatre, on June 29th, 1837. The ballet was in two acts and the principal characters were taken as follows: Herminie Elssler (Medora), Pauline Duvernay (Gulnare), Albert (Conrad), and Dauty (Seyd).

Duvernay made a hit as Gulnare. *The Times* says: "There is much of originality about Duvernay; her style is far removed from the poetical one of Taglioni, and may be called the *naïve* style of dancing. She bounds about in the most playful manner, and falls into her various attitudes as if by accident, and with a general air of good humour that is highly pleasing. The scenery was beautiful, and the grouping gives the greatest credit to the arranger." [16]

Albert's ballet was revived at the Theatre Royal, Drury Lane, on September 30th, 1844, with Clara Webster (Medora), Adeline Dumilâtre (Gulnare), and Albert (Conrad).

[16] June 30th, 1837.

In case the reader may desire to compare the two themes, I quote from a notice of the revival.[17] "Act I gives us the departure of Conrad (Albert) from his island to attack Seide, with the grief of his wife Medora (Miss Clara Webster). Act II shows us how Conrad and his band disturb Seide in the midst of his odalisques, and how the leader is at last captured. By Act III we learn that Gulnare supplicates Seide to save Conrad, and are informed by Conrad's dream in his dungeon, how Seide is murdered by Gulnare, and Medora is lying dead at home in the Pirate's isle. A grand attack on the palace by the corsairs, with a most dazzling conflagration, in the midst of which Conrad may be seen with Gulnare in his arms, apparently balancing himself on a single rafter, and liberally besprinkled by a shower of fire, concludes the piece.

"We have seen better ballets, and we have seen worse, than the *Corsaire*. There is some bustle about it, but the incidents are of a common-place character, and the non-dancing portion is unreasonably long, compared with the *pas*.

"On Dumilâtre as Gulnare," says the same writer "the most unqualified praise may be bestowed. Combining in a remarkable degree great firmness and excessive lightness, she executes with a grace and finish, and floats through her steps with an ease and a freedom from effort which is seldom seen. Her style is perfectly ethereal, and when Desplaces, who dances with her in a *pas de deux,* lifts her from the ground, it is as if the atmosphere alone were sufficient to buoy her up. The slightness of her figure contributes towards this impression, and for the quality of elegance in her art she could scarcely be surpassed; her countenance is very pleasing and expressive, and a beautiful series of elegant attitudes were produced when, reclining on the ottoman at the feet of her lord, she supplicates for Conrad's life.

"Of the scenic effects, the best was the tableau in Conrad's dream representing the dead body of Medora, over which young girls are strewing flowers. The grouping here was exceedingly good, and the purple light gave an appropriate tone to the scene."

*

The first performance of Mazilier's *Le Corsaire* was honoured by the presence of the Emperor Napoleon III and his Empress, both of whom highly praised the production. The director of the Opera was summoned to the Imperial box where the Empress commented on the production in the following terms: "I have never

---

[17] *Times,* Oct. 1st, 1844.

seen in all my life and probably shall never see again anything at once so beautiful and so moving."

"The new ballet," asserts *La France Musicale*, "is a great and brilliant success. The settings alone have an irresistible attraction; all Paris will go to see the scene of the ship sinking beneath the waves amid the lightning flashes and violence of the storm. It is a fantastic sight and the most moving that has yet been seen on the stage.

"The music of Adolphe Adam is worthy of him. The most graceful and captivating themes succeed one another in rare profusion. The whole of the last scene is the work of a master, it is not only ballet music, it is dramatic inspiration of the first rank.

"*Le Corsaire* has been a triumph for La Rosati who displayed in it all her poetry, all her grace, all her seductive passion. At each *pas* of the enchantress the whole house burst into applause."

"It is impossible nowadays to praise La Rosati," says the critic of *Le Théâtre*. "What is there to be said which has not been said already? She played her part with an infinite grace, intelligence, and wit. During the second act the enthusiasm of the house was at its height, and she had to appear at the end of the act in response to the demands of an audience which recalled her with loud shouts. This ovation continued throughout the next act and became a real triumph.

"Segarelli made a happy debut. He rendered the role of Conrad with grace and feeling. He has all that is required to succeed, his features are very expressive and well render the thoughts that move him.

"The part of the slave, Gulnare, taken by Mlle. Couqui, could not fall into better hands. Her reputation cannot but gain by this creation in which she revealed the measure of her real talent. In the scene in which she ridicules her master's ill humour and mocks at his threats, she was much applauded, and deservedly."

*

At London, in the eighteen-fifties, the old grand ballets were giving place to the shorter *ballet-divertissements,* which became increasingly popular with the opera audiences. But Lumley, the director of Her Majesty's Theatre, tempted by the Paris success of *Le Corsaire,* decided to present the ballet, with Rosati in her original part as Medora. The other members of the cast were Ronzani (Conrad), Dauty (Seyd), Vaudois (Birbanto), Mlle. Rosa (Gulnare), and Mlle. Clara (Zulmea). The first performance was given on July 8th, 1856.

It is of interest to quote the director's impressions. "Rosati danced—she acted. Her ethereal bounds across the stage were once more marvels of that apparently effortless power which constituted one of her distinguishing charms. By turns sporting with a cajoling grace, which was the very poetry of coquetry, and bursting forth into melodramatic vigour when the exigencies of the stirring story demanded a more powerful display, she proved herself a pantomimist worthy of the experienced Italian mimic, Ronzani, who acted the *Conrad* to her *Medora*.

"The dancing of Rosati and of the other principals—the general choreographic ensemble—the gorgeous dresses—Marshall's beautiful scenery—the grouping and the *mise en scène*—all was enchanting! The manœuvres of the Corsair's vessel in a storm; the foundering of the ship in the wild waves; and the final rescue of *Conrad* and *Medora* from the wreck, formed *the* great attractive *tableau,* which, in more modern parlance, would have been called 'the grand *sensation* scene' of this ballet of the 'good old school.'

"But the 'Corsaire,' in spite of all its splendour—in spite of all the enormous expense bestowed upon it—was not a source of remuneration to the Theatre. To say that it was a failure would be erroneous. It could not, perhaps, be called a '*demi-fiasco*'; but, as certainly it was only a demi-success . . . the grand *ballet d'ac-tion* had now lost its power of attraction. The majority of the male supporters of the ballet (as a mere display of dancing) had long decided upon eschewing all pantomime. They disliked the trouble of understanding a 'story,' however lucidly set forth in mute action before them. They shut their eyes, and said, 'We *cannot* understand it'; when the fashion of the day simply meant to say 'We *will not* understand it.' They wanted only dancing, not acting, they said. They should, to tell the truth, have said, 'We only want legs, not brains.' And so it was that the mere *divertissement* obtained an undue position on the great choreographic stage of London.[18] "

The critic of the *Illustrated London News* acclaimed the ballet as "one of the most splendid and beautiful spectacles ever put on the stage—a masterpiece of exquisite painting, rich decoration, skilful and striking *tableaux vivants,* and all the appliances of scenic art. They will see the queen of the ballet, the charming Rosati, more lovely than ever, dancing with a beauty which no tongue can describe, and acting with an intelligence, grace, and truthfulness which cannot be excelled—whose every look and gesture is instinct with meaning, which stands in no need of language to be

---

[18] *Reminiscences of the Opera.*

understood. And they will hear some of the prettiest and most animated music that Adolphe Adam has ever composed."

The *Sunday Times* declares that "the *pas* in which the *corps de ballet* dispose their fans at her (Rosati's) back to resemble the wings of a beautiful butterfly, the dance which she executes in the second tableau, flitting like a bird, now on the table, now on the back of the couch on which Conrad reposes; now bending over him in an attitude that seems a study for a classic gem, with the coquettish gambols by which she fascinates the old pasha, might be signalized as the perfection of choreographic art."

The Times[19] critic was much impressed by the fifth scene, which he declares to be "a complete novelty in the way of theatrical effect. The boards are covered by a rolling sea, on which floats the corsair's felucca. Floating vessels on carpet seas have been seen frequently enough, but the peculiarity of this felucca is that it is large enough to contain the whole of the corsair's crew, with Medora and a number of dancing-girls who execute a *pas d'ensemble* on the deck, while a moving panorama at the back of the stage denotes the progress of the voyage. In the midst of the merriment the noise of a tempest is heard, the ropes are crowded with clambering sailors, and amid flashes of lightning and peals of thunder the huge vessel, with all the crew struggling to the last, sinks into the water. . . .

"This awful catastrophe comes as a striking contrast to the early part of the ballet, during which the stage is perpetually crowded with all the lightest and gayest of Oriental attire. The graceful assemblages that appear before the mosques in the market-place of Adrianople, in the cave of the corsair, in the harem of the Pasha, seem to consist of unsubstantial gauzy beings who live but to fall into elegant groups which they form with military precision. A so-called '*pas d'eventail*,' in which each of the corps de ballet holds a fan made of peacocks' feathers, and unites her companions in creating a variety of beautiful combinations, is one of the happiest effects ever achieved by choreographic art.

"As for Mlle. Rosati, nothing can be more perfect than her impersonation of Medora, who, far from being the sentimental being imagined by Lord Byron, is a lively creature, whose very soul consists in dance, and who captivates every heart by her fairy-like evolutions. The ethereal bounds along the stage in the '*pas d'eventail*' are marvels of effortless power, while the sportive gambols with which she cajoles sometimes the corsair, sometimes the Pasha, are exquisite displays of mimetic art—the very poetry of

[19] July 9th, 1856.

coquetry. A group which she forms with Conrad by leaning over him like a Hebe, and filling his goblet from the tiniest of flagons, is of itself a study, and the manner in which with extended pistols she keeps the Pasha at bay in the fourth scene is a grand exploit of the Fidelio kind."

*

Le Corsaire was produced at the Bolshoy Theatre, St. Petersburg, in January, 1858, the production being by Jules Perrot. The parts were distributed thus: Mmes. Fridberg (Medora), Troitskaya (Zulmea), Radina (Gulnare) and MM. Petipa (Conrad), Perrot (Seyd Pasha), Pichaud (Isaac Lanquedem), Frédéric (Birbanto), and Stukolin (Chief Eunuch).

The best dances were the *Pas des Eventails, Pas des Odalisques,* and *Scène de Seduction,* danced by Radina, who in one of the succeeding performances, was replaced by Kosheva. The character dances pleased the audience, but the *ballerina* Fridberg was received with reserve. The ballet was handsomely produced and had a great success; the scene of the shipwreck, designed by Roller, was highly praised.

Le Corsaire was continually revived and passed into the permanent repertory of the Imperial Theatres. The part of Medora, so full of opportunities for the artist dancer-mime, was a great favourite with the Russian *ballerine,* and is associated with a long line of illustrious interpreters, for instance: Fridberg, M. Taglioni, E. I. Andreyanaova, M. S. Petipa, K. Grantsova, E. O. Vazem, H. D'Or, E. P. Sokolova, A. Pavlova, T. Karsavina, and so on.

LES ELFES

Fantastic Ballet in 3 Acts and 4 Scenes. Book: V. de Saint-Georges and Mazilier. Music: Count Gabrielli. Scenery: Desplèchin, Nolau, Rubé, Thierry, and Martin. Choreography: Mazilier. First produced: Théâtre Impérial de l'Opéra, Paris, August 11th, 1856.

CHARACTERS

Albert of Hungary, the reigning Duke, aged twenty	MM.	PETIPA
Count Frederick of Hapsburg, a Palatine nobleman, aged thirty-five . .		SEGARELLI
The Grand Elector, Princess Bathilde's father		LENFANT

A Stone Statue . . . . . Mlles. Amalia
                                              Ferraris
The Queen of the Elves . . . .   Legrain
A Youthful Elf . . . . .   Nathan
Princess Bathilde . . . . .   Marquet

The action passes in the mountains of Hungary.

Lords, Ladies, Huntsmen, Guards, Pages, Musicians,
Villagers, Elves, etc.

*Act I. A forest cross-road at the summit of a mountain. In
the background a ruined temple, closed by a rustic door.*

Hunting-horns herald the approach of a party of huntsmen.
Behind them come Prince Albert of Hungary and his friend,
Count Frederick, attended by a numerous suite. The Prince rallies
his friend for his melancholy air and his lack of attention to the
ladies. He replies: "I am indifferent to love."

Peasant girls offer fruit and flowers to the Prince and his suite,
and entertain them with a dance. Meanwhile the Count wanders
about the temple. He opens the door and sees a beautiful statue
representing a dryad, the base of which is inscribed Sylvia.

The Prince and his suite share the Count's admiration for this
work of art, so much so that the Prince announces his intention
of placing the statue in his palace. He calls an officer who throws
a purple veil over the statue in sign of possession. The hunting-
horns sound the *hallali,* and the Prince and his suite hurry off to
the chase.

The Count remains behind. Overcome by fatigue and the heat
of the day he falls asleep.

A hoary oak parts and from the interior steps Adda, Queen of
the Elves, who traverses the glade, delighting in the solitude. Es-
pying the Count, she flits about him, then makes a signal, and from
every brook and tree comes an elf. They join the Queen and
gaze upon the sleeping stranger.

At this moment the Count awakens and is stupefied to see all
the fairy creatures. Adda tells him that the forest is her kingdom
and that the fairies are her subjects. The Count asks forgiveness
for trespassing on her domains. The Queen smiles assent and
gives him a tender glance. But the Count observes that the only
woman he could love would be one whose heart did not beat.

Adda runs to the temple and, indicating the statue, says to
her companions: "Only a woman of stone can please this handsome stranger."

"Could you love her?" asks the Queen, laughingly.

"Yes, if she were alive," replies the Count.

"Your wish is granted," says the Queen. "This figure will be a woman by day, but a statue by night."

The Queen commands an elf to stand by the statue. She touches the elf with her wand and she swoons to the ground. A little flame leaps from her side and alights on the head of the statue. The stone features become luminous, the breasts rise and fall, and the figure comes to life.

Astonished at this miracle, the Count kneels in terror before the Queen.

Fingers of light mark the approach of dawn and the elves depart, taking with them the dead body of their companion.

The Count, uncertain whether he is awake or dreaming, watches the dryad attempting to leave her pedestal. When she succeeds she is dazzled by the light and overwhelmed by the height of the trees. Overcome with emotion she swoons.

Frederick runs to her side but stops on seeing her studying her reflection in a pool of water. She touches her image and is astounded by the coldness of the water.

When the Count approaches she flees in terror. But he takes a pipe left by one of the peasants and plays a few notes which bring the girl to his side. He offers her some flowers, whose perfume she inhales with delight. He tries to take the nymph in his arms, but she runs to the shelter of the temple.

The air of the peasants' dance is heard in the distance and the nymph begins to dance. The sound of the hunt grows nearer and the Count is fearful lest the Prince should see his prize, but she runs in the temple and closes the door.

The light fades and the hunt is over. The Prince orders the statue to be taken to his castle. The Count, alarmed, rushes to the temple. The door is open, but, with the coming of night, the lovely dryad is once more a thing of stone. He gives a sigh of relief.

The Prince and his companions leave the forest to the fanfare of trumpets, their way lighted by torch-bearers.

Act II. Scene I. A magnificent room in the Prince's palace at Buda. In the background is a splendidly furnished boudoir, closed at the rise of the curtain by great doors. To the left a rich curtain conceals the entrance to a gallery containing pictures and statues.

All is ready for the betrothal of Prince Albert and Princess Bathilde, the Grand Elector's daughter.

The Prince presents the lords and ladies of his Court to his future father-in-law and to his fiancée. He offers Bathilde magnificent presents and rich dresses, which are placed on various tables. Then the Prince offers to show his guests a beautiful statue which he discovered in the mountains. He raises the curtain to disclose an empty pedestal. The Prince is amazed at this extraordinary event.

At this juncture the ladies-in-waiting to the Princess announce that all is ready, and she goes into the boudoir. The Prince goes out with the Elector and his suite to discuss the marriage contract.

While Bathilde is being dressed the dryad peeps out from behind the pedestal. She comes into the room and displays a child-like delight in all the dresses. Noticing how Bathilde is attired, she makes a choice of the dresses and jewels and achieves a splendid appearance. She is watched by the Count who has fallen in love with her. He tells her of his passion, but she does not understand. He places his hand on her heart and withdraws in fear, for it is motionless.

Enter the Prince who is charmed at the sight of the unknown girl, whom the Count presents as his ward. The Prince vainly tries to recall where he has seen her before. He kisses her hand, and she bursts into laughter. The Prince, astonished, compliments her on her beauty, but she turns her back on him and plays with the flowers in a vase.

The Princess enters with her maids-of-honour and the Prince goes to greet her, but he appears pre-occupied by the beautiful unknown whom he presents to his betrothed. Count Frederick is jealous.

The ladies of the Court entertain the Prince with dances, but all at once the dryad bounds in the midst of the dancers and dances a *pas* so original and so unusual that it occasions the greatest surprise. An attempt is made to restrain her, but she eludes all pursuit. The Count follows at her heels. The Elector and his suite conduct his daughter and the Prince to the palace, for the ceremony of betrothal.

Act II. Scene II. The gardens of the Prince's palace at Buda. To the left is a flight of steps leading to the palace; to the right is a green arbour. In the background is a cascade spouting in a marble basin.

Sylvia runs in, breathless from her endeavour to evade pursuit, and sinks exhausted on the greensward. The Count hurries to her side and tries to calm her, but she escapes from his embrace and runs to the arbour, and is about to leap into the water, when the Count restrains her in the nick of time. Overcome with emotion she swoons, and the Count places her on a mossy bank. He is distressed that she lacks both heart and brain.

A fantastic melody is heard, the cascade glows and dies down to give place to the Queen of the Elves, who holds three roses. She points to a piece of overhanging rock on which appears in glowing letters the following words: "These three roses confer reason, grace, and love. But each gift will cause the donor to age ten years."

The Count grasps the three charms. The Queen retires and the fountain plays again.

The Count goes to Sylvia and presents her with the rose that confers reason. Immediately she changes; she is full of maidenly shyness and modesty, and refuses his attentions. He is sad at this miscarriage of his plan.

The Prince enters and Sylvia, contrasting the two men to the Count's disadvantage, goes to the former, who kisses her hand and is surprised to find it so cold.

Princess Bathilde enters with her ladies and is pained to find her betrothed talking to the beautiful unknown. The Prince reassures her. Now Sylvia is jealous and would part the Prince from the Princess, did not the Count restrain her.

The ladies dance and the Prince dances with his fiancée. Sylvia tries to imitate Bathilde, but her ungainly efforts are greeted with laughter. The Count, unable to bear her humiliation, gives her the rose that confers grace. In a flash her clumsiness vanishes to be replaced by an ethereal lightness. The Prince is ravished and almost forgets his betrothed in his admiration. But the Elector reminds him of his daughter and the company stroll towards the palace. The Count and Sylvia are alone.

The Count, unable to contain his feelings, falls on his knees and declares his love, which declaration Sylvia receives with astonishment. The Count, perplexed, realizes that she does not know the meaning of love. So he decides to give her the rose that awakens love.

No sooner does she receive it than she is conscious of a new emotion. The Count, unaware that he has become white-haired and bent, goes to her full of hope. But at the same moment the Prince returns and Sylvia throws herself into his arms.

The Count, enraged, draws his dagger and tries to stab the
Prince, who easily pushes aside the old man, whom he fails to
recognize.

At this juncture the Elector and his daughter, followed by the
Court, return in search of the Prince, for the marriage ceremony
is about to commence. The Count tells Sylvia that Bathilde is
the Prince's fiancée. The Prince, ill at ease, goes to Bathilde and
almost unwillingly takes her hand to lead her to the altar.

Sylvia is overcome with despair. She is minded to make one
last appeal to the Prince, but night falls and she gradually changes
into a statue.

Meanwhile the wedding procession continues on its way to the
Church. The Count, with a wild gesture of triumph, falls at the
foot of the statue.

*Act. III. The valley of roses in the light of the dawn. To the
right is a raised grotto, closed by a movable rock. Below the grotto
is a granite bench. To the left is a mound covered with flowers.*

The Queen of the Elves enters as though borne on the breeze.
She makes a sign and her subjects range themselves at her side,
while another group come flying through the air, carrying, by
means of golden scarfs, the body of the elf whose spirit entered the
statue.

The Queen indicates a bank of roses as a place of burial. The
flowers part and the fairies lower the body of their sister into the
hollow. The elves shower roses over the grave and vanish.

The Count runs in and, rolling back the rock, reveals the grotto
which contains the statue. He waits anxiously for the statue to
come to life.

But the silence is broken by footsteps and the Prince enters.
The Count hastens to guard the entrance to the grotto. But the
Prince has already recognized the statue.

"So it is you who stole it from me," cries the Prince.

"She belongs to me," replies the Count.

They draw swords and a duel begins. But the statue comes to
life and Sylvia interposes herself between the combatants. The
Prince, terror stricken, drops his sword, and the Count seizes the
opportunity to attack him. But Sylvia protects him with her body.
In a rage the Count turns on her. But the Prince succeeds in disarming him, calls for his guards, and bids them take the Count
away.

Left alone with Sylvia, the Prince is afraid, but he takes her
hand, which is now warm, and carries it to his lips. Then follows

a charming love scene which is interrupted by pages who announce the arrival of the Elector and the Duchess. The Prince takes leave of Sylvia to greet his wife.

Hardly has the Prince departed, when the elves fill the valley. On seeing Sylvia they reproach her for the death of their sister. They snatch from her the roses which confer reason and grace, but the third rose she presses to her breast. Immediately she becomes her former self, a creature of caprice.

Rustic music is heard and the elves disappear. Peasants carrying flowers run before the Elector, Bathilde, and the Prince. But Sylvia, to the intense surprise of the bystanders, goes to the Prince and places her hand in his. Bathilde asks him who the stranger is. He bids Sylvia begone, but she clasps his feet and sobs. He leaves her and rejoins Bathilde. Sylvia, overcome with despair, swoons and is carried to the granite seat.

The Prince and his wife tend the unfortunate girl who, with the approach of night, grows colder and colder. There is a loud uproar and the Count, obviously demented, bursts through the crowd who give way and withdraw. He seizes a mace from one of the soldiers and crashes it down on the statue, which shivers into fragments. The Count falls unconscious. The bystanders, horrified, flee in terror.

A tiny flame rises from the statue, hovers in the air, and settles on the elf's flowery tomb. The roses lift their heads, the mound opens, and the elf, radiant and happy, springs to life.

The Queen welcomes her with delight and the elves dance for joy at her return.

*

Les Elfes is associated with the Paris *début* of the celebrated Italian dancer Amalia Ferraris.

"The score . . . is a little masterpiece of attractive and original melodies," says the critic of *La France Musicale.*

"The settings are magnificent," comments *Le Théâtre,* "and the transformation scenes are carried out with magical precision, that rapidity which is the monopoly of the machinists at the Opera. Similarly the greatest care has governed the choice of the costumes, which are of the utmost richness and novelty."

What of the ballet? "To be frank," says *Le Théâtre,* "we must say that the ballet *Les Elfes* does not appear to us to be destined to have the vogue of *Le Corsaire,* and that the admirable *danseuse* who has created the principal role on this occasion owes all her triumph to her own talent.

"We should certainly like to give our readers some impression of that marvellous dancing, which leaves one dazzled, enchanted, and stupefied. Does there exist a voice, a language, a manner of painting to render the agile flight of the butterfly, the grace of the humming-bird, the breath of a gentle breeze, in short, all that is ethereal and impalpable in nature?

"Mme. Ferraris does not dance; she runs, she flies, she bounds, she darts, hardly does her foot skim the ground, scarcely does she glide over the boards. Like the Amazon Camilla, in walking she does not bend the undulating ears of wheat, she does not bedew her tiny shoe on the foaming crest of the waves; her body, supple and slender, seems fashioned of air and dew, and animated by that intangible Fairy soul which provides the central theme of her ballet.

"However, choreographers . . . have technical terms to describe that breeze turned woman, that peri, still more fairy-like than her sisters. They know how to analyse her dancing, to name her steps, to define her poses. Thanks to their help we could inform you that Mme. Ferraris excels in *poses renversés avec battements de jambes;* that she rises with a great deal of *ballon* and elasticity; that, thanks to her supple and sinewy foot, she raises herself with an incomparable strength *sur les pointes,* without apparent effort, and that she beats the *entrechat huit* to perfection, and as it has not yet been seen.

"The mimed part of the ballet *Les Elfes* demands an interpretation as skilful as the dancing part, and only a great artist could make clear those gradual transformations of the statue into a woman, those successive stages of sensibility, comprehension, and passion, depicted in turn in her features, those alternations of artless surprise, joy, uncertainty, annoyance, love, and depair, which form a whole mute drama, of which the glance and facial expression must render the meaning and variations. . . .

"Mme. Ferraris proves herself as perfect in this part of her role as in her marvellous and expressive dancing. Her features spoke, her eyes served as a faithful mirror of the struggle between her feelings and passions, of the storm in her heart, of the ebb and flow of the various sensations and emotions which she had to portray. Never can silence have been more eloquent, never can a gesture, glance, and pose have spoken more plainly, more movingly, more deeply, and more admirably. . . .

"The Parisian public was astonished at the lightness of her dancing, and at the grace of her poses and gestures, which recalled the statues of antiquity. She was regarded as one of the finest exponents of the pure Italian classic school and achieved a triumph."

MARCO SPADA OU LA FILLE DU BANDIT

Pantomimic Ballet in 3 Acts and 6 Scenes. Book: Mazilier. Music: Auber. Choreography: Mazilier. First produced: Théâtre Impérial de l'Opéra, Paris, April 1st, 1857.

CHARACTERS

Prince Osorio, Governor of Rome . . MM.		LENFANT
Federici, his nephew		PETIPA
The Marchesa Sampietri, his niece . . MME.		AMALIA
		FERRARIS
Count Pepinelli, her *cicisbeo,* Captain of		
Dragoons . . . . . . MM.		MÉRANTE
Marco Spada		SEGARELLI
Angela, his daughter . . . . MME.		CAROLINA
		ROSATI
Genario, a Roman bandit . . . M.		CORALLI
Fra Borromeo, the convent treasurer M.		GARNIER-
		BERTIER

Peasants, Village Girls, Servants, Dragoons, Musicians, Lords, Ladies, Guides, Bandits.

Act I. Scene I. A large village near Rome. It is situated at the foot of a mountain, which forms the background. To the left are some houses; to the right is a Franciscan monastery.

A village wedding is in progress. The bride, bridegroom, and young people dance, while the heads of the families are seated to right and left. Enter Prince Osorio, the Marchesa Sampietri, his niece, and her *cicisbeo,* Count Pepinelli, captain of dragoons. The bride is presented to them.

Village dignitaries receive the Governor and complain of the depredations made by the mountain brigands. He shows them his police posting a notice offering a reward for information that will lead to the arrest of the chief of the brigands, Marco Spada. At the same time a party of dragoons are seen moving towards the mountain.

The bride and bridegroom enter a church, followed by the Governor. Meanwhile Pepinelli makes love to the Marchesa, who accepts his attentions, but announces that she is engaged to her cousin, Count Federici. The newly-married couple leave the church and the dances become general.

At the end of the dance a young man, carrying an artist's impedimenta, makes his appearance. The Marchesa recognizes her fiancé who tells her that he is going to finish a painting of the mountain. A lay brother comes out of the monastery and invites the party to visit it, which they do, with the exception of Federici, who climbs the mountain.

Enter Marco Spada, dressed as a gentleman in hunting costume, and attended by two valets. He approaches the dancers and invites them to spend an evening with him at his castle.

Suddenly there is a roll of drums and the Governor announces that the tithes owing to the monastery and long overdue will now be collected. The lay brother, called Borromeo, seats himself at a table while the police remind the debtors of their dues. Seeing Marco Spada he asks him for his contribution, but he replies that he does not reside in the parish. Borromeo studies his features and agrees. The tithes collected, Borromeo dismisses the police who go into the monastery.

There is a clap of thunder and the frightened peasants hasten to their homes. Borromeo takes up his weighty money-bag and goes to the monastery to find the door barred by Spada's two men, who menace him with their muskets. Spada relieves him of the bag, gives him a receipt, and, doffing his hat, ironically takes his departure.

The Governor's party comes out of the monastery just as Borromeo observes that the receipt is signed "Marco Spada." The Governor departs for Rome to send his troops in pursuit.

Act I. Scene II. An elegant drawing-room. The background is circular with several doors opening on to a gallery. Between each door is a large painting. To the right is a table bearing a lighted branched candlestick and some musical instruments.

The Governor, his niece, and Pepinelli enter, seeking shelter from the storm, which has forced them to break their journey. Surprised to find the room unoccupied, Pepinelli takes up the candlestick and disappears into a room on the right. The Governor, despite the semi-darkness, goes to the room on the left, but, just as he opens the door, a young girl embraces him. Pepinelli returns with the candlestick and the room is light again. The girl, frightened at the presence of strangers, explains that she was expecting her father. Seeing their plight, however, she offers them shelter, and, summoning several domestics, invites her visitors to change their clothes.

A guitar is heard outside and Angela, such is the young girl's name, opens the window, when Federici appears. There is a love scene between them which is interrupted by the sound of approaching hoof-beats. Federici is forced to take his departure.

Marco Spada enters and is welcomed by his daughter. He is touched by her affectionate greeting, and asks her if he can help her to realize any cherished ambition. She tells him of Federici and of his desire to marry her, to which he gives his consent.

Now the Marchesa comes into the room and Angela presents the stranger to her father, explaining the reason for her presence. She is followed by the Governor and Pepinelli, to whom Spada is unknown. He invites his guests to stay the night, which invitation is accepted.

Spada rings and his lieutenant, Genario, appears, astonished to see the Governor and Pepinelli. He counsels his chief to take this opportunity to rid himself of his enemies. Spada tells him that after midnight, when the guests have retired, Genario may do as he pleases, but the Marchesa is to be spared.

While the repast is being prepared, the hosts and guests converse. The Governor invites Spada and his daughter to a ball which he is to give on the morrow. At a sign from his daughter, the brigand accepts, but she recalls that she does not know how to dance. The Marchesa offers to teach her before dinner. Pepinelli takes the violin off the table and plays the airs, while the Marchesa shows Angela the steps and figures. During the lesson Spada takes the Governor on a tour of inspection.

At the end of the dance Pepinelli becomes alarmed by strange noises which seem to come from beneath the floor. Angela and the Marchesa go in search of Spada and the Governor. Pepinelli hides behind the hangings covering a door. A trap opens in the centre of the room and twelve brigands climb into the room. Each hides behind one of the large pictures.

The hosts and guests return followed by Genario. Pepinelli tells of the mysterious noises and of the twelve brigands. A far-off trumpet sounds. "It is my soldiers," cries Pepinelli, "I will bring them here." Genario is about to stab him with his dagger, when Spada restrains him. "Not in front of my daughter," he whispers.

The guests sit down and Spada gives an order to Genario, who disappears. The chief observes that Pepinelli must have been mistaken and that the noise came from the kitchens. There is a nearer trumpet-call and Pepinelli enters with a party of dragoons. He orders them to level their muskets at the trap which again rises to reveal a table richly laid. Pepinelli is astonished.

Spada invites his guests to be seated. They take their places and mock Pepinelli's fears. Unconvinced, he orders his dragoons to level their muskets at the pictures. As they do so the pictures disappear and from each frame steps a girl, who offers flowers to the ladies and to the Governor. Pepinelli is amazed. At the same moment the villagers, invited by Spada, arrive carrying baskets of flowers.

Act II. A ballroom in the Governor's palace, Rome.

Enter the Marchesa in evening dress, followed by Pepinelli. She tells him that she is to be married to Count Federici. He is so distressed by the news that he falls on his knees, to the surprise of Federici, who comes in at this moment. The Marchesa goes out leaving the rivals together. Federici tells Pepinelli that he does not intend to marry the Marchesa since he loves another. Pepinelli expresses his delight in a lively dance.

The Marchesa returns with her uncle, the Governor, who receives the guests including Marco Spada and his daughter. Federici is delighted to see Angela who tells her father that he is her fiancé. The ball begins and there follow a succession of *pas de caractère*.

Towards the end of the *divertissement* Borromeo appears and goes towards the Governor. At the sight of the monk, Spada is troubled. He wishes to leave at once with his daughter, but she is so happy that she entreats him to say. Borromeo tells the Governor that the Brotherhood is penniless and asks if he may take a collection among those present. This request is granted.

Pages announce that supper is ready and the guests pass out of the room, all save Spada and his daughter. He goes to the door and tells Genario, disguised as a lackey, to bring up his carriage.

Borromeo and Pepinelli come out of another door. The monk, seeing a possible contributor in Spada, goes to speak with him. While the brigand takes out his purse Borromeo recognizes him and calls him by name.

Angela swoons. Spada menaces the monk with a pistol and summons Genario, who appears with other lackeys and carries off Borromeo. Spada restores his daughter to consciousness just as Federici enters and asks the chief for his daughter's hand in marriage. She struggles between love and duty and finally decides to stay with her father. Federici swears vengeance.

The guests come back into the ballroom. Federici goes to the

Marchesa and announces that he will wed her on the morrow. The dances are resumed. Pepinelli is in despair, and Angela, sad at heart, leaves with her father. The remaining guests offer their congratulations to the Marchesa.

Act III. Scene I. The Marchesa's boudoir. To the left is a mirror and a large wedding-basket covered in satin and adorned with ribbons. To the right is a wardrobe.

Enter Pepinelli, desirous of a last interview with the Marchesa. If she refuses his love he has decided to kill himself. Hearing voices he wishes to escape from the room, but since there is only one door, by which he entered, he hides in the wardrobe.

Young girls enter bearing materials and veils. They are followed by the Marchesa clad in a simple gauze dress. She is going to try on her wedding dress. Her attendants hand her a veil which she tries on before the mirror. While she takes various poses, the girls form different groups about her. Other girls come in carrying floral bouquets and chaplets of orange blossom. She wears these in different ways while the young girls form admiring groups.

Pepinelli, stifled in the cupboard, opens the door and is spellbound by the vision that greets his gaze.

The girls take out jewels and ornaments and soon the Marchesa is arrayed in all her glory. Pepinelli, unable to restrain his passion, rushes towards the Marchesa and falls at her feet.

At the same time a dozen brigands glide into the room. Pepinelli and the girls are terrified while the Marchesa swoons. In the confusion Pepinelli steps into the marriage-basket which shuts on him.

Spada leaps into the room and orders two men to carry off the Marchesa. Others pick up the jewels and lace, and the marriage-basket. As soon as the brigands have vanished the girls run to the door and cry for help.

Act III. Scene II. A forest lighted by the rising sun.

Spada, surrounded by his sleeping men, is leaning against a rock. He touches Genario and bids him blow his horn to awaken them. Everyone rises, fires are lit and breakfast prepared. After the meal there are lively dances.

Two dancers quarrel over a girl, who proves to be Angela. Spada asks her why she has left home, and she tells him that her place is with him. Then she sobs and when he asks her why she is sad, she tells him that Federici is being married to the Marchesa that very morning.

Their meditations are interrupted by a blare of trumpets. The brigands, alarmed, disappear into the forest just as a picket of dragoons enters from the opposite direction.

Act III. Scene III. The upper portion shows the forest, the lower a secret cavern known only to the brigands.

Overhead the dragoons scout through the forest and pass from view. A little later another band of brigands bring the Marchesa and the basket, and descend into the cavern. Pepinelli is released from the basket and the Marchesa is told that she must marry him. When she protests Genario orders his men to level their muskets at her, whereupon she consents. Borromeo is brought in to perform the ceremony. At the same time the wedding procession of the first act passes through the forest overhead. The newly-married couple are led to a cavern and a guard placed over them. Angela thanks her father and the brigands join in a number of dances which are interrupted by a series of musket-shots.

Some brigands arrive and inform Spada that the Governor and Federici have entered the forest and are followed at a distance by a strong party of dragoons.

Spada leaves the cavern with a number of his men. Angela listens in fear and presently the sound of firing is heard.

The Governor and Federici are captured by the brigands and forced to descend. Genario, seeing the Governor, orders his companions to shoot him on the spot, but Angela countermands the order.

Further shots are heard and Pepinelli and the Marchesa, seized with fright at the noise, run into the centre of the cavern and are astonished to see the new prisoners. The Marchesa informs Federici that she has been married to Pepinelli by Borromeo.

At the same moment dragoons fill the forest path to be led to the secret cavern by a brigand turned traitor. They tell the Governor that Spada has been mortally wounded. Angela, about to swoon, is caught by Federici.

The dying chief is carried in by soldiers and his daughter runs to his side. To ensure his daughter's happiness he announces that Angela is not his daughter. "Do you swear that is the truth?" asks Borromeo. "I do," is the reply.

The Governor gives his consent to the marriage of Federici and Angela, and Spada expires. As the rest of the band are brought in by dragoons, Genario gives a cry of joy, for, before being wounded, he had set fire to the forest, which now glows red in the light of the mounting flames.

*

Marco Spada, first produced at Paris on April 1st, 1857, is the comic opera of the same name, originally given at the Théâtre de l'Opéra Comique on December 21st, 1852, adapted as a ballet. The critics, while in two minds as to the success of the production, were unanimous in the view that the principal attraction was the choreographic duel fought by the two *danseuses,* Amalia Ferraris and Carolina Rosati, respectively the interpreters of the Marchesa Sampietri and Angela, the bandit's daughter.

The music, according to the critic of *La France Musicale,*[20] consisted of popular airs taken from *Fra Diavolo, La Barcarolle, L'Enfant Prodigue,* and other operas.

"There are many new settings in *Marco Spada,*" observes the same writer; "the last in particular achieves a certain effect, but it is far from having the attraction of the famous vessel which was shipwrecked in *Le Corsaire.*

"Apart from the *pas* danced by the two heroines, M. Mazilier did not tax his imagination. These tarantellas and *ensembles* which run through the ballet are very crude and prove once more that the management of the Opera must seek out young and intelligent *maîtres de ballet.*"

Our critic gives an interesting description of the qualities of the two rivals. Ferraris is "a feather floating between two breezes. Never have we seen fairies of the dance run *sur les pointes* so boldly and so gracefully. In one of her *pas,* La Ferraris circles the stage, grazing the boards with the tips of her toes. This seems like magic. And then you must follow her in all her frolics; she flits like a bird and in two bounds crosses from one side of the stage to the other, to come to rest in front of the footlights; there she pirouettes swiftly and more agile than the fleetest squirrel; she leaves, and, in one bound, falls, quivering, into her partner's arms. La Ferraris is extraordinary, prodigious; she is one of those marvellous ideal beings which pursue you in dreams, and whose existence you cannot credit when you see them with eyes open. The whole house greeted the great artist with a thousand acclamations. La Ferraris can never have been present at a more beautiful festival.

"Rosati, too, was amazing, extraordinary, wonderful. In style quite different from Ferraris, she has fascination, irresistible allurement. At the close of the ballet she dances, musket in hand, with a dexterity, poise, and artistry that are truly fairy-like. And what a charming mime is La Rosati! She was overwhelmed with applause."

[20] April 5th, 1857.

JULES PERROT

JULES JOSEPH PERROT was born at Lyon in 1800. In his youth he toured for several years with a travelling show in which he played characters requiring an unusual acrobatic ability, such as a monkey, Polichinel, and so forth. It was doubtless this early training which procured him the rare grace and elasticity he displayed when he later became a dancer. He had almost all the natural gifts that a dancer requires—a fiery temperament, ease and lightness of movement, and excellent muscles which gave him extraordinary powers of elevation and earned for him the nickname of *l'aérien*—but nature had betrayed him by neglecting his figure.

After studying under Vestris he made his *début* at the Opéra, Paris, on June 23rd, 1830, in *Le Rossignol*. Later he danced with Taglioni in *Flore et Zéphire*. In 1840, when visiting Naples, he met and fell in love with a young dancer, Carlotta Grisi, whom he married. They studied, travelled, and danced together. On returning to Paris the couple secured an engagement at the Théâtre de la Renaissance, where they appeared on February 28th in *Le Zingaro*.

Gautier, in a review contributed to the *Presse,* of March 2nd, 1840, says of the dancer: "Perrot is not handsome, he is extremely ugly. From the waist upwards he has the proportions of a tenor, there is no need to say more; but, from the waist downwards, he is delightful to look at. It hardly accords with modern views to discourse on a man's physical proportions; however, we cannot keep silent regarding Perrot's legs. You must imagine that we are talking of some statue of the mime Bathyllus or of the actor Paris lately discovered during an excavation of Nero's Gardens or at Herculaneum. The foot and knee joints are unusually slender and counterbalance the somewhat feminine roundness of contour of his legs; the legs of the youth in red trunks, who breaks the symbolic wand across his knee, in Raphael's painting *The Marriage of the Virgin,* are quite in the same style. Let us add that Perrot, in a costume by Gavarni, has nothing of that feeble and inane manner

which, as a rule, makes male dancers so tiresome; his success was
assured before he had made a single step even; it was not difficult
to recognize the quiet agility, the perfect rhythm and the easy
grace of the dancer's miming, Perrot the aerial, Perrot the sylph,
Perrot the male Taglioni." Similar contemporary appreciations
suggest that Perrot was the greatest male dancer of his time, and
a mime without rival.

The success of the two dancers at the Théâtre de la Renaissance
secured them a position at the Opéra. From time to time Perrot
made many tours, during which he arranged dances and ballets,
and soon acquired a great reputation as a choreographer. He produced variously at London, Paris, and Milan, a number of excellent ballets, for instance, *Alma* (1842), *Ondine ou La Naïade*
(1843), *La Esmeralda* (1844), *Eoline ou la Dryade* (1845), *Le Pas
de Quatre* (1845), *Catarina ou La Fille du Bandit* (1846), *Lalla
Rookh or The Rose of Lahore* (1846), *Le Jugement de Paris*
(1846), *Les Eléments* (1847), *Faust* (1848), *Les Quatre Saisons*
(1845), *La Filleule des Fées* (1849).

In 1848 he was engaged at St. Petersburg in the capacity of
dancer, and thus, though he produced many ballets, it was not
until 1851 that he received the official title of *maître de ballet,* which
he retained until 1860, when he retired owing to ill-health. He
created and revived a number of ballets at St. Petersburg, such as
*Esmeralda, Catarina, La Filleule des Fées, The Naiad and the
Fisherman* (*Ondine*), *Gazelda, Faust, Marco Bomba, Armida, La
Vivandière, Le Corsaire, The Rose, The Violet, Le Diable à
Quatre, Le Papillon, Eoline,* and *La Débutante.*

Charles de Boigne, in his *Petits Mémoires de l'Opéra,* 1857, gives
an interesting account of Perrot's method of devising *ballabili.*[1]
"When the moment of inspiration seized him, he squatted on the
stage, his head between his hands. He might have been a china
monkey. When the *corps de ballet* saw him seated on the ground
like a tailor, they knew it would be for a long time, and so every
one made themselves comfortable accordingly; some embroidered,
some lunched, some read, the solo dancers had refreshments
brought to them. After a long interval a certain noise was heard.
It was Perrot snoring. He was awakened; the *ballabile* was finished; it had arrived with the snoring."

Perrot's compositions were distinguished by their rare poetic
feeling and artistic conception. His ballets were a carefully contrasted combination of unusual dances and mimed scenes, often

---

[1] A dance executed by a large number of persons, such as the *corps de ballet;* the
term is derived from the Italian *ballare,* to dance.

of considerable dramatic interest. He considered his whole company from the *ballerina* to the least member of the *corps de ballet*, and tried to give each an opportunity to distinguish herself. The greatest dancers of the day—Marie Taglioni, Fanny Elssler, Grisi, Cerito, Grahn, to name a few only—were all honoured to dance in his ballets.

ALMA OU LA FILLE DE FEU

Ballet in 4 Scenes. Book: Deshayes. Music: G. Costa. Scenery: W. Grieve. Choreography: Fanny Cerito and J. Perrot. First produced: Her Majesty's Theatre, London, June 23rd, 1842.

CHARACTERS

Periphite	
Belfegor	M. JULES PERROT
Emazor	M. DESPLACES
Alma	MLLE. FANNY CERITO

Belfegor strikes a rock with his sceptre: the statue of a lovely girl appears. The marble becomes animate; Alma, its living form, is destined to enchant and fascinate mankind. So long as she resists the passion she excites, her vitality will endure; if she yield to love, she turns again to stone. The genius of evil will attend to attempt her; and he promises himself as well to en'sure her fall.

Alma, led by her guide, arrives at a town in Germany. The burgomaster and the guards would prevent her entering its gates, but she fascinates them by her steps; and, when they yield to the influence of her charm, she leaps into a boat and disappears.

The scene changes and we see her in a salon of a French city. Alma, queen of the fête, inspires all with admiration. Each gallant knight follows her enthralled; and Emazor, most impassioned of them all, obtains access to her apartment. She commands him to leave her; but, touched by his devotion, yields to his supplication to be permitted to remain, on condition that to be near her is all that he desires, and that he asks not her love in return. Belfegor, alarmed, comes to bid her quit the town; so, to avoid her admirers, she appoints a meeting with each at the same time and place. They meet accordingly in darkness, draw their swords, and are about to engage, when Emazor appears to inform them he has seen Alma enter a chamber with her lover. They behold her in flight, and would pursue her, but are stopped by flames, except Emazor, who traverses them fearlessly.

We are now in Granada, where Alma, a captive, presides over a tournament, of which she is to be the prize. Emazor and Lara fight, the former triumphs, but his fallen casque reveals him as a Moorish prince exiled from Granada. Alma obtains his pardon of the king. Emazor, aided by the Moors, attacks and defeats the Spaniards. He is proclaimed king, and offers his throne to Alma. Belfegor comes again to endeavour to save his daughter, but she prefers love to life. Transported with delight, Emazor crowns his bride; but as she mounts the steps of the throne the earth trembles, nature is in convulsions; Alma again becomes a statue, and Emazor in despair breaks the crown he cannot share with his beloved.

*

The opera season of 1842 was particularly successful from the viewpoint of ballet, for it opened with the production of *Giselle,* with Carlotta Grisi, and closed with *Alma,* with Fanny Cerito in the title role. Lumley, the director of Her Majesty's Theatre, tells us that it was the talent displayed by Perrot in the composition and execution of the *Pas de Fascination* which inclined him to select that dancer to be his choreographer, while the *Pas de Trois* "raised to its height what the colder spirits of the time were pleased to call the *Ceritomania.*"

The Times' critic observes of *Alma*: "There is nothing weak about it—there is no appearance of vamping up: all is fresh, new, and glittering, and it seems the inventor of the ballet (M. Deshayes), the inventors of the *pas* (Cerito and Perrot), the scene-painter (Grieve), and the composer (Costa) had all set their very superior wits together to produce a work that should be perfectly complete in its kind."

The same critic describes the *Pas de Fascination* thus:

"Quickly does she go through the waltz step—there is a calm resolution in her glance—she has determined on victory. But the dance has its effect on herself—she warms with it, she becomes energetic, and fresh fire is infused into her at every blow which Perrot strikes on her tambourine. The girls become delighted, the dancer leads them on, and thus is formed the *Pas de Fascination.*"

Of the *Pas de Trois* in the third act *The Times* remarks: "There seemed to be no limit to the number of elegant attitudes into which Cerito dropped, sometimes supported by M. Desplaces, and sometimes appearing balanced in air. There is a certain look of

Cerito in these slow movements, a certain tenderness of expression, that gives them a character that is attained by no other *danseuse* whatsoever. Every group in the slow movement of this *Pas de Trois* told well, and met with marked applause. Of course it was followed by a quick movement, and Cerito raised fresh acclamation by one of her brilliant revolving steps."

ONDINE OU LA NAIADE

Ballet in 6 Scenes. Book: Jules Perrot and Fanny Cerito. Music: Cesare Pugni. Scenery: W. Grieve. Choreography: Jules Perrot and Fanny Cerito. First produced: Her Majesty's Theatre, London, June 22nd, 1843.

CHARACTERS

Ondine	MLLE. FANNY CERITO
Hydrola	MME. COPÈRE
Matteo, a young fisherman . . .	M. JULES PERROT
Theresa, his mother	MME. CAMILLE
Giannina, an orphan, betrothed to Matteo	MLLE. GUY-STEPHAN

Villagers, Peasant-Girls, Ondines, Naiads, etc.

Scene I. A portion of the sea shore on the coast of Sicily, with a huge arched rock in the background.

At the rise of the curtain the peasants and fisher-folk are seen making preparations for the Festival of the Madonna. Matteo, a young fisherman, is present with Giannina, his betrothed, and he invites his friends to the wedding, to be held on the morrow. Giannina is overwhelmed with congratulations which end in a general dance. Then all depart, save Matteo, who wishes to catch a fish for his supper.

He casts his net and draws it to the shore. As he does so a shell rises from the water. It contains a lovely being who has often haunted his dreams. The Naiad, who is called Ondine, has fallen in love with Matteo, and has chosen this means of making her presence known to him.

Matteo, however, loves Giannina, and resists the tempting Naiad. But she fascinates him in a dance so that he follows her along the shore and up the rock until, arrived at the highest point, she drops gently downwards into the waters, her arms outstretched towards him, inviting the infatuated Matteo to follow.

Regardless of danger, he is about to do so, when some peasants enter and save him. Their intervention breaks the spell and he kneels and offers a prayer of thanksgiving for his escape.

Scene II. Matteo's cottage.

Theresa and Giannina anxiously await the return of Matteo, who presently enters, musing on his recent adventure. Giannina soothes away his melancholy and both she and his mother try to fathom its cause. He tells them of the Naiad, but his mother dismisses the matter as a day dream. Then she sits down to her spinning wheel, and Giannina, taking up a skein of silk, gives it to Matteo to hold, while she winds it.

A sudden gust of wind blows the window open and Ondine bounds into the room. Jealous of Matteo's attention to his future bride, she snaps the thread which Giannina is winding and strikes the distaff from his mother's hand. Then the Naiad makes herself visible to Matteo. Dazzled by her rare beauty he vainly pursues her. She is next discovered by Giannina, who also tries to secure the Naiad, but she darts to the window, and leaps through it into the water beneath, inviting Matteo to follow.

He is withheld by Giannina, who reproaches him for his inconstancy on the eve of their wedding. But his mother restores the situation and retires with Giannina, while Matteo flings himself down on his simple couch.

The Naiad, determined to possess Matteo, resolves to reveal to him in a dream something of the lovely world beneath the sea.

Scene III. A submarine cavern peopled with nymphs in pale blue, their hair unbound and adorned with branches of coral.

Ondine rises in their midst and dances a *pas de six*. Believing she has secured Matteo's affection, she lies at his feet.

At this moment Hydrola, Queen of the Waters, appears. She warns her daughter against the fleeting existence of mortals, to which Ondine replies by plucking a rose and declaring that she would willingly perish *with* and *as* it, were Matteo hers alone. In vain does the Queen chide her daughter, the wilful Naiad is resolute and is most reluctantly led away from the sleeping fisherman.

Scene IV. The eve of the Festival of the Madonna, whose statue is in a shrine, and at whose feet the assembled peasants place their gifts and offer their prayers.

After prayers the company join in a tarantella in which "all is wild, animated, and in picturesque disorder, and the colours of the various dresses, rapidly intermingled, flash upon the eyes most brilliantly." Suddenly the dance is interrupted by the bells for vespers, when the dancers kneel and join in the evening prayer.

While the fisher-folk are at their devotions, Ondine rises from a fountain near the shrine and attracts the attention of Matteo who, springing to his feet, vainly pursues her in and out of the maze formed by the kneeling throng. But Giannina perceives her lover's agitation and brings him back to his devotions. He gazes on the face of the Madonna which suddenly changes to the features of the Naiad. An instant later Ondine disappears.

The prayer ended, the dance is resumed until sunset when the peasants retire, leaving Matteo and Giannina to themselves. They, too, make preparations for departure and Matteo goes to unmoor his boat to row her home.

Meanwhile, the wicked Ondine contrives to lure Giannina into the water. As she vanishes from sight, the Naiad, having stolen the form of Giannina, leaps exultingly to the shore.

The moon rises. The light is strong enough for the Naiad to see her shadow, which fills her with wonder "She first thinks it to be her rival, who pursues her; but soon she finds it is one token of her mortality, and then return, in her assumed form, all the caprice, vivacity, and joyousness of her naiad temperament."

When Matteo arrives with his boat, the Naiad has assumed Giannina's cloak and hat. She takes her place and is rowed across the stream, while the real Giannina is seen beneath the water, borne by naiads to the palace of Queen Hydrola.

Scene V. Giannina's bed-chamber.

The Naiad is asleep in Giannina's bed; the alarmed Hydrola watches her sadly. Presently Ondine opens her eyes and the Queen vanishes.

Already the Naiad feels weak and exhausted. She seeks strength in prayer. Hydrola reappears and urges her daughter to relinquish her mortality before it is too late, but she obstinately refuses. The Queen vanishes.

Matteo and his mother enter and now the lovers dance the *Pas de la Rose Flétrie,* a tarantella in which Ondine, wearied by dancing, continually strives to overcome that exhaustion. The fisherman, believing Ondine to be Giannina, is sorrowful at the thought that he must wed an ailing bride, for whose sake he has renounced an immortal.

Scene VI. The Wedding.

The scene opens with the wedding-procession. The Naiad, hardly able to support herself, advances with difficulty, assisted by Matteo.

Hydrola and her attendant naiads make one last effort to rescue Ondine. The Queen has restored Giannina to life and now leads her forward. Matteo recovers his true love and is happy once more, while the wayward Naiad resumes her immortal state and is borne in triumph by the Queen and her subjects to her home beneath the sea.

*

Ondine, despite its title, has little in common with De la Motte Fouqué's *Undine.* The ballet is principally associated with the charming conception of the *Pas de l'Ombre,* made famous by the interpretation of Fanny Cerito.

The Times' critic styles *Ondine* a ballet "unrivalled for the magnificence of its decorations, but certainly not equal to *Giselle* in beauty of idea, nor to *Alma,* in novel and characteristic features. It is, in fact, a work completely produced, rather than a complete work." [2]

Pugni's music is said to be "singularly appropriate, quite descriptive, and adds a charm to the perfection of the ballet. In the scene where the young fisherman, Matteo, is conveyed into the depths of the river, and the ondines dance their many fascinations around him, the musical accompaniments which describe the rise and fall of the waves are eminently characteristic and beautiful: the very ripple of the flow, and the rushing sound of the ebb over the pebbly strand, are heard, and fully satisfy the ear." [3]

Some impression of Cerito as Ondine may be gained from the following prose pictures, taken from *The Times.* The first describes the *pas de six* at the beginning of Matteo's dream of the kingdom beneath the waters; the second, the *Pas de l'Ombre.*

"Cerito rises . . . and dances a *pas de six* with St. Léon, Camille, Scheffer, Galby, and Bernard. The slow movement is a pretty shawl dance of somewhat a novel description, and a pleasing effect is produced by the shawls being waved before Cerito while dropping into her serious attitudes with St. Léon, and thus forming a kind of undulating mist. In the quick movement St. Léon was wonderful, flinging back his legs as he bounded in the air, in a manner which we have never seen before. Cerito introduced many

[2] January 23rd.
[3] *Beauties of the Opera and Ballet.*

of her brilliant steps in this dance . . . but altogether there was a want of unity in the *pas,* and although composed by Cerito, it is by no means equal to the *pas de trois* which she invented for *Alma.*

"The mountains in the background, which shone with the light of day, become red with the tints of sunset, and at last the moon rises, and a full blue light is thrown upon the stage. This is strong enough to show the shadow of Cerito, who having assumed substantial form for the first time, views the outline of herself with wonder. The *Pas de l'Ombre* in which she wildly dances to the shadow, and tries to catch it, is one of those things which none but Cerito could do. The conception is charming, and we only regret the *pas* is not somewhat longer."

*

Ondine, with Grisi in the leading role, was produced under the title of *The Naiad and the Fisherman* at St. Petersburg in 1851. On July 11/23 of the same year, which was the name day of the Grand Duchess Olga Nikolaevna, a Gala Performance was given at Peterhov in the open air. On this occasion the ballet was produced by Perrot on a specially-built platform, raised just above the surface of the water, in the lake by the Ozerky Pavilion. The naiads glided to the platform in boats shaped like shells. The natural scenery of the trees, with the addition of a few tropical plants, made a charming setting. The weather was fine and a beautiful moon shone down upon the scene.

LA ESMERALDA

Ballet in 3 Acts and 5 Scenes. Book: Jules Perrot. Music: Cesare Pugni. Scenery: W. Grieve. Machinery: D. Sloman. Costumes: Mme. Copère. Choreography: Jules Perrot. First produced: Her Majesty's Theatre, London, March 9th, 1844.

CHARACTERS

La Esmeralda	MLLE. CARLOTTA GRISI
Fleur de Lys, betrothed to Phœbus . .	MLLE. ADELAIDE FRASSI
Mme. Aloise de Gondelaurier, her mother	MME. COPÈRE
Diane }Companions of Fleur	{ MLLE. FERDINAND
Beranger } de Lys . . .	{ MLLE. BARVILLE
Phœbus de Chateaupers	M. SAINT-LÉON
Claude Frollo	M. GOSSELIN

Pierre Gringoire, the poet . . . M. Jules Perrot

Quasimodo, the bell-ringer of Notre }
  Dame . . . . } M. Coulon

Clopin Trouillefou . . . . . . M. Gouriet

Truands . . . . Mm. Venafra, Baras-
                                 chini, and Bertram

The action passes at Paris in the 15th century.

Act I. The Cour des Miracles. Sunset.

At the rise of the curtain the stage is seen thronged with Truands. Their monarch, Clopin, seated upon a board, presides over this unruly assembly. While the mad gaiety is at its height, a poet, Pierre Gringoire, rushes to the feet of Clopin, pursued by a party of marauding Truands. Clopin bids him rise, but the poet shrinks to the earth when he perceives that he is in the terrible Cour des Miracles. The savage Truands proceed to go through his pockets, but his sole possession is a much loved poem. Clopin, indignant at this discovery, sentences Gringoire to be hanged.

In vain does he plead for pity. His anguish provokes laughter alone, when the king recalls a law which permits any woman who chooses, to marry to respite the sentence. He calls forward his female subjects; they examine the poet and unanimously reject him. Mad with fear Gringoire casts himself at their feet, but in vain. At this moment a stifled clamour announces the arrival of Esmeralda.

Bounding lightly among the crowd, she passes before Gringoire and at once comprehends the meaning of his agony. Touched by his position, she consents to wed him. The poet is overjoyed at his escape from death. An earthen pot is brought in, which Esmeralda presents to Gringoire, bidding him cast it on the ground. As the vessel shatters into fragments Clopin bestows his blessing upon the young gypsy and her husband, who join in the dances with which the marriage is celebrated.

The sound of the curfew breaks upon the general joy and the crowd suddenly disperses. During the latter part of the dance, Claude Frollo has been watching Esmeralda, who has shrunk from his gaze. He takes Clopin aside and tells him that he is passionately in love with the young Truand, and that she must be his that night. Clopin consents and informs him that she is about to pass through the Cour des Miracles. Frollo summons Quasimodo, and they conceal themselves. A gentle footstep is heard, Esmeralda appears, and Claude springs upon his prey. As she struggles with Claude and Quasimodo, the march of the Patronelle Guard is heard. Phœbus enters at the head of his troop, Frollo escapes, and Quasimodo is seized by the archers.

Freed from danger, Esmeralda approaches Phœbus and gazes at him with a curious admiration. Struck by her beauty the Captain questions her, and learns that she is an orphan; while engaged in this recital she plays with the end of his scarf. Phœbus gives it to her, but, as she receives it, her gaze is attracted by the unfortunate Quasimodo. She intercedes for the prisoner, and, seeing him ready to faint, takes a gourd from her girdle that he may drink. Phœbus orders the archers to release the hunchback, who retires with his eyes fixed upon his benefactress.

Now the Captain asks Esmeralda for a kiss in exchange for his submission to her wishes. She recoils and asks him to take back his scarf; Phœbus refuses and pursues her. She slips from his arms and takes to flight. The disappointed soldier places himself again at the head of his troop.

Act II. Scene I. A small vaulted chamber, with a little couch, a table, and a chair.

Esmeralda enters, gazing sadly upon the scarf Phœbus gave her. She seats herself at the table and, taking some ivory letters, forms them into the name of Phœbus, which she contemplates with love. While she is deep in sweet thoughts, Gringoire enters. He gazes on his wife with admiration, imagining that her love for him is the cause of her abstraction.

He advances with an air of timid triumph and passes his arm round her waist, but she shrinks from him. He pursues her, but when on the point of again seizing her, he sees the blade of a dagger glittering before his eyes. It is now his turn to shriek. Esmeralda explains that she only married him out of pity; he may become her companion and accompany her in her street dances, if he wishes, but no more. He consents and they practise a dance. But, in spite of the pleasure with which Gringoire watches the girl sweeping through the dance, the excitement of the day makes him desire rest. Esmeralda leads him to a chamber, and he retires with an air of disappointed resignation.

Alone, Esmeralda throws herself upon her couch. Scarcely has she done so, than Frollo enters the room. Quasimodo remains motionless upon the threshold. The girl rises hurriedly to call Gringoire. Frollo kneels and implores her to listen to his passion. She bids him leave her; and, showing him the name of Phœbus, tells him that she loves the soldier.

Enraged, Frollo rushes towards the girl, who shrinks at his feet and begs him to have pity on her. Quasimodo does not intervene, although gratitude urges him to do so; but Frollo turns for a moment to see that the door of Gringoire's chamber is fastened, and Esmeralda seizes the opportunity to escape through a secret entrance. As Frollo follows, the door of Gringoire's room is burst open. Claude threatens to stab him if he dare approach. Quasimodo stays his arm and swears vengeance on Phœbus.

Act II. Scene II. The garden of the Gondelaurier mansion, with the preparations for the marriage of Fleur de Lys and Phœbus.

Fleur de Lys enters, accompanied by her bridesmaids, two of whom bear baskets of flowers. Fleur de Lys occupies herself with her companions in making garlands for the festival. Madame de Gondelaurier enters and all curtsy to her. Fleur de Lys runs to her mother and shows her the preparations she has made.

Phœbus de Chateaupers appears. He kisses the hand of his betrothed with an air of indifference, and Fleur de Lys perceives that he is no longer wearing the scarf she had embroidered for him. The guests arrive and the festival begins.

Esmeralda comes to dance, accompanied by Gringoire, who carries her guitar and tambourine. Fleur de Lys is astonished at Esmeralda's beauty and strange costume and speaks to her. The dancer tells her that she can read the future and predicts happiness for the forthcoming marriage. Delighted, the bride gives her a ring and induces her to dance. When she is about to commence she notices the troubled glance of Phœbus who, forgetting the presence of his betrothed, asks her to dance with him. Her love overcomes her prudence and she delights in the presence of her beloved.

Astonished at Phœbus's conduct, Fleur de Lys reproaches him. In his shame he makes some cold protestations to his bride. Esmeralda dances with Gringoire, but, to show Phœbus that she still loves him, she shows him the scarf he had given her. Fleur de Lys springs forward, snatches the scarf from Esmeralda and, reproaching her faithless lover, falls fainting to the ground. She is borne away. Meanwhile Gringoire, protecting Esmeralda from the fury of the guests, leads her off, followed, after a moment's hesitation, by Phœbus.

Act III. Scene I. An apartment in a cabaret, with a window opening on to a river. Night.

Clopin enters with a torch in his hand, followed by Frollo. He points out a hiding place and retires. Frollo draws Esmeralda's dagger and, hearing a noise, conceals himself. Phœbus and Esmeralda appear. The soldier declares his love for her. She asks him how he can love two people at the same time and flings his ring upon the ground. When Phœbus renews his attentions she takes a piece of down from his plume and, blowing it away, tells him that such is his love.

Then, kneeling at his feet, she leans her head on his arm and looks at him with admiration. Frollo, unable to contain his jealousy, springs upon the two lovers, dagger in hand. Phœbus draws Esmeralda into a chamber, but Frollo follows. A blow and a groan are heard, then the fall of a body. Frollo rushes out of the room, and, opening the window, disappears. He is followed by Esmeralda who sinks, fainting with terror, upon the floor. Strangers enter the cabaret. Clopin goes into the chamber, returns, states that a murder has been committed, and denounces Esmeralda as the criminal. She is seized and carried away, despite her protests.

Act III. Scene II. The banks of the Seine: a prison to the right, the towers of Notre Dame in the distance.

Esmeralda is conducted to prison by archers and preceded by Frollo. A crowd follows her. Soon Gringoire enters. He listens before the prison gate and is horrified as he hears the girl condemned to death. He addresses the people who are about to break into a tumult, when the procession of the King of the Fools appears. Quasimodo is borne on the shoulders of the Truands. The crowd mingles with the revellers and their rage and pity turn to joy. Frollo, who enters, tears the royal robes from Quasimodo. The prison-doors open and Esmeralda is led to execution. The procession stops for her to bid Gringoire good-bye. She begs that Phœbus's scarf may be buried with her. Frollo approaches the girl and promises to save her if she will marry him. In her anguish she turns away and calls down divine vengeance upon him. As he commands them to lead her on, Phœbus, whose wound was not fatal, appears among the crowd. Esmeralda swoons on seeing him.

Flinging himself on his knees he declares Esmeralda innocent and points out Frollo as the assassin, who is seized by the archers. Esmeralda recovers her senses and sees Phœbus at her feet. Joy lights up her countenance. But the happiness of the two lovers drives Frollo to madness. He rushes forward and tries to stab Esmeralda, but is arrested by Quasimodo who forces the dagger from his hand and plunges it into his breast. The ballet concludes with the crowd rejoicing at Esmeralda's deliverance.

*

La Esmeralda is based on Victor Hugo's well known romance, *Notre Dame de Paris.* *The Times'* critic describes the piece as "a perfect model of ballet building. Never did we see those parts of a long story that might be dramatically effective selected and arranged with such skill as in this ballet. The catastrophe of the novel is altered. The incidents selected are greatly modified, but the tact with which five *tableaux* have been taken out of the romance, and combined into a neat pantomime of action, without a gap, deserves unqualified praise."

Of Grisi as Esmeralda the same writer observes: "In her representation . . . there was something of the innocent playfulness of Cerito—of the arch coquetry of Elssler—and of the quiet poetry of Taglioni. Yet all was so attuned as to produce a perfect representation of the graceful, the tender, the impassioned Esmeralda.

"The achievements she performs in her *pas* frequently astonish less, because she has acquired such a mastery over her art that she can perform them without effort. . . . All the resources of her art were employed dramatically, all were illustrations of the character. The first bound on the stage with the tambourine was the rush of youthful spirits; her tantalizing *pas de deux* with Gringoire was a compound of good humour, a mild sort of malice. She could not help pitying the poor wretch, and yet she was amused at his trouble.

"When alone with her lover—Phœbus, nothing could be more exquisitely managed than her pantomime. The timidity with which she recoiled from him; and which gradually gave way to the overpowering effects of her love, the contest between two feelings, which gradually subsided, was most beautifully managed. . . . Of the despair when Phœbus is stabbed, and Esmeralda is apprehended, Fanny Elssler would have made more. In the highly tragic the German *danseuse* is unapproachable. The tender, the lyrical, is Carlotta's element."

*

La Esmeralda was presented at St. Petersburg in 1848, with Fanny Elssler (Esmeralda), Didier (Quasimodo), Perrot (Gringoire), and Goltz (Frollo). A contemporary informs us that Elssler's miming was so touching in the scene where Esmeralda bids Gringoire farewell and crosses to the scaffold, that many spectators shed tears.

When Elssler gave a farewell performance at Moscow on March 2/14, 1851, at the Bolshoy Theatre, the ballet chosen was *Esmeralda*. The great dancer was accorded a wonderful reception. An eye-witness, Prince Engalytchev, records his impressions thus: "During the first act, 300 bouquets were thrown on the stage. In the second act the sofa for Esmeralda was made of these flowers, with a large bouquet instead of a cushion placed upon it. This act begins with the scene when Esmeralda, dreaming of her beloved Phœbus, writes his name on the wall. In performing this part, the artiste usually pretends to write and then a small, lettered board is shown. Elssler, however, always wrote the word with chalk, in Russian, but that evening she wrote Москва (Moskva) as if to show how she liked this hospitable town. Her action was received with an unheard-of ovation."

La Esmeralda is one of the great dramatic ballets, while the title-role affords splendid opportunities for the artist dancer-mime. Curiously enough, the ballet has been much neglected in France, Italy, and England, yet it has been constantly performed with success in Russia, where it still figures in the present repertory. Among the numerous successors to Grisi may be cited F. Elssler, M. S. Petipa, Lebedeva, Rosati, Bogdanova, Cucchi, E. P. Sokolova, Grantsova, Zucchi,[4] and Kshesinskaya.

EOLINE OU LA DRYADE

Ballet in 6 Scenes. Book: Jules Perrot. Music: Cesare Pugni. Choreography: Jules Perrot. First produced: Her Majesty's Theatre, London, March 8th, 1845.

CHARACTERS

Rubezhal, the Gnome	MM. Jules Perrot
Edgar, betrothed to Eoline . . .	Toussaint
The Duke, brother to Eoline . . .	Gosselin
Woodcutters	{ Venafra Gouriet
Eoline, the Dryad	Mlle. Lucile Grahn

A Prince of Silesia loved, and was loved in return by, a wood nymph, whose existence depended on that of a magnificent oak tree. A daughter blessed their union; but, shortly after her birth,

[4] Svetlov regarded her interpretation of Esmeralda as the finest of her dramatic portraits.

the tree was shattered by a thunderbolt, and the roots torn up by the whirlwind. From that moment the Dryad appeared no more; but a slip of the tree had taken root, and as it expanded in strength and beauty, so grew the fair child, her daughter, into exceeding loveliness; her life, like her Dryad mother's, dependent on that of the tree beneath whose shade she loved to sit.

The Prince soon fell a martyr to his grief, bearing with him to the grave the strange secret of his child's birth. It was unknown to all, including herself, and, as years rolled on, the fame of her charms spread far and wide; the castle was crowded by claimants for her hand. One only found favour with the lovely Princess, Edgar was his name, and the day was fixed for her nuptials.

Strange rumours, however, were circulated. The castle was said to be haunted by spirits obedient to Eoline's command. In the dark avenues of her park, phantoms were seen to wander, and when the moon spread her silver mantle abroad, a fairy form resembling that of the fair chatelaine, was seen to come forth from an oak tree in the park, and sport in the woods, or float on the lake.

The lovely girl laughed with her guests at their wild tales. Ignorant of her supernatural origin, she was not conscious that, when the shades of evening fell, her spirit, unrobed of its earthly mantle, and assuming the form of a Dryad, gave rise to them.

Eoline's nuptial day approaches, but other spirits than those of the gentle Dryads are in league to oppose her union with Count Edgar. She is loved by Rubezahl, Prince of the Gnomes. This demon-sprite exerts all his magic power to obtain her, but, finding his efforts in vain, he, on her wedding day, sets fire to Eoline's oak tree. She dies; but in her Dryad form yet waves one last adieu to the unhappy Edgar.

*

Eoline is founded on the story of Libussa by Musäus. "Libussa," asserts *The Times*, "is a mythic personage in the early history of Bohemia, and is supposed to have been the daughter of a Dryad and a sage named Crocus, who was a kind of Lycurgus among a rude people. The Dryad perished with the oak to which she was attached, this being the condition of her existence, and Crocus afterwards dying of old age, Libussa succeeded her father in the government of Bohemians, being elected by the popular voice in preference to her two sisters, and displayed the wisdom she inherited from her supernatural mother. The people being soon dissatisfied with female government, she married Premeslaus, and ruled her people in his name."

Perrot has introduced into the story of Libussa an evil element in the person of Rubezahl, who appears in another tale by Musäus. Rubezahl is a gnome who is supposed to haunt the Reisengebirge.

"The ballet wants compression," observes The Times,[5] "but there is more novelty and originality about it than in any work of the sort that has appeared for some time. The constructor has caught the spirit of the tale, and has been most' fertile in his expedients for illustrating the position, half human, half supernatural, of Eoline. His 'effects' show poetical and original innovation, and are complete departures from the beaten track.

"The faint transparent figure which is seen to glide along the waters to Eoline's palace at daybreak, and which represents her returning from her natural sports as a Dryad, beautifully indicates the subject of the story which is to follow. The sense of the shadowy and uncertain is preserved throughout.

"The wood, the haunt of the Dryads, is brought before us by no vulgar method. The trunks of the trees and the highest branches become semi-transparent, and female forms are seen through them by a sort of flickering light. This is a charming idea—the best realization of the spiritual that we have seen. The doubtful point between existence and its contrary is exactly hit, and the trees seem animated by a sort of indefinite life, that fades if we would apprehend it. The grouping of the principal Dryads, who occupy the front of the stage during this scene, and form themselves into little knots, to break them again, in a pas d'ensemble, is admirable."

The principal dances in the ballet were the Valse Silesienne, an ensemble; Pas de la Fiancée, danced by Grahn and Touissant; Mazurka d'Extase by Grahn and Perrot; and the Grand Pas des Dryades, by Grahn and the corps de ballet. The greatest success was the Mazurka d'Extase which, according to The Times' critic, "exhibited mental qualities worthy of the greatest names of the profession. The gnome Rubezahl, by a fascinating power, makes Eoline dance with him against her will, and the point of the pas is to show the horror with which she is obliged to perform it. The play of Mlle. Grahn's countenance, denoting repugnance and agony, the struggle to free herself, the despair with which she fell into the arms of her tormentor, were finished to the highest degree. . . . It is the best thing of the sort that has been done since the Valse de Fascination in Alma, and is marked by greater profundity of thought than that.

"Lucile Grahn's personation of the Dryad was, in our estima-

[5] March 10th, 1845.

tion, perfect. . . . Though a *danseuse* capable of performing astonishing feats—witness some of her revolving bounds—there is a quiet air about her that disguises her own merit. The light easy gracefulness of her movements approaches an appearance of nonchalance, and as she does not take her spectators by storm, they are disposed to overlook her consummate skill. . . . The slight figure, the innocent sportiveness of her dancing, the neatness without effort of every step, completely realized the notion of a fairy creation of the most amiable kind."

LE PAS DE QUATRE

Divertissement. Music: Cesare Pugni. Choreography: Jules Perrot. First produced: Her Majesty's Theatre, London, July 12th, 1845.

ARTISTS

MARIE TAGLIONI
CARLOTTA GRISI
FANNY CERITO
LUCILE GRAHN

Among the many important engagements made for the opera season of 1845 by Benjamin Lumley, director of Her Majesty's Theatre, were arrangements for the appearances of four great *danseuses:* Marie Taglioni, Carlotta Grisi, Fanny Cerito, and Lucile Grahn. With such great talents at his command, he conceived the daring plan "to unite them all in one striking *divertissement.*"

Lumley has recorded in his *Reminiscences*[6] the successive stages in the progress and achievement of his ambitious conception, which it is of interest to quote. "No one," he confesses, "could be more aware than myself of the difficulties I should have to encounter. The government of a great state was but a trifle compared to the government of such subjects as those whom I was *supposed* to be able to command; for these were subjects who considered themselves far above mortal control, or, more properly speaking, each was a queen in her own right—alone, absolute, supreme! . . .

"Material obstacles were easily overcome. When it was feared that Carlotta Grisi would not be able to leave Paris in time to rehearse and appear for the occasion, a vessel was chartered from the Steam Navigation Company to waft the sylph at a moment's notice across the channel; a special train was engaged and ready at Dover; relays of horses were in waiting to aid the flight of the *danseuse,* all the way from Paris to Calais. . . .

"In the execution of the project the difficulties were again manifold. Every twinkle of each foot in every *pas* had to be nicely weighed in the balance, so as to give no preponderance. Each *danseuse* was to shine in her peculiar style and grace to the last stretch of perfection; but no one was to outshine the others— unless in their own individual belief. Lastly, the famous *pas de quatre* was 'composed' with all the art of which the distinguished ballet-master, Perrot, was capable. . . .

"All was at length adjusted. Satisfaction was in every mind; the *pas de quatre* was rehearsed—was announced; the very morning of the event had arrived. . . . Suddenly, while I was engaged with lawyers . . . poor Perrot rushed unannounced into my presence in a state of intense despair. Without regard for the serious conclave assembled, he uttered frantic exclamations, tore his hair, and at last found breath to say that all was over—that the *pas de quatre* had fallen to the ground and never could be given! . . . The explanation came, as follows:

"When all was ready I had desired Perrot to regulate the order in which the separate *pas* of each *danseuse* should come. The place of honour, the *last* in such cases (as in regal possessions), had been ceded without over-much hesitation to Mademoiselle Taglioni. Of the remaining ladies who claimed equal rights, founded on talent and popularity, neither would appear before the other. '*Mon dieu!*' exclaimed the ballet-master in distress, '*Cerito ne veut pas commencer avant Carlotta—ni Carlotta avant Cerito, et il n'y a pas moyen de les faire bouger; tout est fini!*'

" 'The solution is easy,' said I to poor Perrot. 'The question of talent must be decided by the public. But in this dilemma there is one point on which I am sure the ladies will be frank. Let the oldest take her unquestionable right to the envied position.'

"The ballet-master smote his forehead, smiled assent, and bounded from the room upon the stage. The judgment of the manager was announced. The ladies tittered, laughed, drew back, and were now as much disinclined to accept the right of position as they had been before eager to claim it. The *ruse* succeeded. The management of the affair was left in Monsieur Perrot's hands. The order of the ladies being settled, the *grand pas de quatre* was finally performed on the same night before a delighted audience, who little knew how nearly they had been deprived of their expected treat."

The success of this unique *Pas* was immense, in the fullest sense of the word. "The theatre was crowded to suffocation," recalls Lumley, "not only on the first, but on every night when it was given." It was the one universal topic of the day; even ambassadors described the *Pas* at length in their dispatches. *The Times* styles the *Pas de Quatre* "the greatest Terpsichorean exhibition that ever was known in Europe—we repeat the phrase—that ever was known in Europe." The *Illustrated London News* acclaims the *divertissement* as "an event unparalleled in theatrical annals, and one which, some two score years hence, may be handed down to a new generation by garrulous septuagenarians as one of the most brilliant reminiscences of days gone by."

Something of the appearance and reception of the *divertissement* may be gleaned from the following two accounts by eye-witnesses. The first is by the critic of the *Illustrated London News*,[7] the second by that of *The Times*.[8]

"Every other feeling was merged in admiration when the four great dancers commenced the series of picturesque groupings with which this performance opens. We can safely say we have never witnessed a scene more perfect in all its details. The greatest of painters, in his loftiest flights, could hardly have conceived, and certainly never executed, a group more faultless and more replete with grace and poetry than that formed by these four *danseuses*; Taglioni in the midst, her head thrown backwards, apparently reclining in the arms of her sister nymphs. Could such a combination have taken place in the ancient palmy days of art, the pencil of the painter and the song of the poet would have alike been employed to perpetuate its remembrance. No description can render the exquisite, the almost ethereal, grace of movement and attitude of these great dancers, and those who have witnessed the scene, may boast of having once, at least, seen the perfection of the art of dancing so little understood. There was no affectation, no apparent exertion or struggle for effect on the part of these gifted *artistes*; and though they displayed their utmost resources, there was a simplicity and ease, the absence of which would have completely broken the spell they threw around the scene.

"Of the details of this performance it is difficult to speak. In the *solo* steps executed by each *danseuse,* each in turn seemed to claim pre-eminence. Where every one in her own style is perfect, pecu-

[7] July 19th, 1845.
[8] July 14th, 1845.

liar individual taste alone may balance in favour of one or the other, but the award of public applause must be equally bestowed; and, for our own part, we confess that our *penchant* for the peculiar style, and our admiration for the dignity, the repose, and exquisite grace which characterize Taglioni, and the dancer who has so brilliantly followed the same track (Lucile Grahn), did not prevent our warmly appreciating the charming archness and twinkling steps of Carlotta Grisi, or the wonderful flying leaps and revolving bounds of Cerito. Though, as we have said, each displayed her utmost powers, the emulation of the fair dancers was, if we may trust appearances, unaccompanied by envy.

"Every time a shower of bouquets descended, on the conclusion of a *solo pas* of one or the other of the fair *ballerine,* her sister dancers came forward to assist her in collecting them; and both on Saturday and Tuesday did Cerito offer to crown Taglioni with a wreath which had been thrown in homage to the queen of the dance."

*

"When the curtain rose for the impossible *pas de quatre,* and the marvellous four entered, all in a line, hand holding hand, as a testimony of amity, the house burst forth into a tumult, not only of admiration, but of amazement. . . . All came forward and curtsied—and then, what a portentous pause! The audience were all in expectation as to what would happen under circumstances so unparalleled, and the partisan feeling doubtless worked high in many a bosom! A large shower of yellow papers descended into the pit, apparently from the gallery slips, but whether these contained an epic poem, an ode, or a pastoral drama, in honour of the occasion we are unable to say, not having had the felicity to catch one.

"The slow movement of the *pas* began, and the four ladies formed in a series of groups, matchless for taste and elegance, Taglioni usually occupying the central position. Then came the quick movement with the *variations* . . . now was the question to be decided how each would put forth her strength. Taglioni displayed all her commanding manner, relying much on that advancing step, of which, we believe, she was the inventor, and astonishing by some of her bounds. Lucile Grahn, a disciple of the same school, danced with a breadth and vigour which showed a determination not to be outdone by her elder competitors. Cerito entered into the contest with that revolving step which invariably delights; and Carlotta Grisi, forming a striking contrast, gave a piquant, coquettish sort of *variation,* with her wonted fascination.

"Perrot, the inventor of this wonderful *pas,* conducted it at the wing, and might be seen from the left side of the house. The exertions of the *danseuses* were certainly equalled by his own. He beat time, he fumed, he fidgetted in an agony of zeal, the weight of his own work being heavy to bear. Never was such a *pas* before.

"The excitement which a competition so extraordinary produced in the artists roused them to a pitch of energy which would have been impossible under other circumstances, and hence every one did her utmost, the whole performance being a complete inspiration.

"The manifestation of enthusiasm on the part of the audience was scarcely less remarkable than the manifestation of energy on the part of the artists. The whole long *pas* was danced to a running sound of applause, which, after each variation, swelled to a perfect hurricane, the power of partisanship being added to the weight of general admiration. Bouquets flew from every point, an immense profusion, as each *danseuse* came forward, so that they had to curtsy literally in the midst of a shower of floral gifts. Cerito's wreaths and nosegays were more than she could hold in both her arms. Many of the bouquets were demolished by the fall, and scattered their particles about, so that the front of the stage was almost covered with flower leaves."

*

The *Pas de Quatre* was revived at the same theatre during the season of 1847, Lucile Grahn being replaced by Carolina Rosati, and again the famous *divertissement* achieved a triumph.

CATARINA OU LA FILLE DU BANDIT

Ballet in 3 Acts and 5 Scenes. Book: Jules Perrot. Music: Cesare Pugni. Scenery: Charles Marshall. Choreography: Jules Perrot. First produced: Her Majesty's Theatre, London, March 3rd, 1846.

CHARACTERS

Catarina, the youthful leader of a band
of robbers . . . . . . MLLE. LUCILE GRAHN
Diavolino, her lieutenant . . . M. JULES PERROT
Salvator Rosa, a well-known painter . M. GOSSELIN
Florida, a young Spanish widow, Salvator's *fiancée* . . . . . MME. PETIT-STEPHAN
A Chief Judge . . . . . . M. VENAFRA

An Officer . . . . M. Di Mattia
A Sailor . . . . M. Gouriet
Filipuccio, an inn-keeper . . . . M. Bertrand
Principal Model to Salvator Rosa . . Mlle. L. Taglioni
Judges, Bandits, Citizens, Masks, Salvator Rosa's
Models, etc.

The action passes in the suburbs of Rome during carnival
time, in the middle of the seventeenth century.

*Act I. Scene I. A wild and picturesque place among the hills
near Rome. In the distance are two rocks—connected by a bridge
—between which runs a stream. The rock on the left has steps
cut into it. At different heights caves can be distinguished.*

Salvator Rosa, on one of his hazardous expeditions into the Ap-
ennine Hills, has fallen into the hands of a party of bandits from
the Abruzzi. His pictures are being passed from hand to hand
and are commented on with interest, giving rise to a succession of
groups. The painter, forgetful of danger, sketches the various
types in his note-book.

Enter Catarina, a beautiful girl, who, on the death of her father,
has become the leader of the bandits. She asks Salvator if he is
the author of such beautiful pictures, and, on receiving a reply in
the affirmative, orders his property to be restored to him. The
artist is greatly interested in Catarina and entreats her to renounce
her dangerous mode of living and go with him. But she declines
to forsake her companions. Salvator repeats his proposal and, not
entirely adverse to the suggestion, she begins to dance.

The clamour brings forth Diavolino, her lieutenant, who has
just returned from Rome. He offers her various trinkets which he
has pilfered, and which she accepts with shyness.

Surprised at her manner, Diavolino tells how he observed an
officer separated from his men and captured him. He orders the
captive to be brought in for sentence to be passed. The officer asks
to speak with Catarina in secret.

She orders the band to stand back, when the officer produces a
letter from the governor of the province, offering her a pardon if
she will surrender her band to the police. She refuses this des-
picable proposal. Salvator tries to make her agree, and, when
she again declines, the officer points out that her little band cannot
hope to withstand a superior number of troops. But she refuses
to alter her decision.

She gives a signal and women and girls armed with muskets

dash in. Then Catarina asks Salvator to be present at a spectacle she has organized in his honour. At her command they dance the *Pas Stratégique,* in which she joins them. In this *pas* the Amazons represent guerilla warfare. First, general merriment and preparations for battle; then the attempt to surprise the enemy; the general attack; the defence; and the retreat. Several mountaineers descend the hills and begin to dance the Saltarella.

During this dance Catarina and Salvator cannot escape the jealous glances of Diavolino. Catarina, observing her lieutenant's anger and fearing a fight, begins to dance the Romanesca. During this gay measure she contrives to turn his anger to delight.

At this moment Catarina is warned of the approach of a band of soldiers. Salvator urges her to accept the proffered terms, but she swears to fight to the death. Orders are given and immediately obeyed. The officer is placed out of the line of fire and the bandits prepare to surprise the enemy. Catarina urges Salvator to leave, but he determines to remain and protect her from danger. She thanks him with a tender look.

Soldiers appear on the hills, cross the bridge, and slowly descend one of the rocks. As they descend, fighting begins (this is heard, but not seen). A little later Catarina appears accompanied by Salvator, who urges her to go with him, but she replies that if victory is not possible she would rather die with her followers. Salvator confesses his love for her and declares that he could not live if she were to be killed. Catarina is moved and does not know what to do.

Salvator, profiting by her indecision, takes her with him into the hills, across the bridge. Then she cuts the bridge with an axe to prevent pursuit. Soldiers see the fugitives and open fire, but Salvator throws himself in front of Catarina and receives the shot intended for her. He falls wounded into her arms.

At the same moment Diavolino surprises the soldiers and puts them to flight. Only then does he see Catarina, and, realizing her danger, runs to her aid. He clears the abyss at a bound and forcibly takes her away, despite her wish to defend Salvator. The bandits, forsaken by their leader, are everywhere defeated and made prisoners.

Act I. Scene II. The hall of an hotel in a suburb of Rome. In the background is a window through which can be seen a village. There is a side-door, tables, furniture, etc.

The day is just breaking when the quiet is interrupted by an imperious knock at the door. The inn-keeper opens it. Catarina

and Diavolino enter and quickly close the door, for they are in
fear of pursuit. The inn-keeper, disliking the appearance of his
visitors, is minded to give the alarm. But Diavolino follows him
to the door and threatens to pistol him if he leaves the hall. The
inn-keeper, terrified, recoils near Catarina who likewise threatens
him with a pistol, and at the same time proffers a bag of money.

The inn-keeper asks his guests what they desire. "Shelter," replies Diavolino, "a change of clothes, and silence." The inn-keeper
takes the money and shows Catarina into a room.

There is another knock and Filipuccio, at Diavolino's order,
goes to the door. It is a page from the Duke di Col-Albano[9] who
desires a collation, which the inn-keeper busies himself in preparing.

Diavolino also wishes a change of dress. Seeing one of the inn
servants, he compares his height, then smilingly suggests he should
order a bottle of wine and asks him to play a game of cards with
him. The servant agrees and the bandit takes him into an adjoining room so that he can carry out his plan.

The hotel is just open to the public when a masked woman runs
in, pursued by the Duke di Col-Albano and his friends. They insist on her unmasking, but she refuses and tries to evade them.
The Duke tries to snatch off her mask but at this moment Salvator appears. Seeing the artist the domino implores his protection.
Salvator consents and on approaching her tormentors recognizes
the Duke, his patron, who is delighted to meet his favourite
painter. The Duke introduces him to his friends and asks about
his travels.

Salvator tells him of his adventures and how he risked his life
in defence of a beautiful woman. This account is nervously followed by the domino who, on hearing his last words, swoons into
a chair. Everyone goes to her aid and raises her mask. Salvator
is surprised to see that she is a Spanish widow whom he loved
before he met Catarina.

Florida recovers consciousness and forgets the unpleasantness
caused by the Duke in her joy at seeing her lover. The Duke begs
her forgiveness and invites her to join in the repast which he orders
to be served. The inn-keeper informs him that all is ready in an
adjoining room.

Diavolino enters wearing the servant's clothes. Salvator recog-

<hr>

[9] There is a slight discrepancy in the cast as compared with the characters in the
synopsis. The cast is that of the first performance, the synopsis is based on a later
Russian script, which, it will be observed, includes one character, the Duke di Col-
Albano, who does not appear in the original cast.

nizes the bandit and asks him where Catarina is. Diavolino pretends that he does not understand. At this moment Catarina herself appears, dressed as an inn-servant. The lovers are delighted to meet again, but Diavolino evinces intense displeasure. Salvator gives a warning glance to Catarina and follows his friends. Diavolino warns her that soldiers are approaching with their captives.

Several soldiers enter the hotel for refreshment, others remain outside on guard. At the sight of her captured comrades Catarina is sad and plans to free them. Sure that she will not be recognized she jokes with the soldiers. One of them finds a mandoline on the table and begins to strum it. Catarina takes the instrument from him and begins to play with such emotion that Salvator is attracted to her side. Diavolino watches the pair with increasing jealousy. He reminds Catarina of the sad fate of her comrades, and she determines to risk her life for their sake. She dances a Saltarella which creates such enthusiasm that the soldiers guarding the prisoners creep in one by one to watch the proceedings. Diavolino takes the opportunity to free the prisoners and signs to Catarina that her plan has succeeded. He joins in the dancing and the soldiers, carried away by the compelling rhythm, fling themselves into the dance.

Meanwhile the inn is surrounded by another body of soldiers under the command of the officer captured by Diavolino. Seeing him enter, Catarina fears to be recognized and implores Salvator to save her. The artist, seeing the Duke come to inquire into the uproar, passes Catarina to him. The Duke leads her out of the hall.

The officer orders the inn to be searched and noticing Salvator asks him if he has seen the leader of the bandits. He shakes his head. Diavolino, in attempting to escape, is caught.

The Duke comes in with Catarina wearing Florida's domino and is allowed to pass. Florida and the Duke's friends also leave. Diavolino breaks from his guards and, leaping through the window, dashes after Catarina whom he has recognized under her mask. The curtain falls on a scene of wild confusion.

Act II. A hall in the palace of the Duke di Col-Albano, Rome, which Salvator is permitted to use as a studio. Here and there are paintings, some completed, others half-finished. Several canvases depict picturesque sites in the Abruzzi. A large full-size portrait represents Catarina as leader of the banditti. The studio is thronged with students who admire the master's works, others practise a menuet with music, others fence with foils.

Florida comes to see her fiancé and his absence grieves her. The students go in search of the artist. Left alone she examines the paintings and finds one covered with a cloth, which she finds to be the portrait of a beautiful woman unknown to her.

Catarina enters, breathing heavily, and sits on a chair. Observing Florida she entreats her aid, for she fears that she will be captured. Florida promises to help her, then recognizes her as the original of the portrait. Still doubting, she takes her into an adjoining room.

Now comes the Duke arm-in-arm with Salvator and followed by his friends. All admire the new picture. The Duke makes love to Florida, but she disdains his advances and goes to Salvator. She tells the artist that he seems to love her no longer. He swears that she is mistaken and gives her a miniature of himself. A little appeased she suggests a grouping which appeals to the artist.

At a sign from Florida, models dressed as mythological characters enter the studio. While Salvator is planning the group, Florida brings Catarina, dressed as Venus, from the room, and introduces her into the centre of the group. The artist steps back to view the composition as a whole and is astonished to see Catarina, who is equally surprised to see him. But he signs to her not to move as he is conscious of Florida's jealous eyes upon him.

Florida, her suspicions confirmed, flings down the miniature. The Duke tries to soothe her, but she disdains his sympathy. Salvator, deceived by Florida's outward calm, composes another group. Catarina, now carefree, does not notice the grief she has occasioned Florida, and is delighted to take part in Salvator's compositions. The groups change more quickly and the serious work concludes with a number of dances.

After the dancing Catarina perceives the discarded miniature. She picks it up and presses it to her lips. At this moment the officer appears, accompanied by a party of soldiers. Salvator hides the fugitive, but Florida, mad with jealousy, betrays her hiding-place. The artist tells the widow that he never wishes to see her again.

Catarina asks the officer to grant her a few moments' respite. She asks Florida to pardon her for the grief she has brought upon her and begs that she may retain the miniature, as her rival has the living original. She gives a farewell look to Salvator and leaves. Florida asks Salvator to forgive her, but he turns away and runs after Catarina. The Duke endeavours to calm Florida.

Act III. Scene I. A room in a tower which adjoins the court-

room. In the background is a window overlooking the Tiber. On the right is a door leading to the cell in which Catarina is confined.

Catarina is brought in to hear the judges' decision. They enter and she is informed that she has been condemned to death. The judges bid her confess and prepare for execution. Everyone leaves and she is left with a monk who asks her several questions in a sympathetic manner. She answers calmly and shows the monk the miniature. The monk, unable to conceal his agitation, raises his hood and reveals the features of Salvator.

A noise outside the window stops their conversation. Salvator informs Catarina that a man is coming to save her. At the same moment Diavolino climbs through the window. He tells her that all is ready and that the carnival time is well suited to their plans. Catarina is delighted that she can be with Salvator.

Hearing these words Diavolino sheds bitter tears. He notices the miniature in her hand and, enraged that she should love another, threatens to kill Salvator. But the latter reminds him that every moment is precious. Diavolino fixes a rope-ladder and assists Catarina to climb through the window and descend.

Act III. Scene II. A deserted square in Rome. In the background is the Church of St. Peter, other buildings and ruins. To the right are ancient gates leading to the suburbs.

It is the last day of carnival. The square gradually fills with masked revellers, some dancing, some courting, some gossiping. All is in movement. In the distance is a chariot filled with allegorical persons and surrounded by crowds of people. Presently the crowds move on.

Enter Catarina and Diavolino who have changed their clothes and are seeking refuge among the crowd. Dancing begins in which the maskers join. Catarina, dressed as a magician, searches for Salvator, for she wishes to warn him of the danger he runs. At this moment a mysterious mask, representing a bravo, joins the throng. Catarina recognizes Salvator and warns him that he is in danger. Diavolino, dressed as a devil, draws near the couple. Catarina tears off his mask and reveals the bandit.

The police arrest both the bandits but, just as they are about to be taken away, the Duke appears on the scene and hands the officer a pardon for Catarina. She thanks the Duke on her knees and then embraces Salvator. Florida, realizing the situation, accepts the Duke's proposal of marriage and makes him happy. Meanwhile Diavolino escapes from the police and is lost among the maskers.

*

Catarina is said to be founded on an incident in the life of Salvator Rosa, the famous Italian painter (1615–1673).

A contemporary styles *Catarina* as "a true *ballet d'action;* the story is admirably told, with all the additional effectiveness which picturesque costumes and scenery, and admirable dancing, can bestow."

"The first tableau," observes *The Times'* [10] critic, "showing the whole troop of female brigands dispersed about masses of rock, has a very rich and picturesque effect; and in the scene of the carnival, a sedulous attention to the costume of the motley group has given an aspect of novelty to such a hackneyed thing as a masquerade. The view of Rome, before which this festivity takes place, undergoes various dioramic changes, and the last, when St. Peter's and the other buildings become illuminated, is most magnificent."

Here are two impressions of Lucile Grahn as Catarina, the first is from a Press cutting in the Gabrielle Enthoven Collection, the second is from *The Times.*

"Lucile Grahn is charming in this ballet. Her proud and fearless look; her gestures so natural, and, it might be imagined, unstudied; and her expressive pantomime, inspire even more admiration to us than her wonderful flying leaps, and apparent defiance of the laws of gravitation. . . . The first dance in this ballet, the *Pas Stratégique,* is very peculiar and effective. The military evolutions of the 'female brigands' are highly amusing, and are executed with wonderful precision. There is one movement in which Lucile Grahn bends forward shouldering her gun, and poising herself on her left foot, all her comrades imitating her example, which is extremely graceful. There is something piquant in the contrast between the feminine gentleness and softness of appearance and the abrupt precision of military movement, and the handling of deadly weapons, which has in all times proved successful on the stage.

"The small rapid steps of Grahn, when she commences alone the *Pas de Cinq Tems* [*sic*], are very graceful; but we must confess this dance appears to us, despite the applause it meets with, more novel than pleasing; there is something in the eccentricity of the measure which offends the sense of time.

"Perrot's pantomime in this ballet is, as usual, inimitable. In the scene where he relates his escape from his pursuers, his gestures

[10] March 9th, 1846.

convey a silent description which no language could equal. The music at this moment is also very expressive."

"Lucile Grahn is the sole support of the ballet, and she is brought before the public in a character and costume entirely new. The *Pas Stratégique* which she executes, accompanied by a troop of red-attired bandit damsels, who with muskets on their shoulders dance through a number of evolutions, is the most striking in the piece. Throughout the progress of this *pas*, the character of the female brigand is admirably preserved; the musket is employed to produce various effects, as Lucile Grahn gracefully changes its position, and from time to time drops into a beautiful pose, in which is idealized one of those picturesque attitudes which, painters and statuette-makers tell us, belong to brigand life.

"The grace and vigour with which she goes through the *pas* are obvious to all, and, indeed, 'grace and vigour' are associated with the very name of Lucile Grahn; but it is worth while to watch her countenance as she falls into the successive poses. There is a quiet confident intelligence in her face which shows that she not only executes them as *danseuse*, but understands the situation as an actress.

"The saltarelle, which is a near kin to the tarantelle, and which consists of rapid evolutions, and threatening advances with one foot forwards, towards the male dancer (Perrot), displays the power of Grahn in a style of dancing in which fire and piquancy are the chief requisites.

"The *Pas de Masque*, in which, with the assistance of some *coryphées*, she fascinates the folks at the carnival, is one of those grand *pas* which fully exhibit the capabilities and training of the *danseuse*, and Lucile Grahn passed through the ordeal triumphantly. The force with which she flew across the stage at the commencement of this *pas* was wonderful, and the more so, as it was never obtained at the expense of gracefulness."

Catarina was produced at the Teatro alla Scala, Milan, on January 9th, 1847, with Fanny Elssler in the title-role, and was revived on January 25, 1853, with Sofia Fuoco as the leader of the banditti.

The ballet was given at St. Petersburg in 1849 with Fanny Elssler in the title-role. The ballet achieved a considerable success and was frequently revived. Among other interpreters of the celebrated dramatic role may be mentioned K. Fridberg, M. S. Petipa, C. Cucchi, and E. O. Vazem.

SCENE FROM "LE MARCHÉ DES INNOCENTS"
As presented at Théâtre Impérial de l'Opéra, Paris, 1861

MARIUS PETIPA

SCENE FROM "LE LAC DES CYGNES", ACT II.

As presented by the Vic-Wells Ballet, with Alicia Markova & Robert Helpmann

SCENE FROM "LE LAC DES CYGNES", ACT II.
Revival, as presented by Soviet State Ballet

VERA NEMCHINOVA AND ANATOLE OBUKHOV IN "LE LAC DES CYGNES"

ALEXANDRA DANILOVA AND PAUL PETROV IN "LE LAC DES CYGNES"

SCENE FROM "THE SLEEPING PRINCESS", LAST ACT

From the drawing of Prof. Randolph Schwabe

THE PORCELAIN PRINCESSES
Pas de Deux from "The Sleeping Princess"

RED RIDING HOOD AND THE WOLF
Pas de Deux from "The Sleeping Princess"

SCENE FROM "COPPÉLIA", ACT II. SC. I.
Revival, as presented by Les Ballets de Monte Carlo

NICHOLAS LEGAT

Photo: Vajda M. Pal, Budapest

SCENE FROM "CARNIVAL AT PEST"

MICHEL FOKINE

SCENE FROM "LES SYLPHIDES"
Showing the original setting by Alexandre Benois

THAMAR KARSAVINA IN "LES SYLPHIDES"

Photo: Raoul Barba, Monte Carlo

SCENE FROM "LE CARNAVAL"
Revival, as presented by Les Ballets de Monte Carlo

SCENE FROM "SKYSCRAPERS", ACT I.

SCENE FROM "SCHÉHÉRAZADE"

Revival, as presented by Les Ballets de Monte Carlo

SCENE FROM "PETROUCHKA," SC. IV.
Revival, as presented by Les Ballets de Monte Carlo

Photo: Koosen, Paris

SCENE FROM "LE SPECTRE DE LA ROSE"

VASLAV NIJINSKY IN "LE SPECTRE DE LA ROSE"

THAMAR KARSAVINA IN "PETROUCHKA"

VASLAV NIJINSKY IN "PETROUCHKA"

THAMAR KARSAVINA IN "THAMAR"
From the painting by Glyn Philpot, R.A.

SCENES FROM "LE COQ D'OR"
Revival, as presented by Col. W. de Basil's Ballets Russes

Photo: Van Riel, Buenos Aires

ANNA PAVLOVA IN "LE CYGNE"

ANNA PAVLOVA AND AUBREY HITCHINS IN "AUTUMN LEAVES"

COSTUMES WORN BY SOME OF THE DANCERS IN
"IRON FOUNDRY"
From the sketches by Robert Lee Eskridge

VASLAV NIJINSKY

BRONISLAVA NIJINSKA AND VASLAV NIJINSKY
In a pose from "Prélude à l'Après-Midi d'un Faune"

BRONISLAVA NIJINSKA

Coll. Anton Dolin

SCENE FROM "LES NOCES"

Photograph taken during rehearsal at Monte Carlo. Note the architectural
character of the choreography

LALLA ROOKH OR THE ROSE OF LAHORE

Ballet in 4 Scenes. Book: Jules Perrot. Music: Cesare Pugni.
Scenery: Charles Marshall. Choreography: Jules Perrot. First pro
duced: Her Majesty's Theatre, London, June 11th, 1846.

CHARACTERS

Lalla Rookh	MLLE. FANNY CERITO
The Emperor Aurungzebe, her father	M. VENAFRA
Fadladeen, Grand Nazir	M. PERROT
Aliris, the King of Bucharia. Under the name of Feramorz, the poet . .	M. SAINT-LÉON
His Ambassador	M. DI MATTIA
In Attendance on Lalla Rookh . .	MLLES. DEMILISSE, CASSAN, JAMES, LAMOUREUX, JULIEN, and HONORÉ
Princess of the Court of Bucharia . .	MLLE. LOUISE TAGLIONI

The great Emperor of Hindustan, Aurungzebe, has promised the hand of his lovely daughter in marriage to Aliris, the young King of Bucharia, and the story opens with the approaching departure of the young Princess with her suite, for Cashmere, where she is to meet the youthful monarch, and where the nuptials are to be celebrated. The King of Bucharia has a numerous suite to escort his bride, and among the other attendants is a young poet named Feramorz, renowned for his minstrelsy.

During the journey, the latter has many opportunities of interesting the feelings of the Princess, first, by his exquisite performances and his graceful bearing; and lastly, by the services he renders her when placed in imminent peril by a fearful tempest, during which she is abandoned by the frightened attendants, and owes her life to his devoted care.

It follows that Lalla Rookh bestows her young affections on the poet, despite the watchful vigilance of Fadladeen, the great nazir or chamberlain of the Princess, whose envious feelings are all called into play by the pleasing manners and talents of the young poet, and by the preference testified for him by Lalla Rookh.

The Princess arrives at Cashmere; despite her reluctance and despairing entreaties, she is compelled to fulfil her promise; she is dragged, an unwilling victim, into the presence of the young monarch, to whom she can only give her hand, for her heart is with Feramorz.

But what is her astonishment, when her destined bridegroom comes forth to meet her, to find that it is he who, in the disguise of a simple minstrel, had won her affections, and thus assured himself of the real and constant attachment of his destined bride.

*

Lalla Rookh is inspired by Thomas Moore's well known Oriental romance of the same name. It will be recalled that the journey from Delhi to Cashmere forms the setting of the poems with which Feramorz entertains Lalla Rookh, when the convoy encamps for the night.

The ballet is based on the journey alone, which here begins at Lahore and ends at Cashmere. The episode of the storm does not occur in the romance, and this is presumably introduced as a basis for theatrical spectacle, and as a background for the interpolation of several numbers from Félicien David's *Ode Symphonique of the Desert,* the ballet music proper being by Pugni.

Apart from the structure of the ballet, the poems have contributed to the style-atmosphere; for instance, the festivities of the first scene, and the Feast of Roses, which occurs in the last scene, are derived from "The Light of the Harem."

"The great and striking merit of this ballet," asserts the *Illustrated London News,* "is that all engaged—composers, choreographic and musical, the scene-painter, and the fair Cerito herself —seem to have imbibed the inspiration of the poet. The dances— entirely Indian in character, and in the manner in which they are executed; the music, partly selected from Félicien David's 'Desert,' an Oriental composition *par excellence;* and the scenery, which has all the warm Eastern colouring, and is, moreover, faithful to the descriptions and sketches of travellers to those interesting regions—all are in harmony with the design of the great poet. No expense has been spared to render the mounting of the ballet perfect, and we are assured that, in one scene, there are no less than two hundred dancers on the stage." [11]

The Times acclaims *Lalla Rookh* as "the most splendid ballet since *Alma,*" although it "is not a ballet of dramatic character, not one that calls forth the pantomimic powers of the *danseuse* more than *Alma,* but it is splendid spectacle, with some excellent dances.[12]

[11] June 13th, 1846.
[12] June 12th, 1846.

"The representations of the Oriental courts, the splendour and variety of the costumes, the taste and invention displayed in the novel groupings can scarcely be surpassed. The first scene, especially, with Aurungzebe seated on the throne in the form of a peacock's tail, while over his head is a canopy brought forward in bold relief, and his numerous attendants are gathered before him, presents a picture of the most gorgeous magnificence. The dances also in this scene and the last are beautiful in themselves, and just adapted to the enthusiastic style of Cerito.

"The *Pas Symbolique* of Hindoo girls . . . may be pronounced one of the most elegant scarf dances ever yet contrived, and show what new combinations are possible in a style apparently so hackneyed. The last figure in this *pas,* in which Cerito stands as a statue on a pedestal, and the girls with pink scarfs form a series of steps, is entirely novel in its effect, and admirably conceived." The following is a list of the figures represented in this *pas*: Hermes, The Shell, The Kiosks, The Cage, The Mirrors, The Harp, The Framed Picture, The Morning Breeze, The Stars, The Pineapples, The Car of the Rising Sun, The Butterflies, The Sun's Rays, The Living Statue, and The Pedestal.

The second scene, according to the critic of the *Illustrated London News,* "presents to us the dreary waste across which the Princess and her suite are travelling. Here the well-known 'March of the Caravan' from David's 'Desert' is most happily introduced; the peculiar rhythm and the wild character of this march, give a striking originality to the whole scene—a most novel one for ballet. Then comes on a fearful tempest, and again the 'Storm' of Félicien David magnificently describes the warring of the elements. Then follows the preservation of Lalla Rookh by the devotedness of the poet, and the return of calm. Then we have the wild Arabian air of the Chibouk, played by Feramorz, to the tune of which Cerito executes a striking and peculiar dance, while Fadladeen is sent to sleep by the fumes of his pipe. Then follows the 'Sunrise,' the music of which every amateur remembers with pleasure."

The Times' critic comments on this scene thus: "On the whole, we must say we like the beginning and end of the journey better than the journey itself. . . . We must, indeed, admit that some of the groupings of the travellers were admirably managed. The fall at the approach of the sandstorm, the mass of sleepers at sunrise, were worthy of the genius of Perrot. But there is no dancing in the desert, people carry banners and palanquins, and sleep and wake, but they don't dance."

The Feast of Roses forms the last scene, during which the recognition of the lovers takes place. This is followed by the *Pas de Corbeilles,* in which the maidens of Cashmere dance with gilt baskets, and a *Pas de Neuf* danced by Cerito and her attendants. *The Times'* critic terms this *pas* "One of the best dances of the grand style that has been composed. Here Cerito can exhibit all her power, dropping into her most voluptuous poses in the slow movement, and executing her brilliant variations with that fire in which she has no compeer. Those rapid revolutions that seem to spring from the suggestion of the moment, never fail to produce their effect."

LE JUGEMENT DE PARIS

Ballet Divertissement in 1 Act. Music: Cesare Pugni. Choreography: Jules Perrot. First produced: Her Majesty's Theatre, London, July 23rd, 1846.

CHARACTERS

The Goddesses	MLLE. MARIE TAGLIONI
	MLLE. LUCILE GRAHN
	MME. FANNY CERITO
The Graces	MLLE. LOUISE TAGLIONI
	MLLE. JAMES
	MLLE. HONORÉ
Paris	M. ARTHUR ST. LÉON
Cupid	MLLE. LAMOUREUX
Hymen	MLLE. JULIEN
Nymphs	MLLE. CASSAN
	MLLE. DEMELISSE
Mercury	M. JULES PERROT

The success of the *Pas de Quatre* in 1845 induced Lumley to attempt another *divertissement* in which several great dancers would appear in concert. "The glories of that famous group were not to be surpassed, it is true," admits the director, "or even equalled. But the *Pas des Déesses,* combining the attractions of Taglioni, Cerito, and Lucile Grahn, produced in a *divertissement,* called *Le Jugement de Paris,* was nevertheless one among the 'great sensations' of the year; was chronicled in enthusiastic terms, and pictured all over London, insomuch that its renown proved scarcely inferior to that of its more commanding precursor." [13]

[13] *Reminiscences of the Opera.*

A curious point in connection with this *divertissement* is the fact that in *The Times* of March 4th, 1841—five years prior to Perrot's *Jugement de Paris*—under the list of attractions to be presented at Her Majesty's Theatre, there is announced as being in preparation "a grand new ballet in which the characters of Juno, Pallas, Venus, will be supported by Mesdames Taglioni, Fanny Elssler, and Cerito." This promise, however, was not realized that season.

In the present production the principal *pas,* the *Pas des Déesses,* is set in a small ballet, and not given separately as in the case of the *Pas de Quatre.* The theme is the well-known Greek legend of the Judgment of Paris. Here are two descriptions of the ballet by eye-witnesses, the first by the critic of the *Illustrated London News,* the second by that of *The Times.*

"Those who have seen the *Pas de Quatre,* may form some idea of the extraordinary excitement and enthusiasm this *pas* creates; But . . . for poetry of idea and execution the *Pas des Déesses* has decidedly the advantage. Besides this, though the attention is principally directed to the three great *danseuses,* yet the grouping is rendered far more effective by the addition of other actors.

"The *Pas des Déesses* has another recommendation; it is longer; and the intervals while the three 'stars' are resting themselves, are filled up by the charming butterfly steps of Louise Taglioni and the most incredible feats on the part of St. Léon and Perrot. In fact, all here surpass themselves—of Taglioni, Grahn, and Cerito, each in turn seems to obtain the advantage—though of course the palm is finally adjudged by each spectator accordingly as his taste is originally inclined. . . .

"Though the styles of Taglioni and Lucile Grahn, at first sight would seem to be identical, yet they have both their own peculiar characteristics. The buoyant energy of Grahn contrasts with that peculiar quietness that marks Taglioni's most daring feats, while Cerito, who by her very smallness of stature, seems fitted by nature for another style of dancing, bounds to and fro, as though in the plenitude of enjoyment. We have never seen either of these great *danseuses* achieve such wonders as in this *pas.* The improvement of Lucile Grahn is above all marvellous: she introduces a step entirely new and exquisitely graceful; and, though it must be of most difficult achievement, she executes it with an ease and lightness which gives her the appearance of flying. It is a species of *valse renversée* on a grand scale. One of the most effective moments with Cerito is that in which she comes on with St. Léon, executing a *jetés batters* [*sic*] in the air, and, at the same moment, turning her head suddenly, to catch a sight of the much-desired apple. This never fails to elicit thunders of applause.

"As for Taglioni, after taking the most daring leaps in her own easy and exquisitely graceful manner, she flits across the stage with a succession of steps, which, though perfectly simple, are executed with such inconceivable lightness, and such enchanting grace, as invariably to call forth one of the most enthusiastic encores we ever remember to have witnessed; in fact, from beginning to end of the *divertissement,* all the spectators are kept in a state of excitement, which finds vent in clappings, in shoutings, and bravos, occasionally quite deafening."

"The glories of that *Pas de Quatre* which so astounded the operatic world last year are rivalled by the *Pas des Déesses* in a new *divertissement* called *Le Jugement de Paris.* The same emulation among the artists, bounding and revolving against each other, one trying to gain all the suffrages by the breadth and vigour of her movements, another to dazzle by sparkling Elsslerisch [*sic*] steps, the third to twirl herself into supreme eminence—the same emulation among the audience. Nothing like one of these emulative *pas* to produce a sensation—the feeling of general admiration is spiced with the power of partisanship—cheer is intended to drown cheer—and garland to eclipse bouquet.

"The three *danseuses* are—rare combination!—Taglioni, Cerito, Grahn; the two principal male dancers, Perrot and St. Léon, with several others, who help to form the most elegant groups. The three great 'stars' enter separately to dance before the Olympians, who sit in august row along the clouds in the background, and it is curious to see what a distinctive character each gives to her entrance.

"First Grahn darts on with all that audacity and vigour for which she is famous, ever spirited and ever thoroughly in earnest. Then comes Cerito, with equal force, but with a playfulness and, we may say, a heedlessness of manner that are perfectly charming, and form a striking contrast to the intense ardour of Grahn. Lastly appears Taglioni, with the command of an established favourite, and a sense of *prestige* in her movements and her countenance.

"The 'variations' are most numerous and most brilliant. Cerito introducing those evolutions which have always elicited thunders, now executing her favourite rotatory movement, now bounding across the stage in the arms of St. Léon—Taglioni rejoicing in her favourite steps—and Lucile Grahn coming out with a 'variation' which seemed to us entirely new, and remarkable alike for its difficulty and the spirit with which it was executed.

"At the conclusion there was a roar of applause, and all the artists were called and appeared. This did not satisfy the audience, who were determined that Perrot should come and receive honours as composer of the *pas,* in addition to those which he had received as a dancer. The ladies endeavoured to drag him forward, but the modest Perrot resisted, and shrank from the proposed glory. At last Cerito forced him to kneel, and placed a huge wreath of flowers upon his head to the tune of renewed acclamations."

The final tribute to success came in the burlesque entitled *The Judgment of Paris*; or *The Pas de Pippins,* produced at the Theatre Royal, Adelphi, on August 17th. A contemporary informs us that "Wright's imitation of Taglioni's step and Cerito's manner is excellent, the business of bouquet-throwing is comically caricatured, the bouquets finally taken off in a wheelbarrow by a little winged divinity."[14]

LES ELEMENTS

Divertissement. Book: Jules Perrot. Music: Bajetti. Choreography: Jules Perrot. First produced: Her Majesty's Theatre, London, June 26th, 1847.

CHARACTERS

The Fire	MLLE. CARLOTTA GRISI
The Water	MLLE. CAROLINA ROSATI
The Air	MLLE. FANNY CERITO
The Earth	MLLES. CASSAN, JAMES, THEVENOT, and HONORÉ

Les Elements, designed as a successor to the *Pas des Déesses,* united Carlotta Grisi, Carolina Rosati, and Fanny Cerito in a single *pas,* and was one of the principal attractions of the opera season of 1847.

The Times' critic[15] gives an interesting account of this *ballet-divertissement* as follows:

"The scene represents an ornamental garden, with one of those clumps of foliage at the back which one is sure will change into something. It opens—little clusters of leaves flutter away from

[14] *Times,* August 18th.
[15] June 28th, 1847.

each other, and out come a party of nymphs, clad in yellowish
dresses, who represent the earth. The clump sinks and leaves behind it an aquatic car, with a dolphin or two, whence issue the representatives of water, with Rosati at their head, all attired in bluish
raiment.

"Anon arises a volcano, from which proceed some reddish
nymphs, symbolizing fire, while a special whiff of smoke sends
forth Carlotta Grisi.

"Down goes the volcano, three masses of cloud are discovered,
and when these are opened several groups of air nymphs, quite
white, are seen, with Cerito standing in a pose as their queen. . . .

"And be it remarked that the different contrivances of rising,
and sinking, and opening, and discovering, whereby the elements
are necessarily made manifest, evince great taste and ingenuity.
There is none of the sudden slapping transformation of a pantomime trick, but the dissolving fragments separate themselves
slowly, and arrange themselves with elegance.

"The dancing was exquisite. When all the nymphs had exhibited
themselves, they began by dancing an *adage,* while the *corps de
ballet* accompanied their movements, and formed picturesque
groups, to which the assemblage of the four colours—all distinct,
yet none glaring—gave an appearance at once effective and delicate. The *adage* ended, a splendid series of 'quick' variations commenced, each of the three *danseuses* creating, in turn, a hurricane
of applause. One of these 'variations,' in which Cerito and Carlotta Grisi appeared, and executed precisely the same step together,
was encored with enthusiasm, and so also would have been
each of those executed by a single dancer, had not the fair artistes
appealed to the mercy of the admiring spectators."

A charming and most interesting sidelight on this *divertissement* is contained in a letter (dated July 1st, [1847]) written by
Grisi, then staying at 71 Haymarket, which is addressed to "My
dear Fiorentino."

"Since Saturday last, we have at last given the *Pas des Quatre
Elements.* I think this is one of Perrot's best compositions. Cerito
represented Air; Rosati, Water; and I, Fire. We have each a separate entry, then a scene in which Water rushes to extinguish
Fire; this is short but very pretty. Afterwards comes the *pas* in
which I make my entrance out of a flame, which is most effective,
as it all takes place so quickly that no one can understand how I
arrive on the stage. Then I have a very brilliant *variation* which
procures me an immediate and magnificent success. As to the
actual *pas,* if I am not mistaken and from what I hear, it is I who

have made the greatest success of the three. I dance a good deal with Cerito, which she does not like very much, although it pleases me. We have a *variation* together in the *allégro* part of the *pas,* which we always have to repeat. This *pas* has been very helpful to the success of the performance, because, even without Lind, we have had two magnificent houses, and the Queen has honoured us with her presence."

FAUST

Ballet in 3 Acts and 7 Scenes. Book: Jules Perrot. Music: Panizza, Costa, and Bajetti. Scenery: Carlo Fontana. Machinery: Giuseppe Ronchi. Choreography: Jules Perrot. Produced: Teatro alla Scala, Milan, February 12th, 1848.

CHARACTERS

Dr. Faust, an alchemist	M. Effisio Catte
Wolger, his pupil	M. Della Croce
Marguerite	Mlle. Fanny Elssler
Berta, her mother	Mme. Bellini-Casat'
Valentine, Marguerite's friend . .	M. Gaspare Pratesi
Peters, his friend	M. Luigi Righini
Martha, Marguerite's friend . .	Mlle. C. Bagnoli-Quattri
Bambo, Queen of the Demons . .	Mlle. Caterina Costantini

Students, Villagers, Peasant Girls, Nobles, Ladies, Pages, Guards, Spirits of the Air, Heavenly Angels, Evil Spirits, Witches, Fantastic Creatures, Headsman, Judges, Citizens, etc.

The action passes in Germany.

Act I. Scene I. Dr. Faust's laboratory.

As the curtain rises Faust is concluding a lecture on physics to his pupils. When they have left he becomes depressed at his inability to fulfil his ambitions. At this point an ancient tome falls from one of the book-shelves. He picks it up and idly turning the leaves observes that it is a compilation of instructions for summoning the spirits of the underworld.

In his state of intense dissatisfaction, he decides to put these precepts into practice. Flames rise from the ground and Mephistopheles appears. Faust shrinks back in fear and orders the evil

spirit to depart. When he refuses, Faust pronounces a certain incantation and forces him to vanish.

Wolger, hearing the noise in the doctor's study, hastens to his
help. Faust, annoyed at his intrusion, tells him he was merely
trying an experiment. Wolger, however, is inclined to investigate,
when the Demon spirits him away and takes his place disguised
as a student.

Astonished at the presence of the stranger, Faust enquires his
business. Mephistopheles replies that since the doctor objected to
his previous appearance, he has assumed a guise which he thought
would please him better. Faust fears to have dealings with the
powers of evil but, unable to quell his curiosity, enquires how he
can accomplish his desires.

The Demon replies that he has only to seal a pact with his blood
when all his wishes will be granted, but after his death he in return
must serve the powers of evil. Faust declines the offer.

A mist fills the room and disappears to reveal Marguerite's bedroom. The young girl is seen plaiting a garland of flowers with
which she decks her mother's portrait; then she kneels and prays.
The Demon, unable to bear the sight of virtue, vanishes.

The mist returns and Marguerite's room disappears to give place
to a cemetery. At the Demon's command an evil spirit in the
guise of Marguerite appears. The cemetery changes to a fantastic
garden filled with lovely visions.

Mephistopheles, observing that Faust is attracted by these apparitions, again produces the pact, which Faust refuses. Then the
Demon summons the female spirit and, giving her a cup, directs
her to induce Faust to drink from it.

She succeeds and as Faust lifts the cup to his lips he feels a
molten fire course through his veins. Again the Demon presents
the pact and this time Faust consents to sign it. The female spirit
vanishes. Faust reproaches Mephistopheles, who counsels patience.
He spreads his cloak on the ground and signs to Faust to stand on
it, when they both disappear.

*Act I. Scene II. A village market-place. On one side Mar-
guerite's house, on the other an inn.*

Village-folk gradually fill the square; some go to the inn, others
gossip. On this day a prize is to be awarded to the maiden judged
to be the most virtuous in the village. Members of the nobility
and the Mayor are assembled to take part in the ceremony. A
number of girls enter for the competition.

A visitor arrives in the person of a young soldier who excites curiosity by his questions regarding the village. At last a villager called Peters recognizes him as Valentine, a friend of his youth. He enquires about his old sweetheart Marguerite and seeks for her among the damsels. At this moment Marguerite arrives. He goes to greet her and they are joined by her mother, Berta.

Distant music is heard and Mephistopheles enters disguised as a charlatan; he is accompanied by Faust, who has recovered the appearance of youth. The latter indicates Marguerite as the woman he desires.

Meanwhile the Demon has observed Marguerite's friend, Martha, who has been endeavouring to attract the attention of the strangers, for he conceives her to be a useful aid to his plans.

The Mayor is suspicious of the charlatan and inclined to send him packing, but he declares that he is only there to amuse the people and suggests that everyone should join in a dance. He assumes the guise of a carefree youth and induces Marguerite to dance with him. She is visibly disturbed by his captivating manners and tries in vain to master her emotions.

The Demon leaves her and dances in turn with the other damsels, who all fall under his spell. Marguerite grows calm or animated at the Demon's wish while the other maidens dance at his will. She stops breathless near Faust, who watches the proceedings with the greatest interest.

Mephistopheles, with a rapid gesture, seems to tear from his breast some of the fire that consumes him and places it on Marguerite's heart. She is so overcome with emotion that she is about to faint; but the Demon catches her in his arms and whirls her in a mad dance at the end of which she is left breathless.

Now the Mayor calls on everyone to vote as to the award of the prize. The voting is unanimously in favour of Marguerite. Valentine and Berta are delighted. The young men approve, but the other competitors are filled with envy. Mephistopheles, with a sardonic smile, congratulates Marguerite, but she ignores him and turns homewards, escorted by Berta and Valentine.

The Demon takes a glass and, filling it with wine, proposes a toast to the peerless Marguerite. The company raise their glasses but, finding them empty, call for wine.

"Here you are, friends!" cries Mephistopheles, plunging his dagger into the table at which he is sitting. Wine gushes forth from the holes and the young men run to fill their glasses. Faust is annoyed at this delay, but the Demon bids him be patient.

Suddenly the wine changes to gouts of flame. The villagers

draw back in fear. The Demon gives a mocking laugh and vanishes with Faust, while the crowd take to flight.

Act I. Scene III. Marguerite's bedroom, with an alcove in the background.

Faust and Mephistopheles appear in the room where the young girl lies asleep in bed. While Faust gazes upon her, the Demon places a casket in a cupboard.

Marguerite begins to stir and Faust is about to kneel at her feet, when the Demon drags him away, although not before he has picked up her handkerchief and thrust it in his doublet.

Marguerite leaps from her bed as though fleeing from some dreadful dream; the tune of the dance with the stranger still lingers in her ears. She recalls the other fair stranger with whom she did not dance, and, to banish him from her thoughts, tries to think of Valentine. There is a knock at the door. She looks for her handkerchief and unable to find it goes to the cupboard where she discovers the casket. The knocking is renewed. She dresses quickly and opens the door.

It is Martha, who tells her that one of the strangers has given her a beautiful ring. Marguerite shows her the casket, which proves to be filled with gems. Martha feigns surprise although she has already spoken with the stranger, and urges her to adorn herself with the jewels; but Marguerite's modesty prevents her from doing so.

Mephistopheles enters and signs to Martha to leave. Marguerite, wishing to dispel her thoughts, sits at her spinning-wheel. Now the Demon summons his familiar evil spirits—Pride, Gluttony, Sloth, Envy, Anger, Avarice, and Lust, who, unseen by the young girl, pour their evil counsels in her ear. Sloth induces her to stop spinning; Pride and Envy tempt her to put on the jewels. She notices the contrast between the rich gems and her homely dress and, at the bidding of Anger, tears off the jewels and flings them to the floor. But Pride and Avarice counsel her to keep the gems, which she gathers up and conceals in her dress. The Demon and his spirits rejoice in her downfall.

At the Demon's command the room becomes a fantastic garden full of strange flowers and fruit. It is Lust who now whispers in her ear and fills her body with strange yearnings. She sees a vision of the youthful Faust and becomes enamoured of him. Suddenly the voice of Virtue warns her of danger and in an instant everything becomes horrible to her. She utters a prayer and the spell is broken, the spirits vanish, and Marguerite throws herself into the arms of her mother who enters at this moment.

Act II. Scene I. A room in an enchanted palace.

Faust sits at a banquet in which he takes no pleasure, for he is haunted by thoughts of Marguerite. The Demon, having failed to dispel his melancholy, causes a vision of Marguerite to appear as if she were going to receive her prize for virtue. Faust greets her with joy and together they watch a dance which precedes the prize-giving. As the garland of white roses passes through the hands of Vice the flowers wither and blacken. The onlookers are troubled by this evil transformation.

Act II. Scene II. This scene is divided into two, so that Marguerite's room is on the left and the garden on the right.

Faust and Mephistopheles enter the garden, the former reproaching the latter for his failure to induce Marguerite to fall in love with him. The Demon assures him that his desires will soon be fulfilled, but first it will be necessary to put Berta to sleep, and to this end he gives him a vial containing a sleeping potion. Faust accepts the vial on being assured that the contents are harmless.

Footsteps are heard and Marguerite and Berta enter the garden, followed by Valentine and Martha. The Demon bids Faust hide while he keeps watch.

Valentine is in high spirits for Marguerite has agreed to marry him on the morrow. Berta blesses the lovers and tells Valentine that they must part as the hour grows late, but she and the two girls will see him on his way.

Valentine and Berta go first, the two girls follow. Mephistopheles reveals himself to Martha who shrinks back in fear. Marguerite turns to see what is the matter, but is assured that all is well. The Demon whispers to Martha that he must speak with her. Meanwhile Faust appears and kneels at Marguerite's feet, but she takes fright and runs to the house. Martha wishes to follow, but the Demon holds her back.

Faust implores Marguerite to permit him to speak with her. When she answers that her mother would disapprove, Faust shows her the vial, saying that a few drops will make her sleepy.

Suddenly, Martha runs in with the news that Valentine and Berta, alarmed at not seeing the girls, have returned in search of them. But Faust refuses to leave until Marguerite has given her promise to see him later. The Demon touches his arm and they vanish as the others come into the house.

In response to their enquiries Martha declares that she was taken ill. Marguerite, ashamed of such an untruth, looks away. Berta tells Martha that she must stay with them and tells Valentine that he must leave for they will see him on the morrow, and she hands him the key of the garden-gate.

Valentine bids his friends good-night but, on passing through the garden, has a presentiment of evil; he is half-minded to guard the house, but finally decides to leave. As soon as he goes the Demon tells Faust, who is overjoyed.

Martha has retired and Marguerite and her mother are alone. But the latter, instead of going to bed, asks for a book and settles herself to read. Marguerite is frightened at the promise she has given to Faust and is about to confess all to her mother when she sees the hateful stranger.

Berta asks for a cup of water. Marguerite fills a cup with water into which, at the Demon's direction, she empties the vial. She hands the cup to her mother who drinks, becomes seized with trembling, and falls back, inert. Mephistopheles places his hand on her heart and expresses his satisfaction. Then he leads Marguerite into the garden where Faust awaits her.

The Demon goes to Martha and they leave together. Marguerite awakes from the spell to find herself in her lover's arms. She wishes to go, but is forced to stay by Faust's entreaties and avowals of love, and finally confesses that she loves him. At last she tells him that they must part and, seeing Martha and the stranger return, implores her lover to break off his friendship with the latter whom she detests, but he declines.

Martha warns Marguerite that Valentine is approaching and she immediately goes into the house. The young soldier dashes at Faust, sword in hand, while Martha calls for help. They fight, but the Demon guides Faust's blade and his opponent falls mortally wounded. Faust and Mephistopheles vanish. Neighbours, bearing torches, hurry in; they tend the dying man.

Marguerite hears the noise but, finding her mother still asleep, becomes seriously alarmed. She kisses Berta and tries to revive her, but in vain, she is dead. The door opens and she sees Valentine's prostrate body.

She runs to his side but, gathering his strength, he repulses her. The bystanders draw away in horror, while he curses Marguerite with his failing breath. She falls on her knees and vainly pleads for forgiveness. Valentine is dead.

Marguerite rises and, moving as if in a trance, goes towards the onlookers, laughing wildly. Finally she disappears among the trees.

The bodies of Berta and Valentine have vanished and all is confusion.

Act III. Scene I. A bleak part of the Harz Mountains.

Faust enters with Mephistopheles who tells him that he is leading him to a great festival where he will find Marguerite. Weird and fantastic spirits invade the scene. Screams are heard and Faust listens. The Demon, who has recognized Marguerite's voice, urges Faust in the opposite direction from which she approaches, pur- suing a will o' the wisp. She kneels and carries her arms to her breast as if she were nursing a child, which she holds out to an imaginary Faust. But that vision appears to vanish, for weeping and kissing her imaginary child she covers it with the folds of her dress. Then she goes to the edge of a deep stream and, again kiss- ing the child, drops it in the water. She is about to leap in herself when she swoons.

Faust, unable to witness the dreadful witches' sabbath, returns. He sees the prostrate Marguerite and, taking her in his arms, presses her to his heart. Recognising her lover, she tells him of her sufferings, and of the death of their child. He takes Marguerite by the hand and tries to lead her away, but she shrinks from his touch.

The Demon returns and seeing Faust urges him to fly, for sol- diers are approaching to apprehend Marguerite. Faust implores Mephistopheles to save her and, when he refuses, swears that he will die with her. But she repulses him saying that she belongs to God. The soldiers arrive and seize the girl. "Come!" cries the Demon, "she is lost." They vanish as Marguerite is led away.

Act III. Scene II. Another part of the Harz Mountains.

Witches and necromancers are preparing incantations while other evil spirits dance. The dancing grows wilder and wilder. Devils play weird instruments while witches give vent to eldritch screeches. On the entrance of Mephistopheles the dancing abruptly ceases. He places Faust, who is fast asleep, on the ground.

Beckoning to one of the witches the Demon orders her to assume the likeness of Marguerite for Faust's entertainment. She changes her shape and captivates him so that he follows her. But soon he returns, pale and trembling.

A great noise attracts everyone's attention. The clouds lift and on the topmost peak can be seen Marguerite surrounded by soldiers and people. She kneels and prays. A headsman appears with his axe which he raises in the air. The vision fades. Faust wipes the sweat of anguish from his brow, while the witches resume their infernal festival.

A tiny flame flickers over the ground. Faust believes it to be the soul of his beloved. Reproaching Mephistopheles for his failure to save her from a shameful death he attacks him with his sword which snaps in two at a sign from the Demon, who reminds him that his soul is his.

Faust kneels and prays for divine forgiveness, but Mephistopheles draws the fatal pact from his breast and cries: "You are mine, Faust, mine for all eternity!" Suddenly the flame lengthens and burns up the agreement. The Demon is furious at being deprived of his prey.

The flame travels towards the mountain and is followed by Faust who reaches the peak. Mephistopheles summons all the powers of Hell to his aid. The earth opens, flames shoot forth, terrible screams are heard, and a black vapour hides everything from view, as the Demon fights to regain possession of Faust.

Gradually the evil vapour clears to reveal Marguerite, surrounded by angels, who is seen holding out her arms to welcome Faust who is carried towards her, while Mephistopheles vainly continues to rage.

*

Faust was one of Perrot's most successful ballets. So far as I can ascertain it was first produced at Milan in 1848, when it was revived the following year. It is of interest to note that Fanny Elssler, who apparently created the role of Marguerite, which she must have found admirably suited to her rare gifts both as dancer and mime, chose this ballet for her farewell performance at Vienna on June 21st, 1851.

Faust enjoyed its greatest popularity in Russia when it was produced by Perrot in 1854, with himself in his old part of Mephistopheles, Yella as Marguerite, and Marius Petipa as Faust. Among the many interpreters of the role of Marguerite (in Russia) may be mentioned N. K. Bogdanova (1855), A. Ferraris (1858), W. Salvioni (1868), A. F. Vergina (1868), and E. P. Sokolova (1878).

In January, 1869, *Faust* celebrated its hundredth performance at the Bolshoy Theatre, St. Petersburg, and the artistes of the ballet company sent a telegram of congratulation to Perrot, then at Paris.

LES QUATRE SAISONS

Ballet in 1 Act. Book: Jules Perrot. Choreography: Jules Perrot.
First produced: Her Majesty's Theatre, London, June 13th, 1848.

CHARACTERS

Summer	MMES. CARLOTTA GRISI
Autumn	CAROLINA ROSATI
Winter	MARIE TAGLIONI
Spring	FANNY CERITO

The scene[16] is remarkably beautiful, and represents a lovely conservatory with a fountain and exquisitely laid-out garden, about which are statues of rural and floral deities disposed in admirable taste. There is evidently great rejoicing and festivity going on— the garden teems with lady guests, rivalling the flowers in their beauty; and all wears the air of a fête.

Presently the four principal ladies meet, and plan a masque. These four are Cerito, Carlotta Grisi, Rosati, and Marie Taglioni; and they agree, in the above order, to assume the characters of Spring, Summer, Autumn, and Winter. Nothing can be more delicious than their appearance in their costumes, nor more appropriate than the very effective manner in which these are arranged with the symbols and trappings of the season of the year they represent.

Followed by a train of nymphs, arranged in a similarly attractive guise, they perform a series of the most charming groupings. Endless combinations of tints and poses, each of which seems to have exhausted the strange invention of Perrot, only to be followed by something more beautiful, form a perfect human kaleidoscope, if we may be allowed the simile; and then a grand *pas de quatre* takes place, for the four goddesses of the dance.

They first dance singly, Cerito bounding round in her own inimitable style, catching up flowers from baskets presented to her, and throwing them above and around her with most joyous abandon, and Carlotta looking more lovely and dancing with greater elegance—for every attitude speaks for itself—than ever. Rosati performs all her choicest feats, and Marie Taglioni[17] does wonders in her peculiar line. At last they unite in an ensemble, and the

---

[16] The description of this ballet is taken from the *Illustrated London News,* June 24, 1848.

[17] Niece of the great Taglioni.

delight of the spectators reaches its climax, the applause coming like a thunderstorm upon the festival.

On May 16th, 1856, a new version of *Les Quatre Saisons* was produced at Her Majesty's Theatre. This was founded on the *ballet-divertissement* of that name by Lucien Petipa in the opera *Les Vêpres Siciliennes,* and has a particular interest in being the vehicle for the London *début* of the Italian *ballerina,* Anima Boschetti, who took the role of Winter.

LA FILLEULE DES FÉES [18]

Grand Fairy Ballet in 2 Acts and 7 Scenes, preceded by a Prologue. Book: Vernoy de Saint-Georges and Jules Perrot. Music: Adolphe Adam and de Saint-Julien. Scenery: Cambon, Despléchin, and Thierry. Choreography: Jules Perrot. Produced: Théâtre de l'Opéra, Paris, October 8th, 1849.

CHARACTERS

Prince Hugues de Provence	MM. L.	PETIPA
Alain		PERROT
Jobin, a seneschal		BERTHIER
Guillaume, Ysaure's father		LENFANT
A Farm-Lad		ADICE
A Churchwarden		BION
Notary		DARCOURT
1st Witness		ROUYER
2nd Witness		CARRÉ
The Confidant		DAUTY
Two Gamekeepers	{	MORAND / BÉGRAND
Ysaure	MLLES.	CARLOTTA GRISI
The White Fairy		EMAROT
The Pink Fairy		TAGLIONI
The Black Fairy		MARQUET
Nurse		ALINE
Godmother		LAURENT
Two Friends	{	GOUGIBUS / AMELINE
Two Servants	{	GUÉNOT / DESCAMP

Peasants, Peasant Girls, Fairies, Spirits, Nobles, People, etc.

[18] *The Fairies' God-child.*

Prologue. Scene. A large room in a farm-house with wide folding doors the whole length of the background, opening on to a landscape. In the distance is a hill leading to the village church, of which the main door is visible. There is a side door and to the left a great gothic fire-place.

At the rise of the curtain farm-hands are seen decorating the room with flowers. Bells ring out from the church and down the hill comes a happy crowd escorting Father Guillaume, whose little daughter, Ysaure, has just been baptized.

The godfather and godmother join hands and lead the procession. They are followed by Berthe, the nurse, carrying the child in her arms. The godfather distributes sugared almonds and Father Guillaume invites his friends to supper.

The table is laid, the guests take their seats, and the repast is served. The godfather and godmother begin to dance a saraband when there is a knock at the door. Guillaume orders the door to be opened and an old woman enters and begs hospitality. He orders her to be placed at the end of the table.

The dancers recommence when there is another knock. The visitor proves to be another beggar woman who is likewise invited to sit at the table.

The dancers resume when there is yet another knock at the door. The newcomer is another beggar woman whom the farmer again invites to the table. But the godfather notices that this makes thirteen at table. Thereupon the farmer asks her to leave. She refuses and has to be forcibly ejected.

The repast ended, Guillaume proposes the health of little Ysaure and the festival is at an end.

At nightfall the guests depart. Guillaume kisses his child in her cradle and leaves, telling the two old women that they may rest until daybreak.

The nurse rocks the cradle and presently falls asleep. At this moment the two old women each stand beside the cradle and make various signs, which cause the room to be filled with a swarm of little old women who suddenly shed their drab clothes and appear in splendid dresses. The White Fairy and the Rose Fairy—for so they are called—arch their arms over the cradle and the background fills with mist. All the fairies surround the cradle and confer their gifts. "She shall be white as a lily," declares the White Fairy, throwing a lily into her cradle. "And fresh as a rose," adds the Rose Fairy, placing a rose beside the lily. The fairies dance about the cradle then take off their shining belts and place them on their god-child to preserve her from evil.

Suddenly there is a clap of thunder and the third old woman emerges from the fireplace. The other fairies are terrified at her approach. She flings off her cloak and is seen to be dressed in black. She goes to the cradle and waves her wand, of serpents intertwined, over the cradle. She waves her wand again and there passes across the background a black cloud inscribed in letters of fire: "Fear for her. I shall withhold my gifts until her fifteenth year."

The good fairies leave in dismay, then the Black Fairy disappears amid a black mist. The atmosphere of magic clears and the nurse, awakening with a start, lifts Ysaure from her cradle and clasps her tenderly in her arms.

Act I. Scene I. A pleasant countryside with Ysaure's house; opposite, a cistern with a curb. In the background a hill leading to a plateau covered with trees and flowers. In the distance the castle of the Prince Hugues de Provence. Sunrise.

It is the festival of Spring and villagers are busy culling flowers and fashioning them into garlands. They play games and dance.

Enter Ysaure, now fifteen, who is followed by Alain, in love with his foster-sister. The village girls offer him flowers but he disdains their advances, saying that he loves Ysaure. When they mock him, he tells Ysaure of his love for her, but she laughs at him. Remarking his sadness she tells him that if she cannot love him, she will always be his friend. A trumpet sounds and the girls run to take part in the festival, while Berthe takes Ysaure into a hut to change her dress.

Alain, alone, gives way to despair. Suddenly a little old woman leaps out of the cistern. She inquires the reason for his grief and on being told promises to make him happy if he will kiss her.

At first he hesitates then kisses her, when immediately she changes into a beautiful fairy—the Black Fairy seen at Ysaure's baptism. Alain leaves with her as a distant hunting-horn is heard.

Presently a young huntsman enters, weary from the chase. No sooner does he rest on a seat than two old women ask him for alms. He gives them some pieces of gold and they tell him that soon he will fall in love and they point to Ysaure's hut.

The huntsman laughs and wishes to knock at the door, but the old women hold him back. Then they point their crutches at the hut, the wall of which becomes transparent, to reveal Ysaure dressing.

Seized with admiration the huntsman wishes to break through

the fragile wall of the hut, but the Black Fairy appears and, raising her crutch, causes the wall to become opaque.

The huntsman knocks at the door but the Black Fairy renders the knocks noiseless. Foiled in his efforts he blows his horn and huntsmen run in from all sides. He orders them to force the door. While they go to fetch trees for battering-rams, the Black Fairy causes the hut to vanish and re-appear at the summit of the hill.

The huntsman returns and is amazed to find the hut vanished. But the two old women tell him to have patience. They leave, taking him with them.

Enter the village girls dressed in their best and led by Jobin. Ysaure and Berthe descend the hill. Alain also arrives but is surprised to find Ysaure's hut vanished. Sure of the Black Fairy's protection he attempts to dominate Ysaure, who is much amused by his behaviour. Jobin is about to crown Ysaure Queen of Spring, when he vanishes to be replaced by the huntsman, who is none other than the Prince Hugues de Provence. Ysaure is much troubled by the sight of the handsome nobleman. Fanfares are heard and the Prince's suite enters.

The Prince invites Ysaure to dance a *pas* with himself and Alain. This is followed by a general dance until nightfall, when huntsmen appear with torches to escort the Prince to his castle. He begs Ysaure to grant him another meeting, but, before she can reply, Alain steps between them and takes Ysaure's arm in his. The Prince is in despair but the good fairies wave their wands and the Prince vanishes to re-appear in Ysaure's chamber.

Meanwhile Ysaure climbs the hill to return to her dwelling.

The huntsmen, who cannot find the Prince, run hither and thither searching everywhere by the light of their flaming torches.

Act I. Scene II. Ysaure's chamber. To the right an entrance door. In a slope of the wall is the window seen in the previous scene. The room is furnished with rustic seats and cupboards. In the background a mirror hangs on the wall.

The Prince emerges from the window-curtain where he had been hidden. Hearing footsteps the Prince returns to the shelter of the curtain. The door opens and Ysaure enters accompanied by Berthe and Alain. The last-named peers behind the curtain, but the Prince moves to one side so that he is not seen.

Alain offers a bouquet to Ysaure who disdains it. The youth, saddened, picks the flowers to pieces. Ysaure, seeing his distress, offers to take the bouquet. But he shows the spoilt flowers and runs out of the room, telling her that he will make another bouquet.

The Prince emerges from his hiding-place and, kneeling at Ysaure's feet, implores her to marry him. Ysaure, delighted, accords him a kiss. The Prince leaves to make arrangements for the wedding.

Ysaure calls Berthe and tells her of her good fortune. Then she feels ashamed of her simple dress; at the same moment her dress becomes a bridal gown. She goes to the mirror, but it is so small that it only reflects a portion of her. Suddenly it grows larger and become a full length mirror. Fairy music is heard and the simple room becomes a richly-appointed apartment in a splendid palace. Trumpets sound and Ysaure, overjoyed, opens the door expecting to see the Prince. Instead, she is confronted with the Black Fairy who congratulates her on her fifteenth birthday and promises her a gift.

The Rose Fairy and White Fairy appear as if to protect their god-child. The Black Fairy says: "You have made her so beautiful that no man shall look upon her without losing his reason." The Black Fairy vanishes leaving Ysaure and her fairy godmothers overcome with fear.

The fanfares are repeated and the Prince's heralds appear. Ysaure, fearful lest she should harm her beloved, runs into a side room.

The Prince enters in search of his bride, but Berthe and the fairies dare not tell him where she is. He orders his men to find her and presently they lead in Ysaure, who covers her face with her hands. The Prince raises her hands but she turns aside to face Alain who, at that moment, returns with a bouquet. Immediately he loses his reason.

The Prince goes to Ysaure who runs away from him, while Alain, whose jealousy has been intensified, prevents the Prince from following her. They struggle violently until the Prince flings Alain aside and clasps Ysaure in his arms.

Ysaure, in despair, leaps through the window, to the terror of the bystanders. But her fairy godmothers wave their wands and the young girl is saved from falling by a group of fairies who bear her through the air.

Act II. A wooded park. In the background is a lake with a central fountain. Here and there are statues. To the left is a grotto. Moonlight.

Two women are seated by the water. They are the good fairies awaiting their god-child. They wave their wands and the statues come to life, forming graceful groups about her.

On the far side of the lake a charming group looms out of the mist, to reveal Ysaure resting on a swan and surrounded by fairies. Light scarves, fluttering in the wind, serve as sails to the graceful bark which carries Ysaure to the bank.

She is welcomed by the fairies who try to console her for the loss of the Prince. "You must not show yourself to him," they counsel, "or he will lose his reason." They wave their wands and Alain appears. At the same moment the fairies vanish.

Alain looks curiously at his surroundings, then recognizes Ysaure, who appears as a shadow to his fevered brain. He pursues her but always she evades him, and, while he hurries into the wood in search of her, she has already returned.

Ysaure is much troubled by Alain's unhappy lot, of which she is the unwilling cause. At this point the fairies return, accompanied by a group of nymphs who surround her with affection. Her fairy godmothers decide to admit her to this fairy sisterhood, in token of which she is accorded a magic wand. So she shares in their frolics and, like them, leaps over the sward or glides over the water.

With the first rays of sunrise Ysaure cannot resist the desire to see her beloved. She waves her wand and a group of fairies part to reveal the Prince asleep in their midst. She repeats the gesture and the fairies disappear, leaving her alone with her lover.

Ysaure, at first confused, looks tenderly at the youth, then dances about him, covering him with rose-leaves. At this juncture Alain returns and is furious at the sight of his rival. He seizes Ysaure's wand which she tries to recover; in the struggle Alain touches the Prince with the wand. He awakes and runs to Ysaure, who, terror-stricken, flees towards the park.

Alain, inspired by the Black Fairy, touches Ysaure with the wand, when she changes into a statue. Thus the Prince must see Ysaure and lose his reason. But, at the same moment, one of the fairies seizes her arm, thus breaking the enchantment, then hurls her into the grotto which closes upon her.

Alain, enraged, drags the Prince towards the grotto and, waving the wand, causes the rocks to open before them.

Act III. Scene I. A deep cavern carpeted with flowers and aquatic plants. Several springs, which fill the lake, have their sources in this cavern.

The Spirits of the Springs are resting. They are interrupted by the entrance of Ysaure and her fairy godmothers, who come to hide in the cavern.

Ysaure is alone when Alain and the Prince appear in the background. She is seated plucking the leaves of a rose when the madman drags the Prince towards her. Ysaure looks towards the noise, but her fairy protectors cause the Prince to become blind.

At his cry of anguish Ysaure goes to her lover and tries to soothe his despair. Meanwhile Alain looks on in astonishment. Ysaure contrives to recover her wand and is about to restore his sight when the wand breaks in her hand. At the same moment the Black Fairy appears and reproaches the other fairies for having prevented the accomplishment of her vengeance. Ysaure beseeches the Black Fairy to have pity upon her, her godmothers add their entreaties. The naiads re-appear and at last she consents to the Prince's recovery on condition that he will recognize her among all the young girls present. Ysaure accepts the trial.

Act III. Scene II. Clouds invade the scene and a tribunal of fairies assemble to pronounce judgment.

A number of young girls surround the blind Prince. They overwhelm him with caresses and try to lead his thoughts astray by the most captivating endearments. Alain tries to hold back Ysaure each time the Prince is likely to discover her. Meanwhile she suffers agonies of suspense at the dangerous test which may prove fatal to her happiness.

But when Ysaure, making a supreme effort, drives him towards her and presses herself against him so that their hearts beat together, the Prince hesitates no longer. He recognizes his true love, falls at her feet, and clasps her in his arms.

Act III. Scene III. The clouds dissolve to reveal the fairies' paradise. Banks of golden clouds lead to a magnificent temple, glittering with jewels, and from every side come the fairies of the earth, each with her attributes, to celebrate the marriage of their godchild and the Prince de Provence.

Alain, thanks to the united power of the fairies, recovers his senses and deplores his follies as he sees the happiness of the two lovers, who take him by the hand.

MARIE TAGLIONI

MARIE TAGLIONI was born at Stockholm on April 24th, 1804. Her father was the well-known *maître de ballet*, Filippo Taglioni; her mother was the daughter of a Swedish singer called Karsten.

Marie received her first lessons in dancing from her father, and at eight studied at Paris under Coulon. She made her *début* at the Kaernther Thor, Vienna, on June 10th, 1822, when she appeared in a new ballet composed for the occasion by her father and appropriately entitled *La Réception d'une Jeune Nymphe à la Cour de Terpsichore*. She danced beside two reigning stars, Mlle. Millière and Mlle. Héberlé, and by no means to disadvantage. The *Wiener Theater-Zeitung* greets the newcomer as a young person of the highest ability. . . . Her pleasing features, her graceful movements, the convincing quality of her technical perfection already make her an accomplished dancer and show her capable of still further development. . . . The public accorded her a favourable reception which she well deserved."

Taglioni next appeared at Paris, in 1823, at the Théâtre de la Porte Saint-Martin, but, apparently, without exciting any particular interest. She went on to Italy and Germany, where she made a definite success; for at Stuttgart she gained the notice and friendship of the Queen; and, at Munich, King Max held her up to his wife and daughters as a model of grace and deportment.

In 1827 she returned to Paris for a series of performances which began on July 23, and this time attracted considerable attention with her new style of dancing, with its flowing grace and precision of line. Almost for the first time a dancer began to interest the public in the dance as a means to beauty, and not merely as an excuse for seductive movements and alluring poses. A new word—*taglioniser*—was coined to define this new style of dancing.

The next year Taglioni returned to Paris and appeared with success in *Les Bayadères, La Belle au Bois Dormant,* and *Guillaume Tell,* so much so that she received and accepted an invitation to become the *ballerina* at the Opera. The famous old ballet *Flore et Zéphire* was revived for her.

Since, however, the public clamoured to see her in new ballets, Scribe and Auber were commissioned to provide a work, which resulted in *Le Dieu et la Bayadère* (1830); a year later Meyerbeer introduced into his opera, *Robert le Diable,* a ballet for Taglioni, the famous "Ballet of the Nuns."

Then, on March 12th, 1832, the ballet *La Sylphide* was produced and Taglioni's rendering of the title-role made her name a household word, inaugurated the new school of Romantic Ballet, and placed her among the immortals. In the year of her triumph she married the Comte Gilbert de Voisins, but the union was unhappy and the parties separated early in 1835.

In 1837 Taglioni and her father left for St. Petersburg where she achieved a tremendous success. The enthusiasm of the spectators rose to fever-pitch and flowers were thrown to the dancer from the boxes, a manner of homage unknown in Russia before her coming.

The gloomy Emperor, Nicholas I, was conquered by this vaporous dancing and, with two exceptions, was present on every evening that Taglioni danced, throughout the whole five seasons of her successive engagements. While in Russia she appeared in *La Sylphide* and *La Fille de Danube,* also in *La Gitana* (1838) and *L'Ombre* (1839), two new ballets composed for her by her father. Her farewell performance took place on March 18th, 1842, when she was recalled 18 times.

From 1831 to 1847 Taglioni's name was sufficient to draw a full house at any theatre in Europe. The "Sylphide" blazed a trail of triumph wherever she appeared. At Vienna, in 1839, she was recalled 42 times. At Milan, in 1841, the orchestra of La Scala serenaded her at her hotel, and a medal was struck in her honour. At London there were the great days of the *Pas de Quatre* (1845) and the *Pas des Déesses* (1846). These three instances alone will suffice to show in what regard her art was held.

The charm of Taglioni's dancing was due to the spiritual quality with which she invested all her movements, her purity of line, her effortless grace and lightness, and her rare elevation, which enabled her to make those great soaring bounds that never failed to enchant. She, too, like her predecessor, Vestris, and her successor, Nijinsky, was possessed of that unique quality which enabled her, while in flight, to remain momentarily suspended in mid-air, so that she seemed able at will to defy the laws of gravity.

In 1847 she retired after twenty-five years on the stage, a long life for a dancer, whose average rarely exceeds a decade. But, of all her triumphs, only memory remained; her resources were as immaterial as her dancing; the fantastic sums she earned had vanished.

The cause of her comparative poverty remains a mystery to this day. Did she speculate? Was she robbed? Did she fall into the hands of moneylenders? We do not know. It seems incredible that a woman who was so strict in money matters as sometimes to demand payment in cash on the very night she was billed to appear, and refuse to dance without it, should have been induced to follow the will o' the wisp of financial adventure.

Whatever the reason, she was forced to eke out a bare living by giving lessons in dancing and deportment, now at Paris, now at London. She had a particular affection for one of her pupils, Emma Livry, a rising young *danseuse* at the Paris Opera, for whom she planned and composed *Le Papillon*—her sole venture into choreography—the ballet in which she hoped to see herself reborn. Her wish was granted.

But a year later Livry met with a fatal accident and died. Few things could have been more heartrending to the dancer in retirement than that bitter news.

In her last years Taglioni went to stay with relations at Marseilles, where she died on April 27th, 1884, at the age of eighty.

LE PAPILLON

Pantomimic-Ballet in 2 Acts and 4 Scenes. Book: Marie Taglioni and V. de Saint-Georges. Music: Jacques Offenbach. Scenery: Cambon, Thierry, Despléchin, Nolau, Rubé, and Martin. Choreography: Marie Taglioni. First produced: Théâtre Impérial de l'Opéra, Paris, November 26th, 1860.

CHARACTERS

Farfalla	Mlles.	Emma Livry
The Fairy Hamza		Louise Marquet
Prince Djalma, the Emir's nephew . .	MM.	Mérante
Patimate, a woodcutter in Hamza's service		Berthier
Mohamed		Dauty
Zaidée	Mlle.	Stoikoff
Ismaïl Bey, Emir	M.	Lenfant
Leila, Farfalla's friend	Mlles.	Lamy
The Diamond Fairy		Simon
The Pearl Fairy		Mauperin
The Flower Fairy		Schlosser
The Harvest Fairy		Troisvallets

Butterflies, Members of the Sultan's Court, Guards, Ulemas, People, Gypsies, Sprites, Bayadères, Odalisques, Eunuchs, etc.

Act I. Scene I. The Fairy Hamza's abode: situated amid picturesque ruins. In this strange dwelling attributes of the Fairy's power are mingled with golden vases and rare furniture. In the background are the mountains of the Caucasus.

A distant fanfare is heard and, attracted by the sound, the aged Fairy, Hamza, appears, walking painfully with the help of her magic crutch. She divines by magic that a handsome prince is hunting in the forest, and tries to make herself more attractive.

Farfalla, her maid, enters and is much amused at her mistress's coquetries, which she imitates. The Fairy touches her mirror with her crutch, and it reflects the features of Prince Djalma. Farfalla cannot resist a cry of admiration, which reveals her presence to the Fairy, who attempts to beat her, but Patimate, coming in at this moment, receives the blow intended for the maid. The Fairy goes out leaving Farfalla to soothe Patimate.

He tells the maid that the Emir's nephew and his suite are hunting, and that Hamza wishes to entice him to her house so that he may fall in love with her, for if he kisses her she will become a young and beautiful girl.

There is a knock at the door. Patimate opens it and discovers the Prince and his suite, who request refreshment. Farfalla and Patimate open a chest from which they take cups and plates and proceed to lay the table. Suddenly the Fairy enters and frightens the couple so that they drop the dishes.

Hamza, seeing the handsome prince, thanks him for the honour of his visit, and, touching the table with her crutch, changes the simple repast into a magnificent banquet. The Prince is astonished. But the tutor, who has been studying Hamza, tells him that she greatly resembles a woman who kidnapped the Emir's daughter in days gone by.

Gay music is heard and a village wedding procession passes the dwelling. The Prince and his suite invite the party into the house. There is high festivity in the course of which the Prince asks Farfalla to dance with him. Time passes quickly and the Prince and his suite take their departure, after he has bestowed a farewell kiss on the pretty maid, greatly to the Fairy's annoyance.

Hamza vents her ill humour on Farfalla, then sits in her armchair and turns her spinning wheel, while the maid holds the distaff. Presently the Fairy falls asleep and the mischievous Farfalla rises and tickles her mistress's face with a flower, darting to and fro like a butterfly. The Fairy catches her in the act and, rising in a fury, threatens the maid with her crutch. Farfalla, in a moment of fright, leaps into a chest which the Fairy locks.

But Patimate, who has witnessed this scene, goes to free Farfalla, which the Fairy forbids. Since Patimate insists, Hamza touches him with her crutch; he becomes motionless. Then she revenges herself upon Farfalla by changing her into a butterfly. She taps the chest with her crutch and Farfalla, now a butterfly, flutters out.

Hamza, fascinated by her movements, restores life to Patimate. Now a swarm of butterflies come through the window and, led by Farfalla, drive the Fairy from the house. Patimate follows Farfalla and the curtain falls on a scene of wild pursuit.

Act I. Scene II. The scene changes to a clearing in the forest. With the exception of one shaded corner, the trees are bathed in sunlight.

A party of gypsies are camped on some rising ground. The wedding procession enters from one side, while the Emir's nephew and his suite come in from the opposite direction.

The gypsies dance before Djalma. When they have concluded, the ladies of the Court take little nets and take pleasure in hunting for butterflies. One of the ladies makes a capture and offers her prize to the Prince, who gives her a ring in exchange. Then she joins her companions and all disappear into the forest.

Alone, Djalma looks at his charming prisoner. The butterfly has wings and body of the same colour as Farfalla. To secure his prisoner, the Prince plucks a needle from his headdress and pins the butterfly to a tree. To his horror, the butterfly changes into a young girl, her head downcast, her eyes brimming with tears.

The Prince withdraws the pin from her breast and the fantastic being sinks exhausted to the ground. He goes to her help and recognises the features of the pretty maid. But she flutters her wings, takes to flight, and disappears among the trees. Djalma follows in pursuit.

A swarm of butterflies disport themselves in the sunny glade, when they are joined by Farfalla. But, at the sound of footsteps, they flee into the forest. It is the Prince's tutor, Mohamed, and his suite, come in search of the Prince. Djalma informs Mohamed of his adventure, but the tutor thinks his pupil mad. Patimate arrives and tells the tutor about the Fairy and Farfalla. Stranger still, Hamza herself comes to question the tutor about her maid; Mohamed, almost bereft of his senses, departs, taking the Prince with him.

Patimate is furious with the Fairy and threatens to denounce her if she does not restore the Emir's daughter. The Fairy laughs at his threats, then suddenly espies Farfalla. She commands her to come to her. But Farfalla mocks her. Then the Fairy waves her crutch and a net stretches between the trees. The butterfly is caught in it.

Farfalla's winged companions come in quest of her and perceive her plight. They beg Hamza to liberate her; she refuses. But Patimate, who has watched the scene from behind the trees, creeps to the seat where the Fairy has placed her crutch and seizes it. He points the crutch at the net and frees Farfalla, then thrusts it at the Fairy who is rendered motionless. Alas! Patimate drops the crutch and an evil sprite swoops down and bears it away.

The butterflies cover Hamza with the net in which she caught Farfalla, and while she vainly strives to free herself, the butterflies fly away. Patimate calls to Mohamed and his suite and shows them the Fairy imprisoned in the net.

Act II. Scene I. The Palace of the Emir Ismaïl.

Mohamed tells the Emir that he has found the person who kidnapped his daughter. He orders Hamza to be brought in. The Emir questions and threatens her until she admits her misdeed, which she cannot set right for want of her magic crutch. Ismaïl orders the Fairy to be imprisoned, but, as she is being led away, the evil sprite appears and places the crutch in her hand.

"Stop!" she cries, "I will restore to you the daughter I took away."

She waves her crutch towards the east. Music is heard and there appears a rich procession—Circassian girls followed by black slaves bearing a rich palanquin which is set down before the Emir. The curtains are drawn back and a beautiful princess steps to the ground. The Fairy presents Farfalla to her father, who clasps her in his arms.

Djalma comes to greet his uncle, who leads him to Farfalla, who is veiled, and declares that she is the bride he had destined for him. When Djalma observes that he does not wish to marry, the Emir smiles and goes out. Zaïdée, Farfalla's maid, points out the Prince to Farfalla, and draws her veil aside. Djalma thinks he must be dreaming, then clasps the princess in his arms, but the pain of her old wound makes her swoon.

Presently she recovers consciousness, but the memory of her wound makes her repulse the Prince. Djalma tries to kiss Farfalla, but the Fairy glides between them and receives the kiss instead. In a moment she is changed into a beautiful young woman. The Prince, annoyed at Farfalla's indifference, pays his addresses to

Hamza, hoping to arouse the former's jealousy. The ruse succeeds, but the Fairy is furious at being tricked.

Now the Emir returns, followed by his suite, and commands a festival to celebrate his daughter's return. There is a number of dances followed by a combat between Circassian Amazons. Then the Emir announces the betrothal of his daughter and his nephew. The dancing is about to continue when Hamza, who is standing beside Farfalla, touches her cheek with her crutch. Once more she is changed into a butterfly who darts hither and thither among the frantic lords and attendants, who follow in swift pursuit.

Djalma, stupefied at this transformation, is about to rush in search of his *fiancée,* when the Fairy begs him to share her power. He refuses, but she extends her crutch towards him. His eyes close and he falls asleep. Then she strikes the ground with her crutch. The palace disappears to give place to magnificent gardens gleaming with gold and light.

Act II. Scene II. The enchanted gardens. In the background is a cascade of silver flowing into an immense pool, in which grow rushes and aquatic plants mingled with coral. The pool is surrounded by a huge flower-bed.

Tiny sprites precede their mistress, the beautiful Fairy, Hamza. She looks lovingly at the sleeping Prince then, followed by her attendants, goes to prepare fresh delights.

Djalma awakes and believes himself to be under the influence of a dream. Butterflies flutter about the pool and flowers, and among them he distinguishes his beloved Farfalla, who hovers over him. With a sudden movement he catches her in his hand. Music announces the Fairy's return and, fearful for the butterfly's safety, he hides her in a rose-bush.

Hamza enters accompanied by her sisters, the Diamond Fairy, the Pearl Fairy, the Flower Fairy, and the Harvest Fairy, whom she has invited to her wedding with Prince Djalma. Behind follows a brilliant Court.

A beautiful child advances with a lighted torch, symbol of Hymen. Attracted by the light, Farfalla darts towards the torchbearer. Alas! the flame shrivels her wings and she falls into the Prince's arms.

But the enchantment is broken and Farfalla is once more a beautiful princess. Hamza makes a threatening gesture, but her sisters take the part of the lovers and change her into a statue. At the same moment a fairy palace rises behind the gardens to which

the fairies, forming a canopy with their upraised wands, conduct
Farfalla and Djalma.

*

Le Papillon has many interesting associations. It is the only
ballet of which Marie Taglioni was part author, and the only
ballet for which she composed the choreography; it is the first
ballet for which Jacques Offenbach composed the music; and it is
the ballet in which Emma Livry made her first great triumph.

Livry was a *protégée* and pupil of Taglioni, who watched over
her development like a second mother, hoping to see her own art
flower again in Emma. The ballet of *Le Papillon* was devised as a
vehicle to display Livry's capabilities.

Commenting on the score, the critic of *La France Musicale*[1] remarks: "In the first act may be mentioned a pretty theme of a
pastoral nature in march time, during which a village wedding
crosses the stage; the waltz danced by Mérante and Mlle. Livry; a
very witty buzzing of flies at the moment when the roguish maid
tickles the fairy's face; and, lastly, a ravishing waltz theme, the
Valse des Rayons, played on muted violins, which had been applauded in the overture.

"In the last act there was the 'March of the Young Circassian
Women,' the *pas de trois* danced by Mlles. Fiocre, Barate, and
Beaugrand, the *ensemble* of the Butterflies, and the *pas* danced by
Mérante and Mlle. Livry."

Albéric Second[2] reports: "I can still see and hear a certain waltz,
admirably danced by Mlle. Livry, and for which Offenbach has
found a love of a tune, without taking count of many other melodies which could be sung as well as danced. On the other hand
there is a *Pas de Châle* which I did not particularly care for, and a
Pas de Boucliers which I did not like at all."

"The settings," declares the same writer, "are very pretty, except
that of the second scene, which is very beautiful. It depicts a forest
glade on a splendid summer day. As for the fourth scene, there
were great devils of vases which seemed a little like nougat about
to melt."

Of Livry as Farfalla there exist two charming impressions in
prose; the first is by Paul de Saint-Victor,[3] the second by Paul
Smith.[4]

"Mlle. Emma Livry, launched by Mme. Taglioni into the

[1] December 2nd, 1860.
[2] *La Presse,* December 2nd, 1860.
[3] *La Presse,* December 2nd, 1860.
[4] *Revue et Gazette Musicale de Paris,* December 2nd, 1860.

rarefied air of the ideal dance, has raised herself among the stars. What modest grace! What airy lightness! Never did German moonlight be-silver a more diaphanous elf or wilis. She has an elevation which soars and a bound which carries one away. There are moments when we almost hear the wings on her shoulders quiver and rustle. It is an enchantment, a magic spell, to see her bound and rebound in the forest amid the play of light. She might be the queen of motes circling about the sun. When, in the last scene, she darts into the pool of the cascade, gliding over the waters, skimming the lilies, breaking her flight at sharp angles, as do swallows and dragon-flies,

> L'herbe la porterait, une fleur n'aurait pas
> Reçu l'empreinte de ses pas.

"Her success was immense. The public showered upon her flowers, applause, and recalls. Not only her talent but her courage was applauded, because, in the second act, she was seized with a painful attack of cramp in the foot. Nevertheless the brave child completed her dance. Indeed, her anguished expression made a distressing contrast with her dancing feet."

"First Emma Livry was elevated to the rank of sylphide and now she passes to the state of butterfly. Did Mlle. Emma Livry not exist, the Butterfly would not be possible. For this role, so ethereal and so diaphanous, an intangible artiste is imperative, an artiste with whom *ballon* is a natural gift, and Mlle. Emma Livry has a *ballon* which has never been equalled. Marie Taglioni herself must be astonished at seeing herself surpassed, but doubtless she will console herself with the reflection that she had grace, which is even more charming than beauty. Her true heiress has not yet acquired all that is best in her inheritance. In the meantime she bounds and leaps as no one else could do. She skims over the ground, the water and the flowers, apparently without touching them. She rises like a feather, and falls like a snow-flake."

Livry received an ovation at the end of the ballet, but what must have pleased her most of all was the gift she received from Taglioni herself. who sent her a photograph bearing the following touching inscription: *Faites-moi oublier. Ne m'oubliez pas.*

PAUL TAGLIONI

PAUL TAGLIONI, surnamed Paul the Great, was born at Vienna on January 12th, 1808, where his parents resided until 1813. His father was the dancer and choreographer, Filippo Taglioni, while his sister, Marie, was to establish the Romantic Ballet with her creation of the title-role of *La Sylphide*.

He was given a good general education and received dancing lessons from his father; and when the latter's company visited Paris, Paul also studied under the French dancer, Coulon.

Paul made his *début* at Stuttgart in *Zemire et Azor* on November 4th, 1825. Later he danced at Vienna, Munich, Paris, and Berlin, with increasing success. He was a great favourite with the Berlin public and received an excellent engagement at the Opera House there. At this time his dancing-partner was Amalia Galster, whom he married, and by whom he had three children, Marie, Charles, and Augustina.

The first achieved considerable success as a dancer and, owing to her having the same Christian name, is frequently confused with her celebrated aunt; the second entered the diplomatic service; the third became a talented actress.

Paul Taglioni composed a great many ballets, some writers place the number as high as forty, such as *La Nouvelle Amazone* (1831), *Les Jeunes Pensionnaires* (1832), *Le Pauvre Pêcheur* (1836), *La Fille aux Roses* (1838), *Thea* (1847), *Coralia* (1847), *Fiorita* (1848), *La Prima Ballerina* (1849), *Les Plaisirs de l'Hiver* (1849), *Les Metamorphoses* (1850), *L'Ile des Amours* (1851), *Satanella* (1855), *Les Joyeux Mousquetaires* (1857), *Ballanda* (1857), *Morgana* (1858), *Flik and Flok* (1862).

A particular feature of his compositions is his ingenuity and foresight in adapting new inventions for the contriving of novel effects to enhance the attraction of this ballet—for instance, the employment of electric light in *Electra*, and the use of roller-skates in *Les Plaisirs de l'Hiver*.

He retired from the stage on October 1st, 1883, and died on January 6th, the following year.

CORALIA OR THE INCONSTANT KNIGHT

Ballet in 5 Scenes. Book: Paul Taglioni. Music: Cesare Pugni. Scenery: Charles Marshall. Costumes: Miss Bradley and Mr. Whales. Choreography: Paul Taglioni. First produced: Her Majesty's Theatre, London, February 16th, 1847.

CHARACTERS

Coralia, Daughter of Troisondin, the King of the Waters, and adopted child of the fisherman, Ulrich	MLLE. CAROLINA ROSATI
The Knight Hildebrand	M. PAUL TAGLIONI
His Squire	M. GOURIET
Bertha, the Duke's adopted daughter .	MME. PETIT-STEPHAN
Her Page	MLLE. HONORE
The Duke	M. GOSSELIN
Troisondin, King of the Waters . .	M. VENAFRA
Ulrich, the fisherman	M. DI MATTIA

Sir Hildebrand, of Ringstetten, a guest at a tournament given by the Duke, attracts the attention of the latter's adopted daughter, Bertha. She presents him with a magic scarf, but requires him in return to enter the "Enchanted Forest." Sir Hildebrand obeys and takes the road to the forest. Troisondin, a potent spirit of the waters, directs the knight towards the hut of a poor fisherman.

The latter receives him hospitably; and the knight meets the fisherman's adopted daughter, the lovely Coralia, who is at once fascinated by the youthful knight. Coralia, a water nymph, is Troisondin's niece, and, though reared by mortals, retains all the sportiveness of her heedless nature. Her conduct in presence of the stranger draws upon her a reproof, but the playful girl is unwilling to bear restraint, and bounds out of the cottage. A storm arising, the fisherman and the knight become alarmed for the safety of Coralia, and go in search of her.

She is found by Hildebrand reposing on a bed of leaves in the middle of a large lake. By the aid of Bertha's scarf he draws her to the bank. Their mutual love is now avowed, and the nymphs appear to celebrate the happiness of their sister. The fisherman and his wife arrive, when Sir Hildebrand declares his intention to marry Coralia, which union takes place without delay.

Sir Hildebrand's return to Court rejoices everyone except Bertha. Her chagrin is increased by the fisherman and his wife, who come to claim her as their daughter, lost at the time when they found Coralia. Indignant at the contempt with which Bertha treats her parents, the Duke determines to abandon her. Coralia, pitying her condition, offers her a residence at Sir Hildebrand's castle, which Bertha accepts.

At Ringstetten the knight's former love for Bertha revives, and he treats his wife with coldness. Troisondin is angered at this, and, in his character of a water-sprite, visits the castla through a fountain. Coralia has suspected a rival in Bertha, and is confirmed in this idea on seeing the magic scarf, by the possession of which she maintains the passion of the knight. Overwhelmed with grief and indignation, Coralia tears off her wedding-ring, and disappears into the fountain; while the avenging Troisondin drags Sir Hildebrand to destruction.

*

Coralia is based on De la Motte Fouqué's *Undine,* the earlier ballet of *Ondine* having little connection with the romance beyond its title. This ballet has the distinction of having introduced Carolina Rosati to the English stage; while Marie Taglioni, the choreographer's daughter, made her English *début* at the same time, in a solo dance called *Pas de la Rosière,* placed in the fouth scene.

Lumley, the director of Her Majesty's Theatre, records in his *Reminiscences* that "the *ensemble* of the acting, the story, the beauty of the scenery, the lavish richness of the appointments, ensured for *Coralia* a triumphant reception which seemed to have restored for a time the ancient prestige of the lately-discredited ballet pantomime."

The Times' critic states: "This well-devised ballet plays with sorrow and infuses a dash of the pathetic into joy; it is the ironical sport with dramatic interest. Therefore let Undine be regarded as the symbol of the Terpsichorean drama, her sportive courtship of the knight is redolent of a pantomimic drama, her wrongs are teeming with a Giselle-like sorrow. There is nothing about her that choreographic action cannot express." [1]

The settings were much admired, particularly the lakeside scene. The critic of the *Illustrated London News* observes: "The moonlight sheds over it a sort of mysterious hue, which gives a shadowy resemblance to the figures of the Naiads, whose graceful, stealthy movements seem rather like the embodiment of a dream than living reality." [2] *The Times'* critic describes the scenery as "very

[1] February 17th, 1847.

beautiful, especially a concluding picture of the rising waters, with a strong assemblage of Tritons." [1]

"Rosati," says the former writer, "is young and very handsome. Her dark eyes sparkle with fire and intelligence; her countenance varies with every shade of feeling she expresses; her movements are graceful, her pantomime vivacious and impassioned; and her peculiar style of person and air renders her slower *pas* above all highly effective."

Marie Taglioni is described as "very young; her face, and, in fact, her whole person, are *piquante* and original. Her countenance is full of character and intelligence; and, as a dancer, she is light, agile, graceful, and, at the same time, possessed of remarkable power of muscle."

THEA OU LA FÉE AUX FLEURS [3]

Ballet in 1 Act and 2 Scenes. Book: Paul Taglioni. Music: Cesare Pugni. Scenery: Charles Marshall. Machinery: D. Sloman. Costumes: Miss Bradley and Mr. Whales. Choreography: Paul Taglioni. First produced: Her Majesty's Theatre, London, March 17th, 1847.

CHARACTERS

Thea, the favourite slave of Prince
    Hussein . . . . . . MLLE. CAROLINA ROSATI
The Flower Fairy . . . . . MLLE. MARIE TAGLIONI
Prince Hussein . . . . . . M. PAUL TAGLIONI
    Odalisques, Slaves, Animated Flowers, and Aerial Genii.

A magnificent garden of Bagdad. Within an oriental kiosk, reposes the youthful Prince Hussein, surrounded by odalisques. Near the kiosk is Thea, regarding with passionate and tender looks the Prince, who, all unmoved by the music of his slaves and the voluptuous dances of his odalisques, is absorbed in the contemplation of some flowers which he holds in his hand. Nothing can withdraw him from his reverie, and Thea becomes dejected at his indifference. Hussein desires to be left alone. Thea entreats that she may remain; but the Prince commands her to leave him. She feigns acquiescence, but conceals herself behind one of the columns of the kiosk. Hussein appears delighted at his solitude, and goes with rapture from flower to flower, while Thea follows him with

[2] February 20th, 1847.
[3] *Thea or the Flower Fairy.*

all the marks of jealousy. She again attempts to tear him from his ecstasy; but the Prince appears to have eyes for his flowers only. At last he quits the scene.

The neglected beauty weeps in despair; but a sudden thought brings smiles to her lips. She approaches the statue of the Flower Fairy, and entreats the restoration of her lover's heart. She then forms a crown of flowers and throws it in the air; the crown alights on the head of the statue. Thea becomes motionless, and disappears, as does also the kiosk—in the place of which arises a lovely rose-tree, surrounded by every variety of flower. The Prince returns, and sees with joy the change which has taken place. He kisses the flowers, savours their perfumes, and is about to pluck a rose, when, behind the tree, appears the Flower Fairy. She seems in anger, and reproaches Hussein for his audacity. The Prince throws himself on his knees and implores pardon; but the Fairy will grant it only on condition of his marrying the flower which shall have conceived a passion for him. Surprised at this proposal, he nevertheless consents. The Fairy conducts him to a bank of turf, places on his head a crown of poppies, and the Prince sleeps.

It is night; a blue flame issues from each floral group, the flowers become animated and are changed to nymphs, who smile, walk, dance, and form a garland round the Flower Fairy. While the flowers dance, Thea, who represents the rose, escapes, takes the poppy crown from the Prince's head, and returns to mingle with her companions. Hussein awakes; he is dazzled by the tableau which presents itself, but seeks the rose, the object of his dream, falls at the feet of Thea, and offers her his heart and hand. The Queen of Flowers appears to sanction their union.

*

The Times[4] describes *Thea* as "one of the most beautiful ballets ever seen at the Opera-house . . . one of those happy *media* between ballet and *divertissement* which are so much better than those long pieces of action in which the public is worn out with processions and non-dancing magnificence. It is, in fact, one blaze of brilliant dancing from the beginning to the end, the costumes and scenic effects being of the most novel and poetical character. Fancy a *corps de ballet* attired in costumes of the hues of various flowers, from the white lily to the many-coloured tulip, and an elaborate last scene, which combines all the richness and mechanical ingenuity of the last scene of *Coralia,* with a floral instead of an aquatic splendour.

[4] March 19th, 1847.

"Mlle. Rosati has achieved a success to which that which she gained in *Coralia* is not to be compared for a moment. Combining in herself the most striking qualities of all the great *danseuses* of the age, she kept the audience in one continued state of enthusiasm, and two of her 'variations' were rapturously encored. There is also a *pas seul* for the admirable Marie Taglioni.[5] . . . Never was a more brilliant display of scenic decoration and choreographic art. Nothing has approached it since the days of *Alma*."

FIORITA ET LA REINE DES ELFRIDES [6]

Ballet in 4 Scenes. Book: Paul Taglioni. Music: Cesare Pugni. Scenery: Charles Marshall. Costumes: Miss Bradley and Mr. Whales. Choreography: Paul Taglioni. First produced: Her Majesty's Theatre, London, February 19th, 1848.

CHARACTERS

Fiorita	MLLE. CAROLINA ROSATI
Hertha, Queen of the Elfrits . . .	MLLE. MARIE TAGLIONI
Toniello	M. LOUIS D'OR

Toniello, a young Sicilian villager, is about to marry the lovely Fiorita. The happy couple, accompanied by their relations, are already on their way to the village church, when the terrible Hertha, Queen of the Elfrits, or Evil Elves, casts an eye of love on the bridegroom.

The power of Hertha is great, she can raise storms by her incantations; she can cause human beings to lose their vitality and become senseless statues. A tempest separates the lovers, and Hertha, assuming the dress of Fiorita, lures Toniello to a cottage, and, when discovered, bears him to her enchanted gardens.

These are delightful to look upon, but evil lurks beneath their beauties. They are adorned with seeming statues, the victims of Hertha's hate; they are watered with the stream of oblivion, one drop of which produces forgetfulness of the most sacred ties.

But the powers of evil are not suffered to work without impediment. Anar, the genius of good, takes pity on the forlorn Fiorita, and conducts her to the gardens, when she appears to her bridegroom among the other statues. With a rose branch, given to

---

[5] Niece of the great Taglioni.
[6] *Fiorita and the Queen of the Elfrits.*

him by Anar, Toniello disenchants them all, and the sight of his
Fiorita dispels at once the effect which the Elfin Queen had produced on his heart. The sudden appearance of Hertha causes
Fiorita to retire; but before she departs she drops a nosegay as a
token of remembrance.

Hertha must now have recourse to the stream of oblivion, if
she would secure the affections of Toniello. The elves immerse
his cap in the fatal water, and all thoughts of his Fiorita are at
once obliterated from his mind.

But Anar is not unmindful; and, just as Toniello is about to resign himself to the charms of the Elfin Queen, the good genius
removes from the head of the villager the cap that causes the delu-
sion, and transforms Hertha into a statue, that she may stand an
inanimate witness of the happiness of the Sicilian lovers.[7]

*

The story, says the critic of the *Illustrated London News,* "is
slight, greatly differing in this respect from the 'ballet pantomime'
of former years; a change, perhaps, few will regret, but still we almost wish there were greater scope given for the remarkable pantomimic powers of Rosati. It is, however, a charming ballet, and
perfect in all its details." [8]

The Times' critic likewise acclaims the treatment of the subject
as "exceedingly good." "M. Paul Taglioni," he continues, "has
not paused too long in the pantomimic part of the entertainment,
but has interrupted the succession of dances as little as possible,
while, by alternating the lively earthly dances of the Sicilian
peasants with the aerial movements of the fairies, he has achieved
a most agreeable variety. A Tarantella . . . by the villagers, and
a dance by Anar, the good geni, all personated by children, are to
be ranked amongst the prettiest effects which have been produced
by a *corps de ballet.*" [9]

The settings were highly praised, particularly that of the enchanted garden full of statues, and the final scene where the background was formed by a fountain of real water. A contemporary[10]
asserts that this was the first occasion on which real water was
used with success in a theatrical production, a view which is confirmed by *The Times'* critic who observes that "the introduction
of real water as a means of scenic effect has generally proved a

[7] This description is taken from a synopsis in a contemporary programme.
[8] February 26th, 1848.
[9] February 21st, 1848.
[10] *Lady's Newspaper,* August, 1848.

failure, but here the intersecting streams are managed with so much taste and skill that the result is both novel and beautiful." [9]

Commenting on the two principal *danseuses,* the same writer observes: "The consummate art with which Rosati (*Fiorita*) executes those brilliant steps which are peculiar to herself created the wonted enthusiasm, and Marie Taglioni[11] again delighted everybody by the juvenile vigour of her movements. The easy execution of obvious difficulties marks Rosati, the daring accomplishment of *tours de force* distinguishes Marie Taglioni." [8]

The critic of the *Illustrated London News* states that Rosati "executed several new *pas,* one of which, in the first *tableau,* is exceedingly graceful, and obtained an immediate *encore;* she advances to the front of the stage with a sort of *demi-pirouette,* on the point of her toe, alternately reversing from right to left, and ending with a bounding step *à la* Taglioni." [12]

ELECTRA OU LA PLÉAIDE PERDUE [13]

Ballet in 5 Scenes. Book: Paul Taglioni. Scenery: Charles Marshall. Choreography: Paul Taglioni. First produced: Her Majesty's Theatre, London, April 19th, 1849.

CHARACTERS

Electra	MLLE. CARLOTTA GRISI
Queen of the Stars	MME. PETIT-STEPHAN
Alcyone	MLLE. MARRA
Maia	MLLE. TOMASSINI
Merope	MLLE. AUSSANDON
Tayeta	MLLE. JULIEN
Sterope	MLLE. LAMOUREUX
Celeno	MLLE. PASCALES
Nilsson, host of the inn . . .	M. GOURIET
Edda, betrothed to Ehrick . .	MLLE. MARIE TAGLIONI
Jenny, cousin to Edda . . .	MLLE. MARRA
Stenbock ⎱ hunters, friends of	M. DI MARRIA
Berger ⎰ Ehrick . . .	M. VENAFRA
Ehrick, a hunter, betrothed to Edda .	M. PAUL TAGLIONI

[11] Niece of the great Taglioni.
[12] February 26th, 1848.
[13] *Electra or the Lost Pleiad.*

A Norwegian shepherd has been betrothed to a village maiden, but, in his solitary wanderings and contemplations of the heavens, his imagination has become excited into a sort of adoration for "a bright particular star"; and this same star happening to be a pretty woman, is not insensible to his flame.

Electra, so the star is named, comes down from the firmament to meet him in the wood, and a great deal of lively flirtation ensues between them, in the midst of which, unfortunately, the pair are surprised by a whole bevy of stars, with the Queen at their head.

The poor star, as a punishment for her fault, is degraded from her starry state, and condemned to remain on earth. Thus reduced to the condition of a mere village maiden, she accompanies her lover home; but she proves a most unwelcome guest. For her sake the faithless swain deserts his betrothed, who straight runs mad and dies.

But the "starry divinities," moved to pity by this catastrophe, restore the star to her station in the firmament, and the dead maiden to life. The shepherd returns to his old love, and the stars shed their brightest rays, and join in the rejoicings, which conclude amid all the splendour of the Empyrean.

*

"In the whole composition," observes *The Times'* critic, "there is a great deal of poetical feeling. The thoroughly terrestrial dances of the Norwegian peasants are strikingly contrasted with the light airy costumes of the stars,[14] and even these, by the employment of a variety of soft colours, are tastefully distinguished from each other." [15]

The production has a particular interest in that it is presumably the first ballet in which the new invention of electric light was used. "The last scene," says the *Times'* critic, "in which the restoration of the Pleiad is represented, is perfectly original, and is one of the most remarkable ever exhibited. A peculiar haziness is diffused over the whole picture, and through this the personified Pleiads appear as ethereal, indistinct forms, each bearing a lamp. In the midst of them rises their repentant sister, who now surpasses them all in lustre, and whose pre-eminent brilliancy is caused by the use of the electric light." [15]

Another contemporary, describing the same scene, declares: "The stars are seen incarnated in the forms we behold in heavenly ascents in Raphaël and Andrea del Sarto, although here nothing

[14] A device much favoured by this choreographer. Cf. *Fiorita*.
[15] April 18th, 1849.

is painted but the finely transparent azure sky, and the figures are rendered effulgent by the aid of electric light. The audience was mute with astonishment at this startling sight."

The two most successful dances were the *Pas de l'Etoile,* rendered by Grisi, in which she "is deprived by Ehrick of the star which adorned her forehead, and endeavours to regain it with all that playful vivacity in which she is unrivalled." [16] The other dance was the *pas de deux, La Lutte,* by Grisi and Taglioni,[17] in which "each contends with the other to win the affections of Ehrick. In this *pas* . . . the *adage* is marked by a number of new and graceful poses, and the quick movement by the skilful manner in which the styles of the two *danseuses* are contrasted." The critic of the *Illustrated London News* observes of *La Lutte* that "the extraordinary grace displayed, the sprightly twinkling movements, and the daring bounding, almost flying, steps elicited by this contest, baffle description."

LA PRIMA BALLERINA OU L'EMBUSCADE[18]

Ballet Divertissement in 1 Act. Book: Paul Taglioni. Music: Cesare Pugni. Choreography: Paul Taglioni. First produced: Her Majesty's Theatre, London, June 16th, 1849.

CHARACTERS

Mlle. ———, *prima ballerina* . .	MLLE. CAROLINA ROSATI
Virgine, Mlle. ———'s maid . . .	MLLE. MARRA
Passolo, *maître de ballet* and *premier danseur*	M. D'OR
Rinaldo, chief of the bandits . . .	M. PAUL TAGLIONI
Astolfo, his lieutenant	M. DI MATTIA

Bandits of both sexes, Ladies of the Corps de Ballet.

The scene of the ballet is placed in the mountainous borders of the Roman states. The brigands are rejoicing after a successful foray, but are interrupted by Astolfo, who dispatches all those who are unarmed to a festival in the neighbourhood. Hardly have they departed, when a whistle warns the rest that a carriage is approaching. The robbers cut down trees, throw them across the road, and conceal themselves.

[16] April 18th, 1849.
[17] Niece of the great Taglioni.
[18] *The Principal Dancer or the Ambush.*

The carriage approaches, and the bandits seize the postilion, the maid, and the courier, and bind them to the trees. Rinaldo hands down from her carriage, the fair passenger within. This lady is Mlle. —— who is travelling with her *maître de ballet*. She vainly implores the chief to permit her to continue her journey. Her boxes, by their direction, soon reveal to Rinaldo that she is a *prima ballerina,* no less a dancer than the celebrated Mlle. ——. She once more implores her captors to allow her to depart; and he consents to her request on condition that she will execute some of her *pas* before she departs. She cheerfully consents to this proposal.

The boxes are restored to their places, and, while she retires to her carriage to put on her dancing-costume, the trembling Signor Passolo is compelled to execute a new *pas* with the maid, the inspiration for which is dictated by the robbers' pistols, which are constantly pointed at him.

Mlle. —— now reappears in costume, the bandits form a circle, and amid their admiration she performs some of the most celebrated steps of her repertory. At the conclusion of her dancing the bandits clear the road for her to proceed. At this moment the dragoons arrive in pursuit of the robbers.

Mlle. ——, flattered by the triumph she has achieved, silences Passolo, and assures the officer that she has met with no obstruction. Hardly has he conducted her back to her carriage than a procession of black penitents is seen crossing the mountain path, the soldiers set aside their carbines and kneel. The penitents drop their cloaks, reveal their bandit costumes, raise their guns, and the curtain descends.

*

La Prima Ballerina, said to have been founded on an incident in the life of the famous dancer, Marie Taglioni, is acclaimed by *The Times'* critic as "one of the neatest works of the ballet kind that has been produced for some time, and is not at all tedious." [19]

"Mlle. C. Rosati plays the *danseuse,* and with much grace and versatility imitates all those *pas* which Taglioni has immortalized. M. Paul Taglioni, who has composed the *divertissement,* plays the brigand chief with spirit and a perfect knowledge of picturesque effect. The groups of brigands are exceedingly well managed, and at the rise of the curtain a striking *tableau* is formed by the sets of dancers appearing at different elevations among the mountains."

[19] June 15th, 1849.

LES PLAISIRS DE L'HIVER OU LES PATINEURS[20]

Ballet Divertissement in 1 Act and 2 Scenes. Book: Paul Ta-glioni Music: Cesare Pugni. Choreography: Paul Taglioni. First produced: Her Majesty's Theatre, London, July 10th, 1849.

The principal characters by MLLES. CAROLINA ROSATI, MARRA, TOMASSINI, JULIEN, LAMOUREUX, AUSSANDON, and MM. CHARLES, VENAFRA, GOURIET, DI MATTIA, and D'OR.

The first scene is the celebration of a Polish marriage amid flowers in a Winter Garden. In this episode Rosati and the leading dancers of the company display their grace and animation in attractive *pas.* Having disported themselves within until sunrise, the gay votaries join the country people without, in another pastime of their own.

The second scene shows a frozen lake, over which the sun rises. Crowds of skaters throng the ice, attended by vendors of every species of ornament and refreshment. On one side befurred ladies are seen gliding along on sledges; in another direction the men are enjoying the Montagne Russe. Presently room is made for the dances of the mummers.

First there is the *Pas des Frileux.* The laughing, but shivering, crowd dance themselves into warmth. Next comes the *Pas à la Hussarde.* This is followed by the *Grand Quadrille des Patineurs,* wherein every detail is executed by skaters with the most remarkable effect. In the minute pauses between each figure of this *pas* are solos, entries, intermèdes—representing alternately feats of skating, agility, mimed episodes, and dramatic situations: and thus amid the snow-capped icebound scene the most picturesque effects are obtained.

*

Les Plaisirs de l'Hiver was brought out in the middle of an exceptionally hot summer, so that the first aspect of the stage, "with the misty veil extended over the ice-bound waters," had a refreshing effect on the audience.

The new *divertissement,* says *The Times'* critic, "stands out in strong relief to the general platitude. There is about it that great requisition—a distinctive character. Story there is none, not even so much as an attempt to represent a little flirtation, but the sports

[20] *Winter Pastimes or The Skaters.*

of a Hungarian winter are set forth with such liveliness and in such a fresh and genial spirit that the spectator cannot help being carried away by the excitement of the scene.

"The stage, which is covered with a sheet of some smooth material, is supposed to be the Danube, and all sorts of movements are performed upon it by the dancers, who dart along on skates fashioned with small wheels at the bottom. This expedient for skating on a stage was adopted in a Covent Garden pantomime years ago; but the elaboration of the idea with a *Pas de Patineurs,* with an incessant variety of grouping and of attitude, belongs to M. Paul Taglioni." [21]

The music, according to the critic of the *Illustrated London News,* "graphically describes every episode, even imitating the sound of gliding on the ice."

Here is a description of the second, and principal, scene by the same writer. "First are seen isolated individuals, in Hungarian costume, crossing the stage, the early risers of the village rapidly gliding along in the pursuit of business or of traffic—some carrying their merchandise to market. One by one the pleasure-seekers (previously beheld in the Jardin d'Hiver) arrive on the stage— some feeling their way on the ice with hesitating step, others gyrating with the certainty and the enjoyment of the mastery of a practised art.

"The crowd of youths and maidens, attracted by curiosity, who are not supplied with skates, determine to resist the cold by dancing and exercise of their own: they blow on their fingers, clap their hands, foot the measure, and beat their breasts—crossing from side to side, and running from one bank of the lake to the other, to the time of a sprightly characteristic mazourka. Then comes the exquisite *polka à la hussard* on the ice, executed with more than even her ordinary spiriting by Rosati, dressed in the most fascinating costume.

"Upon this ensue the feats of the skaters. Here the illusion is complete; the mechanism entirely concealed, the mazes varied, intricate, fantastic, and original, in appearance inextricable, find their solution in simple movements that fill the audience with delight and surprise, and keep up constant laughter and applause. Then appear on the stage the most renowned skaters of the district, and M. Charles' movements, as their leader, combining vigour and dexterity with attitude and mimic action in the highest degree graceful, elicit at each new episode outbursts of the loudest applause. Then the sun begins to decline, the assemblage

[21] July 5th, 1849.

of skaters, or traders, of ladies drawn by horses in their sledges, throng the stage in the most varied and characteristic groups.

"The power of illusion and of invention of the balletmaster, the painter, and the musician can go no further, and the curtain drops amidst the cheers and applause of the audience, of whom the most austere, for once, find the ballet too short." [22]

The Times' critic praises the ballet no less warmly, but makes an adverse comment on the lighting. "The representation of the sun by electric light," he states, "was the weakest part of the exhibition. In the ballet of *Electra,* where the stage was almost fitted up like an orrery, and no figures were plainly offered to the sight, this light produced an excellent effect, but when dancers are to be observed it dazzles the eye rather unpleasantly, and, moreover, it does not greatly harmonize with the general scenic direction."

LES METAMORPHOSES

Ballet in 1 Act. Book: Paul Taglioni. Music: Cesare Pugni. Choreography: Paul Taglioni. First produced: Her Majesty's Theatre, London, March 12th, 1850.

CHARACTERS

The Sprite, who successively appears as a Page, a rustic Coquette, a Will o' the Wisp, a Folie, a Domino, a Cavalier	MLLE. CARLOTTA GRISI
Karl, a student	M. PAUL TAGLIONI
Ida, his betrothed	MLLE. ROSA
Parents of Ida and Karl	MM. GOURIET and DI MATTIA
Momus	M. CHARLES
Elves	MLLES. AUSSANDON

Karl, a student and an enthusiast, has made himself an abode among the ruins of the Castle of Heidelberg He divides his time between love and study—his betrothed, Ida, and learning—each with him is equally a passion. Not satisfied with literature, sacred and profane, he has passed the bounds of hallowed knowledge, and has endeavoured to penetrate the mysteries of the shadowless kings of perdition.

One of those good-humoured elves or sprites, who mix, invisible, in the haunts of men, and laugh at their follies, discovers the

[22] July 14th, 1849.

peculiar tendency of Karl's mind, and determines to disgust him of the dangerous pursuit by a practical exemplification of the ends of magic power.

Assuming every shape in turn, he makes the student fall in love with him in the form of a lady; he renders him furious from jealousy, by making love to his betrothed, in the shape of a handsome and gallant officer, and so on.

Thus, thanks to a little wholesome mischief, Karl is corrected and becomes wise and happy at last.

FLIK AND FLOK

Fantastic Ballet in 2 Acts and 6 Scenes. Book: Paul Taglioni. Music: Hertel. Choreography: Paul Taglioni. First produced: Teatro alla Scala, Milan, February 13th, 1862.

CHARACTERS

Flik, an alchemist's son	M. Effisio Catte
Marta, his grandmother	Mlle. Pierina Sassi
Nella, Marta's god-daughter . .	
Topazza, daughter of the King of the Gnomes	Mlle. Amina Boschetti
A Sea-Nymph	
Flok, Flik's friend, a street musician	M. Teodoro Gasperini
Van Bett, a Burgomaster . . .	M. Federico Ghedini
Peterson, a peasant	M. Cesare Vismara
The King of the Gnomes . . .	
The Queen, his wife . . .	Mlle. Regina Banderali
Amphitrite	
A Police Officer at the bottom of the sea	M. Giovanni Mauri

The Spirits of Truth, Fortune, Destiny, the Spree, the Thames, the Seine, the Neva, and the Venetian Lagoon. Burgomaster's Officers, Peasants, Gnomes, Nymphs, Inhabitants of the Sea, Cupids.

Act I. Scene I. The interior of Marta's house.

It is Marta's birthday. Flik and Nella enter and embrace her, and give her a present. The Burgomaster arrives and congratulates Marta, then tries to flirt with Nella, who disdains his attentions.

Peasants and fishermen arrive with their presents and a dance follows.

The Burgomaster dances with Marta, then asks Nella for a dance, but she and her youthful companions make fun of him. He complains to Marta that Nella has refused his offer of marriage. Marta replies that she cannot compel her god-child to marry against her will. The Burgomaster, furious with rage and aware that Marta has not paid her rent, orders his officers to seize her furniture. Her friends protest so vigorously that the Burgomaster is obliged to withdraw. The peasants and fishermen continue their dance until he and his officers return. After some altercation they are again forced to leave.

Flik and Nella try to reassure Marta that nothing will happen; at this moment Flok enters.

He admires a miniature which portrays Marta as a young girl. Flik, who has been wondering how he can find some money, remembers that his father, who was an alchemist, may have hidden some gold in the house; immediately everybody begins to turn the house upside down in order to find it.

Flok discovers a large portrait of the alchemist let into the wall. The friends are about to remove it when the Burgomaster's officers enter and take away all the furniture, including the picture. Flik and Flok discover that the picture concealed a door, which gives on to a dark corridor. As soon as the officers have left, the friends enter the corridor.

Nella, who has gone out with her god-mother, returns, and, looking into the corridor, finds the half of a ring. She picks it up and rushes away.

Act I. Scene II. The Kingdom of the Gnomes.

Flik and Flok enter very cautiously. They touch a golden cord. A carillon of bells is heard and the room glows with light. Gnomes appear, welcome the intruders, and begin to dance. They are led by Topazza, with whom Flik falls in love. At the height of the dance the King and Queen enter, attended by courtiers and their executioner.

The friends are seized and the King, refusing to listen to their explanation, decides that they must die. They are brought before a statue of Destiny, but, before the executioner can behead them, the statue comes to life and shows them an inscription on the pedestal, which declares that any stranger who can find the other half of the gold ring shall have love and wealth. The King frees the prisoners and orders them to be taken back to the house.

Act II. Scene I. A Beach.

A ship appears on the horizon and is about to sink in a dreadful storm. In a little while the vessel disappears beneath the waves.

Act II. Scene II. The Palace of Amphitrite.

Flik and Flok are seated at the bottom of the sea, enchanted with their surroundings. A police officer asks them for their passports.

When the friends are left alone they begin to explore. In the sunken ship they find a box which contains a mandoline.

Flok begins to play the mandoline and awakes a sleeping sea-nymph, who approaches them. Inhabitants of the sea come from every side and, led by the nymph, begin to dance. The Queen, Amphitrite, followed by her attendants, appears. The nymph bows to her and explains the plight of the two strangers. Flik tells his adventures and asks the Queen where he can find the other half of the gold ring. She offers to take him to different parts of the world to help him in his search.

At the back of the stage appear figures symbolic of the Spree, the Neva, the Thames, the Seine, and the Venetian Lagoon.

Amphitrite returns and invites Flik to consult the Spirit of Truth, who appears from the Well of Youth. The Spirit asks him what he desires to know. He replies that he wishes to find the woman that Fate has destined for him. The Spirit answers and vanishes.

Flik is astonished at the vision revealed to him, for he recognises Marta and Nella. He notices that the latter has in her hand the half of the gold ring. He entreats the Queen to let them return to earth. Flok thinks of Marta when she was a young girl and steals a small phial from one of the cupids. Amphitrite agrees to their leaving her kingdom, and causes a column of water to rise and bear them upwards.

Act II. Scene III. The interior of Marta's house.

Marta, sad at heart, is sitting by her spinning-wheel. Nella is reading a letter which informs her that the ship on which the two friends were sailing has sunk. Marta endeavours to console her god-child when Flok enters and announces that Flik will arrive immediately. Nella hurries out to meet him.

Flok, in love with the miniature of Marta, offers her the phial he took from the cupid. Eager to recover her youth she drinks too much of the elixir.

At this moment a messenger from the Goddess of Fortune appears and summons all four to go with him to the Temple of Fortune.

Act II. Scene IV. The Temple of Fortune.

Here the lovers are reunited and all ends happily.

ARTHUR SAINT-LÉON

ARTHUR MICHEL SAINT-LÉON was born in 1815. Probably the first ballet arranged by him was *La Vivandière*, which he produced at London in 1844 for Fanny Cerito, who later became his wife, but separated from him in 1850.

He composed a number of successful ballets, of which the following are the best known: *La Vivandière* (1844), *La Fille de Marbre* (1847), *Le Violon du Diable* (1849), *Stella* (1850), *Paquerette* (1851), *Graziella* (1860), *Le Metéore* (1861), *The Orphan Theolinda* (1862), *Diavolina* (1863), *Fiammetta* (1864), *The Humpbacked Horse* (1864), *La Source* (1866), *The Lily* (1869), *Coppélia* (1870), and *Saltarella*. These ballets were created at London, Paris, or St. Petersburg.

Saint-Léon was in great demand both as dancer and choreographer, and received invitations to visit Lisbon, Bordeaux, Vienna, Berlin, Madrid, Rome, Florence, Turin, Brussels, Venice, Pest, and other important cities, when he revived many of his ballets as well as such established favourites as *La Sylphide, Giselle, Esmeralda,* and so on.

In 1852 he wrote a treatise on a new method of dance notation which he had devised—*La Sténochorégraphie*, published at Paris, 1852—and which he used to record his ballets. He made his *début* at St. Petersburg on October 7/19, 1859, in *Saltarella,* a very diverse ballet composed by himself.

Saint-Léon was a talented mime, a dancer of a good school, and a violinist; the last accomplishment he turned to good purpose in *Le Violon du Diable.* He also composed some forty pieces for the violin.

LA VIVANDIÈRE

Pantomime ballet in 1 Act. Book: Arthur Saint-Léon. Music: Cesare Pugni. Scenery: Despléchin, Séchan, and Diéterle. Choreography: Arthur Saint-Léon. First produced: Her Majesty's Theatre, London, May 23rd, 1844.

CHARACTERS

Kathi, a vivandière	Mme. Fanny Cerito
Bibermann, a tavern-keeper . . .	M. Quériau
Hans, his son	M. Saint-Léon
Robintzel, a Burgomaster . . .	M. Berthier
Mme. Robintzel	Mlle. Aline
Baron de Grindberg	M. Fusch
Baroness de Grindberg	Mlle. Louise Marquet
Jacob, a postilion	M. Adice
A Light Infantryman	M. Cornet

Villagers.

Scene. The market square of Wieselbourg, a little village in Hungary. It is a holiday and peasants are enjoying themselves in various ways: some are loosing bows; others are dancing; still others are dining at tables set up before the posting-inn.

Robintzel, the burgomaster, strolls with his wife, bidding everyone enjoy themselves. But, whenever he speaks to a young girl, his wife evinces signs of jealousy.

A light infantryman, travel-stained, dashes through the streets, asking for Mr. Bibermann. The girls point to the inn, from which the proprietor is just emerging. The soldier hastens to hand him a letter.

The girls surround Bibermann and try to read over his shoulder. To satisfy the general curiosity, he announces that Kathi, his ward, Kathi the *vivandière*, is returning home. This news is acclaimed with delight.

The Burgomaster tells his wife that Kathi's beauty has been greatly missed and grows so enthusiastic at the thought of her return that his wife speaks her mind.

A rolling of drums heralds the arrival of Kathi, who enters with a number of soldiers, also returned to their native village. Bibermann asks his ward to sit down and all the inhabitants greet her in turn.

Robintzel kisses her hand and declares that she is more beautiful than ever. His wife reminds him of her presence with a tap of her fan.

"But where is Hans?" asks Kathi.

"He will soon be here," replies Bibermann. "I can hear his horn and the crack of his whip."

Hans drives in a carriage from which descend the Baron de

Grindberg and his wife. The Baron is a captain in Kathi's regiment and asks her why she is staying in the village.

"It is my birth-place," she replies. "I am leaving the army and shall stay here."

The Baroness is also jealous and finds it very strange that her husband should leave her to chat with a *vivandière*.

"Let us be off," says she.

"Well, aren't you going to change the horses?" inquires the Baron of Hans.

The postilion replies that Jacob will take his place as he wishes to join in the dances. But Jacob, whose intentions are similar, pretends that he has hurt his arm. The Baroness orders Hans to continue. But he begs the travellers to wait for the arrival of another postilion, since Kathi has just returned and he has not seen her for two whole years. The Baron takes Hans's part and the travellers decide to stay in the village, although the Baroness is very concerned at the way her husband looks at the pretty *vivandière*.

Hans takes Kathi by the arm and, going to Bibermann, asks him to give his consent to their marriage.

The inn-keeper is about to agree when the Baron and the Burgomaster raise objections. It would be absurd, they argue, that a rich post-master should permit his son to marry a penniless *vivandière*. Bibermann agrees.

"Why have you wrecked my happiness?" asks Kathi of the Baron and the Burgomaster.

They each reply: "Hans is only a clod; he is unworthy of you. I know of a far better man than he."

"Who is it then?" asks Kathi.

The Baron and Burgomaster reply with significant glances which their wives intercept. They reproach their husbands for their guilty intentions. But the Baron and Burgomaster protest their innocence.

The wives ask pardon for their suspicions and suggest that their husbands' thoughts would be less likely to stray if they wore something to remind them of their spouses. The Baroness gives her husband a ring, while Mme. Robintzel places a medallion round the Burgomaster's neck.

The *vivandière* observes all that takes place. She goes to Bibermann and asks him if he would object to her marrying his son if she had a dowry.

"No," replied that worthy.

"Very well," comments Kathi, "I will have one by this evening."

Looking at the Baron and the Burgomaster, she says in an aside. "These two will provide me with one."

The two wives go into the inn, but the Baron says he will follow shortly. He writes a note addressed to himself and offers Jacob a gold piece if he will find someone to deliver it to him at a time he will indicate.

The Baron joins in the dancing and is pleased to notice that Kathi looks at him with a friendly gaze; but Hans reproaches his sweetheart for being a flirt.

"I love you," replies Kathi, "have no fear."

The dance ended, Jacob brings the note to the Baron.

"How unfortunate," he observes on reading it. He tells Hans that his colonel has recalled him and he must leave immediately.

Bibermann goes to tell the Baroness to make ready for the journey.

"No, it is useless," says the Baron. "You may tell her that I shall be back by midnight."

Hans brings in the postchaise and mounts his horse. The Baron climbs in, but gets out the other side and hides behind a tree. Jacob draws the curtains and tells Hans to drive on. The postilion whips up his horses and leaves at a gallop.

Darkness falls and the merry-makers go inside the inn. Kathi is about to follow when the Burgomaster tells her that he must speak with her alone.

"But won't your wife object?" observes Kathi.

The Burgomaster replies that he does not love his wife, but if Kathi could forget Hans and love him, he would make her a handsome present.

She asks him to prove his love by giving her the medallion his wife gave him. The Burgomaster is alarmed, foreseeing the difficulty of explaining its disappearance. He kneels at Kathi's feet and begs her to choose another test. As he kneels she slips the chain from his neck. Then, hearing a footstep, she whispers: "Someone is coming, perhaps it is your wife!"

Robintzel, in a rare fright, hurries away, but not before saying that he must meet her again. Kathi asks him to return when she claps her hands.

The newcomer is the Baron. Kathi expresses surprise that he should be there and he explains his ruse. He declares his love for Kathi and she repeats her tactics, as a result of which the Baron gives her his wife's ring.

Suddenly she pretends to listen and declares that she can hear the crack of the postilion's whip. She urges the Baron to leave her as Hans will be furious.

"But I must see you again," he protests.

"I will clap my hands when you may come," replies Kathi.

The postchaise returns at a gallop. Hans dismounts, furious at the trick played upon him. He accuses Kathi of being a party to it. In reply she claps her hands when her two admirers run out and each take her by the hand.

Hans is about to curse Kathi for having betrayed him, when she takes a soldier's musket left lying on the table and fires it into the air. Everyone rushes to the market-place.

"What is the matter?" cries everyone.

"Two men tried to carry me off," Kathi replies. "But it was so dark I could not see their faces."

"You saw them distinctly," declares Hans. "I'll tell their names if you won't."

"Be quiet," urges Kathi.

"I won't," counters Hans.

"Be quiet, I implore you," entreats Kathi, "our marriage is assured."

The Baron and the Burgomaster reproach her for having fooled them, and swear to have their revenge.

"You will revenge yourselves by giving me that dowry which you told Mr. Bibermann I lacked," declares Kathi.

"Never," they reply.

Then the *vivandière* tells them that she will inform their wives—who are seen approaching—that they have given her a ring and a medallion. The stupefied culprits each give Kathi a well-filled purse, upon which she restores the ring and the medallion. Then she turns to Bibermann and, announcing that the Baron and the Burgomaster have honoured her with a dowry, asks if he still has any objection to her marrying his son.

"No," replies the inn-keeper. "I will even marry you to-day."

*

La Vivandière owed much of its success to the captivating *Redowa,* introduced into the ballet by Cerito and Saint-Léon. "This *Redowa,*" observes the *Times'* [1] critic, "is a capital thing of its kind, the best since the *Pas Styrien*—full of life, character, and 'fun.' The gentleman first assumes a kind of awkwardness; he goes lumbering about the stage, and seems indifferent to dancing. Then the lady pats him into compliance, and all sorts of coquetries

[1] May 24th, 1844.

begin, and are carried on during a pretty sort of stamping movement. Now the pair seem infinitely pleased with each other; now they seem determined to try each other's temper, and the ill humour of the one is always vanquished by the growing kindness of the other. Cerito thoroughly entered into the humour of this very amusing dance, and went through all its varieties with admirable *naïveté* and playfulness."

La Vivandière was produced at Paris on October 20th, 1848, at the *Théâtre de la Nation,* with Cerito and Saint-Léon, and obtained, according to the critic of the *Journal des Théâtres,*[2] a success "almost approaching that of *La Fille de Marbre."*

This little ballet included four successful *pas*: the *Pas de la Vivandière,* "perfectly mimed and danced by Cerito"; the *Pas de l'Inconstance,* "in which the two spouses make the house shake with calls of bravo"; the *Pas de Six,* which achieved a similar success; and, finally, the *Redowotchka,* danced by Cerito and Saint-Léon, which had an overwhelming reception. "Everything that we have seen up to now of *pas styrien, en redowa, en cachuca,* in short, no matter what *danse de caractère,* is surpassed by the production of this picturesque *Redowotchka,* which is, moreover, rendered by its two inimitable interpreters with an incredible spirit, precision, and gaiety."

The critic of *Le Corsaire*[3] is inclined to cavil. "Fanny Cerito in *La Vivandière,"* he says, "is what she was in *La Fille de Marbre,* an elegant woman, well formed, ethereal, who has always the same smile, the same searching glance, the same bow in acknowledgment of applause. Nevertheless, it must be stated that the public seems bored with her talent, and all the bravos are now given to Saint-Léon's unusual lightness. . . . This year we no longer have eyes for the woman, we have admiration for the husband alone."

When Cerito came to St. Petersburg in 1855, *La Vivandière* was produced for her by Perrot. In 1860 the ballet was revived with Alexandra Prikhunova as Kathi.

A ballet of the same name—*La Vivandiera*—and presumably the same theme, was produced at the Teatro alla Scala, Milan, on March 12th, 1854, with choreography by Borri, and the title-role interpreted by Carolina Pochini.

[2] October 25th, 1848.
[3] October 23rd, 1848.

LA FILLE DE MARBRE

Pantomimic Ballet in 2 Acts and 3 Scenes. Book: Arthur Saint-Léon. Music: Cesare Pugni. Scenery: Cambon and Thierry. Choreography: Arthur Saint-Léon. First produced: Théâtre de L'Académie Royale de Musique, Paris, October 20th, 1847.

CHARACTERS

Alyatar, a Moorish Prince . . . MM.	H. Desplaces
Manasses, a sculptor	A. Saint-Léon
Cadaval	Elie
Belphegor, leader of the Salamanders	Quériau
The Governor of Seville	Berthier
Dom Sandoval	Toussaint
An Officer	Adice
A Penitent	Lenfant
The King of Spain ⎱	Monet
A Peasant ⎰	
Fatma	Mme. Fanny Cerito

The action passes at the end of the fifteenth century.

Act I. Scene I. The Palace of the Spirit of Fire, a flaming cavern. The salamanders who inhabit it are grouped in an attitude of surprise.

Satan enters leading by the hand Manasses, whose features express fear. Belphegor, leader of the salamanders, asks the strangers the reason for their visit.

At a sign from his dread companion the sculptor explains that he has fashioned a beautiful female statue with which he has fallen in love, and he is willing to barter his soul with the Devil if he will cause the Spirit of Fire to endow his masterpiece with life. Satan displays a parchment which the sculptor has written with his blood.

Belphegor extends his sceptre towards a giant metallic rock and the statue rises into view. Flames leap from the rock and flicker about the statue. The Lord of Fire commands that the statue shall come to life and fascinate all mortals, yet her own heart shall ever be insensitive to love; should she ever fail in this respect she will revert to a marble statue.

Manasses, shocked at this injunction, entreats Belphegor not to give life to the statue, but already the miracle is accomplished:

the features become animated; the mouth parts in a smile; the bosom rises and falls.

The sculptor delights in the transformation, and Fatma, such is the name of the statue, wishes to embrace her creator; but Manasses steps back in fear. Satan places his taloned hand on the sculptor's brow and his features take on a demoniacal expression, while his dress changes to a fantastic costume.

The rear of the cavern parts and reveals a youth asleep near an arbour. Fatma appears before him but withdraws as he extends his arms towards her. Belphegor informs Manasses that the youth is a Moorish prince, named Alyatar, whom the Spaniards have dispossessed. He dreams of Fatma and loves her without knowing it.

The rear of the cavern closes and Manasses and Fatma are carried earthwards.

Act I. Scene II. A square in Seville. There is an arbour to the right; houses to the left; and in the background the Guadalquivir.

Alyatar sleeps on a bench near the arbour, as in the preceding scene. Satan, disguised as a scholar, contemplates his features. Suddenly the Moor awakes, looking round for the enchanting being of his dream, until he realizes that he was only dreaming.

Satan approaches and asks if it would please him to see the woman of his dream.

"Yes," replies the Moor, "but what do you know of my dream?"

Satan stretches out his hand in sign of friendship, but Alyatar recoils at the searing touch. The Devil departs and Alyatar goes into the arbour.

It is a holiday and the young people of Seville come from the other bank of the Guadalquivir to promenade the square. There is dancing to mandolines, but their pleasures are interrupted by a musician who tells how he has just seen a most terrifying figure. Hard on his words comes Manasses, who enters with grotesque leaps. The frightened girls shrink from his presence, but he tells them that a beautiful gypsy is going to dance to them.

Fatma appears and holds everyone spell-bound by her beauty. Now a halberdier goes to the couple and, indicating a notice that mountebanks and gypsies are forbidden to enter Seville, curtly orders them to leave. But, melted by Fatma's beauty, he invites her to read the notice, on which the word "forbidden" has suddenly changed to "permitted." The halberdier is astonished.

Enter the Governor of Seville who, seeing the gypsies, reprimands the soldier for neglecting his duty. The soldier points to the notice, but it has changed back to its original form. The Gov-

ernor orders the soldiers to eject the gypsies, but Fatma's glance
is so disarming that both Governor and soldiers allow the gypsies
to remain and dance. The enthralled spectators dance too.

Attracted by the noise Dom Sandoval and his friends appear on
a balcony. Alyatar emerges from the arbour and is delighted to
see the original of his dream.

Alyatar darts towards Fatma and declares his love for her. The
sculptor, seeing the prince, wishes to take the young girl away,
but she refuses to go and begins to dance. Dom Sandoval and his
friends surround Fatma and load her with compliments.

Excited by the captivating dancer the bystanders fail to notice
a procession of penitents crossing the river. The leader reprimands
the Governor for his shameless conduct and orders the soldiers
to arrest the gypsies and carry them to prison. But Fatma fascinates both guards and penitents with her glance so that they are
powerless; then the two gypsies enter a boat and put off. Dom
Sandoval and his friends hire other boats to follow the alluring
beauty. Alyatar, seeing all the boats taken, leaps into the river
and swims towards Fatma's boat. Manasses, alarmed, seizes the
oars and rows with fury.

Act II. The Alhambra.

The King of Spain holds high festival in honour of his final
victory over the Moors.

The noblemen, who have pursued Fatma, come to ask the King's
permission for her to dance before him, which is granted.

She enters, accompanied by Manasses. The King is immediately captivated by her beauty and presents her with a magnificent necklace, then leaves with his suite.

Dom Sandoval and his friends pay court to Fatma. Manasses
pays little heed for he sees none whose love is likely to be fatal to
her. But Alyatar, concealed behind a column, watches Fatma with
impassioned gaze. As the couple are about to leave, she sees Alyatar and, suddenly preoccupied, places her hand on her heart.

Alone, Alyatar shows his joy at Fatma's responsive gesture.

Very soon she returns, eager to see the Moor. He tells her of
his love and of all the dangers he has run in order to be near her.
Fatma is conscious of a sympathy which fills her with fear, and
she orders Alyatar never to see her again. But, so touching are
his entreaties, that she permits him to remain, on condition that
he speak no word of love. The Prince tells her that his future
will be decided very soon, for the Moors are to attempt a rising.

Satan enters and warns the young man that the moment has come. Thereupon Alyatar draws his scimitar, trumpets ring out, and, taking farewell of his love, he goes forth to battle.

Fatma anxiously awaits for the result of the contest. Manasses suddenly enters and inquires the reason for her emotion. But her reply is drowned by a terrible uproar and the noise of clashing swords. The Spaniards are routed and Alyatar is proclaimed King of Granada. He asks Fatma to share his throne and the young girl, conquered by love, consents to be his bride. In despair, Manasses reminds Fatma of the terrible danger she runs. She replies that she prefers love to immortality.

Alyatar, in fulfilment of his vow, conducts Fatma up to the steps leading to his throne. But, just as she reaches it, the sky grows dark, thunder rolls, the earth trembles, and Fatma is changed into a statue. Enraged, Alyatar breaks the crown that he cannot share with his beloved.

Manasses is struck dead. Satan places a foot on his corpse in token of possession.

*

The student will find it of interest to compare the theme of this ballet with that of *Alma,* of which it is simply a condensed version, the episode in France being omitted. Since Cerito made one of her greatest successes in *Alma,* produced at London, and, moreover, composed several of the dances in it, doubtless she suggested to her husband the advisability of reviving the ballet under another name.

*

A ballet, called *The Marble Maiden,* with music by Adolphe Adam, was produced at the Theatre Royal, Drury Lane, in 1845. The theme, by V. de Saint-Georges and Albert, has some resemblance to the Pygmalion-like element of the first scene of both *Alma* and *La Fille de Marbre,* otherwise it would seem to be the first sketch for Saint-Georges's later ballet, *Les Elfes,* first produced at Paris, 1856, with choreography by Mazilier.

As a matter of interest I give a transcription of the plot of *The Marble Maiden* as recorded in the *Illustrated London News*[4]:

"A celebrated sculptor of Florence, Massachio (M. Albert) has become enamoured of a very beautiful statue of Hebe (Mlle. Adèle Dumilâtre) which he has produced. In the delirium of his passion he appeals to a statue of the Evil Angel in his *atélier,* to assist him; and from this incarnation learns that the statue shall be animated

---

[4] October 4th, 1845.

by day for his destruction. To counteract this threat, another statue, that of the Good Angel, decrees that the statue shall be marble by night for his safety. Upon these two conditions the ballet turns.

"The Prince Cosmo de Medicis (M. Petipa), discovering that the beautiful figure is in the possession of Massachio, contrives to possess himself of it, and carries it to the palace of his uncle, the Duke Laurent de Medicis (M. Pichler), where he also falls in love with it, although he is betrothed to the Princess Beatrice (Mlle. Adèle). The Hebe, now animated, returns the passion of Cosmo; but, feeling that she is, in duty, bound to Massachio, leaves the palace with him during a *fête,* and returns to the sculptor. Cosmo attempts to regain her, but night approaches, and she is turned to marble.

"Cosmo is, however, so madly in love with her, that, having traced her to a villa wherein Massachio resides, on the Arno, he contrives to gain admittance, with a number of students, and prevails on her to fly once more with him to the Duke's palace, where a splendid festival is about to be given in her honour. The Duke, enraged at the passion of his nephew, orders Hebe to be driven from the palace. Massachio has pursued her there, and arrives during the *fête.* The commands of the Duke are about to be obeyed, when the hour arrives for Hebe to become marble again; and when the change takes place, Massachio, in a delirium of rage, love, and jealousy, seizes a hammer and knocks the statue to pieces. Hebe is then borne to Heaven by the Good Angel, and the ballet concludes."

The Marble Maiden was highly praised for its lavish production, which evoked loud applause, but it was found over long and the action frequently dragged. The ballet was considerably cut after the initial performance.

Dumilâtre received many tributes for her interpretation of Hebe. "Nothing could be more artistically conceived or executed than her animation," observes the critic of the *Illustrated London News,* "and her general dancing and pantomime through the ballet was of the highest order."

LE VIOLON DU DIABLE

Fantastic Ballet in 2 Acts and 6 Scenes. Book: Arthur Saint-Léon. Music: Cesare Pugni. Scenery: Despléchin and Thierry. Choreography: Arthur Saint-Léon. First produced: Théâtre de l'Opéra, Paris, January 19th, 1849.

CHARACTERS

Urbain, a celebrated violinist . . . MM.	ARTHUR
	SAINT-LÉON
Grégoire, his servant	BERTHIER
The Comte de Vardeck	LENFANT
The Baron de Saint Ibars . . .	FUSCH
Doctor Matheus	CORALLI
Father Anselme	CORNET
Hélène de Vardeck . . . . . MLLES.	FANNY CERITO
Beatrix, her governess . . .	PAULINE
	LAURENT
Ursule, an inn-keeper . . .	ALINE DORSE
Solange, Urbain's nurse	DELAGUET

Act I. Scene I. The interior of the White Horse Inn at Roscoff in Brittany.

The inn is crowded with villagers determined to spend a happy Sunday evening. Some are drinking and playing cards, while others dance to the bagpipe. Suddenly the gaiety is interrupted by a loud clap of thunder, and a pale, sinister-looking man, dressed entirely in black and shrouded in a voluminous cape, appears on the threshold.

He walks towards the company who recoil in fright. He endeavours to calm them by explaining that he is merely a traveller seeking shelter from the storm, and entreats everyone to continue their pleasures. While the couples are forming for the dance the stranger takes a pinch of snuff and sneezes three times; at each sneeze the company quakes.

Amused at their fright the stranger goes to the fireplace and shakes his cloak, which sends the cards flying and overturns the glasses and bottles. "What a wind!" cries the mistress of the inn, crossing herself. But the company fear to stay longer and, despite her remonstrances, leave in disorder.

"Who are you, sir?" inquires the inn-keeper of the stranger sitting by the fire-side.

"I am Dr. Matheus," he replies, "and shall be staying the night."

Just as the hostess is about to give orders for a room to be prepared, there enters a young man, accompanied by a servant, carrying a bag and a violin-case. The young man is Urbain, a celebrated violinist. He asks Ursule if a beautiful young girl and her father have changed horses there. She replies in the negative and Urbain is distressed.

Dr. Matheus rises and, greeting the young man, announces that the Comte de Vardeck's daughter will soon arrive. The young man, surprised and alarmed, asks the Doctor how he knows this. "I have divined it," replies Matheus.

At the same moment the Comte and his daughter enter the inn, followed by Father Anselme. As soon as the last-named observes Urbain, he embraces him affectionately. At the sight of the monk, Matheus is visibly disturbed and vanishes through the wall.

The Comte inquires who Urbain is, and Anselme informs him that he is an orphan whom he has brought up and who has become a great artist. The Comte then remembers that he heard Urbain play at a concert given by the King and compliments him on his art. Urbain hopes that Hélène will likewise congratulate him, but she affects to ignore the violinist.

At this point an elegantly-dressed young man comes out of one of the rooms. Astonished to see the Comte and his daughter, he goes towards them and is greeted by Hélène, now all smiles. Urbain asks Anselme the name of the newcomer, and is informed that he is the Baron de Saint Ibars, who is shortly to marry Hélène.

The inn-keeper tells the travellers that their rooms are ready and all retire, save Father Anselme and Urbain. The latter is very distressed and the monk, who has divined his secret, bids Urbain leave, since it is impossible for him to marry the daughter of a rich nobleman. The violinist promises to leave immediately.

At this moment a footman arrives with a message that the Comte wishes to speak with Father Anselme; the monk follows the footman.

Urbain, overcome with despair, resolves to commit suicide. He is about to leave the room to carry out his project when his way is barred by Matheus.

The Doctor smilingly begs a moment of his time, but Urbain replies that he has no time to lose.

"Are you so anxious then to end your life?" inquires Matheus.

"Who told you that I wished to commit suicide?" asks the stupefied young man.

"I divined it," answers the Doctor. "So you are going to renounce Mlle. de Vardeck merely because a monk has told you that you are cherishing a hopeless love, when, if you wished, she might be yours."

"If the wish be sufficient, I have succeeded," answers Urbain.

"A woman may be captivated by music," pursues Matheus. "Will you hand me your violin. Now, are you willing to venture all to achieve your object?"

Urbain hesitates, then assents.

At this moment thunder rolls and midnight strikes on the village clock. Matheus takes his stick and describes a magic circle about Urbain. He makes a commanding gesture and immediately the inn is crowded with women in pale grey dresses. Urbain would like to fly from these fearsome shades.

"Master, what is thy will?" cry the women.

"I desire the rose that inspires love, the laurel that bestows glory, and the serpent that confers the power of fascination."

The women point to the window which opens to reveal three more women dressed in red. They glide towards Matheus. The first carries a rose, the second bears a laurel crown, while the third has a serpent twined about her arm.

Matheus strikes the ground with his stick and a cauldron appears into which he throws Urbain's violin, then the rose, the crown. and the serpent, which are consumed in a fierce flame.

The three women watch the accomplishment of this evil work, while the others dance about the cauldron, from which a demon leaps out, holding in his hand a violin, which he hands to Matheus. Then the demon disappears into the ground. The women and the cauldron vanish, and the thunder ceases.

Matheus offers the violin to Urbain and invites him to try his power. At first he passes the bow mechanically over the strings, then, becoming animated, he plays with passion.

At the head of the stairs appears Hélène, dressed in a white gown and carrying a lighted candle. She listens intently, as if spellbound by the melody. Then she descends the stairs and goes towards the violinist, as if impelled by some magic force.

Urbain gazes at her tenderly, but Hélène remains silent. At this juncture Father Anselme enters and, seeing Hélène, asks the reason for her presence at such an hour. She tells him how she was awakened by a charming melody. The monk counsels her to return to her couch. As she goes she drops a ribbon, which Urbain picks up and presses to his lips.

"You promised to go!" observes the monk to Urbain.

"I was waiting till daylight," stammers the young man.

"You have forgotten to thank me," remarks Matheus.

"My gratitude will be eternal," replies Urbain, pressing his hand.

"He is mine!" exults Matheus.

Act I. Scene II. The ballroom in the Château du Poulighein.

The Comte de Vardeck is giving a ball to celebrate his daughter's birthday. Guests arrive in succession and, having offered their presents to Hélène, mount the staircase which leads to a vast gallery. The Comte accompanies them. Hélène lingers behind on the plea that she wishes to supervise the preparations for the ball, but in reality she wishes to talk with Urbain, who has climbed to the window.

She begs him to withdraw but he leaps into the ballroom instead, saying he cannot live without seeing her. Hélène gives him an invitation card for the ball and entreats him to return. He thanks her and, later on, enters with other guests.

The Comte observes the passionate glances which his daughter exchanges with the violinist and remarks to his friends: "I shall shortly give another festival to celebrate my daughter's marriage with her cousin, the Baron de Saint Ibars." The lovers are greatly distressed by this announcement.

Hélène tells her father that she does not wish to marry.

"But Monsieur de Saint Ibars has my promise," replies the Comte.

"And I have yours," adds the Baron to his cousin.

"I cannot love you," replies Hélène, "because I love another," and she indicates Urbain.

The Comte, indignant, upbraids Urbain, who replies that his intentions are honourable. The Baron, with a gesture of contempt, throws his purse to Urbain, while the Comte orders his footmen to remove the violinist.

Hélène, furious at this insult to Urbain, immediately follows her lover.

Act II. Scene I. The farm belonging to Urbain's cousin, Solange.

Hélène is resting on a couch in the summer-house, attended by Urbain and Solange.

Peasants bring in sheaves of corn and celebrate the harvest with dances and laughter, until Urbain bids them cease, so that Hélène may rest.

As he returns to the summer-house, Matheus passes through the closed door and confronts the terrified musician. He reminds him of his aid and now asks a service in return—to give him his soul.

Urbain refuses, but Matheus, declaring that he is Satan, tells him that it is too late to draw back. The violinist prays to heaven for forgiveness. Satan warns Urbain of his displeasure. A demon emerges from a tree-trunk and smashes his violin. Then Satan shows Urbain the Baron coming towards the farm. The latter knocks at the door. Hélène half rises, then sinks back on her couch. Father Anselme appears from behind her and stretches out his arms in protection.

Satan, baulked of his vengeance, conjures up a woman, resembling Hélène, who leaves with the Baron. Urbain tries to restrain her, but Satan holds him back. "Give me your soul," he cries, "and I will restore your sweetheart." But Urbain refuses. Satan, furious at his defeat, disappears into the ground.

Urbain rushes to the summer-house and rattles the door. Hélène goes to him and is horrified at his wild expression.

Father Anselme comforts the violinist. He tells him that the woman who went with the Baron was only a demon created in her likeness, and offers him a new violin. Urbain recoils in terror.

The monk, believing Urbain to have lost his reason, bids Hélène and Solange pray for him. Old Grégoire wishes to join them, but Father Anselme bids him watch over his master.

When the violinist has finished rushing about in the greatest disorder, Grégoire offers him the violin. He takes it mechanically and plays some strange chords, until at last he evolves a glorious melody which he suddenly ends.

Grégoire urges him to continue. An angel appears and tells Urbain that he may vanquish any evil spirit by playing the melody. The angel vanishes to give place to a demon who menaces the violinist. Urbain takes up the violin and repeats the melody, which causes the demon to vanish. Father Anselme praises the young man and assures him that he is delivered from evil.

Enter the Comte de Vardeck, who thanks the monk for having watched over his daughter. Father Anselme promises that Hélène will be restored to him, and at the same time asks the Comte to give his consent to her marriage with Urbain, assuring him that he is of noble birth. The Comte consents and all ends happily.

Act II. Scene II. A great hall in the Château du Poulighein.

The Comte welcomes his guests and invites them to witness a new *divertissement* in two scenes, called *Les Fleurs Animées,* in which Hélène and Urbain are to play the principal roles.

The flowers revolt against a gardener who keeps them captive in a green-house, and carry him off to the kingdom of roses. There the handsome gardener pleases the queen of that enchanted land and becomes her consort.

*

Le Violon du Diable was well received. Gautier, in his notice of *La Fille de Marbre,* an adaptation of *Alma* by Saint-Léon, produced at Paris in 1847, concludes: "In addition to his talents as choreographer and dancer, Saint-Léon plays the violin in a masterly manner, according to those who have heard him. It should be simple, it seems to us, to find a theme in which he could display his skill both as dancer and musician." [5]

Whether Saint-Léon took the hint, or whether he had already conceived such a ballet, it is difficult to say, but in *Le Violon du Diable* he not only danced but played the violin.

"M. Pugni's score," says the critic of *Le Corsaire*,[6] "is very pleasing. In the second act may be mentioned a charming waltz and a good number of captivating themes.

"The settings are very fine. The inn at Roscoff, the Château du Poulighein, the farm, the green-house, and the rose kingdom are pictures full of colour, splendour, and attraction.

"The first scene of The Animated Flowers seemed a little long, it could be pruned to advantage.

"The dances, in general, are delightful."

Another critic[7] observes that "Saint-Léon plays the violin like he dances.

"M. Coralli is a little plump for a devil, and had he not taken care to insert two little horn-tips in his wig and make his eyes stare in a terrifying manner, he might have been taken for an abbé.

"Mme. Fanny Cerito displays in the new ballet the rarest and most diverse qualities. Perhaps she is not dramatic enough in her first appearance. You would call her a pale and cold statue moving on a marble pedestal, rather than a young girl, till then unfeeling, attracted to her lover by an irresistible and supernatural charm. It seems to us that Elssler would have made a wonderful thing of this scene.

"In the last *pas de deux* with her husband, all her attitudes are charming. It is difficult to have more grace, freshness, lightness, and elevation, impossible better to satisfy the senses without detracting from the ideal."

STELLA OU LES CONTREBANDIERS[8]

Pantomimic Ballet in 2 Acts and 4 Scenes. Book: Arthur Saint-Léon. Scenery: Cambon and Thierry. Music: Cesare Pugni. Choreography: Arthur Saint-Léon. First produced: Théâtre de l'Opéra, Paris, February 22nd, 1850.

[5] *La Presse,* October 25th, 1847.
[6] January 22nd, 1849.
[7] January 29th, 1849.
[8] *Stella or The Smugglers.*

CHARACTERS

Gennaro Vitelli	MM.	ARTHUR SAINT-LÉON
Vitelli, an revenue officer . . .		LENFANT
Petrucio, chief of the smugglers . .		CORALLI
Jacoppo Balbi, his nephew . . .		FUSCHS
Gracioso, a notary		BERTHIER
Stella, Petrucio's daughter . . .	MMES.	FANNY CERITO
Catharina, a farmer		ALINE DORSE
Louiselle, her daughter		TAGLIONI-FUSCHS
Regina, a smuggler		MATHILDE MARQUET

Smugglers, Revenue Officers, Jewish Merchants, Fishermen, Maidens.

Act I. Scene I. Some Neapolitan smugglers have just unloaded their French goods on the coast of Pozzuola, and hide them in a grotto. Their women are crouched about brushwood fires.

Petrucio, their chief, bids his men rest, and the women offer them wine. He asks where his daughter is. His nephew, Jacoppo Balbi, tells him that Stella will soon arrive.

"I think she will be pleased," says Petrucio, "when she sees the necklace I have brought her from France. In the meantime hide it in the secret cleft in the rock."

Stella dances into the grotto and embracing her father congratulates him on having made a successful crossing. She invites the women to dance with her in celebration, which they do, while the smugglers light the scene with lanterns held on high.

Dawn breaks and Petrucio reminds the band of the necessity of selling their goods, and warns the women that, if any revenue officers try to enter the cave, they are to frighten them away by wearing long white veils.

While the women watch the smugglers depart with their chief, Stella is lost in reverie. Her friend, Regina, inquires the reason for her preoccupation, and she confides to her that she is in love with a revenue officer. Regina is horrified at this confession but, hearing footsteps, the women hide in the cave.

Enter a party of revenue officers led by Vitelli, who is accompanied by his son, Gennaro, fearful of the haunted grotto. As they are about to enter, Stella and the women advance, wearing

shrouds. The party take to flight, all save Gennaro, who is par-
alysed with fright.

Stella informs Regina that Gennaro is her lover and, telling her
companions to leave her, takes off her veil and goes to speak with
him. She asks him what troubles him; he replies that he has seen
a number of phantoms. She soothes him and he asks her whence
she has come. She replies that she has just left her father, who was
fishing. Gennaro urges Stella to leave the grotto with him, but
she tells him that she will regard him as a coward if he does not
stay with her.

She proposes a game of dice to which Gennaro agrees. He wins
and she opens her purse to pay him. He tells her that he was playing for a kiss. She kisses her hand to him, but he demands a real
kiss. When he tries to take one she runs away. He follows in
pursuit but, just as he catches up with her, a trumpet sounds announcing the return of the smugglers.

Stella tells Gennaro to flee, but, remembering that he is bound
to be seen, takes him into the grotto and indicates a hiding-place.
Almost immediately the smugglers arrive with the Jewish merchants to whom they have sold the goods. When the last bale
has been handed over, Petrucio tells his men that he will sail as
soon as it is dark. He then goes to the place where Gennaro is
hidden.

"Where are you going?" asks Stella. "I am going to put my
cloak away." "Let me do it for you," says Stella, and gives the
cloak to Regina.

Petrucio thanks her and then observes that he has not given her
his usual present. This time it is a necklace. He is about to procure it when Stella remarks that she would prefer to get it herself.
He tells her that she could not find it, then, scrutinizing her, remarks that she looks very pale.

Filled with surprise he enters the cavern. Alarmed, Stella tries
to hold him back, but he pushes her aside. Presently he emerges
with Gennaro, whom he accuses of being a spy. The smugglers
level their muskets.

"Stop!" cries Stella, "I love him."

"You love him," says Petrucio. "Very well, let him change his
calling for ours and become your husband." He takes off Stella's
ring and places it on Gennaro's finger. "You will leave with us
to-night, say good-bye to your betrothed." Gennaro gives Stella a
kiss which overwhelms her.

A horse is brought in. At the same time Jacoppo notices the uniform belt worn by Gennaro. The article is torn off and burned in

the fire. In the confusion Gennaro leaps on the horse and sends it off at a gallop.

"He has forsaken me," cries Stella.

Act I. Scene II. Vitelli is seated in front of a house on the seafront. Near him sits Catharina, the farmer, and Louiselle, her daughter.

Vitelli is bewailing the loss of his son in the fatal grotto, when Gennaro appears, pale and exhausted. Vitelli and the two women run to his assistance. He tells them of his adventures, but, catching sight of Stella's ring, says nothing of his betrothal to Louiselle. He tries to take off the ring but cannot do so.

The father, overjoyed at his son's return, promises that he shall wed Louiselle on the morrow.

"You do not seem pleased," observes Vitelli.

"I am delighted," replies Gennaro.

"Now go and tidy yourself," says Vitelli, "and we can go and take part in the Blessing of the Oars."

At his father's request Gennaro goes into Catharina's house.

Fishermen enter by the rocky road, bearing oars decked with ribbons. By other paths come the inhabitants of the surrounding districts. They all take part in the dances which precede the ceremony.

But, while everyone is happy, Gennaro is gloomy and thoughtful.

"What ails you?" asks Louiselle.

"Nothing," he replies. "I am only tired."

But she is dissatisfied and leaves Gennaro to himself. She is stopped by Stella, who asks her to accept a bouquet as a little betrothal gift.

Gennaro recognizes Stella and, yielding to an irresistible attraction, goes to her.

"You traitor!" cries Stella, "you have forgotten the oath you took in the grotto. But I will have my revenge."

Louiselle asks them what is the subject of their conversation.

"Your fiancé," replies Stella, "wishes that all three of us should dance the Saltarella."

She takes Gennaro into the middle of the quadrille. Louiselle follows and dances the Saltarella with them. But the honours are with Stella, and everyone wishes to know whence comes this charming girl; but no one can answer.

The dances are interrupted by the arrival of the father superior.

The fishermen kneel and raise their oars while he pronounces his blessing.

When the ceremony is ended Vitelli says to his son:

"We are dining with Catharina, give your fiancée your arm."

Gennaro gazes bewildered at Stella and Louiselle, then takes the latter's arm.

At this moment Petrucio appears and, pointing to Gennaro, says to Stella:

"Do you wish him to die?"

"No," she replies, "his marriage will never take place. Leave it to me."

Act II. Scene I. Catharina is sitting at her spinning-wheel in a room in her house. Louiselle holds a piece of embroidery, but only stares in front of her.

"What are you thinking about?" asks her mother.

"Of Gennaro," she replies. "I do not believe he really loves me."

"How can you be so silly," says Catharina.

There is a knock at the door and Stella enters. She tells Catharina that she has heard of her daughter's wedding and has come to offer her services as a maid.

Louiselle agrees to engage her, but declares that she is the girl that danced with Gennaro and herself. Stella asserts that she is mistaken.

A revenue officer brings a marriage-basket for Gennaro. Louiselle opens it and is delighted with the contents, while Stella bites her nails to stifle her rage. Catharina and Louiselle go out after having told Stella to tidy up the room.

Left to herself she looks at the wedding-dress, the veil, and the chaplet of orange-blossoms, and becomes so mad with jealousy that she is minded to tear them to pieces. But she tries them on and is so pleased with her appearance that she dances for joy. Then she remembers that her rival is to be married in them. Her rage returns, she stamps on the gifts, throws them in the basket, and takes flight through the window.

Hardly has she gone when Louiselle returns to admire her presents. Imagine her surprise when she finds them spoilt.

Stella comes quietly into the room holding a dish of fruit and is immediately accused of having ruined her wedding-dress. But she plays the innocent and suggests that some enemy who came through the window must be responsible.

This scene is interrupted by the arrival of the notary with the marriage contract. Gennaro, Vitelli, and the guests enter in turn. Catharina wishes Gennaro and her daughter to exchange rings. Gennaro pulls off Stella's ring which he throws away, but Stella picks it up. Louiselle offers Gennaro a ring, which he accepts, at the same time receiving from him one in exchange.

Catharina invites the guests to drink to the health of the couple. Stella offers a serviette to Gennaro. To conceal his agitation, he pays Louiselle every attention. Stella, mad with jealousy, drops the plates, upsets a dish of macaroni on the notary, and ends by overturning the salt-cellar. The guests look grave at this portent of ill-fortune.

The notary opens his portfolio to take out the marriage-contract, but it is missing, since Stella has stolen it. However, he discovers the counterpart; but when he asks for a candle, as he is short-sighted, Stella brings the light so near that the paper catches fire. Now the contract cannot be signed.

Catharina dismisses Stella, but she rejoices in having succeeded in her plan. The guests make the sign of the cross, believing Stella to be a force for evil, and drive her away.

The notary departs to draw up a new contract and the guests follow, all save Gennaro, who holds his aching head in his hands. He begins to doze. Stella appears at the window, glides by his side, removes Louiselle's ring from his finger and substitutes her own.

Act II. Scene II. It is the feast of Piedagrotta and, according to custom, betrothed couples go to pray at the Virgin's shrine. Gennaro is about to enter with Louiselle on his right arm when Stella grasps his left.

The bystanders are astonished at this action and demand the reason for it. Stella declares that Gennaro has two fiancées and points to her ring, which is on his finger.

"What a scandal," exclaims Louiselle.

"Why do you pursue my son?" demands Vitelli of Stella.

"I only wish him to keep his promise," replies Stella.

"But who are you?" protests Vitelli.

Petrucio steps forward and answers:

"You know me, Vitelli. My name is Petrucio. I have just returned from France where I made a fortune. This is my daughter."

"Of course I remember you," says Vitelli.

Petrucio turns to Gennaro and remarks:

"I am rich enough to give up smuggling."

"But what about Louiselle?" asks Gennaro.

"Tell me the truth," says Louiselle, "it is Stella you love, is it not?"

"Yes. Will you forgive me, Louiselle?"

"I forgive you and release you from your vows," declares Louiselle. "Although we have been brought up together, I love you as a brother rather than as a husband. I wish you every happiness."

"Thank you," cries Gennaro, embracing Louiselle.

*

Stella, says the *Journal des Théâtres,*[9] consists of "four delicious pictures which successively reveal to our surprised gaze groups of fishermen, maidens, smugglers, revenue officers, Neapolitans, and jolly sailors. The situations, all very choreographic, are treated with an incredible freshness of pattern and style. These picturesque *pas* surpass in effect all that has been attempted hitherto. You can hardly believe what a relief this is to the eye.

"Saint-Léon is a great fancifier who does not wish to follow well-trodden paths; he creates a style and seems to blend all that the dances of Europe possess in the way of piquant originality and dainty coquetry, while conforming to the traditions of the French School. There are suggestions of Spain, Sicily, Calabria, and Moscow in his compositions, of which he alone has the secret; rejuvenated memories brought to perfection which, in truth, are inventions.

"The production is lavish; there is that famous Festival of the Piedigrotta, which immediately recalls an old painting of a Neapolitan Fair. . . .

"The Festival of the Blessing of the Oars is no less unexpected in its happy confusions, ordered and festooned with the most pleasing effect to the eye."

Of Saint-Léon as dancer the same critic[10] declares: "He has never ascended so high. He soars to the 'flies' like a rocket, he twirls like a leaf in a whirlwind—the stage might be made of indiarubber.

"Stella is Fanny Cerito's finest role, which she likes best because it brings her immense honour. The enthusiasm rose to such a pitch that she was even asked to repeat *pas* which had left her momentarily exhausted."

[9] February 27th, 1850.
[10] March 2nd, 1850.

PAQUERETTE

Pantomimic Ballet in 3 Acts and 5 Scenes. Book: Théophile Gautier and Arthur Saint-Léon. Music: Benoist. Scenery: Despléchin, Cambon, and Thierry. Choreography: Arthur Saint-Léon. First produced: Théâtre de l'Académie Nationale de Musique, Paris, January 15th, 1851.

CHARACTERS

François	MM.	ARTHUR SAINT-LÉON
Job		CORALLI
Bridoux		BERTHIER
Sergeant Durfort		ADIN
Martin		LENFANT
The Mayor		CORNET
A Soldier		DAUTY
Paquerette	MME.	FANNY CERITO
Catherine, 1st Cantinière . . .	MLLES.	ALINE
Marthe, 2nd Cantinière . . .		LACOSTE
Marie, 3rd Cantinière . . .		LACOSTE
Two Sheriff's Officers . . . . {	MM.	BEGRANDET LEFEVRE

Act I. A village in the north of France, which reveals many traces of Flemish influence. An air of gaiety and leisure indicates a day of festival.

A young man called François, dressed in his best, comes out of his house to go to the festival. His father remonstrates with him for leaving off work as he has to meet the claims of a rapacious creditor. But François pays no heed, promising to work twice as fast on the morrow.

At this point Durfort, the dreaded creditor, enters and threatens Martin with prison if he does not pay. Martin pleads for time to go to town and arrange a loan. François takes off his best clothes, puts on an apron, and planes and saws with redoubled vigour. Durfort, seeing that little is to be gained by carrying matters too far, consents to Martin's seeking his fortune in town.

The village becomes animated and Paquerette enters with a jug of milk on her head, thinking of all the dances she will dance. Surprised to see François working, she asks him how much longer he will be. François waves her away. Astonished to learn that he is going to work all day in preference to waltzing with her, she is piqued and concludes that he loves her no longer.

The villagers, young and old, dressed in their best, throng into the street. Among them is Durfort's son, Job, a lanky booby, whose every movement excites ridicule. He carries a flower-pot on his head which he offers to Paquerette, who, wishing to spite François, accepts this gift with a charming smile. François flushes with annoyance, which delights Paquerette, since it proves that he still loves her.

Now the games begin. The first contest is shooting at a target with a crossbow; the prize is a gold necklace. The general marksmanship is so poor that Paquerette entreats François to try. He does so and wins, placing the necklace about his sweetheart's neck. Then follows the scissors game. Girls with bandaged eyes try to cut a ribbon from which is suspended a beautiful dress. Paquerette wins and goes into her house to put on the new dress.

While she dresses there is a procession of four cars symbolical of the four seasons. Paquerette returns in all the splendour of her new clothes and François, unable to resist the temptation to dance with her, takes off his apron and leads her out.

After the dance there is a sack-race. Job continually falls on his face, and François has already achieved half the course when his father returns. He has a sad tale to tell, for not only has he been unable to raise any money, but there is to be a draw for the militia. The villagers are greatly alarmed by the news.

A trumpet sounds and Bridoux, the recruiting-sergeant, enters with his soldiers, accompanied by a mayor and his officers carrying the wheel and numbers, which is set up on a table.

Job and François are among those who must draw lots, a prospect which pleases neither. Job pretends to be lame, but when the sergeant draws his sword and threatens him, he flees with the swiftness of a gazelle.

François feigns to be deaf, until the sergeant takes Paquerette behind him and imitates the sound of a kiss.

Now follows the draw. Job picks a low number and must turn soldier, but François has the good fortune to draw a high number and is therefore exempt.

Job is greatly distressed, but his father promises to buy him a substitute. Since he cannot find anyone to take his son's place, he orders the sheriff's officers to take possession of Martin's cottage. Then François offers to become a soldier in discharge of his father's debt. Durfort is delighted but Paquerette is sad. She gives her lover her gold cross as a keepsake and bids him fare-

well. The trumpets ring out and recruits and veterans march
away, led by Bridoux.

*Act II. Scene I. A town in central France. Soldiers sitting
astride benches are playing cards; others, with drums for tables,
are shaking dice; still others are practising sword-play. The veterans smoke or drink, with appraising eyes on the* cantinières *who
pass among the men.*

François tries to kiss Catherine, but she tells him that he is only
pretending. He agrees and shows her Paquerette's cross. François's
comrades are highly amused at this sentimental episode.

Now Bridoux gives the recruits a lesson in dancing and treads a
measure with Catherine for their edification. François burlesques
the sergeant's deportment to the great amusements of his fellows.
Bridoux asserts his authority by sending his men to the mess.

Catherine, left alone, makes merry at the sergeant's pretensions,
when a short, smart, good-looking youth enters with an assumed
ease. He says that he wishes to enlist and asks where he should
apply.

"You are very short," observes Catherine.

"I shall grow," counters the newcomer.

"You are very young," continues the *cantinière*.

"But I shall get older. In ten years time I shall be twenty-six."

Catherine is convinced that the young man is a woman, nevertheless she introduces him to Bridoux.

"You are not tall enough," comments the sergeant.

But Paquerette, who has disguised herself as a man, stands on
her toes and protests that she is almost as tall as the sergeant.

Bridoux, feeling that he has made a mistake, looks more favourably on the would-be recruit. He asks her to walk, then march.
Finally he orders Paquerette to strip.

Filled with consternation, Paquerette seizes a musket, and does
some exercises in the hope of putting the order out of Bridoux's
mind; but, not accustomed to weapons, she drops the musket on
the sergeant's toe, causing him to swear with rage. He repeats the
order to strip, but Paquerette refuses. The sergeant, thinking the
young man is embarrassed by Catherine's presence, sends her
away. But still Paquerette refuses.

"Are you a hunchback?" snaps the sergeant. "Come, off with
your clothes." So saying, he tries to drag off Paquerette's trousers.
But, when she obstinately keeps them on, he shouts: "Are you
bandy-legged?" With a view to finding out he feels her leg and

pinches her calves. Paquerette, alarmed, escapes from Bridoux, but, in doing so, forgets to maintain her masculine deportment. The sergeant, observing that the young man is a woman, claims a kiss as forfeit for attempting to deceive him.

François enters at this moment and, furious at seeing his fiancée in the sergeant's arms, rates her soundly. When Bridoux tries to make peace he turns on him and in a fit of rage threatens him with his sword. A corporal's guard rush in and Bridoux orders them to disarm François and arrest him. They do so and drag him away. Paquerette gives way to tears.

Catherine comes in and upbraids Paquerette, telling her that her lover is like to be shot. Paquerette entreats Bridoux to save her sweetheart, but he informs her that discipline must be maintained. Then she offers to be very nice to him if he will save François from being shot. Bridoux asks her to meet him that evening at seven o'clock and prove her words. She agrees. A trumpet sounds and Bridoux goes out.

Catherine, who loves Bridoux, reproaches Paquerette. But she explains that she only loves François and that she is going to meet the sergeant merely to try and secure the key of François's prison. Catherine is pleased with this explanation and promises to help her. They agree to meet again at seven and Paquerette goes to change into clothes fitting to her sex.

A little later Job enters. He asks Catherine if she has seen a young woman dressed as a man. "Yes," replies Catherine, "she will be back at seven."

At this moment François shows his face at the bars of his cell. Job is delighted to see his rival so situated, and promises himself to return at seven and press his suit.

Bridoux enters and avoids Catherine, who feigns to depart.

Seven strikes. Paquerette returns, dressed as a woman and carrying a parcel which she slips through the bars of François's cell, while the sergeant's back is turned.

Now follows an amusing *pas de deux* in which Paquerette tries to filch the key of the cell from Bridoux, while he tries to kiss her. To keep up with Paquerette's quick movements, Bridoux throws his tunic on a bench. Paquerette dances towards the bench, knocks the tunic to the ground and secures the key as she replaces it.

Bridoux, thinking that Paquerette is too modest to let herself be kissed in view of the passers-by, extinguishes the solitary lantern that illumines the scene. Catherine creeps out of her hiding place and, taking Paquerette's place, receives the kiss intended for the latter. Meanwhile Paquerette opens the door of the cell. François, dressed as a peasant, steps out and together the lovers make their escape. Bridoux is furious at the trick played upon him and when Job appears he is seized and forced into François's discarded uniform.

Act III. Scene I. A wretched inn far from the main road. From the blackened rafters hang kitchen utensils.

A number of peasants, seated at tables, are lively with wine. They would like to dance, but have no music. While the women sulk the sound of a raucous hurdy-gurdy is heard in the distance. The peasants are delighted, and, opening the door, hail the wandering player, who is none other than François, disguised as a Tyrolean.

The girls clap their hands with joy and wish him to play at once, but François says he must rest awhile for he is tired out. The peasants give him refreshment and bid him repose on a form. He thanks them and inquires if they have seen a girl called Paquerette. They answer that they have seen no one. Gradually the peasants go out and let François rest.

As he sleeps a greyish mist fills the room. Three shades materialize and summon forth the spirit of François, who asks them what they desire. The shades reply that they will take him to see Paquerette if he will follow them. He obeys, but, hardly has he taken a few steps, when the floor gives way beneath him and he vanishes from sight.

Some clouds which have gradually filled the scene give place to a fantastic land fashioned of rivers of diamond, lawns of emerald, and mountains of sapphire. From banks of reeds and irises come forth women in robes of muslin shot with silver; they group themselves about Paquerette who symbolizes the ideal.

As soon as François sees his beloved he stretches his arms towards her, but always she eludes him. In desperation he climbs a rock and is about to grasp the fugitive when he slips and falls into the lake. At the same moment the fantastic landscape disappears and François is seen back in the inn, just fallen from his bench to the ground. He rubs his eyes as if waking from a dream and replaces the overturned bench.

Now the peasants return and, giving François his hurdy-gurdy, ask him to play. He is about to begin when a trumpet is heard. Alarmed, he is anxious to be off.

"What are you afraid of?" ask the peasants.

"Nothing," replies François, "only I must be moving on."

But the girls surround him and insist on his playing so that they can dance.

At this juncture Bridoux and his men enter, stating that they are searching for a deserter. While the interrogation proceeds François tries to appear unconcerned. Unfortunately Paquerette chooses this moment to enter and Bridoux concludes that her lover cannot be far away. Catching sight of the musician he bids him play a tune.

François asks the sergeant if he is looking for a deserter.

"I am," replies Bridoux, "have you seen one?"

"Yes, he is dead," declares François.

"Nonsense!" observes the sergeant.

"Yes," continues François, "he has drowned himself, and gave me this gold cross to give to his sweetheart."

Job is horrified at this news, since he will be doomed to remain a soldier.

Bridoux, seeing that Paquerette is little distressed by this tragic news, and, intercepting a glance between the lovers, has his suspicions aroused. He pulls off François's false hair and beard and unmasks him. The soldiers close round François but he snatches a snuff-box from his pocket and, flinging the contents in their faces, escapes with Paquerette.

Act III. Scene II. The town of Ujhaz in Hungary, during the War of the Palatinate.

François and Paquerette have married and built up a modest fortune, the former as carpenter, the latter as a florist.

Paquerette overhears a conspiracy on the part of certain nobles who plan to kill the French officers during a festival given in their honour. She reveals the plot to the French commander who in return obtains a pardon for her husband, whom a court-martial had condemned to death.

*

The critic of *Le Théâtre*[11] acclaims the choreographer of *Paquerette,* Saint-Léon, as "a man of immense talent, an artist in the fullest acceptance of the word. He has invention, considerable tact and originality, he writes, he observes, he composes a *pas,* he arranges an *ensemble,* he makes use of his resources and orders his people with unequalled aptitude and skill. The whole house, like we, was delighted with a *pas de quatre* which adorns the first act, and which he danced with Mmes. Cerito, Robert, and Emarot. As a dancer he shines by his suppleness, airiness, and youthful muscles,

[11] January 22nd 185

and he executed *sur place* a famous *pirouette* which lasted nearly a minute, which is enormous, incredible for a spinning man."

Commenting on the scenery, which is highly praised, the critic of *La France Musicale* [12] observes: "There is a very original setting which depicts the moon or the sun amid blue clouds."

"M. Benoist's score," says the same writer, "is the work of an experienced musician. You feel that the writer should compose more serious music than that for a ballet. Among a thousand themes may be mentioned a charming waltz in the first act, and the whole of the dream scene, which is treated in a masterly manner."

Of Cerito as Paquerette, *Le Théâtre* [13] declares: "She has never portrayed a part which suits her better. When you admire her dancing, you think it is the easiest thing in the world, because everything she does betrays no sense of difficulty or labour: her dancing is firm, precise, smooth; she bends and curves like a reed swaying at the mercy of a breeze. You ask yourself whether it is the stage which moves, or whether it is her arched foot which floats rapidly over the boards. In that misty horizon of the dream scene, she is a winged Giselle who flies about the foliage, and, with the sprightliness of a bee, loses herself in the greenery.

DIAVOLINA

Pantomimic Ballet in 1 Act. Book: Arthur Saint-Léon. Music: Cesare Pugni. Scenery: Cambon and Thierry. Choreography: Arthur Saint-Léon. First produced: Théâtre de l'Opéra, Paris, July 6th, 1863.

CHARACTERS

Diavolina, a wealthy peasant girl . .	MLLE. MARTHA MURAVIEVA
Dona Marianna, her cousin . . .	MLLE. MARQUET
Don Peppino, Diavolina's guardian .	M. DAUTY
Vzula, his niece	MLLE. BRACH
Don Fortunato, a citizen of Caserta .	M. LENFANT
His wife	MLLE. ALINE
Gennariello, a fisherman . . .	MM. MÉRANTE
Don Chichillo, a wealthy citizen . .	CORALLI
Bridoux, a French sergeant . .	BERTHIER

[12] January 19th, 1851.
[13] January 22nd, 1851.

A French Drum-Major . . . . . PETIT

Two Zambogari . . . . . . $\left\{\begin{array}{l} \text{CORNET} \\ \text{ESTIENNE} \end{array}\right.$

A Notary . . . . LEFEBVRE

Neapolitan Fishermen, Peasant Girls of Caserta, Boatmen, Calabrians, French Soldiers, People, Musicians.

The action passes near Caserta, about 1805.

Diavolina is to marry Gennariello, a rich fisherman, and the countryside is *en fête*. Some *zambogari* arrive to give a *matinata* before Diavolina's house; their music is purposely discordant in order to induce the object of their attentions to bribe them to go away.

Marianna, Diavolina's cousin, does her best to drive the "musicians" away, but in vain. Her admirer, Sergeant Bridoux, arrives, and, seeing the situation, calls his friend, a drum-major, to help; between them they put to flight the unwelcome visitors.

Don Peppino, Diavolina's tutor, comes to bring his ward a number of gifts intended to bring good luck: some linen and bread, a medal containing indulgences, and a fine pair of horns as a protection against the *Jettatura*. Don Peppino is waylaid by the *zambogari* and obliged to give them a few pence.

He clasps Marianna in his arms, then goes to Diavolina's abode, where he encounters a number of young girls come to congratulate the bride. Marianna goes to call Diavolina who appears in her bridal dress. She thanks her godfather for his gifts and acknowledges the compliments of her friends, who enter the house with Marianna.

Diavolina grows impatient at Gennariello's non-arrival, but at last he comes, breathless and annoyed at being late. Diavolina, to punish him, runs and sits on a bench and pretends to be asleep. Gennariello, conscious of his fault, resolves to awaken his beloved with a kiss, but she chooses that moment to awake, much to his confusion. She pretends to have been in the middle of a lovely dream. She was dressed as a great lady surrounded by noblemen; one danced with her and gave her a kiss. She does not know why, but it made her very happy.

Gennariello, furious at this recital, reveals his presence, whereupon Diavolina reproaches him for having broken his vow. He replies that she was being unfaithful, even though it were a dream. Diavolina pretends to be astonished and inquires what duty she owes him, for she cannot remember.

Gennariello, distressed at this attitude, picks up his net and is about to go, when Diavolina steps on the trailing strands and stops him. They kiss and become friends again, and seal the reconciliation with a dance.

Now some Neapolitan fishermen enter to congratulate the couple. Gennariello invites them to dance *La Scarpetta*. In this, the youth, in love with a maiden, places a shoe on the ground; if, while dancing, she can put on the shoe without upsetting it, he will become her husband; failing this, she must abandon hope. The fishermen consent and the young girls, who have completed the wedding dress, take part in the dance.

Bridoux pays his attentions to Marianna, but is interrupted by Don Fortunato and his wife, Francesca, who are followed by numerous peasants and sailors. Don Fortunato is a rich citizen who is to be a witness at the wedding.

Next comes Chichillo, a clumsy old dandy, who is always anxious to show off. He has himself followed by a band of rustic musicians whom he leads with a squeaking clarinet. In his hurry he treads on people's feet and dresses, and makes himself a great nuisance.

Tables are brought out and all the guests take their places, the bride and bridegroom last. A repast is served. Chichillo, always in a flurry, appoints himself cup-bearer and pours the wine on the table instead of in the glasses, but this mishap, thanks to a local superstition, is applauded as an augury of prosperity. Delighted at this success Chichillo racks his brain to find a second joke which will achieve the same success. Seeing the lovers clasping hands under the table, he waits until their healths are being drunk, then glides under the table and betrays their secret. Diavolina, greatly annoyed, rises from the table and the guests follow suit while Chichillo, roaring with laughter, gets up with the table on his back.

Don Fortunato tries to relieve the situation by giving the signal for dancing.

Later, the notary arrives to read the marriage contract, when the guests retire or go into the neighbouring house.

Gennariello and his bride stand at the entrance to Diavolina's house and listen to the clauses. He does not wish his wife to make friends with the neighbours as he is very jealous. Diavolina, on the other hand, is fond of company and wishes to know everyone. And so each has a different conception of a partner's duties. Tempers become so high that it seems that no marriage can take place; moreover, Diavolina goes indoors and forbids Gennariello to follow.

Chichillo comes out of the house and asks Gennariello the cause of his despair. He explains and entreats his advice. While he considers the matter, Gennariello is horrified to see Diavolina coming towards them, arm in arm with Bridoux, who is paying her fulsome compliments.

Gennariello, at first dismayed, wonders if Diavolina is mocking him. So he pretends to be ill and falls down unconscious. Chichillo, believing his friend dead, calls for help. Immediately Diavolina rushes towards Gennariello who takes her hand and whispers: "May you be happy; pray for me."

Diavolina, seized with fright, falls on her knees, and, bursting into tears, protests that all she said and did was only in fun, and that she has never ceased to love him.

Gennariello, overjoyed, takes Diavolina in his arms, and, rising, kisses her, to the astonishment of the bystanders.

The reconciled lovers agree to the contract and the dances recommence. Bridoux demands a kiss from Marianna as the price of his having helped Diavolina, but she declares that a true French soldier should be satisfied with the opportunity to do a good deed, without expecting a reward for it.

Bridoux agrees, somewhat ruefully and proposes that the national Rigaudon be danced. The suggestion is applauded and there follows a military *divertissement,* entitled the Good Old Times, in which Diavolina takes part, dressed as a French *vivandière.* The contract is signed and all ends happily.

*

"The ballet was perfectly mimed and warmly applauded," asserts the critic of *La France Musicale.*[14] "Mlle. Muravieva is ravishing in it; she was recalled four times the first evening, which was merited, for in addition to the qualities observed in her Giselle,[15] she has revealed new qualities, although she has not yet been able completely to free herself from that stiffness which is a little antipathetic to the inherent grace of the French. . . .

"M. Saint-Léon is a celebrated *maître de ballet* worthy of his reputation; none know better than he how to compose *pas* and fit groups into a frame."

"Neapolitan customs," declares the critic of the *Ménestrel,*[16] "have furnished two *zambogari,* who play havoc with their bagpipes, and several *pas,* one of which in particular is very original—the *Pas de la Scarpetta* . . . which La Muravieva executes with the most charming sprightliness. . . .

[14] July 12th, 1863.
[15] Muravieva made her Paris *début* in this year in *Giselle.*
[16] July 12th, 1863.

"I do not know if the *Pas de la Niania* is also of pure Neapolitan origin; it is most comical in its foolishness. Its persistent rhythm ends by dominating everyone: there is not a foot which does not beat in time, not a head which does not nod involuntarily. . . .

"As for the music of the new ballet by M. Pugni . . . on the pretext that the action passes at Naples, he has thought fit to pillage the celebrated collection of popular airs called *Passatempi Musicali*, which, starting from Naples, its birthplace, has toured the world. M. Pugni, with an admirable candour, has literally transcribed from it half a dozen well-known airs.

"He has added others no less well known, such as *Le Roi Dago-bert* and *Marlborough*, a proceeding which cannot be excused on the ground of local colour. At least let it be recognized that all the music which M. Pugni has written or which has passed through his hands is essentially danceable.

"A pleasing musical *hors d'œuvre* to mention is the *Danse des Pêcheurs*, which is none other than the *Chasse aux Hirondelles*, a polka-galop by Maximilien Graziani, from whom Saint-Léon has often borrowed airs for his ballets."

FIAMMETTA

Fantastic Ballet in 4 Acts. Book: Arthur Saint-Léon. Music: Minkus. Choreography by Arthur Saint-Léon. First produced: Bolshoy Theatre, St. Petersburg, February, 13/25, 1864.

CHARACTERS

Cupid, the God of Love	
Fiammetta	MLLE. MARTHA MURAVIEVA

Mercury . . . . . .
Terpsichore . . . . .
Coquetry . . . . . .
Count Friedrich Sternhold . . .
Molari, tutor and guardian to the Count
Martini, servant to the Count . . .
Princess Millefleurs . . . .
Ragonda, her daughter . . . .
Eolinda ⎱
        ⎰ Ragonda's friends . .
Margharita ⎰
Otto, an officer . . . . . ∘
Three Friends of the Count . . ∘

A Gypsy . . . .
Four Gypsy Women . . . .
     The Three Graces, Nymphs, Cupids, Muses, Gypsies,
         Tyrolean Peasants.

Act I. The kingdom of Cupid.

The goddesses of Olympus do homage to Cupid. Terpsichore and her nymphs entertain the inhabitants of Olympus with dances. The festivities are interrupted by Mercury, who tells Cupid of the existence on earth of a youth who does not believe in the God of Love. This youth is a rake who has squandered his patrimony in dissipation and hopes to retrieve his fortune by marrying the daughter of the wealthy Princess Millefleurs. But the daughter is in love with Otto, who returns her love, and both entreat Cupid's aid.

At a sign from the God, Ragonda and Otto appear at one side of the stage, while at the other is seen a house with the notice "Love Forbidden Here." This pavilion is occupied by several young men, including the Count, who are surrounded by gypsy women. They are drinking, playing cards, and dancing.

Cupid resolves to take Ragonda under his protection, and punish the Count. Cupid summons his followers about an altar on which burns the flame of love. He extinguishes the flame and produces Fiammetta, a girl of surpassing beauty, whom he orders to fascinate the Count and cede him nothing. Fiammetta flies away with Cupid.

Act II. The Count's estate in the Tyrol. To the left is the pavilion with its notice; to the right is a barn. In the background is a fence, beyond which is a beautiful landscape.

Sternhold and his friends, surrounded by gypsy-women, are carousing and making mock of love. Suddenly a shot is heard. The Count's friends run to the fence to see what has happened. There they meet Cupid disguised as a huntsman. They ply him with questions. He says that he does not wish to annoy them, on the other hand they would be unwise to interfere with him. They laugh at his warning and invite him to join them, but he refuses. Then he observes the notice and is amused by it. He agrees to join them, and the company drink his health. Then he recalls that he has left his gypsy-girl nearby and suggests that she shall join them. The company agree.

Cupid returns with Fiammetta disguised as a gypsy-girl. Dancing begins followed by a mimed scene during which Fiammetta arouses the Count's interest to such an extent that he is the butt for his friends.

Tyrolean peasants are seen returning to their homes. Cupid asks them to rest and refresh themselves. They accept with glee and entertain the company with their national dances.

Cupid, remarking a peasant couple with a lovely baby, draws the Count's attention to them. Sternhold, charmed by this picture of parental happiness, wishes to kiss the baby. Cupid smilingly reminds the Count of the notice on the pavilion. The God observes another couple who are deeply in love but have not the means to marry; he gives them money which they receive with heartfelt thanks. The Count is again interested and again Cupid points to the notice on the pavilion.

Martini, the Count's servant, noticing the change in his master's manner, laughs at him. But Cupid punishes him for his impertinence by making him fall in love with an old woman whom he momentarily causes to appear young. When Martini pays her court, Cupid makes him the laughing-stock of the company by restoring the woman to her natural age.

Now follows a dance—"*Berceuse*"—after which Martini announces the imminent arrival of the Count's tutor. The guests disperse and hurry away, and only Cupid and the Count remain.

The tutor reproves his charge for his mode of living and urges him to hasten his marriage with Ragonda, otherwise he will be ruined. Sternhold refuses at first, but afterwards consents to follow the tutor's instructions, after he has had one final orgy. The tutor agrees and departs.

Sternhold notices Fiammetta and asks her to become his mistress. She receives his suggestion so coldly that he kneels for forgiveness. At this moment Cupid calls the Count's friends and threatens to teach him a lesson for trying to secure possession of Fiammetta. But the latter intervenes and the quarrel is patched up.

The Count becomes sad and Fiammetta tries to cheer him with her dancing.

The gypsy-women return and the orgy is resumed with a drinking-song. The tutor returns, orders the carousers to leave, and reminds his charge of his promise. The Count takes leave of his friends, conscious of a passionate love for Fiammetta. Cupid goes to the pavilion, removes the notice-board, and replaces it with another inscribed: "The Abode of Pure Love."

Act III. A gothic hall in Princess Millefleur's castle.

The Princess is attended by Otto and several ladies-in-waiting.
She receives news of an imminent visit from Sternhold and summons her daughter. Ragonda enters and, on being told that her
future husband is expected, tries vainly to conceal her distaste.
The Princess and Otto receive the guests, and the former instructs
her ladies to entertain Ragonda, who is filled with sadness.

Her friend, Yolande, takes two bouquets, one of scabious, the
flower of sadness, the other of roses, the flower of joy. She asks
Ragonda to close her eyes and make her choice. She consents, but
the ladies, not wishing to disappoint her, offer her the roses.

At this moment Otto appears on the balcony; he is grief-stricken.
Ragonda consoles him and tells him that she will never marry another. Her friends warn her of the Princess's return. Otto disappears and the ladies tie the flowers together.

Enter the Princess and her guests, followed a little later by the
Count. Ragonda greets Sternhold coldly, while the Count, thinking of Fiammetta, omits to pay Ragonda proper respect. The
Princess, believing this to result from the Count's being tired from
his journey, suggests that the marriage contract be signed on the
morrow, and that he rest that night at the castle. The Count accepts and, left alone with Martini, falls asleep on a couch.

Martini is much impressed by his surroundings. He observes
another couch in an alcove where he decides to rest. But, as he
approaches it, he is startled by an apparition. Terrified, he awakes
his master. The Count, disbelieving his story, goes to investigate.
He sees a succession of ghostly pictures. First, Cupid and Fiammetta embracing; then, Otto and Ragonda; and, lastly, Fiammetta alone, who tells him that she can never be his. The visions
leave him exhausted and he calls for help. Guards rush in followed by the Princess, Ragonda, and their friends. They try to
soothe the Count, unaware of the reason for his fear.

*Act IV. The castle grounds. In the background is a terrace with
tables set out for the wedding. Seated at the table are the Princess,
Ragonda, the Count, and his tutor.*

Peasants enter to present the bride with flowers, after which they
dance in her honour. A notary enters with Fiammetta, who gives
Ragonda a bouquet. The Princess, amazed by the girl's beauty,
asks who she is, but no one can answer her. The notary is seen to
be Cupid, who tells the Princess that Fiammetta is his daughter.

Now follows a scene of mime and dance during which Ragonda resolves to tell her mother of her love for Otto. Fiammetta induces Sternhold to break off his proposed marriage with Ragonda. The notary tears up the contract, and, to the surprise of everyone, unites Otto and Ragonda, who, he observes, are true lovers; while the Count only wished to marry Ragonda for her money, and really loves Fiammetta, who is not of this world. At the same moment Fiammetta dissolves into flame and vanishes. The Count rushes at the notary, who changes into the God of Love. Everyone does him homage while the Princess gives her blessing to the union of Otto and Ragonda.

*

Fiammetta, first produced at St. Petersburg on February 13/25, 1864, is said to have been given a little earlier under another title, *The Salamander,* but I have not yet been able to trace this.

Martha Muravieva made a great success in the part of Fiammetta, so much so that Perrin, then director of the Opéra, Paris, invited her to dance there. Later Russian interpreters of the title-role were P. P. Lebedeva (1865), A. Grantsova (1868), E. P. Sokolova (1869), and M. Ogoleyt (1874).

According to Pleschayev,[17] the production of *Fiammetta* was notable for the introduction of many new stage devices, such as shadow effects with the aid of convex mirrors and electric light.

Muravieva repeated her success at Paris on July 11th of the same year, when she appeared in a condensed two-act version of *Fiammetta,* called *Néméa ou L'Amour Vengé,* which was adapted by Meilhac and Halévy. The cast was as follows—it will be observed that the names of the characters have also been changed:

Count Molder	MM.	Mérante
Moko, the Count's friend . . .		Dauty
Istwann, a gypsy		Chapuy
Kiralfi, Hermiola's fiancé . . .		Rémond
Minden, Hermiola's father . . .		Lenfant
Néméa, a village maiden	Mmes.	Muravieva
Cupid		Eugénie Fiocre
Katerina, Hermiola's mother . . .		Caroline
Ilka, a gypsy		Aline
Hermiola		Marie Sanlaville
Yolanda		Marie Pilatte
A little Faun		Verne

[17] *Nash Balet,* 1897.

THE HUMP–BACKED HORSE [18]

Ballet in 5 Acts and 10 *Scenes. Book: Arthur Saint-Léon. Music: Cesare Pugni. Choreography: Arthur Saint-Léon. First produced: Bolshoy Theatre, St. Petersburg, December* 3/15, 1864.

CHARACTERS

Starinoushka	
Gavrila ⎫	
Danila ⎬ his sons . . .	
Ivanoushka ⎭	
A Merchant	M. Troitsky
A Mayor	
A Town Crier	
An Innkeeper	
A Small Boy	
A Waiter	
An Old Woman . . .	
A Young Man with a Balalaika . .	
The Hump-backed Horse . .	
The Khan	
The Khan's favourite Wife . .	
The Tsar-Maiden	Mlle. Martha Muravieva
A Young Slave	
The Khan's Counsellor . . .	
Members of the Khan's Suite.	

Act I. Starinoushka is seen complaining to the bystanders in a bazaar that he cannot make any purchases, since the wheat he was hoping to sell has been trampled down by an unknown person. He tells his sons to watch out for the culprit.

Ivanoushka, his youngest son, accepts this duty and goes to the fields, where he catches a mare. She entreats him to release her, and, in exchange for her freedom, promises him two horses with golden manes and a hump-backed horse. Ivanoushka agrees, but the horses he receives are stolen from him by his two elder brothers.

Act II. Ivanoushka's brothers, Gavrila and Danila, take the stolen horses to the Khan. But they are confronted by Ivanoushka

[18] The synopsis of this ballet is based on a script issued by the Soviet Ballet.

*who declares that the horses are his. The Khan buys the horses
and appoints Ivanoushka his chief groom. The hump-backed
horse gives him a whip and tells him that he has only to crack it
and he will attain the fulfilment of any wish.*

One of the bystanders, a young slave, is seen telling the story
of a dream, in which the beautiful women seen on certain carpets
came to life and danced before him.

Ivanoushka, overhearing this story, cracks his whip and the
slave's dream becomes true. Beautiful women enter and dance.

The Khan, who has also been dreaming of a beautiful woman,
hearing from his courtiers that Ivanoushka made the beauties on
a carpet come to life, asks him to do likewise with his dream.
Ivanoushka shows him several pictures of beautiful women, one
of whom the Khan recognizes and accordingly asks him to produce.

Ivanoushka entreats the aid of the hump-backed horse, who
takes him to the Isle of the Mermaids, where lives the Tsar-Maiden
whom the Khan saw in his dream.

On her appearance the hump-backed horse causes beautiful
fountains to spring from the ground; these surround the maiden
and enable her to be captured.

*Act III. Ivanoushka delivers the Tsar-Maiden to the Khan. She
entreats the latter to set her free. He begs her to remain and promises her many rich presents, then orders his favourite wife to
dance for her delight.*

Ivanoushka's brothers try to play on a pipe, but without success.
Ivanoushka takes the pipe and as a result of his music the Tsar-
Maiden begins to dance. The Khan invites her to become his
wife. She consents on condition that he obtain for her a certain
ring which lies at the bottom of the sea. The Khan commands
Ivanoushka to find the ring.

*Act IV. Ivanoushka goes in search of the ring. The ever-re-
sourceful hump-backed horse contrives that the ring is brought
to him by an eel.*

*Act V. While Ivanoushka has gone on his quest, the Tsar-
Maiden is kept in prison. The Khan tries to induce her to marry
him without waiting for the ring, but in vain.*

Ivanoushka returns and gives the ring to the Khan, who presents it in turn to the Tsar-Maiden. Immediately the Khan presses

for the wedding to take place, but the Tsar-Maiden makes a new condition—the Khan must become as youthful and as beautiful as herself. To accomplish this he has only to immerse himself in boiling water.

The Khan, cautious in such matters, resolves to test the efficacy of her cure on Ivanoushka. The latter bravely enters the boiling water and emerges a handsome young man. The Khan, reassured, likewise enters the water, only to die in agony.

The Tsar-Maiden marries Ivanoushka.

*

The Hump-Backed Horse has a particular interest in that it is the first ballet to be based on a Russian theme; it is founded on a fairy-tale by Ershov. The part of the Tsar-Maiden was the last creation of Martha Muravieva. Her *pirouettes* and *pointe* work left nothing to be desired and the success of the ballet was complete. It became one of the most popular items in the repertory and was given at St. Petersburg well over two hundred times. It is included in the repertory of the Soviet Ballet.

The part of the Tsar-Maiden is associated with a long line of interpreters, from Martha Muravieva, M. N. Madaeva, E. O. Vazem, A. Grantsova, M. I. Amosova, Carolina Rosati, E. P. Sokolova, and so on, to the artistes of the present day.

LA SOURCE

Ballet in 3 Acts and 4 Scenes. Book: Charles Nuitter and Arthur Saint-Léon. Music: Minkus and L. Delibes. Scenery: Despléchin and Lavastre, and Rubé and Chaperon. Choreography: Arthur Sain-Léon. First produced: Théâtre Impérial de l'Opéra, Paris. November 12th, 1866.

CHARACTERS

Naïla, Spirit of the Spring . . .	MMES.	SALVIONI
Nouredda		E. FIOCRE
Morgab, a gypsy		L. MARQUET
Zail, a goblin		SANLAVILLE
Dadje, the Khan's favourite . . .		ALINE
Djémil	MM.	MÉRANTE
Mozdock, Nouredda's brother . .		CORALLI
The Khan		DAUTY

Sindjar, Attendant on the Khan .   .   CORNET
Ismail   .   .   .   .   PLUQUE
   Butterflies, Insects, Flowers, Circassians, Slaves,
      Baggage-Porters, Palanquin-Bearers, etc.

*Act I. A defile in the middle of lofty mountains. In the back-
ground, at the base of a rock, flows the silver thread of a spring,
about which flourish plants and lianas coiled about the branches of
trees. It is not quite daybreak.*

Woodland folk frolic about the spring and seem to render it
homage. Moths and insects flutter about the flowers. Goblins pursue them, robbing one of a wing and another of an antenna, with
which they adorn themselves.

A day-fly is born among the flowers. Butterflies and goblins
regard it with curiosity; another sprite appears and kisses the fly,
which dies under the caress. The scene grows lighter and the
fantastic creatures disappear.

Djémil, a hunter, cups his hands and slakes his thirst with water
from the spring. Meanwhile, Morgab, a gypsy, enters; she picks
poisonous plants which she intends to throw in the water for some
sinister purpose. But Djémil snatches the plants from her and
drives her away. She insists on reading his hand and seems surprised at what she finds written on his palm.

A caravan approaches and passes through the defile. Morgab
tells the hunter that this is a fiancée being conducted to her husband, and that he, Djémil, will fall in love with her. Morgab
departs.

Djémil hides and watches the travellers camp. Nouredda takes
a gúsla and begins an oriental dance. Morgab returns and offers
her fruit which she accepts, then veils.

The camp is struck and at the moment of departure Nouredda
sees a lovely flower overhanging a precipice. She desires it, but
none of her escort will risk his life to obtain it.

Djémil goes to Nouredda and offers to obtain the flower. He
climbs to the summit of the rock and crawls along a branch, but,
just as he is about to grasp the blossom, the branch snaps and he
vanishes from sight. Presently he re-appears and lays the flower
at Nouredda's feet. She signs to Mozdock, her brother, and asks
him to reward Djémil. He throws him a purse which the hunter
indignantly refuses.

What reward does he seek? To gaze for an instant on Nouredda's face. He raises her veil, but Nouredda steps back among
her women, at the same time throwing away the flower.

Mozdock orders Djémil to be bound with osiers, which grow by the spring, and left to die in the desert. The caravan moves on, accompanied by the gypsy, who has obtained permission to follow.

Djémil, left alone, vainly strives to break his bonds. Devoured by a raging thirst he cannot reach the spring. Suddenly the water stretches towards him. It becomes a transparent sheet through which can be seen Naïla, the goddess of the spring. The damp osiers stretch and fall to the ground. Djémil is free.

Naïla thanks him for having protected the spring from the gypsy, but reproaches him for having plucked the blossom, which is a talisman. She picks up the flower, and nymphs and goblins run to her side.

"What is your wish?" asks Naïla.

"To rejoin Nouredda and be avenged," declares Djémil.

"Go!" replies Naïla, "your wish shall be granted."

She gives the magic flower to Zail, her favourite goblin, and orders him to watch over Djémil.

The hunter sets out, guided by Zail.

Act II. The gardens of the palace of the Khan of Ghendjib.

The Khan impatiently awaits Nouredda's arrival and refuses all endeavours to entertain him.

At last the agreed signal is heard in the distance and Nouredda enters, accompanied by Mozdock, her women and his guards, and Morgab. The Khan is dazzled by Nouredda's beauty, which provokes jealous looks among his other wives. But, at the Khan's command, they are forced to prostrate themselves before the new favourite and entertain her with dances.

A trumpet call announces the arrival of another visitor, who proves to be Djémil, splendidly attired. He is accompanied by Zail and two slaves who bear coffers.

Djémil bows low to the Khan and orders the coffers to be presented to Nouredda. He begs her to choose a gift from their contents. Among the glittering jewels she espies a flower similar to that which grew by the spring. She wishes to take it but Djémil observes that he cannot give her the flower, which is a talisman of infinite power. So saying, he casts the bloom into a mass of foliage. Immediately the plants grow taller and thicker, and through the leaves bursts a sheet of water from which appears Naïla.

The goddess of the spring darts from the flowers. The Khan, enraptured with Naïla, loses all interest in Nouredda. He kneels at Naïla's feet and implores her to be his wife. She agrees on condition that she reign alone.

The Khan consents, gives his wives to his officers, and dismisses Nouredda. Her brother, furious at this insult, threatens the Khan, but is forced to leave by the guards.

Nouredda, disconcerted and ashamed, leaves with Morgab, who offers her the shelter of her tent, and promises her vengeance.

Act III. Scene I. Morgab's tent, which is lit by a ray of light from the roof. In the background an idol, which reflects the dying embers of a fire. Here and there instruments of magic.

Morgab enters, then signs to Nouredda and Mozdock to join her. She tells Nouredda that Djémil is protected by a supernatural power, but she has stronger forces at her disposal and can vanquish him. She will induce Djémil to visit the tent then summon Mozdock to kill him.

Morgab prays to the idol and throws a handful of magic herbs on the fire. A bluish mist rises and almost immediately there is a scratching at the door.

The gypsy makes Mozdock leave by another door and Djémil enters. Nouredda asks him by what right he intrudes on her privacy. Djémil throws off his mantle and appears in his simple hunting garb. Nouredda recognizes him and is frightened. He reminds her how cruelly she treated him, although his only offence had been to find her beautiful.

Nouredda conceals her resentment and gazes at him with tear-filled eyes. Djémil cannot resist her spell, and tells her that he loves her still. If she does not wish to hear him, he will go. But Nouredda lays a restraining hand on his arm. He begs her not to mock his love and, taking a dagger from his belt, threatens to kill himself if she deceives him. Nouredda takes the dagger from him and throws it away, and also relieves him of his pistols. Morgab approaches noiselessly and hides the weapons. Then she retires unobtrusively to a corner.

The back of the tent emanates a bluish radiance and reveals Naïla and Zail. The latter shows Djémil kneeling before Nouredda. Naïla looks sadly upon this scene.

Suddenly the vision disappears and Mozdock enters with his men. He flings himself upon the hunter, but Zail appears holding the magic flower, which renders Mozdock and his men motionless, while Djémil carries off Nouredda.

Zail vanishes and Morgab, Mozdock, and his men recover from their stupor. Unable to find Djémil or Nouredda they run out in search of them.

Act III. Scene II. The mountain valley. The flowers are with-ered, the water brackish, the foliage parched. Evil mists drift over the valley.

Naïla is sitting on the rock from which gushes the spring; she seems overwhelmed with sadness. She waves her hand and Djémil and Nouredda appear. She makes a sign and they fall asleep.

Naïla summons Zail and her fairies who threaten the lovers, but she orders them to be spared. She bids Zail waken Djémil who is surprised to find himself in Naïla's presence. Seeing Nouredda unconscious he begs the goddess to forgive her.

Naïla reproaches Djémil for having sacrificed her to Nouredda, who will never love him. The hunter takes Nouredda's hand and, placing it on his heart, asks her if she does not love him. She shakes her head.

The goddess tells Djémil that Nouredda has only made pretence of loving him. The hunter, remarking the magic flower in Naïla's girdle, observes that if she wished she could make Nouredda love him.

Naïla replies that he speaks truly, but the flower is linked to her existence, and if she uses it she will surely die. Djémil remains motionless.

The goddess watches him intently then suddenly draws forth the flower and places it on Nouredda's heart. Immediately she recovers consciousness and throws herself in Djémil's arms.

At the same moment Naïla becomes faint. She summons her subjects and Zail to watch over the lovers and put them on the right road. Djémil and Nouredda climb the path which overlooks the rock.

Naïla grows weaker and weaker and dies beside the spring, which gradually ceases to flow. Her subjects expire with her.

High above the rock can be seen the lovers, exchanging sweet vows.

*

"This ballet is brilliant, well staged, and well danced," says the critic of the *Ménestrel*,[19] "it is lavish and picturesque, but a little long. Three acts is a third too much. . . .

"The language of mime is too imperfect and too vague to hold the interest for long; very few themes are suited to it, and the more involved the plot the greater the number of occasions for it to be incomprehensible. . . .

[19] November 18th, 1866.

"The second act would be improved by being cut by half; and, by condensing the action here and there where it drags a little, a very pleasing ballet would result.

"The final scenes are very well done, and as moving as the simple mime permits."

Turning to the musical aspect, it may be noted that the first and last scenes were composed by Minkus, and the second and third by Léo Delibes. "The style of the two composers," asserts the critic of *La France Musicale*,[20] "is essentially different and easily recognizable at a first hearing. M. Minkus's music has a vague, indolent, and melancholic character, full of grace and languor. That of M. Delibes, fresher and more rhythmic, is much more complicated in orchestration, and sometimes a little more ordinary. I should add that this difference in style is perfectly justified by the contrasting character of the two parts of the ballet."

The critic of the *Ménestrel* declares that "the first act, despite several pretty details, seemed a little thin, but the music of the last scene contains some charming and often very expressive melodies. The second act is brilliant and does great credit to M. Delibes; it is certainly the most successful and most noteworthy portion; the whole of the score could have been entrusted to the young composer, and this will doubtless be done on another occasion."

"The role of the Spring (Naïla)" says *La France Musicale,* "is . . . very well filled by Mlle. Salvioni . . . a most intelligent artist, whose dancing is full of fire and intrepidity, and whose mime is most remarkable. . . .

"M. Mérante plays Djémil. He is a conscientious artist . . . who knows how to invest his roles with their appropriate character and likeness."

La Source was revived the following year with Adela Grantsova, who came from Russia to take the part of Naïla; she achieved a considerable success.

Coppélia

Note. Through an oversight, this ballet is erroneously included in the section devoted to Louis Mérante. For a description of *Coppélia,* see pp. 483-489.

[20] November 18th, 1866.

LUCIEN PETIPA

JOSEPH LUCIEN PETIPA, known as Lucien Petipa, was born at Marseille on December 22nd, 1815. His father, Jean Petipa, was engaged at the Théâtre Royal de la Monnaie, Brussels, in the double capacity of *premier danseur* and *maître de ballet,* and himself trained his son in the art of dancing. But, although Lucien made excellent progress, his father did not hasten his *début,* desiring to await a propitious moment for the venture.

Now it happened that a well known Paris singer, Lafonte, had been appearing in Brussels with success, and when he announced a benefit performance at the theatre to which Jean Petipa was attached, the house was quickly sold out. Here was a golden opportunity for his son to win his spurs and it was arranged that he should dance with Mlle. Ambrosini, a dancer much beloved of the Brussels public. The youthful artist was warmly applauded and the director of the Theatre Royal, The Hague, who happened to be present that evening, offered him an excellent engagement and so he became *premier danseur* at that theatre.

He danced at The Hague for three months when he accepted a new engagement at the Grand Theatre, Bordeaux. There he charmed the public with the lightness, gaiety, and precision of his dancing. From time to time some of the stars of the dance visited Bordeaux, among them being Fanny Elssler and the sisters Noblet, who, delighted with Petipa's ability, urged him to go to Paris.

Cautious by nature he waited some time before he decided to leave the security of Bordeaux for Paris. Arrived at the capital he found that his reputation had preceded him; and, on June 10th, 1840, he made his *début* at the Opéra in *La Sylphide,* with Fanny Elssler in the title-role. That evening was the beginning of a long series of successes in which he danced variously with Carlotta Grisi, Adelina Plunkett, Amalia Ferraris, and Carolina Rosati.

As a choreographer, Lucien did not achieve the fame of his celebrated brother, Marius, but he produced the *divertissements* for several operas such as *La Fronde* (1853), *La Nonne Sanglante* (1854), and *Les Vêpres Siciliennes* (1855), and composed a number of ballets which enjoyed a measure of success, such as *Sacountala* (1858), *Graziosa* (1861), and *Namouna* (1882).

SACOUNTALA

Pantomimic Ballet in 2 Acts. Book: Théophile Gautier. Music: Ernest Reyer. Choreography: Lucien Petipa. First produced: Théâtre Impérial de l'Opéra, Paris, July 14th, 1858.

CHARACTERS

Dushmata, King of India . . .	MM.	L. PETIPA
Madhava, the King's favourite . .		MÉRANTE
Kanu, a Brahmin, Sakuntala's adopted father		LENFANT
Durwasa, a fakir		CORALLI
An Executioner		CORNET I
A Fisherman		CORNET II
Sarnagrava		ESTIENNE
Saraduta		MILLOT
A Courtier		LEFÉVRE
Sakuntala	MMES.	AMALIA FERRARIS
Hamsati, the King's favourite . .		MARQUET
Gautami, superintendent of the young priestesses		ALINE
Priyamwada ⎤		SCHLOSSER
Anusuya ⎟ Sakuntala's friends		POUSSIN
Parabhritica ⎟		CELLIER
Tchaturica ⎦		MAUPERIS

Courtiers, Grooms, Jugglers, Bayadères, Priestesses, Nymphs, Goddesses, Genii, Apsaras, etc.

Act I. A sacred forest on the banks of the Malini. It contains banyan trees, amras, malicas, and madharis, linked together by lianas. To the right is a little shrine; to the left, through the trees, can be seen the reed huts of the hermits. In the background is a flight of steps leading to a sacred pool.

Kanu, head of the Brahmins, attended by *brahmatcharis,* is praying before the temple, when his devotions are interrupted by the sounds of the chase. He sends a *brahmatchari* to see who dares violate the sanctity of the forest.

Enter Dushmata, bow in hand, on horseback, followed by a number of huntsmen. He dismounts, raises the kneeling Kanu, and sends his men away. Then the King himself prays at the altar and makes offerings of fruit and flowers.

Hearing the sound of voices, Dushmata hides in the temple, when young girls come to fill their pitchers at the sacred well. They are followed by Sakuntala, who comes in dancing and is affectionately greeted by her friends.

All at once a bee, taking her for a flower, alights on Sakuntala. In dismay she flees towards the temple, where Dushmata drives away the insect and receives the panting girl in his arms.

Confused by his unexpected appearance, she asks who he is. He replies that he is a young *brahmatchari* come to study the holy writings. Then Sakuntala and her friends lead the King to a bed of moss and bring him fruit and flowers. Dushmata does not take his gaze from Sakuntala and he induces her to dance with him, at the end of which he embraces her passionately.

A huntsman runs in and, bowing before the King, tells him that a wild elephant is ravaging the forest. Dushmata takes his bow and follows the huntsman, intimating that he will soon return.

Sakuntala, now alone, is conscious of her love for the King and is sad at the thought that he must soon forget so humble a maiden. In despair she falls to the ground. Her friends try to calm her with floral offerings until, seeing her asleep, they steal away.

Dushmata returns and, seeing Sakuntala asleep, extends his arms towards her in rapture. She, still sleeping, rises in an ecstatic dream, and involuntarily goes towards the King, until suddenly she awakes and finds herself in his arms. Frightened that someone may see, she glides from his grasp and seeks refuge in the temple. But Dushmata induces her to come forth, when he kneels at her feet and promises to marry her. He kisses her brow and places on her finger a ring, which will admit her to his palace and cause her to be received as his betrothed.

During this scene the hermit Durwasa enters. Tired, hungry, and thirsty, he claims hospitality, but the lovers, absorbed in each other, are indifferent to the world outside.

The hermit, angered by his reception, and displeased that so holy a place should be profaned by love, reprimands the lovers, who awake as if from a dream. Sakuntala tries to soothe Durwasa. The King adds his own apologies, but when the hermit proves indifferent, he loses his temper and threatens him. Thereupon, Durwasa pronounces a terrible curse. Dushmata is distressed and repulses Sakuntala. The sky darkens, the leaves of the trees tremble, and horrible spirits creep along the branches and mock the King and Sakuntala.

The returning huntsmen find the King in a state of delirium and bear him away, while Sakuntala swoons at the foot of a tree.

Durwasa draws the ring from her finger and flings it into the sacred pool. Kanu returns with his disciples and the young girls, finding Sakuntala, manage to revive her. She points to the hermit and tells Kanu all that has occurred. Durwasa interrupts her story by declaring that Sakuntala shall never marry the King.

Kanu calms the distressed girl and, after praying before the temple, the altar fire blazes up and the shape of the flames shows Dushmata crowning Sakuntala.

Then the vindictive Durwasa goes to the temple and invokes Shiva, the God of Destruction, who causes the fire to smoke and reveal a picture of Sakuntala burning on a funeral pyre.

Sakuntala, not knowing what to make of these two opposed presages, resolves to go to Dushmata's palace, a plan which is approved by Kanu. She is distressed at having no fine clothes, but Kanu tells her that heaven will provide. Then, to her horror, she finds that her ring is gone. But a friend persuades her that she is bound to be recognized and so she decides to go on her journey.

Sakuntala is of celestial origin and is the recipient of divine help. *Apsaras* descend from heaven bearing cloths woven from sunlight and moonlight, while shrubs extend their flowing branches and offer jewels, pearls, and necklaces of gold.

Ready for her journey, Sakuntala sets out, accompanied by Kanu and some *brahmatcharis*. From time to time she turns round to bid her friends good-bye. Durwasa goes a little ahead of the procession to offset Kanu's influence.

Act II. The façade of Dushmata's palace, which crowns a succession of vast terraces. In the gardens are masses of exotic flowers.

At the rise of the curtain Dushmata is seated on his throne with Queen Hamsati beside him. The favourite, Madhava, plays her guitar and the *bayadères* dance the King's favourite dance, but he displays no interest in their movements.

The dance over, Dushmata strolls moodily among the women. Madhava tries to interest him, but in vain. The Queen is inclined to reproach her consort, but Madhava declares that the King is suffering from melancholy arising from disappointed love, and must be diverted.

Hamsati bids the *bayadères* dance again.

A messenger informs the King that strangers have arrived and crave an audience. The boon is granted. Sakuntala and her friends walk modestly towards the throne. The Queen is troubled by her beauty, but the King seems surprised to see Sakuntala. Meanwhile, Durwasa casts a spell on the King, which prevents his recognizing her.

Sakuntala kneels before the King and lifts her face so that he may remember her, but he makes no sign of acknowledgment. The Queen tries to persuade him to send the girl away. Then Sakuntala mimes the scene in the wood, but to no avail, and she is forced to leave, defeated. Madhava signs to her to remain nearby.

The Queen bids her women dance again, but the King signs that he wishes to be alone. No sooner has Hamsati departed than Madhava ushers in Sakuntala, who tries once more to stimulate the King's memory, but to no purpose.

All at once Durwasa appears. He calls the Queen who, seeing Sakuntala alone with the King, commands that she shall be put to death with the utmost torture. The executioner is summoned. He throws a black veil over his victim's head and bears her away. Everyone goes out. Hamsati proudly resumes her seat beside Dushmata, who has suddenly discovered that his ring is missing.

There is an outcry at the door and a fisherman tries to force his way in. The King orders him to be admitted, when he tells Dushmata that he found his ring inside a fish he caught and desires to sell it. Dushmata recognizes his ring and purchases it. The more he studies it, the more his memory returns. He recalls his recent visitor and her likeness to Sakuntala. He asks where the visitor is and Hamsati answers that she has been put to death. Dushmata, mad with rage, orders Hamsati to be punished in the same way.

At this juncture celestial music is heard. In the background Sakuntala is seen bound to a pyre, but an *apsara* descends from heaven and the flames change into flowers. The palace is flooded with mystic light and swarms of *apsaras* appear on the terraces.

Sakuntala falls into the arms of the King, who kneels at her feet and entreats her forgiveness. Hamsati, escaping from her guards, kneels before Sakuntala, who pardons her.

Lastly, Dushmata replaces his ring on Sakuntala's finger and kneels before the *apsara* Misvahesi, who ascends to heaven.

The ballet concludes with a *pas de deux* and *divertissement*.

*

Sacountala is founded on the famous play of the same name by the Indian poet, Kalidasa.

The critic of the *Figaro-Programme*[1] declares that "the honours of the evening fell to Mme. Ferraris. What distinguishes her from her companions is the admirable ease with which she executes the most difficult *pas*. With her there is never any sense of effort, you would say that she does not touch the ground, and that she sports with aerial sylphs, her vanquished rivals.

"M. Reyer's music," says the same writer, "is perfectly suited to the theme. It is animated or slow according to the requirements of the poem, and full of novel gradations."

The critic of *La France Musicale*,[2] commenting on Ferraris, declares: "Nothing could be more elegant than those velvet eyes; those eyes in turn full of confessions and promises, full of flashing glances and tears. Nothing could be more expressive than those features which mirrored joy, fear, gratitude, tenderness, melancholy, and despair, because all those emotions follow in quick succession in the fine role of Sakuntala.

"Now for the dancer. At each new role of this daughter of the air, you think that Mme. Ferraris has said her last word, or rather achieved the apparently impossible, and with each new role she throws down a new challenge. The *Pas de l'Abeille* leaves nothing to be desired—on the contrary—in comparison with the *Pas de la Rose;* and the *Pas de Deux* at the end has nothing in common with all the other *pas de deux* in which she had seemed to achieve the zenith of her powers. Who has taught this privileged person to combine so well grace and strength, and abandon of pose and purity of line?"

GRAZIOSA

Pantomimic Ballet in 1 Act. Book: J. Derley and Lucien Petipa. Music: Théodore Labarre. Scenery: Cambon and Thierry. Choreography: Lucien Petipa. First produced: Théâtre de l'Opéra, Paris, March 25th, 1861.

CHARACTERS

Graziosa	MME. AMALIA FERRARIS
Don Manuel, the Governor	MM. CORALLI
The Podesta	DAUTY
Don Rodrigo	ESTIENNE

[1] July 15th, 1858.
[2] July 18th, 1858.

Pietro, a muleteer		CHAPUY
Sergeant Moscatello		BERTHIER
Carraolana ⎫		PETIT
Piniento ⎪ Soldiers . . .		REMOND
Cristobal ⎬		CORNET
Angulo ⎭		JULES
An Alguazil		MILLOT
A Trumpeter		LEFÉVRE
A Clerk		MONTFALLET
Nunziata, an inn-keeper	MMES.	ALINE
Dona Elvira		THIBERT

Lords, Peasants, Soldiers.

The action passes near Naples at the time of the Spanish domination.

Scene. A public square in a small town near Naples.

At the rise of the curtain a number of young girls are dancing the tarantella. One of them, Graziosa, stands out above all the rest. She tells the inn-keeper, Nunziata, that she is expecting a party of muleteers, including Pietro, her sweetheart.

The muleteers arrive; Pietro runs to greet Graziosa and shows her a purse of gold which he has earned. Gradually the bystanders depart. Pietro urges his fellows to leave and rest, as he is anxious to be alone with Graziosa.

In the distance pass a number of Spanish nobles and ladies, who are in the suite of the Viceroy. The ladies are masked as is customary. Among the various groups is a cavalier called Don Manuel, who gives his arm to a lady, with whom he converses in low tones. They cross the square and are about to leave when another cavalier bars their way. The newcomer, Don Rodrigo, asks Don Manuel to permit his lady to unmask. Don Manuel draws his sword and Don Rodrigo does likewise. Except for Pietro and Graziosa, who are chatting, the square is empty.

Hearing the clash of swords, the lovers look round and see the duellists, with the lady clasping her hands in fear. Pietro vainly tries to part them, then goes for help. Meanwhile, Graziosa, unseen by the duellists, leads away the masked lady. Presently the veiled lady returns and entreats the duellists to cease. When they refuse she raises her mask and, to their astonishment, reveals the unknown features of Graziosa.

Don Rodrigo seems to deplore his fatal jealousy and is profuse in his excuses to Don Manuel. The latter, restraining his surprise, accepts them. Graziosa replaces her mask, takes Don Manuel's arm and leaves, while Don Rodrigo departs in the opposite direction.

Pietro returns with the Podesta, followed by Moscatello and his men. Pietro, unable to account for the disappearance of the combatants, tries to escape, but the soldiers seize him and take him before the Podesta. The last-named, indignant that his authority should be flouted, orders Pietro to be placed in a cell and closely guarded. The soldiers, having confined their prisoner, call the innkeeper to serve wine and then play at cards.

Graziosa returns but cannot find Pietro. He calls to her from his cell and makes her aware of his situation. She watches the soldiers playing and then begins to dance. Gradually they notice the dancer and try to catch her; Moscatello, seeing what is happening, orders Graziosa to depart, but she only smiles and finally succeeds in calming him.

He commands the soldiers to keep guard while he dances with her. He pursues Graziosa and tries to kiss her, but she evades him with a coquetry which charms him the more. The soldiers applaud. She leads them to a table and pours out their wine. They entreat her to dance and, kneeling at her feet, beg her to choose a partner. During this moment she signs to Pietro, who loosens one of the bars and, lowering himself to the ground by means of his belt, makes his escape.

Graziosa then laughs at her admirers and declares that she does not wish for any partner and runs away. They dash in pursuit, but give up the chase and return to their post.

The Podesta returns with his clerk and surprises Moscatello trying to recall the steps used by Graziosa. He upbraids him for his frivolity and orders him to produce the prisoner. The sergeant sends soldiers to the prison but they return with the news that he has escaped.

Moscatello explains to the furious Podesta that a charming girl had entertained the soldiers with dances and meanwhile the prisoner must have escaped. But he will recapture both the prisoner and the girl.

"If you fail," threatens the Podesta, "I will have you shot."

The soldiers, alarmed, hastily depart in search of the fugitives.

The Podesta remains as he must attend the Governor, who has promised the Neapolitans a bullfight. The square fills with people and presently the Governor, Don Manuel, and his suite arrive.

The toreadors enter and represent all the stages of a bullfight. First come the chulos with their splendid cloaks, then the banderillas, the picadors, and, finally, the espada, who ends the struggle.

Follow dances by young girls. They are closely watched by the Podesta. Graziosa enters in her bridal dress, for she is about to be wed to Pietro. The Podesta observes the charming newcomer and asks her to dance with him. She pleads inability to dance but when the Podesta insists, dances clumsily. The Podesta leaves her, convinced that she cannot be the brilliant dancer of whom he is in search.

Pietro appears, and Graziosa dances with him with her customary grace. The Podesta, returning with some soldiers and seeing Graziosa's fine dancing, orders her to be arrested. Pietro offers to give himself up, but the Podesta is inexorable. In despair she runs to the Governor and finds him to be the nobleman to whom she had rendered so important a service. He recognizes her in turn and requests the Podesta to pardon the young people.

The Podesta consents and departs with Moscatello and his soldiers.

Everyone applauds the Governor and celebrates the happiness of Pietro and Graziosa.

*

"Here is a ballet such as we understand and love," says *Le Ménestrel*,[3] "a ballet in which the action agreeably interrupts the *pas* and the dances, a ballet in one act, that is to say not very long, in the right proportion . . . a discreet, dainty, gay, sprightly, and entertaining ballet.

"The music is . . . sometimes Italian, sometimes Spanish, ever melodious, which is no disadvantage, and always of good quality.

"The setting . . . represents a splendid Italian landscape."

Ferraris made a great success in the title-role. "You have seen *Orfa, Les Elfes, Marco Spada, Sacountala,* and so on," observes the critic of *La France Musicale*," [4] and you know what Mme. Ferraris is capable of, when she wishes, and she always wishes. Well, add up all her successes, raise the total to the third power, and I doubt if you will arrive at the success she obtained in the new ballet.

"She is a whirling feather, a floating scarf, a fluttering butterfly; she is grace and lightness, she achieves the impossible by proving that difficulties are easy to surmount.

"One moment the stage seems to alarm her so much that she rises in the air, and in that element (which moreover is her own) she gives way to all kinds of capricious flights.

[3] March 31st, 1861.
[4] March 31st. 1861.

"It is true that she allows M. Chapuy, her excellent partner, to support her by the waist, but the audience is undeceived, and sees in it merely an act of good comradeship on the part of Mme. Ferraris. Surprise was evinced that he raised her so high . . . I rather believe he holds her back for fear that she does not fly away for good.

"You should see her when she fascinates the first soldier with her arch and provocative wheedlings, and the second, the third, the fourth, and, lastly, Sergeant Moscatello."

NAMOUNA

Ballet in 2 Acts and 3 Scenes. Book: Charles Nuitter and Lucien Petipa. Music: E. Lalo. Scenery: Rubé, Chaperon, and J. B. Lavastre. Costumes: Eugène Lacoste. Choreography: Lucien Petipa. First produced: Théâtre de l'Opéra, Paris, March 6th, 1882.

CHARACTERS

Namouna	MLLE. RITA SANGALLI
Don Ottavio	M. MÉRANTE
Adriani	M. PLUQUE
Ali	M. CORNET
Andrikès	MLLE. ALICE BIOT
Kitzos	M. AJAS
Iotis	MLLE. SUBRA
Hélène	MLLE. INVERNIZZI
Khaïnitza	MLLE. MERCÈDES

Time: The 17th century.

Act I. Scene I. A casino at Corfu. A hall in an ancient palace which retains something of its original splendour. In the background a large window, overlooking the sea, shows a glimpse of the masts of a tartan moored to the terrace. The night is fine and starry.

The dances have just finished and Count Ottavio is throwing dice with Lord Adriani, whose ship and following suggest a pirate rather than a honest merchant. Adriani, having lost his money, stakes his ship and loses that too. Then he orders one of his men to bring in Namouna, whom he offers to hazard against everything he has lost. The slave entreats her master to renounce this wager, but he refuses. Ottavio declines the stake, but Adriani observes that he cannot refuse him an opportunity to take his revenge. So the game proceeds and Adriani loses.

Ottavio goes to Namouna and gives her the ship and money he has won. He is minded to raise her veil, but confesses that he dare not do so lest he might not let her go.

Namouna, overwhelmed with gratitude, kisses Ottavio's hand, then, taking a posy in her girdle, offers him half, which he accepts. The Count bids Adriani's men accompany the young woman and obey her. Namouna leaves with them, attended by Andrikès.

The bystanders praise Ottavio for his chivalry, but his thoughts are elsewhere. The masts move past the window.

Adriani remains motionless, overwhelmed with disaster, and indifferent alike to mockery and sympathy.

Act I. Scene II. A square in Corfu. In the background the sea; to the right a palace, with large windows and balconies. To the left an inn with terrace and portico.

It is dawn and musicians are serenading Hélène, beloved of Ottavio. She appears at the window. The Count pays the musicians and, climbing on a bench, pays court to Hélène, who leans over and presses his hand.

Adriani approaches and, seeing Ottavio, takes the opportunity to start a quarrel by striking the musicians with the flat of his sword. Ottavio leaps to the ground and recognizes Adriani, who deliberately insults him. Ottavio draws his sword. The fight is joined when a slave asleep in a corner takes to flight. He returns with a veiled woman, who dances between the combatants and offers them flowers. More and more people fill the square and the duel is rendered impossible. The combatants separate. The musicians return and tell their woes to Ottavio, who soothes them with money.

It is a day of festival and now an allegorical car appears, filled with musicians. Hélène returns to the balcony and receives a tender greeting from Ottavio. A veiled woman dances before the Count and seems to imply that Hélène does not love him. Ottavio, attracted by the girl, who is Namouna, dances with her, to the great annoyance of Hélène, who goes indoors.

The dancing continues and the crowd follows the car which passes from sight. At this moment Ottavio sees Hélène, who is going out attended by a lackey. The Count offers her his arm and attempts to justify his conduct.

Adriani reappears and, recognizing Namouna, declares his love for her. She replies that she loves Ottavio, who delivered her from slavery. Adriani is furious and, summoning several ruffians, whispers to them and indicates Ottavio. But Namouna has heard all and gives instructions to Andrikès.

Ottavio escorts Hélène to her abode and, preoccupied with many cares, inhales the perfume of the flowers given to him by Namouna. He turns to go but finds his way barred. He draws his sword just as the sailors summoned by Andrikès come to his aid. The bandits retire in disorder.

The Count thanks his rescuers, who courteously ask him for his sword, and surprise him still more by requesting him to go with them on board a ship. Such, they explain, are their mistress's orders. Half-amused and half-annoyed, Ottavio obeys. As the boat puts off, Adriani makes a vain attack on Ottavio.

A burst of gay music heralds the return of the merrymakers, dancing gaily.

Act II. An island. Oriental carpets suspended from the branches of a giant tree provide a protection from the sun. A dwelling in the eastern manner stands amid the ruins of an antique temple.

This island belongs to Ali, a rich slave-dealer. Slaves of all nationalities are reclining on carpets. Iotis, the prettiest of the slaves, rises and reproaches her companions for their indolence.

Ali arrives and surveys his wares with satisfaction. He is received with deep obeisances. Iotis alone refuses to bow and he pursues her among her friends, who try to hide her. Finally she makes a deep obeisance which soothes Ali's wrath. Iotis dances and her companions dance with her.

These diversions are interrupted by the arrival of the tartan. Ali orders the slaves to put on their veils as Ottavio is led by Namouna, who is veiled, accompanied by Andrikès.

The dealer, with an eye to business, invites Ottavio to rest awhile and take refreshment in his house. The Count follows Ali, when Namouna raises her veil and reveals herself to her former companions. They embrace her and become so excited that Ali returns to quiet them. Then Namouna, to the surprise of the merchant, orders gold and jewels to be brought and purchases all the slaves. The women discard their veils and dance for joy. Then, at her request, they leave her.

Ottavio re-appears and asks Namouna why she has brought him to the island; she shows him the half of the posy she shared with him; then he understands.

The women return bearing flowers which they offer to Namouna and Ottavio. Suddenly they are interrupted by Andrikès who announces the landing of Adriani and a number of men. Ottavio prepares to fight, but Namouna begs him to follow her and sends the women away.

Adriani enters and, having posted sentinels, goes with the rest to reconnoitre. The sentinels perceive a woman dancing before them; she is followed by others. The delighted pirates discard their weapons and dance with the women. One of the soldiers, Kitzos, is captivated by a Moorish girl called Khaïnitza. Suddenly each pirate finds himself threatened by two women, who have seized the discarded weapons.

When Adriani returns, Namouna points triumphantly to the success of her ruse. But the pirate chief has captured Ottavio in his turn. She begs Adriani to free his captive, but he refuses.

Then Namouna orders the women to wait on the pirates and serve them with wine. She herself waits on Adriani and continually fills his cup until he begins to lose his senses, when she frees the Count.

Ottavio throws money to the pirates and while they dispute among themselves, Namouna and he regain the boat; Andrikès follows in the rear.

Suddenly Adriani realizes what is happening and aims his pistol at Ottavio, but Andrikès quickly stabs the chief with her dagger. The pirates, seeing their leader fall, are filled with fear.

Andrikès seizes the oars and the boat puts off with the lovers, to whom the women wave farewell.

*

Namouna appears to have owed its success to certain individual dances rather than to the conception of the ballet as a whole.

The critic of the *Ménestrel*,[5] after reminding his readers that M. Lalo had written several successful symphonies and operas, declares that he "is not a composer of ballet music. He lacks the gift of improvisation and his music delights in details which do not easily harmonize with choreographic requirements.

"Having made these reservations, let us cite . . . the pages of M. Lalo's score which have attracted the attention of musicians." The pieces noted are: the whole of the beginning of the second scene, the prelude-entr'acte of the tartan, the *Pas de la Charmeuse,* the overture to the third scene, the *Pas des Fleurs,* and the flute solo, "scanned by a light clash of cymbals," which latter achieves "a very picturesque effect."

[5] March 12th. 1882.

The scenery and costumes are particularly praised for their beauty and the harmony of their relationship.

The first scene, according to the critic of the *Figaro*,[6] was in the nature of a prologue and played in a small setting. In this scene Sangalli wore "a white Moldavian costume, embroidered in gold, a large white veil spangled with gold, and a silver-embroidered apron with a heavy fringe of red silk."

The second scene, declares the same writer, represents the sea coast. "The setting is ravishing, very warm in tone, with a quay vanishing into the distance, which affords the happiest effect.

"The duel scene is the most humorous duel that we have witnessed at the theatre since the famous duel in *Le Petit Faust*. Not that it is ill arranged, on the contrary, it has been very well organized by the *maître d'armes* of the Opera. But what distinguishes this assault-at-arms from all others is the intervention of Mlle. Sangalli as a flower-girl, who flings herself between the swords, intercepts the thrusts and parries, and replies with a *pirouette*.

"The *Pas des Ioniennes* lacks invention. We have seen and heard this cymbal effect a hundred times.

"*La Charmeuse* and *La Roumaine*, which conclude the act, gain for Mlle. Sangalli many rounds of thoroughly deserved applause.

"The setting of the second act is . . . very pretty and very fresh. . . .

"The lascivious awakening and the little dance of disarmament which occurs in the middle of this act are, in my opinion, the best in the whole ballet. Mlle. Subra . . . is prettier than ever with her little blue bodice and her muslin skirt adorned with a blue and gold border.

"Despite Mlle. Subra and the charm of her companions, a certain sleepiness began to invade the house. Mlle. Sangalli vanquished it decisively with one of those delightful *pas* of which she has the secret, a solo accompanied by the flute alone, which recalls the *pizzicato* from *Sylvia* and the *pas des harpes* from *Yedda*." This *pas*—an interpolated number by Delibes—was encored with acclamation.

[6] March 7th, 1882.

FANNY CERITO

FANNY CERITO was born at Naples in 1821. She made her *début* at the San Carlos Theatre, Naples, in 1835, in a ballet called *The Horoscope*. She then toured most of the Italian towns. Next she spent two years at Vienna, then left for London, where she made many appearances from 1840 onwards. In May, 1841, she danced at Her Majesty's Theatre in *Le Lac des Fées;* in June, *La Sylphide* was revived for her. Afterwards she returned to Vienna. Her two greatest ballets were *Alma* and *Ondine.* The former she first danced in London in July, 1841. The next year she appeared at Her Majesty's Theatre in *Ondine,* in which she danced the famous *Pas de l'Ombre.* In 1844 she danced in *La Vivandière.* In 1845 she took part in the celebrated *Pas de Quatre,* with Grahn, Grisi, and Taglioni; and in 1846 she appeared in the *Pas des Déesses,* with Grahn and Taglioni.

A contemporary describes her thus: "Short of stature, and round in frame, Cerito is an example of how grace will overcome the lack of personal elegance, how mental animation will convey vivacity and attraction to features which, in repose, are heavy and inexpressive. With a figure which would be too redundant, were it not for its extreme flexibility and abandon, Cerito is yet a charming artiste, who has honourably earned a high popularity and deservedly retained it." Her particular forte appears to have been *grands jetés* and *jetés en tournant.*

She made her Paris *début* at the Opera, in 1847, in *La Fille de Marbre,* arranged by her husband, Arthur Saint-Léon; other successes in which she enacted the leading roles were *Le Violon du Diable,* and *Stella.*

Cerito was engaged by the management of the Imperial Russian Theatres and appeared at St. Petersburg in 1855. There she danced in many short ballets such as *Le Rêve du Peintre* and *La Vivandière,* and at her benefit on February 19th, 1856, appeared in *La Fille de Marbre,* revived by Perrot. She made a fine success in a Spanish dance but, failing to achieve further triumphs, left Russia in the same year.

Cerito is one of the very few women dancers who have attempted choreography and doubtless her marriage with Saint-Léon facilitated her studies. She collaborated with Perrot in the composition of *Alma* and *Ondine,* and later produced two ballets by herself: *Rosida* (1845) and *Gemma* (1854), both of which enjoyed success.

Cerito died in Switzerland in 1899.

ROSIDA OU LES MINES DE SYRACUSE

Ballet in 5 Scenes. Book: Fanny Cerito. Music: Cesare Pugni. Scenery: Charles Marshall. Choreography: Fanny Cerito. First produced: Her Majesty's Theatre, London, May 29th, 1845.

CHARACTERS

Rosida, a young Sicilian	FANNY CERITO
Alman, a sailor	M. A. SAINT-LÉON
Queen of the Mines	MLLE. MONCELET
Torbern, the evil Genius of the Mine	M. DI MATTIA
Ottomir	M. GOSSELIN
A Hermit	M. VENAFRA

Sicilian peasants, sailors, persons of different nations.

A Greek vessel has arrived at Syracuse, after a long voyage; the sailors celebrate their safe return, with guests, gay and young, they have invited from the shore. Alman, a young sailor, is discontented with his present mode of life, and is persuaded by Torbern, a miner, who has ingratiated himself into the young man's friendship, and Rosida, a beautiful maiden, to quit a seaman's life, and become a miner.

Before separating, Rosida, who has fallen in love with Alman, gives him an amulet as a charm to preserve him from misfortune. In despair at not being able to follow him into the mines, she confides her love to Torbern, who appears to take an interest in her; he arranges that at a certain hour she shall meet him, disguised as a miner, and that they will descend together into the mines.

Alman is assiduously working in the mines, when he is startled by the vision of a lovely woman. Torbern explains to him that this is the Queen of the Mines, who has taken him under her protection; that if he will serve her faithfully, and never quit these rocks, he will become rich and powerful; if not, her vengeance will be terrible. Alman, allured by the prospect of riches and power, proffers his allegiance to the Queen, who immediately appears with her attendants, receives his oath, and disappears.

He is not long alone before he is joined by a young miner, whom he soon discovers to be Rosida; she tells him that if he refuses to accompany her to the upper earth, she will remain and die with him, for she cannot live away from him. Alman is about to yield to the maiden's love, and she is on the point of ascending the steps that lead from the mine, when suddenly a sulphurous vapour fills the cavern. Rosida is carried away fainting and Torbern has just time to save Alman from the vengeance of the Queen.

What is Alman's horror on rejoining Rosida to find that she has lost her sight! A pilgrimage is undertaken to offer prayers for her recovery—by a miracle she recovers her sight. In the midst of their rejoicings, however, Torbern reminds Alman of his promises to his Queen, he feels himself drawn to the rocks by some super-natural power. Torbern is rejoicing in the accomplishment of his plans, when Alman draws forth the talisman he received from Rosida, and he is at once set free. The happy couple are united; suddenly the darkness is illuminated, and Torbern is seen under the form of an evil spirit, with enormous wings, hovering over the mines.

*

Rosida was noted for its striking and unusual scenic effects. It is also the first and only ballet in which poison gas—sulphur dioxide—is used as an expression of displeasure on the part of the evil genius.

"As far as concerns dramatic merit," observes *The Times'* critic, "it is inferior to many works of the kind. The plot wants the inter-est and striking character which have so often distinguished our modern ballets, and that blindness which appears as an important feature (in this story) comes out with little effect." [1]

Of the settings, a writer in the *Illustrated London News* declares: "Nothing can be more novel and brilliantly effective than the first scene, where the stage is supposed to be transformed into the deck of a ship, crowded with peasants and sailors, clad in the brightest and warmest colours—the masts hung with garlands— the blue waters of the Mediterranean sea beyond. But the last scene, in variety of grouping, colouring, and motion, is a triumph of pictorial art. It represents the port, with vessels lying at anchor, crowds of people of different nations on shore, and devotees come to offer their vows to the Madonna and sea." [2]

[1] May 30th, 1845.
[2] June 7th, 1845.

Commenting on Cerito as choreographer and dancer, *The Times'* critic states: *"Pas* more felicitous, more beautiful, more admirably suited to their charming inventor, were never devised. The 'Sicilienne' with which the ballet commences, and which is danced by Cerito and Saint-Léon on the deck of the vessel, in form somewhat resembles the Cachuca, but it has the tone, the spirit, the mischief of the Redowa. There is all that pursuit and flying, that coquetting and tantalizing in which Cerito is inimitable. The drop upon Saint-Léon's arm as for a pose, and then the hopping in of the two together, preserving the attitude, produced a most novel effect; and all was done with that playful manner, with that genuine merriment, with that perfect naturalness which belongs to the 'realist' school.

"The delight expressed at the sight of the miner's clothes might have been insignificant with an inferior artist, but the little *pas,* executed by Cerito, as she surveyed the attire, was the pure spontaneous expression of unchecked joy.

"A *pas de deux* with Saint-Léon, on the grand scale, formed a contrast to these native dances. This promises to rival the *pas de trois* in *Alma,* Cerito having lavished upon it all her resources in the higher walk of her art. The groups are exquisite, and the voluptuous repose with which Cerito drops into the most elegant attitudes in the slow movement could not be surpassed. The quick movement was as remarkable for its boldness and brilliancy—a rapid step round the stage, producing a perfect tumult of delight among the spectators, and drawing down a shower of bouquets."

GEMMA

Ballet in 2 Acts and 5 Scenes. Book: Théophile Gautier and Fanny Cerito. Music: Count Gabrielli. Choreography: Fanny Cerito. First produced: Théâtre Impérial de l'Opéra, Paris, May 31st, 1854.

CHARACTERS

Gemma	MLLE. FANNY CERITO
Santa-Croce, a mesmerist . . .	MM. MÉRANTE
Massimo, an artist	L. PETIPA
Count of San-Severino, Gemma's guardian	LENFANT
Giacomo, a major-domo	BERTHIER
Beppo, a bridegroom	BAUCHET

Bonifaccio, a peasant . . . . .   PETIT
Angiola, the artist's sister . . . MLLES. L. MARQUET
Marietta, a bride . . . . . .   L. TAGLIONI
Barbara, Gemma's maid . . . .   ALINE

Lords, Peasants, Ladies.

The action takes place at Tarenta, Naples, at the beginning of the 17th century.

Act I. Scene I. A richly-furnished boudoir. In the background are large pier-glasses; to the right and left are doors.

The youthful Countess Gemma, surrounded by her women and friends, is trying on the dress she is to wear at the ball to be given in celebration of her leaving the convent.

The maids in turn hand her flowers and diamonds, and the groups they make are reflected in the mirrors. Gemma has a particular reason for wishing to be beautiful, for the celebrated painter, Massimo, is coming to complete his portrait of her, and she has fallen in love with him.

While the women go out in search of other ornaments a door opens mysteriously and Gemma sees in the mirror two burning eyes gazing at her. She turns round, but the strange visitor has disappeared. This man is the Marquis de Santa-Croce, a debauchee, who dabbles in alchemy and hypnotism in the hope of retrieving his fortunes. He has resolved to dominate Gemma and marry her.

Presently the Marquis returns and, seeing the young girl half swooning in a chair, hypnotizes her with a few skilful passes. Under his influence she makes love to him. At this juncture Giacomo enters to announce Massimo's arrival and is astonished to find the Countess in an ecstatic pose. He retires discreetly. The Marquis awakens Gemma and escapes through a secret door.

Massimo enters to complete his painting. Gemma poses with her companions. While the artist works she leaves her pose and leans on his shoulder. Her beauty and proximity trouble him greatly.

Now the Marquis is announced. He is interested to see how Gemma will receive him. But when he bows and wishes to kiss her hand, she draws away in aversion and contemptuously refuses the rose he offers her. The Marquis, unabashed, maintains a haughty demeanour and courteously saluates the Count of San-Severino, Gemma's guardian, who invites him to the forthcoming ball, also Massimo and his sister, Angiola.

Santa-Croce picks up the rose and magnetizes it. Then, hiding in the shadows, he watches Gemma retrieve the flower, which she kisses and places in her bosom.

Act I. Scene II. A terrace with colonnades and arcades, through which can be seen gardens faintly illumined by the moon.

The guests fill the ballroom, and dance follows dance. Gemma wears the magic rose and under its influence welcomes the Marquis. Massimo, angered that she should wear another's gift, induces her to give it to him. After their dance Massimo conducts Gemma to her seat, when the Marquis begs the favour of a dance. She declines, pleading faintness, and, rising, begs her guardian's permission to retire. But as she is about to leave, Santa-Croce, by means of his will-power, forces Gemma to return and dance with him. The Count shrugs his shoulders at his ward's caprice while Massimo is greatly mystified.

In the meantime Gemma and the Marquis dance together as one. There is something supernatural and magical about this dance, at once animated and lifeless. Slowly Santa-Croce guides the semi-somnolent Gemma towards the terrace, which is now lit up with vivid flashes of lightning. There his men, till then concealed, seize Gemma and carry her off, while Santa-Croce menaces the horrified guests with satanic gaze. Massimo, distraught, rushes forward, but the Marquis whips out his sword and, threatening all who approach, walks backward towards the steps of the terrace and disappears. The major-domo follows at his heels.

Act II. Scene I. The laboratory in Santa-Croce's castle.

Gemma, still in a trance, wears a wedding-dress. Santa-Croce presents her to his friends. Suddenly the door opens violently and Massimo enters. When he wishes to question Gemma, she goes to the Marquis as if for protection. Santa-Croce asks the artist not to press his attentions where they are undesired and shows him a marriage-contract bearing Gemma's signature. Massimo, astounded, and half-demented at the downfall of all his hopes, dashes out of the room.

The Marquis, eager to test his power, awakens Gemma, who, now in her right mind, trembles with fear, and is filled with despair when Santa-Croce displays the contract bearing her signature.

Conscious that he cannot keep his wife in a state of trance, the Marquis tries to conquer her by normal methods. He kisses her hand and tries to embrace her, but she evades his grasp and tries to escape. Alas, the doors are shut fast. They struggle and Gemma snatches a dagger from the Marquis's belt, which is wrested from her by her maid, Barbara, who aids Santa-Croce in his plan in the mistaken belief that she is furthering her mistress's wishes.

In despair, Gemma sees that a window is open. She runs towards it and, seizing a tree which grows beside it, lets herself drop down. At the bottom of the wall waits her faithful major-domo, who could not gain access to the castle. He lifts her up on his horse and gallops away.

Act II. Scene II. A rustic interior adapted to serve as an artist's studio. There are sketches on the walls, easels, and in one corner stands a large covered frame.

Massimo, in despair, refuses to listen to Angiola, who tries to soothe him. He cannot take his eyes off a sketch representing Gemma, but his sister at last induces him to go into the garden. Now the Countess, in search of a refuge, arrives with Giacomo.

Gemma recognizes Angiola and tells her of her escape and how she has always loved Massimo, although she feels that she has been under an enchantment. She devises a plan to restore the artist to his senses. She takes the picture out of the frame and, standing behind it, assumes the same attitude. Massimo enters and see the painting smile at him, hold out its arms, step from the frame, and go towards him. After a series of captivating poses, Gemma makes Massimo realize that she is not a phantom but a woman of flesh and blood. Slowly Massimo recovers his reason.

Suddenly there is a violent knock at the door. Gemma, frightened, resumes her place in the frame and pulls the veil over the picture. Santa-Croce enters but, seeing only a picture, goes out to look elsewhere. The danger averted, Gemma, Massimo, Angiola, and Giacomo disguise themselves as peasants and depart from the Countess's home. Barbara, who has been pardoned, is permitted to accompany them.

Act II. Scene III. A mountainous region with a deep ravine, through which pours a great torrent, spanned by a bridge. To right and left is a footpath cut in the rock. In the foreground is a locanda.

A wedding procession comes down the mountain-side. Beppo and Marietta have just been married and the wedding-feast is to be held on the locanda. Gemma, Massimo, Angiola, Barbara, led by Giacomo, arrive in the midst of the festival. Giacomo plays his pipes, and Gemma and Massimo dance.

Now Santa-Croce enters, followed by his friends, and recognizes the Countess in spite of her disguise. He fixes his magnetic gaze upon her and forces her to come by his side. Massimo tries to restrain the Marquis, but he displays the marriage-contract.

As Santa-Croce leads Gemma up the mountain path, Massimo cries out that the Marquis is a sorcerer and incites the peasants against him. A fight ensues in which Massimo wrests a sword from one of Santa-Croce's friends. Then he runs up the opposite footpath to prevent Santa-Croce from crossing the bridge. The Marquis attacks Massimo with his sword, but, receiving a fatal blow, topples over the bridge and is carried away by the plunging torrent.

The peasants carry Gemma down the path and Massimo takes her in his arms.

*

Gemma, first produced at Paris in May 31st, 1854, is the first and only ballet to be based on the power of hypnotism. "Rarely have we seen such a success," declares the critic of *La France Musicale.*[3] New scenes which . . . have not yet been ventured at the Opera, piquant details, gracious incidents, charmed the audience without cease, by bringing before their eyes the most captivating pictures.

"Let us mention the great mirror scene at the first rise of the curtain. An immense mirror is suggested in the background and accurately reproduces all the poses and all the movements of Gemma and her maids-of-honour.

"The music . . . seemed to us elegant and carefully worked out. The rustic colour of the themes in the last scene is particularly remarkable; the *Valse Magnétique* and the *Abruzzaise* will soon be heard on every piano."

The critic of the *Figaro*[4] states, "The mirror scene is not new, but it has never been attempted with so many persons; it is composed with great taste and rendered with a precision which affords complete illusion. That is the pleasant part . . . the part for criticism will have its turn.

"For instance, a *balletomane* who is very strong in choreography, asserts that the second act of *Gemma* is borrowed 'word for word' from a ballet by Perrot, *Le Délire du Peintre,* and that the final *tableau* is that of the *Forlana* in *Stella.* I have not seen *Le Délire du Peintre* . . . but I have witnessed *Stella,* and it seems to me that my *balletomane* is by no means at fault.

[3] June 4th, 1854.
[4] June 4th, 1854.

"But if I should vex Fanny Cerito, the able choreographer, I hasten to applaud Gemma with both hands. Cerito is better than a *Ballerina;* she is grace personified. With her there is never an abrupt movement or attitude; each angle is 'blurred,' if I may so express myself, by the adorable *morbidezza* of her poses. There are *danseuses* who have more style and greater firmness of execution; but, when you watch her dance, she can be compared with no one."

The critic of *La France Musicale* says of Cerito as Gemma, "You should see her in the *Pas de Deux* or in the *Valse Magnétique* of the second act, to which she brings that fresh and smooth style of dancing, that innate taste, that selection and purity of pose and movement which belongs to Italian *danseuses* alone. Her mime is most intelligent, and is sometimes elevated to power, to drama.

"In the second act, at the moment when Santa-Croce, setting aside his hypnotic power, tries to seduce her by more ordinary means, she was magnificent in her agitation, her terror, and her despair. The whole house was oppressed by this scene, so thrilling, and so well rendered.

"In the fourth scene, in the artist's studio, she mimed with an adorable grace and coquetry, and with a sensitive ability which one is not accustomed to find at the Opera, and which, in the case of Mme. Cerito, seems to add a new and charming quality to those she already possesses.

"The *Abruzzaise,* danced in the fifth scene by Petipa and Cerito, completed the enchantment and raised the enthusiasm of the public to the highest pitch."

MARIUS PETIPA

MARIUS PETIPA was born at Marseille on March 11th, 1822. His father, Jean Antoine Petipa, was a teacher of dancing and *maître de ballet;* his mother was a tragic actress called Victorine Grasseau. Marius's childhood was passed in travelling with his parents, as their professional engagements took them from town to town. He received a general education at the Grand College, Brussels, and also attended the Conservatoire, where he studied music and iearned to play the violin.

At the age of seven his father gave him his first lessons in dancing and, although he disliked the art in his early years, he achieved such progress that, in 1831, he made his *début* at the Théâtre de la Monnaie; he took the juvenile role of a Savoyard in his father's production of Gardel's *La Dansomani.* Then came the Belgian Revolution and the Petipa family was reduced to sore straits.

But, in 1834, Jean Petipa secured the post of *maître de ballet* to the theatre at Bordeaux and took his family with him. Here Marius completed both his general and his dancing education, and, at the age of sixteen, became *premier danseur* at the theatre at Nantes. There he produced several short ballets.

In 1839 he left Nantes to accompany his father on an American engagement which was a fiasco. Marius took advantage of a ship's sailing to France to return to Paris. In 1840 he made his *début* at the Comédie Française, when he danced with Carlotta Grisi at a performance held for the benefit of the celebrated actress, Rachel. As a result he received an engagement for Bordeaux, where he produced several ballets, but the impresario failed. Fortunately, Petipa at once received an engagement for the King's Theatre, Madrid.

He remained in Spain for four years producing several ballets and acquiring a good knowledge of Spanish dancing. Then, as the result of a love affair, he became embroiled with a prominent member of the French Embassy, the Marquis de Chateaubriand, and was forced to leave Spain at the end of 1846. He returned to Paris where he took part in a performance for the benefit of Thérèse Elssler and danced with her famous sister, Fanny.

In 1847 he accepted an offer to fill the post of *premier danseur* to the St. Petersburg branch of the Imperial Russian Ballet—rendered vacant by the departure of Emile Gredlu—at which city he arrived on May 24th. He made his *début* in *Paquita* and in 1858 produced his first ballet in Russia; it was called *Un Mariage au Temps de la Régence.* But it was not until four years later that he was appointed *maître de ballet* in recognition of his having composed in the short space of six weeks a long ballet called *La Fille du Pharaon,* which achieved a considerable success.

Petipa exerted a remarkable influence on the classical ballet of the latter half of the 19th century. One of his contributions was the development of the purely dance element in ballet, which he emphasised not only with beautifully composed *ensembles,* but with the introduction of *soli* designed expressly to exploit the particular virtuosities of his principal artistes.

This led to an incessant and unswerving effort to develop technique. He demanded from his principals the highest standard of execution and insisted that the young dancers training in the schools should be fitted to take their place. Italian dancers possessed of extraordinary technique, such as Ferraris, Salvioni, Brianza, Cornalba, and Pierina Legnani—famous for her thirty-two *fouettés*—were added to the company, and the continual raising of the technical standard, the constant incentive given to competition, caused dancing to tend to transgress the boundary line of acrobatics.

It must not be thought, however, that Petipa was favourably disposed towards an *acrobatic* technique, for, in fact, contrary to the majority of the *maîtres de ballet* of his time, he admired most the classical traditions of the French school of which he himself was a fine example. The truth is that he only fought half-heartedly against the invasion of the Italian dancers and even allowed acrobatic "numbers" to be introduced into his own productions.

Mme. Karsavina has described the Petipa ballets as follows: "At the outset of my career, Marius Petipa was coming to the end of his profession as *maître de ballet.* He had had a long experience and had done much useful service to choreography. He had a remarkable command of mass on the stage and sometimes the form taken by his *ballabiles* showed considerable imagination. But his productions were all founded on the same formula. An inevitable *divertissement* brought his ballets to an ever happy conclusion; while such of his heroes, for whom anything but a tragic end was an historical impossibility, found themselves crowned in a final apotheosis. His ballets tended to be '*féeries.*' In his later years he made some attempts to modernise his art to accord more nearly with the present time, but he never felt at ease when making these efforts and they were unsuccessful. His ballets, which even now have not disappeared from the repertory of the Maryinsky Theatre, were crowded with marches and processions which often interrupted, without any kind of logical excuse, long, continuous scenes of pantomime and beautifully composed dances." [1]

Petipa was a very methodical worker who planned out his ballets stage by stage, making copious notes and sketching the arrangement of the "groups" before he called a rehearsal. Although he had composed twelve ballets prior to his Russian engagement, he learned a great deal respecting choreographic composition from the famous Jules Perrot, who was *maître de ballet* at St. Petersburg in 1847 and remained in that post for twelve years. Perrot was very interested in the young dancer and frequently selected him for his assistant when producing new ballets.

In Petipa's time, custom and tradition reigned supreme. No ballet was composed as the result of collaboration between librettist, composer, *maître de ballet,* and decorative artist. Everyone worked independently, shut up, as it were, in his own office, until music, dances, costumes and scenery were complete when the whole was assembled with results that sometimes were far from satisfactory.

*

Let us consider the production of a ballet at this period. The author of the theme who frequently had little acquaintance with either music, choreography, or painting, selected a legend or story which he happened on by chance and which took his fancy. This he transposed into a ballet, dividing the action over five or six acts, regardless of whether the interest was sufficiently strong to warrant such a treatment.

The sole requisite for success was that everything should centre on one principal character to be interpreted by the *prima ballerina;* for the slightest incident, the feeblest action, served as excuse for bringing in a dance.

There never existed a stranger world than that imagined by the writers of *scenarii;* the course of history was completely changed, the inhabitants common to one land were transported thousands of miles to a place for which their physical characteristics and dress totally unfitted them, rivers which geography has stated to be in Russia and Spain found themselves in Egypt. Never was there

---

[1] *"Souvenirs d'Enfance." Musica,* Dec., 1912.

such a topsy-turvy world, unimagined by the greatest of romancers.

Next a composer was instructed to write the necessary music. There must be so many dances, so many marches in this act, so many in that, and the number of bars each dance was to contain was laid down in detail by the *maître de ballet*.[2] In general, the dances were composed to familiar, easy rhythms like the polka, mazurka, waltz, or galop. If the ballet were Spanish the melodies recalled well-known airs seasoned with the indispensable castanets; if Russian, the composer turned to a Russian folk dance, and so on. If no particular style were specified, a good waltz, march, or polka was certain to ensure success. And, since it often happened that the composer was little acquainted with the *scenario*, the music sometimes afforded a ludicrous comment on the action of the piece. Finally, it would seem that the *maître de ballet* was rarely acquainted with the principles of orchestration, for the music to which the choreography was generally worked out was rendered by one or two violins. The result of this was that when the ballet was finally rendered in conjunction with the full orchestral score, the dancing sometimes provided a strange contrast with the music, *ensembles* being danced to airs lightly scored for the strings, and ethereal movements accompanied by the brass.

The *maître de ballet* worked, again independently, on the dances. The ballet was never conceived as a whole, but simply as a framework on which to hang a number of dances, the style and sequence of which were governed by established tradition. The *prima ballerina* must have her *pas de deux* with its *variations* and *coda,* while the ballet must contain at least one *pas d'action* for the dancer to display her miming abilities. Then there must be a *variation* for the *premier danseur,* and *ballabiles* for the *corps de ballet* to give the former time to rest and change. It was usual, too, to introduce a number of *pas de caractère* for the soloists. Lastly, it was necessary to devise opportunities for the processions in which a crowd of supers marched and counter-marched like soldiers,

[2] An interesting example of this is to be found in *The Life and Letters of Peter Ilich Tchaikovsky* by Modeste Tchaikovsky (English version, translated by Rosa Newmarch, *Lane,* 1906). In Appendix A the author gives an example of a programme prepared for Tchaikovsky by Petipa in connection with the music desired for the ballet, *Casse Noisette.*

No. 1. Soft music. 64 bars.
No. 2. Tree is lit up. Sparkling music. 8 bars.
No. 3. Enter children. Animated and joyous music. 24 bars.
No. 4. Moment of surprise and admiration. Few bars of *tremolo.*
No. 5. *Entrée des Incroyables,* 16 bars. rococo (*tempo di menuetto*).
No. 7. Galop.
No. 8. Enter Drosselmeyer. Awe-inspiring but comic music. A broad move ment, 16-24 bars. . . .

in geometrical figures, finally to form in a mass to serve as a background for the *ballerina* to display her technique.

The scene-designer also worked by himself. He had a competent knowledge of historic ornament and the styles of architecture characteristic of different epochs, but his chief aim was to achieve richness and spaciousness, and with adroit managing of perspective to suggest effects of distance. In almost every ballet there was a lake-side scene, from which convention the members of the last row of the *corps de ballet* came to be known as *les ballerines près de l'eau*. The scene-designer's work then was generally lifeless, devoid of style-atmosphere, and inartistic. It must be admitted, however, that there was little encouragement for a real artist to design artistic scenery, because there was no demand for it.

The costume-designer proceeded in like manner. Although the supers were frequently dressed in historically correct costumes according to the period of the ballet, convention required that the dancers should wear the ballet-skirt, pink *maillot,* and rose-coloured ballet-shoes. If the costume were to be Greek, a Greek key pattern was added to the edge of the skirt; if Egyptian, a lotus flower; if German, that was conveyed by the addition of a dark velvet bodice, a small silk apron, and a few bands of coloured ribbon sewn to the edge of the skirt; if Polish, a few pieces of gold and silver braid were stitched horizontally across the bodice in Hussar fashion and the edges of the sleeves and skirt tipped with fur. The dancer's *coiffure* followed the prevailing fashion, whatever character was interpreted, and was often decorated with a diamond crescent or tiara. Ballet-goers saw nothing incongruous in this, or nothing strange in that a dancer, interpreting a humble slave, should wear jewelled bracelets and pearl necklaces.

If the *ballerina* were satisfied with her dances, well and good; if not, it was easy to cut the offending numbers, regardless of whether the musical sequence were interrupted or not. Again, there were few scruples at borrowing favourite numbers of proved success from old ballets in order that the *ballerina* should repeat her former triumphs; the possibility that they might not accord with the new production was immaterial.

*

Petipa was twice married, in 1854 and 1882. His first wife, Marie Sergeyevna Surovshchikova, became a distinguished *ballerina,* and danced in many of her husband's ballets. She had three children by him, one of whom, Marie Mariusovna, became a well-known dancer. Petipa's second wife was Lubova Leonidovna (Savitsky), a member of the Moscow ballet.

Petipa possessed an almost Napoleonic capacity for work. New *variations, pas de deux, pas de trois, ballabiles,* poured from him like water from a running fountain, and he rarely repeated himself. Those who saw the revival of *La Belle au Bois Dormant* (The Sleeping Princess) at the Alhambra Theatre in 1921, or have seen excerpts from it which have been, and are still being, given from time to time in London and abroad will have a good idea of the technical beauty of his compositions.

A full record of his achievements presents a catalogue of almost incredible labour. He controlled the Russian ballet for over fifty years, during which time he composed 54 new ballets (generally of four, or five acts, and often containing seven or eight scenes), reconstructed 17 old ones, and supplied the dances for 35 operas. Among his best known ballets are the following: *Le Marché des Innocents* (1859), *La Fille du Pharaon* (1862), *Floride* (1866), *Le Roi Candaule* (1868), *Don Quichotte* (1869), *Trilby* (1870), *Camargo* (1872), *La Bayadère* (1875), *Les Aventures de Pelée* (1876), *Roxana* (1877), *La Fille de Neige* (1879), *Mlada* (1879), *Zoraiya* (1881), *La Nuit et la Jour* (1883), *La Vestale* (1888), *The Talisman* (1889), *La Belle au Bois Dormant* (1890), *Le Lac des Cygnes* —with L. I. Ivanov (1895), *Halte de Cavalerie* (1896), *Barbe Bleue* (1896), *Raymonda* (1898), *Ruses d'Amour* (1900), *Les Saisons* (1900), and *Les Millions d'Arlequin* (1900).

Petipa died on July 1/14, 1910.

LE MARCHÉ DES INNOCENTS

Ballet-Pantomime in 1 Act. Book: Marius Petipa. Music: Cesare Pugni. Scenery: Cambon and Thierry. Choreography: Marius Petipa. First produced: Maryinsky Theatre, St. Petersburg, April 23rd/May 5th, 1859.

CHARACTERS

Gloriette . . . . MME. MARIE PETIPA
Denise
Coraline
A Market Woman
Pierrette
Arlequine
Polichinella

Jar
The Captain
Simon
Lindor
Pantaleone
Narcisino
A Gardener
  Market Women, Porters, Flower Girls, Grisettes, Ravaudeuses,
  Incroyables, Soldiers, Citizens, Negro Musicians, Precieuses,
  etc.

The action takes place at Paris, at the time of the Directoire.

Scene. The square called the Marché des Innocents. To the right Gloriette's shop, in front of which is a cask, fitted with a seat and surmounted by a large umbrella. To the left Simon's shop.

At the rise of the curtain, dealers in fish, vegetables, fruit, and flowers cross and recross. Purchasers thread their way through the various groups and make purchases. Simon opens his shop and sets out his wares. He selects from them a basket of cherries which he places on the ledge of Gloriette's cask. Seeing her in the distance he returns to his shop. A bell sounds and the market empties.

Gloriette dances in and sees the love-letters which her admirers have left for her and the cherries. She thanks Simon for his gift and they dance together.

A troupe of strolling players arrive who dance and mime a little play in which the characters are the Captain, Pantaleone, Narcisino, and Coraline.

At the conclusion of the *pas* Lindor appears. He is an *incroyable,* notorious for his extravagant dress and strange fancies. He forces his way through the bystanders with blows from his stick. Seeing Gloriette he is greatly taken with her beauty. He bows low and takes out his purse to bribe the players to leave; but, while he looks for money, Gloriette removes his purse and gives it to the mountebanks. Simon re-enters his shop.

Gloriette sits in the cask making lace as if oblivious of Lindor's presence. He pays her a few high-flown compliments and tries to hold her hand, but she pricks it with her needle. He kneels at her feet and offers to marry her, but she repulses him. Then she draws his attention to a tear in his stocking and offers to mend it. Delighted, he rests his leg on the ledge of the cask and she sews up the rent. But, whenever he tries to kiss her, she pricks him with her needle. Simon watches the proceedings and, while Lindor tries to out-stare him, Gloriette sews a little flag to his calf. Lindor thanks the milliner for her kindness and promises soon to return.

Suddenly a violent dispute breaks out between the women who sell fish. Tempers rise and there is a fight which is ended by the intervention of the other dealers. A general dance completes the reconciliation.

Lindor returns with an enormous bouquet which he offers to the milliner. But Denise, Lindor's mistress, appears and reproaches him with a blow from her fan. Lindor explains that Gloriette has simply mended his stocking. But Denise points to the flag on his calf and proves that he has been fooled. She sends Lindor away and approaches Gloriette who signs to Simon not to interfere.

"Not so quick," observes Gloriette, "I have something to soothe you."

"What you!" sneers Denise.

Gloriette takes a little purse from the cask and says: "Do you recognize this?"

"It is my purse," [3] cries Denise, in a fright. "Do not ruin me!"

Gloriette gives her the purse.

Denise thanks her warmly and asks her pardon, then enquires if she can help her.

Gloriette replies that she wishes to marry a fine young man, but he is poor and she has no dowry.

Denise calls Lindor and forces him to give her his note-case, which she hands to Gloriette, saying:

"Here is your dowry."

Simon and Gloriette thank Denise for her gift, which action is applauded by the bystanders.

Lindor declares that he has been ruined, but consoles himself with the thought that Simon is not handsome and later on—who knows? The ballet ends with a general dance.

*

This ballet is best known as *Le Marché des Innocents,* although it was originally entitled *A Parisian Market.* It was produced at a benefit for Marie S. Petipa, who achieved considerable popularity in the piece, and frequently danced in it when touring abroad with her husband.

[3] The importance of this purse is not clear from the original synopsis. M. Volinine, however, who once danced in this ballet, declared that the purse is supposed to contain compromising letters, which prove that Denise has other lovers besides Lindor.

The ballet was first produced at Paris, at the Théâtre Impérial de l'Opéra, on May 29th, 1861, when Marie Petipa appeared in her original role.

LA FILLE DU PHARAON[4]

Ballet in 3 Acts and 7 Scenes, with Prologue and Epilogue. Book: Vernoy de Saint-Georges and Marius Petipa. Music: Cesare Pugni. Choreography: Marius Petipa. First produced: Maryinsky Theatre, St. Petersburg, January 18th/30th, 1862.

CHARACTERS

PROLOGUE

Lord Wilson	M. MARIUS PETIPA
John Bull, his servant	M. T. A. STUKOLKIN
Mummy of the Pharaoh's Daughter	MLLE. CAROLINA ROSATI
Keeper of the Pyramids	
A Geni	
A Negro	
Three Bayadères	

Camel-drivers, slaves, Armenian merchants, Arabs, bayadères, mummies, etc.

BALLET

Aspicia, Pharaoh's daughter . . .	MLLE. CAROLINA ROSATI
Pharaoh, King of Egypt	M. N. O. GOLTZ
The King of Nubia	M. F. KSHESINSKY
Ta-Hor, an Egyptian youth . . .	M. MARIUS PETIPA
Passifont, his servant	M. T. A. STUKOLKIN
Ramseya, Aspicia's favourite slave . .	MLLE. RADINA I
A Fisherman	M. L. IVANOV
His Wife	MLLE. A. N. KEMMERER
King of the Nile	M. FRÉDÉRIC
High Priest	
Master of the Hunt	
A Courtier of the King of Nubia	
A Slave of Pharaoh	
A Monkey	

Pharaoh's suite, King of Nubia's suite, slaves, huntsmen, priestesses, fishermen and fisherwomen, undines and naiads.

---

[4] *Pharaoh's Daughter.*

Prologue

Scene I. The Egyptian desert. To the right a clump of palm trees; to the left a fountain surrounded by bushes. In the background a pyramid with an entrance door. In the distance a range of hills and a road by which caravans descend into the valley. It is night and the sky is full of stars.

The strains of a march are heard and gradually a caravan of Armenian merchants comes into view. The procession stops in the shade of the palms. Slaves prepare a camp and serve the evening meal. The travellers kneel in prayer then sit down to the repast.

New travellers are seen climbing a little hill. They have only one camel between them and appear to be exhausted. The newcomers are the young Lord Wilson and his servant, John Bull. The latter seems more weary than his master, who stops to examine the pyramid.

Bull, seeing the camp, tells his master, whereupon Lord Wilson approaches the merchants and asks if he may join them. They gladly consent and invite the newcomers to be seated, while slaves offer them refreshment. Bull eats greedily and drains a cup of wine at a draught. The leader of the merchants orders the slave girls to dance for the entertainment of the guests. The dance begins slowly then grows in passion and intensity. Bull, who is now slightly inebriated, attempts to join in the dance. Suddenly there is a terrific thunder-clap, the sky glows with a strange red light, and a simoom breaks.

The merchants hastily rise, the camp is struck, and the caravan reformed. But the simoom grows more and more violent; tents are blown away; palm trees snap and crash to the ground; the whole desert quivers beneath the mighty wind. Everyone runs to find shelter in the pyramid, all save Lord Wilson, who attempts to sketch the scene, while his servant, stricken with fear, urges him to join the others. The simoom grows terrifying in its violence and the young nobleman unwillingly goes towards the pyramid with Bull, constantly buffeted and bowled over by the wind, leading the way. At last they arrive at the door of the edifice.

Scene II. The interior of the pyramid. To the left a statue of a Pharaoh, seated on a granite throne; in the background other sculptured objects. In the centre of the stage is a niche containing a

*royal mummy case, covered with gold leaf and painted in bright
colours. It is flanked by other mummy cases ranged round the
walls.*

The merchants are seated, smoking long pipes of opium. Lord
Wilson enters with his servant, who immediately makes himself
comfortable on some pillows prepared for one of the merchants,
who good-humouredly reclines a little distance away.

An old man clad in rags emerges from the depths of the vault.
He is the keeper of the pyramid, and is amazed to see so many
visitors. Lord Wilson gives him some gold coins and bombards
him with questions. The old man replies and leads the nobleman
to the centre mummy case; he explains the hieroglyphics which
prove the occupant to have been the favourite daughter of one of
the Pharaohs.

Afterwards Lord Wilson asks the merchants if he may smoke a
pipe of opium. The leader offers no objection but, pointing to one
of the smokers, who is in a troubled trance, warns him of the effects
of the drug. The nobleman shrugs his shoulders and, taking the
pipe from the sleeper's hand, slowly inhales the smoke. Bull follows his master's example and presently the two Englishmen fall
into a deep sleep. Light transparent clouds fill the chamber and
an entrancing series of pictures follow—the result of indulgence
in opium.

A beam of light pierces the mist and falls on the centre mummy
case. There is a clap of thunder and from the case steps a young
girl, the beautiful Aspicia, Pharaoh's favourite daughter. She
tries to recall the past and is frightened to find herself in the hall
of the pyramid. She takes a metal mirror, suspended from her
girdle, and, looking into it, is pleased to find that she is as
beautiful as ever.

The old man throws off his rags and becomes a handsome
youth, the geni of the pyramid. He waves his sceptre and the remaining mummies come to life in the full tide of their beauty.
Warriors come forth from the shadows and the pyramid gleams
with fantastic lights.

The young girls make obeisance to Aspicia who observes the
sleeping nobleman and points him out to her friends. The Englishman, tossing in his sleep, extends his arms towards her. Aspicia
places her hand on his heart, then presses it against her breast.
The geni appears, seizes Aspicia, and together they vanish amid
the clouds. The lights grow dim, the clouds become denser, and
in fiery letters appear the words: *The Dream of the Past.*

BALLET

*Act I. Scene I. A thickly wooded valley bathed in sunlight.
In the distance is a winding road which crosses a bridge. To the
right a little hut covered with wild flowers and furnished with a
mossy seat. Before the curtain rises, the sound of horns and trumpets can be heard. The Pharaoh is hunting lions with his daughter,
Aspicia.*

Enter the Princess, attended by women and huntsmen. She
wears a quiver and carries a golden bow. Her women dance a
warlike measure in which she takes part. Then, weary from her
exertions, she goes into the hut and reclines on the seat. Ramseya,
her favourite slave, sits beside the Princess and supports her head
on her breast.

The huntsmen form a group about their mistress, and one of
the slaves sits at Aspicia's feet and plays a lute. Lulled by the
melodious strains, Aspicia and her friends fall asleep; lastly, the
musician drowses too, the lute slipping through her fingers.

A monkey creeps along a tree whose branches overhang the hut.
It climbs down and approaches the Princess, who wakes, rises, and
aims an arrow at the animal. The monkey, seeing its danger, takes
to flight.

In the distance appear two men. They are Lord Wilson and
his servant who, under the influence of opium, have entered this
fantastic world. The former calls himself Ta-Hor, the latter, Passifont.

The servant pleads for a rest and, sitting down, eats fruit and
cakes from his wallet. Ta-Hor, seeing Aspicia, tries to remember
where he has seen her, then, approaching to the music of the
prologue, places his hand on her heart. Huntsmen run in and
Ta-Hor and his servant hurriedly depart.

The huntsmen inform Aspicia that they have found a lion
which is roaming the wood. A lion's roar is heard and the terrified
girls run in all directions. Aspicia also flees, but quickly returns
and warns the girls of the lion's approach. She hurries into the
wood and, almost immediately, the lion bounds across the clearing
in pursuit of Aspicia.

Ta-Hor runs in and asks what has happened. While the attendants explain the situation, he sees Aspicia running across the
bridge with the lion bounding after her. Ta-Hor seizes a bow
and looses an arrow at the lion, which topples over, mortally
wounded. Then Ta-Hor runs to the help of Aspicia who has

swooned. He lifts her up in his arms and carries her to the hut where her women tend her.

Fanfares herald the arrival of the Pharaoh, who enters in a chariot drawn by negroes, and surrounded by huntsmen and guards. He is surprised and angered to see his daughter in Ta-Hor's arms, but Aspicia presents him as her saviour.

The monarch's anger changes to gratitude and he requests Ta-Hor to join his retinue. Pharaoh and his daughter step into the chariot. Passifont follows his master, whom the Pharaoh has placed in a palanquin of honour, and assumes an exaggerated air of consequence. The company set out for the palace.

Act I. Scene II. The Pharaoh's Palace at Thebes, a magnificent hall with an exit into the gardens. On each side is a portico; in the distance a large dais where servants are setting out a feast. Around the walls are caryatides holding torches. A wide staircase leads to a raised platform where stands the Pharaoh's throne.

Enter Ta-Hor and Passifont. The former, overjoyed at the thought of seeing Aspicia again, looks anxiously for her. Presently she comes in attended by young girls and female slaves. She goes to Ta-Hor and offers him caskets of gold and precious stones as a reward for saving her life. But he refuses the gift and declares his love. Passifont, alarmed at his master's boldness, warns the lovers of the Pharaoh's arrival.

The monarch enters with a magnificent suite. A herald approaches and announces that his lord, the King of Nubia, has come to ask for the hand of his daughter, Aspicia. The Princess is overwhelmed at this news, but Ta-Hor maintains an outward calm.

The Pharaoh receives the King of Nubia, who enters with a splendid retinue. He presents him to Aspicia, whose beauty amazes him. He falls on one knee and asks her hand in marriage. Her father is pleased but Ta-Hor is about to draw his dagger, when he is calmed by a look from Aspicia. She whispers to him that she will never belong to the King of Nubia. Then she slips a ring from her finger and gives it to Ta-Hor, who can scarcely credit his good fortune.

The Pharaoh ascends to his throne and orders the festival in honour of Aspicia's escape to begin. Dancing commences, during which the lovers and Ramseya converse in whispers. Ta-Hor urges Aspicia to flee with him; he shows her a key given to him by Ramseya which opens a secret door in the hall, leading to the

Nile, where a boat awaits them. Aspicia is seized with indecision, but finally consents.

Now slaves enter bearing baskets of flowers on their heads. They form groups and dance, then children leap out of the baskets and bring the dance to a conclusion. The two monarchs proceed to the feast, their path strewn with flowers, while the hall is misty with burning incense.

The torches simultaneously burst into flame and the people bow low before the Pharaoh. When the monarchs are seated, the dancing is resumed. Meanwhile, Ramseya flings a mantle over Aspicia's head and the lovers escape through the door opened by Passifont, who follows at their heels.

A slave reports their flight to the Pharaoh who orders his daughter to be brought back. He summons Ramseya before him and threatens her with his anger if she refuses to tell him where Aspicia is. While the Pharaoh issues his commands, the King of Nubia discovers the secret door and hastens after the lovers. All is commotion and uproar.

Act II. Scene I. The interior of a fisherman's hut on the banks of the Nile. To the left the entrance door, above which is a window, with steps leading to it. To the right are doors leading to an inner room. Fishing-nets are hanging on the walls.

Fishermen and fisherwomen run into the hut bearing bunches of grapes. They squeeze the fruit and drink the juice. Dancing begins. Suddenly there is a knock at the door; it is three peasants who crave shelter. They are Ta-Hor, Passifont, and Aspicia in disguise. The fisherfolk welcome the newcomers and offer them refreshment, after which the lovers join in the dances.

At nightfall the fishermen prepare their nets. Ta-Hor offers to help them with their fishing and, bidding Aspicia a tender farewell, takes his departure.

Aspicia, now alone, becomes frightened. She locks the entrance door and is about to pass through the right-hand doors when, to her terror, a cloaked figure steps into the room. He flings off his cloak and reveals himself to be the King of Nubia. Kneeling before her he tries to soften her anger, but the Princess commands him to leave. Then he announces that he has come to claim her.

Aspicia entreats him to leave and declares that she will never be his. The King, enraged, tries to seize Aspicia, but she runs towards the window and, pointing to the river flowing below, threatens to leap into the water if he takes another step. The

King, afraid, stops, but, unable to curb his passion, again rushes towards her. Then the Princess flings herself into the river.

The King, stupefied at Aspicia's action, sobs with grief. His servants run in. He shows them the open window and, half-hysterical, is about to leap into the river himself, when he is stopped by his servants. At this moment Ta-Hor and Passifont return. The King orders them to be arrested.

Act II. Scene II. Beneath the Nile. Aspicia's body is seen slowly sinking. As it nears the bed of the Nile, the scene gradually lightens, to reveal a lovely grotto fashioned of corals, plants, and stalactites.

In the centre, on a jasper throne, sits the King of the Nile, holding a golden trident. He is surrounded by naiads, undines, and other underwater folk. He notices Aspicia's beautiful body which the rivers have brought him and recognises her as the daughter of the stern ruler of Egypt. He bows in homage and orders the naiads to tend her. They carry Aspicia into the grotto. Meanwhile the King commands a magnificent festival in honour of his guest.

He summons the Guadalquivir, Thames, Rhine, Congo, Neva, and Tiber, together with their tributaries and rivulets. They dance the national dances of the countries they water. Follows a dance of naiads and undines, amid whom appears Aspicia, in the guise of an underwater fairy. At the end of the dance she implores the King to let her see Ta-Hor.

The King waves his trident and causes a vision of her lover to appear. Aspicia is delighted, but when she approaches Ta-Hor the apparition fades. Then she begs the King to restore her to the earth where Ta-Hor has remained. The King tells her that his power is bounded by the river, but, after her continued entreaties, promises to fulfil her wishes. At his command a mother-of-pearl shell floats out of the grotto.

Aided by the naiads, Aspicia sits in the shell, which is lined with flowers and lotus leaves. The waters ripple and the shell rises to the surface, when Aspicia throws flowers to her friends below, among whom is the King, who directs her course to the earth.

Act III. The gardens of the Pharaoh's palace. On the right a statue of Osiris. The monarch is seen seated on a granite throne, surrounded by wives, courtiers, and slaves.

The Pharaoh asks the priests and soothsayers to divine Aspicia's fate. The High Priest opens a book, supported by a slave, and cries out to the gods, while the lesser priests and priestesses dance a religious rite. But the oracle remains silent. The High Priest bows to the Pharaoh and declares that he cannot say what has happened to Aspicia. The angry monarch rises from his throne and everyone prostrates themselves before him.

The King of Nubia enters and announces that he has captured Ta-Hor and his servant. The prisoners are led in. But the King says nothing of Aspicia's fate.

Ta-Hor walks in proudly, but Passifont shivers with apprehension. Pharaoh asks Ta-Hor what has happened to Aspicia. He replies that he does not know, but is willing to give his life to see her alive and happy. The Pharaoh orders Ta-Hor to restore his daughter, but he only repeats his previous reply.

The monarch signs to the High Priest who brings in a basket of flowers. Two other priests bring in a black slave with his chest bared; he is made to kneel before the basket.

The High Priest utters an incantation. A thunder-clap is heard and a mist rises. A soft radiance appears and everyone falls on their knees. The flowers in the basket move and an emerald green snake raises its head. The High Priest makes a sign and the snake darts at the negro, who falls and writhes in pain. The priests place the basket on a pedestal. Ta-Hor, although moved by the scene, does not lose his courage; but Passifont grovels on the ground.

The Pharaoh threatens Ta-Hor with the negro's fate if he does not instantly reveal where Aspicia is. Suddenly joyful music is heard. Everyone rises as peasants and peasant-women enter bearing flowers and oak branches.

Ramseya tells the Pharaoh that his daughter has returned. Peasants carry in a litter decked with flowers on which reclines Aspicia. She greets her father from a distance then steps down from the litter and throws herself into his arms. He returns her embrace and asks what has happened to her.

Seeing the King of Nubia she clings to the Pharaoh and tells him what occurred in the fisherman's hut. He is incredulous, but, when she calls on the gods to bear her witness, the King of Nubia confesses his crime. Then the Pharaoh tears up the treaty and orders the King of Nubia to leave. The latter, threatening vengeance, departs with his suite.

Aspicia looks for Ta-Hor and observes the priests leading him to death. Passifont, as an accessory, is to receive the same punishment. Immediately she falls at the Pharaoh's feet and implores him to release Ta-Hor or she will die with him. Seeing that her father is adamant she throws herself before the basket and is about to plunge her hand within.

The Pharaoh, horrified at his daughter's action, drags her back and orders the prisoners to be released. Ta-Hor kneels before Aspicia, but the Pharaoh bids him rise and gives his consent to their marriage.

Aspicia, overjoyed, embraces her father. General happiness, followed by a festival. Towards the end of the dancing the scene is covered with magic clouds.

Gradually the clouds disperse to reveal the interior of the pyramid. Lord Wilson, John Bull, and the Armenian merchants are sleeping. The statues and mummies are still standing in their places. In a corner slumbers the keeper of the pyramid.

The roof of the pyramid opens and, lit with fantastic lights, reveals a magnificent apotheosis. Osiris and Isis are seen surrounded by the lesser gods. Isis opens her arms for the soul of the beautiful Aspicia which, all luminous, is seen floating towards her. The deities rise to greet Aspicia.

At this moment Lord Wilson and his fellow sleepers wake up. The dream is ended.

*

La Fille du Pharaon, inspired by Théophile Gautier's Le Roman de la Momie, played an important part in Petipa's career, for soon after its production he was appointed second maître de ballet.

Rosati, at this time a guest ballerina at the Maryinsky Theatre, had reached the age of thirty-six, and had resolved to leave St. Petersburg, and retire. She expressed a wish that her final ballet should be devised by Petipa. But A. I. Saburov, the Assistant Director of the Imperial Theatres, was short of funds, and refused to authorise the production of the new ballet.

Then Rosati, accompanied by Petipa, made a second call on the director. Petipa pointed out that, in accordance with his contract, he must produce a new ballet. "Tell me," said the director, "can you produce a ballet in seven or eight weeks?" "Yes," replied Petipa, "if I do my best." The director gave way and the ballet was ready in six weeks. It achieved a great success, although Rosati was not very suited to the part of Aspicia. Her mime was excellent, but her dancing left much to be desired.

The role of Aspicia has a long line of interpreters, among whom may be mentioned A. N. Kemmerer, M. S. Petipa, H. d'Or, E. A. Vazem, V. Zucchi, M. Kshesinskya, A. Pavlova. D'Or presented Aspicia as a woman who loves wildly and unrestrainedly, and, although her performance had nothing of the majesty of Rosati's rendering or of the coquetry of Marie Petipa's portrait, it made a considerable impression on the audience.

Zucchi would appear to have been magnificent in this role. Kshesinskaya declares that Zucchi's performances are among her most vivid recollections. The painter, Benois, recalling his memories for the benefit of his friend, Prince Lieven, asserts that Zucchi's acting as Aspicia was admirable, especially in the first act when she is attacked by a lion, an obvious product of the stage carpenter. "Zucchi had only to appear, even with this caricature of a lion, to send a shiver down the spine of the spectator." [5]

LE ROI CANDAULE

Ballet in 4 Acts and 6 Scenes. Book: Vernoy de Saint-Georges and Marius Petipa. Music: Cesare Pugni. Choreography: Marius Petipa. First produced: Maryinsky Theatre, St. Petersburg, October 17th/29th, 1868.

CHARACTERS

Pythia
Gyges
Clytia
Candaules, King of Lydia
Nisia, his wife . . . . MLLE. HENRIETTA D'OR
    Peasants, Shepherds, Shepherdesses, Candaules's Ministers, Priests, Officers and Soldiers of the Army of Lydia, Courtiers, Waiting-Women, Slaves, Dancers, etc.

Act I. Scene I. A forest glade. In the background is the cave of Pythia of Sardis.

The kings and people of Lydia come to this spot to question the oracle as to the future.

At the rise of the curtain, peasants, shepherds, and shepherdesses come to rest on the grass after their toil. Among them is a shepherd called Gyges, who plays on his pipe and induces the company to dance. Near him is his betrothed, Clytia, who looks at him tenderly. Gradually the light fades. The peasants look fearfully at the cave and take their departure. Night falls.

Follows the hooting of owls and the whistling of bats. Pythia emerges from the cave amid clouds of smoke, and, knowing that

[5] Lieven (Prince Peter) *The Birth of Ballets Russes*, 1936.

King Candaules is about to consult her, commands everyone to
leave.

Enter King Candaules escorted by his followers. Gyges, whom
the King encountered in the forest, acts as his guide. He informs
the King that if he wishes to consult the oracle he must strike the
shield that hangs beside Pythia's cave. Gyges and the King's attendants retire. Candaules strikes the shield and Pythia appears.
He entreats her to cast his future.

She tells him that he kidnapped the true king in his infancy,
placed him in a forest at the mercy of wild beasts, and seized the
crown himself. Candaules, alarmed, protests that she is mistaken.
Pythia offers to retract her words if he will submit to the judgment
of heaven. She raises her arms in readiness but Candaules, afraid,
implies his guilt. Then Pythia informs him that the true king
lives and will seize his throne and power. Candaules swears to kill
the king if he be alive.

Pythia bids Candaules walk in fear of the gods. Owls appear
carrying in their claws a roll of papyrus which predicts that Candaules will die an unnatural death. Terrified, he flees into the
forest.

Enter Gyges, who is surprised not to find the King. But Pythia
takes him by the hand, bids him put on the armour left by Candaules, and foretells that he will soon be king. Gyges obeys her
and, becoming conscious of his destiny, waves his sword and disappears into the forest.

*Act I. Scene II. King Candaules's camp on the borders of Libya
and Misia. There are numerous tents with the King's abode in
the centre. In the distance are mountains. Night.*

There is considerable activity. Sentries are being changed, soldiers are furbishing armour, and officers are passing in and out of
the King's tent for their orders.

The flap is thrown back and Candaules emerges. His Queen,
Nisia, with the aid of her women, puts on armour. She is attended
by amazons, and, under her direction, warlike games are played;
meanwhile Candaules's warriors practise the *testudo*. The games
end and silence reigns. Suddenly a messenger gives warning of a
night attack. Candaules orders everyone to be on the alert and a
warrior, Gyges, is placed at the entrance of the tent.

In the half-darkness troops can be seen creeping along the
ground. They surprise the guards and gradually near the King's
tent. Then the enemy leap to their feet and begin to destroy the
tents. They are impressed by the splendour of the King's tent,

which Gyges forbids them to enter. Nisia raises the flap and faces the enemy. Two of her assailants endeavour to capture the Queen, but Gyges cuts them down. Other soldiers attack Gyges, who is almost overcome when a party of Candaules's men come to the rescue, led by the King.

Seeing his wife in Gyges's arms, Candaules takes the warrior for an enemy and rushes upon him with upraised dagger. But Nisia explains that Gyges has saved her life. Candaules thanks Gyges warmly and announces that henceforth he shall rank next to him. Everyone does homage to Gyges, who, however, cannot accustom himself to this high honour.

Act II. Scene I. An arena with a triumphal arch. In the background is a statue of Venus Victrix. On either side are tiers of seats with places of honour for the King and Queen, and their suite.

Citizens of all rank, carrying laurel wreaths and flowers, are seen arriving to greet the King, whose approach is heralded by fanfares. The Lydian warriors enter through the arch, followed by captive chiefs in chains and captive soldiers of various nations. The rear of the procession is formed by the notables of Lydia, and a gold chariot drawn by slaves. In this chariot are King Candaules, Gyges, and the principal ministers. Nisia follows on a magnificently accoutred elephant. She is surrounded by girls who rain down flowers.

The triumphal procession stops in the centre of the arena. The nobles offer their King the keys of his capital, then the captives are paraded before him. Finally Candaules, accompanied by Nisia, takes his seat, and the festival begins.

First, there is a dance by nymphs, *bayadères,* graces, negroes, and half-castes. Just before the dance ends, a Lydian, representing a sunflower and surrounded by other dancers representing roses and forget-me-nots, treads a measure. Nisia is entreated to take part and represent Venus.

At first she refuses, then consents. A new dance begins in which Nisia, cupids, nymphs, and sylphs takes part. Everyone does homage to the new Venus, and Candaules, drunk with pride, declares his consort to be the true Venus. Nisia declines these compliments, but Candaules orders the statue of Venus to be removed from its pedestal and Nisia lifted in its place. Candaules and his courtiers acclaim her as a goddess. The warriors present arms and the women strew flowers at her feet. All at once, the sky grows dark and the priests and people look away in fear, while Candaules, in his arrogance, seems to defy the powers of heaven.

Act III. Scene I. The Queen's bathing place. Splendid tables are laid with gold dishes. In the background is a bathing-pool of pink and white marble, adorned with a fountain and surrounded with flowers.

Nisia is seen standing beneath a curtain and attended by female slaves. They dress her hair and remove her jewels. Others hold up a mirror in which she admires herself. To the music of harps the slaves take up a series of attitudes and afterwards Nisia dances. During the last group, a curtain falls and masks the bathing-pool.

Enter the Queen's ladies who prepare to receive her. Nisia arrives, splendidly attired and attended by many slaves. The arrival of Candaules is announced. He kneels before the Queen whom he has elevated to a goddess. He is surrounded by the women who attempt to fascinate him.

Suddenly Gyges runs in distraught, for he is the bearer of evil news. He is followed by the priests of Venus who demand audience with the King. Candaules, alarmed, orders them to be admitted. The priests are afraid, for Venus has already given signs of her displeasure, since hunger, pestilence, and other miseries have fallen on the land and are spreading throughout Lydia.

The King asks the High Priest how the goddess can be appeased. He replies that the goddess insists that Nisia shall be punished by being forced to renounce her title of Queen. Nisia is terrified and the King refuses the demand. Then the Priest warns him to beware of the anger of the gods. The sky darkens, thunder rolls, lightning flashes, and the tremor of an earthquake is felt.

Candaules induces Nisia to renounce her title, and she flings her gold circlet to the ground. The King falls on his knees and swears eternal love. The sky clears and the Priest returns thanks to heaven. But Nisia looks contemptuously at Candaules and seeks consolation from her women.

Act IV. Scene I. The bed chamber of King Candaules.

The King is seen asleep on a couch. Nisia sits beside a table on which rests his crown. She gazes sadly on this symbol of earthly power, conscious of the gloomy future that lies before her. Then she looks at Candaules, the cause of her fall.

In her anger she menaces the sleeping King. At the same

moment a curtain parts and Pythia appears, bearing a golden cup. She tells Nisia that it contains poison and urges her to satisfy her revenge, for Gyges will marry her and she will again become a Queen. A vision of Gyges is seen at the far end of the room.

Candaules awakes and Pythia disappears. Courtiers enter, including Gyges. All pass by Nisia without noticing her, save only Gyges who bows before her as usual. Nisia conceals her displeasure, but vows vengeance. Candaules, still in love with his wife, tries to calm her. He asks her to dance for him. She consents but asks him to send everyone away, since she is a slave now and only he may see her dance. At Candaules's command the courtiers retire.

Nisia dances and soon captivates the amorous king. He tries to embrace her but she eludes him. Meanwhile Pythia watches behind a curtain and points to the poisoned cup. Nisia takes it and presents it to Candaules with averted eyes. The King drains the cup. He feels the effects of the poison and strikes a gong, but Pythia appears. As Candaules writhes in the throes of death, Gyges and his courtiers rush in. Gyges goes to help the King, but Pythia forces him to confess that Gyges is the rightful monarch. Gyges takes the King's crown and presents it to Nisia who, surprised, looks at Pythia, who reminds her of her prediction.

Act IV. Scene II. A hall in the palace of King Candaules. On the terrace is a table laid with gold dishes. The hall is lit with bronze sconces.

A betrothal feast is in progress, for Gyges has become King of Lydia and is to wed Nisia. Courtiers and nobles are present. The priests enter to conduct the marriage ceremony. They bring in a sacrificial table. Gyges, crowned, leads his bride towards the table, places a hand over the holy flame and take a vow, Nisia does the same, but the flame expires and there is a clap of thunder. The people are astonished at this portent and the priests withdraw from the table. Gyges, enraptured with Nisia, ignores the warning, takes the Queen towards the gardens and commands the festival to begin.

The proceedings open with the Dance of Diana, in which Endymion and a satyr take part. Slaves wait on the guests who are reclining at tables, and fill their cups with wine. Gyges asks the Queen to join in the dancing. She takes a cup and empties it as if to drown her thoughts. She dances in a trance and empties another cup, which is filled by the ghost of Candaules, who suddenly tears the crown from her head. Terrified, she swoons, and

Gyges hurries to her side and endeavours to lead her to her throne, but again the ghost appears. Nisia, panic-stricken, runs among the dancers who cannot see the reason for her fear. At last, exhausted, she falls in Gyges's arms, but the ghost points to his grave, where he awaits his guilty wife. A deathly pallor steals over her features and she sinks to the ground dead. Gyges, overcome with grief, tries to restore her to life. At this moment Pythia appears. She tells Gyges not to grieve but to thank heaven for having preserved him from death, and she indicates a cup of poison which Nisia had prepared for him.

Gyges and all present withdraw from Nisia's body. A blue sky appears and in a diamond temple Venus is seen surrounded by cupids. The jealous goddess, with an expression of triumph, points to Nisia's lifeless body, as if to warn those who seek to rival the goddess of eternal beauty.

*

Le Roi Candaules is based on the history of Gyges, King of Lydia, and is a clever combination of the sequence of events as recorded by Herodotus and by Plutarch. The ballet was produced for Henriette d'Or, of French descent although born in Vienna. The sensation of the evening was the *"Pas de Venus,"* in which d'Or executed a series of five *pirouettes sur la pointe* on the right foot. There were many classic dances and a number of beautiful groups. The Lydian *ballabile* was considered to be a masterpiece of ensemble composition.

This ballet, produced with the utmost splendour, achieved an outstanding success, the first 22 performances being played to packed houses and constituting a record in ballet attendances.

DON QUICHOTTE

Ballet in 4 Acts and 8 Scenes, and a Prologue. Book: Marius Petipa. Music: L. Minkus. Choreography: Marius Petipa. First produced: Bolshoy Theatre, Moscow, December 14th/26th, 1869.

CHARACTERS

Bachelor Sampson Carrasco
Antonina
Don Quixote
Sancho Panza
Lorenzo, an innkeeper

Kitri, his daughter . . . . Mlle. A. I. Sobeshanskaya
Gamache
Basil, a barber
A Gypsy Chief
Graziosa, his daughter
   Villagers, Toreadors, Gypsies, Fairies, Gnomes, Monsters, etc.

Prologue. Don Quixote's study.

Bachelor Sampson Carrasco is seen covering a bookcase with wallpaper, while Antonina is putting into a cupboard some rusty armour and a helmet made of pasteboard.

Don Quixote enters reading a book. He goes to the bookcase and, not finding it, believes that it has been stolen by evil magicians. Then he settles down into an armchair and continues reading. He delights in stories of brave knights and fabulous giants, but gradually his head nods and he falls asleep to dream of their romantic adventures.

Darkness falls and through the study window climbs his servant, Sancho Panza, followed by several angry women, from whom he has filched a chicken. Don Quixote wakes and, sending the women away, tells Sancho that he is determined to seek adventure as a knight-errant. He shows him the pasteboard helmet he has made, which, at one sweep of his sword, becomes a shapeless mass.

Antonina suggests that he should use a basin, which would make a splendid helmet. Don Quixote enthusiastically agrees and, placing it on his head, orders Sancho to bring him his armour, sword, and spear.

Act I. A market-place in Barcelona.

Kitri, an innkeeper's daughter, steals out of her house to meet her lover, Basil the barber. Her father, Lorenzo, sees the lovers and sends Basil away. Kitri gives way to tears.

Now comes a rich nobleman called Gamache, who, likewise in love with Kitri, goes to Lorenzo and asks for his daughter's hand. The innkeeper accepts with delight and asks his future son-in-law into the house.

Dancing begins in the square and some toreadors try to kidnap the girls they fancy, but their relatives and lovers hasten to their aid. At this moment Don Quixote arrives, mounted on his horse, Rosinante, and followed by Sancho, riding a donkey. At his master's command, Sancho sounds a horn.

Lorenzo runs out of his inn, and Don Quixote, taking him for the lord of a famous castle, dismounts and, falling on his knees, begs to be allowed to serve him. Lorenzo invites the knight to sit on his balcony. Sancho remains in the square where he is surrounded by young girls who induce him to take part in a game of blindman's buff.

Then some youths bring in a blanket on which they place Sancho and proceed to toss him into the air. Don Quixote hurries to his assistance and finally sets him free.

Noticing Kitri, the knight acclaims her as his Dulcinea, whom evil magicians have reduced to low estate. Peasants collect in the square and dancing is resumed. Kitri and Basil take the opportunity to run away, but the knight sees them and, ordering his horse to be brought, sets out in pursuit.

Act II. Scene I. The interior of an inn.

Kitri enters with Basil and joins with those who are dancing. At the height of the merriment, Lorenzo and Gamache come in. The former, seeing his daughter, decides to give his blessing to her union with the nobleman. Basil is very annoyed and, reproaching Kitri for her unfaithfulness, draws a sword and stabs himself. As he lies dying he begs Lorenzo to unite him to Kitri, but Lorenzo and Gamache refuse.

The knight approaches Gamache and challenges him for having refused to fulfil a dying man's wish. Gamache declines to fight and the merrymakers drive him out of the inn. Then Lorenzo agrees to unite Basil and Kitri. At this moment Basil pulls out the sword and tells everyone that he was only playing a joke.

Act II. Scene II. Among the windmills outside the village. Here is a camp of gypsies and a marionette theatre.

A clown is seen walking with Graziosa, the gypsy chief's daughter. A gypsy tells the chief of the approach of Don Quixote. The chief plans a trick for his benefit and, putting on a mantle and crown, sits down as though he were a king upon a throne.

Don Quixote is deceived and kneels to the chief in homage. The latter bids his guest sit beside him and orders a festival to be given in his honour. This begins with gypsy dances and is followed by a performance of the marionette theatre.

The knight is delighted with the entertainment but, mistaking the marionette soldiers for real ones, he attacks them. The gypsies are terrified. At this moment the clown and Graziosa run away.

Don Quixote, flushed with victory, renders thanks to heaven.

Seeing the moon he takes it for Dulcinea and tries to get to her. Coming nearer to the windmills he can see the moon no longer and thinks the magicians have hidden his mistress. So, spear in hand, he tilts at the wings of the windmills, which he mistakes for giants. Alas, the knight is caught by one of the wings, and flung into the air to fall unconscious at Sancho's feet.

Act III. Scene I. A forest.

Through the trees appears Sancho leading his donkey, upon which sits the wounded knight. The servant lifts his master down and places him on the grass, so that he can rest. Then, tying up the donkey, he goes to sleep. Don Quixote also tries to sleep, but is troubled by fantastic dreams.

Act III. Scene II. Dulcinea's garden.

Fairies appear surrounded by gnomes. Then come a succession of fearsome monsters, the last being a gigantic spider, who spins a web. Don Quixote attacks the spider, which he slashes in half with his sword. At the same moment the spider's-web vanishes to reveal a beautiful garden, at the entrance of which stands Dulcinea, surrounded by beautiful girls. All at once everything vanishes.

Act III. Scene III. The Duke's hunting-grounds.

The sound of hunting-horns is heard and through the clearing appears the Duke surrounded by a numerous retinue. Don Quixote falls on his knees before the Duke, who invites the knight to accompany him to his castle.

Act IV. The Duke's castle.

A magnificent festival is held in honour of Don Quixote. Suddenly the Knight of the Silver Moon challenges him to a duel, which results in the latter being vanquished.

The victorious knight proves to be none other than Bachelor Sampson Carrasco who forces Don Quixote to give a vow that he will not unsheath his sword for a whole year. The sorrowful knight, true to his vow, takes off his warlike gear and, followed by Sancho, sets out for home.

*

The ballet of *Don Quichotte* is founded on the celebrated novel by Cervantes. This theme is not new to ballet, for Noverre produced a *Don Quichotte* at Vienna in the seventeen-fifties. Again, Milon presented at the Opera, Paris, on January 18th, 1801, a ballet called *Les Noces de Gamache,* which is also derived from Cervantes's romance, although the plot centres on Lorenzo, the innkeeper, Kitri, his daughter, and Gamache, a wealthy nobleman. Lastly, Paul Taglioni produced his *Don Quichotte* at Berlin in 1850. All these productions, like that of Petipa, were mainly a vehicle for the introduction of Spanish dances.

As we have seen, Petipa's ballet was first produced at Moscow in 1869; that version contained 4 acts and 8 scenes. The ballet was presented at the Maryinsky Theatre, St. Petersburg, in 5 acts and 11 scenes, on November 9/21, 1871, when the cast included Alexandra Vergina (*Kitri*), T. A. Stukolkine (*Don Quixote*), N. O. Goltz (*Gamache*), L. I. Ivanov (*Basil*), and M. Bogdanov (*Lorenzo*). In 1902 the choreography was considerably revised by the Moscow ballet-master, A. Gorsky. The ballet is still part of the repertory and, as given to-day, contains 3 acts and 7 scenes. Pavlova added to the repertory of her company a new and condensed version of *Don Quichotte*—with choreography by L. Novikov and scenery and costumes by Korovine—which was well received.

A contemporary, reviewing the first St. Petersburg production, states that Stukolkine was excellent as the apostle of knight-errantry, but the part of Kitri was beyond Vergina's powers, although she had a success with her *double tours* in the *"Grand Pas d'Adage."* She was very dainty and coquettish in the *Pas de l'Eventail,* and in a *pas* with a bouquet. Radina I was brilliant in a *Chica,* Kshesinsky and Tshislova danced a Mexican dance well, and Gerdt and Prikhunova had a success in a *pas de demi-caractère.* Some Spanish dances with a mock bullfight were executed by Simskaya II and eleven *danseuses* dressed in men's clothes. There was also a *"Jota Aragonesa"* danced by Kemmerer I and Ladaeva.

The part of Kitri has been taken by many famous dancers, for instance, Evgenia Sokolova, Anna Pavlova, and Thamar Karsavina.

The necessity of providing a lean horse and plump donkey for the ballet has led to many amusing incidents. When *Don Quichotte* was given at St. Petersburg in 1875 Sancho Panza had to walk on foot, for it was impossible to find a donkey. M. Dandré [6] tells us that the horses hired in London for the Pavlova Company's production of the ballet were generally much too well-fed for the part of Rosinante and had to be made up accordingly, often to

<hr />

[6] *Anna Pavlova in Art and Life,* 1932.

such good effect that there were visits from officials of the R.S.P.C.A.

CAMARGO

Ballet in 3 Acts and 5 Scenes. Book: Vernoy de Saint-Georges and Marius Petipa. Music: Minkus. Scenery: Roller. Costumes: Ponomarev. Choreography: Marius Petipa. First produced: Maryinsky Theatre, St. Petersburg, December 17th/29th, 1872.

CHARACTERS

Marie Camargo .   .   .   .   .   MLLE. ADELE GRANTSOVA
Madeleine Camargo, her sister
Camargo, their father
Vestris, *maître de ballet* and dancer
  to the Court
Comte de Melun
Don Hernandez
His Wife
King Louis XIV.
Duc de Mayenne
An Abbot
A Town Mayor
His Wife
An Alderman
His Wife
First Maid
Second Maid
A Parlour-maid
  Courtiers, Lords, Ladies, Members of the King's suite, suite of
    the Duc de Mayenne, Citizens disguised for the carnival.

The action takes place in Paris at the beginning of the 18th
century.

Scene I. The garden of M. Camargo's house. To the left a terrace with flowers, and a summer pavilion. In the background, a wall with a low gate-way. Above the wall rises the back of the house, with windows overlooking the garden.

Servants are seen laying the table in the summer house. Marie's sister, Madeleine, is giving instructions. She seems anxious for the maids to go, for she keeps looking at the windows of the house next door. At last the servants leave. A window of the next house opens and there appears a youth who is in love with Madeleine. He throws her a bouquet with a letter asking if he may come into the garden and speak with her. Hearing her father coming, she signs to her lover to hide.

Enter Camargo, Madeleine's father, who tells his daughter that he thinks her dress too coquettish. A servant informs Camargo that his guests have arrived. The host leads them to the summer house. At this moment Marie runs in, armed with a net, with which she pursues butterflies, quite regardless of her father's friends.

During this pastime she accidentally strikes one of the guests with her net. Her father apologises and presents his daughter to his friends, who overwhelm her with compliments. The guests sit down to dine, meanwhile Vestris arrives, accompanied by a violinist. Madeleine recognises her lover in the violinist, who is none other than the Comte de Melun, well known for his amorous escapades.

Vestris, unwilling to disturb the dinner, suggests that he give Marie her dancing lesson on another day, which sentiment M. Camargo approves. But Marie insists on having her lesson, whereupon the violinist produces a kit and the lesson begins with a *pas de deux*. Marie finds the tempo much too slow and continually accelerates her steps. The Comte is most interested in Marie and already has almost forgotten Madeleine, whom he has promised to marry. Camargo is rather shocked by Marie's animated steps and observes that such a style of dancing is ill-suited to a modest young girl. To give point to his remark he takes one of the ladies present by the hand, and, together with the other guests, they dance a formal pavane.

The light fades and the guests take their leave of their host who sees them off. Vestris, the Comte, and the two sisters remain behind. The *maître de ballet* produces a bill announcing a fancy-dress ball at the suburb of Saint-Germain. The two men invite the sisters to accompany them to the dance, but they are undecided. The Comte tries to conquer Madeleine's fears, while Vestris tries to arouse Marie's interest. At last the sisters agree to go and ask the two men to return for them at nightfall. Camargo returns. He bids the two remaining guests good night and leads his daughters inside the house.

The curtain is lowered to mark a short interval of time.

The garden gate opens and in step Vestris and the Comte, disguised in long cloaks. They wait for the sisters. But in their place comes Camargo, attended by a servant bearing a lantern, making the round before locking up for the night. The two visitors hide.

Camargo finds the bill on the ground and, reading it with surprise, places it in his pocket. Hardly has he done so when the sisters walk stealthily from the house. After some moments of indecision they run out of the garden, followed by their cavaliers, who emerge from their hiding-places.

Camargo reappears. He locks the garden gate and goes inside his house.

Scene II. A conservatory at Saint-Germain, lit by vari-coloured lamps. All around are tables at which all classes of people are feasting. A number of persons in masks fill the conservatory.

At the rise of the curtain a quadrille is in progress. This varies according to the people arriving and departing, who dance different types of dances.

Enter Vestris and De Melun, nervously followed by the two sisters, wearing dominoes and half-masks. The Comte has lost interest in Madeleine and now devotes all his attention to Marie. At the sight of all this dancing Marie wishes to take part. Unnoticed by the others she disappears into the crowd. Madeleine, not seeing her sister, goes to look for her. At last the dancing ends and the crowd wanders off. De Melun, now alone, decides to carry off Marie, with whose beauty he is enraptured. For this purpose he calls two servants who are present in disguise, and whom he orders, at a certain moment, to kidnap a person he will indicate to them. The servants leave.

Madeleine, unable to find her sister, returns. She asks the Comte if he has seen Marie. He answers rather evasively. Madeleine prepares to continue her search when the crowd enters in triumph, escorting Vestris. They ask him to dance for them. He consents and his dance is received with great applause. Suddenly everyone is startled by the appearance of Marie who now wears another dress and dances a seductive krakoviak. A number of young men go to thank her. Vestris is delighted at his pupil's success. De Melun is no less pleased and is seen kneeling at her feet and declaring his love.

At this moment Camargo appears. Vestris hastens to warn the Comte. The latter, seeing that every moment is precious, indicates Marie to his servants, who take her away. Camargo threads his way through the crowd and, finding Madeleine, upbraids her for coming to such a place. Unable to find Marie the old man becomes very worried. He asks various bystanders if they have seen her but, failing to obtain any satisfactory information, leaves with Madeleine. The dancing resumes its wonted merriment.

Scene III. Marie Camargo's dressing room.

Marie, kidnapped by De Melun, but reassured by his kindness, is concerned that she has been unable to communicate with her father. While she is engaged in her toilet her sister, Madeleine, runs in. They embrace each other. "How did you get here?" asks Madeleine. Marie explains that the Comte is madly in love with her and has sworn to marry her in a few days. "But I love him myself," protests Madeleine, "and he has made the same promise to me." Thereupon she shows her sister a letter from De Melun. Marie is minded to leave the house immediately but resolves to be revenged for the insult offered to herself and her sister.

Marie declares that she will revenge herself publicly. A servant enters and announces the arrival of some guests—friends of the Comte. Marie sends Madeleine into an adjoining room and tells her maid not to say where her sister is. The guests arrive and each tries to court her. She asks them to lunch with her in another room. They pass to this room and Vestris enters. He is anxious to know whether the Comte has forbidden his pupil to go on the stage. He offers her an invitation from the Duc de Mayenne who is giving a garden festival. She accepts in the belief that this festival will afford her an opportunity of being revenged. Vestris, delighted, thanks Marie and asks her to rehearse a *pas* which he wishes her to dance at this festival. A dancing-lesson begins before a mirror. Just before the lesson ends a disturbance is heard and Vestris is anxious to be off, but, at Marie's suggestion, he hides beneath the table. The Comte enters.

Marie asks him the date of their wedding, but he tries to change the conversation. Then he notices Vestris beneath the table, but pretends not to have seen him. De Melun takes Marie by the hand and makes her lunch with him at the table; the repast is served by the maid. During the meal De Melun hands portions of the dishes to Vestris, who unwillingly accepts them. At last, unable to keep from laughing, the Comte orders Vestris to come out from under the table. He asks him his business and Vestris shows him the invitation from the Duc de Mayenne. "Of course you will not go to the festival," says the jealous lover. "That depends on you," observes Marie. The Comte kneels and swears eternal fidelity to her. Marie, unable to pretend any longer, shows him the letter he wrote to her sister. He is at a loss for an excuse and begs her to pardon his flirtation, but she repulses him. Then he vents his anger on Vestris and orders him to leave. But Marie insists that he shall remain, and declares that she will devote herself to art, as she despises the Comte. Then she runs out.

Now the Comte attacks Vestris but, at this moment, the Comte's friends enter and tell him that Camargo has arrived, and that the servants have forbidden him to enter. But he forces his way through them and suddenly appears in the doorway. Hearing the noise Madeleine runs in and, seeing her father, entreats him to be calm, as he is alone and likely to be insulted. He asks where Marie is and demands the name of her kidnapper. Madeleine is just about to point to the Comte when the latter entreats her to remain silent. Then Camargo draws his sword and demands satisfaction.

Now Marie enters and hastens to her father, who pushes her aside saying that she is unworthy to bear his name. Marie swears that she is innocent. The courtiers support her in endeavour to calm her father. Marie begs her father's forgiveness and says that she is going to devote herself to dancing.

Vestris shows Camargo the Duc de Mayenne's invitation and tries to persuade him to allow Marie to take part in this festival. At last he consents. Then he leaves, taking with him his two daughters and Vestris. De Melun is heartbroken at the loss of the one woman he real y loved. His friends try to console him.

Scene IV. The festival at the house of the Duc de Mayenne. A magnificent garden full of variously shaped kiosks, statues, and vases with flowers.

The Duc's friends are seen walking about the shaded avenues. Among them may be observed a tall Spaniard, Don Hernandez, dressed in a strange costume and walking with his wife, who wears an expensive domino and half-mask. Nearby is a young gentleman who closely watches the couple. It is the Comte de Melun who has already forgotten Marie and is now interested in the Spanish lady. The garden gradually fills with guests.

Donna Hernandez, observing the Comte, signs to him with her fan. Seeing this signal the Comte draws near, escorting a woman who is wearing the same disguise as the Donna Hernandez. The Spaniard is seen bowing to different courtiers, with whom he converses. At this moment his wife slips her arm out of his, when her place is immediately taken by the other woman.

The Comte and the Spanish lady hurry out of the garden, but meet the Duc de Mayenne, who asks the Comte to sit beside him. De Melun, although displeased at the suggestion, is obliged to accept, and, accompanied by the Donna, sits down in the special stand. Opposite them sits the Spaniard with the other woman. The courtiers take their places, the Duc raises his hand, and the festival begins.

The entertainment begins with two *tableaux,* representative, respectively, of Summer and Winter. In both there are many *danseuses* who try to captivate the guests in turn. But the greatest success is achieved by Marie, who attracts all eyes save those of the Comte, who is already preoccupied with Donna Hernandez.

Marie remarks the Comte and resolves to take her revenge. The Comte is passionately kissing his companion's hand. Marie, furious, takes off her mask. The jealous Don Hernandez, recognising his own wife, takes her away and menaces the Comte. The Duc asks Marie to explain her action. She replies that she wishes to revenge her sister to whom the Comte promised marriage. The Duc forces the Comte to ask Camargo for the hand of his daughter, Madeleine. The Comte agrees and the Duc promises to present them to the King and ask for their marriage to be approved. Marie and Vestris are invited by the Duc to take part in the King's festival.

Scene V. Interior of the palace at Versailles.

The Comte de Melun, Madeleine, and her father are waiting for the entrance of the King. Presently he enters, attended by a splendid suite. The Comte and Madeleine ask the royal permission to marry, which is granted. The King then invites them both to the festival at which Marie is to make her first appearance.

An entertainment at the palace.

Different groups of *danseuses* present a *grand divertissement* in which Marie plays the principal part. Her success is enormous and from that day she appears on the stage and becomes a famous dancer.

*

Camargo is based partly on historical fact, for one night in the month of May, 1728, Marie Camargo and her sister were abducted by the Comte de Melun and taken to his mansion.

The ballet was splendidly produced in connection with a benefit for Adele Grantsova. The mimed scenes were well arranged, and there were some fine *variations* and wonderful *ballabiles*. *Camargo* was enthusiastically received by press and public alike.

LA BAYADÈRE

Ballet in 4 Acts and 7 Scenes. Book: S. N. Khudekov. Music: Minkus. Choreography: Marius Petipa. First produced: Maryinsky Theatre, St. Petersburg, January 23rd/February 4th, 1877.

CHARACTERS

The Rajah Dugmanta
Gamsatti, his daughter
Solor, a warrior
Nikia, a *bayadère* .   .   .   .   . .   MME. E. O. VAZEM
A Brahmin Priest
Magdaveya, a fakir
Aiya, a female slave
A Servant of the Temple
An Indian dancer (male)

Act I. An Indian Temple.

A young warrior, Solor, after a successful hunt, sends his servant to the Rajah with the present of a tiger, which he has killed. Solor remains by the temple, hoping to see his beloved Nikia. A Brahmin priest tries to gain Nikia's love, but she refuses him. He swears to be avenged.

A fakir, Magdaveya, tells Nikia that Solor awaits her. She comes out of the temple, accompanied by a servant. Solor tries to induce Nikia to go with him. She consents but forces Solor to swear his troth by a holy fire. The Brahmin overhears their conversation.

Act II. The Rajah's palace.

The Rajah is delighted with Solor's gift and offers him his daughter's hand in marriage. Solor, afraid to refuse this great honour and captivated by Gamsatti's beauty, forgets his vow to Nikia. A Fire Festival is arranged in celebration of the betrothal.

Among the dancers who take part in the entertainment is Aiya, Gamsatti's confidant, and Nikia who dances with a partner. The guest of honour is the Brahmin priest.

The last-named contrives to tell the Rajah of the conversation between Solor and Nikia. This disclosure is overheard by Gamsatti. She summons Nikia and, announcing her betrothal, tells her the name of her future husband. Nikia refuses to believe that Solor could break his vow. Gamsatti tries to bribe Nikia to give up Solor. She refuses and the rivals quarrel. Nikia attacks Gamsatti with a dagger, but the old servant holds her back. Aiya soothes Gamsatti and offers to rid her of the insolent *bayadère*.

Act III. The wedding of Solor and Gamsatti.

The Rajah orders Nikia to dance with the other *bayadères*. During the dance Aiya presents her with a basket of flowers in which a venomous snake is hidden, and Nikia is bitten. The fakir kills the snake. The Brahmin offers to save Nikia if she will be his. She refuses and continues to dance until she falls dead.

Act IV. The Kingdom of Shades.

Solor is grief-stricken at Nikia's death. The fakir, wishing to distract him from his pessimistic mood, summons snake-charmers. During the performance Solor falls asleep and dreams that he visits an unknown country accompanied by Nikia. The ghosts of dead *bayadères* appear before him. At last he finds Nikia among them and swears that he will never forsake her again.

*

La Bayadère was produced on the occasion of a benefit for Vazem, who made a great impression as Nikia, especially in the scenes of jealousy and death.

The version of the ballet which I have given is that in use to-day by the Soviet Ballet, which is reduced from 7 scenes to 5. In the original production the ending was different, in that Solor, after his visit to the Kingdom of Shades, marries Gamsatti, and the *bayadère's* prophecy is fulfilled. There is a terrible thunderstorm and the palace falls in ruins under which everyone is crushed to death.

ZORAIYA OR THE MOORISH WOMAN IN SPAIN

Ballet in 4 Acts and 7 Scenes. Book: S. N. Khudekov. Music: L. Minkus. Choreography: Marius Petipa. First produced: Mary-insky Theatre, St. Petersburg, February 1st/13th, 1881.

CHARACTERS

Caliph Abderraman
Zoraiya, his daughter . . . . MLLE. EKATERIN*
                                       VAZEM
Tisbath, her faithful companion
Ali-Ben-Tamarat, an African Chief
Hazdai-Ben-Shaprut, a vizier and
    famous doctor at the Caliph's Court
Abu-Soliman, the Caliph's adopted son
    and a pupil of Shaprut
Pedro Cordoba   ⎱
Houan Pantoka   ⎬ gypsies
Pedro's Wife   ⎰
Her two little daughters
The Governess of the Harem
The Harem Jester and Story-Teller
Alguazil
Master of Ceremonies at the Caliph's
    Court

Ambassadors, Caliph's Suite, *Odalisques,* Bodyguard, Moors,
Arabs, Berbers, Bedouins, Gypsies, Slaves, Spaniards, Houris
                of Mahomet's Heaven.

The action passes in Spain during the Moorish occupation.

Act I. Scene I. The Garden of the Caliph's Harem.

The curtain rises with the *odalisques* engaged in various occu-
pations; some are listening with an air of boredom to the jester.

The Governess announces the arrival of the Caliph's daughter
and the chattering ceases. Enter Zoraiya, attended by Tisbah. The
former dances gaily and asks the other *odalisques* to join her,
which they do with pleasure, and the quiet of the harem is given
up to laughter and merrymaking. Presently the jester reminds the
odalisques that it is time for the dancing to stop. Zoraiya intimates that she wishes to stay and enjoy the lovely evening. The
Governess leads the *odalisques* away and Zoraiya remains behind
with her faithful Tisbah. Suddenly the latter notices Soliman
climbing over the garden wall and points him out to her mistress.

Half-afraid and high-delighted Zoraiya begs Tisbah to keep
guard. Soliman falls on his knees and swears his undying love
for Zoraiya. She asks him how he contrived to come to her since

every step is fraught with danger. He replies that, for her sake, he is prepared to venture all.

Tisbah warns the lovers that the Governess is approaching, and Zoraiya bids Soliman depart. She throws him a flower and hurries away. Soliman entreats Tisbah to arrange another meeting, which she promises to do, then follows her mistress. Soliman climbs back over the wall.

Act I. Scene II. The throne room of the Caliph's Palace.

The scene opens with a splendid procession of the Caliph's ministers, followed by ambassadors and distinguished persons. Enter Abderraman and Tamarat, attended by Hazdai, Soliman, and a number of guards. When the Caliph is seated on his throne he receives gifts and addresses from the representatives of foreign powers. Afterwards he presents Tamarat to the assembled company and announces that he has done him the honour to ask for his daughter's hand. Soliman is stupefied at this unwelcome announcement.

The Caliph commands the Master of the Ceremonies to bring in Zoraiya and the *odalisques.* They enter and sit down, then he presents his daughter to Tamarat, telling her of his proposal. Zoraiya is astonished at the news and can hardly conceal her agitation. On the other hand Tamarat is delighted with her beauty, and Soliman shows signs of jealousy and anger.

The Caliph asks his daughter to dance his favourite *pas,* whereupon Tamarat conducts Zoraiya to her place, paying her compliments; but she is filled with sadness. Touched by Soliman's silent sympathy she resolves to dance. *Odalisques* and negroes bear in gold platters piled with fruit. Against this living background Zoraiya enchants everyone with her dancing.

Twice during the dance Soliman approaches her and whispers words of love. His actions are observed by the jealous Tamarat, who, on the second occasion, in a fit of rage, almost draws his dagger on his rival. But he controls his temper, promising to revenge himself at another time. The Caliph invites all present to the betrothal feast. Everyone leaves and only Zoraiya and Tisbah remain.

The former asks Tisbah to tell Soliman to come to her so that she may asks his forgiveness. Soliman enters and kneels at Zoraiya's feet. At the same time, Tamarat, in search of Zoraiya, comes upon the scene. Hiding behind a column he hears his betrothed bid farewell to Soliman, declaring that since she is her father's ward she must marry Tamarat. Soliman declares that life has lost all attraction for him and runs out in despair; Tisbah leads Zoraiya away.

Mad with rage, Tamarat comes from his hiding-place and swears that Soliman shall die.

Act II. A public square.

Soliman, overcome with grief, is seated by the wall of a house. He thinks only of death, while gypsies pass by, some offering their wares, some telling fortunes, some attempting to pilfer from the passers-by.

Tamarat, disguised in a cloak, observes Soliman. His jealousy revives.

Two poor gypsies ask him for alms and, on seeing them, an evil thought strikes him. He gives them some money and asks them to look well at Soliman. They do so and return to Tamarat who shows them a purse of gold which he offers to give them if they will kill Soliman. They accept and Tamarat bids them await him that evening at an appointed place. Tamarat goes out.

Gradually the square becomes crowded with sightseers eager to catch a glimpse of Tamarat and his bride. The wedding procession approaches and Soliman runs to see his love once more before he dies. In the principal carriage are seated the Caliph, Tamarat, and Zoraiya, followed by a numerous bodyguard. As the carriage passes Soliman he throws himself under the wheels. Zoraiya shrieks, but Tamarat orders the carriage to drive on. When the procession has passed, Hazdai alone hurries to help his favourite pupil. The crowd surrounds them.

Act III. Scene I. A long narrow room, lit by arched windows. On the left is the main door; to the right is a door leading to the Caliph's palace. By this door is a divan.

Hazdai directs Soliman to be carried in and placed on the couch. Tisbah manages to creep in, for she is anxious to tell Zoraiya how Soliman is. Hazdai hastens to examine his unconscious pupil and remarks that he has sustained no serious hurt. Tisbah hears the verdict with delight and hastens back to her mistress. Hazdai sends everyone out of the room then leaves too, after a final glance at his patient.

Act III. Scene II. Soliman's dream. Mahomet's heaven full of wonderful treasures. A fantastic divertissement.

Zoraiya, in the guise of a houri, and surrounded by attendant visions, tries to win Soliman's love.

Act III. Scene III. Same as Act III. Scene I.

The shades have vanished and Soliman is seen fast asleep. Tisbah cautiously enters then leads in Zoraiya, assuring her that there is no danger of her being seen. Zoraiya, with tearful eyes, gazes tenderly at her beloved. Tisbah, who is watching, hears footsteps and warns her mistress. In fear they hide behind a curtain.

Through the balcony comes Tamarat, followed by two terrified gypsies. He points to Soliman and shows them his purse. But, horrified at entering the Caliph's palace, they refuse to attack Soliman. Then Tamarat threatens that if they do not do his bidding he will order them to be put to death. They beg for mercy. Seeing their uselessness Tamarat decides to kill Soliman himself. But Zoraiya rushes out of her hiding-place and defends her lover. Surprised at her action, Tamarat stands rigid. The gypsies take to flight while Tisbah runs for help.

At this moment Soliman awakes and thinking that Zoraiya is in danger wishes to help her. But Hazdai and his servants rush in with torches in answer to Tisbah's call for help. They are followed by the Caliph and his bodyguard.

Zoraiya tells the Caliph of Tamarat's intention to kill Soliman. The Caliph asks Tamarat if this is true. He replies that Zoraiya has invented the story to conceal the fact that she was alone in the room with Soliman. The Caliph looks angrily at Soliman and Zoraiya but, at this moment, the servants bring in the two gypsies, who have been found in the palace.

Tamarat is terrified at the sight of the gypsies. Zoraiya asks the Caliph to question them. They fall on their knees and confess that Tamarat bribed them to kill Soliman, and, when they refused, would have killed him himself, but for Zoraiya.

The Caliph asks Tamarat what he has to say. He confesses his guilt. The Caliph then tells him that he cannot consent to his marrying his daughter. Mad with rage, Tamarat threatens the Caliph, but the latter orders him to leave the palace immediately. Tamarat departs, vowing vengeance.

Zoraiya embraces her father and tells him that she loves Soliman, and he loves her no less. But the Caliph is too distracted to reply. Hazdai reminds him of Soliman's noble birth and entreats the Caliph to give his consent to their union. Zoraiya and Soliman add their entreaties to his and finally the Caliph approves and takes the lovers in his arms.

Act IV. The gardens before the Caliph's palace.

The Caliph makes a state entry accompanied by his daughter,

Hazdai, and Soliman, and announces that he has given his consent to the marriage of Zoraiya and Soliman.

The scene ends with dances in honour of the happy event.

LA NUIT ET LE JOUR

Ballet in 1 Act. Book: Marius Petipa. Music: L. Minkus. Scenery: Botcharov and Waltz. Costumes: Charlemagne, Baron Klodt, and Grigoriev. Choreography: Marius Petipa. First produced: Bolshoy Theatre, Moscow, May 18th/30th, 1883.

CHARACTERS

The Queen of Night	MME. E. SOKOLOVA I
The Night Star	MLLE. GORSHENKOVA
A Swan	MLLE. OGOLEYT I
A Naiad	MME. SHAPOSHNIKOVA
A Dryad	MLLE. LARIONOVA
A Wilis	MLLE. PETROVA
The Queen of Day	MME. E. VAZEM
The Morning Star	MLLE. JOHANNSEN
A Fly	M. GERDT I
A Dove	MLLE. NIKITINA
Butterflies	MLLE. STANISLAVSKAYA / MLLE. MONOKHINA
The Queen Bee	MLLE. VINOGRADOVA

Comets, Planets, Stars, Ferns, Swans, Naiads, Dryads, Wilis, Nereids, Time, Twelve Hours of Night, Spirits of Day, Birds, Butterflies, Bees, Ondines, Six Hours of Day, Representatives of the different Provinces of Russia.

Scene. A rustic landscape, the edge of a forest bordering upon a lake. At the rising of the curtain, the moon shines through the dark foliage. Spirits of Day, enervated by the sun, are chained near a sanctuary, where burns the sacred fire of the sun.

All nature is at rest.

Night's messenger, a star, heralds the arrival of her sovereign. The star persuades her sisters to descend from the sky and take part in the feast of darkness.

Then, from the depths of the lake, rise a swarm of naiads and nereids; whole, from the hollow trunks of hoary oaks, come

dryads who dance in the moonlight. Wilis, the ethereal daughters
of the clouds, and swans transformed into women, dance a misty
round, while living ferns clasp them with their green arms.

In the midst of this fantastic whirlwind appears the Queen of
Night. Divided between pleasure and joy, she joins in the frolic,
always watching the Spirits of Day, whose awakening is the signal
for her disappearance.

The moon disappears behind the mountains; the last hour of
night passes silently and then the horizon is lit with the first rays
of dawn. The morning star sunders the chains of the captive
spirits and the legions of the sun assail the Divinities of Night.

The battle is obstinate, but Time appears and puts an end to the
conflict. Night must surrender to Day.

Dawn tinges the horizon with red and disperses the Spirits of
Darkness.

The radiant run rises into view, flooding the country in its
golden rays.

The Queen of Day and her companions greet the Star of Light.
All nature comes to life; the plants awake; leaves thrill at the
contact of the luminous ray; flowers nodding on their stalks rise
erect and open.

Vari-colored birds play and dart in the air, while insects and
butterflies of a myriad hues sport in the golden haze, voicing their
song of peace and love.

A hive opens to free a swarm of bees who plunder the flowers.

A distant song announces representatives of the different provinces of Russia, come to celebrate the feast of light.

The Spirits of Day vanish. The frightened birds and insects
fly away.

The slopes become covered with people. Boats of all kinds fur-
row the surface of the lake.

The nations of the Empire unite to do homage to the Star of
Day, which shines in all its dazzling splendour, radiating happiness and abundance. Every province is represented.

Dancing begins and joy attains its height.

Borne by an eagle, the spirit of Russia hovers over her people
and other groups symbolical of the arts, sciences, and industries.

Fame with her hundred tongues proclaims the country's glory.

Luminous clouds form an aureole which vanishes to give place
to an immense vista of the principal Russian towns.

THE TALISMAN

Fantastic Ballet in a Prologue, 3 Acts, and 6 Scenes. Book: K. A. Tarnovsky and Marius Petipa. Music: Richard Drigo. Choreography: Marius Petipa. First produced: Maryinsky Theatre, St. Petersburg, January 25th/February 6th, 1889.

CHARACTERS

PROLOGUE

Amravati, Goddess of the Heavenly Spirits
Niriti, her daughter
Vayou, God of the Wind
Manmata, a Heavenly Spirit
Heavenly Spirits.

BALLET

Akdar, King of Delhi
Dannayanti, his daughter, betrothed to Noureddin
Noureddin, Maharajah of Lahore
Djemil, his bodyguard
Niriti, daughter of Amravati
Vayou, God of the Wind
Chief Eunuch
Kadoor, an old weaver
Nal, his son
Nirilya, betrothed to Nal
    Rajahs, Courtiers, Warriors, Weavers, Hindu Girls, Spirits of the Earth, Bengal Roses, *Bayadères,* Hindu *Danseuses,* Slaves, Fakirs, Snake-Charmers, Date-Sellers, Bodyguard, Maharati, Parsees, Bengali, Sinhalese, Merchants, Porters, Beggars, etc.

PROLOGUE

Scene. In the Clouds.

The spirits of heaven descend to meet Amravati, their goddess. She is sad and a spirit asks her the reason. She replies that today, in accordance with the wish of her immortal husband, her daughter, Niriti, must descend to the earth, and perhaps may never return.

Music heralds the arrival of Niriti who runs in and embraces her mother. She tells her daughter that the time has come for her to visit the earth. She warns her that the test is to endure for a week during which time her heart must remain locked against all earthly love. Should she fail she will forfeit for ever her right to immortality.

"But must I go alone?" enquires Niriti.

"No," replies the goddess. "I have chosen a companion for you who will arrive immediately."

Vayou flies in bringing a storm in his wake. He bows to Amravati and craves pardon for his tardiness, since some mortals wished to fathom the secrets of the Poles and he has been forced to sink their ships.

The goddess gives Vayou instructions and hands him her golden mace, which makes him ruler of the spirits of all the elements. Then Amravati takes a star from her diadem and gives it to Niriti, telling her that it is a talisman against all danger, but, should she lose it, she will never see again her mother or her heavenly home.

"But," says Niriti, "surely the mace will force the talisman to be returned to me."

"No," replies her mother; "a star lost by a maiden of the air must be freely returned to her by whatever mortal may come to possess it."

Amravati bids her daughter farewell. Niriti and Vayou descend to the earth.

Act I. The hut of the old weaver, Kadoor.

Nal is working busily at a loom so that he may go and meet Nirilya, his betrothed. But he is distracted by a sun-beam which dazzles his eyes so that he decides to cover the window with his cloak. As he goes towards it Nirilya appears. He begs her to enter, but she refuses. Nal, annoyed, returns to his work. Nirilya creeps behind him and covers his eyes with her hands.

Enter Kadoor, accompanied by his friends and relatives. The lovers are embarrassed. He tells them they have nothing to be ashamed of, for are not they to be married on the morrow. He reminds them of their friends who have come to wish them happiness.

The young people begin dancing while the old weaver and some of his guests decorate the hut with flowers and garlands.

Towards the conclusion of the dances a handsome youth appears —Noureddin, the young Maharajah of Lahore. He has lost his way while hunting and asks shelter for the night.

Kadoor welcomes the visitor and places refreshments before him. Noureddin begs the young people to continue dancing. So

Nal and Nirilya perform a gay dance which delights the noble visitor, who gives Nirilya a necklace and Nal a purse of gold. Then, feeling tired, he asks to be shown to his room. The guests leave and darkness falls. There is distant thunder and lightning. Enter Niriti and Vayou. Niriti enquires where they are. Vayou asks her to remain while he goes to explore.

Niriti is nervous and apprehensive. She finds it difficult to walk, but gradually gains confidence. Everything about her is strange and unexpected. She feels an unwonted tiredness and weakness. She lies down and falls asleep.

Noureddin comes out of Kadoor's room, rubbing his eyes. He has been disturbed by the noise. He catches sight of Niriti and is amazed at her beauty.

She opens her eyes and sees Noureddin. She rises and tries to escape, but Noureddin holds her firm and demands a kiss.

Struggling violently, she calls to Vayou for help. During the contest the star falls from her head. Suddenly Vayou appears, seizes Niriti, and brandishes the mace. There is a violent gust of wind and Vayou and Niriti disappear. A storm rumbles and all is dark.

Noureddin searches vainly for Niriti and discovers the star. Convinced that he has met his ideal love, he swears to find the beautiful girl.

Enter Akdar and Damayanti, attended by a magnificent retinue. The King expresses his delight at seeing Noureddin, declaring that his betrothed had been greatly troubled at his disappearance.

Noureddin had forgotten that he was betrothed.

Akdar announces the chase at an end and requests Noureddin to follow him. The company depart.

Niriti and Vayou appear, followed by the spirits of the earth. They search anxiously for the star, but in vain.

Act II. The gardens of Akdar's palace. To the right is the King's throne, with a fountain beside it. In the distance the city of Delhi.

Servants are completing the preparations for the feast which is the prelude to the wedding of Damayanti and Noureddin. The chief eunuch makes a final approving inspection and orders his men to their places.

Enter Akdar and his daughter who sit upon the throne. They are attended by rajahs and notabilities. To the left assemble *bayadères,* eunuchs, and Damayanti's attendants.

Noureddin comes in followed by Djemil and his guards. He greets Akdar and sits at Damayanti's feet.

The festival begins with a Nautch Dance at the end of which the chief eunuch announces that the feast is ready in the great hall. The King offers his hand to Damayanti and they leave, attended by Noureddin and a numerous suite.

Noureddin, although invited to follow, lingers behind. He cannot forget the beautiful stranger he met in the weaver's hut. He takes the star from his breast and kisses it passionately.

The chief eunuch returns, followed by a number of servants. The eunuch bows and tells Noureddin that the King is surprised that he has not joined them for the wedding feast.

Noureddin is so absorbed in his thoughts that he does not hear the eunuch, who calls to the other servants, when they all repeat the same phrase, but still without success. The chief eunuch then ventures to touch Noureddin's arm. The young man leaps to his feet and, without permitting a word of explanation, drives the servants away.

Moonlight filters into the hall and music announces the beginning of the feast. Noureddin, recalled to the present, is about to hasten to the great hall when a rose-bush springs from the ground and bars his way.

Other bushes appear and from each emerges a rose in human form. From the centre rose-bush comes Niriti, in the guise of the goddess of flowers, and from each side appear the spirits of the earth. With bewitching glances they beg him to give up the star, but when Noureddin refuses they vanish.

There is a fanfare of trumpets and Akdar and his daughter, preceded by torchbearers, enter the hall.

"Come!" cries the King, "the priests are waiting to perform the wedding ceremony."

Noureddin, unable to forget Niriti, confesses that he loves another and must refuse Damayanti's hand.

Damayanti faints into the arms of her waiting-women and the enraged Akdar draws his sword; his guards follow suit. At the same moment Djemil's youths place themselves in a posture of defence to protect Noureddin.

A terrible struggle is imminent when tongues of flame rise from the earth and separate the antagonists. Vayou has devised this means to save Noureddin so that he can return Niriti her talisman.

Niriti appears in the fountain and, unseen by Noureddin, wafts him passionate kisses. Her heart has been melted by his indomitable love.

Act III. Scene I. A large village on the banks of the river Ganges. A bazaar, with stalls and tents.

It is market-day and the bazaar is crowded with types of the numerous races of India. Noureddin passes with his troops on his way back to Lahore. He calls a halt and lies down to rest. The star can be seen glittering on his breast.

At a sign from one of the slave-dealers dancing begins.

Vayou and Niriti, disguised as a Brahmin and his slave, are seen among the crowd. Recognising Noureddin they decide to steal the star, but Noureddin recognises Niriti who tries to hide in the crowd. Noureddin pursues her but is stopped by Vayou, who reproaches him for annoying his slave.

"Will you sell me your slave," asks Noureddin.

"Yes, in exchange for the star on your breast," replies the Brahmin.

Noureddin refuses; Vayou and the supposed slave depart.

The noble youth is suspicious that the star should be preferred to the wealth he could have offered and feels that there is some mystery connected with the star. He wonders if the slave-owner's tongue might be loosened by wine and, calling Djemil, whispers his orders.

Niriti and Vayou return. Noureddin goes to them and asks the Brahmin to taste a new European drink; perhaps it will help them to come to an understanding.

Vayou drinks and, finding the wine greatly to his taste, continually asks for his glass to be refilled. So he becomes communicative and confides that his slave is really Amravati's daughter and that, so long as Noureddin possesses the star, she must remain on earth. To emphasise his words he strikes the table with his mace, which snaps in two. He continues to drink until he falls to the ground.

Noureddin orders Djemil to seize Niriti who calls on Vayou to help her. He awakes but, stupefied with the wine, is helpless. Niriti is caught and led away.

Act III. Scene II. Some ruins. Night.

Niriti is brought in by Djemil's guards and placed on the ground. Noureddin orders his men to keep strict watch and bends over the unconscious Niriti.

She awakes and, after reproaching Noureddin, beseeches him to restore her star.

He replies that if he gives back the star she will return to heaven.

She admits that he speaks the truth, but implores him to help her to return to heaven and her mother.

Noureddin refuses, because, he declares, he wishes her to remain on earth and be his wife and queen. It is her turn to refuse. Noureddin renews his pleading on his knees. Niriti again refuses. Then he reminds her that she is in his power and has no choice but to cede to his wishes.

Niriti plucks a dagger from Noureddin's belt and threatens to stab herself. He quickly wrests the weapon from her and, furious that she should hold his love so lightly, snatches the star from his breast and throws it at her feet. There is a deafening clap of thunder.

Act III. Scene III. Same as that for the Prologue.

Amravati, surrounded by the spirits of heaven, awaits Niriti's return. Niriti, clasping her talisman, is about to ascend, when she resolves to bid Noureddin farewell. Seeing his eyes filled with tears she is oppressed with sadness herself. She begins to wonder whether celestial delights can equal the earthly happiness which Noureddin offers, and which she is about to sacrifice. She wavers, then drops the star, and throws herself into Noureddin's arms.

The star ascends to heaven.

Apotheosis.

KALKABRINO

Fantastic Ballet in 3 Acts. Book: Modeste Tchaikovsky. Music: L. Minkus. Choreography: Marius Petipa. First produced: Maryinsky Theatre, St. Petersburg, February 13th/25th, 1891.

CHARACTERS

Marietta	}	MLLE. CARLOTTA
Draginiatza	}	BRIANZA
René, an innkeeper, Marietta's father		M. KSHESINSKY I
Olivier, a peasant youth		M. LEGAT
Kalkabrino, a smuggler		M. P. A. GERDT
Cigala	} Two	{ MLLE. PETIPA
Agalia	} female smugglers	{ MME. G. CECCHETTI
Reuben	}	{ M. E. CECCHETTI
Pierre	} Three smugglers	{ M. STUKOLKINE
Jean	}	{ M. BEKEFFI
A Monk		M. AYSTOV

Ujel	⎫		MLLE. FEDOROVA II
Silvina	⎬ Marietta's friends		MLLE. KRUGER
Vincenetta	⎭		MLLE. VORONKOVA

Janilla . . . . MLLE. GRUZDOVSKAYA

Malacorda, an incubus . . . . M. BULGAKOV

Two Succubi . . . . . ⎰ MLLE. ZHUKOVA
⎱ MLLE. JOHANNSEN

Peasants, Peasant-Women, Monks, Smugglers, Inn-Servants, Evil Spirits.

Act I. A village in Provence. René's inn is situated among a grove of olive-trees. In the distance a little chapel can be seen, framed by the foliage.

Peasant men and women are seen gathering olives and grapes under René's supervision. Olivier is among the workers. Since the morrow is a day of festival René orders his people to stop work earlier than usual. The young men propose a dance to which the girls agree, and with such enthusiasm do they enjoy themselves that the dancers fail to hear the church-bells calling them to vespers.

A monk enters and, seeing the young people dancing, rebukes them. René asks his pardon. The monk goes into the church and everyone follows save Olivier who awaits Marietta's return from town. Since René does not favour him as a suitor, Olivier hides behind a tree. Marietta, a flower-vendor in the town, arrives. She waits for her lover and is disappointed at his non-appearance. Suddenly a shower of leaves falls on her. At first alarmed, she sees Olivier among the trees, and greets him with delight. Afterwards they express their joy in a dance.

René and his workers emerge from the church. The innkeeper is very annoyed to see his daughter with Olivier and declares that she shall never marry one so poor. Marietta tries to soothe her father but he refuses to listen and orders her indoors. Several of Marietta's friends sympathize with her and lead her into the house.

René, observing a number of strangers approaching his inn, resolves to refuse them admittance. Kalkabrino, Cigala, Reuben, Agalia, and other smugglers make their way to the inn and call for wine. When the innkeeper declines to serve them, Kalkabrino produces a belt full of gold, whereupon René withdraws his objection and Marietta and her girl friends bring in wine.

Kalkabrino is amazed at Marietta's beauty, but she takes no interest in the smuggler, whose men are seen flirting with her friends. Cigala is very jealous. René, overawed by the smuggler's dominating manner, offers no opposition to Kalkabrino's wish that the girls should dance.

Dancing begins and Kalkabrino is seen to become more and more captivated by Marietta. He orders Agalia to tell her fortune and to say that she shall belong to him. Then the smuggler, fired with wine and love, asks Marietta for her hand.

René is alarmed, and the young girl is overwhelmed with grief. She implores her father not to give his consent. Kalkabrino, however, declares that the wedding shall take place immediately. When the innkeeper replies that this is not a day for a wedding, Kalkabrino promises to arrange everything.

Seeing the monk emerging from the church he asks him to marry him to Marietta. The monk refuses. Then the smuggler offers him money if he will do his bidding. When the monk again refuses, he tells him who he is. Everyone is terrified at this disclosure. When the monk still declines, Kalkabrino, furious with rage, threatens vengeance. But the monk exorcises him.

The sky darkens and thunder rolls. Evil spirits whirl about the smuggler and claim him as their victim. But he remains unperturbed.

When the monk will not marry him he tries to make René give him his daughter. Marietta entreats the monk to help her. René also comes to her aid and returns the money to the smuggler, who then attempts to take Marietta by force. But Olivier and his friends range themselves beside her and drive away Kalkabrino and his band who threaten dire revenge.

Act II. A forest bathed in the rays of the setting sun.

Evil spirits, led by Malacorda, fill the glade. They rejoice in the thought of securing possession of the soul of a great sinner, Kalkabrino, who, having been cursed by a monk, is beyond redemption.

Follows a round danced by the demons. Anxious to secure Kalkabrino before he has had time to repent, Malacorda orders one of the female devils to assume the likeness of Marietta. For this purpose she chooses Draginiatza.

Footsteps are heard and the evil spirits vanish. Kalkabrino enters with his band. Unable to banish Marietta from his thoughts, he swears to possess her by fair means or foul.

Cigala and the other female smugglers endeavour to distract him by dancing. Out of the thicket comes Draginiatza in the form of Marietta. Some members of the band pursue her and bring their captive to Kalkabrino who is amazed by her resemblance to Marietta. The demon pretends to be shy and implores the chief to set her free. When she is questioned as to her identity she asserts that she is an orphan, a relative of René, the innkeeper.

The smugglers beg her to join them, and the chief gives her splendid presents to induce her consent. Finally she agrees, and a diabolical smile passes over her lips. The modest maiden suddenly becomes a bold and forward girl, who delights everyone by her dancing. The smugglers lead her to their camp.

Again the forest is filled with evil spirits who revel in the successful beginning of their plot.

Act III. The ruins of an ancient amphitheatre, in one part of which is pitched the smugglers' camp, bathed in moonlight. Members of the band are seen sitting about the camp-fires awaiting the return of their chief.

Enter Kalkabrino with Draginiatza and his comrades. He presents her to the band as his wife to be, and orders a wedding festival to be held in her honour.

The smugglers roll out barrels of wine and arrange torches which they light. The chief bestows more gifts on his bride who amuses herself trying on her presents.

One of the bandits joins Kalkabrino's hand with that of Draginiatza and the feasting and dancing begin.

The demon appears in a magnificent costume sewn with precious stones. When the smugglers ask her where she obtained her dress, she tells them that she has made it out of Kalkabrino's presents. She dances and captivates everyone. The chief is intoxicated with her beauty.

Draginiatza thinks it is not light enough so she seizes a torch when all the ruins radiate an eerie glow. Some of the bandits flee in terror, but Kalkabrino is so blinded by Draginiatza's beauty, that he has eyes for nothing else.

Swarms of evil spirits fill the clearing and begin a maddening dance. With the coming of dawn the dancing ends.

Draginiatza beckons to the chief who tells her of his love and entreats her to go with him. He embraces her with passion. At the same moment she loses her likeness to Marietta and becomes a fearsome demon. With an evil smile she conjures up a vision of Marietta and Olivier being united by the monk. Then she seizes Kalkabrino and takes him with her down to Hell.

CINDERELLA

Fantastic Ballet in 3 Acts. Book: Lydia Pashkova. Music: B. Shell. Scenery: G. Levogt, M. Shishkov, and M. Botcharov. Choreography: Marius Petipa, E. Cecchetti, and L. I. Ivanov. First produced: Maryinsky Theatre, St. Petersburg, December 1st/13th, 1893.

CHARACTERS

The King	M. Aystov
The Queen	Mlle. Ogoleyt I
Prince Charming	M. P. A. Gerdt
Chamberlain	M. Bulgakov
Master of Ceremonies . . .	M. Voronkov I
The Cavalier Pignerolle	M. Stukolkine
Henrietta, his wife	M. E. Cecchetti
Cinderella	Mlle. Pierina Legnani
Odette	Mlle. Kshesinskaya II
Aloisa	Mlle. Andersen
The Good Fairy	Mlle. Johannsen
Jeanne, a cook	Mlle. Zhukova

Court Ladies, Knights, Pages, Guards, Heralds, Servants, Princesses of the Night, Sparks, Fairies Assistant Cooks.

Act I. A large kitchen.

At the rise of the curtain the cook's assistants, under Jeanne's supervision, are busy preparing the evening meal. But whenever she is not watching them they stop and dance with the kitchen utensils. On her return she follows their example and joins in the dancing. Suddenly a bell rings and Jeanne orders the assistants back to work.

Odette and Aloisa enter in search of Cinderella, whom they wish to help them prepare for the King's ball. Greatly annoyed at her disappearance they dispatch the cook's helps to find her.

Cinderella runs in carrying a bundle of firewood. The sisters, seeing her, push her and pinch her and order her to help them with their dressing, which she does to the best of her ability.

The sisters are pleased at their appearance and forecast the success they will attain at the ball. They mock Cinderella and force her to dance with them.

Their parents come in to bid their daughters hurry. Cinderella entreats them to take her to the ball, but her sisters laugh in derision, while her father bids her attend to the work he has given her.

Cinderella is sad and lonely. She pictures the wonder of the ball but, realising such delights are not for her, begins to work. She lights the fire and is surprised to see sparks fly from the fire and dance about her.

Now her fairy godmother appears and is pleased to see how Cinderella does her work without complaint. Cinderella asks her aid to go to the ball. She consents on condition that her god-child will leave before midnight, after which everything she gives her will disappear.

The fairy waves her hand and conjures up a crystal coach and horses, with fairy servants who help Cinderella to dress. When she is ready her godmother gives her a lesson in deportment and hurries her off to the ball, with one final warning to leave before midnight.

Act II. The throne room in the King's palace.

The Master of Ceremonies advises the courtiers of the arrival of the royal family, and they hasten to take their places.

Enter the King and Queen who walk to their thrones. Prince Charming stands beside them. The guests pay homage. Among them is the Pignerolle family. The King is impressed by the charm of the daughters and invites them to sit near him.

Fanfares are heard and guests from Moscow and Poland enter and bow to the King. The Chamberlain announces the arrival of an unknown Princess accompanied with a splendid suite. The Prince goes to welcome her.

Enter Cinderella. The Prince offers her his hand and presents her to the King and Queen and their court. The Pignerolle family observe the likeness of the Princess to their youngest daughter. The King invites her to sit beside him, which greatly offends the jealous sisters.

The Prince orders the Master of Ceremonies to open the ball and continually dances with the Princess. Odette and Aloisa dance too and try to attract the Prince's attention, but without success.

Suddenly a clock strikes midnight. Cinderella is so engrossed with the Prince that she forgets the fairy's warning. As the last stroke sounds she remembers and hurries away. Her mother converses with the Prince. Meanwhile Cinderella's lovely dress has changed to her simple frock and she manages to leave the place unnoticed.

The Prince, observing the disappearance of the Princess, orders the Chamberlain to follow her. At the same moment a page enters with one of the Princess's shoes that he has found on the stairs. The Prince admires the shoe and proclaims that he will marry whomever the shoe fits. Everyone is anxious to try on the shoe.

Act III. A fantastic garden in the Prince's palace.

Servants and pages are busily preparing for the Prince's festival. The Prince enters with his suite and enquires if his wishes have been carried out and whether the Princess has been found. The Chamberlain replies that she will probably be among the guests. The Prince, pleased with this answer, hurries to invite the King and Queen to his ball.

Cinderella, in the double hope of seeing the Prince and recovering her shoe, steals into the garden. Hearing footsteps she hides in the bushes. Not knowing what to do she prays to her fairy godmother to help her.

She appears and upbraids Cinderella for having neglected her warning. Cinderella implores her forgiveness. At this moment fanfares are heard and a herald reads out the Prince's proclamation. Cinderella implores her godmother to make it possible for her to be present at the Prince's ball. She agrees and both leave the garden.

The King and Queen enter with the Prince and their guests. The Prince invites all the most beautiful women to try on the shoe, but not one will it fit. A herald announces that a Good Fairy has arrived with a splendid suite. She enters with Cinderella.

The Prince asks her to try on the shoe and, to everyone's surprise, the shoe glides towards her foot. The Prince declares his love, while her sisters ask her to forgive their ill treatment of her.

She pardons them and a herald proclaims her the Prince's *fiancée*. The whole Court hasten to offer their congratulations.

LE LAC DES CYGNES [7]

Ballet in 4 Acts. Book: V. P. Begitchev and Geltser. Music: P. I. Tchaikovsky. Choreography: Marius Petipa and L. I. Ivanov. First produced in its entirety: Maryinsky Theatre, St. Petersburg, January 15th/27th, 1895.

[7] *The Swan Lake.*

CHARACTERS

Prince Siegfried
His Mother
Wolfgang, the Prince's tutor
Benno, the Prince's friend
Odette . . . . MLLE. PIERINA LEGNANI
Odile
Von Rotbart, an evil magician
    Huntsmen, Peasant Girls, Attendants on the Princess,
      Cygnets, Swans, Court Ladies, Guests, Pages, etc.

Act I. A magnificent garden with a castle in the background.

Prince Siegfried is holding high festival in honour of his coming of age. Village girls and youths arrive to congratulate their lord and there is much gaiety and dancing.

Enter the reigning Princess, Siegfried's mother, accompanied by her suite. She reproaches her son for the company he keeps and reminds him that at the next ball he must choose a wife. The dancing, momentarily ceased, is resumed on the Princess's departure, and includes a *pas de trois* and several *variations* rendered by a youth and two girls.

The Prince's tutor, who has imbibed too well, becomes quarrelsome and expresses his displeasure at the dances, which he considers to be poorly rendered. When he is asked to show how they should be done, he clumsily dances an old-fashioned measure, which excites general laughter.

A flight of swans passes overhead and the Prince's friends propose a hunt. Siegfried agrees, but bids his jester detain the tutor, of whom he wishes to be rid.

Act II. A lake-side with a ruined chapel in the distance. Midnight.

A group of swans, led by one wearing a crown on her head, glide over the surface of the lake. But when they reach the bank they become changed into beautiful young women. Over the chapel hovers the enchanter, Rotbart, in the guise of an owl.

One of the Prince's friends enters the glade and seeing the swans calls to his companions. Siegfried is the first to arrive. But the swan-girls and their leader, Odette, entreat him not to loose his crossbow, explaining that an enchanter has transformed the girls into swans; only at midnight are they permitted to resume for a short space their human form.

Siegfried falls in love with Odette. He is about to embrace her when Rotbart comes between the lovers who fall back in fear. Now the Prince's friends arrive, eager to shoot down the birds; but the Prince reveals to them the secret of the enchanted girls, who surround the huntsmen and begin to dance.

The Prince invites Odette to the ball at which he must choose a bride, and vows that she shall be his choice. But Odette declares that she cannot be present at the ball until Rotbart's spell is broken. She warns Siegfried that the enchanter will do all in his power to separate them and that if the Prince breaks his vow she and all her friends must surely die.

A faint flush of light heralds the dawn. The girls resume their existence as swans and glide away over the surface of the lake.

Act III. A splendid ballroom prepared for a festival. The Princess and her son are enthroned and surrounded by courtiers and guards.

The guests arrive and the mother and her son consider possible brides. Six young ladies of high degree dance before the throne, but none are to Siegfried's liking.

Now the guests in their various national costumes render the dances of their country.

Fanfares announce the arrival of a new guest who proves to be the enchanter, Rotbart, dressed to represent a black swan, and his daughter Odile, whom he has caused to assume the likeness of Odette.

Siegfried, deceived by the resemblance, pays court to Odile, with whom he dances, without noticing the meaning glances that she exchanges with her father.

At the end of the dance the Prince announces that he has chosen for wife the daughter of the Knight of the Black Swan. The enchanter is delighted, because Siegfried has broken his vow to Odette whose spirit beats vainly at one of the castle windows in vain endeavour to warn the Prince. Suddenly the magician and his daughter vanish, and Siegfried, now conscious of his error, hurries out of the castle in search of Odette.

Act IV. Same scene as Act II.

The girl-swans are dancing while awaiting the return of Odette who has gone to the castle. She enters in despair at Siegfried's betrayal of his troth.

Now comes the Prince who hurries to the lake-side full of

anxiety for his beloved. Odette refuses to greet him and hides behind her companions. But when he explains how the enchanter had tricked him, she forgives him and they dance together.

Rotbart causes a storm to spring up. The lake overflows its banks and the frightened girls are filled with terror at the thought of being drowned. Siegfried carries Odette to a neighbouring hill an announces his readiness to die with her. This sacrifice breaks the spell, and the lake returns to its proper boundaries.

Again the dawn gleams faintly, but this time the girl-swans retain their human form, freed for ever from their evil enchantment.

*

Tchaikovsky, in a letter to N. A. Rimsky-Korsakov, dated September 10/22, 1875, says: "The directorate of the Opera have commissioned me to write the music for the ballet *Le Lac des Cygnes*. I accepted the work, partly because I need the money and partly because I have long cherished a desire to try my hand at this type of music."

Le Lac des Cygnes was first produced at the Bolshoy Theatre, Moscow, on February 20th/March 4th, 1877, for the benefit of a *danseuse* called Karparkova; the choreography was by Julius Reisinger. The ballet, however, achieved such little success that after a few performances it was taken out of the repertory. The costumes and scenery are said to have been poor, while the conductor was almost an amateur. N. Kashken asserts that "several numbers were omitted on the ground that they were not sufficiently danceable; their place was taken by dances borrowed from other ballets." It would seem that quite a third of the music was altered in this way.

Tchaikovsky attributed the failure of this ballet to his music and promised to devise a new score for production at St. Petersburg, but his death in 1893 prevented the realisation of this plan. Petipa sent for the original score at Moscow and immediately realised the importance of the material. He was so inspired by the music that he at once drafted a plan for the revival of the ballet which he submitted to the director, I. A. Vsvelojsky.

Since, however, the directorate were anxious to give a special memorial performance of Tchaikovsky's work it was decided to produce the second act only for the time being. Petipa outlined the general style and character of the dances and entrusted the details to his assistant, L. I. Ivanov. The second act was presented at the Maryinsky Theatre, St. Petersburg, on February 17/29, 1894.

The first complete production of the ballet took place at the same theatre on January 15/27, 1895, for the benefit of Pierina Legnani. Here again Petipa roughed out the dances and left their elaboration to Ivanov, for at that time he was very busy with the production of an anacreontic ballet called *Le Réveil de Flore*.

Le Lac des Cygnes has a well-constructed plot, presumably based on some German legend, which not only affords every opportunity for the introduction of both *soli* and *ensembles* based on the technique of the pure classical ballet, but also, in the ballroom scene, permits of the presentation of character dances which provide a useful contrast.

The exact proportion of the choreographic contribution made by Petipa and by Ivanov will probably never be known, nor is it easy to ascertain how much of the 1895 production remains to-day, nevertheless the fact remains that *Le Lac des Cygnes* is one of the great ballets of the Romantic School.

Viewed as a whole the ballet is a lovely conception and the dances attractive and varied. The dances of Odette and her companions are conceived in a bird idiom which, generally speaking, is used with skill and taste, from the preening movements made by the arms to the succession of *petits battements* which, by the delicate tremor of the beating foot, suggests the quivering of a bird's wing. These suggestions of bird behaviour are, however, purely incidental to the theme, and the wise spectator will not seek to pursue the analogy too far.

The first act is little more than a prologue and is rather overweighted with mime, but the *pas de trois, variations,* and particularly the *ensemble,* are well arranged.

The second act, except for the *scène d'action* between Odette and the Prince, is practically all dancing, and the choreography of this portion is remarkable for its sustained quality, which sometimes, as in the *variation* when Odette first encounters the Prince, attains the height of genuine poetry of movement. For all these reasons this act is frequently presented apart from its context, since it forms a ballet in itself. There are some fine *adages* for Odette, and among the other numbers a special favourite is the *pas de quatre,* danced by the four cygnets, which requires considerable precision of execution; yet, attractive dance though it is, its exuberance seems to me to be quite out of keeping with the mood required by the theme.

The third act contains the traditional group of character dances rendered by guests presumed to have come from various countries. Choreographically considered, the *"Dance of the Court Ladies"* is the weakest and the *"Csárdás"* the best. The scene includes many

brilliant dances for Odile, including the famous thirty-two *fouettés*
—purely a *tour de force*—originally created by the Italian *ballerina,*
Pierina Legnani.

The final act, while the best from the musical standpoint, has no
special dance interest.

Tchaikovsky's music includes some lovely melodies; for instance,
the plaintive air which heralds the approach of the swans, first
heard at the end of the first act, and Odette's theme.

The double role of Odette–Odile, originally composed for two
dancers, was formerly so interpreted. For some time, however, it
has been customary for one dancer to take the two parts, since the
story requires that Odette shall exactly resemble Odile.

The mimed portion of Odette–Odile is a study in dual personality. It is the Dr. Jekyll and Mr. Hyde of ballet-roles. As Odette,
the dancer must be tender and loving; as Odile, she must contrive
to convey, without any exterior aid, that she is an influence for
evil. The dual role then is a part that must be built up piece by
piece with a thousand little touches evolved from hours of study
and reflection, and from the experience gained from many performances.

From the technical standpoint the part of Odette–Odile demands
a first-rate dancer, because it is the most arduous of all roles in the
classical ballet repertory, for in the second act, as Odette, the dancer
must execute many difficult *adages* invested with a poetic lyricism
of movement, while in the third, as Odile, she has to perform a
whole series of brilliant *enchaînements,* including the thirty-two
fouettés, the *manège de petits tours,* and a series of thirty-two
échappés travelled from the front to the back of the stage. And
her technical equipment must be such that she can do all those
difficult and exhausting movements and yet retain sufficient control
of her mental faculties to convey two persons whose natures are
diametrically opposed.

The role of Odette–Odile is associated with a host of *ballerine*—
Legnani, Pavlova, Karsavina, Kshesinskaya, Preobrazhenskaya,
Spessivtseva, Nemchinova, Markova, to mention a few names only.

The part of Siegfried likewise boasts a long line of interpreters,
the more modern representatives being Nijinsky, Mordkin, Lifar,
Idzikovsky, Dolin, and Helpmann. The role however, apart from
the solo and *pas de deux* in the third act, is practically all mime
except when the dancer is called upon to support the *ballerina* in
her *adages.*

Le Lac des Cygnes is still included in the repertory of the Soviet

Ballet [8] and has been performed at one time or another by most ballet companies of importance. The Diaghilev Company presented a two-act version of the ballet, beginning with Act II, at the lake-side, then passing to the palace scene in Act III, and concluding with a short excerpt from Act IV, in which the enchanter carried off Odette, and Siegfried fell unconscious. Col. de Basil's "Ballets Russes" have presented the second act only, the part of Odette being brilliantly rendered by Alexandra Danilova.

The Vic-Wells ballet presented a revival of the complete ballet, which was staged by N. Sergeyev, with Markova and Helpmann as Odette–Odile and Siegfried respectively, at the Sadler's Wells Theatre, London, on November 20th, 1934.

HALTE DE CAVALERIE

Character Ballet in 1 Act. Book: Marius Petipa. Music: Armsheimer. Scenery: Levogt. Costumes: Ponomarev. Choreography: Marius Petipa. First produced: Maryinsky Theatre, St. Petersburg, January 21st/February 2nd, 1896.

[8] The present rendering conforms to the original theme. In 1934, however, the Soviet Ballet presented an unusual version in 3 acts and 4 scenes, in which the action was transferred from the Middle Ages to the romantic eighteen-thirties.

Siegfried becomes a German Count residing in an ancient castle. A storm rises and some of the Count's friends enter with a dead swan, the sight of which inspires him to thoughts of hunting. But some young people arrive and beg the Count to stay with them. He consents but, not given to merry-making, soon grows bored. The guests dance a Polonnaise and leave. The Count, left alone, takes a musket and goes hunting. His friends see him in the distance and decide to follow him.

The second scene of the first act takes place by the lake-side, with much of the action associated with Act II, except that the Count is armed with a musket in place of a crossbow.

The second act shifts the action to the castle hall, the Count having planned a fancy-dress ball in which all the guests are to come in mediæval costume. Here again the theme follows the usual course. Rotbart becomes Duke Rotbart, a penniless nobleman, who hopes to improve his position by marrying his daughter, Odile, to the Count. Among the guests is a girl dressed to represent a swan. The count goes towards her but she disappears. Then Odile asks him to dance with her, which he does. But the swan-girl reappears and the Count, pushing Odile aside, goes in search of her. In his eagerness he hurries out of the castle to the amazement of his guests.

The final act returns to the lake-side. A swan enters in great distress for Rotbart has been hunting and wounded her. Now comes the Count still searching for the swan-girl. He runs towards the wounded swan and taking her into his arms tries to tend her, but she dies. The Count, greatly distressed, stabs himself and leaps over a cliff.

Later, the guests find his body.

CHARACTERS

Headman of the Village . . .	M. Gellert
Marie, his daughter	Mlle. Marie M. Petipa
Theresa	Mlle. Pierina Legnani
Pierre	M. P. A. Gerdt
Colonel of Hussars	M. Lukyanov
Captain of Hussars	M. Bekeffi
An Officer of Lancers . . .	M. Kshesinsky II.
A Cornet of Lancers . . .	M. S. Legat

Peasants, Village Girls.

Scene. A village in Austria.

The headman of the village tells the villagers that it is time they set out for work. Marie, unnoticed by the others, gives Pierre a light blue ribbon and arranges to meet him. A little later Theresa gives him a red ribbon and also plans to meet him. The peasants move off to the fields, the women return to their homes. Pierre pretends to go with the peasants but stays behind to keep his trysts.

Pierre, left alone, considers the two ribbons and tries to guess which of the two girls will arrive first. He is still uncertain as to whom he prefers. Seeing Theresa enter he quickly produces the red ribbon and passionately kisses it. Theresa, delighted, permits him to kiss her.

Marie arrives at this moment. The lovers, surprised, try to separate. The newcomer reproaches Pierre and Theresa in turn. The former tries to soothe Marie, but with little success. The bickering is interrupted by a trumpet call. The girls hastily retire.

A troop of hussars and lancers enter, led by a Colonel. Pierre, seeing them, tries to steal away unobserved, but the troopers drag him before their leader, who asks him where the villagers are and calls for wine. When he refuses to reply, the soldiers blindfold Pierre and lock him in a hut. The Colonel orders the trumpeter to blow a call, when the women begin to peer from their windows or emerge from their dwellings. The soldiers flatter them, but the women, suspicious, depart, followed by the soldiers.

Marie, who has evaded the soldiers, is apprehensive at Pierre's disappearance. Hearing a knocking from the hut, she opens the door and is surprised to find her lover, who tells her how he came there. She cannot conceal a smile at his plight.

Enter the Cornet who, seeing Marie, tries to flirt with her. Pierre hides behind her, and she does her best to conceal him while trying to get rid of the Cornet.

The hussar Captain enters and, seeing Marie, sends the Cornet on a mission, thus clearing the field for himself. Meanwhile, Pierre manages to escape to the fields, where he warns the villagers of the arrival of the soldiers.

The Captain's flirtation does not last long for the Colonel arrives and likewise sends the Captain on a mission. Then he makes advances to Marie who allows him to kiss her.

The peasant women and soldiers return. The Colonel and Marie, surprised, are forced to listen to the congratulations of both parties. The soldiers, following their leader's example, make the women dance with them.

The latter, hearing their men returning in response to Pierre's warning, are filled with alarm. The Colonel suggests that Marie, Theresa, and the peasant women should arm themselves with brooms and pitchforks, while the soldiers pretend to attack them.

The peasants, seeing their wives and mothers bravely defending the village, are duped by the scene enacted for their benefit.

The Colonel goes to the headman and announces that the officers, as a peace offering, will give a dowry to Marie on condition that she is betrothed to her true love. She immediately throws herself in Pierre's arms.

The Colonel orders wine to be brought and hands the headman the promised dowry. The betrothal is celebrated in a joyous festival in which the soldiers take their part.

BARBE–BLEUE

Ballet in 3 Acts and 7 Scenes. Book: L. Pashkova. Music: Schenck. Choreography: Marius Petipa. First produced: Maryinsky Theatre, St. Petersburg, December 8th/20th, 1896.

CHARACTERS

Ysaure de Renoualle
Anne, her sister
Ebremard ⎱ her brothers
Raymond ⎰
Arthur, a Page, in love with Ysaure
Bluebeard
A Knight
The Spirit of Curiosity
    Bluebeard's retinue, Astrologers, and Dancers representing Vessels of Gold, Jewels, Precious Stuffs, Planets, Stars, etc.

Act I. A garden in front of the castle owned by the De Renoualle family. To the left, the castle with machicolated towers, and a large window and door leading on to the terrace. In the depths of the garden is an elaborate gate and railing, through which can be seen a beautiful landscape dominated by Bluebeard's castle. It is a morning in early spring.

Arthur, a page, who is in love with Ysaure, steals into the castle belonging to her brothers. Having made certain that he has entered unobserved, he signs to his fellow pages, who creep in masked and bearing musical instruments. Under Arthur's direction they prepare to serenade Ysaure.

During the serenade Ysaure appears; she listens with pleasure to the music. Arthur entreats her to descend. She agrees and the lovers embrace. Meanwhile her brothers, Raymond and Ebremard, watch the proceedings from the shelter of a gallery. A dance is formed in which the lovers take part, and at this point the brothers enter and the merriment abruptly ceases.

They order Arthur to unmask. The page and his friends remove their masks. Arthur tells the brothers that he is passionately in love with Ysaure and asks for her hand. They point out his poverty and the stupidity of his request. Arthur admits his lack of wealth, but continues to urge his love, which only arouses the brothers' laughter.

Raymond and Ebremard go to their sister and inform her that Bluebeard, a wealthy neighbour, is a suitor for her hand; they counsel her to accept him. Ysaure is filled with grief but accedes to her brothers' wishes and enters the castle to prepare for her suitor's visit.

Trumpets are heard and the major-domo announces the arrival of an important visitor. Through the garden-gates winds a magnificent procession, which includes the sad-faced Arthur and finally Bluebeard himself. The brothers accord him every honour, while Ysaure descends the steps and offers him a cup of wine.

Bluebeard asks Ysaure for her hand. She hesitates, then consents. Arthur cannot disguise his sorrow. Bluebeard offers Ysaure his arm and together they mount the terrace, where members of his retinue are presented to her.

The betrothal is celebrated by a succession of dances contributed first by village children, then by peasant girls and youths, and concludes with a *pas d'action* danced by Ysaure, Bluebeard, her two brothers, her sister Anne, Arthur, and two ladies.

Ysaure is delighted to see Arthur among the dancers and they exchange words of love. Ysaure's brothers, seeing her happy mood, attribute it to her pleasure in the match they have made. Bluebeard gazes passionately at his *fiancée,* so that Arthur's jealousy is aroused, but he is helpless.

When the dances finally end, Ysaure's ladies bring in a wedding-gown in which they clothe their mistress, who then takes her place in a litter, which is borne in procession for the wedding ceremony.

Arthur, left alone, gives way to tears.

Bluebeard and Ysaure return and the married couple, attended by their retinue, go towards the former's castle. Arthur wishes to offer Ysaure a flower, but her sister stays his hand. As the unhappy page bestows a farewell glance on his beloved, the curtain falls.

Act II. Scene I. Ysaure's chamber. The rear wall is adorned with a large mirror screened by a curtain. To the left is a rich four-poster bed with hangings. To the right a couch. Ysaure is making her toilet, while her ladies offer her flowers and other articles of adornment. Arthur entertains Ysaure by playing on a lute.

Anne and Arthur dance a passepied. Then Ysaure orders the curtain to be drawn and she dances in front of the mirror.

Footsteps announce the approach of Bluebeard who, entering the room, hurries to his wife. Meanwhile Anne and Arthur withdraw.

While Bluebeard converses with Ysaure, Arthur enters and announces that a knight desires an audience with him. Surprised and annoyed, Bluebeard consents to receive him. The knight enters and, having delivered a warlike message from his lord, flings down his gauntlet. Bluebeard picks up the gage and accepts the challenge. The knight departs.

Bluebeard tells his wife that he must set out on a military expedition but promises soon to return. Ysaure expresses her sorrow, but is secretly delighted at the thought of his departure. He bids her not to languish in his absence, but to amuse herself with games and dances. He also gives her a collection of keys fashioned of various metals which afford access to his underground treasure-chambers. She may use all these keys save one, which is made of iron, and if she disobeys him in that respect, he warns her of his severe displeasure.

Distant horns are heard. Bluebeard's retainers enter with a suit of armour which they buckle on their lord. Ysaure passes her scarf over his shoulders. He kisses her and departs.

Ysaure, left alone, is all eagerness to try the keys, especially the forbidden one. In the distance can be heard the fading tones of a military march.

Ysaure is now visited by a strange person called Curiosity, who tries to make her follow him underground. She opens a door on the left with a gold key and descends the stairs.

Act II. Scene II. The first underground chamber. The walls are lined with glittering vessels of gold and silver; there are gold candelabra with candles, and caryatides bearing baskets of flowers on their heads.

Curiosity leads Ysaure through the right-hand door into the chamber. She is amazed at the treasures it contains.

Suddenly the caryatides become alive, and the candles burst into flame. The gold and silver vessels become animated and cause a vast clanging as they jostle together.

At the conclusion of their dance Ysaure opens another door with a silver key.

Act II. Scene III. The second underground chamber. Here the walls are covered with wonderful materials of all shapes and sizes, and from every country.

All these precious stuffs come to life. There is a Japanese dance with a fan, a Hindu dance, an Eastern *variation,* a *coda,* and a final *ensemble.*

Then Ysaure opens the left-hand door with a diamond key.

Act II. Scene IV. The third underground chamber.

Ysaure, urged by Curiosity, enters from the right.

The room is in semi-darkness, but gradually it lightens, and is seen to contain heaps of precious stones which come to life and enter into a dance.

First there is a waltz by Diamonds; then a dance by Emeralds, Coloured Diamonds, Rubies, and Sapphires. Follows a *variation.* Last of all comes another waltz when the Jewels disappear and complete darkness ensues.

Ysaure notices another secret door, which is heavily barred. Curiosity urges her to insert the iron key. Unable to resist his pleading she goes half-eagerly, half-fearfully, towards the door. With trembling hand she slips the key in the lock and turns it. Then she takes a candle and, lighting it, moves towards the chamber which is seen to contain the bodies of Bluebeard's numerous wives whom he has killed as a punishment for their disobedience. Horrified, Ysaure drops the candle and falls senseless on the threshold.

Act III. Scene I. The terrace of Bluebeard's castle. To the right a large tower with steps leading to the top of it. The castle entrance has an iron sconce, to the left is a low stone wall. On the right a fountain with a stone basin.

Ysaure, pale and distraught, comes out of the castle. She calls her sister Anne and tells her of her discovery behind the fateful door. "Look!" she cries, holding up the key, "it fell into some blood and I cannot wash away the stain."

The sisters hurry to the fountain and vainly strive to clean the key in the running water. At the same moment distant trumpets announce the return of Bluebeard. The sisters are filled with terror.

Arthur, who has been watching the scene, runs to Ysaure in the hope of saving her. She entreats him to fetch her brothers immediately. He hurries away on his mission and is seen on horseback galloping towards their castle. Ysaure watches him until he is lost to view and fervently prays for help.

Anne mounts the tower so that she can watch for the coming of her brothers.

The trumpets sound nearer and presently Bluebeard enters in triumph, having vanquished his enemy.

Ysaure goes to meet him. Bluebeard kisses his wife and asks her how she has fared during his absence. She, trying to maintain outward calm, expresses joy at his return, but he observes her nervous manner and is filled with suspicion.

He asks for the keys which Ysaure tremblingly restores to him. Remarking the absence of the iron key, he demands to know where it is. Shaking with fear, she gives it to him. He examines the key and asks Ysaure how it has come to be blood-stained.

When she professes her ignorance of the cause, Bluebeard tells her that she has disobeyed his commands and must suffer the penalty. Ysaure pleads for forgiveness, but Bluebeard unsheathes his sword.

Ysaure begs for time to say her prayers.

Bluebeard consents, but bids her hurry.

Overwhelmed with grief, she can hardly walk to the tower. She asks her sister if her brothers are in sight. Anne replies that nothing can be seen.

Bluebeard orders Ysaure to descend from the tower. Once more she asks her sister if she can see any signs of her brothers.

Anne replies that she can now see some horsemen.

Bluebeard, raging with impatience, begins to mount the steps leading to the tower.

Ysaure, trying to gain time, hurries to the topmost step. Bluebeard follows and drags her down to the terrace. Then, lifting his sword, he prepares to cut off her head.

At this moment the brothers dash through the castle-gates, followed by Arthur. They rescue Ysaure, and Ebremard challenges Bluebeard to single combat. The contest is waged with varying fortunes, until, finally, Ebremard mortally wounds his opponent, who topples over the wall into the moat.

Ysaure swoons into her brother's arms.

Anne thanks her brothers for coming in time. They declare that Ysaure would have been killed but for Arthur.

The page again asks for Ysaure's hand which is granted and the curtain falls on the happiness of the reunited lovers.

Act III. Scene II. A magnificent garden, the centre of which contains a temple in honour of Saturn, with a colonnade in three parts: the temples of the past, of the present, and of the future. At the side are staircases leading to the temples, decorated with fantastic marble sphinxes.

The wedding guests enter in a splendid *ensemble*. Next come four astrologers with their trains supported by pages. At their command Uranus descends from the skies, then the planets Venus and Mars, and lastly Stars of various grades.

The Stars form groups and dance. Then there is a *variation* by Venus, followed by a waltz rendered by the Stars.

The door of the Temple of the Past opens and there emerges a procession of characters typical of an ancient period of France, who render several early dances such as the Gaillarde.

The door of the Temple of the Present opens and now come characters representative of the present, who dance contemporary dances.

Finally the door of the Temple of the Future opens and two dancers present the *Pas de Deux Electrique*.

The ballet ends with a final *ensemble* and apotheosis.

*

The theme of *Barbe–Bleue* is based on Perrault's well-known story.

RAYMONDA

Ballet in 3 Acts and 4 Scenes. Book: Lydia Pashkova and Marius Petipa. Music: Alexander Glazunov. Choreography: Marius Petipa. First produced: Maryinsky Theatre, St. Petersburg, January 7th/19th, 1898.

CHARACTERS

Raymonda
The Countess Sybille
Jean de Brienne, betrothed to Raymonda
Abderam, a Saracen knight
Beranger }
Bernard de Ventadour } Troubadours
Henriette }
Clemence } Raymonda's Friends
King Andrew II of Hungary
The White Lady, Protectress of the Castle
A Seneschal
Visitors, Knights, Soldiers, Pages.

It is Raymonda's birthday and the seneschal is planning the celebrations. Some troubadours are practising sword play; others are playing on viol and lute. The maids of honour, attracted by the music, dance with the pages.

Enter Raymonda's aunt, the Countess Sybille. She reproaches the company for their idleness, but no one heeds her. Then the Countess draws their attention to the statue of the White Lady, an ancestress, who is reputed to visit punishment on those unfaithful to the family traditions. But the young people mock the superstitious Countess and dance round her.

A trumpet sounds and the seneschal announces the arrival of a messenger from Jean de Brienne, Raymonda's *fiancé,* who has been away at the wars. The Countess calls her niece who receives the letter. She reads it and tells her aunt that De Brienne is to arrive on the morrow.

The seneschal again enters and announces the arrival of Abderam, a Saracen knight. The Countess and Raymonda are surprised by the unexpected visit, but nevertheless welcome the knight and his following. He tells Raymonda he has heard of her beauty and offers her rich presents and his love, which she indignantly rejects.

The Countess, out of courtesy, invites Abderam to the birthday festival, which invitation he eagerly accepts, for he had decided to carry off Raymonda. Other guests arrive and there is a general dance. As the day draws in, the guests take their leave. At last Raymonda is alone, except for her ladies and two friends and the two troubadours.

Raymonda reclines and plays a lute while her friends dance. Then she hands the instrument to one of her companions and herself dances a solo. Fatigued she rests and the little group gradually fall asleep, all save Raymonda who, terror-stricken, sees the statue of the White Lady become animated and descend from its pedestal. She signs to Raymonda, who feels compelled to follow her on to the terrace. The room fills with clouds.

Act I. Scene II. Gradually the clouds disperse and it is possible to make out the misty outline of a park, with a distant view of the castle terrace.

The White Lady, followed by Raymonda, is seen descending a staircase leading into the garden.

At a signal from the White Lady the mist clears and reveals a vision of Jean de Brienne, surrounded by his knights. Raymonda runs to her lover's arms and dances with him. But the White Lady dispels the vision and Raymonda finds herself confronted by Abderam, who ardently renews his advances. Raymonda entreats the White Lady to save her. Abderam tries to embrace Raymonda and in a moment of thwarted love resolves to kill her. Suddenly the scene is filled with elves and goblins.

Raymonda swoons and the visions disappear.

With the coming of dawn, ladies and pages come in search of their mistress, whom they carry to the castle.

Act II. The courtyard of the castle of the Countess de Doris. On a dais are seated the Countess and Raymonda, attended by pages and ladies-in-waiting.

Trumpets announce the arrival of the guests, whose titles are declaimed by heralds. Among the arrivals is Abderam, whom Raymonda recognises with horror. She begs the seneschal to dismiss this undesirable guest, but the Countess informs her niece that the traditions of family hospitality must be maintained.

Abderam again pays court to Raymonda, and, in the hope of dazzling her, commands the varied members of his suite to entertain her with dances. Then he orders cups of wine to be distributed, and offers one to Raymonda. The dances grow wilder and wilder and the Saracen knight takes the opportunity to have Raymonda carried off by his slaves.

Suddenly Jean de Brienne enters with King Andrew II of Hungary. De Brienne rescues Raymonda and is about to punish Abderam when the King orders the knights to settle their differences in single combat. The contest is furious, but the White Lady appears and causes Abderam to be seized with weakness and slain; then she vanishes.

The King joins the hands of Raymonda and De Brienne and blesses their union.

Act III. A park on the estates of Jean de Brienne. In the distance can be seen the castle, gleaming in the sunlight.

A festival is to be held in celebration of the marriage of Raymonda and De Brienne.

The proceedings open with a ceremonial procession of noble guests and their attendants, and concludes with the King, the Countess, and the newly wedded couple.

The festival begins with a Hungarian *divertissement* which ends with a galop and an apotheosis depicting a brilliant tourney.

RUSES D'AMOUR

Ballet in 1 Act. Book: Marius Petipa. Music: Alexander Glazunov. Choreography: Marius Petipa. First produced: Hermitage Theatre, St. Petersburg, January 17th/29th, 1900.

CHARACTERS

The Duchess Lucinde
Isabelle, her daughter . . . . MLLE. PIERINA LEGNANI
Marinnette, her maid
The Marquis, Isabelle's *fiancé* . .

Guests, Players.

Scene. A shady park with a lawn in the centre. In the left foreground is a great staircase leading to the castle of the Duchess Lucinde.

Young noblemen and ladies form several groups reminiscent of Watteau's paintings. It is a little festival given by the Duchess in honour of her daughter Isabelle, who is betrothed. Her *fiancé* is expected momentarily, but Isabelle knows him only by hearsay. He is said to be handsome and of noble birth, but not rich.

As the guest of honour is late in arriving, the Duchess invites her friends to dance. Isabelle dances with a young Count. Then four couples take up their position for a saraband, and, lastly, most of the guests join in a gay farandole.

At this point there passes in the distance a small band of strolling players. They stop and a player begs the Duchess to be permitted to give a marionnette performance. She consents. The marionnettes dance, the guests are delighted, and the players depart, well rewarded for their pains.

Marinnette, the maid, brings Isabelle a letter from her *fiancé* announcing his imminent arrival. In a spirit of fun Isabelle proposes that she should change places with her maid, for then, she remarks, I shall be able to judge whether I am courted for myself or for my fortune. The guests are delighted with this intriguing suggestion and the Duchess, Isabelle, and Marinnette go into the castle to make the necessary preparations.

Enter the Marquis accompanied by his valet, who points out the staircase. But just as the former is about to mount the steps, Isabelle appears, dressed as a maid. The Marquis asks if the Duchess and her daughter can receive him. She answers in the affirmative and replies so courteously to all his questions that he hopes the mistress is like the maid. She tells him how beautiful her mistress is and how gracefully she dances. At his request she attempts to show him how her mistress dances. He is so charmed that he is minded to kiss her, when the Duchess and Marinnette, dressed as her daughter, descend the staircase, followed by a number of guests. There is a ceremonial presentation but the Marquis finds the mistress far from what the maid had led him to expect. The company, noticing the Marquis's chagrin, can scarcely conceal their smiles.

Refreshments are served and the Marquis is left to converse with the supposed Isabelle, who bores him more and more. A dance is proposed and here the false Marinnette moves with a captivating grace while the supposed Isabelle appears clumsy. This painful exhibition determines the Marquis to break off the marriage.

The Duchess invites him to inspect the castle and they mount the staircase together. But the Marquis manages to elude his hostess for a moment and descends to speak with the maid, who has changed her costume and veiled her features, and is really Marinnette. The young man tells her he can never marry her mistress, but that he loves her dearly. He implores her to fly with him. She consents.

At this moment the Marquis's valet tells his master that his carriage is waiting. The Marquis puts his arm about Marinnette and is about to lead her away when the Duchess and Isabelle, veiled like Marinnette, suddenly appear with the other guests.

The Marquis whispers to Marinnette that he will meet her again at night.

The Duchess begs the Marquis to take his *fiancée* into dinner. He hesitates, but Isabelle raises her veil. In amazement he looks at the maid, who likewise raises her veil. He divines the trick that has been played upon him and can scarcely contain himself for joy.

The guests congratulate the happy couple and a number of villagers arrive, bringing with them offerings of flowers. The villagers dance. The betrothed couple, carried away by the general merriment, join in and the festival concludes with a solo by Isabelle followed by a gay *ensemble*.

LES SAISONS

Ballet in 1 Act and 4 Scenes. Book: Marius Petipa. Music: Alexander Glazunov. Choreography: Marius Petipa. First produced: Hermitage Theatre, St. Petersburg, February 10th/23rd, 1900.

Scene I. *A winter landscape.*

At the rise of the curtain Winter is seen surrounded by his faithful companions: Hoar-Frost, Ice, Hail, and Snow. This group is the centre of a whirling band of snow-flakes. The fairies of Hoar-Frost, Ice, Hail, and Snow, disport in the fog, when two gnomes enter. The newcomers strike a light and set fire to some faggots. Winter, distressed by the warmth, vanishes. Soon the fairies follow suit.

Scene II. *The landscape is covered with flowers.*

Spring enters joyously, escorted by Zephyr, Birds, and Flowers. The Flower–Fairies dance and Spring joins them. Then a Bird dances. The sun sheds its golden beams and the merry band take to flight.

Scene III. *A vast field of wheat nodding in the breeze.*

The field is dotted with cornflowers and poppies, in the midst of which appears the Spirit of the Corn. Exhausted by the dancing and the heat, the flowers drowse on the ground.

Now the Naiads appear. They carry azure veils symbolical of the streams, whose coolness is eagerly sought by the flowers. The Spirit of the Corn dances with the flowers and Naiads.

Satyrs and Fauns enter, playing their pipes. They attempt to carry off the Spirit of the Corn, who is protected by the flowers. The latter are almost vanquished when Zephyr disperses their enemies.

Scene IV. The landscape takes on an autumnal aspect.

Bacchantes dance beneath stray falling leaves. The Seasons take part in the Bacchanale and then there are *variations* for Winter, Spring, the Bird, and Zephyr. Afterwards the Bacchantes, Satyrs, and Fauns, and Spirit of the Corn resume their frenzied dance. A rain of falling leaves descends upon the revellers. The dances come to an end.

Apotheosis. Against a sable sky, constellations of stars sparkle above the earth.

THE SLEEPING PRINCESS

Ballet in 5 Scenes. Book: Marius Petipa. Music: P. I. Tchaikovsky, with Prelude to 3rd Scene and Aurora's Variation in Scene III orchestrated by I. Stravinsky. Scenery and Costumes: Léon Bakst. Choreography: Marius Petipa and B. Nijinska. First produced: Alhambra Theatre, London, November 2nd, 1921.

CHARACTERS

King Florestan XXIV	M. LEONARD TREER
The Queen	MME. VERA SUDEIKINA
Cantalbutte, Master of the Ceremonies	M. JEAN JAZVINSKY
The Fairy of the Pine Woods . . .	MME. FELIA DUBROVSKA
Her Page	M. ERROL ADDISON
The Cherry Blossom Fairy . . .	MME. LYDIA SOKOLOVA
Her Page	M. LEON WOIZIKOWSKY
The Fairy of the Humming-Birds . .	MME. NIJINSKA
Her Page	M. NICHOLAS ZVEREV
The Fairy of the Song-Birds . . .	MME. LUBOV EGOROVA
Her Page	M. NICHOLAS KREMNEV

The Carnation Fairy	MME. VERA NEMCHINOVA
Her Page	M. TADEO SLAVINSKY
The Fairy of the Mountain Ash . .	MME. LUBOV TCHERNICHEVA
Her Page	M. ANATOLE VILZAK
The Lilac Fairy	MME. LYDIA LOPOKOVA
Her Page	M. STANISLAS IDZIKOVSKY
Carabosse, the wicked fairy . . .	MME. CARLOTTA BRIANZA
Her Two Pages	MM. FEDOROV AND WINTER
Her Four Rats	MM. SAVITZKI, KARNECKI, YALMOUZHINSKY, LUKINE
Royal Nurses	MMES. ALLANOVA, KRASSOVSKA, MAJCHERSKA, KOMAROVA
Ministers of State	MM. SEMENOV, SINGAIEVSKY, C. STEPANOV
Royal Pages	MM. MIKOLAICHIK, BOURMAN, OKHIMOVSKY, PATRIKEEFF
The King's Herald	M. KOSIARSKY
The Royal Physician	M. PAVLOV
Maids-of-Honour	MMES. KLEMENTOVICZ, BEWICKE, MORETON, SUMAROKOVA
The Princess Aurora	MLLE. OLGA SPESSIVA
The Spanish Prince	M. ANATOLE VILZAK
The Indian Prince	M. LEON WOIZIKOWSKY
The Italian Prince	M. TADEO SLAVINSKY
The English Prince	M. ERROL ADDISON
Countess	MME. LUBOV TCHERNICHEVA
Prince Charming	M. PIERRE VLADIMIROV
Pierrette	MME. NIJINSKA
Columbine	MME. VERA NEMCHINOVA
Pierrot	M. NICHOLAS ZVEREV
Harlequin	M. ANATOLE VILZAK
Puss-in-Boots	M. ERROL ADDISON

The White Cat . . . . . . MME. LUDMILLA SHOL-
                                        LAR
The Blue Bird . . . . M. STANISLAS IDZIKOW-
                                        SKY
The Enchanted Princess . . . . MME. LYDIA LOPOKOVA
Red Riding Hood . . . . . . MME. LYDIA SOKOLOVA
The Wolf . . . . M. MIKOLAICHIK
Bluebeard . . . . M. FEDOROV
Ariana . . . . MME. LUBOV TCHERNI-
                                        CHEVA
Sister Anne . . . . MME. FELIA DUBROVSKA
Scheherazade . . . . . . MME. MARIA D'ALBAI-
                                        CIN
The Shah . . . . M. PAVLOV
His Brother . . . . . . M. SINGAIEVSKY
The Porcelain Princesses . . . . MMES. BEWICKE, MORE-
                                        TON
The Mandarin . . . . M. NICHOLAS KREMNEV
Innocent Ivan and his Brothers . . MM. LEON WOIZIKOW-
                                        SKY, TADEO SLAVIN-
                                        SKY, KORNEZKY

Ladies-in-Waiting, Lords, Pages, Negro Lackeys, Village
Maidens, Village Youths, Duchesses, Dukes, Baronesses,
Marchionesses, Marquises, Huntsmen, Nymphs, Beaters,
Servants, Princess Aurora's Friends, Ladies of the Court,
Dignitaries of the Court, etc.

The period of Scene I is the 17th century, and that of subsequent scenes, the 18th century.

SCENE I. THE CHRISTENING.

*The interior of the palace of King Florestan XXIV. To the right
and left are serried groups of lofty marble columns which support
great stone architraves encrusted with gilded mouldings. These in
turn sustain an immense domed roof. There are several entrances
to the apartment, the principal being formed by a central gap in the
back row of columns. It is bridged by a short flight of steps set at
an angle. Negro guards are stationed about it, armed with halberds
and richly dressed in long tunics and baggy trousers of red, black,
and gold. Beyond is a grand staircase which extends as far as the
eye can reach. At regular intervals these steps wind into broad*

*landings. Distant red dots and lines indicate musketeers of the
royal guard on duty at their several posts.*

*To the left of this scene is a large double door enriched with
ormolu. Immediately above this doorway is one of those deeply-
inset, circular leaded windows, termed "œil-de-bœuf," which serves
to throw into greater relief a bronze classic figure disposed on the
pediment. In the left background is a similar door and window.
To the right-hand side is a short flight of steps bounded by a broad,
curved balustrade. On the topmost stair rests a gold cradle wherein
lies the royal infant invested already with the symbols of power—
a gold crown upon her head, and the blue ribbon of a noble order
pinned across her swaddling clothes. Over the head of the cradle is
a high canopy of velvet lined with ermine and surmounted with a
gold crown. To the right of this stairway is a dais set with two gilt
stools.*

Grouped about the cradle are the royal nurses, some in blue,
some in pink, who by means of golden cords cause it to sway
rhythmically to and fro. The royal physician stands near by in
watchful attendance. Dark spectacles are perched on his nose.
Filled with a due sense of responsibility he moves restlessly with a
shuffling gait, rubbing and waving his white-gloved hands in
delight as he contemplates the sturdy limbs of the subject of the
ceremony.

In the centre of the apartment stands Cantalbutte, Master of the
Ceremonies. He is a tall, bowed old nobleman in coat and breeches
of deep orange over which falls a voluminous, dull gold robe
fringed with ermine. His lined and troubled visage is framed in a
grey wig. He, too, wears spectacles, having long ago weakened his
sight through overmuch examination of parchment deeds and pat-
ents. He is a model courier; learned and unbending in the rigid
etiquette of ceremonial; officious, overbearing, and obsequious as
occasion demands. With one hand he sways the folds of his robe,
in the other he bears a parchment scroll.

The trumpets blare in announcement of the arrival of the guests,
and the arched roof echoes to the loud strains of a pompous march.
Presently a stream of arrivals flows down the short central flight of
steps: ladies of high degree dressed in brocades and satins, their
powdered wigs crested with gold crowns or ostrich plumes; they
are attended by nobles in costumes of black and crimson.

As each guest descends into the apartment, Cantalbutte peruses
his scroll and registers their presence. He greets each with a sweeping bow which is acknowledged with a low curtsey or graceful
doffing of feathered hat. Then the Master of the Ceremonies

directs them to the position vouchsafed by their rank. He rolls up the scroll and prepares to do homage to the King whose imminent arrival is proclaimed by a resounding fanfare of trumpets.

From the right-hand side enters a gentleman in light blue who bears a white wand. He is followed by four king's pages in rose. Then comes the King, a tall, imposing figure enveloped in a long robe of dark blue velvet fringed with ermine. His train is supported by two pages. A short interval, and then follows the Queen dressed in a gown of white satin, while over her shoulders falls a robe of light blue velvet patterned with silver. Behind her walk two pages. She is attended by four maids-of-honour and several ministers. The rear of the procession is comprised of negro guards in black and gold, their waists bound with wide blue sashes. As the royal couple make a slow tour of the apartment, the assembly bow in homage, which greeting is acknowledged by a grave inclination of their heads.

The King makes his way to the cradle and bends over the sleeping infant, then retraces his steps and stands in front of his throne. The Queen follows his example, kisses her little daughter, and stands at his right side. The ladies sink to the ground in a sweeping curtsey while the gentlemen doff their hats. The King and Queen take their seats, whereupon the pages arrange their robes and kneel at their feet.

Again a fanfare of trumpets and Cantalbutte shuffles forward to the royal presence to announce the arrival of the fairies. First, the Fairy of the Pine Woods; she is dressed in a short skirt fashioned of pine leaves laden with snow, but here and there the snow has fallen to reveal a glimpse of the green leaves otherwise hidden beneath their winter covering. From her shoulders depends a long green cloak glistening with hoar frost. Her friends follow in quick succession. The Cherry Blossom Fairy, also in white, her dress adorned with little bunches of cherries; her train is white, decorated again with cherries. Then the Carnation Fairy, in white fringed with gold, and upon her head a trio of rose-coloured plumes; her train is silver. Now the Fairy of the Song-Birds, in yellow, her hair threaded with orange feathers; her train is yellow. The Fairy of the Humming-Birds, in white patterned with red and black; her train is orange red. Lastly, the Fairy of the Mountain Ash, in white striped with vertical lines of little coral bows; her train is crimson. Each fairy wears an eight-pointed gold crown, and is attended by a page who bears her christening present.

As each fairy enters she bows low before the King, then makes her way up the stairs which lead to the cradle. Each bends over

the sleeping child and breathes upon her a magic spell. One promises that she shall be the most beautiful being in all the world;
another that she shall dance more gracefully than the most light-
footed midsummer elf; a third, that she shall sing more sweetly
than the nightingale; a fourth, that she shall rival Orpheus in her
playing of instruments of music . . . so that the Princess of a few
months is endowed with all those coveted accomplishments to
attain only one of which the ordinary mortal must toil for a life-
time. The pages come forward bearing on silken cushions the
christening gifts which they proffer on bended knee. Each is
peculiar to the donor. There is the youngest baby pine-tree, the
choicest carnation, the prettiest song-bird in a gilded cage—each
is acclaimed with delight.

The music changes to a lively measure and the maids-of-honour
commence to dance. They advance two abreast, while their arms
wreathe slowly to and fro; then each pair sweeps in a circle to
right and left. Arrived at the foot of the central staircase they form
into one line and again advance with rapid movements of either
foot and graceful poses of their arms. They step from side to side,
then conclude in a charming group. The fairy pages spring into
the centre of the apartment and vault into the air. Now each steps
behind a maid-of-honour, takes her hand, turns her slowly round,
raises her high in the air, lowers her *sur la pointe,* and again turns
her slowly round. The music becomes more and more animated,
impelling the dancers to move with agile steps and bounds. They
separate, melt into a starlike formation, separate again to stop in
the centre of the apartment, grouped in a pose of chaste abandon.

A fanfare of trumpets and a newcomer steps down the broad
stairway—the Lilac Fairy. She is costumed in a short, pale lilac
skirt, fringed with a broad band of deeper hue figured with silver
leaves. A gold crown rests on her head, and from her shoulders
falls a purple train borne by two pages. Cantalbutte receives her
with a deep obeisance and leads her to the King. She inclines her
head in homage. Her pages remove her train. The other fairies
cluster about her in friendly greeting.

Then all spread into a single line of which the Lilac Fairy forms
the centre. Behind each stands a page. In turn each fairy twirls in
a swift *pirouette* whereupon each page drops on bended knee to
receive her in his arms. All rise, *pirouette,* and finish *en attitude.*
They move their arms *en arabesque,* rise *sur la pointe,* and turn
slowly round with the assistance of their pages. The Lilac Fairy,
accompanied by her page, steps into the centre of the apartment,
while the other fairies form a hollow square about her.

Each rises *sur la pointe, en arabesque,* to turn slowly in the same pose, while the Lilac Fairy is raised high in the air by her page, then lowered to the ground to revolve in a *pirouette.*

A sudden blast of trumpets and the tempo rapidly increases. The fairies form into line abreast and flit to and fro with quick vivacious steps, while their pages, similarly disposed behind them, bound from side to side, leap upwards and revolve in the air. The fairies *pirouette* then combine in a group which brings the dance to a conclusion. They pass to the left of the King's throne, and now each fairy honours the court with a *pas seul.*

The music changes to a languid melody and the Fairy of the Pine Woods advances slowly *sur les pointes* with her arms raised *en attitude.* She moves to right and left, to pause now and again with a graceful backward pose of her head and arms. She revolves slowly in a succession of *pirouettes,* poses *en attitude, pirouettes* and falls to the ground on one knee with her head lowered and her arms clasped to her breast.

The theme becomes gay and lively, and the Cherry Blossom Fairy appears. She advances with rapid bounds on either foot while the raised leg flashes in a circular movement. Now she whirls in a series of *pirouettes,* at first slow, then quicker and quicker until the dance is brought to a conclusion.

The third dance is that of the Carnation Fairy. To a melodious, well-marked *pizzicato,* she trips quickly with neat accentuation of the rhythm, then darts forward on the left foot while the other sweeps forward at right angles to her hip. Her arms are arched above her head. Swiftly the raised leg sweeps backward and her arms are lowered *en arabesque.* With each forward bound she effects the same brilliant change of pose. Now she rises *sur les pointes* and swerves, first to left, then to right, her toes moving so quickly that one is reminded of the twittering movements of a small bird. She stops with her arms extended and one leg raised.

The melody changes to a curious trilling followed by the silvery tinkle of a triangle and the Fairy of the Song-Birds dances quickly to and fro with quick little nods of her head and fluttering movements of her arms.

She is followed by the Fairy of the Humming-Birds, who moves with incredible speed. The tempo is continually accelerated while she dances faster and faster; her head jerks from side to side while the index finger of each hand is extended, withdrawn, pointed upwards and downwards, so that its path recalls the erratic movements of a bird in swift flight.

From the left-hand side glides the Fairy of the Mountain Ash, who dances in a diagonal line across the floor, the while one foot sweeps slowly upwards at right angles to her hip, to be lowered and raised again. Presently she *pirouettes,* leaps sideways with her arms extended *en arabesque, pirouettes* again and rises *sur la pointe* with her arms *en attitude.*

The theme changes and from the opposite side comes the Lilac Fairy. She leaps lightly forward on one foot while the other traces a circle in the air. She turns sideways and rises *en arabesque.* She rises *sur les pointes* and leaps in the air, while her feet swiftly interchange in the execution of an *entrechat.* Now she retraces her steps with little bounds alternately on each foot, then vaults upward to twirl in the air. She softly alights to rebound and revolve again and again. She stops, advances with quick little steps, and concludes. The music is expressive of her movements. It resembles the tinkle of little bells, the liquid melody of a running brook. At the conclusion of her dance the other fairies walk to her side, and together they commence to ascend the steps leading to the cradle. Suddenly there is the far-off boom of a clap of thunder. The guests gaze questioningly at each other at this evil omen, but the fairies smile at these misgivings, and proceed upon their way. Again the thunder peals, this time near at hand. It is followed by the scuffling noise of people fleeing in disorder.

The King and Queen rise from their thrones indignant at this outcry, when the White Stick in Waiting leaps down the steps. He is the bearer of grave tidings, for he reports the imminent arrival of the wicked fairy Carabosse. He leans on his wand and imitates her dragging gait and bent figure. The guests are seized with fear. The nobles finger their sword-hilts. The ladies take counsel in trembling whispers; distraught and unnerved, the royal presence alone prevents their instant flight.

The ears are pierced by a blare of discordant trumpets, followed by eerie squeaks and shrill whistling, and there dashes into the apartment a sinister black coach drawn by four giant grey rats, each wearing a gold crown upon its head. This strange vehicle is canopied in black, trimmed with silver; at the corners are funereal plumes. Four young rats squat upon the forepart of the coach, and behind stalk two creatures in blue. Their faces are livid red and rendered stranger still by a hooked nose and projecting chin overhung with fangs; their arms, too, are red, and hairy, and their fingers tipped with long talons.

The rats scamper from the shafts and assist their mistress to descend. She is an old, shrivelled-up little woman, with a beak-like nose. Wisps of grey hair fall over her brow, and long, straggling hairs sprout from her chin. Her expression is fierce and vengeful. She walks with difficulty, leaning on a crooked stick. She is dressed in a long black coat, bordered with gold and powdered with silver moons; and from her shoulders falls a long black train mottled with ugly orange spots. She surveys the company with a malicious leer and low chuckles of ill humour. With menacing jerks of her head she approaches the King and exclaims: "I, too, bring a christening gift for your child," whereupon one of her creatures lurches towards the dais to deposit at the King's feet an oblong gold cage. The King regards it with fear. A dark shape moves within. Horror! It contains a rat. The witch breaks into a delighted sinister chuckle.

Her rats support her train and she moves towards the guests. She espies Cantalbutte and enquires why she was not included in the invitations. The hapless old man pores over his scroll as if to repudiate her insinuation. Impatient at his sighs and fumbling fingers, Carabosse regards him with so furious a glance that he becomes panic-stricken and can only gibber and shake his wig in unavailing excuse. The witch signs to one of her creatures who beckons him nearer with a grim, clawing gesture of his taloned hand. In a great fright Cantalbutte shuffles forward with quaking limbs, for the witch grinds her teeth, bites her lips, and menaces him with a crooked and wrinkled finger. She beats the ground with fretful bows of her stick, and threatens him with dreadful punishment. Terrified, Cantalbutte falls on his knees and pleads for pardon. The witch stoops over him and snatches off his wig, which is caught up and thrown away by the delighted rats. Again the witch is convulsed with rage, and plucks out the solitary grey lock which adorns his bare poll. Humbled in pride, he can only mumble a feeble protest at this last indignity.

Carabosse turns from him and limps toward the cradle; but before she can approach the stairs, six of the fairies wind about her. She stops, then capers to and fro while the music becomes harsh and full of evil presage. The rats scamper and shuffle in her wake, brush one forepaw against the other, scratch their ears, comb their long whiskers, and writhe their long tails. The witch approaches the King and describes how each year the Princess shall grow in beauty and accomplishment. The King listens with a sigh of pleasure, bemused by her flattering words, but the Queen is filled with misgivings and creeps closer to her spouse who soothes her with soft caresses. The rats lift the witch in the air, and suddenly she changes her tone and cries: "But one day she shall prick her finger, and on that day she shall surely die!" The rats lower her to the ground. The Queen, fearful for her child, throws herself at the witch's feet and implores her pity. She is greeted with derisive laughter. The King steps to her side and leads the Queen back to her throne.

Again Carabosse becomes imbued with the desire to ascend the steps leading to the cradle. As she limps forward the nurses draw back in dismay. Suddenly, from behind the cradle, appears the Lilac Fairy who bears a glittering wand in one outstretched hand. The witch recoils reluctantly before this unexpected protector. Then with cunning wiles she strives to elude and pass this obstacle, but the wand ever describes a dazzling arc which forces her back and back. Enraged, she summons her rats, but they are crouched low on the ground, a huddled swarming group, each member of which vainly seeks a hole through which to make its escape from the blinding, torturing coruscations of the magic wand. Foiled and impotent, the witch scrambles into her coach. The rats scamper to the shafts, the two creatures take their places behind. Carabosse sweeps her arm in a furious gesture and the vehicle, rocking and swaying from side to side, dashes from the palace.

The Lilac Fairy, attended by her friends, goes to the King and Queen and bids them be of good heart, for she promises them that, instead of dying, the princess shall fall into a deep slumber until a king's son shall come and awaken her with a kiss. With tears of gratitude the royal couple thank her for her protection, Cantalbutte kisses her robe, and the fairy ascends the steps leading to the cradle. Then, as she turns and faces the assembly, her face illumined with a happy smile, and her wand raised high above her head so that it glitters like a celestial star—the mighty company of ministers, nobles, and fair dames fall upon their knees and bow their heads in fervent thanksgiving.

SCENE II. THE SPELL.

The garden of King Florestan's palace. To right and left are tall masses of foliage. The background is formed by a graceful colonnade behind which rises tier upon tier of turreted box, flanked by pointed yews of a darker green. Through these hedges and trees is just visible a wealth of balustrades and columns, which indicates the exterior of the palace. To the right of the garden are placed two gilded stools.

Sixteen years have passed since the witch Carabosse cast her dread spell, and the Princess Aurora has become a lovely maiden, far-famed for her beauty and the manifold variety of her accomplishments. Four princes have arrived to seek her hand in marriage. One from Spain, one from England, another from Italy, and one even from distant India. The King has decreed that high festival be held in their honour. The villagers have been invited to contribute their folk-dances, and it is at this moment that the curtain rises.

The air is filled with the lilting strains of a melodious waltz, to which the village youths and lassies, with linked arms, dance gaily round and round—a kaleidoscope of red, orange, and green. To the right of these brightly-coloured revolving circles is a group of four girls, who are occupied in threading spindles.

Presently Cantalbutte enters, bows to the company and, in high good humour, nods his head to the swinging rhythm. Suddenly he stops, for he has remarked the girls who carry spindles. His mouth opens wide with astonishment, for this is an infringement of the stern law made immediately after the visit of Carabosse, by which it became a criminal offence for any person to bring spindles within a mile of the palace. He shuffles towards them as fast as his doddering legs will permit, snatches away the spindles, and warns them of the consequences of their foolish action. The unhappy culprits kneel and entreat pardon for their fault. The other villagers cease their dance and surround the frightened girls with gestures of dismay. Cantalbutte pauses for breath, and at the same moment the proceedings are graced by the arrival of the King and Queen, who enter arm in arm.

They are attended by the four princes and four maids-of-honour to the Princess, each of whom bears a freshly plucked rose. The princes are all young, handsome, and richly dressed. The Spaniard is attired in doublet and hose of white and brown, the Englishman in coat and breeches of crimson, and the Italian in a similar costume of white piped with pale blue. The Indian wears coat, trousers and turban of pale rose. Cantalbutte turns towards them and, fearing for the four girls, passes the incriminating spindles behind his back.

Alas, the King remarks with surprise this strange disposition of his hands, and demands the reason, whereupon Cantalbutte is forced to reveal the cause. In high temper the King seizes the spindles and, easily guessing the offenders by their shrinking forms, approaches them, flings the spindles at their feet, and rates them soundly. He reminds them that the penalty is instant execution. The Master of the Ceremonies vainly pleads pardon for their fault, but his enraged Majesty commands him to be silent. In despair, Cantalbutte falls on his knees before the Queen and beseeches her intercession for the lives of the villagers. The princes, too, pray her clemency. She turns to the King and, with kindly words, so softens the royal anger that at last the penitents are forgiven. Their Majesties take their seats, and the villagers manifest their gratitude in joyful leaps and bounds.

The maidens go to the colonnade, to reappear shortly with baskets of wild flowers. Each holds her basket on her arm, the other she links in that of her swain. Thus they dance to the captivating rhythm of the waltz. Presently the men retire, to return with branches fashioned in an arch and festooned with flowers, with which they form a flowered archway. The village girls wind about them, then thread their way through the archway with rhythmic swaying of their heads and graceful, flowing movements of their arms. The arches are raised and lowered continually, so that a myriad winged petals appear to hover over the nodding heads. Now the girls melt into a serried line abreast, followed by the youths, who dexterously ply their garlands so that they ever encircle or frame the forms of their sweethearts. Swiftly the maidens drop on one knee, their arms outstretched, so that the baskets are extended in offering. They rise, lay the flowers at the feet of the royal couple, and withdraw in whispering groups.

The Queen dispatches four maids-of-honour in search of the Princess. Soon they run back and cross to the left, where they remain in attendant pose, for the rising breeze carries the gay, trilling notes of a song which betokens the arrival of the Princess. The princes turn expectantly in the direction of the sound, and swiftly running through the colonnade comes the beautiful Aurora. She wears a dress of rose-coloured silk embroidered with silver, her hair is dressed with a short white wig bound with a fillet of flowers. She bursts into the garden with a succession of gay leaps and bounds, then trips to the Queen, who presses her to her breast, kisses her and lightly taps her cheek, as if in reproof of her high spirits. The Queen informs her daughter of the arrival of the four princes, then takes her by the hand and presents her to each in turn. They bow in deep homage and politely dispute the honour of being the first to kiss her hand.

Aurora greets the princes with a pleasant smile and permits each in succession to assist her while she rises *sur la pointe* and turns slowly round to conclude in an *arabesque*. The maids-of-honour walk towards the colonnade attended by three of the princes. Meanwhile the Princess turns to the Spanish Prince, who supports her in a series of *arabesques,* then raises her in the air while she arches her arms above her head. Now he lowers her to the ground.

The maids-of-honour cross over to the left, followed by the princes who beguile from each a rose. The Spanish Prince presents his flower to the Princess, who receives it while slowly turning round. With his assistance she continues to turn while each of the remaining princes presents in turn his flower. She poses *en arabesque* and, with an enchanting smile at her several suitors, proffers her bouquet to the Queen, who embraces her affectionately and accepts the roses with smiling compliments on her grace. Then the Princess flees into the garden.

The princes mark with sorrow her departure, and each searches in his own language for a word that expresses adequately her beauty and charm. The music strikes up a lively measure and the maids-of-honour trip lightly *sur les pointes*. They cross, form into pairs, *pirouette,* merge into line abreast, separate, *pirouette,* dance in a circle and trip forward in single file.

Aurora reappears and approaches the Queen who entreats her to dance again. With a smile of assent she executes a series of *arabesques,* then poses with head and arms inclined backwards in a graceful attitude, *pirouettes,* rises *sur les pointes,* and dances in a circle. The music is accelerated and she traces a broad circle with a brilliant succession of ever-quickening *pirouettes.* The princes stand by her friends and watch her with every sign of admiration, then, as her *pirouettes* cause her to pass in front of them, each drops on bended knee and presents her with a rose. She throws the flowers to the Queen and again turns slowly round, assisted by each prince in turn. At the conclusion of her dance the princes bow in homage.

Again the maids-of-honour break into a lively dance, while the Princess trips in a diagonal line across the garden. A newcomer glides furtively among the watching villagers—a strange old woman with a humped back. Stealthily she draws closer and closer to the Princess, then she slightly opens her cloak to reveal a spindle. The Princess surveys it with astonishment. With a cunning smile the old woman covers it with her cloak. She fondles the Princess's arm and again opens her cloak to display the spindle. Impelled by curiosity, the Princess snatches the spindle from her grasp; then, like a child delighted with an unusual gift, she dances gaily the while she waves aloft the spindle. The onlookers regard her in fearful trepidation, particularly Cantalbutte, who recalls the evil threats of the witch Carabosse. The music grows louder and louder, mingled with a frenzied thrumming of tambourines.

Suddenly the Princess is conscious of a sharp pain in her finger. She flings down the spindle in disgust. The slight wound quickly grows more and more painful, so that she drops on one knee, her hand pressed to her lips, her eyes dimmed with tears. The King and Queen hurry to her side and soothe and kiss her wounded hand. Slowly she rises with faltering steps, then whirls in a mad dance of hysteria. The bystanders draw near in frightened groups. The Princess stops and swoons to the ground, inert, as if dead. Her parents gaze sadly upon her closed eyes and motionless form.

The King draws himself erect, turns about, raises his arms in a gesture of rage, and demands that the person who brought the spindle shall be secured instantly. Hardly has he spoken when he is confronted by the strange figure in black. He raises his clenched fist as if to dash her to the ground, but, with a swift movement, she throws back her hood to reveal the malevolent visage of Carabosse. Appalled, the King shrinks back. The princes clasp their sword-hilts and, in response to his command, draw their weapons and dash upon the witch. But ere they can approach, with a mocking laugh, she disappears in a mass of smoke and flame. The princes stamp the ground with vexation and sheathe their swords. They return to the prostrate Princess and lament her fate.

A plaintive melody whispers about the trees, and the Lilac Fairy glides from behind a pillar of the colonnade. She comforts the heart-broken parents and directs that the Princess be carried into the palace. As the sad procession moves slowly away she waves her hand in a glittering arc. There is a crash of thunder, and darkness supervenes. For a moment she remains still, then she stoops over the ground with little caressing gestures of her wand. Slowly there spring upward little tufts of green plants gay with violet blossoms. They raise their heads, grow taller and taller, broaden, until the fairy is lost to view behind the impenetrable wall that ever rises. Through the interstices of the foliage can be seen other plants climbing to the skies, while flashing pin-points of light indicate the fairy moving to and fro in her beneficent task. A tiny gap appears at the roots of the first wall of flowers. It widens slowly to form a narrow arch through which can be seen the Lilac Fairy, now motionless, her cloak outspread by two child pages, her eyes raised heavenwards, her arms arched above her head to sustain her gleaming wand, her form luminous in the silvery rays of the rising moon.

Scene III. The Vision.

A hundred years have passed and the action takes place at the close of an autumn day. The curtain rises to reveal a forest glade fringed by a narrow stream, its course dotted with stones and islets.

To right and left stretch serried groups of massive oaks, their gnarled roots lost among giant boulders. As the eye looks upward one is astonished at the length of the groping boughs; so inextricably mingled, so intertwined, as to form a natural roof. It is the hour of sunset for the water is rendered iridescent by the fading ray that falls aslant its surface.

The woods echo to the merry tarah-ti-rarah-ri-rarah of lustily-blown hunting-horns. The call is repeated again and again; now near, now far off. The snapping of twigs and crunching of under-growth gives warning of the approach of a party, and soon there appears a band of servants in red uniforms, who stumble under the burden of a heavily-laden basket. Behind them comes Gallison, tutor to Prince Charming, and a host of guests evidently just dis-mounted, to judge by their spurred boots and the riding-switches they carry in their hands.

All are dressed in rich riding-habits. There are baronesses in blue and green, barons in blue and gold, duchesses in gold and fawn, dukes in green and gold. . . . The soft colours are thrown into sharp relief by the brilliant red coats of the beaters who pass by in the distance, some armed with heavy muskets, others stagger-ing under long poles from which hang the spoils of the chase—birds, hares, and even a wild boar.

Now comes Prince Charming himself in broad feathered hat and red coat and breeches laced with gold. By his side walks a beautiful Countess. The gentlemen bow and the ladies curtsey in homage. Gallison approaches the servants and orders them to pre-pare a meal; they spread the ground with white cloths upon which are set the contents of the basket—platters, various dishes of meat and game, silver cups, and dusty bottles of wine. While they are thus engaged, Gallison struts among the guests and submits them to a severe quizzing through his raised eyeglass.

Now the Countess, accompanied by the more adventurous of the ladies, suggests a game of blindman's buff and prevails upon Gallison to be the hunter. It is doubtful if this is a suitable role for him, since his rolling gait and exaggerated good humour sug-gest that he has endeavoured already with some success to lighten the burden of the provisions, at least so far as the wine is concerned.

Nevertheless they bind his eyes with a lace handkerchief, turn him round, and dare him to make a capture. Supremely confident, he staggers to and fro with widely extended arms, only to be flicked with switches and pushed and tapped with the butts so that his equilibrium is in momentary danger. Try as he will, his merry tormentors always evade his clumsy embrace until he stumbles against one of the huntsmen, and with a shout of triumph envelops him in his arms. He is speedily convinced of his mistake and goaded to try again. This time he clutches the Prince, who bids him quit a game which is not to his humour. Profuse in apologies, he tears off the bandage and angrily shakes his head in response to the wheedling entreaties of the ladies to resume the play. Some of the nobles invite him to take a cup of wine, a proposal which he accepts with alacrity. He pushes back his wig and mops his heated forehead with a handkerchief while he slakes his thirst with greedy and appreciative sipping of the wine.

Now the dukes and duchesses dance; then the Prince and Countess; and finally the barons and baronesses. Excited by the attractive rhythm, Gallison lurches to and fro with a wine bottle held in one hand. He stamps from side to side, raises his bottle high in the air, and discourses on the rival pleasures of women and wine. As the dance concludes he bends forward in a sweeping bow and, with a wild attempt to retain his balance, falls heavily to the ground. He is surrounded by laughing friends who raise him to his feet. The guests join in a brilliantly executed Farandole.

Again the hunting-horns ring out in chorus. It is time for the company to depart, and so they commence to leave in chattering groups. The Prince seems ill at ease, for he pays little heed to the languorous glances of the Countess. He flicks the ground with his riding-switch, his head sunk upon his breast in deep thought. Tiring of his neglect the Countess leaves his side and moves slowly away. A nobleman steps forward and offers her his arm, which she accepts. At the edge of the clearing she stops for a moment and regards sorrowfully the moody, preoccupied, and restless figure of the object of her love.

Gallison, who has remained to the last, approaches the Prince and informs him that he must hasten, for the hunt is well forward. The Prince bids him begone, whereupon Gallison quizzes him through his raised eyeglass and hints only too clearly at the cause of his desire for solitude. Then, as he remarks the Prince's rising ill-humour, he staggers away with faint chuckles and sly shakes of his bewigged head.

The light fades slowly and presently the stillness is broken by the plaintive melody which signifies the approach of the Lilac Fairy. Along the limpid waters of the pool glides a little gondola fashioned of mother-o'-pearl, in the prow of which stands the Lilac Fairy. The boat draws near to the bank. The Fairy steps out and glides towards the Prince. He confides to her his sense of boredom, his lack of ambition, his disgust at the daily monotony of his life. The Fairy listens with sympathy and relates to him the story of the Sleeping Princess. He is incredulous, whereupon she offers to reveal to him the Princess in a vision. He falls on his knees and entreats her to grant him this boon. She waves her wand and the glade is peopled with fairies. All are in white and so light, so graceful, that they resemble a band of fleeting snowflakes.

She waves her wand a second time and with a bound there appears the vision of the lovely Aurora. The once disconsolate Prince is imbued with passion, an intense love for this ethereal creature. He strives to clasp her in his arms, but the Lilac Fairy waves her wand and two of the fairies hold his arms. As the vision darts away the fairies loosen their grasp. He clasps his hands in rapture and the vision glides to his side and softly rests one hand upon his shoulder. A moment later and she vanishes into the woods. The fairies form into two parallel diagonal lines. The vision reappears and flits in and out of this gossamer avenue. The Prince follows in swift pursuit, but whenever his ardour seems about to be crowned with success the Lilac Fairy intercepts him with a commanding flourish of her wand.

Now the fairies melt into a circle which contains the vision and the Lilac Fairy. So beautiful, so harmonious, is this mass of commingled muslin that one is reminded of the opening of a white rose. In despair the Prince wanders about this unassailable fortress until the vision comes from her hiding-place and dances about the fairy ring. Now the Prince holds her fast in his arms. She sways backward and forward, then slips from his grasp and floats into the woods like a feather carried by a sudden breeze.

The fairies form into a lovely group of interlaced arms so arranged that the centre provides a natural arch. Again the Lilac Fairy waves her wand and the vision appears in the centre. She tip-toes to and fro, rises into the air, alights, winds in a seemingly never-ending series of *pirouettes,* poses for an instant, then flees into the woods pursued by the Prince. The fairies form into two lines and incline their heads so that they resemble masses of swansdown. The Lilac Fairy dances down this avenue of fluttering skirts. She vaults into the air, alights, and rebounds, the while she waves her wand with a caressing gesture over her friends. The dance ceases and the fairies vanish, all save the Lilac Fairy.

The Prince returns disconsolate and woebegone at the loss of the enchanting vision. The Lilac Fairy comforts him and promises to take him to the castle where the Sleeping Princess awaits the kiss of a king's son. She leads him to her little boat, steps inside, and invites him to follow. She stands on the prow and as she waves her wand the boat glides slowly down the stream. The Prince nestles closely to her side, fearful of losing one word of her instructions, while his eyes strain for the sight of the promised land.

The scene grows darker and darker. A mist rises about the boat which soon enshrouds it from view. Presently, trees, boat, stream—all are rendered invisible by the pall of opaque vapour. In imagination one pictures the boat drifting ever forward to the uncharted coast. A silvery light streaks the mist and it commences to lift. Again, it is possible to see the little boat with its eager occupants. A vague silhouette appears on the horizon. Its outline becomes sharper and more pronounced, to resolve itself into masses of giant boulders, then a row of tall poplars, in the centre of which rise the vertical lines and turreted spires of a castle. The boat grates against the bank. The occupants step to the ground and commence to scale the heights.

SCENE IV. THE AWAKENING.

The hall of King Florestan's palace. Everything is in deep shadow, and a monstrous web guarded by two enormous spiders hangs from the ceiling to the floor. A dusty beam of light illumines the centre of the apartment where is set a grey stone tomb. Upon the top of this reclines the Princess Aurora, fast asleep.

The air seems to vibrate to faint, melodious music. Presently a dim figure emerges from the left. As it draws closer it is possible to recognise the red coat and feathered hat of Prince Charming. He picks his way with cautious steps the while he peers wonderingly at the evidences of decay and neglect that everywhere confront him. He espies the tomb and walks towards it. He climbs the steps at its base and regards with sorrow the incarnation of the vision of the forest. He bends over and kisses her lips. There is a crash of thunder, the Princess opens her eyes and slowly sits upright. The Prince takes her hand and lifts her to the ground.

A burst of triumphant music, and in a moment the palace is ablaze with lights. The tomb disappears below the floor, and the web and the spiders crumble to powder. Now, the scene presented is one of unparalleled magnificence. The apartment is bounded by towering groups of gilded columns. The background is occupied by a flight of broad curved steps which leads to a massive colonnade. Here, at regular intervals, are high arched doorways which afford entrance to further rooms. To the left of the hall is a winding stairway bordered by a stone balustrade. To the right is a high dais set with two thrones.

The Prince and Princess walk toward the dais, where they are greeted by Cantalbutte, who wears a rich gown of gold brocade. The lofty roof echoes to triumphant fanfares and an imposing procession files down the left-hand staircase. First, four pages in green followed by a White Stick in Waiting. Then the King, resplendent in half-armour damascened with gold, his helmet crested with purple plumes; from his shoulders depends a purple train supported by two pages, and in his hands he bears the symbolical orb and sceptre. Now follow two negroes in white and gold. Behind walks the Queen, her hair dressed with a high fan of ostrich plumes. She is attended by pages and negroes who support her train of emerald velvet. The rear is composed of a body of Polish ladies and gentlemen. The former are attired in short, brocaded skirts, bodices of silver tissue, and tasseled czapkas. The latter wear gold-embroidered white coats which fall over baggy, green breeches; black velvet ermine-lined capes hang from their shoulders; on their heads are bronze helmets decorated with green and black plumes. The Polish contingent stand in two rows in front of the colonnade. The King and Queen welcome their beloved daughter and give her in marriage to the Prince who has freed them all from enchantment.

A joyous peal of many trumpets heralds the guests come to pay honour to the newly-betrothed couple. They are the familiar and beloved friends of childhood, the inhabitants of Perrault's *Cabinet des Fées*. First, from the left, comes Harlequin, Columbine, and Pierrot, who execute a lively *pas de trois*. From the right comes Pierrette. She leaps into the air with her body swaying from side to side and concludes with a *pirouette*. All retire. Presently Columbine returns to an air played *pizzicato,* and accompanied by the tinkling of triangles, to which she dances gaily with quick little nods of her head. Pierrot and Harlequin enter. Pierrot dances alone while Harlequin and Columbine perform a *pas de deux*. The trio exit then return close to the colonnade. Each bounds to a corner of the room, then they unite in pairs; first Pierrette and Harlequin, then Pierrot and Columbine. At the conclusion of the dance they take their departure.

Now comes the White Cat—a dancer dressed in a short skirt trimmed with white fur. On her head is a white cap adorned with two short ears. She moves with little bounds, followed by Puss in Boots, a big grey cat who walks on his hind legs. He wears tall brown boots and red breeches, while his left shoulder is crossed by the broad red ribbon of a noble order. As he pursues her she excites him with every wile of feline coquetry. She leans her head on one side, lightly paws her chin and darts away. Her lover follows, proudly stroking his long whiskers. They circle about each other with wary steps, then rub their backs together until the White Cat becomes spiteful and scratches him. He leaps back with a trembling paw upraised in self-protection, then attempts to fondle her. She scampers from view and Puss in Boots, with a frantic leap, bounds after her.

The music changes and the Enchanted Princess enters, followed by the Blue Bird. The former dances with quick little steps. Now, supported by the dancer who personifies the Blue Bird, the Princess turns on one foot, while she beats the raised foot against it. The Blue Bird leaps away and the Princess tip-toes forward, *pirouettes,* and, as her partner comes to her side, falls into his arms. With a quick movement he lifts her upon his shoulders, then lowers her to the ground so that she falls on one knee. Now the Blue Bird dances. He walks to the colonnade, and, as the melody changes to a broad, swinging rhythm, traverses the apartment with great bounds. He leaps upwards and his legs cross rapidly in a series of *brisés.* He alights, leaps again, and whirls round in the air. He retraces his steps and traverses the room in a diagonal direction. Again he leaps upward, performs an *entrechat,* alights and rebounds while the fingers of his outstretched arms flutter in semblance of the wings of a bird.

The Princess returns and dances slowly in a series of *arabesques.* She *pirouettes,* dances quickly *sur les pointes,* and falls on one knee with one hand raised gracefully to her lips.

The Blue Bird again crosses the room, this time in a series of *cabrioles.* The Princess whirls in many *pirouettes.* Now the two dancers unite in a *pas de deux.* They move with quick short leaps so that they go forward, retreat slightly, and go forward again. The Princess runs off. The Blue Bird leaps upward, whirls in the air, alights, and with a single bound disappears from sight.

Four soldiers walk in carrying branches of trees. These provide the forest setting for the episode of little Red Riding Hood. Presently, basket on arm, she trips through the forest. She sets her basket on the ground and steps to and fro. The measure is accelerated and a travesty of a Wolf bounds to her side. Terrified, she runs about the trees, but the Wolf lies in wait and suddenly confronts her. He threatens her with a fierce gesture of his forepaws. She points behind him and he turns his head to ascertain the reason. At the same moment she darts away, stops to retrieve her precious basket, when, alas, the Wolf, quickly undeceived, springs upon her and, despite her struggles, carries her off.

Ariana and Sister Anne enter with a joyful dance. Bluebeard arrives and doffs his feathered cap with a ceremonious flourish. He asks Ariana for the keys confided to her in his absence. She bows and with an air of misgiving hands them to him. He counts them over and discovers that one is missing. He gives way to a fit of rage, flings the keys on the ground and demands the one missing key. Ariana, trembling and fearful, plucks at her corsage and produces another key. He snatches it away and examines it closely to find it stained with blood. He rushes upon her, drags her by the arms until she shrieks for mercy, then throws her to the ground. Sister Anne waves her handkerchief in a despairing appeal for succour. As Bluebeard fumbles for his dagger the crash of hoofs is heard and two knights armed *cap-à-pied* and mounted on horse-back, bear down upon him with levelled lances. Bluebeard lifts his hands in dismay and flees. Sister Anne raises Ariana to her feet, and they express in a lively dance their joy at the timely rescue.

The sixth episode is an Eastern tale. A curious procession files in to the music of the *Danse Arabe* from Tchaikovsky's *Casse Noisette*. First, a Shah richly dressed in orange, red, and gold; then his brother in pale blue and silver. Each bears a drawn sword. Behind follows a Moorish litter borne on stout poles by two negroes. Arrived in the centre of the room, the two princes step aside while the negroes carefully lower their burden to the ground and fling open the doors. Scheherazade steps from the interior of the great box and walks forward with vibrating heel-taps of her feet. She is magnificently attired in wide filmy trousers striped pale pink and green, over which falls a broad skirt brocaded in rose, green, and gold. The two princes march slowly to the near opposite corners of the apartment. Now they close in, raise their swords and cross them in front of her. They return to their corners each with his hand on his sword-hilt. Scheherazade faces about and glides towards the Shah. She leans over him and tries to kiss his lips, but he repulses her with a threatening sweep of his sword. With the same pattering of her heels she crosses to his brother, who also refuses her attentions. Again the princes close upon her. They cross their swords and force her towards the litter. Then, with a quick movement they seize her wrists, turn her round, and thrust her into her prison. The negroes close the doors, raise their poles on their shoulders, and the procession passes out, headed by the two brothers, who march in single file, their heads erect, their naked swords held upright.

This Persian miniature is succeeded by a pseudo-Chinese dance based on the designs characteristic of Chinese lacquer. The music is the *Danse Chinoise* from *Casse Noisette.* There are three personages: A Mandarin in pink, green, and gold, with a gold pagoda-like headdress and a tasselled gold umbrella; and two Porcelain Princesses in black, white, and gold, with quaint conical hats. First the latter enter with dainty steps and much fluttering of their fans. They are followed by the Mandarin, who moves with agile bounds. He threads his way about them with nods of the head, jerks of his umbrella, and the upraised forefinger of his other hand. As the dance concludes he falls down with his legs crossed beneath him.

The final episode is a boisterous Russian dance by Innocent Ivan and his two brothers. All wear short blue breeches, white caftans embroidered with enormous red roses, and red top-boots. They dance with fierce stamps of their feet and swift jerks of their bodies. Now Ivan leaps upward in a high jump and alights on the heel of one foot while the other foot slides along the ground. His brothers bend down their backs and he jumps upon each in turn. Now they squat on the ground and propel themselves forward with sharp kicks of their feet. Ivan sweeps his foot on the ground in a wide circle. Suddenly the two brothers turn sideways back to back and with a great bound Ivan leaps on their shoulders.

The Prince comes forward leading the Princess and together they dance a charming measure. The Polish ladies and gentlemen walk forward in pairs and execute a mazurka. They dance in a circle, then file down the centre. Now all the folk of fairyland join them—the Shah and his brother with Ariana and Sister Anne; the White Cat and Puss in Boots; Red Riding Hood and the Wolf; the Blue Bird and the Enchanted Princess . . . they swing into line and accent the rhythm of the music with fierce stamps of the feet and upward fling of the arms. They break into four circles which revolve ever quicker, then they melt into four lines, advance, and suddenly drop to the ground with one leg outstretched.

*

The Sleeping Princess, first produced at the Alhambra Theatre in 1921, was a revised version of what is perhaps the greatest of all Petipa's ballets—*La Belle au Bois Dormant,* originally produced at the Maryinsky Theatre, St. Petersburg on January 3/15, 1890.

The theme is based on Perrault's well-known story and the final scene is devoted to the traditional set of character dances, here suggested by other fairy tales by that charming writer. The revival was based on the notes made by Sergeyev, formerly producer at the Maryinsky Theatre, and by enquiries and consultations with dancers who had once taken part in the ballet.

The ballet was produced with great care by Léon Bakst, and Sir Oswald Stoll spared no expense that the production should be worthy of its great traditions. The costumes designed by Bakst were conceived in that spirit of florid magnificence characteristic of theatrical entertainments given by the French nobility of the late 17th and early 18th centuries. The scenery was inspired by the splendid architectural conceptions of the Bibienas.

I could have confined myself to the theme of *La Belle au Bois Dormant,* but since the revival may be regarded as having considerable resemblance to the original, I have preferred to describe this glorious ballet in detailed action as I saw it night after night for some three months. This production was a landmark in the history of ballet in this country and many years will pass before its like is seen again.

The Sleeping Princess was divided into three acts and five scenes corresponding to the plan of the *"Belle,"* but, a little later, the fourth scene, in which Prince Charming awakens the Princess with a kiss, and the fifth scene, the wedding scene, were merged into one. I have followed this arrangement in my description of the ballet.

The revival did not differ greatly from the *"Belle,"* the principal changes occurring in the last scene, when the dances *"Cinderella"* and *"Hop o' my Thumb, his Brothers, and the Ogre"* were omitted, and their places taken by the *"Danse Arabe"* and *"Danse Chinoise"* borrowed from *Casse Noisette,* the *"Tale of Bluebeard,"* and the number called *"Innocent Ivan and his Brothers."* Another introduction was the *"Danse de la Fée Dragée"* from *Casse Noisette,* which was rendered by the Lilac Fairy in the first scene. The last-named *variation* followed the standard version by Ivanov, but the several numbers mentioned above, together with the mimed scene, *"Hunting Dance,"* and Aurora's *variation* in Scene III, were arranged by B. Nijinska.

Of the several ballets composed by Tchaikovsky there is no doubt that *La Belle au Bois Dormant* was his favourite. He began work on it in December, 1888, and by January 18/30, 1889, had sketched out the first four scenes.

There was a gala rehearsal of the ballet on January 1/13, 1890, at which the Imperial Court was present. The courtiers were pleased, but not enthusiastic. When the composer was presented to the Emperor expecting to receive his congratulations, he was received with the dry comment: "Very nice." Tchaikovsky was greatly chagrined by this cool reception of what he considered to be his finest composition for ballet, and justly, for the score is full of lovely melodies, sparkling silvery music, entrancing to listen to and a joy to the dancer, who seems borne on waves of glorious rhythm. There is no composer whose work is more danceable than that of Tchaikovsky.

Yet gradually the ballet became a great favourite and, with the exception of *Le Lac des Cygnes,* there is none other which Russian ballet-goers held, and still hold, in such affection and esteem. Bakst has written of his first introduction to the *"Belle":* "I lived in a magic dream for three hours, intoxicated with fairies and princesses, splendid palaces flowing with gold, in the enchantment of the old tale." Again, when the revival was decided upon, Stravinsky wrote to Diaghilev: "It gives me great pleasure to know that you are producing that masterpiece *La Belle au Bois Dormant."* If these expressions should be thought mere puffs for the Press, I can vouch for their honesty. I had the honour of being present at many of the rehearsals. It was a revelation to witness the smiles, the chuckles, the rapt attention of Bakst, Diaghilev, Stravinsky, and their companions, as each day saw the ballet carried a little nearer to completion.

I have recorded some impressions[9] of those rehearsals which I think it may be of interest to quote, not only for their special reference to *The Sleeping Princess,* but because the proceedings are in the main characteristic of all ballet rehearsals.

"The production of a ballet falls into three main divisions. First, practice in the rehearsal-room, where the dancers learn their roles and rehearse the steps designed and continually perfected by the choreographer. When all thoroughly understand what is required of them, the rehearsals are transferred to the stage of the theatre selected for the production. This is the second stage and the point at which the real difficulties arise.

"It is then that the dances are sorted and classified in their order of sequence. What in the rehearsal-room appears beyond improvement may be woefully inadequate when tried on the stage. The 'groups' may appear weak or confused. Everything must be revised according to actual conditions. It is the difference between a field day and active service. Meanwhile the scenery has been made. Its appearance involves further revision. A 'group' alto-

[9] *Dancing Times,* December, 1921.

gether delightful when viewed against a plain background, appears totally different when scored by the vertical lines of a colonnade, or when silhouetted against a mass of trees.

"You enter the Alhambra Theatre on a rehearsal night, about 8 p. m. The auditorium is without lights, empty, cold, gloomy—altogether cheerless. Seated in the stalls are at the most a dozen people. You will recognise the broad back of Diaghilev; to his right, Léon Bakst, dapper, keen, leaning forward with his chin supported on the back of the fauteuil in front of him; to his left, Stravinsky, coat-collar turned up and felt hat pulled over his eyes. Next to him is the choreographer, Sergeyev, short, spare, and grim of expression.

"Only the stage is lit, and here are grouped the company. Everyone looks very cold. The costumes are varied to an infinite degree. The *danseuses* wear pink tights, and short ballet-skirts, generally white; the men tight-fitting black knickers, white shirts, white socks, and black shoes. . . . To the right of the stage, where later will be the 'wings,' is a piano. Near by is the *regisseur*, Grigoriev, very tall and suave, who seems unable to move without a graceful inclination of his body or an expressive sweep of his arms. A little distance from him stands Nijinska in a long black cloak. She has a pale face and big slanting eyes framed in straw-coloured hair. To glance at her is to be reminded of her famous brother. Their movements and actions are extraordinarily similar.

"The pianist renders the theme of the movement, which echoes strangely in the vast empty space, while the dancers perform evolution after evolution which Nijinska controls and directs with dramatic gestures of her arms. The dancers swirl into long sinuous lines, melt into one throbbing mass, divide, form circles, revolve and then dash from sight.

"Meanwhile Diaghilev consults with his lieutenants. Sergeyev whispers that such a 'group' might be improved thus. Stravinsky is displeased with the tempo; it must be accelerated; and he emphasises his remarks with a flourish of his cigarette. Bakst regards everything with a cold penetrating glance. He says very little, and when he does speak, pronounces each word with a precise intonation and very definite significance. He has the air of a prosecuting counsel.

"Now and again Diaghilev rises from his seat, throws off his long overcoat, pulls it over his shoulders, and strides towards the footlights. He regards the scene with his head curiously inclined to one side, then he sharply claps his hands. The dancers cease. He shields his mouth with is hands and shouts directions to the *regisseur,* who transfers his instructions to the troupe. It is extraordinary how difficult it is to make the voice carry from the auditorium to the stage. The dance is repeated with the prescribed alterations. Presently the dancers, panting from their exertions, are permitted to rest. In little whispering groups they walk to the 'wings.' Now it is a *pas seul.* Lopokova steps forward . . . She dances with a precise technique and such piquant vivacity as to draw from the famous critics a loud 'brava!' a high mark of appreciation. She smiles, crosses one hand over her breast, and makes a mock obeisance. The *corps de ballet* resume their labours. . . .

"A few days later we arrive at the third stage of the rehearsal. The dances are repeated, but now the piano is replaced by an orchestra. Then the costumes must be considered. This time Diaghilev is seated in an armchair placed in the centre of the stage. Each dancer finds in his dressing-room his costume and the original drawing mounted on card and protected by a sheet of transparent talc. When dressed he walks on the stage and hands the design to the director, who compares it with the realisation. Nothing is left to chance. The dancer is required to perform such and such a *variation.* Does the costume prevent free movement of the arms? Does its weight prevent the execution of such a step? Notes are made and orders given for the necessary alterations.

"Few spectators realise what it means to produce a ballet, even of one act. The selection of the theme, the music, the designs; the casting of the roles, the planning of the choreography, the making of the costumes, the painting of the scenery, the arrangement of the finances—and then the million and one things that have still to be decided when everything seems accomplished."

And here is my impression[10] of the famous night of the first performance.

"The occasional costume trials at the rehearsals were unimportant. It was only on the first night that one could receive a true conception of that superb production. Diaghilev had produced an eighteenth century ballet in a manner worthy of Fouquet's entertainments at his palace of Vaux. The house was packed, the promenades almost obliterated by the throng of expectant bystanders. Everywhere tobacco-smoke, chatter, and surmises.

"I hurried on to the stage because I was anxious to renew acquaintance with the green-room. The contents of the room were a strange admixture of poverty and wealth. To the left, a much-used sewing-machine; to the right, along the whole side of one wall, a row of faded deck-chairs. Every conceivable space was

[10] *Fanfare,* December 1st, 1921.

piled high with beautiful flowers and gigantic laurel wreaths. The floor was ankle-deep in torn tissue wrappings.

"The stage was filled with scene-shifters and workmen putting the finishing touches to the scenery. The machinist, Komishov, very tall with an imposing red beard, was transforming a wooden balustrade into stone by means of a brush filled with grey paint. Some of the dancers appeared. Lopokova, serious and reserved. Spessiva, a beautiful, shy creature, thin and frail as an ivory statuette. They passed to the centre of the stage to rehearse a few difficult steps.

"Until then, there was always the atmosphere of behind the scenes. Yet in a moment all was transformed. It became impossible to move. Everywhere one encountered proud and richly costumed ministers of state, courtiers, maids-of-honour and ladies-in-waiting. As the bewigged figures strutted to and fro one was reminded of a page of Dumas awakened to life, a picture by Vanloo or Charles le Brun. There was nothing of the tawdriness, the unreality that invariably greets the spectator who, charmed by the stage picture, seeks to touch only to have the illusion destroyed. . . .

"Despite the rapturous reception of the ballet by the general public the first performance was marked by a failure of the stage machinery at two critical moments in the development of the theme, a serious and distressing event for the director and his lieutenants who for weeks had worked far into the night in order to ensure the smooth working of the complicated dances."

The presentation of the ballet itself was a bold experiment made in the belief that it could run for a season of six months. Unfortunately this proved to be impracticable. An audience used to the concentrated one-act ballet which, with Diaghilev's large repertory, permitted a continual variation of the evening's entertainment, found it difficult to accustom themselves to the same ballet night after night which, moreover, was an exposition of pure academic technique in opposition to the many developments in presentation and modernist experiments to which the average spectator was accustomed.

At one time there was a plan to give *The Sleeping Princess* a modern twist by having each scene introduced by a boy and girl of to-day, who were to speak appropriate lines, and it was intended to invite Mr. G. B. Shaw to write the dialogue. This plan, however, was abandoned.

One new and interesting feature was provided by allotting the principal roles to different dancers in succession. For this purpose a rare collection of *ballerine* was assembled. Thus one evening

Trefilova would enact the Princess Aurora; at another perform-
ance, the part would be taken by Egorova, Lopokova, or Spessiva.
It was extremely interesting to compare the various interpretations.
Trefilova and Egorova were typical products of the Petipa *régime*.
The first displayed an extraordinary technical ability, but, while in
both cases the eye was enchanted, the heart remained unmoved.
Spessiva was a delightful dancer and a stylist of the first rank.
Lopokova did not evince such a great technical ability, but she
invested her performance with that charm and feeling characteris-
tic of all her work. She gave also a delightful rendering of the role
of the Lilac Fairy, which alternate evenings she exchanged with
Nijinska.

The principal roles of Princess Aurora and the Lilac Fairy are
comparatively simple from the standpoint of mime, but the part
of the Princess Aurora includes several difficult dances, particularly the "Rose" *adage* in Scene II, and the *variations* which follow
it; and the *"Grand Pas de Deux"* in the final scene.

Among the other dances the most attractive are those of the
Carnation Fairy, the Fairy of the Song-Birds, and the Fairy of the
Humming-Birds in Act I, Scene I, and the dances in Act III ren-
dered by Columbine, the White Cat and Puss in Boots, Little Red
Riding Hood and the Wolf, the Porcelain Princesses and the Man-
darin, and the Blue Bird and the Enchanted Princess.

Of all these the Blue Bird stands pre-eminent and this famous
"Grand Pas de Deux" is frequently given as a separate number
apart from its context. There are very few dancers who have not at
one time or another danced in it. The best rendering I have seen
was given by Karsavina and Nijinsky, but among other interesting
performances may be mentioned those of Idzikowsky, Lifar, Dolin,
Turner, and Helpmann as the Blue Bird, and those of Lopokova,
Danilova, Markova, Savina, Nikitina, Shollar, Dubrovska, Hyman,
and Honer as the Enchanted Princess. The *pas* was originally
danced by Enrico Cecchetti and V. A. Nikitina.

The dance is cast in the traditional four-part form: an *adage*
for two, girl's *variation,* man's *variation,* and *coda,* which last is an
exhibition of virtuosity gradually increasing in tempo towards a
climax which brings the whole to a triumphant conclusion.

The original interpreters of the Princess Aurora and the Lilac
Fairy, that is in *La Belle au Bois Dormant,* were Carlotta Brianza
and Marie M. Petipa; while Prince Charming, originally called
Prince Desiré, was taken by P. A. Gerdt. It will be noticed that
the part of Carabosse in the revival was taken by Brianza, the
Aurora of some thirty years before; the original Carabosse was

Cecchetti, the disappearance of the witch in Scene II enabling him to appear in the final scene as the Blue Bird.

The performance of Thursday, January 5th, 1922, was marked by the reappearance of the Maestro Cav. Enrico Cecchetti. This was to celebrate the fiftieth anniversary of his appearance on the stage in a principal role. On this occasion he played his old part of Carabosse. Few of those spectators privileged to be present will ever forget that magnificent exhibition of the art of mime.

At the end of the second act he was the recipient of many souvenirs of the occasion presented by his fellow-artists. Then, when the curtain was finally lowered, a moving scene was enacted upon the stage. He was surrounded by the company, one of whom read out a long address in Russian, which set forth his history, his triumphs, the love and honour they bore him as a great artist and kindly teacher, and, lastly, their congratulations to him on this night of his jubilee.

The old man listened with bent head and quivering lips. Then, as the words conjured up vision after vision of theatres, some no longer existent; of *maîtres de ballet;* of dancers—some dead, some old and in retirement, some of whom he knew as children and who even then stood by his side—his eyes became dimmed and the surface of his grease paint was furrowed by a tear. He was embraced and kissed by all, then lifted shoulder-high and carried in triumph to his dressing-room.

The Sleeping Princess has never been revived but some impression of it has been preserved in the one-act ballet called *Aurora's Wedding,* which consists of the following numbers taken from it: *"Polonnaise," "Pas de Sept of the Maids of Honour and their Cavaliers"* (actually the *Pas de Sept* of the Fairies and their Pages from Act I, Scene I), *"Dance of the Duchesses," "Dance of the Marquesses," "Farandole," "Florestan and his two Sisters," "Little Red Riding Hood and the Wolf,"* the *"Blue Bird,"* the *"Porcelain Princesses,"* the *"Three Ivans," "Pas de Deux by the Princess Aurora and Prince Charming,"* and a final *"Mazurka."* In the version given by the Diaghilev Company the ballet was given against the backcloth of Bakst's setting for Act I, Scene I. The original Bakst costumes were damaged in storage and the dancers were attired partly in 18th century costumes made for *Le Pavillon d'Armide,* and partly in new dresses designed by N. Gontcharova.

Aurora's Wedding has been revived by De Basil's "Ballets Russes," and is presented sometimes with the backcloth of Bakst's setting for Act I, and sometimes with his backcloth for the last scene.

LOUIS MÉRANTE

L OUIS FRANÇOIS MÉRANTE was born in 1828. He was only six years old when he made his *début* at the Théâtre Royal, Liége, in the ballet in Auber's opera, *Gustave III*. In 1846 he became *premier danseur* at the Grand Theatre, Marseille, and two years later accepted an engagement at the Paris Opera, where he understudied Lucien Petipa.

As a dancer, Mérante was almost always the *jeune premier;* he created a number of important roles such as Gianni in *L'Etoile de Messine*, Count Molder in *Néméa*, Djémil in *La Source*, Nori in *Yedda*, Lilèz in *La Korrigane*, and Don Ottavio in *Namouna* (1882). He married the Russian dancer, Zina Richard.

As a choreographer, he was responsible for a number of ballets produced at the Opera, for instance: *Gretna Green* (1873), *Sylvia* (1876), *Le Fandango* (1877), *Yedda* (1879), *La Korrigane* (1880), *La Farandole* (1883), *Les Jumeaux de Bergame* (1886), and *Les Deux Pigéons* (1886).

The French poet, François Coppée, has recorded a brief sketch of him as follows. "He was a very dignified man of simple and precise manners, who excelled in his art and who knew how to make himself loved and respected by his regiment of short skirts, from the staff of *premiers sujets* to the *rats* . . . He gave them his orders with a quiet Napoleonic decisiveness, and for the *premier quadrille* he had the paternal half-smile of the Emperor reviewing his Grenadiers." [1]

Mérante died at Asnières (Seine) on January 6th, 1887.

COPPÉLIA OU LA FILLE AUX YEUX D'EMAIL [2]

Ballet in 2 Acts and 3 Scenes. Book: C. Nuitter and A. Saint-Léon. Music: L. Delibes. Scenery: Cambon, Despléchin, and Lavastre. Choreography: Arthur Saint-Léon. First produced: Théâtre Impérial de l'Opéra, Paris, May 25th, 1870.

[1] *Figaro Illustré*, February, 1895.
[2] *Coppélia or The Girl with Enamel Eyes.* See note to *Coppélia*, p. 359.

CHARACTERS

Swanilda . . . . MLLES. G. BOZACCHI
Frantz . . . . E. FIOCRE
Coppelius, a toy-maker . . . . MM. DAUTY
The Burgomaster . . . . . CORNET
The Lord of the Manor . . . . F. MÉRANTE
Nettchen . . . . MME. ALINE
Peasants, Automata, Lords, Ladies, Pages, etc.

Act I. A square in a little town on the borders of Galicia. The high wooden houses with pointed gables are painted in gay colours. One house stands out from the others by reason of its low barred windows and massive door. It is the abode of Coppelius.

A girl looks out of a dormer window of one of the houses. A little later she comes out of the dwelling and, making sure that she is not watched, steals towards Coppelius's house and gazes up at the window, in front of which sits a young girl, apparently reading a book. Swanilda is interested in this girl, said to be Coppelius's daughter, for she believes her sweetheart, Frantz, to be in love with her. She tries to attract the girl's attention, but in vain.

Then she hears footsteps and hides. Coppelius appears at a low window while Frantz steals towards the mysterious house. He kisses his hand to Coppelia, who seems to reply and then abruptly sits down.

Swanilda, pretending to have seen nothing, runs after a butterfly. Frantz joins in and catches the insect, which he triumphantly pins to his collar. Swanilda reproaches him for having been unfaithful to her. She asks him if he prefers Coppelia to her. Frantz makes a vigorous protest, but she refuses to listen and declares that she loves him no longer.

Now a happy crowd fills the square and the burgomaster announces that the lord of the manor has presented a bell to the town, and this will be celebrated by a festival to be held on the morrow. He whispers to Swanilda that many couples are to be wedded then and that all will be given dowries. He enquires if she is not going to be married.

"Oh, not yet," she replies, and, taking up a little sheaf of corn, she listens to it and passes it to Frantz.

"Does it not say that you love me no longer?" she asks.

Frantz replies that he heard nothing.

Then Swanilda presents the corn to one of Frantz's friends, who laughingly declares that he can hear quite well. Frantz protests, but Swanilda snaps the corn-stalks and tells him that all is over between them.

Frantz departs in vexation, while Swanilda dances a *Csárdás*[3] with her friends.

Night falls and the merry-makers gradually depart.

Coppelius comes out of his house and is immediately jostled by a number of youths, who try to make him dance. It is some time before he can free himself from their unwelcome attentions.

Swanilda, on her way home with some girl friends, sees a key on the ground outside the door of Coppelius's house. She picks it up and shows it to her companions, who suggest a visit to the mysterious abode. Swanilda unlocks the door and the party go inside.

Hardly have they entered than Frantz arrives with a ladder, which he places against Coppelius's window. He has just begun to mount the rungs when Coppelius returns in search of his key. He sees Frantz and voices his anger. Frantz, alarmed, leaps to the ground and takes to his heels.

Act II. Scene I. Coppelius's workshop. A large room fitted up with all kinds of tools. Here and there are mechanical figures in various stages of construction: a bearded old man in Persian costume, turning over the pages of a book, a tall negro with raised scimitar, a Moorish cymbal-player seated on a cushion, and a Chinaman playing on a dulcimer. The room is faintly lit with a single lamp.

The girls steal into the room, half defiantly, half in fear, uncertain of what lurks in the fitful shadows. Swanilda draws back the window curtain to reveal Coppelia, still sitting in a chair, book in hand.

Swanilda bows to her, speaks to her, but there is no reply. The girls are astounded. Swanilda touches the girl's arm which is quite cold; she places her hand on Coppelia's heart, but it does not beat. This lovely girl, then, is nothing but a piece of clockwork. Swanilda and her friends are highly amused at this discovery, especially Swanilda, who promises herself a fine awakening for Frantz.

[3] *Coppélia* is the first ballet in which this Hungarian folk-dance was danced; its success did much to popularise the introduction of 'numbers' based on national and folk dances.

Their fears vanished, the trespassers set the figures in motion. All at once Coppelius, furious at this invasion, dashes up the stairs and pursues the girls who gradually evade him and run downstairs, all save Swanilda who hides behind the window curtain.

The old man goes to inspect his precious Coppelia, and finds the toy undamaged. Hearing a. noise he looks through the window and sees Frantz climbing up the ladder. Coppelius hides. But, as soon as Frantz leaps into the room, the old man seizes him and asks him what he means by breaking into his house.

Frantz confesses that he is in love. Coppelius makes light of the matter and invites him to take a glass of wine, which he accepts. The old man does not drink himself, although he contrives continually to fill the youth's glass. Very soon Frantz falls asleep.

Meanwhile, behind the curtain, Swanilda has put on Coppelia's costume and taken her place.

Coppelius decides to carry out a long-contemplated experiment, to invest the inanimate Coppelia with Frantz's life-force. He places Coppelia under various spells in accordance with the precepts recorded in a book of magic which he possesses. Presently, to his great delight, Coppelia rises from her chair, drops her book, and steps slowly down from her pedestal. Gradually she walks less stiffly and her features, till now expressionless, become mobile. She smiles and begins to dance a waltz.

Then Coppelia turns capricious. She tries to drink the wine, turns over the pages of the precious book with her toe, takes up a sword which she thrusts through the Moor, and prepares to do the same with Frantz. Coppelius becomes alarmed and succeeds in stopping her. He finds it difficult to cope with her changes of mood. He puts a tambourine in her hand and she dance a Spanish *pas*. Then she picks up a plaid and dances a jig. Coppelius tries to hold her, but she runs away from him, destroying everything in her path.

Meanwhile, Frantz wakes up and tries to collect his thoughts. The toy-maker seizes Coppelia, forces her into her chair, and wheels her behind the curtain. He goes back to Frantz and forces him to leave by the window.

Then Coppelius is startled by a curious little tinkle which he recognises as the air which regulates Coppelia's movements. He pulls back the curtain and sees the figure sitting stiffly as usual. At the same moment Swanilda glides away, setting two other figures in motion.

Coppelius goes to the window and sees Swanilda arm in arm

with Frantz. Half-puzzled, half-conscious that he has been fooled, he faints in the midst of his clockwork figures, which seem to mock him with their mechanical movements.

Act II. Scene II.[4] *A shady lawn before the residence of the lord of the manor. In the background is the bell, suspended from poles, decked with flags. In front of the bell is an allegorical car, filled with players. Stands have been built to accommodate the lord and his friends. Guards contain the expectant crowd.*

The priests have blessed the bell and now the parties to be married are presented to the lord of the manor. During these proceedings, Frantz and Swanilda make up their differences and join the couples.

Coppelius forces his way through the bystanders. He demands restitution for the damage done to his inventions. Swanilda, who has just received her dowry, offers it to Coppelius. But the nobleman tells her to keep it, and announces that he will make good any losses that the toy-maker has suffered. Placing a purse in the old man's hand, the nobleman mounts a platform and gives the signal for the festival to begin.

The bell-ringer is the first to descend from the car. He calls the morning hours who enter, followed by Dawn, surrounded by little wildflowers.

The bell rings the hour of prayer. Dawn flees, followed by the hours of day. Spinners and harvesters begin their labour.

The bell rings again to announce a marriage and Hymen appears, attended by a little Cupid.

Suddenly the bell sounds the tocsin, and fire is reflected in the sky.

But soon all is calm again and the bell announces the return of peace.

A final *divertissement* brings the ballet to a close.

*

Coppélia is one of the earliest, if not the earliest, of ballets to be based on the theme of a doll's coming to life. The synopsis was adapted by Nuitter, then archivist to the Paris Opera, from Hoffmann's story, *Der Sandmann*.

It was towards the end of 1866, or early in 1867, that Nuitter

[4] This scene contributes little or nothing to the theme and would seem to have been added simply as an excuse for a *divertissement* to lengthen the ballet. For this reason this episode is frequently omitted in later productions.

began work on *Coppélia,* and had mentally cast for the title-role a rising young *danseuse* called Léontine Beaugrand. The management approved the theme and, Delibes having composed the score, the ballet was put into rehearsal. But Perrin, the director of the Opera and a keen business man, felt that Beaugrand's reputation was not sufficient to attract the large audiences essential to success. In short, he wanted a name, a star that would be certain to "draw."

So Mlle. Grantsova was imported from Russia and the choreography entrusted to Mérante. But the rehearsals were so prolonged that the *ballerina* was obliged to return without having danced the part for which she had been engaged. Beaugrand was again passed over in favour of Guiseppina Bozacchi, a youthful Italian *danseuse* in the company. The ballet, after having been three years in rehearsal, was finally given on the date recorded, when the piece and its principal interpreter achieved a considerable success.

The music has a most infectious charm and gaiety, and includes many attractive melodies admirably suited to the dance. Commenting on the music, the critic of *Le Figaro*[5] observes: "M. Leo Delibes has composed for the three scenes of *Coppélia* a distinguished, piquant, and colourful score, excellently orchestrated. . . . It is very difficult to write for legs with a little artistry, taste, and style. For instance, ballets such as *Giselle* are not improvised by the dozen. M. Delibes has avoided the commonplace in a piece where it has every right to succeed."

Of Bozacchi, the critic of *Le Ménestrel* [6] declares: "The title of child prodigy should be devised for her, had it not been abused in so many other cases; although scarcely fifteen years old she is already a very skilful dancer, what is better still in our opinion, she is a graceful and witty actress; add to that a well-proportioned, dainty little body, and that she bids fair to have the prettiest features in the world. If she fulfils all her first promises, she will be a power in her profession."

But Bozacchi's triumph was short-lived for on July 19th the Franco-German War broke out, Paris was invested, and little Bozacchi died of a virulent siege fever.

On October 16th, 1871, *Coppélia* was revived and Beaugrand was awarded the title-role. Her lightness, her precise technique, the rhythm of her movements, and her roguish and vivacious miming procured her a triumph. Gautier hailed her as the suc-

[5] May 28th, 1870.
[6] May 29th, 1870.

cessor of Carlotta Grisi, and what tribute could be greater, coming from the author of *Giselle?*

*

It seems incredible that thirty-six years should pass before *Coppélia* was given in England and then had to submit to the interpolation of additional numbers by the conductor, C. J. M. Glaser. The ballet was first produced at London, at the Empire Theatre, on May 14th, 1906, as a vehicle for Adeline Genée, then in the full tide of popularity.

The Times[7] reviewed the event as follows: "Londoners are at present so little accustomed to follow the plot of a *ballet d'action* that they may be excused if they find some of the piece a little difficult to follow. Whether Coppelius, the inventor of all the automata, imagines that he has actually given life to one of his figures is not easy to say; but as mimed by Mlle. Genée (the representative of Swanilda, the girl who, to regain her swain's affections, pretends to be the doll he admires) the general gist is perfectly clear, and her exquisite dancing in the first act, and her really comic movements as the doll, with her admirable play of posture, wins her a new triumph. . . .

"The playing of the lovely music, like the dancing of all concerned, is admirable; but we may point out that the mazurka differs from the waltz, not merely in the rate of speed, but in the position of the secondary accent in each bar, which difference is not brought out."

Coppélia has been frequently revived both here and abroad. Among recent productions may be mentioned that of the Vic-Wells Ballet (based on choreography by L. I. Ivanov) first presented at Sadler's Wells Theatre, London, on March 21st, 1933, with Lydia Lopokova as Swanilda[8]; and the version given by René Blum's Ballets de Monte Carlo (choreography by Nicholas Zverev) in which Nemchinova danced the famous role.

SYLVIA OU LA NYMPHE DE DIANE

Ballet in 3 Acts and 4 Scenes. Book: Jules Barbier and Baron de Reinach. Music: Léo Delibes. Scenery: Chéret, Rubé, and Chaperon. Costumes: Lacoste. Choreography: Louis Mérante. First produced: Théâtre de l'Opéra, Paris, June 14th, 1876.

[7] May 15th, 1906.
[8] Later the role was taken by Ninette de Valois.

CHARACTERS

Sylvia, a nymph of Diana . . .	MLLE. RITA SANGALLI
Diana	MARQUET
Eros	SANLAVILLE
Two Ethiopian Slaves . . . {	MOLLNAR
	GILLERT
A Young Shepherd	RIDEL
A Peasant	ALINE
A Negress	
Amyntas, a shepherd	MM. MÉRANTE
Orion, the black huntsman . . .	MAGRI
First Sylvan	REMOND
First Satyr	AJAS
Two Satyrs . . . . . {	FRIANT
	F. MÉRANTE
A Peasant	PONÇOT

Sylvans, Satyrs, Naiads, Dryads, Nymphs of Diana, Shepherds, Shepherdesses, Villagers, Bacchantes, Priests of Bacchus, Slaves, Sailors, etc.

Act I. A sacred wood. In the background, to the left, a little marble hemi-cycle with a statue of Eros in the centre. To the right a water-course overhung with intertwined branches. Here and there are masses of rock and clumps of myrtle and laurel bushes. Moonlight.

Fauns and woodland folk emerge from the bushes. Dryads come out of the water. Together they disport in the moonlight. The woodland folk dispute with one another for the love of the dryads who laughingly evade them. Finally they are caught with garlands of flowers. Suddenly a footstep is heard and all seek safety in concealment.

Enter the shepherd, Amyntas, who slowly makes his way, listening intently. But all is silent. He throws down his crook and mantle and meditates. It was on just such a night when, hidden in the break, he espied a beautiful woman in the guise of a huntress, whose image has remained impressed on his heart. Perhaps she was one of Diana's nymphs far beyond earthly love, but he yearns to see her again. The sound of a distant horn is heard. Amyntas, conscious of the approach of his beloved, hides behind the statue.

Sylvia enters, followed by her nymphs. They dance in honour of the chase, then, passing before the statue, seem to defy Eros in the name of their goddess, the chaste Diana. Weary from the ardours of the chase, some recline on the greensward, others bathe in the stream. Sylvia seats herself on a bough and swings lightly over the water. Orion, the dark huntsman, the terror of the forests, appears among the rocks, but, seeing the nymphs, watches them in secret.

Suddenly one of the nymphs catches sight of Amyntas's crook and mantle. She quickly takes them to Sylvia. The nymphs are furious at the thought that they have been watched by a man. Some search for Amyntas whom they discover and drag before Sylvia. At the same moment Orion disappears, with a threatening gesture at his rival.

The shepherd forgets his peril in the joy of seeing Sylvia. The nymph is minded to loose an arrow at the presumptuous mortal, but reflects that a simple shepherd is unworthy of her vengeance, and that it is rather Eros who should be punished. She draws her bow at the statue but Amyntas runs to protect the god against such sacrilege. The arrow flies and strikes the shepherd who staggers and falls to the ground, with a last tender glance at Sylvia.

The nymph, unmoved, curses the statue. In turn the statue looses an arrow. Sylvia trembles and places her hand to her heart. The nymphs run to her side. One picks up a golden arrow and asks if she is wounded. She shakes her head and smilingly places the arrow in her quiver.

Dawn approaches and there is heard the distant music of pipe and tabor. Sylvia blows her horn and vanishes into the wood, followed by her companions. The sun rises, gilding the tree-tops, and village girls and peasants dance in on their way to the harvest. They are followed by shepherdesses carrying baskets of fruit and amphoras of wine. They all kneel before the statue and pass on their way.

One young shepherd lingers behind but hides at the approach of Orion.

The dark huntsman loves Sylvia and resolves to be avenged on the insolent shepherd who dares to be his rival. At this moment he perceives the prostrate Amyntas and rejoices at his death. He has a plan to ensnare the rebellious nymph and to this end prepares a length of gold chain which he carries with him. Hearing a light footstep he pricks up his ears and, overjoyed, hides behind the hemi-cycle.

It is Sylvia who, separated from her companions, is drawn towards Amyntas whom she regards with tenderness. She takes the golden arrow from her quiver and presses it to her lips, and seems to demand pardon for having struck him.

Orion creeps towards the nymph and casts his chain. She evades it and flees. He follows in pursuit, launches the chain a second time, and captures Sylvia, whom he carries off, despite her struggles.

The young shepherd emerges from his hiding-place and, terrified at what he has seen, calls to his friends, who hasten to his side. They recognise Amyntas and vainly strive to revive him. An old sorcerer comes forward and, plucking a rose, presses it to Amyntas's lips. Gradually the stricken shepherd recovers his senses, only to be filled with despair at his fruitless longing for Sylvia. The sorcerer tries to soothe him by suggesting that perhaps Sylvia has been wounded by an arrow such as Eros alone can launch. He points to the statue, of which the bow is no longer arched and the arrow vanished.

Amyntas asks where Sylvia is, whereupon the sorcerer bids him listen to the wild calls which, he informs him, is Orion celebrating the nymph's capture. At this juncture the young shepherd returns, accompanied by his companions, bearing Sylvia's torn mantle. Amyntas swears to rescue his beloved, in spite of attempts to restrain him.

Before departing, he prays to the statue of Eros. Suddenly the statue disappears and the god himself takes his place on the pedestal, bow in hand. The peasants bow down in homage before the god, radiant in the sunlight. Eros points to the path taken by Orion, and Amyntas sets out on his quest.

Act II. A rocky grotto with a narrow entrance. To the right a winding passage which communicates with another part of the cavern. Pieces of rock serve as stools and table.

Sylvia lies unconscious on a bed of moss. Orion takes her bow and quiver and hangs them on the wall. While he contemplates his captive she revives and opens her eyes. Seeing Orion she recoils in terror and tries to flee, but he bars her way. She threatens him with Diana's vengeance, but only arouses his derision. Again she attempts to escape, but Orion blocks the entrance with a boulder.

He declares his love for her, but Sylvia repulses him. Furious, he threatens her with a hatchet, but she remains impassive. Then he offers her food which she accepts. He claps his hands and two little slaves bring in fruit and drink.

Sylvia, remarking that Orion has only milk and water, takes the grapes and asks the slaves to squeeze them into an amphora, which they bring to her. Then she fills Orion's cup and her own with the juice. Orion drinks and finds the beverage greatly to his taste. He drinks cup after cup and grows more and more passionate.

To gain time, Sylvia proposes to dance to him. The slaves play on a pipe and tabor and the chaste nymph imitates the dance of the bacchantes, at the end of which she offers Orion another cup of wine. He drains it at a draught and tries to embrace her. She evades his grasp and he pursues her, but the wine mounts to his brain and he falls asleep. The slaves follow suit.

Sylvia tries in vain to escape from the grotto. She finds her bow and implores Eros to grant her his protection. The god appears and leads her out of the cavern. Then he makes a sign and the grotto and its occupants disappear into the ground. Sylvia thanks her deliverer.

A horn sounds in the distance. The nymph wishes to join her companions when Eros points out Amyntas, overcome with sadness, sitting among the rocks.

Act III. A wooded landscape on a sea-coast. To the left a Temple of Diana.

Villagers enter bearing a statue of Bacchus and another of Silenus. The former is placed on an altar improvised at the foot of an oak tree. Silenus is stood before the altar. The peasant girls place offerings of grapes before the images of the gods and dance a bacchanale.

Amyntas returns, exhausted from his fruitless search for Sylvia. The girls strive vainly to calm his sadness, when a ship is sighted. Gradually it approaches the shore.

Eros, disguised as a pirate, steps to the ground, followed by a number of slaves, whom he seeks to sell. At his command the slaves approach Amyntas, who tries to flee, but is drawn by an irresistible attraction towards one of them. She dances for his delight and raising her veil proves to be Sylvia. Amyntas, overjoyed, falls at her feet.

At this moment Orion appears. He threatens the lovers with his hatchet. Amyntas seizes a thyrsus and awaits his onslaught. Sylvia runs to the temple to invoke the protection of the goddess Diana. The temple-doors close behind her.

Orion ignores Amyntas and crashes his axe three times on the doors. The villagers recoil in terror. The sky darkens, thunder rolls, and clouds fill the background.

At the third blow the temple-doors fly open and Diana is seen on the threshold, holding a drawn bow. Sylvia kneels beside her. Orion draws back. Diana's nymphs group themselves about the temple.

Suddenly Orion leaps at Sylvia. At the same moment Diana looses her bow and Orion falls dead. Clouds invade the scene and hide the temple and the huntsman's corpse.

Then Diana turns on Sylvia and asks her why she strayed from her companions and how she came to lose her bow. Sylvia explains that Eros wounded her with his arrow as a punishment for insulting his statue. She confesses that she has fallen in love and indicates Amyntas. The lovers implore the goddess's forgiveness, but she refuses to pardon them.

A clap of thunder sounds and, while all present bow their heads, Eros goes towards the angry goddess, and cries:

"Why are you so unbending? Look!"

The clouds part and reveal a vision of Diana visiting the sleeping Endymion.

The goddess, confused, asks the pirate how he knows the secrets of the gods. For answer, he throws off his pirate's garb and reveals himself in his costume as the God of Love.

Diana agrees to pardon the lovers, whereupon Eros makes a sign and the vision disappears.

The goddess raises Amyntas and Sylvia and forgives them. The clouds vanish and the sunlight returns, so that Diana's temple reappears in all its splendour.

Diana ascends towards the background and, supported by Eros and surrounded by nymphs and deities, smiles down upon the lovers, who bow in homage. The villagers look on in amazement.

*

Sylvia, apart from its skilfully devised theme and its association with Rita Sangalli, the creator of the title-role, is remarkable for the beauty of its score. Not only is it fresh, strikingly rhythmic and melodious, and full of dramatic colour, but it has a symphonic quality then new to ballet-music. It is far above the average score which frequently served as little more than a metronome to regulate the dancers' steps.

Delibes has been aptly described as "the father of modern ballet-music," and with good reason, for there is no doubt that Tchaikovsky and many of his successors were inspired by this new method of treating ballet-music, which, henceforth, was no longer regarded as something approaching hackwork, so that in course of time the greatest contemporary composers were pleased to write for the ballet.

Here is a contemporary view taken from *L'Opinion*.[9] "M. Leo Delibes has written a score which reveals the hand of a master symphonist. The picturesque choice of themes, the expressive variety of melodies, the attractive improvisation of harmonies, and the highly-coloured orchestration make this ballet, to my mind, an exquisite work, perhaps too refined and too delicate for the glare of the footlights."

Sangalli, the critic of *Le Ménestrel* [10] declares: "Showed herself at once marvellously graceful and energetic in each of her *pas*. She is a dancer of the classic school which makes us the envy of all the foreign theatres where ballet flourishes. . . .

"The *pas* danced by Mlle. Sangalli which were acclaimed by the audience were the valse lente, L'Escarpolette; the Danse Bacchique in the second act; and her two big *variations* in the *divertissement* in the third act, the scherzo-polka pizzicato and the captivating valse which follows.

"Mérante, the choreographer of *Sylvia,* partners Mlle. Sangalli in person and supports her in a masterly manner.

"Praise is also due to M. Magri, the black huntsman, an Italian dancer who is also a talented choreographer.

"Among the stars of the second rank we must mention Mlle. Sanlaville, the most charming Eros you could imagine, and Mlle. Pallier, a naiad such as poets dream of."

The settings are said to be "genuine masterpieces," while M. Lacoste's costumes are also highly praised.

*

Sylvia was produced at London, at the Empire Theatre, in a one-act version arranged by C. Wilhelm, on May 18th, 1911. Delibes' music was arranged and supplemented by Cuthbert Clarke, while the production was by Fred Farren.

The cast was Fred Farren (*Pan*), F. Martell (*Artemis*), Unity More (*Eros*), C. Mossetti (*Amyntas*), Phyllis Bedells (*Ianthe*), and Lydia Kyasht (*Sylvia*).

The Times[11] said of the ballet: "The movement is delightfully varied, and the music with it; the mixture of gods and mortals, of Mr. Fred Farren as the shaggy goat-foot at one end of the scale, and so alluring a nymph turned mortal as Mlle. Lydia Kyasht at

[9] June 15th, 1876.
[10] June 18th, 1876.
[11] May 19th, 1911.

the other; the cold moonlight of Diana, terrible in her wrath against her defaulting nymph, the rosy glow of the God of Love, the sun-browned mirth of the villagers, all makes up a ballet of peculiar vitality and charm, with just a taste, too, of a pleasant old fashion, when ballet, and even burlesque, were bound to have a pagan god or two in them. . . .

"We have never seen Mlle. Lydia Kyasht at once so dramatic as last night and so secure in the mastery of the very difficult displays of pure dancing which she gave. Her *pirouettes* specially roused the audience to great enthusiasm. Miss Phyllis Bedells improves constantly. In Ianthe's solo-dance, as well as in all her pantomime, she showed an advance in knowledge, besides an increase in those qualities of grace and swiftness which made her a favourite when she was still a little girl. Last night her roguishness and gaiety were irresistible. Mr. Fred Farren was a first-rate Pan—extraordinarily nimble, at once grotesque and graceful, and full of character in his pantomime; and Miss F. Martell as Artemis, Miss Unity Moore as Eros, and Miss C. Mossetti as Amyntas were all at their best."

YEDDA

Ballet in 3 Acts. Book: Philippe Gille, Arnold Mortier, and Louis Mérante. Music: Olivier Métra. Scenery: J. B. Lavastre, Lavastre Senior, and Carpezat. Costumes: Eugène Lacoste. Choreography: Louis Mérante. First produced: Théâtre de l'Opéra, Paris, January 17th, 1879.

CHARACTERS

Yedda	Mmes. Rita Sangalli
The Princess	L. Marquet
Sakourada, Queen of the Spirits of Night	Righetti
Nori, betrothed to Yedda . . . MM.	L. Mérante
The Mikado	Rémond
Tô, the Mikado's Jester	Cornet
Yedda's Father	F. Mérante

Basket-Makers, Rice Cultivators, Peasant Women, Lords and Ladies of the Mikado's Court, Porters, Spirits of the Night, Jugglers, Jesters, etc.

The action passes in the Southern Japan of legend.

Act I. Entrance to a Japanese hamlet on the borders of a sacred lake, which can be seen in the distance winding among trees and blue mountains. To the right the fringe of a forest, with a block of granite in the foreground. To the left, the farm of Yedda's father, with a view of the interior of the house. A little in front of the farm is a small fountain of carved wood, surmounted by a cock with plumage outspread.

Basket-makers and their women are busy plaiting baskets. Near the lake other peasants are threshing rice straw, which is brought to them in armfuls. Still other groups are eating out of dishes of lacquer and porcelain.

Young girls adorn Yedda's hut with lanterns and flowers, for this day she is to be betrothed to Nori, a young peasant. Her father invites the peasants to join in the celebration. But where is Yedda? Her friends call her name.

Yedda enters carrying rushes and reeds. The girls turn their backs in pretended ill-humour. She questions them anxiously and they end by smiling and showing her the flower-decked house. She thanks them warmly and seeks her *fiancé,* who presently appears, carrying a lacquer chest. He runs to Yedda but the villagers restrain him, while the girls similarly hold Yedda.

The men tell Nori that he must remove the bow from Yedda's dress without using his hands, when they will leave the lovers to themselves. He adroitly removes the bow with his lips and the villagers depart.

Nori embraces Yedda and shows her the presents he has brought her; among them is a metal mirror. Yedda is delighted with her reflection. Suddenly a trumpet sounds and a stately procession approaches. It is the Mikado and his cousin, a Princess. Tô, the court jester, helps the Mikado to alight from his litter and indicates the rock as a resting place. The Princess goes to speak with her cousin, but the jester quickly steps between them, until the Mikado dismisses him with a tap of his fan.

The Mikado enquires the reason for the flower-decked house and, on being told, summons Yedda before him. Tô presents her and the Prince is charmed with her beauty. "And she dances beautifully," adds the jester. Thereupon the Prince asks her to dance.

Yedda calls her companions and they give several dances. At the end they offer the Prince baskets of flowers. Nori offers a flower to the Princess who takes instead the bow he had detached from Yedda's dress. Tô, who loves the Princess himself, plans to make use of the Mikado's admiration for Yedda, to serve his own interest.

Yedda, dazzled by all this unaccustomed splendour, becomes filled with envy. Tô, fathoming her thoughts, tells her that if she has courage she can be the equal of any of the court ladies. She entreats his counsel.

The jester replies: "At the far end of the lake, at the hour of midnight, the Spirits of the Night assemble at the foot of the tree of life. They are the daughters of the gods who bestow good and evil upon human beings. When the nightingale sings, step on one of the giant leaves which float on the lake, it will carry you to the Spirits."

Tô departs and the villagers call to Yedda from the farm. She is about to go when the nightingale begins to sing. She listens and walks slowly towards the lake. Fearfully she steps on to a leaf, which floats away.

Nori emerges from a hut. He looks for Yedda and sees her form disappear into the night mist. He calls to her in vain. Peasants hurry in with lanterns. Nori is in despair, convinced that Yedda is lost to him for ever.

Act II. A romantic misty lakeside, dominated by the tree of life.

As the moon rises the Spirits of the Night appear from rocks, the tall grass, and the branches of the tree of life.

Sakourada appears and summons her subjects to dance a measure which grows wilder and wilder. A pale figure looms out of the mist; it is Yedda.

The Spirits watch her leap to the bank and kneel at the foot of the sacred tree. The Queen asks her the reason for her visit. She replies that she desires wealth.

"But how would it help you, who are but a peasant?" asks Sakourada.

"Then confer upon me the power to charm," answers Yedda.

"So be it," replies the Queen.

She and her companions teach Yedda some dance steps which she reproduces so well that they promise her their protection. Sakourada breaks off a branch of the tree of life and gives it to her, saying:

"This branch will render you rich, powerful, and of surpassing beauty, but with each wish a leaf will wither, and when there are none you will die."

The Spirits point out the road to Yedda, who, radiant, sets out for the palace, where she hopes to realise her ambitions.

Act III. A hall in the Mikado's palace. To the left tall square columns, raised on three steps, which lead to the private apartments: in the middle of these columns is a throne. To the right are plants and flowers. The background is formed by immense screens decorated with images of the gods and Japanese heroes. These screens, when raised, reveal the principal street of the capital.

The Mikado is seen surrounded by courtiers, in the midst of whom is seated the Princess. The court dancers vainly strive to interest the bored monarch.

"Is there no woman among those present who pleases you?" enquires Tô.

"None," replies the Prince, "the one I desire is the peasant I saw yesterday. I shall never see her again."

"Who can tell," observes the jester. "Command that we be alone and I will show you the person in your thoughts."

At a sign from the Mikado, everyone withdraws, including the Princess. But, before going, she calls the Captain of the Guard, and, showing him the bow she took from Nori, commands him to find the man from whom she took it.

When the courtiers have departed Tô makes a sign and retires. The flowers part and Yedda enters the room.

The Prince runs towards her, but she evades him to inspect all the treasures in the room, then she takes the branch and whispers, "I wish him to love me." The Prince falls on his knees and declares his passion.

At this moment the Princess returns. Mad with jealousy, she reproaches the Prince and reminds Yedda of the lover who awaits her in her village. The Prince intervenes and declares that he will marry Yedda. In desperation the Princess snatches a dagger from his belt and tries to stab him. But Yedda utters the wish that he may suffer no injury and the dagger breaks in the hands of the Princess; she is about to take to flight when the Captain of the Guard returns with Nori.

"There is your *fiancée*," whispers the Princess. Nori remains motionless, stupefied. The Princess goes out.

Officials enter for the coronation of the Prince, who leaves to dress after bidding Yedda prepare for the ceremony. She is overjoyed at the thought of realising her highest ambitions. Then she perceives Nori whose love she is about to betray. He implores her to go away with him. She is about to surrender to his entreaties when there is a fanfare of trumpets. Her ambition revives and, to strengthen her decision, she expresses the wish that she may forget Nori. A leaf flutters from the magic branch and she departs.

Tô and the Princess return and ask Nori if he has won back his betrothed. He shakes his head sadly and is about to leave the palace when he decides to hide behind the flowers and see Yedda for the last time.

The Princess seeks another instrument for her vengeance. Tô offers to remove Yedda if the Princess will give herself to him. She consents.

There is a burst of music and the people surge into the palace. The screens are raised to reveal the city prepared for the festival. The imperial procession enters, led by pages disguised as jesters. Tô tells the Princess that he will profit by the resemblance of costumes to stab Yedda without being recognised.

Jugglers arrive and are performing their tricks when a man runs towards Yedda with uplifted dagger. But Nori rushes forward and receives the blow intended for her.

Yedda, horror-stricken, throws herself on her lover's body. In despair at the dread consequences of her ambition she takes the fatal branch from her sash and snaps it in two. At the same moment she is stricken in her turn. She tries vainly to reach her lover's body and falls dead in the midst of the splendour for which she has sacrificed her true happiness.

*

Yedda was written expressly to inaugurate Sangalli's reappearance and provide her with opportunities to display her abilities both as dancer and mime. The setting of the ballet was doubtless inspired by the success of the Japanese Exhibition then lately held in Paris.

Lacoste, the designer of the costumes, made a special study of the articles in the Exhibition, but his main difficulty was to retain the Japanese characteristics while avoiding the traditional robe, which was not suited to the demands of classical ballet.

A contemporary[12] declares that the third act was the most Japanese in spirit, for in that scene "there were represented Japanese nobles in their splendid robes of ceremony. . . . No description can render the effect of these masses. The whole effect is genuinely magical. The colours, although very decided in tone, combine in exquisite harmony. There is a modulation of hues which the intensity of gradations renders almost inexplicable."

The Japanese *coiffures* did not please the *corps de ballet* who, used to wearing a curl or two on the forehead, found the head-

[12] *Figaro*, January, 1879.

dresses very tiring. Moreover, their features were so changed that they could hardly recognise one another.

The scenery was highly praised, particularly that of the second act, which the same writer asserts was "an inspiration at once grandiose and poetic. The sacred lake with its extraordinary perspective, affords the spectator an indescribable emotion; on seeing the silvery waters extending towards, and vanishing among, the mountains, you experience a mysterious sensation of infinity. On the far bank the tree of life extended its gigantic and innumerable branches."

Métra's music, says the critic of *L'Universe Illustré*,[13] "is too fluent, too simple, perhaps we should have preferred more originality and an oriental element which is lacking."

Mlle. Sangalli as Yedda "displays that rare suppleness and strength, that perfect precision and elegance which we have praised elsewhere; she mimes the last scene in a very dramatic manner."

"Mlle. L. Marquet is a very beautiful and noble Princess, Rémond plays the Mikado with much grace and feeling, while Cornet, very alert and refined, amusingly makes clear the dual nature of Tô the jester, who passes from jester to lover and *vice versa* with a captivating alacrity."

The writer in the *Figaro* records an amusing incident relating to the first performance. He tells us that Sangalli was obsessed with the fear that she might go on without the famous branch from the tree of life which is indispensable to the action of the third act. At the dress rehearsal the property-master had forgotten to return to her the precious talisman which she had received in the second act. Such an omission at the first performance would have had the most fatal consequences for, once the dancer had glided upon the stage, it would be too late to hand her the branch. To guard against such a calamity, authors and dancers placed a branch by every possible entry, while the ballerina herself kept a stock of branches in her dressing-room. Even so, when she was about to make her entrance, a dozen voices anxiously enquired if she had her branch.

LA KORRIGANE

Fantastic Ballet in 2 Acts. Book: François Coppée and Louis Mérante. Music: Ch. M. Widor. Scenery: Lavastre, Rubé, and Chaperon. Costumes: Eugène Lacoste. Choreography: Louis

[13] January 25th, 1879.

Mérante. First produced: Théâtre National de l'Opéra, Paris, December 1st, 1880.

CHARACTERS

Yvonnette, first a tavern-maid, later a korrigane	MLLES. ROSITA MAURI
Queen of the Korriganes . . .	SANLAVILLE
Janik, a beggar boy	OTTOLINI
Lilèz, a player of the *biniou* . .	MM. L. MÉRANTE
Pascou, a Hunchback, the town-crier .	AJAS
Loïk, a tavern-keeper	M. CORNET
A Sergeant of Police	M. PLUQUE
His Wife	MME. LAURENT
The Mayor	M. PORCHERON
His Wife	MME. WAL
A Chaplet-vendor	M. PONÇOT

Korriganes, Moths, Elves, Peasants, Soldiers, and Beggars.

The action passes in Brittany of the 17th century.

Act I. A village square. To the right is an old well. To the left is a tavern and tables. A little further back is a gothic church, flanked by a little clock-tower. In the background is a village street, with a view of rocks and the sea in the distance.

It is the Day of Pilgrimage and all is bustle and animation. Pots of cider are being drained, old crones are gossiping, children are playing, peddlers are sorting out their wares, limping beggars are whining for charity. A malicious hunchback, the village town-crier, enters followed by mocking children. Loïk, the tavern-keeper, greets the hunchback, who joins those drinking. Exit all.

Yvonnette, a poor orphan who is Loïk's servant, comes out of the tavern. Distant strains of a gay dance are heard. Sad because she cannot join the merry-makers, Yvonnette essays a few steps, but Loïk sees her, rates her for her laziness, and is about to strike her, when the hunchback intervenes. Loïk retires and the hunchback takes advantage of his absence to make advances to Yvonnette, who is frightened and takes to flight. Janik, a beggar-boy and dependant of Yvonnette's, threatens the town-crier, who repulses him.

The first stroke of vespers sounds and the peasants prepare for church. Yvonnette reappears and gives Janik a meal at one of the tables. The sound of a *biniou* announces the arrival of Lilèz, the most handsome youth in the village, who has an affectionate greeting for everyone save the hunchback, whom he despises. On the second stroke of vespers a peddler offers him a sacred rosary, a certain protection against korriganes. The hunchback mocks Lilèz's credulity but Janik induces him to purchase the charm.

On the last stroke of vespers the mayor and his wife, the sergeant of police and his wife, and other village notables go into the church, followed by the crowd. Meanwhile Yvonnette looks in admiration at Lilèz. He is about to drink at the well, but she brings him a glass of cider. He asks her why she does not join the others and she shows him her tattered clothes. Thereupon he gives her a crown and goes into the church. Yvonnette is offended and cries. The hunchback mocks her, but Janik consoles her. She insists on his taking the money.

At this moment an old woman in a cowl, carrying a load of wood, slips and falls. Yvonnette goes to her help and the latter declares that she knows of her love for Lilèz and will aid her. Suddenly the old woman changes into a fairy. She is the Queen of the Korriganes.

She extends her hand towards the well and summons a band of strange dwarfs, who dance a fantastic measure. Next come a number of handsome youths and girls. Some of the dwarfs place before Yvonnette a basket filled with beautiful clothes and lovely jewels. She may have all these treasures if Lilèz proves his love for her before the Angelus rings. If not, then Yvonnette will belong to the Queen and become a korrigane.

Unable to resist this temptation Yvonnette consents and is immediately dressed in her fine clothes. The Queen reminds her of her promise and departs, followed by her attendants. The hunchback, half afraid, half curious, is a witness of this scene.

The villagers come out of the church and are astonished at Yvonnette's appearance. Lilèz can hardly take his eyes off her. But it is time for the festival to begin and, to dance with greater ease, he takes off his waistcoat, from which the hunchback filches the rosary. Gradually night falls and the dancers depart.

Lilèz, left alone with Yvonnette, tries to kiss her. But she resists him, saying that he is only in love with her clothes. He replies that he is willing to marry her that very minute. Yvonnette falls into his arms, but the hunchback, who has watched this scene, moves the hands of the clock and causes the Angelus to ring. The korriganes rush in, surround Yvonnette, and seize her. She protests that the hunchback has altered the time, but the Queen is relentless. Lilèz rushes to Yvonnette's aid, but the dwarfs restrain him while the korriganes bear away his betrothed.

Act II. A deserted heath in the moonlight. To the right a path winding beneath some oak-trees. In the background is a marsh, on the farther bank of which can be seen the silhouette of a village with its belfry.

Korriganes dart over the heath and disappear. They are succeeded by moths and elves who vanish likewise. Strange music is borne on the breeze.

The hunchback and Janik enter, accompanied by some drunkards. Frightened by the strange voices the latter take to flight. But the hunchback is unafraid because he has the rosary. He accepts the flask which Janik offers him. He grows sleepy and sinks to the ground. Janik takes advantage of his condition to deprive him of the rosary and departs.

Suddenly a dwarf emerges from behind a rock, leaps upon the sleeper, and calls his fellows. The hunchback wakes up in a fright and hurriedly searches for the rosary, which he cannot find. The dwarfs force him to dance until he kneels and begs for mercy. Then a little dwarf leaps on his shoulders and the hunchback, terrified, takes to flight, pursued by his tormentors.

Fairies and korriganes come from all parts and assemble on the heath. The Queen calls for Yvonnette, who appears dressed as a korrigane. But she is so downcast that the Queen asks the reason. She explains that the hunchback altered the hands of the clock, causing her to become a korrigane.

The Queen orders her dwarfs to bring in the hunchback who is astounded to see Yvonnette. Then the Queen touches him with her wand and causes two asses' ears to grow. Yvonnette mocks him in a dance, then the dwarfs seize Pascou and force him to take part in a furious measure until he tumbles into a hole.

Lilèz's *biniou* is heard in the distance and Yvonnette is delighted, believing that her lover will rescue her. But the Queen gives an order and the korriganes disappear.

Enter Lilèz in despair at being unable to find Yvonnette. All at once the korriganes surround him. He asks the Queen to restore him his sweetheart.

"Here are my subjects," she replies, "find her if you can."

Each fairy approaches Lilèz in turn and tries to captivate him, but he disdainfully repulses them. It is Yvonnette's turn and she throws her arms about his neck. He is about to respond when the Queen extends the magic branch in her hand, and he fails to recognise his love. The Queen is delighted, for she is certain now that Yvonnette cannot leave her.

But the young girl has a sudden inspiration and begins to dance the very steps that captivated Lilèz at their first meeting. None of the fairies can copy such difficult steps and Lilèz, convinced that the dancer is Yvonnette, embraces her. The korriganes are furious and try to separate the lovers.

But now Janik arrives with the precious rosary. Lilèz seizes it and forces the korriganes to withdraw. Moreover the hour of dawn approaches when all evil things must flee.

Peasants homeward bound from the pilgrimage find Lilèz shaking hands with Janik in gratitude for his timely aid, while with the other arm he enfolds his beloved.

*

La Korrigane was one of the most successful ballets to be given at the Opera, and was performed over one hundred times. Coppée has recorded that his association with ballet was the outcome of a chance meeting with an actor friend called Régnier, who said to him: "Would you like to write the 'book' for a ballet? We have a delightful 'star' at the Opera, Rosita Mauri, who made such a success in Gounod's *Polyeucte*. We must have an important ballet for her, a work in two acts. . . . Vaucorbeil hoped that the theme would be devised by a poet and he thought of you." [14]

At first Coppée refused, but, on thinking the matter over, the task did not seem so formidable, and he accepted the commission. After due cogitation he actually wrote two ballets, one called *Fleurs Mortelles,* based on a story by Hawthorne, and one entitled *La Korrigane,* inspired by a Breton legend. The latter was chosen. Widor was asked to write the music, while the choreography was assigned to Mérante.

Widor, an excellent musician and a distinguished organist, thoroughly enjoyed composing the music. Coppée recalls that "on twenty occasions, between one day and the next, often on the vaguest suggestion from the choreographer, he would bring a page of exquisite melody. If that did not suit, he would immediately write another without a trace of weariness or a sign of ill-humour." [14]

"The music," declares the critic of *Le Ménestrel,*[15] "is of such symphonic importance that we have no hesitation in assigning it first place in our notice of *La Korrigane.* . . . The score of *La Korrigane* is a work of art, perhaps too delicately written for a house like that of the Académie Nationale de Musique, where

---

[14] *Figaro Illustré,* February, 1895.
[15] December 5th, 1880.

coarse effects blend better with the demands of choreography" . . .
The writer then goes on to praise in particular the waltz-mazurka,
La Sabotière, danced by Mauri; the *adage* which follows, also
danced by Mauri "with a wonderful artistry," and the *Gigue
Bretonne,* danced by her to a giddy rhythm.

The critic of *La Revue et Gazette Musicale de Paris*[16] observes:
"The score achieved complete success; its great qualities are originality, vigour, clarity, and rhythm. The orchestration is treated
with great lightness, due in large measure to the frequent use of
harmony, and offers a variety of colours and effects which are
wonderfully suited to the various pictures M. Widor wishes to
depict.

"This orchestration, in which the sonorous mass of the strings
seems relegated to second place, makes the instrumentation sometimes seem a little thin, but it also has the advantage of giving the
pictures a variety of colours and the most pleasing gradations. . . .

"The melody follows the dancer's movements and the expression of the gesture; one thought is hardly expressed than another
comes to take its place. It is at once an improvised and studied
art; it is a special art in which symphony is wedded to drama."

"Two scenes, very different from each other," says the same
writer, "constitute the plan of the new ballet at the Opera. In one
there are clumsy peasants marking the rhythm of the traditional
dance with stamps of their sabots; our solemn Bretons entering
piously under the porch of the little church, surrounded by tombs,
or following with slow steps the procession, headed with banners,
which winds over the heath. Then, on the other hand, there are
airy sylphides, korriganes, all those little beings which dwell in the
old mysterious menhir and dance on the plain without bending the
stalks of that purple heather.

"The double scene takes place in two settings, one in daylight,
the other at night-time . . . this dual picture gives M. Coppée's
ballet the charm and originality which distinguish it, and nothing
is more pleasing than this combination of the real and the fanciful,
of darkness and light. Add that up to now Brittany has been little
exploited at the Opera; the women with their bright dresses
adorned with bands of gold, silver, or velvet, according to the
station of their wearers, with their varied caps; the men with their
great hats, and black and white clothes studded with pewter buttons; all this gives the collection of costumes an effect of originality in the best taste. . . .

"This little tale, very clear and very well arranged, affords ample

[16] December 5th, 1880.

material for picturesque and animated scenes. In the first act there is the struggle for the stick, and, above all, the Sabotière, a sort of quaint and brilliant Bourrée, which was encored; in the second act the scene of the gnomes and Pascou, the ballet of the korriganes, and the procession; are pictures which reflect the greatest honour on the choreographer."

Coppée tells an amusing story of the *corps de ballet's* first sight of the Breton caps they were required to wear. "Accustomed to represent flowers, butterflies, or stars, they could not bring themselves to put the Breton caps on their heads, notwithstanding their prettiness and diversity. 'We shall look like servants,' they said, in indignation. Some even dissolved in tears." [17] But these were soon dried when it was seen that the ballet was a complete success.

Here is Coppée's impression of Mauri as Yvonnette. "La Mauri is divine, seen from the audience with or without the aid of operaglasses. Indeed, I regard it as one of the greatest events in my life as a dramatist to have seen that extraordinary artist, that ethereal being who after a prodigious bound—I put it badly—after soaring in the air, returned to the stage, so lightly, so delicately, that you could not hear a sound, no more than when a bird descends and alights on a twig.

"La Mauri is dancing personified. To the trials of rehearsal, so tedious and wearing for all the artistes, but particularly exhausting for the *prima ballerina* who must expend so much strength and dexterity, la Mauri brought a kind of physical enthusiasm, a kind of joyous delirium. You felt that she loved to dance for nothing, from instinct, for the love of dancing, even in a dark and empty theatre. She whinnied and darted like a young foal; she soared and glided in space like a wild bird; and, in her sombre and somewhat wild beauty, there is something of both the Arab steed and the swallow."

While accomplishing one of her *tours de force,* Mauri hurt her foot and was obliged to remain several weeks with her foot extended on a couch. Despite the care of the best doctors she made such little progress that her father decided to go on a pilgrimage to his native Spain, and invoke the aid of a church noted for its miracles. As a votive offering he took with him and laid on the altar a little foot made of solid gold. In the meantime the famous Dr. Labbé did not relax his treatment. Soon after the pilgrim's return, Mauri improved, and was able to don Yvonnette's sabots and repeat her triumphs.

[17] *Figaro Illustré,* February, 1895.

LES DEUX PIGEONS

Ballet in 3 Acts. Book: Henry Régnier and Louis Mérante.
Music: André Messager. Scenery: Rubé, Chaperon, and J. B.
Lavastre. Costumes: Bianchini. Choreography: Louis Mérante.
First produced: Théâtre de l'Opéra, Paris, October 18th, 1886.

CHARACTERS

Gourouli	MLLES.	ROSITA MAURI
Pepio		SANLAVILLE
Mikalia[18]		MONTAUBRY
Djali		HIRSCH
Queen of the Gypsies . . .		MONNIER
1st Gypsy Girl		WAL
2nd Gypsy Girl		LAURENT
Zarifi, Chief of the Gypsies . .	MM.	PLUQUE
Franca-Trippa, a Gypsy . . .		DE SORIA
1st Gypsy		MÉRANTE
2nd Gypsy		VASQUEZ
The Captain		AJAS
Stefano, an old servant . . .		PONÇOT
The Syndic		HOQUANTI

Gourouli's friends, Gypsies, Children, Servants, People.

The action passes in Thessaly, on the sea-coast bounded by the Aegean Sea. The period is the 18th century.

Act I. The principal room in a country house. The interior is rustic, but indicative of ease and comfort. A large window framed in climbing plants overlooks the countryside. Facing the window is a large dove-cot with many pigeons sitting on the roof.

At the rise of the curtain, servants are busy decorating the room with country flowers in honour of their mistress, Gertrude. The youngest of them, roguish by nature, goes from group to group, upsetting everything, borrowing flowers to put in her hair, until, grumbled at by her companions, she goes away sulking.

Discovering a wicker basket she takes a handful of grain which she flings at the pigeons.

Gertrude enters leaning on a stick, for age has robbed her steps

---

[18] Gourouli's mother was originally called Gertrude; this name was changed to Mikalia as given in the cast.

of their firmness. The servants greet her with affection and help her to an armchair. Then she asks for her daughter, Gourouli, whom she does not see, nor her daughter's *fiancé,* Pepio.

At the same moment the door opens and Gourouli comes in with a bouquet which she offers to her mother, who receives it sadly. Gourouli asks if anything is the matter. She replies that she is worried because Pepio seems moody and dissatisfied. Gourouli is greatly alarmed.

Pepio enters with an air of boredom. Gourouli goes towards him. Pepio pulls himself together, smiles at his *fiancée,* greets Gertrude, then goes to the window and peers into the distance.

Gertrude urges her daughter to talk to Pepio. So she points out the pigeons which she tells him are happy because they love one another. Inspired by their example they imitate their manners of courtship, then pretend to quarrel and peck each other. Finally, they separate, return, and become friends again.

But Pepio soon grows weary and, sitting down, gives himself up to his day-dreams. Gourouli is disappointed at this abrupt end to their game.

Suddenly strange music is heard and everyone runs to the window. It is a band of gypsies on their way to a neighbouring village. Gertrude bids a servant ask them in, that they may give their performance.

The servants are delighted at the possibility of entertainment and even Pepio seems to cheer up. The troupe give a number of dances in which Gourouli joins, but her chaste dancing leaves Pepio indifferent. On the other hand he is quite carried away by the fire and attractiveness of the gypsy dances. In fact he is obsessed with the idea to join the troupe.

He informs Gourouli and her mother of his intention to travel. They warn him of the dangers that may befall him. But Pepio announces that if he goes for a few days he will be satisfied. Gourouli agrees and declares that she will accompany him. But Pepio tells her that she must not forsake her mother. Gourouli is about to insist when Gertrude signs to her to give way. So she sits down in desperation while her mother helps Pepio with his preparations.

Ready at last he kisses Gourouli and Gertrude good-bye. A turtle dove coos plaintively and Pepio takes his sweetheart in his arms. Then he departs.

Gertrude bids her daughter follow at a distance and watch over him. Gourouli, accompanied by Stefano, follows on the heels of the traveller.

Act II. The sunlit entrance to a village. In the centre is an immense oak-tree which casts a deep shadow. To the left is a gypsy tent; to the right, an inn.

The gypsies are preparing for a festival which is about to begin. Enter Pepio who is recognised by the band. He enters into conversation with the gypsy girl who had already attracted his attention.

Meanwhile a young girl arrives. She wears a hooded cloak and approaches Zarifi, the chief, who recognises Gourouli. She produces a purse which she offers in return for his aid. He tells her to keep her purse saying that he will be happy to be of service to so charming a girl.

Gourouli reproves him sharply and he asks how he can serve her. She indicates Pepio as her *fiancé,* saying that he has left her to indulge in adventures, and she wishes him to be sorry for his action and return to her.

"But how can I help?" enquires Zarifi.

"First, by letting that young girl lend me her costume."

Zarifi consents and tells the gypsy indicated to go with Gourouli into the tent.

At the same moment the village bells ring out, drums beat, and trumpets blare. The villagers enter dressed in their best, with various officials at their head.

Now follows a *grand divertissement* to which the gypsies contribute dance after dance. But the chief honours fall to Gourouli, who, disguised as a gypsy and dancing with the utmost vivacity, turns the heads of all the men. Even Pepio, failing to recognise her, is carried away by her attractions.

No sooner does Gourouli pause for breath than Pepio is surrounded by gypsies who force him to play cards and lose his all. He has no time to bewail his lot before Gourouli overwhelms him with her gaiety.

However, the sky darkens, rain begins to fall, and everyone hastens to seek shelter before the threatened storm breaks. The gypsies retire into their tent, where Pepio enters in search of Gourouli, only to come face to face with Zarifi, who orders him out. Pepio shudders at having to go out into the rain and tries to gain shelter at the inn, where he is refused admittance as he is penniless.

Pepio, greatly distressed at being unable to find shelter, remembers with regret the warm house he has forsaken. Suddenly he thinks of the oak tree and takes shelter beneath it, but a blinding flash of lightning strips a branch from the tree and Pepio, terrified, runs hither and thither until he falls exhausted to the ground.

Presently the storm abates, the rain stops, and the village children venture out. One of them espies Pepio who, forlorn and wet through, thinks of returning home. The band of imps surround him and assail him with shrill cries. He tries to escape but one boy lassoes him with a cord, and he becomes a butt for their sport. They pay no heed to his cries for mercy until Stefano comes out of the inn and drives away the children with his stick. Then, having made certain that their victim is unhurt, he leaves before Pepio has time to thank his deliverer.

Act III. Same as Act I.

Gertrude, surrounded by Gourouli's friends, bewails her deserted home. The young girls vainly strive to console her, but she is full of evil presentiments. Suddenly a girl, who has been looking out of the window, announces that she can see one of the stray birds returning to its nest—Gourouli.

Gertrude rises from her chair and just reaches the door when her daughter enters and embraces her. She tells her that Pepio, too, will soon be back. "Well," laughs Gourouli, "he has had his lesson, and you will see whether he has profited by it."

At this juncture Pepio appears on the threshold. He hangs his head, fearing to be received with derision, but, remembering all the kindness he has received, is secretly overjoyed to be back.

Gertrude welcomes him and he melts under her tenderness. He asks whether Gourouli will forgive him. For answer, her mother pushes him towards her daughter who holds him in her arms. Then the re-united lovers, surrounded by their friends, kneel and receive Gertrude's blessing.

*

Les Deux Pigéons is based upon the well-known fable by La Fontaine. A writer in the *Figaro*[19] reveals that when the ballet was first conceived "it was the male pigeon which remained at home and the female pigeon which set out in search of adventure. The two roles have since been transposed and this happy change enables us to appreciate Mlle. Mauri under two different aspects, dark or fair, chaste or lascivious, and from this contrast she draws, from the double viewpoint of *plastique* and choreography, the most unexpected effects.

"In the first act the female pigeon is charming without her clouds of muslin and with her fair wig . . . but this is no more

[19] October 19th, 1886.

Rosita Mauri. By good fortune we find her again in the second act, with her magnificent black tresses flowing over her shoulders, whose whiteness emerges from a fire-coloured bodice, which gives her an air of diabolical wantonness. In this guise, to a *pizzicato* which is a near relation of that in *Sylvia,* she dances an intoxicating *variation* which, owing to the applause, she has to repeat."

LEV IVANOV

L EV IVANOVICH IVANOV was born in Russia, February, 1834. His father was a man of business. At the age of eight young Ivanov was sent to school where he remained for two years, when he joined the Imperial School of Ballet, St. Petersburg. He was placed in a class conducted by Pimenov. Later he studied under Gredlu, Frédéric, and Jean Petipa.

Ivanov was transferred to the ballet troupe in February, 1850, and was regarded as one of the most promising of the rising male dancers. Even before he had completed his schooling he danced with M. N. Muravieva in a *pas de deux* in *La Péri,* and with Fanny Elssler in *Catarina, Esmeralda,* and *La Filleule des Fées.*

However, Perrot, then *maître de ballet,* was not very partial to Russian dancers and made little attempt to advance Ivanov. His first opportunity came in 1855 when T. P. Smirnova invited him to dance with her in *La Fille Mal Gardée,* in connection with a benefit performance. This would appear to have been his first appearance as a solo dancer, and his success on this occasion caused him to be cast for roles.

In a similar way he was given an opportunity to demonstrate his ability as a mime, for Petipa was suddenly taken ill and he had to deputise for him in *La Vivandière.* He rehearsed the mime and dancing with Prikhunova on the morning of the day of the performance and in the evening appeared with success.

During his long career he took part in most of the important ballets such as *Faust, Esmeralda, Le Roi Candaule, La Fille du Pharaon, La Bayadère, The Wilful Wife, Zoraiya,* and so on. He was excellent both as classical and character dancer.

In 1858 he was appointed to conduct two junior classes in the School of Ballet. His colleagues were Pichaud, Johannsen, and Stukolkin, all of whom later became famous. Among Ivanov's pupils were E. P. Sokolova, Vazem, Vergina, Gorshenkova, A. F. Nikitina, and Preobrazhenskaya.

When the *régisseur* Bogdanov retired, the post was offered to Ivanov. He accepted the position but resigned in 1885 in order to become second *maître de ballet,* in which he acted as assistant to Marius Petipa. Ivanov produced a number of short ballets such as *Cupid's Pranks, The Enchanted Forest, The Beauty of Seville,* and *The Boatmen's Festival,* as well as several long ballets for instance, *La Tulipe d'Haarlem* and *Casse Noisette.* He also collaborated with Petipa in the famous *Le Lac des Cygnes.*

In 1897 he was invited to Warsaw when he produced *Halte de Cavalerie* (Petipa), *Le Marché des Innocents* (Petipa), *The Magic Flute,* some dances for an opera called *The Demon,* and some numbers for a *divertissement.*

For many years he annually composed ballets for the Tsar's private theatre at Krasnoe Selo.

A contemporary asserts that his ballets were distinguished for their artistry, and that he made good use of his experience as dancer and stage manager. He was endowed with pleasant manners and considerable personal charm, which made him a great favourite with everyone with whom he came into contact.

He was always hard at work and, on the day of his fifty years' jubilee, declared that his dearest wish was to "die in harness," an ambition which was fulfilled. In November, 1901, he was busy on a revival of *Sylvia* when he was seized with periods of intense fatigue. He became ill and died in December of the same year.

THE MAGIC FLUTE

Ballet in 1 Act. Book: L. I. Ivanov. Music: Richard Drigo. Choreography: L. I. Ivanov. First produced at Annual Pupils' Display in Small Theatre of Imperial Ballet School, St. Petersburg, March 10th/22nd, 1893.

CHARACTERS

The Marquis, a rich lord of the neighbourhood
A Countrywoman
Lise, her daughter
Luc, a country youth . . . . . . M. MICHEL FOKINE
Footman
Oberon (disguised as a hermit)
The Judge
Lise's Friends

Scene. A village in France in the reign of Louis XV.

A well-to-do countrywoman, pleased with the work achieved by her farmhands, rewards them with beer and bids them dance.

Her daughter, Lise, beckons to her sweetheart, Luc, and invites him to join in the celebrations. Alas, her mother sees Luc, whose poverty does not commend him to her as a suitor, and she bids the youth begone.

Enter the Marquis's footman who announces that his master desires to choose a bride from the village maidens. Hard on his heels comes the nobleman himself, who, after due inspection, selects Lise. She, however, scorns his proposal; but her mother forces her to accept the attentions of the Marquis, who entreats her hand on bended knee. But when he tries to kiss her hand he caresses that of Luc.

The Marquis, eager to demonstrate his grace, offers to teach Lise the Menuet, and she in turn shows him a village dance. Afterwards, at her mother's invitation, he enters her house to take a little refreshment.

The villagers leave, but Luc returns and sits upon the step of the judge's house nearby. While waiting he sees Lise's mother drive away an aged hermit. Pitying his plight, he goes to the hermit and gives him his last coin.

The hermit, observing his sorrow, enquires the cause. On being told his story he presents him with a flute which is inscribed with the words: "Play on this and everybody will be forced to dance. It will bring you luck." Luc turns to thank the hermit for the gift, but he has vanished. The youth puts the flute to his lips and pipes a tune which brings Lise dancing to his side. As he explains to her the magic properties of his gift, Luc's mother and the Marquis appear, followed by servants armed with brooms and sticks. But when Luc plays his flute they are forced to dance.

The Marquis charges Luc with sorcery and orders gendarmes to arrest him. But as soon as he puts the flute to his lips, everyone, including the gendarmes, is obliged to dance. In the end the magic flute is wrested from him and he is haled before the judge. That worthy orders the flute's power to be tested, but since he himself is compelled to dance, his dignity is outraged and he condemns Luc to death.

Now the magic notes are heard in another quarter and Oberon in all his splendour stands before the company. He reveals that he was the hermit, and when Lise's mother beseeches his forgiveness, he agrees only on condition that she will consent to the union of Luc and Lise.

As the Marquis and his footman steal away, the villagers celebrate the happiness of the re-united lovers.

*

This ballet was a favourite item in the repertory of the Pavlova Company, the part of Lise being taken by Pavlova, that of Luc by Volinine, and that of the Marquis by Cecchetti.

CASSE NOISETTE

Ballet in 2 Acts and 3 Scenes. Book: L. I. Ivanov. Music: P. I. Tchaikovsky. Scenery: M. I. Botcharov. Choreography: L. I. Ivanov. First produced: Maryinsky Theatre, St. Petersburg, December 5th/17th, 1892.

CHARACTERS

President . . . . M. KSHESINSKY I.
His Wife . . . . MLLE. BILINSKAYA
Clara ⎫
Franz ⎬ their children
Drosselmeyer
Aunt Marianna
Governess
Butler
Vivandière ⎫   ⎧ MLLE. ANDERSEN
Soldier   ⎬ Clockwork ⎨ M. LITAVKIN
Columbine ⎥   toys   ⎨ MLLE. OLGA PREOBRA-
Harlequin ⎭   ⎪ ZHENSKAYA
King of the Mice   ⎩ M. KYAKSHT
Nutcracker . . . . M. LEGAT
Sugar-Plum Fairy . . . . . MLLE. ANTONIETTA
                               DELL 'ERA
Prince Koklush . . . . . M. P. A. GERDT
Children, Guests, Parents, Incroyables, Merveilleuses, Mice, Biscuits, Soldiers, Snowflakes, Fairies.

Act I. Scene I. Clara's Home.

The President and his wife are giving a Christmas party and are seen receiving their many guests. When they have all arrived there are dances for the grown-ups and dances for the children. One of the guests, Drosselmeyer, brings four clockwork toys as presents, and to Clara, the host's daughter, he gives a toy Nutcracker, which her brother Franz covets, and there is a quarrel. He snatches the toy from her and throws it on a couch. One final dance, the *"Grosvater,"* brings the festivities to an end, when the guests depart and the children go to bed.

Clara, however, cannot sleep for thinking of her Nutcracker, and at midnight she comes to seek her toy. But, by one of those metamorphoses common to fairyland, the familiar room becomes a battlefield, for toy soldiers come to life and, under the command of the Nutcracker, wage war against an invading horde of mice led by their king. Clara fights beside her beloved Nutcracker and helps him to victory. This act of devotion causes him to transform into a handsome boy, and he invites Clara to go with him to the Kingdom of Sweets.

Act I. Scene II.

The youthful lovers are seen passing through a storm of snowflakes on their way to that delectable country.

Act II. The Kingdom of Sweets.

The lovers arrive in a small boat. A sugar-kiosk melts under the sun's rays and disappears.

Clara and the Nutcracker are received by the Sugar-Plum Fairy and her attendants who honour them with a festival, which affords opportunity for the traditional series of character dances: *"Chocolate: Danse Espagnole"; "Café: Danse Arabe"; "Thé: Danse Chinoise"; "Bouffon"; "Danse des Mirlitons"*; a *Grand Pas de Deux* by the Sugar-Plum Fairy and her Cavalier; and a final *ensemble*.

The ballet ends with an apotheosis which represents a bee-hive guarded by flying bees.

*

Casse Noisette is based on Dumas's version of Hoffmann's tale, *The Nutcracker and the King of Mice*.

Tchaikovsky found the theme of this ballet decidedly inferior to that of *La Belle au Bois Dormant* and disliked it. Gradually, however, he became interested. He began to compose in January, 1891, and completed his draft score on July 7th of the same year.

The choreography was begun by Petipa, but soon afterwards he became ill and entrusted the work to Ivanov.

The ballet was finely conducted by Drigo and splendidly staged. It was received with considerable applause and yet there was a feeling that it was not entirely successful. The theme was thought to be weak and the delicate beauties of the music did not appeal to the audience during the first few performances. In fact, some time passed before the ballet became a favourite.

The part of the Sugar-Plum Fairy was brilliantly rendered by

Dell' Era; at the second performance the role was taken by A. F. Nikitina.

Casse Noisette was presented by the Vic-Wells Ballet at the Sadler's Wells Theatre, London, on January 30th, 1934, the revival being staged by N. Sergeyev. It is always difficult to assess the exact relation of a revival to an original which one has not seen, but, since it is presumably based on Ivanov's choreography, it can provide a basis for criticism.

The opening scene possesses little of interest save a pleasant old-world charm, for the dances by the dolls, and the fight between the soldiers and the mice, are frankly undistinguished and only suited to a juvenile audience.

The scene of the snowflakes in which the fairies wave branched sticks tipped with fleecy balls of snow, and perform their evolutions amid falling snowflakes, is a charming spectacle. In the original production this *ballabile* was given by fifty-nine *danseuses*.

The final scene is merely an excuse for the traditional series of character dances which, in this instance, are seldom appropriate to the situation and, generally speaking, are of indifferent quality. It passes the understanding that "Coffee" should be conveyed by a Stomach Dance in the manner of a dancer of the Ouled-Naïl, and that "Tea" should be suggested by a couple of ridiculous Chinese whose "number" seems to have been borrowed from a pantomime version of Aladdin.

Yet, amid so much that is mediocre, there are three beautiful "classical numbers"—the *pas de deux* danced by the Sugar-Plum Fairy and her Cavalier, the latter's *variation,* and the *"Dance of the Sugar-Plum Fairy."* At the "Wells" these were well rendered by Markova and Turner, particularly the last dance, which Markova danced with a dignified grace and technical brilliancy that were positively sparkling.

The Markova-Dolin Ballet gave the third scene of *Casse Noisette* as a *divertissement;* there the dances I have praised were rendered by Markova and Dolin.

SCENE FROM "LES BICHES"

LEONIDE MASSINE

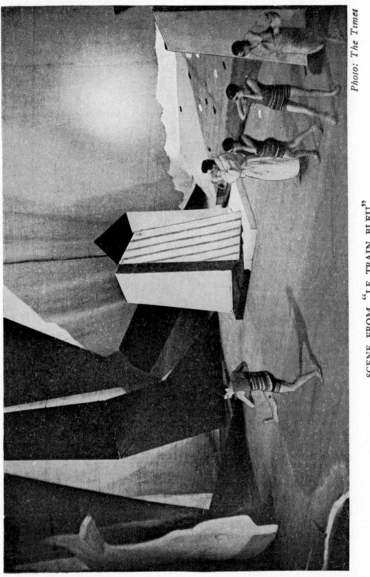

SCENE FROM "LE TRAIN. BLEU"

Anton Dolin

SCENE FROM "SKATING RINK"

SCENE FROM "LA CRÉATION DU MONDE"

As presented by les Ballets Suédois, Théâtre des Champs-Elysées, Paris, 1923

SCENE FROM "LA BOUTIQUE FANTASQUE"

Revival, as presented by Colonel W. de Basil's Ballets Russes.

SCENE FROM "LE TRICORNE"

Revival, as presented by Colonel W. de Basil's Ballets Russes

Leonide Massine   *Tamara Toumanova*

SCENE FROM "LES PRÉSAGES"

Photo: Raoul Barba, Monte Carlo

ALEXANDRA DANILOVA AND LEONIDE MASSINE IN "LE BEAU DANUBE"

LEONIDE MASSINE IN "UNION PACIFIC"

SCENE FROM "SYMPHONIE FANTASTIQUE", PART II.

Photo: Lipnitzki, Paris

A BATTLE SCENE FROM "THE GREEN TABLE"

SCENE FROM "THE BIG CITY"

Photo: *Anthony*

KURT JOOSS

SCENE FROM "THE GREEN TABLE", SC. I.

SCENE FROM "HEAR YE! HEAR YE!"
Ruth Page

Photo: Maurice Seymour, Chicago

Photo: Angus McBean

ANTONY TUDOR

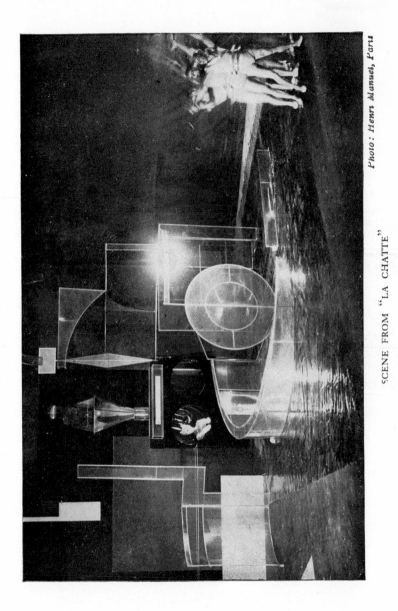

SCENE FROM "LA CHATTE"

Photo: Henri Manuel, Paris

SCENE FROM "THE GODS GO A-BEGGING"

As presented by the Vic-Wells Ballet

Photo: J. W. Debenham

SERGE LIFAR IN "ALEXANDRE LE GRAND"

FREDERICK   ASHTON

SERGE LIFAR IN "ICARE"

SCENE FROM "DAVID TRIOMPHANT"

SCENE FROM "THE LADY OF SHALOTT"

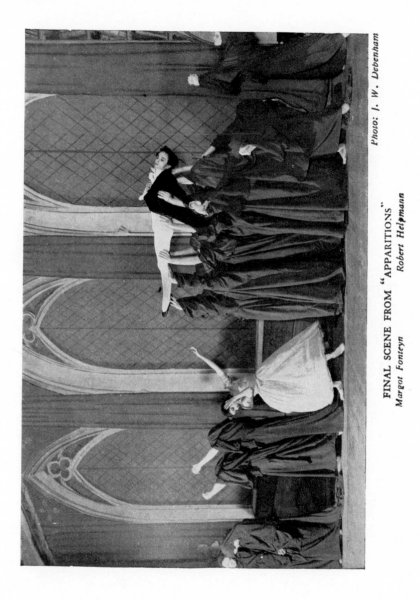

FINAL SCENE FROM "APPARITIONS."
Margot Fonteyn   Robert Helpmann

Photo: J. W. Debenham

SCENE FROM "THE DESCENT OF HEBE"

MAUDE LLOYD AND HUGH LAING IN "LE JARDIN AUX LILAS"

Photo: Paul Hansen

GEORGE BALANCHINE

SCENE FROM "THE RED POPPY", ACT I.

SCENE FROM "THE GOLDEN AGE"

SCENE FROM "THE FLAMES OF PARIS"

Coll.: Archw. Inter. de la Danse, Paris

LUIGI MANZOTTI

L UIGI MANZOTTI was born at Milan on February 2nd,
1835. His father was a merchant who dealt in fruit and
vegetables, and Luigi assisted him in the capacity of accountant.

His hobby was the theatre, for which he had an intense love,
and he delighted in watching the performances of the great actors
of his day, such as Salvini and Ernesto Rossi. In 1857 he fell in
love with a certain Rachele who was a pupil of Bocci, a well-
known mime. She induced him to leave his father's business and
learn to dance and mime.

He made his first appearance as a mime at the Canobbiana
Theatre, in 1858, in Borsi's *L'Incoronazione di Corinna in Roma*.
His efforts were applauded and he received other engagements
which took him to the Pergola Theatre, Florence, and the Alibert
Theatre, Rome. An impresario called Jacovacci engaged him for
the Argentina and Apollo Theatres and suggested that he should
devote himself to choreography. Manzotti accepted the suggestion and composed a one-act ballet, *La Morte di Masaniello,* in
which he took part as a mime. This production was praised and
he contrived other ballets: *Il Moro delle Antille, Michelangelo
e Rolla* (afterwards known as *Rolla*), *Pietro Micca,* and *Galileo
Galilei*.

Manzotti resided in Rome for fourteen years where he worked
assiduously to gain a knowledge of dance technique, music, literature, architecture, costume, history, and similar subjects which
might help him towards the realisation of his ambitions. In the
light of his later productions it is not unlikely that he planned to
achieve success by combining in his ballets the two elements which
were most likely to appeal to his fellow-countrymen—patriotism
and spectacular effect. He had seen the dawn of the Italian Risor-
gimento in 1848, and the reawakening of an intense pride in the
national achievements of the past, coupled with a profound belief
in the future growth of Italy; the love of spectacle was inherent.

In 1872 Manzotti returned to Milan to be *premier mime* in
Bianca di Nevers, a mediocre ballet by Pratesi, given at the Scala.

In 1875 Manzotti himself produced at the Scala a new version of his *Pietro Micca,* a ballet based on the story of the Italian patriot, and *Rolla.* The following year he went to Turin to reproduce *Rolla* and was also asked to devise a new ballet; this commission resulted in the ballet *Sieba,* which had a considerable success and was frequently revived abroad. Manzotti was engaged to reproduce *Sieba* at Lyon, and it was the industrial activity of that city which gave him the inspiration for *Excelsior,* a kind of Jules Verne ballet recording the progress of science and invention and glorifying its latest achievements. *Excelsior* achieved a wonderful success and brought the choreographer both fame and riches.

Dazzled by the flattery lavished upon him, Manzotti conceived the grandiose plan of producing a choreographic version of Dante's *Divina Commedia,* but eventually renounced the project.

Excelsior was followed in 1886 by *Amor,* a ballet on the power of love, illustrated with episodes from Italian history, and concluding with an appeal for universal peace.

The trilogy was completed in 1897 with *Sport,* a glorification of sport in every form: skating, fishing, boat-racing, horse-racing, cycling, fishing, duelling, big game hunting, athletics, and so on. This ballet was given forty-four times. Some idea of its popularity may be gleaned from the fact that the well-known firm of Liebig issued as an advertisement of their product a series of cards consisting of coloured reproductions of scenes from *Sport.* This was Manzotti's last important production for his energies gradually declined until his death on March 16th, 1905.

*

What did Manzotti contribute to the ballet? In reality he commercialised it; he transformed what had been a vehicle for poetic conception into a stupendous spectacle, where the aim first and last was theatrical effect. In *Amor* he used both elephants and horses on the stage.

Manzotti's ballets were not ballets in the present understanding of the term, but a succession of related episodes expressed in mime, varied with simple but effective *ensembles* by dancers, and striking processions by well-drilled supers.

He had the merit to impose a strict discipline upon his *corps de ballet.* He perfected those female cohorts which Filippo Taglioni had introduced into his *Révolte au Sérail,* and which have since attained their zenith in the Tiller Troupes and similar organisations.

But while Manzotti, generally speaking, subordinated the dance proper to spectacular effect, he invariably afforded opportunity for a few good *soli* or *pas de deux* executed by dancers of the first rank; for instance, the principal dancers in *Excelsior* were Giovannina Limido and Enrico Cecchetti. The themes were frankly propagandist. Manzotti was, in fact, the inventor of the propaganda ballet which later gave rise to such London productions as *Under One Flag* 1897, and *Our Crown,* 1901 (both given at the Empire Theatre); and *The Entente Cordiale* (1904), and *Under Two Flags* (1908), presented at the Alhambra Theatre.

SIEBA

Ballet in 6 Acts and 8 Scenes. Book: Luigi Manzotti. Music: Romualdo Marenco. Scenery: Alfredo Edel. Choreography: Luigi Manzotti. First produced: Turin, 1876.

CHARACTERS

Wotan
Surtur
Harold, King of Thule
Sieba, a Valkyrie
Kafur, Prime Minister of Thule
Meuhor, his friend and confidant
Holerut, chief of the Danish pirates
Cadmo, a Lusitanian youth, Holerut's slave
Obola, Danish pirate
Wolf, a Danish pirate

Valkyries, Alfings, Liasalfar (good spirits), Dohalfar (evil spirits), Soldiers of Thule, Gantars, Heroes of Wingolf and of Asgard, Scalds, Priests, Danish Pirates, Dancers, Musicians, Minstrels, Shield-Bearers, Mercenaries, Pages, Citizens, Water-Nymphs, Jugglers, etc.

Period: 640 A.D.

Act I. A ruined temple on the banks of the Teuta, close to the sea. Dawn.

Some Danish pirates are making ready for a raid, forging and sharpening weapons, preparing stores and rigging. Among the band is a Lusitanian youth, Cadmo, kidnapped from his mother when he was a baby. He tells the chief, Holerut, that two strangers desire speech with him.

Enter Kafur and Meuhor, the treacherous ministers of Harold, King of Thule. Kafur, taking advantage of Harold's war with the Gantars, wishes to seize the crown, and offers Holerut a large bribe if he will carry off Harold. The chief accepts.

Act II. The Gardens of the King's Palace at Thule. Along the sides of a wide avenue, tables have been placed ready for a banquet. In the distance can be seen the sea. Day.

Soldiers, summoned to defend their country, are seated at the tables. They feast and dance before the battle. Harold enters attended by his ministers. The soldiers are stirred by his presence and exhortations. But the King, aware of the enemy's strength, invokes the aid of Wotan.

The God grants Harold's prayer and resolves to send him his magic sword by one of his Valkyries. Sieba accepts the mission, although there is a risk of her falling in love with a mortal, with its attendant punishment.

She appears on the sea standing on a golden shell and gives Harold the magic sword. The King, amazed by Sieba's beauty, falls in love with her, while she, on her side, is conscious of a strange new emotion. Sieba wishes to leave, but Surtur, Wotan's rival, urges her to join in the dances.

Suddenly a messenger arrives with news of the enemy's approach. The soldiers seize their weapons and prepare for battle. Harold is about to follow when, seeing Sieba, he declares his love. Fearful, she tries to leave, but Surtur urges her to stay. Then Harold rushes to join his troops. Sieba, distracted by Surtur, hastens after him.

Act III. The King's camp. To the left is Harold's tent; to the right that of Kafur.

Cadmo steals to Kafur's tent and informs the minister that all is ready. He leaves and the two ministers creep towards the King's tent. Finding Harold asleep, Kafur seizes the magic sword and cries "I shall be King." The ministers depart.

Sieba enters. She goes to Harold's tent and, bending over the King, kisses him. Harold awakes and, seeing the object of his thoughts before him, clasps the Valkyrie in his arms. Meanwhile the pirates glide through the trees, led by Kafur, who points out the King's tent. Sieba, conscious of having violated her oath, is fearful of the consequences and hurries away. Harold is about to follow in pursuit, when the conspirators seize the King and carry him off.

Trumpets give warning of the Gantors' approach, and officers run up to warn the King, who, to their consternation, cannot be found. Kafur enters and, declaring that the King has forsaken his troops, offers to lead them against the enemy. The soldiers, encouraged, follow the minister.

Act IV. Valhalla with Wotan enthroned.

Sieba returns, hoping that her sin has remained undiscovered. But Wotan, gazing sternly upon her, orders Sieba to take off her armour of which she is unworthy. She withdraws.

The Valkyries and Heroes do homage to Wotan, who orders Sieba to return and receive sentence. He condemns her to the darkness and horror of the pit of serpents.

Act V. Scene I. Askur—the Pit of Serpents.

Sieba is terrorised by Surtur and his demons.

Act V. Scene II. A Grotto leading to Askur. In the distance, through a cleft in the rocks, can be seen the sea.

Sieba emerges from the fearsome pit and attempts to throw herself into the sea. Surtur tries to drag her back, but Wotan sets her free, for she is destined to live among mortals.

Seeing a ship, Sieba waves her scarf. A small boat appears and Cadmo steps from it. She tells him her story and begs him to take her to King Harold. Cadmo tells her that the King is a prisoner on the distant vessel. She enlists the youth's help and together they row out towards the ship.

Act VI. Scene I. The hold of Holerut's ship.

The pirates are waiting for Kafur to bring them their reward. Harold emerges from his den to breathe the fresh air. Hearing footsteps he retires.

Sieba enters and fascinates the pirates. While they toast her beauty a distant horn is heard. Holerut, hearing Kafur's agreed signal, orders his men to go with him and receive the minister.

Cadmo and Sieba, left alone, search for Harold. They near

his hiding place when Kafur and the pirates return. The minister, having vanquished his enemies with the magic sword, has decided to proclaim himself King, and wishes Cadmo to kill Harold.

When Cadmo refuses, Holerut rushes to do the deed himself. Sieba tries to defend the King, but is thrown aside. Cadmo opens the trapdoor when Harold emerges.

Sieba flings herself into his arms while the ministers hide their faces. She points out the traitors who have betrayed him. Harold tears away Kafur's cloak and, recognising his minister, calls down upon him the curse of Wotan. Kafur, enraged, orders Holerut to kill the King. But Sieba seizes the magic sword and forces the pirate to stand back.

Suddenly the sky darkens and a vivid flash of lightning almost strikes the ship. The terrified pirates rush on deck. Kafur orders Meuhor to prepare to leave.

Cadmo, pretending to lower the boats, brings one near a port-hole, through which he climbs into the ship and urges Sieba and Harold to escape. At this point, Kafur returns and attempts to stay the fugitives, but Sieba wounds him with a sword-thrust.

Cadmo is about to leap into the boat when he is attacked by Holerut. After a tense struggle the chief is hurled to the deck and the youth, finding the boat gone, leaps into the sea. Kafur tries to leave but, overcome with exhaustion, falls into Meuhor's arms. Holerut curses with rage when suddenly the ship shivers, as if it had struck a rock, and begins to sink.

Act VI. Scene II. The City of Thule decorated for Harold's return.

The people of Thule, having learned of Kafur's villainy, rejoice at the return of their rightful King, who presents to them his wife Sieba, who has sacrificed all for love, and to whom he owes his life.

EXCELSIOR

Ballet in 6 Parts and 12 Scenes. Book: Luigi Manzotti. Music: Romualdo Marenco. Scenery and costumes: Alfredo Edel. Choreography: Luigi Manzotti. First produced: Teatro alla Scala, Milan, January 11th, 1881.

CHARACTERS

Light	MLLE. BICE VERGANI
The Spirit of Darkness	M. CARLO MONTANARA

Civilisation	MLLE. ROSINA VIALE
Papin	M. CARLO COPPI
Volta	M. ANGELO CUCCOLI
George, an inn-keeper	M. CESARE RAZZANI
Cunigonda, his wife	MLLE. GIUSEPPINA GENINAZZI
Valentine, a boatman, their son . .	M. CESARE COPPINI
Laura, his sister	MLLE. GILDA MAY
Fanny, betrothed to Valentine and daughter of	MLLE. GIULIA HOFSCHULLER
William, a farmer	M. LUIGI RADICE
Fritz, a boatman	M. ACHILLE BALBIANI
An Italian Engineer	M. CARLO COPPI
A French Engineer	M. CESARE RAZZINI
An Italian Second Engineer . . .	M. ANGELO CUCCOLI
A French Second Engineer . . .	M. CESARE VISMARA
An Italian Foreman-Miner . . .	M. ACHILLE BALBIANI
A French Foreman-Miner . . .	M. LUIGI RADICE

The Genii of Civilisation, Perseverance, Invention, Concord, Fame, Force, Glory, Science, Agriculture, Industry, Valour, Union. Boatmen, Peasants, Musicians, Postillions, Telegraph-messengers, Engineers, Miners, Navvies, Europeans, Asiatics, Africans, Americans, Sailors, Officers, etc.

Part I. Scene I. A Spanish town in ruins. A bell tolls for those about to be burnt at the stake.

The Spirit of Darkness rejoices, for at his feet lies a woman, Light, in chains. Gradually she revives, breaks her chains, and informs the Spirit of Darkness that his reign is over and that the future belongs to her.

Part I. Scene II. The abode of Genius and Light. The walls are inscribed in gold with the names of those associated with the greatest achievements.

Science, Power, Industry, Love, Civilisation, Perseverance, Union, Concord, Courage, Glory, Invention, the Fine Arts, Agriculture, Commerce—all inhabit this abode. Civilisation and the Spirit of Light meet in triumph.

Part II. Scene I. A village on the banks of the Weser. To the left a tavern; to the right, a post-house.

The inn-keeper and his wife greet their son, Valentine, a boat-man who has won all the prizes at the regattas. His betrothed and his friends congratulate him and drink his health. But the unsuccessful competitors are downcast and do not care to join in the rejoicings. A quarrel is averted by the arrival of a party of postillions and country lasses who dance a mazurka.

The dance concluded the losers propose a new trial of strength, which Valentine accepts. As they go to the river the Spirit of Darkness draws their attention to a strange craft, the invention of Papin, which moves by itself. He declares it to be inhabited by demons, and that it will ruin their trade. The boatmen seize their weapons and smash the steam-boat. The Spirit of Darkness is triumphant; but Light appears, saves Papin, and declares that his invention will attain full success at the hands of Watt and Fulton.

Part II. Scene II. The Brooklyn Viaduct, New York.

Two promontories are connected by an iron bridge over which express trains pass, while a steamer forges through the stormy sea below.

Part III. Scene I. Volta's laboratory at Como.

Volta is seen engaged in various experiments. After some fail-ures an electric spark appears. He kneels and offers thanks to God.

The Spirit of Darkness attempts to destroy the battery but is hurled backwards by an electric shock. Light shows Volta the benefits of this discovery and the curtain descends to the ringing of electric bells.

Part III. Scene II. Telegraph Square, Washington.

Light and the Spirit of Darkness are borne to the Central Tele-graph Office, Washington. Little telegraph-messengers pour out of the office. Light is triumphant, but the Spirit of Darkness swears vengeance.

Part IV. Scene I. A desert simoom.

Clouds of sand arise and hold up a caravan. Robbers attack the caravan and pillage it. The wayfarers struggle vainly against the storm and gradually all are buried beneath the sand. The Spirit of Darkness arises in triumph, but Light points to the horizon.

Part IV. Scene II. The Isthmus of Suez.

The desert is replaced by the Suez Canal along which pass numerous vessels. In the meantime there are great festivities in honour of De Lesseps's achievement.

Part V. Scene I. The Tunnelling of Mount Cenis.

The Spirit of Darkness watches in anger the work of tunnelling go forward. The mine is ready and fired, but the Italian engineer's men do not hear the pickaxes of the French. There is consternation.

A distant detonation is heard and an engineer listens intently. He hears the French at work and orders his own men to attack their end of the tunnel. Soon Mount Cenis is pierced and the French and Italians embrace in triumph. Light glories in the achievement.

Part V. Scene II. A bust of De Lesseps supported by Fames.

The Spirit of Darkness attempts to flee, but Light tells him that it is his turn to tremble. Clouds fill the stage and, through them, all the nations are seen at peace. At a gesture from Light, the earth opens and engulfs the Spirit of Darkness.

Part VI. Scene I. The clouds vanish and there follows a Grand Festival of the Nations.

Part VI. Scene II. Apotheosis of Light and Peace.

*

Excelsior was the most popular of all Manzotti's ballets. It was given 103 times during the year 1881, the hundredth performance being on October 29th. It was revived at the Scala in 1883, 1888, and 1894 when 31, 45, and 27 performances respectively were given. The ballet was given in many other Italian theatres and was reproduced at the principal European theatres with considerable success.

Excelsior was first produced at London, at Her Majesty's Theatre, on May 22nd, 1885, the production being by Carlo Coppi, while the principal dancers were Giovannina Limido and Enrico Cecchetti.

The critic of the *Illustrated Sporting and Dramatic News*[1] gives an interesting account of the ballet, although written in a half-humorous vein.

[1] August 1st, 1885.

"At the outset we have Light in chains, and oppressed by Darkness—a kind of pantomimic Iago given to mephistophelian posturing and folded arms. Light having shattered her chains, and astonished the oppressor considerably, announces 'the grand mission of Enlightenment and Civilisation' on the light fantastic toe. Result: a change of scene to 'The Temple of Light—the abode of Genius and Science,' a 'Grand Ballabile,' in which the stage is thronged with brilliant figures: the fall of the act drop, and a dreary interval of 15 minutes.

"Act the Second opens with a view of a village on the banks of the River Weser. Here Dionisio Papin . . . appears in the character of the pioneer of steam navigation. . . . Of course Darkness, with a due amount of mephistophelian attitude, urges the boatmen of the Weser to destroy the new invention, and, of course, Light, arising from the waves, changes the scene to the tableau of 'Steam Power in all its Glory,' a suspension bridge with two trains running over it, and a steamer passing beneath.

"Then we have what I thought was the laboratory of Faust, but what turned out to be that of Alessandro Volta at Como. The *ballerino* entrusted with the part of Volta renders it somewhat remarkable by quivering like a jelly during the whole of the time that he is on the stage. . . . With much quivering he indicates his discovery of the pile that bears his name. He then goes out personally to proclaim this result to the world at large, and Darkness, more mephistophelian than ever, steals on and 'endeavours in vain to destroy the great discovery.' He ignominiously burns his fingers . . . and lo! the scene changes to 'The First Electric Telegraph Office at Washington.'

"Here we have another 'Grand Ballabile' of the telegraph-messengers. Such dainty messengers. . . . A picturesque attack upon a caravan in the desert by Arab robbers, mounted on real horses, would have gladdened the heart of George Sanger, but the simoom subsequently enveloping the combatants was rather too obviously the product of the loom. The 'Inauguration of the Suez Canal' was remarkable for being accomplished to the accompaniment of a 'Grand Egyptian Ballabile,' excellently staged, and a clever 'Allegorical Pas de Cinq,' typifying 'The Emancipation of Slavery.'

"The third act shows the piercing of 'The Tunnel of Mount Cenis,' presented with a degree of realism and a working up of the excitement resulting in thunders of applause, 'The Temple of All Nations,' with yet another 'Grand Ballabile', and the vanquishing of Darkness for good and all by Light, and a final 'Apotheosis' . . .

"The lean and lissom *primo ballerino* Signor Enrico Cecchetti not only fairly astounds by his wondrous pirouetting, but dances throughout in such finished and graceful style as fairly to conquer the prejudices I have generally entertained against the masculine ballet dancer. In the plump and pleasing *prima ballerina,* Signora Adelina Rossi, he has a worthy co-adjutor."

A feature of particular interest in the London production was the appearance of Kate Vaughan, who danced a Turkish Dance in the Suez episode. She proved a great attraction. A contemporary says of her. "She does not beat the stage with her feet; she floats about it. Others perplex themselves with effort; she glides unconsciously. With her it is not a dance but a dream. And all London goes to see it."

A curious survival of the popularity of *Excelsior* is the *pas de deux* expressive of the contest between Darkness and Light, which, rendered by marionettes, still figures in the repertory of Dr. Podrecca's famous *Teatro dei Piccoli.*

AMOR

Ballet in 2 Parts and 16 Scenes. Book: Luigi Manzotti. Music: Romualdo Marenco. Scenery and costumes: Alfredo Edel. Choreography: Luigi Manzotti. First produced: Teatro alla Scala, Milan, February 17th, 1886.

Part I. Scene I. Chaos.

The Elements are seen struggling with one another. Gradually they are dominated by a new force—Love.

Part I. Scene II. Love introduces Order into the Universe.

At a sign from Love the glowing earth is cooled and becomes covered with trees and flowers. Animals come into being, bears and monkeys dance, stars appear in the sky, and the sun bursts into radiance.

Part I. Scene III. The First Kiss.

Enter Man, the Lord of Creation, who gazes in mingled astonishment and fear upon the illimitable marvels of Nature. The sun sets and feeling tired he goes to sleep. On awakening he finds near him a woman, who has been created to be his companion. Love makes each enamoured of the other.

Part I. Scene IV. The Arrival of other Human Beings.

From their union humanity is born. Men and women are seen travelling towards other climes. Love guides them and teaches them that God is the source of all good things.

Part I. Scene V. The First Labour of Man.

Love causes the Spirits of the various Arts to appear to the mortals and teach them the properties of different metals and how to extract them from the earth.

Part I. Scene VI. Parnassus.

From the symbolical mountains of Parnassus, where reside Apollo and the Muses, poetic inspirations flow into the world. Love teaches men to become artists and poets.

Part I. Scene VII. The Pantheon of Arts in Greece.

Here are seen all the masterpieces of Greek sculpture. All the Greek poets are present followed by the personages they have created. After a dance by the Spirit of the Arts the Pantheon falls into ruins and Greece succumbs to Roman domination.

Part I. Scene VIII. The Triumph of Caesar.

Rome is seen in all its splendour. Julius Caesar is to pass down the Via Sacra on his way to the Capitol to render thanks to the Immortal Gods.

Brutus wishes to overthrow Caesar and quarrels with Antony, who is Caesar's friend. Calpurnia, Caesar's wife, helped by Love, calms the contestants.

The triumphal procession comes into view; monarchs of the vanquished races follow the car in which Caesar is seated upon a throne.

Part II. Scene I. The Temple of Venus, Rome.

A number of people are seen drinking and making merry. The Guards bring to the Emperor Galerius a young Christian girl. He is smitten with her. In the distance the Christians can be heard singing hymns. The girl kneels and prays. She is recognised as a follower of the new religion.

Some Christians enter, among them being the girl's father. The crowd mock and beat them. They are asked to renounce their religion and, when they refuse, the revellers demand that they shall be thrown to the lions. The Christians depart singing. The crowd resume their orgy.

Part II. Scene II. The Destruction of Rome.

The orgy is interrupted by Love. Armed with a sword he entreats the Romans to rise in defence of their country, which is invaded by barbarians. Nobody heeds his appeal.

The flames of the fire which is destroying Rome are seen in the distance. The barbarians arrive and invade the Temple.

Part II. Scene III. Barbarossa.

The smoke of the fire drifts away to reveal a panorama of the Alps. Barbarossa arrives at Susa and is well received by the inhabitants who hope to save their town. The greatest ladies of Susa offer him the Town Banner in submission, but he tears it to pieces and, dismissing them, swears that he will destroy Milan and every town in the Lombard League. The soldiers and camp-followers dance and finally depart.

Love appears and encourages the peasants and inhabitants to resist the invader, assuring them that Barbarossa will fail in his plans.

Part II. Scene IV. The Lombard League at Pontida.

The representatives of the various towns in the Lombard League assemble at Pontida and elect as their chief the Marquis Obizzo di Malaspina. A bishop blesses the company. The Marquis asks all present to swear that they will resist Barbarossa to the last. They take the oath to fight Barbarossa and rebuild Milan. Then they depart, taking with them the Carroccio.

Part II. Scene V. On the road to Legnano.

The bells of the villages peal, for everyone is taking up arms. One of the representatives of Milan is brought in, fatally wounded. His wife sends her only son to take the place of his father. As the latter expires the trumpets sound in honour of victory.

Part II. Scene VI. The Victory of Legnano.

Now is seen the Lombard plain and in the middle of it the Carroccio flanked with the banners of the towns of Lombardy; over all waves the red cross of Milan. The field is strewn with the wreckage of the battle. The invaders are retiring in the distance.

Part II. Scene VII. Liberty brings joy into the World.

Liberty brings light and joy into the world.

Part II. Scene VIII. The Triumph of Love.

The Gods celebrate the triumph of Love.

*

Amor was given 44 times in 1886. It was revived in 1902 when it achieved a total of 48 performances.

MARIQUITA

MARIQUITA, said to have been of Italian extraction, was born near Algiers in the eighteen-thirties. While still quite a young child she became a member of a band of strolling players, and at the age of seven arrived in Paris. In 1845 she played at the Funambules, then renowned for its association with the famous mime, Deburau.

In 1855 Mariquita was engaged at the Bouffes Parisiens and from there she went to the Théâtre de la Porte St. Martin, at which latter theatre she created many dancing roles in plays and eventually became the wife of the manager, Marc Fournier. She achieved a considerable reputation as a character dancer.

Later, Mariquita was appointed *maîtresse de ballet* at the Gaité and afterwards filled the same post at the Folies-Bergère. In 1898 she was appointed *maîtresse de ballet* at the Opéra Comique, a post she filled for twenty-two years; she was also responsible for the training of the *corps de ballet* attached to that theatre and proved herself to be an admirable teacher.

She arranged the dances in *Aphrodite, Marouf, La Danseuse de Pompéi,* and in many well-known operas. She also devised several ballets, one of the most popular of which was *Javotte.*

Mariquita died at Paris on October 7th, 1922.

JAVOTTE

Ballet in 1 Act and 3 Scenes. Book: J. L. Croze. Music: Camille Saint-Saëns. Scenery: Amable. Costumes: Marcel Multzer. Choreography: Mariquita. First produced: Grand Theatre, Lyon, December 3rd, 1896.

CHARACTERS

Jean	MM. SOYER DE TONDEUR
Javotte's Father	BURGAT
The Village Constable	FERRENBACH

Judges	{ BRIALOU { PIANAZZI
The Lord of the Manor	
Javotte	MLLES. ELISA DAMIANI
Her Mother	DUMONT
Three Young Girls	{ A. PEUGET { ALICE CHERY { VARASI

Peasant Girls, Villagers.

Scene I. The village square decked with flowers and greenery. To the left, near a tree, is a bench; to the right, a platform. In the background is a church and belfry, which can be seen above the tree-tops.

It is a holiday and dancing couples fill the stage. Some young girls invite Jean, who is seated on the bench, to dance. But he declines as he is waiting for his sweetheart, Javotte. Tired of their importunities he strolls among the trees.

Javotte's parents arrive in a great rage, asking everyone if they have seen their daughter, but to no avail. A constable offers to find Javotte and they follow at his heels.

Jean returns and Javotte, breathless, runs to his arms. A bourrée begins in which the lovers take their part. Suddenly the church bell announces the hour of vespers. The dances cease and the young men and girls pray. The scene is empty save for Javotte and Jean, and a group of men drinking at a table.

Jean, noticing that his sweetheart is preoccupied, asks her what is the matter. She confesses that she has come out against her parents' wishes, and, full of remorse, begins to cry.

Noticing her parents she goes towards them, while Jean slips away. Her father wishes to beat her, but Javotte confesses her fault and is forgiven.

Jean watches his sweetheart being escorted home by her parents. He departs when the dances recommence.

Scene II. A room in the house of Javotte's parents.

Javotte enters with her parents. Her mother gives her various household tasks to do and tells her that, as a punishment for disobedience, she must work while they go and enjoy themselves at the festival. Javotte's father shuts the window and then the parents leave, after carefully double-locking the door.

Javotte, left to herself, begins to clean the dishes but drops a plate and breaks it. She takes from her sash a posy which Jean has given her and presses it to her lips. "Ah," she thinks, "how I should love to dance." She dances a few steps, but her conscience pricks her and she resumes her work.

Now she sits at her spinning-wheel but, with her mind on dancing, the thread breaks. Then she tries to knit, but the impulse to dance is too strong and she begins to dance gaily.

Suddenly there is a knock on the window. She goes to see what it is and finds it is Jean, who has climbed up on the sill. The reunited lovers dance for joy. Then Javotte becomes the hostess and shows him the picture, clock, and other articles in the room. Again they dance madly, knocking over anything that is in their path. Jean whispers words of love and the lovers dance passionately to a slow waltz theme.

Jean urges his sweetheart to return to the ball and, one after the other, they leave by the window. Hardly have they gone when the parents return, in festive mood. They are amazed to find the room in disorder and the prisoner flown—evidently by the window.

There is a knock on the door and the constable enters. He announces that he has found Javotte and her young man. The parents prepare to administer correction, but the couple the constable pushes towards them are strangers!

Furious at what they believe to be an ill-timed joke, the parents belabour the constable with stick and broom.

Scene III. Same as Scene I. Night has fallen and the square is lit with venetian lanterns.

The great event of the day is about to take place—the election of the Queen of the Ball. This title is to be awarded to the best *danseuse,* who will also receive a money prize and gifts presented by the lord of the manor.

There are three competitors, but after they have danced the judges find themselves unable to agree. Jean and Javotte arrive and there are loud cries for Javotte to dance. She does so and is proclaimed Queen of the Ball.

At this moment the parents return in company with the constable, with whom they have made peace. They search for Jean and Javotte who, with the assistance of their friends, play hide and seek behind their backs. At last they are caught.

The constable upbraids Javotte for having disobeyed her parents, and censures Jean for having incited her to do so.

Jean acknowledges his fault and begs to be allowed to marry Javotte, whom he loves so dearly. The father is indignant, but his wife reminds him that Jean is a hard-working young man, while Javotte's prize will be a great help towards setting-up house. Finally the father gives his consent and unites Javotte and Jean.

The lord of the manor and his family arrive. He congratulates the lovers and begs them to dance. There is a *pas de deux* and the ballet ends with a gay *ensemble* and a procession in which Javotte is triumphantly borne shoulder-high.

*

Javotte was produced at the Opera, Paris, on February 5th, 1909; it is a popular ballet and still figures in the repertory.

NICHOLAS LEGAT

NICHOLAS GUSTAVOVICH LEGAT was born at Moscow on December 27th, 1869. His father, of mixed French and Swedish descent, was *premier danseur* at the Bolshoy Theatre, Moscow, and instructor in classical ballet to that branch of the Imperial Ballet; his mother, a Russian, was a dancer at the same theatre.

Nicholas entered the Imperial School of Ballet, Moscow, in 1880. He began his studies under Volkov and early gained the Didelot Scholarship. In 1888 he completed school with the rank of *premier danseur* and continued his studies under his father and the famous pedant, Johannsen. Later on, when the latter retired through ill-health, Legat replaced him as director of the Class of Perfection.

Legat made his *début* in 1887 in a *pas de deux* with M. K. Andersen, and danced with most of the famous *ballerine* of his day, achieving considerable fame both as dancer and mime. In 1896 he receives the coveted title of Soloist to His Majesty.

Legat was very musical and studied to good purpose both the violin and the piano. He also had a very definite talent for drawing, which he sometimes exercised in caricaturing his fellow-dancers. A collection of these under the title *Russky Balet v Karikatura* was published at St. Petersburg in 1891. He was none the less interested in all forms of sport, in several branches of which he was himself an expert.

He was twice married, first to A. I. Tchumakova, a dancer at the Maryinsky Theatre, St. Petersburg; second, to N. A. Nicolaeva, a *ballerina* of the Bolshoy Theatre, Moscow.

Apart from his accomplishments as dancer and teacher, Legat composed a great number of dances and several ballets, among which latter may be mentioned *The Blood Red Flower, The Two Thieves,* and *The White Lily.* He also revived several earlier ballets, for instance: *The Fairy Doll, The Talisman, Barbe-Bleue,* and *The Magic Flute.*

At the period of the Russian Revolution, Legat was attached to the Bolshoy Theatre, Moscow, as *maître de ballet* and instructor to the senior class of classical ballet. In 1922 Legat suffered from ill-health and he and his wife were granted permission to leave Russia. The next year saw them in London when they opened a School of Dancing at Cricklewood, later transferred to Baron's Court.

Legat died at London on January 24th, 1937.

THE BLOOD-RED FLOWER

Fantastic Ballet in 6 Scenes. Book: Marzhetsky, adapted from the story by S. T. Axsakhov. Music: F. A. Hartmann. Choreography: Nicholas Legat. Scenery and Costumes: C. A. Korovine.

CHARACTERS

Marco Lugano, a rich Venetian merchant
Annunziata ⎫
Flaminia ⎬ his daughters
Angelica   ⎭
Olivia Solarino, a distant relative of Marco Lugano
Orsino del Sato   ⎫
Lucentio Fabiani ⎬ *fiancés* of the two elder daughters
A Monster
A Prince
Vasiano Gennaro, a merchant
Mustapha ⎫
Ben Kyram ⎬ Algerian merchants
Tranio Biondello, harbour-master
Giovanni Podesta, Lugano's man of business
Abu-Bekr, a notary
A Ship's Captain
Master of Ceremonies
An Old Dervish
A Jew
A Slave of Abu-Bekr
       Courtiers, Warriors, Merchants, Slaves, Sailors,
               Troubadours.

Scene I. A part of the merchants' harbour at Venice. The distant horizon is half-veiled in a bluish mist. A few ships are seen anchored close to the quay, which is crowded with slaves, sailors, flower-sellers, charlatans, pilgrims, and so on.

A captain and several sailors go to Lugano's house and are met by Podesta, who gives the captain money and tells him that the merchant will receive him shortly. Lugano appears and is saluted by the captain, who tells him that the ship is ready and only awaits the order to sail.

Lugano goes up the ship's gangway followed by the captain. Podesta wishes to follow, but the sailors ask him to reward their labours with money for wine. Podesta agrees, wine appears, as if by magic, and a toast is drunk to their benefactor. The sailors invite him to witness their dances. He consents and sits on the steps of Lugano's house, accompanied by several musicians armed with lutes and mandolines. The sailors invite the flower-girls to join them in a furlana.

Lugano returns and instructs Podesta to watch over everything during his absence. Annunziata and Flaminia, escorted by Olivia di Solarino, approach their father; he asks them what they would like him to bring them back. The first asks for a tiara, jewels, and a girdle; the second for ear-rings and a jewelled fan. He promises to bring them and asks where Angelica is. They are about to seek for her when she enters. Lugano hides behind the elder daughters and Angelica, unable to see her father, is about to leave when he catches her hand and asks her why she is so late.

She tells him that she could not recover from a dreadful dream which haunted her during the night. "I saw a monster who wished to kiss me. I was so terrified that I swooned. When I awoke I found myself in a beautiful garden. Before me was a bush bearing a single flower of magical beauty. I stretched out my hand towards it and awoke."

Lugano soothes Angelica and tells her that she must not distress herself over a dream, and now, what would she like him to bring her for a present.

"Bring me the flower I saw in my dream," she replies.

Lugano asks her where he can find a flower she saw in a dream. But when she insists he agrees to do his utmost to gratify her wish.

In the meantime the sailors have gone on board their ship, while the captain has received a pass from the harbour-master and followed them.

Lugano kisses his daughters, bids Olivia good-bye, and bows to the servants. He goes on board, the gangway is removed, the sails unfurled, the anchor raised. Hats, scarves and cloaks are waved in the air as the ship glides away.

Scene II. A bazaar in an Eastern town. Tents and stalls are arranged to form a square. In the distance can be seen crooked streets and dazzling minarets. In the left foreground is a canopy beneath which sits Abu-Bekr. To the right are snake-charmers. In the middle of the square all is activity. Some passers-by are choosing shawls, others gold articles; one is waiting for a tailor to mend his dressing gown, another is having his head shaved. At one of the tents several people are drinking coffee.

Two merchants come to Abu-Bekr to draw up an agreement. Several persons look at the snake-charmers and ask them to give their performance. One collects money while the other fetches a number of *Odalisques* who dance a veil dance. In the centre of the group is a snake-charmer who plays before a small basket. A snake appears from it and sways its head in rhythm to the music. An assistant takes the snake and hangs it round his neck. The dancing grows wilder. Suddenly the man throws the snake back into the basket and the dancing abruptly ends.

Through the square passes a religious procession, led by a horseman in white bearing a white flag. There is a strange music of wailing pipes and drums which gradually dies away as the procession fades into the distance. Everyone runs towards the procession. The sellers have forgotten their customers; the latter have left behind their purchases.

Out of the crowd comes Lugano with several Algerian merchants. They approach Abu-Bekr and gradually business is resumed. When Lugano has completed his business with Abu-Bekr he tells him of the flower desired by his youngest daughter. The merchants express surprise, but Abu-Bekr says he knows of a dervish who may be able to say where the flower can be obtained. He sends for the slave.

Some strolling players appear and ask Lugano to witness their dances. The first is danced by men and women bearing branches of coconut palm, and finishes with a picturesque group about a palm tree. Next comes a dance by wild men. Then a few women dance with fans. Several men join them with peacock feathers in their hands. While dancing they balance the feathers and the women try to knock them over with their fans, which they succeed in doing at the end of the dance. Afterwards several men dance with curved swords. Their dance is interrupted by a girl who bears flowers on long stalks which she plants in the ground, then she dances round them and falls on her knees. One by one the warriors jump towards her and try to knock over a flower with a single stroke of their swords. The first to be successful takes the dancer.

At this point the dervish arrives. Lugano describes the flower he seeks. The dervish tells him of an island surrounded by great rocks, on which there is a beautiful garden, where the flower desired may be found. Lugano rewards the dervish, throws money to the dancers, bids the merchants farewell, and departs.

A slave-dealer approaches the merchants and offers them two male and two female slaves. They dance and one merchant is so pleased that he buys all four. The leader of the dance troupe, ill-pleased at the dealer's success, orders his company to dance, and the curtain falls at the height of their exertions.

Scene III. A beautiful, fairy-like garden. Aromatic grasses are mingled with narcissi, roses, orchids, and tulips, which form a gigantic bank of flowers. Here and there are bright red peonies. In other parts are ugly cacti, extraordinary trees, and straggling lianas.

In the depths of this silent garden, high up, is a prominent green bush, on which can be seen a broken branch and not one flower. To the right is a marble staircase, leading to a castle.

Lugano enters with Angelica who bears a golden ewer containing a flower. Both peer from side to side; the latter with excited interest, the former with apprehension. He takes her to the bush and points to where he plucked the flower.

"As I did so," he declares, "there was a clap of thunder and I fell unconscious. When I opened my eyes I saw a dreadful monster who called me a thief and declared I must die. But when I explained that I only picked the flower for my favourite daughter, the monster agreed to let me go, on the condition that I would induce you to live with him on the island. If you refused, then I had to promise that I would return. You, my darling, agreed to save your father."

Lugano blesses Angelica and expresses the wish that she will soon return home, then departs, sad at heart.

Angelica takes the flower from the ewer and places it by the broken stem; they join immediately. At the same time the monster quietly descends the staircase and, amazed at Angelica's beauty, remains on the last step.

Angelica continues to inspect the garden. Raising her head she sees the monster, who politely invites her to visit the castle. But she falls unconscious. The monster, cursing his ugliness, kneels beside Angelica and kisses her dress. Then he commands the flowers to weave sweet dreams for her delight.

The bush parts and the flower becomes a handsome cavalier. The other flowers also come to life. In her dream Angelica sees herself surrounded by flowers and being invited by the cavalier to take part in the dance. The whole flower bed begins to move, forming a beautiful bouquet, in the centre of which is Angelica and her cavalier.

The flowers form groups which gradually change. Meanwhile, Angelica dances with her cavalier, occasionally glancing up at the monster who stands at the head of the staircase. Gradually she becomes accustomed to his presence. At the end of the *adage* there is an *ensemble* by the flowers, which represents different types of dancing. The peonies court the roses and lilies; the narcissi annoy some other flowers, who shyly close up at each touch; the tulips delight in their smart appearance; the ivy weaves about everyone; the orchids run about or join in the groups. The flowers form a garland and now enters the cavalier. The orchids follow him and dance their own dance. When the cacti join in, all the other dancers move away. During Angelica's solo the cacti ring little blue-bells; gradually the flowers surround her and finish with a lively galop, after which they resume their original places.

The monster enters the castle and Angelica, still asleep, remains alone. Presently she wakes and, still under the influence of the dream, runs to the bush where glows the flower. Then she mounts the steps and, seeing the monster shyly approaching, asks if he will show her the castle. He kneels and begs her to consider him her slave.

Scene IV. A magnificent but gloomy hall in Lugano's house. Near one wall, part of which is covered by a Persian rug, can be seen a chess-table and other objects collected by the merchant during his Eastern travels.

Troubadours are playing on lutes, to which music the company dance, including the two daughters and their *fiancés*. But Lugano is sad at Angelica's absence.

Suddenly, to everyone's surprise, she enters. Lugano faints. But Angelica kisses him and with the assistance of her sisters, restores him to consciousness. Her father is overjoyed and asks her about the island. She tells him that the monster is very kind to her and has given her a ring which she only has to change from one finger to another to be transported whither she will.

Everyone congratulates her, thinking she has returned for good.

Lugano's neighbours enter with their daughters and sons and share in the general happiness. Retainers bring in refreshments and the young people begin to dance.

The guests ask Angelica to dance. She does so and charms all with her grace and skill. Her sisters and their *fiancés,* accompanied by some of the guests, dance different figures about her. Meanwhile Angelica sees in the depths of the hall a vision of the lovely garden, where, close to the bush, the monster lies on the ground, gasping for breath and imploring her return. (*The vision is seen by her alone.*)

Quickly she runs to her father and announces her immediate return. The monster is unhappy and may die. Lugano begs her to stay. Her sisters join their entreaties. But Angelica refuses. She changes her ring and disappears. Everyone seeks in vain for her. Lugano, broken-hearted, sinks back in his chair.

Scene V. Same as Scene III.

Beside the bush with the blood-red flower lies the monster motionless. Angelica runs in and seeing him, as she thinks, asleep, tries to wake him, but in vain. Full of pity for the monster she bends down and kisses him.

Immediately he changes into a handsome young prince who thanks her warmly for having freed him from the enchantment of a magician. He asks Angelica to be his wife. She consents and he leads her into the castle.

Scene VI. A white marble hall with colonnades stretching into the distance where they meet another colonnade set at right angles. Through the arches can be seen a magnificent staircase leading into the hall. At the right is a golden throne, flanked by chairs.

Heralds blow fanfares. The Prince and Angelica, followed by a splendid retinue, enter the hall. Everyone bows to the Prince and his bride and wishes them happiness.

Angelica remembers her father and sisters and tells the Prince that she is sorry they are not present. The Prince points to the ring. She changes it from one finger to another, and Lugano with his two daughters and their *fiancés* appear before her. Lugano is overjoyed at being restored to his daughter. Angelica presents her father to the Prince and explains how the enchantment was broken.

The Prince invites Lugano to sit beside him. The Master of Ceremonies receives permission for the festival to begin. A ball commences in which all the company takes part. On this gay scene the curtain falls.

*

A ballet in 7 scenes, called *The Beauty and the Beast,* with a similar theme to *The Blood-Red Flower,* was produced at the Alhambra Theatre, London, in 1898. The music was by Georges Jacobi, the choreography by Carlo Coppi. The cast was as follows: Miss Casaboni (*Beauty*), Miss Julie Seale (*The Beast*), and Signor Egidio Rossi (*the Merchant*); the *première danseuse* was Cecilia Cerri.

LEO STAATS

LEO STAATS was born in 1877. He studied dancing under Francis Mérante, a dancer at the Opéra, Paris, and is said to have made his *début* when still a child on January 7th, 1887. In *La Maladetta,* produced at the Opéra, Paris, in 1893, the name of Staats figures among those of the twelve children who appear in the first act. That same year he produced his first ballet, *Ici l'on Danse.*

As a dancer Staats is best known for his interpretation of the role of Jean in *Javotte.* As a choreographer he has composed or revived a great many ballets. At the Opéra, Paris, he produced *Namouna* (1909), *Javotte* (1909), *Bacchus* (1909), *La Fôret* (1910), *España* (1911). From 1910-1914 he was responsible for the artistic direction of all plays and spectacles produced at the Théâtre des Arts under the direction of Jacques Rouché.

In 1915 Staats returned to the Opéra, Paris, and produced the following ballets: *L'Offrande à la Liberté* (1915), *Les Contes de Ma Mère l'Oye* (1915), *Hommage à la Belgique* (1915), *Mademoiselle de Nantes* (1915), *Les Virtuosi de Mazarin* (1916), *Le Roman d'Estelle* (1915), *Les Abeilles* (1917), *Fête Triomphale* (1919), *Taglioni chez Musette* (1920), *La Légende de Saint Christophe* (1920), *Antar* (1921), *Maimouna* (1921), *Les Troyens*—opera—dances only (1921), *La Péri* (1921), *Hérodiade* (1921), *Falstaff*—opera—dances only (1921), *Frivolant* (1922), *Cydalise et Chèvrepied* (1923), *La Khovanchina*—opera—dances only (1923), *Padmavâti* (1923), *Le Jardin du Paradis* (1923), *Esclarmonde*—opera—dances only (1923).

In addition, Staats has arranged ballets and dances for almost every theatre and music-hall in Paris. He is still actively engaged at the Opéra, and teaches daily at his school in the Rue Saulnier.

545

CYDALISE ET LE CHÉVRE-PIED [1]

Ballet in 2 Acts and 3 Scenes. Book: G. A. de Caillavet and Robert de Flers. Music: Gabriel Pierné. Choreography: Leo Staats. First produced: Théâtre de l'Opéra, Paris, January 15th, 1923.

CHARACTERS

Cydalise	MLLE. CARLOTTA ZAMBELLI
Mnesilla	MLLE. DE CRAPONNE
Slaves	MLLES. ROSELLY, LORCIA, CEBRON, S. DAUWE, SIMONI
The Governess of the Nymphs . .	MLLE. YVONNE FRANCK
The Spirit of the Spring	MLLE. DELSAUX
Styrax	M. AVELINE
The Old Faun	M. FEROUELLE
The Sultan	M. FEROUELLE
The Farmer-General	M. P. BARON
Captain of the Gardes-Françaises . .	M. PERICAT
The *Maître de Ballet*	M. MARIONNO
The Intendant	M. CHATEL
1st Doctor	M. DENIZART
2nd Doctor	M. CUVELIER
The Little Negro	MLLE. MARIA LOPEZ

Dryads, Hamadryads, Nymphs, Fauns, Attendants on Cydalise, *Danseuses, Danseurs,* Apothecaries, Pirates, Gardes-Françaises, Workmen, Dressmakers, Wig-Makers, Slaves, Children.

Act I. A quiet corner of the grounds at Versailles, decorated with a grotto made of rock, marble vases, and an ivy-covered statue of Cupid bending his bow. In the background a pond and a road. Night.

The moon rises and as it reaches the tree-tops dryads and hamadryads emerge from the undergrowth. Parched with thirst they go to the grotto in search of water. The Spirit of the Spring appears, bearing an urn, and gives them water to drink. The

---

[1] *Cydalise and the Faun.*

sound of a flute is borne on the breeze and the dryads seek shelter while the Spirit of the Spring returns to her grotto.

Enter a number of young fauns led by an old satyr. He makes them sit in a circle and gives them a lesson on the pan-pipes. One of the fauns called Styrax is very frolicsome and has to be constantly reprimanded by his mentor.

Now a band of nymphs arrive in charge of an older one who gives them lessons in dancing. They join the young fauns and dance with them.

Styrax has Mnesilla for partner and since his pranks provoke disorder the old faun punishes him by tying him to a tree.

With the approach of dawn the nymphs and fauns depart, forgetting their prisoner.

Mnesilla returns to liberate Styrax. She wishes him to go with her, but, since he prefers to stay, leaves him.

Left to himself Styrax inhales the scent of the flowers and tastes the fruit. He espies the statue of Cupid. At first frightened he becomes interested and ends by pelting it with fir-cones and chestnuts. One missile strikes Cupid's bow and causes the arrow to fall. Styrax picks it up and dances in triumph, during which he pricks himself with the barb. He is assailed by a vague uneasiness.

There is a rumble of wheels and a coach lumbers into view. Styrax surveys this strange object with amazement. It is seen to be filled with the King's dancers. As the coach passes, Styrax leaps up behind and is carried away.

Act II. Scene I. Another part of the grounds at Versailles prepared for a ballet performance. To the right a dais erected for the Court; to the left a view of trees and statues.

Workmen and soldiers are busily erecting a post bearing the notice:

LA SULTANE DES INDES
Comedy Ballet
Danced by Mlle. Cydalise
In Honour of the Betrothal of the Dauphin

Styrax darts out of the wood but, finding he is not alone, takes shelter behind a tree.

Enter the *maître de ballet* and the dancers wearing wraps and cloaks. Baskets are brought in and the contents—properties and costumes—distributed among the dancers, who go behind a tent to prepare for the dress rehearsal. One costume—a nobleman's dress —is left on the basket.

The workmen leave and the stage is empty. Styrax peeps out and, seeing everyone gone, amuses himself by putting on the costume. Hearing footsteps, he leaps into the basket.

The *maître de ballet* returns, impatient to begin. Cydalise arrives, dressed as a sultana, and attended by her maids, with whose aid she puts the final touches to her toilet, while Styrax watches the proceedings from his basket.

Cydalise's lovers arrive—a farmer-general and a captain of the Gardes–Françaises. She wheedles a purse from the former which she hands to the latter. Now the *maître de ballet* orders the rehearsal to begin.

The theme concerns a sick sultan whom his physicians and apothecaries are unable to cure. Some pirates arrive and offer the sultan the prizes they have captured: a number of Arab women and the beautiful Cydalise. She dances and the sultan, charmed, approaches her. But she strikes him with her fan. Everyone falls down in terror at the consequences, but the sultan pardons the affront, and all ends happily.

Cydalise's lovers congratulate her. Feeling cold, she asks the captain to fetch her cloak. He goes to the basket and out jumps Styrax, who runs to Cydalise and embraces her.

There is an uproar. Styrax dances a frenzied dance in which he is joined by Cydalise. Their gaiety is communicated to the other dancers. But the young faun grows so passionate that her lovers hastily intervene. Cydalise gives Styrax a rose as a parting gift, while he offers her Cupid's arrow. Styrax, waving the rose, dances in triumph.

Act II. Scene II. An attic in the Palace of Versailles improvised as a bedroom. A large window overlooks the park.

Cydalise enters attended by her admirers. The performance is over and, greatly fatigued, she sends them away. Maids bring her flowers and prepare her for the night.

She finds in her sash the arrow given her by Styrax. Closing the shutters she lies on the bed, and composes herself to rest.

Styrax enters and, seeing Cydalise asleep, pricks her lightly with the arrow. She plays the coquette while the faun examines with delight the articles on her toilet-table.

She asks him to write her a love-letter, but he cannot write. She offers him one to read, but he cannot read.

"What can you do?" she enquires.

"I can play the pipes," he replies.

He does so and she begins to dance. Presently he joins her and the dance grows more and more passionate. They swear never to leave each other.

She opens the window to breathe in the cool morning air and ushers in the faint whispers of the forest stirring to life. Styrax yearns to return to his native element, while Cydalise implores him to stay.

As the day grows lighter, nymphs and fauns appear at the window. Some leap into the room carrying flowers and leaves, whose perfume Styrax inhales with delight.

He lays Cydalise on the bed and, taking a bunch of poppies from a faun, places it near her lips. The other wood-folk cover her with flowers and she falls asleep.

The wood-folk glide through the window one by one. The last to leave is Styrax, who wafts a kiss as he departs.

*

Cydalise et le Chèvre-pied was very successful. "Undoubtedly," records André Levinson,[2] "what one sees is not a monumental and pathetic masterpiece such as a painting by Poussin, a group by Rude, or a tragedy by Corneille. But the ballet by Caillavet and De Flers is a charmingly French thing in the manner of Sèvres bisque, a carpet from La Savonerie, or *Les Trois Sultanes* played by Mme. Favart.

"The choreographic scenes proper are rare and brief. At the beginning the rhythmic evolutions of the dryads and the Spirit of the Spring arouse some apprehensions, but their stylished weariness is dissipated by the march of the young fauns.

"The entrance of that group of dancers, with their droll deliberate steps and their bent arms with separated thumbs and palms placed in profile in the manner of Nijinsky in *L'Après–Midi d'un Faune,* produced a great sensation. . . .

"The flute-lesson interrupted by Styrax's pranks is very well done; musically, it is unconstrained, petulant, and new. I like the dancing-lesson less, the plan of which is too clever, too symmetrical."

Of the rendering of Styrax in this scene Levinson declares: "Impudent, frolicsome, artless, insinuating, and savage, the faun is perfectly played by M. Aveline. But this master dancer is obliged to contend with insurmountable obstacles: a thick-set figure, and consequently limited *parcours;* his foot, which wears the cloven shoe, cannot convey the mad bounds of the capricious Styrax. This makes the action appear, at times, to drag.

[2] *Comoedia,* January, 1923.

"The second scene . . . resembled a delightful concoction of molièresque memories. How charming is the rehearsal when the young folks give way to *cabrioles* and *pirouettes*. Nothing could be wittier than those *entrechats-six* executed in shoes with heels and buckles in the Richelieu manner, accompanied by flying perukes, lace sleeves, and the skirts of ceremonial costumes; here is another desirable and happy anachronism.

"But the entrance of Mlle. Zambelli effaces everything by that radiance which is the appanage of choreographic royalty, and which distinguishes the Star from a thousand dancers of merit. Those firm and sharp *pointes* which emerge from the sultana's long transparent flowing pantaloons, borrowed from *Schéhérazade,* do wonders.

"The final scene brings . . . Mlle. Zambelli's soliloquy, the reading of the love-letters—when one perceives that the *ballerina* is intelligent to the tips of her toes. Do you not remember those bursts of laughter echoed in the orchestra, mimed by the arms, emphasized by the agile *pointes!*

"Follows a delicately sensual dialogue, when experience swoons in the arms of innocence, a dialogue whose structure is reminiscent of *Le Spectre de la Rose*—and all is at an end."

EDE BRADA

E DE BRADA was born at Vienna on March 11th, 1879. On completing his training as a dancer he became soloist at the Opera, Vienna, and later filled the same post at the Royal Opera, Budapest. He was appointed *maître de ballet* in 1921 and continued in that position until his recent retirement. During that period he produced 54 ballets at the Royal Opera, of which the following are the best known: *Princess Malve* (Mader), *Prince Argyl* (Gajary), and *Carnival at Pest* (Liszt).

Brada was teacher of dancing for eleven years to the children of the Archduke Joseph. To-day he is teacher of dancing to the Franz Joseph Institute and the Ludoviceums, both at Budapest.

CARNIVAL AT PEST

Ballet in 1 Act. Book: Ede Brada. Music: Franz Liszt. Scenery and costumes: Gusztáv Oláh. Choreography: Ede Brada. First produced: Royal Hungarian Opera, Budapest, December 6th, 1930.

CHARACTERS

The Patroness	MLLE. JÓZSA SZABÓ
Her Husband	M. REZSÖ KOVÁRY
Her Three Daughters	MLLE. BELLA BORDY
	MLLE. ILONA VERA
	MLLE. IRÉN MÁTRAY
Her Son, a Lieutenant of Hussars . .	M. FERENC KÖSZEGI
A Colonel of Hussars . . .	M. A. KODOLANYI
A Young Lady from Vienna . .	MLLE. KAROLA SZALAY
A Gentleman from Vienna . .	M. GY. HARANGOZO
Master of the Ceremonies . .	M. REZSÖ BRADA

Members of the County Gentry, Officers, Students, Servants.

Scene. The ballroom of the Hôtel de l'Europe, Budapest, 1867.

Distinguished members of the county gentry are assembled in

the great ballroom of the Hôtel de l'Europe, and university students and officers of Hussars await the arrival of the Patroness who is to open the ball. Presently she enters, attended by her husband, her three daughters, and her son, who is a lieutenant of Hussars.

The ball opens with the Palotás, for centuries the favourite dance of the Hungarians. At the conclusion new guests arrive: a young lady from Vienna, escorted by a gentleman. They bring with them a Viennese dance—the Waltz.

The lieutenant dances with the Viennese lady and falls in love with her. But the Hungarian gentry regard the foreign dance with disfavour, and the students ostentatiously withdraw.

The young man from Vienna tries to stop the dance, which leads to a quarrel between the two men. But peace is restored through the intervention of the lieutenant's vivacious sisters.

The next dance is the Grand Mazur, during which the Viennese couple become reconciled, much to the annoyance of the lieutenant, who is intensely jealous. And when he sees them embrace his despair is such that he is about to blow out his brains.

Fortunately, his colonel observes his intention and forces him to surrender his weapon. Having administered a reprimand, he sympathises with him until the young officer regains his good humour, and delights everyone with his spirited dancing of the Csárdás, which carries everyone with him.

His youngest sister, to the delight of the Hungarian party, teaches the dance to the young man from Vienna.

Now supper is announced and the guests file into an adjoining room, all save the lieutenant who takes his shako and cloak and is about to leave, when he finds his way barred by the young lady from Vienna, who tells him that her escort is her brother; the lieutenant has nothing to fear, for she loves him dearly. They kiss and are surprised by the guests who whirl in to a lively measure.

Midnight strikes and the mothers express a desire to go home, but the fathers plead for the party to continue. The Patroness, touched by the genuine love of the young people for each other, gives them her blessing, upon which the whole company resume the Csárdás, which they dance till dawn.

*

This ballet is very popular at Budapest. The music for the ballet consist of Liszt's IXth Rhapsody and portions of the IInd, VIth, Xth, XIth, and XIIIth Rhapsodies, with the addition of a few piano pieces.

MICHEL FOKINE

MICHEL MIKHAYLOVICH FOKINE, the son of a well-to-do business man, was born at St. Petersburg on April 26th, 1880. At the age of nine he entered the Imperial School of Ballet attached to the Maryinsky Theatre and began his studies under Platon Karsavin, the father of the *ballerina,* Thamar Karsavina.

The new pupil made rapid progress and two years later was transferred to the class of Volkov, a martinet for technical precision. From time to time Fokine danced in the school *corps de ballet* and in 1891 took part in the Annual Pupils' Display, when he was allotted the important role of Luc in Ivanov's ballet *The Magic Flute,* which was the piece chosen that year for study.

From his first years Fokine surprised his teachers with his versatility and his particular aptitude for dancing, mime, music, and painting. He spent his leisure hours in reading or in visiting the Hermitage and other galleries to study Russian and foreign art.

Volkov died some months after Fokine had joined his class, and that teacher's place was taken by Shirayev, with whom Fokine studied until 1893, when he was transferred to the highest class conducted by the famous dancer-mime, P. A. Gerdt. In 1896 the last-named resigned and was succeeded by N. Legat, with whom Fokine continued his studies.

Two years later he passed his final examination and was admitted to the ballet company, and at once cast for important parts, notwithstanding the rule that every artiste must begin his career in the *corps de ballet.* He made his *début* at the Maryinsky Theatre on April 26th, 1898, when he danced with Egorova, Syedova, and Obukhov in the *pas de quatre* from *Paquita.*

He next studied with Johannsen, whose class was a school of choreographic counterpoint, and in 1902 was appointed to take the ballet class for junior girls. In 1905 he was promoted to teach the senior class.

As Fokine pursued his studies he began to feel that ballet had

553

reached a point beyond which it could not advance while fettered by tradition. He formed the opinion that it must be freed of the conventional costume and gesture, and the set order of steps; that technique must be employed as a means and not as an end; and, finally, that there must be unity of action and unity of style in accordance with the music used, which should be expressive.

In 1904 he happened to read the *Daphnis and Chloë* of Longus, upon which he based a *scenario* for a ballet, which he submitted to the director of the Imperial Theatres with explanatory notes for the production of the piece. These observations included a plan for the reform of ballet. It is important to quote some of his opinions:

"Dancing should be interpretative. It should not degenerate into mere gymnastics. The dance should explain the spirit of the actors in the spectacle. More than that, it should express the whole epoch to which the subject of the ballet belongs.

"For such interpretative dancing the music must be equally inspired. In place of the old-time waltzes, polkas, *pizzicati,* and *galops,* it is necessary to create a form of music which expresses the same emotion as that which inspires the movements of the dancer.

"The ballet must no longer be made up of 'numbers,' 'entries,' and so on. It must show artistic unity of conception. The action of the ballet must never be interrupted to allow the *danseuse* to respond to the applause of the public.

"In place of the traditional dualism, the ballet must have complete unity of expression, a unity which is made up of a harmonious blending of the three elements—music, painting, and plastic art."

The only outcome of this plea for reform was the issuing of an order to the effect that, in view of the necessity for preserving the illusion and theatrical impression, artistes were forbidden to bow during the performance of an opera. Evidently the management considered the preservation of illusion in ballet of no importance.

In 1905 Fokine composed for the Annual Pupils' Performance his first ballet, *Acis et Galatée.* In the same year he composed a solo dance for Anna Pavlova, *"Le Cygne,"* a plastic poem which is known the world over, and is perhaps the best known of all dances.

In 1906 he composed two more ballets: *A Midsummer Night's Dream* and *La Vigne,* which latter brought him a warm message of congratulation from Marius Petipa. The following year he produced *Eunice* and *The Animated Gobelins.* In 1908 he created *Une Nuit d'Egypte* and *Chopiniana.*

This same year he accepted an invitation from Serge Diaghilev to be choreographer in connection with the proposed season of Russian Ballet, which it was the latter's intention to stage at Paris in 1909. This association, which gave Fokine his first opportunity to show his work abroad, laid the foundation of his international renown, a reputation which has been worthily sustained for over twenty-five years by the many fine ballets he has continued to create.

In arranging a ballet Fokine's first care is to study the music in relation to the theme. He works for days until he has the sequence of music to his liking, and has established a balance of mood which satisfies him. Then he studies the music in relation to movement, and the movement in relation to the mood and style-atmosphere required by the theme, which is finally considered in relation with the scenery and costumes. Gradually he conceives a mental picture of each stage in the development of the action, which becomes more and more detailed.

On the day of rehearsal he requires only dancers to bring into being the phantom pictures and movements that people his brain. He knows what phrase of movement is to be interpreted in such a movement, where there is to be a pose, and for how long. He composes like a painter, sketching a few movements here, arranging a few details of a pose there; it is one of the most entrancing experiences to see these apparently isolated elements gradually set in their proper order and combined to form a beautiful dance. The sensation received can only be compared to the witnessing of a film of a growing flower.

Fokine has produced ballets on almost all the great stages of Europe and America. His original creations to date number sixty-four, as follows:

Examination Performances of the Imperial Ballet School: *Acis et Galatée* (1905), *The Animated Gobelins* (1907), *A Midsummer Night's Dream* (1906), *Chopiniana*—second version, better known as *Les Sylphides*—(1908), *Les Quatre Saisons* (1909).

Charity Performances, Russia: *La Vigne* (1906), *Eunice* (1907), *Chopiniana*—first version—(1908), *Une Nuit d'Egypte,* later known as *Cléopâtre* (1908), *Le Carnaval* (1910), *Venusberg* (1910), *Papillons* (1912), *Islamei* (1912), *Le Rêve* (?), *Francesca da Rimini* (1915), *Eros* (1915), *Stenka Razin* (1915), *Jota Aragonesa* (1916), *L'Apprenti Sorcier* (1916).

Productions for the Imperial Russian Theatres: *Le Pavillon d'Armide* (1907), *Orpheus and Eurydice* (1916), *Judith* (1912), Dances in *Russlan and Ludmilla* (1917).

Productions for Serge Diaghilev: *Polovtsian Dances from Prince Igor* (1909), *L'Oiseau de Feu* (1910), *Schéhérazade* (1910), Dances in *Sadko* (1910), *Narcisse* (1911), *Petrouchka* (1911), *Le Spectre de la Rose* (1911), *Le Dieu Bleu* (1912), *Daphnis et Chloë* (1912), *Thamar* (1912), *Midas* (1914), *Le Coq d'Or* (1914), *La Légende de Joseph* (1914).

Productions for Anna Pavlova: *Les Preludes* (1913), *The Seven Daughters of the Mountain King* (1918).

Productions for America and London, 1919–1924: Dances in *Aphrodite* (1919), Dances in *Mecca* (1920), *Russian Toys* (1921), *The Adventures of Harlequin* (1922), Ballet in the play *Johannes Kreisler* (1923), *Return from the Carnival* (1923), Dances in *The Miracle* (1923), *Frolicking Gods* (1923), *Farlandjio* (1923), Dances in *A Midsummer Night's Dream* (1924), Dances in *Hassan* (1924), Prologue to *Faust* (1927), *The Thunder Bird* (1921).

Productions for the Fokine Ballet: *Le Rêve de la Marquise* (1921), *Medusa* (1924), *Ole Toro* (1924), and *Elves* (1924).

Production at Stadium, Stockholm; *The Moonlight Sonata* (1918).

Productions for Ida Rubinstein: *Diane de Poitiers, Semiramis, Bolero,* and *La Valse.*

Production for the Scala Theatre, Milan: *The Love of the Three Pomegranates.*

Productions for René Blum: *L'Epreuve d'Amour* (1936), *Don Juan* (1936), *Les Eléments* (1937).

Fokine has three claims to fame: as dancer, as reformer, and as choreographer.

He was well known in Russia as a fine mime and excellent dancer, and appeared with most of the great *ballerine* of his time, commencing with Anna Pavlova. He danced the leading roles in many of his own ballets, for instance, the Vicomte de Beaugency in *Le Pavillon d'Armide,* Harlequin in *Le Carnaval,* Polovtsian Chief in the *Polovtsian Dances from Prince Igor,* Daphnis in *Daphnis et Chloë,* the Gold Negro in *Schéhérazade,* Amoûn in *Cléopâtre,* the Marquis in *Le Rêve de la Marquise.* He also danced at many of the recitals given by him and his wife, Vera Fokina, in various countries.

As a reformer he is to the twentieth century what Noverre was to the eighteenth, for he has exerted a profound and beneficial influence in every branch of the art of ballet. He has instituted important reforms in ballet costume. He has made mime in ballet expressive in place of the former series of conventional gestures; he has proved the importance of using good music; he has stressed the necessity for a dance to conform to the theme; he has insisted on correct style-atmosphere.

As a choreographer he is certainly the greatest living exponent of the very difficult art of dance composition. His acute sensitiveness to music is extraordinary. If a ballet by Fokine be examined as it has left the hands of its creator, it will be found that the relation between music and movement is inseparable and complete, so much so that it is difficult to believe that any other form and sequence of movement could so perfectly express that particular phrase of music.

His ballets are always worked out to a logical conclusion. There is always a beginning, a middle portion, and a climax. There are no weaknesses, no loose ends; when the ballet is at an end one receives the impression that the final word has been said. Lastly, through all Fokine's ballets there is an ever-present sense of harmonious rhythm which is as characteristic of his compositions as the association of a certain fragrance with a particular flower.

How well they are constructed is proved by their continued popularity, for, although many of the several Fokine ballets revived by various companies leave a good deal to be desired in comparison with the original productions, and some of the characters have strayed far from their original conception and presentation, still, there are several ballets such as *Le Carnaval, Les Sylphides, Petrouchka,* and so on, which, although given year after year, never fail to draw appreciative applause from the public.

Consider, too, the variety of Fokine's work—the German romanticism of *Le Carnaval,* the pure classic ballet of *Les Sylphides,* the barbaric strength of the *Polovtsian Dances from Prince Igor,* the ineffable poetry of *Le Spectre de la Rose,* the exotic voluptuousness of *Schéhérazade,* the tragi-comedy of *Petrouchka,* with its vivid glimpses of a vanished Russia, the recapturing of the beauty of ancient Hellas in *Daphnis et Chloë,* the mordant burlesque of *Le Coq d'Or,* the delicate wit of *L'Epreuve d'Amour.* Here is not one masterpiece, but many masterpieces, a record of successful achievement which cannot be matched by any other choreographer, past or present.

LE PAVILLON D'ARMIDE

Ballet in 1 Act and 3 Scenes. Book: Alexandre Benois. Music: Nicholas Tcherepnine. Scenery and costumes: Alexandre Benois. Choreography: Michel Fokine. First produced: Maryinsky Theatre, St. Petersburg, November 25th, 1907.

CHARACTERS

Armide	Mlle. Anna Pavlova
Vicomte de Beaugency	M. P. A. Gerdt
The Marquis	M. Soliankov
Slave of Armide	M. Vaslav Nijinsky

Friends of Armide
Master of the Ceremonies
    Dancers, Captive Knights, Ladies-in-Waiting, Gentlemen,
  Chief Buffoon, Buffoons, Harpists, Pages, Negroes, Saturn,
      Cupid, Servants, Postillions, etc.

Period: Louis XIV.

Scene I. Armide's pavilion.

The Vicomte de Beaugency, while travelling on a visit to his betrothed, is caught in a storm which forces him to break his journey and seek refuge.

He finds himself in the grounds of a castle belonging to a certain Marquis de Fierbois, who is a magician. The Marquis receives his guest with every courtesy and invites him to rest the night in an annex, known as Armide's pavilion, where lived in former times the beautiful Marquise Madeleine, whose memory is preserved in a Gobelins tapestry representing her as Armide, surrounded by her Court. This tapestry is the glory of the pavilion.

At the rise of the curtain the Vicomte is seen entering the pavilion, which servants are preparing for his comfort. His first thought is the tapestry, which he examines with intense interest. The material seems to glow, while the face of Armide appears to smile. The Vicomte is filled with alarm, but at this moment the valets assist him to undress and go to bed. Then they bid him good night and depart.

The pavilion is gradually flooded with moonlight which illumines the domed ceiling, the tapestry, and the giant clock, supported by figures of Love and Time, which stands beneath it. The Vicomte cannot rest; he remains gazing at the tapestry. At last he falls asleep.

On the stroke of midnight Time reverses his hour-glass and the supporters of the clock step down from their pedestal. Love drives away Time, and, one by one, a dozen little boys in gold and silver trip from the clock-case and render the Dance of the Hours, after which they return to the clock.

A strange mysterious music is heard. The Vicomte wakes up,

listens, rises, and goes to the tapestry, but, finding nothing unusual, returns to bed. The music is repeated and the Vicomte is minded to flee, only he is afraid of appearing ridiculous. The tapestry grows, the music becomes more and more seductive, and the figures seem to come to life.

Scene II. *The Animation of the Gobelins.*

The Gobelins changes into a superb palace set in a garden of enchantment, in which Armide appears, attended by her suite. At a sign from the mysterious Marquis, the Vicomte is transformed into René, her lover.

Armide reproaches the Vicomte for his long absence; and, under her irresistible charm, he grows passionate. She commands a festival in honour of his return. Her ladies and courtiers dance, then her friends, and, lastly, herself.

Enter King Hydrao who bears a striking resemblance to the Marquis. The friends resume their dance; this gives place to Bacchus and his attendant Bacchantes. They are followed by several magicians who propose to conjure visions, but Hydrao waves his wand and they disappear, to be replaced by some gay buffoons.

The festival reaches its climax. René is madly in love with Armide, who makes him wear her embroidered scarf.

Day dawns and the nocturnal visions disappear.

Scene III. *Same as Scene I.*

The first rays of sun have dispelled the visions as suddenly as they came. A flock of sheep with their shepherd and shepherdess pass by the window. The Marquis appears. The Vicomte is disquieted by his cynical smile which recalls the nocturnal vision of King Hydrao.

The Vicomte prepares to resume his journey when the Marquis shows him Armide's scarf, resting on the clock. The Vicomte gazes fearfully at the tapestry and observes that Armide no longer wears a scarf. Realising that what he took to be a dream was reality, he falls unconscious.

*

The theme of *Le Pavillon d'Armide* is based on Gautier's short story, *Omphale*.

One scene from the ballet, that entitled *"The Animated Gobelins,"* was staged at St. Petersburg by Fokine on April 15/28, 1907, in connection with the Annual Pupils' Performance, simply as a composition to display the abilities of his pupils. It happened that while Fokine was at a concert he heard a piece entitled *Suite from "Le Pavillon d'Armide"* and, being attracted by the music and in search of a theme for a short ballet, he asked the composer, who was present, if he might produce the piece as a ballet, although it was only for a Pupils' Performance. The composer assented and explained that the suite was a scene from a contemplated ballet in three acts written by the painter, Alexandre Benois.

After the Pupils' Performance, Fokine was invited by the director of the Imperial Theatres to produce the whole ballet on the Imperial stage with real artistes. He accepted and suggested that Benois should be commissioned to furnish the scenario, to which the director agreed. After various difficulties the ballet was produced in its entirety in November and achieved a brilliant success.

When Diaghilev planned his first season of ballet to be given at the Théâtre du Chatelet, Paris, in 1909, *Le Pavillon d'Armide* was among the ballets he selected, and this composition, with the *Polovtsian Dances from Prince Igor* and a series of *divertissements* called *Le Festin,* formed the programme of the memorable opening night on May 19th.

It was in 1911, some twenty-five years ago, that I first saw this ballet, when the roles of Armide and her Slave were taken respectively by Karsavina and Nijinsky. Of that evening I can recall four things which impressed me: the melodious music with its seductive quality and hint of mystery; the grace and beauty of Karsavina as Armide; the wonderful dancing of Nijinsky as the slave, particularly in a *variation* in which he crossed from one side of the stage to the other by means of a series of vertical bounds, *entrechats,* and *tours en l'air,* in which he rose and fell and rose again with the softness and ease of a bouncing indiarubber ball; and, lastly, that glorious *"Buffoons' Dance,"* with its fascinating broken rhythm.

I believe the ballet was last performed in 1914 at the Theatre Royal, Drury Lane, London, when the cast was as follows: Thamar Karsavina (*Armide*), Adolph Bolm (*Vicomte de Beaugency*), Enrico Cecchetti (*The Marquis*) and Vaslav Nijinsky (*Slave of Armide*).

PRINCE IGOR

Ballet in 1 Act. Music: Alexander Borodine. Scenery and costumes: Nicholas Roehrich. Choreography: Michel Fokine. First produced: Théâtre du Chatelet, Paris, May 18th, 1909.

CHARACTERS

A Young Polovtsian Girl	. . .	MLLE. SOPHIA FEDOROVA
A Polovtsian Woman	. . . .	MLLE. HELEN SMIRNOVA
A Polovtsian Chief .	. . . . .	M. ADOLPH BOLM

Polovtsian Girls, Slaves, Warriors, Youths.

Scene. A Polovtsian camp at dawn. On a rising plain is a semi-circular group of rude, dome-shaped tents made from the hides of animals, tanned and dyed to varying shades of red and brown. On the slope of the eminence are further tents which spring up like giant mole-hills. In the distance, half-obscured by a damp haze and the smoke from the dying camp-fires, stretches a dreary range of violet hills, their bases lapped by a broad river. The whole scene is bathed in the fitful glare of glowing embers.

Grouped about the tent-flaps are maidens and women of the tribe, while on the ground sprawl the still slumbering warriors. Now they rise from their hard couches to bend and stretch their aching limbs, and greet one another with rough shoulder-clap and uncouth jest. Ferocious of aspect, their faces smeared with soot and mud, their coats green and mottled red and ochre, their trousers striped in bright hues, one is reminded of a lair of wild beasts rather than a camp of human beings.

A mournful chant fills the air and several women wend their way forward in single file. They dance with slow languorous movements, their bodies swaying rhythmically to the fluttering of the rose-coloured veils which they hold above their heads between outstretched hands. They turn round and fall on one knee. Another group of women dance forward in the same manner. Now they sway their bodies from side to side with rippling movements of their arms. They incline their heads backward and forward, then rise to their feet. They renew their graceful dance and gradually merge into two circles between which comes a new-comer, a woman clad in scarlet with her hair dressed in two dark plaits threaded with a string of pearls. She glides softly to and fro, now advancing, now retreating, her body swaying with a soft rounded grace, her arms extended in an undulating line.

At the conclusion of the dance the women melt into one quivering mass, above which the veils wave and writhe like wind-blown points of flame, and retire to the shelter of their tents. There they sink to the ground and raise themselves on one elbow, each face half-concealed with a veil-draped arm.

Swiftly the wailing chant gives place to a fierce, throbbing rhythm. A flash of scarlet and there vaults into the centre of the clearing a dazzling figure in striped costume of red and ochre. It is the chief. His whole being pulsates with a burning excess of savage exultation in his strength. He continually whirls round, springs upward, spins in the air and crashes to the ground. His brows are contorted, his head flung back, his mouth opened wide in a hoarse, gasping shout of triumph.

Fired by his example, his lieutenants dart to his side. They maintain one line and step quickly to right and left, now as if in pursuit of a foe, now as if in retreat, the while they bend their bows and twang the strings in simulated loosing of an arrow. Now they dash forward in two lines. Those in front drop swiftly to the ground, while those behind spring over their recumbent figures. Suddenly they rise in a splendid posture of defiance. Some are kneeling, some standing, but each bow is bent with the string drawn taut to the ear. One is reminded of some classic heroic frieze. They rise, divide into little groups, and exchange congratulations on their prowess.

Again the women glide forward to inflame the heated warriors with the voluptuous swaying of their veils. They merge into two lines, between which dances the chief's favourite. The avenue dissolves into a circle and the women fall on their knees, their heads thrown backward, their arms extended in a gesture of abandon. Their passions awakened by this spectacle, the warriors bound in and out of their midst, stamping their feet and shaking their bows aloft with incredible ferocity.

Now the warriors collect into two bands disposed at the left- and right-hand corners of the encampment, while the women rise to their feet, form into a serried mass, and slowly retreat.

Again the music reverberates in impetuous, fiery rhythm. One group of warriors surges forward in a diagonal line from right to left. A moment later their path is crossed by the remaining band, who pass in a diagonal line from left to right. Now the warriors turn about and, with catlike step and sinister crouching attitude, surround the women, a quick movement—and they fling them on their shoulders with a facility born of long practice. They lower the women to the ground and withdraw to the tents.

The music changes to a swift theme played *pizzicato,* and four youths spring forward. They emphasize the measure with loud slaps of their hands on their muscular thighs. Now each pair links arms and whirls round and round. They separate, bound high in the air, and fall flat on their stomachs.

The maidens come forward in serried line, their arms out-stretched, their bodies quivering with the frenzied shuffling of their feet. Suddenly they fall to the ground on one knee, each with an arm flung aloft to curve gracefully over the head.

The young men spring to their feet to bound into the air with wild grimaces and rhythmic claps of their hands. The maidens repeat their former dance. Then they spin to right and left, their garments fluttering, their dark plaits swinging with the velocity of their movements. Again they fall to the ground on one knee, with bodies arched and one arm held above their heads.

Two of the youths leap into the air with a convulsive bound and loud claps of their hands. Exactly as they descend, their companions repeat their movements. The women pass to each side of the encampment and the chief dashes into their midst. He leaps forward, spins in the air, and crashes to the ground. The other warriors, their primitive passions stirred by this war-like display, hurl themselves into the dance—feet thudding to the maddening, pulsating rhythm of the music, bows flourished aloft. They flow into two lines, cross and recross, every step affording occasion for a frenzied leap. Now they wind about their chief in a circle which alternately narrows and widens. They inflame their flagging spirits with hoarse cries and goad their tired muscles with frenzied lashing of the ground with their bows. The movement becomes a seething tumult of brutal rage, ever faster, ever more violent, until the dancers, breathless, soaked in sweat, and staggering from exhaustion, cease from sheer physical inability to continue. The women dash forward in four long lines, spin on one foot alternately to right and left, whirl in three successive turns, and retreat to the shelter of the tents. The chief and his lieutenants dash forward with mighty bounds, heads thrown back, bows shaken on high, mouths opened wide in a shout of triumph.

*

No one who has seen this dance will deny its right to be acclaimed a masterpiece. Nothing could be more removed from the traditions of the Petipa epoch and nothing could be more indicative of Fokine's genius as a choreographer. After its first performance it was greeted with a veritable tempest of spontaneous applause which seemed never-ending. There were no less than six curtain calls.

The *Polovtsian Dances from Prince Igor* were composed by Fokine at the instance of Diaghilev, who, planning his first season of ballet at Paris, 1909, asked the choreographer to arrange a series of dances to an excerpt from the second act of Borodine's opera, *Prince Igor*. The ballet was composed and rehearsed in a small theatre near the Ekaterininsky Canal, St. Petersburg.

There have been many interpreters of the Polovtsian Chief, the two best [1] being Adolph Bolm and Leon Woizikowsky. So savage were the early performances that it was no uncommon occurrence for bows to be smashed, so forcibly did the dancers lash them against the stage.

Fokine has reproduced *Prince Igor* for companies other than that of Diaghilev, in the course of which the ballet has received new settings and costumes, some by Roehrich, some by Korovine.

LES SYLPHIDES

Ballet in 1 Act. Music: Chopin. Scenery and costumes: Alexandre Benois. Choreography: Michel Fokine. First produced in Western Europe: Théâtre du Chatelet, Paris, June 2nd, 1909.

DANCES

Nocturne . . .	MMES. PAVLOVA, KARSAVINA, BALDINA, M. NIJINSKY and *corps de ballet*
Valse	MME. THAMAR KARSAVINA
Mazurka . . .	MME. ANNA PAVLOVA
Mazurka . . .	M. VASLAV NIJINSKY
Prelude . . .	MME. BALDINA
Valse	MME. ANNA PAVLOVA and M. VASLAV NIJINSKY
Valse	MMES. PAVLOVA, KARSAVINA, BALDINA, M. NIJINSKY and *corps de ballet*

Scene. A sylvan glade. On one side rises the grey ruins of a monastery, on the other a little group of leafless trees, while in the centre background the outline of a tomb emerges faintly. It is night and the scene is correspondingly dark, except where the moon sheds quivering patches of light. The general colour is a glowing dark green.

When the curtain rises the *corps de ballet,* a shimmering mass of white, are seen grouped against the background in a semi-circle; in the centre are the four dancers who will render the *variations.* The dancers are dressed in the traditional ballet skirt of the

[1] I have not seen Fokine's interpretation of this role.

period of Taglioni, the edge of the skirt reaching mid-way between ankle and knee; their hair is adorned with a little fillet of white flowers, at the breast there is a tiny posy of forget-me-nots. Silvery wings are attached to the dancers' waists.

The effect of these floating white clouds against the cold atmosphere of the scene reminds one of snowflakes whirled hither and thither by the wind in the moonlight of a winter's eve. At other times they resemble wisps of mist, the surf on a breaking wave, and perhaps best of all a phantom poet and his muses, at play beneath the waning moon in the shadow of a frosted glade.

Apart from the first mazurka, all the dances breathe an intense sadness, save only the last, which is full of rapture, a joy of quick movement; and, just as the spectator feels he must join in to free himself from the intense strain on his emotions, the curtain falls. Then, so torn is he between the conflicting emotions of sadness and rapture, that a few moments elapse before he can applaud.

The phantoms, the glade, the moonlight—all have faded away, but an unforgettable memory remains, and a regret that the vision has passed, and so quickly.

*

The idea of arranging a ballet to Chopin's music came to Fokine when, on turning over some pieces at a music-seller's, he found a Suite entitled *Chopiniana,* orchestrated by Glazunov. It consisted of four pieces—a Polonaise, Nocturne, Mazurka, and Tarantella. To these, Fokine decided to add a Waltz which, at his request, Glazunov also orchestrated.

At this first presentation of the ballet, on March 8/21st, 1908, the *Polonaise* was danced as such by a number of artistes dressed in rich Polish costumes; the scene represented a ballroom.

The theme for the *Nocturne* was suggested to Fokine by an incident in the life of Chopin. The scene showed the interior of a deserted monastery, the dreary expanse of wall broken by the sombre outlines of the tombs of dead monks. Chopin is seen seated at a piano engaged in composition. He is very ill and cannot concentrate his thoughts. Becoming assailed with vague fears, he rises from his seat and peers into the distant gloom. Now the ghosts of the dead monks come forth and torment him with menacing gestures. He recoils in terror, clings to the piano, strikes a few chords with trembling fingers and collapses, half-fainting, on the keys. Presently, Chopin's Muse, represented by a dancer in white, comes from the darkness, drives away the haunting visions, and comforts him. He raises his head and resumes his place at the piano. At peace, he continues his composition.

The theme for the *Mazurka* was a Polish wedding. A young girl is to be married to an old man. While the festivities are at their height, the young girl's lover enters and begs her to go away with him. She throws away her engagement-ring and grants his prayer.

The *Waltz* was the first sketch for a new conception of *Chopiniana* (*Les Sylphides*). It was a purely classical *pas de deux* danced by Pavlova and Obukhov. The danseuse wore a long ballet dress in the manner of Taglioni.

The *Tarantella* was an *ensemble* danced by several artistes and was given a realistic atmosphere by the presence of a number of small children. The scene represented Naples with a distant view of Vesuvius.

Note that the first version of *Chopiniana* was danced by artistes of the Imperial Ballet.

On April 6th (1908), at a Pupils' Annual Performance, Fokine presented a new version of *Chopiniana,* now transformed into a purely classical ballet, and danced in the long muslin skirts characteristic of Taglioni's epoch. This second *Chopiniana* was orchestrated by Maurice Keller, with the exception of the Waltz taken from the first *Chopiniana,* which, it will be remembered, was orchestrated by Glazunov. *Chopiniana* was chosen for Diaghilev's first Paris season, when it was re-named *Les Sylphides,* a title suggested by the first romantic ballet, *La Sylphide.*

Les Sylphides begins with an overture (Prelude, op. 28, no. 7) which induces an appropriate mood for the ballet. The ballet proper begins with a Nocturne (op. 32, no. 2) danced by the whole company, a Valse (op. 70, no. 1) executed by one of the *premières danseuses,* a Mazurka (op. 33, no. 3), danced as a *pas seul* by the *danseuse étoile,* another Mazurka (op. 67, no. 3) *pas seul* by the *premier danseur,* a Prelude (same as that used for the overture) by one of the *premières danseuses,* a Valse (op. 64, no. 2) *pas de deux* by the *danseuse étoile* and *premier danseur,* and a final Valse (op. 18, no. 1) by the entire company.

Les Sylphides is a composition in the manner of the pure Romantic Ballet—a series of four *variations* and a *pas de deux* framed in two *ensembles,* one with which the ballet opens and another which brings the work to a conclusion.

All the *soli* are conceived in a spiritualised mood, with the exception of the first Mazurka, which is gayer in tone. The *pas de deux* is a lovely composition, the preparation for the first movement of which is made off stage, so that the *danseuse* makes her entrance as if soaring into the air, her partner supporting her at the waist in a manner which suggests that he is lightly restraining her lest she should vanish into the skies. Sometimes he clings lightly to her while she soars into the air, sometimes she descends to the earth and permits him to dance with her. The concluding *ensemble* is a gay animated movement which suggests stream uniting with stream to burst into a cascade at the very edge of the footlights, then ebbing backstage to return to form again the group with which the ballet opens.

Les Sylphides is certainly the most poetical of ballets of the 20th century and, perhaps, of all time. It demands faultless execution, the purest sense of line, and perfect expressiveness, timing, and mood. The movement of the arms is very important in this ballet; they require to ripple with the softness and smoothness of still water set in motion by the casting of a stone. So often the ripple becomes an ugly writhing which in itself can mar the whole work. There is another lovely arm movement in the Man's solo. I remember how Nijinsky, when making a *développé,* extended his arm in a caressing movement which passed over the raised leg from thigh to instep; this is rarely seen nowadays, the movement ending short at the knee. I should like to mention another blemish; some of the soloists in later performances have a tendency in certain positions to jerk the head back over the shoulders in an exaggerated pose which I find most disagreeable. The whole ballet is conceived in such a purity of style that any form of excess or exaggeration, which might pass unnoticed in some ballets, here strikes a note of blatant vulgarity.

There have been several settings for *Les Sylphide* by A. Benois, by A. Socrate, by Léon Zack, also adaptations of paintings by Corot, and, on one occasion, I saw the ballet given in the pinewood scene borrowed from Mussorgsky's opera *Ivan the Terrible.* But, to my mind, the original scene designed by Benois is still incomparably the best.

Fokine revived *Les Sylphides* for René Blum in 1936, when many of the ballet's graces, which had been lost in the years succeeding its original production, were restored; the Man's solo, however, was re-arranged to new music, which is a pity, for the new *variation* is not equal to the solo as presented at the first Paris season.

CLÉOPÂTRE

Ballet in 1 Act. Book: Michel Fokine. Music: Arensky, with additional numbers by S. Taneyev, Rimsky-Korsakov, Glinka, and Glazunov. Scenery and costumes: Léon Bakst. Choreography:

Michel Fokine. First produced in Western Europe: Théâtre du Chatelet, Paris, June 2nd, 1909.

CHARACTERS

Ta-hor	MLLE. ANNA PAVLOVA
Cleopatra	MLLE. IDA RUBINSTEIN
Amoûn	M. MICHEL FOKINE
Favourite Slaves of Cleopatra . .	{ MLLE. THAMAR KARSAVINA { M. VASLAV NIJINSKY

High Priest of the Temple
Servants of the Temple, Egyptian Dancers, Greeks, Satyrs, Jewish Dancers, Syrian Musicians, Slaves, Suite of Cleopatra, People.

Scene. The exterior of a temple formed by massive figures hewn out of rock. In the distance gleams the blue water of the Nile.

The curtain rises on an empty stage. Presently a group of young girls enter, walking two by two, and bearing on their shoulders great pitchers which they have doubtless replenished from the waters of the Nile. Scarcely have they passed when there arrives Ta-hor in search of her lover, Amoûn, who bounds to her side. They dance a *pas de deux* expressive of their love. Their dance is interrupted by the dignified entry of the High Priest, to whom they kneel to receive his blessing.

A messenger arrives hot-foot with the news of the immediate arrival of Cleopatra and her suite. A triumphant burst of music heralds her approach, and the head of the procession comes into view. The rear is brought up by a kind of sarcophagus borne on the shoulders of many slaves, and escorted by Greek maidens who bear timbrels and roses.

The chest is lowered to the ground. A slave darts forward. Having bowed three times, he flings open the doors to reveal a mummy case. This is raised to disclose a tightly swathed mummy. Slave girls advance and commence to unwind the wrappings. The figure moves and bursts through the final veil to reveal Cleopatra. She indolently poses against the background of vari-coloured veils, while maidens arrive bearing a divan for her repose. Assisted by her two favourite slaves she glides to the divan upon which she reclines, her hands resting sphinx-like on the head of the couch.

Amoûn, half-concealed in the shadows, gazes intently upon the Queen, at first curious, then admiring, finally madly enamoured. Ta-hor, wounded by his indifference, plucks at her lover's arm.

He angrily shakes her off and tries to approach the couch, but the slaves drive him away.

The Queen commands the ceremonial dances to begin, and while the dancers move to the rattle of the sacred *sistra* clasped in their hands, Ta-hor leads Amoûn away. He begs her forgiveness and disappears into the shadows.

Custom demands that Ta-hor shall lead the dance, so, filled with evil foreboding, she throws herself into the swiftly moving throng. Meanwhile Amoûn tries to obtain a clearer view of the alluring Queen, who drives him to distraction. He busies himself with his bow then looses an arrow which falls at the foot of the couch. A wave of indignation ripples over the assembly. In an instant he is surrounded by guards and dragged before the Queen, tell-tale bow in hand. A slave retrieves the arrow whose barb carries a strip of papyrus. A love message this, which Cleopatra scans with languid interest. Amoûn, indifferent, awaits sentence. The Queen, attracted by his handsome features, offers him a night of ecstasy, to be paid for with his life. Amoûn bows his head in consent and rapturously kisses her feet.

Ta-hor, in a frenzy of desperation, beseeches Amoûn not to forsake her, but he remains indifferent to her supplications. Then she begs mercy of the Queen, who ignores her. Embittered by a sense of failure, Ta-hor's grief turns to anger and by sheer strength of her fury she forces Amoûn from the Queen's presence. He soothes Ta-hor with caressing touches, then, freeing himself from her grasp, dashes back to where his enchantress calmly awaits him.

Cleopatra gazes into his eyes and, gliding an arm about his neck, leads him to the divan, the while her slaves pile high the furs. As she reclines, Amoûn sinks on one knee, then, slowly drawing him towards her, she offers a deliberate and voluptuous embrace.

Follows a dance by Cleopatra's slave boy and slave girl, who celebrate the amorous triumph of their mistress in movements of the greatest abandon. A new melody is heard and in pour the Greek maidens, accompanied by two satyrs. It is the Bacchanale!

The music grows more insistent, the measure continually accelerated as wave after wave of melody beats on the ear until all blends in one maddening crescendo of rhythm. Before the couch flow the dancers in a seemingly endless stream, one confused mass of whirling garments, streaming tresses, and gleaming limbs, until they fall exhausted to the ground, the while the satyrs stroke their bearded chins with cunning leer.

Now the High Priest enters bearing the cup of death. The Queen rises, and, taking the cup, advances with slow step to the centre of the temple, driving Amoûn before her. Confronting him, she proffers the cup.

Amoûn gazes at her intently, seeking in vain some remission of the penalty. Taking the cup he drains it at a draught. The poison is swift, for the cup slips from his nerveless grasp and he sinks to his knees, clutching spasmodically at the Queen's robe. For a moment she recoils, then, placing her hands beneath his chin, slowly raises him to his full height, intently peering into his eyes as if unwilling to lose sight of the death throes of her victim. Suddenly, his arms fly upwards and he falls headlong.

Cleopatra remains motionless, as if lost in some strange ecstasy, then slowly makes her way out of the temple, followed by her suite. As the last figure departs the Priest enters accompanied by two slaves who throw over the body a sombre cloth. He utters a brief prayer and strides into the desert.

A dark figure steals past the great figures. It is Ta-hor in search of her lover. Fearfully, her gaze roves about her to rest upon the sinister object that encumbers the ground. She approaches with slow, faltering steps, then rolls back a corner of the cloth, to reveal the cold staring eyes of Amoûn. She kisses the still warm lips, caresses the stiff arms. Then, suddenly conscious of her powerlessness, she rends her hair and beats her breast in the agony of her grief.

*

Cléopâtre is largely based on a ballet called *Une Nuit d'Egypte,* first produced by Fokine at the Maryinsky Theatre, St. Petersburg, on March 8/21, 1908. The plot is very similar, the chief differences being as follows. First, when Amoûn has paid the penalty, Antony appears in his trireme; after an exchange of greetings a feast is held, with dancing as part of the entertainment; then Cleopatra and Antony, with their suites, embark on the ship, which sails away. Second, the ending of the older ballet is a happy one, for the High Priest substitutes a harmless sleeping draught for the poisoned cup, and when Berenice—called Ta-hor in *Cléopâtre*—bewails her lover, the High Priest bids her take heart and awakens Amoûn.

The music of *Une Nuit d'Egypte* is by A. Arensky, that of *Cléopâtre* is basically Arensky, with a few alterations. First, for the arrival of Cleopatra and the dancing by the female slaves, the music written by Rimsky-Korsakov for the appearance of Cleopatra in his opera-ballet *Mlada* was substituted. Second, for the veil dance of the two slaves, Glinka's *Danse Orientale* from his opera *Russlan and Ludmilla,* was taken. Third, for the final dance, the *Danse*

Persane from Mussorgsky's *Khovanchina* was used. In each case the music was matched with the rhythm, character, and length of Arensky's original numbers; the choreography remained almost unaltered.

Finally there was added a Bacchante dance arranged to the *Bacchanale* from Glazunov's *Les Saisons*.

When first given *Cléopâtre* achieved a furore. Something of this was due to Bakst's setting, whose giant figures hewn out of tawny rock produced an overwhelming effect of grandeur and solemnity; and something was due to Rubinstein, who made a great success as Cleopatra, her profile, with its enigmatic smile, being very suited to the part.

In London the role, which is pure mime, was taken first by Seraphina Astafieva and later by Tchernicheva. The former gave a voluptuous rendering; the latter's portrait had a calculating, half-sinister, half-enigmatic quality.

The role of Ta-hor has had many interpreters, the most impressive renderings being those of Pavlova and Sophie Fedorova.

When the ballet was revived by Diaghilev in 1918 it was given new scenery by Robert Delaunay. This conception was very modern, almost blinding in the brilliance of its violently contrasted colours, and very effective as a spectacle; but the sombre mood which had contributed so much to the drama of the original production had vanished with Bakst's setting.

LE CARNAVAL

Ballet in 1 Act. Book: Michel Fokine. Music: Robert Schumann. Scenery and costumes: Léon Bakst. Choreography: Michel Fokine. First produced in Western Europe: Théâtre National de l'Opéra, Paris, June 4th, 1910.

CHARACTERS

Columbine	MLLE. THAMAR KARSAVINA
Chiarina	MLLE. VERA FOKINA
Estrella	MLLE. L. SHOLLAR
Papillon	MLLE. BRONISLAVA NIJINSKA
Harlequin	M. VASLAV NIJINSKY
Pierrot	M. ADOLPH BOLM
Eusebius	
Pantalon	M. ENRICO CECCHETTI
Florestan	M. KUSSOV

Waltzers, Philistines.

Scene. The ante-chamber of a ballroom—a deep blue curtain, at the top of which runs a broad black and gold frieze. The sole furniture: two quaint little striped settees.

As the curtain rises to the lively *Préambule,* three ladies flit across the scene in quick succession, each hotly pursued by an enraptured swain. They are followed by other couples swaying delightfully to the rhythm of the waltz. Enter Chiarina, then Estrella, each followed by an infatuated admirer. Vanishing, they are replaced by two lovers walking arm-in-arm. A stolen kiss and they, too, whirl away to the mysterious realms beyond.

Suddenly the curtain parts to reveal the head of a Pierrot. Peering anxiously from side to side, as if fearful of being seen, he steps forth with grotesque strides. Flapping his long sleeves with a dismal air, he wanders aimlessly to and fro, opening and shutting his mouth as if hungering for someone to kiss, while the music, now slow, halting, and melancholy, renders his thoughts aloud. Then, as it changes to joyful melody, Harlequin bounds before us. Gaily he capers about the woebegone Pierrot, now mocking him with pointed finger, now dragging him by his sleeves, until, angered by his stupidity, Harlequin flicks him smartly with his hand, disappearing with another agile leap as Pierrot, losing his balance, falls clumsily to the ground.

Again the scene is occupied by six couples dancing merrily. As they pass from sight, Pierrot drags himself away with shambling gait and listless air. Now through the curtain glides the romantic Eusebius who, sitting on a sofa, muses on his mistress until his vision takes shape in the form of the lady herself, who presents him with a rose. In a whirlwind of silk and lace comes Estrella followed by the ardent Florestan. He falls on his knees and avows his love, but the mischievous coquette raises her hands in feigned horror at this unseemly proceeding. Then, relenting, she slips an arm into his and away trip the happy pair. Now follows a *pas de deux* between Eusebius and Chiarina, who dances on tiptoe while her lover follows her every movement with rapt adoration.

Enter Papillon, a vivacious lady all high spirits and fluttering ribbons, tip-toeing and pirouetting in a maze of varied movement, closely watched by Pierrot, now wearing his tall, conical hat. Half-concealed behind a sofa he becomes transported with the excitement of the chase. Emerging from his hiding-place, he launches in clumsy pursuit, but his hapless efforts are met with mocking raillery. Then, certain of his quarry, he flings down his hat, but, as swiftly as it falls, so the lady flits away. Pierrot, elated by his skill, hugs his breast in triumph, but on opening the cap finds it empty.

Now come three masked ladies, Chiarina and her two friends, who waltz merrily to and fro when there appears Florestan in quest of Estrella. They bar his way, but he slips under their arms and takes his departure. As the music changes to a slow, pathetic movement—*Chopin*—Chiarina tip-toes to the centre of the curtain, while the friends each move to her right and left. With raised finger Chiarina beckons to one who receives a charming embrace. The other lady advances and the two turn slowly round her, separating again as they sadly pass from view.

The melody changes to the lively *Reconnaissance,* and with quaint steps there enters Columbine attended by the sprightly Harlequin. Evidently he is in her good graces, for as they bow to each other she bestows on him a kiss. With beckoning finger he beseeches her to elope with him, but laughingly she refuses. Brisk, important footsteps announce the arrival of Pantalon, a pompous little man, who, twirling his carefully-waxed moustache, withdraws from his pocket a folded note which he peruses with great care and then consults his watch. He seats himself on a sofa and re-reads the note. While he is thus occupied Columbine leaps on the sofa and places her hands over his eyes. Chuckling with delight, Pantalon strives to free himself from these pleasant bonds, while Harlequin, creeping to his side, snatches the note from his hand. Struggling to his feet, Pantalon loses no time in paying attentions to his visitor, but the fickle lady is no easy victim; she repulses him with playful smacks on the cheek. Then with a graceful curtsey she introduces him to Harlequin. Pantalon, raising his hat, extends his hand, whereupon Harlequin displays to his astonished gaze the compromising missive. Crestfallen, he claps on his hat and retires in high dudgeon, while Harlequin leaps in the air and tears the note to pieces.

Now Columbine, tripping after Pantalon, detains him with outstretched hands and soothes his feelings with a kiss. Harlequin bounds to her side and the three perform a *pas de trois,* from which Pantalon is dismissed with a push. Harlequin performs a *pas seul* and sits on the ground. Columbine comes to his side when he makes as if to take out his heart and lay it at her feet. Columbine retires to a sofa and Harlequin sits on the ground beside her, lost in contemplation of her beauty.

Again the room is filled with revellers, who hasten to offer their felicitations to the newly-betrothed pair. Pantalon is charmingly pardoned, Pierrot may kiss her hand, and the auspicious event is

celebrated in a joyful dance, interrupted all too soon by some decidedly proper-looking dames and their consorts. But even the spoil-
sports, despite their protestations, are bandied to and fro in the
whirl of the dance, while Harlequin, unable to refrain from further
mischief, contrives with the assistance of his partner to throw into
collision Pierrot and Pantalon. Before they can recover from their
surprise, he deftly flings the former's sleeves around the latter, and,
fastening the ends, succeeds in binding together the ill-assorted
pair. As they vainly struggle to extricate themselves, the entire
company group themselves about Harlequin and Columbine in an
admiring circle, in which *tableau* Pierrot and Pantalon reluctantly take their places.

*

Le Carnaval is a study in romanticism, a festival of joy, an evocation of pretty sentiment, light intrigue, and high spirits seen in a
Victorian mirror.

This ballet was first produced at St. Petersburg, at the Pavlova
Hall, in Lent, 1910, in connection with a charity entertainment. It
was composed very quickly, in three rehearsals, the original cast
being: Leontiev (*Harlequin*), Cecchetti (*Pantalon*), Nijinska
(*Papillon*), Fokina (*Chiarina*), Shollar (*Estrella*), Karsavina
(*Columbine*), Meyerhold (*Pierrot*), and Kshesinsky (*Florestan*).

The original conclusion was a little different from the standard
version in that, during the *Marche des Davidsbündler contre les
Philistins,* the artistes left the stage and executed their dances
among the audience. At the final *Galop* they all ran back to the
stage, while Pierrot and Pantalon only returned during the fall of
the curtain, in front of which they remained.

The original scene represented a little garden which, in the later
productions, was changed to a curtain surround, sometimes ultra-
marine blue, sometimes emerald green, with a broad dado, relieved
by two preposterous striped settees.

The ballet has suffered several innovations since its original production. Then it was a sparkling light comedy with an undercurrent of subtle humour varied with moments of pathos. But
when Diaghilev revived the ballet at the Coliseum Theatre, London, in 1918, with Lopokova and Idzikowsky respectively as
Columbine and Harlequin, in place of Karsavina and Nijinsky,
the ballet was seen to have changed. The old satirical humour had
evaporated to be replaced by a child-like mood.

Some technical changes, too, have crept in. When Harlequin
outwits Pantalon by producing the compromising note, he used to
leap into the air and tear the note to pieces to the accompaniment

of *entrechats,* now the dancer frequently assumes a pose and tears up the note. In Harlequin's *pas seul* which follows his *pas de trois* with Columbine and Pantalon, both Nijinsky and Idzikowsky executed a dazzling series of *pirouettes à la seconde,* then, gradually bringing in the working leg and sinking on the supporting knee, each ended sitting on the ground; this is a very difficult movement which demands a fine balance. Now, the Harlequin frequently limits himself to a few *pirouettes* and then sits on the ground.

The *pas de deux* when Columbine and Harlequin make their entrance to the lively *Reconnaissance* is an interesting example of contrapuntal arrangement in choreography—Columbine travelling with swift little steps in contrast to Harlequin's big movements, yet both move together in perfect harmony.

Le Carnaval is one of the most popular of ballets, and the seeming simplicity of its choreographic structure makes it an alluring vehicle for aspiring dancers. Unfortunately, its very simplicity is its difficulty, the movements are so clear-cut that the execution and timing must be perfect, and defects in these qualities are immediately visible.

Most contemporary performances tend to be frivolous rather than gay; there is too much shaking of the head on the part of Harlequin, too much beckoning of the forefinger from Columbine. Pantalon is no longer that brisk, lovable little lady-killer of uncertain age as presented by Cecchetti, he has become something between a Napoleonic officer on half-pay and a type which suggests affinity with the Baron from a pantomime version of *Cinderella.* Pierrot, once a great tragic figure, as portrayed by Bolm, a pathetic figure of unrequited love and frustrated hopes, has almost faded away into an aimless weakling who inspires contempt rather than pity.

SCHÉHÉRAZADE

Ballet in 1 Act. Book: Alexandre Benois. Music: N. Rimsky-Korsakov. Scenery and costumes: Léon Bakst. Choreography: Michel Fokine. First produced: Théâtre National de l'Opéra, Paris, June 4th, 1910.

CHARACTERS

Zobeida	MME. IDA RUBINSTEIN
Zobeida's Favourite Slave . . .	M. VASLAV NIJINSKY

Shahryar, King of India and China . M. Alexis Bulgakov
Shah–Zeman . . . . M. Basil Kissilev
The Chief Eunuch . . . . . . M. Enrico Cecchetti
An *Odalisque* . . . . Mlle. Sophie Fedorova
   Odalisques, Sultanas, Dancers, Negroes, Youths, Ladies and
  Gentlemen of the Court, Aide-de-Camp to the Shah, Members
               of the Shah's Suite.

The overture at once creates an Eastern atmosphere—mysterious, voluptuous, and misty with the perfumed wreaths of burning incense—while underlaying the wistful cadence of the dance, the joyous call of the hunting-horns, and the frenzied sense of unbridled passion, booms the ever-insistent, ever-menacing, warning note of impending tragedy.

The curtain rises to reveal a marvellous scene, dominated by a voluminous emerald green curtain caught up to reveal Shahryar's harem. In the centre, set a little way back and at a slight angle, is a smaller apartment pierced by three scintillating blue doors. To the right are tall, orange columns serving to support the ceiling of blue and gold. To the left, set on a dais provided with a short flight of steps, is a sumptuous divan piled high with vari-coloured cushions.

The Shah Shahryar is seated on the divan with his favourite wife, Zobeida, on his left hand, and his brother, the Shah Zeman, on is right. Around the room are grouped the women of the harem. Zobeida solicits the caresses of her lord, but he is in an angry mood, for his brother has hinted that his wives are unfaithful.

Suddenly Shahryar summons the Chief Eunuch, who, grovelling before him, awaits his commands. Then, in response to his directions, there enter three *odalisques* who entertain their lord with dances. Tiring of their efforts, he dismisses them with an impatient gesture, and, springing to his feet, descends the steps to stride restlessly to and fro, pausing now and again to cast a questioning glance at Zobeida.

Zobeida goes to him and beseeches him to return to the comforts of his divan, but he announces his intention of starting on a hunting expedition. The women shake off their mask of lassitude, and subtle smiles suggest that they will not languish in his absence. But, for the moment, such thoughts must remain secret, and, practised in deceit, they simulate overwhelming sorrow at his proposal and seek to detain him with seductive arms. Zobeida, however, is annoyed at her lord's unexpected whim, and suspects that the journey is a pretext to seek the favours of another. But Shahryar is not to be deterred, and, pacing the ground with haughty mien, commands that arms for the chase be brought. Meanwhile, he becomes deep in whispered converse with his brother.

Eunuchs shuffle out of sight to return with cuirass and spear. The women surround the Shah and buckle on his armour. Huntsmen and guards arrive and the Shah takes his departure. The music quickens, the shrill notes of the hunting-horns blare out and fade into the distance.

The Shah's absence assured, the women throng about the blue doors, then bring out caskets of jewels, with which they adorn themselves. Presently two of their number depart and return with the Chief Eunuch, whom they bribe to open two of the doors. From the first issues a group of negroes attired in rose, from the second a similar group in green. With ingratiating leers they soon make love to the women and, seizing the objects of their admiration, disappear among the shadows.

The Chief Eunuch, his fat face wreathed in smiles and bubbling over with delight, collects his treasures and prepares to depart, when his way is barred by Zobeida, who imperiously demands that he shall open the last door. This time he is adamant, the risk is too great. Anxiously he seeks an outlet for escape, by turns angry, apologetic, cringing. At last, her patience exhausted, Zobeida snatches a rope of pearls from her neck, and, forcing it into his hands, commands him to open the door, failing which she threatens to dispatch him herself. Finding his prayers of no avail, the wretched Eunuch mechanically opens the last door. Even as he does so, four of his underlings glide from the harem like serpents, to carry the tidings to Shahryar.

From the mysterious depths of the opened door comes a flash of gold and a negro leaps to Zobeida's side. Momentarily he hesitates, blinded by the sudden transition from darkness to light, then, uttering little dumb cries of pleasure, he grimaces at his mistress and together they fall upon the divan, but lately vacated by her lord.

Immediately there enter youths, prancing in with grotesque strides and balancing on outstretched hands platters heaped with fruit; then come women bearing wine; lastly, *almées* inspiring passion with the thrumming of their tambourines. The music reverberates in dance-compelling rhythm. The youths, their hands alternately flung above their heads and resting on their hips, bound gaily to and fro, while from the mysterious recesses of the harem emerge the negroes and their paramours. Soon the floor is covered with a mad revolving throng, drunk with wine and consumed with passion.

Zobeida rises languorously from her couch, followed by the gold-clad negro who, with raised hands trembling with excitement, and gleaming teeth chattering in ecstasy of delight, hangs over her like a bee poised on some honeyed flower. Zobeida becomes motionless, her heaving breasts plain evidence of the strength of her emotion.

Suddenly the negro leaves her side and bounds into the turmoil of motion, whereupon the dancers form into two long lines, when, to the rhythmic clapping of their hands, he makes his way down the human avenue, now springing into the air to fall upon one knee, now spinning like a top; to plunge a second later into another frenzied movement. The dancers grow wilder and wilder in their actions, with raised arms undulating like serpents, and close about him so that he becomes the centre of this living wheel, the hub about which they revolve, swifter and swifter, circle within circle, until the eye is almost blinded with the glittering vortex of colour and motion.

As the movement declines in intensity, Zobeida darts upon her lover, to sway with him to the measure of the dance. Some of the revellers link arms, and through this series of oscillating arches, other dancers thread their way with bewildering rapidity. Feet thud and shuffle to the maddening rhythm of the dance. The gold-clad negro and his mistress return to the divan.

With the orgy at its height, the four eunuchs return, amazed at the spectacle that greets their eyes. Quick at their heels appears Shah Shahryar, in a rage so terrible as to leave little doubt as to the result of its unloosing. Behind him walks his brother.

The gold-clad negro springs to his feet and is about to fling himself into the dance when he observes the Shah. Terrified at this spectre of wrath, the dancers regard him panic-stricken, unable to move hand or foot. Then with one mind they turn to flee.

With a dramatic gesture Shahryar raises his hand, and there pour into the harem wave on wave of armed men, brandishing gleaming scimitars. The negroes and women dash blindly hither and thither in their frantic endeavour to escape. Soon the floor is heaped with the bodies of the slain. As for the unfaithful Chief Eunuch he merits a crueller fate and is choked to death by four of his underlings. Now returns the gold-clad negro. Suddenly he is confronted by the Shah. Even as he darts away a scimitar flashes. He falls, his legs shoot upwards, thud to the ground, and as he rolls over on his side a convulsive shudder proclaims the passing of his spirit.

There remains but Zobeida, surrounded by a glittering circle of weapons. Shahryar gazes sternly at her, sad at heart that she, too, has proved unfaithful. He is minded to pardon her, when his brother, with a contemptuous kick at the negro's body, reminds him of her lover. At this, his rage rekindles, and he motions to the guards, but Zobeida snatches a dagger from the belt of the nearest and kills herself. As she expires, Shahryar buries his face in his hands.

*

Schéhérazade is based on the first tale in the book of *The Thousand and One Nights.* It is the most voluptuous of all the ballets that were presented by the Diaghilev Company and, as originally given, presented a marvellous spectacles which for sheer sensuousness of colour and mood has probably never been equalled.

The music used is that of Rimsky-Korsakov's symphonic poem *Schéhérazade.* The complete work was found to be too long, hence it was decided to use Part I as an overture, and Parts II and IV for the ballet.

At this period Fokine had not seen any Oriental dances, so he sought inspiration by studying Persian miniatures, and made use of expressive pantomime in place of gesticulation.

When *Schéhérazade* was first given there was a great outcry from certain musical authorities, who criticised Fokine for having used the symphony to illustrate certain incidents in the ballet which differed considerably from the design the composer had in mind when writing the music. These objections were answered by Henri Ghéon who wrote:

"Is it fitting to regard as sacrilege the changing of the purpose of a piece of music? The first culprit is the composer who did not explain to us the literary or artistic dream, in every case unconnected with music, which he wishes to translate into pure music. I should not advise anyone to imitate Bakst and Fokine in this, but I consider that the manner in which they have translated Rimsky-Korsakov's poem, without regard to the original plan, is perfectly justifiable. The music had a certain significance, but it had a great many others, and, in a more general way, without the aid of synopsis or a picture, no music by itself can express an idea or feeling, still less colour or form—nothing but movement. The movements in *Schéhérazade* are correct and that is sufficient."

M. D. Calvocoressi, the musical critic of the *Comoedia Illustré*,[2] replied in a similar strain:

"The suppression of one of the four movements is the only

[2] July 1st, 1911.

thing that has taken place. We need not decide the question whether there ensues from this a break in the musical balance; there remains the question whether, if at different moments in the music a new meaning be attributed to them, the result be artistically false. I am well aware that the negroes are massacred at the moment when Rimsky-Korsakov's music refers to Sinbad's shipwreck, but I cannot help feeling envious of those whose sense of rhythm and notes is so precise that any different meaning is intolerable to them.

"How far are they from that German professor, both learned and authoritative, who, in his analysis of *Schéhérazade,* terms 'Shahryar's theme' what another commentator of no less merit styles 'sea theme,' with other curiosities of the same kind, from Johann Sebastian Bach himself who accords to an identical piece of music the duty of expressing in one case the pleasures of hunting, and in another the religious fervour of a soul exalted by prayer!"

The principal roles in *Schéhérazade* are Zobeida, the Chief Eunuch, and the Gold Negro. I did not see Rubinstein's rendering of Zobeida, which she created; in London the role was first taken by Karsavina, but she was not so impressive as the favourite sultana as in so many other roles. The best rendering of Zobeida that I have seen is undoubtedly that of Lubov Tchernicheva, who gives a most dignified performance. It is, however, open to criticism, in that while her whole bearing is indicative of her high place in Shahryar's household, it is difficult to believe that a woman so aloof could fall in love with her negro slave; moreover, she receives his attentions as homage rather than as a token of a passionate affection which she reciprocates.

Cecchetti was excellent as the Chief Eunuch, a doddering old man who waddled to and fro, his fat cheeks creased in a fatuous smile. How cunningly he allowed himself to be bribed, and how terrified he was at the unexpected return of the Shah. Of late there has been a regrettable tendency on the part of certain interpreters to make the Chief Eunuch a comic personage, which detracts from the dramatic balance of the ballet.

But the whole ballet was dominated by Nijinsky's performance as the Gold Negro. I can still see his astounding first entrance when, the last blue door having been flung open, he darted towards Zobeida with the swiftness of a bolt from a crossbow, a flashing parabola, to stretch his arms wide in a gesture of possession, like some indolent animal awakened from sleep. His performance ended on a high note, and thrilling death scene, when, having run and swerved and doubled in frantic endeavour to escape his murderous pursuers, he was cut down, to fall headlong and spin on the back of his neck with his legs flung upwards, until he subsided like "a fish tossed on to the sand." [3]

L'OISEAU DE FEU

Ballet in 1 Act and 2 Scenes. Book: Michel Fokine. Music: Igor Stravinsky. Scenery and costumes: Golovine. Choreography: Michel Fokine. First produced: Théâtre Nationale de l'Opéra, Paris, June 25th, 1910.

The Bird of Fire	MLLE. THAMAR KARSAVINA
Ivan Tsarevich	M. MICHEL FOKINE
Köstchei, the Immortal	M. ENRICO CECCHETTI
The Beautiful Tsarevna	MLLE. VERA FOKINA

The Enchanted Princesses, Youths, Kikimoras, Indians, Bolebochki, Köstchei's Women, Monsters, Pages, etc.

The ballet commences with an overture which soon creates an atmosphere of witchcraft, goblins, and attendant magic. The music has a peculiar timbre. There are low mutterings, mysterious long-drawn wails as of one unknown creature calling to another, the tramp of gnomes underground, strange rustlings, moans, the rumble of distant thunder, the music of a stream coursing over stones—and above all can be heard, at first faintly, then with increasing distinctness, the tremulous whirr of the wings of a bird soaring in circular flight.

When the curtain rises all is dark, a land of shadows, save only in the centre, where, bathed in a circle of amber light, grows a tree, its branches laden with golden fruit. The music increases in volume and the scene lightens slightly to reveal the depths of a forest. Not a breath of air stirs in the trees. Presently a bird, gleaming with orange radiance, flashes across the background of foliage. Now it is possible to discern a high wall to the right, over which a youth in hunting-dress clambers. It is Ivan Tsarevich. In one hand he holds a crossbow with bolt ready in the slide, with the other he parts the bushes as he peers anxiously to right and left. The whirr of wings is heard and the Bird of Fire flits to the tree. The Prince raises his weapon, takes aim, and looses the bolt,

[3] Nijinsky (Romola) *Nijinsky.*

but he misses and the startled bird flies away into the depths of the forest.

The Prince remains concealed and soon the bird returns to play amid the gleaming leaves of the magic tree. He approaches with stealthy steps and catches it in his arms. The bird struggles until exhausted, then offers him a golden feather for ransom. Ivan assents and allows it to go free. The scene grows lighter, and it is possible to see that through the trees runs a light palisade, ending in two gates through which is visible a flight of steps lost in shadow. Ivan is about to depart when a plaintive melody is heard and twelve maidens wind their way across a sloping eminence and down the steps. The Prince, amazed, steps into the shadow.

The gates open and the maidens go toward the tree, where they are presently joined by another whose rich dress proclaims her rank. They shake the tree so that the apples fall to the ground and roll in all directions. The maidens career in pursuit, and each casts her prize high in the air to catch it and throw it to a companion. Ivan comes from his hiding-place and doffs his cap to them. But the leader of the maidens warns him to depart, for he is before the castle of Köstchei, an enchanter of mighty power, who captures all who trespass on his domains. The Prince, however, already in love with the maiden, wishes to stay.

Suddenly there sounds a discordant note which is repeated. The startled maidens run through the gates, which close after them. The Prince is about to take his departure when darkness descends and he is unable to find an outlet. He runs to and fro in terror, then turns to the gates and strives to open them. He shakes them. They fly open, the forest blazes with light, and down the eminence pours a motley horde of demons and goblins. They fall on the Prince and hold him fast, to await the coming of Köstchei.

The maidens come down the steps, then more guards, and finally the enchanter himself. He glares at his victim and strives to cast a spell upon him, but Ivan remembers the golden feather and waves it aloft. To his aid flies the glorious Bird of Fire, who scatters his enemies and begins a dance of closely increasing measure. The demons are compelled to follow her until, exhausted, they sink to the ground and fall into a deep slumber. The Bird of Fire bids Ivan take the chief of the maidens to a place of safety, then shows him a root which marks the base of a hollow tree. He crawls inside to reappear with an iron-bound casket.

He raises the lid and withdraws an enormous egg, which he throws into the air and catches as it falls, while Köstchei, who knows that it contains his soul, trembles with fear and apprehension. In desperation he clutches at the precious object, but Ivan dashes it to the ground. There is a deafening crash and darkness falls.

Presently the stage lightens, showing the palisade broken asunder while Köstchei, his court, and the Bird of Fire have vanished. In their place is a group of young men dressed richly, who pay homage to Ivan. Down the steps comes a beautiful Princess, the maiden to whom he pledged his troth, and in her train a group of nobles and fair dames, now freed from enchantment by the death of Köstchei. They are followed by a procession of pages, who bear in their midst a crown, sceptre, and ermine robe. Ivan is invested with these symbols of power and the assembly acclaim him as their deliverer and sovereign lord.

*

The theme of *L'Oiseau de Feu* is an adaptation from several Russian fairy-tales—*The Tale of Ivan Tsarevich* and *The Bird of Light and the Grey Wolf* combined with the legend of the enchanter, Köstchei, and his soul hidden in an egg.

Lyadov was originally invited to compose the music for the ballet, but, as he worked slowly and seemed very uncertain as to when he could complete the score, Diaghilev took back the commission and gave it to Stravinsky, then a rising young composer whose work he greatly admired.

Stravinsky visited Fokine and they worked in the closest collaboration. Fokine explained his conception of the mimed scenes, then the composer devised appropriate themes, and the two collaborators discussed them in detail from the choreographic and musical view-points.

The dances for the Bird of Fire were likewise the result of this consultation. The Bird of Fire gives each group of demons a theme to which she forces them to dance again and again, then she gives another group a different theme and so forth. Stravinsky was greatly pleased with this plan, which is accurately expressed in the music. As Stravinsky completed each section of the music, so Fokine worked on the choreography.

The role of the Bird of Fire has a long line of interpreters, of which I prefer Karsavina's rendering. She wore a costume which was far more charming and far more fantastic than the orange and yellow bodice and short skirt which succeeded it. Of present-day renderings of the role that of Danilova is the best.

With the exception of the costume for the Bird of Fire and that for the Tsarevna, which were devised by Bakst, the original dresses and settings were designed by Golovine. Unfortunately this scene was destroyed by damp in 1922. In 1926 the ballet was revived with new scenery and costumes by N. Gontcharova. These are very decorative in colour and design, but they lack the fairy-like beauty which distinguished Golovine's work.

LE SPECTRE DE LA ROSE

Ballet in 1 Act. Book: J. L. Vaudoyer. Music: Weber. Scenery and costumes: Léon Bakst. Choreography: Michel Fokine. First produced: Théâtre de Monte Carlo, 1911.

CHARACTERS

The Young Girl . . . . MLLE. THAMAR KARSAVINA
The Spirit of the Rose . . . M. VASLAV NIJINSKY

Scene. A young girl's bedroom. The room, octagonal in shape, is pure white, except where the walls are covered with a deep blue paper on which stands out, in sharp relief, a simple floral design, also in white. Between the two windows is placed a sofa covered in blue and white chintz, at the side of which is a round table, on which stands a bowl of roses. To the right, situated in an alcove, is a small wooden bed, the sheets of which are thrown back as if awaiting to enfold their dainty mistress. At the foot is a comfortable leather arm-chair and her sketching easel. On the left side is her dressing-table with looking-glass and powder-puff carefully arranged. Everything indicates the neatness and simplicity of the owner. In the left and right back corners are tall french windows thrown wide open to reveal a garden with high clusters of rose-bushes almost covered with pink and red blossoms. Overhead can be seen the warm blue sky of a summer's evening, and through the open window streams the moonlight, flecking the floor with bright patches of green and yellow.

From the garden comes a gentle breeze laden with the fragrance of roses, and into the room steps a young girl, sweet and demure in her high-cut ball-dress of creamy white, over which is lightly fastened a little cloak. In her hand she gently holds a rose, fearful lest her tiny fingers should crumple its fragile beauty. She raises it to her lips and imprints on it a loving kiss. What tender secrets does it hold, this lover's gift? She gazes upon it with downcast eyes. Surely it is not wrong to be loved? Her lips quiver and seem to murmur his name. She glances around the room, so friendly, so dear to her, with all its innocent treasures. Now that her face is upraised how tired she looks. Perhaps, little accustomed to worldly pleasures, the excitement of the ball has proved too great for her. She throws off her wrap and walks slowly to her arm-chair. She sinks into it with a sigh of content, her eyes close and in a few moments she is fast asleep. Her limp hands fall and through her fingers the rose slips, caresses her dress, and glides to the floor.

The music quickens to a rapturous movement and through the open window alights the object of her dream, the spirit of the rose. With what joy, with what abandon, does he dance, blown hither and thither like a rose petal in the wind.

At his magic touch she is spirited out of her chair to join him in the ever-quickening, soothing melody of the waltz. How high she leaps, yet so gracefully that it seems as if she, too, had forsaken her mortal body. Together they float through the still air, impelled everywhere by the fairy-like touch of his hand. Then the music slowly dies away and ceases. A moment and she is again in her chair, her features still calm in repose, unruffled, as if what had just transpired was but an elfin touch of our imagination. Bending over her for a brief instant, the rose-coloured sprite disappears through the open window just as the first rays of dawn trace curious shadows on the wall.

The maiden stirs, and, smoothing her sleep-laden eyes, looks about her as if what was in truth but a dream were reality. The room is empty. Still doubting, she bends and picks up her precious rose. Then she remembers, her face lights up in a sad half-smile, and as she presses the rose to her bosom the curtain falls.

*

The theme of *Le Spectre de la Rose* was suggested by the French poet, J. L. Vaudoyer, during the Diaghilev Company's first visit to Paris. It is an adaptation of Gautier's little poem, the subject of which is the evocation of the spirit of a rose given to a young girl at a ball. The dance was set to Weber's well-known piece, *L'Invitation à la Valse*.

Fokine's intention was to use Nijinsky's rare *élévation* to create a poetical picture of the rose-coloured sprite, so that the dance executed by the sleeping girl, rendered by Karsavina, should afford a charming contrast to the energetic movements of the male dancer who represented the spirit of the rose.

This composition in the style of the Romantic Ballet illustrates exactly Fokine's contention that the technique of the classical ballet should be used only where it is applicable. *Le Spectre de la Rose* is a *classical pas de deux* and Nijinsky's wonderful *élévation* was employed in such a manner that his leaps and bounds seemed the embodiment of grace and ease, the natural attributes of an ethereal being, and not the product of an extraordinary technique.

Everyone who saw Nijinsky in this ballet will recall that wonderful leap by which he entered from the rose-garden, through the open french window, to alight beside the young girl asleep in her chair. There was a rose-coloured flash and he was seen to describe a graceful parabola with the ease of a grasshopper leaping from one blade of grass to another. There was no flurry, no strained features, no thud as the feet came to the ground; it was just as though a rose-petal had been caught up by a night breeze and wafted through the open window.

Le Spectre de la Rose achieved a furor wherever it was given. On one occasion when it was danced at an official charity performance held at the Grand Opera, Paris, it achieved so overwhelming a success that, in response to the clamours of the audience for an encore, the whole was repeated—an unprecedented event for Paris.

This miniature ballet, as it left Fokine's hands, and as it was presented by Karsavina and Nijinsky, was a genuine choreographic poem, so beautiful and so intangible that, when it was at an end, you were uncertain as to whether you had seen the ballet or had momentarily been dreaming.

Le Spectre de la Rose is so linked with the two artists who gave it life that it should be sacrosanct. All the revivals I have seen not only lacked the fragrance of the original, but choreographic details were missing, the lighting left much to be desired, and, in one instance, in place of the famous leap, the dancer stood on the window-ledge and jumped into the room. *Sic transit gloria mundi.*

PETROUCHKA

Burlesque Ballet in 1 Act and 4 Scenes. Book: Igor Stravinsky and Alexandre Benois. Music: Igor Stravinsky. Scenery and costumes: Alexandre Benois. Choreography: Michel Fokine. First produced: Théâtre du Chatelet, Paris, June 13th, 1911.

CHARACTERS

The Ballerina . . . . Mlle. Thamar
Karsavina

Petrouchka	. . . . . .	M. Vaslav Nijinsky
The Moor	. . . . . .	M. Alexander Orlov
The Old Showman	. . . . .	M. Enrico Cecchetti
The Bibulous Merchant	. . . .	M. Kussov
The Gypsies	. . . . . .	{ Mlle. Schollar { Mlle. Reysen
Street Dancers	. . . . . .	{ Mlle. B. Nijinska { Mlle. L. Shollar

Nurses, Coachmen, Grooms, First Organ-Grinder, Second Organ-Grinder, The Old Father of the Fair, The Picture-Showman, Masks and Masqueraders, Vendors, Officers, Soldiers, Gentlemen, Ladies, Children, Policemen, A Bear-Leader, etc.

Scene I. The Admiralty Square, St. Petersburg, in the year 1830, during the revels which take place on the last three days before Lent, Maslenitsa—Butter Week—a period of peasant holiday and debauch before the abstinence of the forty days. Two curtains are used in the performance of this ballet; the first is the usual barrier between the audience and the dancers, the second is that which screens the interior of the Showman's booth from both the real and the stage audience.

Prior to the raising of the curtain there is a brief overture extraordinarily descriptive of the sounds of a fair—the bustle of a seething mass of people bent on amusement, the raucous invitations shouted by the owners of side-shows, the jargon of noise produced by innumerable instruments all playing a different tune, while, above all, can be heard the grinding melody of a combined mechanical organ and roundabout.

The scene depicts a fair held in mid-winter. To the left is a booth hung with red and white striped curtains upon the top of which is a yellow boarded platform. Here, sheltered under a coarse blue awning, is an old man who calls attention to the length of his beard, and two gypsies who entreat onlookers to have their fortunes told. To the right, backing on to the side of a wooden hut, is a collection of stalls loaded with sweets and trinkets. In the centre is another booth, rectangular in shape, the contents of which are screened by a blue curtain. Behind loom the top of a roundabout and the misty outline of the Admiralty spire. Over the snow-covered ground comes and goes a multi-coloured throng, laughing, shouting, dancing, as full of fun as can be. In turn they make way for a band of peasants, who noisily stamp to the lively strains of a concertina, and a street dancer who steps to the accompaniment of a hurdy-gurdy. Suddenly, two drummers emerge from the interior of the centre booth, and commence to beat a vigorous tattoo. A whistle sounds and the bearded head of a showman appears through the curtain. He steps forth, then, striding to the side of the booth, causes the curtain to fly back revealing three compartments, in each of which grotesquely sprawls a puppet. The first is a Moor, the second a Ballerina, the third Petrouchka. At a signal from the showman they break into a quick, automatic dance and presently come out of the booth into the snow. The crowd applauds heartily. Suddenly the puppets collapse to the ground and all is dark.

Scene II. Petrouchka's cell, a triangular apartment of deep black lightly powdered with silver stars, at the left of which is a low double door.

Presently this flies open and Petrouchka is impelled through the opening by the Showman's cruel boot. He tries in vain to escape from his prison. Again the door opens and the Ballerina enters, to him a figure of surpassing beauty. He seeks to gain her favour by an exhibition of wonderful leaps, but he is coldly received and the Ballerina departs. Again he tries to find an outlet, tears at the wall, then falls headlong to the ground. The light vanishes.

Scene III. The home of the Moor, a very luxurious apartment decorated with red wall paper patterned with gigantic palm-trees.

In the centre stands a divan upon which the Moor sprawls, playing with a cocoa-nut. Then he tries to break the nut with his scimitar and, failing to do so, believes it to be a fetish. He prays to it, when the door opens and the Ballerina enters carrying a toy trumpet, with which she dances. The Moor drops the cocoa-nut and watches her with delight. Presently he pulls her on to his lap when the door again opens and Petrouchka appears. The guilty pair separate and the Moor chases Petrouchka, and eventually dispatches him through the door with a kick. Triumphant, he pulls the Ballerina again on his knee. All is dark.

Scene IV. Same as Scene I; but time has passed, the sky is darkening and nightfall is imminent.

Some sightseers are preparing to depart while a few more boisterous spirits, several coachmen, invite some nursemaids to dance, an attempt which is frustrated by the ladies' escorts. Now the nursemaids decide to dance among themselves. Meanwhile the crowd is distracted by new arrivals: a performing bear, a vendor of ribbons, a merchant with a gypsy girl on each arm. The coachmen begin a lively dance in which the girls join until interrupted by a group of revellers with their faces concealed by grotesque masks. The scene grows darker and now a terrible commotion is heard in the booth where the puppets live.

The curtain is violently agitated and out leaps Petrouchka followed by the Moor with upraised scimitar; at his heels runs the frightened Ballerina. With a vicious sweep of his blade the Moor fells Petrouchka to the ground, then runs away, accompanied by the Ballerina. A crowd quickly collects and a policeman is summoned who returns with the Showman. He seizes the corpse and points out its stuffed body and wooden limbs. The crowd, relieved, departs homewards, while the Showman drags the useless puppet behind him. Suddenly there is an unearthly shriek and on the top of the booth appears the head and shoulders of the wraith of Petrouchka. The Showman looks upward, starts back in terror, drops his burden and flees.

*

The music of this ballet came to be written as the result of an unusual chain of circumstances. In 1909 Stravinsky was at St. Petersburg putting the finishing touches to his score of *L'Oiseau de Feu,* when he suddenly conceived the idea of a ballet based on a primitive pagan rite, which he decided to call *Le Sacre du Printemps.* He told Diaghilev of his conception; his friend was enthusiastic and urged Stravinsky to begin work.

The composer, however, decided that he would first write a short composition which had been taking shape in his mind for some little time; it was to express a kind of burlesque duel between an animated puppet and an orchestra, in which the puppet was finally slain by a terrific burst of cacophony. This piece he intended to call *Petrouchka.*

When Diaghilev visited Stravinsky he was greatly taken aback to be greeted with some of the themes for *Petrouchka,* instead of the airs for the promised *Sacre du Printemps.* But he delighted in the novelty of the *Petrouchka* music, which he saw as material for a fascinating ballet.

Who was responsible for the "book" of *Petrouchka?* The programmes give the names of Stravinsky and Benois as joint authors. Prince Lieven confirms this statement. On the other hand Stravinsky[4] himself suggests that much of the theme was the outcome of a collaboration between Diaghilev and himself. The probability is that the theme was the product of all three.

If ever any ballet had the right to be acclaimed a masterpiece, it is certainly *Petrouchka,* for its music, its choreography, and its settings and costumes are impeccable. What a fine ballet this is! It is impossible to describe the vivid sense of life which animates the whole. The crowd is quite extraordinary, it does not march methodically to and fro like soldiers at review in the manner of the old ballet; the people jostle and push each other, struggle to obtain the best view of the peep-show, exchange greetings, compare opinions of the merits of the rival street-dancers, banter the proprietors of the stalls—one may see this ballet a score of times and yet find some new by-play which in the wealth of various incidents offered had hitherto passed unnoticed.

The steps for the dolls are worked out with the same loving care; there are clumsy steps and florid movements for the Moor; dainty, *pizzicato* steps for the Ballerina; and stiff, wooden gestures for the hapless Petrouchka. Yet, though all the movements of these puppets are essentially doll-like, by some cunning art Fokine has succeeded in investing them with a certain mystic symbolism. The spectator, from his first introduction to them feels that for all their expressionless faces, their bodies of sawdust, they possess a soul. The dances, too, are full of variety and national character. Who can forget the hand-claps and lusty rhythmic stamps of the fat coachmen, the semi-stupid movements of the nurses, the frenzied dances of the gypsies—red and orange skirts flashing, hips swaying; all executed with a fine devilry—and the terrifying gestures of the masked revellers who pretend to frighten the women. *Petrouchka,* as the eminent critic Vuillemin stated, is "a miracle of choreographic art."

There have been many interpreters of the title-role—for instance, Massine, Idzikowsky, Woizikowsky, Zverev, Obukhov, to mention only a few—but, to my mind, not one of them approaches Nijinsky who, curiously enough, had some difficulty at the first performance in remembering certain of the movements set for his part, and Fokine, at the dancer's request, had to prompt him from behind the scenery during the whole of the episode in Petrouchka's room.

There was a definite puppet-like quality about Nijinsky's Petrouchka. He seemed to have limbs of wood and a face made of plaster, in which his eyes resembled nothing so much as two

[4] See *Chronique de ma Vie.*

boot-buttons. Only now and again did he make you aware that beneath this façade there was a tiny spark of human life, which you caught sight of by accident, as though it were something you were not meant to see. Gone were those fascinating features with the slanting eyes, that marvellous *élévation*—all had vanished, to be replaced by this wretched puppet—beaten, humiliated, and the sport of its fellows—a victim of cruel injustice which moved by jerks and starts and hardly left the ground. Nijinsky's Petrouchka was a puppet that sometimes aped a human being; all the other interpreters of the role that I have seen suggested a dancer who was imitating a puppet.

Many dancers have portrayed the Ballerina, and among the best I should place Karsavina, Lopokova, and Nijinska. This is not such a simple part as it appears, because the steps require a particular crispness and tautness of execution, without which the performance loses that piquancy which is its prime attraction. One episode that is frequently lacking in quality occurs in the third scene—the entrance of Petrouchka at the moment when the all-conquering Moor has the Ballerina sitting on his knees. Karsavina made this a delicious study of mock modesty and protesting innocence, but, as generally given nowadays, the scene has lost its savour.

THAMAR

Ballet in 1 Act. Book: Léon Bakst. Music: Balakirev. Scenery and costumes: Léon Bakst. Choreography: Michel Fokine. First produced: Théâtre du Chatelet, May 20th, 1912.

CHARACTERS

Thamar, Queen of Georgia .   .   MLLE. THAMAR KARSAVINA
The Prince .   .   .   .   .   M. ADOLPH BOLM
Friends of Thamar, Lesghins, Servants.

Scene. Interior of Thamar's castle. It is a large, rectangular room with a high roof which slopes to an acute angle. The walls are of brick, shaded from rose to deep violet. Around the base of the walls, for about the height of a man, runs a broad crimson tapestry, decorated with large circles rimmed with a blue and white chequer. At the back, to the left, is a heavily-studded green door, at the side of which is an ikon set in a tryptych. To the right is a large turret window, half-covered by a heavy curtain, which

reveals a glimpse of snow-clad mountains. The last rays of a pale
sunset lighten the green-carpeted floor. From the centre of the
roof hangs a crude candelabrum set with candles which smoke
and flicker under the gales that sweep about the castle. The room
is strewn with rich carpets and costly skins, but, despite the splen-
dour of the appointments, there is an atmosphere of gloom and
unrest.

Near the window is a table loaded with flagons. Beside this
stands a couch upon which reclines Thamar, Queen of Georgia.
She is attired in a light crimson caftan while her hair is gathered
into two long plaits threaded with a string of pearls.

To the left of the room, in a recess, a band of musicians is
seated. Women and guards are grouped about the walls. Some
converse in low tones, others are silent and impassive. Thamar
turns uneasily on her couch. An attendant inclines her head as if
straining at a sound. She darts forward on tip-toe, bends over the
queen and whispers in her ear. Thamar languidly raises herself
on one elbow and peers intently through the darkening window.
Then she gropes among her cushions and withdraws a scarf.
With a jerk of her wrist it waves in the air—once, twice, and
thrice. A pause. The signal has been observed and answered.

A ripple of expectation passes over the waiting men and women.
The queen rises and steps to the floor. With an imperative gesture
she summons three of her guards who fling long, black cloaks over
their shoulders and pass out to welcome the guest. The music, till
now almost unnoticed, becomes more insistent, even ominous, as
the guards return accompanied by a tall stranger, cloaked from
head to foot, his face half-hidden by a scarf drawn tight about his
throat and chin.

Thamar gazes at him with intensity as if in endeavour to divine
his features. Impatient, she flings back the scarf to reveal a handsome youth. They look steadfastly at each other, then he extends
his arms as if to embrace her, but she eludes his grasp and signs
to the guards to relieve him of his cloak. She offers him wine
which he drinks. The traveller bends over her, but the women
close about him and usher him from the chamber.

The queen remains standing, deep in thought. She summons
her warriors to dance. In single file the guards sweep forward in
a semi-circle. With a jerk of their hands they pluck daggers from
their sheaths and whirl their arms in a circular movement, so
that the bright steel describes a series of glittering arcs. They
dance with frenzied bounds, with fierce stamps of the feet; the

measure becomes wilder and wilder. The music throbs and pulsates with a maddening rhythm. Soon they lose all restraint. The daggers are raised in the air to be hurled viciously into the floor. But scarcely have they ceased quivering when they are wrenched from their sockets, to be hurled down again. The music swells in an ever-increasing volume of sound. Thamar, a little apart, surveys the scene with outward signs of increasing passion. Unable to restrain her impatience, she imperiously stamps her foot.

The door opens and the stranger enters, clad in a splendid caftan. He is surrounded by a group of women who bear large tambourines. They wind about the room with languorous movements the while they strike their tambourines. The stranger quickly espies the queen and strives to approach her, but she affects to ignore him. She retreats through her waiting women and makes her way to the couch, with her lover following hard at her heels. He seeks to win her favour with a dance. He springs into the air, jerks his head to and fro, and curves his legs under him so that, with every leap, his body is arched like a strung bow. He bounds higher and higher, his feet stamp, twist, and turn, faster and faster, to the frenzied throbbing of the tambourines. The queen marks with satisfaction his feverish looks, his savage movements. She joins in the dance and their lips meet in a passionate kiss. Then she twists from his grasp and runs through the green door. He follows in pursuit.

Their disappearance is an excuse for the resumption of the mad dance of a short while since. The eye can scarce support the turmoil of nodding hats, wind-blown garments, gleaming daggers— the vivid purples, greens, and reds of the costumes intermingled in one scintillating, revolving mass. The floor echoes to the pulsating rhythm of the measured stamp of heel and toe. At last, overcome with exhaustion, the dancers cease and lean against the walls to rest their weary, aching limbs.

Again the youth reenters. He staggers backward into the room as if his legs were incapable of supporting his frame. Now Thamar appears, her eyes lowered, her nostrils dilated, her features set in a grim and sinister mask. She comes to him, leans over his face with a seductive smile, then throws an arm about his neck and drags him to and fro. Meanwhile, two attendants pull back a cunningly-devised panel set in the wall through which, sparkling in the pearl-grey light of dawn, can be seen the swiftly-falling waters of the Terek. Stealthily she unsheathes the dagger at her girdle. She draws him closer, kisses his eyes and, with a quick movement of her arm, stabs him to the heart. The wretched youth struggles from her embrace, totters from side to side and falls backward through the panel. The attendants close the door.

The queen steps towards her couch and summons her women who loosen her hair and divest her of her outer garments. She flings herself upon the couch and closes her eyes. Again a woman inclines her head in an attitude of listening. She lightly touches the slumbering queen and whispers in her ear. Thamar half-rises and gazes through the turret window. She fumbles among her cushions and withdraws the scarf. Again it writhes in the air —once, twice, thrice. . . .

*

Thamar is a fine example of a dramatic ballet. Fokine had visited the Caucasus in his youth, and he drew on those memories for his inspiration for the dances, which are extraordinarily fierce and thrilling. He has no equal in the arrangement of dances which require to be imbued with a mad frenzy. The wonderful manner in which he combines movement with rhythm, the endless combinations of colour which he evolves from the varied order and movement of the costumes, so excite the spectator that it requires the greatest effort for him to observe the social conventions which demand that he shall remain quietly seated in his place.

The mimed scenes are most impressive and it is remarkable how the queen, though never rendered obtrusive, is made to dominate the whole like some evil spirit drawn by Vrubel. From the moment the curtain rises, the action, swift and tense, keeps the spectator enthralled to the end.

Those who have seen *Thamar* as rendered by De Basil's "Ballets Russes" in 1936 may consider my praise of this ballet's splendid barbaric quality to be excessive. The explanation is simple, the latest revival was a drawing-room version compared with the original production; again, the lighting had little of the mystery of the original, and the timing of certain of the dramatic episodes was faulty.

In the original production Karsavina and Bolm were superb. It was a stirring experience to watch that fine figure of a man, radiating energy in every line, making his first entrance on the rising tide of excitement in the music, to be gradually enmeshed in the snares of the beautiful vampire with her dark, glowing eyes and bloodless face. You could almost feel the heat of the mutual passion that consumed them—the hot pursuit, the surrender, then, for the Prince, the kiss of betrayal, the sudden thrust of an unsuspected dagger, and the victim's reeling fall through the open panel.

That manner of disposing of the Prince was much more effective, theatrically, than the later version which crept in and still persists, in which the Prince is stabbed in the middle of the stage, raised on the shoulders of servants, and borne ceremoniously to the open panel to be hurled into the waters below.

DAPHNIS ET CHLOË

Ballet in 1 Act and 3 Scenes. Book: Michel Fokine. Music: Maurice Ravel. Scenery and costumes: Léon Bakst. Choreography: Michel Fokine. First produced: Théâtre du Chatelet, Paris, June 8th, 1912.

CHARACTERS

Chloë	MLLE. THAMAR KARSAVINA
Daphnis	M. VASLAV NIJINSKY
Darkon	M. ADOLPH BOLM
Lisinion	
Old Man	
Nymphs	

Greeks, Brigands with Lances, Brigands with Bows, Young Brigands.

Scene I. A grove sacred to Pan and his Nymphs. The background is formed by a group of cypresses bounded by large boulders; in the distance can be seen rising fields dotted with scattered bushes. To the right and left of the foreground are similar groups of cypresses, that on the left being flanked by a rocky eminence upon which stand out in sharp relief the sculptured forms of three nymphs, marking the rough altar erected to the glory of the God Pan.

Soon there arrives a procession of graceful maidens bearing on their heads baskets and oval jars which contain offerings for the altar—wine pressed from the choicest grapes, fruit plucked from the finest orchards, flowers culled from the fairest fields. Slowly, with infinite variety of pose and gesture, the maidens wind about the altar. Now they are joined by young men who also take part in these solemn measures.

The rites ended, the worshippers break up into little groups. Among the throng can be seen the handsome Daphnis and the fair Chloë, lovers from their tenderest years. Daphnis casts many spells over the hearts of the young girls present. Soon, ever willing to please, he joins them in a dance which arouses Chloë's jealousy. In revenge, she wanders among the young men and becomes in consequence the object of the attentions of Darkon, a boorish herdsman whose sole claim to admiration lies in his immense physical strength.

He becomes bolder and attempts to snatch a kiss, which inclination is prevented by the timely intervention of Daphnis. It is clear that the rivals will soon fall to blows, but the shepherds will have none of it and bid them match their prowess in a dance. Darkon, already convinced of his superiority, executes a clumsy dance with much stamping of feet, shaking of head, and wild flinging of his arms. The onlookers burst into laughter, and Darkon, seeing that his efforts excite only derision, retires in scornful humiliation. Then it is the turn of Daphnis who, taking in his hand a white wand, performs a graceful dance which is received with applause. Chloë, her anger past, bestows on him a kiss. Now all leave the grove save Daphnis who, spent with the exertion of the dance, composes himself on the ground to rest. No sooner is his head pillowed on the turf than evil befalls him in the guise of the temptress Lisinion. She unveils and with languorous dance seeks to captivate him, but Daphnis angrily repulses her and bids her begone. She departs in dismay.

Suddenly there is heard the noise of running feet, the clash of warlike weapons, the hoarse cries of lawless men, mingled with the pitiful shrieks of women who, fleeing in terror, seek to escape from the merciless pirates who have just landed in quest of plunder. The voices come nearer, and Chloë, gasping for breath, seeks sanctuary in the sacred grove. But the pirates have no scruples and one of their number seizes Chloë, throws her over his shoulder, and disappears.

All has passed in an instant and before Daphnis, stupefied by the clamour, can run to her aid, the grove is empty and in place of Chloë there remains only her torn scarf trodden deep into the earth. Distraught, he curses the gods and falls in a swoon.

The shadows fall and dusk deepens into night. A mysterious light illumines the altar and out of the darkness appear the three Nymphs who with reverent gesture and solemn dance invoke the aid of Pan.

Scene II. The pirates' camp, a vast clearing, almost surmounted by great, orange-brown cliffs. Between two of these can be seen a glimpse of the Aegean Sea where their ship rides at anchor. Overhead glows a blue sky across which float sun-streaked masses of cloud as if to imitate the motion of the ship below.

Again that awful tumult falls on the ears and the pirates arrive, laden with booty and dragging in their midst the trembling Chloë. They call for a dance, and, shouting with drunken glee, seize their bows and spears and bound and leap in a circle. They quarrel and wrestle among themselves, howling and struggling like a pack of dogs. But at a signal from their chief they cease their dangerous play and all is quiet. With a grin he beckons to Chloë but, unwilling, she has to be half-carried, half-dragged to his presence. She begs for pity, but the chief only grins the more, and stretching out his arm pulls her on to his knee.

Suddenly a strange shadow falls over the cliffs, at the sight of which the pirates tremble with superstitious fear. The shadow comes nearer and the pirates, relinquishing their captive, flee in terror. Chloë falls on her knees and offers up a prayer of thanksgiving.

Scene III. Same as Scene I.

Here Daphnis, awakened from his trance, ponders deeply on the loss of his beloved. But how can he avail against a score of fierce pirates? He is about to leave when Chloë runs to his arms. They embrace, their friends return, and there are mutual congratulations. Now together, hand in hand, the happy couple are betrothed before the altar consecrated to Pan, and the scene ends with a joyful dance in celebration.

*

The theme of *Daphnis et Chloë* is the same as that originally written by Fokine in 1904, which it will be remembered was in two acts. The present ballet consisted of the first act only, which falls into three scenes. The second act was never finished, nor has the music been written for it.

The score of this ballet is musically of great importance and is regarded by competent critics as one of the finest achievements in modern French music.

I first saw this ballet in 1914 when it was given in London by the Diaghilev Company then at the Theatre Royal, Drury Lane. The title roles of Daphnis and Chloë were taken respectively by Fokine and his wife, Vera Fokina, who gave a most artistic rendering. The production was full of poetry and showed a careful study of the arts of ancient Hellas. I remember that the opening procession was particularly beautiful and that the struggle between the pirates was a vigorous conception, brilliantly phrased with the music.

Fokine revived this ballet with French artistes at the Opera, Paris, on June 20th, 1921.

LA LÉGENDE DE JOSEPH

Ballet in 1 Act. Book: Hugo von Hofmannsthal and Count Harry Kessler. Music: Richard Strauss. Scenery: J. M. Sert. Costumes: Léon Bakst. Choreography: Michel Fokine. First produced: Théâtre National de l'Opéra, Paris, May 14th, 1914.

CHARACTERS

Potiphar's Wife	MME. MARIA KUSNETZOVA
The Shulamite Woman . . .	MME. VERA FOKINA
Potiphar	M. ALEXIS BULGAKOV
Joseph	M. LEONIDE MASSINE

Master of the Ceremonies, Potiphar's Male and Female Slaves and Bodyguard, A Sheik and his Attendants, Three Veiled Women, Three Unveiled Women, Female Servants of the Veiled Women, Boxers, Joseph's Playmates, Executioners, A Male Archangel.

Scene. A great pillared hall. The walls, a little higher than a tall man, are built of rectangular bricks, seemingly of solid gold. Along the top of the wall runs a loggia composed of massive, convoluted columns, which scintillate with a metallic green lustre like the wing-case of a scarabeus. Through these can be seen a deep blue sky, here and there obstructed by the tops of tall palms. At the left is an ached doorway, to the right is a flight of steps leading to the loggia.

At the back, against the wall, runs a long table, set on a raised platform and flanked on the left by a short table raised on three broad steps. Both are covered with white cloths on which gleam gold beakers and crystal flagons of wine, and gold platters piled high with fruit and viands. Behind the long table sit the guests, ladies in gorgeous brocades, nobles in costly doublets and slashed trunks.

At the raised table Potiphar is seated, an imposing figure in velvet and ermine. Beside him is his wife, dressed in a robe of red brocade, heavy with gold embroidery. Grouped about the walls stand Potiphar's bodyguard, tall negroes in black and yellow, their breasts protected with gold corslets. For arms they bear gold halberds and long whips with short handles.

The scene presents a marvellous spectacle of the wealth and might of Potiphar. Bored to the last degree, he lazily sips from a tall beaker that stands in front of him. Satiated with all that life can offer, it is certain that for him there remains no pleasure untasted, no sensation unrealised. His is indeed a world "in which the air seems charged with gold dust." A sheik advances and begs permission to display his wares. In quick succession he disposes of a bowl filled with precious stones, a carpet of wondrous colours, and a pair of greyhounds.

At a gesture from Potiphar slaves advance and lay the gifts at his wife's feet. Another slave comes to the sheik carrying scales and bags of gold. For a moment little is heard but the trickle of the gold dust in the pan as the sheik receives the amount of Potiphar's purchases. He bows low and prepares to depart, but at a signal from Potiphar remains. Now enters a band of women, some veiled, some unveiled. Together they perform a slow, languid dance swaying gently from the hips. Suddenly a single dancer detaches herself from the group and dances alone. At the conclusion she advances to Potiphar's wife, but with an impatient gesture is dismissed. The dancers file out slowly while along the loggia passes a band of men, nude except for a short skirt about their loins, who descend into the hall.

They are boxers who, after massaging their muscles, commence to give an exhibition of their art. Slowly, walking with stealthy, cat-like tread, they move around each other in a circle, seeking to take their opponent at a disadvantage. At first the dance is a display and nothing more, but gradually their brutish instincts come to the fore and they begin to fight in earnest, intent only on the killing of their opponent. But at a sign from Potiphar the men-at-arms separate them with lashes from their long whips. The boxers cower like beaten dogs and flee through the arched doorway.

Potiphar nods to the sheik who makes a sign in the direction of the loggia. Enter two negro slaves bearing a hammock on their shoulders. Behind them follow a group of shepherd boys, some with cymbals in their hands, others with flutes. The hammock is lowered to the ground. It contains a sleeping boy. The sheik awakens him and assists him to his feet. It is Joseph. He stands there clad in a short white goatskin, his eyes open to their fullest extent at the splendour that surrounds him.

His companions sit on the ground and play simple airs, to

which he dances round and round. At first the measure is clum-sily performed and his whole attitude expresses innocence and freedom. Gradually he becomes hypnotised by the circular move-ment and his actions become more pleasing, more regular, as if he had received divine inspiration. Again the dance changes, expressive of the supreme joy of spiritual comfort; then it ceases and he assumes the simple demeanour of a shepherd boy.

During his dance the guests whisper one to another in endeavour to determine what lies behind his rude exterior. For the first time Potiphar's wife relaxes her haughty mien and shows deep interest in Joseph's dances. Her quivering lips and gleaming eyes betoken her agitation. Potiphar makes a sign; he will buy this wonderful youth. Again a slave goes to the sheik and the trickle of gold dust in the scale pan is heard once more.

Potiphar's wife rises to her feet and, drawing the bowl of precious stones towards her, takes a jewelled collaret from it. A slave leads Joseph to the dais which he slowly mounts. As he approaches she rests her left hand on his neck and with the other clasps on the collaret. Then, as if ashamed of her weakness, she turns from him. Potiphar frowns suspiciously at his wife, rises, and signs for the feast to end.

They descend from the dais and mount the steps leading to the loggia, behind them follows the train of guests. The sheik and his slaves bow low and pass through the arched doorway. Joseph remains standing in a respectful attitude.

*

The scene remains unchanged except that now it is dark. In the centre of the wall at the back is a recess, dimly lit, containing a low couch. Joseph kneels beside it in prayer, then lies on the couch and falls asleep.

A light flickers at the far end of the loggia and a woman in white, carrying a small lamp, approaches and descends into the hall. She goes to Joseph's couch and raising the lamp so that its rays fall on his features, contemplates them in ecstasy. She touches his cheek and as if aghast at her temerity extinguishes the lamp.

Joseph awakes and, seeing in the woman before him the vision of his dreams, believes her to be an angel. He stretches out his hand towards her. She falls on her knees and loosening her hair covers her face. Then she bends down and kisses him. At this Joseph leaps up and flees into the centre of the hall, where he cowers, covering himself with his cloak. She follows and tries to raise him to his feet. For an instant he remains in prayer, then draws himself up, extends a hand as if to ward off a blow, and looks at her in horror. She clutches at his cloak but he holds it firm. Then with a quick movement he steps to one side and casts it from him, gazing at her in contempt. She falls to her knees and seems to implore pardon, but he remains unmoved. Overcome with rage, she leaps to her feet and tries to strangle him. They struggle, then she is forced slowly to her knees.

Again a light appears at the far end of the loggia, and attendants, alarmed at the noise, run down the steps into the hall. Potiphar's wife rises and with a regal gesture commands them to arrest Joseph. He who disdained pleasure may now taste torture. There is an ominous silence, then with measured tread Potiphar enters with his men-at-arms. They advance and chain Joseph hand and foot.

Potiphar turns to his wife who, with half-closed eyes, offers him her lips to kiss. He caresses her to soothe her agitation. Then she points dramatically at Joseph. At this Potiphar stamps his foot with fury. Now several executioners enter bearing in their midst a gigantic brazier. They busy themselves about it, reviving the dying embers with the bellows. The embers glow and burst into flame. The men stir them about and begin to heat pointed irons. Joseph remains calm, his face uplifted. Suddenly a radiant light shines and across the loggia and down the steps walks a glittering angel. He advances, touches Joseph on the shoulder, and his chains fall from him; then the angel takes the youth by the hand and leads him up the steps.

The frightened attendants seem rooted to the ground. Then some fall prostrate, others shield their eyes, fearful lest a ray from the glorious being should strike them dead. Potiphar's wife, astonished at the interruption, becomes terrified, then stretches out her arms as if seeking to follow Joseph and the angel. But suddenly her face becomes drawn, her teeth clench, and clutching at the rope of pearls about her neck, she draws it tighter and tighter, strangling herself. A last gasp and she falls dead.

*

La Légende de Joseph was not so much a ballet as a wordless play in the manner of *Sumurun*. It contained many dances, but these were more in the manner of embroidery than a necessary adjunct to the plot.

Though founded on the ancient legend which remains in its entirety, the action was transferred to Venice of the 16th century. Bakst's costumes were all in the manner of Paolo Veronese with the exception of those worn by Joseph and the dealers, which were Oriental dresses of the same period.

This ballet has a special association in that it marks Massine's first introduction to the public.

LE COQ D'OR

Opera-Ballet in 3 Acts. Book: V. Bielsky, revised by Alexandre Benois. Music: N. Rimsky-Korsakov. Scenery and costumes: Natalia Gontcharova. Choreography: Michel Fokine. First produced: Théâtre Nationale de l'Opéra, Paris, May 21st, 1914.

CHARACTERS

Queen of Shemâkhan . . .	MLLE. THAMAR KARSAVINA
Amelfa	MME. JEZIERSKA
King Dodon	M. A. BULGAKOV
Astrologer	M. ENRICO CECCHETTI
General Polkan	M. KOVALSKY
Guidone	M. SERGE GRIGORIEV
Afrone	M. FROHMAN

Prologue and Act I. Before the piece begins there is a short prologue, in which an old astrologer, in characteristic conical hat and black gown, informs the audience that the piece about to be presented, though a fairy tale, is not without its moral.

Barely has he departed when the curtain rises to unfold a scene which, for wealth of colour, fantasy, and imagination, it would be difficult to surpass. To right and left of the stage, grouped in tiers like an oratorio choir, are male and female singers, dressed in crimson. These choirs remain seated throughout the play. In regard to the scene proper, the background is formed by a low, yellow wall, upon which are depicted curious animals in a fighting attitude, while along its base grow miniature bushes of a vivid green. In the centre of the wall is a gate, let into a lofty arch, bounded on each side by a high pointed tower, lavishly decorated with a broad floral design in reddish brown. Above the wall rise the varied towers and spires of a town.

The left wing is formed by enormous brown houses, and a tall green tree, bearing white blossoms of monstrous size, in appearance not unlike a giant narcissus; to the right are similar houses and another giant tree, deep brown in hue, with fronds like those of a palm tree, from which depend green, rose, and yellow flowers.

*At the left centre stands a four-poster bed of fantastic design,
which, like the floor, is of reddish-brown.*

The aged King Dodon with his sons and advisers are taking
council together as to the best means of defending the kingdom
against a threatening neighbour. After much foolish advice has
been proffered and discussed, the company, unable to find a satisfactory solution to the problem, fall to quarrelling among themselves, when suddenly the Astrologer of the prologue appears. He
offers the King the gift of a magic golden cockerel which will
always give warning of the presence of danger.

At first the King refuses to believe him, until the bird, having
been brought in, commences by telling the King to reign at his
ease, at which he is so delighted that he promises the Astrologer
what he will. The latter, satisfied with such munificence, departs
to ponder over the form his reward shall take, while the King,
relieved of responsibility, intimates a desire to slumber and is put
to bed. The court, unable to think of anything better to do, go
to sleep likewise. Meanwhile, the ladies-in-waiting, grotesquely
attired, dance round the King's bed, waving handkerchiefs as they
go, to drive away the flies.

All at once the cock crows: "Danger, beware!" The King
awakes with a start, despatches the unwilling princes in charge of
a select body of troops to deal with the menace, and resumes his
sleep. There is much humour in the departure of the warriors.
All are bearded, ferocious of expression, and armed to the teeth.
They march off with slow jerky movements like those of a clockwork toy.

Again the cock crows: "Danger!" and this time the King, having
no one else to send, is forced to undertake the business himself.
This episode is no less amusing in the actions of the portly monarch
who grumblingly tries to mount a huge wooden horse. First he
drops his sword, then his shield, until at last, after a period of utter
exasperation, he succeeds in mounting his charger, to the relief of
all concerned, and, accompanied by the remainder of the army,
sets forth to defend his country, amid the acclamations of the court.

*Act II. The frontier, a scene in sharp contrast to the first, for all
is black, dismal, and veiled in mist.*

Here Dodon and his followers wander over what has evidently
been the field of battle. Corpses are piled thickly and in the centre
lie the bodies of his two sons, a sword standing upright in each.
At this miserable sight the doddering old man is reduced to tears,

when suddenly the mist clears and a large green tent, seemingly risen from the ground, is revealed to the astonished onlookers.

With considerable apprehension the soldiers prepare for battle, but the curtains are softly drawn back and from the interior emerges the beautiful Queen of Shemâkhan, so fascinating a vision that the King thinks of nothing but other kinds of conquests. Now a band of women come from the tent and seating themselves on the ground begin the prelude to a dance. The Queen dances slowly with languorous movements, swaying to the rhythm of the music, her lips parted in a mocking smile.

The King, hopelessly infatuated with such beauty and scarcely knowing whether he is on his head or his heels, soon surrenders, while the visitor further strengthens her position by inducing him to dance too. In high humour he assents, but only succeeds in making himself a lamentable and ridiculous spectacle, at the sight of which even his hardened court give way to laughter. At last, breathless and exhausted, he sinks to the ground. At his request the Queen consents to be his bride and accompanied by the court and army they set out for the capital.

Act III. The exterior of the palace of the first act. There is seen the fronts of two huge palaces, with turrets and steeples protruding at all manner of queer places. Except for the shaded pink bricks composing the buildings, the whole is carried out again in reddish-brown, green, and yellow. The assembled populace await the return of their beloved monarch and his bride.

Soon the procession enters, headed by an advance guard of warriors, followed by the King and Queen seated in an extraordinary chariot, heavily gilt and guarded by a grotesque band of slaves, waiting women, and further warriors. The King, despite his anxious and careworn appearance, gazes with loving tenderness at his consort while she looks the picture of utter boredom.

A clap of thunder resounds and again the Astrologer enters. Dodon receives him with great goodwill and expresses his willingness to bestow the promised reward for the present of the golden cockerel, whereupon the Astrologer demands the Queen of Shemâkhan. At this the King's anger passes all bounds and, in a rage, he strikes him on the head with his sceptre.

The Queen laughs cynically at this untoward incident, but Dodon, fearful of his deed, begins to bemoan the consequences. He begs sympathy from his bride, but now, no longer simulating affection, she reproaches him. Suddenly the golden cockerel flies to the King and, striking him down with a blow of its beak, lays him dead. Again is heard a clap of thunder followed by a short period of darkness. When all is light both bird and Queen have disappeared, and the curtain falls on the sorrowing populace.

Again the Astrologer appears before the curtain and informs the audience that, with the exception of himself and the Queen, there were no real people in the piece, the rest was but a dream.

*

Le Coq d'Or is based on the well-known poem by Pushkin. It possesses not only a legendary character, but also an undercurrent of pointed satire which contributes considerably to its remarkable originality.

The Fokine production was conceived in a manner then probably unique, for the cast was divided into two parts, operatic and choreographic, that is to say, while one character acted and danced, the words "spoken" by the character were sung by his or her counterpart in the vocal cast, producing a most unusual effect. The ballet was conceived in a spirit of lively good humour and burlesque which aroused roars of laughter from the delighted spectators.

The costumes and settings by Gontcharova were remarkable for their fantasy, brilliant colour, and richly decorative quality.

In September, 1937, Fokine revived *Le Coq d'Or* for the De Basil Company; in this version there was no singing.

L'ÉPREUVE D'AMOUR

Ballet in 1 Act. Book: André Derain and Michel Fokine. Music: Mozart. Scenery and costumes: André Derain. Choreography: Michel Fokine. First produced at the Théâtre de Monte Carlo, April 4th, 1936.

CHARACTERS

Chung-Yang	MLLE. VERA NEMCHINOVA
The Lover	M. ANDRÉ EGLEVSKY
The Mandarin, Father of Chung-Yang	M. JEAN JAZVINSKY
The Strangers	M. ANATOLE OBUKHOV / M. LEBERCHER / M. ARVO
The Butterfly	MLLE. HELENE KIRSOVA

Friends of Chun-Yang, Monkeys, Soldiers, Friends of the Lover, Servants, etc.

Scene. A Chinese landscape. To left and right is a pale blue pagoda with a bright red roof; the pagoda on the right is built on a slight eminence. In the distance is a stretch of grass land, dotted with an occasional pagoda, which borders a river. In the far dis-tance are ranges of violet hills. The whole is dominated by a cobalt blue sky, relieved with drifts of fleecy cloud.

At the rise of the curtain a number of grey monkeys are seated together. They nod their heads and scratch themselves, lope in a circle, and dance a round.

Enter the mandarin in yellow and blue. His thoughts concentrated on the difficult problem of how to achieve wealth, he resents the chattering monkeys, and drives them away with a stick. Another trial besets the mandarin in the form of a blue and purple butterfly which flutters about him. Finally the insect departs and the mandarin follows.

A number of maidens enter and dance a graceful measure. From the opposite side comes a youth who, after a brief dance, retires. Now comes Chung-Yang, the mandarin's daughter. The youth, who is her lover, returns. He dances and takes Chung-Yang in his arms. The maidens hide their eyes from modesty. Suddenly the mandarin enters. He has made a plan to marry Chung-Yang to a rich husband and, furious at seeing the poor suitor courting his daughter, indignantly drives him away.

Now arrives an ambassador from the Western world, with two aides-de-camp. They enter with slow, mannered steps, followed by pages bearing treasure. The mandarin marks the ambassador's arrival with delight. Coolies pass in the background bearing baggage and tents, which latter are speedily erected.

The ambassador distributes presents to the maidens. The mandarin invites his distinguished visitor to be seated, and the maidens, led by Chung-Yang, dance before him. The lover appears and retires, highly displeased at the mandarin's manœuvres.

The ambassador decides to repay his host's courtesy by dancing himself. So, with the two aides-de-camp providing a discreet background, he launches into a dazzling series of florid steps. Overwhelmed by this display, the maidens and coolies kneel in admiration. At the end of the dance the ambassador and his aides-de-camp retire to the tents prepared for them.

The mandarin dismisses his attendants, but, before leaving, orders his daughter to remain behind, in case the ambassador might wish to converse with her. Frightened of being alone with these strange foreigners in the vicinity, she kneels in prayer.

The ambassador has observed the girl, and, half-dressed, steals out of his tent. The two aides-de-camp, imbued with the same plan, emerge from their tents, but the ambassador angrily waves them back. Then he approaches Chung-Yang and makes love to her; she is very alarmed. The mandarin, who has watched the scene from a place of concealment, rubs his hands with delight. But the Chinese lover, another eye-witness, is filled with rage.

Just as the ambassador carries Chung-Yang to his tent a curious trumpeting is heard. The ambassador quickly sets down his burden, for a monstrous dragon with gigantic head, lolling tongue, and bloated frame, attacks the foreigners, who, terrified, hide in the depths of their tents.

Chung-Yang goes to the dragon and caresses it for having saved her. Suddenly the giant head rises and her true lover steps forth; the reptile, for all its fearsome appearance, is only wire and paper.

The reunited. lovers dance a charming measure, expressive of their mutual love, and, softly gliding to the ground, so that they rest face to face, their lips meet in a kiss.

Then the youth summons four of his friends, who don ferocious masks. Next they remove the tents and attack the foreigners, who, after a brief defence, are captured and bound. The coffers of treasure and the foreigners' coats are also removed.

The mandarin, horrified at this blow to his plans, calls his soldiers to arrest the robbers. Presently they return with the youth, who is hemmed in by lances. Chung-Yang implores her father to spare her lover, but he indignantly drags her away, and forces her to release the ambassador with her own hands. Meanwhile her maidens unbind the two aides-de-camp. The soldiers go to the ambassador in anticipation of reward, but he is penniless, as are also his friends.

The mandarin, seeing the ambassador's plight, consents to his daughter's marrying her lover, whose friends restore the foreigners' clothes and treasure.

The mandarin, observing that the ambassador is rich again, revokes his consent, and, taking Chung-Yang from her lover, again offers her to the ambassador, who, seeing clearly that it is only his wealth and not his handsome person that is covered, angrily declines the honour.

So the lovers are united once more. They are placed in a palanquin, lifted high in the air, and borne to the place of marriage, followed by officials and soldiers who step briskly to a gay wedding march.

The mandarin, left alone, bewails the downfall of his plans. The monkeys return to jeer; and even the butterfly flutters about him in derision for seeking so useless a commodity as wealth, until, roused to anger, he flings his stick at the insect, which promptly flies away.

*

L'Epreuve d'Amour is based on a score by Mozart recently discovered at Graz. The present theme owes much to the ingenuity of Derain and Fokine, for Derain designed a number of costumes for characters that might well be found in a China depicted on porcelain vases or painted screens, then, in collaboration with Fokine, built up a story round them.

The scenery and costumes are charming, even though the Chinese maidens have their hair dressed *à la Japonaise*.

There are very few ballets which have the subtle wit and refinement of this production. It has the fragrance of a blend of rare Pekoe, in which every ingredient is rightly proportioned and combined.

The ballet-goer who is interested in choreography for its own sake will find this ballet a whole education in itself. The manner in which the movements are combined with the music, and the way in which every gesture, every step, arises simply and naturally from the development of the action is really extraordinary.

The Chinese have a beauty of movement which is in sharp contrast with the stilted, ultra-refined dances of the foreigners. Look, too, at the flowing movements of Chung-Yang's friends, who are so many porcelain princesses come to life. And, finally, observe the grouping of the figures when it is necessary to provide a stage audience for certain of the incidents; notice how one person stands here, and another there, while there is a little group at this point and a cluster of figures at that—all is so seemingly the impulse of the moment, yet with what cunning art is it all planned.

Where everyone is so excellent, it seems invidious to choose a name for special mention. Yet it must be stated that the piece, as given last year, was dominated by Obukhov, whose dancing and miming were in the finest tradition of the Imperial Ballet; in short, he was superb.

DON JUAN

Choreographic Tragi-Comedy in 1 Act and 3 Scenes. Book: Eric Allatini and Michel Fokine. Music: Gluck. Curtain, Scenery, and Costumes: Mariano Andreù. Choreography: Michel Fokine. First produced: Alhambra Theatre, London, June 25th, 1936.

CHARACTERS

Don Juan	M. Anatole Vilzak
Dona Elvira	Mlle. Jeanne Lauret
The Commander, Dona Elvira's father	M. Jean Jazvinsky
Sganarelle, Don Juan's valet . .	M. Louis Lebercher
The Gitana	Mlle. Marie Ruanova
Chief Fury	Mlle. Helene Kirsova
Chief Jester	}M. André Eglevsky
Chief Demon	
Tambourine Dancers . . .	{ Mlle. Tatiana Semenova Mlle. Raisse Kusnetsova Mlle. Lucia Nifontova
Jesters	{ Mm. Panayev, Sobichevsky, Beriosov, Kroller
The Duenna	Mlle. Marie Zarina

Musicians, Guests, Pages, Mourners, Furies, Demons, Valets, Lackeys, etc.

The stage curtain rises to disclose a blue-grey curtain—decorated with bold devices in red, black, and green—before which is a little group of musicians, seated on a short flight of steps. They play their instruments until a light glows through the back of the curtain, which parts to give entrance to four lantern-bearers in buff and yellow. They draw back the curtain to reveal a street scene, faintly gleaming in the moonlight.

The musicians, directed by Sganarelle, Don Juan's valet, prepare to serenade the central house, at present shrouded in darkness. A cloaked figure enters. It is Don Juan. A light appears at an upper window, to which he gracefully sweeps his hat; a young woman's face looks down into the street.

Don Juan knocks for admittance, then steps into the shadow. A duenna opens the door, steps out, and peers into the darkness. At the same moment Don Juan slips inside the house. A little later he is seen in the upper room whispering words of love to the woman.

Enter Elvira's father, the Commander, who drives away the musicians. At this point Elvira and her lover emerge from the house. The Commander orders his daughter indoors and challenges Don Juan to a duel. Swords are drawn, they fight, and the Commander is killed.

Soldiers enter and mourn the death of their lord, while Don Juan, Sganarelle, and the musicians make their escape. The duenna comes out of the house accompanied by Elvira, who is horrified at the spectacle that greets her eyes. She kneels beside her father and finds that he is dead.

The blue-grey curtain is slowly closed by black-clothed figures who ooze over the material like dark stains.

When they have passed from sight a nobleman and his lady cross the scene, followed by torch-bearers who break into a lively dance; this is succeeded by another dance by Don Juan's jester.

The torch-bearers draw back the curtain to reveal the banqueting-hall of Don Juan's house, ablaze with light and filled with guests.

Some ladies give a formal dance on a raised dais. Then four gentlemen dance in the foreground, in the course of which they cross and recross from opposite corners. The ladies dance again and Don Juan himself dances a measure, which is lavishly applauded by the company. The guests mingle and converse, and Don Juan dances among them, greeting his mistresses in turn with a kiss or a caress. He signs to Sganarelle for the banquet to begin. The valet claps his hands. A table is brought in, chairs ranged about it, and fruit and wine brought in by negro servants.

In the midst of the feast there is a loud unearthly knocking at the door, and the ghost of the Commander appears. The guests withdraw from the table and huddle together in fear. But Don Juan invites the newcomer to take wine with him. The Commander refuses and vanishes.

The guests return to the table and resume the interrupted repast. Don Juan summons his valet and, giving him money, sends him on a secret mission.

The host then turns to his guests, bids them make merry, and orders dancers to show their skill for the entertainment of his guests. First, there is a lively buffoon dance; then a seductive dance by three bacchantes; and, last of all, a fiery, passionate dance by a Spanish gypsy girl.

At this point Sganarelle and his men bring in a veiled figure, who is placed at the table. Don Juan bids his guests retire for a moment, then he withdraws the veil to reveal the features of Elvira. She looks about her in amazement. Don Juan reveals his presence and avows his love. The guests return and he has the impudence to present her to his mistresses. She recoils in horror. The guests sit beside her at the table.

Again there is a loud knocking. The ghost of the Commander reappears and vanishes. After a momentary hesitation the guests, reassured by their host, begin to dance.

Once more the knocking is heard, this time louder than before. Don Juan sends his valet to see who it is. Sganarelle goes out and returns pale and trembling, speechless from fright.

His master takes up a branched candlestick, determined to solve the mystery, and is confronted by the ghost of the Commander. Don Juan fills a glass with wine and offers it to the ghost. He refuses the wine, but, in turn, invites Don Juan to visit him in the cemetery. Elvira swoons. Don Juan throws a parting glance at Elvira and his terrified guests, then drinks the wine and orders his valet to fetch his hat and cloak. He puts them on and, accompanied by Sganarelle, sets out for the cemetery. The musicians close the curtains.

Buffoons enter with lanterns and draw back the curtains, to reveal the cemetery, a gloomy vista enclosed in tall cypresses; to the left is the Commander's tomb, guarded by an equestrian monument which gleams dully in the waning moonlight.

Don Juan enters, accompanied by his valet. He boldly challenges the statue, which nods its head in greeting. The valet, terrified, takes to his heels.

The Commander seems to reprove Don Juan for his dissolute life. He calls up the spirits of his dead mistresses, a melancholy procession, and entreats him to mend his ways. But the libertine only mocks his victims.

He goes towards the statue and is caught up by its stone arm. The Commander, seeing him to be past salvation, looses the furies upon him. In they burst, an eager, writhing mass, a sea of tossing arms and streaming hair, a pack of hunters disputing their prey. They pull down Don Juan, who is flung from one to another, and almost torn to pieces, until he expires.

*

The production of *Don Juan* was the outcome of a sequence of events which it is of interest to relate. In February, 1936, the Blum Ballet was rehearsing at Paris in the Studio of the Salle Pleyel. Blum and his lieutenant, Allatini, had left the rehearsal-room and were on their way to attend to other matters, when at the entrance they encountered Desormières, the well-known conductor. The greetings over, the latter asked Blum what ballets he had in preparation. And when the details had been given he suggested: "Why not produce Gluck's *Don Juan*? That was always one of Diaghilev's ambitions." Blum was intrigued and asked Allatini to search for the music.

Allatini found a score which contained four numbers. He

played it to Blum, who was delighted with the music. Fokine was called and the music played to him. Everyone agreed that it was ideal for ballet.

Allatini, however, thought the score seemed very short for a ballet and became filled with doubts as to whether it was complete. He made enquiries of various music-publishers, but was told that no other music for *Don Juan* existed. Still unable to calm his misgivings, he consulted M. Prod'homme, the curator of the Bibliotheque de l'Opéra, who produced a MS. volume relating to Gluck's productions, which mentioned that his *Don Juan* contained an overture and 31 numbers, and had been originally produced at the Burgtheater, Vienna, in 1761, with choreography by Gaspare Angiolini, and that MS. copies of the score were filed in the Vienna Opera House, at Darmstadt, at Berlin, at the British Museum, and at the Paris Conservatoire.

Allatini hastened to the Conservatoire to discover that the copy there was dated 1850 and contained only 15 numbers. He went to others centres and at last secured from Germany a tattered old score which had the full number of pieces. From a careful study of the music in connection with certain MS. annotations he was able to work out the relation of the music to the plot. This was further revised in course of consultations with Fokine.

The theme of *Don Juan* derives from Spain, the first dramatic version being by a Spanish prior, one Gabriel Tellez, who wrote under the name of Tirso de Molina. This play was very popular in Italy and spread to France, when it was re-adapted by Molière under the title, *Don Juan, ou le Festin de Pierre*. Gluck's ballet is based on the Molière script.

Gluck's *Don Juan* has a special interest in being one of the earliest, perhaps the first, of dramatic ballets with dramatic music to fit the various situations and to be composed with careful regard for style-atmosphere. Several of the numbers are Spanish themes worked out into a dramatic form. One of the best numbers musically is the "Furies' Dance," which recurs in Gluck's *Orfeo*.

The ballet, from the manner of its treatment, falls into two parts —Scene I forming Part I, and Scenes II and III forming Part II. Scene I contains no dancing in the general acceptance of the term, it is pure choreodrama, a mimed scene not "walked," but one in which every movement flows in harmony with the mood and rhythm of the music.

Scene II contains a number of dances, the most interesting being the Torch Dance, the Jester's Dance—admirably danced by Eglevsky—and the long solo by Don Juan himself. This last shows obvious traces of careful study of contemporary technique, and, in accordance with the custom then prevailing, Don Juan is given more elaborate steps than those of the women who precede him, so as to emphasise the superiority of the male sex. The dances with tambourines and the gypsy dance are, to my mind, not quite in keeping with the general period of the piece.

Scene III is notable for the Dance of the Furies, one of those stirring compositions in which Fokine has no equal. Effective as this is, it contains some elements of modern "adagio" work which do not accord with the general style-atmosphere.

The outstanding creation is Vilzak's Don Juan, a portrait so fascinating in its combination of noble grace, bravado, and polished wile, as to induce strong sympathy for the villain in the hour of his downfall.

The settings by Andreù are beautiful, but the dresses range over several centuries, a period roughly covered in our own history from Elizabeth to Anne. Despite this anachronism, the costumes are splendidly decorative.

The first performance of Fokine's *Don Juan* was originally intended and announced to be given on June 19th, but the whole of the 120 costumes, which were in course of completion at a London workroom, were accidentally destroyed by fire on June 16th. Fortunately the designs were undamaged and all the dresses were re-made in time for the new ballet to be presented on June 25th.

HEINRICH KRÖLLER

HEINRICH KRÖLLER was born at Munich on July 25th, 1880. His father was the works manager of a glove factory. Young Kröller had a cousin who was second soloist at the Royal Court and National Theatre, who took him to see a ballet class. At this time Heinrich was nine years old. He was very interested in what he saw and determined to become a dancer like his cousin. To this end he spent his weekly holidays from school in the junior ballet class attached to the Royal Theatre, his teacher being the *maîtresse de ballet,* Flora Jungmann. When he was eleven years old he was selected as pupil soloist by Ritter Ernst von Possart, the director of the Munich Opera. One of Kröller's earliest appearances was in *Kinder Weihnacht's Traum;* he also danced a solo in *Puppen-Fée.*

In 1896 the *premier danseur,* Otto Herz, fell ill and Kröller was given his part in *Le Carnaval de Venise.* A director from Leipzig happened to see his performance and offered him an engagement at the Opera House. Possart, however, refused to grant him permission to accept the engagement; at the same time he promoted him to the rank of *premier danseur* and instructed him to double the principal parts in the theatre's repertory of ballet.

Kröller was considered so promising a dancer that he was granted exemption from military service. A new intendant arrived and when Jungmann retired owing to ill health, he, viewing matters in the light of military procedure, directed that the oldest solo dancer should be appointed *maître de ballet.* Kröller was very offended by this decision and requested permission to resign. Since this was refused he had to wait until the expiration of his contract in 1906.

He first went to Paris, where he studied with Zambelli at the Opera. Leo Staats, who was impressed by his ability, proposed him as *premier danseur* to the director, M. Messager, who courteously expressed his inability to accept the recommendation owing to the regulation which states that the *premier danseur* of the Opera must not be of German nationality.

Kröller then obtained the post of *premier danseur* at the Dresden Opera House, where he remained for seven years. He was always at work writing stories for ballets and planning all the details of their production, but, owing to difficulties with the *maître de ballet,* he was unable to present any of his conceptions. Tiring of this situation he wrote to the directors of several theatres offering his services as choreographer, but without success.

It happened, however, that Clare Gabler, who was *prima ballerina* at the Dresden Opera, left to take up the same position at Frankfurt, and she recommended Kröller to the director of that theatre as a talented choreographer. As a result he received an invitation to produce a ballet which was so successful that he was appointed *maître de ballet.*

In 1917 Baron von Frankenstein, the director of the Munich Opera House, offered Kröller an engagement as *maître de ballet,* a post which he eagerly accepted, since it meant returning to his native town. Later he became, in addition, guest choreographer to the State Operas of Berlin, and of Vienna, and occasionally produced ballets at Copenhagen and Prague.

Kröller devised a great many dances and over forty ballets, of which the following are the best known: *Bachusfest* (1915), *Josefslegende* (1921), *Sylvia* (1922), *Die Ruinen von Athen* (1925), *Don Juan* (1925), *Pagoden* (1927), *Mammon* (1927), *Wolkenkratze (Skyscrapers)* (1928), *Casanova* (1929). He also arranged the dances in several operas such as *Schwanda, Die Drei Musketiere, Die Vögel, Zigeunerbaron, The Mikado.*

Kröller died at Würzburg on July 25th, 1930.

SCHLAGOBERS [1]

Ballet in 2 Acts. Book: Richard Strauss. Music: Richard Strauss. Scenery and Costumes: Ada Nigrin. Choreography: Heinrich Kröller. First produced: Operntheater, Vienna, May 9th, 1924.

CHARACTERS

The Young Communicant . . .	THEIMER
The Mother	MLLE. LOITELSBERGER
The Godfather	M. BUTTULA
A Dandy	M. RUNPEL
Another Godfather	M. SCHREITTER

[1] A type of pastry, filled with whipped cream, which is very popular in Vienna.

Princess Teaflower . . . . . MLLE. LOSCH
Prince Coffee . . . . . . MLLE. PFUNDMEYER
The Vision . . . . . . MLLE. MINDZENTY
Prince Cocoa . . . . . . M. NEMETH
Don Sugaro . . . . . . M. BIRKMEYER
The Doctor . . . . . . M. DUBOIS
Princess Praline . . . . . MME. PICHLER
Prince Santa Claus, Marshal of the
Court . . . . M. SCHNEIDER
Mlle. Marianne Chartreuse ⎫   MLLE. KRAUSENECKER
Ladislav Slivovitz   ⎬ Liqueurs M. BIRKMEYER
Boris Vodka   ⎭   M. RUDI FRANZL

The Court of Princess Praline, Sweets, Christmas Crackers, Chocolate Sausages, Four Heralds with Trumpets, Gingerbread, Marzipan, and Sugar-Plum Soldiers, Chorus of Sponge-Cakes, Roly-Polies, Plum-Cakes, Pretzels, Eclairs, Ginger-Snaps, Wafers, Turkish Delight, Whipped Cream, etc.

Act I. A famous confectioner's shop in the Kärntnerstrasse, Vienna.

It is Whit-Sunday and a number of boys and girls who have just been confirmed arrive in carriages, decked with lilac and roses, to partake of the traditional feast of cakes and pastries. The children, accompanied by their god-parents, step out of the carriages, and select the pastries they fancy, which they eat at little tables. Having satisfied their hunger the children dance a gay measure, during which one little boy feels sick and is taken away by his godfather.

The stage gradually darkens to permit of a change of scene showing the interior of the confectioner's shop, which contains an assortment of tins lettered according to their contents. From one tin come marzipan archers; from another, sugarplum spearmen; from another, gingerbread soldiers bearing swords and shields. After a fantastic march they are swept out of the kitchen by means of gigantic shovels.

From another tin comes Princess Teaflower and her four ladies, who dance and then group themselves about a Chinese tea-pot. They are followed by Prince Coffee and his companions who dance a Brazilian Maxixe, and Prince Cocoa who burlesques a well-fed bourgeois.

Enter Don Sugaro, who seeks the favour of these three influential personages. Disdained by Princess Teaflower and coldly greeted by Prince Coffee, he is warmly received by Prince Cocoa,

with whom he dances. Presently they are joined first by Prince
Coffee and later by Princess Teaflower.

They vanish to be replaced by a giant cook, who begins to whip
an enormous basin full of cream, which froths over in the form of
a *corps de ballet,* clad in white, who dance a captivating waltz
which becomes more and more animated.

Act II. A sick room.

The little boy of the first act is seen ill in bed and attended by
his mother. The doctor comes, makes an examination of the
patient, and administers a soothing medicine, which he pours out
of a large medicine bottle. The little boy falls asleep.

The stage darkens to permit of a change of scene.

Enter Princess Praline in a coach, attended by crackers and
chocolates. She steps from the coach and dances a solo. The
chocolates dance a peasant dance, after which the crackers follow
with their springing dance, in which the Princess and the whole
company take part. Then she steps into her coach and departs.

The stage darkens to permit of another change of scene, which
shows a glass case filled with giant bottles of liqueur. One, labelled
Chartreuse, inclines forward, and from the neck of the bottle
emerges Mlle. Marianne, who dances a menuet. Slivovitz likewise
comes from his bottle and pays court to the lady, who repulses him,
half attracted, half frightened. Vodka approaches her in turn, but,
since he seems inebriated, she turns to Slivovitz and invites him to
dance a *pas de deux,* during which they exchange vows of love.
Vodka is enraged.

Again the stage darkens and when it lightens you see a number
of sponge-cakes, roly-polies, plum-cakes, pretzels, and eclairs, led
by ginger-snaps and turkish delight, making preparations to revolt.
Marianne, Slivovitz, and Vodka join the rioters, in which action
they are supported by the soldiers of marzipan, gingerbread, and
sugar-plum. The insurgents march on the town.

The arrive in front of the confectioner's shop in the Kärntnerstrasse and become threatening. An attempt is made to quell the
rioters by pouring tea on them from a giant tea-pot; this is followed
by coffee; then by cocoa, which proves very effective.

Four heralds enter and blow a fanfare. Then, by means of two
great mugs of "Hofbräubier," the crowd becomes so orderly that
Princess Praline is able to appear. She descends from her palace of
glass attended by her chocolate negroes, and attaches Marianne,
Slivovitz, and Vodka to her suite. Her Marshal of the Court, Santa

Claus, invests the turkish delight with the Order of St. Plutus, and her negro boys distribute largess in the form of chocolate coins wrapped in silver paper.

The ballet ends with a general reconciliation and final *ensemble* led by the Princess, during which her palace changes into a gigantic cake-stand, upon which the whole company form a group, surmounted by the Princess.

SKYSCRAPERS [2]

Ballet in 2 Acts. Music: John Alden Carpenter. Choreography: Heinrich Kröller. First produced: Opernhaus, Munich, 1929.

Act I. The rising of the curtain reveals a skyscraper in course of construction. In the foreground a group of workmen are engaged in a series of mechanical movements; in the background the endless chain of an everyday crowd in the capital passes by in silhouette.

Presently the workers exit through an opening in the curtain surround, moving with a heavy dragging step. But almost immediately they return by another opening, stepping gaily, each with a girl on his arm. These simultaneous actions heighten the contrast.

Act II. Coney Island.

Various amusements are in progress and groups of merrymakers appear and depart. Suddenly, lightning flashes and thunder rolls; all stop and remain motionless, while out of the darkness the groups of workers appear and perform their duties mechanically, as though the sudden thought of their work had flashed through the minds of the crowd.

Soon they disappear, the storm passes, and all is bright and joyous again. A very unusual mirror dance is executed in a rotatory movement. A dancer appears through a trap. First he dances alone, then he is joined by four girls. The dance ended, he exits by jumping over their bent backs. Some of the women begin to quarrel, their friends take sides, and a fight ensues. It ends with the police marching off the brawlers. Only a road-sweeper remains, a negro clad in white. His work finished, he lies down and sleeps.

The back-cloth rises and through gauze curtains his dream is revealed. Far down south where his own folk live, types long forgotten sing a chorus and perform their religious dances. These become more and more fanatical. The negro begins to stir in his

[2] I am indebted to Miss Derra de Moroda for particulars of this ballet—C.W.b.

sleep. He tosses from side to side, until, finally, he jumps up and joins in the mad dance. Suddenly the light fades and a procession of sandwichmen crosses the stage. As the scene lightens the action returns to Coney Island with merriment at its height.

The black surround re-appears and this time the men and girls exit through one opening and the serious-faced workers enter by the other. A factory whistle screams shrilly, and the skyscraper is again seen, with men at work on the scaffolding. As another group moves to the front, the curtain slowly falls.

SOME ALHAMBRA
BALLETS

TWO London theatres, the Alhambra and the Empire, were long known as "homes of ballet," due to the fact that they each made use of ballet as their principal attraction. The typical evening programme contained one or two ballets, according to length, varied with music-hall turns.

The term "English ballet" was a figure of speech, for there was no institution corresponding to the State Schools of Ballet possessed by France, Russia, Italy, and Denmark for so many years; moreover, the principal dancers were almost invariably foreign artistes engaged from abroad for the run of the piece.

The form of ballet associated with the Alhambra and the Empire theatres was in reality a combination of extravaganza, spectacle, and revue, with dancing, planned on certain set lines. Prettiness and spectacle were the two qualities sought—pretty music, pretty scenery of the realistic order, and pretty costumes of the florid type then fashionable.

The theme was expressed in a conventional system of mime, varied with effective dances, spectacular marches and countermarches by the *corps de ballet,* and *soli* by the *première danseuse.* Every endeavour was made for the action of the ballet to shift from one country to another with each successive scene, since this afforded occasion for a complete change of costume and the introduction of character or speciality dances.

Male dancers were at a premium, and it was rare for a male dancer to attempt anything beyond a national dance or an eccentric number, for the majority of the general public, having never seen a dancer of quality of the pure classic school, regarded dancing of this type as effete, unmanly, and even loathsome. For this reason the role of *jeune premier* was generally taken by a *danseuse* dressed to suggest a male character. This transformation had to be accepted as a convention like the "principal boy" of pantomime, for the curvilinear female form characteristic of this period could not easily be mistaken for that of a man.

There were occasional exceptions as there are to all rules, but the foregoing is a fair picture of the conditions obtaining in London in the second half of the nineteenth and the first few years of the twentieth centuries.

The Alhambra opened in 1854 under the imposing style of "Panopticon of the Arts and Sciences," but, failing in its self-appointed mission to instruct, it turned to the provision of entertainment. In 1870 the "Panopticon" became the Alhambra and offered a music-hall programme. Towards the end of the year certain riots caused the theatre to lose its music-hall licence, when it became a regular theatre and re-opened in April, 1871, as the Alhambra Theatre. The programmes given consisted of light opera, farces, pantomimes, and ballets, which last gradually became the management's chief attraction.

Among the principal ballets presented at the Alhambra may be mentioned *The Golden Wreath* (1878), *Salandra* (1890), *Temptation* (1891), *Aladdin* (1892), *Beauty and the Beast* (1898), *Soldiers of the Queen* (1900), *Britannia's Realm* (1902), *The Devil's Forge* (1903), *Carmen* (1903), *All the Year Round* (1904), *Parisiana* (1905), *The Queen of Spades* (1907), *Les Cloches de Corneville* (1907), *Femina* (1910), *The Dance Dream* (1911), and *1830* (1911).

Most of the music of the Alhambra ballets was composed or arranged by G. Jacobi, who became musical director in 1872 and was associated with the production of some hundred ballets; and G. W. Byng who succeeded him in 1898.

The costumes were designed by, or executed under the supervision of, M. Alias, who supplied every costume for every production for well over a quarter of a century.

The principal dancers[1] at the Alhambra during 1871 to 1914, in chronological order, were E. Pertoldi, Emma Palladino, Lucia Cormani, Pierrina Legnani, Emma Bessone, Maria la Bella, Mlle. Britta, Carlotta Mossetti, and Catherine Geltzer, and MM. de Vicenti and Tichomirov.

The choreographers were A. Bertrand, Carlo Coppi, and Alfredo Curti.

The Alhambra differed in one respect from its rival, the Empire, in that it possessed its own permanent *corps de ballet* whose precision and coördination was a feature of the productions at the

---

[1] The list does not pretend to be exhaustive.

former theatre, while the Empire specialized in its *premières danseuses*.

The two ballets which follow have been chosen as typical examples of the Alhambra spectacles.

FEMINA

Grand Spectacular Ballet in 5 Scenes. Book: Alfredo Curti. Music: George W. Byng and Valverde. Scenery: Amable and E. H. Ryan. Costumes: Comelli. Choreography: Alfredo Curti. First produced: Alhambra Theatre, London, May 30th, 1910.

CHARACTERS

The Spirit of Vanity . . .	MLLE. BRITTA
Spanish Espada	SENOR FAICO
Spanish Dancer	SENORA LOLA LA FLAMENCA
High Priest	MR. CHARLES RAYMOND
Keeper of the Posada . . .	MR. TOM COVENTRY
An Old Chief	MR. R. VALLIS
Femina	MLLE. LEONORA

Alhambra Corps de Ballet

Scene I. The first garden. Moonlight.

The Spirit of Vanity comes upon Femina as she lies asleep and awakens her with a shower of petals. When she resists his advances, he fashions a costume for her from leaves and flowers. Fascinated by the manner in which it enhances her beauty, she can resist Vanity no longer.

Scene II. The Stone Age.

Femina is Queen of the Tribes, whose chiefs are rivals for her hand. It is agreed that the prize shall fall to the strongest. The contest is joined and the victor comes to claim his reward. But Vanity appears in the person of a young chief who has been away on a hunting expedition. He offers the Queen a number of lovely furs, spoils of the chase, which she accepts with pleasure, and, rejecting her former suitor, bestows her hand on the young chief.

Scene III. The interior of a temple in ancient Assyria.

The temple-dancers are worshipping the God of the Temple. The High Priest is enamoured of Femina, a Priestess, who refuses his advances.

Vanity arrives in the guise of a Prince who bears offerings of jewels and flowers ostensibly for the God of the Temple, but in reality for the conquest of Femina. Fascinated by the jewels she consents to fly with him, but the High Priest bars their way. He orders the Prince to leave the Temple and renews his advances to Femina, who promises to accept him as her lover, if he will give her the jewelled necklace from the neck of the God. The Priest refuses, horrified at this suggestion of sacrilege.

The sacred dances begin and, when they are about to end, the Priest, distracted at the thought that he may lose Femina, removes the coveted necklace that adorns the God. There is a crash of thunder and the Temple falls in ruins. In the confusion Femina seizes the necklace and is assisted to escape by the Prince.

Scene IV. Interior of a wayside inn in Andalusia.

Femina, now a gitana, dances and coquets with a young gypsy. A number of toreadors enter, including a famous Espada, renowned both for his skill in the ring and for his dancing. Femina, attracted by the toreador, deserts her lover and accepts the gifts of the newcomer.

Scene V. The Kingdom of Fashion.

This scene consists of a parade of women dressed in contemporary and fantastic costumes which ends with them all gazing up at a giant cobweb, in the centre of which is a woman regarding herself in a mirror held at arm's length.

THE DANCE DREAM

Ballet in 7 Scenes. Book: Alexander Gorsky. Music: Brahms, Glazunov, Tchaikovsky, Luigini, Rubinstein. Scenery: Amable and E. H. Ryan. Choreography: Alexander Gorsky. First produced: Alhambra Theatre, London, May 29th, 1911.

CHARACTERS

The Ideal	
A Cloud	
An Amazon	MLLE. CATERINA
A Tzigane Girl	GELTZER
A Young Russian Noblewoman	

Tamaragua, a warrior
A Scythian
A Tzigane   } M. Tichomirov
A Young Russian Noble
A Bayadère Sorceress   .   .   .   . Miss Marjorie Skelly
Two Slaves   .   .   .   .   .   . { Miss Gina Cormani
                                        Miss Agnes Healy

Alhambra Corps de Ballet.

Scene I. The Temple.

Tamaragua, an Indian warrior, while under the influence of opium, dreams of a beautiful girl who becomes his ideal.

A Bayadère, who is a sorceress, and in love with the warrior, tries to captivate him with her dances. As he continues to inhale the precious smoke he imagines himself transported to the Himalayas.

Scene II. The Himalayas.

The summit of the mountains is veiled in a mist which gradually resolves into a number of dancers, among whom is the cherished Ideal. But the dancers vanish to give place to a starlit sky.

Scene III. India.

Now Tamaragua believes himself to be the Rajah of a splendid palace filled with dancers, who strew his path with flowers. The Bayadère Sorceress uses all her arts to captivate him, but cannot disperse the memory of his Ideal.

Scene IV. The Temple.

The Warrior wakes and, seeing the Sorceress with arms outstretched towards him, remembers her power and entreats her to conjure up for him a vision of his Ideal. She refuses, and in a fit of jealousy tries to stab him; but he is saved by the timely intervention of one of his slaves.

The Sorceress, filled with remorse and hoping to regain his favour, consents to grant him his wish. As she dances before him his Ideal is revealed. He goes towards her, but the Sorceress causes him to fall asleep and he dreams that he is living in the Bronze Age.

Scene V. Scythia.

Here Tamaragua finds his Ideal who entertains him with savage dances.

Scene VI. A valley in Hungary.

Now Tamaragua believes himself in Hungary, a member of a camp of gypsies. His Ideal is a beautiful Tzigane girl with whom he wanders among the flowers.

Scene VII. Old Russia.

Finally the Warrior imagines that he is in Old Russia. A number of young ladies are dancing the Khorovod in which they are joined by several youths. Among the women he distinguishes his Ideal; alas, she is still beyond his reach, for all is but a dream.

SOME EMPIRE BALLETS

THE Empire Theatre opened in 1884 with a musical spectacle called *Chilpéric,* founded on Hervé's opera of the same name. This production included three ballets by M. Bertrand. The costumes were designed by Bianchini, Faustin, and Wilhelm. The last name is of particular importance, for Wilhelm was to play an important part in the production of ballets at the Empire.

During its first three years the Empire essayed various types of theatrical entertainment—light opera, ballet, burlesque, extravaganza, and opera; then, in December, 1887, it became a theatre of varieties under the joint management of George Edwardes and Sir Augustus Harris.

The first step in establishing the Empire as a centre of ballet was the engagement as *maîtresse de ballet* of Katti Lanner, the daughter of the famous Viennese composer of waltzes, who was principal of the then well-known school of dancing, which served as a source of material.

During the next ten years Mme. Lanner was responsible for the production of many successful ballets—*Sports of England* (1887), *Dilara* (1887), *Rose d'Amour* (1888), *Cleopatra* (1889), *The Dream of Wealth* (1890), *Cecile* (1890), *By the Sea* (1891), *Nisita* (1891), *Versailles* (1892), *Round the World* (1892), *Faust* (1895), *La Danse* (1896), *Monte Cristo* (1896), and *Under One Flag* (1897). Among the dancers who appeared in these productions were Mlles. Adèle Rossi, Santori, Bettina de Sortis, Aenea, Palladino, Malvina Cavallazzi, and Giuri; and MM. Enrico Cecchetti and Luigi Albertieri, and Mr. Will Bishop (an eccentric dancer).

On November 22nd, 1897, the Treasure Island scene from *Monte Cristo* was revived and Mlle. Genée, a dancer new to this country, made her London *début.* She next appeared as the Spirit of the Liberty of the Press in *The Press* (1898) and her success in this role established her as a potential star. Originally engaged for six weeks she remained for ten years, with re-appearances after that. The following is a list of the principal Empire ballets in which she appeared—*Alaska* (1898), *Round the Town Again* (1899), *Les*

Papillons (1900), *Old China* (1900), *Our Crown* (1901), *The Milliner Duchess* (1903), *Vineland* (1903), *High Jinks* (1904), *The Dancing Doll,* a version of *Die Puppenfee* (1905), *Cinderella* (1906), *Coppélia* (1906), *Fête Galante* (1906), *The Débutante* (1906), and *The Belle of the Ball* (1907) in which Phyllis Bedells made her *début*.

Among the dancers who appeared in these productions were Mlles. Malvina Cavallazzi, Zanfretta, D. Craske, Elise Clerc, and Messrs. Fred Farren and W. Vokes.

Genée retired from the Empire on November 22nd, 1907, when her place was taken by an English dancer, Topsy Sinden, who made her *début* in *The Belle of the Ball*. *Coppélia* was revived on June 10th, 1908, and Genée was persuaded to return to the stage and take up her old part of Swanilda. In August, it is of interest to note that Lydia Kyasht and Adolph Bolm made their London *débuts* in a series of dances. In September *The Dryad* was produced at the Empire with Genée in the title-role. But since she found the two parts too much of a strain, Kyasht took over her role in *Coppélia*. Soon afterwards Genée left London to fulfil an American engagement.

The next productions at the Empire had mainly a topical interest, and many of them resembled the type of entertainment now known as revue: *A Day in Paris* (1908), *Round the World* (1909), *Ship Ahoy* (1910), *Sylvia,* one act version (1911), *New York* (1911), *The Water Nymph* (1913), *Titania* (1913), *Europe* (1914).

The Empire ballets had something in common with the Alhambra ballets in that they too, had a patriotic, historical, or topical basis. But the Empire ballets were, in general, more refined in conception and manner of presentation, due to the dancing of Genée and the influence of C. Wilhelm as librettist and designer of costumes and settings.

The name of Genée is almost a synonym for the Empire Theatre, so closely were their successes linked together, and, although many other dancers of merit succeeded her, for instance, Topsy Sinden, Lydia Kyasht, and Phyllis Bedells, her fame remained undiminished.

Adeline Genée was born on January 6th, 1878, at Aarhus, Jutland, Denmark. She was eight years old when she began to study dancing at the school conducted by her uncle and aunt, M. and Mme. Alexander Genée. In 1895 she made her *début* as principal dancer at the Opera House, Copenhagen. A little later she achieved an important success at the Royal Theatre, Berlin, in *The Rose of Shiraz*. She then went to the Opera House, Munich, when the post of *première danseuse* was offered to her, but she declined it. She returned to Copenhagen and danced Swanilda in *Coppélia* before the King and Court. In November, 1897, she came to London for a short engagement at the Empire which was the beginning of a long series of successes.

Among the roles particularly associated with her are the Queen of Butterfly Land in *Les Papillons,* the solo hunting dance in *High Jinks,* Cinderella in *Cinderella,* Swanilda in *Coppélia,* Delphine Duvet in *The Débutante,* and the Dryad in *The Dryad.*

"There is something essentially of the North in Genée's dancing." says J. E. Crawford-Flitch[1], "a freshness and energy like that of the north wind, a hint of the athlete in the vigorous clean-limbed movements, an absence of passion, a purity, shall we say a coldness? Her spirit seems to belong to the heights rather than to the depths. It is bright rather than subtle. It is full of high lights but lacking in half-tones."

Max Beerbohm, reviewing her performance in *Coppélia,* says: "Perfect though she be in the '*haute école*', she has by some miracle preserved her own self. She was born a comedienne, and a comedienne she remains, light and liberal as foam. A mermaid were not a more surprising creature than she—she of whom one half is as that of an authentic *ballerina,* whilst the other is that of a most intelligent, most delightfully human actress. A mermaid were, indeed, less marvellous in our eyes. She would not be able to diffuse any semblance of humanity into her tail. Madame Genée's intelligence seems to vibrate in her very toes. Her dancing, strictliest classical though it is, is a part of her acting. And her acting, moreover, is of so fine a quality that she makes the old ineloquent conventions of gesture tell their meanings to me, and tell them so exquisitely that I quite forget my craving for words."

C. Wilhelm, whose association with the Empire began in 1887, when he designed the costumes for *Dilara,* was responsible for the costumes and many of the settings for the majority of the ballets presented at that theatre until 1915. In addition he wrote the themes of a number of ballets, the most successful being: *Faust, The Press, Les Papillons, Old China, The Débutante, The Vine,* and *Camargo,* nearly all of which were given at the Empire.

He had a keen eye for theatrical effect which enabled him to visualise at once the possibilities of Dresden china, a Watteau painting, and so on as a basis for a ballet.

As a designer he had made a careful study of historical costume which he adapted to his requirements. His drawings were very

[1] *Modern Dancing and Dancers,* 1912.

detailed and the colourings soft and delicate, but his conceptions were inclined to be pretty-pretty. Wilhelm died on March 2nd, 1925.

The five ballets which follow have been chosen as typical examples of the Empire productions.

THE PRESS

Ballet in 3 Scenes. Book: C. Wilhelm. Music: Leopold Wenzel. Scenery: Joseph Harker. Costumes: C. Wilhelm. Choreography: Katti Lanner. First produced: Empire Theatre, London, February 14th, 1898.

CHARACTERS

Caxton	MLLE. MALVINA CAVALLAZZI
King Edward IV	MR. ROCKLIFFE
Queen Elizabeth Woodville	MISS GUEST
Edward, Prince of Wales	MISS GARSTANG
The Duke of York	MISS M. HAYES
Princess Margaret	MISS E. HAYES
A Monk	MR. PERKINS
The Duke of Clarence	MR. G. GRIFFITHS
Richard, Duke of Gloster	MR. LEWINGTON
The Liberty of the Press	MLLE. ADELINE GENÉE
The Daily Mail	MISS M. EASTON
Father Times	MR. F. ARTELLI
The Sun	MISS E. JENKINS
The Star	MISS E. SLACK
The Referee	MLLE. CORA
The Man of the World	MISS SHEPHERD
The Sporting Times	MISS ADA VINCENT
The Illustrated London News	MISS SHROEDER
The Sketch	MISS COURTLAND
The Graphic	MISS KAYGILL
The Golden Penny	MLLE. PAPUCCI
The Army and Navy Gazette	MISS MILTON
The Regiment	MR. GEO. VINCENT
The War Cry	MISS F. BANBURY
Fashion	MLLE. FRANCESCA ZANFRETTA
The Xmas Number	MISS HIND
The Summer Number	MISS WILLS

Fun . . . . Miss E. Tree
Pick-me-Up . . . . Miss Gradella
Moonshine . . . . Mr. C. Perkins
Punch . . . . Mr. John Ridley
Alley Sloper . . . . Mr. Will Bishop

Printers' Devils, Typewriters, War Correspondents, Special Artists, Newspaper Boys' Chorus, The Daily Telegraph, The Standard, Sunday Papers, Theatrical Papers, The Financial News, The Financial Times, Pearsons, Answers, Tid-Bits, Black and White, and Society Papers.

Scene I. Westminster, A.D. 1471. *Caxton's printing-press in the Almonry.*

The curtain rises on a scene based on the well-known painting by Maclise. Caxton is seen receiving a visit from Edward IV and the royal family. The father of English printing displays the wonders of his press and, when his guests have departed, muses on the possible development of printing. But his thoughts are rudely disturbed by the entrance of a band of printers' devils who wreck his printing-press. From the ruins rises the spirit representing the liberty of the Press who promises him a vision of the progress of printing.

Scene II. Fleet Street, A.D. 1898. *The offices of "The Metropolitan Press."*

The scene shows some of the stages in the production of a newspaper.

Scene III. The Hall of "The Fourth Estate."

This in an ingenious spectacle in which dancers costumed to represent the different newspapers take part. Father *Times* enters to a march, the *Daily Telegraph* whirls in to a waltz, the *Standard* arrives to another march. Then come the Morning Papers and the Evening Papers, who have a difference of opinion which ends with a reconciliation between the *Sun* and the *Star*. Then come the Sunday Papers led by the *Referee*.

The Man of the World introduces the *Sporting Times,* which affords occasion for a Hunting Galop by the Sporting Papers. These are succeeded by the Theatrical Papers who indulge in a *Polonaise*.

Lastly come the Society Papers, the Financial Papers, the *Regiment,* portrayed by a private soldier, who is captured by a Salvationist damsel who represents the *War Cry,* the gay pranks of the Comic Papers, and a final *tableau* in which Caxton is supported by Father *Times* and Mr. *Punch.*

LES PAPILLONS

Fantastic Ballet Divertissement in 2 Scenes. Book: C. Wilhelm. Music: Leopold Wenzel. Scenery: Joseph Harker. Costumes: C. Wilhelm. Choreography: Katti Lanner. First produced: Empire Theatre, London, March 18th, 1901.

CHARACTERS
Mortals

Mathurin, a miller	MR. GEORGE VINCENT
Yvonne, his daughter . . .	MISS A. VINCENT
Petit Jean, her little brother . .	MISS R. HARRINGTON
Herve, her fiancé, a young farmer .	MISS M. PASTON
Babette, Mathurin's housekeeper .	MISS BANNISTER
Gaspard, a notary	MR. MAINWARING
Noel	M. AMEDEO SANTINI
An Old Beggar	MR. C. PERKINS

Villagers and Farm Labourers, Musicians.

Immortals

Vanessa Imperialis, Queen of Butterfly Land	MLLE. ADELINE GENÉE
A Moth	MLLE. Q. PAPUCCI
Ladybird	MLLE. CORA
Grey Moths	MISSES K. HEWITT, THOMAS, N. VINCENT and WEGNER
Captain of the Glow-Worm Patrol .	MISS E. CLERC
Grasshopper, Master of the Revels .	MR. WILL BISHOP
The Spider	MR. MAINWARING
Stag Beetle, public executioner .	MR. GEO. VINCENT
Court Chamberlain . . .	MISS E. TREE
Chrysoris, chief officer of the Royal Dragonfly Guard . . .	MISS M. FORD
A Little Fly	MISS R. HARRINGTON
Mayflies	MISSES D. CLARKE, L. COLLIER, KAYGILL, and TREVESICK

Tortoise-Shell Butterflies   .   .   .   MISSES M. HAYES, GAR-
                                                STANG, WILLS, and
                                                McFARLANE
Flower Elves, Glow-Worms, Butterflies, Moths, Grasshoppers,
                    Bees, Dragonflies.

Les Papillons, says the *Times'* [2] critic, "is a fairy ballet, and the
scene, laid as it is in fairyland at the bottom of a cornfield surrounded with giant blades of corn, corncockles, convolvoluses,
and briars, is one of the most beautiful that has ever been staged
at this theatre. The inhabitants are butterflies of every size and
hue. The dresses are beautifully done with great fidelity to nature.
Peacocks, tortoiseshells, red admirals, and a number of other
butterflies are reproduced, besides a host of gnats, bees, grasshoppers, glow-worms, and other small members of the insect
world. . . .

"The soloists include Mlle. Adeline Genée who, as the Queen of
Butterfly Land, gives a number of very charming dances, and Mr.
Will Bishop, who, as the Grasshopper, conducts the revels with the
greatest spirit and drollery, while the Stag Beetle of Mr. George
Vincent, the Ladybird of Mlle. Cora, and the Spider of Mr. Main-
waring are all as good as could be devised."

CINDERELLA

*Fairy Ballet in 5 Scenes. Book: C. Wilhelm. Music: Sidney
Jones. Choreography: Fred Farren (Mlle. Genée's dances by
Alexander Genée). Scenery: Hawes Craven, Joseph Harker, E.
Banks, and H. Brooke. Costumes: C. Wilhelm. First produced:
Empire Theatre, London, January 6th, 1906.*

CHARACTERS

Fortunée, Cinderella's fairy godmother	MLLE. ZANFRETTA
Crystal, the little glass slipper fairy .	MISS F. CRASKE
The Baron de Sans-Sous	MR. W. VOKES
Fi-Fi, the Baroness, his second wife .	MR. FRED FARREN
Brunette ⎱ her daughters . . .	⎰ MISS ELISE CLERC
Blondine ⎰	⎱ MISS MAY PASTON
Sambo, their black page	"LITTLE JIMMY"
Prince Fleur-de-Lys	MISS D. CRASKE

[2] March 19th, 1901.

The Count Dandini, his secretary . .	Miss L. Collier
Celadon ⎫	⎧ Miss F. Martell
Bel-Amour ⎪ gentlemen-in-	⎪ Miss B. Trevesick
Mutine ⎬ waiting	⎬ Miss F. Mansell
Mignonne ⎭	⎩ Miss E. Collier
Pavane, Lord Chamberlain . . .	Miss Courtland
Rigodon, the Court dancing-master .	Miss Shepherd
Jasmin, officer of the Guard . . .	Mr. P. Sundberg
Equerries	Misses Dawson, Kay-gill, Roullright and Swanton
Court Ladies	Misses Badham, Osmond, Shaw and Hill
Watteau Dancers	Misses N. Banbury, G. Tree, Banks, Reeves and Beacon
Flunkeys and Housemaids . . .	Misses Ruby, Willey, C. Craske, Lyons, Rushton, Bosetti, Arigoni and Evans
Head Forester	Mr. Lewington
Toupet, a perruquier	Mr. Marsland
P'tit Bleu, a milkman	Mr. Oram
Veronique, a donkey	Mr. Ford
Epinard, a greengrocer	Mr. Perkins
Canardot, a poulterer	Mr. A. Young
Cinderella, daughter of the Baron . .	Mlle. Adeline Genée

Court Dancers, Guards, Huntsmen, Guests, Cooks, Sedan Bearers, Pages, Fairy Milliners, Daisies, and Butterflies.

Cinderella, an arrangement by C. Wilhelm of Perrault's fairy tale, fell into five scenes, the titles of which almost suggest the development of the action: I. A Glade in the Royal Park. II. Kitchen at the Baron's. III. The Baronial Hall. IV. On the Road to the Palace. V. Conservatory and Ballroom in the Palace.

The piece is best described in the words of the *Times'* [3] critic: "The period is Louis XV, which, owing to the sartorial fashions of that day, is eminently suitable, but the ballet in its more boisterous moments becomes frankly 20th century. Cinderella's family consists of the Baron de Sans-Sous, Mr. W. Vokes, and his spouse, who is admirably portrayed in the methods of modern

[3] January 8th, 1906.

pantomime by Mr. Fred Farren. Of course there are the two unkind sisters, and Mr. C. Wilhelm, who has designed the ballet, adds considerably to the gaiety of the household by providing it with a little black page. For the rest there is a display of courtiers, ladies, guards, and all the usual multitude arrayed in gorgeous attire and harmonizing well with the magnificence of the scenery, and Mr. Banks's scene 'On the road to the Palace' is especially deserving of mention. There is rather too much of the old-fashioned harlequinade style of fun in the performance, and the breakdown of the motor on its way to the ball is reminiscent only of a more amusing breakdown 'turn' which was to be seen not long ago, but when Mlle. Genée is on the stage these trifles are forgotten."

The production was chiefly remarkable for two things, the opening scene and Genée's interpretation of the title-role. The former, which represented "a park with a lake, a classic temple in the distance, a hint or two of florid stonework in the foreground," was an evocation of a Watteau painting, in which elegantly-clad youths and ladies disported themselves in a menuet to the soft strains of lutes.

Of Genée's performance as Cinderella a contemporary asserts: "If this is not a flawless performance, we have never seen one. Perhaps performance is not the best word, because it suggests a conscious art, whereas Mlle. Genée's quiet charm is something wholly apart from her technical skill, wonderful as that is. It is a charm of native, even homely simplicity; a charm that is never mutinous, coquettish, 'disquieting,' as the French say; the charm of a child blithely yielding, without a thought of onlookers, to the play-impulse.

"See her when 'Cinderella' is left alone in the kitchen, after the others have gone to the ball. At first she sits forlorn; then the picture of the ballroom takes hold of her and her face beams with delight at the idea of improvising a little ball-room scene all to herself. Up she jumps, plucks a couple of feathers from her broom and sticks them in her hair, snatches up the table-cloth to make a train, and whirls round with her broom for an imaginary partner. The dainty grace with which she makes believe to eat an ice, to bow to her partner, to yield to a pressing invitation for just one dance more! To every little endearing detail she brings some quaint touch of humour, some ingenuity of invention. As to technical skill, we have called it wonderful. It is dancing without the slightest trace of effort, every step—in reality, no doubt, calculated to a hair's breadth and assiduously practiced—having the air of a happy impromptu."

The first scene of *Cinderella* was later expanded into a Watteau ballet called *Fête Galante,* which was produced on August 6th of the same year. The ballet opened with a menuet. Later a troupe of dancers arrived for the entertainment of the noble hostess and her guests. This *divertissement* permitted the introduction of Camargo. Later the whole company took part in a stately dance which, seen in the fading light, took on the misty texture of a dream. Gradually the dancers melted into the group with which the ballet opened, when the curtain fell.

THE DÉBUTANTE

Ballet Divertissement in 3 Scenes. Book: C. Wilhelm. Music: Cuthbert Clarke and G. J. M. Glaser. Scenery and costumes: C. Wilhelm. First produced: Empire Theatre, London, November 14th, 1906.

CHARACTERS

Scenes I and II

M. Pirouette, *maître de ballet* at the Opera House	Mr. Fred Farren
Celestine, his wife, second dancer at the Opera	Miss B. Trevesick
Isidore, their son, assistant ballet-master	Miss D. Craske
Mlle. Lutine, head pupil	Miss Elise Clerc
Mlle. Florita, principal dancer at the Opera	Miss E. Collier
Baron Salomon, a patron of the ballet	Mr. Paul Sundberg
Rafael, his son	L. Greville
Coulisse, call-boy	W. Garraway
Labrosse, scenic artist . . .	Mr. H. Huntly
Signor Pesante, *chef d'orchestre* . .	Mr. Lewington
Chevalet, first violin	Mr. C. Perkins
Perruquier	Mr. T. Vincent
Mme. Duvet	Miss Paston
Mlle. Delphine Duvet, a *débutante* .	Mlle. Adeline Genée

Friends of the Baron, Pupils.

Scene III

The Sultan	Mr. Fred Farren
The Sultana	Miss B. Trevesick

Hassan, Captain of the Guard . . Miss D. Craske
Zulma, Confidante of the Sultana . . Miss Elise Clerc
Mesrour, grand vizier . . . . Miss F. Jenkins
Chamberlains . . . . . . Misses Courtland and
                                    Dawson
Court Ladies . . . . . . Misses E. Collier and
                                    G. Tree
Mustafa, slave dealer . . . . Mr. Paul Sundberg
Azalea, chief odalisque . . . . Mlle. Adeline Genée
    Pages, Fan Bearers, Pupils, Flaneurs, Bayadères, Guards,
                        Boatmen, Slaves.

The action takes place in Paris, 1835.

Scene I. Rehearsal Room at the Opera House.

M. Pirouette, the *maître de ballet,* is seen taking a class. Friends
of the dancers watch proceedings or try to exchange confidences
with the objects of their admiration. Instruction at an end, M.
Pirouette tells the company of his intention to produce a new
ballet, to be called *Azalea, or the Odalisque,* which he proceeds to
outline.

But the temperamental *première danseuse,* Mlle. Florita, is
displeased with the role allotted to her, and, in a pet, throws up
her part. M. Pirouette, seeing his cherished ballet deprived of its
shining star, is overcome with despair. His wife gallantly offers her
services, but she, alas, is no longer in the flower of her youth.

At this point a certain Baron Salomon, a well-known patron of
the ballet, arrives and introduces his *protegée,* Mlle. Delphine,
whom he regards as a dancer of promise. M. Pirouette gives her a
trial and is delighted with her rare charm and accomplishments.
The ballet is saved.

Scene II. Behind the scenes, a month later.

This scene affords a glimpse of the hectic last few minutes
before the curtain goes up on the first performance of *Azalea.*
M. Pirouette is the centre of a frenzied throng of musicians,
dancers, wig-makers, and the rest, all clamouring for last minute
instructions.

Scene III. The gardens of the seraglio.

A slave-dealer brings a number of female slaves for the inspection of the aged Sultan. He is delighted with a certain Azalea

whom he desires to purchase, but she resents the suggestion that she should be added to the Sultan's harem. A young officer attempts to protect her from the brutal slave-dealer and is arrested for his pains. Azalea pleads for him to be released and finally the Sultan agrees, subject to the condition that she can wile the signet-ring from his finger. Azalea achieves this object by means of her dancing, and all ends happily.

The Times[4] acclaims this ballet as "one of the most delightful recent years have produced, full of contrast, not overlaid with incident, gracious, bright, and interesting."

Of Azalea the same writer observes: "She achieves . . . a display of dancing . . . which even Mlle. Genée has never in our recollection equalled."

A *ballet-divertissement* called *The Dancing-Master*, founded by C. Wilhelm, on the first act of *The Débutante*, was produced at the Empire Theatre in July, 1910. The cast was as follows: Fred Farren (*M. Pirouette*), Lydia Kyasht (*Mimi the Débutante*), and Phyllis Bedells (*Mlle. Lutine*). In August, Kyasht went on holiday and Bedells took her part of Mimi, in which she made a considerable success.

THE DRYAD

Pastoral Fantasy in 2 Scenes. Book: Dora Bright. Music: Dora Bright. Choreography: Alexander Genée. First produced: Empire Theatre, September 7th, 1908.

CHARACTERS

The Dryad . . . . MLLE. ADELINE GENÉE
The Shepherd . . . . . . MR. GORDON CLEATHER

A certain Dryad, loveliest of the Wood Nymphs, who subdued all mortals by her beauty and the charm of her dancing, aroused the jealousy of Aphrodite who caused her to be imprisoned in an oak tree. Once in every ten years she was permitted to leave the tree between the hours of sunrise and sunset, and if she could find a mortal faithful to her for a decade, her freedom was to be restored to her.

On one of these occasions a shepherd spies her dancing in the moonlight. He falls in love with her and vows eternal faithfulness.

[4] November 21st, 1906.

With the coming of dawn she bids her lover farewell and vanishes into the tree.

Ten years pass and again the Dryad emerges from the prisoning tree in search of her lover. But he has long since forgotten her and the wood is empty. She dances sadly, always hoping that he will keep the tryst, but in vain, and she is compelled once more to enter the bondage of the tree.

*

The Dryad, the theme of which appears to be inspired by the story of Libussa by Musaüs, provided an excellent vehicle for Genée's gifts, since it gave her many opportunities to show her abilities both as dancer and mime. There was her radiant joy on her release from the tree. How she loved to dance on the greensward, to flit about the flower-girt glade in the light of the moon! Then she must exercise her wiles to ensnare the handsome shepherd and capture his heart, so bound up with her future freedom. At last came the sad parting and her return to the tree.

The years pass and again she emerges from the tree. Imagine her joy, her eager longing to greet the lover whose constancy means so much to her! But, unable to find him, she grows faint and anxious. Then she hears his voice lifted in song and is filled with a great joy. Alas, he passes her by and she is stricken with grief, well knowing that she is doomed to return to the fatal tree.

ANNA PAVLOVA

ANNA PAVLOVNA PAVLOVA was born at St. Petersburg on January 31st, 1882. She was the only child of poor parents and had the misfortune to lose her father when only two years old. At the age of eight she was taken by her mother to see a performance of *La Belle au Bois Dormant,* which delighted her so much that she resolved to become a dancer.

She entered the Imperial Ballet School when ten years old. Her principal teachers were C. Johannsen, P. A. Gerdt, Evgenia Sokolova, and Enrico Cecchetti. She made her *début* at the Maryinsky Theatre on June 1st, 1899, and was cast for small parts without having to pass through a period of service in the *corps de ballet.* In the course of time she became a soloist and finally attained the rank of *prima ballerina.*

After various tours beginning in 1907 she made her London *début* on April 18th, 1910, at the Palace Theatre, supported by Mordkin and a company of eight dancers. In a single night Pavlova and Mordkin became the talk of the town. She returned to the Palace Theatre the next year on April 17th, and, in October, appeared with the Diaghilev Company, when she portrayed the title role in *Giselle,* Cleopatra's Slave in *Cléopâtre,* Armide in *Le Pavillon d'Armide,* and danced in *Les Sylphides* and in the *pas de deux "L'Oiseau Bleu."*

In 1912, 1913 and 1914 she again visited London, increasing her repertory and enlarging her company, which gradually became virtually British. From 1914 onwards her life was a series of extended tours all over the world, broken only by periodical returns to London for fleeting appearances, refitment, and rest. Her musical director, the late Theodore Stier, declares in his Memoirs that in the course of his 16 years' association with her, he travelled 300,000 miles, conducted 3,650 performances, and over 2,000 rehearsals.

These tours were of inestimable value to the art of dancing and, while Pavlova's dancing gave great pleasure to the general public, she became the model and inspiration to many young dancers.

In January, 1931, she went to The Hague to begin a fresh tour, but contracted a severe cold which developed into pneumonia, from which she died on the 23rd of the same month.

*

Those who never saw Pavlova dance may ask what it was she did that made her so wonderful. It was not so much what she did, as how she did it. Perhaps the most subtle and happiest definition of her dancing was the phrase coined by a French writer who styled it: *"la danse de toujours, dansée comme jamais"* —the dance of every day as it was never danced before.

Pavlova danced with her whole body, from the crown of her head to the tip of her toe. She danced with such abounding vitality, with such ecstasy of the spirit; she surrendered herself so completely to the mood of the dance; that she became a being transformed. She glowed, became almost incandescent, as it were, from the lavish outpouring of her nervous energy and muscular force. Sometimes there was just a pale luminosity which filled the spectator with an exquisite sadness as in *"Le Cygne,"* sometimes the glow burst into flame as in *"L'Automne Bacchanale."* These two dances are poles apart and prove the immense scale of her accomplishment.

Pavlova was also a great dramatic artist with a range as wide as in her dancing.

Although at one time or another she had portrayed most of the celebrated roles in the repertory of the Imperial Russian Ballet, and appeared with success in many of the ballets in the repertory of her own company, for instance, *The Fairy Doll, Amarilla, Autumn Leaves,* and so on, she is best known for her *soli* and *pas de deux,* such as *"Le Cygne,"* L'Automne Bacchanale," "Les Coquettries de Colombine," "La Libellule," "Papillon," "Gavotte Pavlova,"* and *"Valse Caprice."*

Pavlova rarely ventured into choreography, her achievements being limited to a few *divertissements,* and one ballet—*Autumn Leaves.* She made no attempt to increase the vocabulary of the dance; she found it sufficient and devoted all her energies to learning to speak the language to perfection. That she succeeded, few, if any, will dispute.

AUTUMN LEAVES

Choreographic Poem in 1 Act. Book: Anna Pavlova. Music: Frédéric Chopin. Scenery: Castro. Choreography: Anna Pavlova. First produced: Rio de Janeiro, Brazil, 1918.

CHARACTERS

A Chrysanthemum . . . . . MLLE. ANNA PAVLOVA
A Young Poet . . . . . . M. ALEXANDER
                               VOLININE
The Autumn Wind . . . . M. HUBERT STOWITTS
         Autumn Leaves

The scene, conceived in appropriate tints of russet and gold, depicts a park, of which the chief adornment is a beautiful chrysanthemum.

A boisterous Autumn Wind sweeps through the grounds, scattering the fallen leaves and uprooting the chrysanthemum. A Poet, strolling through the park, perceives the flower, which he picks up and tends with loving care.

But the Wind returns and dashes it from his hand. This time the Poet carries the flower to a fountain, places it on a soft bank of moss, and composes himself to read.

Again the Wind fastens on the poor flower and flings her among a cloud of leaves, which whirl about her, until, cold and exhausted, she expires in the last rays of the setting sun.

The Poet tries to revive the fading flower, but, finding his efforts of no avail, departs with his betrothed, who has come to meet him.

*

Pavlova had a special affection for this ballet and took particular pains to ensure that a high standard of performance was maintained. The leaves were represented by the *corps de ballet*.

The ballet was a charming conception in which Pavlova gave a fine performance as the Chrysanthemum.

ADOLPH BOLM

A DOLPH RUDOLPHOVICH BOLM was born at St. Petersburg. His father was first violin and assistant conductor at the Mikhailovsky Theatre and so he grew up in the atmosphere of the theatre. At the age of ten, at the suggestion of his godfather, he presented himself at one of the periodical entrance examinations held in connection with the Imperial Ballet School and was accepted as a student.

His teacher was Platon Karsavin, who, at the beginning, was not too pleased with his pupil's progress, but, by dint of perseverance and assiduous application, he gradually improved, and when he finished school in 1904 gained the first prize. On being transferred to the Imperial Ballet at the Maryinsky Theatre he soon attracted attention by his brilliant dancing and ability to mime, and his highly developed sense of the theatre. In the summer holidays he obtained permission to go abroad and travelled through Germany, France, and Italy, visiting museums and art galleries and attending performances at local theatres. On one occasion he made a special visit to Turin to study under Maestro Enrico Cecchetti.

These travels suggested to him the possibility of making a tour with a company of dancers from the Imperial Theatre, a dream which he brought to realisation in 1908. With an excellent troupe which included Anna Pavlova, Lubov Egorova, Elsa Will, Obukhov, Legat, and Shirayev, and a select *corps de ballet,* he toured with success Riga, Copenhagen, and Stockholm, and at the last-named town King Gustave conferred upon him the gold medal *Literis et Artibus*. In 1909 Bolm made a second successful tour, again with Pavlova, this time visiting Berlin.

Bolm next went to London where he appeared with Lydia Kyasht at the Empire Theatre. He was offered a three years' contract as choreographer but, on consideration, preferred to throw in his lot with Diaghilev, with whom he remained until 1914. Those who have not seen Bolm's interpretation of Pierrot in *Le Carnaval,* of the Chief in *Prince Igor,* of the Stranger in

Thamar, of Prince Ivan in *L'Oiseau de Feu,* of the Moor in *Petrouchka,* cannot conceive to what heights these roles can be raised. During his association with Diaghilev he produced at Monte Carlo, in 1912, Rameau's opera-ballet *La Fête d'Hebé,* with Carlotta Zambelli; the Persian dances in Rimsky-Korsakov's *Khovanchina* (1914), and the russalka dances in the same composer's *Nuit de Mai* (1914).

When the Great War broke out in 1914 Bolm was at Lausanne, where he later received an invitation from Sir Oswald Stoll to come to London and stage a season of ballet with Karsavina as *ballerina* and Bakst as artistic collaborator. But Diaghilev, who had also arrived at Lausanne, was planning an American tour and invited Bolm to join him. Again he chose to accompany Diaghilev and, since it proved to be impossible to enlist the services of either Karsavina, Fokine, or Nijinsky, Bolm found himself laden with the double responsibility of *premier danseur* and choreographer. The American venture was very successful and was followed by a tour of Spain. During this period Bolm composed a ballet based on one of the scenes from Rimsky-Korsakov's *Sadko* (Madrid, 1916).

Plans were made for a second American tour, and after some hesitation Bolm agreed to go with the troupe, which this time was not to have the controlling presence of Diaghilev. While dancing in *Thamar* in California, Bolm slipped and injured himself, as a result of which he left the company. On his recovery he decided to remain in America and established himself in New York. There he formed the Bolm Ballet Intime, consisting of twelve dancers—including oriental artistes such as Roshanara and Michio Ito, and fourteen musicians, with which he gave many successful programmes.

Then he accepted an invitation from the Metropolitan Opera to produce *Le Coq d'Or,* which was given in 1918. Next he produced a version of *Autumn Leaves* for Ziegfeld. In 1919 he staged *Petrouchka*—with himself in the title-role—for the Metropolitan Opera, and towards the end of the year produced *The Birthday of the Infanta*—music by John Alden Carpenter; scenery and costumes by Robert Edmond Jones—for the Chicago Opera Co. This ballet, based on the well known story by Oscar Wilde, with Ruth Page as the Infanta and himself as the Dwarf, definitely established his reputation as a choreographer of considerable distinction.

When the opera-houses closed, he continued with his Ballet Intime and was the first person to introduce dance prologues for

New York cinemas, a feature which has since become elaborated into stupendous spectacles.

In 1920 Bolm brought his Ballet Intime to London for a successful season at the Coliseum Theatre. On his return to New York he produced a ballet called *Krazy Kat* (Carpenter), the forerunner of Mickey Mouse. At this same period he made the first dance film synchronised to music rendered by an orchestra, the music being the *Danse Macabre* of Saint-Saëns.

Two years later Bolm left New York to become *maître de ballet* and teacher of dancing to the Chicago Civic Opera, a post he filled with distinction until 1924, when he joined the Chicago Allied Arts as *maître de ballet*. During the next three years he produced *Elopement* (Mozart), 1924; *Foyer de la Danse* (Chabrier), 1924; *El Amor Brujo* (De Falla), 1925; *The Rivals* (Eichheim), 1925; *Mandragora* (Szymanovsky), 1925; *Bal des Marionettes* (Satie), 1925; *Pierrot Lunaire* (Schönberg), 1926; *Parnasse au Montmartre* (Satie), 1926; *La Farce au Pont Neuf* (Herscher), 1926; *La Tragédie du Violoncelle* (Tansman), 1927; *Christmas Carol* (Vaughan Williams), 1927. In addition he created numerous dances.

During 1925 Bolm returned to New York to restage *Petrouchka,* after which he went to the Colon Theatre, Buenos Aires, where he produced *Le Coq d'Or, Petrouchka, The Rivals,* and *Bal des Marionettes.* Three years later he was engaged to mount several ballets in connection with programmes given by the Chamber Music Society of Washington. This led to the production of Stravinsky's *Apollon Musagète,* specially composed for this festival, *Arlechinata, Alt Wien,* and *Pavane pour une Infante Défunte* (Ravel).

In 1931 Bolm was invited to Hollywood to produce a ballet for *The Mad Genius,* a film with a ballet background. Rodzynsky, the conductor of the Los Angeles Orchestra, drew his attention to Mossolov's *Spirit of the Factory,* the very type of music he had been seeking, and he eagerly set to work on the mechanical ballet he had in mind. Unfortunately the film proved to be so long in itself that the ballet was cut to such an extent as to make it almost incomprehensible. Later, however, the complete work was given at the Hollywood Bowl, where it attracted audiences of fifteen and twenty thousand spectators at a time.

In November, 1933, Bolm staged *Le Coq d'Or* for the San Francisco Opera, and the success of the production led to the establishment of a School of Ballet with Bolm as director. Among the ballets given may be mentioned *Patterns* (Tansman) and *Bach Cycle*. May, 1935, saw the production of three choreographic works to music by Bach—*Danse Noble* (Fugue in G minor), *Lament* (Prelude No. 8), and *Consecration* (Toccata and Fugue in D).

Adolph Bolm has done a great deal for the advancement of the Dance, particularly in America, where his labours as dancer, choreographer, and teacher have achieved excellent results, not only in the staging of artistic ballets and the introduction of good music, both classic and modern, but in fostering an understanding and appreciation of the true ideals of ballet as opposed to mere spectacle.

FOYER DE LA DANSE

Pantomimic Ballet in 1 Act. Book: Adolph Bolm. Music: E. Chabrier. Scenery and Costumes: Nicholas Remisov. Choreography: Adolph Bolm. First produced: Eighth St. Theatre, Chicago, November 27th, 1927.

CHARACTERS

Wig-maker	PAUL DU PONT
Property Man	LORNE BALSLEY
Ballet-Master	MARK TURBYFILL
Wardrobe Mistress	RUTH ALBERT
Musicians	{ CHARLES MILLHOLLAND { FRANK LISCHERON
Director of the Opera . . .	CAIRD LESLIE
Composer	CHARLES MORRIS
Prima Ballerina	RUTH PAGE
Premier Danseur	ADOLPH BOLM
Solliste	MARCIA PREBLE

Coryphées, Corps de Ballet, Peasant Dancers, Mothers, Children.

Scene. The rehearsal-room of the Grand Opera, Paris, 1870.

A ballet rehearsal is in progress with all the accompanying activities of ballet-master, director, wardrobe mistress, property man, and "stars," major and minor. No one is missing, not even the mothers of the dancers and their children, the next generation of dancers.

The ballet was inspired by the well-known painting by Degas, "*Foyer de la Danse,*" which is in the Louvre, Paris.

There is an English ballet called *Foyer de Danse,* with choreography by Frederick Ashton and music by Lord Berners, which was inspired by the same painting. This composition was presented by the Ballet Rambert at the Mercury Theatre, London, in 1932. There are three principal roles in *Foyer de Danse* which originally were taken thus: L'Etoile—Markova; Le Maître de Ballet—Walter Gore; Un Abonné—William Chappell.

IRON FOUNDRY

Ballet in 1 Act. Book: Adolph Bolm. Music: A. Mossolov. Costumes: That of Elise Reiman by N. Remisov, all other costumes designed by A. Bolm. Choreography: Adolph Bolm. First produced: Hollywood Bowl, California, August, 1932.

CHARACTERS

Principal Dynamos { ELISE REIMAN   ROBERT BELL

Switches (first line)
Gears (second line)
Pendulars (back line)
Fly Wheel (circle to right)
Principal Pistons (boys with long poles)
Piston Rods (girls with poles)
Spring Valves (line to extreme right)

The ballet opens with a blast on a steam siren which is the signal for the dancers representing various units of machinery to begin to move. The immense stage reflects a red furnace-like glare into which the dancers, clad in close-fitting metallized fabrics, make their way in various groups, their movements exactly synchronised with the music.

Enter the Dynamo, a *danseuse* in gleaming silver and cellophane, whose whirling causes her pleated silver skirt to spread out and form a wheel. Her dance, which is rapid and graceful, and full of spinning motions, represents the magic of electricity.

She is followed by another Dynamo, a male dancer dressed in black, scored with silver spirals and bound at the waist with a red sash. His dance is expressive of the might of electricity.

The groups continually change in accordance with the pounding rhythm of the music, each group a complete unit in itself, yet all contributing to present a tremendous spectacle of concerted rhythm.

*

This ballet, first conceived as a feature of the film *The Mad Genius,* was there shown in a fragmentary form only. The complete ballet was given for the first time at the Hollywood Bowl, when it was rendered by fifty dancers. The music is Mossolov's *"The Spirit of the Factory."*

Bolm received his inspiration for the composition while touring with his Ballet Intime, when he visited the Ford factory in Detroit, and saw the giant printing-presses of the *New York Times* in motion. The units of the machinery suggested to him moments of whimsicality, gaiety and pathos. He was impressed, too, by the similarity of the movements made by the machines and the technique of the classical ballet—the *battements* of levers, the *pirouettes* of fly-wheels, the *glissades* of worm-gears, the *fouettés* of pendula, and the *jetés, cabrioles,* and *entrechats* of springing valves.

The light effects in this ballet were very important, and special iron poles, some fifty feet high, were erected to carry certain lights in order that they should not obstruct the view of the audience.

Iron Foundry achieved an enormous success and attracted audiences of thousands. It was revived the following season and is frequently in demand. *Iron Foundry* is now known as *Ballet Mécanique.*

VASLAV NIJINSKY

V ASLAV FOMICH NIJINSKY was born at Kiev, South Russia, on February 28th, 1890. His parents were of Polish origin.
His mother was a former student of the Imperial School of Ballet,
Warsaw; his father was a first-rate exponent of classical ballet, and
also an excellent character dancer.

It was decided that Vaslav should be trained as a dancer, and,
on August 20th, 1900, he presented himself at the Imperial School
of Ballet, St. Petersburg, where he was chosen with five other boys
from a group of 150 candidates. For this success he was partly
indebted to Nicholas Legat, one of the examiners, who was
impressed by the unusual development of his thigh muscles. Legat
was his first master, under whom he made great progress, and
in 1902 he was permanently admitted to the School of Ballet. One
evening Nijinsky took part in a Court performance when he was
presented with a gold watch bearing the Tsar's initials, the highest
mark of His Majesty's pleasure to a pupil of the Imperial School.

In 1906, Obukhov, then Nijinsky's teacher, reported that he
could teach him no more and it was resolved to make him a member of the Maryinsky Theatre two years before the normal period
for graduation. Nijinsky, however, wished to continue at the
school for two more years, a request which was granted.

In May, 1908, Nijinsky made his *début* in the ballet in Mozart's
opera, *Don Giovanni*. So popular did he become that he was given
more and more difficult parts. He became the regular partner for
Matilda Kshesinskaya, the *prima ballerina assoluta,* and was
acclaimed as the Vestris of the North. Now he began to study
hard with Maestro Cecchetti.

During the winter of the same year Nijinsky made the acquaintance of Serge Diaghilev, then in supreme authority concerning all
artistic matters. The acquaintance developed into a strong mutual
attachment and Diaghilev guided his young friend's taste in literature, art, and music. A little later the plan of presenting Russian Ballet to Western Europe was conceived and Diaghilev bent
all his efforts towards the fulfilment of that dream. The ballets

and dancers were selected and permission obtained for the latter to appear at Paris in connection with the contemplated season.

The first performance took place at the Théâtre du Chatelet, May 17th, 1909. Nijinsky's dancing as the Slave in *Le Pavillon d'Armide* and his subsequent appearances in *Cléopâtre* and *Les Sylphides* made him the idol of the town. When the troupe returned the following year Nijinsky won fresh laurels with his performances as the Slave in *Schéhérazade* and as Harlequin in *Le Carnaval.*

On Nijinsky's return to St. Petersburg his success at the Maryinsky continued unabated until a certain day when he appeared in *Giselle,* wearing white tights and velvet tunic, but without the customary small slip. The director ordered him to change but, since there was insufficient time, Nijinsky refused. As a result he was suspended. Diaghilev persuaded him to resign, promising to form a permanent company.

The troupe was formed and new ballets were evolved by the fertile genius of Fokine. Nijinsky's fame grew and grew. His two greatest creations at this time (1911) were his dancing with Karsavina in *Le Spectre de la Rose,* the rare beauty of which cannot be realised by those who never saw the original, which included the famous leap he made at his entrance and at his exit, a leap so wonderful that it was thought to be the product of specially prepared shoes or some mechanical contrivance. The other famous character was his rendering of the title-role in *Petrouchka,* in regard to which it is sufficient to quote the words of Sarah Bernhardt who, on witnessing his miming said: *"J'ai peur, j'ai peur, car je vois l'acteur le plus grand du monde."* Nijinsky, with his remarkable sense of line and his rare technical ability, his wonderful *ballon,* and his astounding *élévation,* was one of those supreme artists who appear but once in many score years.

In 1912, Nijinsky, who had pondered on the subject for some time, turned choreographer. He sought to employ dancing as an absolute medium, so that even when his subject was not an excuse for dancing, the action was to be expressed through that medium. His first effort was *Prélude à L'Après-Midi d'un Faune* in which he used straight lines and angles in opposition to the curvilinear conceptions which, until then, had mainly dominated ballet.

The success of his first composition induced Nijinsky to go a step further. He stated his disapproval of the grace, softness, and roundness characteristic of the classical ballet, and asserted that ballet must be angular, tense, and virile; while for lightness he proposed to substitute heaviness. He also came under the influence of the teaching of Jacques Dalcroze who required each note in the music to be expressed by a corresponding movement on the part of the dancer. Nijinsky applied his theories in two ballets: *Jeux* and *Le Sacre du Printemps,* both given in 1913. The first had a lukewarm reception, owing to the dancers being reduced to clockwork figures, and soon disappeared from the repertory. The second, a most iconoclastic work, was given only six times.

In 1913 the troupe went on tour to South America, but Diaghilev, obsessed by some ill omen, remained behind and went to the Lido instead. During the voyage out Nijinsky and a young Hungarian *danseuse* in the company became engaged. They were married at Buenos Aires on September 16th. Diaghilev was exceedingly displeased and informed Nijinsky by cable that his services were no longer required.

Under these circumstances Nijinsky accepted an offer to appear the following spring at the Palace Theatre, London. He assembled his company and arrived at London, but, after three performances, he became ill, the contract was declared void, and the company had to be disbanded.

Nijinsky was in Vienna when the Great War broke out and there he was interned. In due course, as the result of high-placed intervention, he and his wife were allowed to go to America on parole. It had been arranged that he should take part in a New York season organised by Diaghilev. But, although the latter was outwardly cordial, it was clear that Nijinsky had not been forgiven.

The season over, Nijinsky received an offer from an American impresario for a coast-to-coast tour. The company had to be rented from Diaghilev, and Nijinsky was to be artistic director. He agreed, and began to prepare a new ballet, *Tyl Ulenspiegel,* with music by Richard Strauss, but the ballet was only given a few times owing to various difficulties that arose.

There was another tour of South America and then Nijinsky and his wife returned to Europe and settled at St. Moritz. There he began to develop strange moods. He would draw at lightning speed weird figures—butterflies which resembled himself, and spiders with the face of Diaghilev. There were other untoward incidents culminating in a dance recital, where he astonished and terrified the audience by his attempt to express in dancing the War with its misery and suffering. He was found to have lost his reason.

Among all the tragedies in the history of dancing—Mlle. Aubry, who fell from a *gloire* and was doomed to a life of inactivity; Emma Livry, who died as a result of her ballet-skirt catching fire;

poor little Bozacchi, the creator of Swanilda in *Coppélia,* who died at sixteen from plague during the siege of Paris, 1870—to recall but a few examples—that of Nijinsky is the greatest.

PRÉLUDE À L'APRÈS-MIDI D'UN FAUNE[1]

Choreographic Tableau in 1 Act. Book: Vaslav Nijinsky. Music: Claude Debussy. Scenery and Costumes: Léon Bakst. Choreography: Vaslav Nijinsky. First produced: Théâtre du Chatelet, Paris, May 29th, 1912.

CHARACTERS

The Faun . . . M. Vaslav Nijinsky
Nymphs . . . Mmes. Nelidova, Nijinska, Tcherepanova, Hokhlova, Maicherska, Klementovicz, Kopycinska

A faun, day-dreaming on a hillside in the summer heat, finds simple delight in playing on a flute and partaking of a bunch of grapes. A group of nymphs emerge into view as they stroll along a path at the base of the hill, with intent to bathe at a pool hard by.

The faun, glancing downwards, espies the nymphs, and, filled with curiosity, descends the hillside and goes towards them. At first they are swayed between fear and curiosity; then they take to flight. Presently they return and the faun seeks to woo them. Again they run away. But one, bolder or more curious than the rest, returns. They link arms, but the nymph, suddenly afraid, escapes from his grasp, leaving behind her scarf. From a point of vantage she hesitates, divided between the hope of retrieving her scarf and the fear of being seized by the faun. Caution prevails and she, too, follows her companions.

The faun, disconsolate at the loss of such desirable playmates, is filled with sadness until he perceives the scarf, which he takes up in his arms and bears to his retreat. Arrived there, he consoles himself for the loss of the nymph by fondling her scarf.

*

The theme of the *Faune* is usually ascribed to Nijinsky, yet on this point, as in the case of other matters having reference to him, the evidence of contemporaries is diametrically opposed.

[1] The title of the ballet was later altered to *L'Après-Midi d'un Faune.*

Stravinsky[2] declares that Diaghilev suggested the theme, which was to be a kind of tableau in which an amorous faun would pursue a group of nymphs; and that this idea was changed by Bakst, who advised the director to present the ballet in the form of an animated bas-relief, with figures in profile. Stravinsky further states that Bakst inspired the actual choreography down to the least detail.

On the other hand, Mme. Nijinsky, in her biography[3] of her husband, states that the theme of the Faun was first conceived by Nijinsky when he was staying with Diaghilev at Carlsbad in 1911. According to her, the original subject was concerned with a youth's awakening to adolescence, his clumsy attempts to caress some passing girls, who take to flight, leaving behind some article of dress, which enables the youth to imagine that the young girl is by his side. Nijinsky, however, realising the difficulties of presenting this theme on the stage, transferred the action to archaic Greece. He imparted his plan to Diaghilev who heartily approved, and, after much searching, found for him suitable music in Debussy's *Prélude à l'Après-Midi d'un Faune.*

When the 1911 London season had ended, Diaghilev and Nijinsky went to Paris and there the young choreographer began work on the *Faune.* Mme. Nijinsky asserts that he was loaned A. Gavrilov, then a promising young dancer in the company, as material on which to work out the steps and movements he had in mind, the rehearsals taking place at the top of the Chatelet Theatre, where the work went on for two months, *only the pianist being admitted.*[4]

Later, when the troupe reassembled in Monte Carlo, the cast of seven *danseuses* was selected and Nijinsky began to teach them the ballet. The artistes, however, accustomed to the technique of the classical ballet, found great difficulty in moving in profile and many hours were occupied in acquiring this new mode of progression. Mme. Nijinsky asserts that from first to last the production of the ballet entailed an extraordinary number of rehearsals!

*

L'Après-Midi d'un Faune, arranged to Debussy's music, in turn intended as a prelude to Mallarmé's poem of the same name, was an attempt to adapt the figures on Greek vases to the service of ballet. Not to use them as poses in a three-dimensional composi-

---

[2] *Chronique de ma Vie.*
[3] *Nijinsky.*
[4] The italics are mine.—C.W.B.

tion, but to preserve the two-dimensional surface characteristic of Greek vases and friezes. The actual result corresponded to a frieze of living figures—their bodies facing the audience, their head and limbs in profile—which moved at different speeds. When it was necessary for the dancers to recross their tracks, they made an abrupt half-turn on place and moved in the opposite direction, so that the impression of a two-dimensional surface was always retained. The arms and hands, with the palms parallel to the spectators, were used with particular effect.

It may be that the combination of static poses suggestive of movement with actual movement was occasionally inharmonious, and, from a pedantic standpoint, artistically wrong, but, as a spectacle, the ballet had both novelty and charm, enhanced by Debussy's silvery music and Bakst's lovely costumes, which, in the original designs, themselves forshadowed the dancers' movements. In this ballet the music was employed simply as an accompaniment, and how admirably suited it was, with its sweet piping and its hint of rustling leaves and singing streams.

The ballet aroused considerable protest when first produced, principally on account of the movements made by the faun at the close of the ballet, which overstressed the fetichist aspect. This gesture was afterwards modified.

Nijinsky gave a remarkable performance as the Faun, which he presented as a half-human, half-animal creature, his movements being deliberate and brutish. One of the most charming of his poses, which Rodin justly compared to living sculpture, occurred at the beginning of the ballet, when the faun is seen sunning himself on the hillside, half-reclining on one elbow, while with the other hand he presses his reed flute to his lips and trills out a fascinating melody.

The ballet, as given nowadays, when the only decoration is a low painted hill in profile, or a few steps covered with a painted cloth, has lost a great deal. For instance, the opening scene, when the faun espies the nymphs and descends the hillside in search of them, has no point when the reclining faun can almost touch the nymphs with his hand. Again, the ballet, if ballet it can be called, is quite meaningless if given, as sometimes happens, without the essential nymphs.

LE SACRE DU PRINTEMPS [5]

[5] *The Rite of Spring.*

A Picture of Ancient Russia in 2 Acts. Book: Igor Stravinsky and Nicholas Roehrich. Music: Igor Stravinsky. Scenery and Costumes: Nicholas Roehrich. Choreography: Vaslav Nijinsky. First produced: Théâtre des Champs-Elysées, Paris, May 29th, 1913.

CHARACTERS

An Old Woman 300 years old . . . MME. GOULUK
A Wise Man . . . . . . M. WORONZOV
The Chosen Maiden . . . . MLLE. MARIE PILTZ
Maidens, Women, Elders of the Tribe, Youths, Ancestors.

Le Sacre du Printemps was an attempt to show the birth of human emotion in a primitive age. It is a story of herd reaction under the tribal rites of prayer and sacrifice in worship of the earth and the sun. Just as the Aztecs sacrificed the handsomest young man among them in honour of the god Tezcatlepoca, so one spring evening, after initial ceremonies, we see the fairest maiden of the tribe forced to dance until she dies from exhaustion, as an offering to the goddess of spring, the season of fertility, that the crops may be good and the tribe fruitful.

The first act is devoted to ritual movements in which the members of the tribe, at the direction of the aged seer, dance crudely in adoration of the earth. The second act turns on the selection of the victim, the initial rites before the sacrifice, and ends with the tremendous dance by the Chosen Maiden which culminates in her death.

The second episode provides the peak of the ballet, for the movements made by the Chosen Maiden work up to an incredibly forceful rhythm which borders on delirium, and is certainly the most exhausting dance, both physically and mentally, in the whole history of the choreographic art. The creator of this role was Marie Piltz, whose superb interpretation forced an angry, excited, rebellious audience to silence.

*

This ballet was successful in creating an extraordinary atmosphere of savagery, mingled with a deeply-felt religious atmosphere. Coming after the romantic beauty of Fokine's ballets, it was a tremendous shock to one's conceptions of ballet. It was so extraordinary that Nijinsky, the personification of grace and a true child of the air, should replace speed and elevation by slow, uncouth movements in which the dancers were so seemingly obsessed by the earth that they appeared unable to stand upright. Stravinsky's music, with its insistent, throbbing rhythm, emphasised by the dancers' feet pounding on the stage, became as irresistible and dominating as the remorseless thudding of the drum which sets the atmosphere for O'Neill's *The Emperor Jones*. The music and choreography of the *Sacre* were united not by steps danced to notes, but by the immense force of rhythm.

There were many new ideas in the choreography; for instance, the variety and quality of sound provided by the music were expressed in the variety and quality of the dancer's movements. The feet were turned inwards and movements made inwards in complete opposition to the traditions of classical ballet. There was also a kind of counterpoint in mass movement, in that now and again one group of dancers danced heavily in opposition to another group which danced lightly. The movements generally were symbolic rather than emotional, and, on account of their complexity, sometimes carried to a fantastic degree, required the greatest precision in execution. It may be mentioned that this ballet required one hundred and twenty rehearsals and was given at Paris and London only six times in all.

At first acquaintance, this ballet was so completely novel in its outlook, so starkly primitive in its conception, so brutal in its movements, that many found it utterly repellent. No other Diaghilev production roused such a storm of protest and furious indignation. So great was the tumult on the first night that Diaghilev stood up in his box and called out, *"Je vous en prie, laissez achever le spectacle!"* Behind the scenes, the dancers, harassed and over-wrought, were on the verge of tears. When the second act began, the tumult in the theatre was so great that the music could not be heard, and Nijinsky had to stand in the wings and beat out the rhythm with his fists. But after the first shock had passed, and the ballet had been witnessed a second and a third time, it was seen to possess much primitive beauty and to evoke a deep inner emotion.

In 1920 *Le Sacre du Printemps* was revived with new choreography by Massine, which aroused considerable interest. This time the part of the Chosen Maiden was taken by Lydia Sokolova, who gave a fine interpretation of that difficult role.

BRONISLAVA NIJINSKA

B RONISLAVA FOMICHINA NIJINSKA was born on January 8th, 1891. She first studied dancing with Maestro Cecchetti, from whom she had private lessons. In 1900 she entered the Imperial School of Ballet, St. Petersburg, her first teachers being Cecchetti and Gellert. At the end of a year she was transferred to the class conducted by Michel Fokine, where she remained for three years. Then she passed to the class directed by Kulichevskaya, and in the summer holidays received lessons from her brother, Vaslav Nijinsky.

Before Nijinska had completed her training she was invited to dance a *pas de trois* in the Imperial Ballet, with Georgevskaya and Bolm, but, having sustained an injury to her foot, she was unable to accept. She completed her school training under Cecchetti and Nicholas Legat, and passed into the Imperial Ballet on May 30th, 1908. On leaving school she received the first prize for studies and the first prize for dancing.

Among the many ballets in which she took part may be mentioned: *Le Réveil de Flore* (Goddess), *La Belle au Bois Dormant* (Sapphire Fairy), *Le Roi Candaule* (*Pas de Quatre*). She also created the role of Papillon in *Le Carnaval,* first produced by Fokine at St. Petersburg in 1910.

Nijinska took part in Diaghilev's first season of opera and ballet at Paris in 1909, and appeared in subsequent seasons during which she danced, among other roles, those of Papillon in *Le Carnaval* (1910), the Street Dancer in *Petrouchka* (1911), Bacchante in *Narcisse* (1911), and the Dancer in *Petrouchka* (1912).

When her brother formed his own company she appeared with him at the Palace Theatre, London, in 1914. Then she returned to St. Petersburg, but, owing to the outbreak of the Great War, was unable to rejoin Diaghilev. During this period she composed for herself a dance called *La Tabatière,* which was her first essay in choreography. She next opened a school of ballet at Kiev where she composed many other dances and *ensembles* for the instruction of her pupils.

In 1921 Nijinska was able to leave Russia and join Diaghilev in Paris, to assist in the production of a revival of *The Sleeping Princess* (*La Belle au Bois Dormant*), which was to be presented in November at the Alhambra Theatre, London. Afterwards she composed many ballets for Diaghilev: *Le Rénard* (1922), *Les Noces* (1923), *Les Biches* (1924), *Les Facheux* (1924), *Les Tentations de la Bergère* (1924), and *Romeo and Juliet* (1926).

She was *maîtresse de ballet* at the Colon Theatre, Buenos Aires, during the seasons 1926-27 and 1932, where she produced *Daphnis et Chloë, Ala et Lolii,* and *Etude* (2nd version), and revived *Le Train Bleu* and *Petrouchka.*

Nijinska returned to Paris in 1928 to produce several ballets for Mme. Ida Rubinstein: *Nocturne* (1928), *Bolero* (1928), *Les Noces de l'Amour et Psyche* (1928), *La Bien Aimée* (1928), *La Princesse Cygne* (1928), *Le Baiser de la Fée* (1928), *La Valse* (1929), and, for the Comte de Noailles, *Aubade* (1929).

For the "Russian Opera at Paris" (1930–31) she composed the dances in *Sadko, Russalka,* and *Russlan and Ludmilla,* and two ballets—*Capriccio* and *Etude* (3rd version).

In 1932 Nijinska founded her own "Théâtre de Danse" at Paris and produced the following ballets: *Variations* (a ballet composition in three parts—"Pyrrhique," "Pastorale," and "Pathétique"), *Les Comédiens Jaloux, Bolero* (2nd version), *La Princesse Cygne* (2nd version), *Etude* (4th version), *Les Biches,* and, in 1934, *Hamlet* and *Le Baiser de la Fée.*

In 1935 she produced for Col. de Basil's Ballets Russes: *Les Cent Baisers* (1935), *Les Noces* (revival, 1936), and *Danses Slaves et Tziganes* (1936); in the same year she arranged the dances in Reinhardt's film *A Midsummer Night's Dream.*

In 1937 she revived *Les Biches* and *La Bien Aimée* for the Markova-Dolin Ballet.

NOCES[1]

Russian choreographic episodes in 4 scenes. Words and music Igor Stravinsky. Scenery and Costumes: Natalia Goncharova. Choreography: Bronislava Nijinska. First produced: Théâtre Gaité-Lyrique, Paris, June 14th, 1923.

[1] *Wedding.*

CHARACTERS

The Bride	MLLE. FELIA DUBROVSKA
The Bridegroom	
The Bride's Parents	
The Bridegroom's Parents	

Match-makers, Friends of the Bride, Friends of the Bridegroom, Guests, etc.

Scene I. Benediction of the Bride.

Scene II. Benediction of the Bridegroom.

Scene III. Departure of the Bride from the parental home.

Scene IV. The Wedding Feast.

Les Noces is an attempt to express in the simplest terms the inner spirit of the semi-pagan rites and century-old ceremonies associated with a marriage of peasants in provincial Russia.

The choreographic treatment is very modern, the dancers being moved and massed in a manner which is part geometrical, part architectural in conception. The use of dancers as a kind of building material with which to construct human pyramids is quite new to ballet, and is often effective and impressive.

The glowing colours characteristic of so many Diaghilev productions are here rejected and replaced by a sombre scheme in black and white, the dancers wearing stylised peasant costume in black and white.

*

The ballet had a mixed reception at Paris, some critics being as much in favour of it as others were violently opposed.

Noces was not given at London until 1926 when it again aroused considerable controversy. *The Times,*[2] reviewing the production at His Majesty's Theatre on June 14th, asserts: "There are no heart flutterings about the drear ceremonies of this village wedding. . . . The bride with her maidens, the bridegroom with his companions, each goes through a long series of calisthenics before receiving the benediction of her lugubrious parents. The bride lives in a house with one tiny window in it, the bridegroom in one with two windows. That and the nature of the calisthenics is the only difference between scenes one and two. We return to the

[2] June 16th, 1923.

one tiny window for the departure of the bride, and then are transported to an equally drab scene, with the bridal bed piled with pillows inside a rabbit hutch, for the scene of the barmecidal love feast. Through it all four solo singers and a chorus are chanting, wailing, crying, shouting, and their chants, wails, cries and shouts are pierced by tremendous drummings or other percussion noises. Two double grand pianos, terrible engines of war with a keyboard at each end of them, are banged, thumped, tickled, and titillated by four serious musicians, each of whom has composed ballets of the modern kind and only consents to perform "in token of the deep admiration all modern musicians have for the composer."

This notice may be regarded as a fair example of the generally hostile reception which the ballet received from the Press. *Noces,* however, found a vigorous champion from an unlikely quarter, in the person of Mr. H. G. Wells, who, in an open letter[3] to the Press, expressing his astonishment at their findings, observed: "I do not know of any other ballet so interesting, so amusing, so fresh or nearly so exciting as *'Les Noces.'* I want to see it again and again."

Nijinska has revived the ballet abroad with considerable success, but it has never been a favourite with London audiences. It was reproduced by her in 1936 for De Basil's Ballets Russes, during the company's American tour, when it had a mixed reception.

*

The idea of *Noces* originated with Stravinsky early in 1914, and was one of several compositions to be based on Russian folk-themes. Stravinsky began work on *Noces* at Clarens, Switzerland, late the same year. In the spring of 1915 Diaghilev visited the composer, who played to him the music of the first two scenes of the new work, which aroused his whole-hearted admiration. It was apparently completed at Madrid late in 1917. But Diaghilev postponed the production of the ballet from year to year, doubtless awaiting a favourable moment to launch so iconoclastic a work.

At last it was decided that *Noces* should be given in June, 1923, and Nijinska was chosen as choreographer. The rehearsals began at Monte Carlo in March. In the meantime Stravinsky was preoccupied with the question of its orchestration. He resolved that the orchestra should consist of a piano, timbals, bells, and xylophones; the instrumentation was begun in the winter of 1922 and completed at Monaco on April 6th, 1923.

[3] June 18th, 1923.

The composer, in his Reminiscences,[4] asserts that the stage production was quite different from what he had pictured. He wished the ballet to be in the nature of a *divertissement,* a kind of scenic ritual based on the traditional ceremonies associated with the celebration of Russian marriage, and desired both musicians and dancers to take part in the theatrical action. Thus the members of the orchestra would be on the stage. The fact that the dancers would be in Russian dress and the musicians in evening dress did not present any incongruity to him, since he regarded this as part of the suggestion of masquerade which he wished to convey.

LES BICHES [5]

Ballet with Chorus in 1 Act. Music: Francis Poulenc. Curtain, Scenery and Costumes: Marie Laurencin. Choreography: Bronislava Nijinska. First produced: Théâtre de Monte Carlo, 1924.

Rondeau	MMES. DUBROVSKA, DEVALOIS, NIKITINA, MAIKERSKA, GEVEROVA, SUMAROKOVA, CHAMIE, KOMAROVA, ZALEVSKA, NIKITINA II, CLEMETSKA, SUMAROKOVA II.
Chanson Dansée	MM. LEON WOIZIKOWSKY, ANATOLE VILZAK, NICHOLAS ZVEREV
Adagietto	MME. VERA NEMCHINOVA
Jeu	MME. VERA NEMCHINOVA, MM. LEON WOIZIKOWSKY, ANATOLE VILZAK, NICHOLAS ZVEREV, and Ensemble
Rag Mazurka	MME. BRONISLAVA NIJINSKA, MM. LEON WOIZIKOWSKY, NICHOLAS ZVEREV
Andantino	MME. VERA NEMCHINOVA, M. ANATOLE VILZAK
Chanson Dansée	MMES. LUBOV TCHERNICHEVA, ALEXANDRA DANILOVA
Finale	MMES. VERA NEMCHINOVA, LUBOV TCHERNICHEVA, BRONISLAVA NIJINSKA, ALEXANDRA DANILOVA, MM. ANATOLE VILZAK, LEON WOIZIKOWSKY, NICHOLAS ZVEREV, and Ensemble

Scene. A large white walled room, the background formed by a large window, looking on to a balcony, shaded by a pinkish blue

[4] *Chronique de ma Vie.*
[5] English title is *The House Party.*

curtain. There are entrances to right and left. Near the window is a large lavender colored sofa. The room has an air of expensive simplicity while the sophisticated colouring suggests the height of fashion.

Enter a number of young girls, dressed in summery frocks of palest pink, who delight in a dance. When they leave, three young men dressed in bathing costumes come in and dance a gay *pas de trois.* The girls return and the youths, placing themselves in a line at right angles to the window, resume the dance, while the girls wind about them in chains of fluttering muslin. The girls rest from their exertions, while the men dance and form groups.

At this point a new arrival enters, a very sophisticated young lady in white tights and gloves, set off by a short, close-fitting coat of blue velvet. She crosses the room with dainty steps *sur les pointes.*

The men exchange glances with the girls, who dance and then sit down.

The girl in blue velvet recrosses the room.

The girls in pink flirt with the youths. One group goes off with one young man, another set with another, while the remaining male is left sitting on the sofa.

The girl in blue velvet returns and dances a charming *pas seul,* in which she is later joined by one of the young men, who slips his arms over hers and walks away with her.

The girls in pink return with two young men, who sit with them on the sofa. They turn the sofa at right angles to the audience and dance about it, when it is again turned so that it is placed back to the audience.

The girl in blue velvet returns with her admirer, with whom she dances. The girls in pink peep cautiously over the back of the sofa. The couple go off.

Then two young men dance in together and the girls hide behind the sofa. Afterwards they come from their hiding-place, push the sofa to a corner of the room, and run off.

Now the hostess herself enters, one hand toying with the end of her pearl necklace, the other flourishing a long cigarette-holder. Tiring of this exercise she flings herself on the sofa and composes herself in a seductive attitude.

Two of the youths enter and are attracted by their hostess, who induces them to join in a dance (*Rag Mazurka*), of which she takes the fullest opportunity to flirt with them. They leave with her.

The other young man comes in just as the girl in blue enters from the opposite side. They dance together a modern *adage* (*Andantino*), at the end of which he picks her up in his arms, raises her on his shoulders, then lowers her to the ground and they go off together.

Two young girls in grey arrive and dance together (*Chanson Dansée*). They kiss, then, a little nervous of being seen, go off opposite ways.

The girls in pink return, followed by the three young men, who seem to revel in the sheer joy of movement. They are succeeded by their hostess, who attracts the same two young men to her. The girl in blue returns and is joined by the other young man. The girls in pink dance away, and while the three young men, the girl in blue, and the hostess dance a final measure, the curtain falls.

*

Les Biches is a half-playful, half-malicious comment on that form of contemporary social entertainment known as the house-party. There is no story. The elements composing the party are as light-hearted and care-free as a group of butterflies sporting in the sunlight. So these human particles circle, converge, meet, and separate. Amid these desirable young women and athletic young men glides the hostess, who keeps young by surrounding herself with youth.

The music, setting and dances are all conceived in the essence of sophistication. The ballet is subtle and beneath all the froth of muslin and choreographic badinage there are many piquant comments for those who choose to look below the surface.

One of the most attractive dances is the *Adagietto,* danced by the girl in blue, which introduces a new style of choreography. Although the steps have a classical ballet foundation, the placing of the arms in angular positions which have a strange and unexpected grace, and the novel use of the shoulders which dip and rise in a wave-like rhythm, are quite new. Nemchinova gave an inspired performance as the girl in blue which definitely placed her in the front rank of modern dancers. In after years her role was taken by Alice Nikitina and Olga Petrova.

Other dances of particular interest are the two *Chansons Dansées,* the *Rag Mazurka* and the *Andantino.* The part of the Hostess was later taken by Lydia Sokolova, who gave a fine performance of this difficult role.

Mme. Nijinska regards *Les Biches* as the *Sylphide* of our age, the romantic ballet of our own time.

Les Biches, under the title of *The House Party,* was recently revived by Nijinska for the Markova-Dolin Ballet, when Markova took Nemchinova's role and Dolin took the part of her admirer. The part of the Hostess was taken alternately by Diana Gould, Beatrice Appleyard, and Helen Forbes.

LE TRAIN BLEU

Operette Dansée in 1 Act. Book: Jean Cocteau. Music: Darius Milhaud. Scenery: H. Laurens. Costumes: Chanel. Curtain: Pablo Picasso. Choreography: Bronislava Nijinska. First produced: Théâtre des Champs-Elysées, Paris, June 20th, 1924.

CHARACTERS

La Championne de Tennis . . MME. BRONISLAVA NIJINSKA
Perlouse . . . . . . MLLE. LYDIA SOKOLOVA
Beau Gosse . . . . . M. ANTON DOLIN
Le Joueur de Golf . . . . M. LÉON WOIZIKOWSKY
Poules, Gigolos.

Scene. On a beach, 1924.

This ballet is best described in Diaghilev's own words: "The first point about *Le Train Bleu* is that there is no blue train in it. This being the age of speed, it has already reached its destination and disembarked its passengers. These are to be seen on a beach which does not exist, in front of a casino which exists still less. Overhead passes an aeroplane which you do not see. And the plot represents nothing. Yet, when it was presented for the first time in Paris, everybody was unaccountably seized with the desire to take the blue train to Deauville and perform refreshing exercises. Moreover, this ballet is not a ballet; it is an *operette dansée.* The music is composed by Darius Milhaud, but it has nothing in common with the music which we associate with Darius Milhaud. It is danced by the real Russian Ballet, but it has nothing to do with Russian ballet. It was invented for Anton Dolin, a classical dancer who does nothing classical. The scenery is painted by a sculptor, and the costumes are by a great arbiter of fashion who has never made a costume."

*

Le Train Bleu, the second of the topical ballets inaugurated by Nijinska with *Les Biches,* was expressive of fashionable life on a

French *plage*. In a sense it might be called a musical comedy which was danced instead of being sung. The ballet has an interesting origin. In November, 1923, Dolin joined the Diaghilev Company, then at Monte Carlo. One day, while the young dancer was practising in the rehearsal-room some exercises in acrobatic technique which he had set himself, he was watched with interest by Jean Cocteau, who received the inspiration for a ballet which gradually evolved into *Le Train Bleu*.

Nijinska's choreography was based on movements associated with swimming, golf, tennis, and beach games. The honours went to Dolin for his interpretation of the role of Beau Gosse, in which he had to execute a most difficult and dangerous series of movements.

Dolin has recorded his impressions of the first performance at London at the Coliseum Theatre, which are revealing of the dancer's mental state in moments of stress. "Nothing seemed to hurt me. My body for that half hour did not belong to me. Someone other than myself, someone far greater, had taken control of it and those senses were telling it what to do. It was not then to feel the cuts and bruises it was sustaining." [6]

One of the most popular numbers was the waltz danced by Sokolova and Woizikowsky which, according to Dolin, was partly suggested to Nijinska by the dancing of Marjorie Moss and her partner, Georges Fontana, who, at the time of the production of the ballet, were appearing at the Metropole Hotel.

LA BIÉN-AIMÉE

Ballet in 1 Act. Book: Alexandre Benois. Music: Schubert and Liszt, arranged by Darius Milhaud. Scenery and Costumes: Alexandre Benois. Choreography: Bronislava Nijinska. First produced: Théâtre National de l'Opéra, Paris, 1928.

CHARACTERS

La Bien-Aimée	MME. IDA RUBINSTEIN
The Poet	M. ANATOLE VILZAK
Shades	
Peasants	
Grisettes	
Students	
The Lioness	
Her Admirers	
Carnival Masquers	

[6] *Divertissement.*

A poet, seated at a piano, conjures up his memories through the medium of the music he plays. His Muse has appeared to him but departed. Pursuing his reflections he recalls the village loves of his tender years, then the gaiety of his student days, and his encounter with the fatal woman. He banishes that memory with the thought of his Muse, who again appears to him only to vanish once more.

*

The most attractive parts of this ballet are the dances by the peasants, and the Carnival masquerade with which the piece ends; a most inspiriting and attractive choreographic picture.

La Bien-Aimée, under the title of *The Beloved One,* was recently revived by Nijinska for the Markova-Dolin Company. This production has a new setting and costumes by George Kirsta, whose dresses for the masquerade are particularly charming. In the revival the parts of the Well-Beloved and the Poet were respectively taken by Markova and Dolin.

LA VALSE

Choreographic Poem in 1 Act. Book: B. Nijinska. Music: Maurice Ravel. Setting and Costumes: Alexandre Benois. Choreography: Bronislava Nijinska. First produced: Théâtre de l'Opéra, Paris, 1929.

CHARACTERS

She . . . . Mme. Ida Rubinstein
He . . . . M. Anatole Vilzak
Guests: Ladies, Girls, Officers of Hussars, Lancers, Dragoons, and Court Chamberlains.

Scene. A splendid ballroom of the Third Empire.

The curtain rises on a scene which suggests a painting by Eugène Lami, a crimson and gold ballroom lined with enormous mirrors and lit with groups of candelabra. At the far end folding doors thrown back give on to a second ballroom. The suggestion of a painting is enhanced by the gauze curtain which at present screens the scene.

The ballroom is almost unoccupied except for two or three ladies seated on a long settee, while opposite them sits another lady with a Court Chamberlain bending over her hand in greeting. Slowly the figures rise to their feet and begin to waltz. The gauze curtain

rises and now other dancers enter through one of the large doors—
beautiful ladies in billowing crinolines and handsome officers in
their splendid dress uniforms. The dancers form various figures,
sometimes in small groups, sometimes in massed formations.

At another stage dancers are seen in the distant room, and a
very interesting form of choreographic counterpoint is provided by
the dancers in the second room moving quickly in a chain, while
those in the foreground slowly revolve to the languorous strains of
the waltz; later, the rhythms are reversed.

La Valse was a lovely conception and is well worth revival.

JEAN BORLIN

JEAN BORLIN, the son of a captain in the mercantile marine, was born on March 13th, 1893, at Haernoesand, in the north of Sweden. His education was undertaken by an aunt and uncle, with whom, at the age of six, he went to live. He was a handsome little boy with very fair hair and bright blue eyes, but given to moodiness and introspection.

Above his uncle's flat lived a musician who frequently played the piano. The little boy, fascinated by the rhythm of the music, would often break into an artless dance. At the age of seven he was sent to school, but his solitary nature made him dislike his school-fellows with their rough games.

Then he began to learn to play the piano and tried to invest his dancing with a greater variety of steps and movements. This was a curious trait in a boy who had never been to a theatre nor seen anyone dance on the stage. His guardians began to consider seriously whether he should be trained as a dancer. After some discussion they sent him to Gunhild Rosen, who, at that time, taught dancing to the school attached to the Theatre Royal, Stockholm. This was in 1902. There he revelled in a new fantastic world and learned both to dance and sing. In 1905 he was admitted a member of the *corps de ballet*.

One day he was given a role and became filled with apprehension as to his ability to achieve success. This form of stage-fright never left him, even in after years, and each time he appeared on the stage had to be reconquered by a great exertion of will power.

Having taken part in several operas he began to concentrate on singing; then his voice broke and he sang no more; instead, he studied harmony and musical composition. He still kept up his dancing, but rather in a spirit of duty, for something of his early enthusiasm had evaporated. By the time he was eighteen he had acquired a good technique, and a definite grace and nobility of style, in accordance with the tradition of Bournonville.

Then, in 1911, Fokine arrived at Stockholm, to produce several of his ballets for the Royal Opera. The company began rehearsals and when Borlin for the first time saw the great choreographer at work, his flagging interest revived and he became filled with a new zeal for the Dance.

Fokine, in his memoir[1] of the dancer, recalls how he gave him the part of a faun in *Cléopâtre,* and how, while rehearsing, he saw a fair youth with blue eyes who "crossed the stage with great bounds, landed with all his force and glided over the boards among the group of bacchantes. What character! What ecstasy! The fanatical sacrifice of a bruised body in order to produce the maximum of choreographic effect. It was a revelation to me."

In 1913 Borlin was promoted *second danseur.* In 1918 he would have been made *premier danseur,* had he not elected to leave the Opera and study with Fokine, who then resided at Copenhagen.

It was about this time that Borlin made the acquaintance of a wealthy landowner and farmer, by name Rolf de Maré, whose hobby was the arts and who took a particular interest in folk and national dances. This farmer was no dilettante. He had made a scientific study of agriculture and applied his knowledge to the constant improvement of his estates.

Now and again he sought respite from his labours by travelling both at home and abroad, where he delighted to visit the museums, converse with artists and musicians, and study at first hand the local folk-dances and costumes. This led quite naturally to an interest in design for the theatre. Gradually he conceived an ambitious plan for founding a company of dancers who would be able to render the Swedish national dances and later be able to express, in terms of the dance, contemporary movements in art. He decided that it was essential that such an experiment should be made outside Sweden; Paris seemed the best point of departure.

He imparted something of his plans to Borlin, who suggested means by which they might be realised. De Maré was interested, but not yet convinced that the young dancer was the "animator" he sought. There were further meetings, more discussions. Then he had a final consultation with Fokine. As a result he embarked on his voyage of adventure. Borlin was engaged as *premier danseur* and choreographer to the troupe to be.

It was not easy to form a company, for male dancers were scarce in Sweden, so it became necessary to include a number of Danes. A programme was planned, scene designers chosen, and rehearsals began. A reconnaissance was made on March 24th, 1920, when Borlin gave his first dance recital at the Théâtre des Champs-Elysées, Paris. He was well received and, on October 25th of the

---

[1] *Borlin: Mon Élève.*

same year, returned in force with his troupe, the opening performance consisting of *Jeux, Iberia,* and *Nuit de Saint-Jean.* The saga of the "Ballets Suédois" had begun.

The company remained in being until March 17th, 1925, a little over four years, a period of almost incredible activity and experiment, during which the following ballets were produced, all having choreography by Borlin: *Jeux, Nuit de Saint-Jean, Iberia, Maison de Fous, Le Tombeau de Couperin, El Greco, Derviches, Les Vierges Folles, Boite à Joujoux*—all 1920; *L'Homme et son Désir, Les Mariés de la Tour Eiffel, Dansgille*—all 1921; *Skating Rink,* 1922; *Marchand d'Oiseaux, Offerlunden, La Création du Monde, Within the Quota*—all 1923; *Le Roseau, Le Porcher, Le Tournoi Singulier, La Jarre, Relâche*—all 1924. During this period the ballet toured the principal towns of France, Spain, Belgium, Germany, Denmark, England, Sweden, Switzerland, Italy, Austria, and the United States of America.

From the beginning the repertory included several unusual ballets, such as *El Greco* and *Maison de Fous,* which contrasted sharply with the refined *Tombeau de Couperin* and the ingenuous charm of *Les Vierges Folles.* The novelty of the company's productions combined with the use of good music and the artistry of the settings and costumes was highly praised. The dancing, however, was invested with a certain coldness and reserve, derived from the national temperament, which provided a marked contrast to the liveliness of the Russian dancers.

The director and his choreographer did not relax from their determination to enlarge the field of ballet, and re-invigorate it, by bending to its service the newest tendencies in art, music, and literature, yet never allowing any of these elements to dominate the dance, which was to remain pre-eminent. Experiment succeeded experiment, each bolder than the last. Some names chosen at random may suggest how forceful those experiments were: Fernand Léger, Francis Picabia, René Clair, Erik Satie, Jean Cocteau, Paul Claudel, Darius Milhaud . . . and Borlin was on fire to create.

Such novelties were acclaimed with rapture by the advance-guard just as they were ferociously attacked by the conservative critics. In after years it is sometimes difficult to understand the clamour excited by certain productions, so often is the sensation of to-day the commonplace of to-morrow. But the pioneers are sacrificed on the altar of progress, and Borlin suffered from being in advance of his time. His activity was so feverish there was no time to prepare the public for these iconoclastic productions.

Borlin found it difficult to work in the atmosphere of recrimination engendered by his ballets, and each new production demanded a new avenue of approach. Again, the company had continually to be reconstructed; for some members of the troupe were tempted away by the offer of seductive contracts, others resigned from lack of sympathy with modernist ballets.

The strain of reconstructing the repertory and rehearsing the new members of the troupe weighed heavily on Borlin. He was divided between his immense responsibilities as choreographer and his duty to himself as *premier danseur,* and often the former had to give place to the latter.

With the production of *Relâche*—the quintessence of challenge and provocation—it seemed impossible to go further. It was equally undesirable to go back. Therefore De Maré cried a halt. A few months later he disbanded the "Ballets Suédois."

Borlin, however, continued to give dance recitals both in France and abroad. While at Brazil he contracted jaundice which his constitution, weakened by the struggles and trials of the previous years, failed to repel. His medical advisers insisted that he must renounce dancing. He refused and determined to dance in New York. Before leaving he gave a recital at Paris, assisted by certain of his pupils.

But the Apollo of 1920 had begun to tire, and he lacked the support of his seasoned company. His enemies did not fail to seize the opportunity to attack him in terms which far exceeded the grounds of legitimate criticism. Borlin, who never refused the critics' right to criticize, revolted. He instituted proceedings but, before the case could be heard, his illness grew worse and he passed away in New York on December 6th, 1930. His body was taken to Paris where it was interred on January 8th, 1931.

Borlin rests in the cemetery of Père Lachaise. His memory is perpetuated in a splendid and unique monument—the Archives Internationales de la Danse—erected to his memory by his friend and collaborator, Rolf de Maré. At this institution students may profitably pursue their researches, and dancers and choreographers seek inspiration in the achievements of the past for the ballets of the future.

NUIT DE SAINT-JEAN

Ballet in 1 Act. Book: Jean Borlin. Music: Hugo Alfuén. Scenery and costumes: Nils de Dardel. Choreography: Jean Borlin. First produced: Théâtre des Champs-Elysées, Paris, October 25th, 1920.

CHARACTERS

A Farmer
His Wife
Their Daughter . . . . . MLLE. JENNY HASSELQUIST
A Country Youth . . . . M. JEAN BORLIN

In Sweden, St. John's Eve is a time of great rejoicing. Youths and maidens gather about a flower-decked maypole and dance to the airs of old folk-songs. Between the dances they toast one another and clink glasses in true Scandinavian fashion.

The night is short and affords but a sweet spell of rest which ends with the rising of the sun.

Again the strains of music are heard. The dances are resumed and the merrymakers go from village to village, dancing their way.

*

This was an *ensemble* ballet, with choreography based on Swedish folk-dances.

LES VIERGES FOLLES

Ballet Pantomime in 1 Act. Book: Kurt Atterberg and Einar Nerman. Music: Kurt Atterberg. Scenery and costumes: Einar Nerman. Choreography: Jean Borlin. First produced: Théâtre des Champs-Elysées, Paris, November 18th, 1920.

CHARACTERS

The Bride . . . . . MLLE. JENNY HASSELQUIST
The Bridegroom . . . . M. JEAN BORLIN

Five Foolish Virgins . .
{
MLLE. CARINA ARI
MLLE. KLARA KJELLBLAD
MLLE. DAGMAR FORSLIN
MLLE. BERTA KRANTZ
MLLE. IRMA CALSON
}

Five Wise Virgins . . . .
{
MLLE. HELGA DAHL
MLLE. MARGARETA JOHANSON
MLLE. MARGIT VAHLANDER
MLLE. TORBORG STJERNER
MLLE. GRETA LUNDBERG
}

Two Angels . . . .
{
MLLE. ASTRID LINDGREN
MLLE. JOLANDA FIGONI
}

A Musician . . . . . M. NILS OSTMAN

The bride comes forth accompanied by wise and foolish virgins; the former carefully tend the trimming of their lamps and shield their flames; the others are careless, thinking solely of pleasure. They pay no heed to the remonstrances of their wise sisters. One after another the young girls are overcome by fatigue and go to sleep round the bride.

The latter, in a dream, sees her affianced husband. The vision disappears. The bride wakes in radiant spirits and rouses her friends. The foolish virgins are alarmed because the oil in their lamps is exhausted. Vainly do they try to obtain some from the wise virgins; vainly do they search everywhere for a supply of the precious fluid.

Now, in realisation of the bride's dream, the bridegroom comes to meet her. He takes her hand and leads her into the church, preceded by the wise virgins.

When the foolish virgins return from their fruitless search, angels bar their way and they can only gaze from afar upon the procession as it leaves the sacred precincts.

*

Les Vierges Folles is based on a tapestry in the Nordiska Muséet, Stockholm, which depicts the familiar parable of the wise and the foolish virgins. The music, scenery, and costumes were conceived in the same spirit of peasant art.

This ballet, with its puppet-like virgins in their striped dresses of black and green and their black steeple-crowned hats, possessed a quaint simplicity and old-fashioned charm which captivated all who saw it. It was the most popular work in the repertory and was given in all 375 times.

EL GRECO

Dance Drama in 1 Act. Book: Jean Borlin. Music: D. E. Inghelbrecht. Scenery: Mouveau. Costumes after paintings by El Greco. Choreography: Jean Borlin. First produced: Théâtre des Champs-Elysées, Paris, November 18th, 1920.

CHARACTERS

A Christian Girl	MLLE. JOLANDA FIGONI
Her Attendants	⎰ MLLE. TORBORG STJERNER ⎱ MLLE. MARGARETA JOHANSON
A Young Man	M. JEAN BORLIN
His Brother	M. NILS OSTMAN

Scene. A market-square in Toledo.

Lightning flashes and thunder peals. The crowd, terrified, regard the storm as a token of divine wrath and pray for forgiveness.

But one of the bystanders, a young man, appeals in turn to the Lord of Heaven and the Powers of Hell.

Monks approach and watch him in silence.

At the far end of the square a funeral procession is seen passing. The young man's brother, who has been struck by lightning, is being taken to his last rest.

A Christian girl comes forward and the crowd—suddenly silent —make way for her.

She goes to the young man who tells her of his grief and curses Heaven. She tries to comfort him and speaks to him of the eternal life hereafter. But he has lost faith and is incredulous. She counters his doubts with statements of her own beliefs and gradually convinces him so that faith re-enters into his heart.

Now the skies clear, the storm passes, and the glorious light of day once more illumines the square.

*

El Greco was an evocation of the sombre mood that is characteristic of that artist's work. Few persons can have witnessed that stark, gloomy picture expressed in terms of movement and music without being deeply moved. It was a fine essay in the difficult art of producing style-atmosphere.

Borlin and Figoni were highly praised for their respective performances as the Young Man and the Christian Girl.

L'HOMME ET SON DÉSIR

Plastic Poem by Paul Claudel. Music: Darius Milhaud. Scenery and costumes: Andrée Parr. Choreography: Jean Borlin. First produced: Théâtre des Champs-Elysée, Paris, June 6th, 1921.

CHARACTERS

The Man	M. Jean Borlin
The Woman	Mlle. Margareta Johanson
The Other Woman . . .	Mlle. Torborg Stjerner
The Pipes of Pan . . .	M. Kaj Smith
The First Golden Cord . .	Mlle. Carina Ari

The Moon. The Servant of the Moon. The Reflection of the Moon. The Reflection of the Servant of the Moon. The Black Hours. The White Hours. The Bells. The Golden Cords. The Cymbals.

Scene. The scene is vertical, perpendicular to the eye like a painting, or a book one is reading. The scene resembles a sheet of music in which each action is inscribed on a different staff. On the highest plane pass the black hours of Night, wearing their golden haloes. Below them is the Moon, led across the sky by a cloud, as a servant precedes a great lady. At the base, in the waters of the vast primitive marsh, the Reflections of the Moon and her Servant follow the measured step of the heavenly pair. On the middle platform between sky and water, the drama takes place.

The principal character is Man, recaptured by elemental powers, whom Night and Slumber have robbed of name and personality. He comes in led by two forms exactly alike beneath their veils. They bewilder him by making him turn round and round like the child who is caught in the game of hide-and-seek. One of these forms is Imagination, or Memory; the other, Desire, or Illusion. They sport with him a moment, then vanish.

He remains standing. His arms outstretched, he sleeps in the refulgence of the tropical moon like a drowned man in deep waters. All the wild animals, all the sounds of the eternal forest, rise from the orchestra. They come to look at him and to sound in his ears Bells, Pipes of Pan, Cords, and Cymbals.

The Man grows animated in his dream. He stirs and begins to dance. It is the eternal dance of Nostalgia, of Desire, of Exile, the dance of captives and cast-off lovers, of those feverish souls tormented by insomnia who spend entire nights pacing from one end to the other of their verandahs, of caged animals who ceaselessly hurl themselves against impassable bars. Sometimes it is a hand from behind which draws him back, sometimes a perfume which robs him of all energy. His obsession grows more violent and frantic, and, in the solemn deeps of the darkness which precede the day, one of the women returns and revolves, as if fascinated, about the Man. Is she dead? Is she living?

The sleeper seizes a corner of her veil while she turns and unveils herself, pivoting about him, so that he is enveloped like a chrysalis while she becomes almost nude. Then, joined by the last shred of a veil as tenuous as our dreams, the woman places her hand on his face and both exit.

Of the Moon and her Servant we see only their Reflections below. The black Hours have passed and the first white Hours appear.[2]

*

L'Homme et son Désir, declares M. Claudel, "is the fruit of the collaboration of three friends who, during 1917, exchanged ideas, music, and drawings on the heights of the Serra which dominate Rio de Janeiro.

"This little plastic drama grew out of the ambiance of the Brazilian forest in which we were, so to speak, submerged, and which has almost the uniform consistency of an element. How strange is the glowing night when it begins to be filled with cries and movement! It is one of these tropical nights that our poem is intended to present.

"We have not tried to reproduce with photographic exactitude the inextricable confusion of the 'floresta.' We have simply thrown over the four levels of the scene a veil in which violet, green, and blue move about a central point of black." [3]

The ballet, with its unusual philosophical content and novel presentation, roused considerable controversy. Some critics praised De Maré and Borlin for the skilful manner in which they had penetrated the mystic qualities of Claudel's plastic poem, others regarded the production as a piece of pure extravagance.

Gradually, however, the significance of the ballet as a definite contribution to artistic presentation was recognised, and it was given in all 56 times during the company's existence.

Margareta Johanson gave an outstanding performance as the Woman.

LES MARIÉS DE LA TOUR EIFFEL

Ballet in 1 Act. Book: Jean Cocteau. Music: Georges Auric, Arthur Honegger, Darius Milhaud, Francis Poulenc, and Germaine Tailleferre. Scenery: Irène Lagut. Costumes and Masks: Jean Hugo. Choreography: Jean Borlin. First produced: Théâtre des Champs-Elysées, Paris, June 18th, 1921.

CHARACTERS

First Phonograph . . . . M. Pierre Bertin
Second Phonograph . . . M. Marcel Herrand

[2] This description is taken from *La Danse,* June, 1921.
[3] This description is taken from *La Danse,* June, 1921.

The Ostrich	MLLE. GRETA KAER
The Sportsman	M. KAJ SMITH
The Manager of the Eiffel Tower	M. HOLGER MEHNEN
The Photographer	M. AXEL WITZANSKY
The Bride	MLLE. MARGIT VAHLANDER
The Bridegroom	M. PAUL ELTORP
The Mother-in-law	MLLE. IRMA CALSON
The Father-in-law	M. KRISTIAN DAHL
The General	M. PAUL WITZANSKY
First Bridesmaid	MLLE. HELGA DAHL
Second Bridesmaid	MLLE. KLARA KJELLBLAD
First Bridesman	M. NILS OSTMAN
Second Bridesman	MLLE. DAGMAR FORSLIN
The Cyclist	MLLE. ASTRID LINDGREN
The Child	MLLE. YOLANDA FIGONI
The Bathing-Girl from Trouville	MLLE. CARINA ARI
The Lion	M. ERIC VIBER
The Collector	M. ROBERT FORD
The Picture-Dealer . . .	M. THOR STETTLER
First Telegram	MLLE. TORBORG STJERNER
Second Telegram	MLLE. MARGARETA JOHANSON
Third Telegram	MLLE. GRETA LUNDBERG
Fourth Telegram	MLLE. BERTA KRANTZ
Fifth Telegram	MLLE. ASTRID LINDGREN

Scene. The first platform of the Eiffel Tower.

An ostrich enters with measured steps to the accompaniment of a solemn air. The ostrich has escaped from the apparatus of a photographer who, before an exposure, is accustomed to cry: "Watch the little bird come out!" Imagine his surprise when an ostrich really does emerge!

A sportsman pursues the new chimera; he is foolish and stubborn like everyone who undertakes a stupid plan.

In turn intervene the manager of the Eiffel Tower and the photographer himself. All these types are introduced by two human phonographs, which fulfil the role of the antique chorus.

Now a wedding party arrives on the Tower. The men are dressed like tailors' dummies, the women rival the men in their elegant attire. This procession is a satire on our disgraceful clothes and customs.

It is the Fourteenth of July, and the wedding party has chosen this day to lunch in triumph at the Eiffel Tower.

Tne photographer prepares to take the group, but, from his apparatus, which is evidently out of order, appears a bathing-beauty. Assuming picture-postcard poses, she parodies the fashionable ladies of yesterday.

Then, from the same mysterious apparatus, emerges a lion, which devours the General who presides at the wedding. Then a child slays the guests, who revive an out-of-date quadrille, by pelting them with tennis balls.

And each time the photographer speaks it is unwillingly to keep back a new surprise.

*

Les Mariés de la Tour Eiffel completes the trilogy of experiment by Cocteau, of which the two previous works were *Parade,* the ballet written for Diaghilev, and *Le Boeuf sur le Toit.* The *Mariés,* a trenchant satire on bourgeois traditions, caused an uproar on its first performance, but, the first shock over, it gradually won its way to success.

Just as the antique Greek Theatre made use of gigantic masks, so the characteristics of the types in the ballet were stressed and magnified by the dancers' wearing special masks and padded costumes; the photographer's costume is a very interesting example. The use of masks, however, involved many difficulties for the choreographer, since the dancers could neither hear the music nor the voice of the announcer. All the movements, therefore, had to be worked out with mathematical precision.

Another innovation was the use of the human phonograph. At each side of the stage was placed a two-sided booth, fitted with a megaphone, in which the announcer, hidden from the audience, made the necessary introductions for the entrance of each character.

M. Cocteau, invited by the editor of *La Danse*[3] to describe his ballet, offered some entertaining comments from which I quote the following:

"Ballet? No. Play? No. Revue? No. Tragedy? No. Rather a kind of secret marriage between the antique tragedy and modern revue, between chorus and music-hall number. Everything is seen from afar, in perspective, modern antiquity, people of our childhood, wedding-parties that are dying out—an episode in the Eiffel Tower which, having been discovered by painters, becomes again what it should never have ceased to be: a charming person in mittens whose one aim was formerly to dominate Paris and who has now become a simple telegraph operator.

[3] June, 1921.

"What happens? Nothing is described. People such as you encounter on Sundays move about while two human phonographs to right and left of the stage, comment on their actions. Thanks to Jean Hugo, these types, instead of being too small, as they always are on the stage, too pitifully true to life to stand out from the luminous and decorative mass of scenery, are constructed, stuffed out, rectified, and artificially brought to a resemblance and a scale which do not flame like straw in the fire of the footlights and the spotlights. Thanks to Irène Lagut, our Eiffel Tower brings to mind those Parisian post-cards at the sight of which I have even seen little Arabs sigh in Africa. . . .

"Georges Auric's overture 'The Fourteenth of July' evokes the powerful charm of the streets, the people on holiday, the little band-stands that resemble guillotines and about which drums and cornets incite clerks and girls and sailors to dance. His soft trills accompany the miming in the same way that a circus orchestra repeats a tune interminably during an acrobatic act.

"This same atmosphere abides in 'The Wedding March,' 'The Funeral March,' 'The Telegram Dance,' 'The Bathing-Girl,' and the 'Quadrille' of Germaine Tailleferre, Arthur Honegger, Francis Poulenc, and Darius Milhaud."

SKATING RINK

Ballet in 1 Act. Book: Riciotto Canudo. Music: Arthur Honegger. Scenery and costumes: Fernand Léger. Choreography: Jean Borlin. First produced: Théâtre des Champs-Elysées, Paris, January 20th, 1922.

The Madman	M. Jean Borlin
The Woman	Mlle. Yolanda Figoni
The Man	M. Kaj Smith

Over the skating rink glide, in leisurely procession, the swaying figures of typical devotees of the pastime—workmen, factory-girls, ultra-fashionable young men, and other characteristic types. This whirlwind of skaters is symbolic of the vortex of life itself. The figures mingle and separate, and from this moving mass emerge a man and a woman drawn to each other by the strongest and most elemental of all forces. They express in dancing and mime their desire for each other.

The woman's lover tries to regain his sweetheart, but they are separated by the whirlwind of skaters.

Gradually the discarded lover is caught up in the swirling mass, while the newcomer carries off his mistress, consenting or filled with anguish.

The skaters circle round and round in complete indifference.

*

This ballet is the first to be based on impressions of a skating rink; the choreography, music and setting were all conceived in a very modern style. Borlin and Léger derived inspiration for the choreography and music by visiting apache balls at Paris.

LA CRÉATION DU MONDE

Ballet in 1 Act. Book: Blaise Cendrars. Music: Darius Milhaud. Scenery, curtain, and costumes: Fernand Léger. Choreography: Jean Borlin. First produced: Théâtre des Champs-Elysées, Paris, October 25th, 1923.

CHARACTERS

The Man . . . . M. JEAN BORLIN
The Woman . . . . . . MLLE. EBON STRANDIN
   Deities, Insects, Monkeys, Birds, Herons, Men, Women

The curtain rises very slowly on a dark stage. In the centre of a clearing can be seen a confused mass of intermingled bodies. Three giant Deities move slowly about it. They are Ngama, Medere, and N'kva, Masters of creation. They hold council and pronounce magical spells as they move about the shapeless mass.

The centre of the mass moves and starts. A tree shoots up little by little, becomes larger, stands up, and when one of its seeds falls to the ground, a new tree rises into view. When one of the leaves of the tree touches the earth the leaf swells, vibrates, begins to walk, and becomes an animal—an elephant which remains suspended in mid-air, a slow tortoise, a crab, and monkeys which glide down from above. The stage gradually lightens during the creation to flare up at the birth of each new animal.

Each creature, whether *danseur* or *danseuse,* bursts from the mass, turns round by himself or herself, takes a few steps, then quietly joins a round dance which gradually encircles the three Deities. The circle parts, the three Deities cast fresh spells, and the shapeless mass quivers. Everything shakes, a monstrous leg appears, backs tremble, a hairy head is seen, arms are stretched forth. Two torsos rise into view, each close against the other. It is

Man and Woman. They recognise each other and stand face to face.

While the two dancers execute the dance of desire, the shapeless mass gradually merges into the dance, which quickens to a delirious frenzy. These are the N'guils—male and female soothsayers, sorcerers, and witch-doctors.

The dance grows calmer, slows down, flags, and comes to a stop. The circle breaks up into little groups. The couple are isolated, absorbed in a kiss which seems to carry them away on a wave. It is the springtide of human life.[4]

*

For some years previous to the production of this ballet, Borlin had taken a great interest in native dances, and in 1919 had arranged for himself a solo dance which he called *"Sculpture Nègre."* From that day he always contemplated the production of a negro ballet.

La Création du Monde is the story of Creation and the birth of Man as an aboriginal might conceive it. There were several new elements in the choreography, for instance, the dancers who suggested herons moved on stilts, others who took the part of animals walked on all-fours. Again, the action took place in semi-darkness, with occasional dimming and lightening which produced an interesting play of light and shade.

*

La Création du Monde, with new choreography by Ninette de Valois, was presented in London, at one of the Camargo Society's performances, on April 20th, 1931. In this production the theme was simplified and expressed in the form of a negro dance-drama.

This version forms part of the repertory of the Vic-Wells Ballet, and was first given at Sadler's Wells Theatre on April 30th, 1932.

WITHIN THE QUOTA

Ballet in 1 Act. Book: Gerald Murphy. Music: Cole Porter. Scenery and costumes: Gerald Murphy. Choreography: Jean Borlin. First produced: Théâtre des Champs-Elysées, Paris, October 25th, 1923.

[4] This description is based on the original scenario.

CHARACTERS

The Immigrant	M. Jean Borlin
The Millionairess	Mlle. Klara Kjellblad
The Puritan	M. Toivo Niskanen
The Coloured Gentleman . . .	M. Kaj Smith
The Jazz-Baby	Mlle. Ebon Strandin
The Cowboy	M. Paul Eltorp
The World's Sweetheart	Mlle. Edith Bonsdorff

An immigrant lands in America and before him pass, against a giant reproduction of an American "daily," a cavalcade of American types—part real, part mythical—with which he is already familiar through visits to the cinema. His pleasure in these types is interrupted by a figure who assumes in turn the character of Social Reformer, Revenue Agent, Uplifter, and Sheriff. Finally the immigrant makes the acquaintance of the World's Sweetheart with the inevitable result, which brings the ballet to its conclusion.

*

Within the Quota, although first produced at Paris, was originally planned for America. It is the first ballet to have an American theme set to music by an American composer.

The ballet is a satire on contemporary life, the choreography being based on characteristic steps from American dances, combined with well-known gestures from American daily life.

The music is gay, and full of parody and entertaining exaggeration.

LA JARRE

Ballet in 1 Act. Book: Luigi Pirandello. Music: Alfredo Casella. Scenery and costumes: Giorgio de Chirico. Choreography: Jean Borlin. First produced: Théâtre des Champs-Elysées, Paris, November 19th, 1924.

CHARACTERS

Don Lollo, a wealthy farmer	
Nela, his daughter	Mlle. Inger Friis
Zi'Dima a hunchback	M. Eric Viber
A Youth	M. Jean Borlin
Farm-hands, villagers.	

Scene. Don Lollo's farm in Sicily.

The day is drawing to a close and Don Lollo's farm-hands are seen returning from their work, dancing gaily. Suddenly, three young girls arrive in the greatest agitation. They are followed by a number of men who carry an enormous oil jar, which has a piece freshly broken out of it. The peasants, knowing the store their master sets on this treasure, are filled with dismay. They decide to acquaint him with the accident. Don Lollo's rage is unbounded, but his daughter hastens to his side and succeeds in calming him.

The peasants decide to send for Zi'Dima, a hunchback, who is the village tinker. He arrives, steps inside the jar, and successfully repairs it. Then he discovers that he cannot get out for his hump. The peasants are highly amused at this development.

They discuss breaking the jar, but the farmer warns them that the tinker must pay if the jar is broken. Furious, Don Lollo gives the jar a violent shaking but, finding this of no avail, goes into his house.

Zi'Dima holds out his pipe, which a peasant fills with tobacco, then lights and returns it to him. The prisoner resigns himself to the situation and philosophically puffs at his pipe. The peasants depart.

Darkness has fallen and moonlight floods the scene. A young man serenades Nela, who comes out of the house. She calls the peasants, who bring wine and drink to the tinker's deliverance. Excited by the wine they dance lustily about the jar until Don Lollo, enraged by the noise, dashes out of the house and hurls over the jar and its contents. The peasants rescue Zi'Dima, who becomes the centre of a triumphal dance, while Don Lollo, exasperated, goes back into his house.

*

The theme of this ballet is founded on Pirandello's short story, *La Giarra*. The ballet was much admired for its robust good humour. The choreography was based on Sicilian folk-dances which Borlin had studied when on holiday in Italy, in company with Pirandello and Casella. The composer of the music derived his inspiration from the same source.

La Jarre, with new choreography by Ninette de Valois, and scenery and costumes by William Chappell, was first produced at London, at Sadler's Wells Theatre, on October 9th, 1934.

Although primarily an *ensemble* ballet, this version contained two *soli* of interest, that danced by Nela, originally taken by

Beatrice Appleyard, which has attractive arm movements; and the grotesque Tinker's Dance, originally taken and admirably rendered by Walter Gore, which forms the prelude to the piece.

De Valois's version is full of life and characterisation, but the high key is over-sustained and apt to become a little strident for want of sufficient relief.

Chappell's setting is charming alike in colour and design.

RELÂCHE

Instantaneous Ballet in 2 Acts and a Cinematographic Entr'acte, and a "Queue de Chien." Book: Francis Picabia. Music: Erik Satie. Cinematographic Entr'acte: René Clair. Production: Francis Picabia and Jean Borlin. First produced: Théâtre des Champs-Elysées, Paris, December 4th, 1924.

CHARACTERS

A Woman	MLLE. EDITH BONSDORFF
A Man	M. JEAN BORLIN
The Other Man	M. KAJ SMITH

The curtain rises to disclose an act-drop inscribed with the names of the collaborators in the production, which are painted in transparent letters lit from behind. The names continually flicker,[5] giving the impression of a cluster of electric nightsigns, such as may be seen in the principal streets of any modern city.

The act-drop is replaced by a screen, then follows a cinematographic prologue which shows a series of fleeting images suggestive of the dance, but having no logical basis for their sequence.

The film ends to be replaced by a dazzling scene expressive of the wings of a theatre: a group of metal discs arranged in a vertical plane.

A fireman enters and strolls about the stage, incessantly smoking the while.

A woman in evening dress passes through the auditorium and on to the stage. She dances and smokes a cigarette.

Then eight men in dress suits enter and dance with the woman; at the conclusion one of the men carries her off the stage.

The second act is preceded by a film representing the most extraordinary objects—a dancer's feet seen at a curious angle; a group of chess-players; a sportsman who hits an egg sustained by a waterjet, thus releasing a pigeon which alights on a man's hat; the sports-

[5] Effect produced by introducing a flasher into the electric circuit.

man fires at the bird but kills the man; there is a nightmare funeral with a hearse, decorated with hams, which breaks loose from the camel which draws it, and rolls away at full speed; the relatives follow in pursuit; landscapes are seen upside down; finally, the hearse parts from the coffin, from which emerges a polished and smiling man of the world.

The second scene consists of a number of broken lines and notices couched in arresting and provocative language, for instance: "Those who are dissatisfied can go to the devil!" "Fancy, there are people who prefer the ballets at the Opera, poor fools!"

The dancers return, take off their dress clothes, so that they appear in fleshings, when they resume their antics, while the fireman ceaselessly and methodically pours the water out of one bucket into another, only to return it to its original receptacle.[6]

*

Relâche was the first ballet to make use of the cinematograph to project a series of images intended to evoke a mood in accord with the spirit of the piece, as was later done in Massine's *Ode*.

The production was largely the conception of Picabia, who had worked out his plans in great detail while the company were on tour in America, so that when Borlin returned the piece was so near completion that his contribution as choreographer was rendered necessarily slight.

Relâche was an experiment in ultra-modernism and is certainly the most advanced example seen to date. *Relâche,* declares Picabia, in one of his half-explanatory, half-mystifying manifestoes, is "life, life as I like it; life without a morrow, the life of to-day, everything for to-day, nothing for yesterday, nothing for to-morrow. Motor headlights, pearl necklaces, the rounded and slender forms of women, publicity, music, motor-cars, men in evening dress, movement, noise, play, clear and transparent water, the pleasures of laughter, that is *Relâche*. . . .

"Erik Satie, Borlin, Rolf de Maré, René Clair, Prieur, and I have created *Relâche* a little in the same way that God creates life. There are no scenes, no costumes, no nudity, only space, space in which our imagination loves to roam." [7]

It is easy to conjure up the mingled howls and applause which greeted this iconoclastic production. Its purpose is best explained in Picabia's own words: *"C'est beaucoup de coups de pied dans beaucoup de derrières consacrés ou non."*

[6] I am indebted to Dr. Pierre Tugal for many details regarding this ballet.
[7] *La Danse,* November-December, 1924.

LEONIDE MASSINE

LEONIDE FEDOROVICH MASSINE was born at Moscow on March 26th, 1896. He studied both drama and ballet at the Moscow Imperial School for the Theatre. It was there that Diaghilev found him in 1913 when, having broken with Nijinsky, he searched St. Petersburg, Moscow, and Warsaw in the hope of finding some young and promising dancer who might be trained to take Nijinsky's place.

Massine, having become a member of the Diaghilev Company, was placed in the care of Maestro Cecchetti who proceeded to prepare him against the day when he would make his *début*. He was an attractive, well made youth with glossy black hair, swarthy features, and lustrous brown eyes. His first solo part was in Fokine's ballet, *La Légende de Joseph* (1914), in which he played the title-role. His success decided Diaghilev to devote his energies to the creation of this new potential star.

To this end he placed him in contact with modern painters such as Larionov and Picasso, from whom Massine imbibed the principles of the newest movements in art; and while Diaghilev supervised his training as a dancer he encouraged him to attempt the composition of dances.

Massine's first ballet, *Soleil de Nuit* (1915), was in the nature of an *ensemble* founded on Russian folk-dances, varied by a few *soli*. His next productions were *Las Meninas* (1916), *Les Femmes de Bonne Humeur* (1917), and *Parade* (1917), the first cubist ballet, which, with scenery and costumes by Picasso, aroused considerable controversy as a result of its unusual choreography and novel presentation. This was followed by *Contes Russes* (1917), a further composition based on Russian folk-dances, with scenery and costumes by Larionov and Gontcharova.

Massine's principal choreographic works may be conveniently grouped into four parts:—FIRST DIAGHILEV PERIOD, 1915–1920, which includes the four ballets mentioned together with *Les Jardins d'Aranjuez* (1918), *La Boutique Fantasque* (1919), *Le Tricorne* (1919), *Pulcinella* (1920), *Le Chant du Rossignol* (1920),

Le Astuzie Femminili (1920), and *Le Sacre du Printemps* (1920)[1];
SECOND DIAGHILEV PERIOD, 1924–1928, with *Les Facheux* (1924),
Les Matelots (1925), *Zéphyre et Flore* (1925), *Le Pas d'Acier*
(1927), and *Ode* (1928); and the present DE BASIL PERIOD, begin-
ning in 1932, with *Le Beau Danube* (1933), *Scuola di Ballo* (1933),
Jeux d'Enfants (1933), *Les Présages* (1933), *Choreartium* (1933),
Beach (1933), *Union Pacific* (1934), *Le Bal* (193?), *Jardin Public*
(1935), and *Symphonie Fantastique* (1936).

In addition Massine has appeared in, and composed ballets and
dances for, the following Cochran productions: *On With the
Dance* (1925), *Still Dancing* (1925), *Cochran's Revue* (1926),
Helen (1932), and Reinhardt's *The Miracle*. He was choreographer at the Roxy Theatre, New York, for three years beginning
in 1926, and has also produced ballets for the Ida Rubinstein Company at Paris and for the Scala Theatre, Milan.

The sources of Massine's choreographic inspiration derive from
his study of modern art, fostered by the influence of his friends
Goncharova, Larionov, and Picasso; so cubism is the basis of
Parade, constructivism that of *Le Pas d'Acier,* and surrealism that
of *Jeux d'Enfants.*

Most of the ballets in the first period, and several of those in the
second, are characterised by angular lines and a jerky, distorted
style of movement quite opposed to the curved lines and flowing
movement associated with Fokine's choreography. Massine also
contrives to give a strong individuality to the characters in his
ballets by investing them with burlesqued movements and attitudes, reinforced by special facial make-up. It is very likely that he
acquired his taste for caricature partly from his interest in the
music-hall and partly from his studies of the Commedia dell'Arte,
for the latter influence is very marked in *Les Femmes de Bonne
Humeur, La Boutique Fantasque, Le Tricorne,* and *Pulcinella.*
This passion for the grotesque has sometimes led Massine to commit minor breaches of good taste, for instance, the assistant's picking of his nose and the behaviour of the poodles in *La Boutique
Fantasque,* and the simulated emptying of bedroom slops on the
gallants at the early performances of *Pulcinella.*

The First Group is composed entirely of *ballets d'action,* that is
to say, ballets with a theme, and his productions of this period have
a robust humour and richness of characterisation which enable
them to wear well even when rendered by artistes not always equal
to the creators of the roles. These ballets, too, have a sustained

---

[1] Ballet by Stravinsky originally produced in 1913 with choreography by
Nijinsky. This is a new version with choreography by Massine.

freshness and spontaneity which, with a few exceptions,[1] I find lacking in Massine's later productions, which are so studied, so reasoned, so scientifically constructed that, while they may have greater value as works of art and do at times rise to the height of pure poetry, they do not communicate that glow to the spectator which for a glorious half-hour makes him one with the ballet.

The Second Group—with the exception of *Les Matelots,* which is really a witty *ballet de moeurs*—might be termed cerebral ballets, since they demand for their success a considerable measure of understanding from the spectator, who must be able to appreciate the modernist idiom in which they are conceived. In short, they are highly sophisticated. Of this group *Les Matelots* and *Le Pas d'Acier* are the best, but I should qualify the last selection by the addition—second scene. Today, only *Les Matelots* persists.

The Third Group contains ballets which belong to one or other of the two preceding groups—for *Le Beau Danube* belongs to the first group just as *Jeux d'Enfants* is in the manner of the second—and also introduces what, for Massine, is a quite new type of ballet, the philosophic manner, which aims at the transmutation of music into pure dancing, the creative impulse being directly derived from the music alone or from the music interpreted in the light of a chosen philosophical theme. It is not an entirely new conception, for the reader will have observed the philosophical tendency in the ballets of Viganò, produced some hundred years before, but it is a field which has been little explored in modern times. In these symphonic ballets of Massine there is both flowing and angular movement, with an unusual accentuation of the dominant links in the rhythmic chain produced by the raising and lowering of certain of the dancers in a vertical plane.

A general characteristic of Massine's ballets is his endeavour to make them all dancing. From beginning to end the dancers, so long as they are on the stage, are continually in movement. The *tempo* varies considerably but the ballet hardly ever comes to a definite stop, and, if it be necessary to mime, that miming is an integral part of the dancer's movements. This is quite different from miming while dancing; the movements of the limbs, the tilt of the head, the inclination of the trunk, are all co-ordinated to convey a message or series of messages. The Miller's Dance before the birdcage in *The Three Cornered Hat,* Niccolo's entry with refreshments in *The Good-Humoured Ladies,* and the Barman's Dance in *Union Pacific* are examples in point. Massine's groups

---

[1] For instance Parts I. and II. of *Les Présages,* Part I. of *Choreartium,* and Scene IV, of *Symphonie Fantastique.*

follow the same principle, they suggest a "still" from the film of a ballet, a kind of suspended animation rather than a definite pause. In short, to adapt a simile from punctuation, Massine prefers the semi-colon to the rounded period of a full point.

How does Massine compose his ballets? In an interview accorded to the *Dance Journal* [2] he revealed many interesting details of his methods which it is important to reproduce:

"I have no fixed method of arranging my ballets or dances. It is quite individual if I prefer to arrange them to music already written, or to have the music specially composed to my choreographic idea. If I have to work with a new composer, with whose work I am not familiar, I prefer the first way. If, on the other hand, the composer and the style of his music are known to me, I like to get my choreographic idea first and then discuss it with the composer in detail. The next person I consider very important is the designer of the setting and costumes, for, if he is a man of ideas, he can be of great assistance. I keep constantly in touch with my collaborators to ensure the closest co-ordination in our work, and I discuss all my plans and ideas with them.

"The actual scenes and dances I do not work out before I commence my rehearsals; but I generally visualise them in my mind and form just a hazy outline of them, somewhat like the outline of houses seen through a London fog. I do not discuss the ballet with my dancers, unless it is of such an unusual character that I find it imperative for them to understand it, in order that they may grasp the situations. I regard the dancers as the elements for the realisation of my ideas, and as such I must be able to inspire them with the same feeling for my work that I have.

"When I begin to rehearse I may start with any scene or dance in the ballet; only gradually do I place the scenes and dances into their proper order. I work separately with my principal artistes and the rest of the company, and it is only when the scenes take definite shape that I rehearse them altogether. During the rehearsals I create the dances and work out every detail for every member of my company; and I expect them to remember these details, as I may forget them when I get other ideas. . . .

"I prefer modern music to arrange to, but I am also fond of classical music. In some sort my method of arranging ballets has many points of similarity with musical composition. I regard solo dances as melodies written for a single instrument; just as group dances correspond to a piece orchestrated for a given number of instruments. And, just as an orchestration should contain colour

[2] February, 1932.

and contrast, so do I seek to invest my group and mass dances with similar qualities.

"It is not always the music that inspires me to arrange a ballet; sometimes it is the theme, or the period in which the action takes place. To make my meaning clearer, I must mention a few of my ballets. In *Le Sacre du Printemps* the predominant element was the music, then the theme; in *Les Femmes de Bonne Humeur* the period was the principal consideration; in *Parade* the music was supreme, although the theme, too, interested me. Whichever element influences me the most, that is the aspect from which I work. If it is the music, I commence by studying the score and receive my choreographic inspiration from that source; if it is the theme, I concentrate upon that and afterwards arrange it to the music.

"The ideals to strive for in the production of a ballet are (1) the highest power of expression possible to obtain; (2) the attainment of a perfect balance between dynamic movement and pure *plastique,* and an interesting counterpoint of mass movement as opposed to that of the individual.

"To my mind the general movement is the most important part of a ballet. Light and shade are essential. My style of ballet-composition is closely connected with the musical theme, and I have my own method for contrasting the movements. If the music does not give it to me, I contrive opportunities for the introduction of light and shade.

"Whether I compose an imaginative or a period ballet, I make use of the same method, because these two types are in a sense the same; the only difference is that in the first case the movements are purely imaginative, while in the other they must be controlled by a sense of period."

Another important factor in the production of a Massine ballet is the presence of the choreographer himself, for he has danced and still dances the leading roles in his ballets. He has a most delicate sense of style-atmosphere which is reflected in his dancing; he can assume the poet's dreaminess in *Symphonie Fantastique,* acquire a dashing elegance as the Hussar in *Le Beau Danube,* be deliciously raffish as the Can-Can Dancer in the *Boutique,* or grotesque to the point of caricature as the Barnum in *Union Pacific.* Apart from his burlesque roles his movements have a cat-like elegance and sinuousness; his timing of step and gesture is superb; and his personality so vital and so compelling that he can force the spectator to follow the least crook of his finger.

LES FEMMES DE BONNE HUMEUR [3]

Choreographic Comedy in 1 Act. Music: Domenico Scarlatti. arranged by Vincenzo Tommasini. Scenery and costumes: Léon Bakst. Choreography: Leonide Massine. First produced: Teatro Costanza, Rome, April 12th, 1917.

CHARACTERS

The Marquise Silvestra	MME. GIUSEPPINA CECCHETTI
Mariuccia, her maid	MME. LYDIA LOPOKOVA
Constanza, Silvestra's niece . . .	MME. LUBOV TCHERNICHEVA
Felicita ⎫	⎧ MLLE. KOKHOVA
Dorotea ⎬ Friends of Constanza	⎨ MLLE. CHABELSKA
Pasquina ⎭	⎩ MLLE. ANTONOVA
Leonardo, Husband of Felicita . .	M. LEONIDE MASSINE
The Marquis di Luca	M. ENRICO CECCHETTI
Battista, betrothed to Pasquina . .	M. STANISLAS IDZIKOWSKY
The Count Rinaldo, betrothed to Constanza	M. SIGMUND NOVAK
Niccolo, Waiter at the *Café* . . .	M. LÉON WOIZIKOWSKY
Captain Faloppa	M. MASCAGNI
A Beggar	
Street Musicians	

The action takes place at Venice in the 18th century.

Scene. The setting by Bakst is altogether reminiscent of a street scene by Francesco Guardi. It represents an open space in a small town near Venice. The background is formed by a collection of broad villas and wide sloping roofs, above which rises a white campanile. A café with rude trestle-table and chairs forms the right wing, and on the left is a house whose main feature is a curved balcony overhanging a doorway. A fountain with a stone figure, some dilapidated palisades, and a ponderous oaken seat complete the scene.

When the curtain rises, seated upon the balcony is the Marquise Silvestra, attended by her niece's winsome maid, Mariuccia. As

[3] *The Good-Humoured Ladies.*

eager for the Carnival as any young gallant the old lady is busily engaged in repairing by artifice the ravages made by time.

Near to her elbow stands a round box of ample proportions, into which she continually dips a powder-puff: now dabbing her nose, now her cheeks, anxiously surveying the result in the mirror proffered by the maid.

There is no shadow of doubt regarding the thoroughness of the good dame's endeavours. Now the dress demands attention; then the lace ruffles on her corsage; so that the titivation seems endless. Absorbed in her fascinating occupation, she fails to notice the movements of her maid, who, with youth's mockery of old age, mimics her every action with grossly exaggerated gesture.

During this by-play there enters a beggar in brown rags, who, Callot-like in his grotesqueness, doffs his feathered cap to the old lady; then, with a shrug of the shoulders, as quickly disappears. Her labours at an end, the Marquise goes indoors, followed by the maid.

Upon their departure appears the Count Rinaldo, a very exquisite of exquisites. Passing his hand over his forehead as if fatigued, and stifling a yawn, he sinks into one of the *café* chairs with an air of indolent ease.

To his summons appears Niccolo, the waiter, balancing on one hand a tray piled high with wine and glasses, who, bustling in with a whimsical side-way shuffle, sets it down in the centre of the table with a magniloquent sweep of the arm. As the waiter returns inside the *café,* the Count pours himself out a glass of wine.

To him comes the dainty figure of Constanza's maid, who, significantly pressing a finger to her lips, hands him a sealed missive, intimating with insinuating smile and roguish glance the delicate nature of the contents.

Now you must know that Constanza—the betrothed of Count Rinaldo—desirous of proving the depth of his affection, has conceived a very pretty plan for his undoing.

Opening the note the Count is delighted to find it to be a *billet-doux,* informing him that a lady, infatuated with his good looks, longs for the pleasure of his acquaintance. As a sign, she will wear in her hair a pink rose.

Now through the doorway come the actors in the comedy—Constanza and her young friends, Felicita, Dorotea, and Pasquina, the features of each concealed beneath a pale blue mask; while adorning each head is a pink rose.

While Constanza departs in search of her aunt, the old Marquise—to whom also is assigned a role—the three friends, one after the other, pirouette before Rinaldo. With enraptured smile and courtly bow he declares to each the ardour of his love. But each in turn, with averted face and hands raised in mock indignation, disdains his amorous advances, serving only to increase them the more, until at last, despairing and exhausted, he falls back into his chair.

Courage! Here approaches yet another lady, bearing the same love token, for, through the doorway, with fluttering fan and mincing step, comes the proud Marquise, a majestic figure in her voluminous black bustle, largely patterned with gold stars, and her corsage of bright green silk; her snow-white hair built up into a marvellous head-dress that would have excited the admiration of Léonard himself.

Once again the gallant Count presses his suit; all graceful bows and tender smiles. This time there is no mistaking the success of his attack, and the lady, enraptured with his agreeable words and charming manner, is easily persuaded to join him in a glass of wine preparatory to setting out for the Carnival. Alas! Just as the Marquise lifts her mask to drink, Rinaldo perceives the magnitude of his error. Pressing a hand to his forehead in endeavour to soothe his fevered brow, he becomes the unwilling recipient of the old lady's tender ministrations, which, so far from assuaging his despair, only serve to increase it.

Vainly does he struggle to escape from the rueful bargain, but the Marquise will have none of it, and, reminding him that love vows once made are not so easily broken, slips his arm into hers and drags him—still feebly protesting—to the Carnival, to which the young people have already repaired.

In the absence of her mistress, little Mariuccia takes advantage of the opportunity to plan a supper for her admirer, Leonardo, Felicita's husband, who soon arrives upon the scene, followed by his friend, Battista, in love with Pasquina. The invitation is extended to him, so that now the supper must needs be for three. Free from restraint the happy trio carry out a table, setting it in the shadow of the balcony. In a trice it is covered with a lace-edged cloth. Now follow the knives and forks, the platters and dishes, while Battista, burlesquing the deportment of a court chamberlain, brings in the wine. Seating themselves, they attack their feast with the greatest of gusto, while the table rocks to the laughter of their merry quips and pranks.

As the fun flies fast and furious there appears the old Marquis di Luca. His still handsome features, though marred with ample traces of rich living and good company, become wreathed in smiles at the sight of Mariuccia, for whom he cherishes a warm corner in his heart.

For a moment the merriment subsides at this unexpected intrusion, then with one accord the company invite the old nobleman to join them. Nothing loth, with many catches of the breath and painful twinges, he seats himself. Glass after glass is emptied and the behaviour of the party speedily passes all bounds of decorum. Clapping their hands and stamping their feet, first they toast the maid and then in turn each other, banging their glasses and clashing their knives and forks to some tuneful air of the day. Then, having exhausted every available means of relieving the exuberance of their spirits, they propose a dance.

In response to a noisy burst of approval, Mariuccia rises and, gracefully spreading out her frock, tiptoes to and fro in the most ravishing manner, from time to time indulging in a delightful pirouette, which is encored by the further clinking of glasses.

Now it is Battista's turn, and gleefully he vaults and leaps in a succession of bewildering *entrechats*.

With the conclusion of his dance Mariuccia goes to each in turn, coquetting with one, then another, with much murmuring of pretty confidences and merry sallies, which are evidently to the company's taste, to judge by the mirthful smiles which illumine every countenance. Even the Marquis coughs and chokes delightedly as the pert little maid whispers into his upraised ear-trumpet.

He, too, wishes to exhibit his prowess as a dancer, and, taking Mariuccia's hand, the oddly assorted couple step to the opening bars of a menuet, while the old nobleman bows and flourishes his handkerchief with all the grace of his youth. But hardly have they taken a dozen paces when the Marquis begins to stagger under the combined effects of the wine and unwonted exercise, so that he has to be escorted back to his chair.

Then follows a triumphant *pas de trois*. The Marquis approvingly nods and shakes his head, whose movements lessen as he falls to sleep. Still the dance goes merrily on, until suddenly interrupted by the arrival of Felicita and Dorotea.

Catching sight of his wife, Leonardo takes to his heels, while the ladies tell Battista that Pasquina has been flirting all the evening with the brave Captain Faloppa. Incredulous and indignant, he refuses to believe them until their story is confirmed beyond all doubt by the appearance of the guilty pair themselves, as, arm in arm and chattering gaily, they pass by on their return from the Carnival.

Mad with jealousy, Battista runs after them, knocking over the table in his excitement; the loud crash awakening the snoring Marquis.

As he gazes about in bewilderment, the vivacious ladies—seeing in him another butt for their fun—fasten a mask over his eyes, and, exulting in their jest, flee through the doorway. While he fumbles at the string with sleeping fingers, the town clock solemnly booms out the hour of four.

Presently, through the doorway, comes the gentle Constanza, expressing in a graceful dance her grief at the ease with which her aunt has enticed away her lover. Even while she deplores her loneliness there passes the Marquise, glowing with triumph and good humour, supported on each arm by Rinaldo and Faloppa. Now come Leonardo and Battista disguised in feminine attire, their faces covered with long black veils. They are followed by the sprightly ladies. Together they determine to fool the Marquis and Marquise.

First the two pretended ladies delight the old nobleman by inviting him to join them at the *café*. Upon his eagerly accepting they indulge in a stately *pas de trois,* at which his gestures are even more elaborately courteous than before. At the conclusion of the dance, one arranges his lace ruffle, while the other smooths the nap of his coat, until, overwhelmed with such fascinating attentions, the poor old man hardly knows whether he is on his head or his feet.

Motioning them to be seated, he goes in search of a bottle of wine, but, no sooner is his back turned, than the two accomplices in this roguish villainy give way to unbridled mirth at the success of their stratagem. Suddenly catching sight of their faces, now freed of the veils, their identity is revealed to him. Horror-stricken and cursing his gullibility he collapses into a chair, while his tormentors caper around him, poking fun and flapping their veils in fiendish glee.

In the meantime the genuine ladies have prevailed upon Niccolo, the *café* waiter, to dress up as a Prince, and, thus disguised, to offer his hand to the Marquise. On his consenting they furnish him with rich apparel, in which he speedily arrays himself. His features concealed with a green mask, they pose him in an attitude of rest against the doorway.

At this juncture comes a poor masked musician, a picturesquely cloaked figure, who, moving with a dragging gait, plays on his fiddle the plaintive melody of the "Cat's Fugue," which heralds the arrival of the Marquise and her gay companions.

With arch smile and subtle gesture, they point out the gorgeously transformed Niccolo, who, advancing with exaggerated princely bows and sweeping off his feathered hat, declares his love and asks for the old lady's hand. Amazed and delighted beyond measure, the Marquise turns to all present and pompously announces her marriage to the supposed Prince.

But, with a quick movement, Mariuccia slips forward and smilingly plucks off the mask, revealing the unhappy Niccolo. Now it is the Marquise's turn to be tricked, and, furious with rage at her discomfiture, she soundly rates the miserable waiter, boxing his ears to the accompaniment of peals of laughter from the assembled company.

This last noise is too much for one slumberer, for, speechless with anger and brandishing a stick, comes the Marquis in nightcap and gown. Laying about him with the greatest of vigour, he seeks to drive away these disturbers of his night's repose; unfortunately, with fatal precision, the stick falls on the old lady's head, to send flying her magnificent array of hair, now shown all too plainly to be a wig. The Marquise, feeling only the blow and unaware of the enormity of the injury, raises her hands in anxious endeavour to set matters aright, only to come into contact with her pate, round and bald as an egg.

With her features expressive of the utmost bewilderment, she drops to the ground, overcome with chagrin and ridicule, at which the jubilation of the delighted onlookers bursts out anew; and with this crowning triumph of youth over old age, the curtain falls.

*

The theme of *Les Femmes de Bonne Humeur* is based on Goldoni's comedy *Le Donne di Buon Umore,* to which selections of music by Scarlatti were most skilfully adapted.

The atmosphere of the 18th century is wonderfully conveyed both by Bakst's settings and costumes, the choreography, and the music; and enhanced by the spinet which at one time was introduced into the orchestra, for, as the quaint tinkling notes of the old-world instrument fell upon the ear, the illusion was complete.

This ballet is a masterpiece and one of the best examples of Massine's ability to make dancing mimetic: Niccolo's first entry with his tray, the scene of the supper-table, the *pas seuls* danced in turn by Mariuccia and Battista, and the triumphant *pas de trois* by Mariuccia, Leonardo, and Battista are all as gay and as sparkling as the dialogue of the best of Goldoni's comedies. In contrast there is Constanza's dance, that lovely lament on the loss of her lover, which is one of Massine's most poetic compositions.

But to savour this ballet to the full you must have seen Lopokova, Tchernicheva, M. and Mme. Cecchetti, Massine, Idzikowsky, and Woizikowsky in their original roles. The ballet as revived by the De Basil Company is pleasing, but it has not the wit and sparkle and pace of those early performances.

Most of all I miss Lopokova, that rare combination, an artist-dancer who was also a comedienne. How good she was as Mariuccia, pert, winsome, seducing everyone with her gay chatter, bright eyes, and merry laughter. How eager she was to take part in every fun and frolic! How she flirted with Leonardo and Battista! Those who were privileged to see her will not have forgotten the joy of that tomboy *pas de trois,* that coquettish elbowing of each in turn, and the uproarious fun at the supper-table set to the music of clashing knives and forks, the dances, the kisses, the naughty whispering into the speaking-trumpet of the amorous old Marquis! Was she not adorable, that little minx?

PARADE

Realistic Ballet in 1 Act. Book: Jean Cocteau. Music: Eric Satie. Curtain, scenery and costumes: Pablo Picasso. Choreography: Leonide Massine. First produced: Théâtre du Chatelet, Paris, May 18th, 1917.

CHARACTERS

The Chinese Conjurer	M. LEONIDE MASSINE
The Acrobats	{ MLLE. LOPOKOVA M. ZVEREV
The Little American Girl . .	MLLE. CHABELSKA
The Manager in Evening Dress .	M. WOIZIKOWSKY
The Manager from New York .	M. STATKEWICZ
The Manager on Horseback . .	{ M. OUMANSKY M. NOVA

The overture has hardly begun with a few, deep-toned chords in the manner of a classic fugue, when the curtain parts to reveal a crude and sombre drop-curtain which depicts the interior of a booth in which, seated about a table, is a motley group of performers awaiting their "call."

Now there fall upon the ear the half-muffled, mellow sounds that proclaim the proximity of a church—the rich, quivering notes of a hymn played on a great organ, the rustling stir of many people rising from their seats as one, and the brush of slippered feet against stone as the acolytes glide to and fro in the service of the priest. The overture concludes with a scale of bells that tinkle and echo like tiny marbles dropped into a wine-glass. The curtain glides upwards to reveal the scene proper: the simple curtained entrance to a booth.

From right to left paces an extraordinary figure, seemingly a wooden head and body poised on human legs. The head is formed by a horizontal flange-like arrangement of thin sheets of wood on one of which is placed a strip of card, twisted to suggest a moustache. The body resembles a rectangular box at the back of which is fixed a house; the legs are clothed in black breeches and shoes, with white woollen stockings stretched over the most preposterous calves. From each shoulder hangs a limp and flattened arm; one serves to support an enormous clay pipe at which the figure puffs contentedly, the other holds a white cane. This is the French manager.

The orchestra strikes up a monotonous march composed of flute-like notes and the figure moves slowly across the stage with a series of short steps and staccato stamps of the feet. Arrived at the centre, the manager faces the audience, stops, and twists his left foot to and fro on its heel as if in indecision. Again he resumes his march with vigorous stamps of the feet and tapping of the floor with his stick. A shrill whistle sounds and again he turns to face the audience. The curtains of the booth are withdrawn and at the right hand side is exhibited a card which announces 1.

Quickly the music changes to a pompous march interspersed with lively flourishes, and from the booth there stalks a mysterious figure whose costume suggests that he is a Chinese conjurer. Everything about him is intended to convey and strengthen the opinion that he really is what he purports to be, though there is a lingering suspicion that he may be a European. Yet he has a voluminous, short-sleeved coat, striped to resemble the rising sun; baggy trousers tucked into broad-soled shoes; and, above all, the plaited pigtail so necessary to a Chinaman's exterior. His face is sallow, the eyebrows curved in an expression of bland surprise, and the thick red lips are parted in a faint smile at once mysterious and secretive.

He marches round the stage in a circle, his stiffly-held head jerked backwards and forwards as after each exaggerated step he throws back his knee so high as to be on a level with his chin. Arrived at the point from which he started, he bows majestically three times—to the left, centre, and right of the audience. He points with his finger first to one leg and then the other, and violently shakes his coat. Then, with a jerk of his head, he throws his pigtail over his shoulder and pretends to extract from it an egg. He stamps his feet, opens wide his mouth, and places the egg inside. He closes his mouth with his finger-tips and opens it again. The egg has vanished. He smiles mysteriously and extends his arms to show that there is "no deception." Now he slides out his left foot sideways until he is almost seated on the ground, slowly extends his left hand, and from the toe of his shoe gracefully extracts the imaginary egg. He rises slowly to his feet, his lips parted in an enigmatic smile.

Now the music quickens and he bounds in the air, leaps across the stage, and breathes from his mouth imaginary smoke and flame. He stops and with a commanding gesture causes imaginary flame to issue from the ground. He fans it with his hands so that gradually it becomes a pillar of fire. Tiring of his exertions he yawns wearily. Suddenly the orchestra strikes up the music of his entrance and he again marches grotesquely round the stage. Arrived before the booth, he enters it, falls on his knees and flings back his head. The curtains are swiftly closed.

From the left side of the stage enters the manager from New York, a figure conceived on similar lines to the French manager. His exterior is suggestive of America by reason of the skyscraper he bears on his back, his red shirt, and cowboy riding-boots. In one hand he bears a megaphone, in the other a placard blazoned with the word PARADE. He approaches his fellow-manager who, furiously stamping his feet, expresses his disgust at the public who have failed to appreciate the genius of the Chinese conjurer. The American listens sympathetically, then struts to and fro, waves his placard, and, raising his megaphone, bellows the praises of the American dancer he is about to present.

The curtains of the booth fly back and a card announces 2.

The orchestra strikes up a lively two-step which commences in the treble and is repeated in lower octaves, when a dark-haired girl makes her way across the stage by means of a succession of convulsive bounds, her hands extended in front of her as if she were mounted on a mettlesome horse. She is attired in a sailor coat, white skirt, and short white stockings and black shoes; her hair is bound with a white ribbon à l'Americaine.

The music changes to a syncopated melody and she assumes the curious stilted walk associated with Charlie Chaplin. The melody merges into a plaintive chant and she pretends to cry. Now the music and her corresponding actions change with incredible rapidity and variety. She pretends to jump on a moving tram, drive a motor-car, swim a river, and, for a few moments, affords a glimpse of a film drama, in which she drives away a robber at the point of a revolver. Again the music changes to a lilting rag-time tune to which she shrugs her shoulders and sways her body with undisguised zest. Thunder rolls and she believes herself at sea in a storm; she imitates the rolling motion of the ship, then, terrified, closes her eyes and falls to the ground. She opens her eyes in the belief that she is at the sea-side and with a finger traces figures in the sand. The music returns to the lively air that marked her entrance, and she gallops away through the curtains of the booth.

Evidently the public are unimpressed for no one comes forward, and the two managers give vent to their disappointment in furious stamps of the feet.

Now comes the third manager, evidently in charge of the equestrian section of the troupe. He is suggested by a dummy negro, faultlessly attired in evening dress, and mounted on a horse of unusual equine intelligence, for it trots in with a very affected air, paws the ground, and then calmly proceeds to sit down, regardless of the peril to which it exposes his rider. The horse rises, shuffles to and fro, and creates much amusement by jumping alternately on its fore-legs and hind-legs. Then, tossing its head with deep knowing, it trots disdainfully out of sight.

The orchestra strikes up a waltz and a card announces 3.

At once a pair of acrobats launch themselves through the curtains to perform a bewildering succession of vaults and leaps, twists and turns. One is a fair young man, the other a girl with dark hair flowing over her shoulders. Both are dressed in tights, patterned in blue and white. The man poses in a variety of *arabesques* while the girl pirouettes on her toes. He slides out one foot, keeping the knee bent, upon which his partner steps to pose with one foot extended and her head thrown back over his shoulder. She leaps to the ground and again they dart to and fro in a maze of varied movement. Now he clasps her about the waist and swings her in the air, the while she imitates with her arms the fluttering wing-actions of a bird in flight, then, with a quick movement he lifts her on to his shoulder and carries her from the scene.

The orchestra reverts to rag-time and through the curtain comes a quaint trio composed of the two managers and the American girl. They emphasise each bar of the melody with magnificent swaying of the shoulders and swinging of the arms. The horse follows at a gallop and proceeds round the stage, plunging with its hoofs, tossing its head, and pawing the air with all the humour of which it is capable. The Chinese conjurer glides forward, profuse in bows and smiles, while the acrobats reappear at the back of the booth in a succession of wonderful leaps.

The public refuse to come forward.

In desperation, the American girl leads the horse across the stage and the company form in line. The managers shout themselves hoarse in endeavour to explain that the parade is only a glimpse of the performance to be witnessed inside. The public are incredulous, convinced that they have seen all that there is to be seen. Why should they pay for mere repetition? The artistes are saddened at this tragedy of misunderstanding. The managers droop under the weight of their cares, the American girl tearfully extends her arms, the acrobats tremble plaintively from their exertions, the conjurer, true to his disguise, views the matter with Oriental calm, while the horse, utterly exhausted, collapses to the ground.

The orchestra returns to the fugue of the overture and the drop-curtain slowly falls.

*

Parade was a satire on the doings of a small French touring company, part music-hall, part circus, and the action takes place on a Sunday in a Paris street. Following the practice of time immemorial, such companies endeavour to attract attention and custom by performing without charge an excerpt from their repertory; this is called a parade.

Everyone has seen the frock-coated, silk-hatted manager who bawls the merits of his show and emphasises each remark with a crashing blow on a big drum, the while an acrobat performs marvels of equilibrium on a wooden sphere, a strong man lifts slowly upwards immense weights, and an equestrienne, in fleshings and spangled skirt, blows kisses to a gaping crowd—that is the atmosphere of *Parade*.

The ballet was really a tragi-comedy in miniature, a satirical comment on a phase of contemporary life, in which the professional gestures and movements characteristic of certain well-known music-hall types were used as the inspiration for a series of dances. The best of these was the "Dance of the Chinese Conjurer," rendered by Massine with a fine sense of style and caustic observation. The "Acrobats' Dance" was interesting in its pathos, for their movements suggested the incessant, purposeless activity which one associates with a performance by caged white mice.

A minor artistic sensation was provided by dressing the managers in cubist costumes which, to my mind, detracted from, rather than contributed to, the general effect. Moreover, they created a curious illusion of false realism so that the real dancers seemed puppets.

Satie's score was part ironic, part fanciful, and part burlesque; and was novel in that an attempt was made to provide each character with a background of appropriate sound, for instance the click of a typewriter for the American girl, and the humming of an aeroplane engine for the acrobats.

Although *Parade* has never been revived, the "Dance of the Chinese Conjurer" has been given as a solo, principally by Woizikowsky, in a programme of *divertissements*.

CONTES RUSSES

Ballet in 1 Act and Scenes. Music: A. Liadov. Scenery and costumes: Michael Larionov. Choreography: Leonide Massine. First produced in its entirety: Coliseum Theatre, London, 1919.

CHARACTERS

Dance Prelude	M. Léon Woizikowsky
Kikimora	Mlle. Lydia Sokolova
The Cat	M. Stanislas Idzikowsky
The Swan Princess . . .	Mlle. Lubov Tchernicheva
Bova Korolevich . . .	M. Leonide Massine
Baba-Yaga	M. Nicholas Kremnev
The Little Girl	Mlle. Antonova
Baba-Yaga's Hut . . .	{ M. Okhimowsky / M. Maximov
Devils	{ M. Jazvinsky / M. Statkiewicz / M. Pavlov

The Princess's Sisters, Peasant Girls, Village Youths.

The ballet commences with an overture whose simple folk-tunes, set to the accompaniment of drums and tambourines, radiate the spirit of peasant holiday.

The curtain rises to reveal a bright blue drop-curtain, patterned in red and lighter blue, with entwined flowers and their stems.

At first the scene is empty, then, as the overture fades into a thinly-piped little dance, a street-vendor enters with quick, sliding steps, his lively demeanour reflected in his gay white and crimson costume and smiling bearded face. He holds under each arm a doll, one representing Kikimora, the embodiment of wickedness;

the other, her protector the cat, the symbol of human malice. He holds out the dolls at arms' length, shakes and gazes at each in turn, and beats a merry tattoo with his feet. Now he squats on his heels and propels himself forward by alternately kicking out each foot. With his departure the drop-curtain rises to reveal the home of Kikimora.

Scene I. A large room dominated by three cylindrical beams which support the roof. The walls are bright yellow and pierced by a single window, whose frame is painted deep red. To the right stands a tall, green-enamelled stove; the sole furniture is a low form and two square stools.

In a wooden cradle, decorated with gigantic flowers, reposes the terrible Kikimora. Her face presents a grotesque appearance for each cheek is disfigured by a broad black stripe, and her dark tangled hair is piled up on the top of her head in a great bunch which nods at her every movement. Even in her sleep she plans fresh misdeeds, for her teeth snap together and her clenched fingers, with their cruel nails, claw spitefully at the air.

A little distance from her is her faithful protector, a big white cat with an orange handkerchief tied about its neck. Perched upon a stool, it dozes quietly as if fatigued with its vigil. Suddenly, it awakes with a start, stretches itself and leaps to the floor, where it stands alternately on each hind-leg and slowly strokes its stomach. Then, as it wearily yawns, Kikimora awakes in a rage, claws the air, gnaws her thumbs, and shrieks imprecations.

Alarmed the cat bounds to her side, gently rocks the cradle, slowly waves its fore-paws over her, and purrs a soothing lullaby until it succeeds in putting her to sleep. It returns to the centre of the room, passes its fore-paws over its ears, resumes its position in front of the cradle, rolls itself up into a ball, and falls fast asleep.

Restless and tossing in her cradle, Kikimora again opens her eyes, and, furious at the cat's non-appearance, flings back the counterpane and clambers out of her cradle. Now it is possible to see that the witch is attired as a woman, but her pink blouse spotted with sinister brown patches, her blue skirt, and horrible red stockings make her repulsive in the extreme. She gnashes her teeth, bites her thumbs, and calls down the most terrible curses upon the unfortunate animal, as she stamps up and down the room in a frenzy of rage. She goes to a low form near the stove and takes up a pair of sticks, connected together by a twist of straw; then she dashes up to the cat to torment it with fierce lashes of the straw rope, a proceeding which is also invested with a deep symbolical significance, for, according to Russian superstition, to be touched by straw forbodes great evil.

Astonished and frightened at such treatment, the cat leaps to its feet, bounds from side to side, and endeavours to soothe the angry witch, but, filled with malice and spite, Kikimora repeats her threats and continues to menace the cat with her long nails. Now she stamps furiously on a stool employing each foot in turn, whereupon the cat leaps upon an adjacent stool and again endeavours to pacify the witch with frantic waving of its fore-paws. Kikimora leaves the stool and springs at the terrified animal which, seeing its efforts of no avail, defends itself to the best of its ability while it continually bounds convulsively into the air from sheer anxiety. Enraged at the cat's resistance, the witch rushes to her cradle and draws from it a gleaming axe, then she dashes up to the cat, grasps it by the throat, and crashes the weapon on its skull—once, twice, thrice! Powerless against such a brutal attack, the animal collapses to the floor, shoots out its legs, becomes rigid and rolls over dead. Kikimora disappears and an instant later flies out through the roof to cast her evil spells upon the world.

The jolly street-vendor enters at this juncture and, forgetful of the play, becomes so horrified at the thought of Kikimora's escape, that he commences to crack his whip lustily across the cat's back which, naturally alarmed at the strange conduct of its fellow-actor, scrambles to its feet and scampers on-all-fours out of the room.

The drop-curtain descends and there enters a procession of peasant-girls in brightly-coloured skirts who slowly step sideways across the room, each with a yellow handkerchief held above her head and drawn tight between her finger-tips. A group of sturdy peasants follow, who bear shoulder-high the two actors who have acquitted themselves so well. First four men gaily costumed in red and yellow, who form a guard of honour, and, finally, another group of four men bearing Kikimora in her cradle, who still bites her thumbs and gnashes her teeth. The rear is brought up by the street vendor who squats on his heels and propels himself forward on his toes.

As they pass from view the scene becomes darker and darker, and the drop-curtain rises on a second play, which tells of a beautiful princess who has fallen a victim to the enchantment of a terrible dragon. With each sunset she cherishes a faint hope of succour for, at night, in the guise of a swan, she is free to watch on the borders of a lake, near the palace, for the rescuer of her dreams. But with the first rays of dawn she reassumes her natural shape, when her sisters come to clothe her in the royal mantle and restore her to the palace of the dragon.

Scene II. The banks of the magic pool, lit by the pale green rays of the moon. Strange reeds lift their fan-shaped heads and so thick is the growth of water-lilies that the limpid water seems carpeted with flowers.

Against this sombre background the Swan-Princess dances sadly. Her costume is entirely white, faintly tinged with pearl-like shades of palest pink and blue; her skirt is adorned with masses of swansdown and fringed with feathers. Her face gleams silver amid the dark oval frame of her hair, which falls over her breast in two long plaits. Upon her head she bears the royal *kokovschnik,* deeply sewn with pearls.

Slowly she moves to and fro, her arms undulating gently as some ripple traced by a stray breath of wind on the placid surface of the pool. In despair she sinks to the ground, her body quivering with the plaintive movements of a wounded bird. Gradually the light fades and the scene vanishes from sight.

Scene III. The courtyard of the palace. The background is formed by the open sky, red with the rising sun. To the left is a flight of great pink and white steps which give entrance to the palace. On the far side of these the dragon lies couched, a terrible writhing mass of scaly coils, from which stands erect the powerful neck which bears its three heads, each with their complement of gleaming, bulging eyeballs, jagged teeth, and fiery tongues.

The Swan-Princess reclines in the courtyard, attended by two of her sisters, dressed in long gowns, red and purple, blue and green, their heads crowned with tall, mitre-shaped hats. They gently raise the Princess to her feet and drape over her shoulders a long robe, embroidered in silver and fringed with ermine. Immediately behind stand her six other sisters, who hold on high a ceremonial robe, of which at present only the orange lining can be seen. The sisters conduct the Princess to this garment, fasten it about her throat, and creep under its voluminous folds. Then, as she majestically walks towards the steps, the robe is displayed in its full beauty of blue silk, broadly fringed with silver and patterned with arabesques of the same precious metal. Borne thus by the figures who glide concealed beneath its train, it billows out so gracefully that one is reminded of the passage of some proud galleon of old.

Arrived at the foot of the steps, she mounts each in turn, while the robe flows behind her to reveal the sisters in its wake. As the Princess reaches the head of the steps, four of the sisters bow low in her honour, but the remaining four perceive something unusual, for they beckon with their hands. Now there arrives, mounted on a white charger, the famous knight, Bova Korolevich, a Russian Sir Galahad, who travels the vast plains with no other thought than the doing of brave deeds in the righting of wrong.

He is a gallant figure in his rich costume of green and gold, while his strong personality is expressed in the stern bronzed face that looks out beneath his pointed helmet. His right hand grips the reins, his left bears his sword and shield.

The knight dismounts, takes his sword in his right hand, and defies the dragon. Then he steps towards the sisters, makes deep obeisance, and prepares to do battle, while the agitated sisters cross themselves and pray for the success of their champion. For a moment the knight falls to his knees and joins them in prayer, then, with sword upraised, and lowered shield guarding his face, he advances boldly to the attack, his feet twisting and turning to avoid entanglement in the monster's coils. His flashing sword describes glittering arcs of light—he crouches for the supreme effort —then the blade sweeps upwards in a mighty blow and the dragon's three heads sway and fall to the ground, severed at a single stroke.

Quietly he makes his way up the steps to greet the Princess, while the sisters acclaim the victor with joyful clapping of their hands. As he confronts her, they circle about each other and slowly descend the steps. The Princess, already in love with the valorous knight, holds out her arms to clasp him to her breast, but he quickly mounts his charger, waves his hand in farewell, and rides away. The sisters bow their heads in sorrow, while the Princess covers her tear-stained face with her hands.

The drop-curtain of the interlude descends, and, to a burlesque of a funeral march, there enters the cat, who walks on his hind-legs with faltering steps, his body bent in an attitude of grief, his limbs shaking from the violence of his sobs. As his drooping head dolefully shakes from side to side, he dries his tears with his orange handkerchief. Behind him solemnly stride four peasants with bowed heads, who bewail the dragon's death with trembling hands raised to heaven. Now, borne aloft on a pole by three stalwart men, come the dragon's three heads. The mock funeral procession is completed by a further group of peasants accompanied by Kikimora.

The dragon's remains pass from view, and the company form into a single line and kneel with their hands held to their ears. Suddenly the music changes to a lively melody, and a laughing girl and her sweetheart dance in with swift, staccato steps. He tries to clasp her waist, but she repulses him with playful slaps of her hands. Now she glides behind his back, slips an arm about his neck, and, heedless of his struggles, forces him to continue the dance. Then she repents of her cruelty and releases him, whereupon he sits on his heels, seizes her foot, pulls her after him, gaily kicks out his toes, and, with his free hand, slaps the sole of her foot with the utmost amusement. They pass from view, followed by the entire company.

The drop curtain rises on the third and last play which deals with the story of Baba-Yaga, a terrible ogress who lives with her attendant demons in the depths of a thick forest. She possesses a magic house which is supported on four hen's feet and follows her wherever she goes. According to legend, she feeds on the bodies of little children who, having lost their way and fallen into her clutches, are killed, boiled, and eaten.

Scene IV. A forest glade, surrounded by sinister trees and almost roofed in by the drooping fronds of their giant leaves. The trees are deep brown and covered with a scaly bark like snake-skin; the leaves are alternately dark and light green, broad at the base and narrowing to a point, from which depends an evil-looking red flower.

To the right is a fearsome-looking cottage supported on four webbed claws, while in the centre stand three loathsome wood demons, half-animal, half-human. Their bodies are covered with coarse brown hair after the manner of ourang-outans; their heads are tall, very narrow, and deathly white, grotesque as some distorted carving of a South Sea Islander. Black feathers sprout from their crowns, long pointed moustaches fall over their lips, and from their chins hang immense, stringy beards which reach to their knees.

The demons face each other in turn, swing their great arms and, leering and shaking with diabolical laughter, roll over on their backs with a horrid squirming of their gross bodies. They lurch to their feet as there enters the terrible Baba-Yaga, a horrible old woman with hooked nose and humped back, further deformed by one foot which is longer than the other owing to a pointed bone which grows out of the base of her heel. In one hand she bears a knotted stick. She shakes her talons, shrieks imprecations at the demons, and stamps angrily to and fro. From time to time she rises on her bony foot, upon which she twists and twirls with incredible ferocity.

Now comes a young girl who, having lost her way, rests her tired head on her arm, weary at her vain efforts to find the true path. All unconscious of the dangers that beset her, she limps through the dreadful glade. Suddenly the ogress bars her way. Terrified, the girl tries to flee, only to meet the three demons, who immediately drive her back to their mistress, who stamps her bony foot, strikes the ground with her stick, and utters the most frightful threats of what is in store for them if they permit so succulent a morsel to escape. For a few moments the poor girl struggles to evade their clutches, but in vain, for the demons unite and bear down upon her. Soon their hairy arms paw at her dress, their beards brush her very face. Horrified, she begs for mercy, while the delighted ogress beats her with blow after blow of her stick.

In despair she makes the sign of the cross. Startled and amazed, the demons gaze at each other in alarm and tremble with fear; they fall to the ground and roll off into the depths of the forest. The ogress, confronted with a power that none dare dispute and thus baulked of her meal, stamps away viciously, her features contorted with the bitterness of her thoughts.

Overjoyed at her rescue from the fate that so nearly claimed her, the girl composes herself in a prayer of thanksgiving. Suddenly there is a burst of joyous music and she extends her arms to whirl in a breathless pirouette. This is evidently the pre-arranged signal for the commencement of festivities, for the glade resounds to the laughter and shouts of merry peasants who seek to forget their labours in the rapture of a country dance. Handkerchiefs leap from sleeves and bosoms to flutter gaily in the wind.

Fresh arrivals come to swell the throng. First, the cat, who gleefully bounds in the air, then the knight, and lastly the Princess, her train supported by the three demons, now as jolly as the three good bears. They thread their way though the dancers, climb upon a mossy bank, and, from this high point of vantage, urge the company to greater efforts. The men spring into the air, then sit on their heels, and kick out their toes; and as the girls twirl round in a seemingly never-ending pirouette, the curtain falls.

*

Contes Russes, as its title suggests, is based on Russian fairy-tales and folk-lore. As originally conceived the ballet consisted solely of the story of Kikimora, under which title it was presented by the

Diaghilev Company in 1916 at the Teatro Victoria Eugenie, San Sebastian, Spain. It proved so successful that later in the same year the miniature ballet was enlarged by the addition of the stories of the Swan-Princess and Baba-Yaga, and concluded with a Khorovod. It was produced in this form, under the title *Contes Russes,* at the Teatro Constanza, Rome, and performed at the Théâtre du Chatelet, Paris, in 1917. On the company's return to London in 1919, the ballet was revised and enlarged still further by the addition of two comic interludes, in which final state it formed one of the chief attractions of the Diaghilev Company's first season—since the War—at the Coliseum Theatre.

Contes Russes is a fine piece of composition, full of varied incident and contrasted types of movement. The first episode, which is the most original in treatment, is almost an epic of spitefulness. The movements of Bova Korolevich in the second scene are based on ikon paintings. The final episode conveys a rare sense of horror which is banished by the joyous *ensemble* which brings the ballet to a conclusion.

The piece is presented as a People's Play, in which the roles are presumed to be played not by professional actors but by peasants, as in the Miracle Plays of the 14th century, which have a modern survival in the Passion Play of Oberammergau.

Of the principal roles the following were the best interpreters: *Kikimora,* by Nijinska or Sokolova; the *Cat,* by Idzikowsky; *Bova Korolevich* by Massine or Vilzak; and *Baba-Yaga* by Kremnev.

Larionov's settings and costumes are remarkable for their richness of fantasy, colour and design. The horse ridden by Bova Korolevich is a finely painted two-dimensional animal, for Diaghilev detested the use of real horses on the stage, on the ground that they never looked real.

LA BOUTIQUE FANTASQUE

Ballet in 1 Act. Music: Giacomo Rossini, arranged and orchestrated by Ottorino Respighi. Curtain, setting, and costumes by André Derain. Choreography: Leonide Massine. First produced: Alhambra Theatre, London, June 5th, 1919.

CHARACTERS

The Shopkeeper	M. ENRICO CECCHETTI
His Assistant	M. ALEXANDRE GAVRILOV
Two Porters	MM. PAVLOV & KOVALSKY

A Thief	M. Okhimovsky
An English Old Maid . . .	Mlle. Klementowicz
Her Friend	Mme. Mikulina
An American	M. Jazvinsky
His Wife	Mme. Alanova
Their Son	M. Bourman
Their Daughter	Mme. Evina
A Russian Merchant . . .	M. Serge Grigoriev
His Wife	Mme. Giuseppina Cecchetti
Their Son	M. Lukine
Their Four Daughters . .	Mmes. Nemchinova, Zalevska, Potapovich, Mascagno
Dolls—Tarantella Dancers . .	{ Mme. Lydia Sokolova { M. Leon Woizikowsky
Mazurka:—	
The Queen of Clubs . . .	Mme. Lubov Tchernicheva
The Queen of Hearts . . .	Mme. Vera Nemchinova
The King of Spades . . .	M. Statkiewicz
The King of Diamonds . . .	M. Novak
The Snob	M. Stanislas Idzikowsky
The Melon Hawker . . .	M. Kostetsky
A Cossack Chief	M. Nicholas Zverev
Five Cossacks	MM. Kostrovsky, Kegler, Okhimowsky, Ribas, Mascagno
A Cossack Girl	Mme. Istomina
Dancing Poodles	{ Mme. Vera Clark, { M. Nicholas Kremniev
Can-Can Dancers	{ Mme. Lydia Lopokova { M. Leonide Massine
Twelve of their Friends . .	Mmes. Klementowicz, Vera Nemchinova, Kostrovska, Slaviska, Istomina, Wassilevska, Radina, Grantzeva, Olkhina, Petipa, Pavlovska, Mikulina

The ballet opens with a brief overture in the Russian vein, a Slav march played *pizzicato,* then repeated to the brisk accompaniment of rolling drums. Soon the curtain glides upwards to reveal a drop-curtain depicting two figures, a guitar-player and a dancer in short skirts posed against a pale, terra-cotta coloured curtain background, slightly parted to reveal a severe landscape.

With the raising of this curtain the spectator is admitted to the interior of the "Boutique Fantasque." This is a large dignified apartment bounded by terra-cotta walls pierced by broad windows. The small windows at the side are decorated with bowls filled with flowering plants, while the large windows at the rear afford a charming view of Nice harbour; calm blue sea—upon which lazily rocks a paddle-steamer surrounded by smaller craft—bounded by a landscape in the style of Henri Rousseau le Douanier.

The shop is empty except for two ordered rows of chairs and an oblong box upon which stand two dolls—dressed as peasant girls— resplendent in blue and yellow, and red and pink, brocade. Entrance to the shop is provided by a tall doorway at first closed by a pair of iron gates.

The period is about 1865. It is early afternoon and the sun streaming through the windows radiates an atmosphere of warmth and happiness. Now through the doorway can be seen two men, who stop before the gates, unlock them, and enter the shop with lively steps as if anticipating good business. These are the shop-keeper and his assistant.

The former is a quaint old gentleman, dressed in white drill, his head half concealed under a wide-brimmed Panama hat. His face is round, chubby, adorned with side-whiskers and rendered con-spicuous by the enormous spectacles perched on his nose. His assis-tant is a youth in grey trousers and velvet coat, from one pocket of which dangles a spotted handkerchief. With a whimsical air he bustles round the room, dusting and arranging a chair, and re-pleat-ing the dresses of the two dolls. Then he trots into the interior of the shop.

No sooner is his back turned than a shabbily-dressed boy glides swiftly through the open door. He tip-toes up to the dolls and is about to despoil them of their gold lace when the assistant returns and, seeing the thief, drags him before the shopkeeper. The thief drops to his knees, begs for mercy, then, finding prayers of no avail, leaps to his feet and offers a strenuous resistance. For a few minutes there is a wild rough and tumble, but between them the shopkeeper and his assistant bestow on him a sound drubbing until forced to relax their efforts from sheer exhaustion, when the wretched youth makes his escape by dashing through the door, nearly colliding with two old ladies about to enter the shop, who, overcome with consternation, open their tiny parasols in a posture of defence.

All danger past they sweep into the shop with a magnificent air of patronage, upon which the shopkeeper and his assistant bound

forward—bowing and scraping and beseeching the honour of
their custom in the most obsequious manner. Rendered haughtier
than ever by this display of servility, they raise their lorgnettes and,
after rudely quizzing them from top to toe, express their desire to
inspect the dolls of which they have heard some slight account.
Bowing again at this tribute to his reputation, the shopkeeper
guides them, with many flourishes of the hand, to the oblong
box, upon which stand the two dolls. Now the assistant shuffles
forward and, as he turns a handle operating the mechanism, the
figures begin to revolve slowly. Suddenly they shake their heads
and arms and come to a standstill. Delighted with the performance, the ladies, with much giggling and whispering, compare their
impressions.

Soon the novelty wears off and they demand to see more. The
shopkeeper beckons to the assistant who returns with a long pole
at the end of which dangles a bunch of miniature dolls representing the range of the stock. As the pole is lowered, so that the
figures dance under their noses, the shopkeeper requests the pleasure of their selection. Their deliberations are interrupted by a
party of new arrivals.

First, an American with a wealth of side-whisker, sporting a
loud suit of brown checks; his wife, a frigid, overbearing lady in
yellow crinoline; and their two children—a little boy in grey Nor-
folk suit and brown gaiters, and a little girl in a light blue frock,
trimmed with ruchings of dark blue silk. Evidently the two
parties are well acquainted, for, ignoring the pressing attentions
of the shopkeeper, the old ladies go forward to meet them, bowing
and shaking hands with the parents and embracing the children
with much kissing of both cheeks and friendly pats on the back.
Puffing at his pipe and affecting an air of a man of the world, the
American instructs the shopkeeper to display his goods so that he
may judge if they are worthy of purchase.

Meanwhile the two children, chaperoned by the two old ladies,
are taken to see the two dolls. They go into raptures over the
figures, finger their dresses, feel their limbs, and implore the assistant to set them going. Again the figures perform their dance.
Recalled by their parents, the two children sit down with them,
for the dancing peasants are nothing to the feats of mechanical
ingenuity that are about to follow.

With knowing smiles and nods of the head the shopkeeper
instructs his two porters to bring in the Tarantella dancers. The
porters disappear, and return wheeling a light trolley on which are
rigidly posed two figures: an Italian peasant girl attired in short

stays and an ample silk skirt of the national colours, and her lover
a bronzed youth in tightly-fitting grey trousers, white shirt, and
red cap. The customers rise quickly from their seats to inspect
the dolls, while the shopkeeper enlarges on their beauties. As the
company resume their seats there is a rattle and jingle of tambourines, the dolls step to the floor and break into a lively Tarantella.
The youth clasps his sweetheart's waist whirling her round and
round. Then they circle about each other, their arms alternately
flung into the air. They face about, rest their arms behind their
backs, and advance and retire with quick steps. Suddenly they
fall to the ground on one knee, their bodies arched and one hand
curved back over their heads. The spring has run down; their
performance is at an end.

While the porters are occupied in replacing the dancers upon
the trolley and removing them to the interior of the shop, the
mischievous children, excited by the dance, seize the maiden ladies,
pull them off their chairs, and whirl them round in imitation of
the dolls, then, releasing the hot and indignant victims, breathless
from the unwonted exercise, they excitedly embrace and return to
their seats, restlessly swinging their legs while their parents sternly
reprove them for their naughtiness.

The porters reappear with four new dolls, attired as court cards,
in red, blue, and yellow. They represent the Queen of Clubs, the
Queen of Hearts, the King of Spades, and the King of Diamonds.
Again the customers rise from their seats to crowd round the
new arrivals, the parents and the two ladies inspecting the quality
of the materials, the children rapturously clasping their hands in
delight at the brilliantly-coloured skirts of the queens and the
twirling moustaches of the kings. They resume their seats and
await the performance.

With mechanical precision the four figures step to the lively
strains of a mazurka. The dance begins in a grandiose manner
with such stately bows and sweeping curtseys as befit the counter-
feits of royalty. Now they form partners, then, again quickly
dividing, cross and recross with bewildering rapidity. The dance
is continually accelerated until finally they whirl round and round
and, as the kings drop on one knee and carry their partner's hand
to their lips, the movement is arrested. The porters come forward, raise the kings to their feet, and the four figures are removed
from sight.

During this performance the customers display ample proof of
their appreciation. The children rock on their chairs, swinging
their legs and clapping their hands in sheer delight; the American,

who till now has maintained a languid air of boredom, sticks his fingers in his arm-holes and leans back, beating time with his pipe, while the ladies bounce up and down in their seats, as if they themselves were mechanical dolls.

A slow stately march intimates the arrival of a new party of customers: a Russian merchant, a gigantic bearded man in long fur coat and top boots; his wife, a stout lady in ample blue crinoline, her shoulders covered by a gaudy yellow shawl; and their four daughters in traditional furred costume. He carries one of the children whom he now sets down, mopping his brow with evident relief. Their presence is ill received by the other customers, particularly by the maiden ladies who announce their departure, and endeavour to induce their friends to accompany them. Failing in this they leave by themselves, expressing by their manner the loftiest disdain.

Now the porters return with one of those curious combination toys, which aim at uniting in a single toy two or more figures which not only each possess a distinct movement of their own, but are grotesquely opposed in costume and station. In the present instance, it consists of a snob, the acme of fashion in his smart grey suit, tall top-hat, flowered buttonhole and waxed moustache, behind whom stands a quaint figure in green coat and brown trousers, half valet, half gardener, who wheels before him a barrow upon which is displayed a stock of melons.

At a signal from the shopkeeper they are set in motion to the tinkle of a musical box. The snob nods his head, jerks his hands, and propels himself by a quaint sideway swing of his legs which causes him to slide forward on his toes; behind him runs his companion with the barrow. The latter takes a knife and cuts a slice of melon which he hands to his master, who eats it in a manner suggesting the playing of a mouth-organ, while the hawker busies himself in pretended brushing of his boots. Now the snob replaces the melon slice, and, as the hawker obediently follows with his barrow, nearly running over him, he falls to the ground in pretended dismay. He springs up into the air, turns round and round, and, as his feet touch the floor, he comes to rest with one hand raised in the action of twisting his moustache. The performance is at an end. Again the porters come forward and while one carries off the snob in his arms the other wheels away the hawker.

Mutually pleased with the exhibition, the two parties of customers become more friendly in their manner, and, while the grown-ups exchange polite greetings, the children, laughing, shouting, dancing, and imbued with the spirit of escapade, dash hither and thither on a tour of inspection. Suddenly they espy a green sheet draped over a collection of figures whose angular outlines suggest the possibility of further dolls. With youthful inquisitiveness they draw back the cover to see—a slender regiment of six cossacks. Shouting and pointing them out to their parents they insist on seeing them work. Amused at their eagerness the shopkeeper instructs his assistant to bring out the toy soldiers.

Magnificent in their green and red uniforms, with their officer in bright blue at their head, they march with true military precision. Each carries a rifle—represented by a short stick—with which they perform their exercises. They kneel, spring to attention, about-turn with the ease of veterans. They double, point their sticks, and pretend to shoot. Then, as they shoulder arms, marking time with exaggerated shaking of the head and raising of the knees, the officer is joined by a pretty Cossack girl who steps to his side with the liveliest animation. He clasps her waist and for a few minutes the lovers dance together, the soldiers behind them twirling their sticks with incredible facility. Now the officer snatches a kiss from his sweetheart, and, as her head appropriately falls on his breast, the whole party comes smartly to attention. The porters walk forward and, causing each figure to take a right turn, march them to the interior of the shop.

Now the shopkeeper and his assistant lead forward by the ears a pair of dancing poodles, who, in the manner of performing animals, walk upright on their hind legs. The first is a big male dog, so closely shaved that his pink skin is far more in evidence than his woolly head and the narrow bracelets of white curls around his middle and his limbs, which are all that remains of his original covering. He is a quiet, self-satisfied animal in sharp contrast to the playful animated female that leaps and paws behind him. She bounds in front of him and endeavours to attract attention by throwing back her head and lifting up her hind leg so high that the two almost meet. Excited by this display, the white dog jumps into the air, shakes his fore-paws, scratches the ground, and voices his delight in short gruff barks. Finally he wildly dances round her and they come to a standstill.

During this exhibition the American and his wife, ever careful of their high moral standard, bandage their unwilling children's eyes that they may not be aware that the same passions regulate the lives of lower animals as those of human beings.

With the departure of the dogs the shopkeeper announces that he has but one more toy to exhibit, but this is his finest work, a triumph of mechanical resource and ingenuity. He beckons to the porters who wheel into the shop a pair of Can-Can dancers. The man is a dark youthful rake, dapper to an exaggerated degree, in a tight-fitting cut-away coat and trousers of black velvet, check waistcoat, and patent shoes, while his crimped and curled glossy hair, pomaded side-whiskers and curling moustache, would excite the envy of a barber's model. His companion is a dainty little lady in a pale blue bodice and short white skirt, fringed with black lace which ill conceals a wealth of lace petticoat, adorned with bows of blue ribbon.

They slip to the floor and advance on one foot, the other raised in the air, twisting, turning, pointing to the lively air of the Can-Can. Now they separate, confront, and retreat from each other. The man flaps his hands, throws back his head, falls forward on his toes, balances himself with a swift backward spring of his body. The lady alternately flings into the air each leg, which writhes, twists, turns, revolves amid a foaming sea of lace and ribbon. They retreat, turn their back on each other, and, while the lady flaunts her petticoats in mischievous abandon, the gentleman, alternately posed on each foot, throws himself backwards with such verve that his body almost assumes the horizontal.

Now each extends a leg and, supporting it with outstretched hand, they perform a dazzling series of pirouettes. Suddenly the man falls to the floor and as the lady dances round, continually whirling a leg over his head, he lowers his eyes and flaps his hands in mock horror at her naughtiness. He rises; there is a brief repetition of the Can-Can and the lady falls to the ground in a magnificent *écartement*. He quickly leaps to her side and as he whispers in her ear the figures become rigid and the performance comes to an end.

The toy achieves an enormous success. The two American children behave like imps of mischief, the boy anxious to pull up his mother's dress, the girl kicking up her legs in imitation of the dancer. Even the stolid American, despite the severe expression of his wife, raises his eyebrows and watches the dancer with ill-disguised interest. For a few moments the shop is a veritable pandemonium. The Russian children are vociferous in their entreaties that their father will buy them the little lady, while the other children are equally insistent in their demands that their parents will purchase the splendid gentleman. The heads of the two families enquire the price, but the shopkeeper, by no means anxious to part with his treasures, demands a heavy sum. After some consultation the purchase is effected. Each indulgent father withdraws a bulging pocket-book and the notes are counted out one by one. The children, impressed with the value of their new toy, carefully dust and smooth the clothes of the figures. The porters arrive with their cylindrical boxes and pack up the dolls, placing them on each side of the entrance to the shop.

Pleased with their purchases the two families arrange to call for them in the morning and depart their separate ways. As the children file out, each secure in the belief that their own doll is the best, they express their contempt by making faces and rudely putting out their tongues.

Enchanted with this fine stroke of business, the shop-keeper and his assistant waltz round the room, kissing and rubbing their hands, and chuckling with delight. Now they clear away the chairs, draw the blinds, lock up the gates and depart for the night.

*

It is the dolls' hour, the hour when they forsake the darkness of their homes, those pent-up boxes in which they live.

The music becomes sad and wistful, as if expressing the parting of the lovers, who, having found two purchasers, must for ever be separated. From each side glides a group of toy ballet-dancers, altogether charming in their white skirts trimmed with red bows, their arms linked overhead in a graceful curve. As the two groups approach they form a single line, crossing and recrossing, to rest now and again poised on one foot, one hand pressed to their lips. Again they melt into one glorious arch of interlaced arms.

A burst of triumphant music heralds the arrival of the cossacks, who crouch and spring into the air again and again. They divide into pairs, and arrange their sticks to form a series of horizontal bars. Now comes the snob who dashes up to the bars and swings himself over each in turn. Follow the two poodles, bounding and leaping, succeeded by the Tarantella dancers, who merrily stamp across the room, while the court cards bring up the rear.

The melon-hawker comes forward with quaint, mechanical strides, and releases the lady Can-Can dancer from her box, then guides her to her friends. She performs a little *variation,* slowly pirouetting with an air of sadness as if oppressed with the terrible thought of separation from her lover. At the end of the dance she falls on one knee with her arms curved above her head.

But now some noise disturbs them, for the dolls huddle together for safety, then softly tip-toe up and down the room, straining their ears to catch the slightest sound. Again seized with fright they dash into the interior of the shop, followed by the gentleman Can-Can dancer who has slipped out of his box.

For a few moments all is quiet, the scene is empty. Now the ballet-dancers tip-toe back into the shop, and the Can-Can dancer reappears bearing his sweetheart on his shoulders. He crosses the room with quick strides then bends to the ground to enable her to step to the floor. She pirouettes and falls on to his knee. The cossacks enter in single file, followed by the ballet-dancers, winding slowly about the lovers; then, falling on their knees, they raise the lady on crossed sticks, higher and higher, so that as the dancers rise with outstretched arms one is reminded of a pistil rendered visible by the opening petals of a flower in bloom. Now, held above their heads, she resembles some classic goddess, some Venus enthroned. Gliding forward on tip-toe the dancers escort her to the interior of the shop.

Her lover re-enters with quick, short strides. For a moment he remains posed—a magnificent silhouette—in a listening attitude, then he calls his friends. It is the signal for the cake-walk, the dance that concludes the evening's frolic. The shop is quickly filled with delighted dolls stepping gaily to the syncopated music —heads thrown back, hands flapping, knees jerked high in the air. Flowing into three lines, up and down the room they go, passing so quickly that it is impossible to tell where they end and where they begin.

Now the re-united lovers, the Tarantella dancers, and the poodles fall out and step to the front, still dancing merrily. For a moment the dance is arrested as they gaily clap their hands. Again they whirl in frenzied movement when suddenly the principal dancers proceed into the interior of the shop. The remaining dolls form a circle, and, as they slowly revolve, the ballet-dancers swing backwards on their partners' arms, indulging in a display of high-kicking. Now they divide into pairs, each ballet-dancer escorted by a cossack. They form two lines and, as the cossacks fall on one knee, the dancers step up and lean back on their shoulders, pointing one leg stiffly in the air. They jump down and dash out of the room.

*

With the approach of dawn the shop gradually lightens. The gates swing back on their hinges and there appear the shopkeeper and his assistant, who, yawning and lazily stretching his arms, begins to draw back the curtains.

The shop is hardly opened when the two families arrive to collect their dolls. Bowing and scraping, the shopkeeper and his assistant whisk off the boxes to reveal—nothing! There is a moment of amazement, then the indignant and furious customers spring on the unfortunate youth and his master. Bowed down under the fierce blows of the enraged Russian merchant, the poor old man is subjected to the swishing cuts of the American's stick. The assistant is in a terrible plight, the centre of a swarm of vindictive children, who, pushing him to the ground, kick and stamp on him to their heart's content. Leaving their victims to rub ruefully their aching backs and bruised limbs, they break into the interior of the shop, bent on the destruction of the dolls. Here, however, an unpleasant surprise awaits them, for the wife of the Russian merchant speedily returns, pursued by the two poodles, who bite and snap at her dress, while the snob subjects her to his unwelcome embraces. The American children are seized by the two porters, flung across their knees and soundly spanked. The Russian merchant and his daughters are assailed by the court cards, while the American and his wife retire before the shockingly high kicks of the ballet-dancers, and, as the cossacks return in a semblance of a dashing bayonet charge, the whole party is driven out of the shop.

Peeping in at the broad windows, the dishevelled customers witness a strange sight, for the dolls are gathered together in two groups, dancing in triumph, while the Can-Can dancers congratulate the delighted shopkeeper; then, as their legs fly into the air in three high kicks, the curtain falls.

*

La Boutique Fantasque is based on an old German ballet, for which the music was written by Bayer. It was also given at St. Petersburg with new choreography by Sergey and Nicholas Legat, and, some years ago, the ballet was revived by Anna Pavlova under the title of *The Fairy Doll*, with herself in the title-role. This production had a setting by Dobuzhinsky and choreography by Ivan Clustine, and was presented with considerable success at the Forty-fourth Street Theatre, New York. Later, the ballet was given a new setting by Sudeikin and added to the repertory of the Pavlova Company. In the Diaghilev version only the outline of the original theme was retained; the new ballet differed in every other respect.

Of first importance was the music; the old score of Bayer was replaced by an arrangement of little-known, but delightful fresh and piquant, compositions of Rossini. It will be recalled that after the success of *William Tell*, the composer deserted music, almost entirely, for the space of forty years. His life was divided between

Florence and the Parisian suburb of Passy. In the latter town he maintained a boundless hospitality. He gave epicurean banquets which often concluded with a concert. Youthful composers rendered their works for the approval of the master who on particular days would grace the company with a performance of his own compositions written for the occasion. Diaghilev found a number of these pieces collected in an album bearing the disarming inscription *"Les Riens"*. The gaiety of these numbers is reflected in their titles, for instance: *Four Hors-d'Oeuvre; Radishes, Anchovies, Gherkins, and Butter themes in variations"*, *"Almonds"*, *"Abortive Polka"*, *"Castor Oil"*, and *"Capriccio Offenbachique"*, which last supplies the air for the famous Can-Can dance.

The scenery and costumes were assigned to André Derain. This was a marked development for, in contra-distinction to the rich, glowing and barbaric colours of the Russian painters, Derain employed the most restful of hues.

Massine's choreography was founded on a critical study of the period of 1865, and the drawings and lithographs of Toulouse-Lautrec.

I have recorded some of my impressions of the stages leading up to the first performance and now invite the reader to accompany me behind the scenes.

At the Alhambra Theatre, recently demolished, situated between the left-hand side of the stage and the dressing-rooms, was a small, rectangular, and low-ceilinged apartment to which access was gained by a short flight of steps. This room served as auxiliary property-store, office, and green-room. It was here that members of the directorate used to repair during the intervals between the ballets. The furniture was simple: a large mirror and two small tables at the far end of the room; a large table in the centre and a few chairs. At one of the smaller tables it was usual to see the conductor Ansermet running through the score of some ballet. He would mark time with one upraised hand and with the other he would swiftly turn the leaves, while he hummed the melody which he emphasised with an excellent imitation of the various types of musical instrument represented. Another evening there would be the other conductor Defosse; slight in figure, dark, clean-shaven, with his hair worn *en casque*. He was dapper, quiet, and had the dreamy pre-occupation of a poet.

At a corner of the centre table was the stage manager, Grigoriev, discussing business details with Diaghilev. The former was tall, spare, with a high forehead, pale face, and sad eyes. The latter was majestic, imposing, with iron-grey hair and the suspicion of a white lock that recalled Whistler's self-portrait. But there the resemblance ended; the veiled, half-closed eyes that flickered to and fro, the air of mystery, of power, of infinite calm, suggested the attributes of an Oriental potentate.

It was on one of these occasions that Diaghilev informed me that the first few days in June (1919) would at last see the new ballet, for Massine had completed his choreography and Derain would shortly arrive in London to superintend the realisation of his designs. A little later I met the distinguished artist. In appearance he was as little like the popular conception of an artist as it is possible to be. He was fair, clean-shaven, very tall and broad, with a massive chest and shoulders and large hands. In dress he affected a broad-brimmed felt hat set at a jaunty angle, soft collar, loose jacket, wide trousers and heavy brown boots. He had the most delightful, unassuming manners and radiated the naïve good humour of a child.

He was very secretive in regard to his work. Whenever he was asked for details he would reply, *A bientôt, vous verrez des choses merveilleuses*. But one night he offered to show his *projet* for the drop-curtain. Very solemnly he withdrew from his waistcoat pocket a minute, folded piece of paper. He laid it on the table and slowly opened it, carefully pressing out each fold with the air of a conjuror engaged in a difficult feat of legerdemain. At last the paper was opened out and in the centre, hardly more than an inch square, were a few lines covered with a wash of Venetian red. When he saw the blank looks on the eager faces about him, he laughed with glee at the success of his little trick.

As the eagerly awaited date approached, the room received new properties—a barrow filled with green melons, a wooden knife and a long pole to which was attached a collection of varied dolls. It is hardly necessary to state how these novel objects excited one's imagination.

On the first performance every seat had been taken and the promenades filled to overflowing. Everywhere one looked, there was the same shimmer of white faces, now and again rendered hazy by the smoke from lighted cigarettes which rose upward like incense burnt in honour of some goddess of ancient mythology.

The first ballet was *L'Oiseau de Feu*, yet, although Lopokova danced the title-role, the performance received but moderate applause. It was plain that everyone had eyes and ears only for *La Boutique Fantasque*.

Behind the scenes there was a sense of nervous calm. Derain was passing in review the dancers as they emerged from their dressing-rooms. He was very particular on the subject of make-up and each artiste had placed on his or her table a tiny sketch showing what was required. There was a shout of *orchestre!* and, to the shrill scraping of bows, Defosse threaded his way through the musicians to his seat. Three metallic raps of his baton on the iron frame of his desk and there commenced the lively pizzicato notes of the *Marche Slav* which forms the overture. The heavy curtain swung upwards to reveal the drop-curtain. The naïve treatment of the two figures posed against the broad masses of harmonious reds and browns recalled the decoration of an early Victorian pencil-box. One received an impression of complete, all-satisfying joy. One felt conscious of that youthful, delicious happiness experienced when on a seaside holiday one takes off one's shoes and stockings and paddles in the sea.

The drop-curtain rose and there was the shop, bathed in the warm sunlight that streamed through the windows. The customers arrived and the dolls were brought out and set in motion. The applause was unceasing. It came in volleys of hand-claps, of stamps of the feet, which died away only to be renewed with greater vigour. When the Can-Can dancers appeared there were shouts of "Lopokova!" "Massine!"

The ballet was a complete success. But when the collaborators came forward to take a call, Derain was frightened at the warmth of his welcome and had to be dragged upon the stage; Massine made repeated graceful bows; while Lopokova, half-laughing, half-crying, seemed divided between sadness and delight.

The *Boutique* has been a favourite with audiences the world ever since its inception. The reason is not hard to find, for the ballet is so replete with good humour, joy, and happiness that it pleases both the serious devotee of dancing and the seeker after amusement. The quiet, harmonious scenery, the simple sparkling melodies of another age that better understood the difficult art of enjoyment of life, and the merry dances of the artistes, set free those memories of youth which lie, however deeply concealed, in the heart of every spectator.

From the purely choreographic standpoint the ballet has not the artistic merit of *Les Femmes de Bonne Humeur* or *Le Tricorne,* but the dolls' dances go with a swing, the *ensembles* are well contrived, and the finale is excellent. The best composed dances are that of the Snob and the Melon-Hawker, originally created and admirably rendered by Idzikowsky and Kostetsky, and the Can-Can Dance executed by Lopokova and Massine.

Lopokova was delightful. Her resemblance to a doll was extraordinary. It was a totally different conception from the angular, stiffly-jointed puppet of the Dancer in *Petrouchka*. Her rounded limbs, pale face, full cheeks, curved pouting lips, and innocent expression recalled one of those china dolls so beloved by children of the Victorian era.

Not only was the resemblance complete; her every action, her every pose, were subordinated to the demands of the character. She danced with incredible precision and verve. She flaunted her petticoats in the most mischievous abandon and, without altering the expression of her features, contrived to convey by the pose of her head and arms, the fleeting emotions of disdain, surrender, coquetry, and pique.

Massine was equally superb. He danced with all that sinuous, cat-like grace and seemingly india-rubber limbs which history has accorded to the notorious Valentin le Désossé, and radiated a sinister raffishness which at once suggested a background of gas-lit globes and the glare of chandeliers reflected in countless mirrors.

The *Boutique* has been revived by the De Basil Company where it continues its triumphant course, but it has not the bouquet of the ballet I first saw eighteen years ago. The Tarantella Dancers have not the fire of Sokolova and Woizikowsky; the Court Cards have not the crispness of that first hand; the Snob is still good when rendered by Shabelevsky; but, although Massine still dances in the Can-Can, it is not the same without Lopokova.

How many of her successors in that role have I seen—Karsavina, Nemchinova, Danilova, Zorina, to mention a few names only—but not one of them can recapture for me that delicious piquant blend of ingenuousness and naughtiness which was Lopokova's creation, that—dare I say it?—entrancing suggestion of the innocent doll who had momentarily taken the wrong turning, which went to one's head like a glass of sparkling champagne.

LE TRICORNE [4]

Ballet in 1 Act. Book: Martinez Sierra. Music: Manuel de Falla. Choreography: Leonide Massine. Scenery and costumes: Pablo Picasso. First produced: Alhambra Theatre, London, July 22nd, 1919.

CHARACTERS

The Miller	M. LEONIDE MASSINE
The Miller's Wife . . .	MME. THAMAR KARSAVINA

[4] *The Three Cornered Hat.*

The Corregidor . . . . M. Léon Woizikowsky
The Corregidor's Wife . . Mlle. Alanova
The Dandy . . . . . M. Stanislas Idzikowsky
Neighbours, Police, Peasants, Footmen, etc.

The ballet commences with a triumphant fanfare of trumpets, the motif similar to that which announces the *torero's* entrance during a performers' parade into the bull-ring, followed by slow, distinct, thunderous beats of a big drum. Suddenly the ears are startled by a roar of enthusiastically shouted *olés,* immediately succeeded by a burst of heel-tapping, and the crashing *tr-r-r-ra tak-ta* of lustily shaken castanets.

The curtain parts to reveal a grey drop-curtain which serves to frame a small rectangular picture set in its centre. The picture depicts a group of spectators in their box at a *corrida*. It is evidently the interval between the removal of one slain animal and the entrance of a newcomer, for there is just visible to the eye a group of gaily-caparisoned, galloping horses dragging a hurdle across the sanded floor of the arena.

Now is heard the plaintive melody of a distant chant which forewarns the approach of evil in the person of the devil. As the last trill dies away there is a renewed drumming of heels. Again the trumpets blare in a furious crescendo. They cease—the big drum booms out once, twice, thrice—silence. The drop-curtain glides slowly upward.

Scene. A magnificent archway through which can be seen a semi-circular stone bridge; behind this lies a broad, flat plain crowned in the distance by the vague, angular outlines of a small village shadowed by two high mountains. To the left is a gorge and a few deep-toned houses. To the right is another house provided with a porch hung with a striped awning. By the side of the door is fixed a wooden cage which contains a black and white bird. Near to the house stands a well. Overhead burns a deep blue sky, and the white-washed walls of the houses gleam white under the fierce rays of the sun.

In front of the bird-cage stands the miller, a dark, bronzed youth clad in tight-fitting black trousers and short velvet waistcoat which serves to set off his open shirt, gaily-striped in blue and white. He is engaged in trying to teach the bird to sing. He places his hands on his head with the fore-fingers pointing stiffly upward and impatiently jerks his body back and back, as if in endeavour to drag out forcibly the required notes from the throat of the reluctant bird. Finding his efforts are productive only of discordant shrieks, he brings himself erect and stamps his feet in exasperation.

The music changes swiftly to a languorous melody, and from the rear of the house glides his wife, coquettish, insinuating, her body swaying with that soft rippling grace inherited from the Moors. She sweeps to and fro while her hands excitedly shake the rustling folds of her ample pink silk skirt, adorned with black lace and brilliant with iridescent sequins.

She playfully evades her husband's intended embrace and, smiling over her shoulder, tempts him to follow; so begins the merry comedy of escape and pursuit. They break into a dance to circle about each other and quickly pass and repass in the light, captivating steps of the *koradin*. Then, like children overflowing with high spirits, they run to the well and the miller busies himself in the drawing of a pail of water by the laboured turning of a loudly-creaking handle.

Across the bridge comes a gay young spark in coat and knee-breeches of spotless white faced with pale green satin, his cravat and cuffs adorned with a plentiful fall of black and white ribbons. His mischievous face is framed in a green wig crowned by a three-cornered hat. In one hand he carelessly trails the string of a low flying kite. As he catches sight of the miller's wife, he leans over the parapet of the bridge, presses his fingers to his lips, and throws her kiss after kiss.

Perceiving her spouse intent on his task, she accepts the compliment with a provocative smile and sideway tilt of the head, then she daintily raises her skirt ever so slightly and offers to his admiring gaze the entrancing spectacle of a well-turned ankle. Delighted at this favour, the young nobleman performs for her benefit a few steps of the *bolero*. He leaps upward, twists his hands outward, and swings his legs sideways in mid-air, then falls lightly to the ground and again leaps upward to swing his legs in the opposite direction.

Unhappily for the progress of this wordless flirtation the miller lifts down the pail, raises his head to make a remark, and perceives the situation. With a muttered exclamation, he dashes on to the bridge, but it is too late, for the young rascal gaily wafts a parting kiss and laughingly takes to his heels.

Unable to conceal his annoyance the miller stamps his feet with rage. The music changes to a slow, pompous march, and husband and wife shade their eyes and gaze intently in the direction of the sound. The music increases in volume and there enters a small procession composed of the Corregidor's wife, carried in a green and yellow sedan-chair supported by tall bewigged footmen, richly dressed in coat and breeches of red velvet. The rear is brought up by six alguacils or policemen, arrogant representatives of their master's power and authority, who march stiffly in double file, their arms folded upon their breasts. Their faces are white with powder which ill conceals the evil spots and lines that scar their cheeks, while their breeches and pleated cloaks, striped in black and yellow, give them the appearance of monstrous bats.

By the side of the sedan-chair hobbles the Corregidor himself, a vicious old gentleman in black satin, who alternately leers at his wife and feasts his gaze on the number of his servants. Seeing the miller's wife, who has drawn near to watch the unusual spectacle, he blinks his red-rimmed eyes and rudely quizzes her. Finding her greatly to his taste he bestows a meaning smile upon her and carelessly pretends to drop his handkerchief, which she, conscious only of the respect due to his rank, hastens to pick up and, with the accompaniment of a low curtsy, restore to him.

Delighted at this proof of submission he thanks her with an exaggerated bow and continues on his way, his mind already occupied in the devising of stratagems for her seduction. The procession passes from sight, followed for a short distance by the miller's wife.

Enter three of the miller's men who each bear on their shoulders a weighty sack of flour. The miller encourages them with amiable smile and friendly gesture until the supplies are carried safely into his storehouse.

Follows an attractive young girl who bears on her head a large pitcher. The miller, who seems no less susceptible than his wife to the charms of the opposite sex, pauses to bid her good-day and playfully chucks her under the chin. The girl smiles good-humouredly, upon which he dances round her. At this moment the wife returns. Enraged, she stamps her foot and shakes her skirt, then sobs on her arm and bewails his unfaithfulness. He is profuse in apologies, loads her with caresses until he is forgiven, and the episode is forgotten in a brief dance of reconciliation. The music soars upward on a brilliant scale and the miller runs into his house.

Left to herself his wife dances quickly to and fro with brisk little stamps of the feet. Now she extends her arms in a parallel line. They ripple, flow, and undulate while the fingers expand and close, at once repellent, warning, and inviting. Exulting in her skill she exerts herself to the utmost, little dreaming that she has an audience in the person of the Corregidor, who watches intently from the far side of the gorge. In one hand he holds an ebony cane with which he softly taps the ground in time to the measure; in the other he holds a lace handkerchief, which he continually presses to his lips to stifle the delighted chuckles that follow each swaying of her hips, each flash of rounded arm, each palpitation of her breasts. The music increases, and now her hands beat swiftly in counter-time, then her petticoats whirl upward in a pirouette and she falls to the ground on one knee.

The Corregidor departs only to re-appear at the near side of the gorge. He advances, greets her with a sweeping bow, and compliments her upon her performance; then he playfully pats her cheek and begs the honour of her company in a few steps of the *menuet.* Flattered at such gracious approval she smilingly consents. The old roué, anxious to please, glides backward and forward, flings back his head, and flutters his coat-tails in the most distinguished manner.

But the miller's wife soon tires of the slow and ceremonious measure and, running to the bird-cage, takes a bunch of grapes and invites him to join her in a dance, which has its counterpart in the old English dance of "bob-apple". So she steps to and fro dangling the grapes from her outstretched hand while the Corregidor, with hands placed behind his back, vainly essays to bite it. Now the dance enters on another phase when the Corregidor turns his back to her, and, with head tilted backward, strives again to bite the fruit held so tantalisingly beyond his reach. Desirous of making greater effort, he throws back his head still further, only to lose his balance and fall heavily to the ground. Groaning with pain he rolls feebly from side to side. The miller appears, runs to the help of his wife, and together they succeed in raising him to his feet. The husband, who has doubtless watched the whole of the proceedings from the concealment of his house, makes no pretence at withholding his pleasure at the Corregidor's discomfiture, and, jumping with glee, the miller and his wife snap their fingers in derision and turn their backs upon him. The Corregidor perceives that he has been the butt for their fun and departs in a terrible rage, shaking his fists, and swearing speedy vengeance.

They pay little heed to his threats and leap high in the air. The purring of the castanets falls on the ear and they launch themselves into the opening movements of the *fandango.* They tease, entreat, and pursue each other by turns. They whirl about each other, faster and faster. Suddenly the miller drops to the ground on one knee. He maintains his stooping position and bounds from side to side. Again he leaps to his feet, and again the couple revolve, pass and repass in rapid *traversias*. Their eyes gleam, droop, and flash up again like an expiring flame. Each time they face, their legs sweep forward and upward, the jacket flaps, the shawl writhes, and the skirt rustles and flutters in the breeze of their movements. All is a madness of rhythmic animation—seductive, fiercely passionate, inflaming. *Olé! Olé!* Now their feet beat in time to the measure, louder and louder, faster and faster—suddenly they both fall to the ground on one knee, each with an arm flung aloft to curve gracefully above the head. *Olé! Olé! Bien parado!*

As they rise to their feet, newcomers enter upon the scene. First, three girls in ample dresses, striped pale-blue and black, accompanied by three men in red and one in blue and white. The miller and his wife greet each with a pleasant smile and low bow. Now come other friends, girls in white and green, men in blue and brown. The afternoon is to be devoted to a *festa,* for all are dressed in their best.

Four of the men commence to enliven proceedings with a burst of reverberating heel-taps. Fired by their example another quartette, composed of two girls and two men, step briskly to a quick measure. Now the whole company dispose themselves in two long lines, a necessary preparation for the execution of the *sevillianas,* the classic dance of Andalusia.

The opening measures consist of turns, advances, and retreats performed in a grand and majestic manner to the *tr-tr-tr* of castanets. Gradually the movement increases in speed and the arms move in simple opposition; the left extended in a line with the shoulder as the right falls across the chest, then, as the right arm leaps above the head, the left forearm falls across the back. The dance concludes with a pirouette and each falls to the ground on one knee with one hand curved above the head.

They smooth their clothes and sit in a semi-circle. The miller's wife advances, holding in her hands a heavy black shawl which she swings from side to side, then with a quick upward sweep of her arms she causes it to wind about her head and shoulders.

Meanwhile, the miller goes into the house and returns bearing on his head a large bundle tied up in a white sheet. He sets it down, unties the knot, and takes out a supply of cups and a distended wine-skin. The cups are filled and distributed among the guests. His wife unwinds the shawl and takes her place among her friends. The miller holds the wine-skin in his hands, lifts it to his lips, and takes a deep draught. Then he flings it to the ground, draws himself erect and commences the fiery movements of the *farucca*.

He slowly snaps his fingers and moves forward with little, brisk steps—each advance punctuated by a resounding thump of the feet. Now he winds one hand about the other while his feet crash to each beat of the measure. The pace quickens—he leaps—revolves in mid-air—crashes to the ground with another savage stamp of the feet. He swings on one foot alternately to right and left, then raises the free foot to slap the heel sharply with the palm of each open hand. He whirls in a swift pirouette, falls to the ground on his hands, and a second later leaps to his feet. The movement slows and he holds his hands parallel to his chest, the palms facing, the fingers slightly parted. Now he turns slowly on one foot and gradually raises and lowers his hands with a plaintive fluttering of the fingers. Again the measure increases in speed—bursts into fiery rhythm. He moves with short convulsive bounds—forward —backward—forward—backward—the street echoes to the swift chop of his feet as they continually strike the ground. One of his friends, with ever-quickening hand-claps, urges him to still greater efforts. So he leaps—faster—faster—the stamps grow louder— louder—the frenzy of rhythm quickens the pulse—fires the blood —a sudden deafening thud of the feet and the miller stops dead —quivering, breathless, streaked with sweat. *Olé! Olé! Bien parado!*

The guests rise and congratulate the miller on his prowess while some of the more adventurous spirits dash hither and thither in simulated reproduction of a *capea*. The afternoon passes quickly in such pleasant diversions and soon the light fades and darkness overshadows the scene. It is time for the guests to depart. Again the cups are filled and raised in a parting toast when there falls on the ear the menacing, staccato stamp of swiftly-marching feet. The company lower their cups and gaze at each other in amazement. What can be abroad at such an hour?

The question is soon answered by the entrance of the Corregidor's repulsive henchmen. With all the overbearing insolence of the petty official they push their way through the astonished guests and surround the miller. One of their leaders confronts him, and, with a swift jerk of his wrist, unrolls a warrant for his arrest, which he maliciously dangles before his frightened eyes. The miller trembles and shakes in every limb and seems bereft of his reason. Hemmed in by the hideous, striped cloaks he can only see the white parchment which authorises the seizure of his person. He pleads piteously for an explanation. That is none of their business. His wife, distracted by this bitter end to their holiday, makes a despairing effort at rescue, only to be pushed roughly aside. Then the policemen close about their prisoner and bear him away. In sorrow the miller's friends take their departure.

The moon rises to bathe the bridge in cold, grey-green shadow and to illumine the drawn face of the miller's wife. Her features reflect with unmistakable clarity the conflicting thoughts that flee through her mind—the desire for vengeance and the anguish of fear for her husband's fate.

Emotion follows emotion with lightning rapidity. Now the nostrils dilate and the eyebrows contract in a vengeful frown, now the eyes half-close as if filled with tears. Again is heard the poignant chant which, like Dodon's cockerel, forewarns of the approach of danger. The miller's wife walks slowly to and fro, tears at her skirts and stamps the ground in impotent rage, then sorrow wells up in her throat and she falls on her knees and buries her face in her hands.

The humorous theme employed to mark the Corregidor's entrance is heard again and a muffled figure appears on the bridge, who moves with so insolent an air and so complacent a swagger as to leave little doubt concerning his identity. Half-way across, he flings off his cloak, lays it on the parapet and continues on his way with short mincing steps.

Hearing the patter of footsteps the miller's wife quickly rises and wheels round to find herself face to face with the Corregidor.

Unabashed, he greets her with an ingratiating smile and elaborate bow, and begs the honour of her company in a *menuet*. With an angry gesture she intimates that she will have nothing to do with him. He pursues her relentlessly with specious argument and whining avowals, while she continually stamps her feet with rage and draws her skirts about her as if his contact would defile them. Distracted with the fever of his passion, the Corregidor becomes forgetful of his rank, his birth, even of his manhood, and drags himself after her on his hands and knees, crawls in the dust, willing to undergo any humiliation if only she will listen to his entreaties.

Disgusted and irritated at this degrading spectacle the miller's wife seeks escape by running on to the bridge. The Corregidor struggles to his feet and totters after her. Now, greatly daring, he endeavours to clasp her waist, but she savagely shakes herself free and gives him so fierce a push that he overbalances and falls with a resounding splash into the river below.

Forgetful of her fears she rushes to the parapet, extends her arms, and assists him to clamber back to safety. Then she retraces her steps and gives vent to her delight in peal on peal of laughter as she repeatedly surveys the miserable, bedraggled, dripping figure that limps disconsolately in her wake.

Arrived in front of the house the Corregidor, maddened at his plight and the continued set-back to his desires, resolves upon more forceful measures. He quickly throws his arms about her, but with a sudden movement she disengages herself and, with a scornful glance, moves away. Undaunted, the old *roué* follows at her heels as fast as his tottering limbs will permit, until at last he has her fast in his arms. Now several peasants glide upon the bridge, interested spectators of the struggle below. Resisting with all her might she forces his arms apart and twists from his grasp. Then, thoroughly alarmed for her safety, she rushes to the house, snatches up a musket that hangs by the door, points the muzzle at her persecutor, and thus effectually bars his pursuit while she walks backward through the gorge.

The Corregidor, no longer buoyed up with the excitement of the chase, begins to reflect seriously on the consequences of his rashness. His limbs tremble from the strain of the unwonted exercise, his teeth chatter as a result of his unlucky immersion. Cursing his folly he takes off his dripping hat and laboriously frees his arms from his sodden coat. He shakes the clothes and hangs them up to dry. Then he puts on the miller's coat, which is suspended from a nail, pulls aside the striped awning, and wearily throws himself on to the miller's bed.

Across the bridge comes the miller, evidently escaped from his captors. He notices the striped cloak, stops short, takes it up, and makes his way to his house. Hearing the footsteps the Corregidor totters to his feet, to see to his horror the vengeful, grinning face of the miller. As the latter sees the cause of his troubles he waves the cloak in the manner of a *torero* and baits him like a bull. He dashes the cloak into his face, winds it about his head, forces him to the ground, and proceeds to kick and trample upon him to his full content.

Then he circles about the prostrate figure and triumphantly dances the grotesque steps of the *chuflas*. His face distorted in a malevolent grin, his body is arched and rocks from side to side, his hands loudly slap his muscular thighs. He makes his way to the near side of the house and scribbles on the wall: *Your wife is no less beautiful than mine.* Then he snatches up the wet clothes as a trophy and blithely takes his departure.

Aching in every limb and groaning with pain the Corregidor struggles to his feet. Then he notices the writing on the wall which he anxiously reads. As the significant meaning of the lines dawns upon his dazed brain he claps his hands to his ears in dismay, falls on his knees, and in utter misery bangs his head upon the ground.

Suddenly he hears the noise of running feet. He is seized with panic at the thought of his appearance—his breeches stained with water and soiled with mud; the rough brown cloth and ridiculous pompoms of the miller's coat. In despair, he returns to bed just as his myrmidons enter, enraged at the loss of their prisoner. They dash up to the house, push aside the awning and drag out the wretched inmate. Heedless of his protestations, they force him into their midst and assault him with insults, kicks, and blows of their fists. Felled to his knees, he unavailingly beseeches, begs, prays for mercy and recognition.

And now the reunited couple return, accompanied by their friends. The husband and wife quickly thread their way through the astonished policemen, and, before the latter have recovered from their surprise, the Corregidor is the recipient of another stream of blows. The crowd becomes more and more menacing, and finally so threatening, that, fearing for their own safety, the policemen depart in haste, dragging in their midst the once splendid, now battered, stiff, and unconscious figure of their master.

From all quarters come the villagers eager to celebrate the downfall of the Corregidor and his despotic sway. Bounding idiots with hair and beards of enormous length; beggars; old crones who, despite their crutches, contrive to swing themselves in the semblance of a dance; then the dandy who bears on his shoulder the stuffed effigy of the Corregidor; finally a procession of peasants headed by a banner scrawled with a rude caricature.

The castanets, now suspended from the two middle fingers, ring out with their pulse-quickening *tok-tok-tok,* and the company surge to and fro in the broad, rolling movements of the *jota.* The eye is dazzled with the flash of bare arms and twinkle of white petticoats, bewildered by the crossing and recrossing of the striped costumes; the ear echoes to the rhythmic stamping of feet and the clatter of castanets; and the joyous lilt of the melody sweeps upward like a mighty wave—pauses for an instant—and again soars. The effigy is thrown away, to be picked up and tossed in a blanket so that it ever bounds and rebounds to a greater height—the miller's wife and two of her friends are hoisted in triumph on stalwart shoulders—and the reign of the three-cornered hat is at an end.

*

Diaghilev had long meditated the production of a Spanish ballet. The most obvious difficulty was the selection of a composer, but the choice would surely have been made from among Granados, Albeniz, Turina, or De Falla. It is possible that the last-named would have seemed the most suitable for two reasons. First, the production of De Falla's opera, *La Vida Breve,* proved him to possess a remarkable sense of dramatic values; second, Stravinsky had expressed so great an admiration for the composer's work as to baptise him the "Liadov of Spain".

When, during the War years, Diaghilev and his company arrived at Spain, after their tour in America, the director took immediate steps to make the composer's acquaintance. At their first meeting De Falla played the first part of a "pantomime" which he had written to a theme supplied by his friend, Martinez Sierra. Diaghilev suggested that he should adapt the score to the requirements of the dance, for though it had been produced already with considerable success under the title of *El Corregidor y la Molinera* at the Eslava Theatre, Madrid, the theme was so minutely expressed as to leave little or nothing to the art of the choreographer. De Falla consented to rearrange his composition and added the *Farucca* and also the magnificent *Jota,* which brings the ballet to its conclusion.

While engaged in collaboration, the director, composer, and Massine, anxious to obtain the correct atmosphere, paid a visit to the less-frequented parts of Andalusia. One night, as they walked in the streets, they encountered a blind man, chanting a melody to the accompaniment of a broken guitar, an episode which has its romance, for this same melody is recorded in the score of the ballet.

From the choreographer's point of view, Massine was enraptured with the grace, precision, and beauty of the native dances of Andalusia. He spent his evenings in out-of-the-way cafés, organised fetes, travelled here, there, and everywhere, and, in order to obtain a still more detailed knowledge of the movements comprised in the dances, caused them to be recorded by cinematography.

During a visit to Seville, Diaghilev visited a gypsy dance festival; one of the dancers, a youth known as Felix, impressed him greatly, although, when not dancing, he was of a sullen disposition, and even a little unbalanced. Diaghilev realised the boy's value as a source of material for his new ballet and engaged him to teach his steps to Massine. The youth assented eagerly, believing that he was to be the star of the production in preparation. When, later, he was disillusioned, the shock was such that he grew strange in his manner and ultimately became mentally deranged.

Such were the sources of the choreographic material. Massine had two courses open to him, to make an exact reproduction of the Spanish dance, or else employ it as a means of inspiration. He chose the second and more artistic course.

Le Tricorne is entitled to be called a masterpiece; it abounds in passion, colour, and comedy-action, and while there are charming *soli* and *pas de deux,* there are also excellently orchestrated *ensembles,* particularly the final *Jota.*

The theme by Martinez Sierra is based on the play, *El Sombrero de Tres Picos,* written by the Spanish poet, Pedro Antonio de Alarcon. Born in 1833 his life of fifty-eight years was divided between soldiering and writing, and the material of his tales is based largely upon personal experiences.

Picasso's scenery is admirable alike for its simplicity and the charm of its proportions. The costumes are not so happy. Many of them are based on the paintings of Goya, but the too-frequent introduction of the stripe as a decorative pattern tends to monotony and causes certain of the dancers to acquire an importance in the choreographic arrangement beyond their allotted role.

The music is conceived in a rare spirit of subtle wit and delicate satire, intensified with a deep, psychological insight. There can be few themes more expressive of feminine caprice and coquetry than those which illustrate the gestures of the miller's wife. Finally, the whole score is so impregnated with the spirit of humour that the music is humorous in itself. Consider the elfish fun contained in the theme that accompanies the brief flirtation between the dandy and the miller's wife; the laughter-provoking effect produced by the contrast between the courtly and graceful measure of the *menuet* and the Corregidor's version of the steps that should accompany it; and the merry, whimsical, swaggering air employed to mark the Corregidor's entrance. De Falla proves in such themes as these that music, which has been more or less restricted to the expression of passion and tragedy, is no less capable of interpreting the more widely diffused emotion of humour.

Karsavina, Massine, and Woizikowsky each made a considerable success in their respective roles of the Miller's Wife, the Miller, and the Corregidor.

Karsavina gave a brilliant performance from the viewpoints of both dancing and mime, and the only criticism that could be made is that she was perhaps too elegant for the part. Among her successors in the role may be mentioned Sokolova, Tchernicheva, and Toumanova. Of these the best was Tchernicheva.

Massine is magnificent as the Miller, a most difficult role with all its subtle variations and its several styles of dancing. In the Farucca he is superb and his dancing never fails to rouse the audience to the highest pitch of enthusiasm. Woizikowsky has danced this role on many occasions, but, although he gives an excellent performance, his interpretation lacks the sinuousness and subtlety of Massine's rendering.

Woizikowsky was at his best in the part of the Corregidor, which he danced and mimed with a fine appreciation of the various situations.

PULCINELLA

Ballet in 1 Act. Music: Igor Stravinsky-Giambattista Pergolesi. Curtain, scenery, and costumes: Pablo Picasso. Choreography: Leonide Massine. First produced: Théâtre National de l'Opéra, Paris, May 15th, 1920.

CHARACTERS

Pulcinella	M. LEONIDE MASSINE
Pimpinella	MME. THAMAR KARSAVINA
Prudenza	MME. LUBOV TCHERNICHEVA
Rosetta	MME. VERA NEMCHINOVA
Fourbo	M. SIGMUND NOVAK
Caviello	M. STANISLAS IDZIKOWSKY
Florindo	M. NICHOLAS ZVEREV
Il Dottore	M. ENRICO CECCHETTI
Tartaglia	M. STANISLAS KOSTETSKY
Four Little Pulcinellas . . .	MM. BOURMAN, OKHIMOV-SKY, MIKOLAICHIK, LUKINE

Scene. The entrance to a narrow street in Naples. It is night and the low full moon throws up the houses in sharp relief. The view is presented from an angle which permits the spectator to see two sides of the end house on the left. There are windows and two doors; the outer one gleams white in the moonlight, the inner is dark in shadow. The end house on the right is also in shadow. The street leads down to the water-side where in the foreground is a moored boat, and, in the distance, the vague outline of a volcanic mountain.

The music rises and falls in a plaintive melody and from the left enters Caviello, a gallant in plum-coloured doublet and white hose. He wears a white curly wig, crowned by a large feathered hat. With broad leaps and agile turns in the air he dances slowly round the square in front of the houses. Arrived again in front of the house to the left, wherein resides Rosetta, he bows low with an eloquent sweep of his hat, then falls on one knee, clasps his hands, and regards the window with intent gaze.

From the right side comes another gallant, his friend Florindo, similarly attired, but in blue. He too dances about the square and stops in front of the other house, the dwelling of Prudenza. He likewise expresses his love in courtly bows and imploring gestures of his outstretched arms.

At each window appear the objects of their infatuation: Rosetta, in pink, Prudenza, in green. They lean over the sills and contemplate their admirers with half-amused, half-disdainful smiles. Suddenly the ladies disappear, to return each with a pitcher, the contents of which they throw upon the unfortunate gallants below, who immediately withdraw in dismay. The ladies leave the windows.

From the right-hand house comes the old Doctor who is Prudenza's father. He is dressed in a fawn-coloured jacket, white breeches and stockings; on his head is perched a high black conical hat and in his hand he carries a stout stick. His wide-rimmed horn spectacles proclaim his shortsightedness, but his long protruding nose would imply an excellent liking for interfering in other people's business. He roundly upbraids the dishevelled gallants, and strikes at them with his stick. They easily escape his ill-directed blows and take to their heels while the old man stamps up and down after them in a paroxysm of rage. He then stalks away.

From the inner door of the left-hand house comes Pulcinella, a figure at once mysterious and attractive with his voluminous white blouse and trousers, red socks and tie, and sugar-loaf cap. His features are concealed by a close-fitting black half-mask. He takes off his cap with a flourish, replaces it, and, from the depths of his blouse, produces a small violin and bow. With frenzied glee he scrapes a lively air to which he executes a merry dance. He springs into the air, pirouettes, leaps on one foot, then on the other. He stamps one foot in time to the measure, kicks his feet out sideways, bounds upwards, twists to right and left, then moves in a circle with a slow dragging gait, while he takes the violin in one hand and whirls it up and down in a circular movement.

Again he emphasises the theme with a rhythmic stamp of his foot, then stops and throws away the violin.

Prudenza comes from her house and steps into the street. She tip-toes toward Pulcinella with winning smiles and gracefully extended arms. Pulcinella looks upwards and, with a protecting gesture towards his heart, implies that it is not for her. She tries to embrace him, but he slips from her grasp and turns his back on her. Again she pays him court, but he withdraws with a shrug of his shoulders. She pursues him, but he scuttles to and fro with lowered head and crouching body. Now he glides behind her, snatches off his cap, holds it low and with little jumps drives her into her house. Vastly amused at his defeat of Prudenza, he breaks into an animated dance; he twists his body from side to side, shrugs his shoulders, and nods his head.

From the left-hand house comes Rosetta and her father Tartaglia, a foolish old man with a pompous up-turned nose. He is dressed in white coat and breeches, laced with red, and wears a black hat with red feathers. Rosetta informs her father of her love for Pulcinella, but he refuses to countenance it, and roundly abuses her for casting her thoughts so low. Rosetta bows her head, then, with a disdainful shrug of her shoulders, goes to Pulcinella and tries to embrace him.

He receives her advances with indifference, whereupon she essays to capture his fancy in a charming dance. Pulcinella becomes more complaisant. He kisses Rosetta, takes off his cap, and places it on her head. He lifts her on his shoulder, carries her a little way, then sets her down. He pushes her behind him, slips his arm into hers, and, as she raises the other arm above her head, dances her to the right-hand side of the square. Then he quickly glides from her side, snatches his cap from her head, and retraces his steps.

From the inner door of the left-hand house comes Pimpinella, a peasant girl in red skirt and white bodice. Now you must know that she is Pulcinella's mistress. It is plain from her looks that she has witnessed the diversions of her lover. Pulcinella is alarmed, ill at ease. In nervous trepidation he hastily pulls his cap over his eyes, then, deciding to brave out the matter, drags off his cap, places it in his blouse, and approaches her with fair words and glowing accounts of his indifference to everyone but her sweet self.

Pimpinella sets her hands on her hips and shrugs her shoulders in incredulity at his statement. She stamps her foot with vexation. Pulcinella protests his affection, but she turns away from him. He caresses her, whispers in her ear, and pats her bare arms. His arm glides round her waist and the two lovers, now reconciled, walk slowly across the square. Now they dance a lively measure which they emphasise with claps of their hands. Then they squat on their heels and glide along the ground with a quick sliding movement of their feet. He lifts her on to his shoulders, sets her down, and they resume their vows of love.

From the left comes Caviello who espies Pulcinella. He retires and returns with Florindo. Keeping in the shadow they make their way behind Pulcinella. Suddenly, with a concerted movement, they spring upon him and drag him from Pimpinella. He wriggles, strains his body backwards and forwards, but to no avail. They seize him by his long sleeves so that, pinioned thus, he is powerless to retaliate. They beat him with their fists so that he cowers beneath their blows. They force him to his knees.

Pimpinella wrings her hands in anguish and loudly calls for help, whereupon Rosetta and Prudenza run from their houses and, with threats of their displeasure, drive away the furious gallants. Then the three women run to the help of Pulcinella, raise him to his feet, and soothe his injuries with caresses and endearments. But Pimpinella resents the attentions of the two noble ladies so that Pulcinella, still groaning, is like to be torn into pieces by the jealous trio, each determined to claim him for her own. In endeavour to escape the clutches of his new captors he drags himself to and fro in utter helplessness, while the women clutch his blouse so tightly that it is in immediate danger of being stripped from his back.

Hearing the uproar, the Doctor and Tartaglia come upon the scene and drive their daughters indoors. Pulcinella, exhausted by his struggles, falls on his knees while Pimpinella, half-fainting from excitement, falls backward on top of him. He makes a wry face at this unexpected burden, groans, then slowly raises himself and sets his mistress on her feet. She looks round with wondering eyes, while he pats her and restores her to her senses. Now he moves to and fro with a sliding step, spins round and falls on one knee, then claps his cap on his head. Pimpinella tip-toes a little distance away then returns in a series of big steps. Pulcinella lifts her on his shoulders, carries her about the square, sets her down, and kisses her hand.

From the right enter Caviello and Florindo, disguised in long black cloaks and each bearing a sword. They glide stealthily round the square, then conceal themselves in the doorways. It would seem that the astute and wary Pulcinella has some glimmer of their intentions for he swiftly rises, crosses himself, seizes Pimpinella, and flees through the inner door of the left-hand house. But the door is small so that Pimpinella must enter first; as Pulcinella follows, Florindo steps forth and thrusts at him with his sword. Pulcinella totters backward, his knees tremble, his head shakes from side to side, he drags himself wearily along the ground, then collapses as if dead. The two gallants approach the body with slow, majestic steps. They point with outstretched forefingers at the prostrate form and raise their hands on high as if to suggest that heaven has visited due punishment on this villain. Then, sadly nodding their heads, they solemnly take their departure, their hands set on their sword-hilts.

As soon as they have gone, Pulcinella rolls over on his stomach. He remains motionless for a while, then slowly rises to a kneeling position, and devoutly crosses himself. He shades his eyes with one hand and peers anxiously to right and left. Reassured, he rises, presses his hands to his stomach, and extends his arms in a wide, circular sweep; a self-compliment to the success of his stratagem. Then he walks away with slow steps and all-meaning sweeps of his arms.

Now enter four little Pulcinellas, similarly attired in white, but wearing masks in which the pendulous nose is cruder and more pronounced, while their eyes are rimmed with white. They march in single file and bear on their shoulders another Pulcinella, his arms folded on his breast. Arrived before the left-hand house, they set down the body and regard it with outstretched arms. Then they form into line, shield their eyes with upraised hand, and peer alternately to right and left. They walk quickly to and fro with jerky movements. They shake their shoulders in an outburst of grief, nod their heads, then turn round on one foot and jump into the air with an upward swing of their arms. They dance in a circle, divide into pairs, and take off their caps.

Now come the Doctor and Tartaglia accompanied by their daughters, who approach the body with reverent demeanour and gestures of profound sorrow. Prudenza, unable to restrain her tears, covers her eyes with her hand. Tartaglia shuffles behind, raising his hands in horror. Rosetta contrives to raise the prostrate Pulcinella, while Prudenza takes his hand and rubs it; but the body falls back, limp and inert. The Doctor drops on one knee and after a brief examination pronounces life extinct.

Enter a quaint personage whose costume suggests a magician. He walks slowly with the aid of a long pole. Approaching the grief-stricken group he boldly announces that he can bring to life the seeming dead. He motions them to stand back and regard him with attention. The two fathers retreat, half in gratitude, half in fear, and converse in whispers. Prudenza kneels and offers up a prayer for their success. The four little Pulcinellas doff their caps to the magician and crowd together in excited expectation.

The magician walks round his pole, then stands on one foot and slides the other up and down the pole. Now he places the pole in front of him, seizes it with both hands, places his feet together, and thus propels himself round the body with a series of convulsive leaps. He beats the body with his hands, rises, places one foot on the Pulcinella's chest, and, with a commanding wave of the hand, orders him to rise. To the astonishment of the onlookers, the Pulcinella shakes himself and staggers to his feet. The Pulcinellas sit on the ground and wave their caps in triumph. The Pulcinella flings wide his arms and with a jerk of his legs stands on his heels. Rosetta and Prudenza offer their fervent congratulations and renew their vows of affection, which the happy trio celebrate in a dance. The four Pulcinellas bound in the air with delight and take their departure.

But the Doctor and Tartaglia remain immobile; one points with trembling finger in a gesture of profound surprise while his mouth gapes wide in astonishment; the other raises his hands in mute astonishment at this seeming miracle.

The magician takes off his wig and gown and reveals the costume of a Pulcinella, but with a mask that closely fits his face. It is evident that Pulcinella has masqueraded as the magician, while he in turn has been impersonated by a friend, whom you must know as Fourbo. The four little Pulcinellas whisk off their caps and circle about the motionless Doctor and Tartaglia. They divide into couples, in which one Pulcinella sits on his heels while his partner seizes his hand and whirls him round. They rise and take their departure.

Pulcinella takes off his cap, rolls it into a baton, and pushes it under the Doctor's nose. The latter peers at the object with anxiety, but the length of his nose prevents him from inspecting it closely. He strives to obtain a nearer view but Pulcinella gently withdraws it from him. So the old man, consumed with curiosity, follows the droll object just as a donkey is unable to resist the sight of a succulent carrot held tantalisingly just beyond its reach. Similarly, Fourbo rolls up his cap and attracts Tartaglia. Thus each is respectively drawn off to right and left.

Now comes Pimpinella who tip-toes on one foot with the other raised *en arabesque*. She falls on one knee, again rises on her toes, and, with a whipping movement of one foot, impels herself in a graceful pirouette. Meanwhile Pulcinella and Fourbo enter from the right and watch her movements. Suddenly she notices the two friends. Frightened at this apparition she flees through the inner door of the left-hand house. Pulcinella dispatches Fourbo in pursuit.

From the left of the square come Florindo and Caviello with their features concealed by Pulcinella-masks. They dance to and fro with broad leaps and high bounds. They play little tricks upon each other, then, feeling secure in their disguise, decide to renew their attentions to Prudenza and Rosetta. They clasp their hands in mutual exchange of good wishes then quarrel as to who shall first essay his luck. They part and enter the houses of their respective loves.

Presently Prudenza emerges from her dwelling followed by Florindo. They dance a graceful measure at the conclusion of which he lifts her high on his shoulder and swings her in the air. Rosetta enters, pursued by Caviello, who likewise raises her into the air, then kneels down, pulls her to him, and kisses her hand. Now Pimpinella returns leaning on the arm of Fourbo, who sits on the ground and draws her to him. At the height of these love episodes Pulcinella bounds in their midst.

The three women run to greet the object of their affections, but Fourbo and the two gallants are terrified at his unexpected appearance. Pulcinella dances with the three women, then breaks from their embrace, and skips furiously round the square. In turn he approaches the three men and with a powerful kick bids them take themselves elsewhere. They retreat in dismay. Fourbo hastens to envelop himself in the magician's robe while Pulcinella pursues the trembling gallants. He seizes them by the neck and with a quick movement unmasks them and leads them to Prudenza and Rosetta.

At this point the Doctor and Tartaglia return. The magician goes to them and suggests that the happy couples should be united in marriage. The fathers agree and, while their daughters kneel, bestow their blessings on the union. Pulcinella crosses the square, gaily swinging above his head the two masks. He approaches Pimpinella who falls into his arms and rests her head on his breast. He soothes her with caresses and playfully pats her hair.

The magician reads the marriage lines over the two gallants and their fiancées and exhorts them to good conduct, which homily they receive with upraised hand and numerous genuflections. Pulcinella informs the magician of his desire to be wedded to Pimpinella. Prudenza, Florindo, and the Doctor link arms and dance; Rosetta, Caviello, and Rosetta follow suit. They separate and the newly-married couples dance by themselves while Fourbo steps a measure with the Doctor and Tartaglia. Again they divide and the Doctor and Tartaglia encircle Pimpinella. The four little Pulcinellas return. There is a lively fanfare of trumpets and, as the dancers quickly clap their hands, spin round on one foot, and swing their bodies backward and forward to the rhythm of the music, the curtain slowly falls.

*

The success of *Les Femmes de Bonne Humeur* with Scarlatti's music prompted Diaghilev to prepare another ballet with music by an Italian master, in this case, Pergolesi, whose compositions he much admired. During his many visits to Italy, Diaghilev was always on the look-out for unpublished MS. compositions of this composer, and, in course of time, he had accumulated a considerable store of material, which he handed to Stravinsky as the basis for the score of a new ballet to be founded on the adventures of Pulcinella.

The theme was taken from a manuscript book of comedies, dated 1700, which was found in Naples. It is a collection of *scenarii* and dialogues written round Pulcinella, one of the famous masks of the Commedia dell'Arte. The play selected is entitled *The Four Pulcinellas*. The other two principal characters are Il Dottore and Tartaglia, also well known masks.

Stravinsky tells us in his Memoirs[5] that Massine composed the ballet from a piano arrangement made from his orchestral score, which was sent to the choreographer by instalments as each number was completed. The discussion between Diaghilev, Stravinsky, Massine, and Picasso of the work in progress seems to have been lively and even stormy, but it must be admitted that the final result was well worth the labour, for the dancers' movements are admirably knit with the music and well express the action. This ballet is much more than a *pastiche,* it breathes the very spirit of the Commedia dell'Arte, so far as it can be assimilated from a study of the plays and engravings of the period.

There are charming numbers for all the *danseuses*; those of Pimpinella being cast in a peasant form as opposed to the modish dancing of Rosetta and Prudenza. Il Dottore and Tartaglia are mime parts. But the whole ballet is dominated by the character of Pulcinella who is hardly ever off the stage, and who has to express all kinds of varied emotions while dancing, partly by movement, partly by the expressive line of his body. In this role Massine's

[5] *Chronique de ma Vie.*

faculty for making dancing mimetic is developed to a considerable degree, for Pulcinella's face is almost obscured by his mask, yet, by the tilt of his head and body, he makes his thoughts easily intelligible.

The role of Pulcinella was largely worked out on Woizikowsky, who sometimes took the part. Excellent as Massine is in this character, the writer prefers the interpretation of Woizikowsky which, a little coarser in presentation, is even more in the tradition of the famous Neapolitan mask.

Pulcinella was revived in 1935, under the title of *Les Deux Polichinelles,* by Woizikowsky and his own company at the Coliseum Theatre, London, when he took the title-role.

LES MATELOTS

Ballet in 5 Scenes. Book: Boris Kochno. Music: Georges Auric. Curtains, Scenery, and Costumes: Pedro Pruna. Choreography: Leonide Massine. First produced: Théâtre Gaité-Lyrique, Paris, June 17th, 1925.

CHARACTERS

The Young Girl	MLLE. VERA NEMCHINOVA
Her Friend	MME. LYDIA SOKOLOVA
First Sailor	M. LEON WOIZIKOWSKY
Second Sailor	M. TADEO SLAVINSKY
Third Sailor	M. SERGE LIFAR

The Musician

I. Three sailors, about to leave on a voyage, visit a young girl and her friend. The young girl becomes engaged to one of the sailors who promises to marry her on his return.

II. The young girl, left alone, longs for the return of her lover.

III. The three sailors return home and, donning false beards, test the young girl's fidelity by making love to her.

IV. Her friend tries to induce her to go to a tavern and meet the sailors, but she refuses.

V. The three sailors return and remove their disguise. The young girl embraces her lover to whom she has been faithful.

*

Such, in outline. is the theme of *Les Matelots,* a gay, lively conception with a background which hints at brothel and bar, a ballet very much in the Massine idiom of angular poses and spasmodic movements, but full of the atmosphere of a Marseille dockside, tricked out in the Picasso-like colours favoured by Pruna.

Massine has devised very attractive dances for the three sailors, including a particularly ingenious number in which the sailors, perilously balanced on tilted chairs, play a game of cards. In contrast with the sailors' gaiety there is the piquant dance of loneliness rendered by the young girl at the departure of the beloved, and the sly ways of her friend who tries to turn her from the path of duty.

This ballet is particularly associated with Serge Lifar who made his first important success as one of the sailors, which was his *début* in a leading role.

The music is Auric's lively fantasia on circus themes.

*

Les Matelots was first produced at London, at the Coliseum Theatre, on June 29th, 1925, when the cast received a temporary addition in the form of Mr. G. P. Dines, an ex-bluejacket who entertained theatre queues by dexterously manipulating tablespoons in the manner of a performer on the bones. Massine saw Mr. Dines in the Haymarket and, delighted with his performance, offered him an engagement to play the spoons in the tavern scene of *Les Matelots,* in which he appeared with success.

JEUX D'ENFANTS

Ballet in 1 Act. Book: Boris Kochno. Music: Georges Bizet. Curtain, Scenery and Costumes: Joan Miro. Choreography: Leonide Massine. First produced: Théâtre de Monte Carlo, April 14th, 1932.

CHARACTERS

The Spirits who govern the Toys . . .	{ MLLE. LUBOV ROSTOVA { M. ROLAND GUERARD
The Top	MLLE. TAMARA TOUMANOVA
The CHILD . . .	MLLE. TATIANA RIABOUCHINSKA
The Wooden Rocking-Horses , .	MM. PETROV, HOYER, KATCHAROV, LIPATOV, DOLOTINE, SHABELEVSKY

Two Rackets . . .	MM. Borovsky, Jasinsky
A Shuttlecock . .	Mlle. Valentine Blinova
Amazons . . .	Mlles. Obidenna, Marra, Kervilly, Strakhova
Soap Bubbles . . .	Mlles. Slavinska, Kirsova, Tresahar, Chabelska, Morosova, Lipkovska, Sonne, Blanc, Valenska
The Traveller . .	M. David Lichine
Three Sportsmen . .	MM. Leon Woizikowsky, Guérard, Ladre

A little girl, inspired perhaps by Hans Andersen's tales, wishes to share in that mysterious life which playthings are said to enjoy in the silent hours of the night. Two spirits, the animators of toy-folk, enter about their magic. First they set in motion a striped top. At this juncture the little girl comes into the mysterious room and delights in this new aspect of beloved objects at games of their own devising.

There are rocking-horses, a pair of rackets disporting with a shuttlecock, toy amazons who fight with bucklers and scimitars, some athletes, and an agile traveller. The little girl takes a fancy to the last-named and dances with him. Then the athletes attract her attention with the beauty of their exercises. She transfers her affections to one of them, but the jealous top twirls between and separates them. The scene lightens and with the coming of dawn the spirits return, to take back the life they had temporarily bestowed on the playthings.

*

Jeux d'Enfants is a kind of miniature revue with the little girl as *commère,* and the choreography has a freshness which is enchanting. The character of the Top enables Baronova (or Toumanova, as the case may be) to launch into a bewildering succession of admirably executed *fouettés en tournant,* the effect being emphasised by her striped costume. Then there is Woizikowsky as the superb athlete, Lichine as the bounding traveller, and Riabouchinska as the little girl. Her portrait has a fascinating artlessness all her own, at once ingenuous and all-understanding. It is said to be her favourite character because she feels it to be almost a part of herself, and that is exactly the impression she conveys.

Miro's surrealist scenery and costumes are most successful from a decorative standpoint, and also at conveying the essence of play-things and the abstract quality of the whole episode. All the objects have the simple bright colouring which, gleaming in the light, brings back childhood memories of the polished feel and resinous odour of enamelled surfaces.

SCUOLA DI BALLO [6]

Ballet in 1 *Act. Book: Leonide Massine. Music: Françaix-Boccherini. Scenery and Costumes: Comte Etienne de Beaumont. Choreography: Leonide Massine. Produced:*[7] *Théâtre de Monte Carlo, April 25th,* 1933.

CHARACTERS

Rigadon, a professor of dancing	M. Leon Woizikowsky
Ridolfo, Rigadon's friend. .	M. Vania Psota
Fabrizio, an impresario . .	M. Edouard Borovansky
Count Anselmi	M. André Eglevsky
Rosina	Mlle. Tatiana Riabouchinska
Josephina, the favourite pupil .	Mlle. Irina Baronova
Felicita, the bad pupil . .	Mlle. Evgenia Delarova
Bianca	Mlle. Natalia Branitska
Rosalba	Mlle. Olga Morosova
Carlino	M. Leonide Massine
Philipino	M. Yurek Shabelevsky
Nicoletto	M. Marjan Ladre
Lucrezia, Rosina's mother . .	Mlle. Eleonora Marra
The Notary	M. Jan Hoyer

Carabiniers.

Scene. The dancing-school of Professor Rigadon.

Rigadon, a dancing-master, agrees to find an excellent engagement for one of his pupils, Lucrezia's talented daughter, Rosina. An impresario, Fabrizio, introduced by Ridolfo, visits Rigadon in search of a "star." The dancing-master suggests Felicita, the most backward of his pupils, and, by insisting that she is too important an artiste to give an audition, tricks the impresario into signing a contract for her engagement.

Count Anselmi arrives with Josephina, with whom he dances a measure indicative of their mutual affection.

Later Fabrizio returns and desires Felicita to dance, to ascer-

[6] *The Dancing School.*
[7] This ballet was first produced for the Comte de Beaumont in 1924?. It was revived by *Les Ballets Russes de Monte Carlo* in 1932.

tain how best her talent may be presented. She dances and he perceives that he has been duped. Rosalba arrives for a lesson; Fabrizio, recognising her talent, insists upon her replacing Felicita. Since Rigadon refuses, he summons a notary and forces the dancing-master to return the commission paid to him. Meanwhile Rigadon's pupils take their departure, telling him that they have obtained much better engagements elsewhere.

*

Scuola di Ballo is based on Goldoni's five-act comedy of the same name. The music is an arrangement by J. Françaix of airs by Boccherini. This is the third ballet which Massine has based on the elements of 18th century Italian comedy, but it is not so successful as either *Les Femmes de Bonne Humeur* or *Pulcinella.* The choreography is pleasing and well adapted to Boccherini's flowing melodies, and many little touches of comedy and character—suggesting Longhi's paintings have been studied to some purpose—are adroitly introduced. One of the most successful numbers is Felicita's solo, a delicious satire on faults in ballet technique, charmingly danced by Evgenia Delarova. But the theme is too involved to be compressed into a single act and inclined to be over-prolonged, an impression which is heightened by two or three false climaxes which suggest that the ballet is about to end before it does.

LES PRÉSAGES

Choreographic Symphony in 4 Parts. Music: Tchaikovsky's Fifth Symphony. Book: Leonide Massine. Scenery and Costumes: André Masson. Choreography: Leonide Massine. First produced: Théâtre de Monte Carlo, April 13th, 1933.

CHARACTERS

Part I.

Action	MLLE. NINA VERCHININA
Temptation	{ MLLE. NATALIA BRANITSKA { MLLE. NINA TARAKANOVA M. ROLAND GUERARD
Movement	ENSEMBLE

Part II.

Passion	MLLE. IRINA BARONOVA
	M. DAVID LICHINE

Fate	M. LÉON WOIZIKOWSKY
Destinies	ENSEMBLE

Part III.

Frivolity	MLLE. TATIANA RIABOUCHINSKA
Variation	ENSEMBLE

Part IV.

Passion	MLLE. IRINA BARONOVA
Frivolity	MLLE. TATIANA RIABOUCHINSKA
Action	MLLE. NINA VERCHININA
Fate	M. LÉON WOIZIKOWSKY
The Hero	M. DAVID LICHINE
Destinies	ENSEMBLE

The ballet portrays Man's contest with his destiny, and falls into four parts: I. Action, or life with its amusements, ambitions, and temptations. II. Passion, or the contest between sacred and profane love. III. Frivolity. IV. War.

The whole production takes place against a simple back-cloth, coloured red, green, yellow, mauve, and brown, on which a sinister mask, shooting stars, and kris-shaped tongues of flame, are combined in a curvilinear design.

The first scene was dominated by Nina Verchinina's dance as Action. Clad in a classic, pleated robe, she moved with a noble statuesque grace reminiscent of a Tanagra figurine. But her luminous eyes and the commanding poise of her head had something of that unearthly, mystical quality characteristic of Blake's angels. Her arms played a great part in this dance and were remarkable for their varying quality of movement. Sometimes they described beautiful curves, moving with a gentle rhythm like the ripple of a wave; sometimes they darted forwards or backwards with the sudden swiftness of the flick of a whip-lash; and sometimes, held almost rigid, one arm was flung forwards or backwards with such emphasis that it suggested the stroke of a double-edged sword. So dynamic were her movements that she seemed to radiate power, and this impression was intensified by the complete contrast afforded by the dancer's being poised, or travelling, *sur les pointes.* The dance is executed partly solo, partly against a moving background of dancers.

The second scene, which opens with an almost religious solemnity, is full of lovely movement. The entrance of Irina Baronova and David Lichine as the lovers provides a moment of rare beauty. Their ecstasy is interrupted by a group of destinies and by a sinister, bat-like figure of Fate, who makes a grotesque exit by walking backwards on his heels.

The third scene has a gay dance by Tatiana Riabouchinska as Frivolity, and is noteworthy for many beautiful groups. An effective finale is provided when the men, moving in single file parallel to the audience, each raise aloft a woman, whose arched bodies and tunics billowing in the breeze of their movements suggest giant birds in flight.

The last scene is a stylised representation of war in which Fate, the evil genius, urges mankind on to destruction until reason prevails and peace is restored.

*

The ballet, if a little protracted, is a homogeneous work, expressive of the theme and closely attuned to the music. The student of ballet will find it of interest to compare Massine's handling of his fourth scene with the treatment of the battle scenes in Jooss's *The Green Table*. There is an element of weakness in the dances arranged for Fate, which, although intensely dramatic at certain movements, sometimes verge on the commonplace.

Finally, some of the surrealist costumes are not too happy and tend to mar rather than enhance the dancers' beauty of line. Subject to these qualifications, *Les Présages* is a work of great interest, conceived on a high plane, and containing many choreographic passages invested with a true poetic beauty and intellectual appeal.

LE BEAU DANUBE

Ballet in 1 Act. Book: Leonide Massine. Music: Johann Strauss. Scenery: V. and E. Polunin, after Constantin Guys. Costumes: Comte Etienne de Beaumont. Choreography: Leonide Massine. First produced: Théâtre de Monte Carlo, April 15th, 1933.

CHARACTERS

The Street Dancer	. .	MLLE. ALEXANDRA DANILOVA
The Daughter	. . .	MLLE. TATIANA RIABOUCHINSKAYA
The First Hand	. . .	MLLE. IRINA BARONOVA
The Hussar	. . . .	M. LEONIDE MASSINE

The King of the Dandies	M. David Lichine
The Athlete	M. E. Borovansky
The Manager	M. J. Hoyer
The Mother	Mlle. A. Krassnova
The Father	M. V. Psota
The Artist	M. M. Ladré
The Gardener	M. J. Hoyer

Modistes, Needlewomen, Ladies of the Town, Salesmen, Dandies.

The scene is laid in the Prater, time 1860, and one of Constantin Guys's sketches of the aristocracy driving in the Bois, has provided the inspiration for the setting by V. Polunin.

It is a public holiday and all is liveliness and good humour; a child plays with a skipping-rope, milliners and salesmen dance, and young bloods make merry. Now a young hussar enters, meets his sweetheart, and dances a gay mazurka with her. A comic interlude is afforded by the arrival of a strolling troupe: a dancer, a strong man, and their "barker," who demonstrate their skill. But the dancer recognises a former lover in the hussar and an awkward moment ensues. The young girl faints and her affronted parents lead her away. The dancer takes the opportunity to endeavour to recapture the hussar's affection, but the young girl returns and vanquishes her would-be rival. The parents, returning in search of their daughter, view the reunion with disfavour, but the young girl's little sister induces her father and mother to bestow their blessing. The ballet concludes with a general dance.

*

Le Beau Danube is a reconstruction of a ballet with the same name, originally produced for the series of performances entitled *"Soirée de Paris,"* presented at that capital from May 17th to June 30th, 1924, by the Comte Etienne de Beaumont. The present version has entirely new costumes and occupies one scene, instead of two, as formerly. The music is an arrangement of airs by Johann Strauss, orchestrated by Roger Desormière. The Street Dancer in the original production was Lydia Lopokova.

The scenery and costumes of *Beau Danube* combine to form a pleasing harmony of varying shades of brown, ranging from palest beige to sepia. In considering the music it seems curious that the famous Blue Danube Waltz, from which the ballet derives its name,[8] should be allotted so minor a role in the score.

[8] In the printed repertory of the company as issued at Monte Carlo, 1933, this ballet is styled *Le Beau Danube Bleu.*

The choreography, if nothing unusual, is pleasing, and the *soli* and ensembles are well contrived. Danilova and Riabouchinska are delightful as the Dancer and Daughter, and contrive to invest their dancing with a certain contrasted raffishness and innocence which the respective characters demand; Massine makes a gallant hussar. His *pas de deux* are executed with a delicate appreciation of poise and rhythm, the martial elegance of the hussar being well set off by the yielding graces of his companion. Mention must also be made of Borovansky's excellent characterisation of the Strong Man—complete with quiff, cigarette behind ear, and panther-like gait. But the whole production radiates an air of spontaneous gaiety—light-hearted, but never boisterous—which is most infectious.

CHOREARTIUM

Choreographic Symphony in 4 Parts. Music: Brahms's Fourth Symphony. Scenery and Costumes: Constantine Terechkovich and Eugene Lourie. Choreography: Leonide Massine. First Produced: Alhambra Theatre, London, October 24th, 1933.

PRINCIPAL DANCERS

Part I	MLLE. IRINA BARONOVA M. DAVID LICHINE MLLE. VERA ZORINA
Part II	MLLE. NINA VERCHININA
Part III	MLLE. ALEXANDRA DANILOVA M. YUREK SHABELEVSKY MLLE. TATIANA RIABOUCHINSKA M. ROMAN JASINSKY
Part IV	MLLE. IRINA BARONOVA M. DAVID LICHINE M. PAUL PETROV MLLE. ALEXANDRA DANILOVA M. YUREK SHABELEVSKY MLLE. TATIANA RIABOUCHINSKA M. ROMAN JASINSKY

Part I. The first, and by far the best, episode takes place against a vague landscape dominated by a rainbow. There is something extraordinarily fresh about the choreography. It is as though a deity had chosen a mountain-top, fashioned a number of youths and maidens, breathed life into them, filled the air with music, and then set them down to dance. The result is a wonderful kaleidoscopic panorama of dancing figures—sometimes two, sometimes four, six, a dozen, a score—continually changing in number and always forming some new and still more beautiful pattern. The dancing, the formation of the groups, the exits and entrances, the varying quality of movement are all so natural, so spontaneous, and in such perfect accord with the music, that without advance knowledge it would be difficult to say which inspired the other.

Part II. The background is formed by a blue curtain which a change of lighting deepens to green. In contrast with the gaiety of the previous scene the dancers, clad in robes of sombre crimson, enter slowly, with bent heads, in a long chain, which later separates into three groups, sometimes forming varied poses, sometimes in movement. Against this shifting background moves a solo dancer—a tragic muse.

Part III. The background is an expanse of yellow, beige, and grey, which suggests a Japanese print. The costumes—white, pink, or pale blue—are somewhat sugary. The dancing is lively, with a hint of folk-dance.

Part IV. The background is a gloomy grey, relieved by a suggestion of window and doors outlined in a darker grey. The scene opens most unexpectedly with six male dancers in black, separately and successively executing *tours en l'air*. There is a fine *adage* in this part and many beautiful groups, ingeniously revealed as from time to time the curtain of dancing figures is drawn aside.

*

Viewed as a whole the ballet is too long, and the standard of choreographic invention is not maintained at so consistently high a level as in *Les Présages*. The first part, however, is superbly arranged, and worth going many miles to see. The second part is associated with Verchinina, who gave a fine performance of a difficult role—a restless, brooding, tragic figure who seems to battle vainly against some power that holds her in thrall.

The costumes for the first two scenes are very pleasing, particularly a band of dancers in brown tunics who bear green scarves.

UNION PACIFIC

*Ballet in 1 Act and 4 Scenes. Book: Archibald MacLeish.
Music: Nicholas Nabokov. Scenery: Albert Johnson. Costumes:
Irene Sharaff. Choreography: Leonide Massine. First produced:
Forrest Theatre, Philadelphia, 1934.*

CHARACTERS

The Surveyor of the Irish Work-men	M. ANDRE EGLEVSKY
The Lady Gay	MLLE. EVGENIA DELAROVA
The Surveyor of the Chinese Workmen	M. DAVID LICHINE
The Barman	M. LEONIDE MASSINE
His Assistant	MLLE. SONO OSATO
The Mormon Missionary . .	M. VALENTINOV
The Mexicans	MLLE. TAMARA TOUMANOVA M. VANIA PSOTA M. EDOUARD BOROVANSKY
The Capitalists	M. EDOUARD BOROVANSKY M. JEAN HOYER M. VANIA PSOTA
The Cameraman	M. ROLAND GUERARD

Irish Workmen, Chinese Workmen, Gamblers, Girls.

The curtain rises to show an enlarged blue-print, which forms
the act-drop for each scene, before which a surveyor dances.

*Scene I. The curtain act-drop rises to reveal a stretch of waste
territory east of Promontory Point.*

A number of Irish workmen are building the eastern section of
the new railroad. Rigid figures in close-fitting dresses are carried
in to form sleepers, and others set across them to serve as rails.
The workmen seize the arms of the recumbent figures and swing
them as though using tap-hammers and ratchet spanners.

*Scene II. Another stretch of waste territory west of Promontory
Point.*

A number of Chinese workmen are seen engaged in the construction of the western section of the new railroad. Their labours

are directed by another surveyor, whose attention is partly occupied by the amorous advances of a certain Lady Gay, one of those flashy belles invariably to be encountered in the vicinity of construction camps.

Scene III. An enormous tent, part dance-hall, part gambling saloon.

Workmen and dancing-girls are drinking at various tables, while a group of Mexicans dance their version of the Jarabe Tapatio. This is followed by a dance of gamblers. Now the barman himself resolves to entertain the house with an impromptu number, which, at first indifferently received, ends by winning the company's complete approval.

The Lady Gay is much in evidence during these proceedings, endeavouring to complete her conquest of the surveyor of the Chinese workmen, an action which is bitterly resented by the rival surveyor. Presently the latter interferes. Tempers rise and matters grow serious. Attempts are made to separate the two men, but now the workmen take sides and join in the dispute. The scene ends with a general fight in which chairs and stools are freely used.

Scene IV. The meeting of the two lines at Promontory Point.

The last rail is laid and the railway completed. Two engines puff in from opposite sides bearing a load of top-hatted officials. There are congratulations all round, the assembled company form into a group, and a photographer records the auspicious event.

*

This ballet has a clear-cut theme which affords opportunities for many "amusing" touches of which Massine takes full advantage. But, although the choreography is full of life and character, the actual result suggests musical comedy rather than ballet. The production also suffers from being a mixture of styles, for some portions are treated in a realistic manner, while others are abstract in presentation.

The ballet, however, has one supreme moment, that is Massine's dance as the barman, which evokes such a storm of applause that the action is held up for several minutes. He employs an unusual make-up which, with its staring white features, bushy eyebrows, drooping moustache, and shocklike hair, suggests a savage mask rather than a human face. The actual dance is a strange succession of step dance, cake walk, and similar movements—just the mixture that an uncouth, half-demented, half-inebriated creature might be expected to contrive. But it is not so much the material as the way Massine uses it that makes the number a little masterpiece of characterisation. The timing and placing of every step and gesture, and their resultant effect, have been minutely calculated, and afford a picture which sears itself into the mind as deeply as some of Daumier's lithographs and certain etchings of Rops and Callot.

SYMPHONIE FANTASTIQUE

Choreographic Symphony in 5 Scenes. Book: H. Berlioz. Music: Hector Berlioz. Scenery and Costumes: Christian Bérard. Choreography: Leonide Massine. First produced: Royal Opera, Covent Garden, London, July 24th, 1936.

CHARACTERS

A Young Musician	M. LEONIDE MASSINE
The Beloved	M. TAMARA TOUMANOVA
The Old Shepherd	M. MARC PLATOV
The Young Shepherd	M. GEORGE ZORICH
The Deer	M. ALEXIS KOSLOV
The Jailer	M. YUREK SHABELEVSKY

Visions of Gaiety, Melancholy, Reverie, and Passion; Guests at the Ball; The Picnic Party, The Children, Winds; Executioners, Judges, Crowd; Monsters, Witches, Ghouls, Vampires, Spectres, Furies.

Part I. The curtain rises to reveal a bare room in which a young musician, whose dress belongs to the Romantic Period, is seated at a table, wrestling with his thoughts. In a fit of love-sick despair he takes a dose of opium which, insufficient to kill him, causes him to sleep; but, although his body is at rest, his mind is filled with fitful visions, some gay, some sad, some terrifying, some horrible.

Gradually the scene lightens to reveal the fantastic country where at present he roams in spirit, a bleak landscape dominated by a sphinx-like statue with ghostly wings outspread. Here, in succession, he is visited by shades which induce a succession of moods—gaiety, melancholy, reverie, and passion—and woven into all these patterns of movement is the figure of the woman he loves, whose white ball-dress and pale face framed in her dark hair from time to time loom out of this mist of ghostly forms, ever-present, yet always tantalisingly beyond his reach.

Part II. The scene changes to a ballroom, a vivid conception in black and red, peopled with dancers, the women in white, the men in black. The young musician strays into the room in search of his beloved. To his great joy he finds her and for a few moments enjoys the ecstasy of dancing with her, then, evasive as ever, she vanishes from his sight.

Part III. The scene changes to a sunny countryside dominated by the ruins of an ancient aqueduct. A solitary deer gambols lightly in this peaceful spot, in which the musician at last finds repose. Seated on a broken column he contemplates the beauties of nature. He watches two shepherds, one young, one old, who call to their flocks by sounding a rustic instrument.

Some young girls come to picnic, and children play happy games and frolic with the deer. One of the girls is attracted by the handsome young shepherd with whom she dances, and as they dance each becomes conscious of a deep love for the other. Across the sky floats a vision of the musician's beloved. His peace is troubled; he is filled with the fear that she may not be faithful to him. The old shepherd resumes his quaint calling to his flock. The sun begins to set and the serenity is disturbed by the sullen rumble of distant thunder.

Part IV. The scene changes to the courtyard of a prison. The musician's fears for his beloved's constancy have borne evil fruit, for he imagines that in a fit of jealousy he has murdered her, and must now pay the penalty for his crime.

The bleak empty courtyard with its sinister background of iron bars slowly fills with a winding stream of gossips, male and female, who, nodding and gesticulating, covertly discuss the criminal and gloat over the punishment that is to be meted out to him.

A jailer brings in the prisoner who walks slowly with set features; he is followed by the executioners in red. Behind come a phalanx of judges in official dress, studying their books of law. The executioners' movements are deliberate, remorseless; those of the judges are perky and puppet-like, as though they danced to the letter of the penal code.

While the latter pore and nod over their books to find some fresh horror to which the prisoner must be subjected, he is scourged by the executioners; then they seize him by the arms and legs and pull him in opposite directions, as though he were stretched upon a rack. The crowd delight in the spectacle as if they, too, wished to be personally revenged on the criminal. Then he is held up with arms and legs outspread and turned round in a vertical plane, as though tortured on the wheel. He is lowered and the crowd press forward. He becomes the centre of a clamouring mob, but gradually he is again raised, so that he is waist-high above the struggling throng. Once more he sees a vision of his beloved, then suddenly he drops downwards like the fall of a doomed man from the gallows, and disappears from sight.

Part V. The scene changes and now the musician dreams that he is present at a witches' sabbath. His body is carried in and set down in a dark fearsome place filled with evil spirits, some black, some green, some red, who dance an unholy round about their victim. Some of the ghouls assume the likeness of monks and parody the *Dies irae* with its tolling bells. More witches arrive and now they begin to crawl about the ground like an army of ants. Among the latest arrivals is the beloved, who is seen to be a witch, and who is greeted by the others as one of themselves. The satanic round increases in intensity and amid the mingled melodies of the *Dies irae* and the orgy the curtain falls.

*

In the grandeur of its conception and its considerable range, the *Symphonie Fantastique* is the most important of all Massine's choreographic symphonies, and it is easy to understand that the ballet required over two years of preparation before it assumed final shape in his mind. Some parts of the music are well suited to parallel expression in dancing, others, however, are not so adaptable, and there are moments when one feels that the choreographer has been hard pressed to devise a movement corresponding to the music.

The first scene is principally remarkable for Massine's inspired miming and for the succession of lovely groups formed by the various visions, which are finely composed.

The second scene, though effective theatrically, is not particularly interesting from the choreographic standpoint.

The third scene has never been surpassed as an expression of a sober mood. The setting, the mime, and the dancing are combined to convey a sense of serenity which is indescribable and can only be fully appreciated by those who have seen it. The rendering of a deer by a dancer is also new, very successful at first, but not so happy in the later passages. The final touch of poetry is produced by the *pas de deux* of the young girl and the shepherd, which, as rendered by Verchinina and Zorich, is a lovely pastoral and most moving in its evocation of first love.

The fourth scene is the most dramatic of all. In the writer's view, the entrance of the gossips is a composition of sheer genius, which gains strength from the horrible jigging of the judges; both these episodes suggest that Daumier's mordant satires of life at the French law courts have been studied to some purpose.

The fifth scene is perhaps the least successful in the ballet; the witches are a little difficult to believe in and the scene generally tends towards the melodramatic.

The whole ballet is dominated by Massine's rendering of the Young Musician. Although is is a purely mimed role, he quietly and unobtrusively becomes the focal point of all the changing moods of the several scenes, and gives a superb performance. The part of the Beloved is rendered by Toumanova with an appropriate sense of poetry and appreciation of her ghostly character.

NINETTE DE VALOIS

NINETTE DE VALOIS, *née* Edris Stannus, was born in Ireland on June 6th, 1898; her father was the late Col. T. R. A. Stannus, D.S.O. She studied dancing under several teachers, principally under Enrico Cecchetti, with whom she remained for five years.

She made her *début* as principal dancer in 1914, in a pantomime presented at the Lyceum Theatre, when her success was such that she appeared there annually until 1919. She appeared with the Beecham Opera Co. (1918), and also danced in several revues. In 1919 she was *première danseuse* at the Royal Opera, Covent Garden.

In the autumn of 1923 she became a member of the Diaghilev Ballet, in which she rose to the rank of soloist. She left the company definitely in 1925, but, at Diaghilev's request, made occasional appearances with it in 1926, during the summer and autumn seasons, when Lydia Sokolova was ill, taking her parts of the Hostess in *Les Biches,* and that of Felicita in *Les Femmes de Bonne Humeur;* she also danced in the *pas de trois* in *Le Mariage d'Aurore* with Nikitina and Lifar.

During the whole of her association with the Diaghilev Ballet she danced various roles in the following ballets: *Narcisse, Daphnis et Chloë, Petrouchka, Papillons, Le Carnaval, Les Sylphides, Cléopâtre, Prince Igor, Schéhérazade, Thamar*—all by Fokine; *Le Sacre du Printemps, Soleil de Nuit, Les Femmes de Bonne Humeur, Contes Russes, La Boutique Fantasque, Le Tricorne, Chout, Cimarosiana, Zéphyre et Flore*—all by Massine; *Le Lac des Cygnes* and *Le Mariage d'Aurore*—both by Petipa; *L'Après-Midi d'un Faune*—by Nijinsky; *Les Biches, Les Facheux, Les Tentations de la Bergère, Le Train Bleu, Les Noces*—all by Nijinska; and *Le Chant de Rossignol,* arranged by Balanchine. It is of interest to study these details for they reveal that De Valois acquired a practical acquaintance with the works of six choreographers, and a considerable experience of the several styles of ballets composed by Fokine, Massine, and Nijinska, in the case of the two last-named learning her role direct from the choreographer.

In May, 1926, De Valois opened an Academy of Dancing at South Kensington, London, and in the autumn of the same year she made the acquaintance of Miss Lilian Baylis, director of the South London theatre popularly known as the "Old Vic," who was then seeking a suitable person to give classes in stage movement to her dramatic students, and to arrange the dances for the productions of certain of Shakespeare's plays.

At Christmas, 1928, Miss Baylis gave her permission to mount a small ballet, *Les Petits Riens*. The production was a success and Miss Baylis agreed that a new ballet should be produced occasionally and at each succeeding Christmas. This decision led to the production of *The Faun* (1928), *Hommage aux Belles Viennoises* (1929), and the Bach-Goossens *Suite de Danse* (1930).

In January, 1931, De Valois closed her academy and established a school of dancing at the then newly-built Sadler's Wells Theatre, also managed by Lilian Baylis. The nucleus of the school was formed by her own pupils, who constituted a small *corps de ballet* for short dance compositions in the repertory of popular opera given at that theatre.

From then onwards the proportion of ballet performances given at one or other of the two theatres was gradually increased from an occasional evening to a definite performance once a fortnight, to reach the present plan of two performances a week. The company has been continually enlarged and strengthened, and now consists of a well trained *corps de ballet* and a picked group of soloists, both sexes being well represented.

De Valois has produced the following ballets at the "Wells": *Création du Monde* (1931), *Cephalus and Procris* (1931), *Job* (1931), *Fête Polonaise* (1931), *Italian Suite* (1931), *The Jew in the Bush* (1931), *The Nursery Suite* (1932), *The Origin of Design* (1932), *Douanes* (1932), *The Scorpions of Ysit* (1932), *The Birthday of Oberon* (1933), *The Wise and the Foolish Virgins* (1933), *The Haunted Ballroom* (1934), *The Jar* (1934), *The Rake's Progress* (1935), *The Gods Go a-Begging* (1935), *Barabau* (1935), *Prometheus* (1936), *Checkmate* (1937). She also produced *Bar aux Folies-Bergère* for the Ballet Rambert in 1934. Of all these the following are the most important: *La Création du Monde, Job, The Haunted Ballroom, The Rake's Progress, The Gods Go a-Begging,* and *Checkmate*.

Although Ninette de Valois is the leading contemporary British choreographer, it is probable that in after years she will be best known for her great services in the foundation and development of the Vic-Wells Ballet, fast becoming a national institution, where, in addition to composing many of its most successful ballets, she has built up a strong company of British dancers, given opportunities to British choreographers, and invited and secured the collaboration of British musicians and British decorative artists. In the short space of barely seven years, with the unfailing support of Miss Baylis, she has raised the Vic-Wells Ballet to a state of efficiency and artistry which commands both respect and admiration.

JOB

A Masque for Dancing in 8 Scenes. Book: Geoffrey Keynes. Music: R. Vaughan Williams. Scenery and Costumes: Gwendolen Raverat. Wigs and Masks: Hedley Briggs. Choreography: Ninette de Valois. First produced: Cambridge Theatre, London, July 5th, 1931.

CHARACTERS

Job	JOHN MACNAIR
His Wife . . .	MARGERY STEWART
His Three Daughters .	MARIE NEILSON, URSULA BORETON, DOREEN ADAMS
His Seven Sons . .	WILLIAM CHAPPELL, HEDLEY BRIGGS, WALTER GORE, CLAUDE NEWMAN, ROBERT STUART, TRAVIS KEMP, STANLEY JUDSON
The Three Messengers .	ROBERT STUART, CLAUDE NEWMAN, TRAVIS KEMP
The Three Comforters .	WILLIAM CHAPPELL, WALTER GORE, HEDLEY BRIGGS
War, Pestilence, and Famine . . .	WILLIAM CHAPPELL, WALTER GORE, HEDLEY BRIGGS
Elihu	STANLEY JUDSON
Satan	ANTON DOLIN
The Children of God .	BEATRICE APPLEYARD, FREDA BAMFORD, JOY NEWTON, NADINA NEWHOUSE, PHYLLIS WORTHINGTON, JOAN DAY, WENDY TOYE, MARLEY BELL
Sons of the Morning .	JOY ROBSON, MONICA RATCLIFFE, MOLLIE BROWN, ELIZABETH MILLER
Job's Spiritual Self . .	JOHN LOFTUS

Scene I. Job is sitting in the sunrise of prosperity with his wife, surrounded by his seven sons and three daughters. They all join in a pastoral dance. When they have dispersed, leaving Job and his wife alone, Satan enters unperceived. He appeals to Heaven, which opens, revealing the Godhead (Job's Spiritual Self) enthroned within. On the steps are the Heavenly Hosts. Job's Spiritual Self consents that his moral nature be tested in the furnace of temptation.

Scene II. Satan, after a triumphal dance, usurps the throne.

Scene III. Job's sons and daughters are feasting and dancing when Satan appears and destroys them.

Scene IV. Job's peaceful sleep is disturbed by Satan with terrifying visions of War, Pestilence, and Famine.

Scene V. Messengers come to Job with tidings of the destruction of all his possessions and the death of his sons and daughters. Satan introduces Job's Comforters, three wily hypocrites. Their dance at first simulates compassion, but this gradually changes to rebuke and anger. Job rebels: "Let the day perish wherein I was born." He invokes his vision of the Godhead, but the opening Heaven reveals Satan upon the throne. Job and his friends shrink in terror.

Scene VI. There enters Elihu who is young and beautiful. "Ye are old and I am very young." Job perceives his sin. The Heavens then open, revealing Job's Spiritual Self enthroned.

Scene VII. Satan again appeals to Job's Godhead, claiming the victory, but is repelled and driven down by the Sons of the Morning. Job's household build an altar and worship with musical instruments, while the heavenly dance continues.

Scene VIII. Job sits a humbled man in the sunset of restored prosperity, surrounded by his family, upon whom he bestows his blessing.

*

Job had its origin in Mr. Geoffrey Keynes's long study of the designs of William Blake, upon whose life and works he has long been a distinguished authority. The simplicity and power of the drama portrayed in Blake's *Book of Job* suggested to him a possible theme for a ballet, or rather, a masque with dancing. The synopsis which Mr. Keynes finally evolved is that cited above, which synopsis figures in all printed programmes of the ballet. The principal dramatic climax occurs midway in the work when, to quote Mr. Keynes, "Job summons his vision of the God-head, and Satan is revealed upon the throne." The action gains strength from the several contrasts presented; for instance, the calm characters of Job and his Spiritual Self as opposed to the fiery nature of Satan; the false-faced Comforters as opposed to the pure Elihu; and the "Dark horror of Satan's enthronement and the severe beauty of the scene when the Godhead is restored to his place by Job's spiritual enlightenment."

Mr. Keynes next obtained the collaboration of Mrs. Gwendolen Raverat as decorative artist, who devised several scenes and costumes based on Blake's designs.

The author then pondered on the selection of a composer for the music. His choice fell on Dr. Vaughan Williams who was full of enthusiasm for the task.

In the meantime, Mr. Keynes prepared a French version of his scenario which, accompanied by a collection of reproductions of Blake's designs, he submitted to Diaghilev for his consideration. The last-named, however, rejected the ballet [1] as being "too English" and "too old-fashioned."

It now looked as though *Job* would end as a concert piece and accordingly Dr. Vaughan Williams scored his composition for a large orchestra, the work being completed early in 1930. It was first performed by the Queen's Hall Orchestra on October 23rd of the same year.

Then Ninette de Valois took an interest in the ballet and proposed it to the Camargo Society for production. The suggestion was approved and she was entrusted with the choreography. In the meantime Constant Lambert re-scored the piece for a small orchestra. The first performance of the ballet was most favourably received and, in September, 1931, the production was added to the repertory of the Vic-Wells Ballet, by whom it is still frequently given and always with success. The part of Satan is now generally rendered by Robert Helpmann.

*

Job undoubtedly reflects the deeply religious feeling of Blake's drawings, but the choreography shows evidence of the influence of the Central European School, which has tended to cause the angular and jerky elements of movement to be overstressed, and is therefore at times opposed to the spirit of Blake's compositions, which are based on curves massed like a serpent's coils.

---

[1] The Blake reproductions, dryly records Mr. Keynes, were not returned. *Vide: Illustrations of the Book of Job* by William Blake. Edit. Laurence Binyon and Geoffrey Keynes, 1935, p. 60.

Miss De Valois has clearly studied Continental stagecraft to some purpose, for an excellent effect of supernatural power is conveyed by setting Job's Spiritual Self on a throne placed at the head of a flight of broad steps, the varying levels being most effectively employed in the grouping of the Sons of the Morning and in the dramatic scene where Satan, cast out of heaven, rolls headlong down the steps. The two levels of steps and stage are also used symbolically, the spiritual beings moving about the steps while the mortals are restricted to the stage.

Job, with the exception of a few minor parts, is an *ensemble* ballet with one dominant role—that of Satan. Anton Dolin, who created this part, was excellent. His dancing and mime were most impressive and he contrived to surround his movements with a tangible, if invisible, radiance which really did suggest an immortal.

The role of Satan has since been taken with success by Robert Helpmann.

THE HAUNTED BALLROOM

Ballet in 1 Act and 2 Scenes. Book: Geoffrey Toye. Music: Geoffrey Toye. Scenery and Costumes: Motley. Choreography: Ninette de Valois. First produced: Sadler's Wells Theatre, London, April 3rd, 1934.

CHARACTERS

The Master of Tregennis . . .	ROBERT HELPMANN
Young Tregennis	FREDA BAMFORD
Alicia	ALICIA MARKOVA
Ursula	URSULA MORETON
Beatrice	BEATRICE APPLEYARD
The Stranger Player	WILLIAM CHAPPELL

Ghosts, Butler, Footmen.

The appropriate atmosphere is established with the first few notes of the music and retained unbroken until the final lowering of the curtain. The overture commences with the solemn tolling of a bell, which is succeeded by a disturbing melody, from time to time broken with ghostly sounds—heavy thuds, the liquid notes of running water, and the faint whispers of a waltz tune. A sense of impending tragedy invades the dark theatre.

The curtain rises to disclose a large bare room, which has clearly not been used for many years. From the centre of the ceiling hangs a chandelier with thick ropes of cobweb stretching from its branches to the topmost corners of the surrounding walls.

Enter young Tregennis, followed by three ladies in ball-dress, each carrying a large fan. The boy, in granting their wishes to be shown the room, is not without deep misgivings. But the ladies mock his fears and fluttering their fans begin to dance. While he entreats them to desist, his father enters and sternly orders him to bed.

His son absent, he relates the tragic story of the ballroom in which so many of his ancestors were found dead. The tale ended, the ladies nervously take their departure; but the Master of Tregennis remains gazing into space, obsessed with the fear that he is doomed to the fate of his ancestors.

*

After a brief musical interlude, which intensifies the eerie atmosphere, the curtain rises on the second scene. Gradually the prevailing gloom lightens and the walls are seen to be hung with faded portraits. Then, strange happening, the walls become semi-transparent and give place to a dark sky powdered with stars.

A sombre cloaked figure steals into the room and opens wide the door. Clad entirely in black, masked, and wearing a tall hat crowned with nodding sable plumes, he presents an awe-inspiring figure. The Stranger lifts an ivory pipe to his lips and summons an array of spectral dancers, who tread the measures of a weird dance.

The Master of Tregennis, unable to sleep, appears in the doorway, drawn to the ballroom by an irresistible power. He asks the Stranger who his companions are, and is told that they are dancers waiting for the Master to lead them. He flings off his dressing-gown and bounds and spins in a mad dance. Enter three more ghostly dancers, who resemble the three ladies who had invaded the ballroom. They dance with fans. The music grows more mysterious and threatening; and through the turgid melody emerge snatches of a waltz tune, mingled with the hiss of driving sleet and the rattle of falling stones.

One of the ghosts with a fan dances alone, and now all her companions recede into the night. The Master, attracted by this beautiful phantom, dances with her. But soon the spectres return, followed by the spirits of the Master's ancestors, to take their part in the gruesome measure. The waltz melody grows more insistent, louder, and wilder, to become a mad inferno of dance-compelling rhythm from which the Master cannot escape. Struggle as he will, he is urged on by these relentless whirling wraiths. But exhaustion fast reaches its limit and suddenly he drops dead. The ghostly company fades from sight, the stars vanish, and the ballroom takes on its wonted gloom.

*

A ghostly bell awakens the sleeping house to a sense of tragedy. The youthful heir bursts into the room, followed by the startled guests. Then he sees his father's lifeless body, and his horror is echoed by the ladies.

As the latter sadly take their departure, retainers bear the Master away. Young Tregennis, pale and distraught, stares into space, conscious that one day he, too, must fall victim to the same dread fate.

*

This ballet is one of the most popular of De Valois's compositions. The choreography is interesting and musical; the mimed passages are effective and easily comprehensible; and the eerie atmosphere is maintained throughout. The most effective part of the composition is the final *ensemble,* ending in the Master's death.

De Valois has made use of the technique of the classical ballet for the dances arranged for the Master and his guests, but the *ensembles* are conceived in the spirit of the modern German school of mass movement. While the actual result is admirable, the mixture of styles, artistically considered, must be accounted a fault. Finally, the concluding scene, in which the heir finds his father's body, is too long drawn out and comes almost in the nature of an anti-climax.

Markova gave a fine performance as Alicia and invested the role with a remarkable phantom-like quality which has not been attained so far by her successors. Freda Bamford's portrait of Young Tregennis is still the best. William Chappell, as the dignified Stranger Player, continues to give a dignified rendering of a difficult part.

Robert Helpmann as the Master of Tregennis dominates the ballet throughout. Not only does he dance well, but he is possessed of a real dramatic sense and appreciation of character which combine to produce an inspired portrait which lives in the memory.

The scenery and costumes are excellent; indeed, the first scene deserves high praise for the manner in which the maximum of effect is obtained by the simplest means.

BAR AUX FOLIES-BERGÈRE

Ballet in 1 Act. Book: Ninette de Valois. Music: Emmanuel Chabrier. Scenery and Costumes: William Chappell. Choreography: Ninette de Valois. First produced: Mercury Theatre, London, May 15th, 1934.

CHARACTERS

La Goulue, *étoile du Can-Can* . .	ALICIA MARKOVA
La Fille au Bar	PEARL ARGYLE
Grille d'Egout ⎫	DIANA GOULD
Hirondelle ⎪ Can-Can . .	MARY SKEAPING
Nini Patte en l'air ⎬	TAMARA SVETLOVA
La Môme Fromage ⎭	MONA KIMBERLEY
Valentin, *garçon*	FREDERICK ASHTON
Adolphe ⎫	WILLIAM CHAPPELL
Gustave ⎬ *habitués du Bar* . . .	WALTER GORE
Le Vieux Marcheur	OLIVER REYNOLDS
Servante	SUZETTE MORFIELD

Scene. The bar at the Folies-Bergère, about 1870. Along the rear wall, which is mirrored, runs a marble-faced counter, holding a collection of vari-shaped bottles. In the left foreground chairs and small round tables.

When the curtain rises, the barmaid is seen standing behind the counter, gazing vacantly into space. Recalling herself with an effort, she finds occupation in dusting the bottles, polishing the glasses, and arranging her hair.

Enter Adolphe and Gustave, two frequenters of the bar, who already seem to see things through a haze. They subside into chairs by the counter and order drinks.

Valentin the waiter bustles in. He is succeeded by Grille d'Egout who, after a spirited display of high spirits, seats herself at one of the small tables. Valentin serves her with a drink, steals a kiss, pats her knee, and strokes her arms—all in a twinkling. The other Can-Can girls come in and are soon busy exchanging confidences. The two friends at the bar begin telling each other interminable stories of their successes as anglers.

Meanwhile, Valentin has transferred his attentions to the barmaid. At his entreaty she leaves the counter and dances with him. It is plain that she is in love with the handsome waiter.

A gay old gentleman arrives on the scene and, seeing the girls, chucks them under the chin. They go out and return with La Goulue, the star of the Folies-Bergère. The old gentleman, excited by all this beauty, claps his hands and offers to stand champagne all round. For his benefit the girls dance a spirited Can-Can, which meets with his cordial approval.

Now La Goulue renders a solo. The susceptible Valentin, carried away by her flashing eyes, mincing steps, and frothy petticoats, forsakes the barmaid for the star.

Gradually the dancers and habitués take their departure until there remain only Adolphe, Gustave, and the barmaid. A slatternly woman comes in with a pail and floor-cloth. Seeing the two men dozing by the counter, she throws a little water on them. They awake with a start, place each a visiting-card on the counter, and, staggering to their feet, go off arm-in-arm.

The barmaid slowly tears up the cards, places her elbows on the counter, and, resting her chin on her knuckles, stares fixedly into space.

*

Mme. Rambert, the director of the Ballet Club, had long thought of Manet's painting, *Bar aux Folies-Bergère,* as the focal point of a ballet, and much credit is due to Ninette de Valois for the way in which, while retaining the Fille au Bars as the central character, she contrived to build up a succession of appropriate and reasonable incidents which afforded excuse for dancing and mime. It should be stressed that this is definitely a chamber-ballet designed for the miniature Mercury Theatre with its intimate atmosphere, for the production undoubtedly loses when given under different conditions.

The piece is particularly associated with Pearl Argyle, who gave an inspired performance as the Fille au Bar. She had the features of a Manet and she evoked the jaded air of a young woman who is weary of her tawdry surroundings, and has no illusions left.

Another interesting portrait was Markova's La Goulue, a period impression, purged of the crudity of the original, a portrait at once piquant and harmless as a salted almond, if such a comparison be permitted. She had little to do, but she did it perfectly, with such artless naughtiness, and with so engaging an air, as to be irresistible.

Ashton was brilliant as Valentin—dapper, suave, deft, lively as quicksilver, and he treated the girls with an easy familiarity which succeeded by its very audacity.

Of the several Can-Can dancers, Diana Gould's Grille d'Egout was the nearest to reality.

So far as the choreography is concerned, the mimed portions are more interesting than the actual dances. Miss De Valois wisely restricted the latter to the simple expression of gaiety, for the Can-Can which was the delight of Toulouse-Lautrec and his contemporaries, might prove startling seen *au naturel*.

THE RAKE'S PROGRESS

Ballet in 6 Scenes. Book: Gavin Gordon. Music Gavin Gordon. Scenery and Costumes: Rex Whistler. Choreography: Ninette de Valois. First produced: Sadler's Wells Theatre, London, May 20th, 1935.

CHARACTERS

The Rake	WALTER GORE
The Tailor	CLAUDE NEWMAN
The Jockey	RICHARD ELLIS
The Fencing-Master . . .	JOHN BYRON
The Bravo	MAURICE BROOKE
The Horn-Blower	FRANK STAFF
The Betrayed Girl	ALICIA MARKOVA
Her Mother	AILNE PHILLIPS
The Dancing-Master . . .	HAROLD TURNER
The Dancer	URSULA MORETON
The Servant	JILL GREGORY
The Rake's Friend	WILLIAM CHAPPELL
Ladies of the Town	SHEILA McCARTHY
	GWYNETH MATHEWS
	ELIZABETH MILLER
	PEGGY MELLISS
	DORIS MAY
The Ballad Singer	JOY NEWTON
Musicians	FRANK STAFF
	LESLIE EDWARDS
The Creditors	CLAUDE NEWMAN
	MAURICE BROOKE
	LESLIE EDWARDS
The Gamblers	RICHARD ELLIS
	LESLIE EDWARDS
	FRANK STAFF
The Gentleman with a Rope . . .	HAROLD TURNER
The Violinist	JOHN BYRON

The Sailor . . . . . . CLAUDE NEWMAN
The King . . . . LESLIE EDWARDS
The Pope . . . . MAURICE BROOKE
Visitors . . . . GWYNETH MATHEWS
                        PEGGY MELLISS
                        DORIS MAY

Scene I. The Rake at Home.

The Rake, having inherited a fortune, is surrounded by a group of importunate representatives of the arts proper to a man of fashion, anxious to enter his service. While he dabbles in these several pursuits a mother arrives with her daughter, whom the Rake has ruined under promise of marriage, and whom he now offers to buy off.

Scene II. A house of ill-fame.

The Rake makes merry in the company of ladies of the town, drinks heavily, and joins in the songs contributed to the company by a tattered ballad-monger.

Scene III. A street.

The Rake, having squandered his patrimony, is about to be arrested for debt, when the girl he has betrayed pays his creditors with her savings.

Scene IV. A gaming-house.

The Rake attempts to retrieve his position at the gaming-table, only to lose his all.

Scene V. The debtor's prison.

The Rake is committed to the debtor's prison, but the girl promises to help him.

Scene VI. The mad-house.

The Rake, ruined in body and mind, dies in a mad-house.

*

The Rake's Progress is based on the well-known series of paintings by William Hogarth, which are in the Soane Museum, London. The eight episodes which form the subject of the original pictures have been reduced to six, by combining the first two and omitting the fifth, in which the Rake marries for wealth, which would obviously complicate an otherwise simple tale.

The scenery is constructed on lines similar to those employed by the late Claud Lovat Fraser in his setting for *The Beggar's Opera,* and consists of a permanent setting with an act-drop, depicting a street in the neighbourhood of Covent Garden, and a back-drop changed with each scene.

The Rake's Progress is not so much a ballet as a mime play with dances. In the first episode the best numbers are the Tailor's Dance, the Horn-Blower's Dance, and the Dancing-Master's long solo, which latter is so well rendered by Harold Turner. It must be observed, however, that this conception depicts a ballet-dancer rather than the affected, stilted creature typical of so many dancing-masters of the period.

The scene of the orgy is very lively and the nearest of any to the Hogarth spirit.

The fourth episode is well devised, but is purely a mime play set to music.

The sixth episode is far too long and needs to be shortened considerably, first because it drags and secondly because it is inadvisable to prolong this type of situation, the sole purpose of which is to bring the tale to its final stage of awful retribution. This scene includes a remarkable dance with a rope, which, as rendered by Turner, is a genuine creation, and, in its way, as macabre as Massine's "Barman's Dance" in *Union Pacific.*

The principal roles of the Rake and the Betrayed Girl have had several interpreters, the best so far being Robert Helpmann and Elizabeth Miller respectively.

KURT JOOSS

KURT JOOSS was born on January 12th, 1901, on the family estate at Wasseralfingen, Würtemburg, Germany. At the age of nine he went to school at the Realgymnasium at Aalen, a town nearby, and in 1919 he became a student at the High School for Music at Stuttgart, where he studied singing, piano, and harmony. In June 1920 he took an additional course of study at a Dramatic School.

In July he made the acquaintance of the German dance innovator, Rudolf von Laban, whose views interested him profoundly. Then he was faced with the problem of choosing between the theatre and returning to the family estate. He decided to study farming and to this end went to Ulm, where he remained until November, 1921, when, unable to resist his passion for the arts, he renounced the family estate and joined Laban, then attached to the National Theatre, Mannheim. He studied with Laban for some three years, first as pupil, and later as his principal dancer and assistant.

In June, 1924, Jooss was appointed *Bewegungsregisseur* (producer for all movement used in Dancing, Drama, and Opera) at the State Theatre, Münster, at that time the most modernist theatre in all Germany. Among his fellow-workers in the Dance Group (which gave separate performances as well as danced in Opera and Drama) were Aino Siimola and Sigurd Leeder. Fritz Cohen, a young composer, joined the theatre to study opera production. The Dance Group became known as the "Neue Tanzbühne."

During the period July, 1924, to October, 1926, Jooss produced several ballets, some with stories by himself—*A Persian Ballet* (Wellesz), 1924, *In Search of a Wife* (1925), *Dido and Aeneas* (Purcell), 1926, *Tragedy* (Cohen), 1926. In September, 1925, the "Neue Tanzbühne" toured Germany.

In October, 1926, Jooss left that organisation to study in Paris and Vienna. In 1927 he returned to Germany, and, in September, founded at Essen the "Folkwang-Schulen," with himself as director and Leeder as head instructor.

A year later Jooss founded the "Folkwang-Tanztheater-Studio," whose original members included Aino Siimola, Sigurd Leeder, Fritz Cohen, and his wife Elsa Kahl. In August, 1929, Jooss married Aino Siimola.

The following month he was appointed supervisor of the Dance Group at the Opera House, Essen, and the "Folkwang Tanz-bühne" gave its first public performances. In August, 1930, Jooss was appointed *maître de ballet,* and his organisation became the Ballet Group of the Opera House.

When Rolf de Maré, the director of the *Archives Internationales de la Dance,* announced his intention to stimulate the art of choreography by the offer of a number of monetary prizes for the three best ballets submitted to a Board of Judges, Jooss resolved to enter for the competition. His ballet was called *The Green Table.* The Essen Opera House bore the expense of the costumes and, after a performance in the nature of a dress rehearsal, Jooss and his company left for Paris. His composition was awarded the first prize.

Then *The Green Table* was presented publicly at Paris, where its success led to a succession of tours first in Germany, then Belgium and Holland, Paris again, and Switzerland, to conclude in June, 1933, with the first London season at the Savoy Theatre.

About this time the members of the company seceded from the Essen Opera to form a new self-supporting organisation styled "Ballets Jooss." The company went on a first world tour, September, 1933–June, 1934. In April of the latter year the school was transferred from Essen to Dartington Hall, Totnes, England, to form the Arts Department of that experimental organisation founded by Mr. and Mrs. L. K. Elmhirst. Here, too, the company study and rehearse new productions in preparation for forthcoming seasons. The "Ballets Jooss" went on a second world tour from September, 1935–June, 1936, to be followed by a third world tour, which began on October, 1936.

Jooss has composed the choreography for a number of ballets as follows: *A Persian Ballet* (1924); *In Search of a Wife*, The Demon* (both 1925); *Tragedy*, The Den,* Ballets in *Dido and Aeneas* (all 1926); *Drosselbart*, Room No.* 13*, *Pavane for a Dead Infanta*, Suite* 1929* (all 1929); *Petrouchka, Gaukelei, Le Bal, Danses Polovtsiennes, Coppélia, Die Puppenfee* (1930); *Le Fils Prodigue** (1931); *Pulcinella*, The Green Table*, Big City*, Ball in Old Vienna*,* (all 1932); *The Prodigal Son*, The Seven Heroes** (both 1933); *Ballade*, Johann Strauss—to-night*, The Mirror** (all 1935). Those ballets for which Jooss is also responsible for the theme are denoted by an asterisk.

Jooss's choreography is largely influenced by his early collaboration with Laban, to which he has united certain elements of the technique of the classical ballet. He is at his best in dramatic themes, and his later work shows a distinct partiality for the use of modern sociological problems as a basis for choreographic expression.

His ballets are remarkable for the inter-relation between music and movement, the fine grouping, and forceful miming. The majority of his productions are given against a black velvet surround, the requisite atmosphere being produced by skilful lighting.

THE GREEN TABLE

Dance of Death in 8 Scenes. Book: Kurt Jooss. Music: Fritz Cohen. Costumes: Hein Heckroth. Choreography: Kurt Jooss. First produced: Théâtre des Champs-Elysées, Paris, July 3rd, 1932.

CHARACTERS

Death	M. KURT JOOSS
The Leader	M. ERNST UTHOFF
The Young Soldier	M. WALTER WURG
The Old Soldier	M. RUDOLF PESCHT
The Young Girl	MLLE. LISA CZOBEL
The Woman	MLLE. ELSA KAHL
The Old Mother	MLLE. FRIDA HOLST
The War-Profiteer	M. KARL BERGEEST

Gentlemen in Black, Soldiers, Women.

The "green table" is the long table covered with baize at which diplomats are wont to confer. The opening scene shows a number of gentlemen in morning dress engaged in discussion. The arguments for and against are vigorously developed by the opposing sides. There are moments of rage, misunderstanding, conciliation, fresh provocation, menaces, and passionate disagreement which flares up into a declaration of war, symbolised by the diplomats' drawing revolvers from their breast-pockets and firing them at each other.

The action passes to the world outside. We see the young men in uniform taking their places in the ranks and the tearful farewells with mothers, sweethearts and wives; scenes of battle; refugees; a brothel; and the home-coming of the survivors. And through all these scenes stalks the grim figure of Death wearing the trappings of Mars—ponderous, patient, remorseless—claiming the young soldier, the old soldier, the aged mother, and the young man, in turn.

The action switches back to the first scene when peace is symbolised by the diplomats' firing their revolvers in the air. The conference is resumed.

*

The Green Table is a modern Dance of Death, conceived in the mordant humour of a Rops, a Daumier, or a Forain. It owes its inspiration to the events of the Great War and doubtless something of its extraordinary success is due to its topicality, for there are many members of the audience who can savour the ballet's grim humour with a zest sharpened by personal acquaintance with similar scenes. The legendary glory of war is proved to be a hollow sham, a diplomats' game in which Death, the looker-on, takes all.

The ballet sprang into fame through winning the first prize of 25,000 francs in a choreographic competition organised by the *Archives Internationales de la Danse,* Paris. This success was followed by a Paris season in which *The Green Table* was the principal attraction. Since then the ballet has been given all over the world, everywhere making a deep impression.

It is part dance, part dramatic movement, very modern in treatment, and presented with a sure feeling for design in the construction of its groups and ground patterns; while the executants play their part with a delicate sense of the harmony of rhythm and movement, and a dramatic intensity in keeping with the tragic theme. The orchestration of movement in the opening scene is a first-rate piece of composition, its satirical content heightened by the very ingenious masks, designed by Heckroth, which are worn by the dancers. The whole production is dominated by Jooss's impressive performance as Death.

IMPRESSIONS OF A BIG CITY

Ballet in 1 Act and 3 Scenes. Book: Kurt Jooss. Music: Alex-ander Tansman. Choreography: Kurt Jooss. First produced: Opera House, Cologne, November 21st, 1932.

CHARACTERS

The Young Girl . . . . . . MLLE. MASCHA LIDOLT
The Simple Young Man . . . . M. SIGURD LEEDER
The Libertine . . . . . . M. ERNST UTHOFF

Children	{ Karl Bergeest Mlle. Frida Holst Mlle. Lisa Czobel M. Heiz Rosen
Mothers	{ Mlle. Trude Pohl Mlle. Aino Siimola

The ballet opens with a suggestion of a busy street at night-time, with typical figures passing by. Anyone who has stood at the corner of Piccadilly Circus must have received that sensation of watching the turning of an enormous wheel, whose rim is dotted with figures which sweep into view and then pass from sight. That is the impression produced by this scene.

Among the crowd are two sweethearts of the working class, but a well-dressed libertine lures the girl from her lover, by inviting her to a dance-hall.

The second scene shows the couple visiting the workers' quarter, where the girl goes to her dwelling to return, clad in evening dress, to her admirer, followed by the half-curious, half-cynical glances of the neighbours.

The third scene shows the dance-hall filled with dancing couples. While the two newcomers join in the whirling throng, the girl's sweetheart arrives to look on with rage and resentment. The dancers depart and he is left alone.

*

The choreography is again part dance, part dramatic movement, with just a hint of the mechanical in the action to suggest that the dancers are puppets directed by Fate. The choreography is simple in structure and highly effective, owing to the skilful lighting and the adroit timing of the action.

The music used is Tansman's *Sonatine Transatlantique*.

RUTH PAGE

R UTH PAGE was born at Indianapolis. Her father was a well-known surgeon; her mother is devoted to music. Their daughter first studied dancing when she was twelve years old, with local teachers. Then, learning that the Pavlova Company was at Chicago, she went to study with their *maître de ballet,* Ivan Clustine. Eventually she became a member of the company during their tour of South America, Central America, Cuba and Mexico.

On her return to Chicago she studied with Adolph Bolm, who did much to develop her dance talent, and when he produced Carpenter's *Birthday of the Infanta* for the Chicago Opera Company he gave her the leading role of the Infanta, in which she made a decided success. Later, he founded his Ballet Intime and she became his *première danseuse.*

In 1922 Ruth Page went to New York as *première danseuse* in the second Music Box Revue, where she remained for a year, then toured America the year after. In 1924 she returned to Chicago to join Bolm in a new organisation called the Chicago Allied Arts, which was devoted to the production of modern ballets. The following year Bolm went to Buenos Aires as guest choreographer to the Colon Theatre, and there Ruth Page appeared as the Queen of Shemakhân and the Ballerina respectively in *Le Coq d'Or* and *Petrouchka.*

On her return to Chicago, Ruth Page was engaged as *première danseuse* for the Allied Arts performances for the seasons of 1925 and 1926, and in the summer of the latter year she became both *première danseuse* and *maîtresse de ballet* to the Ravinia Opera Company, a post she retained until 1931. It was during this period that she began her first essays in choreography.

In 1926 and 1927 Ruth Page was engaged as *première danseuse* to the Metropolitan Opera Company, of New York; and in the spring of 1928 she danced in the first production of Stravinsky's *Apollon Musagète,* which was given at Washington.

Soon afterwards she visited Tokyo, where she gave a series of performances; and, in 1930, she presented a number of her dances in Russia. The same year she effected an artistic partnership with Harald Kreutzberg with whom she toured for three years.

In 1934 the Chicago Grand Opera Company was reorganised, and as a result Ruth Page became its *première danseuse* and *maîtresse de ballet*. She has already produced many dances and a number of ballets, for instance: *Sun Worshippers* (Loomis); *La Guiablesse* (Still), 1934; *Iberian Monotone* (Ravel), 1934; *La Valse* (Ravel); *Hear Ye! Hear Ye!* (Copland), 1934; *Love Song* (1935); *Gold Standard* (Ibert), 1934; *Americans in Paris* (Gershwin), 1936; *American Pattern* (Moross), 1937. The Russian artist, N. Remisov, has provided interesting settings for many of her ballets and has collaborated with her in several of their themes.

Ruth Page is undoubtedly a choreographer with a modern out-look and a flair for adapting current topics to the purpose of ballet. She has also done much to foster interest in native music by commissioning American composers to write the scores of several of the ballets she has produced.

LA GUIABLESSE

Ballet in 1 Act. Book: Ruth Page. Music: William Grant Still. Scenery and Costumes: Nicholas Remisov. Choreography: Ruth Page. First produced: Grand Opera House, Chicago, June 23rd, 1933.

La Guiablesse is a she-devil who haunts the folklore of Martinique, a fatal siren that tempts men to cast themselves down from pinnacles, a siren who wails for an earthly love.

The scene is an island where tropical heat incubates a world of awesome and vaporous beings. It is a writhing garden of the earth wherein the twisted rocks, the fleshy plants, and swaying trees are evil personalities which terrify the simple folk. Here sunset explodes with quivering colours that stupefy the mind; here a population of spirits disturb the night. Men are never secure. Even at dazzling noon stroll the most sinister of all—beings who work ruin with the appearance of beauty.

Such a being is La Guiablesse who, with her subtle deceit, comes to separate and destroy dark-skinned lovers. Intangible as she is, it is not against flesh and blood, but against powers, against darkness that they wrestle. With the promise of her strange kiss she lures men to dizzy precipices under the dying and crimson sun. Then with eldritch laughter she reveals her real and hideous face. From her incredible height she stoops to embrace her follower, who finds escape only in death on the rocks below.[1]

*

La Guiablesse was a negro ballet with an all-negro cast, although on two occasions Ruth Page danced the title-role.

In this ballet a singer behind the scenes sings a weird song.

HEAR YE! HEAR YE!

Ballet in 1 Act. Book: Ruth Page and Nicholas Remisov. Music: Aaron Copland. Scenery and Costumes: Nicholas Remisov. Choreography: Ruth Page. First produced: Chicago Opera House, Chicago, November 30th, 1934.

CHARACTERS

A Prosecuting Attorney	MARK TURBYFILL	
A Defending Attorney	PAUL DU PONT	
The Judge	ROBERT ROBINSON	
A Defendant ⎱ a night-club dance	⎰ RUTH PAGE	
The Victim ⎰ team	⎱ BENTLEY STONE	
A Maniac ⎱ two other defendants	⎰ RAYMOND WEAMER	
A Chorus-Girl ⎰	⎱ MARGOT KOCHE	
A Night-Club Hostess ⎱	⎰ VIOLET STRANDZ	
A Bride ⎬ witnesses	BETTINA ROSAY	
A Groom ⎰	WALTER CAMRYN	
A Negro Waiter ⎰	⎱ DON ROBERTO	

Jury, Chorus-Girls.

The ballet begins with an overture, during which headlines reminiscent of sensationalist journalism are flashed upon the curtain, for instance: "Murder in a Night-Club," "Who is Guilty?" "Three Versions of the Crime."

The curtain rises to reveal a stylised court-room with the judge seated at a raised desk in the centre, the jury to the left, members of the general public—represented by dummies—to the right, and the witness stand.

The male dancing star at a night-club has been murdered. The court proceedings begin with arguments presented by an emotional attorney for the prosecution, and opposed by a nonchalant attorney for the defence.

---

[1] This description is adopted from the original scenario.

The first witness is the night-club hostess, the essence of sophistication, who gives her account of the crime. As she begins her story the lights dim and there is a flash-back of the scene at the night-club on the fatal evening.

A number of chorus-girls enter and dance to a jazz rhythm. They are followed by the star team, a male dancer and his partner. A chorus-girl produces a revolver, which she aims at the male dancer, but his partner snatches the weapon from her and shoots him herself.

(*There is a black-out and the scene returns to the court-room*).

The jury are asked to give their verdict. They point to the male dancer's partner and the word "guilty" is flashed on the walls of the court-room.

The two attorneys resume their arguments and the next witness is called—a honeymoon couple. They give their version of the crime, seeing everything through a rose-coloured mist.

(*Again the lights dim and there is a flash-back to the night-club*).

The chorus-girls enter and dance, and this time their work takes on a sentimental character which is stressed in the sugary number given by the star and his partner. A chorus-girl produces a revolver and shoots the male dancer.

(*There is a black-out and the scene returns to the court-room*).

This time the jury find the chorus-girl guilty.

The two attorneys resume their arguments and the third witness is called—a negro waiter. He dramatises everything he describes.

(*Again the light dims and there is a flash-back to the night-club*).

The chorus-girls dance their number which now becomes a jungle jazz, while the star and his partner dance a Blues. A maniac glides in, dances with the male partner, and shoots him.

(*There is a black-out and the scene returns to the court-room*).

This time the jury find the maniac guilty.

The lawyers resume their arguments and finally shake hands.

The judge calls the next case with a loud rap of his hammer.

ANTON DOLIN

ANTON DOLIN, christened Patrick Healey-Kay, was born of
English parents at Slinfold, Sussex, on July 27th, 1904; there
was, however, a strain of Irish blood in him derived from his
grandmother. He was a hardy youngster who delighted in violent
exercise. When he was ten the family went to live at Brighton,
where he was seized with a desire to learn dancing. He studied
first with Miss Clarice James, then under the Misses Gracie and
Lily Cone, who visited Brighton weekly. In due course he
appeared in a display organised by the Misses Cone at the Brighton
Hippodrome. The manager expressed his approval of the young
dancer, and it was decided that he should go to London and receive
a thorough training for the stage.

At first a series of professional engagements led him away from
ballet into drama. He played the part of Peter in *Bluebell in Fairyland,* and that of John in *Peter Pan.* He became a pupil at the
Conti School and won the first prize for elocution given by the
British Empire Shakespearean Society. This success secured him
further engagements for minor parts in other plays.

In August, 1917, he saw Astafieva's production of *The Swin-
burne Ballet* at the London Coliseum and decided that he must
learn dancing from her. Before the month was out he had his first
lesson. Some four years later Diaghilev visited the school in search
of some extra dancers for *The Sleeping Princess,* then in rehearsal
at the Alhambra. Dolin was chosen and danced in the *corps de
ballet* during the thee months' run of the piece.

On August 26th, 1923, he made his first success at the Albert Hall
in an evening of ballet devised by Astafieva, when he appeared in
two solo dances composed by himself: *"Hymn to the Sun"* and
"Danse Russe." Reports of his favourable reception reached Diaghilev's ears and, in September, Dolin went to Paris to give him an
audition. He was offered and accepted a contract and joined the
company in November at Monte Carlo.

Diaghilev was interested in his new acquisition and arranged for
him to have both class and private lessons with Nijinska, then

maîtresse de ballet. A few months later he was cast for the role of Daphnis in *Daphnis et Chloë,* in which he made his *début* on January 1st, 1924. In June he made a big success as the Beau Gosse in *Le Train Bleu,* a ballet created specially for him. During his association with the company he appeared in *Cimarosiana, Les Tentations de la Bergère, Le Lac des Cygnes, Le Spectre de la Rose, Les Facheux, Zéphyre et Flore, Pulcinella,* and *Le Carnaval,* and danced the famous *"L'Oiseau Bleu"* in *Aurora's Wedding.* But, early in 1925, he quarrelled with Diaghilev and declined to remain in the company.

In July, Dolin appeared in *The Punch Bowl* revue, for which he arranged the dance *"Alabamy Bound,"* and in another revue, *Palladium Pleasures* (February, 1926). Next followed a season with Phyllis Bedells at the Coliseum Theatre, for which Dolin devised several dances—*"Exercises," "Raguette," "Little Boy Blue," "Ring o' Roses,"* and *"Jack and Jill."* Afterwards Dolin danced in the *Charlot Show for* 1926, in which he arranged two dance scenas— *"The Pedlar"* and *"See-Saw."*

In 1927 Dolin danced with Karsavina at the Coliseum in a revival of *Le Spectre de la Rose,* and then appeared in the short-lived *Whitebirds* revue, after which he founded the Nemchinova-Dolin Ballet with Vera Nemchinova and himself as principals. For their opening season at the Coliseum he produced the ballet, *The Nightingale and the Rose* (music by H. Fraser-Simson), founded on the well-known story by Oscar Wilde.

In February, 1928, the company gave a Paris season at the *Théâtre des Champs-Elysées,* where Dolin produced a new ballet, *Rhapsody in Blue,* to Gershwin's music of the same name, which, with *The Nightingale and the Rose* and a newly composed dance *"Espagnol,"* became the most popular items in the repertory. In October, Dolin produced another ballet, *Revolution,* to an Etude by Chopin. After various tours the two partners decided to end their business association and early in 1929 the company came to a conclusion.

During the January of that year there had been a suggestion that Dolin should rejoin the Diaghilev Ballet. Now negotiations were opened and Dolin finally decided to return. He danced in many of the ballets of the repertory and created important roles in the new productions by Balanchine—*Le Bal* and *Le Fils Prodigue.* Then, in August, Diaghilev died and the troupe was disbanded.

After some dance recitals with Anna Ludmilla as his partner, Dolin went to New York to appear in *The International Revue.* Later in 1930 he returned to London and took part in the productions of the newly established Camargo Society, when he danced Vertumnus in Ashton's *Pomona* and made a great success as Satan in De Valois's *Job*.

From 1931–35 Dolin was principal dancer at the Vic-Wells Ballet, when he left to become a director of, and the principal dancer in, the newly formed Markova-Dolin Ballet, sponsored by Mrs. Henderson, two positions which he still retains.

Dolin has danced the principal role in most of the well known classical and modern ballets. He has a fine technique and is equally at home in pure ballet, character, and modern work. For some years he has been, and still is, the leading English exponent of the classical ballet.

RHAPSODY IN BLUE

Ballet in 1 Act. Book: Anton Dolin. Music: George Gershwin. Scenery and Costumes: Gladys Spencer-Curling. Choreography: Anton Dolin. First produced: Théâtre des Champs-Elysées, Paris, April 16th, 1928.

CHARACTERS

Classic	MME. VÉRA NEMCHINOVA
Jazz	M. ANTON DOLIN
Barman	M. NICHOLAS ZVEREV

Les Mannequins, Les Jazz.

The theme of this ballet is the contest for supremacy between jazz and classical music. Jazz, temporarily vanquished by classical music, eventually triumphs because it is an expression of modern life.

*

This ballet has an interesting origin. Dolin had planned a special attraction for his Paris season, an Egyptian ballet called *The Wings of Horus*. But, when he began work on it, he found the choreography required much longer time for its composition than he had at his disposal. So, thinking over an alternative, he suddenly remembered Gershwin's *Rhapsody in Blue* which he had heard at a party at which Diaghilev was present.

Learning that the composer was in Paris he told him of his plan. Gershwin was so interested that he promised to play the piano part at the first performance, a promise which circumstances prevented his keeping. Nevertheless, he contrived to be present and to share in the numerous calls accorded the production.

The ballet was composed in seven days and proved very successful.

KEITH LESTER

K EITH LESTER was born at Guildford, Surrey, in 1904. He
first studied dancing with Anton Dolin and made his *début*
in the dances arranged by Fokine for Basil Dean's production of
Flecker's *Hassan* (1923).

Lester next studied with Nicholas Legat. He was selected by
Lydia Kyasht as her partner, a position he filled for two years,
when he accepted an invitation from Thamar Karsavina to become
her partner. He joined the *ballerina* at Riga and danced with her
throughout Central Europe for some three years, when he returned
to England.

Lester resumed his studies with Legat and next became the partner of Olga Spessiva in connection with her engagement at the
Colon Theatre, Buenos Aires. During this period Fokine produced
a number of his ballets at that theatre, when Lester danced the
principal roles in *L'Oiseau de Feu, Les Sylphides, Schéhérazade, Le Spectre de la Rose,* and *Thamar.*

At the end of the season, Lester returned to London and danced
in Reinhardt's production of *The Miracle* at the Lyceum Theatre
(1932) for which Massine arranged the dances. When the production went on tour Lester took the part of the Knight. He next
joined the Ida Rubinstein Ballet for its season at the Opera, Paris,
which included the Valéry-Honegger-Fokine ballet, *Semiram's,* in
which he took the part of the Captain, and the Gide-Stravinsky-
Jooss ballet, *Persephone,* in which he took the dual roles of Servi-
teur de Pluton and Triptolème.

Lester toured North America with Ernst Matray in a ballet-
revue and returned to London to join in the formation of the
Markova-Dolin Company (1935), in which he not only danced,
but also composed the choreography of *David* (1935); *Pas de
Quatre* (1936)—a ballet inspired by the celebrated lithograph by
A. E. Chalon and danced to the airs of the famous *Pas de Quatre*
of 1845; *Bach Suite No. 2 B Minor* (1936); and a *"Lament of the
Swans"* interpolated in the company's abbreviated version of *Le
Lac des Cygnes.*

DAVID

Ballet in 6 Episodes. Book: Poppaea Vanda. Music: Maurice Jacobson. Curtain: Jacob Epstein. Scenery and Costumes: Bernard Meninsky. Choreography: Keith Lester. First produced: Theatre Royal, Newcastle-on-Tyne, November 11th, 1935.

CHARACTERS

Jesse	PETER MICHAEL
Eliab	JOHN CRANSTON
Abinadab	JOHN REGAN
Shammah	JOHN THORPE
The Younger Sons of Jesse . . .	FREDERIC FRANKLYN TEDDY HASKELL TRAVIS KEMP ROBERT DORNING
Samuel, the Prophet	ALGERANOFF
David	ANTON DOLIN
Saul	KEITH LESTER
Abner, Captain of the Host . . .	STANLEY JUDSON
Jonathan, son of Saul	GUY MASSEY
Attendant on Saul	NORMAN WALLER
Michal, Saul's daughter . . .	PRUDENCE HYMAN
Abishai	PETER MICHAEL
Ahimelech	ALGERANOFF
Abigail	NATASHA GREGOROVA
Three Priests	BERNARD DE GAUTIER PETER MICHAEL FREDERIC FRANKLYN
Two Prophets	TRAVIS KEMP TEDDY HASKELL

Maidens of Michal, Soldiers, Congregation of Israel.

Episode I. At the house of Jesse.

Jesse sits brooding before his home in Bethlehem. Samuel arrives and asks to see Jesse's sons. He shows him Eliab, his eldest. Samuel approves, but the voice of God warns him that this is not the one. Then Jesse presents Abinadab and Shammah, who are rejected. Samuel is about to depart when Shammah brings forward the younger children, who are also rejected. Samuel asks Jesse if these are all his sons. He shakes his head and summons David, his youngest. Samuel bows his head in prayer and, immediately aware that David is the chosen of God, blesses him to the mingled feelings of David's brothers.

Episode II. Saul's camp.

Saul, Abner, and Jonathan face each other in despair, for each and all fear Goliath. Eliab, Abinadab, and Shammah sit apart from them. Attendants bring Saul his armour. Jonathan climbs to the look-out and scans the enemy. David enters and, going to Saul, offers to fight Goliath. The king replies that he is only a stripling. But David, suddenly conscious of his power, draws himself up to his full height.

Saul offers him his armour and Jonathan his sword, but David declines them, having resolved to trust to the sling he carries at his waist. He leaps on to the parapet and passes from sight. His brothers and Abner kneel in prayer, but Jonathan anxiously watches the combat. Suddenly he gives a shout which brings everyone to the look-out, where they give vent to cries of triumph. Saul dispatches Abner to complete the rout of the Philistines.

David enters, carrying the head of Goliath, which he offers to Saul on his knees. Saul rises and embraces him, his younger brothers dance in triumph, the elder ones depart in jealousy. David is conscious of his power, but Saul, filled with envy, retires to his tent.

David is saddened, but Jonathan sympathises with him and, as they dance together, speaks to him of poetry and music.

Episode III. The House of Saul.

Saul, jealous of David's triumph, tosses uneasily on his couch. Michal, his daughter, tries to soothe him, but in vain. Jonathan also tends his father.

David, at Jonathan's bidding, dances to the sound of his harp, which gradually calms Saul. Michal kneels beside him, looking at David in admiration. Jonathan, too, watches David. When the song is finished, Saul turns his face to the wall. Jonathan goes out.

Michal looks at David. Their glances meet; she looks down and attends to Saul.

Six maidens enter and Michal, looking up, smiles. She will dance to soothe Saul and attract David. So she dances in the midst of her women. David watches and is visibly moved, but he makes no other sign. Saul sleeps.

Michal dismisses her women and remains standing in the centre of the room. David goes to her. They dance together and suddenly he takes her in his arms. They continue their dance, clasped together. Saul wakes and watches them with anger. Michal kneels at David's feet. Saul, furious, flings a javelin at David, but it misses him.

Michal rushes at her father and her cry of distress summons Jonathan, who enters and holds his father. Jonathan signs to David to leave, and, as he departs, Saul sinks down on his couch.

Jonathan studies Saul, then Michal; he cannot reconcile his father's madness, his sister's passion, and David's love.

Episode IV. *The Hill of Hachilah* (*Camp of Saul*).

David awaits Jonathan, while his man, Abishai, keeps watch. The latter calls to David who, going to greet his friend, sees not Jonathan, but Saul. They hide as he enters with Abner and a body of soldiers. Weary and exhausted, the newcomers lie down to sleep, while Abner keeps guard. But even he nods and slumbers.

David and Abishai creep out of their hiding-place. Abishai urges David to kill Saul, but he refuses; instead, he takes Saul's spear and water-bottle and goes to the mountain. From this vantage-point David gives a shout and, displaying his trophies, mocks Abner for his careless watch.

Saul confesses his fault and, calling David down, blesses him. The soldiers close about David but, at a sign from Saul, they stand back and he goes up the mountain-path. Saul watches until David has passed from sight, then gives way to prayer and lamentation.

Episode V. *The Hill of Hachilah* (*Camp of David*).

David and Abigail sit at the tent-door, watching a performance by Abishai. Suddenly, Ahimelech rises and throws something from his belt into a bowl. Smoke rises and through and about this he dances.

Hearing footsteps, David looks up and sees Michal. He signs to Abigail to go into the tent. Abner enters leading Michal. David goes to her while the others quietly efface themselves. She receives him coldly. He dances to her and at last she dances with him.

Abigail watches from the tent and, when she sees Michal's returning love, steps out from the tent. Michal, seeing her, steps back in horror. Abigail kneels to David, then Michal embraces him. Abigail rises and Michal steps back.

David goes to Michal and gently rests his hand on her shoulder, but she casts her eyes down. She looks up and sees Abigail's sneering look. Michal shudders and David sees that she despises him. Abigail takes David's hand and leads him in a daze to the tent. Michal gazes after them and suddenly gives way to tears.

Episode VI. Before the Tabernacle in the City of Zion.

The Ark of God, followed by the king, has passed to the Taber-nacle, to which a gaily-dressed crowd eagerly presses forward. The people return, moving backwards, and last of all comes David, in his royal robes. As the crowd give him passage, he takes off his robe and hands it to two attendants. Then he dances before the Ark. Suddenly he brings the dance to an end. The attendants again drape the robe about his shoulders, and all the populace turn towards the Ark.

Michal watches David from a window and despises him.

*

David has an interesting origin. Miss Vanda formed the plan that David's dance before the Ark would make an interesting theme for a *pas seul,* and Lester found some suitable music in Prokofiev's *"Overture on Jewish Themes."*

When, however, the suggested solo was submitted to Dolin, he proposed that the dance should be expanded into a ballet. Miss Vanda then studied the *"Book of Kings"* and devised five more episodes to lead up to the dance before the Ark, tracing David's life from his humble beginning as a shepherd to his elevation to king-ship. Since Prokofiev's overture was not long enough for the ballet, Maurice Jacobson was invited to compose the music, which he did in collaboration with Lester, who showed him the types of move-ment he wished to use during different stages in the ballet.

Jacob Epstein was invited to design the costumes and scenery but, owing to press of other work, he was unable to accept the com-mission, although he agreed to contribute the curtain. The other designs were entrusted to Bernard Meninsky.

David has an affinity with De Valois's *Job* in that it is a masque rather than a ballet, for the theme of *David* is expressed in terms of dancing, mime, and dramatic movement, sometimes used alter-natively, sometimes combined. The production is founded on clas-sical ballet technique invested with what may be called "local colour" in gesture and pose derived from a study of Assyrian art, which was the dominating influence in the arts of the surrounding countries at this period.

The story is presented with clarity and dignity, and is often full of atmosphere, the choreography being well supported by Meninsky's starkly primitive scenery which is notable for its strength of design.

The best episodes are the calming of Saul's madness, the slaying of Goliath, and David's dance before the Ark. The piece is dominated by Dolin's performance of the title-role, but Lester makes an impressive Saul. Algeranoff both mimes and dances well as Samuel and Ahimelech respectively, while Prudence Hyman gives a charming and sympathetic performance as Michal.

GEORGE BALANCHINE

G EORGE MELITONOVICH BALANCHIVADZE was born at St. Petersburg in 1904. His father, a Georgian, was a well known composer. The son was intended for the army, but since his mother had always wanted a daughter who could be a dancer, it was decided that he should be trained for that profession; if he afterwards failed to make good, he could enter the army.

He presented himself at one of the periodical examinations and, being accepted, entered the Imperial School of Ballet in August, 1914. But he did not care for the life and ran away. He was, however, brought back and this time settled down to his studies. In 1915 he was one of several children chosen to dance beneath the floral garlands held by the villagers in the third act of *La Belle au Bois Dormant*.

This introduction to the actual stage gave the young pupil a new outlook on his studies, and he was as eager now to learn as hitherto he had been unwilling. His teachers were S. C. Andreyanov and P. A. Gerdt. As time passed young Balanchivadze took part in *Esmeralda, Don Quichotte, Paquita, Casse Noisette, Koniok Gorbunok,* and other well-known ballets in the repertory.

In 1917 Tsar Nicholas abdicated and the School of Ballet was closed, although performances of opera and ballet continued to be given throughout the period of civil strife. Meanwhile the dance student worked as a bank-messenger and saddler's apprentice. A year later the school was reopened and the pupils returned to their labours, but there was little fuel and hardly any food.

In 1921 Balanchivadze finished school and entered the ballet company attached to the Maryinsky Theatre. At the same time he entered the Conservatory of Music where for three years he studied piano and theory.

In 1923 he announced a series of performances called "Evenings of the Young Ballet," which were intended to show the development of choreography through the cycles of Petipa, Fokine, and Balanchivadze! But the senior dancers were opposed to the venture and the enterprise was abandoned after the first performance.

Undaunted, Balanchivadze tried his hand at all kinds of dance composition in the intervals of his work in the *corps de ballet* at the Maryinsky Theatre. He produced Cocteau's *Boeuf sur le Toit* as a pantomimic ballet and later contrived a second "Evening of the Young Ballet."

V. Dmitriev, a tenor at the Maryinsky Opera, became interested in Balanchivadze's work and in the dancers associated with him; they included Alexandra Danilova and Tamara Gevergeva. After a considerable difficulty they were accorded permission to go abroad and spread the cause of the new Russian art. Dmitriev, by heroic efforts, managed to arrange a tour of German watering-places, after which the little company went to London, where they appeared at the Empire Theatre at the same time that Layton and Johnstone, the well known American singers, were making their London *début*. Dmitriev obtained an audition with Diaghilev, then in Paris, who was sufficiently impressed to take the company into his own organisation. Since the name Balanchivadze was difficult to pronounce, Diaghilev shortened it to Balanchine.

Not only did he dance for Diaghilev, but he was appointed choreographer in succession to Nijinska. He composed for Diaghilev ten ballets in all: *Barabau* (1925), *La Pastorale* (1925), *Jack in the Box* (1926), *The Triumph of Neptune* (1926), *Le Rossignol* (1926), *La Chatte* (1927), *Apollon Musagète* (1928), *The Gods go a-Begging* (1928), *Le Fils Prodigue* (1929), and *Le Bal* (1929).

When Diaghilev died and the company was disbanded, Balanchine went to Copenhagen as *maître de ballet*. In 1932 René Blum and Col. W. de Basil founded the "Ballets Russes de Monte Carlo" and Balanchine was engaged as choreographer. With a company consisting of promising young dancers, leavened with some former members of the Diaghilev Company, he produced *La Concurrence* and *Cotillon*.

On the conclusion of the first Monte Carlo season, Balanchine left to found a new independent company called "Les Ballets 1933," for which he staged *Errante, Songes, Mozartiana,* and *Les Sept Péchés Capitaux,* given at the Théâtre des Champs-Elysées, Paris. Then followed a London season which, owing to various circumstances, did not achieve the expected success.

At this period Balanchine received and accepted an invitation from Lincoln Kirstein and Edward M. M. Warburg to direct a School of American Ballet which they had in contemplation. The venture materialised and has not only begun to fashion dancers but, under Balanchine's direction, has produced many ballets which have aroused considerable interest, for instance: *Alma Mater*

(1935), *Serenade* (1935), *Transcendance* (1935), *Reminiscence* (1935), *The Bat* (1936), *Orpheus* (1936), *The Fairy's Kiss* (1937), and *The Card Party* (1937).

*

In the course of an interview with the *Dance Journal*,[1] Balanchine gave many details concerning the manner in which he approaches the problem of composing his ballets and dances, which it is of interest to quote.

"When I am about to produce a ballet I approach the task in one of two ways; either I begin with the idea and then look for suitable music, or I hear a certain piece of music which inspires me with an idea.

"In the first case, I much prefer to have the music specially written for me; and to be in constant touch with the composer while he is writing it. I must be able to convey to him exactly what I require, so that the music accords with my action and harmonises with my movements. In the second case, I familiarise myself with the music and try to fathom what the composer had in mind when writing it, or endeavour to conceive a theme which will harmonise with the mood of the music.

"Before beginning any rehearsals I map out an outline of the ballet and the general scheme of the action. I never arrange any of the dances or movements until I am actually rehearsing the artistes. I discuss the setting and costumes with my designer, so that they will accord with my idea; but I do not discuss the ballet with my dancers.

"When I start to rehearse I do not even tell them the plot or anything about the ballet, but, as the work progresses, I may mention the name of a part to one, and say, 'You play the brother of so-and-so.' My dancers do not know what they will have to do, or what characters they will be called upon to portray.

"I have no fixed method of procedure. Sometimes I arrange the end of the ballet first; sometimes I commence in the middle. I have the outline in my head—I never make notes—and then I work out every movement, showing each dancer what he or she must do to the slightest movement, and I expect everyone to copy me in the smallest detail. If I have plenty of time at my disposal I work with each dancer until he or she is perfect in his or her part; if I am pressed for time I expect the soloists to perfect themselves. This was the case with the ballet *The Prodigal Son*, which I had to produce in a fortnight. It was only an hour before the

---

[1] August-October, 1931.

dress-rehearsal that I conceived and arranged the scene where the table is used as a boat. . . .

"To return to the artistes. I expect them to do exactly what I show them and as I wish it to be done. I must make them see a movement as I see it, as if they saw it through my eyes. I do not tell them what they have to portray in their roles, because that would prejudice their conception of them. I make them drop naturally into their parts, so that they gradually come to live them. Nothing is left either to principals or *corps de ballet* to do for themselves; I show them every tiny movement and the least mimetic action; and I count their every step."

THE TRIUMPH OF NEPTUNE

Pantomimic Ballet in 2 Acts and 6 Scenes. Book: Sacheverell Sitwell. Music: Lord Berners. Scenery and Costumes: Adapted from scenes and costumes for the Juvenile Drama, as published by B. Pollock and H. J. Webb. First produced: Lyceum Theatre, London, December 3rd, 1926.

CHARACTERS

The Fairy Queen	MLLE. ALEXANDRA DANILOVA
Tom Tug, a sailor . . .	M. SERGE LIFAR
W. Brown, a journalist . .	M. MICHAEL FEDOROV
Goddess	MME. LYDIA SOKOLOVA
Emerald ⎫ Fairies . .	⎰ MME. LUBOV TCHERNICHEVA
Ruby ⎭	⎱ MME. VERA PETROVA
Sylphs	⎰ MME. LUBOV TCHERNICHEVA
	⎱ MME. VERA PETROVA
Street Dancer	MLLE. TATIANA CHAMIE
The Sailor's Wife . . .	MLLE. BARASCH
The Sailor's Mother . .	MLLE. FEDOROVA
Snowball, a blackman . .	M. GEORGE BALANCHINE
Dandy	M. CONSTANTINE TCHERKAS
Journalists	MM. JAZVINSKY, WINTER
Policemen	MM. HOYER, CIEPLINSKY
Cab Driver	M. PAVLOV
Telescope Keepers . .	MM. BOROVSKY, PETRAKEVICH
Waiter	M. LISSANEVICH
Beggar	M. GEORGE BALANCHINE
Street Hawkers . . .	MM. ROMOV, LADRE
Workmen	MM. STRECHNEV, IGNATOV, HOYER II

Newsvendors	Mm. Jazvinsky, Winter
Newspaper Boys	Mm. Strechnev, Hoyer II, Ignatov
Officer	M. Domansky
Chimney Sweep	M. Gaubier
King of the Ogres . . .	M. Pavlov
Clowns	Mm. Petrakevich, Ladre

Fairies, Harlequins, Pages, Ogres, Attendants on Neptune.

Act I. Scene I. London Bridge.

A crowd of Londoners gather about a magic telescope, by means of which the fairy realm may be observed. Two daring adventurers, a journalist and bluejacket, are about to undertake a voyage to the unknown fairy world.

Act I. Scene II. Cloudland.

The daughters of the air are seen disporting among the clouds.

Act I. Scene III. Farewell.

The two adventurers are seen taking leave of their nearest and dearest. As soon as the sailor is about to take coach for the first stage in their journey, a dandy begins making love to his wife.

Act I. Scene IV. Shipwreck.

A terrible storm ensues and the travellers, now crossing the ocean, are shipwrecked and cast into the sea. They are enabled to cling to a rock from which they are rescued by the goddess.

Act I. Scene V. Fleet Street.

Here we see the staffs of two rival newspapers trying to obtain news of the explorers.

Act I. Scene VI. The Frozen Wood.

In this scene we see a band of fairies at play in an enchanting forest covered with snow, which glitters in the pale moonlight.

Act II. Scene I. The Giant Hand.

The dandy is seen dancing a polka with the sailor's wife, to the strains of a brass band. They go inside her house and their shadows are observed against the blind. They are seen about to embrace when the sailor's spirit hastens back in defence of his honour. The shadow of his hand, bearing a knife, is seen against the blind. Two policemen scurry forward to arrest the sailor but they grasp an empty shadow, his spirit has already returned to fairyland.

Act II. Scene II. The Evil Grotto.

Lurking in a dark grotto are a number of fearsome giants with huge misshapen heads. The explorers, however, are undeterred, and fight their way into the castle.

Act II. Scene III. The Ogres' Castle.

Here the journalist is seized by the attendants of the King of the Ogres and sawn in half. The sailor manages to escape.

Act II. Scene IV. London Bridge.

A drunken negro upsets the magic telescope and so all connection with the fariy world is severed.

Act II. Scene V. The Triumph of Neptune.

The sailor, disgusted by his wife's infidelity, resolves to accept fairy form. Transformed into a Fairy Prince he marries Neptune's daughter.

Act II. Scene VI. Apotheosis.

The wedding.

*

The origin of *The Triumph of Neptune* is a little involved. In July of 1926 Lord Berners had completed a number of pieces of music with a view to their being used for a ballet. Diaghilev liked the compositions and invited Sacheverell Sitwell to write an appropriate book.

Diaghilev first wished for something modern and Sitwell showed him drawings by Wadsworth and Roberts. Then the director expressed a preference for a ballet dealing with the Elizabethan period and suggested that the *Merry Wives of Windsor* or *As You Like It* might be adapted to that purpose. Again he altered his mind and stated that, on consideration, it would be best to have an entirely new work with spoken verses. To this end Edith Sitwell wrote some specimen verses. But still Diaghilev could not make up his mind.

Finally Sitwell proposed a ballet based either on Cruikshank's drawings or upon the "penny plain and twopence coloured" sheets of the Juvenile Drama. The director was attracted by the latter suggestion and, escorted by Sitwell, visited Pollock's historic shop in Hoxton, where Diaghilev spent some time examining the coloured sheets and purchasing a selection for study. A little later Diaghilev went to Florence where he was joined by Sacheverell Sitwell, and there, after further discussion, it was decided that the ballet should be on the lines of an old English pantomime.

The ballet was attractive both in its conception and its presentation; there were charming vignettes of Victorian life; a suggestion of the opening chapter of one of Jules Verne's romances in which the hero prepares to undertake some stupendous journey such as attempting to compass the world in eighty days or planning a rocket voyage to the moon; and a swift tour through a fantastic land of transformation and make believe, a world of burlesque and extravaganza doubtless inspired by Dibdin and Planché.

Two of the most charming scenes associated with dancing were "Cloudland" and "The Frozen Wood" which gave opportunities for dances in the tradition of the classical ballet. Danilova as the Fairy Queen, and Tchernicheva and Petrova as Fairies, were captivating in their crimson bodices and white skirts; and in the Frozen Wood there was a lovely flying ballet which was the best possible argument for its revival. The actual dancing in these scenes lost something owing to the jerky arm movements devised by the choreographer and the angular position of the arms above the head, a position copied from some of the prints of fairies, which Balanchine might have taken for an authentic pose of the period instead of being merely the result of faulty drawing.

The ogres were not very successful, and, unless the writer's memory fails him, that particular episode disappeared at the next performance of the ballet. On the other hand the final transformation scene was a lovely vision of scintillating spangles and tinsel.

There were three outstanding dances: a hornpipe dance by Sokolova in front of an act-drop, in which she wore a glengarry and a real sparkling tunic of the period which consisted of innumerable pieces of cut glass sewn to a foundation, a garment of incredible weight; a wonderful negro dance by Balanchine; and another hornpipe danced by Danilova and Lifar in the last scene, a dance so precisely phrased and rendered with such spirit that it provoked the most enthusiastic applause.

Of the character *ensembles* the best was the "Dance of the Harlequins."

The music was most entertaining, modern yet seasoned with a sense of period, and, in outlook, at once English and Continental.

The Triumph of Neptune was revived with success in 1927.

LA CHATTE

Ballet in 1 Act. Book: Sobeka. Music: Henri Sauguet. Scenery and Costumes: Gabo and Pevsner. Choreography: George Balanchine. First produced: Théâtre de Monte Carlo, April 30th, 1927.

CHARACTERS

The Cat . . . . MLLE. OLGA SPESSIVA
The Young Man . . . . . M. SERGE LIFAR
Companions of the Young Man.

A youth, in love with a cat, prays to Aphrodite to change the animal into a girl. The goddess assents, the cat becomes a girl, and the youth succeeds in winning her affections.

But, during their love-making, Aphrodite puts the girl's constancy to the test, by tempting her with a mouse which scampers across the bridal chamber. The girl immediately forsakes her lover to pursue it. Then Aphrodite changes the girl back into a cat, to the great distress of her lover, who dies.

*

The theme of the ballet is based on one of Æsop's fables. The production was chiefly remarkable for its settings and costumes, and for its exploitation of the beauty of manhood.

The setting—an essay in constructivism—was carried out in a decorative material new to ballet—talc—which has many attractions on account of its flexibility, transparency, and ability to reflect light. This fantastic shimmering edifice was set on, and against, a floor, and walls, of gleaming black American cloth. The cat's head and fore-paws were visible at one of two rounded windows in a dark shrine, above which was a gleaming rhomboidal figure which symbolised the goddess. The mouse was actually a clockwork one which proved so unmanageable that later on its appearance was left to the imagination.

The cast was unusual in that it consisted of seven men and one woman. The choreography appeared to have little connection with the theme which served mainly as an excuse for a series of movements in which a number of lightly-clad, bronzed young men, led by Lifar, then in the flower of his youth, executed a series of movements reminiscent of a gymnastic display, contrast being afforded by the amorous *pas de deux* between Spessiva and Lifar.

Spessiva injured her foot after the first performance and the role was subsequently taken by Alice Nikitina. Later, the part of the Cat was rendered by Markova.

THE GODS GO A-BEGGING [2]

Ballet in 1 Act. Book: Sobeka. Music: Handel. Choreography: George Balanchine. First produced: His Majesty's Theatre, London, July 16th, 1928.

CHARACTERS

The Serving-Maid	Mlle. Alexandra Danilova
The Shepherd	M. Léon Woizikowsky
Two Ladies	{ Mme. Lubov Tchernicheva { Mme. Felia Dubrovska
A Nobleman	M. Constantin Tcherkas
	Ladies, Noblemen, Servants.

Scene. A forest glade.

A serving-maid, assisted by several lackeys, spreads a cloth on the grass and sets out refreshments in readiness for an elaborate picnic. The noble host and his guests arrive and among them strays a shepherd.

Two of the ladies find amusement in enticing the shepherd to dance with them. But he suddenly espies the serving-maid, whom he prefers. They take delight in a dance which is expressive of their mutual affection.

The noblemen are highly indignant at this rebuff to the ladies, and are minded to chastise the shepherd, when the two lowly persons doff their rags and prove themselves to be two divinities, who have descended upon earth in humble guise.

*

This ballet, with its charming evocation of a *fête champêtre* by Watteau or Lancret, was a kind of last-minute production given at the end of the 1928 London season. To a selection of lovely airs by Handel, skilfully woven together and orchestrated by Sir Thomas Beecham, Balanchine contrived a simple direct form of choreography with only the merest touch of modernity. The love-duet between the shepherd and the serving-maid is one of the most poetic of Balanchine's compositions.

[2] At Paris the ballet was given under the better title of *Les Dieux Mendiants*.

The scenery was Bakst's setting for the opening scene of *Daphnis et Chloë,* while the noble guests at the picnic were dressed in Gris's costumes for Nijinska's *Les Tentations de la Bergère;* only the gods' dresses were new.

*

The Gods Go a-Begging has been recently revived by the Vic-Wells Ballet, with new choreography by Ninette de Valois, and scenery and costumes by Hugh Stevenson.

The scenario, too, is slightly different, in that there are two serving-maids and a chief serving-maid. First, the ladies induce the shepherd to dance with the two serving-maids, then the company stroll away into the woods. During their absence the shepherd dances with, and becomes enamoured of, the chief serving-maid. The company return and, displeased, order the lovers to leave.

Suddenly darkness falls and Mercury enters to recall the maid and shepherd who prove to be divinities in disguise and who now appear in their radiant beauty. The company dance in homage and, with the coming of night, take their departure.

The Vic-Wells production is charmingly arranged and the groups are clearly inspired by a careful study of Watteau's paintings. The final scene, in which the lords and ladies pay homage to the god and goddess who look down from the night sky, is a picture that lingers long in the memory.

LE FILS PRODIGUE

Ballet in 3 Scenes. Book: Boris Kochno. Music: Serge Prokofiev. Scenery and Costumes: Georges Rouault. Choreography: George Balanchine. First produced: Théâtre Sarah Bernhardt, Paris, May 21st, 1929.

CHARACTERS

The Prodigal Son	M. SERGE LIFAR
The Father	M. MICHAEL FEDOROV
The Siren	MLLE. FELIA DUBROVSKA
The Servants	{ MLLE. ELEONORA MARRA { MLLE. NATALIA BRANITSKA
Friends of the Prodigal Son . .	{ M. LEON WOIZIKOWSKY { M. ANTON DOLIN

Acquaintances of the Prodigal Son.

Scene I. The Prodigal Son quarrels with his father and departs in the company of his two false friends.

Scene II. The Prodigal Son meets with a number of acquaintances and takes part in their feasting.

Enter a Siren who seeks to captivate him with her dancing. His two friends entertain the guests. Then he dances with the Siren. She and his friends induce him to drink to excess so that he falls into a stupor. His false friends, the Siren, and the guests strip the Prodigal Son of his possessions.

The Prodigal Son, recovered from his debauch, wakes and bemoans his miserable plight, then, distraught, resolves to return home.

When he has departed, his false friends, the Siren, and the guests return to parade their plunder.

Scene III. The Prodigal Son, penniless, heartbroken, and exhausted, returns home to be welcomed and forgiven by his father.

*

It is curious that the *Fils Prodigue* should have followed so soon after Diaghilev's rejection of Mr. Keynes's synopsis of another Biblical theme—*Job*.[3] Did the latter inspire the former, or was the similarity of source pure coincidence?

Kochno's admirable adaptation of the well known parable was not turned to full account by Balanchine, who time and again sacrificed its grandeur to his desire to be novel and "amusing."

The ballet's principal interest was Rouault's setting and costumes, and Lifar's magnificent performance in the title-role.

Rouault's settings, particularly the first scene, had a sombre majestic richness of colour which, if an analogy with music be permitted, may be compared to a deep organ note. And against such a background the artist would place a single colour accent, such as Lifar's blue tunic in the first scene or his wine-red coat in the second episode.

Dubrovska, Woizikowsky, Dolin, and Fedorov were excellent in their respective roles, but Lifar's portrait of the Prodigal Son was a memorable achievement. There was a genuine Blake-like grandeur in that touching last scene when, leaning heavily on a stick, he dragged himself wearily over the ground on his penitent knees to fall, exhausted, at his father's feet. This episode had a

[3] See pp. 760–763.

deep emotional content, which could only have been produced by an artist who realised the situation with his whole being.

COTILLON

Ballet in 1 Act. Book: Boris Kochno. Music: Emmanuel Chabrier. Scenery and Costumes: Christian Bérard. Choreography: George Balanchine. First produced: Théâtre de Monte Carlo, April 12th, 1932.

DIVERTISSEMENTS

The Toilet

MLLES. TAMARA TOUMANOVA, NATALIA STRAKHOVA, M. DAVID LICHINE

The Introductions

MLLE. VALENTINA BLINOVA and ENSEMBLE

The Conductor of the Dance

M. LÉON WOIZIKOWSKY

The Pleasure Garden

MLLE. VALENTINA BLINOVA, M. LÉON WOIZIKOWSKY and ENSEMBLE

Dance of Hats, Harlequins, Jockeys, and Spaniards

MLLES. TAMARA TOUMANOVA, NATALIA STRAKHOVA, BRANITSKÁ, KIRSOVA, LIPKOVSKA, TRESAHAR
MM. DAVID LICHINE, LADRE, SHABELEVSKY

The Hand of Fate

MLLE. LUBOV ROSTOVA, M. VALENTINE FROMAN

The Magic Lantern

MLLES. LUBOV ROSTOVA, TAMARA TOUMANOVA, VALENTINA BLINOVA
MM. DAVID LICHINE, VALENTINE FROMAN

Grand Rond

ENSEMBLE

Scene. A marble-walled ballroom relieved by a single line of floor-level boxes, decorated in red and gold.

The daughter of the house stands upon a gilt stool and, with the aid of a hand-glass, completes her toilet, while an adoring girl friend kneels to arrange her dress. A guest steals beside her, is seen in the mirror, and expresses his admiration. They are interrupted by the arrival of the guests.

Since the Conductor of the Dance has not arrived and time presses, his partner makes the introductions.

At this point the Conductor arrives and, dishevelled and breathless, hurries round the circle as if to make up for his tardiness. But the bustle and anxiety prove too much for him, and, feeling faint, he subsides into a chair, which one of the guests has had the forethought to place under him.

When the Conductor has recovered, the Conductress and he dance the first figure, which is copied by all the guests. Then the guests receive cotillon favours in the form of vari-shaped hats and guitars which provide an excuse for several charming dances.

One of the gentlemen comes to choose his partner from among the ladies, but is met by Destiny, distinguished by her black gloves, who forces him unwillingly to dance with her.

The daughter of the house tells the ladies their fortunes. She seems to be drawn towards the Conductress, but, finding her affection unreturned, takes to flight. The young girl's admirer returns, masked, slightly inebriated, and bearing a glass of champagne.

Destiny reveals herself to be a vampire and her partner takes to flight.

Follows a *Grand Rond* which ends with the dancers whirling off the stage. The young girl enters, takes up her position in the centre of the ballroom, and spins quickly *sur la pointe*. The guests return and encircle the girl who, rising on the points of both feet, continues to turn. The curtain falls.

*

Cotillon is to Balanchine what *Les Biches* is to Nijinska, but it differs from the latter in that it does not introduce any new style of movement. The chief merits of the ballet are, first, its theme, which is admirably contrived and doubtless inspired by the pages of Cellarius's once fashionable guide; second, the atmosphere of the ballet, for, if the analogy be permitted, it emanates a curious bitter-sweet perfume, a mingling of elegant sophistication with the shyness of adolescence which is most attractive; and, last, but not least, Chabrier's music, which is charming.

The compositions which provide the ballet score are *Menuet Pompeux* (overture), *Tourbillon, Mauresque, Scherzo-Valse, Idylle, Danse Rustique, Valse Romantique,* and *Danse Rustique.*

SERGE LIFAR

SERGE LIFAR was born at Kiev, South Russia, in 1905. His schooling was interrupted by sterner matters, first, the Great War of 1914, then the collapse of the Russian Empire and the birth of civil war in 1917. Amid all this strife and the desire to revolutionise every form of human activity, Lifar grew up.

Towards 1920 Nijinska left Petrograd to open a school of dancing at Kiev. One morning Lifar was afforded an opportunity to watch a class, an experience which made a great impression upon him. He suddenly felt that to dance was what he had always longed to do, although, in point of fact, he had never seen anyone dance on the stage.

He became a pupil at Nijinska's school and was put to the bar. One month later Nijinska left Kiev to join Diaghilev at Paris, to assist in the production of the revival of *La Belle au Bois Dormant* to be given at London.

Lifar struggled on in Kiev trying to fit himself for the dance by the assiduous practice of his small repertory of exercises. Then, one day early in 1923, Nijinska sent to the school asking that five of her favourite pupils should go to Paris to join the Diaghilev Ballet. Since one of the chosen had vanished, Lifar, on his entreaties, was allowed to go in his place. After the most terrible experiences he succeeded in crossing the frontier and finally arrived at Paris on January 15th, 1923.

For two whole years Lifar was set to work with the *corps de ballet* in the daily class for technique. There he acquired and practised the rudiments of classical ballet, but, notwithstanding all his efforts, he could not progress fast enough for his liking. One of the older dancers, to whom he confided his distress, advised him to spend his forthcoming holidays in studying with Cecchetti. Learning that the Maestro was at Turin, Lifar obtained permission from Diaghilev to visit the famous old teacher. When Lifar returned, his improvement was obvious to all.

He made his *début* in the *pas de quatre* in *Cimærosiana*, then followed a succession of roles which became more and more important: Boreas in *Zéphyre et Flore* (1925), the Third Sailor in *Les Matelots* (1925), the Officer in *Barabau* (1925), the Young Man in *Les Biches* (1925), Siegfried in *Le Lac des Cygnes* (1926), Ivan Tsarevich in *L'Oiseau de Feu* (1926), Romeo in *Romeo and Juliet* (1926), the Telegraph Boy in *Pastorale* (1926), Tom Tug in *The Triumph of Neptune* (1926), the Young Man in *La Chatte* (1927), in *Le Pas d'Acier* (1927), in *Ode* (1928), Apollo in *Apollon Musagète* (1928), the Moor in *Petrouchka* (1928), in *Le Bal* (1928), and the title-role in *Le Fils Prodigue* (1929).

In 1929 Lifar made his *début* as choreographer in a new version of *Renard*—ballet by Stravinsky, the original choreography being by Nijinska—an unusual conception in which the roles taken by the dancers were doubled by professional acrobats. Then came the sudden death of Diaghilev, which was followed by the disintegration of the troupe, and with it passed Lifar's cherished ambition to compose ballets for the company.

Soon after this sad event, the director of the Paris Opera wished to revive Beethoven's *Promethée,* originally produced by Viganò at Vienna in 1801. Balanchine had been commissioned to compose the choreography, but he fell ill; Lifar received an invitation to produce it in his stead. He accepted, and the success of his composition led to his appointment as *premier danseur* and *maître de ballet* at the Opera, posts which he still occupies.

In 1930 Lifar appeared with success in *Cochran's 1930 Revue,* then returned to the Opera where he successively produced, and danced in, *Prélude Dominical* (1931), *L'Orchèstre en Liberté* (1931), *Bacchus et Ariane* (1931), *Sur la Borysthène* (1932), *Icare* (1936), *David Triomphant* (1936), *Le Roi Nu* (1936), and *Alexandre le Grand* (1937).

In addition, Lifar revived *Le Spectre de la Rose* (1931) with himself as the Sprite, and Spessiva as the Young Girl; *Giselle* with himself as Albrecht, and Spessiva in the title-role; and devised a solo version of *Le Prélude à l'Après-Midi d'un Faune* (1932). Of all these his finest interpretation is that of Albrecht in *Giselle*.

Lifar is undoubtedly one of the greatest dancers of the present century. His movements are as graceful and lithe as those of a wild animal. Equipped with a splendid technique, an unusual elevation, a fine sense of line, and an admirably formed body, he is the personification of manly vigour, while his engaging and striking personality radiate a fire and intensity of feeling which must affect the most unemotional spectator.

As a choreographer his principal achievements to date are *Promethée, Icare,* and *Le Roi Nu.* He is an ardent experimentalist, ever seeking out new ways for the furtherance and development of his art, and at this stage it is impossible to say where they may lead. Already he has published a preliminary statement of his plans for reform, *Le Manifeste du Chorégraphe,* which may be perused with interest, though not everyone will subscribe to the views expressed.

ICARE [1]

Choreographic Legend in 1 Act. Book: Serge Lifar. Rhythms: Serge Lifar, orchestrated by J. E. Szyfer. Scenery and Costumes: P. R. Larthe. Choreography: Serge Lifar. First produced: Théâtre de l'Opéra, Paris, July 9th, 1935.

CHARACTERS

Icarus . . . . M. SERGE LIFAR
M. LEGRAND
MLLES. HUGHETTI, BARBAN, DIDION, GRELLIER
MM. EFIMOV, DOMANSKY, BOZZONI, GUYLAINE

The theme of *Icare* is derived from the well-known Greek legend which relates how Icarus attempted to fly with wings contrived by his father, Dedalus, which were attached to him by means of wax. Icarus flew so high that the sun's rays melted the wax and he was flung to the ground.

When the curtain rises a number of young people are seen disporting in a gorge near the sea, which can be seen in the distance. Dedalus enters, bearing the wings he has just fashioned. The young people make fun of the invention. Now Icarus comes forward, impressed by the grandeur of the project that is to be entrusted to him.

While the merry-makers resume their games, Icarus snares a dove in a net to fathom the secret of how birds fly. Dedalus places the wings on his son, who attempts to fly, but only falls to the ground. The young folk watch his fruitless attempts with astonishment, then begin to leave.

Now Dedalus urges his son to put forth all his strength. This time he succeeds in spreading and fluttering his wings and gradually he soars to the sky. His father and the young people watch his progress in anxious fear. Gradually he mounts towards the

---

[1] The synopsis of this and the two following ballets by Lifar have been adapted from programme notes.

sun, suddenly, one of his wings falls off and he drops down faster and faster to crash to death upon the rocks.

*

Icare has a particular significance in the development of choreography, because it is the first ballet in which Lifar sought to apply his theory that the choreographer had too long been the slave of music, for which he proposed to substitute rhythms devised by him in accordance with the movements and steps he had composed for his ballet.

DAVID TRIOMPHANT

Ballet in 2 Acts and 3 Scenes. Book: Serge Lifar. Music: Debussy and Mussorgsky, with rhythms by Serge Lifar, orchestrated by Vittorio Rieti. Scenery and Costumes: Fernand Léger. Choreography: Serge Lifar. First produced: Gala d'Inauguration du Théâtre de la Maison Internationale des Etudiants, Paris, December 15th, 1936.

CHARACTERS

David	M. SERGE LIFAR
King Saul	M. S. RENN
Melchola, his daughter . .	MLLE. MIA SLAWENSKA
Warriors	MM. EFIMOV, DOMANSKY
The Sorceress	MLLE. VERGINA

Slaves and a Negro.

Scene I. King Saul, having heard of the bravery of the shepherd, David, wishes to send him against his enemies. Hardly is the shepherd youth ushered into his presence when he loads him with the weapons he is to use against the Philistines. David, weighed down by this unaccustomed equipment, puts down the weapons one by one. Surrounded by the soldiers he dances a war-dance; at this moment Goliath and his Philistines are seen. Saul's troops, seized with panic, take to flight, while David, with a stone cast by his sling, kills Goliath, whose head he offers to the King.

Scene II. Summoned by the King, David improvises a dance by the wayside. In his palace, Saul is consumed with jealousy; he cannot support David's continually increasing popularity. His jealousy is heightened because he has promised the shepherd his daughter in marriage. The people can be heard crying, "Saul hath slain his thousands, and David his ten thousands."

Now the shepherd enters with his harp and such is his ability to charm that he captivates the King with his dancing. Spellbound, Saul gives his daughter to David.

While the two young people exchange vows of love, the song in praise of David grows louder and louder. Saul, unable to restrain his fury, throws a javelin at the shepherd, which fails to strike him. David, in his innocence, retrieves the weapon and restores it to Saul. The King's daughter, Melchola, dances for her betrothed and for her royal father.

Again David dances to the accompaniment of his harp, and again is heard the song of praise. His jealousy rekindled, Saul again seizes his javelin to kill the shepherd, but the latter, suddenly realising that his life is endangered, with a bound catches the blade, while Melchola restrains her father.

Scene III. David, who now commands the army, learns that Saul is resolved to have his head at all costs. Believing that the King plans to murder him in his bed, he places a statue of himself in his place, and flees with Melchola.

Saul consults a sorceress: she conjures up the spirit of the prophet Samuel who predicts that the kingdom will pass to David.

Saul immediately goes to slay David, but only finds the statue. At the same time there is heard the menacing advance of the Philistines. Abandoned by all, Saul is attacked and wounded. Concluding that all is lost, he stabs himself to death at the very moment that David arrives to succour him. David, master of his enemies, is proclaimed King.

*

This ballet is based on portions of the first *Book of Kings*. The production is now in the repertory of the Opera, Paris, the roles of Saul, Melchola, and the Sorceress being at present rendered by M. Sauvageau, and Mlles. Chauviré and Darsonval respectively.

ALEXANDRE LE GRAND

Choreographic Epic in 3 Scenes with a Prologue and Epilogue. Book: Serge Lifar. Music: Philippe Gaubert. Scenery and Costumes: P. R. Larthe. Choreography: Serge Lifar. First produced: Théâtre de l'Opéra, Paris, June 21st, 1937.

CHARACTERS

The Queen of Babylon	MLLE. LORCIA
Alexander	M. SERGE LIFAR
A Jewess	MLLE. CHAUVIRÉ
The Oracle	MLLES. BINIOS
An Egyptian Woman . . .	SOL. SCHWARZ
Two Egyptian Slaves	{ KERGRIST { DYNALYX

Egyptian Women, Jewish Women, Warriors, Jews, Generals.

Prologue. Alexander, having resolved to embark on the conquest of the world, takes leave of his generals. The oracle tells him the legend of the Gordian knot, cunningly tied by the father of Midas, and declares that "whosoever shall untie it shall reign over the world."

The curtain rises to reveal the rocky heights which dominate the plain of Gordium. Alexander appears on the heights followed by his soldiers. Meanwhile, in the plain, the Greeks vainly strive to untie the knot. Alexander distributes among his officers his attributes of power and, henceforth freed of all earthly contingency, descends into the plain. There, he draws his sword and cuts the knot.

Scene I. The Temple of Solomon, Jerusalem.

Alexander is about to capture Jerusalem, time-honoured queen of Palestine. Assembled about the High Priest in the Temple of Solomon, the Jews pray and bewail their lot. A messenger arrives with the news that the city is taken; the citizens are filled with panic. At the same moment Alexander and his troops enter the Temple. Magnanimous in the hour of victory, the hero spares the city. The High Priest bids him welcome. Alexander chooses for wife the most beautiful virgin in Palestine and orders his soldiers to leave him.

Scene II. An oasis in Egypt.

Alexander's troops are weary of a campaign which seems to be endless. The hero allows his soldiers to rest in the enchanted oasis. Nevertheless, murmurs of discontent are heard. But a Priest of Zeus appears and crowns the youthful hero "god and son of Zeus." Alexander is raised in triumph by his soldiers.

Scene III. A palace at Babylon.

Alexander feasts, surrounded by his soldiers and the women
captured in the various conquered countries. The Queen of Babylon, who has failed to vanquish Alexander by force of arms, tries
to captivate him with her charms. She begs Alexander to join her
in a friendly cup of wine, which, unknown to him, she has caused
to be poisoned. At a sign from her, men dressed in black bear in
a great cup of wine. Alexander drinks and sinks to the ground.
Feeling the approach of death, he bids his soldiers farewell.

Epilogue. Zeus appears in a blaze of light. All present bow
down their heads in fear. The god has come to claim his son. Follows an apotheosis in which the hero slowly climbs to the summit
of Olympus.

FREDERICK ASHTON

FREDERICK ASHTON was born on September 17th, 1906, at
Guayaquil, Ecuador, South America. When still quite young
he accompanied his parents to Lima where he was educated by
the Dominican Fathers. He remained at Lima until he was fourteen at which time that city was visited by the late Anna Pavlova
and her company. On that occasion Ashton made his first entrance
into a theatre and saw his first ballet. It was an experience that
made a lasting impression upon him, and he became filled with a
burning ambition to dance.

A little later his parents went to England and he was sent to
Dover College to complete his education. During the holidays he
saw performances of the Diaghilev Ballet and told his parents of
his wish to become a dancer, a suggestion which received no
encouragement. Towards 1923 he left school and entered the office
of a London export merchant in the capacity of foreign correspondent, where he remained some eighteen months.

Towards the end of 1924 Ashton saw an advertisement in a
newspaper which stated that M. Leonide Massine was prepared to
give a trial lesson to anyone aspiring to become a dancer with a
view to ascertaining whether he or she had talent. Ashton visited
Massine and as a result went every Saturday afternoon for a
lesson. This lasted for six months.

Then Ashton had the misfortune to lose his father. His mother
returned to England and found her son singularly short of pocket-
money. She investigated the matter and discovered that he had
been taking lessons in dancing. These were promptly stopped but
Ashton became depressed and finally ill. As a result it was decided
to allow him to continue his lessons and he returned to Massine.

But the latter, having to leave London on professional engagement, placed him with Mme. Rambert, with whom Ashton went
to study. She encouraged him to try his hand at the composition
of ballets and this resulted in his first production, *The Tragedy of
Fashion, or The Scarlet Scissors,* included in a revue, *Riverside*

Nights, presented by Sir Nigel Playfair at the Lyric Theatre, Hammersmith, in 1926.

Ashton next joined the Ida Rubinstein Ballet for which Massine and Nijinska had been engaged as choreographers. There he stayed for some twelve months. In *Les Noces de l'Amour et Psyche* he danced in a *pas de quatre* with Lichine, Shabelevsky, and Jasinsky.

In 1929 he returned to Mme. Rambert and worked hard at choreography, composing *Leda and the Swan,* and *Capriol Suite,* both of which were given at a matinée of ballet presented by Mme. Rambert at the Lyric Theatre on February 25th, 1930. In the same year Ashton appeared with Markova in a ballet in Sir Nigel Playfair's production of *Marriage à la Mode,* and this led to a long professional association with that dancer, who took the leading role in many of his later ballets.

Mme. Rambert founded the Ballet Club in October, 1930, and Ashton became principal choreographer to the organisation, for which he composed many ballets: *La Péri* (1931), *Mercury* (1931), *The Lady of Shalott* (1931), *Récamier* (1932), *Foyer de Danse* (1932), *Les Masques* (1933).

For the Camargo Society Ashton produced four ballets: *Pomona* (1930), *Façade* (1931), *Lord of Burleigh* (1931), and *A Day in a Southern Port* [1] (1932).

In 1933-4 Ashton went to America where he produced and devised the choreography for Gertrude Stein's opera-ballet, *Four Saints in Three Acts.*

For Mme. Rambert's season of ballet at the Duke of York's Theatre, 1935, Ashton produced *St. Valentine's Eve.* In 1935 he joined the Vic-Wells Ballet both as choreographer and dancer, for which company he has so far composed the following ballets: *Les Rendez-vous* (1933), *Le Baiser de la Fée* (1935), *Apparitions* (1936), *Nocturne* (1936), *Les Patineurs* (1937), *A Wedding Bouquet* (1937) and a new version of *Pomona* (1937). The works devised by Ashton for the Vic-Wells Ballet previous to 1935 were produced by him in the capacity of guest-choreographer.

FAÇADE

Ballet in 1 Act. Music: William Walton. Scenery: John Armstrong. Choreography: Frederick Ashton. First produced: Cambridge Theatre, London, April 26th, 1931.

[1] This has been revived for the Vic-Wells Ballet under the title *Rio Grande.*

DIVERTISSEMENTS

Scotch Rhapsody .	{ PRUDENCE HYMAN, MAUDE LLOYD, ANTONY TUDOR
Jodelling Song . .	{ LYDIA LOPOKOVA, FREDERICK ASHTON, WILLIAM CHAPPELL, WALTER GORE
Polka	ALICIA MARKOVA
Valse	{ PEARL ARGYLE, DIANA GOULD, MAUDE LLOYD, PRUDENCE HYMAN
Popular Song . .	WILLIAM CHAPPELL, WALTER GORE
Tango Pasadoble .	LYDIA LOPOKOVA, FREDERICK ASHTON
Tarantella Sevillana .	{ LYDIA LOPOKOVA, FREDERICK ASHTON, and ENSEMBLE

Façade was the title given to an entertainment for voice and six instruments. It consisted of a group of poems by Edith Sitwell, which were recited to a musical accompaniment by William Walton. This diversion was first performed at the Æolian Hall, London, on June 12th, 1923. Later a number of the musical pieces were elaborated to form an orchestral suite, also entitled *Façade,* which provides the music for the present ballet from which the name is derived. The suite was first used as a ballet by a young German choreographer called Günter Hess, the performance being given at his Chamber Dance Theatre at Hagen, Westphalia, about 1930.

Façade is a series of seven *divertissements* suggested by the music. It opens with a *"Scottish Dance,"* which is followed by a number based on a milking scene, in which Lopokova as the milkmaid made a big success. Then came a *"Polka"* sur les pointes, a well arranged number notable for the gaiety with which Markova invested it. The next number is a *"Valse"* which has some attractive arm movements. All these dances are conceived in a spirit of light burlesque with little satirical touches which accord exactly with the mood of the music, everything is up-to-date, frivolous, and as light as chocolate éclair.

Then come two numbers of lesser merit. which suggest a comment on the music-hall—a step-dance in the American manner, followed by a burlesque of a Tango which, frankly, borders on low comedy. This latter portrays a raffish-looking dago, who attempts to exercise his fascinations on a bashful maiden, anxious to "see life" but a little doubtful of the propriety of the dance movements he tries to teach her.

*

This ballet was first given under the auspices of the Camargo

Society. Later it was in the programmes of both the Ballet Rambert and the Vic-Wells Ballet. In the latter production (1935) the ballet received an addition in the form of a *"Country Dance,"* placed before the *"Tango."* There are three characters: a Maiden, a Yokel, and The Squire, which were originally taken by Pearl Argyle, Richard Ellis, and Robert Helpmann respectively.

THE LADY OF SHALOTT

Ballet in 1 *Act and* 2 *Scenes. Book: Frederick Ashton. Music: Sibelius. Costumes: William Chappell. Choreography: Frederick Ashton. First produced: Mercury Theatre, London, November* 12*th,* 1931.

CHARACTERS

The Lady of Shalott .	PEARL ARGYLE
Her Reflection . .	MAUDE LLOYD
The Reapers . .	PRUDENCE HYMAN, ELISABETH SCHOOLING, BETTY CUFF, SUZETTE MORFIELD, WILLIAM CHAPPELL
The Lovers . .	{ ANDRÉE HOWARD, WALTER GORE
Sir Lancelot . .	FREDERICK ASHTON

The ballet opens with the Lady of Shalott gazing into her mirror at her reflection, conveyed by means of two dancers placed each side of a gauze curtain in such a way that their movements are synchronised. Then the Lady turns to her weaving and we are shown what she sees in the mirror; the reapers at work in the fields, two lovers lately wed, and the red-cross knight, Sir Lancelot. At the sight of the last-named the Lady tires of pale shadows and, looking through the window towards forbidden Camelot, brings upon herself the threatened curse.

Next we see her wandering by the riverside, imprisoned in a trance of fears which overwhelm her so that she dies. The ballet ends with the knight, the reapers, and the lovers gazing sadly at her still form.

*

The theme of *Lady of Shalott* is based on Tennyson's poem of the same name. The synchronisation of movement to suggest a mirror is a device which the reader will have noted in earlier ballets, but it was here used very successfully. Again, the death of the Lady of Shalott, instead of taking place in a skiff borne by the flowing river—in accordance with the poem—was altered to be the culminating point in a mimed scene of madness a little reminiscent of the end of the first act of *Giselle*. The ballet was admirably conceived and presented, and was exactly suited to the stage of the Mercury Theatre.

The outstanding figure in the ballet was Pearl Argyle in the title-role, whose movements radiated grace and style, while, in the death scene, her miming rose to great heights. Andrée Howard and Walter Gore were excellent as the lovers.

APPARITIONS

Ballet in 5 Scenes, including a Prologue and Epilogue. Book: Constant Lambert. Music: Liszt, orchestrated Gordon Jacob. Scenery and Costumes: Cecil Beaton. Choreography: Frederick Ashton. First produced: Sadler's Wells Theatre, London, February 11th, 1936.

CHARACTERS

The Poet	ROBERT HELPMANN
The Woman in Ball-dress . . .	MARGOT FONTEYN
The Hussar	HAROLD TURNER
The Monk	MAURICE BROOKE

Ladies of Fashion, Dandies, Belfry Spirits, etc.

Prologue. Scene. A lofty room in a Gothic mansion, one wall pierced with glazed, arched windows. It is night and one corner of the room fitted up as library is illumined by an oil-lamp placed on a desk.

When the curtain rises a young poet of the Romantic Era is seen writing at the table. He is working at a sonnet, which, strive as he will, he cannot fashion to his satisfaction. Suddenly the windows light up and each frames a strange figure—a hussar, a monk of sinister aspect, and a woman dressed in ball-dress, who smiles upon the poet. This beautiful vision becomes the symbol of the love the poet is desirous of expressing in his poem. The figures vanish and the poet returns to his composition; but the words dance before his eyes and he finds himself unable to concentrate. In despair he takes a sleeping draught which causes him to slumber uneasily and dream.

Scene I. *A ballroom.*

First the poet imagines himself in an enormous ballroom where beautiful women are dancing with handsome men. He, too, wishes to join in the dance, only to be ignored. The dancing stops and the woman of his vision enters and dances alone. Follows an *ensemble* in which the dancers change partners and miraculously the poet finds himself dancing with her, but it is clear that she has eyes only for the handsome hussar. The guests depart and the poet is left alone with his thoughts.

Scene II. *A snow-clad plain.*

The chiming of bells is heard and in the poet's fevered imagination the bells become animate and take the form of girls, who dance in bell-like skirts and encircle him. They vanish to give place to a funeral procession heralded by a melancholy chant and led by the sinister monk he saw in the window. The poet is curious regarding the still figure borne beneath the purple canopy. He approaches the bier and draws back the coverlet, to reveal the face of the woman of his vision. The monk pushes him aside. The poet, horrified and full of pity, kneels in the snow and offers up a prayer.

Scene III. *A cavern.*

Here the guests, dressed in red, seem to be delighting in an unholy orgy. The poet takes part in the satanic round, which is suddenly interrupted by the arrival of the woman in the ball-dress, who proves to have hideous features. Terrified, he wishes to leave, but now she pursues him. Exhausted, he swoons. Her features resume their normal loveliness.

Epilogue. *Same Scene as for the Prologue.*

The poet awakes from his sleep and realises that his dream is but a reflection of his own life. He goes to the window where he first saw the woman of his vision, but there is nothing. In despair, he stabs himself.

The woman in ball-dress and her companions enter and bear away the poet's corpse.

*

The theme of *Apparitions,* although inspired by Berlioz's synopsis for his *"Symphonie Fantastique,"* has many original touches.

The mimed scenes of the prologue and epilogue are well contrived and clearly expressed. The best episode choreographically is that of the ballroom. In the succeeding scene the dance by the belfry-spirits is too conventional, but the funeral is a most effective piece of theatre. In the cavern scene the costumes of the revellers take on a hint of the Beardsley of *Under the Hill* and introduce a note of frivolity which does not accord with the suggestion of a witches' sabbath.

The principal dancers are Margot Fonteyn, who dances charmingly in the ballroom scene and bears herself gracefully in the succeeding episodes, and Robert Helpmann, whose dancing and miming are excellent throughout, and contribute greatly to the successful evocation of the Romantic Period.

The music is a selection by Constant Lambert of Liszt's later compositions.

NOCTURNE

Ballet in 1 Act. Book: Edward Sackville West. Music: Frederick Delius. Scenery and Costumes: Sophie Fedorovich. Choreography: Frederick Ashton. First produced: Sadler's Wells Theatre, London, November 10th, 1936.

CHARACTERS

A Spectator	FREDERICK ASHTON
A Young Man	ROBERT HELPMANN
A Rich Girl	JUNE BRAE
A Poor Girl	MARGOT FONTEYN

Masquers, Revellers.

Scene. The entrance to a dance hall, the background being formed by a terrace overlooking Paris. Night.

When the curtain rises the scene is empty save for the presence of a man in an evening cloak who, with his back to the audience, stands in the centre of the terrace balustrade, gazing into the distance.

Enter a number of ladies in ball-dress with their escorts. They are followed by an elaborately costumed young girl, accompanied by two male friends, with whom she is conversing gaily. The revellers go into the dance hall but the rich girl remains chatting with one of her admirers.

A flower-girl passes by and looks at the young man in admiration. The rich girl goes into the dance hall; the young man remains gazing after her. The flower-girl shyly offers him a bunch of violets which she places in his hand; impulsively he throws the flowers after the rich girl. Stepping back he collides with the flower-girl. He apologises and, suddenly aware of her beauty, bends down and kisses her. They talk, she sets down her basket of flowers, and they dance together.

During this sentimental passage the dancers emerge from the dance hall to breathe the night air. They are greatly amused at the spectacle which greets them and make fun of the flower-girl. The young man, his pride touched, hastily attaches himself to the rich girl. The flower-girl, unable to withstand the gibes levelled at her, sadly departs.

The revellers go out and the young man dances alone. Presently the revellers return accompanied by a number of masquers. Now the young man dances with the rich girl.

The flower-girl returns and tries to approach the young man, but her way is continually barred by the dancing revellers. Finally she breaks through the moving cordon and does reach him, so that he is the centre of the two women. He hesitates for a moment and leaves with the rich girl, while the flower-girl, broken-hearted, collapses into the arms of the masquers, who leave her and, accompanied by the revellers, enter the dance hall.

Throughout the piece the man in the evening cloak moves slowly in the shadow, watching the human tragedy that is enacted before his eyes. Slowly he makes his way to the flower-girl, raises her and speaks words of sympathy and encouragement. Then he goes to the terrace and, raising his arms, lowers them slowly in a gesture of resignation. The curtain falls.

*

Nocturne, which is arranged to Delius's *Paris,* doubtless derives its name from the composer of the music, who styled his work a Nachtstück or Nocturne. The theme of the ballet, the costumes for which suggest the eighteen-nineties, has the manner of the *Yellow Book,* and might well have been written by Crackanthorpe or Dowson.

The choreography is chiefly interesting for its groups, its *ensembles,* and for the part played by the masquers, who afford a kind of choreographic comment on the development of the action. While Margot Fonteyn and June Brae respectively invest their roles with appropriate shyness and glamour, the turns *en arabesque* which Ashton has allotted to the flower-girl are over-elaborate for such a type. Helpmann is excellent as the Young Man. Ashton provides an effective prologue and epilogue as the Spectator, a character reminiscent of the Stranger in Jerome's *Passing of the Third Floor Back.*

The setting and costumes by Fedorovich are admirably contrived to set off each other, the setting being austere and low in tone, while the dresses are richly coloured and diaphanous.

LES PATINEURS

Ballet in 1 *Act. Music: Meyerbeer. Scenery and Costumes: William Chappell. Choreography: Frederick Ashton. First produced: Sadler's Wells Theatre, London, February 16th, 1937.*

ARTISTES

Entrée . . .	MARY HONER, ELIZABETH MILLER
Pas de Huit . .	GWYNETH MATHEWS, JOY NEWTON, PEGGY MELLISS, WENDA HORSBURGH, RICHARD ELLIS, LESLIE EDWARDS, MICHAEL SOMES, PAUL REYLOFF
Variation . . .	HAROLD TURNER
Pas de Deux . .	MARGOT FONTEYN, ROBERT HELPMANN
Ensemble . . .	MARGOT FONTEYN, MARY HONER, ELIZABETH MILLER, PAMELA MAY, JUNE BRAE
Pas de Huit . .	The same, with HAROLD TURNER and ROBERT HELPMANN
Pas de Trois . .	MARY HONER, ELIZABETH MILLER, HAROLD TURNER
Pas des Patineuses .	JUNE BRAE, PAMELA MAY
Ensemble . . .	MARY HONER, ELIZABETH MILLER, PAMELA MAY, JUNE BRAE, HAROLD TURNER, RICHARD ELLIS, LESLIE EDWARDS, MICHAEL SOMES, PAUL REYLOFF

Les Patineurs,[2] as its title suggests is a series of *divertissements* based on the gliding and spinning movements associated with skating, although Ashton has never visited a rink.

The dances are well devised, particularly the *ensembles,* and serious "skating" is relieved with little humorous touches suggested by possible mishaps on the ice. One particularly amusing

[2] *The Skaters.*

conceit is the way in which a pair of skaters appear to slip and rise up on the tips of their skates, which permits of an assumed unsteady progression *sur les pointes*.

All types of skaters are presented; the beginners, the experts, and the lovers, who find the pastime a fine opportunity for holding hands. In certain "numbers" Mary Honer's *fouettés* and Turner's *pirouettes* are exploited to full advantage. Gradually the skaters depart and the ballet ends with Turner's spinning so perfectly, and with such admirable poise, that real ice seems to be the only logical explanation for such a dazzling succession of *pirouettes sautés*.

The music, selected by Constant Lambert from Meyerbeer's compositions, consists of four numbers from *Le Prophète* and four from *L'Etoile du Nord*. The production has an additional attraction in the charming setting and costumes provided by the ingenuity and artistry of William Chappell.

REZSÖ BRADA

R EZSÖ BRADA was born at Budapest in 1906. His father, Ede Brada, a former *maître de ballet* of the Royal Hungarian Opera House, Budapest, gave him his first lessons in dancing. Later, he studied in America with Albertina Rasch and Chester Hale.

In 1921 Brada joined the ballet company attached to the Royal Opera, and, in 1935, the then director, Nikolaus Radnai, appointed him *maître de ballet*. Later, Brada went on an American tour and also appeared at Berlin and Vienna. As a dancer his principal roles have been in *Schéhérazade, Petrouchka, Sylvia, Coppélia,* and *The Three-Cornered Hat.*

Among the several works produced by him, or for which he has devised the choreography, partly or wholly, may be mentioned: *The Holy Torch, Kuruc Fairy Tale, The Selfish Giant, Lysistrata, The Mirror, La Vida Breve, Venus de Milo, Azra, Rip van Winkle, Hunyady László,* and a number of *divertissements* in opera.

THE HOLY TORCH [1]

Ballet in 11 Scenes. Book: Mme. Dohnanyi-Galafres. Music: Erno Dohnanyi. Scenery and Costumes: Zoltán Fülöp. Choreography: Mme. Dohnanyi-Galafres. Directed: Rezsö Brada. First produced: Royal Hungarian Opera House, Budapest, December 6th, 1934.

CHARACTERS

Buza	MLLE. KAROLA SZALAY
Gypsy Girl	MLLE. BELLA BORDY
Queen of the Evil Fairies	
Osöd	M. F. KÖSZEGI
Guardian Angel	MLLE. KORNÉLIA KLIER
1st Evil Fairy	MLLE. JULIA RAKSÁNYI

[1] The Hungarian title is *Szent faklya.*

820

2nd Evil Fairy	Mlle. Margit Máté
1st Good Fairy	Mlle. M. Ottrubay
2nd Good Fairy	Mlle. Hedvig Hidas

Hetyke (Cheeky)		Mlle. Ilona Vera
Szerelmes (Loving)		Mlle. M. Ottrubay
Szelid (Demure)	Shepherdesses	Mlle. Irén Mátray
Dacos (Proud)		Mlle. Dóra Vágó
Könnyelmü (Light-hearted)		M. Rezsö Brada
Hiu (Vain)	Shepherds	M. László Csányi
Eröszakos (Violent)		M. Gyula Harangozó
Félénk (Timid)		M. K. Zsedényi

Scene I. Marshes.

Osöd, a young shepherd, goes to the well where Buza, his beloved, awaits him. On his way he encounters a gypsy girl—the Queen of the Evil Fairies in disguise—who tries to captivate him, but he drives her away. The gypsy disappears.

Scene II. Shepherds and their sweethearts are seen dancing in the Inn.

Scene III. Shepherds and girls are seen bidding each other goodbye after the dance. The shepherds light a row of bonfires to protect them from the evil fairies. But Buza does not wish to part from Osöd. Then, just as she is about to leave him, she sees the gypsy-girl approach Osöd. He drives her away and she goes off, laughing gaily.

Buza begs Osöd to light a bonfire to keep away the evil fairies and implores him to let her stay with him. So he settles her to rest on his big coat and soon she is fast asleep. Osöd keeps watch and in doing so forgets to attend to the fire, which goes out.

Scene IV. Osöd struggles with the evil fairies.

Scene V. Buza awakes and finds that Osöd has disappeared. Evil fairies gather and threaten her. Suddenly a little torch begins to gleam. Full of hope, Buza kneels in prayer.

Scene VI. Her patron saint appears and hands her the sacred torch.

Scene VII. Buza dances over the marsh, protected by the sacred torch

Scene VIII. The land of the evil fairies.

Osöd is brought in by a band of evil fairies. Shepherds who have been trapped in the marsh call out to him for help, but the fairies hold him fast. The Queen tries to captivate him, then suddenly leaps upon him to suck his heart's blood, like a vampire. Buza appears and saves her lover by means of the torch. Osöd in turn sets free the shepherds and fires the marsh by means of the torch.

Scene IX. The rescued and rescuers return home to find the marsh burnt out and replaced by solid ground. They all kneel and offer prayers of thanksgiving and return the sacred torch to the patron saint.

Scene X. Dance by children on the flowery meadow.

Scene XI. A wedding-dance on the meadow at the marriage of Buza and Osöd.

KURUC FAIRY TALE[2]

Ballet in 3 Acts. Book: Harsányi Zsolt. Music: Zoltán Kordály. Scenery: Gusztav Oláh. Choreography: Aurél Milloss and Rezsö Brada. First produced: Royal Hungarian Opera House, Budapest, March 13th, 1935.

CHARACTERS

The Father	M. Rezsö Brada
The Mother	Mlle. Etel Begovits
The Daughter	Mlle. Karola Szalay
The Stout Aunt	Mlle. M. Köszeghváry
The Thin Aunt	Mlle. Ilona Vera
The Uncle	M. Gyula Harangozó
The Nurse	Mlle. Irén Mátray
The Labanc Suitor	M. László Csányi
The Kuruc Lieutenant	M. Ferenc Köszegi

Szekely Peasants, Kuruc Soldiers.

The action of Acts I and II takes place in Transylvania, that of Act III near Galánta.

Time: End of the 17th century.

[2] Hungarian title is *Kuruc Mese.*

Act I. The hall of a large castle on the shores of the Maros.

A family council is being held to persuade the daughter of the house to accept the marriage proposal of a Labanc[3] suitor, but in vain. The suitor is offended and departs.

Again the family try to persuade the daughter to marry, but without success. Her uncle secretly suggests that she can rely upon him to help her, for he is not in sympathy with the others.

Act II. The castle garden on a summer afternoon.

The daughter confides in her maid how unhappy she is at being unable to marry the man she loves, a Kuruc lieutenant. She picks a rose which she sends to her lover by her servant. The maid hurries away and later returns with a gift from the Lieutenant, a heart-shaped honey-cake which her young mistress presses to her breast.

The family enter the garden and the father informs his daughter that she must accept the Labanc suitor or enter a convent. The family leave and the terrified girl is left alone with her maid.

The uncle makes his way into the garden among a number of peasants and Kuruc soldiers, disguises the daughter as a man and helps her to escape.

The family return to hear of their daughter's escape and are greeted with the derisive laughter of the crowd.

Act III. A Kuruc camp.

The Kuruc Lieutenant is seen dreaming of his beloved. Orders arrive and he departs to carry them out.

The daughter, disguised as a man, enters with her servant and enlists as a soldier.

Later the Lieutenant returns and presently the family are brought in, having been arrested by the Kuruc troops. In exchange for their freedom, the daughter's parents reluctantly consent to her marriage with the Lieutenant.

[3] Kuruc is a difficult word to translate. It refers to a patriotic movement which originated in Hungary, in the 17th century, against the oppression of the Turks and the Habsburgs. Kuruc embodied the spirit of rebellion against tyranny, the spirit of liberty and independence. Those serving the Habsburg cause were called Labanc. For this information I am indebted to the courtesy of Dr. Sima of the Royal Hungarian Legation.—C.W.B.

GYULA HARANGOZÓ

G YULA HARANGOZÓ was born at Budapest on April 19th,
1908. When he was six years old his parents took him to see
a ballet. On his return home he imitated the dances he had seen
and so adroitly that it was plain that he had a marked talent for
the Dance. His parents, however, had other plans for their son.
But later, when he became a student, he secretly joined the chorus
of the Opera House, Budapest.

In December, 1928, M. Gaubier produced *The Three-Cornered
Hat* and selected Harangozó to play one of the principal roles,
which he did with such success that he was immediately offered an
engagement as solo dancer. He persuaded his parents to give their
consent and now began to study under Jan Cieplinsky. In the
meanwhile he danced important roles in *Schéhérazade, Carniaval
at Pest, Coppélia,* and so on.

Harangozó arranged a number of solo dances for the Szeged
open-air performances, as a result of which the directorate of the
Opera House, Budapest, invited him to arrange a ballet to music
by some Hungarian composer. He chose Prof. Jenö Hubay's
"Csárda-jelenet" (Inn Scene) and the ballet was produced on
December 6th, 1936, the name day of the Regent, Admiral Horthy,
which was a gala night at the Opera.

The production was enthusiastically received and Harangozó
was invited to devise further ballets. This resulted in the production of *Sybil* (February, 1937), *Perhaps To-morrow!* (May, 1937),
and *Csizmás Janko (Little Johnny in Top-Boots)*. The success of
the last-named was such that Harangozó was appointed *maître de
ballet* at the Opera House, Budapest.

PERHAPS TO-MORROW!

*Ballet in 1 Act and 3 Scenes. Book: István Juhász. Music: Jenö
Kenessey. Scenery: Aladár Olgyay. Costumes: Klára Szunyogh-
Tüdös and Tivadar Márk. Choreography: Gyula Harangozó.
First produced: Metropolitan Art Theatre, Budapest, May 9th,
1937.*

CHARACTERS

The Girl	MLLE. ILONA VERA
The Officer	M. FERENC KÖSZEGI
The Coquette	MLLE. HEDVIG HIDAS
	M. ZOLTÁN SALLAY
A Sportsman	M. LÁSZLÓ CSÁNYI
A Woman of the Streets . . .	MLLE. MANCI HORVÁTH
A Student	M. KÁROLY ZSEDÉNYI
A Lady	MLLE. ERZSÉBET HORVÁTH
A Gentleman	M. FERENC PINTÉR

Workmen, Soldiers, Passers-by.

Scene I. A street. Prominent among the buildings is the entrance to a Gas-Attack Precautions School, advertised by means of a sinister poster.

Along the street pass many characteristic types of city-folk—workmen, elegant ladies, smartly-dressed gentlemen, courting couples, students, and so on. They stop and examine the new poster with interest. Some regard it as a huge joke; others view it with alarm. Some hastily purchase newspapers in the belief that war has broken out and that a raid is imminent. But there is no news of importance.

An officer, who is in charge of the gas-attack precautions course, arrives and enters the school. He is accompanied by his sweetheart, who stops to buy a rose, then follows him.

Scene II. Interior of the Gas-Attack Precautions School.

The officer enters and awaits his sweetheart, who presently arrives. Various people come in to take the course, more out of curiosity than with a view to paying serious attention to the instruction they are to receive. The girls joke and giggle while the youths do their exercises. Presently the officer loses his temper and warns the class that the time may come when their lives will depend on what they have learned.

His sweetheart is ashamed of her conduct, and, with a view to appeasing her lover, smuggles a rose into his gas-mask without his noticing it.

Suddenly there is a terrific detonation which announces a sur. prise gas-attack from the air. The laughing girls and youths become a panic-stricken mob. Quickly the officer shepherds the pupils to the gas-proof cellar, then he returns to give instruction orally and by telephone, while the crash of bombs is mingled with the screaming of sirens.

It is time for the officer to seek shelter himself. He goes to put on his gas-mask, but it will not fit. He pulls it off and discovers the rose inside. He takes it out and, while he is holding the flower in one hand and the mask in the other, the deadly gas seeps into the room. He sinks to the ground.

Scene III. Same as Scene I. Night.

Passers-by are feverishly rushing to and fro in an endeavour to sheek shelter, while the street resounds to the crash of bursting gas-bombs and the vivid flashes of explosions.

Gradually all becomes quiet and the people emerge from their shelters, including the pupils of the anti-gas school. The officer's sweetheart searches eagerly for her lover but cannot find him. She is about to enter the school when a group of soldiers emerge with a stretcher on which her lover lies dead, still holding her rose in his hand. She flings herself on his body and sobs bitterly. The curtain slowly falls.

*

Perhaps To-morrow! is a well-planned propagandist ballet intended to bring home to the general public the advisability of preparing in time of peace against the possible terrors of the wars of the future. This ballet is, I think, the first to be based on the theme of a gas-attack by air. Its production excited considerable interest both at Budapest and abroad, where it was much commented upon by foreign Press representatives.

LITTLE JOHNNY IN TOP–BOOTS

Ballet in 1 Act and 3 Scenes. Book: Ervin Clementis. Music: Jenö Kenessey. Scenery: Zoltán Fülöp. Costumes: Gusztav Oláh. Choreography: Gyula Harangozó. First produced: Royal Hungarian Opera House, Budapest, June, 1937.

CHARACTERS

Csizmás Janko (Little Johnny in
    Top-Boots) . . . . . M. Gyula Harangozó
The Witch . . . . . . Mlle. Ilona Vera
Ildikó . . . . Mlle. Karola Szalay
Seppi . . . . M. Zoltán Sallay

The Bride . . . . . . Mlle. Bella Bordy
The Bridegroom . . . . . M. László Csányi
The Fairy Queen . . . . Mlle. Hedvig Hidas
The Fairy King . . . . . M. Pál Fekete
Peasants, Witches, Fairies, Dwarfs.

Scene I. *A stretch of pasture-land.*

Janko, a merry shepherd boy, is seen tending his sheep. A wedding-party passes by and among the guests is a beautiful and wealthy girl called Ildikó. Janko immediately falls in love with her, and she with him. But Seppi, a rich peasant youth who loves Ildikó himself, sneers at Janko's poverty and points out that he has not even a pair of boots to his feet. Janko feels ashamed and his one ambition is to obtain a pair of boots.

Scene II. *A forest.*

An old woman, who is a witch in disguise, comes to gather twigs. Janko, seeing that she is weary, goes to help her. In return she gives him a sword which will lead him to fairyland, where great happiness awaits him.

Seppi, armed with a stick, enters in search of Janko, whom he is determined to kill. But the witch causes the stick to become fastened to his hand. Some of his friends arrive and, seeing Seppi's plight, go to his help. The witch warns them that anyone who touches Seppi will become stuck to him. His friends, however, ignore her warning, and a grotesque chain is formed of girls and youths who struggle in vain endeavour to set themselves free. In this way they execute a crazy dance which brings them, like Janko, to the gate of fairyland.

Scene III. *The gate to fairyland.*

Janko and Seppi each receive a bow and arrow from the witch, who informs them that each will receive his deserts accordingly as he shoots. Seppi looses an arrow at the door, which opens to reveal a horde of demons and witches who frighten Seppi and his friends. The door closes and Janko draws his bow. The arrow flies true, and the door opens to reveal the King and Queen of Fairyland with all their fairy folk.

Janko is invited to dance and so charms the fairies that the Queen presents him with a pair of golden boots. Ildikó takes him in her arms and they are happily betrothed.

ANTONY TUDOR

ANTONY TUDOR—he is known only by his professional
name—was born at London on April 4th, 1909. He comes
of a business family and began his career as a clerk. Towards
1928, impelled by curiosity, he went to a performance given by
Anna Pavlova, and then to see the ballets presented by Serge
Diaghilev. These experiences changed the whole course of his
life. He conceived the ambition to become the director of a ballet
company, and, having carefully considered the matter, decided that
the first step towards this end was to spend his leisure hours in
studying the technique of the classical ballet. He studied with
Mme. Marie Rambert and also had lessons from Pearl Argyle and
Harold Turner.

In 1930 Tudor joined a firm of assessors, which work entailed a
certain amount of travelling and so interfered with his dance
studies. When Mme. Rambert founded the Ballet Club in October
of that year, she offered him a two-year contract under which he
was to act as secretary to the club and to dance in the ballets presented. He decided to relinquish his business career, accept the
contract, and concentrate upon the Dance. He also tried his hand
at choreography and in 1931 produced at the Club his first ballet,
Cross-gartered, an interesting composition based on an episode in
Shakespeare's *Twelfth Night.* Tudor's contract was renewed for
a further year.

In September, 1933, he joined the Vic-Wells Ballet where he
served for two years, dancing, among other parts, those of Eusebius
in *Le Carnaval,* the Man in *La Création du Monde,* and the Man
in *Hommage aux Belles Viennoises.* He also arranged the ballets
in the operas *Carmen* and *Faust.*

But he did not sever his connection with the Ballet Club where
he devoted himself more and more to the production of ballets.
The following is a list of his compositions to date: *Lysistrata, or
the Strike of Wives* (Prokofiev), 1932; *Adam and Eve* (Lambert),
1932; *Atlanta of the East* (Seelig), 1933; *The Planets* (Holst),
1934; *The Descent of Hebe* (Bloch), 1935; *Jardin aux Lilas*

828

(Chausson), 1936; and *Dark Elegies* (Mahler), 1937. All these were produced at the Ballet Club, with the exception of *Adam and Eve,* which was composed for the Camargo Society, and *Dark Elegies,* which was first presented at the Duchess Theatre, during a season given by the Ballet Rambert. In each of these ballets Tudor himself danced one of the principal roles.

He also produced *Castor and Pollux* for the Oxford University Opera Club (1934) and, in 1935, in connection with the season of opera at Covent Garden, he arranged the dances in *Schwanda* (Weinberger), *La Cenerentola* (Rossini), *Carmen* (Bizet), and *Koanga* (Delius). In 1937, Tudor produced a new ballet called *Gallant Assembly*—to music by Tartini—at the Playhouse, Oxford.

THE DESCENT OF HEBE

Ballet in 1 Act and 4 Scenes. Book: Antony Tudor. Music: Ernest Bloch. Scenery and Costumes: Nadia Benois. Choreography: Antony Tudor. First produced: Mercury Theatre, London, April 21st, 1935.

CHARACTERS

Hebe	Pearl Argyle
Mercury	Hugh Laing
Night	Maude Lloyd
Hercules	Antony Tudor

Attendants on Jupiter, Attendants on Night.

I. (Prelude). Hebe, while serving the Gods, trips and spills a cup of precious nectar. Overcome with shame she attempts to steal away, hoping that her carelessness may have passed unnoticed. But Mercury arrives with a message from Jupiter, which banishes her to Earth as a punishment for her fault.

II. (Dirge). Night, with her horsed chariot, awaits Mercury's signal to leave for Earth. He arrives, followed by Hebe, whom he presents to Night with the injunction that she be taken to Earth. Hebe, however, refuses to enter the chariot. Thereupon, Night conjures up a vision of Hercules whom Hebe will meet on Earth. Hebe is captivated and, now as eager to depart as formerly she was reluctant to leave, leaps into the chariot.

III. (Pastoral). Hebe arrives on Earth and encounters Hercules who woos her.

IV. (Dirge). Apotheosis.

*

In 1933 Ashley Dukes presented at his Mercury Theatre a play by J. V. Turner entitled *Jupiter Translated,* which was produced by Rupert Doone. In the middle of this play there was a short suite of dances, in which Hercules and Hebe were the principal characters. Beginning with these two characters, Tudor evolved the *scenario* for this ballet which is given to Bloch's *Concerto Grosso.*

The second scene is the most interesting from a technical standpoint, for it is really an *adage* for Night, in which the possibilities of the *pirouette* in various positions are exploited.

The third scene, with its gay leaping movements by Hercules, recalls an episode from one of those anacreontic ballets fashionable at the beginning of the 19th century.

In the final scene Tudor has sought to express in terms of the dance the mood induced by a musical fugue.

JARDIN AUX LILAS

Ballet in 1 *Act. Book: Antony Tudor. Music: Chausson. Scenery and Costumes: Hugh Stevenson. Choreography: Antony Tudor. First produced: Mercury Theatre, London, January 26th, 1936.*

CHARACTERS

Caroline, the Bride-to-be	MAUDE LLOYD
Her Lover	HUGH LAING
The Man She must Marry . . .	ANTONY TUDOR
The Woman in his Past	PEGGY VAN PRAAGH

Guests.

Scene. The lilac-garden of Caroline's house.

At the rise of the curtain, Caroline, the bride-to-be, is seen conversing with her fiancé. It is evident from their demeanour that the marriage is one of convenience. Caroline is to be married at her fiancé's home, but, before leaving, has planned a farewell party to which she has invited her friends. Among the guests are the man she really loves, and a woman who, unknown to her, has been her fiancé's mistress. Since these two characters are unnamed, it will be helpful to style them Hugh and Peggy, after the names of their respective interpreters.

While Caroline and her fiancé are conversing with an air of bored decorum, Hugh enters. He is about to greet Caroline with every affection, when she deters him with a warning gesture. Caroline and her fiancé go out and the guests dance.

Presently Caroline returns alone. She seeks for Hugh only to encounter Peggy, who ignores her proffered hand and goes to look for her lover.

Hugh comes in and meets Caroline. They dance together with every sign of mutual affection, but the bride-to-be, well aware of the dangerous situation, frequently interrupts the dance to keep watch against the return of her fiancé. Whenever Hugh and Caroline pass momentarily from sight in the course of their dance, their place is taken by Caroline's fiancé and Peggy. She wishes her lover to continue with her on the old footing; he, on the other hand, is equally insistent that they must part. And as they dance and quarrel, so now it is the fiancé who fears that Caroline may enter and learn the secret of his past. These two episodes give rise to a series of interrupted *pas de deux*.

The ballet ends in a *pas de quatre* in which Caroline has to leave on the arm of her fiancé, without having had an opportunity to take that final tender farewell of her lover which she had so adroitly planned, and which was the principal excuse for the party.

*

This ballet has an interesting origin. Tudor wished to compose a ballet cast in a certain mood and set in the Edwardian era. This desire was inspired to some extent by his reading a short story by the Finnish author, Aino Kallas, a story in which a peasant couple are to be married when the landowner announces his intention of exercising his *droit du seigneur*. The bride goes to fulfil the law but armed with a dagger. This situation was not practical, so Tudor discussed allied themes with his friends. Finally, he sought a situation in which lovers about to be separated have a desperate longing to kiss each other before parting. This is the main-spring of *Jardin aux Lilas*. For music, Tudor selected Chausson's *Poème*.

This Maupassant-like plot is a rare theme in ballet and offers an example which might be imitated with advantage. The choreography, dancing, setting, and costumes are all charming, and the nervous tension is maintained throughout. The only criticism that might be made is that there are many exits and entrances, but, since the whole ballet depends on the interplay of the two groups, it is difficult to see how that could be avoided.

Jardin aux Lilas is, so far, Tudor's most successful ballet.

DAVID LICHINE

DAVID LICHINE, *né* Lichtenstein, was born on December 25th, 1910, at Rostov-on-Don, South Russia. His father is a composer under the name Michael Olshansky and was formerly a singer at the Narodny Dom, St. Petersburg.

Lichine completed his education at the Russian High School, Paris, and, always fond of dancing, began, in 1926, to train with Lubov Egorova; later, he studied with Bronislava Nijinska.

He danced for short periods in the Ballet Ida Rubinstein, and in the Pavlova Company. In 1932 Lichine joined the company called "Russian Opera at Paris," jointly directed by Col. W. de Basil and Prince Zereteli, and has remained under the former's management ever since. Lichine became a *premier danseur* in the Col. de Basil's Ballets Russes and is best known for his dancing in *Les Présages* and *Choreartium*.

In 1933 Lichine made his first essay in choreography with *Nocturne;* this was followed by *Les Imaginaires* (1934), *Le Pavillon* (1936), and *Francesca da Rimini* (1937). *Le Pavillon* achieved a measure of success, but *Francesca,* despite its inequalities, showed definite promise. His future compositions are awaited with interest.

FRANCESCA DA RIMINI

Ballet in 2 Scenes. Book: David Lichine and Henry Clifford. Music: P. I. Tchaikovsky. Scenery and Costumes: Oliver Messel. Choreography: David Lichine. First produced: Royal Opera House, Covent Garden, London, July 15th, 1937.

CHARACTERS

Francesca	MME. LUBOV TCHERNICHEVA
Gianciotto Malatesta, Frances-ca's husband	M. MARC PLATOV
Paolo, Malatesta's younger brother	M. PAUL PETROV

832

Chiara, Francesca's nurse . . MLLE. ELEONORA MARRA
Girolamo, Malatesta's spy . . M. EDOUARD BOROVANSKY
Domenico, Paolo's friend . . M. YURA LAZOVSKY
Angelic Apparition . . . MLLE. TATIANA RIABOUCHINSKA
Guinevere . . . . . MLLE. ALEXANDRA DANILOVA
Lancelot . . . . . M. ROMAN JASINSKY
  Signors of Rimini, Dwarfs, Francesca's Ladies, Chorus, Musi-
    cians, Soldiers, Servants, Townspeople.

The Lord of Ravenna, desirous of ending the long years of strife
that have existed between his own signory and that of Rimini,
proposes to establish peace by offering his daughter, Francesca, as
wife to Gianciotto, son of the Lord of Rimini. Gianciotto, however, is so deformed that, fearing Francesca may refuse him, he
sends his handsome brother, Paolo, to marry her by proxy and
escort her to him. But the formal ceremony has become reality and
Francesca and Paolo are in love with each other.

*Scene 1. A room in Malatesta's castle. The austere stone walls
are relieved by delicate arches supported on slender columns. In
the background are two windows giving on to a beautiful landscape. To the left is a chair placed on a dais, over which hangs
a canopy.*

At the rise of the curtain, Gianciotto is seated on the dais,
attended by a number of evil dwarfs. Seated below him are a
number of courtiers with whom he debates what action shall be
taken should Francesca refuse him. The discussion becomes so
heated that blows are exchanged between the courtiers.
  In the midst of the confusion news is brought of the arrival of
Francesca, who is accompanied by her nurse, Chiara. Francesca
enters and dutifully kneels in homage to Malatesta. But when he
looks at her and Francesca is made aware of his deformity, she is
overcome with horror.
  Girolamo, Malatesta's spy, informs his master that Francesca is
in love with Paolo. Malatesta is furious with rage, and threatens
Francesca. Chiara tries to protect her charge by extending a crucifix before her, but Girolamo pushes the nurse aside. Malatesta
strikes the spy in reproof, then, gathering Francesca in his arms,
carries her out of the room just as Paolo enters. When he tries to
follow his brother, armed guards bar his way. Chiara, filled with
anxiety for her mistress's happiness, loses her reason.
  Francesca returns. Paolo attempts to escape with her, but is prevented by Girolamo.

Scene II. Francesca's bower. The background is formed by an arched doorway at present closed by an iron-studded door. To the right is a surrounding wall pierced by a fretted window. The left is formed by a delicate building with a portico of small arches balanced on slender columns. Before the portico is placed a settle.

Francesca and Paolo are seated together on the settle, reading from a folio the story of the love of Lancelot and Guinevere—conveyed by two dancers—a tale which so enthralls them that Paolo kisses Francesca and they "read no more." So happy are they in the sweet ecstasy of their love that the room seems filled with angels.

Trumpets announce the approach of Malatesta. Francesca, terror-stricken, bids Paolo hide on the terrace. Hardly has he done so when the great door is flung back and the sinister Malatesta is seen framed in the doorway. He is preceded by his dwarfs who scamper about like rats, peering behind tapestry and furniture in quest of Paolo. While Malatesta rages with a drawn sword, the dwarfs search the terrace, where they discover their victim.

A terrible duel ensues between the two brothers; it is watched beyond the doorway by a group of lords and people, whose excited movements are expressive of the varying fortunes of the combat. At last Paolo is slain.

Francesca, frantic with grief, flings herself upon the sword that killed her lover.

*

Francesca da Rimini is arranged to Tchaikovsky's tone poem of the same name. This is not the first occasion on which it has served as the framework for a ballet, since it was presented in that form with choreography by Fokine at the Maryinsky Theatre, St. Petersburg, in 1915.

The symphonic poem, which is based on Canto V of Dante's *Inferno,* is in three parts. The first describes the second circle of Hell, where a flight of carnal sinners are tossed about ceaselessly by furious winds; the second expresses the episode in which Francesca and Paolo read the chronicle of Lancelot and Guinevere; in the third, the lovers pass from view and the winds resume their fury.

In Lichine's ballet the first part of the symphony provides the music for Scene I, and the remaining parts that for Scene II. The first scene is largely dramatic movement and mime, and is often very effective as orchestration of movement. Tchaikovsky's music, however, is so tremendously dramatic from the start, that the ballet is forced to begin on a high note which, having regard to the theme of debate and quarrelling, tends to become extravagant and, moreover, cannot be sustained. But this first act is stirring from the very intensity of feeling which Lichine has infused into it.

The first half of the second act, which depicts the love of Francesca and Paolo, is far from happy. To begin with, the particular quality of the music at this point is ill suited to interpretation in dancing, and the manner in which the angelic visions are presented tends to make this scene ridiculous rather than moving. Again, dresses based on the visions represented in paintings of Italian primitives do not accord with *pointes,* and the costumes worn by Lancelot and Guinevere have a suggestion of revue.

The second half of the scene improves with the spirited duel between the brothers, which is accompanied by the movements of a group of distant spectators who, like a Greek chorus, provide a constant commentary on the progress of the fight.

There is little dancing by the principals, but some fine miming by Tchernicheva, Platov, Petrov, Marra, and Borovansky in their respective parts. The first scene is ofen dominated by the four dwarfs, whose movements, part buffoon, part sinister, are most exciting to watch, although these creatures seem to belong to the court of Peter the Great rather than to that of Malatesta.

SOVIET BALLETS

THIS section contains a selection of the principal Soviet Ballets, which I have found more convenient to group together.

The Soviet ballets, which are definitely propagandist in theme, are splendidly staged, but, with a few exceptions, such as the work of Petritsky at Kharkov, adhere to the canons of the realistic school of stage decoration, and are seldom marked by any particular distinction of design.

When the new régime came into force, Ballet was caught up in the general urge for drastic change. The old ideals of choreography, based on the traditional technique, were to be replaced by revolutionary ideas in movement. In actual practice the new conception of ballet resolved itself into a few experiments inspired by the clowning and acrobatism of the circus, and some impulses borrowed from the Duncan and similar schools of interpretative dancing. These experiments, however, were found to yield little of material benefit, and there was a reversion to the old school of conventional steps and mime.

Soviet choreography, then, approximates in the main to the epoch of Marius Petipa, and, at best, to Fokine's first period, that of *L'Oiseau de Feu*. It is curious that, in a state where modernism is a god, the Soviet choreographers appear to be unacquainted with the later work of Fokine, and quite unaware of the ballets of Borlin, Balanchine, and Massine.

THE RED POPPY

Ballet in 3 Acts and 6 Scenes. Book: M. T. Kurilko. Music: R. M. Glière. Scenery: B. Erbstein. Production: F. V. Lopukhov. First produced:Bolshoy Theatre, Moscow, 1927.

CHARACTERS

Captain of a Soviet Steamer
Tai-Hoa, a Chinese dancer

Li-Shan-Fu, an adventurer
Sir Hips
Shan-Fan-Lu, a banker
Boatswain of the Soviet steamer
Aide-de-camp to Sir Hips
The Proprietor of an Opium Den
  Sailors of different nationalities, Chinese citizens, Europeans,
    Dock-labourers, Foremen, Chinese servants, Monsters.

Act I. A large Americanized modern treaty-port in China. There is an exaggerated comparison of old Chinese dwellings with modern buildings of concrete and steel. There is a bar with an entrance on the sea-front, which is filled with foreign sailors; some Malay women dance on a stage as an exotic attraction. In the roads are anchored large steamers which have brought goods and passengers from different parts of the world. Among them is a Soviet vessel. The ships are being unloaded.

Wretched, half-starved coolies are being driven to work by their foremen, who urge them on with blows and curses. Meanwhile the frequenters of the bar are growing merry. The entrance of Tai-Hoa is hailed with enthusiasm. She descends from her palanquin and dances with a fan. She is followed by some other turns, such as an eccentric with a donkey, and a troupe of music-hall dancers. Suddenly the audience's attention is drawn to a disturbance among the coolies. One of their number has been felled and voices rise in protest. The Soviet captain goes on to the quay and, seeing the situation, orders his crew to relieve the exhausted coolies. The task of unloading continues.

The coolies are touched by this unexpected act of kindness. A meeting is organised and the matter is discussed. Tai-Hoa comes out of the bar attended by her admirers. She is very impressed by the captain's act and offers him a bouquet of flowers, among which he observes some red poppies. He gives one of them to a coolie as a symbol of liberty. Meanwhile, Tai-Hoa is jealously watched by Li-Shan-Fu. Now she dances with a lance, after which she departs, accompanied by her impresario.

Gradually the sea-front becomes filled with sailors, dock-labourers, and other workers who have finished work. The Malay women join the coolies in a dance-game which represents victory over the oppressors. This is followed by a series of *divertissements* consisting of dances by sailors of different nationalities—a dance by a stolid German sailor, a jolly dance by an English sailor, a dance by a negress boatswain, a dance by a Chinese pirate, and a dance by an Indian. The entertainment concludes with a dance by the Soviet sailors, to the tune of *Ekh Yabolochko,* which is enthusiastically received.

Act II. Scene I. An opium den, with various clients arriving. Many of these are already under the influence of the drug. Tourists arrive on the look-out for sensation, and sailors enter for a lark. This den is also a club.

Here Tai-Hoa is seen dancing with four Chinese women. The commander of the port, Sir Hips, is present incognito, to spy out the land. The Soviet captain's action has incited unrest among the coolies and the peace of the port is threatened. Sir Hips desires to offset this tendency by getting rid of the Soviet captain. Sir Hips speaks with Li-Shan-Fu, who does not like the Soviet captain. They decide to make him responsible for a disturbance in order to have an excuse for getting rid of him. But when they attempt to seize him, the captain summons his men with his whistle, and they run to his aid. Sir Hips glides away while the Chinese in his pay are left to make what excuse they can.

The opium den is gradually cleared of customers; only Tai-Hoa remains. She wishes to help the Soviet captain, but Li-Shan-Fu watches her closely. Sad at heart, she seeks forgetfulness in smoking opium and falls asleep.

Act II. Scene II. Tai-Hoa's dream. Part I.

Tai-Hoa dreams of legendary China. She is haunted by a procession of malevolent monsters, dragons, soldiers in ferocious masks who brandish their weapons, Chinese gods and their priests. Over all looms the bloodthirsty idol, Gouandi.

Act II. Scene III. Tai-Hoa's dream. Part II.

The evil dreams change to peaceful dreams suggested by the beauties of nature, which enables the Chinese element to give place to dances of a classical type. There are dances symbolical of lotuses, poppies, and various small flowers and butterflies. Tai-Hoa imagines that she takes part in the dances herself. She thinks of the Soviet captain whose image appears before her. With thoughts of love she goes towards him, but the apparition disappears.

Act III. Scene I. At the ball given by Shan-Fan-Lu. The flower of Chinese and European aristocracy are received in his magnificent ballroom. Through a window can be seen a city of skyscrapers, bathed in the glare of electric light. The refined pleasures of the oppressed races are strongly contrasted.

There is an entertainment for the guests. First, a female dancer dances on a gigantic dish. This is followed by an eccentric *pas de deux*. Finally, there is a rendering of an ancient Chinese theatrical performance by a Chinese troupe, which includes Tai-Hoa and Li-Shan-Fu, the latter acting as manager. The last item is lengthy and includes many types of dances—dances by Chinese chiefs, dances by girls with scarves, a Chinese devil-dance, a dance by Hai-Hoa, to the accompaniment of drums, and an acrobatic dance.

The entertainment over, dancing in the ballroom is resumed. Among the guests is the Soviet captain, who has been invited for a sinister purpose, for it is hoped to poison him by means of Tai-Hoa. At first, unsuspecting, she observes various preparations and looks for the captain. Follows a mimed scene in which she tells him of her love, and entreats him to leave as his life is threatened. He refuses and asks Tai-Hoa to work with him for the liberty of the masses, and reminds her of the symbolic flower which he gave her.

A supper follows. Li-Shan-Fu hands Tai-Hoa a glass of poisoned wine to give to the captain. As she cannot refuse she pretends to slip, so that the glass falls to the floor and the wine is spilt. Thereupon, Li-Shan-Fu draws a revolver and fires at the captain. This incident creates a panic. But, in his excitement, Li-Shan-Fu misses his aim.

Act III. Scene II. The Soviet steamer is seen leaving Chinese waters. It has already left port and Tai-Hoa is left standing on the sea-front waving farewell.

Enter Li-Shan-Fu, jealous and angry at his unsuccessful attempt to kill the captain. Mad with rage at this exchange of farewells he stabs Tai-Hoa with a dagger. She falls to the ground, unconscious. Some children gather about her. With a great effort she revives and urges them to fight for their liberty, in token of which she hands them a red poppy and dies.

The ballet concludes with an epilogue, in which the stage picture represents the victory of the Chinese proletariat. The musical theme is based on the "Internationale."

*

The Red Poppy has attained a considerable popularity which dates from its initial performance. Its strength lies in the number of dances for men, while, conversely, its weakness is its lack of any outstanding dancing roles for women.

Glière's music is another factor in the ballet's success, and several of his "numbers," such as the Sailors' Dance, have become popular items in concert programmes.

THE GOLDEN AGE

Ballet in 3 Acts and 5 Scenes. Book: A. V. Ivanovsky. Music: D. D. Shostakovich. Scenery and costumes: V. M. Khodasevich. Choreography: E. I. Kaplan and V. I. Vainonen, with speciality dances by V. P. Tchesnakov and L. V. Jacobson. First produced: Bolshoy Theatre, Moscow, 1931.

CHARACTERS

Director of an Industrial Exhibition
Deva, a Danseuse and Fascist
A Fascist
Chief of Police (a Fascist)
Four Secretaries who are also Detectives
Captain of a Soviet Football Team (a Factory Worker)
A Woman of the Communist Soviet Youth (U.S.S.R.)
A Woman of the Communist Soviet Youth (Western Europe)
A Negro Boxer
A White Boxer
Referees, trade representatives

Act I. Scene I. An industrial advertising exhibition, called The Golden Age, in a large capitalist city.

The curtain rises on a procession of guests of honour, among whom a group of Fascists is particularly welcomed, a carpet being laid down before them. In contrast there is the quiet entrance of a Soviet football team, who have been invited by local labour organisations.

Members of the general public inspect the exhibition while the Fascists are wheeled round in splendidly upholstered chairs.

The director and chief of police demonstrate a newly invented gun. The Fascists are displeased by the appearance of the footballers.

Another advertising display. A strange Hindu intrigues the public by various occult passes. Suddenly he throws off his robe and appears in evening-dress—the referee for a boxing match. A crowd of sightseers collect.

A firm of manufacturers of boxing-gloves have organised a boxing match between a white man (a Fascist) and a negro. A secret agent of the Fascists bribes the referee. The police are summoned as a precaution against disorder.

The white man delivers a foul blow, which is ignored by the referee, and the negro, who was winning, is knocked down. The referee quickly counts ten and acclaims the white man the winner, although he immediately faints as a result of the strenuous contest.

The local workmen are furious at the verdict. They climb into the ring intending to assault the referee. The police are ordered to force the workers back. The bourgeois public vent their anger by brandishing their sticks and umbrellas.

Suddenly a woman of the local Communist Soviet Youth emerges from the crowd and slaps the referee's cheek.

Act I. Scene II. A cabaret in the exhibition.

A number of Fascist youths and girls are dancing about the tables. Enter the director of the exhibition, accompanied by the chief of police and various secretaries. Everyone awaits the appearance of Deva, the famous Fascist dancer. At last she enters; the men hurry to kiss her hand, while the women are amazed at her fine clothes.

Deva dances an *adage* which is much applauded.

The footballers enter accompanied by local labour representatives, who are showing them over the exhibition.

Deva is attracted by the captain of the team and dances a passionate number.

The footballers dance a measure full of virile energy. There is much applause and Deva becomes still more interested in the captain.

She induces her partner, a Fascist, to invite the captain to dance with her. The captain courteously refuses. His action is resented by the bourgeois public.

Deva and her partner dance a number expressive of love.

The negro boxer and two footballers dance a *pas de trois* symbolical of good comradeship.

The director and chief of police observe the football captain and invite him to take part in a special dance expressive of peaceful co-operation between all classes.

A placard is shown announcing a dance between a worker and Deva, the Fascist. She offers the captain a glass of wine and asks him to drink the Fascist toast. The captain, momentarily stupefied, refuses. The enraged Fascists are about to attack the captain when he raises his football in defence. The Fascists imagine the football to be a bomb and fling themselves to the ground in preparation for the expected explosion. The captain places the ball beside the director's head and leaves with his comrades.

The Fascists, frightened out of their wits, gradually recover from their apprehensions and perceive their mistake. The director summons the chief of police, who sends for his men. Gradually the excitement subsides and everyone finds relief in dancing a fox-trot.

Act II. Scene I. A street in the same city.

The negro, the football captain, and the woman of the Communist Soviet Youth are seen walking in the street, sight-seeing. They are shadowed by detectives. The chief of police and his men prepare a trap for their victims. After several unsuccessful attempts, the detectives manage to slip counterfeit notes into the captain's pocket. He is stopped and arrested with his companions. They are led through the city.

But the negro resolves to escape. He punches one of his captors, rescues the woman, and flees with her. The captain remains in the hands of the police. The negro is hotly pursued, but in vain.

The chief of police is very annoyed at the negro's escape and strikes those who had charge of him.

Act II. Scene II. A workers' stadium.

Procession of the workers to the stadium, and dance of the pioneers.

Worker-sportsmen are seen going to the sports, while the pioneers play a game called "Find the Fascist."

Now several sports are seen in progress, for instance, boxing, discus-throwing, tennis, fencing, basket-ball, javelin-throwing, and so on.

The Soviet football team are accorded a triumphant reception. Follows a representation of the game of football.

There is an interlude when a film is shown. It is called "Everyone to his own Pleasure," and shows Fascists playing for high stakes and developing evil instincts.

Then comes a dance between a woman of the Communist Soviet Youth and four sportsmen.

General dance symbolical of sport.

Another film is shown in which the police are seen pursuing a negro and the woman of the Communist Soviet Youth, who are running towards the stadium. The workers organise themselves into a Red Front. The police are forced to give up their chase.

Act III. A music-hall in the exhibition. The performance is called Festival of the Golden Age, and consists of a number of divertissements.

First, there is a tap dance number to advertise Superfine Boot Polish.

Then a Polka called "Once upon a time in Geneva." The dance illustrates the talking-machine of Western Europe, with its views on Peace of Nations, Disarmament, and other beautiful things.

Next a touching "Dance of Reconciliation of all Classes," with light falsifications. This is danced by Deva and her Fascist partner who has disguised himself as the captain of the Soviet football team. This number is enthusiastically received.

Afterwards comes a Can-Can. This is an *ensemble* to a quick tempo; it is reminiscent of a bacchanalian orgy and represents the enthusiasm of the bourgeois public for the previous number.

This is followed by a film representing the freeing of prisoners. There is the prison, the prisoners, and their rescue by the Red Front.

The Red Front surround the music-hall. The woman of the Communist Soviet Youth (Western Europe) denounces Deva's partner as a Fascist. The bourgeois public is in a panic.

Lastly, there is a dance expressive of the co-operation between the workers of Western Europe and the Soviet football team; it is also symbolical of various types of work and the joy of labour.

*

In 1929 there was a shortage of new synopses for ballet, and a competition was organised for the best ballet on a Soviet theme. The winning entry was *The Golden Age,* which, however, was subjected to considerable revision before production. A stage-manager was appointed to supervise the ballet, which became a collective production.

This piece has a special interest in being the first ballet score written by the young composer, Dmitri Shostakovich.

As a ballet the production is weak, due to over-emphasis of the Soviet theme.

THE FLAMES OF PARIS

Ballet in 4 Acts and 7 Scenes. Book: N. D. Volkov and V. V. Dmitriev. Music: B. V. Asafiev. Scenery: V. V. Dmitriev. Choreography: V. I. Vynonen. Production: S. E. Radlev. First produced: Bolshoy Theatre, Leningrad, November 7th/20th, 1932.

CHARACTERS

Gaspard, a peasant
Jeanne ⎱ his children
Pierre ⎰
Philippe ⎱ Marseillais
Jerome ⎰
Gilbert
The Marquis Costa de Beauregard
The Comte Geoffroy, his son
The Mayor
Mireille de Poitiers, an actress
Antoine Mistral, an actor
Amour, an actress of the Court Theatre
King Louis XVI
Queen Marie Antoinette
Master of the Ceremonies
Thérèse
A Jacobin Orator
A Sergeant of the National Guard
Marseillais, Parisians, Ladies of the Court, Officers of the
Guard, the Swiss Guard.

The action passes in France, in the summer of 1792.

Act I. Marseille. The square in front of the Marquis de Beauregard's castle. Early morning.

Jeanne and Pierre enter shyly and conceal themselves behind the base of a castle tower.

The Marquis's huntsmen drag in Gaspard and push him through the castle gateway. Jeanne and Pierre discuss how to get into the castle, but, hearing the noise behind the gates, they hide again.

Servants come out quickly carrying luggage; they are followed by the Marquis, his son, and the steward. From the latter's sharp orders the children gather that the family are taking flight to Paris. The family having departed the steward and servants go into the castle and lock the gates.

The day grows lighter and the square begins to fill with excited groups of Marseillais who have decided to abolish all representatives of the King's authority. Philippe, Jerome, and Gilbert, ask the children what they are doing. They recount how they were gathering wood in the Marquis's forest, when his huntsmen seized Gaspard and took him into the castle; and then they tell of the departure of the Marquis and his family.

Furious at the news of the Marquis's escape, the Marseillais prepare to storm the castle. The guards who appear on the walls are received with showers of stones. The gates are broken down and the crowd pour into the castle.

Gaspard runs out, followed by some frightened prisoners who have been kept in the dungeons. The bright sunshine dazzles their eyes. They cannot understand why they have been brought into the square and fear they are to be put to death. The crowd regard the prisoners with horror, then take them under their protection and explain that they are free.

Meanwhile several Marseillais bring out the steward. They take off his waistcoat and beat him. General merriment begins. An inn-keeper rolls out several barrels of wine and offers it to the crowd. Gaspard places a phrygian hat on a pike and stands it in the middle of the square. The crowd dance a farandole. Philippe, Jerome, and Jean dance together and try to out-do one another. Suddenly the tocsin rings and Pierre, Jerome, and Jean run in and explain that they are forming a band of volunteers to go to Paris to help the *sans-culottes.*

A party of the National Guard enter with flags flying and a banner bearing the device "The Country is in Danger." After a short speech by the leader, recruiting begins. Among the first to join are Philippe, Jerome, Gilbert, also Gaspard, Pierre, and Jean. The soldiers sing the *Marseillaise,* the crowd join in, the recruits form into ranks and then march away.

Act II. A great festival in the Palace of Versailles.

At the rise of the curtain ladies of the Court and officers of the King's Guard are seen dancing the sarabande. The dance is cold and ultra-refined, and offers a sharp contrast with the folk dancing of the first act.

The sarabande ended, the officers bow to the ladies. A sudden change in the music announces the arrival at Versailles of the Marquis de Beauregard and his son. They have learned of the happenings at Marseille, and, rather shocked and excited, are telling the news to the Court. The Marquis asks the courtiers to join with him in avenging and upholding the King's authority. The officers swear fealty to the King.

The Master of Ceremonies enters and invites everyone to a theatrical entertainment which is to be followed by a banquet, given by the officers of one of the King's regiments recently arrived in Paris. All take their places in the boxes and there follows a performance by the King's actors.

The setting represents the sea. An actor and actress play an *entr'acte* in the manner of the period. The hero and heroine, wounded by Cupid's darts, fall in love with each other. But he leaves her and she invokes a storm which wrecks the boat in which the faithless lover takes to flight. The waves cast him up on the beach, but even then there is no safety. He is followed by furies who surround him, and dies at the feet of his deserted sweetheart. Above the questioning waves appears a figure symbolical of the sun. The style of the production is a mixture of symbol and allegory borrowed from the ancient world.

The performance ended, the players bow to the public, and men-servants bring in tables and prepare the banquet. The officers take their seats at the tables and different toasts are proposed, occasionally interrupted by Grètry's popular song, *"O Richard, O mon roi."*

Enter Louis XVI and Marie Antoinette and their suite. The officers rise, draw their swords, and acclaim the King and Queen. The King, touched by their greeting, wipes the tears from his eyes. The officers, in their monarchist enthusiasm, tear off their tricolour scarves and put on white bows. One officer pulls down a tricolour flag and tramples on it.

The King and Queen depart, also many of the court ladies, and the banquet gradually loses its formal character.

Comte Geoffroy is seen reading to a group of his friends a petition to the King which he has drawn up, in which the signatories entreat His Majesty to crush the revolution with the Guard regiments. One after another the officers sign. Meanwhile, several enthusiastic officers bring in the actor and actress and invite them to the banquet.

A group of officers and ladies dance a chaconne, but now their movements have lost the coldness of the sarabande. Mireille is asked to dance and she improvises a dance which is enthusiastically received. Then the two players are asked to join in the chaconne.

The effect of the wine grows more pronounced. The ladies disappear and the officers fall asleep at the tables; in the middle of the fading candle-light Mireille continues to dance with several unsteady officers. She does not like them but cannot leave. Mistral tells her to keep calm and not annoy the officers. He tries to remain near the actress, but a group of officers take him to a table, and Geoffroy insists on Mireille's dancing with him.

Standing by the table, Mistral notices the petition to the King and reads it. Geoffroy remarks the paper in the actor's hands and, furious, pushes him away and, drawing his sword, mortally wounds him. He falls to the ground still clutching the paper. Some of the officers surround Geoffroy and make him sit down, when he immediately falls asleep. The officers, thinking Mistral dead, depart. Almost all the candles are out and his body is seen lying in the ballroom.

Mireille vainly tries to recall what happened. Thinking that perhaps Mistral is alive, she calls for help, but all is silent. Mistral makes a few spasmodic movements and Mireille runs towards him, but he is motionless. She believes him dead. She dances to a new theme, investing her dancing with a sense of tense pathos.

In the distance can be heard the Marseillais entering Paris. Mireille takes the paper from Mistral's hand and reads it. The chant of the *Marseillaise* draws nearer. Mireille realises why Mistral was killed and makes a decision. She holds proof of the counter-revolutionary movement among the officers. She will give it to the revolutionaries. She picks up the bedraggled tricolour and hurries out of the palace.

Comte Geoffroy wakes up and, recollecting the train of events, searches for the petition to the King. He runs beside Mistral's body but the paper has disappeared.

Act III. Scene I. A square in Paris. Night.

It has been decided to attack the Tuileries in the morning. A group of citizens have collected by the Jacobin Club and await the signal for the assault. The arrival of the Marseillais is joyously welcomed. In the corner are a group of Basques, full of hate. Among them is Thérèse, an actress-revolutionary. The dancing in this scene has a folk-dance basis derived from the Basque provinces, Auvergne, and so on.

The dancing is interrupted by the arrival of Mireille and several Jacobin leaders whom she has already informed of the plot. Mireille gives the Council the petition which everyone tries to read. The Jacobins sing the revolutionary song "Chant du Départ." The crowd joins in and enthusiastically acclaims Mireille.

Gradually the meeting becomes an anti-royalist demonstration. Two dolls, caricatures of the King and Queen, are brought in. Playing a parody of *Richard, o mon roi,* the crowd bow derisively before the two dolls. In turn the crowd bow, dance, fire off muskets, and jump over bonfires burning in the square.

During the excitement a party of ladies cross the square. They are escorted by several officers, including Comte Geoffroy. Shocked at the insult offered to the King and Queen, the officers snatch the dolls from the demonstrators. The crowd subsides and watches the passing aristocrats. Suddenly Jeanne recognises the person who attacked her in the wood and, running up to him, slaps his face.

Geoffroy draws his sword, Gilbert goes towards him, and they fight by the light of the bonfires. The latter knocks Geoffroy's sword out of his hand. The crowd is ready to attack the little party of aristocrats who are hard pressed. But Gaspard restrains them, goes to Geoffroy and laughingly thanks him for the beating he received at the hands of his father's huntsmen. With derisive shouts the crowd dash at the aristocrats, who just manage to effect their escape.

Thérèse places the head of the doll representing King Louis on a pike and the crowd dance the Carmagnole. Enter a Jacobin speaker who asks the crowd to march to the Tuileries. They reply in the words of the *Marseillaise.* Singing the *Ça Ira* and waving tricolour flags the crowd march off.

Act III. Scene II. The grand staircase in the King's palace. Swiss Guards walk to and fro on sentry duty. The officer of the watch goes the rounds. All is quiet.

Suddenly the distant roll of drums is heard followed by snatches of the song *Ça Ira.* The officer listens with apprehension and orders the guard to turn out. The soldiers enter with slow measured steps and form up across one of the staircases. The singing grows louder.

Enter a group of excited court ladies and officers, among them the Marquis de Beauregard and Comte Geoffroy. They stop by the windows and listen. All at once the singing stops. The guards lay down their arms and refuse to fight for a foreign king. Some of the officers remind the soldiers of their oath of allegiance, others soothe the frightened ladies. The guards take up their muskets and agree to defend the palace.

At the officers' command they take up their positions on the staircase. Suddenly the doors are burst open and the crowd pour ın. But the soldiers repulse them. Then a girl speaks to the soldiers and tells them that no harm will come to them, they require only the King. The guards listen. But the Marquis and one of the officers fire from behind a column and kill the girl. Not knowing where the shooting comes from, both sides come to blows. Gradually the crowd is forced back, but Gaspard and his followers dash forward, at the same time others of the crowd climb through the windows behind the Swiss Guard. The defence is broken, the crowd pour into the palace, and fighting takes place in all parts. Different episodes in the conflict are shown to the audience.

Jerome stops two officers who are trying to escape and after a fierce fight kills both of them; soon afterwards he himself is shot by an officer. Geoffroy runs down the staircase, shooting as he goes, but is met by Jeanne. Recognising her, he swears to be avenged, and seizes her by the throat. But Pierre comes to her aid and stabs the Comte in the neck.

One of the Basques runs in with a flag in his hand, but is killed by a sword-thrust from an officer, who takes the flag. In turn Jeanne captures the flag from the officer and is herself shot by a fleeing courtier. At last the battle is over and the palace is captured.

From all sides enter groups of the victors. Isolated courtiers and officers try to hide, but are caught and disarmed. Down the staircase run panic-stricken ladies, one of whom hides her face with a fan. Gaspard, suspicious, seizes her. The fan contains a dagger with which she attempts to stab him, but without success. The "lady" is found to be the Marquis. He is bound and taken away. The crowd is amused by this incident. Gaspard, taking the fan, burlesques the Marquis. Preceded by triumphant fanfares the crowd dance on the steps of the palace.

Act IV. Scene I. The Reckoning.

To the depressing strains of Gossec's "Funeral March" the Parisians are seen taking away the bodies of those killed in the storming of the Tuileries.

Act IV. Scene II. The official festival of the triumph of the Republic, which is given in the square before the King's palace.

Members of the Government occupy tribunes. The middle of the square is surrounded by revolutionary troops. At a given signal the statue of the King is taken down.

Enter girls dressed in antique costumes, followed by men dressed as Roman warriors. They draw a chariot in which stands Mireille de Poitiers, who represents the Spirit of Victory. She is lifted on to the vacant base of the statue of the King. In contrast with the folk-dancing of other scenes, the dancing is by artistes of the State Theatres. This is the main feature of the celebration. The music is austere in feeling.

Act IV. Scene III. The People's Festival in honour of the taking of the Tuileries.

There is general dancing, intermingled with scenes burlesquing the King and Queen, and the aristocrats. The main dance is a *contre-danse,* executed to melodious music with a well-marked rhythm.

The ballet concludes with a Carmagnole which works up to a tremendous climax.

*

The theme of *The Flames of Paris* is based on a careful study of historical material relating to the French Revolution, and was written in the spring of 1931.

In the autumn of the same year Asafiev began to compose the music, which was completed by November, 1932. The score consists of selections from the works of contemporary composers, for instance, Grètry, Lully, Méhul, Gluck, and the like, skilfully worked into a complete whole. The plan of composition has many interesting features, for instance, the Royalist episodes are expressed in music of a sombre dignity, while incidents associated with the revolutionaries are, contrariwise, allotted fresh and lively airs symbolic of the birth of a new age.

Rehearsals were begun in March, 1932, as a result of which the synopsis was enlarged and revised; by June, the choreography was complete and in course of rehearsal. In the meantime Radlov had planned the mimed portion. Then the rehearsals were transferred to the stage. On June 23rd there was a private performance of the Prologue and the first three scenes. At the beginning of the season 1932–3, the rehearsals of the fourth act were complete and the first three acts had been revised.

The role of Mireille was taken partly by a singer from the State Opera and partly by a member of the ballet company. The song, "Chant du Départ," originally intended to be sung as a solo, was transferred to the chorus, which also sang the "Marseillaise" in Act I.

Act III was performed simultaneously at Leningrad and Moscow on November 6/19th, 1932, the fifteenth anniversary of the October Revolution.

The complete ballet was first performed at Leningrad on November 7/20th, 1932, at Moscow in the spring of 1933, at Dniepropetrovsk in the winter of 1933-4, and at Odessa in the spring of 1934.

THE FOUNTAIN OF BAKHCHISARAY

Choreographic Poem in 4 Acts. Book: N. D. Volkov, after the poem by A. S. Pushkin. Music: B. V. Asafiev. Scenery and costumes: V. M. Khodasevich. Produced: R. V. Zakharov. First produced: Bolshoy Theatre, Moscow, 1934.

CHARACTERS

Marie, a Polish Princess
Prince Adam, Marie's father
Vatslav, a young nobleman
Gierey, a Crimean Khan
Zarema, a Georgian woman, the beloved wife of Gierey
Old Gentlemen, Young Gentlemen, Young Ladies, Seneschal of the Castle, Captain of the Guard, Guests at the Ball, Servants, Soldiers of the Guard, Tartar Princes, a Tartar Spy, Chief Eunuch, Eunuchs, the Builder of the Fountain, Courtiers, Bodyguard, Wives of Gierey, Servants of the Harem, Marie's Attendants, Zarema's Attendants, Polish Women, etc.

The action of Act I passes in Poland, that of Acts II and III in Bakhchisaray.

Act I. An ancient park in a castle in Poland. In the background is the castle, a magnificent building with brilliantly lighted windows. A ball is in progress and snatches of music can occasionally be heard. The curtain rises on an empty stage.

Marie and Vatslav, her lover, enter. They dance lightly and depart.

Enter servants, headed by the seneschal, who prepare a clearing for the continuation of the ball. The Captain of the Guard appears followed by soldiers guarding a Tartar spy, whom they have caught near the castle. The Captain and seneschal express their disapproval of the ball, when the Tartars may arrive at any moment. The soldiers lead the captive away.

The music of the Polonaise is heard and a procession of guests come. The first couple is the grey-whiskered owner of the castle and his daughter, Marie. At the end of the dance Prince Adam lets Marie join the young people. There is general merriment. Now two youths dance with two old men, each age trying to rival the other. Then four ladies dance in the same manner. Follows a *grand pas de deux* for Marie and Vatslav. The father watches the young couple with delight and begins to dance a Krakoviak; the guests join in. During the dance, the Captain of the Guard, greatly alarmed, runs in. He tells the Prince that Tartars have been seen close to the castle. The Prince bids the men draw their swords and prepare for defence; the women disperse.

For a moment the clearing is empty then Marie and Vatslav enter, peering from side to side. Marie is wrapped in a shawl. Suddenly their way is barred by Gierey, surrounded by his body-guard. Vatslav leaps at the Khan who strikes him down. Gierey tears off Marie's scarf and is amazed by her beauty. The castle is now a flaming pile. The glare reveals the motionless figure of Gierey, with Marie kneeling beside the slain youth.

Act II. The Khan's harem. Gierey's wives, superintended by a eunuch, bathe and dress. Zarema, the favourite, is at one side, resting on a splendid divan.

Gierey enters, followed by eunuchs. Zarema dances for him, but his thoughts are full of Marie, and he is indifferent to her efforts. Marie passes through the harem. Now the other wives try to entertain Gierey, but he departs moodily.

Zarema, ignored by Gierey, is mocked by the other wives. She dances again and tries to suggest that she has not lost her power of attraction and can still compete with Marie.

During her dance, Gierey returns. As her dance reaches its climax she tries to fling her arms about the Khan who gently removes them and, looking away, goes out.

Act III. Marie's bed chamber in the harem of the Bakhchisaray Palace where Gierey has allowed her to live, attended by a female attendant.

Marie is seen playing on a small harp. Gierey enters. He tries to approach her, but she evades him. At last he leaves and Marie dances an elegy, reminiscent of happy days in Poland.

The servant leads Marie to bed and lies down on guard. Zarema enters noiselessly. In one hand she bears a light, in the other she holds a dagger to her breast. As she approaches the couch, Marie wakes and stares at Zarema. The latter pleads with Marie to hear her. She relates how she fell in love with Gierey and became his favourite, but since Marie's arrival the Khan ignores it. During her dance the servant wakes up and, seeing Zarema, leaves the chamber unnoticed by the two women. Zarema's pleadings change to threats.

At this moment Gierey enters, followed by the eunuch and the servants. Seeing the dagger in Zarema's hand, Gierey tries to wrest it from her, but she manages to evade him and stabs Marie to death. The Khan tries to seize the dagger to stab Zarema, but, with a happy smile, she offers her breast. Gierey, seeing that death at his hand would be a pleasure and not a punishment, gives her to the eunuchs and plans for her to be killed by torture.

Act IV. A fountain court. In the background a view of Bakhchisaray.

To the sound of trumpets Gierey enters to receive his returning troops, who bring him captured flags and treasure, and women for his harem. But he displays little interest either in the spoils of victory or the women.

Through the court eunuchs lead Zarema to execution. Seeing her, Gierey is reminded of Marie. He tries to efface this sad memory by goading himself to a war-like fury. To this end he orders his Tartars to give a warrior's dance. But the dancing brings him no relief; he orders it to cease and desires to be alone.

Then he summons the builder of the fountain of tears which he has had constructed in Marie's memory. He grows more and more moody and her vision appears before him. She dances an *adage* expressive of mingled sadness and reproachfulness. Gradually the vision fades, the scene grows dark, leaving the gleaming fountain softly playing in the dusk.

THE THREE FAT MEN

Ballet in 4 Acts and 8 Scenes. Book: I. Olecha. Music: V. A. Oransky. Scenery: B. A. Matrunine. Choreography: I. A. Moiseyev. First produced: Bolshoy Theatre, Moscow, 1935.

CHARACTERS

Prospero, an armourer
Dr. Gaspard
Tibul, a gymnast
Suok, a circus artiste

The Balloon-vendor
Razdvatre, a teacher of dancing
The Three Fat Men
The Chancellor
Prince Tutti
Tutti's Teachers
Grandpa Brizak
Circus Artistes

Act I. Scene I. The square in front of Dr. Gaspard's house.

Dr. Gaspard prepares to go for a long walk. He notices the gymnast, Tibul, affix a revolutionary poster to the wall.

The soldiers of the Guard try to arrest Tibul. Comic scenes of pursuit in the manner of the Italian *commedia dell'arte*.

A balloon-vendor stops in front of the poster. The doctor and other curious passers-by also go to it. The poster reads as follows:

To Workmen, Miners, Sailors
and all the Poor Working Classes
Very Soon
Prospero the Armourer will lead the
Workers to the Assault on the Palace of
the Three Fat Men.
To Arms!

Gradually the people fill the square. In the distance is heard the voices and measured tramp of the revolutionary armourers led by Prospero. Tibul marches beside him.

A gust of wind carries away the balloon-vendor. The doctor is amazed to see him fly in the air.

Rain falls. The doctor opens his umbrella and immediately a squall rises and carries him away likewise.

Act I. Scene II. The Palace of the Three Fat Men.

Preparations are being made for a feast in honour of the defeat of the armourers. Scullions hurry incessantly from the palace kitchen to the dining-room. At last everything is ready. An enormous cake is set up in the centre of the room.

A gust of wind blows open the window and wafts in the balloon-vendor, who falls in the cake. Everyone is terrified. There is only one thing to do, to leave the balloon-vendor in the cake and cover it with cream.

Enter the master of ceremonies and professor of dancing, Razdvatre. The guard of honour is mounted. The Three Fat Men, surrounded by ministers and guests, make a solemn entry.

Tutti, the prince apparent, appears with his doll.

The Fat Men send for Prospero, who is brought in chained and confined in a cage. His fiery glance terrifies the bystanders.

The Chancellor pronounces sentence. The key of the cage is placed round Tutti's neck, when the cage disappears below.

Razdvatre opens the festival. The Guards execute a mazurka. The guests are shown dances by the negroes Havai and La Chasse.

At the end of the festival the Guards dance a galop.

One of the Fat Men cuts the cake from which rises the balloon-vendor.

The Guards try to seize him. The balloon-vendor, closing his eyes in fright, brandishes a sword in defence. In the scuffle Tutti's doll is pierced. The doll falls. The balloon-vendor escapes through the window.

Tutti sheds tears over his broken doll.

Act II. Scene I. Tutti's room.

Tutti is bored; he misses his doll. His teachers and servants offer him other toys: the doll Fouetté, a violinist, a *danseuse,* a monkey. But none please him.

Dr. Gaspard, clinging to his umbrella, is blown through the window. The Chancellor is delighted, for the doctor will be able to repair Tutti's doll. He is ordered to mend the doll by the following midday. Gaspard departs with the doll.

Act II. Scene II. The jewellers' square.

There is a joyous festival in the square. The citizens dance a waltz.

Enter a convoy of chained armourers guarded by soldiers.

The citizens threaten the prisoners with their canes and umbrellas. The prisoners are taken away and gradually the crowd disperses.

The town sleeps. The fires are extinguished. The night watch goes its round.

A cab arrives with Dr. Gaspard, who holds the doll on his knees. The old hack can hardly crawl. The doctor is asleep and allows the doll to fall on the pavement.

A distant shot is heard. The horse takes fright but fails to overturn the carriage. The doctor wakes up. He dashes off in search of the doll, which cannot be found.

The doctor arrives at the caravan of Grandpa Brizak. The curtains part and reveal the pretty features of little Suok. Her likeness to the doll deceives the doctor. Tibul clears up the misunderstanding and proposes that Suok shall go as the doll. Tibul disguises himself as a negro.

They accompany the doctor to the palace.

Act III. Scene I. The Palace of the Three Fat Men.

Tutti impatiently awaits the arrival of the doctor. The clock strikes noon. Dances of the hours, animated numbers.

Dr. Gaspard appears with the doll. Little Suok plays her part to perfection. Imitating the doll's gestures, she goes before the soldiers, scullions, ministers, musicians, professors, players, and guests, who run to see her. Dr. Gaspard, with a solemn air, makes the mended doll walk before Tutti. The doll and Tibul execute an *adage*. Then the doll dances a *variation* and offers a rose to the Prince.

Delighted, Tutti begins to dance; his example is followed by all the onlookers.

Act III. Scene II. Tutti's room.

Tutti and Suok are alone. The Prince offers the doll dainties. They dance.

Tired by the day's excitements, Tutti sleeps in his chair. Suok filches the key of Prospero's cage and escapes through the window, which overlooks the palace garden.

Act III. Scene III. The palace garden.

Suok goes down an avenue. The sentry who dozes at the entrance to Tutti's menagerie appears to be dreaming.

Suok takes a lantern and enters the menagerie.

In his dream the sentry sees a number of dolls dancing to sweet music. They waltz and turn about one another, while quarrelling. The sentry fancies he hears the animals growling.

In truth the wild beasts, disturbed by Suok, give vent to awful growls. Guards and ministers hurry in from all sides. Lastly the Three Fat Men enter.

But Prospero appears at the door of the palace, holding little Suok on his shoulder. With the other hand he restrains a panther by its collar. Behind him come Tibul and the armourers.

Act IV. The Place de l'Etoile.

The people celebrate their delivery from the oppression of the Three Fat Men.

A troupe of strolling players performs an interlude. The players mock the Three Fat Men and the Guards; they glorify Tibul, Suok, and Prospero, and praise the wisdom of Dr. Gaspard.

Ballet executed by Tibul, Suok, and the balloon-vendor. The dance becomes general.

KATERINA

Ballet in 3 Acts and 7 Scenes. Book: L. M. Lavrovsky. Music: Anton Rubinstein, arranged by E. A. Dubrovsky (The Music of the serfs' ballet by Adolphe Adam). Scenery and costumes: B. M. Erbstein. Choreography by L. M. Lavrovsky. First produced: Leningrad and Moscow, 1927.

CHARACTERS

A Landowner and proprietor of the Serfs' Theatre
His Sister
Ulinka, his Daughter
Andrey, her fiancé and the Governor's nephew
The Governor
Palkin, an aristocratic owner of a small estate
Poteau, a *maître de ballet* and professor of dancing
The Countess, Ulinka's Aunt
Katerina, a parlour-maid and *première danseuse* of the Serfs' Theatre
Vladimir, a footman and *premier danseur* of the Serfs' Theatre
Visitors, Retainers.

Period. The second and third decades of the 19th century.
The action passes on an estate near Moscow.

Act I. A great hall on the landowner's estate.

Katerina and Vladimir are friends. Vladimir is called and they part. From the garden comes pretty Ulinka, flushed and excited because Andrey has just avowed his love for her. She drops the flowers she is carrying and hides behind a column. Andrey appears and is annoyed not to find Ulinka, but she emerges from her hiding-place and makes him join her in a dance which ends with a kiss.

Her father enters and, leading the lovers to a seat, embraces them affectionately. He rings a bell, which is answered by Katerina and Vladimir. The landowner introduces the servants as the principal dancers in a new ballet which he proposes to show his friends.

The guests gradually arrive and Ulinka, surrounded by other young people, goes into the garden; she sends Katerina for her fan.

The hall is empty save for a number of footmen who are arranging the tables and lighting the candles. Vladimir is sad at the sight of all this festivity when his own life is so unhappy.

Katerina crosses the hall with the fan. She meets Vladimir but the landowner comes in from the garden and, ill-pleased at the friendship of the servants, forbids them to associate with each other.

Katerina moves towards the garden as Ulinka and her friends come into the hall. The young people play blindman's buff and are chased by Andrey, who has his eyes bandaged. Ulinka orders Katerina to stop. Andrey catches Katerina, and, feeling the fan, declares that he has caught Ulinka. He lifts the bandage and discovers his mistake. Annoyed, he snatches the fan from the maid and gives it to Ulinka.

Katerina is so distressed that she can scarcely keep back her tears, and retires.

The games continue until interrupted by the entrance of the Governor. Everyone goes to greet him. He gives Ulinka a costly present and jokes with the landowner.

Now Cossack women serve champagne and Ulinka's engagement to Andrey is announced. General delight and congratulations. The Governor observes Katerina and covets her. The dancing recommences. Katerina is frightened by the Governor, for his eyes follow her every movement.

The landowner invites his guests into the garden, which is now illuminated. Katerina runs in with a scarf belonging to Ulinka and meets Vladimir. They dance together in a mood of evil presentiment, until interrupted by the arrival of some guests. Then Katerina picks up the scarf and goes into the garden, anxiously watched by Vladimir.

Act II. Scene I. The Serfs' Theatre from behind the curtain.

The dancers run in from all sides. The *maître de ballet* grumbles at some for being late. He is about to reprove Katerina when the Governor and the landowner appear. All the dancers bow and remain in that position. The landowner is not pleased at the Governor's interest in Katerina, since she is a good dancer and an excellent servant. He tries to interest him in some of the other *danseuses*, but to no purpose.

The Governor calls Katerina to him. She obeys, full of fear and aversion, while the Governor roars with laughter, knowing that the girl will be sold to him. This difficult situation is relieved by the arrival of Ulinka, who declares that the guests are growing impatient for the performance to begin. The *maître de ballet* orders the troupe to their places, a bell rings and the ballet commences.

Act II. Scene II. The Serfs' Theatre before the curtain.

The name of the ballet is *Admadeya and Dryas,* and the characters are as follows:

Admadeya, a nymph . . . . . KATERINA
Her friends
Dryas, a shepherd . . . . . VLADIMIR
Pan, in love with Admadeya
Eros, God of Love
Boreas, a North Wind, also in
 love with Admadeya
    Nymphs, Zephyrs, Satyrs, Amorini

The scene represents a typical classical landscape.

Pan is seen with the satyrs capering about him. He plots to kidnap Admadeya with their help. Hearing footsteps they all hide. Nymphs enter the clearing and zephyrs follow. Cupids lead in Admadeya and Dryas by means of ropes of flowers.

Suddenly Pan and his satyrs spring on the nymphs and capture Admadeya. Eros appears and, freeing Admadeya, orders the cupids to bind Pan. Eros flies away and the nymphs express their joy at Admadeya's rescue.

But now Boreas comes and with his cold breath drives away the nymphs and himself seizes Admadeya. Dryas contests the prize. During the struggle Pan slips his bonds and tries to kidnap Admadeya. But Boreas is victorious and carries off the nymph. Dryas is broken-hearted at his loss.

Act II. Scene III. The dressing room of the danseuses of the Serfs' Theatre.

Katerina is filled with forebodings, although her friends try to soothe her. Suddenly the landowner and Governor enter; they order everyone to leave, save Katerina, who breaks a mirror in her nervousness. The landowner informs her that she has been transferred to the Governor, and orders her to kiss the hand of her new master. Overwhelmed, she kneels to the landowner and implores him not to send her away from the theatre, but her entreaties are in vain. The landowner departs.

Then she pleads with the Governor and asks him to refuse her. But he declares that she already belongs to him. She walks to and fro in the greatest agitation, and bursts into wild laughter; her happiness as a serf is ended. A bell rings for the *danseuses* to return to the stage. Katerina, grief-stricken, goes to take part in the second act of the ballet.

Act II. Scene IV. The Serfs' Theatre, before the curtain.

Dryas and the nymphs bring offerings and pray to the Gods to restore Admadeya. Eros again comes to their help. Two Zephyrs bring in the freed Admadeya. Eros blesses the lovers and they disappear into a grotto. Pan implores the God to make him happy, so he confers a magic quality on his flute, which, when played, will charm the nymphs' hearts.

Katerina and Vladimir should now dance a *grand pas classique*. She begins to dance, but her strength fails her, because she is haunted by the Governor. She tries to continue but swoons into her partner's arms. The ballet continues around them. Dryas and Admadeya are the centre of an apotheosis. A cipher of Alexander I grows into being and cupids blow their trumpets in triumph The curtain falls.

Act III. Scene I.

In honour of the betrothal of Andrey and Ulinka a bachelor's party is held. Lackeys set out wines and refreshments and *danseuses* are posed on pedestals to represent statues.

The young people, led by Andrey, inspect the *danseuses*. Palkin is particularly interested. Punch is made and the living statues dance. Gradually the guests become tipsy. The curtain parts and gypsies sing and dance.

Next, Katerina appears in a *tableau vivant* called "The Maiden's Prayer." The Governor, who is drunk, passionately embraces Katerina, who tries to escape. Her cries of fear are received with coarse laughter.

Suddenly the door opens and Vladimir runs in to Katerina's help. Forgetting his position he embraces Katerina and, kneeling to the landowner, tells him of their love. His plea is greeted with fresh roars of laughter, meanwhile, Katerina runs from the room.

The landowner, mad with rage, seizes a whip and slashes at Vladimir. But the footman wrests the whip away and strikes the landowner instead. This episode angers the guests, who attack Vladimir and trample him under foot.

Act III. Scene II. The courtyard of the landowner's house. The morning mist is gradually dispelled by the rising sun.

Katerina runs out of the house, pursued by lackeys. She hides while they search for her in the park. Vladimir, who is bruised all over, is led to the stables.

Katerina, seeing his sad plight, cannot resist going to comfort him. The servants, affected by this scene, do not know what to do. At last, fearful of the landowner, they drag the lovers apart. Vladimir is hustled to the stables, but Katerina flees into the park.

Some serfs hurry in and explain what has happened. The ill-treatment of Vladimir and Katerina has roused their hatred. The serfs assemble and voice their anger. The landowner appears with a whip and immediately realises the danger of the situation. At a sign from him the murmurs die down.

He calls out several women and orders them to dance. Afraid to disobey, they make a pretence of dancing. Gradually he calls out more and more to join in the dance until all take part. The tempo increases and the landowner strikes at all those who lag behind the time. A sad song is heard and the dancing stops abruptly.

Serfs run in various directions to make way for a party of drunken youths, headed by the Governor, who come out of the house. The Governor demands Katerina. A procession is seen moving through the park. Very soon lackeys enter carrying the body of Katerina, who has hanged herself. They quietly place her body on the ground before the Governor.

*

Katerina is based on a careful study of the conditions of the Serfs' Theatre[1] at the beginning of the 19th century. The theme is interesting and full of dramatic possibilities, and permits of a ballet within a ballet, as in *Le Diable Boiteux*. The ballet styled *Admadeya and Dryas* is intended to be in the anacreontic style of Didelot.

[1] The *Journal des Archives Internationales de la Danse*, April 15th, 1935, page 38, contains an interesting article on the Serfs' Theatre.

THE BRIGHT STREAM

Comedy Ballet in 3 Acts and 4 Scenes. Book: F. V. Lopukhov and Andrey Pyotrovsky. Music: Dmitri Shostakovich. Scenery: M. P. Bobyshov. Choreography: F. V. Lopukhov. First produced: Bolshoy Theatre, Leningrad, 1935.

CHARACTERS

Zina	Z. A. VASILIEVA
Pyotr, her husband, an agricultural student	P. A. GUSEV
A Female Dancer ⎫	F. I. BALABINA
A Male Dancer, her partner ⎬ Members of an Artistes' Brigade	N. A. ZUBKOVSKY
An Accordion-Player ⎭	A. A. ORLOV
A Dweller—middle-aged—in a Country Bungalow	M. A. ROSTOVTSEV
His Wife, anxious to appear younger than she is	E. V. LOPUKHOVA
Gavrilich, a shock-worker . .	F. I. CHERNICHENKO
Galiya, a school-girl	G. I. ISAEVA
A Highlander	A. V. LOPUKHOV
An Uzbek	S. P. DUBININ
A Kuban Cossack	V. E. NIKOLAYEV
A Milkmaid	N. N. LATONINA
A Tractor-Driver	K. V. TIKHOMIROV
Two Youths . . . . . ⎰	U. U. SAVITSKY
⎱	N. N. FEDOROV

Act I. Scene I. A small wayside halt on one of the branch lines of the North Caucasian Railway. Early autumn.

The local collective farms have completed both their harvesting and autumn sowing. As a reward the workers are to be entertained by a group of artistes from town, and some members of the nearest collective farm, called "The Bright Stream," have assembled to greet their guests. Among the workers are Gavrilich, a jolly old man and a general favourite; Galiya, and some child friends with a bouquet; and Pyotr and Zina.

The last to arrive are two bungalow-dwellers, who, bored to

extinction, have come to see the artistes. Zina, serious-minded, reads a book while waiting. Pyotr tries to cheer her up and induces the others to share in his efforts. At last everyone except Zina proceeds to the platform.

They return with the artistes—a ballet-dancer, her partner, and an accordion-player. Zina greets the first-named with delight, for they recognise each other as old friends, having once studied together at the same dancing-school. Since then Zina has married Pyotr and helped him on the farm. No one knows that she was once a dancer.

The newcomer asks Zina if she has forgotten her dancing and accidentally produces a pair of ballet-shoes. Donning shoes each tries to see who can remember the most of their former lessons; they are interrupted by the return of Gavrilich and Pyotr. Zina introduces her husband to the dancer and goes out chatting to Gavrilich. Pyotr, dazzled by the visitor, begins to court her. At this moment Gavrilich and Zina return; the latter feels her first pang of jealousy.

Act I. Scene II. The day draws in.

The workers of "The Bright Stream," encamped among the sheaves of wheat, joyfully make plans for the morrow, which is to be a day of festival.

The artistes' brigade arrives. Pyotr presents them to the fieldworkers' brigade. The artistes display the presents awarded to the best shock-workers. There is a gramophone for Gavrilich, a silk dress for the best milkmaid, and so on. The prize-winners are lustily applauded and the jollity merges into a dance.

First there is a dance by Gavrilich and some old men; next, the bungalow-dwellers are forced to trip a measure, by way of a joke, they dance a Chaconne. Now follows a number by some young girls who are members of a club organised by Zina. But the main interest is centred on the milkmaid; everyone wishes to see her dance in her new dress. She dances with the tractor-driver. The merriment increases. Gavrilich puts a record on his new gramophone and asks the artistes to dance in their turn.

Not wishing to disappoint the workers they agree, although far from happy at the prospect of dancing in their ordinary clothes. However, they improvise a dance among the wheat-sheaves. The workers watch the dance with pleasure, but the bungalow-dwellers are more interested in the artistes themselves. The husband admires the *danseuse,* while his wife is greatly taken with the male dancer. Zina is jealous. Pyotr is greatly attracted by the *danseuse,* who seems such a glorious being in contrast with his quiet wife. The accordion-player is asked to dance with Galiya.

Now the proceedings are interrupted by some young field-workers from Kuban and the Caucasus, who burst into a gay, warlike dance, which is enthusiastically received.

At last the merriment subsides and everyone is invited to partake of refreshments. During the general exit the bungalow-dweller whispers in the dancer's ear that he would like to see her alone, while his wife conveys a similar intimation to the male dancer. But Pyotr leaves with the *danseuse*. Then Zina begins to sob; the bystanders try to soothe her.

The *danseuse* returns and informs Zina that she has no intention of flirting with her husband. She urges her to tell the young people what her profession used to be. Zina consents and the two friends dance together. Everyone is astounded.

Zina's friend proposes that a joke be played upon Pyotr and the others. She suggests that the male dancer, disguised as herself, shall meet the bungalow-dweller, while she, made up as the male dancer, shall meet the bungalow-dweller's wife; lastly, that Zina herself, wearing one of her theatrical costumes, shall go to the meeting with Pyotr. The plan is approved.

Act II. A very warm southern night. A clearing surrounded with bushes and trees. The young people are assembled. The bungalow-dwellers arrive, late as usual. The accordion-player is attracted by Galiya who danced with him earlier in the day.

The bungalow-dweller, his wife, and Pyotr remind their acquaintances of their engagements. The young people now definitely resolve to teach them a lesson. They quickly dress up: the dancer in her partner's clothes, the partner in one of the dancer's dresses, while Zina puts on one of her friend's theatrical costumes. To add to the fun the tractor-driver wears a dogskin.

All is ready when Galiya remembers that the accordion-player invited her to meet him. This revelation threatens to ruin the whole plot, but the tractor-driver suggests that she keep the appointment while he, pretending to be a dog, will prevent the accordion-player from approaching her. This is agreed.

Galiya, attended by the "dog," is seen awaiting the accordion-player. He appears and is much puzzled by the presence of the dog, which seems very savage and quarrelsome. At last he perceives that he has been tricked, but takes the joke in good part and agrees to help in the main plot.

The old bungalow-dweller arrives, wheeling a bicycle. Anxious to make an impression on the dancer, he has got himself up as a sportsman and is weighed down with a double-barrelled gun and other impedimenta. Now his wife arrives at the same spot. She is wearing ballet-shoes to astonish the male dancer.

Suddenly the bungalow-dweller espies his sylphide through the trees. This episode is observed by the wife who, revealing her presence, drives her husband away with a stick. In turn she is frightened by the tractor-driver who, still wearing his dogskin, rides the bicycle. Then the *danseuse,* dressed as her partner, jeers at the wife. All go out.

Enter Pyotr, who meets Zina, disguised as the dancer. He fails to recognise her and after a little banter they leave arm in arm.

The bungalow-dweller runs in with the supposed *danseuse,* while she, disguised as her partner, emerges from the bushes and makes a scene.

Now follows a comic duel. The first to shoot is the disguised dancer, who misses. Then the bungalow-dweller is handed a pistol. Too frightened to shoot, he contents himself with merely taking aim. Simultaneously, Gavrilich bangs a pail and the old man imagines he has fired. Immediately the supposed *danseuse* falls to the ground as though shot. The bungalow-dweller, horrified at the result of his careless aim, takes to his heels. No sooner has he disappeared than the victim comes to life and dances, amid the laughter of the delighted plotters.

Act III. The beginning of the morning of the following day. The harvest festival.

On the meadow everything is planned for the celebration. There are brightly-coloured swings, and an improvised stage for the artistes to give their performance.

Pyotr is particularly anxious for the show to begin so that he can see the dancer he met last night in the woods. But, to his great surprise, there are two dancers, dressed exactly alike, their faces hidden by masks. At the conclusion of the dance, Pyotr moves towards the stage entrance.

The interest shifts to the bungalow-dwellers who arrive at this moment. The old man kneels to his wife and implores her forgiveness for his crime of last night. At this moment the two dancers approach him. Seeing not only the dancer he shot, but a second one, he suspects that he has been fooled. They raise their veils and the secret is out.

Pyotr, observing that one of the dancers is his wife, asks her forgiveness. The bystanders also exert their efforts to make peace. The festival ends with a general dance in which all, young and old, take part, together with the guest artistes.

INDEX